Money and Capital Markets

The Financial System in an Increasingly Global Economy

Money and Capital Markets

The Financial System in an Increasingly Global Economy

Third Edition

Peter S. Rose
Texas A & M University

1989

BPI
IRWIN

Homewood, IL 60430
Boston, MA 02116

© RICHARD D. IRWIN, INC., 1983, 1986, and 1989

Sponsoring editor: Michael W. Junior
Project editor: Lynne Basler
Production manager: Stephen K. Emry
Designer: Hunter Graphics
Compositor: Graphic World, Inc.
Typeface: 10/12 Century Schoolbook
Printer: R. R. Donnelley & Sons Company

LIBRARY OF CONGRESS
Library of Congress Cataloging-in-Publication Data

Rose, Peter S.
  Money and capital markets : the financial system in an
increasingly global economy / Peter S. Rose.—3rd ed.
      p.   cm.
  Includes bibliographies and index.
  ISBN 0-256-06524-1
  1. Finance—United States. 2. Money market—United States.
3. Capital market—United States. I. Title.
HG181.R66   1989
332'.0973—dc19

88–24101
                                                                CIP

To My Family

Preface

THE STUDY OF MONEY AND CAPITAL MARKETS

As teachers and practitioners of the art and science of financial decision-making are well aware, it would be difficult to find a subject for study that is of greater importance for the welfare of businesses and individuals than the financial system and its markets. The money and capital markets are *the* mechanism for converting the public's savings into investments in buildings, machinery and equipment, public facilities, and inventories of goods and services that make it possible for the economy to grow, for new jobs to be created, and for living standards to rise. It is the financial system that handles most of the payments made for purchases of food, clothing, shelter, automobiles, and tens of thousands of other goods and services. That system also generates credit to sustain the public's spending and standard of living and stores future purchasing power in the form of stocks, bonds, and other securities. And the money and capital markets make possible the liquidation of those securities whenever cash is needed for immediate spending.

The financial system offers risk protection to businesses and individuals through sales of insurance policies and hedging instruments such as options, futures, and swaps. And both domestic and international financial systems today carry the great burden of public policy, serving as the conduit for government actions designed to promote economic growth, a stable international economy, low unemployment, and stable prices of goods and services. A central theme of this book, in all its editions, has been to highlight these essential contributions of the financial system to the economy, hopefully leaving the reader with a clear picture of how money and capital markets around the globe work to fulfill these varied functions and roles.

THE FINANCIAL SYSTEM BESET BY CHANGE

Today's financial system is of great importance to every one of us. Student and teacher, businessman and woman, consumer and investor, government policymaker and private citizen—all depend upon the speed, efficiency, and quality of services that the financial system provides. But, as this book tries to convey in each of its eight sections, that system of markets and institutions is today beset by sweeping change and serious problems—challenges and difficulties whose dimensions and solutions are by no means easily grasped, but whose consequences will affect every individual and institution in the global economy.

There is, for example, the trend toward increasingly intense worldwide competition for financial services as improvements in communications and technology have brought widely separated financial service suppliers into direct competition. In recent years, for example, Japanese banks and investment houses have made substantial inroads into both business and consumer financial service markets in the United States and Western Europe, while U.S. financial institutions have established or acquired affiliates and subsidiary firms in Eastern and Western Europe, in Asia, and around the Pacific Rim. Deregulation of the financial sector by governments in Australia, Canada, Great Britain, the United States, and many other nations has spurred the spread of competition, as noted in the opening chapter of this edition.

The unfolding of worldwide financial services competition may well have benefitted the consumer of financial services with lower prices and better quality, but it has also brought enormous problems that await solutions. Failures of banks and other financial institutions have mushroomed, with even the largest financial institutions vulnerable to collapse. The result is a serious threat to public confidence in the soundness and solvency of major financial service suppliers and the safety of the public's savings. A related problem centers on the huge volume of debt carried by many nations in both the industrially developed regions of the globe and among lesser developed countries of the Third World, including Argentina, Brazil, and Mexico. In the United States, both foreign-held debt and government debt have reached unprecedented levels, so that the interest and goodwill of foreign savers and investors has come to have a potent impact on economic and financial conditions inside the United States and on domestic economic policy. These debt problems are addressed in numerous chapters of the book, from those that focus on public policy to the international chapters in the final section.

One of the factors that makes the huge global debt overhang such a problem is the volatility of the world economy. The past two decades have brought wide and unprecedented swings in the prices of crude oil and natural gas, gold, industrial raw materials, food, and fiber. Key industries, such as agriculture, steel manufacturing, autos, and energy fuels, have fluctuated from unparalleled prosperity to the depths of depression. Not surprisingly, because of the close links between the economy and the financial system, financial markets and institutions have mirrored the ups and downs of these volatile industries. Demands for credit and other financial services first burgeoned, then nosedived. Stock prices on exchanges in London, New York, Tokyo, and other leading financial centers rose to unprecedented heights, only to crash even faster in the wake of persistent economic problems. Loan defaults and business bankruptcies first weakened and then laid low many of the financial institutions that had benefitted the most from the good times, especially those banks that had made large energy and agricultural loans.

FINANCIAL RISK MANAGEMENT

As we will see in this edition, the result today is a financial system of markets and institutions both more sensitive and more alert to *risk* in all its forms. Risk management has become a cornerstone of modern business decision-making, and the financial markets have responded with a rapidly widening array of innovative new services, including security options, financial futures contracts, options on futures, interest rate and currency swaps, and balanced-funds management. This new edition of *Money and Capital Markets* contains an expanded discussion of all these techniques and integrates them more fully into the material in all of the relevant chapters.

ABOUT THIS BOOK

As *Money and Capital Markets* enters its third edition, its goals remain much the same:

- To present a comprehensive yet interesting analysis of the *entire financial system*—both domestic and international—*and its component parts*.

- To acquaint the reader with all the major types of *financial instruments,* including bonds, stocks, mortgages, bills, notes, deposits, and other financial assets, and their uses, principal buyers and sellers, and trading characteristics.

- To provide a clear view of all the major types of *financial institutions* that operate within the financial system.

- To provide a thorough knowledge of *how interest rates and security prices are determined* and what causes prices and rates to change.

- To promote a better understanding of *public policy* issues in the financial marketplace and how government policymakers, working through the central banking system and through government taxation and spending programs, can influence financial and economic conditions and the welfare of businesses, individuals, and families.

- To identify and understand the *current and future trends*—economic, demographic, and financial—that are reshaping the financial system in order to respond to tomorrow's financial service needs and pressures.

FEATURES OF THIS BOOK

These objectives are pursued through a variety of educational methods:

- Each chapter begins with a clear statement of its *learning objectives* and a list of *key terms and concepts* to alert the reader to what is most important in the pages that follow. Each key term and concept is identified in boldface within each chapter so the reader can quickly review the most important points covered.

- Numerous illustrations, tables, and examples appear throughout the book to help emphasize and clarify key points, equations, and ideas.
- Problems to solve are included at the end of many chapters, accompanied by extensive references for readers interested in mastery of the subject.
- Money and Capital Markets Dictionary has been added at the end of the book to provide immediate access to important terms in the field.
- A new chapter, entitled "The Future of the Financial System," attempts to tie together the various economic, demographic, and financial trends that are reshaping the money and capital markets into a global, intensely competitive, and risk-laden environment.

ACKNOWLEDGMENTS

As in earlier editions of this book, the author has benefited from the ideas, criticisms, and data provided by many economists, financial analysts, government agencies, trade associations, and private groups. The author wishes to extend special appreciation to James C. Baker of Kent State University, Ivan T. Call of Brigham Young University, Eugene F. Drzycinski of the University of Wisconsin, Mona J. Gardner of Illinois State University, Timothy Koch of Texas Tech University, David Mills of Illinois State University, John P. Olienyh of Colorado State University, Colleen C. Pontalone of Northeastern University, and Richard Rivard of the University of South Florida for their review and critique of the earlier edition and for numerous suggestions to improve and update the presentation. The author wishes to extend appreciation to Paul Bolster, Northeastern University; Robert M. Crowe, American College; Joseph P. Ogden, University of Tennessee—Knoxville; and Donald A. Smith, Pierce College, for their comments on the third edition. In addition, numerous associations and institutions gave their permission to reprint important data or information, including the American Council of Life Insurance, the *Canadian Banker,* official publication of the Canadian Bankers' Association, the Chicago Board of Trade, the Credit Union National Association, Dow Jones Reprints, Dun & Bradstreet, Inc., the First Boston Corporation, the Insurance Information Institute, Moody's Investor Service, Standard & Poor's Corporation, and the United States League of Savings Associations. The author also gratefully acknowledges the support, patience, and understanding of his family, who made completion of this third edition possible. Nevertheless, any shortcomings that remain belong solely to the author.

A NOTE TO THE STUDENT

The money and capital markets are a fascinating field of study. What happens in those markets affects the quality of our lives every day in many different ways. Moreover, the financial markets are dynamic institutions continually "putting on a new face" in the form of new services, new instruments, and new methods. This text is only an introduction to these vast, ever-changing institutions—one that you will want to build upon throughout your career through both reading and personal experience.

As you begin each chapter of this book, aim for mastery of the material, for making the most of an important opportunity. How can you do that?

Let me suggest that you start with the short list of *learning objectives* that begin each chapter. These are guideposts—a brief description of what I hope you will come away with after you have closed the book. It is a good idea to go over this list of learning objectives as you start to read and then again when you have finished each chapter. If you are still unsure whether you have received any help with any one of these learning objectives, go back and review the part of the chapter that deals with that particular objective. Ask yourself if the goal makes sense to you and if you now feel better informed about it than before.

Next, note the *key terms and concepts* listed just below the learning objectives. Make a pencil list of these key terms on a sheet of notebook paper and then be on the lookout for them as you read the chapter (these key terms are shown in boldface type to make them stand out). Consider writing a definition in your own words for each of the key terms you have listed. Double check your own definitions with those given in the text or with the dictionary of money and capital market terms that appear at the end of the book.

At the end of each chapter is a list of *Study Questions* and *Problems*. Your instructor may assign some of these, but even if that doesn't happen, try to answer them for yourself. If you have the time, writing out an answer to each question and problem is the best approach for mastering the subject. Or you can try to answer each question orally or discuss them in a group study session with other members of the class. If you don't feel comfortable with your answer to a particular problem or question, go through the chapter until you find the right section and review that portion of the chapter again.

Keep in mind that this text is designed with two fundamental purposes in mind: (1) to arm you with *analytical tools* to help you understand why the financial marketplace behaves as it does and how we should make financial decisions; and (2) to *describe* how today's financial markets operate and where they appear to be headed so that you can more easily "speak the language" of the markets and find your way around in them. Chapters 1 through 12 are aimed mainly at the first of these purposes—developing a good set of analytical tools. Chapters 13 through 30 mainly aim at the second purpose—to see how each market operates today and to be able to "speak the language." A successful course in money and capital markets will give you *both* the tools and the language of the financial markets.

Reading this book and successfully completing this course should help you in meeting your long-range career goals and successfully completing your degree program. *Money and Capital Markets* provides essential information for those taking subsequent course work in investments, capital budgeting, business finance, money and banking, macroeconomics, international finance, and government policy. Moreover, this book sensitizes you to the key problems and issues faced by business managers and government policymakers on a daily basis, especially in those problem areas related to borrowing and lending money and to government regulation of the economy and the financial markets. However, just as with every other book and every other course you will take, your future success in using this new knowledge will depend upon the energy and enthusiasm, the commitment to excellence and hard work that you bring to the subject. It is a challenge worthy of your best efforts. Good luck!

Peter S. Rose

Contents

Part One

The Financial System in Perspective

Chapter 1

The Role of the Financial System in the Economy

Learning Objectives in This Chapter

- To explain the functions and roles played by the financial system.
- To define key terms and concepts about the money and capital markets that will be used throughout the course.
- To describe basically how the financial markets operate to fulfill their various roles and functions.

Key Terms and Concepts in This Chapter

Financial system	*Money market*	*Secondary markets*
Financial market	*Capital market*	*Arbitrage*
Savings	*Open markets*	*Perfect market*
Investment	*Negotiated markets*	*Efficient market*
Credit	*Primary markets*	

THIS book is devoted to a study of the financial system—the collection of markets, institutions, laws, regulations, and techniques through which bonds, stocks, and other securities are traded, interest rates determined, and financial services produced and delivered. The financial system is one of the most important inventions of modern society. Its primary task is to move scarce loanable funds from those who save to those who borrow for consumption and investment. By making funds available for lending and borrowing (credit) the financial system provides the means whereby modern economies grow and increase the standard of living enjoyed by their citizens. Most of the credit thus obtained goes to purchase machinery and equipment, to construct new highways, factories, and schools, and to stock the shelves of businesses with goods. Without the financial system and the funds it supplies, each of us would lead a very different and probably less enjoyable existence.

The financial system determines both the cost of credit and how much credit will be available to pay for the thousands of different goods and services we purchase daily. Equally important, what happens in this system has a powerful impact upon the health of the nation's economy. When credit becomes more costly and less available, total spending for goods and services falls. As a result, unemployment rises and the economy's growth slows down as businesses cut back production and reduce their inventories. In contrast, when the cost of credit declines and loanable funds become more readily available, total spending in the economy increases, more jobs are created, and the economy's growth accelerates. In truth, the financial system is an integral part of the economic system and cannot be viewed in isolation from it.

THE ECONOMY AND THE FINANCIAL SYSTEM

Flows within the Economic System

In order to better understand the role played by the financial system in our daily lives we begin by examining its position within the economy.

The basic function of any economy is to allocate scarce material resources in order to produce the goods and services needed by society. The high standard of living most of us enjoy today depends fundamentally upon the ability of the nation's economy to turn out each day the enormous volume of clothing, food, shelter, and other essentials of modern living. This is an exceedingly complex task because scarce resources must first be procured in just the right amounts to provide the raw materials of production and combined at just the right time with labor and capital to generate the products and services demanded by consumers. In short, any economic system must combine inputs—land and other natural resources, labor and managerial skills, and capital equipment—in order to produce outputs in the form of goods and services. The economy generates a flow of production (goods and services) in return for a flow of payments (see Exhibit 1–1).

Exhibit 1–1   **The Economic System**

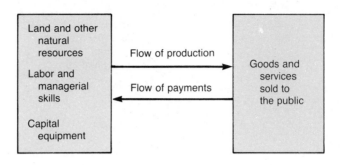

We may also depict the flows of payments and production within the economic system as a *circular flow* between producing units (mainly businesses and governments) and consuming units (principally households). (See Exhibit 1–2.) In modern economies households provide labor, managerial skills, and natural resources to business firms and governments in return for income in the form of wages, rents, dividends, and so on. Most of the income received by households is spent to purchase goods and services. In 1987, for example, about 94 percent of the $3.5 trillion in total personal income received by individuals and families in the United States was spent for consumption of goods and services or paid out in taxes.[1] The result of this spending is a flow of funds back to producing units as income, which stimulates them to produce more goods and services in future periods. The circular flow of production and income is, thus, interdependent and never ending.

The Role of Markets in the Economic System

In most economies around the world, *markets* are used to carry out this complex task of allocating resources and producing goods and services. What is a market? It is an institution set up by society to allocate resources which are scarce relative to the demand for them. Markets are the channel through which buyers and sellers meet to exchange goods, services, and resources.[2]

The marketplace determines what goods and services will be produced and in what quantity. This is accomplished essentially through changes in the prices of commodities and services offered in the market. If the price of

---

[1]In percentage terms, U.S. households in 1987 allocated about 80 percent of their total personal income for consumption expenditures; about 14 percent went for federal, state, and local taxes and fees; and the remainder—about 6 percent—was set aside as personal savings.

[2]Of course, scarce resources may be allocated by government order and central planning as well as by the marketplace. In the Soviet Union, for example, resources flow to those uses predetermined by a central government plan. While most industrialized economies in the Western world use markets to allocate the majority of their scarce resources today, these economies are really *mixed* economies, with market mechanisms and government-directed planning operating side by side.

Exhibit 1–2   **Circular Flows of Income, Payments, and Production
in the Economic System**

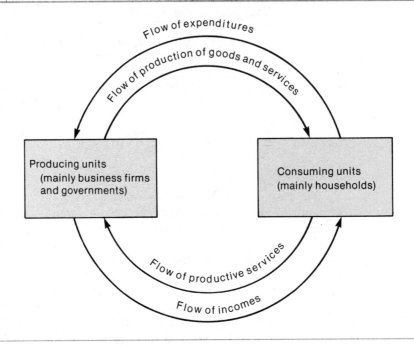

a commodity rises, for example, this stimulates business firms to produce
and supply more of it to consumers. In the long run new firms may enter
the market to produce those goods and services experiencing increased demand and rising prices. A decline in price, on the other hand, usually leads
to reduced production of a good or service, and in the long run some firms
will leave the marketplace.

Markets also distribute income. In a pure market system the income of
an individual or business firm is determined solely by the contributions each
makes to production. Markets reward superior productivity, innovation, and
sensitivity to customer needs with increased profits, higher wages and other
economic benefits.

Types of Markets

There are essentially three types of markets at work within the economic
system: (1) factor markets, (2) product markets, and (3) financial markets
(see Exhibit 1–3). In factor markets consuming units sell their labor, managerial skill, and other resources to those producing units offering the highest prices. The *factor markets* allocate factors of production—land, labor,
and capital—and distribute incomes in the form of wages, rental income,
and so on to the owners of productive resources.

Exhibit 1–3   Types of Markets in the Economic System

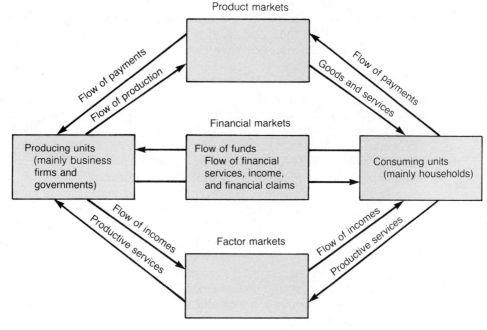

Consuming units use most of their income from the factor markets to purchase goods and services in *product markets*. Food, shelter, automobiles, books, theater tickets, gasoline, and swimming pools are among the many goods and services sold in product markets.

The Financial Markets and the Financial System

Of course, not all factor income is consumed. A substantial proportion of after-tax income received by households each year—$104 billion in 1987—is earmarked for personal saving. In addition, business firms save billions of dollars each year to build up equity reserves for future contingencies and to support long-term capital investment. For example, in 1987, U.S. corporations earned $334 billion in after-tax profits, of which $112 billion was set aside (undistributed) for possible future needs. It is here that the third kind of market—the financial market—performs a vital function within the economic system. The financial markets channel savings—which come mainly from households—to those individuals and institutions who need more funds for spending than are provided by current income. The financial markets are the heart of the financial system, determining the volume of credit available, attracting savings, and setting interest rates and security prices.

As we will see in Chapter 7, the definition of *savings* differs depending upon what type of unit in the economy is doing the saving. For households, savings is what is left over out of current income after current consumption expenditures are made. In the business sector, savings include current net earnings retained in the business after payment of taxes, stockholder dividends, and all other cash expenses. Government saving arises when there is a surplus of revenues over expenditures.

Most of the funds set aside as savings flow through the financial markets to support investment by business firms and governments. Investment generally refers to the acquisition of capital goods, such as buildings and equipment, and the purchase of inventories of raw materials and goods to sell. The makeup of *investment* varies with the particular unit doing the investing. For a business firm, expenditures on fixed assets, such as buildings, equipment, and inventories are investment expenditures. Households invest when they buy a new home. However, household purchases of furniture, automobiles, and other durable consumer goods are generally classified as consumption spending (i.e., expenditures on current account) and not investment (i.e., expenditures on capital account). Government spending for public facilities is another form of investment.

Modern economies require enormous amounts of investment in capital goods—drill presses, warehouses, schools, airports, and thousands of similar items—in order to produce goods and services for consumers. Investment in new equipment increases the productivity of labor and ultimately leads to a higher standard of living. However, investment often requires huge amounts of funds, often far beyond the resources available to a single firm or government. By selling financial claims (i.e., stocks, bonds, etc.) in the financial markets, though, large amounts of funds can be raised quickly, and the loan repaid out of future income. Indeed, the financial markets operating within the financial system make possible the *exchange of current income for future income.*

Those who supply funds in the financial markets receive only *promises* in return for the loan of their money. These promises are packaged in the form of attractive financial claims and financial services, such as stocks, bonds, deposits, and insurance policies (see Exhibit 1–4). Financial claims promise the supplier of funds a future flow of income, which may consist of dividends, interest, capital gains, or other returns. But there is no guarantee that the expected flow of future income will ever materialize. However, suppliers of funds to the financial system expect not only to recover their original commitment of funds but also to earn additional income as a reward for waiting and for the assumption of risk.

The role of the financial markets in channeling savings into investment is absolutely essential to the health and vitality of the economy. For example, if households were to set aside savings and those funds were not returned to the spending stream through investment by businesses and governments, the economy would begin to contract in size. The amount of income paid out

Exhibit 1–4   **The Financial System**

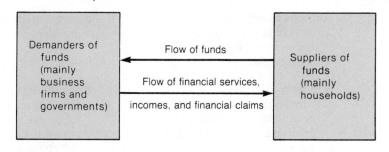

by business firms and governments would not be matched by funds paid back to those same sectors. As a result, future payments of wages and other forms of income would begin to decline, leading to reduced consumption spending. The nation's standard of living would fall. Moreover, with less spending going on, the need for labor would be curtailed, resulting in rising unemployment.

FUNCTIONS PERFORMED BY THE FINANCIAL SYSTEM AND THE FINANCIAL MARKETS

The great importance of the financial system in our daily lives can be illustrated by reviewing its different functions. There are seven basic functions of the financial system in a modern economy. (See Exhibit 1–5.)

Savings Function

As we noted earlier, the system of financial markets and institutions provides a *conduit for the public's savings*. Bonds, stocks, deposits, and other financial claims sold in the money and capital markets provide a profitable, relatively low-risk outlet for the public's savings. Those savings flow through the financial markets into investment so that more goods and services can be produced in the future, increasing society's standard of living. When savings flows decline, however, the growth of investment and of living standards tends to fall.

A good example of this danger is the track record of the U.S. economy in recent years. The average U.S. citizen's personal savings rate has dropped to the lowest levels since World War II, while other nations, such as Japan, continue to maintain high savings rates. The result is rapid increases in living standards among many foreign countries while U.S. living standards have leveled and even declined in some sectors. The savings function of any

Exhibit 1–5   **Functions of the Financial System**

Savings Function—
providing a potentially profitable and relatively low-risk outlet for the public's savings.

Liquidity Function—
providing a means of raising funds by converting securities and other financial assets into cash balances.

Payments Function—
providing a mechanism for making payments to purchase goods and services.

Policy Function—
providing a channel for government policy to achieve the nation's goals of high employment, low inflation, and sustainable economic growth.

Wealth Function—
providing a means to store purchasing power until needed at a future date for spending on goods and services.

Credit Function—
providing a continuing supply of credit for businesses, consumers, and governments to support both consumption and investment spending in the economy.

Risk Function—
providing a means to protect businesses, consumers, and governments against risks to people, property, and income.

financial system supplies the vital raw material of funds to invest so that economic growth and living standards can flourish.

Wealth Function

For those businesses and individuals choosing to save, the financial instruments sold in the money and capital markets provide an excellent way to *store wealth* (i.e., to preserve value or hold purchasing power) until funds are needed for spending in future periods. While we might choose to store our wealth in "things" (e.g., automobiles and clothes), such items are subject to depreciation and often carry great risk of loss. However, bonds, stocks, deposits, and other financial instruments do not wear out over time, usually generate income, and normally, their risk of loss is much less than would be true of other forms of stored wealth. In 1986 well over $21 trillion in securities, deposits, and so on were held by businesses, households, and governments in the U.S. economy. Individuals and families alone held almost $11 trillion in stocks, bonds, and other financial instruments. These holdings represent stored purchasing power which will be used in future periods to finance purchases and increase society's standard of living.

Liquidity Function

For wealth that is stored in financial instruments, the financial marketplace provides a means of converting those instruments into ready cash with little risk of loss. Thus, the financial system provides *liquidity* for savers holding financial instruments but in need of *money*. In modern societies money consists mainly of deposits held in banks. Money is the only financial instrument possessing perfect liquidity; it can be spent as it is without the necessity of converting it into some other form. However, money generally earns the lowest rate of return of all assets traded in the financial system, and its purchasing power is seriously eroded by inflation. That is why savers generally minimize their holdings of money and hold bonds and other financial assets until spendable funds really are needed.

Credit Function

In addition to facilitating the flow of savings into investment and providing liquidity for stored wealth, the financial markets furnish credit to finance consumption and investment spending. *Credit* consists of a loan of funds in return for a promise of future payment. Consumers frequently need credit to purchase a home, buy groceries, repair the family automobile, and retire outstanding debt. Businesses draw upon their lines of credit to stock their shelves, construct buildings, meet payrolls, and grant dividends to their stockholders. State, local, and federal governments frequently borrow to construct buildings and other public facilities and cover daily cash expenses until tax revenues flow in.

The volume of credit extended by the money and capital markets today is huge and growing rapidly. As shown in Exhibit 1–6, total net credit funds raised in U.S. financial markets in 1987 (including issues of corporate stock) exceeded $900 billion, compared to just over $400 billion as recently as 1982. Growth of the economy, inflation, and the tax deductibility of interest payments all appear to have fueled this rapid growth in credit usage by American households and institutions.

Payments Function

The financial system also provides a *mechanism for making payments for goods and services*. Certain financial assets, mainly checking accounts and NOW (negotiable order of withdrawal) accounts, serve as a medium of exchange in the making of payments. Plastic credit cards issued by many banks, credit unions, and retail stores give the customer instant access to short-term credit but also are widely accepted as a convenient means of payment. Another type of plastic card—the debit card—is used today to charge a buyer's deposit account for purchases of goods and services and transfer the proceeds instantly by wire to the seller's account. Debit cards

Exhibit 1–6   **Net Funds Raised in U.S. Financial Markets by Major Sectors of the U.S. Economy, 1987***

Sector and Funding Source		Amounts of Funds Raised ($ billions)	Percentage of Total Net Funds Raised†
Net borrowing by sector:			
Households		$224.0	24.0%
Nonfinancial business firms:			
Farms	$– 19.5		
Nonfinancial corporations	91.2		
Other businesses	92.8		
Total for all business firms		164.5	17.6
Private financial institutions		137.4	14.7
Governments:			
U.S. government	$ 151.4		
Federally sponsored agencies	180.2		
State and local governments	28.6		
Total for all governments in the United States		360.2	38.5
Foreign borrowers in the United States, net		– 12.7	– 1.4
Total net borrowing		$873.4	93.4
Net funds raised by issuing new corporate stock (equities)		61.8	6.6
Total net borrowed and equity funds raised in U.S. financial markets		$935.2	100.0%

*Figures for first half of year at annual rates.

†Column does not add to exactly 100 percent due to rounding.

Source: Board of Governors of the Federal Reserve System, *Flow of Funds Accounts,* 1988.

and other electronic means of payment, including computer terminals in homes, offices, and stores, are likely to displace checks and other pieces of paper as the principal means of payment in the years ahead.

Risk Function

The financial markets offer businesses, consumers, and governments *protection against life, health, property, and income risks.* This is accomplished, first of all, by the sale of life and property-casualty insurance policies. Policies marketed by life insurance companies indemnify a family against possible loss of income following the death of a loved one. Property casualty insurers protect their policyholders against an incredibly wide array of personal and property risks ranging from ill health, crime and storm damage to negligence on the nation's highways. In addition to making possible the selling of insurance policies, the money and capital markets have been used increasingly by businesses and consumers to "self insure" against risk. This simply means building up one's holdings of securities, deposits, etc., as a precaution against future loss. The liquidity of most financial instruments makes it easy to raise spendable cash quickly in an emergency.

Policy Function

Finally, in recent decades the financial markets have been the principal channel through which the federal government has carried out its policy of attempting to stabilize the economy and avoid excessive inflation. By manipulating interest rates and the availability of credit, government can affect the borrowing and spending plans of the public which, in turn, influence the growth of jobs, production, and the prices of goods and services. As we will see in subsequent chapters, this task of economic stabilization has been given largely to central banks, such as the Federal Reserve System.

TYPES OF FINANCIAL MARKETS WITHIN THE FINANCIAL SYSTEM

Charged with many different functions, the financial system fulfills its various roles through *markets* where financial claims and financial services are traded. These markets may be viewed as *channels* through which moves a vast flow of funds, continually being drawn upon by demanders of funds and continually being replenished by suppliers of funds.

The Money Market versus the Capital Market

The flow of funds through the financial markets may be divided into different segments, depending upon the characteristics of financial claims being traded and the needs of different groups. One of the most important divisions in the financial system is between the money market and the capital market.

The money market is designed for the making of short-term loans. It is the institution through which individuals and institutions with *temporary* surpluses of funds meet borrowers who have *temporary* funds shortages. Thus, the money market enables economic units (principally business firms and governments) to manage liquidity. By convention, a security or loan maturing *within one year or less* is considered to be a money market instrument. One of the principal functions of the money market is to finance the working-capital needs of corporations and to provide governments with short-term funds in lieu of tax collections. The money market also supplies funds for speculative buying of securities and commodities.

In contrast, the capital market is designed to finance long-term investments by businesses, governments, and households. Trading of funds in the capital market makes possible the construction of factories, highways, schools, and homes. Financial instruments in the capital market have original maturities of *more than one year* and range in size from small loans to very large, multimillion dollar credits.

Who are the principal suppliers and demanders of funds in the money market and capital market? In the money market commercial banks are the most important institutional supplier of funds (lender) to both business firms and governments. Nonfinancial business corporations with temporary cash surpluses also provide substantial short-term funds to banks, securities dealers, and other corporations in the money market. On the demand-for-funds side the largest borrower in the American money market is the U.S. Treasury, which borrows several billion dollars weekly. The largest and best-known corporations and securities dealers are also active borrowers in the money market through their offerings of short-term notes. Finally, there is the Federal Reserve System, which is charged by Congress with responsibility for regulating the flow of money and credit in the U.S. financial system and keeping the money market functioning smoothly. Due to the large size and strong financial standing of these well-known money market borrowers and lenders, money market instruments are considered to be high-quality, "near money" IOUs.

The principal suppliers and demanders of funds in the capital market are more varied than in the money market. Families and individuals, for example, tap the capital market when they borrow to finance a new home. State and local governments rely upon the capital market for funds to build schools and highways and provide essential services to the public. The U.S. Treasury draws upon the capital market in issuing longer-term notes and bonds to pay for federal government programs. The most important borrowers in the capital market are businesses of all sizes, which issue long-term IOUs to cover the purchase of equipment and the construction of new plants and other facilities. Ranged against these many borrowers in the capital market are financial institutions, such as banks, insurance companies, and pension funds, that supply the bulk of long-term funds.

Divisions of the Money and Capital Markets

The money market and the capital market may be further subdivided into smaller markets, each important to selected groups of demanders and suppliers of funds. Within the money market, for example, is the huge *Treasury bill* market. Treasury bills—a short-term government IOU—are a safe and popular investment medium for financial institutions and corporations of all sizes.

Nearly as large in total dollar volume is the market for *negotiable certificates of deposit* (CDs) issued by the largest, best-known commercial banks and other depository institutions. Depository institutions use the funds raised from CDs and other sources to extend loans to corporations and other borrowers. Two other important money market instruments evidencing loans to corporations are *bankers' acceptances* and *commercial paper*—both short-term IOUs issued by large, well-established borrowers of funds. Still another portion of the money market is devoted to trading in *federal funds*, which are essentially reserve balances of banks held at the Federal Reserve and with other banks that are immediately transferable anywhere by wire. Another segment of the money market reaches around the globe to encompass suppliers and demanders of short-term funds in Europe, Asia, and the Middle East. This is the vast and largely unregulated *Eurocurrency* market, where bank deposits denominated in the world's major trading currencies—the dollar, the franc, the pound, the yen, and the mark—are loaned to corporations and governments all over the globe.

The capital market, too, is divided into several major sectors, each having special characteristics and its own collection of suppliers and demanders of funds. For example, the largest segment of the capital market is devoted to *mortgage loans* to support the building of homes, apartments, and business structures such as factories and shopping centers. State and local governments sell their *tax-exempt (municipal) bonds* in another sector of the capital market. Households borrow in yet another segment of the capital market, using *consumer loans* to make purchases ranging from automobiles to home appliances. There is also an international capital market represented by *Eurobonds* and *Euronotes*.

Probably the best-known segment of the capital market is the market for *corporate stock* represented by the major exchanges, such as the New York Stock Exchange (NYSE) and the Tokyo Exchange and a vast over-the-counter (OTC) market for individual stocks. No matter where it is sold, however, each share of stock (equity) represents a certificate of ownership in a corporation, entitling the holder to receive any dividends that may be paid out of current company earnings. Corporations also sell a huge quantity of *corporate notes* and *bonds* in the capital market each year to raise long-term funds. These securities, unlike shares of stock, are pure IOUs, evidencing a debt owed plus an obligation to pay interest to the holder. A list of the principal financial instruments traded in the U.S. money and capital markets today is shown in Exhibit 1–7.

Open versus Negotiated Markets

Another distinction between markets in the financial system which is sometimes useful is that between open markets and negotiated markets. For example, some corporate bonds are sold in the open market to the highest bidder and bought and sold any number of times before they mature and are paid off. In contrast, in the negotiated market for corporate bonds, securities generally are sold to one or a few buyers under private contract and held to maturity.

An individual who goes to his or her local banker to secure a loan for a new car enters the negotiated market for auto loans. Most state and local government securities are sold in the open market, but a growing number

Exhibit 1–7   **Principal Financial Instruments Traded in the U.S. Money and Capital Markets, 1987** ($ Billions; End of First Quarter)

	Amount
Principal money market instruments:	
U.S. Treasury bills*	$ 406.2
Bank certificates of deposit ($100,000 +)	354.1
Securities issued by federal and federally sponsored agencies*	306.9
Federal funds sold and repurchase agreements	169.1
Eurodollar deposits†	321.3
Commercial paper	338.8
Bankers' dollar acceptances	66.1
Principal capital market instruments:	
Mortgages	$2,622.4
Common stocks‡	2,868.1
Corporate and foreign bonds‡	782.4
U.S. Treasury notes and bonds*	1,214.6
State and local government bonds and notes‡	466.1
Consumer loans‡	666.5

*Data as of April 1987.

†Liabilities owed by foreign branches of U.S. banks, payable in U.S. dollars.

‡Figures as of year-end 1985.

Source: Board of Governors of the Federal Reserve System.

are sold under a privately negotiated "treaty" with one or a few buyers. In the market for corporate stocks there are the major stock exchanges, which represent the open market. Operating at the same time, however, is the negotiated market for stock, in which a corporation may sell its entire stock issue to one or a handful of buyers.

Primary versus Secondary Markets

The financial markets may also be divided into primary markets and secondary markets. The primary market is for the trading of new securities never before issued. Its principal function is the raising of financial capital to support *new* investment in buildings, equipment, and inventories. You engage in a primary-market transaction when you purchase shares of stock just issued by a company, borrow money through a new mortgage to purchase a home, or negotiate a loan at the bank to restock the shelves of your business.

In contrast, the secondary market deals in securities previously issued. Its chief function is to provide liquidity to security investors—that is, provide an avenue for converting existing stocks, bonds, and other securities into ready cash. If you sell shares of stock or bonds you have been holding for some time to a relative or friend or call a broker and place an order for shares currently being traded on the American Stock Exchange, you are participating in a secondary-market transaction.

The volume of trading in the secondary market is far larger than trading in the primary market. However, the secondary market does *not* support new investment. Nevertheless, the primary and secondary markets are closely intertwined. For example, a rise in interest rates or security prices in the secondary market usually leads to a similar rise in prices or rates on primary-market securities and vice versa. This happens because investors frequently switch from one market to another in response to differences in price and yield.

Spot versus Futures, Forward, and Option Markets

We may also distinguish between *spot markets, futures* or *forward markets,* and *option markets.* A *spot market* is one where securities or financial services are traded for *immediate delivery* (usually within one or two business days). If you pick up the telephone and instruct your broker to purchase Telecom Corporation shares at today's going price, this is a spot market transaction. You expect to acquire ownership of Telecom shares within a matter of minutes or hours.

A *futures* or *forward market,* on the other hand, is designed to trade contracts calling for the *future delivery* of financial instruments. For example, you may call your broker and ask to purchase a contract from another investor calling for delivery to you of $1 million in U.S. Treasury bonds six months from today. The purpose of such a contract would be to reduce investor risk by agreeing on a price today rather than waiting six months when Treasury bond prices might have risen.

Finally, *options markets* also offer investors in the money and capital markets an opportunity to reduce the risk of adverse changes in security prices. These markets make possible the trading of options on selected stocks and bonds, which are agreements (contracts) that give an investor the right to either buy from or sell designated securities to the writer of the option at a guaranteed price at any time during the life of the contract. When the option agreement expires, however, it can no longer be used and becomes worthless.

We will see more clearly how and why such transactions take place when we explore the financial futures and options markets in Chapter 12 and the forward markets for foreign currencies in Chapter 28.

Factors Tying All Financial Markets Together

Each corner of the financial system represents, to some extent, a distinct market with its own special characteristics. Each segment is insulated from the others to some degree by investor preferences and by rules and regulations. Yet when interest rates and security prices change in one corner of the financial system, *all* of the financial markets will be affected eventually. This implies that, even though the financial system is split up into many different markets, there must be forces at work to tie all financial markets together.

Credit, the Common Commodity. One unifying factor is the fact that the basic commodity being traded in all financial markets is *credit*. The money market, as we have seen, provides short-term credit, while the capital market provides long-term credit. Borrowers can switch from one market to another, seeking the most favorable credit terms. It is not uncommon, for example, for an oil company to finance the construction of a drilling rig through short-term money market loans because interest rates in the capital market today are unusually high, only to seek long-term financing of the project later on when capital market conditions are more favorable. The shifting of borrowers between markets helps to weld the parts of the financial system closer together and to bring credit costs in different markets into balance with one another.

Speculation and Arbitrage. Another unifying element is profit seeking by demanders and suppliers of funds. *Speculators* in securities are continually on the lookout for opportunities to profit from their forecasts of future market developments or from small differences in prices or interest rates attached to different securities. A temporary rise in yields in one corner of the market, for example, quickly sends funds flowing toward that point. Speculators perform an important function in the financial markets by leveling out the prices of securities, buying those they believe are underpriced and selling those securities thought to be overpriced.

Still another unifying force in the financial markets is the investors who watch for profitable opportunities to arbitrage funds—transferring funds from one market to another whenever the prices of securities in different markets appear to be out of line with each other. *Arbitrageurs* help to maintain consistent prices *between* markets, aiding other security buyers in finding the best prices with minimal effort.

Perfect and Efficient Markets. There is considerable research evidence today suggesting that all financial markets are closely tied to one another because of their perfection and efficiency. What is a perfect market? It is one in which all available information affecting the value of financial instruments is freely available to everyone, the cost of carrying out transactions is zero or nearly so, and all market participants are price takers (rather than being able to dictate prices to the market). In such a market there are no significant government restrictions on trading and the movement of funds.

A perfect market has a very desirable characteristic: *the prices of financial instruments accurately reflect their inherent value and fully reflect all available information.* Moreover, any *new* information supplied to the market will instantly be impounded in a *new* set of prices. A market in which prices fully reflect all the latest available information is an efficient market. Numerous studies of the financial markets, spanning decades, suggest that they very closely approach the ideal of a perfect and efficient marketplace.

The Dynamic Financial System

There is an old saying: "You can't step into the same river twice, for rivers are ever flowing onward." As we shall see in future chapters of this book, that statement can be applied with equal force to the financial system—it is rapidly changing into a *new* financial system. As shown in Exhibit 1-8, powerful trends are underway today converting national financial systems into a global system, at work 24 hours a day to trade securities, attract savings, extend credit, and fulfill other needed roles. Satellites, computer terminals, fiber-optic cables, and thousands of other automated electronic

---

Exhibit 1–8   Key Trends in the Financial System for Today and Tomorrow

Increasing competition among all suppliers of financial services in all countries

Rapid growth of new technologies to produce and deliver financial services (faster and more efficient methods to store, process, and transfer financial information)

Broadening of financial markets to circle the globe (trading 24 hours a day in securities, loans, and other financial services) with many foreign institutions entering domestic markets

Deregulation of financial service firms by national and local governments (letting the free market operate more and more in the financial system to allocate resources and to price services)

Greater risks faced by financial service firms with more failures and government bail-outs

Rapid growth of debt issued by businesses, households, and governments relative to their incomes with more loan defaults and bankruptcies

Increasing consolidation of banks and other financial firms through mergers into larger and larger size companies (to reduce risk exposure, expand markets, and offset rising costs)

Increasing sophistication and awareness of borrowers and lenders of their alternative sources of financial services and a growing sensitivity of lenders to risk

Increasing emphasis on financial innovation (i.e., the development of many new services and new financial firms to produce and sell them)

systems now tie together financial service businesses and trading centers as widely dispersed as London, New York, Tokyo, Sydney, and Hong Kong. The result is intense worldwide competition for customers, the development of many new financial services, increased risks to both financial service firms and many of their customers, and a wave of mergers among banks and other financial institutions. One of the main purposes of this book is to help us understand why these trends are occurring and what they are likely to mean for all of us.

THE PLAN OF THIS BOOK

This text is divided into eight major sections, each devoted to a particular segment of the financial system.

Part One of the book provides an overview of the financial system—its role in the economy, major sectors, and basic characteristics. The emphasis here is on providing the reader with a broad-brush picture of the fundamental nature and purpose of transactions in the financial marketplace. The vital processes of saving and investment, lending and borrowing, and the creation and destruction of financial assets are described. This section concludes with a discussion of the major sources of data available today to students and researchers interested in following movements in interest rates, security prices, and the volume of borrowing and lending going on in the financial system.

Part Two is devoted to the study of financial institutions. Commercial banks, credit unions, savings and loan associations, savings banks, money market funds, insurance companies, pension funds, mutual funds, finance companies—these and other financial firms that dominate our financial system are analyzed in this section. The reader is presented with an overview of their financial characteristics, regulatory environment, and current problems.

Part Three examines the forces that shape and influence interest rates and the prices of financial instruments. Because the rate of interest is the key price in the financial system, this section begins in Chapter 7 with a review of major theories of interest rate determination. The measurement and behavior of interest rates and security prices are then addressed in Chapter 8. The next two chapters in Part Three are devoted to the factors (such as risk and inflation) that cause the interest rate and price of one security to differ from those of another, while Chapter 11 focuses on problems and methods for forecasting interest rates and for protecting against the risk of interest rate changes. Finally, Chapter 12 examines in detail two popular methods of hedging against interest rate risk—financial futures and options.

Part Four is aimed at the money market, beginning with an overview of the principal institutions and instruments that dominate money market activity around the world. Chapters in this section examine the characteristics of U.S. Treasury bills, federal funds, repurchase agreements, bank certificates of deposit, commercial paper, federal agency securities, bankers' acceptances, and Eurodollars. The section concludes with a chapter on some of the newest of short-term financial instruments—financial futures and options.

The borrowing habits and financial characteristics of consumers—families and individuals—are considered in Part Five. Chapter 18 presents an overview of consumer finance, examining the major categories of consumer debt outstanding today and recent changes in laws and regulations affecting the consumer. Chapter 19 is devoted to the largest of all consumer debt markets—residential mortgages—where new financial instruments are being developed today to make home ownership more affordable for individuals and families.

Part Six focuses on the activities of nonfinancial business firms in the money and capital markets. Chapter 20 covers business borrowing, principally the marketing and pricing of corporate bonds. Chapter 21 is concerned with the market for common and preferred stock. This chapter opens with a discussion of the basic characteristics of corporate stock and then proceeds to examine the structure of today's equities market.

The often dominating role of governments—federal, state, and local—within the financial system is taken up in Part Seven of the text. The first three chapters in this section are devoted to monetary policy and the Federal Reserve System. A brief history of the Federal Reserve System is presented along with an analysis of the operating structure of the Fed, its major policy tools, and its policy indicators. The fiscal operations of federal, state, and local governments are then examined in Chapters 25 and 26.

Finally, Part Eight of the text is devoted to the international financial system and future trends within the global financial system. Topics covered here include the economic benefits of international trade and finance, the history of changing monetary standards, and the balance-of-payments accounts. The markets for foreign currencies are examined in considerable detail, including the mechanics of modern foreign exchange trading. International banking institutions are discussed in Chapter 29 with special emphasis on U.S. bank operations abroad and the recent rapid growth of foreign banking activities in the United States. Finally, Chapter 30 concludes the book with an examination of current and future trends that are likely to reshape the financial system for years to come. This concluding chapter pays special attention to ongoing changes in the economy, the population, and technology that even now are bringing about profound changes in the money and capital markets.

Throughout this book there is a strong emphasis on the innovative character of modern financial systems and institutions. There has been a virtual explosion of new instruments and trading techniques within the financial system in recent years. Moreover, the pace of innovation in financial services and methods appears to be accelerating under the combined pressure of increased competition, rising costs, and burgeoning demand. As we will see in the pages that follow, these forces of innovation, competition, rising costs, and growing demand are profoundly reshaping the structure and operations of our whole financial system today.

STUDY QUESTIONS

1. Why is it important to understand how the financial system operates? In what ways is the financial system linked to the economy as a whole?

2. What are the principal functions of the financial system? How do the financial markets fulfill those functions?

3. Explain what is meant by saving and by investment. Why are they important to economic growth and the nation's standard of living?

4. Distinguish between money market and capital market, between open and negotiated markets, primary and secondary markets, and spot, forward, and futures markets. What are the principal divisions of each?

5. Why do interest rates and security prices in the various segments of the financial system tend to move in the same direction? What forces seem to bind the various parts of the financial system together?

6. What is a *perfect* market? An *efficient* market? Identify some features of real-world markets which in your judgment limit their efficiency.

PROBLEMS

1. Please *classify* the following financial transactions as to whether they fit in: (a) the money market or the capital market; (b) the primary or the secondary market; (c) the open or negotiated market; and (d) the spot or futures/forward market. (Note: The transactions below may fit in more than one of the above categories of markets. Be sure to include *all* the appropriate types of markets that each transaction fits.)
   Financial Transactions to Classify:

   a. You visit a local bank today and secure a three-year loan to finance the purchase of a new car and some furniture.
   b. You purchase a new U.S. Treasury bill for $9,800 through the Federal Reserve bank in a neighboring city for delivery today.
   c. Responding to a rise in the price of Texaco common stock, you have just purchased 100 shares of that company's stock by a phone call to your broker who is linked to a major stock exchange.
   d. Concerned about recent trends in the price of the Mexican peso, you contact a large money-center bank in the region and purchase 10,000

pesos at today's dollar-peso exchange rate for delivery in six months when you plan to fly to Mexico City.

  e. Receiving an unexpected windfall, you contact a local savings and loan association this afternoon and purchase a $15,000, two-year CD, bearing an interest rate that you and the association's officer have agreed upon.

  f. The corporation you represent needs to raise $25 million immediately to purchase raw materials. You contact a New York securities dealer who agrees to advertise the sale of $25 million in commercial paper, maturing in 90 days, this afternoon. The dealer expects to sell all the notes within 24 hours.

2. What *functions of the financial system* do the following transactions illustrate or represent? (Note: Some transactions may involve more than one function. Be sure to identify *all* the financial system functions involved in each transaction.)

  a. James Rhodes purchases health and accident insurance policies through the company where he works.

  b. Sharon MacArthur uses her credit card to purchase wallpaper for a home remodeling project.

  c. Fearing a slowdown in the nation's rate of economic growth and increasing joblessness, the Federal Reserve System moves to lower interest rates and accelerate the growth of the nation's money supply.

  d. Dynamic Corporation places some of its current earnings in a bank CD, anticipating a need for funds in about a year in order to build a new warehouse.

  e. The U.S. Treasury sells new bonds in the open market to cover a large deficit.

  f. Cal Lewis hopes to put his three children, ages 7, 9, and 10, through college some day. Accordingly, he purchases an annuity plan from a life insurance company and begins buying U.S. savings bonds at work.

  g. Needing immediate spending power, Hillcrest Corporation sells its holdings of Denton County bonds through a security broker.

SELECTED REFERENCES

Fama, Eugene F., and Merton H. Miller. *The Theory of Finance.* New York: Holt, Rinehart & Winston, 1972.

Polakoff, Murray E., and Thomas A. Durkin et al. *Financial Institutions and Markets.* 2nd ed. Boston: Houghton Mifflin, 1981.

Simpson, Thomas D. "Developments in the U.S. Financial System Since the Mid-1970s," *Federal Reserve Bulletin,* January 1988, pp. 1–13.

Chapter 2

Financial Assets, Money, and Financial Transactions

Learning Objectives in This Chapter

- To examine the different ways in which funds flow from lenders to borrowers within the financial system.
- To explore the nature and characteristics of *financial assets*—how they are created and destroyed in the money and capital markets.
- To examine the critical role played by financial intermediaries and other financial institutions in lending and borrowing and creating and destroying financial assets within the financial system.

Key Terms and Concepts in This Chapter

Financial asset	Balanced-budget unit	Depository institutions
Money	Direct finance	Contractual institutions
Equities	Semi-direct finance	Investment institutions
Debt securities	Indirect finance	Disintermediation
Deficit-budget unit	Secondary securities	
Surplus-budget unit	Primary securities	

THE financial system is the mechanism through which loanable funds reach borrowers. Through the operation of the financial markets, money is exchanged for financial claims in the form of stocks, bonds, and other securities. And through the exchange of money for financial claims, the economy's capacity to produce goods and services is increased. This happens because the money and capital markets provide the financial resources needed for investment. While it is true that the financial markets deal mainly in the exchange of paper claims and bookkeeping entries, these markets provide an indispensable conduit for the conversion of savings into investment, accelerating the economy's growth and development.

This chapter looks closely at the essential role played by the financial markets in converting savings into investment and how that role has changed over time. We begin by observing that nearly all financial transactions between buyers and sellers involve the creation or destruction of a special kind of asset—a financial asset. Moreover, financial assets possess a number of characteristics that make them unique among all the assets held by individuals and institutions. In the next section we consider the nature of financial assets and how they are created and destroyed through the workings of the financial system.

THE CREATION OF FINANCIAL ASSETS

What is a financial asset? It is a claim against the income or wealth of a business firm, household, or unit of government, represented usually by a certificate, receipt, or other legal document, and usually created by the lending of money. Familiar examples include stocks, bonds, insurance policies, and deposits held in a commercial bank, credit union, or savings bank.

Characteristics of Financial Assets

Financial assets do *not* provide a continuing stream of services to their owner as does a home or an apartment, an automobile, or a washing machine. These assets are sought after because they promise *future* returns to their owners and serve as a store of value (purchasing power).

A number of other features make financial assets unique. They cannot be depreciated because they do not wear out like physical goods. Moreover, their physical condition or form is generally *not* relevant in determining their market value (price). A stock certificate is not more or less valuable, for example, because of the size or quality of paper it is printed on or whether it is frayed around the edges. Because financial assets are generally represented by a piece of paper (certificate or contract) or by information stored in a computer file, they have little or no value as a commodity, and their cost of transport and storage is low. Finally, financial assets are *fungible*—they can be easily changed in form and interchanged with or substituted for other assets. Thus, a bond or stock usually can be quickly converted into cash at low cost and then subsequently converted into any other asset the holder desires.

Different Kinds of Financial Assets

While there are thousands of different financial assets outstanding at any one time, they generally fall into one of three categories: money, equities, or debt securities.

Any financial asset that is generally accepted in payment for purchases of goods and services is money. Thus, checking accounts and Federal Reserve currency are financial assets serving as payment media and therefore are forms of money. Later in this chapter we will discuss more fully the special features and importance of money as a financial asset. Equities (more commonly known as stock) represent ownership in a business firm and, as such, are claims against the firm's profits and against proceeds from the sale of any of its assets. We usually further subdivide equities into *common stock,* which entitles its holder to vote for the members of a firm's board of directors and therefore determine company policy, and *preferred stock,* which normally carries no voting privilege but does entitle its holder to a fixed share of the firm's net earnings ahead of the common stockholders.

Debt securities include such familiar financial claims as *bonds, notes,* and *accounts payable.* Legally these financial assets entitle their holder to a priority claim over the holders of equities to the assets and income of an individual, business firm, or unit of government. Usually that claim is fixed in amount and time (maturity) and, depending on the terms of the *indenture* (contract) accompanying most debt securities, may be backed up by the pledge of specific assets as collateral. Financial analysts usually divide debt securities into two broad classes: (1) *negotiable,* which can easily be transferred from holder to holder as a marketable security; and (2) *nonnegotiable,* which cannot legally be transferred to another party. Passbook savings accounts and U.S. savings bonds are good examples of nonnegotiable debt securities. In this book our primary focus is on negotiable (marketable) instruments such as Treasury bonds and corporate notes.

The Creation Process for Financial Assets

How are financial assets created? We may illustrate this process using a very rudimentary financial system in which there are only two economic units—a household and a business firm.

Assume that this financial system is *closed* so that no external transactions with other units are possible. Each unit holds certain assets accumulated over the years as a result of its saving out of current income. The household, for example, may have accumulated furniture, an automobile, books, clothes, and other items needed to provide entertainment, food, shelter, and transportation. The business firm holds inventories of goods to be sold, raw materials, machinery and equipment, a building, and other assets required to produce its product and sell it to the public.

The financial position of these two economic units is presented in the form of balance sheets, shown in Exhibit 2–1. A *balance sheet,* of course, is a financial statement prepared as of a certain date, showing a particular unit's assets, liabilities, and net worth. *Assets* represent the accumulated uses of funds made by economic units, while *liabilities* and *net worth* represent the various sources of funds that economic units have drawn upon to acquire the assets they now hold. The net worth account represents total savings accumulated over time by each economic unit. A balance sheet must always balance, so that total assets (accumulated uses of funds) must equal total liabilities plus net worth (accumulated sources of funds).

The household in our example holds total assets valued at $20,000, including an automobile, clothes, furniture, and cash. Because the household's financial statement must balance, total liabilities and net worth also add up to $20,000, all of which in this instance happens to come from net worth (accumulated savings). The business firm holds total assets amounting to $100,000, including a building housing the firm's offices, equipment,

Exhibit 2–1   Balance Sheets of Units in a Simple Financial System

HOUSEHOLD
Balance Sheet

Assets*		Liabilities and Net Worth†	
Cash	$ 13,000	Net worth (accumulated savings)	$ 20,000
Furniture	1,000		
Clothes	1,500		
Automobile	4,000		
Other assets	500		
		Total liabilities	
Total assets	$ 20,000	and net worth	$ 20,000

BUSINESS FIRM
Balance Sheet

Assets*		Liabilities and Net Worth†	
Inventories of goods	$ 10,000	Net worth (accumulated savings)	$100,000
Machinery and equipment	25,000		
Building	60,000		
Other assets	5,000		
		Total liabilities	
Total assets	$100,000	and net worth	$100,000

*Accumulated uses of funds.

†Accumulated sources of funds.

and machinery, and an inventory of unsold goods. The firm's only source of funds currently is net worth (accumulated savings), also valued at $100,000.

By today's standards the two balance sheets shown in Exhibit 2–1 are most unusual. Neither the household nor the business firm has any outstanding debt (liabilities). Each unit is entirely self-financed, because each has acquired its assets by saving and spending within its current income and not by borrowing. In the terminology of finance, both the household and the business firm have engaged in *internal financing*—the use of current income and accumulated savings to acquire assets. In the case of the household, it has accumulated its savings by taking some portion of each period's income and setting money aside rather than spending all its income on current consumption. The business firm has abstained from paying out all its revenues in expenses (including stockholder dividends). Instead, some portion of the firm's cash inflow each period has been set aside in the form of retained earnings which flow into its net worth account (accumulated savings).

For most businesses and households, internally generated funds are the most important resources for acquiring assets. For example, in the U.S. economy half or more of all investment in plant, equipment, and inventories carried out by business firms each year is financed internally rather than by borrowing. Households as a group save substantially more than they borrow each year, with the savings flowing into purchases of real assets, such as homes, automobiles, appliances, and clothing, and into sizable purchases of stocks, bonds, and other financial assets.

Suppose the business firm in our rudimentary financial system wishes to purchase new equipment in the form of a drill press. Due to inflation and shortages of key raw materials, however, the cost of the new drill press has been increasing rapidly. Internal sources of funds are not sufficient to cover the equipment's full cost. What can be done? There are four likely alternatives: (1) postpone the purchase of the new equipment until sufficient savings can be accumulated to cover its cost; (2) sell off some existing assets to raise the necessary funds; (3) borrow all or a portion of the needed funds; or (4) issue new stock (equity securities).

Time is frequently a determining factor here. Postponement of the equipment purchase probably will result in lost sales and lost profits. In the real world where there is not one business firm, as in our example, but many serving the same market. A competitor may rush ahead to expand its operations and capture some share of this firm's market. Then too, in an environment of inflation, the new drill press surely will cost even more in the future than it does now. While selling some existing assets to raise the necessary funds is a distinct possibility, this may take time, and there is the risk of substantial loss, especially if fixed assets must be sold. The third alternative—borrowing—has the advantage of raising funds quickly, and the interest cost on the loan is tax deductible.[1] The firm could sell additional stock if it hesitated to take on a debt obligation, but equity financing is usually much more expensive than borrowing and requires more time to arrange.

If the business firm decides to borrow, who will lend the funds that it needs? Obviously, in this two-unit financial system the household must provide the needed funds. The firm must engage in *external financing* by issuing to the household securities evidencing a loan of money. In general, if any economic unit wishes to add to its holdings of assets but lacks the necessary resources to do so, it can raise additional funds by issuing financial liabilities (borrowing)—provided a buyer of those IOUs can be found. The buyer will regard the IOUs as an asset—a financial asset—which may earn income unless the borrower goes out of business and defaults on his or her loan.

Suppose the business firm decides to borrow by issuing a liability (debt security) in the amount of $10,000 in order to pay for its new drill press. Because the firm is promising an attractive interest rate on this new IOU, the household willingly acquires it as a financial asset. This asset is *intangible*—a mere promise to pay $10,000 at maturity plus a promised stream of interest payments over time. The borrowing and creation of this financial asset may be shown on the balance sheets of these two economic units. As shown in Exhibit 2–2, the household has purchased the firm's IOU by using some of its accumulated cash. Its total assets are unchanged. Instead of holding $13,000 in non-interest-bearing cash, the household now holds an interest-bearing financial asset in the form of a $10,000 debt security and $3,000 in cash. The business firm has increased its stock of machinery and equipment from $25,000 to $35,000 after purchasing the new equipment, but also has incurred new debt amounting to $10,000. The firm's total assets and total liabilities *increase* due to the combined effect of borrowing and the acquisition of a productive real asset.

FINANCIAL ASSETS AND THE FINANCIAL SYSTEM

This simple example illustrates several important points concerning the operation and role of the financial system in the economy. First, the act of borrowing simultaneously gives rise to the creation of an equal volume of financial assets. In the foregoing example, the $10,000 financial asset held by the household lending money is exactly matched by the $10,000 liability

---

[1]An added advantage associated with issuing debt is the *leverage effect*. If the firm can earn more from purchasing and using the new equipment than the cost of borrowing funds, the surplus return will flow to the stockholders in the form of increased earnings. Earning per share of stock will rise, increasing the value of the company's stock. The result is favorable (positive) financial leverage. Unfortunately, leverage is a two-edged sword. If the firm earns less than the cost of borrowed funds, the stockholders' losses will be magnified as a result of unfavorable (negative) financial leverage.

Exhibit 2–2   **Unit Balance Sheets Following the Purchase of Equipment and the Issuance of a Financial Asset**

HOUSEHOLD
Balance Sheet

Assets*		Liabilities and Net Worth†	
Cash	$ 3,000	Net worth	$ 20,000
Financial asset	10,000		
Furniture	1,000		
Clothes	1,500		
Automobile	4,000		
Other assets	500		
		Total liabilities	
Total assets	$ 20,000	and net worth	$ 20,000

BUSINESS FIRM
Balance Sheet

Assets*			Liabilities and Net Worth†	
Inventories of goods		$ 10,000	Liabilities	$ 10,000
Machinery and equipment:			Net worth	100,000
Existing equipment	$ 25,000			
New equipment	10,000			
Total machinery and equipment		35,000		
Building		60,000		
Other assets		5,000		
			Total liabilities	
Total assets		$110,000	and net worth	$110,000

*Accumulated uses of funds.

†Accumulated sources of funds.

of the business firm borrowing money. This suggests another way of defining a financial asset: *Any asset held by a business firm, government, or household that is also recorded as a liability or claim on some other economic unit's balance sheet is a financial asset.* As we have seen, many different kinds of assets satisfy this definition, including common and preferred stock, corporate and government bonds, and deposits and loans held with a financial institution.

For the entire financial system, the sum of all financial assets must equal the total of all financial liabilities and claims outstanding. In contrast, real assets, such as automobiles, furniture, machinery, and buildings, are not necessarily matched by claims or liabilities somewhere in the financial system.

This distinction between *financial assets* and *liabilities,* on the one hand, and *real assets,* on the other, is worth pursuing with an example. Suppose you borrow $4,000 from the bank to purchase an automobile. Your balance sheet will now contain a liability in the amount of $4,000. The bank from which you borrowed the funds will record the transaction as a loan—an interest-bearing financial asset—appearing on the asset side of its balance sheet in the like amount of $4,000. On the asset side of your balance sheet appears the market value of the automobile—a real asset. The value of the real asset probably exceeds $4,000, since most banks expect a borrower to supply some of his or her own funds rather than borrowing the full purchase price. Let's say the automobile was sold to you for $5,000 with $1,000 of the cost coming out of your savings account and $4,000 from the bank loan. Then, your balance sheet would contain a new real asset (automobile) valued at $5,000, a liability (bank loan) of $4,000, and your savings account (a financial asset) would decline by $1,000.

Clearly, there are two equalities which hold for this transaction and also hold whenever money is loaned and borrowed in the financial system. First,

$$\begin{array}{ll} \text{Volume of financial} & \text{Volume of liabilities} \\ \text{assets created} & = \text{issued by borrowers} \end{array} \qquad (2\text{--}1)$$

$$\begin{array}{ll} \text{In this case a bank} & \text{A borrower's IOU} \\ \text{loan of \$4,000} & = \text{of \$4,000} \end{array}$$

Second,

$$\text{Total uses of funds} = \text{Total sources of funds} \qquad (2\text{--}2)$$

$$\begin{array}{ll} \text{Purchase of a} & = \text{Issue of a \$4,000} \\ \text{\$5,000 automobile} & \text{borrower IOU} + \$1,000 \\ & \text{drawn from a savings} \\ & \text{account} \end{array}$$

Every financial asset in existence represents the lending or investing of money transferred from one economic unit to another.

Because the sum of all financial assets created must always equal the amount of all liabilities and claims outstanding, the amount of lending in the financial system must always equal the amount of borrowing going on. In effect, *financial assets and liabilities (claims) cancel each other out across the whole financial system.* We can illustrate this fact by reference to the balance sheet of any unit in the economy—business firm, household, or government. The following must be true for all balance sheets:

$$\text{Total assets} = \text{Total liabilities} + \text{Net worth} \qquad (2\text{--}3)$$

Because all assets may be classified as either real assets or financial assets, it follows that

$$\text{Real assets} + \text{Financial assets} = \text{Total liabilities} + \text{Net worth} \quad (2\text{--}4)$$

Because the volume of financial assets outstanding must always equal the volume of liabilities and claims in existence, it follows that the aggregate volume of real assets held in the economy must equal the total amount of net worth. Therefore, for the economy and financial system as a whole:

$$\text{Total financial assets} = \text{Total liabilities} \qquad (2\text{--}5)$$

$$\text{Total real assets} = \text{Net worth (i.e., accumulated savings)} \qquad (2\text{--}6)$$

This means that the value of all buildings, bridges, highways, machinery, schools, and other real assets in existence matches the total amount of *saving* carried out by all businesses, households, and units of government. We are not better off in real terms by the mere creation of financial assets and liabilities. These are only pieces of paper or blips on a computer screen evidencing a loan or investment of money. Rather, society increases its wealth only by saving and thus increasing the quantity of real assets, for these assets enable the economy to produce more goods and services in the future.

Does this suggest that the creation of financial assets and liabilities—one of the basic functions of the financial system—is a useless exercise? Not at all. The mere act of saving by one economic unit does not guarantee that those savings will be used to build or purchase real assets which add to society's stock of wealth. In modern economies saving and investment usually are carried out by different groups. In the U.S. economy, for example, the bulk of saving is carried out by households, while business firms account for the majority of investments in productive real assets. Some mechanism is needed to ensure that savings flow from those who save to those who invest in real assets.

The *financial system* provides the essential channel necessary for the creation and exchange of financial assets between savers and borrowers so that real assets can be acquired. Without that channel for savings, the total volume of investment in the economy surely would be reduced, and the growth of investment and production would be diminished. All investment by individual economic units would have to depend on the ability of those same units to save (i.e., engage in internal financing). Many promising investment opportunities would have to be foregone or postponed due to insufficient savings. Society's scarce resources would be allocated less efficiently than is possible with a system of financial markets. Growth in the nation's income, employment, and standard of living would be seriously impaired.

LENDING AND BORROWING IN THE FINANCIAL SYSTEM

Business firms, households, and governments play a wide variety of roles in modern financial systems. It is quite common for an individual or institution to be a lender of funds in one period and a borrower in the next, or to do both simultaneously. Indeed, financial intermediaries, such as banks and insurance companies, are in the business of operating on both sides of the financial markets, borrowing funds from customers by issuing attractive financial claims and simultaneously making loans available to other customers. Virtually all of us at one point or another in our lifetimes will be involved in the financial system as a borrower or lender of funds, and probably both.

A number of years ago two economists, Gurley and Shaw (1956, 1960), pointed out that each business firm, household, or unit of government active in the financial system must conform to the following identity:

Expenditures out of current income − Current income receipts	= − Change in holdings of debt and equity Change in holdings of financial assets during the current period

In symbols,

$$E - R = \Delta D - \Delta FA \qquad (2\text{--}7)$$

If our current expenditures (E) exceed our current receipts (R), we usually make up the difference by: (1) reducing our holdings of financial assets ($-\Delta FA$)—for example, by drawing money out of a savings account; (2) issuing debt or stock ($+\Delta D$); or (3) using some combination of both. On the other hand, if our receipts (R) in the current period are larger than current expenditures (E), we can (1) build up our holdings of financial assets ($+\Delta FA$)—for example, by placing money in a savings account or buying a few shares of stock; (2) pay off some outstanding debt or retire stock previously issued by our business firm ($-\Delta D$); or (3) do some combination of both.

It follows that for any given period of time (e.g., week, month, or year) the individual economic unit must fall into one of three groups:

Deficit-budget unit $E > R$; and so $\Delta D > \Delta FA$
    (net borrower of funds)

Surplus-budget unit $R > E$; and thus, $\Delta FA > \Delta D$
    (net lender of funds)

Balanced-budget unit $R = E$; and therefore, $\Delta D = \Delta FA$.
    (neither net lender nor
    net borrower)

A net lender of funds is really a net supplier of funds to the financial system. He or she accomplishes this function by purchasing financial assets, paying off debt, or retiring equity (stock). In contrast, a net borrower of funds is a net demander of funds from the financial system, selling financial assets, issuing new debt, or selling new stock. The business and government sectors of the economy tend to be net borrowers (demanders) of funds, while the household sector, composed of all families and individuals, tends to be a net lender (supplier) of funds. This is shown clearly in data on purchases of financial assets and increases in liabilities compiled each year by the Federal Reserve System for the U.S. economy. For example, as Exhibit 2–3 reveals, in 1987 households acquired about $270 billion in financial assets and issued about $200 billion in liabilities, making this sector of the U.S. economy a net lender of funds to the financial markets in the amount of about $70 billion. In contrast, nonfinancial businesses were net borrowers of just over $58 billion, while the federal government borrowed net almost $170 billion during the year.

Of course, over any given period of time any one household, business firm, or unit of government may be a deficit-, surplus-, or balanced-budget unit. In fact, from day to day and week to week, our major institutions in the business and government sectors fluctuate from being deficit-budget units to surplus-budget units and back again. Consider a large corporation such as Ford or Exxon. One week such a firm may be a net lender, supplying monies to deficit-budget units in the financial system for short periods of time through purchases of U.S. Treasury bills, bank CDs, and other financial assets. The following week a dividend payment may be due company stockholders, bonds must be refunded, or purchases made to increase inventories and expand plant and equipment. At this point the firm may become a net borrower of funds, drawing down its holdings of financial assets, securing loans by issuing financial liabilities, or selling equity (stock). Most of the large institutions that interact in the nation's financial markets continually fluctuate from one side of the market to the other. This is also true of most households today. One of the most important contributions of the financial system to our daily lives is in permitting businesses, households, and governments to adjust their financial position from that of net borrower to net lender and back again, smoothly and efficiently.

Exhibit 2–3   Net Acquisitions of Financial Assets and Liabilities by Major Sectors of the U.S. Economy, 1987* ($ Billions)

	Net Acquisition of Financial Assets during Year	Net Increase in Liabilities during Year	Net Lender (+) or Net Borrower (−) of Funds
Households	$272.5	$201.9	+ 70.6
Nonfinancial businesses	67.9	126.5	− 58.6
State and local governments	58.1	60.5	− 2.4
Federal government	− 81.2	87.4	− 168.6

*Figures are annualized rates for the first quarter of the year.

Source: Board of Governors of the Federal Reserve System, *Flow of Funds Accounts, 1st quarter 1987*, Statistical Release of the Division of Research and Statistics.

MONEY AS A FINANCIAL ASSET

What Is Money?

The most important financial asset in the economy is *money*. All financial assets are valued in terms of money and flows of funds between lenders and borrowers occur through the medium of money. Money itself is a true financial asset because all forms of money in use today in most countries are a claim against some institution, public or private, and are issued as debt. For example, one of the largest components of the U.S. money supply today is the checking account, which is the debt of a commercial bank. Another important component of the money supply is currency and coin, or pocket money held by the public. The bulk of currency in use today in the United States consists of Federal Reserve notes, representing debt obligations of the 12 Federal Reserve banks. In fact, if the Federal Reserve ever closed its doors (a highly unlikely event), Fed notes held by the public would be a first claim against the assets of the Federal Reserve banks. As we will see in Chapter 24, some definitions of the nation's money supply today include savings accounts at banks and credit unions, shares in money market mutual funds, and even overnight loans between financial institutions and their customers—all forms of debt, giving rise to financial assets.

The Functions of Money

Money performs a wide variety of important services. It serves as a *standard of value* for all goods and services. Without money the price of every good or service we might wish to trade would have to be expressed in terms of exchange ratios with all other goods and services—an enormous information burden for both buyers and sellers. We would need to know, for example, how many loaves of bread would be required to purchase a quart of milk or what quantity of firewood might exchange for a suit of clothes. To trade just 12 different goods and services, we would have to remember 66 different exchange ratios. In contrast, the existence of money as a common standard of value permits us to express the prices of all goods and services in terms of only one good—the monetary unit. In the United States that unit is the dollar; in Japan, it is the yen. But whatever the monetary unit is called, it always has a constant price in terms of itself (i.e., a dollar always exchanges for a dollar). The prices of all other goods and services are expressed in multiples or in fractions of the monetary unit.

Money also serves as a *medium of exchange*. It is usually the only financial asset which virtually every business, household, and unit of government will accept in payment for goods and services. By itself, money typically has little or no use as a commodity (except when gold or silver, for example, is used as the medium of exchange). People accept money only because they know they can exchange it at a later date for goods and services.

This is why modern governments have been able to separate the monetary unit from precious metals like gold and silver bullion and successfully issue fiat money (i.e., pieces of paper) not tied to any particular commodity. Money's service as a medium of exchange frees us from the terrible constraints of barter, allowing us to separate the act of selling goods and services from the act of buying goods and services. With a medium of exchange, buyers and sellers no longer need to have an exact coincidence of wants in terms of quality, quantity, time, and location.

Money serves also as a *store of value*—a reserve of future purchasing power. Purchasing power can be stored in currency or in a checking account until the time is right to buy. Of course, money is not always a good store of value. The value of money, measured by its purchasing power, can experience marked fluctuations. For example the prices of consumer goods represented in the U.S. cost of living index more than tripled between 1967 and 1988. If individuals or families had purchased in each of these years the identical market basket of goods and services represented in the cost of living index, they would have found that the purchasing power of each unit of their money had decreased by about two thirds during this period.

Money functions as the *only perfectly liquid asset* in the financial system. An asset is liquid if it can be converted into cash quickly with little or no loss in value. A liquid asset possesses three essential characteristics: price stability, ready marketability, and reversibility. An asset must be considered *liquid* if its price tends to be reasonably stable over time, if it has an active resale market, and if it is reversible so that investors can recover their original investment without loss.

All assets—real and financial—differ in their degrees of liquidity. Generally, financial assets, especially U.S. Treasury bills, bank deposits, and stocks and bonds issued by major corporations, tend to be highly liquid, while real assets, such as a home or an automobile, may be extremely difficult to sell in a hurry without taking a substantial loss. Money is, of course, the most liquid of all assets because it need not be converted into any other form in order to be spent. Unfortunately, the most liquid assets, including money, tend to carry the lowest rates of return. One measure of the "cost" of holding money is the income foregone by the owner who fails to convert his or her money balances into more profitable investments in real or financial assets. The rate of interest, which is the price of obtaining credit in the financial system, is a measure of the penalty suffered by an investor for not converting money into income-earning assets.

TYPES OF FINANCIAL TRANSACTIONS

Financial systems are never static; they change constantly in response to shifting demands from the public, the development of new technology, and changes in laws and regulations. Competition in the financial marketplace forces financial institutions to respond to public need by developing new, better-quality, and more convenient financial services. Over time, the system of financial markets has evolved from simple to more complex ways of carrying out financial transactions. The growth of industrial centers with enormous capital investment needs and the emergence of a huge middle class of savers have played major roles in the gradual evolution of the financial system.

Whether simple or complex, all financial systems perform at least one basic function. They move scarce funds from those who save and lend (surplus-budget units) to those who wish to borrow and invest (deficit-budget units). In the process, money is exchanged for financial assets. However, the transfer of funds from savers to borrowers can be accomplished in at least three different ways. We label these methods of funds transfer: (1) direct finance, (2) semidirect finance, and (3) indirect finance. Most financial systems have evolved gradually over time toward greater reliance upon indirect finance.

Direct Finance

With the direct financing technique, borrower and lender meet each other and exchange funds in return for financial assets. You engage in direct finance when you borrow money from a friend and give him or her your IOU or when you purchase stocks or bonds directly from the company issuing them. We usually call the claims arising from direct finance *primary securities* because they flow directly from the borrower to the ultimate lender of funds. (Exhibit 2–4 illustrates the process of direct financing between borrowers and lenders.)

Direct finance is the simplest method of carrying out financial transactions. However, it has a number of serious limitations. For one thing, both borrower and lender must desire to exchange the same amount of funds at the same time. More important, the lender must be willing to accept the borrower's IOU, which may be quite risky, illiquid, or slow to mature. Clearly, there must be a coincidence of wants between surplus- and deficit-budget units in terms of the amount and form of a loan. Without that fundamental coincidence, direct finance breaks down.

Exhibit 2–4   **Direct Finance**

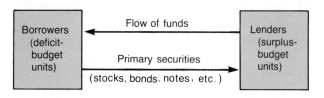

Another problem is that both lender and borrower must frequently incur substantial information costs simply to find each other. The borrower may have to contact many lenders before finding the one surplus-budget unit with just the right amount of funds and a willingness to take on the borrower's IOU. Not surprisingly, direct finance soon gives way to other methods of carrying out financial transactions as money and capital markets develop.

Semidirect Finance

Early in the history of most financial systems, a new form of financial transaction appears which we call semidirect finance. Some individuals and business firms become securities brokers and dealers whose essential function is to bring surplus- and deficit-budget units together, thereby reducing information costs (see Exhibit 2–5).

We must distinguish here between a broker and a dealer in securities. A *broker* is merely an individual or financial institution who provides information concerning possible purchases and sales of securities. Either a buyer or a seller of securities may contact a broker, whose job is simply to bring buyers and sellers together. A *dealer* also serves as a middleman between buyers and sellers, but the dealer actually acquires the seller's securities in the hope of marketing them at a later time at a more favorable price. Dealers take a "position of risk" because, by purchasing securities outright for their own portfolios, they are subject to risk of loss if those securities decline in value.[2]

Semidirect finance is an improvement over direct finance in a number of ways. It lowers the search (or information) costs for participants in the

Exhibit 2–5   **Semidirect Finance**

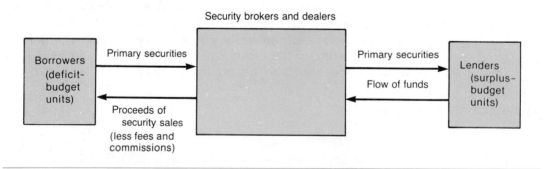

Security brokers and dealers

Borrowers (deficit-budget units) — Primary securities → — Proceeds of security sales (less fees and commissions) ← — Primary securities → — Flow of funds ← — Lenders (surplus-budget units)

---

[2]The meaning of the term *position of risk* is discussed in greater detail in Chapter 14, where the activities of government securities dealers are examined.

financial markets. Frequently a dealer will split up a large issue of primary securities into smaller units affordable by even buyers of modest means and thereby expand the flow of savings into investment. In addition, brokers and dealers facilitate the development and growth of secondary markets where securities can be offered for resale.

Despite the important contribution of brokers and dealers to the functioning of the financial system, the semidirect finance approach is not without its limitations. The ultimate lender still winds up holding the borrower's securities, and therefore the lender must be willing to accept the risk, liquidity, and maturity characteristics of the borrower's IOU. There still must be a fundamental coincidence of wants and needs between surplus- and deficit-budget units for semidirect financial transactions to take place.

Indirect Finance

The limitations of both direct and semidirect finance stimulated the development of indirect finance carried out with the help of *financial intermediaries*. Financial intermediaries active in today's financial markets include commercial banks, insurance companies, credit unions, finance companies, savings and loan associations, savings banks, pension funds, mutual funds, and similar organizations. (See Exhibit 2–6.) Their fundamental role in the financial system is to serve both ultimate lenders and borrowers, but in a much more complete way than brokers and dealers do. Financial intermediaries issue securities of their own—secondary securities—to ultimate lend-

---

Exhibit 2–6   Major Financial Institutions Active in the Money and Capital Markets

Financial Intermediaries

Depository institutions:	Contractual institutions:
Commercial banks	Life insurance companies
Nonbank thrifts:	Property-casualty insurers
Savings and loan associations	Pension funds
Savings banks	Investment institutions:
Credit unions	Investment companies (mutual funds)
Money market funds	Real estate investment trusts
Other financial intermediaries:	
Finance companies	
Government credit agencies	

Other Financial Institutions

Investment bankers	Security dealers
Mortgage bankers	Security brokers

ers and at the same time accept IOUs from borrowers—primary securities (see Exhibit 2–7).

The secondary securities issued by financial intermediaries include such familiar financial instruments as checking and saving accounts; health, life and accident insurance policies; retirement plans; and shares in a mutual fund. For the most part these securities share a number of common characteristics. They generally carry *low risk of default.* For example, most deposits held in U.S. banks and credit unions are insured by an agency of the federal government up to $100,000. Moreover, the majority of secondary securities can be acquired in *small denominations,* affordable by savers of limited means. For the most part secondary securities are *liquid* and therefore can be converted quickly into cash with little risk of significant loss for the purchaser. Financial intermediaries in recent years have tried to make savings as *convenient* as possible through mail transactions services and transfer of funds by plastic card, computer terminal, and telephone in order to reduce transactions costs to the saver.

Financial intermediaries accept primary securities from those who need credit, and in doing so, take on financial assets which many savers, especially those with limited funds and limited knowledge of the market, would find unacceptable. For example, many large corporations require billions of dollars in credit financing each year—sums that would make it impractical to deal directly with thousands of small savers. By pooling the resources of scores of small savings accounts, however, a large bank or other intermediary frequently can service the credit needs of several large firms simultaneously. In addition, many primary securities, even those issued by some of the largest borrowers, are not readily marketable and carry sizable risk of borrower default—a situation usually not acceptable to the small saver. By issuing its own securities, which are attractive to ultimate lenders (savers), and accepting primary securities from borrowers, the financial intermediary acts to satisfy the financial needs of *both* surplus- and deficit-budget units in the economy.

Exhibit 2–7   Indirect Finance

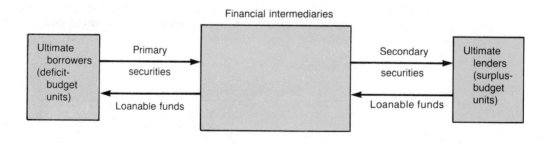

RELATIVE SIZE AND IMPORTANCE
OF MAJOR FINANCIAL INSTITUTIONS

Financial institutions differ greatly in their relative importance within the U.S. financial system. Measured by total financial assets, *commercial banks* dominate the financial system, as shown in Exhibit 2–8. The more than $2.5 trillion in financial assets held by U.S. banks at year-end 1986 represented about two fifths of the total resources of all American financial institutions. A distant second in relative size are *savings and loan associations*—another deposit-type financial intermediary active in the nation's mortgage market. Very similar in sources and uses of funds to savings and loans are *savings banks,* headquartered mainly along the Atlantic Coast, which attract small savings deposits from individuals and families. The fourth major kind of deposit-type financial intermediary, the *credit union,* was also created to attract small savings deposits from individuals and families and make loans to credit union members.

When the assets of all four deposit-type intermediaries—commercial banks, savings and loans, savings banks, and credit unions—are combined, they represent about two thirds of the total financial assets of all U.S. financial institutions. The remaining third of the sector's total financial assets are held by a highly diverse group of financial institutions. *Life insurance companies,* which protect policyholders against the risks of pre-

Exhibit 2–8   **Total Financial Assets Held by U.S. Financial Institutions, Selected Years** ($ Billion at Year-End)

Financial Institutions	1960	1970	1980	1986
Financial intermediaries:				
Commercial banks	$224.2	$488.9	$1,247.9	$2,580.6
Savings and loan associations	70.3	173.1	621.9	1,158.3
Life insurance companies	115.8	200.9	464.2	905.1
Private pension funds	38.1	110.4	412.7	635.0
State and local government pension funds	19.7	60.3	198.1	469.5
Finance companies	27.6	64.0	198.7	412.1
Property-casualty insurance companies	26.2	49.9	174.3	346.4
Money market funds	—	—	74.4	292.1
Savings banks	41.0	79.3	171.5	239.2
Investment companies	17.0	46.8	63.5	413.5
Credit unions	6.3	18.0	71.6	166.1
Real estate investment trusts	—	3.9	5.8	8.5
Other financial institutions:				
Security brokers and dealers	6.7	16.2	36.1	77.9

Source: Board of Governors of the Federal Reserve System, *Flow of Funds Accounts, Financial Assets and Liabilities Year-End*, 1960–86.

mature death and disability, lead the list of nondeposit financial institutions. The other type of insurance firm—*property casualty insurers*—offer a far wider array of policies to reduce risk associated with loss of property, crime, weather damage, and personal negligence. Among the fastest-growing financial institutions are *pension funds,* which protect their customers against the risk of outliving their sources of income in the retirement years.

Other important financial institutions include finance companies, investment companies, money market funds, and real estate investment trusts. *Finance companies* lend money to both businesses and consumers to meet short-term working-capital needs and for long-term investment. *Investment companies* pool the funds contributed by thousands of savers by selling shares and then invest in securities sold in the open market. A specialized type of investment company is the *money market fund*, which accepts savings (share) accounts from businesses and individuals and places those funds in high-quality money market securities. Also related to investment companies are *real estate investment trusts,* the smallest member of the financial institutions' sector, investing mainly in commercial and residential properties.

CLASSIFICATION OF FINANCIAL INSTITUTIONS

Financial institutions may be grouped in a variety of different ways. One of the most important distinctions is between depository institutions (commercial banks, savings and loan associations, savings banks, and credit unions), contractual institutions (insurance companies and pension funds), and investment institutions (investment companies or mutual funds, money market funds, and real estate investment trusts). Depository institutions derive the bulk of their loanable funds from deposit accounts sold to the public, while contractual institutions attract funds by offering legal contracts to protect the saver against risk. Investment institutions sell shares to the public and invest the proceeds in stocks, bonds, and other securities.

PORTFOLIO DECISIONS BY FINANCIAL INTERMEDIARIES AND OTHER FINANCIAL INSTITUTIONS

The management of a financial institution is called upon daily to make *portfolio decisions;* that is, what financial assets to buy or sell, what the institution's sources and uses of funds should be. A number of factors affect these critical decisions. For example, the *relative rate of return and risk attached to different financial assets* will affect the composition of the institution's portfolio. Obviously, if management is interested in maximizing profits and has minimal aversion to risk, it will tend to pursue the highest-yielding financial assets available, especially corporate bonds and stocks. A more risk-averse institution, on the other hand, is likely to surrender some yield in return for the greater safety available in acquiring government bonds and high-quality money market instruments.

The *cost, volatility,* and *maturity of incoming funds* provided by surplus-budget units also has a significant impact upon the financial assets acquired by a financial institution. Commercial banks, for example, derive a substantial proportion of their funds from checking accounts, which are relatively inexpensive but highly volatile. Such an institution will tend to concentrate its lending activities in short- and medium-term loans in order to avoid an embarrassing and expensive shortage of cash (liquidity). On the other hand, a financial institution such as a pension fund, which receives a stable and predictable inflow of savings, is largely freed from concern over short-run liquidity needs. It is able to invest heavily in long-term financial assets. Thus, the *hedging principle*—the approximate matching of the maturity of financial assets held with liabilities taken on—is an important guide for choosing those financial assets that a financial institution will hold in its portfolio.[3]

Decisions on what financial assets to acquire and what sources of funds to draw upon are also influenced by the *size* of the individual financial institution. Larger institutions frequently can take advantage of greater diversification in sources and uses of funds. This means the overall risk of a portfolio of securities can be reduced by acquiring securities from many different borrowers. Similarly, a larger institution can contact a broader range of savers and achieve greater stability in its incoming flows of funds. At the same time, through economies of scale (size), larger financial institutions can often sell financial services to both ultimate borrowers and ultimate lenders at lower cost per unit and pass those cost savings along to their customers.

Finally, regulations and competition, two external forces, play major roles in shaping both the sources and uses of funds for a financial institution. Because they hold the bulk of the public's savings and are so crucial to economic growth and investment activity, financial intermediaries are among the most heavily regulated of all business firms. Commercial banks are prohibited from investing in corporate stock or in speculative debt securities. Insurance companies must restrict any security purchases to those a "prudent man" would most likely choose. Most regulations in this sector pertain to the assets that can be acquired, adequacy of net worth, and services that can be offered to the public. In theory, at least, such regulations are designed to promote competition and ensure the safety of the public's funds.

---

[3]See Chapters 9 and 15 for further discussion of the hedging principle.

DISINTERMEDIATION OF FUNDS

One factor which has influenced the financial assets selected by financial institutions for their portfolios in recent years is the phenomenon of disintermediation. Exactly opposite from the intermediation of funds, disintermediation means the withdrawal of funds from a financial intermediary by ultimate lenders (savers) and the lending of those funds directly to ultimate borrowers. In other words, disintermediation involves the shifting of funds from indirect finance to direct and semidirect finance (see Exhibit 2–9).

You engage in disintermediation when you remove funds from a savings account at the local bank and purchase common stock or Treasury bills through a broker. The phenomenon is more likely to occur during periods of high and rapidly rising interest rates when the higher returns demanded by savers may outpace the interest rates offered by financial intermediaries. Clearly, disintermediation forces a financial institution to surrender funds and, if severe, may lead to losses on its assets and ultimate failure. While intermediaries are forced to be more liquid and reduce their credit-granting activities during periods of disintermediation, there is no evidence that the total flow of credit through the financial system is reduced during such periods. Moreover, disintermediation has become far less a problem for financial intermediaries now that federal interest-rate ceilings on deposits have been phased out, allowing most intermediaries to respond more freely to movements in market interest rates. Correspondingly, however, financial intermediaries today are faced with greater uncertainty about their funds sources and funds costs than ever before.

SUMMARY

In the next section of the book we will explore the role of financial institutions in the money and capital markets. We will discover that their role

Exhibit 2–9   **Financial Disintermediation**

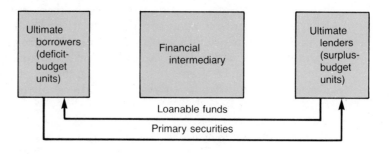

has been expanding rapidly in recent years in response to the rise of the small saver and the massive needs for credit of businesses, consumers, and governments. In most years the process of indirect finance (financial intermediation) accounts for about four fifths of all savings flows in the American economy. Thus, while direct financing and semidirect financing techniques are still important ways of carrying out financial transactions, indirect financing through financial intermediaries is clearly the most important route for financial transactions in the modern world.

STUDY QUESTIONS

1. What is a financial asset? How does it arise within the workings of the financial system? Why must the volume of financial assets outstanding equal the volume of liabilities?

2. Explain the difference between internal and external finance. When an economic unit, such as a business, household, or government, needs funds, what are its principal alternatives? What factors enter into the choice among different sources of funds?

3. How is the creation of financial assets and liabilities linked to saving and investment activity in the economy?

4. Define the terms deficit-budget unit, surplus-budget unit, and balanced-budget unit. Which were you last month? Why?

5. What is money? What are its principal functions within the financial system?

6. Distinguish among direct finance, semidirect finance, and indirect finance. Which is most important today in the financial system? Explain why.

7. What are primary securities? Secondary securities? Give examples of each. What are the principal characteristics of each?

8. List the major kinds of financial intermediaries in the American economy. Which ones can be classified as depository intermediaries? Contractual intermediaries? Investment intermediaries?

9. What is disintermediation? What are its principal causes and possible cures?

PROBLEMS

1. In a recent year the sectors of the U.S. economy listed below reported the following *net* changes in their financial assets and liabilities (measured in billions of dollars):

	Net Acquisitions of Financial Assets	Net Increase in Liabilities
Households	$434.6	$292.0
Farm businesses	2.7	−2.5
Nonfarm noncorporate businesses	8.7	35.0
Nonfinancial corporations	84.9	127.8
State and local governments	74.8	60.6
U.S. government	13.0	236.3
Foreign individuals and institutions	150.7	29.0
Federal Reserve System	32.0	31.2
Commercial banking	256.0	245.7
Private nonbank financial institutions	556.9	590.7

Using the figures listed above, indicate which sectors were deficit-budget sectors and which were surplus-budget sectors for the year under study. Were there any balanced-budget sectors? For all these sectors *combined,* were more funds loaned or more funds borrowed? Why do you think there is a discrepancy between total funds loaned and total funds borrowed?

2. Consider the balance sheets shown below for a household (individual or family), business firm, and government—the only units present in a *closed* economy.

Household				Business Firm				Government			
Assets		Liabilities and Net Worth		Assets		Liabilities and Net Worth		Assets		Liabilities and Net Worth	
Cash	$15	Notes payable	$20	Cash	$10	Bonds	$60	Loans	$20	Securities	$50
Securities	65	Taxes payable	15	Securities	45	Taxes payable	40	Buildings	85	Money	25
Automobile	5	Net worth	135	Truck	25	Net worth	90	Equipment	30	Net worth	140
Home	75			Plant	60			Tax receivables	55		
				Equipment	20						
Other assets	10			Other assets	30			Other assets	25		
Total assets	$170	Total liabilities and net worth	$170	Total assets	$190	Total liabilities and net worth	$190	Total assets	$215	Total liabilities and net worth	$215

Which economic unit above is completely self-financed? Which economic units above are deficit-budget units? Surplus-budget units? Balanced-budget units? Referring to Equations 2–4, 2–5, and 2–6 in this chapter, do these equations hold for the units depicted above? Please demonstrate.

3. In this chapter, a number of different types of financial transactions were discussed: direct finance, semidirect finance, indirect finance (intermediation), and disintermediation. Examine each of the following

financial transactions and indicate which type it is. (*Note:* Some of the transactions described below involve more than one type of financial transaction. Be sure to identify *all* the types of transactions involved.)

a. Borrowing money from a bank.

b. Purchasing a life insurance policy.

c. Selling shares of stock through a broker.

d. Withdrawing money from a savings deposit account and lending it to a friend.

e. Selling shares of stock to a colleague at work.

f. The corporation you own contacting an investment banker to help sell its bonds.

g. Writing a bank check to purchase stock from your broker.

SELECTED REFERENCES

Dougall, Herbert E., and Jack E. Gaumnitz. *Capital Markets and Institutions*. 4th ed. Englewood Cliffs, N.J.: Prentice-Hall, 1980.

Goldsmith, Raymond W. *Financial Institutions*. New York: Random House, 1968.

Gurley, John G., and Edward S. Shaw. "Financial Intermediaries and the Saving-Investment Process." *Journal of Finance,* May 1956, pp. 257–66.

———. *Money in a Theory of Finance*. Washington, D.C.: Brookings Institution, 1960.

Polakoff, Murray E., Thomas A. Durkin, et al. *Financial Institutions and Markets*. 2nd ed. Boston: Houghton Mifflin, 1981.

Pyle, David H. "On the Theory of Financial Intermediation." *Journal of Finance,* June 1971, pp. 737–47.

Chapter 3

Sources of Information for Financial Decision Making in the Money and Capital Markets

Learning Objectives in This Chapter

- To identify the most important sources of data and information on the money and capital markets and the financial system.
- To learn how an observer of or a participant in the financial marketplace can follow the prices of securities and changes in interest rates.
- To explore the concept and content of social accounting as represented by the flow of funds accounts of the United States.

Key Terms and Concepts in This Chapter

Note	*Social accounting*	*Financial investment*
Bond	*National income accounts*	*Real investment*
Bid price	*Flow of Funds Accounts*	*Borrowing*
Asked price	*Flow of Funds Accounts*	*Current saving*
Stocks		*Flow of funds matrix*
Credit bureaus	*Sources and uses of funds statement*	

EVERY day in the money and capital markets, individuals and institutions must make important financial decisions. For those who plan to borrow, for example, key decisions must be made concerning the timing of a request for credit and exactly where the necessary funds should be raised. Lenders of funds must make decisions on when and where to invest their limited resources, considering such factors as the risk, marketability, and expected return on securities available in the financial marketplace. Government policymakers also are intimately involved in the financial decision-making process. It is the responsibility of government to ensure that the financial markets function smoothly in channeling savings into investment and in creating a volume of credit sufficient to support business and commerce.

Sound financial decisions require adequate and accurate *financial information*. Borrowers, lenders, and those who make financial policy require data on the prices and yields attached to individual money and capital market securities today and the prices and yields likely to prevail in the future. A borrower, for example, may decide to postpone the taking out of a loan if it appears that the cost of credit will be significantly lower six months from now than it is today. Those who wish to forecast future interest rates and security prices need information concerning the expected supply of new securities brought to market and the expected demand for those securities. Because economic conditions exert a profound impact upon the money and capital markets, the financial decision maker must also be aware of vital economic data series that reflect employment, prices, industrial output, the volume of savings flows, business capital expansion plans, and related types of information.

What are the principal sources of financial information? Where do financial decision makers go to find the data they need? We may divide the sources of information relied upon by financial decision makers into five broad groups: (1) debt security prices and yields, (2) stock prices and dividend yields, (3) information on security issuers, (4) general economic and financial conditions, and (5) social accounting data. In the following sections we discuss the most important sources of these kinds of financial and economic information.

DEBT SECURITY PRICES AND YIELDS

Among the most important securities traded in the financial system are bonds and notes. As noted in Chapter 2, bonds and notes are debt obligations issued by governments and corporations, usually in units (par values) of $1,000. A note is a short-term written promissory obligation, usually not exceeding 5 years to maturity while a bond is a long-term promissory note, usually at least 5 to 10 years to maturity and often much longer. While bonds and notes generally pay a fixed rate of return to the investor in the form of coupon income, their prices fluctuate every day as interest rates change. Therefore, while bonds and notes are often referred to as fixed-income securities, the investor may experience significant gains or losses on these securities as their prices change. Bonds and notes generally carry a set maturity date, at which time the issuer must pay the holder the security's par value. These securities are generally identified by the name of the issuing company or governmental unit, their coupon (fixed-interest) rate, and their maturity date.

Quotations of prices and yields on bonds and notes actively traded in the financial markets are available from a wide variety of published sources. Major securities dealers trading in bonds and notes publish *quote sheets* showing the market prices, yields, and amounts outstanding. A portion of a sample page from a major bond dealer's quote sheet is shown in Exhibit 3–1. This particular exhibit presents price quotations on U.S. Treasury

Exhibit 3–1 Dealer Quotation Sheet for U.S. Treasury Securities

United States Treasury Securities — **First Boston**, Park Avenue Plaza, New York, N.Y. 10055

NEW YORK (212) 909-2000 · ATLANTA (404) 658-9009 · BOSTON (617) 542-7200 · CHICAGO (312) 372-6840 · CLEVELAND (216) 696-8822 · DALLAS (214) 742-2900 · LOS ANGELES (213) 486-9888 · PHILADELPHIA (215) 972-1700 · SAN FRANCISCO (415) 981-0700

U.S. TREASURY NOTES AND BONDS

Coupon	Maturity	Bid	Asked	Chg	Yield to Mat.*	Yield After Tax ■	Corp Tax Equiv.	Yield Value Par 1/32	1981 Range High	1981 Range Low	Amt Pub Held ◁	Dated Date
N 8	2-15-85	88- 0	88-16	+16	.....13.39	8.20	15.19	.0158	89- 4	83-20	2795	2-15-78
N14 5/8	2-15-85	101- 6	101-10	+ 8	.....13.98	7.55	13.98	.0146	102- 6	98-24	5593	2-16-82
N13 3/8	3-31-85	98-20	98-28	+ 8	.....13.86	7.57	14.02	.0142	99-22	95-16	3408	3-31-81
••B 3 1/4	5-15-85	84- 0	85- 0		..... 9.39	6.18	11.44	.0141	85- 0	82- 0	369	6- 3-58
••B 4 1/4	5-15-85/75	84- 0	85- 0		.....10.50	6.79	12.58	.0143	85- 0	82- 0	515	4- 5-60
N10 3/8	5-15-85	92- 0	92- 4	+12	.....13.61	8.07	14.95	.0144	92-24	68-16	2501	12- 4-79
N14 1/8	5-15-85	100- 8	100-12	+ 8	.....13.94	7.53	13.94	.0136	101-12	98- 2	5250	5-17-82
N14 3/8	5-15-85	101- 8	101-12	+ 8	.....13.75	7.42	13.75	.0135	102- 4	98-24	2458	3- 3-80
N14	6-30-85	98-24	98-28		.....14.47	7.90	14.63	.0134	101- 4	97- 4	3143	6-30-81
N 8 1/4	8-15-85	86-16	86-24	+20	.....13.64	8.34	15.44	.0139	87- 8	82-16	3213	8-15-78
N 9 5/8	8-15-85	89-24	90- 0	+24	.....13.70	8.13	15.05	.0136	90-12	86- 0	3209	6- 5-80
N15 7/8	9-30-85	104- 8	104-16	+16	.....14.06	7.59	14.06	.0120	105-24	101-14	3656	9-30-81
N11 3/4	11-15-85	94-12	94-20	+24	.....13.80	7.82	14.48	.0124	95-12	91- 0	3082	9- 3-80
N14 1/8	12-31-85	100-16	100-24	+20	.....13.84	7.47	13.84	.0116	101-14	97- 8	3276	12-31-81
N13 1/2	2-15-86	96-20	98-26	+20	.....13.89	7.57	14.03	.0114	100- 8	95-20	3171	12- 1-80
N14	3-31-86	100- 8	100-12	+20	.....13.65	7.46	13.65	.0110	102- 2	97- 6	3817	3-31-82
N 7 7/8	5-15-86	83- 6	83-16	+24	.....13.52	8.32	15.40	.0119	84- 0	78-12	4061	5-17-76
N13 3/4	5-15-86	99-20	99-28	+24	.....13.77	7.44	13.76	.0107	100-24	96- 4	3434	3- 4-81
N14 7/8	6-30-86	102-16	102-20	+16	.....13.98	7.55	13.96	.0103	102-20	100- 8	4008	7- 6-82

DECIMAL EQUIVALENTS of 32nds and 64ths per $100

+	$.015625	5+	$.171875	10+	$.328125	15+	$.484375	20+	$.640625	25+	$.796875	30+	$.953125
1	.031250	6	.187500	11	.343750	16	.500000	21	.656250	26	.812500	31	.968750
1+	.046875	6+	.203125	11+	.359375	16+	.515625	21+	.671875	26+	.828125	31+	.984375
2	.062500	7	.218750	12	.375000	17	.531250	22	.687500	27	.843750	32	1.00000
2+	.078125	7+	.234375	12+	.390625	17+	.546875	22+	.703125	27+	.859375		
3	.093750	8	.250000	13	.406250	18	.562500	23	.718750	28	.875000		
3+	.109375	8+	.265625	13+	.421875	18+	.578125	23+	.734375	28+	.890625		
4	.125000	9	.281250	14	.437500	19	.593750	24	.750000	29	.906250		
4+	.140625	9+	.296875	14+	.453125	19+	.609375	24+	.765625	29+	.921875		
5	.156250	10	.312500	15	.468750	20	.625000	25	.781250	30	.937500		

Coupon Rate %	Interest Per Million Per Day*	Nbr Days to Equal 1/32nd	Coupon Rate %	Interest Per Million Per Day*	Nbr Days to Equal 1/32nd	Coupon Rate %	Interest Per Million Per Day*	Nbr Days to Equal 1/32nd
1 1/2	$41.09589	7.6	6 1/4	$171.23288	1.8	9 1/4	$253.42466	1.2
2	54.79452	5.7	6 1/2	178.08219	1.8	9 1/2	260.27397	1.2
2 1/2	68.49315	4.6	6 3/4	184.93151	1.7	9 3/4	267.12329	1.2
3	82.19178	3.8	7	191.78082	1.6	10	273.97260	1.1
3 1/2	95.89041	3.2	7 1/4	198.63014	1.6	10 1/4	280.82192	1.1
4	109.58904	2.9	7 1/2	205.47945	1.5	10 1/2	287.67123	1.1
4 1/2	123.28767	2.6	7 3/4	212.32877	1.5	10 3/4	294.52055	1.1
5	136.98630	2.3	8	219.17808	1.4	11	301.36986	1.0
5 1/4	143.83562	2.2	8 1/4	226.02740	1.4	11 1/4	308.21918	1.0
5 1/2	150.68493	2.1	8 1/2	232.87671	1.3	11 1/2	315.06849	1.0
5 3/4	157.53425	2.0	8 3/4	239.72603	1.3	11 3/4	321.91781	1.0
6	164.38356	1.9	9	246.57534	1.3	12	328.76712	1.0

*365 day basis

CLOSING QUOTATIONS— MON., JULY 12, 1982 **YIELDS FOR DELIVERY—** WED., JULY 14, 1982

U.S. Treasury Notes and Bonds are exempt from state and local income tax. B Bonds, N Notes, WI When Issued. Yield to first call for callable issues quoted at a premium.

◁ As of 2/26/82 Issue Date if later. Amounts in millions.

■ Yield after corporate tax of 46%. For obligations selling at a discount from par, and which are more than twelve months from maturity, effect is given to the corporate capital gains tax of 28%.

Source: The First Boston Corporation, *Handbook of the Securities of the United States Government and Federal Agencies*, 30th ed., 1982, p. 202.

bonds and notes posted by First Boston Corporation, one of the world's leading securities dealers. The prices shown for each security issue—identified by its coupon rate and date of maturity—are based on an assumed $100 par value.

The market prices of bonds and notes generally are expressed in 32nds of a dollar and sometimes in 64ths, indicated by a plus (+) sign. Both bid and asked prices are posted by the dealer, who will purchase securities at the bid price but sell to customers at the asked price. Yields are computed against the asked price and are generally figured to maturity when the security is selling at a discount from its par value. When the security is selling at a premium over par and has various possible maturity dates, the yield is generally figured to the nearest maturity date. New prices and yields must be posted daily by dealers because demand and supply factors continually alter the price and return on individual securities.

To illustrate the kinds of information displayed in a dealer's quote sheet, let us examine the first entry in Exhibit 3–1. The security represented there is a U.S. Treasury note bearing an 8 percent coupon rate. It was issued February 15, 1978, and matured on February 15, 1985. On July 12, 1982, the dealer was willing to buy (bid) the note at 88 0/32 and sell it at 88 16/32. Because each 32nd equals $0.03125 per $100, this coupon security would sell for $88.50 assuming a par value of $100 or $885 for a $1,000 par-value security. Its yield to maturity at that price would be 15.19 percent before federal income taxes and 8.20 percent after taxes for a corporation subject to maximum federal tax rates. A total of about $2,755 million of these Treasury notes was held by the public at the time these price and yield quotations were published. An investor interested in this particular note would, of course, want to compare one dealer's asked price with the prices posted by other dealers.

Financial newspapers report daily quotations on the most actively traded bonds and other securities. Most daily newspapers contain a list of prices for bonds traded on the New York and American stock exchanges. One of the most complete listings of daily price and yield quotations appears in *The Wall Street Journal* (WSJ) published by Dow Jones. WSJ reports the prices of securities traded on the major securities exchanges and also issues sold over the counter (OTC). Exhibit 3–2 shows the prices of corporate bonds traded on the New York Stock Exchange on February 11, 1988, as reported in *The Wall Street Journal*. In these quotations, bonds are priced in dollars and fractions of a dollar (in this case, down to one eighth of a dollar or $0.125), assuming a $100 par value. For example, we note that bonds issued by American Natural Resources (ANR), carrying a coupon rate of 9⅝ percent and due to mature in 1994, traded the previous business day at a closing price of 100. This means that, when trading ended on the date indicated, the ANR bonds were selling for $1,000 (which was also their par or face value). This closing price was unchanged from the price established

Exhibit 3–2 Bond Price and Yield Quotations from *The Wall Street Journal*

NEW YORK EXCHANGE BONDS

CORPORATION BONDS
Volume, $30,440,000

Bonds	Cur Yld	Vol	Close	Net Chg.
ANR 9⅝94	9.6	8	100	...
AVX 8¼12	cv	10	87½	+ 2
AbbtL 9.2s99	9.0	3	102	+ 1
Advst 9s08	cv	63	83⅝	+ ¾
AetnLf 8⅛07	8.8	10	92¾	+ 1¼
AirbF 7½11	cv	5	82	− ½
AlaP 7⅞s02	8.8	14	89½	− 1½
AlaP 9¾s04	9.6	5	101¾	...
AlaP 10⅞05	10.4	5	104¾	...
AlaP 10½05	10.0	5	105	+ ⅞
AlaP 8¾07	9.4	10	93½	...
AlaP 9½08	9.5	10	100	...
AlaP 9⅝08	9.6	15	99¾	+ ⅛
AlaP 12⅝10	11.8	15	107	+ 1⅛
AlskH 17¾91	15.3	36	115⅞	− ⅛
AllgWt 4s98	6.3	10	64	+ 3
Allgl 10.4s02	22.2	139	46¾	− 1⅛
Allgl 9s89	12.8	7	70¼	...
AlldC zr92	...	40	68	...
AlldC zr2000	...	96	32½	+ ⅞

Thursday, February 11, 1988

Total Volume $30,510,000

SALES SINCE JANUARY 1

1988	1987	1986
$946,097,000	$1,230,112,000	$1,283,756,000

	Domestic Thu.	Domestic Wed.	All Issues Thu.	All Issues Wed.
Issues traded	732	704	735	706
Advances	320	390	321	391
Declines	243	179	244	180
Unchanged	169	135	170	135
New highs	19	11	19	11
New lows	7	8	7	8

Dow Jones Bond Averages

−1986− High	−1986− Low	−1987− High	−1987− Low	−1988− High	−1988− Low		−−−Thursday−−− −1988−		−1987−		−1986−	
93.65	83.73	95.51	81.26	90.84	86.92	20 Bonds	90.65	−0.11	95.21	+0.09	86.06	+0.62
95.79	81.85	98.23	79.51	91.61	86.65	10 Utilities	91.46	−0.14	97.35	....	85.61	+0.54
91.64	84.82	93.10	83.00	90.44	86.96	10 Industrial	89.83	−0.08	93.06	+0.17	86.52	+0.71

Source: *The Wall Street Journal*, Friday, February 12, 1988, p. 23. Reprinted by permission of *The Wall Street Journal*

the previous day. The current yield (Cur Yld) is also shown for each bond except for convertible bonds, which are designated with a "cv."[1] The current yield is simply the ratio of the annual interest income each bond promises divided by its current price.

The bulk of bond trades on the major securities exchanges, such as the New York Stock Exchange, are small-volume, odd-lot transactions. Purchases and sales of large quantities of bonds between dealers and major institutional investors generally take place off the major exchanges through direct negotiation or with the aid of security brokers. Prices and yields on such large transactions (round lots) must be gathered from other sources of information, including dealer quote sheets such as the one shown in Exhibit 3–1.

Several other sources of information on bond yields and prices are readily available to investors in published form. *The Daily Bond Buyer,* for example, gives a detailed breakdown of daily prices and yields for a large number of actively traded bond issues, as does the *Commercial and Financial Chronicle,* a financially oriented newspaper. Moreover, a number of bond-yield *indexes* have been compiled in recent years; they pool several bond issues of similar quality and report the average rate of return (yield) to the investor for the entire pool of bonds. In this way bond market investors and companies planning to issue new bonds can see the trend of recent price and yield

[1]See Chapter 10 for a description of convertible bonds.

Exhibit 3–3   **Indicators of Average Bond Yields** (Average Annual Yields in Percent)

Yield Series	1981	1982	1983	1984	1985	1986	1987*
State and local govern- ment notes and bonds:							
Aaa—Moody's Series	10.43%	10.88%	8.80%	9.61%	8.60%	6.95%	7.90%
Bond Buyer Series	11.33	11.66	9.51	10.10	9.11	7.32	8.70
Corporate bonds:							
Seasoned issues, all industries	15.06	14.94	12.78	13.49	12.05	9.71	10.97
Moody's classified by rating:							
Aaa	14.17	13.79	12.04	12.71	11.37	9.02	10.52
Aa	14.75	14.41	12.42	13.31	11.82	9.47	10.74
A	15.29	15.43	13.10	13.74	12.28	9.95	10.98
Baa	16.04	16.11	13.55	14.19	12.72	10.39	11.62

*For the month of October.

Source: Board of Governors of the Federal Reserve System, *Federal Reserve Bulletin,* selected issues.

changes and decide if their plans need to be altered to reflect the latest developments.

Among the most popular bond-yield indexes are those compiled by Moody's Investor Service and the *Bond Buyer* newspaper for both corporate and state and local government bonds. In addition, the U.S. Treasury makes available estimated average yields for its notes and bonds, arrayed by maturity. Dow Jones publishes a daily index of prices for some of the most actively traded corporate bonds, including 10 utility and 10 industrial issues. The Dow bond averages date back to 1915.

These various bond-yield indicators appear in numerous publications, including both private and governmental sources. *The Federal Reserve Bulletin,* published by the Board of Governors of the Federal Reserve System, and the *Survey of Current Business,* published by the U.S. Department of Commerce, report weekly, monthly, and annual average bond yields. Recent changes in various bond-yield indexes as reported in the *Federal Reserve Bulletin* are shown in Exhibit 3–3. We note the marked fluctuations in bond yields between 1981 and 1987, reflecting significant changes in economic conditions and credit demands during this period.

STOCK PRICES AND DIVIDEND YIELDS

Of all securities traded in the money and capital markets, stocks are among the most popular with investors. Stock prices can be extremely volatile, offering the prospect of substantial capital gains if prices rise but also significant capital losses if prices fall. Many corporations issuing stock pay dividends regularly, thus giving the investor a reasonably steady source of income as well as the opportunity to achieve "windfall" gains if the value of the stock rises. Unlike a bond, however, a share of stock is a certificate of ownership in a corporation and not a debt obligation. No corporation need pay dividends to its stockholders, and some never do, preferring to retain all after-tax earnings in the business.

As in the case of bonds, price and yield data on the most actively traded stocks are reported daily in the financial press. Most daily newspapers list current stock prices, especially for those equities traded on the New York and American stock exchanges. *The Wall Street Journal* contains an extensive list of the daily prices and dividend yields of major stocks sold over the counter and on the major securities exchanges, including the New York, American, Midwest, Pacific, Philadelphia, Boston, and Cincinnati stock exchanges in the United States, and the London, Tokyo, Frankfurt, and other major exchanges abroad. An example of WSJ stock price quotations is shown in Exhibit 3–4.

We note that each stock price quotation is identified by the abbreviated name of the company issuing it. High and low prices at which the stock has

Exhibit 3–4 Stock Price Quotations from *The Wall Street Journal*

NEW YORK STOCK EXCHANGE COMPOSITE TRANSACTIONS

Thursday, February 11, 1988

Quotations include trades on the Midwest, Pacific, Philadelphia, Boston and Cincinnati stock exchanges and reported by the National Association of Securities Dealers and Instinet

52 Weeks High	52 Weeks Low	Stock	Div.	Yld %	P-E Ratio	Sales 100s	High	Low	Close	Net Chg.
47 1/4	31 3/8	AllgPw	3.00	7.4	10	374	40 7/8	40 1/4	40 3/8	− 3/8
105 7/8	53 1/8	Allegis		...	12	1932	71	70 5/8	70 5/8	− 1/2
19 3/8	5 1/2	AllenG		...	...	238	8 7/8	8 5/8	8 5/8	− 1/8
24 7/8	9 1/4	Allen pf	1.75	13.5	...	15	13	12 1/2	13	+ 1/2
44	12 3/8	AlldPd		...	8	518	14 1/2	13 1/2	14 1/8	+ 5/8
49 1/4	26	AldSgnl	1.80	5.4	61	5331	34 3/8	33 1/4	33 3/8	...
3 3/4	1	viAllisC		...	...	34	1 1/4	1 1/8	1 1/8	...
10 1/4	8 7/8	AlstMu n	.30e	2.9	...	490	10 1/4	10 1/8	10 1/4	+ 1/8
34 1/8	23	ALLTL s	1.52	5.2	10	212	29 5/8	29 1/8	29 1/2	+ 1/4
64 3/4	33 3/4	Alcoa	1.20	2.8	17	8629	43 1/4	41 1/2	43	+ 1 1/4
32	14	AmxG n	.06e	.3	17	193	18	17 5/8	17 5/8	− 5/8
29 1/4	12 1/2	Amax		...	6	4467	17 1/2	16 3/4	17	− 1/8
47 3/4	34	Amax pf	3.00	7.8	...	12	38 1/2	38 1/2	38 1/2	− 3/4
41 7/8	21 1/2	AmHes	.45e	1.7	10	2010	28 1/4	27 1/8	27 1/8	− 5/8
30 3/8	9 7/8	ABrck s	.05e	...	...	972	18 1/4	17 3/4	18 1/8	+ 3/8
60	36 1/2	AmBrnd	2.20	4.9	10	3744	46	45 1/8	45 1/8	− 5/8
34 3/8	28	ABrd pf	2.75	9.7	...	117	28 1/4	28 1/8	28 1/4	− 1/8
118 3/4	76	ABrd pf	2.67	2.9	...	2	92	92	92	+2
26 5/8	15	ABldM	.90	4.4	16	34	20 5/8	20 1/4	20 1/4	− 1/8
31 1/2	15 1/2	ABusPr	.88	4.0	13	56	22	20 7/8	21 3/4	+ 1 1/8
25 3/8	17 7/8	ACapBd	2.20a	9.9	...	67	22 1/4	22 1/8	22 1/8	+ 1/8
35 3/8	22 3/4	ACapCv	5.61e	23.0	...	13	24 3/8	24 1/4	24 3/8	+ 1/8
22 5/8	7 5/8	ACMR	1.00	7.9	10	23	12 3/4	12 5/8	12 5/8	− 1/8
69	42 1/4	BectDk	.86e	1.5	17	1553	57 3/4	56 3/4	56 7/8	− 1/4
15/16	7/32	viBeker		...	...	35	13/32	3/8	13/32	+ 1/32
28 3/8	18 1/4	BeldnH	.40a	1.7	11	11	23 5/8	23 1/2	23 1/2	...
75 1/4	40 3/4	BelHwl	.62	1.0	11	451	61 5/8	61 5/8	61 5/8	+ 1/8
79 3/4	60 1/2	BellAtl	3.84	5.3	12	1583	73 1/2	72 1/8	72 1/4	− 1 1/8
23 3/8	11 1/4	BellIn s	.28	2.0	21	40	14 1/8	14	14	...
43 1/2	29 1/8	BellSo	2.20	5.3	12	2564	41 3/4	41 1/4	41 3/8	− 3/8
77 1/4	42 1/4	BeloAH	.80	1.7	19	54	47 1/2	47 1/4	47 1/2	...
42	25 1/2	Bemis	.88	2.3	16	136	38 3/8	37	38 3/8	+ 1 5/8
65 1/4	28 1/2	BenfCp	2.00	4.9	...	214	42	40 7/8	40 7/8	− 7/8
54 3/4	38	Benef pf	4.30	9.7	...	6	44 1/4	43 1/2	44 1/4	+ 3/4
55	41	Benef pf	4.50	10.7	...	z130	42 1/4	42 1/4	42 1/4	+ 1/4
30 3/4	23	Benef pf	2.50	10.1	...	z180	24 3/4	24 3/4	24 3/4	− 1/4
9 7/8	2 1/2	BengtB	.05e	1.4	...	131	3 5/8	3 1/2	3 1/2	− 1/8
7 1/8	2 1/8	Berkey		...	...	138	4 1/4	4	4	− 1/8
23 1/4	5 3/4	BestBy s		...	11	108	7	6 7/8	6 7/8	...
13	6	BestPd		...	11	417	9 3/4	9 1/2	9 3/4	+ 1/4
19 3/4	6 3/8	BethStl		...	12	3402	17 3/8	17 1/8	17 3/8	+ 3/8
47 1/2	18 3/8	BethSt pf	1.25k	...	...	96	44 3/4	43 3/4	44 5/8	+ 7/8
24 1/4	9 1/4	BthS pfB	.62k	...	...	58	22 7/8	22 3/8	22 5/8	...
18 7/8	5 1/2	Bevrly	.05i	...	...	8350	7 3/4	7 1/8	7 3/8	...
25 3/8	16 1/2	BevIP n	2.30e	11.7	13	193	19 7/8	19 1/2	19 5/8	+ 1/4
28 3/8	13 1/2	Biocft		...	16	237	17 5/8	17 1/4	17 1/4	+ 1/4

Source: *The Wall Street Journal*, February 11, 1988, p. 38. Reprinted by permission of *The Wall Street Journal* been traded during the past year and the most recent annual dividend declared by the issuing company are given.[2] The dividend yield, or ratio of dividends to current price, appears next, along with the ratio of the stock's current price to the past 12 months of company earnings, or the P-E ratio. All remaining entries provide a summary of the previous business day's transactions in the markets where that particular stock is bought and sold. The one-day sales volume, expressed in hundreds of shares, is shown, as well as the highest and lowest prices at which the stock was exchanged that day. The closing price for which the stock was traded in the last sale of the day is reported, expressed in dollars and fractions of a dollar down to eighths. The final entry gives the net change between the day's closing price and the closing price one business day earlier.

Stock prices for individual companies, covering a period of several years, are provided by *The Value Line Investment Survey,* published weekly by Arnold Bernhard & Company of New York. Each company's business is described and basic financial information, such as sales, net earnings, and long-term indebtedness, is provided for at least a decade. Similar financial and price data for more than 1,100 actively traded stocks are published in the monthly series *3-Trend Security Charts* and in the quarterly series *3-Trend Cycli-Graphs,* both published by Securities Research Company of Boston. Extensive charts showing weekly stock price ranges, earnings, dividends, and number of shares traded appear in each issue.

Stock prices and basic internal financial data for individual companies are also presented in comprehensive reports compiled by Standard & Poor's Corporation (S&P) and published in *Stock Reports*. This monthly S&P series covers shares traded on the New York and American stock exchanges and over the counter. Information is provided subscribers on dividends paid by each company, its principal products, and an analysis of its performance. Daily and weekly stock price movements are also reported in S&P's quarterly publication, the *Daily Stock Price Record,* and in the monthly publication *Trendline's Current Market Perspectives*.

The stock market is watched closely by investors as a barometer of expectations in the business community. A rising trend in stock prices generally signals an optimistic assessment of future business prospects and expectations of higher corporate earnings. A declining market, on the other hand, is often a harbinger of adverse economic news and may signal a cutback in business investment and lower corporate earnings.

Many students of the financial markets follow several broad stock price indexes which reflect price movements in groups of similar quality securities. One of the most popular indexes is the Dow-Jones Industrial Average of 30 stocks, including such major companies as American Telephone &

---

[2]The occasional letters which appear beside certain stocks in the list of quotations refer to footnotes that give special information. All stocks shown are common equity shares unless the symbol *pf* appears, indicating an issue of preferred stock. The symbol *u* indicates a 52-week high in price, while *d* reflects a new 52-week low. The letter *s* refers to a stock split or stock dividend of 25 percent or more in the past 52 weeks.

Telegraph, General Motors, and Exxon. Dow Jones also reports a Transportation Average of 20 stocks (including such industry leaders as American Airlines and Southern Pacific) and a Utility Average of the shares of 15 leading utility companies (such as Consolidated Edison and Pacific Gas and Electric). The Utility Average is of special importance to many investors because it appears to be highly sensitive to interest rate fluctuations, and some analysts regard it as a barometer of interest rate expectations. Recent movements in the Dow Jones Industrial Average reported in *The Wall Street Journal* are shown in Exhibit 3–5. Daily reports on the performance of all the Dow series also may be found in local newspapers, as well as in Standard & Poor's *Daily Stock Price Record*.[3]

Two of the most comprehensive stock market indicators available are Standard & Poor's 400 Industrial Stock Price Index and 500 Composite Stock Price Index, both including the most actively traded U.S. corporate equity shares. The S&P 500 includes the shares of 40 utility companies, 20 transportation firms, and 40 financial stocks not present in the S&P 400 industrial index. All five S&P stock series—the 400 Index, Utility Index, Transportation Index, Financial Stock Index, and the 500 Composite Index—are widely followed and regarded as sensitive barometers of general stock price movements in the United States.[4] An even broader price index than the S&P 500 Composite is the New York Stock Exchange Composite Index, which gives greatest weight to stocks having the highest market values. Considered a useful indicator of total market performance, the NYSE Composite is often used to compare the performance of major institutional investors, such as investment companies and pension funds, against the market as a whole. Two other broad market indicators are the AMEX Index, a weighted average of all stocks traded on the American Stock Exchange, and the NASDAQ OTC Composite, which measures price movements in stocks sold over the counter rather than on the major exchanges.

Many newspapers, including *The Wall Street Journal,* and financially oriented magazines contain a daily stock market diary similar to that shown in Exhibit 3–5. Such summaries of recent market developments indicate both price movements and the volume of trading on the major exchanges. Market diaries usually report the total number of shares traded on a given day or week, the number of stocks advancing or declining in price, and those whose price remains unchanged after recent trading. Many stock analysts chart movements in the ratio of stock price advances to declines as an indicator of "oversold" or "overbought" conditions in the market.

---

[3]The Dow Industrial, Transportation, and Utility averages are combined to form a fourth market indicator—the 65 stock Composite Average. The Dow Industrial Average is the oldest of the four series, dating back to 1897. Probably the most widely followed stock market index in the world, the Dow Industrials is constructed by adding up the current prices of 30 industrial stocks represented and dividing by an adjustment factor designed to account for stock splits and changes in the list of companies represented in the average.

[4]See Chapter 21 for a discussion of the market for corporate stocks and the factors which influence stock prices.

Exhibit 3–5 Daily Stock Market Diary

STOCK MARKET DATA BANK Feb. 11, 1988

Major Indexes

HIGH	LOW	(12 MOS)	CLOSE	NET CH	% CH	12 MO CH		FROM 12/31	
DOW JONES AVERAGES									
2722.42	1738.74	30 Industrials	1961.54	– 0.50	– 0.03	– 204.24	– 9.43	+ 22.71	+ 1.17
1101.16	661.00	20 Transportation	774.14	– 2.72	– 0.35	– 136.71	–15.01	+ 25.28	+ 3.38
222.02	160.98	15 Utilities	184.33	– 1.78	– 0.96	– 34.81	–15.89	+ 9.25	+ 5.28
992.21	653.76	65 Composite	731.15	– 1.86	– 0.25	– 98.94	–11.92	+ 16.88	+ 2.36
NEW YORK STOCK EXCHANGE									
187.99	125.91	Composite	143.99	– 0.25	– 0.17	– 13.59	– 8.62	+ 5.76	+ 4.17
231.05	149.43	Industrials	171.84	+ 0.04	+ 0.02	– 14.10	– 7.58	+ 4.80	+ 2.87
80.22	61.63	Utilities	73.03	– 0.60	– 0.82	– 3.91	– 5.08	+ 5.72	+ 8.50
168.20	104.76	Transportation	123.25	– 0.62	– 0.50	– 10.92	– 8.14	+ 4.68	+ 3.95
165.36	107.39	Finance	123.14	–0.62–	– 0.50	– 32.75	–21.01	+ 8.57	+ 7.48
STANDARD & POOR'S INDEXES									
336.77	223.92	500 Index	255.95	– 0.71	– 0.28	– 19.67	– 7.14	+ 8.87	+ 3.59
393.17	255.43	400 Industrials	293.85	-0.26	– 0.09	– 18.54	– 5.94	+ 7.99	+ 2.80
274.20	167.59	20 Transportation	194.00	– 1.83	– 0.93	– 28.81	–12.93	+ 3.83	+ 2.01
121.11	91.80	40 Utilities	110.73	– 1.22	– 1.09	– 6.28	– 5.37	+ 8.61	+ 8.43
32.56	20.39	40 Financials	22.96	– 0.19	– 0.82	– 6.53	–22.14	+ 1.33	+ 6.15
NASDAQ									
455.26	291.88	OTC Composite	351.04	+ 1.72	+ 0.49	– 58.14	–14.21	+ 20.57	+ 6.22
488.92	288.30	Industrials	350.50	+ 2.48	+ 0.71	– 75.64	–17.75	+ 11.56	+ 3.41
475.78	333.66	Insurance	402.57	+ 2.09	+ 0.52	– 50.50	–11.15	+ 51.51	+14.67
526.64	365.63	Banks	434.39	+ 1.31	+ 0.30	– 60.25	–12.18	+ 43.73	+11.19
195.36	124.98	Nat. Mkt. Comp.	151.58	+ 0.76	+ 0.50	– 23.64	–13.49	+ 8.99	+ 6.31
187.94	110.21	Nat. Mkt. Indus.	135.35	+ 1.00	+ 0.74	– 27.24	–16.75	+ 4.24	+ 3.23
OTHERS									
365.01	231.90	AMEX	274.40	+ 1.75	+ 0.64	– 40.01	–12.73	+ 14.05	+ 5.40
1926.2	1232.0	Fin. Times Indus.	1381.0	+ 12.6	+ 0.92	– 120.0	– 8.00	+ 7.7	+ 0.56
26646.43	19531.52	Nikkei Stock Avg.	Closed	....	.....	....	......	....	......
289.02	181.09	Value-Line	214.35	+ 0.74	+ 0.35	– 43.87	–16.99	+ 12.73	+ 6.31
3299.44	2188.11	Wilshire 5000	2524.85	– 2.08	– 0.08	– 258.72	– 9.30	+ 107.73	+ 4.46

Most Active Issues

NYSE	Volume	Close	Change
Niagara Pwr	24,864,200	13⅝ –	⅛
Atl Richfield	6,472,500	78⅝ –	⅛
Panhndle East	4,890,100	26½ +	⅞
Fed Dept	3,099,900	59⅞ +	2⅜
Consol Ed NY	2,243,100	45⅛ –	¼
Eastman Kod	1,856,400	41⅞ +	⅜
General Elec	1,770,400	43⅛ –	⅛
Exxon Corp	1,525,600	40¼ –	1
Stop & Shop Cos	1,515,200	36⅞ +	½
IBM	1,483,400	111¼ –	⅜

Diaries

NYSE	THUR	WED	WK AGO
Issues traded	1,980	1,979	1,982
Advances	804	1,219	752
Declines	717	354	756
Unchanged	459	406	474
New highs	7	8	6
New lows	6	5	15
Adv Vol (000)	81,321	147,007	98,610
Decl Vol (000)	101,096	19,829	59,559
Total Vol (000)	200,760	187,980	186,490
Block trades	3,443	3,745	3,110

Source: *The Wall Street Journal*, February 12, 1988. Reprinted by permission of *The Wall Street Journal* © Dow Jones & Company, Inc., 1988. All rights reserved.

Finally, with the increasing globalization of financial markets, more and more savers and borrowers are turning to foreign markets to invest their savings and raise needed funds. Therefore, key financial information sources increasingly are reporting the daily changes in security prices and interest rates in foreign trading centers. A good example is Exhibit 3–6, which reports the prices of selected corporate stock as of the preceding day

Exhibit 3–6   **Stock Price Movements in Selected Countries**

FOREIGN MARKETS

Wednesday, September 2, 1987

FRANKFURT (in marks)			TOKYO (in yen)			LONDON (in pence)		
				Close	Prev. Close		Close	Prev. Close
AEG	340	344				Allied Lyons	415	417
Allianz Vers	2,116.5	2,120	Ajinomoto	3,460	3,510	Babcock	n.a.	282
BASF	339.10	343.30	Asahi Chem	1,250	1,290	Barclays Bk	565	569
Bayer	358.50	361.40	Bk of Tokyo	1,630	1,640	Bass Ltd	929	925
BMW	783	785	BridgestnTire	1,180	1,210	BOC Group	536	539
Continental	360	368.50	C. Itoh	743	734	Borland Int'l	226	228
Commerzbnk	307	308.50	Daiwa House	2,300	2,320	British GE	207	212
Daimler-Benz	1,129	1,142	Daiwa Secur	3,12^	3,120	Britoil	323.5	336
Degussa	535	536.50	Eisai	2,320	2,440	BTR PLC	337	338
Deutsche Bk	707	710	Fuji Bank	3,230	3,400	Cable&Wi	430	436
Dresdner Bk	368	368	Fujitsu	1,180	1,220	Cadbury Sch	270	271
Hoechst	329.80	333.50	Isuzu Mot Ltd	432	432	Charter Con	450	450
Lufthansa	184	185.50	Kalima Corp	1,850	1,800	Coats Viyella	353.5	355
Nixdorf	842	846.50	Kansai Elec	3,250	3,320	Consol Gold	1,403	1,383
Porsche	1,010	1,019	Komatsu Ltd	700	711	Dalgety	378	382
RWE	254	256	MaruiDeptStr	3,380	3,370	Glaxo	1,699	1,725
Schering	610	617.50	Marubeni	525	530	Grand Metro	535	534
Siemens	656.50	663.50	Mazda	439	440	GKN	391	392.5
Thyssen-Hut	138.80	140.30	MitsubishiEst	2,680	2,680	Guinness	352	354
Veba	322.50	323.30	MitsubishiInd	633	635			
Volkswagen	406.50	404.30						

Stock Market Indexes

EXCHANGE	WEDNESDAY CLOSE	NET CHG	PCT CHG
Tokyo Nikkei Average	25946.60	− 171.82	− 0.66
Tokyo First Section	2139.47	− 13.73	− 0.64
London FT 30-share	1763.2	− 15.7	− 0.88
London 100-share	2249.5	− 23.3	− 1.03
London Gold Mines	444.9	+ 6.7	+ 1.53
Frankfurt FAZ	655.57	− 4.49	− 0.68
Zurich Credit Suisse	595.4	+ 1.3	+ 0.22
Paris CAC General	426.6	− 3.8	− 0.88
Milan Stock Index	859	− 4	− 0.46
Amsterdam ANP-CBS General	314.5	− 4.0	− 1.26
Stockholm Affarsvarlden	905.1	+ 3.2	+ 0.35
Brussels Stock Index	5297.72	− 13.9	− 0.26
Sydney All Ordinaries	2179.6	+ 21.9	+ 1.01
Hong Kong Hang Seng	3635.86	− 8.42	− 0.23
Singapore Straits Times	1426.31	+ 21.76	+ 1.55
Johannesburg J'burg Gold	2397	+ 38	+ 1.61
Toronto 300 Composite	3977.92	− 4.31	− 0.11

in Frankfurt, West Germany; Tokyo, Japan; and London (all denominated in their respective home currencies). It also reports the previous day's movements in broad stock-price indexes at the major securities exchanges in Western Europe, Canada, South Africa, and around the Pacific Ocean rim.

INFORMATION ON SECURITY ISSUERS

Lenders of funds have a pressing need to secure accurate financial information on those individuals and institutions that seek to borrow funds or to sell their stock. Fortunately, financial information on individual companies and other security issuers is available from a wide variety of published sources. Two of the most respected sources of information on major security issuers are Moody's Investors Service, inc., and Standard & Poor's

Corporation, both headquartered in New York City. In a series of annual volumes, Moody's provides financial data on industrial corporations, commercial banks, insurance companies, investment funds, real estate companies, utilities, and state and local units of government. The most widely known Moody's volumes include the *Industrial Manual, Bank and Finance Manual, Public Utility Manual, Transportation Manual,* and *Municipal and Government Manual.* In the case of individual corporations, Moody's provides information on the history of each firm, including any recent acquisitions or mergers, names of key officers, and recent financial statements. In addition, Moody's assigns credit ratings to selected issuers of corporate and municipal bonds, commercial paper, and preferred stock as a guide for investors. These ratings are published monthly in Moody's *Bond Record.* Standard & Poor's provides similar credit ratings for corporate and municipal bonds, assessing the likelihood of default on a security issue and the degree of protection afforded the investor.[5] The S&P *Bond Guide,* containing relevant financial information on more than 6,000 bond issues, appears once a month.

Even more extensive financial data are provided by the reports and registration statements that corporations must file with the Securities and Exchange Commission (SEC). These SEC reports and statements are available in many libraries on microfiche or microfilm. One company, Disclosure Incorporated, which is under contract with the SEC, provides its subscribers with microfiche copies of more than 100,000 corporate documents filed each year by approximately 11,000 companies.

The most important of these corporate documents is the SEC's *10-K Report*—an annual business and financial report which must be filed by most companies within 90 days after their fiscal year-end. 10-K reports identify the principal products or services and markets served by a firm, provide a summary of its operations for the past five years, note any securities outstanding, include complete audited financial statements, and list the names of key officers. SEC regulations pursuant to the Securities Act of 1933 and the Securities Exchange Act of 1934 also require corporations offering securities for public sale to file registration statements. While these statements vary in content with the type of organization selling the securities, registration statements generally include a prospectus outlining the terms of sale of new securities, marketing arrangements, issue and distribution expenses, and financial reports.

Another useful source of data on business firms seeking credit is the Business Information Report prepared by Dun & Bradstreet, Inc. This credit-rating company collects information on approximately 3 million firms, making detailed financial reports available to its subscribers. A sample page

---

[5]Moody's and Standard & Poor's investment ratings are discussed in Chapter 10 and presented in detail in Appendix A.

from a Dun & Bradstreet Business Information Report is presented in Exhibit 3–7. Dun & Bradstreet also provides industrywide financial data so the financial condition of an individual business borrower can be compared with that of other firms in the same industry. D&B's Key Business Ratios series calculates 14 key operating and financial ratios for more than 800 lines of business, grouped by SIC Code. Similar industrywide performance indicators are prepared and published in *Troy's Almanac,* in Robert Morris & Associates' *Annual Statement Studies,* and in Standard & Poor's *Industry Surveys* and the *Analysts Handbook.* This information can be supplemented with news information on individual industries and firms by checking *The Wall Street Journal Index,* the *New York Times Index,* the *Business Periodicals Index,* and *Barron's Index.*

Information on banks and other financial institutions is available from a wide variety of sources, starting with trade associations in each industry and federal and state regulatory agencies. For example, the American Bankers Association, Life Insurance Association of America, League of U.S. Savings Associations, and Credit Union National Association frequently will provide annual reports or pamphlets describing recent industry trends. Studies of financial institutions' problems are found in specialized journals and magazines, such as the *Journal of Commercial Bank Lending, Journal of Bank Research, Bankers Magazine, Savings Bank Journal, Financial Analysts Journal,* the *Institutional Investor,* and *Euromoney.*

Among key government agencies providing annual reports and special studies of financial institutions' trends and problems are the Federal Deposit Insurance Corporation, Federal Reserve Board and Federal Reserve Banks, Federal Home Loan Board and Banks, and the Comptroller of the Currency. For example, the Federal Reserve Banks publish annually the results of their Functional Cost Analysis study, which presents data on bank costs and returns for a wide variety of bank services and bank sizes. The Federal Deposit Insurance Corporation provides periodic reports on the growth of bank offices and branches, financial statements, and bank failures.

Information on individuals and families who seek credit is assembled and disseminated to institutional lenders such as banks and finance companies by nearly 2,000 credit bureaus in the United States. The files of these bureaus include such information as the individual's place of residence and occupation, marital status, loans and credit charges outstanding, and the promptness with which an individual pays his or her bills. A typical credit file for an individual will indicate whether he or she has filed for bankruptcy or has judgments or liens against either assets or income. Most credit bureaus maintain files on an individual's bill-paying record for up to seven years and may release that information only to those lenders, debt collectors, employers, or licensing agencies who have a legitimate right to know the individual's credit standing. As discussed in Chapter 18, individuals have a right to see their credit files and the right to dispute the information they contain.

Exhibit 3–7   **The Dun & Bradstreet Business Information Report**

```
Dun & Bradstreet, Inc.                          This report has been prepared for

   BE SURE NAME, BUSINESS AND        ANSWERING      SUBSCRIBER: 008-001042
   ADDRESS MATCH YOUR FILE           INQUIRY

        THIS REPORT MAY NOT BE REPRODUCED IN WHOLE OR IN PART IN ANY MANNER WHATEVER

   CONSOLIDATED REPORT                                  {FULL REVISION}
```

DUNS: 06-647-3261	DATE PRINTED	SUMMARY
RETTINGER PAINT CORP.	AUG 13, 197-	RATING CC2
727 WHITMAN WAY	WHOL PAINTS &	STARTED 1950
BENSON, MI 48232	VARNISHES	PAYMENTS DISC-PPT
TEL 313 961-0720		SALES $ 424,612
	SIC NO.	WORTH $ 101,867
CARL RETTINGER, PRES.	51 98	EMPLOYS 5
		HISTORY CLEAR
		CONDITION GOOD
		TREND STEADY

SPECIAL EVENTS   Business burglarized July 3 but $18,000 loss is fully insured.

PAYMENTS   {Amounts may be rounded to nearest figure in prescribed ranges}

REPORTED	PAYING RECORD	HIGH CREDIT	NOW OWES	PAST DUE	SELLING TERMS	LAST SALE WITHIN
07/7-	Disc	30000	17000	-0-	2 10 30	1-2 mos.
	Disc	27000	14000	-0-	1 10 30	2-3 mos.
	Disc-Ppt	12000	4400	200	2 10 30	1 mo.
	Ppt	9000	8000	-0-	30	1 mo.
06/7-	Disc	16000	7500	-0-	2 10 30	2-3 mos.
05/7-	Disc	9000	3800	-0-	2 10 30	1 mo.
	Ppt	1500	-0-	-0-	30	1-2 mos.

FINANCE
06/22/7-   Fiscal statement dated May 31, 197-:

Cash	$ 20,623		Accts Payable	$ 47,246
Accts Rec	55,777		Owing Bank	34,000
Merchandise	92,103		Notes Pay {Trucks}	7,020
	---------			---------
Current	168,503		Current	88,266
Fixts. & Equip.	13,630		Common Stock	35,000
Trucks	8,000		Earned Surplus	66,867
	-------			---------
Total Assets	190,133		Total	190,133

SALES {Yr}: $424,612. Net profit $17,105. Fire ins. mdse $95,000;
equipt $20,000. Mo. rent: $3500. Prepared by Steige Co., CPAs, Detroit, MI.

                              --0--
          06/22/7-Laswon defined monthly payments: $3000 to bank, $400 on notes.
Admitted collections slow but losses insignificant. Said inventory will drop
to $60,000 by December. Expects 5% sales increase this year.

PUBLIC FILINGS
03/25/7-   March 17, 197- financing statement A741170 named subject as debtor and
NCR Corp., Dayton, O. as secured party. Collateral: equipment.
05/28/7-   May 21, 197- suit for $200 entered by Henry Assoc., Atlanta, Ga. Docket
A27519. Involves merchandise which Lawson says was defective.

BANKING
06/25/7-   Account, long maintained, carries average balances low to moderate five
figures. Unsecured loans to moderate five extended and now open.

HISTORY
06/22/7- CARL RETTINGER, PRES.   JOHN J. LAWSON, V PRES.
          DIRECTORS: The Officers
                  Incorporated Michigan February 2, 1950. Authorized capital 3500 shares,
          no par common. Paid in capital $35,000, officers sharing equally.
                  RETTINGER, born 1920, married. Employed by E-Z Paints, Detroit 12 yrs,
          five as manager until starting subject early 1950.
                  LAWSON, born 1925, married. Obtained accounting degree 1946 and then
          employed by Union Carbide, Chicago until joining Rettinger at inception.

OPERATION
06/22/7-   Wholesales paints and varnishes {85%}, wallpaper and supplies. 500
          local accounts include retailers {75%} and contractors. Terms: 2 10 30. Peak
          season spring thru summer. EMPLOYEES: Officers active with three others.
          LOCATION: Rents 7500 sq ft. one-story block structure, good repair.

Source: Dun & Bradstreet.

GENERAL ECONOMIC AND FINANCIAL CONDITIONS

A number of different sources provide market participants with information on developments in the economy, prevailing trends in the money and capital markets, and actions by the government that may affect economic and financial conditions (for a summary, see Exhibit 3–8). For example, many of the world's major commercial banks publish monthly and weekly newslet-

Exhibit 3–8   Summary of Key Sources of Information on the Financial Markets and Market Participants

Information on Securities and Security Prices and Interest Rates (Bonds, Notes, Other Forms of Debt, and Stock)	Information on Individual Borrowers and Security Issuers
The Wall Street Journal	The Wall Street Journal
Daily Bond Buyer	(news stories and journal index)
The New York Times	The New York Times
Dealer quote sheets	(news stories and index)
Broker reports	Dun & Bradstreet
Financial sections of daily newspapers	(Business Information Reports and Key Business Ratios)
Value Line Investment Survey	Moody's Banking and Industrial Manuals
U.S. Financial Data (Federal Reserve Bank of St. Louis) and other data releases of the Federal Reserve Banks and the Federal Reserve Board	Standard & Poor's Reports, Industry Surveys, and Analysts Handbook
Survey of Current Business (U.S. Dept. of Commerce)	Securities and Exchange Commission Reports (Annual Reports, 10Ks, etc.)
Federal Reserve Bulletin (Federal Reserve Board)	Business Periodicals Index
The Treasury Bulletin (U.S. Treasury Department)	DATEXT computer files
Moody's Investor Service (various publications)	Trade associations
Standard & Poor's Corporation (various publications)	Credit bureaus

Information on Economic and Financial Conditions

The Wall Street Journal	Federal Reserve Bulletin
Federal Reserve Bank of St. Louis, National Economic Trends, Monetary Trends, International Economic Conditions	Survey of Current Business
	Industry and government forecasts
	National Income Accounts
Newsletters issued by large commercial banks	Flow of Funds Accounts
Economic consulting firms	

ters for the benefit of smaller correspondent banks and customers. These newsletters frequently contain discussions of recent changes in employment, industrial output, security prices, and interest rates.

The Federal Reserve System releases large quantities of financial information to the public upon request. Statistical releases available on a weekly or monthly basis cover such items as interest rates, money supply measures, assets and liabilities held by banks and nonbank thrift institutions, the federal government's financing operations, and reports on corporate earnings, consumer borrowing, industrial output, and international transactions. Information of this sort is summarized each month in the *Federal Reserve Bulletin* published by the Board of Governors of the Federal Reserve System in Washington, D.C. The board also publishes the results of internal staff studies which examine recent financial trends or address major issues of public policy.

Within the Federal Reserve System, the Federal Reserve Bank of St. Louis publishes large quantities of financial data in its weekly, monthly, and quarterly news releases. One of the most popular is *U.S. Financial Data,* which appears weekly and contains a summary of week-to-week changes in interest rates and in the components of the nation's money supply. Another regular St. Louis Fed publication is *Monetary Trends,* summarizing monthly changes in the money supply and bank reserves. These data series are watched closely by many investors because they often foreshadow broad movements in interest rates, security prices, and national economic conditions.

A number of published sources regularly report on the status of the economy, particularly as reflected in employment, prices, and production. Newsletters published by banks in major money centers, and daily financial newspapers, such as *The Wall Street Journal,* nearly always include important economic data. The Federal Reserve Bank of St. Louis publishes a monthly news release, *National Economic Trends,* which tracks changes in U.S. employment, consumer and wholesale prices, and industrial production.

The *Survey of Current Business,* a monthly magazine published by the U.S. Department of Commerce, contains one of the most up-to-date and comprehensive collections of U.S. economic data available anywhere. The *Survey* reports the latest consumer spending, government expenditures at all levels, changes in business spending, and exports and imports. The *Survey* contains a detailed breakdown of U.S. production volume by market and by different industries. Information on international economic and financial developments is provided by the St. Louis Federal Reserve Bank's monthly publication, *International Economic Conditions.*

Forecasts of future economic and financial developments are available from a wide variety of private financial institutions and management consulting firms. For example, Salomon Brothers, a leading investment banking firm, provides annual estimates of the supply and demand for credit and a forecast of the trend in long- and short-term interest rates for the ensuing year. Other major investment/brokerage houses usually make economic and financial forecasts available upon request. Forecasts of annual capital spending based on repeated industry surveys are prepared regularly by the U.S. Department of Commerce (published quarterly), McGraw-Hill Publication Company Department of Economics, Merrill Lynch Economics, Inc., and Rinfret Associates, Inc. Banks and other businesses often subscribe to the services of one or more of a number of economic consulting firms that prepare detailed forecasts of the nation's GNP and its components, inflation, and interest rates. Among the more prominent of these forecasting firms are Chase Econometrics Associates, Inc., Data Resources, Inc., and Wharton Econometric Forecasting Associates, Inc.

SOCIAL ACCOUNTING DATA

Students of the economy and the financial markets also make use of social accounting systems to keep track of broad trends in national economic and financial conditions. Social accounting refers to a system of recordkeeping which reports transactions between the principal sectors of the economy, such as households, financial institutions, corporations, and units of government. The two most closely followed social accounting systems are the National Income Accounts and the Flow of Funds Accounts.

National Income Accounts

The National Income Accounts (NIA) are compiled and released quarterly by the U.S. Department of Commerce. The NIA accounting system presents data on the nation's production of goods and services, income flows, investment spending, consumption, and savings. Probably the best known account in the NIA series is gross national product (GNP), which is a measure of the market value of all goods and services produced in the U.S. economy within a year's time. GNP may be broken down into the uses to which the nation's output of goods and services is put. For example, Exhibit 3–9, drawn from the *Survey of Current Business* and *Federal Reserve Bulletin,* indicates the size of the U.S. GNP and its major components in 1987.

The National Income Accounts provide valuable information on the level and growth of the nation's economic activity. However, these accounts provide little or no information on financial transactions. For example, one component of the NIA system reports the annual amount of personal savings, but it does not show how those savings are allocated among purchases of bonds, deposits, stocks, and other financial assets. This task is left to the Flow of Funds Accounts, prepared by the Board of Governors of the Federal Reserve System.

Exhibit 3–9   **National Income and Product Accounts: The Components of U.S. GNP, 1987* (Billions of Current Dollars)**

Personal consumption expenditures:		$2,850.7
Durable goods	$ 384.6	
Nondurable goods	961.7	
Services	1,504.5	
Gross private domestic investment:		718.1
Fixed investment	678.1	
Change in business inventories	40.0	
Net exports of goods and services:		−111.9
Exports	391.6	
Imports	503.4	
Government purchases of goods and services:		891.4
Federal	369.2	
State and local	522.2	
Gross national product of the United States		$4,348.4

*First quarter only.

Source: U.S. Department of Commerce, *Survery of Current Business;* and Board of Governors of the Federal Reserve System, *Federal Reserve Bulletin,* July 1987.

The Flow of Funds Accounts

Flow of funds data have been prepared and published quarterly by the Federal Reserve System since 1955. Some data series go back to 1945. Monthly issues of the *Federal Reserve Bulletin* contain the latest summary reports of flow of funds transactions, while detailed breakdowns of financial transactions among major sectors of the economy are readily available on both a quarterly and an annual basis from the Federal Reserve Board in Washington, D.C.

Purposes of the Flow of Funds Accounts. The basic purposes of the Flow of Funds Accounts are to: (1) trace the flow of savings by businesses, households, and governments into purchases of financial assets; (2) show how the various parts of the financial system are related to and interact with each other; and (3) highlight the interconnections between the financial sector and the rest of the economy.

Flow of Funds Construction and Sector Balance Sheets. Construction of the Flow of Funds Accounts takes place in four basic steps. First, the economy is divided into several broad *sectors,* each consisting of economic units (transactors) with similar balance sheets. The 12 major sectors in the current account series include:

- Households, including personal trusts, foundations, private schools and hospitals, labor unions, churches, and charitable organizations.

- Farm businesses.
- Nonfarm noncorporate businesses, including partnerships and proprietorships engaged in nonfinancial activities.
- Nonfinancial corporations.
- State and local governments.
- U.S. government, including government-owned agencies.
- Federally sponsored credit agencies, such as the Federal Land Banks and Federal National Mortgage Association.
- Monetary authorities, including the Federal Reserve System and certain monetary accounts of the U.S. Treasury.
- Commercial banks.
- Foreign banking agencies.
- Savings institutions, including savings and loans, insurance companies, and pension funds.
- Other financial institutions, such as finance companies, investment companies, and security brokers and dealers.

The second step in assembling the Flow of Funds Accounts is to construct *balance sheets* for each of the sectors listed above at the end of each quarter. Like any balance sheet for a business firm or household, sector balance sheets contain estimates of the total assets, liabilities, and net worth held by each sector as of a single point in time. Assets are divided into financial assets and real (nonfinancial) assets. Detailed breakdowns of total financial assets and liabilities outstanding for each sector are made available to the public once a year.

An example of such a partial balance sheet containing financial assets and liabilities for the household sector for the years 1975 through 1985 is shown in Exhibit 3–10. We note, for example, that households held total financial assets of almost $8 trillion at year-end 1985 (shown in line 1)—more than triple their financial asset holdings of a decade before. A substantial part of this total was represented by holdings of demand deposits, currency, and time and savings deposits at commercial banks and nonbank savings institutions. These liquid financial assets totaled nearly $2.7 trillion in 1985 (line 3). The next most important financial asset held by households was corporate stock (equities), totaling about $1.9 trillion in 1985 (line 18), or about one quarter of the household sector's total financial resources. Holdings of debt securities (credit market instruments), including U.S. Treasury notes and bonds, federal agency securities, state and local government bonds, mortgages and similar assets, amounted to about $1.1 trillion (line 8) as of year-end 1985. It is interesting that the total indebtedness of individuals and families in the United States is far less than their holdings of financial assets.[6] Exhibit 3–10 indicates that the household sector's liabilities totaled nearly $2.5 trillion in 1985 (line 25)—roughly a third of its total financial assets. Most of the household sector's indebtedness was in the form of home mortgages (line 27) and installment debt (line 28).

Sources of Data. Data needed to construct sector balance sheets in the Flow of Funds Accounts come from a wide variety of public and private sources. For example, the U.S. Treasury provides monthly statements of its receipts and expenditures. Information on lending, borrowing, and acquisition of securities by nonfinancial businesses is derived from the Securities and Exchange Commission, the Internal Revenue Service, the U.S. Department of Agriculture, the Commerce Department, the Bureau of the Census, and the Federal Reserve itself. Various trade groups provide financial data on their respective industries, while the Securities Industry Association provides selected information on gross offerings of securities. Inevitably, inconsistencies arise in classifying financial transactions due to differences in accounting procedures used by agencies and groups contributing data to the accounts. Moreover, in an economy as vast and complex as that of the United States, some financial transactions fall between the cracks. To deal with problems of consistency and coverage, the Federal Reserve includes a Statistical Discrepancy account which brings each sector into balance.

Preparation of Sources and Uses of Funds Statement. After balance sheets are constructed for each sector of the economy, the third step in the construction of the Flow of Funds Accounts is to prepare a sources and uses of funds statement for each sector. The sources and uses of funds statement shows changes in net worth and changes in holdings of financial assets and liabilities taken from each sector's balance sheet at the beginning and end of a calendar quarter or year. Thus:

Sources and Uses of Funds Statement

Uses of Funds	Sources of Funds
Change in real assets (or net real investment)	Change in liabilities outstanding (or net borrowing)
Change in financial assets (or net financial investment)	Change in net worth (or net current savings)
Change in total assets = Total uses of funds	Change in liabilities and net worth = Total sources of funds

An example of such a statement for the U.S. commercial banking sector for 1980–87 is shown in Exhibit 3–11. The first portion of the sources and

---

[6]The relationship between household debt and holdings of financial assets is examined in more detail in Chapter 18.

Exhibit 3–10   **Statement of Financial Assets and Liabilities for the Household Sector, 1975–1985 ($ Billion; Year-End Outstanding)***

		1975	1976	1977
1	Total financial assets	2,558.9	2,899.7	3,076.5
2	Deposits + credit market instruments†	1,294.8	1,438.9	1,596.2
3	Deposits	940.1	1,062.0	1,189.5
4	Checkable deposits + currency	170.4	186.2	205.2
5	Small time + savings deposits	719.6	835.8	930.9
6	Money market fund shares	3.7	3.7	3.9
7	Large time deposits	46.4	36.4	49.5
8	Credit market instruments	354.7	376.9	406.7
9	U.S. government securities	138.7	145.5	163.4
10	Treasury issues	126.2	129.8	142.3
11	Savings bonds	67.4	72.0	76.8
12	Other Treasury	58.9	57.9	65.5
13	Agency issues	12.5	15.6	21.2
14	Tax-exempt obligations	68.1	70.1	70.1
15	Corporate and foreign bonds	60.9	71.6	71.4
16	Mortgages	76.2	83.6	91.7
17	Open-market paper	10.9	6.1	10.0
18	Corporate equities	646.9	766.0	723.4
19	Mutual fund shares	43.0	46.5	45.4
20	Other corporate equities	603.9	719.5	678.1
21	Life insurance reserves	166.5	175.3	184.8
22	Pension fund reserves	405.6	467.2	513.8
23	Security credit	4.5	6.3	5.3
24	Miscellaneous assets	40.6	46.0	52.9
25	Total Liabilities	808.0	907.4	1,051.7
26	Credit market instruments	778.8	871.2	1,012.2
27	Home mortgages	482.9	544.3	635.1
28	Installment consumer credit	172.3	193.8	230.6
29	Other consumer credit	50.9	54.8	58.6
30	Tax-exempt debt	2.7	4.7	8.1
31	Other mortgages	24.8	25.6	26.7
32	Bank Loans NEC	13.7	14.6	17.4
33	Other Loans	31.5	33.4	35.7
34	Security credit	12.1	17.2	18.5
35	Trade credit	9.4	10.5	11.7
36	Deferred and unpaid life insurance premiums	7.7	8.4	9.3

*Households, personal trusts and nonprofit organizations
†Excludes corporate equities.

Source: Board of Governors of the Federal Reserve System, *Flow of Funds Accounts, Assets and Liabilities Outstanding, 1962–85.*

1978	1979	1980	1981	1982	1983	1984	1985
3,364.5	3,850.0	4,532.0	4,826.3	5,377.3	6,057.5	6,760.8	7,870.8
1,767.5	1,975.1	2,181.0	2,433.9	2,645.6	2,916.4	3,421.2	3,790.6
1,321.5	1,450.4	1,620.7	1,830.2	1,983.3	2,177.6	2,474.9	2,659.8
228.3	249.4	264.0	299.4	315.9	355.7	380.9	428.0
996.9	1,056.9	1,140.2	1,187.1	1,323.8	1,537.6	1,686.8	1,829.7
10.8	45.2	74.4	181.9	206.6	162.5	209.7	207.5
85.5	98.8	142.0	161.7	137.0	121.7	197.5	194.6
446.0	524.8	560.4	603.7	662.3	738.8	946.3	1,130.8
184.1	226.8	240.2	264.8	277.3	323.3	531.8	594.8
156.8	181.6	188.2	208.2	226.2	268.7	432.8	429.1
80.7	79.9	72.5	68.2	68.3	71.5	74.5	79.8
76.1	101.8	115.6	140.0	157.9	197.2	358.2	349.3
27.3	45.2	52.1	56.5	51.1	59.5	99.0	165.8
72.7	83.2	89.9	100.8	132.8	173.8	190.2	249.2
65.2	64.0	53.3	50.4	45.7	45.0	38.5	54.1
105.9	125.9	148.1	171.2	191.7	183.8	151.1	152.2
18.1	24.7	23.8	16.5	14.7	7.9	34.6	80.6
741.0	892.3	1,188.2	1,134.3	1,274.8	1,466.2	1,490.7	1,949.4
45.8	51.2	63.5	63.8	89.5	129.3	162.5	283.0
695.2	841.1	1,124.8	1,070.5	1,185.4	1,336.9	1,328.2	1,666.5
196.0	206.7	216.4	225.6	232.8	240.8	246.0	253.8
592.6	699.6	859.1	941.2	1,122.7	1,322.3	1,477.2	1,737.7
7.8	9.6	14.8	12.7	16.0	19.3	18.1	18.5
59.5	66.7	72.4	78.5	85.3	92.5	107.6	120.5
1,225.8	1,409.8	1,544.3	1,679.3	1,778.7	1,975.7	2,157.5	2,455.0
1,182.5	1,362.5	1,487.0	1,619.2	1,712.1	1,887.5	2,082.0	2,371.2
746.5	869.2	967.5	1,051.0	1,096.9	1,200.1	1,303.4	1,451.5
273.6	312.0	314.9	335.7	355.8	396.1	460.8	543.2
64.3	71.3	74.8	80.7	85.9	96.9	109.0	123.3
10.7	13.6	16.7	21.1	29.4	40.6	51.2	81.3
28.1	29.6	31.5	33.8	36.4	38.9	41.4	43.8
19.9	20.8	26.8	31.2	34.4	38.4	36.7	45.0
39.5	45.9	54.7	65.8	73.2	76.5	79.4	83.1
19.7	20.7	27.2	25.6	28.8	48.1	34.6	41.9
13.2	14.9	17.2	19.8	22.2	24.0	25.8	28.0
10.3	11.7	12.9	14.7	15.5	16.1	15.1	13.9

Exhibit 3-11 **Sources and Uses of Funds Statement for the U.S. Banking Sector, 1980-87** ($ Billions)

| | | **U.S. CHARTERED COMMERCIAL BANKS, SEASONALLY ADJUSTED ANNUAL RATES** | | | | | | |
	1980	1981	1982	1983	1984	1985	1986	1987*
1 Current surplus	7.6	8.9	10.0	14.3	12.8	15.0	18.6	16.6
2 Plant and equipment	9.8	10.7	12.4	14.9	14.7	22.4	19.2	17.2
3 Net acquisition of financial assets	84.2	106.3	112.1	133.7	167.8	193.1	177.5	-9.2
4 Total bank credit	84.2	100.3	106.7	136.6	174.3	133.4	163.9	22.0
5 U.S. government securities	25.0	11.4	26.7	44.2	3.5	4.6	42.4	3.9
6 Treasury issues	15.3	1.8	19.4	43.5	4.1	7.5	5.9	-22.3
7 Agency issues	9.7	9.6	7.3	0.7	-0.6	-2.9	36.5	26.2
8 Tax-exempt obligations	13.2	5.7	4.6	3.8	9.5	57.2	-28.4	-7.5
9 Corporate bonds	0.5	*	1.7	3.6	3.2	2.3	18.4	-7.8
10 Total loans	45.6	83.2	73.7	85.0	158.1	119.3	131.5	33.4
11 Mortgages	17.7	21.4	14.5	28.6	46.2	49.6	67.0	81.1
12 Consumer credit	-6.2	4.0	6.7	22.7	46.0	36.1	23.3	-1.0
13 Bank loans NEC	31.9	53.4	51.0	33.2	58.9	29.6	47.9	-52.7
14 Open-market paper	1.0	-0.2	1.0	-1.5	1.3	-2.8	-0.7	-10.6
15 Security credit	1.2	4.7	0.5	2.0	5.7	6.8	-5.9	16.7
16 Vault cash and member bank reserves	-1.0	-3.4	2.2	-3.6	-2.0	7.4	19.0	-36.2
17 Miscellaneous assets	0.9	9.4	3.2	0.7	-4.5	2.3	-5.4	5.0
18 Net increase in liabilities	76.7	100.1	107.5	125.9	163.3	188.6	167.1	-5.9
19 Checkable deposits	10.7	14.8	20.9	15.6	23.4	51.8	93.2	-200.3
20 U.S. government	-2.6	-1.1	6.1	-5.3	3.8	10.3	1.7	-68.9
21 Foreign	-0.2	-3.0	-2.2	1.4	2.0	0.1	2.7	-4.6
22 Private domestic	13.4	18.9	17.1	19.5	17.5	41.4	88.8	-126.8
23 Small time and savings deposits	44.8	40.3	97.0	130.0	70.7	80.3	71.6	23.5
24 Large time deposits	39.3	43.9	2.3	-38.7	35.9	10.8	-6.6	38.6
25 Fed funds and security RPs	17.8	13.1	10.7	10.2	9.2	37.3	15.9	51.2
26 Net interbank liabilities	-36.7	-18.8	-27.6	7.6	17.1	-0.6	0.4	57.4
27 Federal Reserve float	-2.3	-2.7	1.0	-1.2	-.7	0.1	0.3	19.2
28 Borrowing at Federal Reserve banks	0.4	-0.2	-0.9	0.2	2.7	-0.5	-1.5	-2.6
29 To domestic banks	-12.4	-9.7	-9.5	-1.0	8.1	-9.0	4.1	8.0
30 To foreign banks	-22.3	-6.2	-18.2	9.6	7.1	8.8	-2.4	32.8
31 Corporate equities	0.4	0.5	0.6	0.7	0.8	1.4	1.4	1.5
32 Corporate bonds	0.2	-0.1	0.6	-0.2	1.9	4.5	2.2	1.6
33 Profit taxes payable	-0.5	-0.4	-0.1	-0.1	*	0.1	*	0.1
34 Miscellaneous liabilities	0.8	6.7	3.1	0.9	4.2	3.0	-11.0	20.5
35 Discrepancy	-9.7	-7.9	-7.0	-8.4	-6.4	-11.9	-11.0	2.7
36 Memo: Credit market funds advanced	83.1	95.6	106.2	134.6	168.6	165.6	162.5	6.8

*Figures are for first quarter only.

Source: Board of Governors of the Federal Reserve System, *Flow of Funds Accounts*, First Quarter 1987.

uses statement (lines 1–17) shows changes in the banking sector's net worth (i.e., current surplus, representing net current savings), real assets (net investments in plant and equipment), and net acquisitions of financial assets. The second portion of the statement (lines 18–34) reflects net borrowing as reflected in an increase in the liabilities carried by U.S. commercial banks and their affiliates.[7] We note, for example, that U.S. chartered commercial banks actually reduced their holdings of financial assets by $9.2 billion during 1987 (line 3). Bank loans to consumers, businesses, and other borrowers actually rose $33.4 billion. Commercial bank holdings of U.S. government securities rose just $3.9 billion (line 5). However, banks reduced their holdings of state and local government (tax-exempt) securities and corporate bonds by a total of $15.3 billion (lines 8 and 9) in 1987. And bank holdings of vault cash and reserves, due to changing economic conditions and bank regulations, fell by just over $36 billion (line 16). The nation's commercial banks invested $17.2 billion in plant and equipment (line 2) during the course of that year.

Where did the banking sector get the funds it needed to make loans and increase its investment in plant and equipment during 1987? The necessary funds came principally from retained earnings (current saving), as reflected in the current surplus account (line 1), which rose $16.6 billion during 1987. Liabilities of the banking sector actually fell $5.9 billion, led by a massive decline of $200 billion in demand deposits (checking accounts), as reflected in line 19. As we saw above, there were large-scale sales of securities on the asset side of the banks' balance sheet to provide funds to cover the loss of checking account deposits and make the loans banks wanted to make.

Balancing Out a Sources and Uses of Funds Statement. As we have seen, sources and uses of funds statements in the Flow of Funds Accounts are derived from the aggregated balance sheets of each sector of the economy. Because balance sheets must always balance, we would also expect a sources and uses of funds statement to balance (except, of course, for discrepancies due to inaccuracies in the underlying data). In a sources and uses statement,

$$\begin{array}{c}\text{Net investment} \\ \text{in plant} \\ \text{and equipment}\end{array} + \begin{array}{c}\text{Net acquisitions} \\ \text{of financial} \\ \text{assets}\end{array} = \begin{array}{c}\text{Net increase in} \\ \text{liabilities} + \text{Change} \\ \text{in current surplus account}\end{array} \qquad (3\text{--}1)$$

Net acquisitions of financial assets are frequently referred to as financial investment, while net purchases of plant and equipment may be labeled real investment. Both are *uses of funds* for a sector or economic unit. Net increases in liabilities represent borrowing in the current period. And changes in the

---

[7]All changes on a sources and uses of funds statement are shown *net* of purchases and sales. When purchases of an asset exceed sales of that asset, the resulting figure is reported as a *positive* increase in the asset. When sales exceed purchases, an asset item will carry a *negative* sign. A nonnegative liability item on the sources and uses statement indicates that net borrowing (i.e., total borrowings minus debt repayments) has occurred during the period under study. If a liability item is negative, debt repayments exceed new borrowings during the period covered by the statement.

current surplus account reflect current saving. Both latter items are *sources of funds*. Therefore, the relationship shown above may be written simply as:

$$\text{Net real investment} + \text{Net financial investment} \qquad (3\text{--}2)$$
$$= \text{Net borrowing} + \text{Net current saving}$$

or,

$$\text{Total uses of funds} = \text{Total sources of funds} \qquad (3\text{--}3)$$

For each unit—business, household, or government—and for each sector of the economy, the above statements must be true. For example, in the commercial banking sector during 1987 we have, as shown in Exhibit 3–11:

Uses of Funds ($ billions)		Sources of Funds ($ billions)	
Net investment in plant and equipment (line 2)	$ 17.2	Net borrowing (line 18)	$ −5.9
Net financial investment (line 3)	−9.2	Net current saving (line 1)	16.6
Statistical discrepancy (line 35)	2.7	Total sources	$ 10.7
Total uses	$ 10.7		

Once the statistical discrepancy is taken into account, total uses and sources of funds should be equal for this and for all other sectors in the economy.

Constructing a Flow of Funds Matrix for the Economy as a Whole. The final step in the construction of the Flow of Funds Accounts is to combine the sources and uses of funds statement for each sector into a flow of funds matrix for the whole economy. An example of such a matrix for the U.S. economy is shown in Exhibit 3–12, which shows *borrowings* by each major sector of the economy and total borrowings by all sectors combined, and Exhibit 3–13, which shows funds *loaned* by each major sector to domestic nonfinancial borrowers and total credit extended by all sectors. The majority of funds sought by businesses, consumers, and governments in the nation's financial markets clearly were raised by issuing debt instruments, as shown in Exhibit 3–12. The sum total of all debt instruments outstanding rose a net $1092.1 billion (line 50) in 1986. The U.S. Treasury and various federal agencies were among the heaviest borrowers of funds, issuing about $388 billion in debt instruments (line 51). Next in line for the most borrowed funds were issuers of residential and commercial mortgages who borrowed more than $298 billion in 1986 (line 54). State and local governments borrowed net $49.5 billion (line 52), while domestic corporations and foreign borrowers issued $144 billion net in bonds during 1986 (line 53). Installment credit extended to consumers totaled just about $66 billion (line 55).

Exhibit 3–12 **Funds Raised in U.S. Credit Markets** ($ Billions; Half-Yearly Data at Seasonally Adjusted Annual Rates)

Transaction category, sector	1981	1982	1983	1984	1985	1986ʳ	1984 H1	1984 H2	1985 H1	1985 H2	1986ʳ H1	1986ʳ H2
						Nonfinancial sectors						
1 Total net borrowing by domestic nonfinancial sectors	375.8	387.4	548.8	756.3	869.3	834.0	727.8	784.8	732.6	1,006.1	706.0	962.5
By sector and instrument												
2 U.S. government	87.4	161.3	186.6	198.8	223.6	214.3	181.3	216.3	201.8	245.5	211.3	217.5
3 Treasury securities..............................	87.8	162.1	186.7	199.0	223.7	214.7	181.5	216.4	201.9	245.5	211.4	218.0
4 Agency issues and mortgages	−.5	−.9	−.1	−.2	−.1	−.3	−.2	−.1	−.1	−.1	−.1	−.5
5 Private domestic nonfinancial sectors	288.5	226.2	362.2	557.5	645.7	619.6	546.5	568.5	530.8	760.6	494.7	745.0
6 Debt capital instruments	155.5	148.3	252.8	314.0	461.7	461.7	298.4	329.6	355.4	568.0	392.3	531.2
7 Tax-exempt obligations......................	23.4	44.2	53.7	50.4	152.4	49.5	42.8	58.0	67.5	237.3	15.9	83.0
8 Corporate bonds...........................	22.8	18.7	16.0	46.1	73.9	113.7	31.2	61.1	72.7	75.1	137.0	90.4
9 Mortgages...............................	109.3	85.4	183.0	217.5	235.4	298.5	224.5	210.5	215.2	255.7	239.3	357.7
10 Home mortgages.......................	72.2	50.5	117.1	129.9	150.3	199.2	135.2	124.7	133.1	167.5	156.1	242.3
11 Multifamily residential.................	4.8	5.4	14.1	25.1	29.2	33.0	27.5	22.7	24.6	33.7	30.8	35.1
12 Commercial..........................	22.2	25.2	49.0	63.3	62.4	73.7	62.9	63.7	60.3	64.4	59.7	87.7
13 Farm...............................	10.0	4.2	2.8	−.8	−6.4	−7.4	−1.1	−.5	−2.8	−10.0	−7.4	−7.4
14 Other debt instruments	133.0	77.9	109.5	243.5	184.0	157.9	248.1	238.9	175.4	192.6	102.4	213.9
15 Consumer credit	22.6	17.7	56.8	95.0	96.6	65.8	98.7	91.3	97.3	95.9	70.6	61.6
16 Bank loans n.e.c.	57.0	52.9	25.8	80.1	41.3	71.0	91.9	68.4	24.9	57.7	17.6	124.4
17 Open market paper.........................	14.7	−6.1	−.8	21.7	14.6	−9.3	24.8	18.7	12.3	16.9	−15.7	−3.0
18 Other.................................	38.7	13.4	27.7	46.6	31.4	30.3	32.7	60.5	40.9	22.0	29.9	30.7
19 By borrowing sector	288.5	226.2	362.2	557.5	645.7	619.6	546.5	568.5	530.8	760.6	494.7	745.0
20 State and local governments	6.8	21.5	34.0	27.4	107.8	59.4	25.2	29.6	56.8	158.7	35.7	83.2
21 Households.............................	121.4	88.4	188.0	239.5	295.0	282.1	232.8	246.2	253.6	336.4	222.4	342.3
22 Farm.................................	16.6	6.8	4.3	.1	−13.6	−14.4	−.4	.5	−5.9	−21.3	−15.1	−13.7
23 Nonfarm noncorporate	38.5	40.2	76.6	97.1	92.8	114.6	101.4	92.7	85.6	99.9	94.4	134.7
24 Corporate..............................	105.2	69.2	59.3	193.4	163.7	178.0	187.4	199.5	140.7	186.8	157.3	198.6
25 Foreign net borrowing in United States.................	23.5	16.0	17.4	6.1	1.7	9.7	35.5	−23.3	−4.1	7.5	24.3	−5.0
26 Bonds	5.4	6.7	3.1	1.3	4.0	3.2	1.1	1.5	5.5	2.6	7.1	−.8
27 Bank loans n.e.c.	3.0	−5.5	3.6	−6.6	−2.8	−1.0	−2.2	−11.1	−6.1	.4	1.4	−3.5
28 Open market paper..........................	3.9	1.9	6.5	6.2	6.2	11.5	18.0	−5.6	4.2	8.2	20.6	2.4
29 U.S. government loans	11.1	13.0	4.1	5.3	−5.7	−4.0	18.7	−8.1	−7.8	−3.6	−4.8	−3.1
30 Total domestic plus foreign	399.3	403.4	566.2	762.4	871.0	843.6	763.3	761.5	728.4	1,013.5	730.3	957.6
						Financial sectors						
31 Total net borrowing by financial sectors.................	101.9	90.1	94.0	139.0	186.9	248.4	134.2	143.8	154.8	218.9	185.9	310.9
By instrument												
32 U.S. government related..........................	47.4	64.9	67.8	74.9	101.5	173.7	69.8	80.0	92.9	110.2	129.5	217.8
33 Sponsored credit agency securities..................	30.5	14.9	1.4	30.4	20.6	12.6	29.1	31.8	25.3	15.9	4.4	20.8
34 Mortgage pool securities......................	15.0	49.5	66.4	44.4	79.9	161.4	40.7	48.2	67.6	92.1	124.3	198.6
35 Loans from U.S. government	1.9	.4	.....	.....	1.1	−.4	.....	.....	.....	2.2	.8	−1.5
36 Private financial sectors	54.5	25.2	26.2	64.1	85.3	74.8	64.4	63.8	61.9	108.8	56.4	93.1
37 Corporate bonds............................	4.4	12.5	12.1	23.3	36.5	26.6	17.3	29.3	35.3	37.7	25.5	27.7
38 Mortgages...............................	*	.1	*	.4	.1	.1	.4	.4	*	.1	.6	−.4
39 Bank loans n.e.c.	1.2	1.9	−.1	.7	2.6	4.0	−.1	1.4	.9	4.2	2.4	5.6
40 Open market paper..........................	32.7	9.9	21.3	24.1	32.0	24.2	31.1	17.0	13.9	50.1	14.4	34.1
41 Loans from Federal Home Loan Banks	16.2	.8	−7.0	15.7	14.2	19.8	15.7	15.7	11.7	16.7	13.5	26.2
By sector												
42 Sponsored credit agencies	32.4	15.3	1.4	30.4	21.7	12.2	29.1	31.8	25.3	18.1	5.2	19.3
43 Mortgage pools	15.0	49.5	66.4	44.4	79.9	161.4	40.7	48.2	67.6	92.1	124.3	198.6
44 Private financial sectors	54.5	25.2	26.2	64.1	85.3	74.8	64.4	63.8	61.9	108.8	56.4	93.1
45 Commercial banks	11.6	11.7	5.0	7.3	−4.9	−3.6	15.4	−.9	−9.2	−.6	−6.7	−.5
46 Bank affiliates	9.2	6.8	12.1	15.6	14.5	4.5	23.7	7.5	13.7	15.3	1.7	7.4
47 Savings and loan associations	15.5	2.5	−2.1	22.7	22.3	29.2	20.2	25.1	12.1	32.6	23.1	35.3
48 Finance companies	18.5	4.3	11.4	17.8	52.8	44.1	4.3	31.3	44.8	60.9	37.5	50.6
49 REITs..................................	−.2	*	−.2	.8	.5	.6	.8	.8	.5	.5	.9	.3

Source: Board of Governors of the Federal Reserve System, *Federal Reserve Bulletin*, August 1987, Table 1.57, p. A-42.

Exhibit 3–12   *(concluded)*

Transaction category, sector	1981	1982	1983	1984	1985	1986'	1984 H1	1984 H2	1985 H1	1985 H2	1986' H1	1986' H2
						All sectors						
50 Total net borrowing	501.3	493.5	660.2	901.4	1057.8	1092.1	897.5	905.3	833.3	1,232.4	916.2	1268.5
51 U.S. government securities	133.0	225.9	254.4	273.8	324.2	388.4	251.2	296.4	294.8	353.5	340.0	436.9
52 State and local obligations	23.4	44.2	53.7	50.4	152.4	49.5	42.8	58.0	67.5	237.3	15.9	83.0
53 Corporate and foreign bonds	32.6	37.8	31.2	70.7	114.4	143.5	49.6	91.9	113.5	115.3	169.6	117.4
54 Mortgages	109.2	85.4	183.0	217.8	235.4	298.6	224.8	210.8	215.2	255.7	239.9	357.3
55 Consumer credit	22.6	17.7	56.8	95.0	96.6	65.8	98.7	91.3	97.3	95.9	70.6	61.6
56 Bank loans n.e.c.	61.2	49.3	29.3	74.2	41.0	74.0	89.6	58.8	19.8	62.3	21.4	126.6
57 Open market paper	51.3	5.7	26.9	52.0	52.8	26.4	73.8	30.1	30.4	75.2	19.3	33.4
58 Other loans	68.0	27.6	24.8	67.6	41.0	45.8	67.1	68.1	44.8	37.3	39.4	52.3
						External corporate equity funds raised in United States						
50 Total new share issues	−3.3	33.6	67.0	−31.1	37.5	119.5	−40.1	−22.2	33.3	41.6	146.8	92.3
60 Mutual funds	6.0	16.8	32.1	38.0	103.4	191.7	39.3	36.6	93.6	113.1	198.7	184.6
61 All other	−9.3	16.8	34.9	−69.1	−65.9	−72.1	−79.4	−58.8	−60.4	−71.5	−52.0	−92.3
62 Nonfinancial corporations	−11.5	11.4	28.3	−77.0	−81.6	−80.8	−84.5	−69.4	−75.7	−87.5	−68.7	−92.7
63 Financial corporations	1.9	4.0	2.7	6.7	11.7	7.0	5.9	7.6	11.0	12.4	8.3	5.7
64 Foreign shares purchased in United States	.3	1.5	3.9	1.2	4.0	1.6	−.7	3.0	4.3	3.6	8.5	−5.3

Exhibit 3–13 looks at borrowing in the economy from the *lenders'* point of view—for whatever is borrowed by one sector must be credit extended by other sectors. For example, line 1 in Exhibit 3–13 shows that total funds advanced in U.S. credit markets in the form of loans to domestic nonfinancial sectors amounted to $834 billion in 1986. This amount exactly matches the total net borrowing by domestic nonfinancial sectors shown in line 1 of Exhibit 3–12. Similarly, Exhibit 3–12 shows that corporations retired a net $72.1 billion in outstanding stock (corporate equity shares) in 1986 (line 61), which corresponds exactly to the decline in total funds advanced through stock sales in the U.S. economy during 1986 as shown in Exhibit 3–13 (line 53). The flow of funds matrix reminds us that, for all sectors of the economy combined into one, the amount of saving must equal the total amount of real investment in the economy and the amount of borrowing in total must equal total financial investment (i.e., the total amount of financial assets acquired by all sectors).

Limitations and Uses of the Flow of Funds Accounts. It should be clear by now that the Flow of Funds Accounts provide a vast amount of information on trends in the financial system. They are an indispensable aid in tracing the flow of savings and other funds through the money and capital markets. Moreover, as we will see in Chapter 11, estimates of flow of funds data can be used to make forecasts of savings and investment, lending and

Exhibit 3–13 Direct and Indirect Sources of Funds to Credit Markets
($ Billions, Except as Noted; Half-Yearly Data at
Seasonally Adjusted Annual Rates)

Transaction category, or sector	1981	1982	1983	1984	1985	1986ʳ	1984 H1	1984 H2	1985 H1	1985 H2	1986ʳ H1	1986ʳ H2
1 Total funds advanced in credit markets to domestic nonfinancial sectors	375.8	387.4	548.8	756.3	869.3	834.0	727.8	784.8	732.6	1,006.1	706.0	962.5
By public agencies and foreign												
2 Total net advances	104.4	115.4	115.3	154.6	203.3	311.1	132.5	176.6	201.8	204.9	267.6	354.5
3 U.S. government securities	17.1	22.7	27.6	36.0	47.2	87.8	26.8	45.2	53.1	41.3	85.4	90.1
4 Residential mortgages	23.5	61.0	76.1	56.5	94.6	158.5	52.7	60.2	85.6	103.7	121.0	196.0
5 FHLB advances to savings and loans	16.2	.8	−7.0	15.7	14.2	19.8	15.7	15.7	11.7	16.7	13.5	26.2
6 Other loans and securities	47.7	30.8	18.6	46.5	47.3	45.0	37.5	55.5	51.4	43.2	47.7	42.3
Total advanced, by sector												
7 U.S. government	24.0	15.9	9.7	17.4	17.8	10.9	9.0	25.7	28.8	6.7	12.9	9.0
8 Sponsored credit agencies	48.2	65.5	69.8	73.3	101.5	176.6	74.0	72.5	98.2	104.9	135.3	217.9
9 Monetary authorities	9.2	9.8	10.9	8.4	21.6	30.2	8.8	8.0	23.7	19.5	9.8	50.6
10 Foreign	23.0	24.1	24.9	55.5	62.4	93.4	40.7	70.4	51.0	73.8	109.7	77.1
Agency and foreign borrowing not in line 1												
11 Sponsored credit agencies and mortgage pools	47.4	64.9	67.8	74.9	101.5	173.7	69.8	80.0	92.9	110.2	129.5	217.8
12 Foreign	23.5	16.0	17.4	6.1	1.7	9.7	35.5	−23.3	−4.1	7.5	24.3	−5.0
Private domestic funds advanced												
13 Total net advances	342.3	352.9	518.7	682.7	769.2	706.2	700.5	664.9	619.6	918.8	592.1	820.9
14 U.S. government securities	115.9	203.1	226.9	237.8	277.0	300.6	224.4	251.2	241.7	312.2	254.5	346.8
15 State and local obligations	23.4	44.2	53.7	50.4	152.4	49.5	42.8	58.0	67.5	237.3	15.9	83.0
16 Corporate and foreign bonds	19.8	14.8	14.6	32.6	41.2	79.0	25.6	39.6	49.7	32.7	104.2	53.9
17 Residential mortgages	53.5	−5.3	55.0	98.5	84.8	73.7	109.9	87.0	72.0	97.5	65.9	81.4
18 Other mortgages and loans	145.9	96.9	161.5	279.1	228.1	223.2	313.6	244.7	200.4	255.9	165.0	281.9
19 Less: Federal Home Loan Bank advances	16.2	.8	−7.0	15.7	14.2	19.8	15.7	15.7	11.7	16.7	13.5	26.2
Private financial intermediation												
20 Credit market funds advanced by private financial institutions	320.2	261.9	391.9	550.5	554.4	647.9	581.8	519.1	471.3	637.4	572.4	724.0
21 Commercial banking	106.5	110.2	144.3	168.9	186.3	194.8	184.2	153.5	133.8	238.8	106.9	283.0
22 Savings institutions	26.2	21.8	135.6	149.2	83.4	105.3	173.5	124.9	63.0	103.9	101.4	109.3
23 Insurance and pension funds	93.5	86.2	97.8	124.0	141.0	137.2	144.5	103.5	121.8	160.1	128.6	145.9
24 Other finance	94.0	43.7	14.1	108.3	143.6	210.5	79.5	137.2	152.7	134.5	235.6	185.8
25 Sources of funds	320.2	261.9	391.9	550.5	554.4	647.9	581.8	519.1	471.3	637.4	572.4	724.0
26 Private domestic deposits and RPs	214.5	195.2	212.2	317.6	204.8	242.3	300.2	334.9	203.0	206.6	224.5	260.3
27 Credit market borrowing	54.5	25.2	26.2	64.1	85.3	74.8	64.4	63.8	61.9	108.8	56.4	93.1
28 Other sources	51.2	41.5	153.4	168.8	264.2	330.8	217.2	120.4	206.5	322.0	291.5	370.5
29 Foreign funds	−23.7	−31.4	16.3	5.4	17.7	12.4	3.0	7.8	11.2	24.3	.9	24.0
30 Treasury balances	−1.1	6.1	−5.3	4.0	10.3	1.7	−.1	8.2	14.4	6.1	−5.5	9.0
31 Insurance and pension reserves	89.6	92.5	110.6	112.5	107.0	120.0	146.5	78.5	97.4	116.6	104.5	135.5
32 Other, net	−13.6	−25.7	31.8	46.8	129.2	196.6	67.8	25.9	83.5	175.0	191.5	202.1
Private domestic nonfinancial investors												
33 Direct lending in credit markets	76.6	116.3	153.0	196.4	300.2	133.1	183.1	209.6	210.2	390.2	76.1	190.0
34 U.S. government securities	37.1	69.9	95.5	132.9	150.9	81.0	142.2	123.6	130.8	171.0	41.4	120.9
35 State and local obligations	11.1	25.0	39.0	29.6	59.2	17.8	25.0	34.3	20.5	98.0	−21.8	57.4
36 Corporate and foreign bonds	−4.0	2.0	−12.7	−3.4	13.2	12.3	−26.8	19.9	25.4	1.0	49.3	−24.7
37 Open market paper	1.4	−1.3	15.1	8.9	51.8	1.4	15.7	2.2	7.3	96.3	−13.8	16.7
38 Other	31.0	20.6	16.2	28.3	25.1	20.6	26.9	29.7	26.3	24.0	21.0	19.8
39 Deposits and currency	222.4	204.5	229.7	321.1	215.1	262.7	311.3	330.9	215.9	214.3	241.6	284.0
40 Currency	9.5	9.7	14.3	8.6	12.4	14.4	13.1	4.1	15.8	9.0	10.9	17.9
41 Checkable deposits	18.5	18.6	28.8	27.8	42.0	99.4	29.4	26.3	18.2	65.8	83.1	115.9
42 Small time and savings accounts	47.3	135.7	215.3	150.7	137.5	123.1	136.4	164.9	167.1	108.0	119.5	126.7
43 Money market fund shares	107.5	24.7	−44.1	47.2	−2.2	20.8	30.2	64.2	4.2	−8.6	29.0	12.7
44 Large time deposits	36.0	5.2	−6.3	84.9	14.0	−8.2	93.4	76.5	−.8	28.9	.9	−17.3
45 Security RPs	5.2	11.1	18.5	7.0	13.4	7.2	10.8	3.1	14.3	12.5	−7.9	22.3
46 Deposits in foreign countries	−1.7	−.4	3.1	−5.1	−2.1	6.0	−2.0	−8.2	−2.9	−1.3	6.2	5.7
47 Total of credit market instruments, deposits and currency	299.0	320.7	382.7	517.4	515.3	395.8	494.4	540.5	426.0	604.5	317.8	474.0
48 Public holdings as percent of total	26.2	28.6	20.4	20.3	23.3	36.9	17.4	23.2	27.7	20.2	36.6	37.0
49 Private financial intermediation (in percent)	93.6	74.2	75.5	80.6	72.1	91.7	83.1	78.1	76.1	69.4	96.7	88.2
50 Total foreign funds	−.7	−7.3	41.3	60.9	80.1	105.8	43.7	78.2	62.2	98.1	110.5	101.1

Source: Board of Governors of the Federal Reserve System, *Federal Reserve Bulletin*, August 1987, Table 1.58, p. A-43.

Exhibit 3–13   *(concluded)*

Transaction category, or sector	1981	1982	1983	1984	1985	1986ʳ	1984 H1	1984 H2	1985 H1	1985 H2	1986ʳ H1	1986ʳ H2
Memo: Corporate equities not included above												
51 **Total net issues**	−3.3	33.6	67.0	−31.1	37.5	119.5	−40.1	−22.2	33.3	41.6	146.8	92.3
52 Mutual fund shares	6.0	16.8	32.1	38.0	103.4	191.7	39.3	36.6	93.6	113.1	198.7	184.6
53 Other equities	−9.3	16.8	34.9	−69.1	−65.9	−72.1	−79.4	−58.8	−60.4	−71.5	−52.0	−92.3
54 Acquisitions by financial institutions	19.9	27.6	46.8	8.2	33.3	25.2	−4.1	20.6	54.0	12.6	35.4	15.1
55 Other net purchases	−23.2	6.0	20.2	−39.4	4.1	94.3	−36.0	−42.7	−20.7	29.0	111.4	77.2

NOTES BY LINE NUMBER.
1. Line 1 of table 1.57.
2. Sum of lines 3–6 or 7–10.
6. Includes farm and commercial mortgages.
11. Credit market funds raised by federally sponsored credit agencies, and net issues of federally related mortgage pool securities.
13. Line 1 less line 2 plus line 11 and 12. Also line 20 less line 27 plus line 33. Also sum of lines 28 and 47 less lines 40 and 46.
18. Includes farm and commercial mortgages.
26. Line 39 less lines 40 and 46.
27. Excludes equity issues and investment company shares. Includes line 19.
29. Foreign deposits at commercial banks, bank borrowings from foreign branches, and liabilities of foreign banking agencies to foreign affiliates, less claims on foreign affiliates and deposits by banking in foreign banks.
30. Demand deposits and note balances at commercial banks.

31. Excludes net investment of these reserves in corporate equities.
32. Mainly retained earnings and net miscellaneous liabilities.
33. Line 13 less line 20 plus line 27.
34–38. Lines 14–18 less amounts acquired by private finance plus amounts borrowed by private finance. Line 38 includes mortgages.
40. Mainly an offset to line 9.
47. Lines 33 plus 39, or line 13 less line 28 plus 40 and 46.
48. Line 2/line 1.
49. Line 20/line 13.
50. Sum of lines 10 and 29.
51, 53. Includes issues by financial institutions.
NOTE. Full statements for sectors and transaction types in flows and in amounts outstanding may be obtained from Flow of Funds Section, Division of Research and Statistics, Board of Governors of the Federal Reserve System, Washington, D.C. 20551.

borrowing, and interest rates. However, these social accounts have a number of limitations which must be kept firmly in mind.

First, the Flow of Funds Accounts present *no* information on transactions among economic units within each sector. If a household sells stock to another household, this transaction will not be picked up in the accounts because both units are in the same sector. However, if a household sells stock to a business firm, this transaction will be captured by the flow of funds bookkeeping system. Moreover, the accounts show only *net* flows, not changes or fluctuations that occur between beginning and ending points of the study period.

Finally, all flow of funds data are expressed in terms of current market values. Therefore, these accounts measure not only the flow of savings in the economy, but also fluctuations in the prices of stocks, bonds, and other financial assets (i.e., capital gains and losses). This market value bias distorts estimates of the amount of saving and investment activity occurring from year to year.

Despite these limitations, however, the Flow of Funds Accounts are one of the most comprehensive sources of information available to students of the financial system. They provide vital clues on the demand and supply forces which shape movements in interest rates and security prices. The Flow of Funds Accounts indicate which types of securities are growing or declining in volume and which sectors finance other sectors within the economic system. One of the principal uses of flow of funds data today is to forecast interest rates and build econometric models to simulate future conditions in the credit markets. Coupled with the National Income Accounts and other sources of information, flow of funds accounting provides us with the raw material out of which financial decisions can be made.

SUMMARY

An unimpeded flow of relevant information is vital to the functioning of the financial system. If the scarce resource of credit is to be allocated efficiently and an ample flow of savings made available for investment, financial information must be readily available to market participants. There are really two types of markets within the financial system—an information market and a market for financial claims, evidencing loans and investments. The two markets must work together in coordinated fashion to accomplish the desired end result—a smooth flow of scarce loanable funds toward their most profitable and beneficial uses.

In this chapter we have examined the information market in some detail. Our principal focus has been upon five broad categories of financial information available today—debt security prices and yields, stock prices and dividend yields, the financial condition of security issuers, general conditions in the economy and financial system, and social accounting data. The purpose of this chapter has been to give the student of the financial system a broad overview of the kinds and quality of information currently available. Knowing where to find relevant and up-to-date information is an essential ingredient in the process of solving economic and financial problems.

STUDY QUESTIONS

1. Why is the availability of financial information important to borrowers and lenders of funds? Government policymakers?

2. List several major sources of financial information, and discuss which types of information each contains.

3. If you needed to gather information for a possible stock or bond purchase, where would you look? What information is available on the financial condition of major U.S. companies?

4. What is social accounting? Compare and contrast the Flow of Funds Accounts with the National Income Accounts. What type of information does each provide that might be useful for financial decisions?

5. Explain how the Flow of Funds Accounts are constructed. What is a sources and uses of funds statement?

6. Discuss the principal limitations of flow of funds data and the implications of those limitations.

PROBLEMS

1. Construct sources and uses of funds statements for each sector of the economy and for the whole economy using the following information:

	Households ($ billion)	Business Firms ($ billion)	Banks and Other Financial Institutions ($ billion)	Governmental Units ($ billion)
Current saving	$428.8	$280.0	$35.0	-$35.0
Current real investment	332.5	350.0	17.5	—
Current financial investment	306.3	78.8	43.8	8.8
Current borrowing	210.0	148.8	26.3	43.8

Assume that the four sectors listed above are the *only* sectors in the economy and there are no international transactions. Is there a statistical discrepancy? Where? Referring back to the discussion in Chapter 2, which sectors are deficit-budget, and which are surplus-budget sectors?

2. Suppose you are given the data listed below for the household sector of the economy. From this information, construct a statement of financial assets and liabilities for the household sector.

	($ billion)		($ billion)
Deposits in banks and savings institutions	$540	U.S. government securities................	$110
Home mortgages...........	290	Credit extended by nonbank lending institutions	40
Installment loans extended by banks................	110	Trade credit	5
Holdings of currency and coin	120	Corporate and foreign bonds....................	30
Security credit owed.........	10	Corporate equities...........	680
State and local government bonds....................	50	Life insurance reserves	130
Deferred and unpaid life insurance premiums.......	10	Pension fund reserves	420
Holdings of miscellaneous financial assets	50	Miscellaneous liabilities	35

3. Construct a sources and uses of funds statement for the commercial banking sector for the year immediately concluded. A check of the Federal Reserve's Flow of Funds Accounts indicates that U.S. banks reported a current earnings surplus (after paying stockholder dividends) of $12 billion and made investments in plant and equipment of $11 billion. They acquired net $120 billion in loans to their customers and purchased $3 billion in corporate bonds, $13 billion in state and local government bonds, and $25 billion in U.S. government securities. Miscellaneous assets rose $10 billion. There was a statistical discrepancy in the Flow of Funds Accounts of $8 billion in the banking sector's sources of funds.

SELECTED REFERENCES

Board of Governors of the Federal Reserve System. *Introduction to the Flow of Funds.* Washington, D.C., February 1975.

Cohen, J. "Copeland's Moneyflows after Twenty-Five Years: A Survey." *Journal of Economic Literature,* March 1972, pp. 1–25.

Freund, William C., and Edward D. Zinbarg. "Applications of Flow of Funds to Interest-Rate Forecasting." *Journal of Finance,* May 1963, pp. 231–48.

Goldsmith, Raymond W. *Capital Market Analysis and the Financial Accounts of the Nation.* Morristown, N.J.: General Learning Press, 1982.

Part Two

Financial Institutions in the Financial System

Chapter 4

Commercial Banks and Money Creation

Learning Objectives in This Chapter

- To understand how important commercial banks are in the functioning of a modern economy and financial system.
- To examine the makeup (structure) of the U.S. banking industry in terms of types and sizes of banks.
- To see how and why banks are regulated and to explore the recent trend toward deregulation of this important industry.
- To be able to read and understand bank financial statements and grasp how banks can actually create and destroy money.

Key Terms and Concepts in This Chapter

Banking structure	*Bank holding company*	*Nondeposit funds*
State-chartered banks	*Deregulation*	*Money creation*
National banks	*Primary reserves*	*Legal reserves*
Consolidation	*Transaction accounts*	*Excess reserves*
Branch banking		

THE dominant privately owned financial institution in the United States and in the economies of most major countries is the *commercial bank*. This institution offers the public both deposit and credit services, as well as a growing list of newer and more innovative services, such as investment advice and execution and tax and travel planning. The name *commercial* implies that banks devote a substantial portion of their resources to meeting the financial needs of business firms. In recent years, however, commercial banks have significantly expanded their offerings of financial services to consumers and units of government. The result is the emergence of a financial institution that has rightly been called a financial department store because it satisfies a broad range of financial service needs in the economy.

The importance of commercial banks may be measured in a number of ways. They hold about two fifths of the total assets of all financial institutions headquartered in the United States and hold a major share of all financial assets held abroad as well. Commercial banks are still the principal means of making payments through the checking accounts (demand deposits) they offer. And banks are also important because of their ability to create money from excess reserves made available from the public's deposits. The commercial banking system can take a given volume of excess cash reserves and, by making loans and investments, generate a multiple amount of credit—a process explained later in this chapter.

Banks today are the principal channel for government monetary policy. In the United States, the Federal Reserve System carries out policies to affect interest rates and the availability of credit mainly through altering the level and growth of reserves held by banks and other depository institutions. The same is true in Canada and Great Britain, and in many other nations as well. Today, commercial banks are the most important source of consumer credit and one of the major sources of loans to small- and medium-sized businesses. In most years, banks are the principal purchasers of debt securities issued by state and local governments and one of the major buyers of the new security issues of the U.S. Treasury. For all these reasons, commercial banks play a dominant role in the money and capital markets and are worthy of detailed study if we are to understand more fully how the financial system operates.

THE STRUCTURE OF U.S. COMMERCIAL BANKING

The structure of U.S. banking is unique in comparison with other banking systems around the globe. The term banking structure focuses on the number and different sizes of commercial banks operating in thousands of local communities across the nation. While the banking systems of most other nations consist of a few large banking organizations operating hundreds or thousands of branch offices, the U.S. banking system is dominated by thousands of relatively small commercial banks. For example, in 1988 there were about 15,000 commercial banking institutions headquartered in the United States, compared to only 11 domestically chartered banks in Canada and less than three dozen domestically owned banks in the United Kingdom.

Not surprisingly, most U.S. banks are modest in size compared to banks in other countries. About four fifths of all American commercial banks have total assets of under $100 million each, while only about 2 percent hold assets of a billion dollars or more and actively compete in global markets for loans and deposits (see Exhibit 4–1). While smaller banks predominate in numbers, the larger banks have a disproportionate share of the industry's assets. For example, the roughly 2 percent of all U.S. banks with a billion or more dollars in total assets hold nearly two thirds of all assets in the industry. In contrast, the numerically dominant small banks with less than $100 million in assets hold less than 14 percent of the U.S. banking industry's total assets.

Most commercial banks in the United States are chartered by the states rather than by the federal government. As shown in Exhibit 4–2, of the almost 15,000 commercial banks in operation at year-end 1986, close to 10,000 were state-chartered banks. The remaining one third, classified as national banks, were chartered by the federal government. National banks, on average, are much larger and include nearly all of the nation's billion-dollar banking institutions. All national banks must be insured by the Federal Deposit Insurance Corporation (FDIC) and be members of the Federal Reserve System. State-chartered banks may elect to become members of the Fed and also elect to have their deposits insured by the FDIC if they are willing to conform to the regulations of these two federal agencies. The vast majority of U.S. banks (about 96 percent) are FDIC insured, but only a minority have elected to join the Federal Reserve System. Nevertheless, Fed member banks hold more than two thirds of all bank deposits and assets in the United States. We will have more to say about the roles of the Fed, the FDIC, and other bank regulatory agencies at a later point in this chapter.

Exhibit 4–1   **Number and Size of Insured U.S. Commercial Banks, First Quarter 1987**

Asset Size Group	Number of Banks	Percent of Total	Total Amount of Assets ($billions)	Percent of Total
Less than $25 million	4,765	33.9%	$ 70.4	2.4%
$25 to $100 million	6,585	46.8	333.8	11.5
$100 to $300 million	1,853	13.2	298.0	10.3
$300 million to $1 billion	524	3.7	262.7	9.1
Over $1 billion	334	2.4	1,937.4	66.7
Total	14,061	100.0%	$2,902.0	100.0%

*Columns may not add to totals due to rounding.
Source: Federal Deposit Insurance Corporation, *Quarterly Banking Profile*, First Quarter 1987.

Exhibit 4–2   **Number of Operating Commercial Banks and Branches in the United States, December 31, 1986**

Category	Number of Commercial Banks	Number of Branch Offices
Insured banks:		
National banks	4,882	23,219
State-chartered member banks	1,110	5,179
Members of the Federal Reserve System:		
Total	5.992	28,398
Nonmember state-chartered banks	8,233	15,432
Total	14,225	43,830
Noninsured banks	623	87
Total	14,848	43,917

Source: Federal Reserve Board, *Annual Report*, Washington, D.C., 1986.

A Trend Toward Consolidation

A number of interesting structural changes have affected the banking in-dustry in recent years. One of the most important is the drive toward con-solidation of industry assets and deposits into larger and larger organiza-tions.

As we noted above, the United States is still essentially a nation of small banks. But great pressures are operating to form larger banking organi-zations in order to make more efficient use of resources. Research studies by Benston, Hanweck, and Humphrey (1982) and others suggest that as banks grow, their costs increase more slowly than output, resulting in cost savings. For example, a 100 percent rise in deposit and loan accounts may result in only about a 92 percent increase in the cost of bank operations. When automated bookkeeping and computer processing of accounts are used, substantial economies of size characterize bank installment and real estate lending and the offering of checking accounts. Under pressure from a cost squeeze, declining profit margins, and increased competition from foreign banks and nonbank financial institutions, many U.S. bankers view the strat-egy of growing into larger-sized banking organizations as a possible escape from these pressures.

We hasten to add, however, that scale economies resulting from growth appear to be modest—once a bank reaches perhaps $100 million or so in total assets, its unit production costs stop falling and level out. In fact, some analysts argue that production costs begin rising when banks approach the billion-dollar size because of the difficulty management has in controlling such a large organization and because of the tendency of larger banks to multiply their service offerings. Others argue, however, that large banks enjoy lower costs of raising capital and the risk-reducing benefits of diver-sification which give them a significant advantage over smaller banks. Large banks also seem to have an easier time introducing new services and new technologies.

Branch Banking

The drive toward consolidation of banks into larger organizations is most evident in the shift toward branch banking. Until the 1940s and 1950s, the United States was basically a nation of unit banks, each housed in only a single office. For example, in 1900 there were 12,427 banks, but only 87 of these had any branches. By 1987, however, there were about 15,000 commercial banks, of which more than 7,000 were branch-banking organizations and the number of branch offices has increased dramatically in recent years. In 1950 there were approximately 4,700 branch-banking offices in operation; by 1986, the total reached almost 44,000 (see Exhibit 4–2).

The growth of branching has been aided by the liberalization of many state laws to permit greater use of branch offices as a means of growth. Prominent examples of states liberalizing their branch-banking laws in recent years include Florida, New Jersey, New York, Virginia, and Texas. Another factor is the massive shift of the U.S. population over the last three decades to suburban and rural areas. Many of the nation's largest banks have followed their customers to outlying markets through branching and merger in order to protect their sources of funds.

In the decade of the 1980s expansion of branch offices across state lines became a key issue in American banking. Although the McFadden Act of 1927 and the Banking Act of 1933 (Glass-Steagall) prohibited full-service interstate branching, individual states could vote to allow out-of-state banking organizations to branch into their territory if they so chose (see Exhibit 4–3). Few states endorsed such "invasions" until the 1980s when more than two thirds of the states approved of entry by out-of-state banks, usually on condition their own banks are extended the same privilege. This new trend toward reciprocal branching has put great pressure on Congress to repeal or amend federal restrictions against interstate branching.

Further pressure for greater branching and service powers arose during the 1970s and 1980s with the expansion of financial conglomerates, such as Sears Roebuck, Prudential-Bache, Shearson-American Express, and so-called nonbank banks. The latter are limited-service depository institutions that manage to avoid regulations as commercial banks either by ceasing to make commercial loans or by refusing to accept checkable deposits—the two key services which, under federal law, constitute commercial banking. Many of the nonbank banks and financial conglomerates have elected to concentrate their service offerings in the consumer area. They sell credit, insurance, real estate, and savings plans, either by mail or through conveniently located branch offices not restricted by antibranching laws. The rise of this form of outside competition for commercial banks has brought strong protests from the banking community and from some federal regu-

Exhibit 4–3   **Key Federal Laws Affecting the Structure of the U.S. Banking Industry**

National Bank Act (1863–64)	Set up a procedure for federal chartering and supervision of banks by the Comptroller of the Currency.
Federal Reserve Act (1913)	Created the Federal Reserve System as central bank and guarantor of the banking system's liquidity.
McFadden Act (1927)	Vested the states with authority to limit branch banking within their borders and prohibited interstate branching unless the states involved specifically approved it.
Banking Act of 1933 (Glass-Steagall Act)	Created the FDIC and prohibited commercial banks from paying interest on demand deposits and from underwriting corporate securities.
Bank Holding Company Act (1956)	Multibank holding companies controlling two or more banks were required to register with the Federal Reserve Board and be subject to its rules. Controlling acquisitions of out-of-state banks were prohibited (Douglas Amendment).
Bank Merger Act (1960)	Mergers involving federally supervised banks must have the approval of their principal federal regulatory agency.
Bank Merger Act and Bank Holding Company Act Amendments (1966)	Mergers or holding-company acquisitions could be approved by federal banking agencies if their anticompetitive effects were outweighed by public benefits.
Bank Holding Company Act Amendments (1970)	Holding companies controlling only one bank are subject to Federal Reserve regulation; nonbank business ventures acquired by holding companies are confined to closely related fields.
International Banking Act (1978)	Foreign banks operating in the United States were brought under federal regulation, restricting their interstate branching activities, requiring federal licensing, imposing deposit reserve requirements, and providing FDIC insurance.
Depository Institutions Deregulation and Monetary Control Act (1980)	Granted nonbank thrift institutions broader deposit and credit powers, began the phasing out of federal deposit rate ceilings, and imposed uniform deposit reserve requirements on banks and nonbank thrifts.
Garn–St Germain Depository Institutions Act (1982)	Authorized banks and savings and loans to offer money market deposit accounts, granted savings and loans additional commercial and consumer lending powers, and provided for mergers or government-backed loans for troubled deposit-type financial institutions.

Exhibit 4–3

Competitive Equality Banking Act (1987)	Placed a moratorium on banks offering such new services as insurance, real estate, or securities underwriting and required depositories to make funds deposited by check available more quickly for spending; interstate emergency acquisitions of banks or bank holding companies can be arranged by the FDIC.

latory agencies who fear loss of control over the banking system and loss of public confidence in banking institutions due to increased failures and a blurring of the traditional distinctions between banking and commerce.

Bank Holding Companies

Paralleling the rapid growth of branch banking has been the growth of bank holding companies. The bank holding company is a relatively old organizational form in the industry, having its origins in the nineteenth century. A bank holding company is simply a corporation organized to acquire and hold the stock of one or more banks. The company may also hold stock in certain nonbank business ventures. Holding companies have become popular as vehicles to avoid laws prohibiting or restricting branch banking and as a way to offer services that commercial banks themselves cannot offer.

Fearing danger to the safety of banks, Congress first attempted to regulate the bank holding company movement during the 1930s but was unsuccessful. Then in 1956 the Bank Holding Company Act was passed, requiring all holding companies controlling at least 25 percent of the stock of two or more banks to register with the Federal Reserve Board. In addition, a holding company seeking to acquire additional shares of a bank was required to obtain Fed approval.

The Bank Holding Company Act left an unregulated opening for holding companies that held stock in only one bank. As a result, many of the nation's largest commercial banks formed one-bank holding companies during the late 1960s and began to reach out and acquire nonbank businesses far removed from the business of banking, including steel mills and meat-packing plants. Congress closed this loophole with passage of the 1970 amendments to the Bank Holding Company Act. From this point on, all holding companies seeking to acquire even a single bank had to register with the Federal Reserve Board and gain approval before purchasing any new bank or nonbank business. Nonbank business ventures acquired must now be so closely related to banking as to be "a proper incident thereto."

What business activities are "closely related" to banks? To date, the Federal Reserve Board has approved for holding company acquisition businesses engaged in the making of loans (such as finance, mortgage, or credit card companies), the writing of full-payment leases for personal or real property (e.g., equipment-leasing companies), insuring the repayment of credit (such as firms selling credit life insurance), the recording and transfer of financial information (such as data processing firms), the giving of financial advice (i.e., through a trust company, management consulting firm, or investment adviser), and the execution of some security trading (such as discount brokerage services or assisting in the placement of short-term corporate IOUs with investors)—to name the principal permissible nonbank activities.

Bank holding companies have grown rapidly in the United States. In 1960 there were just 47 registered holding company organizations controlling only about 8 percent of the total assets of U.S. insured commercial banks. By the 1980s, holding companies numbered more than 5,000 and held well over 85 percent of total insured bank assets.The growth of nonbanking business activities of holding companies also has been extremely rapid. Insurance agencies, finance companies, mortgage companies, leasing firms, factoring companies, data processing facilities, consulting firms, and other financially related businesses have been started or acquired in large numbers by bank holding companies in recent years. These ventures represent an attempt to diversify banking operations geographically and by product line in order to reduce risk and gain access to a broader market, often outside a bank's home state.

International Banking

The growth of larger U.S. banking organizations at home has been paralleled by substantial growth of American banks abroad. This expansion overseas has not been confined to the largest institutions in such established money centers as New York, Chicago, and San Francisco, but today includes leading banks in regional financial centers, such as Atlanta, Dallas, and Miami. Several of the nation's largest banks receive half or more of their net income from foreign sources.

These big U.S. banks have penetrated overseas markets for a wide variety of reasons. In many cases their corporate customers expanding abroad have needed multinational banking facilities. The huge Eurodollar market, which spans the globe, offers an attractive source of bank funds when domestic sources are less available or more costly. In most instances, foreign markets have also offered fewer regulatory barriers and less banking competition than are found in the United States.

On the other side of the coin, foreign banks have grown rapidly in the United States, with many of the largest European, Middle Eastern, and Asian banks viewing the 50 states as a huge economically and politically stable common market. Moreover, foreign-based banks are able to offer some services, such as the underwriting of corporate securities or insurance sales, that U.S. banking organizations currently are not allowed to offer. The Japanese banks in particular have grown into global dominance and include 18 of the top 20 banks in the world (see Exhibits 4–4 and 4–7). Congress responded to this invasion by passing the International Banking Act of 1978, bringing foreign banks under federal regulation for the first time.[1]

Bank Failures

One undesirable side effect of all these recent changes in the banking community is an apparent rise in the bank failure rate. For most of its history, the banking industry has experienced an extremely low failure rate (about 1 or 2 percent of the banking population each year) due to extensive gov-

---

Exhibit 4–4   **The Growing Global Competition Faced by All Banks Today—A List of the Largest Banks and Other Financial Institutions in the World**

1. Nomura Securities, Japan	21. Daiwa Bank, Japan
2. Sumitomo Bank, Japan	22. Taiyo Kobe Bank, Japan
3. Dai-Ichi Kangyo Bank, Japan	23. Yasuda Trust and Banking Co., Japan
4. Fuji Bank, Japan	24. Union Bank of Switzerland
5. Mitsubishi Bank, Japan	25. Allianz Aktie, West Germany
6. Industrial Bank of Japan	26. Deutsche Bank, West Germany
7. Sanwa Bank, Japan	27. American International Group, United States
8. Sumitomo Trust & Banking Company, Japan	28. Nippon Credit Bank, Japan
9. Mitsubishi Trust, Japan	29. Swiss Bank Company, Switzerland
10. Long-Term Credit Bank of Japan	30. Kyowa Bank, Japan
11. Daiwa Securities, Japan	31. Bank of Yokohama, Japan
12. Nikko Securities, Japan	32. J. P. Morgan, United States
13. Mitsui Bank, Japan	33. National Westminster Bank, United Kingdom
14. Tokai Bank, Japan	34. Citicorp, United States
15. Tokoi Marine and Fire, Japan	35. Aetna Life and Casualty Co., United States
16. Mitsui Trust and Banking Company, Japan	36. Münchener Rückversi Cherungs, West Germany
17. Assicurazioni Generali, Italy	37. Crédit Suisse, Switzerland
18. Bank of Tokyo, Japan	38. Yasuda Fire & Marine, Japan
19. Yamaichi Securities, Japan	39. General Reinsurance, United States
20. American Express, United States	40. Barclays Bank, United Kingdom

---

[1]The provisions of the International Banking Act and the recent growth of international banking are discussed more fully in Chapter 29.

ernment regulation and conservative management practices. However, the number of commercial bank failures and the average size of failing banks have advanced sharply in recent years. For example, a postwar record for the number of bank failures in a single year was set in 1987, when 184 U.S. banks closed their doors. Moreover, bank failures occurring in the 1970s and 1980s included the largest in U.S. history. Among the most notable were Franklin National Bank of New York in 1974 and Penn Square Bank in Oklahoma City in 1982, both billion-dollar institutions. In addition, several major money center banks got into deep financial trouble and had to be merged with a healthy institution or backstopped by government loans. Most notable in this case was Continental Illinois Bank of Chicago, which in 1984 was propped up by approximately $4.5 billion in federal insurance funds.

The reasons behind this apparent acceleration in bank failures are numerous. Many bankers today are willing to accept greater risk in their operations, in part because of intensified competition from other banks and nonbank financial firms and because of government insurance of bank deposits. More leniency in the enforcement of banking regulations, such as standards for the maintenance of equity capital, also has been a factor in the trend toward more bank failures. The movement toward banking *deregulation* in the 1980s gave banks greater opportunities to market new services and expand geographically without such strict controls, but also increased their opportunities for failure. Some analysts argue that even more important is the increased volatility of *economic* and *financial conditions*, especially interest rates and the prices of foreign currencies. Related to the economic factors are the many loans to energy companies, farm operators, and cash-strapped developing nations that have become delinquent in the wake of falling energy and commodity prices. A growing fear of many bankers as failure rates rose was that the hard-won progress toward deregulation might be overturned by public concern over the safety of the nation's banking system.

Changing Technology

Banking today is passing through a technological revolution. Computer terminals and high-speed information processing are transforming the industry, stressing convenience and speed in handling such routine transactions as making deposits, withdrawing cash, repaying loans, and cashing checks. Most of the new technology is designed to reduce labor and paper costs, making the industry less labor-intensive and more capital-intensive.

Among the most important pieces of technology in the industry are automated teller machines (ATMs). ATMs accept deposits, dispense cash and information, and accept payments. For many banking transactions they perform just as human tellers do, with the added advantage of 24-hour availability. Initially most ATMs were placed on bank premises, but their growth has also extended to retail stores, shopping centers, airports, and train terminals. In these locations they are known as remote service units (RSUs). They lower transactions costs for the customer and reduce the need for conventional branch banking offices.

Related to ATMs are point-of-sale terminals (POS) located in retail stores and other commercial establishments. Connected on-line to the bank's computer, POS terminals accept plastic credit and debit cards, permitting the customer to pay instantly for a purchase without the necessity of cashing a check. For those customers who do want to cash checks, a store can use the POS terminal to verify that a check is good. Customers have not accepted POS terminals as enthusiastically as they have ATMs. Part of the problem is the customer's loss of checkbook float when payments are made instantly.

Another important new piece of machinery in the industry is the automated clearinghouse (ACH). An ACH transfers information from one financial institution to another and from account to account via computer tape. More than 10,000 banks and other institutions are members of about three dozen ACHs that serve the nation. They are used principally for handling payrolls, dispensing welfare payments, and processing federal government transactions. Check truncation systems are also being used alongside the ACH. Such a system transmits images of checks electronically from one financial institution to another, eliminating the need to transfer paper.

The future will bring increased emphasis on in-home and at-work banking via TV screen and telephone, probably coupled with retail shopping information and other convenient services. Using a special keyboard, the customer can punch in a request for information or conduct transactions over the telephone. Even arrangements for a loan can be made by telephone and remote video screen. Such systems in effect make every customer a branch, provide greater convenience, and cut down on paper flow. Home-shopping TV broadcasts offering credit card transactions, deposits, insurance, and other financial services, and credit cards with built-in microprocessors to carry out personal financial transactions ("smart cards") are also service innovations with bright futures.

These recent technological changes have profound implications for bank costs, employment, and profitability. In the future, customers will have less need to enter a bank building, and the need for brick-and-mortar branches will decline. Indeed, many branch offices have recently been closed in a move toward greater economy and efficiency, suggesting that future needs will be met mainly by transferring information rather than by requiring people to move from one location to another. The banker's principal function will be one of providing the necessary equipment and letting customers conduct their own transactions. This development implies fewer but more highly skilled bank employees and more equipment per dollar of deposits. Heavy investment in computers and money machines will result in substantial fixed costs, requiring a large volume of transctions and favoring the largest banking organizations in the nation. The new technology of banking should further intensify pressures for consolidation of the industry into banks smaller in number, but much larger in average size.

THE REGULATORY FRAMEWORK FOR BANKS

Commercial banks, due to their importance in the financial system, are closely regulated. Moreover, in the United States banking is more heavily regulated than is true in most other industrialized countries. From earliest U.S. history there has been a fear of concentrated power in banking, because bank credit is so vital to the well-being of businesses and households. During colonial times several banks were burned to the ground because of public mistrust and misunderstanding of their basic function in the economy. During the nineteenth century and again early in this century severe restrictions were placed on the growth of banks through branching and holding companies.

Another significant restriction on banking's growth and development occurred in 1933 when Congress passed the Glass-Steagall Act, forbidding commercial banks from acquiring or underwriting corporate stock. This step effectively prevented banks from gaining control of nonfinancial corporations through purchases of stock. When banks skirted this prohibition in the late 1960s through the formation of holding companies, Congress again applied the brakes by passing the 1970 amendments to the Bank Holding Company Act. However, as the 1980s began, a significant deregulation trend set in, marked by the passage of two landmark pieces of legislation—the Depository Institutions Deregulation and Monetary Control Act of 1980 (DIDMCA) and the Garn-St Germain Depository Institutions Act of 1982 (Garn bill). As we shall see in this and the following chapter, these new laws granted major new asset and deposit powers to commercial banks and to their principal competitors—savings banks, savings and loans, and credit unions. The net result was to place banks and nonbank thrift institutions on more equal footing, leveling the competitive playing field for all depository institutions.

However, progress toward deregulation of banking in the United States was temporarily halted in 1987 with passage of the Competitive Equality Banking Act. This law temporarily prohibited federal regulatory agencies from allowing banks to offer new insurance, real estate, or securities services and restricted the activities of foreign banks inside the United States. The purpose of the restrictions was to give Congress time to consider the proper role for banks in serving the public. The new law also required banks to accelerate procedures for giving their customers credit for any checks deposited. After September 1, 1990, local checks must become available for customer withdrawal of funds no later than one business day after their deposit, while out-of-town checks must be available no later than four days after deposit. The FDIC was also granted additional powers for dealing with banks and bank holding companies in danger of failure.

Responsibility for regulating U.S. banks is divided among three federal banking agencies and the state banking commissions of each of the 50 states. These regulatory agencies have overlapping responsibilities, so most banks are subject to multiple jurisdictions. The regulatory agencies responsible for enforcing banking's ground rules include the Federal Reserve System, the Comptroller of the Currency, and the Federal Deposit Insurance Corporation—all at the federal level—and the state banking commissions of the 50 states. Exhibit 4–5 provides a brief summary of the principal regulatory powers exercised by these federal and state agencies.

The Federal Reserve System

The Federal Reserve System is responsible for examining and supervising the activities of all its member banks. When a member bank wishes to

Exhibit 4–5   Principal Bank Regulatory Agencies

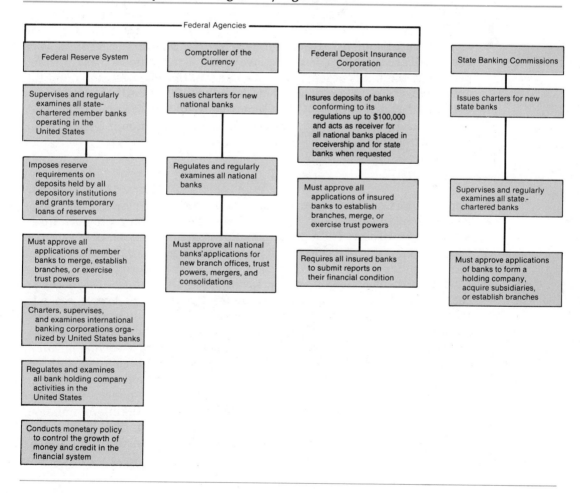

merge with another bank or establish a branch office, it must notify the Fed. The Fed must review and approve the formation of all bank holding companies active in the United States and approve the acquisition of non-bank businesses by holding companies. The Federal Reserve is responsible for U.S.-based international banking corporations (known as Edge Act subsidiaries) and for supervising member bank operations in foreign countries. It is responsible for regulating credit extended by banks and by security brokers and dealers for the purchasing or carrying of corporate stocks or convertible securities. The Fed also sets reserve requirements on both transactions deposits (such as checking accounts and NOW accounts) and time and savings deposits for all depository institutions.

The Comptroller of the Currency

The Comptroller of the Currency—also known as the Administrator of National Banks—is a division of the U.S. Treasury established under the National Banking Act of 1863. The Comptroller has the power to issue federal charters for the creation of new *national banks*. These banks, once chartered, are subject to an impressive array of regulations, most of which pertain to the kinds of loans and investments that may be made and the amount and types of capital which each bank must hold. All national banks are examined periodically by the Comptroller's staff and may be liquidated, merged, or consolidated with another financial institution if deemed to be in the public interest.

Federal Deposit Insurance Corporation

The Federal Deposit Insurance Corporation insures deposits of U.S. commercial banks which meet its regulations. This coverage provides up to $100,000 per depositor if a bank fails. Each participating bank is assessed annually a fraction of its eligible deposits to build and maintain the national insurance fund.

One of the most important functions of the FDIC is to act as a check on the state banking commissions, because few banks today—even those with state charters—will open their doors without FDIC insurance. The FDIC reviews the adequacy of capital, earnings prospects, the character of management, and the public convenience and needs aspects of each application before granting deposit insurance. This agency is also charged with examining insured banks that are not members of the Federal Reserve System. The FDIC acts as receiver for all national banks placed in receivership and as receiver for state banks when requested by a state banking commission. In most cases an insolvent bank will be merged with or absorbed by a healthy one. The FDIC often purchases some of the bankrupt institution's weaker assets to support such a merger.

State Banking Commissions

The regulatory powers of the federal banking agencies overlap with those of the state banking agencies which regularly examine all state-chartered banks. The states also have rules prescribing the minimum amount of equity capital for individual state-chartered banks and issue charters for new banks. One of the areas in which state banking law currently is supreme is that concerning branch banking. Since the McFadden Act of 1927, the federal government has allowed the states to determine whether commercial banks operating within their borders will be permitted to establish any branch offices and if so, under what circumstances. However, as we saw earlier, there is a definite trend toward greater use of branching and holding company activity in most parts of the United States. One recent example is Florida, which until 1978 was a unit-banking state and now permits statewide branching. The State of New York converted to statewide branching in 1976, following an experiment with limited branching in designated regions. Most experts predict that interstate branching in one form or another will continue to spread across the United States as the need for larger banking organizations and new financial services increases.

PORTFOLIO CHARACTERISTICS
OF COMMERCIAL BANKS

Commercial banks are the financial department stores of the financial system. They offer a wider array of financial services than any other form of institution, meeting the credit, payments, and savings needs of individuals, businesses, and governments. This characteristic of financial diversity is reflected in the basic financial statement of the industry—its balance sheet (or statement of condition). Exhibit 4–5 provides a list of the uses of funds (assets) and major sources of funds (liabilities and equity capital) for all FDIC-insured commercial banks for selected years.

Cash and Due from Banks (Primary Reserves)

All commercial banks hold a substantial part of their assets in primary reserves, consisting of cash and deposits due from other banks. These reserves are the banker's first line of defense against withdrawals by depositors, customer demand for loans, and immediate cash needs to cover expenses. Banks generally hold no more in cash than is absolutely required to meet short-run contingencies, however, since the yield on cash assets is minimal or nonexistent. The deposits held with other banks do provide an implicit return, though, because they are a means of "paying" for correspondent banking services. In return for the deposits of smaller banks, the larger U.S. correspondent banks provide such important services as clearing of checks, management of security portfolios, and computer processing of records. Thousands of smaller banks across the United States invest their excess cash reserves in loans to other banks (usually called federal funds) with the help of their larger correspondents.[2] Primary reserves also include reserves held behind deposits as required by the Federal Reserve System.

Security Holdings and Secondary Reserves

Commercial banks hold securities acquired in the open market as a long-term investment and also as a secondary reserve to help meet short-run cash needs. For many banks municipal securities—bonds and notes issued by state, city, and other local governments—represent the largest portion of security investments. Commercial banks are subject to the same tax rates as most nonfinancial corporations and therefore find the tax-exempt interest income paid by municipal securities to be attractive.[3]

About equal to municipals in amount are bank holdings of U.S. Treasury obligations (including bills, notes, and bonds). Banks generally favor Treasury bills (which must mature within one year) and shorter-term Treasury notes and bonds because these securities can be marketed readily to cover short-run cash needs. Moreover, Treasury securities are free of default risk. A closely related form of federal debt—securities issued by federal agencies such as the Federal Land Banks—has rapidly increased its share of bank portfolios. These securities carry yields slightly above those on direct Treasury obligations; yet they appear to involve little additional risk. Commercial banks also hold small amounts of corporate bonds and notes, though they generally prefer to make direct loans to businesses as opposed to purchasing their securities in the open market. Under existing regulations, commercial banks are forbidden to purchase corporate stock. However, banks do hold small amounts of corporate stock as collateral for loans.

Loans

The principal business of commercial banks is to make *loans* to qualified borrowers. Loans are among the highest-yielding assets a bank can add to its portfolio, and they provide the largest portion of operating revenue.

Banks make loans of reserves to other banks through the federal funds market and to securities dealers through repurchase agreements. Far more important in dollar volume, however, are direct loans to both businesses and individuals. These loans arise from negotiation between the bank and

---

[2]A more complete discussion of the operations of the federal funds market is presented in Chapter 15.

[3]Banks also tax shelter their income through the purchase and leasing of equipment to business firms. Another bank tax shelter consists of setting aside a portion of current income as an operating expense for protection against possible losses on loans.

its customer and result in a written agreement designed to meet the specific credit needs of the customer and the requirements of the bank for adequate security and income.

As shown in Exhibit 4–6, most bank credit is extended to commercial and industrial customers. Historically, commercial banks have preferred to make short-term loans to businesses, principally to support purchases of inventory. In recent years, however, banks have lengthened the maturity of their business loans to include term loans (which have maturities over one year) to finance the purchase of buildings, machinery, and equipment. Because the longer-term loans carry greater risk due to unexpected changes in interest rates, banks have also required a much greater proportion of new loans to carry variable interest rates that can be changed in response to shifting market conditions.

Moreover, longer-term loans to business firms have been supplanted to some extent in recent years by equipment leasing plans available from larger banks and the subsidiaries of bank holding companies. These leases are the functional equivalent of a loan: the customer not only makes the required lease payments for using the equipment but is responsible for repairs and maintenance and for any taxes due. Lease financing carries not only significant cost and tax advantages for the customer but also substantial tax advantages for a bank because it can depreciate leased equipment.

Commercial banks are also important lenders in the real estate field, supporting the construction of residential and commercial structures. Major types of loans in the real estate category include farm real estate credit, conventional and government-guaranteed (FHA and VA) single-family residential loans, conventional and government-guaranteed loans on multi-family residences, and mortgage loans on nonfarm commercial properties. Indeed, commercial banks are the most important source of construction financing in the economy.

Probably the most dynamic area in bank lending today is the making of installment loans to individuals and families. The number of new households has expanded rapidly in recent years, and commercial banks have moved to answer this need by offering longer maturities on installment loans and new types of credit arrangements, especially credit card plans. Banks finance the purchase of automobiles, mobile homes, recreational vehicles, home furnishings and appliances, and provide funds to modernize homes and other properties.

Deposits

In order to carry out their extensive lending and investing operations, banks draw upon a wide variety of deposit and nondeposit sources of funds. The bulk of commercial bank funds (80 percent or more) comes from deposits. There are three main types of deposits. *Demand deposits,* more commonly known as checking accounts, are the principal means of making payments

Exhibit 4–6　Assets, Liabilities, and Capital of Insured Commercial Banks in the United States (Year-End Figures)

	1970		1980		1985	
	Millions of Dollars	Percent Total Assets	Millions of Dollars	Percent Total Assets	Millions of Dollars	Percent Total Assets
Assets						
Cash and due from banks (primary reserves)	$ 93,948.1	16.1%	$ 331,909.3	17.9%	$ 340,640	12.5%
Security holdings:						
U.S. Treasury securities	61,617.0	10.7	104,466.2	5.6	118,262	4.3
Federal agency securities	13,277.7	2.3	59,078.3	3.2	127,582	4.7
Municipal securities	69,390.3	12.0	146,263.4	7.9	160,555	5.9
Other securities	2,933.9	0.5	24,637.3	1.3	33,237	1.2
Federal funds sold and securities purchased under agreements to resell	15,952.3	2.8	70,321.8	3.8	133,091	4.9
Loans:						
Real estate loans	73,053.4	12.7	269,111.6	14.5	438,426	16.1
Loans to farmers	11,153.6	1.9	32,259.8	1.7	36,106	1.3
Commercial and industrial loans	112,215.0	19.5	309,930.8	21.1	577,738	21.2
Loans to individuals	66,005.7	11.5	187,375.7	10.1	308,931	11.3
All other loans	35,771.9	6.2	48,940.8	2.6	269,581	9.9
Less: Unearned income on loans	*	*	21,031.7	1.1	17,905	0.7
Less: Allowance for possible loan losses	*	*	10,053.0	0.5	23,216	0.9
Direct lease financing	*	*	13,993.2	0.8	24,312	0.9
Real estate owned	9,550.3	1.7	2,208.4	0.1	47,842	1.8
Other assets	12,381.6	2.1	110,394.6	5.9	162,020	5.9
Total Assets	$576,350.8	100.0%	$1,855,687.8	100.0%	$2,730,498	100.0%
Liabilities						
Non-interest-bearing deposits (primarily demand deposits)	$247,170.4	42.9%	$ 431,539.4	23.3%	$ 471,340	17.3%
Interest-bearing deposits (primarily time and savings deposits, including NOWs and money market accounts and foreign deposits)	235,343.4	40.8	1,049,621.4	56.5	1,646,436	60.3
Total deposits	482,513.9	83.7	1,481,160.7	79.8	2,117,776	77.6
Federal funds purchased and securities sold under agreements to repurchase	16,609.0	2.9	133,290.7	7.2	221,987	8.1
Subordinated capital notes	2,091.9	0.4	6,553.6	0.4	14,659	0.5
Other liabilities	28,359.1	4.9	127,086.3		206,874	7.6
Total liabilities	529,573.9	91.9	1,748,091.3	94.2	2,561,246	93.8
Equity Capital						
Preferred stock—par value	107.3	0.0+	134.6	0.0+	993	0.1
Common stock—par value	11,137.8	1.9	21,672.0	1.2	29,143	1.1
Undivided profits, surplus, and reserves	29,229.4	5.1	85,789.9	4.6	139,116	5.1
Total equity capital	40,474.5	7.0	107,596.5	5.8	169,252	6.2
Total liabilities and capital	$576,350.8	100.0%	$1,855,687.8	100.0%	$2,730,498	100.0%

Note: Figures may not add to totals due to rounding.

*Not available as a separately reported item.

Source: Federal Deposit Insurance Corporation.

because they are safer than cash and widely accepted. *Savings deposits* generally are in small dollar amounts; they bear a relatively low-interest rate but may be withdrawn by the depositor with little or no notice. *Time deposits* carry a fixed maturity and offer the highest interest rates a bank can pay. Time deposits may be divided into nonnegotiable certificates of deposit (CDs), which are usually small, consumer-type accounts, and negotiable CDs that may be traded in the open market and are purchased mainly by corporations.

During the 1970s and 1980s new forms of checkable (demand) deposits appeared, combining the essential features of both demand and savings deposits. These transaction accounts include negotiable orders of withdrawal (NOWs) and automatic transfer services (ATS). NOW accounts may be drafted to pay bills but also earn interest, while ATS is a preauthorized payments service in which the bank transfers funds from an interest-bearing savings account to a checking account as necessary to cover checks written by the customer. Two relatively new transaction accounts—money market deposits accounts (MMDAs) and Super NOWs—were offered in 1983, following passage of the Garn bill in 1982. MMDAs, designed to compete directly with the high-yielding share accounts offered by money market mutual funds,[4] and Super NOWs may carry prevailing market rates on short-term liquid funds. Both can be drafted by check, automatic withdrawal, or telephone transfer, but the number of permissible withdrawals from MMDAs is limited. MMDAs may be held by an individual, business firm, or unit of government, but Super NOWs can be held only by individuals, governments, and nonprofit organizations. Other deposit plans that also offer *market-linked* returns to investors are being developed. For example, Chase Manhattan Bank of New York developed a "market index account" whose return is linked to stock market performance (as measured by percentage increases or decreases in the Standard & Poor's 500 stock index).

The mix of bank deposits has changed dramatically in recent years. Demand deposits and low-yield savings deposits have declined as a percentage of bank funds, while more costly interest-bearing accounts such as MMDAs have grown rapidly. This shift toward more expensive deposits reflects, in part, the growing sophistication of bank customers, especially large corporations, who have developed efficient cash management practices and insist on maximum return on their funds. Banks are well aware today that their customers are more financially sophisticated and have a greater tendency to "shop around" for the highest returns available on both transactions and savings deposits. As a result, the average cost of bank deposits has increased.

Moreover, the cost of attracting customer funds has been further increased in recent years by the tendency of bankers to expand services, offering their customers "one-stop" financial convenience. Thus, to retain old deposits and attract new ones, many banks have developed or franchised:

---

[4]See Chapter 5 for a discussion of the nature and growth of money market mutual funds.

(1) security brokerage services so that customers can purchase stocks and bonds and pay by charging their deposit accounts; (2) insurance counters to make life, health, and property casualty policies, usually sold by nonbank firms, available to their customers; (3) networking agreements with other banks so that customers can access their deposit accounts while traveling; (4) account relocation services and real estate brokerage through local realtors for customers who move; (5) financial and tax counseling centers to aid customers with important personal and business decisions; and (6) merchant banking services that aid major corporations with mergers and other structural changes. Bankers are also pushing Congress and the regulatory agencies for permission to offer *investment banking* services—purchasing corporate securities issued by their business customers and reselling them to investors. While generally prohibited by federal law, a few of the nation's leading banks have received permission to offer short-term corporate notes and selected other securities through subsidiary firms. These new services may have opened up new markets for banks, but they have also created new complexities for bank management and demanded greater efficiency and greater emphasis on marketing and customer analysis.

Nondeposit Sources of Funds

One of the most marked trends in banking in recent years is greater use of nondeposit funds, borrowed to meet bank cash needs, especially as competition for deposits has increased. Principal nondeposit sources of funds for banks today include purchases of reserves (federal funds) from other banks, security repurchase agreements (where securities are sold temporarily by a bank and then bought back later), and the issuance of capital notes. Capital notes are of particular interest because these securities may be counted under regulations as equity capital for purposes of determining a bank's loan limit. Both state and federal laws limit the amount of money a commercial bank can lend to any one borrower to a fraction of the bank's equity capital (net worth).[5] In order to be counted as equity capital, however, capital notes must be subordinated to deposits, so that if a bank is liquidated the depositors have a first claim on its assets.

Recently banks have turned to new nondeposit funds sources, including floating-rate CDs and notes sold in international markets, sales of blocks of loans, and securitizations of selected assets. The floating-rate securities tend to be longer-term borrowings of funds, stretching out from one year to as long as 20 years (or even issued without any maturity date) with an interest rate that is adjusted periodically (usually every three to six months) to reflect changing conditions in international markets. Larger banks (such

---

[5]For national banks the loan limit is a maximum of 15 percent of equity capital and surplus. Most states are more lenient, allowing loans to a single borrower up to a larger maximum percentage—25 percent is common—of equity capital.

as Chase Manhattan and Citicorp) have expanded their sales of top-quality, short-term business loans from their books, usually selling these credits in million-dollar blocks. These loan sales provide new funds to the banks and permit them to replace old lower-yielding loans with new higher-yielding ones. Finally, better-quality loans have been packaged into asset pools and used as collateral for bank security issues that are sold to investors through a broker or dealer. The bank secures additional funds from these securitized assets which have included packages of auto, credit-card, mortgage, and foreign-country loans and trade receivables.

Equity Capital

Equity capital (or net worth) supplied by a bank's stockholders provides only a minor portion (about 6 percent, on average) of total funds for most banks today. In fact, the ratio of equity capital to bank loans and deposits generally declined for several decades, due to falling profit margins, inflation, and efforts by bank managers to employ greater financial leverage. This development has many financial experts concerned, because one of the most important functions of equity capital is to keep a bank open even in the face of operating losses until management can correct its problems. Recently, federal law has mandated minimum ratios of capital to assets for banks and many banks have acted to improve their equity capital positions. There is also a move toward cooperative international capital regulation for major banks by the United States, Great Britain, Japan, and several other nations.

Revenues and Expenses

The majority of bank revenues come from interest and fees on loans, as shown in Exhibit 4–7. Interest and dividends on security holdings are the second most important source of bank revenue after loans. Other minor sources of income include earnings from trust (fiduciary) activities and service charges on deposit accounts (mainly checking accounts).

Bank expenses have risen rapidly in recent years, putting a squeeze on operating income. Greater competition from bank and nonbank financial institutions for sources of funds, especially CDs and transaction accounts, has resulted in dramatic increases in the cost of raising funds. Interest on deposits is the principal expense item for commercial banks, followed by the salaries and wages of their employees. Rising rapidly in importance is the interest cost on nondeposit sources of funds, such as borrowing in the federal funds market or long-term borrowing in the form of mortgages and capital notes.

Commercial banks must be more conscious of expense control and tax management in future years if they are to protect their profit margins, generate sufficient capital to grow, and provide a greater array of financial

Exhibit 4–7   Earnings and Expenses of Insured Commercial Banks in the United States—1970, 1980, and 1985

	1970		1980		1985	
	Millions of Dollars	Percent Total Oper. Income	Millions of Dollars	Percent Total Oper. Income	Millions of Dollars	Percent Total Oper. Income
Sources of revenue:						
Interest and fees on loans	$22,967.4	66.2%	$126,953.5	66.5%	$181,242	64.9%
Interest on balances with depository institutions	*	—	16,256.3	8.5	14,014	5.0
Interest on federal funds sold and securities purchased under agreement to resell	1,006.4	2.9	8,763.8	4.6	9,523	3.4
Interest on investment securities held	6,539.2	18.8	23,076.3	12.1	37,740	13.5
Income from direct lease financing	*	—	1,370.6	0.7	2,347	0.8
Service charges on deposit accounts	1,178.2	3.4	3,186.9	1.7	7,369	2.6
Other sources of revenue	2,302.4	6.6	11,161.4	5.9	27,012	9.7
Total operating income	$34,716.4	100.0%	$190,768.3	100.0%	$279,247	100.0%
Expenses:						
Salaries and employee benefits	$ 7,717.1	22.2%	$ 24,673.2	12.9%	$ 39,986	14.3%
Interest on deposits	10,483.8	30.2	98,419.2	51.6	130,791	46.8
Expense of federal funds purchased and securities sold under agreements to resell	1,400.8	4.0	16,770.6	8.8	16,622	6.0
Interest on other nondeposit borrowings	569.3	1.6	4,932.7	2.6	9,887	3.5
Occupancy, furniture, and fixtures	1,254.5	3.6	7,353.6	3.9	13,290	4.8
Provision for possible loan losses	703.2	2.0	4,478.6	2.3	17,717	6.3
Other operating expenses	5,459.9	15.7	14,635.2	7.7	29,044	10.4
Total operating expenses	$27,588.6	79.5%	$171,263.8	89.8%	$257,337	92.2%
Income before taxes and extraordinary items	$ 7,127.8	20.5%	$ 19,504.6	10.2	$ 23,477	8.4
Applicable income taxes	2,173.8	6.3	5,019.7	2.6	5,643	2.0
Income before extraordinary items	4,954.0	14.3	14,484.9	7.6	17,834	6.4
Extraordinary items, net	− 116.5	0.3	− 475.2	− 0.2	224	0.1
Net income	$ 4,837.5	13.9%	$ 14,009.7	7.3%	$ 18,057	6.5%

Note: figures may not add to totals due to rounding.

*Not available as a separate item in the indicated year.

Source: Federal Deposit Insurance Corporation, *Bank Operating Statistics*, 1980, *Annual Report*, 1970, and *Statistics on Banking*, 1985.

services to the public. They must also contend with increasing competition from both foreign and domestic financial institutions, a shifting customer base to older, higher-income, and better-educated consumers of their services, the ever-changing technology of service production and delivery, and greater risk of failure in a more competitive and volatile environment, as Exhibit 4–8 reminds us. To be a successful banker today demands a unique combination of technical and social skills and the capacity to be flexible and to learn new methods and techniques in an ever-changing, dynamic market.

Exhibit 4–8   **Worldwide Trends in the Banking Industry**

1. Deregulation of banking and other financial service industries in the United States, Great Britain, and in many other nations around the globe, permitting private markets to allocate more resources and financial services instead of governments.

2. Increased penetration of foreign markets by major banks in most countries, so that banking is increasingly becoming a global industry with fewer geographic and territorial boundaries (including the spread of interstate banking in the United States).

3. Growing proliferation of banking and financial services (i.e., financial innovation) as bankers respond to increased competition and develop new service areas, such as investment banking (i.e., securities underwriting), insurance sales, and real estate development and brokerage services.

4. Spreading technological revolution with more and more banking transactions carried out via computer terminals and other automated equipment, satellites, fiber-optic cables, etc., instead of through human labor, tranforming banking into an increasingly fixed-cost industry.

5. Changing sources and uses of bank funds as banking's customer base changes toward older, more financially sophisticated, and more interest-sensitive depositors and investors and more customers from the service sector of the economy. The new sources of bank funds include loan sales (where higher quality, more marketable loans are sold out of the bank's loan portfolio), securitizing of loans (where loans are packaged and used as collateral for borrowings to raise money for other bank activities), and market-linked accounts (where yields to the depositor or supplier of funds fluctuate with credit market or stock-market conditions). In addition, banks are doing more "off-balance-sheet" financing of their customers' credit needs, providing letters of credit and other standby guarantees of customer borrowings in case their customers cannot raise sufficient funds from the financial markets. This device earns fee income for banks, but avoids an immediate drain on scarce bank funds.

6. Increased rate of failures and other financial problems among the world's banks due to the risks of service and technological innovation and to increasing worldwide competition.

MONEY CREATION AND DESTRUCTION BY BANKS

Commerical banks differ from many other financial institutions in one critical respect: *banks have the power to create money in the form of new checkable deposits*. The banking system creates and destroys billions of dollars in money each year at the stroke of a pen. Now an individual bank cannot create any more money in the form of checkable deposits than the volume of excess reserves that it holds. However, the banking system as a whole can create a volume of money equal to a multiple of any excess reserves deposited with it simply by extending credit (i.e., making loans and purchasing securities).

Reserve Requirements and Excess Reserves

Money creation by banks is made possible because the public readily accepts claims on bank deposits (mainly checks) in payment for goods and services. In addition, the law requires individual banks to hold only a fraction of the amount of deposits received from the public as reserves, thus freeing up a majority of incoming funds for the making of loans and the purchasing of securities. We need to look more closely at these so-called reserve requirements banks must meet because they play a key role in the money creation process.

Under current federal law, banks and other depository institutions must hold reserves in cash or in deposit form behind their transaction accounts and nonpersonal time deposits. These reserve requirements are linked to the size of the depository institution and require that a specified percentage (ranging from 3 to 12 percent) of all deposits must be placed either in an account at the Federal Reserve bank in the region or as cash in the bank's vault. As a practical matter, banks hold most of their reserves in the form of deposits with the regional Federal Reserve banks. Vault cash holdings are kept to a minimum; insurance rates increase significantly when large amounts of vault cash are held on bank premises and no interest is earned on these cash holdings.[6] Vault cash and deposits at the Fed constitute a bank's holdings of legal reserves—those assets acceptable for meeting reserve requirements behind the public's deposits.

Each bank's legal reserves may be divided into two categories—required reserves and excess reserves. *Required reserves* are equal to the legal reserve requirement ratio times the volume of deposits subject to reserve requirements. For example, if a bank holds $20 million in transaction accounts and $30 million in nonpersonal time deposits and the law requires it to hold 3 percent of its transaction accounts and 3 percent of its nonpersonal time

---

[6]The current reserve requirements of commercial banks and the role which reserve requirements play in government monetary policy are discussed in Chapter 23.

deposits in legal reserves, the required reserves for this bank are $20 million × 3% + $30 million × 3%, or $1.5 million.

Excess reserves equal the difference between the total legal reserves actually held by a bank and the amount of its required reserves. For example, if a bank is required to hold legal reserves equal to $1.5 million, but finds on a given date that it has $500,000 in cash on the premises and $1.5 million on deposit with the Federal Reserve bank in its region, this bank clearly holds $500,000 in *excess* reserves. Because legal reserve assets earn little or no interest income, most commercial banks try to keep their holdings of excess reserves as close to zero as possible.

The Creation of Money and Credit

The distinction between excess and required reserves is important because it plays a key role in the growth of credit in the economy and the creation of money by the commercial banking system. To understand why, we need to make certain assumptions concerning how banks behave and the regulations they face. To simplify the arithmetic, assume that the Federal Reserve has set a basic reserve requirement of 20 percent behind the public's deposits. Therefore, for every dollar that the public deposits in the banking system, each commercial bank must put aside in either vault cash or deposits at the Federal Reserve 20 cents as required reserves. Assume also that, initially, the banking system is "loaned up"—that is, bankers have loaned out all excess legal reserves available to them. No additional reserves are made available to the banking system from some external source. In addition, assume that all bankers are profit maximizers and will attempt to loan out immediately any excess funds available to them in order to earn the maximum interest income possible.

Suppose that a deposit of $1,000 is made from some source outside the banking system. Perhaps the Federal Reserve has purchased securities from a dealer and paid for its purchase by providing $1,000 in additional reserves to the dealer's bank. Alternatively, the public may have decided to convert a portion of its currency and coin holdings ("pocket money") into bank deposits for greater convenience and safety. Either way, a deposit of $1,000 appears at Bank A as shown in Exhibit 4–9. This exhibit contains an abbreviated balance sheet (T account) for Bank A with changes in its assets shown on the left-hand side and changes in its liabilities and net worth shown on the right-hand side.

Under the assumed Federal Reserve regulations, Bank A would be required to place $200 aside as required reserves (i.e., 20 percent of the $1,000 deposit), leaving excess legal reserves of $800. Because the $800 in cash earns no interest income, the banker will immediately try to loan out these excess reserves. Banks make loans today by bookkeeping entry. The borrower signs a note indicating how much is borrowed at what rate of interest and when the note will come due. In return, the banker creates a checking account in the borrower's name. In our example, assume that Bank A has received a loan request from one of its customers and decides to grant the customer a loan of $800—exactly the amount of excess legal reserves it holds.

Commercial banks find that, when they make loans, the borrowed funds are withdrawn rapidly as borrowers spend the proceeds of their loans. Moreover, it is likely that most of the borrowed funds will wind up as deposits in other banks as loan customers write checks against their accounts. For this reason, Bank A will not loan out any more than the $800 excess legal reserves it currently holds. This way, when the borrower spends the funds and the money flows to other banks, Bank A will have sufficient funds in reserve to cover the cash letters demanding payment which it will receive from other banks.

Assume that the $800 loaned by Bank A eventually winds up as a deposit in Bank B. As indicated in Exhibit 4–9, Bank B must place $160 (20%) of this deposit in required reserves and then has excess reserves of $640, which are quickly loaned out. As this borrower spends the funds, the $640 loan finds it way into deposits at Bank C. After setting aside required reserves of $128, Bank C has excess reserves of $512. It too will move rapidly to loan out these funds if a suitable borrower can be found.

The pattern of these changes in deposits, loans, and required reserves should now be fairly clear. The results are summarized in the bottom portion of Exhibit 4–9. Note that the total volume of bank deposits has been considerably expanded by the time it reaches the third or fourth bank. Similarly, the total volume of new loans grows rapidly as funds flow from bank to bank within the system. If the credit-creation process works through the entire banking system and there are no leakages, then with a 20 percent reserve requirement, the banking system ultimately will hold $5,000 in deposits and will have created loans in the amount of $4,000. Clearly, by making loans whenever and wherever excess reserves appear, the banking system eventually creates total deposits and total loans several times larger than the original volume of funds received.

In the foregoing example each dollar of required reserves supports $5 in deposits, due to the fact that the legal reserve requirement is 20 percent. That is, total deposits created by the banking system are equal to the initial amount of legal reserves deposited in the system—in this example $1,000—times the reciprocal of the reserve requirement ratio—in this case 1/0.20, or 5. The reciprocal of the reserve requirement ratio is known as the *deposit multiplier,* a concept we will discuss more fully in Chapter 23. In the real world, leakages from the banking system greatly reduce the size of the deposit multiplier—probably to no more than two. Among the most important leakages are the public's desire to convert some portion of new demand deposits into currency and coin (pocket money) or into time and savings deposits, and the presence of unutilized lending capacity, which results be-

Exhibit 4–9   **The Creation of Credit and Deposits by the Banking System**

1. Bank A Receives New Deposit

Assets		Liabilities	
Required reserves	200	Deposits	1,000
Cash	800		

4. Loan Made by Bank B

Assets		Liabilities	
Required reserves	160	Deposits	800
Loans	640		

2. Loan Made by Bank A

Assets		Liabilities	
Required reserves	200	Deposits	1,000
Loans	800		

5. Deposit of Loan Funds in Bank C

Assets		Liabilities	
Required reserves	128	Deposits	640
Cash	512		

3. Deposit of Loan Funds in Bank B

Assets		Liabilities	
Required reserves	160	Deposits	800
Cash	640		

6. Loan Made by Bank C

Assets		Liabilities	
Required reserves	128	Deposits	640
Loans	512		

By making loans whenever there are excess reserves, the banking system will ultimately generate a volume of deposits several times larger than the amount of the initial deposit received by Bank A.

Transactions within the Banking System

Name of Bank	Deposits Received	Loans Made	Required Reserves
A	$1,000	$ 800	$ 200
B	800	640	160
C	640	512	128
D	512	410	102
—	—	—	—
—	—	—	—
Final amounts for all banks in the system	$5,000	$4,000	$1,000

cause banks either cannot find qualified borrowers or wish to hold a protective cushion of reserves.

Destruction of Deposits and Reserves

Not only can the money supply expand by a multiple amount as a result of the injection of new reserves, but it can also *contract* by a multiple amount when reserves are withdrawn from the banking system. This is illustrated in Exhibit 4–10, where a depositor has decided to withdraw $1,000 from a

Exhibit 4–10   **Deposit and Credit Destruction in the Banking System**

Depositor withdraws funds:

Federal Reserve Bank		Bank A	
Assets	Liabilities	Assets	Liabilities
	Member bank − 1,000 reserves	Required reserves − 1,000	Deposits − 1,000

If Bank A was loaned up when the withdrawal occurred, it will now have a reserve deficiency of $800 as indicated below.

Total reserves lost at Bank A when depositor withdrew funds	$1,000
Required reserves no longer needed due to deposit withdrawal	− 200
Total reserve deficit at Bank A	$ 800

Bank A sells securities to acquire additional reserves:

Bank A			Bank B	
Assets		Liabilities	Assets	Liabilities
Securities	− 800		Required reserves − 800	Deposits − 800
Required reserves	+ 800			

The sale of securities in the amount of $800 enables Bank A to cover its reserve deficits. However, customers of Bank B bought those securities and that bank was already loaned up. Therefore, Bank B now has a reserve deficiency of $640.Thus:

Total reserves lost at Bank B after deposit withdrawals to purchase Bank A's securities	$800
Required reserves no longer needed due to deposit withdrawals	− 160
Total reserve deficit at Bank B	$640

The actions taken by Bank B to cover its reserve deficit will cause other banks to lose reserves and incur deficits. Deposits will continue to contract until total reserves available to the banking system are sufficient for *all* banks to meet their legal reserve requirements.

---

transaction account at Bank A. Recall that behind the $1,000 deposit Bank A holds only $200 in required reserves. This means that when the deposit is withdrawn, that bank will have a deficiency of $800. If Bank A is loaned up and has used all of its cash in making loans and investments, it will have to raise the necessary funds through the sale of securities or through borrowing.

Suppose Bank A decides to sell securities in the amount of $800. As indicated in Exhibit 4–10, the sale of securities increases Bank A's legal reserves by the necessary amount. However, the individuals and institutions who purchase those securities pay for them by writing checks against their deposits in other banks, reducing the legal reserves of those institutions.

For example, assume that Bank B loses deposits of $800 and required reserves of $800 as Bank A gains these funds. Considering Bank A and Bank B together, total deposits have fallen by $1,800. This deposit contraction has freed up about \$360 (\$200 + \$160) in required reserves. However, if Bank B is also loaned up and has no excess reserves, the \$800 lost to Bank A means Bank B has a net reserve deficiency of \$640. Further contraction of deposits will occur as Bank B attempts to cover its reserve deficiency by drawing reserves from other banks. In fact, with a 20 percent reserve requirement and no other leakages from the banking system, deposits will contract by a full \$5,000 as banks try to cover their reserve deficits by raising funds at the expense of other banks.

Implications of Money Creation and Destruction

This capacity of banks to create and destroy money has a number of important implications for the financial system and for the economy. Creation of money by banks is one of the most important sources of credit funds in the economy—an important supplement to the supply of savings in providing funds for investment so the economy can grow faster. Money created by banks is instantly available for spending and, therefore, unless carefully controlled by government action, can fuel inflation. That is why the Federal Reserve System, the nation's central bank, regulates the growth of the money supply principally through controlling the growth of bank reserves—a subject dealt with at length in Chapters 23 and 24.

SUMMARY

It is clear that the banking industry has undergone significant financial and structural changes in recent years. These changes have been brought about by shifts in regulation and by strong economic and financial pressures. High interest rates, soaring operating costs, and intense competition from nonbank financial institutions have propelled bankers into a new scenario in which the character of their loans, investments, and sources of funds has changed markedly. Moreover, there is no end in sight to many of these trends. Costs of labor and funds continue to rise or remain at high levels. Indeed, many experts looking at the age composition of the U.S. population and the expected rate of family formations ahead expect continued pressure on bankers to find higher yielding uses for their funds in order to offset rising costs. A key factor in the industry's response to these demand and cost pressures, of course, will be the willingness of federal and state regulatory authorities and the Congress to permit banks to respond freely to new and changing public demands.

The drive toward larger and larger banking organizations centered around branch banks and bank holding companies appears to be a continuing trend for the future. One area of growing concern to the banking industry is the proliferation of near-banks which offer credit services and recently have begun to attract the public's funds through sales of deposit-like IOUs. These organizations include such well-known names as Sears, Roebuck Co., Prudential-Bache, Shearson-American Express, and various stock brokerage firms. These organizations offer financial services to customers and yet are not subject to the extensive regulations which commercial banks must satisfy. The future, therefore, promises to foster intense competition not only within the banking industry, but from without. In line with economic theory, stronger competition should mean lower profit margins and a more efficient use of financial resources within the banking system.

STUDY QUESTIONS

1. In what ways are commercial banks of special importance to the functioning of the money and capital markets and the economy?
2. Why are banks so heavily regulated? List the principal bank regulatory agencies. What areas of bank operations are subject to regulation?
3. What are the principal uses of commercial bank funds? Major sources of funds?
4. Two dominant postwar movements in the structure of U.S. banking have been the spread of branch banking and the growth of bank holding companies. Explain what has happened in these two areas and why.
5. Why and how are banks able to create money? Does the ability of banks to create money have important implications for public policy? Please explain.

PROBLEMS

1. Given the following information on the revenues and expenses of First National Bank, determine the bank's net income after taxes for the year just concluded:

Salaries and employee benefits	$ 80,000	Occupancy costs	$11,000
Interest on deposits	170,000	Provision for loan losses	22,000
Interest on loans	320,000	Miscellaneous expenses	8,000
Income from U.S. Treasury securities	75,000	Interest on municipal securities	86,000
Extraordinary items, net	0	Service charges on deposits	10,000
Interest on nondeposit borrowings	30,000	Miscellaneous operating revenues	13,000
Net securities gains	0		
Applicable income taxes	50,000		

2. Construct the Report of Condition (balance sheet) for First National Bank for December 31st of the year just ended from the following information:

Equity capital	$ 50 million	Other assets	$ 50 million
Demand deposits	100 million	Real estate loans	60 million
Savings deposits	150 million	U.S. Treasury	
Time deposits	200 million	securities	25 million
Federal funds		Commercial and	
borrowings	12 million	industrial loans	300 million
Cash and due		Other liabilities	38 million
from banks	20 million	Municipal securities	55 million
		Loans to individuals	40 million

3. A commercial bank holds $120 million in transaction accounts and $240 million in nonpersonal time deposits. Current reserve requirements set by the Federal Reserve Board stipulate that 3 percent of the first $30 million in transaction deposits and 12 percent of any excess transaction deposits over $30 million must be held in a legal reserve account. Similarly, 3 percent of nonpersonal time deposits must be placed in the legal reserve account. What is the bank's total reserve requirement based on the above deposit totals? Suppose the bank's legal reserve account has a current average balance of $20 million. Does the bank have any excess reserves? If so, how much?

SELECTED REFERENCES

Benston, George J., Gerald A. Hanweck; and David Humphrey. "Scale Economies in Banking: A Restructuring and Reassessment." *Journal of Money, Credit and Banking* 14, November 1982, Part I, pp. 435–56.

Chase, Samuel, and John Mingo. "The Regulation of Bank Holding Companies." *Journal of Finance,* May 1975, pp. 282–92.

Eisenbeis, Robert A. "Regulation and Financial Innovation: Implications for Financial Structure and Competition Among Depository and Nondepository Institutions." *Issues in Bank Regulation,* Winter 1981.

Furlong, Frederick T. "New Deposit Instruments." *Federal Reserve Bulletin,* May 1983, pp. 319–26.

Johnson, Sylvester, and Amelia A. Murphy. "Going Off the Balance Sheet." *Economic Review,* Federal Reserve Bank of Atlanta, September–October 1987, pp. 23–35.

Rose, Peter S. "The Quest for Bank Funds: New Directions in a New Market." *The Canadian Banker,* December 1987, pp. 56–61.

White, George C. "Electronic Banking and Its Impact on the Future." *The Magazine of Bank Administration,* December 1979, pp. 39–42.

Chapter 5

Nonbank Thrift Institutions: Credit Unions, Savings and Loan Associations, Savings Banks, and Money Market Mutual Funds

Learning Objectives in This Chapter

- To understand how important nonbank depository institutions, such as credit unions and savings banks, are in the functioning of a modern economy and financial system.

- To examine the principal financial services offered by nonbank thrift institutions.

- To see how credit unions, savings and loan associations, savings banks, and money market funds are similar and how they differ one from another.

Key Terms and Concepts in This Chapter

Credit unions

National Credit Union Administration (NCUA)

Share drafts

Depository Institutions Deregulation and Monetary Control Act (DIDMCA)

Garn–St Germain Depository Institutions Act

Savings and loans

Federal Savings and Loan Insurance Corporation (FSLIC)

Mutuals

Money Market Deposit Accounts (MMDAs)

Savings banks

Money market mutual funds

THERE is a tendency in discussions of the financial system to minimize the role of nonbank financial institutions and emphasize the part played by commercial banks in the flow of money and credit. For many years financial experts did not consider the liabilities of nonbank financial institutions, including deposits in savings and loan associations, savings banks, and credit unions, as really close substitutes for bank deposits. It was argued that interindustry competition between commercial banks and other financial institutions was slight and, for all practical purposes, could be ignored. Beginning in the 1960s and continuing to the present, however, an entirely different view has emerged concerning the relative importance of nonbank financial institutions. We now recognize that these institutions play a vital role in the flow of money and credit within the financial system and are particularly important in selected markets, such as the mortgage market, and in the market for personal savings.

This new awareness of the critical importance of nonbank financial institutions in the economy and financial system stems from a number of sources. One is the rapid growth of selected nonbank financial intermediaries in recent years; some have outstripped commercial banks in the growth of their assets. Still another factor is the increasing penetration of traditional financial service markets by nonbank institutions. For example, credit unions, savings banks, money market mutual funds, and savings and loan associations offer NOWs and other interest-bearing payments services that compete directly with bank checking accounts. For a number of years credit unions have marketed credit cards, many of which have carried lower interest charges than those levied by commercial banks. Moreover, federal deregulation legislation in the 1980s authorized federally chartered savings and loan associations to issue credit cards and greatly expanded the powers of nonbank thrifts to make both consumer installment loans and business loans comparable to many forms of bank credit. Insurance companies, savings banks, and credit unions today are offering new savings plans that compete directly with commercial bank money market accounts.

On both the asset and liability sides of the balance sheet, then, nonbank financial institutions are becoming increasingly like commercial banks and competing for many of the same customers. Moreover, banks themselves are offering many of the services traditionally offered by nonbank financial firms, such as security brokerage and insurance services. This is why financial analysts today stress the importance of studying the whole financial institutions sector in order to understand how the financial system works. In this chapter and the next we examine the major types of nonbank financial institutions that channel the public's savings into loans and investments.

CREDIT UNIONS

Growth of Credit Unions

The characteristics and operations of credit unions have been a neglected area of research in the financial system. Recently, however, there has been a strong revival of interest in credit union behavior and growth. One reason is the rapid growth of this financial intermediary. For example, credit union assets have more than doubled since 1980 (see Exhibit 5–1). Today U.S. credit associations are the third largest institutional supplier of consumer installment credit, behind commercial banks and finance companies, and account for about one seventh of all consumer installment loans in the United States. These institutions are exclusively household-oriented intermediaries, offering their deposit plans and credit resources only to individuals and families. Their rapid growth stems mainly from offering low loan rates and high deposit interest rates to individuals and families.

Credit unions are really cooperative, self-help associations of individuals, rather than profit-motivated financial institutions. Savings deposits and loans are offered only to members of each association, and the members are technically the *owners,* receiving dividends and sharing in any losses that occur. Credit unions began early in the twentieth century to serve low-income individuals and families by providing inexpensive credit and an outlet for their savings. Early growth was modest until the 1950s, when

Exhibit 5–1   **Credit Unions in the United States**

Years	Number of Credit Unions	Number of Members	Total Assets ($ millions)
1940	9,023	2,826,612	$ 253
1950	10,591	4,610,278	1,005
1960	20,456	12,037,533	5,653
1970	23,699	22,797,193	17,960
1980	21,930	45,420,000	72,250
1986	16,910	54,066,729	166,063

Source: Credit Union National Association, Inc., *Credit Union Report 1986* (Madison, Wis., 1987).

these institutions broadened their appeal to middle-income individuals by offering many new financial services and engaging in aggressive advertising campaigns.

The credit union sector remains relatively small compared to other major financial institutions, accounting for only about 6 percent of all consumer savings in the United States placed with depository institutions. However, the industry's potential for future growth appears excellent due to its innovative character and growing public acceptance. For both savings deposits and consumer installment loans, the credit union has become an aggressive competitor of commercial banks and savings associations. Beginning in 1978, credit unions were authorized to offer money market certificates which can carry the same terms as the money market deposit plans sold by banks. In addition, many credit unions offer payroll savings plans where employees can conveniently set aside a portion of their salary in a savings account.

Credit union loans have kept pace with the growth of their deposits. Consumer loan rates charged by credit unions are fully competitive with rates charged by the other two major consumer lenders—commercial banks and finance companies. Moreover, credit unions frequently grant their borrowing members interest refunds up to 20 percent of the amount of the loan. Thus, credit unions often accept a smaller spread between their loan and deposit interest rates; this is possible because their operating costs are usually so low. Many associations provide credit life insurance free to their customers—a service charged for by most other lending institutions. Data released by the Federal Reserve Board show that credit unions accounted for only 4 percent of total consumer installment loans outstanding in 1950, but that by 1986 this figure had risen to 13 percent.

Chartering and Regulation

In the United States, credit unions are chartered and regulated at both state and federal levels (see Exhibit 5–2). Today about three fifths of all credit unions are chartered by the federal government and the remainder by the states. Federal credit unions have been regulated since 1970 by the National Credit Union Administration (NCUA), an independent agency within the federal government. Deposits are insured by the National Credit Union Share Insurance Fund (NCUSIF) up to $100,000. State-chartered credit unions may qualify for federal insurance if they conform to NCUA's regulations.

Credit Union Membership

Credit unions are organized around a common affiliation or common bond among their members. Most credit union members work for the same employer or for one of a group of related employers. In most cases if one family member belongs to a credit union, other family members are eligible as well. Occupation-related credit unions account for about three quarters of all U.S. credit unions. About one sixth of American credit unions are or-

Exhibit 5–2   Government Agencies Regulating the Nonbank Thrifts

Nonbank Thrift Institution	Chartering and Licensing of Thrifts	Setting Up Branches		Mergers and Acquisitions		Deposit Insurance	Supervision and Examination
		Intra-state	Inter-state	Intrastate	Interstate		
Credit unions	National Credit Union Administration/State Banking Departments	No approval required		National Credit Union Administration/State Banking Departments	National Credit Union Administration/State Banking Departments	National Credit Union Share Insurance Fund/State Departments	National Credit Union Administration/State Banking Departments
Savings and loan associations	Federal Home Loan Bank Board/State Banking or Savings and Loan Departments	Federal Home Loan Bank Board/Federal Savings and Loan Insurance Corporation/State Banking or State Savings and Loan Departments	*	Federal Home Loan Bank Board/State Banking Departments/State Savings and Loan Departments	Federal Savings and Loan Insurance Corporation	Federal Savings and Loan Insurance Fund/State Insurance Funds	Federal Home Loan Bank Board/State Banking or Savings and Loan Departments
Savings banks	Federal Home Loan Bank Board/State Banking Departments	Federal Home Loan Bank Board/State Banking Departments	*	Federal Home Loan Bank Board/State Banking Departments	Federal Deposit Insurance Corporation	Federal Deposit Insurance Corporation/State Insurance Funds	Federal Deposit Insurance Corporation/State Banking Departments
Money market funds	Securities and Exchange Commission	No approval required		No approval required		No government programs/some employ private insurance	None

*Generally prohibited for federal thrift institutions.

Source: Based on *Depository Institutions and Their Regulators,* Federal Reserve Bank of New York.

ganized around a nonprofit association, such as a labor union, a church, or a fraternal or social organization. Common area of residence, such as a city or state, has also been used to get credit unions organized.

Size of Credit Unions

There is a strong shift today toward fewer but larger credit unions. For example, the number of associations reached an all-time high in 1969 at almost 24,000 and now totals only about 17,000 (see Exhibit 5–1). However, in 1970 only about one sixth of the nation's credit unions held more than $1 million in assets. Today that figure is about 40 percent. Although the average-size credit union still remains very small compared with other depository institutions, credit union membership continues to grow rapidly, increasing by 1 to 2 million a year. There were fewer than 5 million U.S. credit union members in 1950, but this total exceeded 54 million in 1986. Worldwide, there are more than 60 million members associated with about 45,000 credit unions operating in at least 70 countries.

New Services Offered

Credit unions are rapidly expanding the number of services they offer. Some now sell life insurance, while others act as brokers for group insurance plans where state law permits. Many credit unions are active in offering 24-hour teller services, traveler's checks, financial planning services, retirement savings, credit cards, home equity and mortgage loans, and money orders. Larger credit unions compete directly with commercial banks for transaction accounts by offering share drafts—interest-bearing checkbook deposits. The share draft was first authorized by several states in 1974 and made legal for all federally insured credit unions when the Depository Institutions Deregulation and Monetary Control Act (DIDMCA) was passed in 1980 (see Exhibit 5–3). A substantial proportion of U.S. credit unions also offer credit cards and automated teller machines, many of which are linked nationwide through an electronic exchange network.

U.S. credit unions have been under intense pressure to develop new services and penetrate new markets, due to increasing competition from other financial institutions and a decline in the demand for their most important credit service—automobile loans. Both credit unions and banks have lost ground to finance companies, such as GMAC, as prime auto lenders. In addition, a substantially larger proportion of family income today is spent on food, fuel, and other necessities; credit unions have begun shifting their loan programs into these areas.

Government Regulation of Loans, Investments, and Dividends

Credit unions, like commercial banks, are heavily regulated in the services they are permitted to offer, the rates charged for credit, and dividends paid on members' deposits. Under current federal regulations, these institutions are permitted to make unsecured loans to members, including credit card loans, not exceeding 5 years to maturity, or secured loans out to 30 years. The 1982 Garn–St Germain Depository Institutions Act significantly expanded their real estate lending powers, including their ability to accept second-mortgage loans (see Exhibit 5–4).

Associations' permissible investments in securities are limited to a list prescribed by either state or federal regulations. In the main, credit unions are permitted to acquire U.S. government securities, hold savings deposits at commercial banks, savings and loans associations, savings banks, and

Exhibit 5–3   **Provisions of the Depository Institutions Deregulation and Monetary Control Act (DIDMCA) of 1980 Applying to Credit Unions, Savings and Loan Associations, and Savings Banks**

New Deposit Powers

1. Interest-rate ceilings on deposits will be phased out over a six-year period, permitting rates offered the public to respond to competition in the marketplace.
2. NOW accounts which bear interest and can be used to make payments may be offered to individuals and nonprofit organizations by all federally insured depository institutions beginning December 31, 1980.
3. Federally insured credit unions are authorized to offer share drafts (i.e., interest-bearing checking accounts) beginning March 31, 1980.
4. Savings banks are empowered to offer demand deposits to their business customers.

New Loan and Investment Powers

1. Federally insured credit unions can offer real estate loans.
2. Federally chartered savings and loan associations may issue credit cards, offer trust services, and make investments in consumer loans, commercial paper, and corporate bonds up to 20 percent of their assets.
3. Savings banks with federal charters may invest up to 5 percent of their total assets in commercial, corporate, and business loans within the home state of the bank or within 75 miles of the bank's home office.

federally insured credit unions, and purchase selected federal agency securities. Credit unions rely heavily on U.S. government securities and on savings deposits in other financial institutions to provide liquidity in order to meet deposit withdrawals and accommodate member credit needs.

Credit unions pay dividends to their members, but are considered nonprofit associations doing business only with their owners. Therefore, credit unions are classified as tax-exempt mutual organizations.

A Strong Competitive Force

Credit unions today represent stiff competition for commercial banks, savings banks, and other financial institutions serving consumers. Today, one out of every five Americans belongs to a credit union—roughly double the proportion a decade earlier. The industry has repeatedly demonstrated its capacity for innovation and ability to compete successfully for both consumer loans and savings accounts. With the authority recently granted under deregulation legislation, these nonbank thrifts are likely to be a significant competitive force in consumer credit and savings plans in the years ahead.

Exhibit 5–4   **Provisions of the Garn–St Germain Depository Institutions Act of 1982 (Garn bill; HR-6267) Applying to Credit Unions, Savings and Loan Associations, and Savings Banks**

New Deposit Powers

1. Depository Institutions Deregulation Commission (DIDC) is authorized to develop a deposit account for banks and nonbank thrifts "directly equivalent to and competitive with money market mutual funds" no later than December 15, 1982.
2. Federally chartered savings associations may accept regular checkbook deposits from businesses having a loan relationship to the associations or as a repository for payments.
3. All deposit-type financial institutions are permitted to offer NOW acounts to governmental units.

New Loan and Investment Powers

1. Federal savings associations may make secured or unsecured loans to businesses up to 10 percent of their total assets starting in 1984.
2. Commercial real estate loans may be increased from 20 to 40 percent of total assets at federal savings associations and required loan-value minimum ratios are eliminated. Federal credit unions are granted broader real estate loan powers with longer maximum maturities.
3. Federal savings associations may purchase municipal revenue bonds (up to a 10 percent of capital limitation) as well as general-obligation municipal bonds and invest in time deposits at depository institutions insured by the Federal Savings and Loan Insurance Corporation (FSLIC).
4. Federal savings associations may invest in consumer loans up to 30 percent of their total assets (including loans to businesses to acquire consumer goods inventories).
5. Federal savings associations may lease or lend against personal property up to 10 percent of their assets.
6. State laws and court decisions restricting enforcement of due-on-sale clauses in real property loans (such as home mortgages) are preempted so that when a mortgaged home is sold, the outstanding home mortgage loan becomes due and payable.

Other Provisions of Garn–St Germain

1. Qualified insured depository institutions may issue net worth certificates to their federal insurance agency in return for promissory notes from the agency which can be held as assets to strengthen the depository institution's net worth.
2. Depository institutions can freely change organizational form from mutual to stockholder owned and change their federal or state supervisory agency.

SAVINGS AND LOAN ASSOCIATIONS

Savings and loan associations are similar to credit unions because they extend financial services to households. They differ from credit unions, however, in their heavy emphasis on long-term rather than short-term lending. In particular, savings and loans are the major source in the United States of mortgage loans to finance the purchase of single-family homes and multi-family dwellings. And like credit unions, savings and loans today are developing many new financial services to attract new customers and protect their earnings.

The first savings and loans were started early in the nineteenth century as building and loan associations. Money was solicited from individuals and families so that certain members of the group could finance the building of new homes. The same individuals and families who provided the funds were also borrowers from the association. Today, however, savers and borrowers are frequently different individuals.

Savings and loan associations began as basically a single-product industry—accepting savings deposits from middle-income individuals and families and lending those funds to home buyers—and this situation persisted until the 1970s. More recently, however, competition from commercial banks and credit unions, coupled with unstable interest rates and many failures, have forced savings and loans to diversify their operations and aggressively solicit new accounts.

Chartering and Regulation

Currently savings associations receive their charters from the states or from the federal government. Today about half have charters from state authorities who supervise their activities and regularly examine their books. The remainder have federal charters, and these associations are insured (up to a maximum of $100,000 per depositor) by the Federal Savings and Loan Insurance Corporation (FSLIC) (see Exhibit 5–2). S&Ls chartered by the states also may qualify for FSLIC insurance. Both federally chartered and federally insured state associations are supervised and examined by the Federal Home Loan Bank System—the principal regulator of the industry.

Most savings and loans are mutuals and therefore have no stockholders. Technically, they are owned by their depositors. However, a growing number of associations are converting to stock form. Stockholder-owned S&Ls can issue capital stock to increase their net worth—a privilege that is particularly important when a savings and loan is growing rapidly and needs an additional source of long-term capital. Nationwide, close to one fourth of all S&Ls are stock associations. The stockholder-owned associations, on average, are much larger in size than the mutuals, however, holding just over half of the industry's total assets.

How Funds Are Raised and Allocated

Savings and loans, like credit unions, are gradually broadening their role, with many choosing to offer a full line of financial services for individuals and families. Other S&Ls are branching out into business credit and commercial real estate lending.

Asset Portfolios. Residential mortgage loans still dominate the asset side of the savings and loan business. Exhibit 5–5, showing the industry's assets and liabilities for year-end 1986, indicates that mortgage credit (predominantly home loans) accounted for about three-fifths of total industry assets. But the current era has brought rapid growth in other housing-related investments, such as mortgage-backed securities, mobile home loans, home equity loans, and investments in service corporations which provide funds for land development, and housing-rehabilitation projects. Mortgage-backed securities include pass-throughs issued by the Government National Mortgage Association and participation certificates (PCs) issued by the Federal Home Loan Mortgage Corporation. Both pass-throughs and PCs are investor shares in a pool of mortgages backed by the issuing government agency.

In addition, as shown in Exhibits 5–3 and 5–4, the 1980 DIDMCA law and the 1982 Garn bill granted federal savings associations the power to issue credit cards and invest a substantial portion of their assets in consumer

Exhibit 5–5   Assets and Liabilities of All Savings and Loan Associations in the United States, December 31, 1986*

Item	Amount ($ millions)	Percentage of Total
Assets:		
Mortgage loans outstanding	$ 655,936	56.3%
Insured mortgages and mortgage-backed securities	157,742	13.5
Mobile home loans	7,512	0.6
Home improvement loans	4,921	0.4
Loans on deposits	3,924	0.3
Education loans	4,238	0.4
Other consumer loans	30,040	2.6
Cash and government securities	62.912	5.4
Other investments	101,914	8.7
Investment in service corporations	21,380	1.8
Buildings and equipment	14,901	1.3
Real estate owned	13,308	1.0
All other assets	86,564	7.5
Total assets	$1,165,291	100.0%
Liabilities and Net Worth:		
Savings deposits:		
Accounts of $100,000 or less	$ 772,445	66.3%
Accounts of more than $100,000	117,469	10.1
Federal Home Loan Bank advances	100,048	8.6
Other borrowed money	96,459	8.3
All other liabilities	25,756	2.2
Net worth	53,114	4.6
Total liabilities and net worth	$1,165,291	100.0%

Note: Components may not add to totals due to rounding.

*Preliminary.

Sources: Federal Home Loan Bank Board; United States League of Savings Institutions, *87 Savings Institutions Sourcebook*, Table 69, p. 55.

loans, commercial paper, and corporate debt securities. Restrictions on home mortgage lending were eased to allow adjustable-rate mortgages (ARMS) whose returns vary with market conditions. S&Ls were granted the power to invest in mutual funds and offer trust services. Acquisitions of municipal revenue bonds and time deposits of other S&Ls were also added to the permissible list. The essence of all these changes was to allow associations to become more like commercial banks with flexible asset portfolios, hopefully better able to withstand fluctuations in interest rates and economic conditions.

Liabilities of S&Ls. Savings deposits provide the bulk of funds available to the savings and loan industry. However, there has been a significant shift in deposit mix in recent years from those savings accounts earning the lowest interest rate to deposits earning much higher and more flexible returns. Particularly important among the new higher-rate savings deposit plans offered by the industry are money market deposit accounts, CDs, NOW and Super NOW accounts, and Keogh and IRA plan retirement accounts. Money Market Deposit Accounts (MMDAs) and Super NOWs were authorized with passage of the Garn bill in 1982. Both of these new deposit accounts are draftable by check and carry interest rates that change with money market conditions. One unfortunate side effect of these newer plans is that savings and loans today are faced with a more costly deposit base.

Savings and loans also rely upon several nondeposit sources of funds to support their loans and investments. One of the most important consists of advances (loans) from the Federal Home Loan Bank System, which provides extra liquidity in periods when deposit withdrawals are heavy or when loan demand exceeds incoming deposits. Another rapidly growing source of funds is *securitized assets,* where mortgages or other S&L assets are packaged (often backed by the guarantee of a government agency) and debt securities are issued against these pooled assets and sold to investors to raise longer-term, lower-cost funds. Thrift institutions are making widespread use of securitized assets, issued against a growing list of home mortgage and consumer installment loans, to supplement deposit flows and keep funding costs down.

Another popular nondeposit funds source is *loan sales*—sales of mortgages and other loans to investors in the secondary market. These sales of S&L assets tend to be heaviest in periods when loan demand is high and deposit growth is sluggish and give savings and loans the opportunity to invest in new, higher-yielding loans. They also help S&Ls better diversify their assets, increase the availability of liquid funds, and avoid an increased regulatory burden (such as demands for more equity capital). One danger, however, is that S&Ls and other financial institutions will sell their best-quality loans, leaving them with a more risky loan portfolio.

Equity capital or net worth (i.e., the retained earnings and the general reserves held by individual associations) makes up only about 5 percent of total funds sources, but is very important to the public. It is the net worth account that absorbs losses and keeps the doors open until management can correct any problems. Many S&Ls, particularly in those regions of the nation hit hard by energy and farm problems, have zero or even negative net worth and have relied heavily upon continued government support and patience (forbearance) to keep them afloat.

Trends in Revenues and Costs

Recently, savings and loans have experienced one of the darkest periods in their long history. Many savings associations remain unprofitable or cling to desperately thin net worth positions. Dozens of ailing associations have been helped into mergers by the FSLIC, which has purchased sizable quantities of questionable industry assets. Some observers feared that a continuation of this trend would eventually swamp the FSLIC's deposit insurance fund. But Congress moved quickly with passage of the Garn bill to authorize the FSLIC (as well as the FDIC) to head off outright failures with agency-assisted mergers. A troubled S&L could be merged with a stronger association (even one in another state if suitable in-state associations were in short supply) or with another depository institution (such as a commercial bank) if suitable S&L merger partners could not be found.

For those associations headed toward serious trouble, the FSLIC could provide emergency assistance to restore an S&L's net worth to acceptable levels. This could be accomplished by an exchange of notes. The agency would issue insurance corporation notes and exchange these for net worth certificates of the troubled association. Both the total assets and the net worth of the aided S&L would increase. To further strengthen the FSLIC, Congress authorized the injection of several billion dollars in new capital into that insurance fund in 1987 with passage of the Competitive Equality Banking Act, hoping to strengthen public confidence in both the FSLIC and in savings and loan associations themselves.

What circumstances got the industry into such a troubled state? One cause is the fact that S&Ls historically have issued mortgage loans with fixed interest rates, while accepting deposits whose interest rates are sensitive to changing market conditions. In short, many of their assets are rate-insensitive, while a growing portion of their liabilities are highly rate-sensitive. In periods of rapidly rising interest rates, the industry's *net interest margin*—the difference between its interest earnings on assets and its interest costs on borrowed funds—has been severely squeezed. Indeed, in several recent periods, short-term interest rates paid on deposits exceeded interest rates earned on long-term loans; the industry's net interest margin turned negative.

Other recent trends have also hurt profitability. The individuals and families whose savings provide the bulk of association funds have become more financially sophisticated, withdrawing deposits whenever higher returns were available elsewhere or whenever there was even a hint of trouble in the thrift industry. Unquestionably the savings and loan industry was damaged severely in the 1970s and 1980s by the growth of money market mutual funds—aggressive institutions that offered small savers higher and more flexible yields. Federal regulations in the past limited the interest rates S&Ls could pay on savings accounts, hurting their ability to compete with money market funds. At the same time, other government rules prevented S&Ls from introducing more flexibility into their investments in earning assets so their revenues could grow as fast as their rising operating costs.

Trends in Industry Structure

The pressure of rising costs and the resulting squeeze on earnings have caused many savings and loans to merge or be absorbed by larger associations. As a result, the number of associations in the United States has been declining since 1960. The S&L population decreased from about 6,300 in 1960 to about 3,000 in the latest year. Not surprisingly, with declining numbers the average-size S&L has increased tremendously in recent years; still there are numerous small associations—about 1,600 have assets of less than $100 million each. With large numbers of relatively small S&Ls, continuing increases in costs and competition, and heavy pressures on earnings, more savings and loans are likely to be absorbed into larger financial institutions in the future.

Possible Remedies for the Industry's Problems

If savings and loans are to be viable institutions in the future, they will need help from at least two sources: (1) sound decision making by management to diversify their operations, identifying innovative new services to offer the public; and (2) a further relaxation of government regulations to permit the offering of new services and the merging of smaller associations into larger ones. The classic savings and loan association—investing the bulk of its assets in long-term, fixed-rate mortgages and offering relatively low-yielding savings accounts to the public—cannot survive in today's volatile economic environment.

More aggressive S&Ls are branching out in at least three different directions. Some have followed a *real estate* model, literally becoming mortgage banking firms. These savings associations are selling off their long-term mortgages and converting into real estate service organizations, managing and developing property, and brokering mortgages. Many have become *family financial centers,* offering a full range of retail banking services to the consumer. Services offered range from NOW accounts and home equity loans to financial counseling and even assistance in preparing income tax returns. While home mortgages continue to dominate their asset portfolios, most of these S&Ls offer principally adjustable-rate mortgages (ARMs) whose yield adjusts more readily to changing market conditions. Other S&Ls have adopted a *diversified* model, becoming holding company organizations with ownership and control over retail-oriented consumer banks, mortgage banking firms, and commercial credit affiliates. Only time will tell which of these models can adapt successfully to the changing character of the nation's financial system.

SAVINGS BANKS

Savings banks were started in the United States approximately 150 years ago to meet the financial needs of the small saver. These institutions play an active role in the residential mortgage market, as do savings and loans, but are more diversified in their investments, purchasing corporate bonds and common stock, making consumer loans, and investing in commercial mortgages. The Garn bill of 1982 permitted S&Ls to convert readily into federal savings banks and savings banks to convert readily into S&Ls. For this reason the technical distinction between savings and loans and savings banks will become less relevant in future years.

From their earliest origins savings banks have designed their financial services to appeal to individuals and families. Deposit accounts can be opened for amounts as small as $1, with transactions carried out by mail or, in many instances, through 24-hour automated tellers in convenient locations. Savings banks in Massachusetts and New Hampshire were the first to develop the interest-bearing NOW account, perhaps the most important new consumer financial service of the past two decades. Many savings banks advertise the availability of family financial counseling services, home equity loans, and travel planning as well as a wide variety of savings instruments.

Number and Distribution of Savings Banks

The number of savings banks operating today is small—about 600. Through most of this century, the savings bank population has been on the decline. For example, in 1900 there were 626 of them operating in the United States, but the number had fallen to 424 by 1982. Then, legislation was passed to allow the chartering of federal savings banks (FSBs), resulting in a dramatic increase in the number of savings banks to more than 600. Savings bank assets and deposits also have grown rapidly in recent years. In 1950 total assets of all savings banks stood at $22 billion, but industry assets had climbed toward $500 billion by the late 1980s (including FSBs). Of course, as a result of the long-term decrease in the number of savings banks coupled with rapidly expanding assets, the average savings bank grew tremendously in size and now is far larger than most credit unions and savings and loan associations, and even most commercial banks. This increase in average size has aided savings banks in offering a greater variety of services and in slowing somewhat the growth of their operating costs.

Savings banks are located primarily in New England and the Middle Atlantic states. Massachusetts leads the list, followed by New York. Other states that have mutuals headquartered within their borders include Alaska, Connecticut, Delaware, Indiana, Maine, Maryland, Minnesota, New Hampshire, New Jersey, Oregon, Pennsylvania, Rhode Island, Vermont, Washington, and Wisconsin.

Charters and Regulations

Savings banks can be chartered by either the states or the federal government. Federal chartering of savings banks was authorized by Congress in 1978. Before that time all savings banks were chartered by the states and only by those few states, located principally along the eastern seaboard, that made explicit provision for them in their statutes. The advent of federally chartered savings banks (FSBs) makes possible the nationwide spread of these institutions, overcoming their narrow geographic origins.

State and federal governments also share responsibility for insuring savings bank deposits (see Exhibit 5–2). Most savings banks have deposits insured by the Federal Deposit Insurance Corporation (up to $100,000). The remainder are covered by state insurance programs or by the Federal Savings and Loan Insurance Corporation.

How Funds Are Raised and Allocated

Technically, savings banks are owned by their depositors. All net earnings available after funds are set aside to provide adequate reserves must be paid to the depositors as owners' dividends. Regulations exercised primarily by the states are designed to insure maximum safety of deposits. This is accomplished principally through close control over the types of *assets* which a savings bank is permitted to acquire. For example, state law and the "prudent man" rule enforced by the courts generally limit savings bank investments to first-mortgage loans, U.S. government and federal agency securities, high-grade corporate bonds and stocks, and municipal bonds.

The industry's role in the financial system can be seen by looking at its balance sheet. On the asset side, the key investment is mortgages and mortgage-related instruments, accounting for about half of their total assets (see Exhibit 5–6). Most of the mortgage total represents direct mortgage loans to build single-family homes, apartments, shopping centers, office facilities, and other commercial and residential structures. The remainder is devoted to Government National Mortgage Association (GNMA) pass-

Exhibit 5–6   **Balance Sheet of the Savings Bank Industry, December 31, 1984* ($ Millions for All FDIC-Insured Savings Banks)**

Item	Amount	Percentage of Total
Assets:		
Real estate loans	$ 87,445	51.2%
Commercial and industrial loans	4,581	2.7
Loans to individuals	7,552	4.4
Loans to financial institutions	1,271	0.7
Other loans	423	0.2
Cash and due from depository institutions	5,634	3.3
U.S. Treasury and federal agency securities	28,334	16.6
State and local government securities	2,158	1.3
Corporate bonds	16,855	9.9
Other bonds, notes, and debentures	3,174	1.9
Corporate stock	2,991	1.8
Buildings and equipment	1,562	0.9
Real estate owned	420	0.2
All other assets	8,382	4.9
Total assets	$170,782	100.0%
Liabilities and Surplus Accounts:		
Demand deposits	$ 2,873	1.7%
Savings deposits	65,720	38.5
Time deposits	85,190	49.9
All other liabilities	9,244	4.8
Subordinated notes and debentures	511	0.3
Surplus accounts	8,244	4.8
Total liabilities and surplus accounts	$170,782	100.0%

Note: Columns may not add to totals because of rounding.

*Preliminary data.

Source: Federal Deposit Insurance Corporation.

through securities (also known as Ginnie Maes), backed by a government-guaranteed pool of mortgages.[1]

A distant second in importance to mortgages are savings bank investments in corporate bonds, corporate stock, and government bonds. The volume of corporate bonds held by the industry outnumbers its investments in corporate stock about five to one. Due to the pressures of inflation and higher deposit costs, however, many states have liberalized their regulations to allow savings banks increased purchases of common and preferred stock. Another factor favoring investments in stock has been the industry's growing federal tax burden. Since most of their stock dividend income is exempt from federal taxation, savings banks have taken greater interest in the stock market. State law and tradition, however, severely limit the growth

---

[1]See Chapter 19 for a discussion of GNMA pass-throughs and other mortgage-related securities.

of savings bank investments in the stock market. Savings banks also make loans for the support of education, to fund home improvements, and to cover personal expenses.

The principal source of funds for savings banks is *deposits,* representing close to 90 percent of total funds available. *Savings* deposits carry no specific maturity but may be withdrawn at any time by the customer and carry the lowest rate of interest. *Time* deposits, on the other hand, have fixed maturities, and savings banks are allowed to pay higher maximum rates on these accounts, depending on their maturity date.

Industry deposits have grown rapidly over the past three decades, reflecting the ability of savings banks to appeal to the financial needs of individuals and families. The larger savings banks have established extensive branch office systems and have been highly innovative in offering new services. Nearly all savings banks today offer checkable NOW accounts, money orders, loans against savings accounts, and home equity and home improvement loans. Many savings banks also offer life insurance policies to their customers where permitted by state law.

Like savings and loan associations, savings banks have discovered that the customers they serve have become more financially sophisticated in recent years. The highest yielding deposit accounts have grown much faster than lower yielding savings plans. The most pronounced shift has been out of regular passbook savings accounts to fixed-maturity time deposits and money market accounts that carry contract rates which float with conditions in the money market. Nondeposit borrowings also have grown rapidly. The net result of all these changes has been to push interest costs higher, put pressure on earnings, and increase the volatility of funds flows. Savings banks today must be more concerned with their liquidity (cash) position than has been true in the past. Their checkable NOW and money market accounts in particular are more volatile than savings deposits and require increased investments in liquid assets to back them up.

Current Trends and Future Problems

The savings bank industry faces a number of problems that will significantly affect its future as a conduit for savings and investment. One factor is increasing competition with savings associations and commercial banks offering similar services. Because of the heavy concentration of savings bank assets in mortgage-related investments, savings banks are less flexible than commercial banks in adjusting to changing financial conditions and to the changing service needs of their customers. Many still have severe earnings problems due to inflexible asset structures coupled with sharply higher deposit interest costs. On the other hand, many savings banks have countered this relative inflexibility in asset structure with aggressive competition for funds and innovative new services. The future growth of this industry, like that of most other financial institutions, will depend heavily on the ability of savings banks to gain the necessary changes in federal and state regulations to allow them to respond to changing financial market conditions.

MONEY MARKET FUNDS

A fourth major nonbank thrift institution appeared on the scene as recently as 1972. In that year the first money market mutual fund—a financial intermediary pooling the savings of thousands of individuals and businesses and investing those monies in short-term, high-quality money market instruments—opened for business. Taking advantage of the fact that the interest rates on most deposits offered by commercial and savings banks were then restrained by federal ceilings, the money fund offered share accounts whose yields reflected prevailing interest rates in the nation's money market. Thus, the money fund represents the classic case of profit-seeking entrepreneurs finding a loophole around ill-conceived government regulations.

The growth of money market funds was explosive. As of year-end 1973, there were only 4 in existence, with assets totaling about $100 million. Money funds peaked in 1982 when more than 200 of them held over $200 billion in assets (see Exhibit 5–7). Beginning in late 1982 and 1983, however,

Exhibit 5–7   **Money Market Funds: Assets Held and Total Shares Outstanding, 1975–1986**

Item	1975	1976	1977	1978	1979	1980	1981	1982	1983	1984	1985	1986
Assets:												
Demand deposits and currency	*	*	*	$ 0.1	$ 0.1	$ 0.2	$ -0.5	$ 0.3	$ -0.3	$ -1.2	$ 0.2	*
Time deposits	2.1	1.5	1.8	4.5	12.0	21.0	43.8	40.8	24.0	23.6	16.8	19.1
Security RPs	0.1	0.1	0.3	0.3	2.4	5.6	14.5	16.2	13.0	22.8	26.1	32.2
Foreign deposits	—	—	*	0.5	5.1	6.8	18.8	23.8	21.9	21.2	19.0	22.2
U.S. government securities	0.9	1.1	0.9	1.5	5.6	8.2	31.9	54.6	36.2	42.4	42.7	43.2
Tax-exempt obligations	—	—	—	—	—	1.9	4.2	13.2	16.8	23.8	36.3	63.8
Open-market paper	0.5	0.9	1.1	3.7	19.3	31.6	70.4	69.1	66.2	98.0	99.1	105.3
Miscellaneous assets	-0.1	-0.1	-0.2	0.3	0.7	1.1	2.9	1.8	1.5	3.0	3.6	6.5
Total assets	$3.7	$3.7	$3.9	$10.8	$45.2	$76.4	$186.2	$219.8	$179.4	$233.6	$243.8	$292.1
Total shares outstanding	$3.7	$3.7	$3.9	$10.8	$45.2	$76.4	$186.2	$219.8	$179.4	$233.6	$243.8	$292.1

Note: Columns may not add to totals because of rounding.

*Less than $50 million.

Source: Board of Governors of the Federal Reserve System, *Flow of Funds Accounts, Financial Assets and Liabilities Outstanding, 1963–86.*

a decline set in as banks and other depository institutions fought back with Super NOWs and Money Market Deposit Accounts (MMDAs), both authorized to carry unregulated interest rates by the Garn bill in October 1982. Subsequently, however, money market funds resumed their growth, making sharp gains late in the 1980s.

What factors explain the initial rapid growth and continuing viability of this newest nonbank thrift institution? One is the absence of regulatory restrictions. There are no legal interest rate ceilings and, unless the funds themselves impose it, no mandatory penalties for early withdrawal, as is required by law with many deposit plans offered by banks and thrifts. Another factor is the high quality of assets acquired by the funds. The typical money market fund invests primarily in U.S. Treasury bills, bank certificates of deposit, bankers' acceptances, commercial paper, and securities issued by federal government agencies.[2] All are the highest quality financial instruments with low risk of borrower default and limited fluctuations in price. Contributing to the low-risk character of money fund investments is their short average maturity of only a few weeks or months. The short maturity of fund investments results in a highly liquid security portfolio that can be adjusted quickly to changing market conditions. Many funds declare dividends on a daily basis, crediting the earnings to customer accounts and often notifying the customer by mail monthly of additional shares purchased with the dividends earned. Most are "no load" funds that do not charge their customers commissions for opening an account, purchasing additional shares, or redeeming shares for cash.

One of the outstanding advantages of the money funds for many investors is the ease with which their accounts can be accessed. Most funds allow the customer to write checks in order to redeem shares, provided the amount of each check exceeds a designated minimum ($500 is common). The customer is issued a book of checks and can merely write out and deposit the check in his or her local bank account, often receiving credit for the deposited check from the local bank or thrift the same day, even though it may take several days for the money fund check to be collected. Meantime, daily interest is still being earned on the monies waiting in the customer's share account. Most money funds also offer customers the option of purchasing or redeeming shares by wire or telephone. A toll-free phone number is usually maintained to provide transfer services as well as to answer customer inquiries.

Despite their numerous advantages for customers interested in professional management of their short-term funds, the money funds today possess some competitive disadvantages which many financial analysts believe will limit their future growth. Their share accounts are not federally insured as are bank and thrift deposits, though many of the funds have attempted to deal with this problem by arranging for private insurance or creating funds

---

[2]These various money market securities are discussed in depth in Part Four.

invested solely in U.S. government securities. Moreover, the yield differential between posted yields on money fund share accounts and money market deposits at banks has narrowed in recent years. Certainly, the money funds are not likely to go away; they are an established and potent competitor for both small individual savings accounts and businesses' liquid funds. However, barring further restrictive federal regulation of bank and thrift deposits, *all* bank and nonbank thrift institutions, including money market funds, will continue to compete for savings and interest-bearing transaction accounts on relatively equal terms. Thus, the relative growth of all these competing thrift institutions should be more stable in the period ahead.

SUMMARY

Nonbank thrift institutions—credit unions, savings and loans, savings banks, and money market funds—are expected to grow rapidly in the coming years. But it will not be an era of trouble-free growth and expansion. The volatility in funds flows experienced by nonbank thrifts during the 1970s and 1980s may be accentuated in the years ahead by another powerful force—competition. An intense competitive battle for savings deposits, transaction accounts, and consumer loans is now under way between commercial banks and nonbank thrifts in thousands of local markets across the United States.

This fierce competitive battle is not likely to end in the near future; in fact it should intensify as electronic systems are further developed for the automated transfer of funds and other pieces of financial information. Savings and loans, savings banks, credit unions, and money funds are determined to be a part of the growing "electronic money" network which moves funds almost instantly nationwide via computer tape and terminal. In fact, savings and loans in the Midwest have taken the lead in developing point-of-sale (POS) terminals in retail stores, automated tellers in shopping centers, and branch offices to service their customers' financial needs. Investment in these devices is motivated by the desire to bid transaction accounts away from commercial banks and to open up the markets for a wide variety of new consumer-oriented financial services necessary for the thrifts' future survival. Moreover, federal and state authorities that oversee nonbank thrift institutions have shown a willingness in recent years to liberalize operating rules so that these institutions can expand and improve their services to the public.

STUDY QUESTIONS

1. Credit unions are one of the fastest-growing financial intermediaries in the United States. What factors have contributed to this rapid growth?

2. What are the principal differences between savings and loan associations and savings banks? How are these institutions similar to each other?

3. How and why did money market funds begin in the 1970s? What factors contributed to their rapid growth in the late 1970s and early 1980s? Why did that growth subsequently slow?

4. Competition between commercial banks, credit unions, savings banks, money market funds, and savings and loan associations is increasing rapidly, especially in the markets for savings deposits, payments accounts, and consumer credit. Explain the reasons for this trend toward increasing competition. What are the probable consequences for the consumer?

5. Why is the savings and loan industry in trouble? What solutions have been offered to deal with its problems?

6. What effect would you expect NOW accounts, MMDAs, and share drafts to have on the loan and investment policies of nonbank thrift institutions? Please explain the reasoning behind your answer.

SELECTED REFERENCES

Cargill, Thomas F. "Recent Research on Credit Unions: A Survey." *Journal of Economics and Business,* Winter 1977, pp. 155–62.

Credit Union National Association. *1986 Yearbook.* Madison, Wisconsin.

Cumming, Christine. "The Economics of Securitization." *Quarterly Review,* Federal Reserve Bank of New York, Autumn 1987, pp. 11–23.

Dunham, Constance. "The Growth of Money Market Funds." *New England Economic Review,* Federal Reserve Bank of Boston, September–October 1980, pp. 20–34.

Eisenbeis, Robert A. "New Investment Powers for S&Ls: Diversification or Specialization?" *Economic Review,* Federal Reserve Bank of Atlanta, July 1983, pp. 53–62.

Longrehr, Frederick W. "Money Market Mutual Fund Investors' Savings Account Holdings and Demographic Profile." *Journal of Bank Research,* Autumn 1982, pp. 202–6.

Moran, Michael J. "Thrift Institutions in Recent Years." *Federal Reserve Bulletin,* December 1982, pp. 725–38.

Pavel, Christine, and Harvey Rosenblum. "Banks and Nonbanks: The Horse Race Continues." *Economic Perspectives,* Federal Reserve Bank of Chicago, May–June 1985, pp. 3–17.

United States League of Savings Institutions. *'85 Savings Institutions Sourcebook.* Chicago, 1985.

Chapter 6

Insurance Companies, Pension Funds, and Other Financial Institutions

Learning Objectives in This Chapter

- To examine the roles played by and the financial services offered by a variety of financial institutions ranging from life and property-casualty insurance companies to pension funds, finance companies, security dealers, mortgage banks, and investment companies.
- To explore the principal sources of funds and principal uses of funds for these financial institutions.
- To understand the problems faced by financial institutions operating in the money and capital markets and the current trends in this sector of the economy.

Key Terms and Concepts in This Chapter

Life insurance companies

Property casualty insurers

Pension funds

Finance companies

Investment companies

Security dealers

Investment bankers

Mortgage banks

Real estate investment trusts (REITS)

Leasing companies

Symbiotic

We now turn to a highly diverse group of financial institutions that attract savings mainly from individuals and families and, for the most part, make long-term loans in the capital market. Included in this group are life insurance companies, pension funds, and property casualty insurance companies, which today are leading institutional buyers of bonds and stocks. Finance companies, another member of the group, are active lenders to both business firms and consumers and borrow heavily in the nation's money market. While not generally providing new capital to businesses and other borrowers, investment companies (often called mutual funds) are active traders in corporate stocks and bonds and state and local government securities. As we will soon see, the majority of these financial institutions provide important services to participants in the markets for business and consumer credit.

LIFE INSURANCE COMPANIES

Life insurance companies were present early in the history of the United States. In fact, they were one of the first financial institutions founded in the American colonies. The Corporation for Relief of Poor and Distressed Presbyterian Ministers and of the Poor and Distressed Widows and Children of Presbyterian Ministers, established in 1759, was the first life insurance company in the United States. Life insurance companies offer their customers a hedge against the risk of earnings losses that often follow death, disability, or retirement. Policyholders receive risk protection in return for the payment of policy premiums that are set high enough to cover estimated benefit claims against the company, operating expenses, and a target profit

Exhibit 6–1   **Life Insurance in Force in the United States, 1976–1986** ($ Billions)

Category	1976	1986
Total amount:		
Ordinary	$ 1,178	$ 3,658
Group	1,003	2,801
Industrial	39	27
Credit	124	234
	$ 2,343	6,720
Average amount:		
Per family	$30,100	$69,100
Per insured family	35,000	81,200

Note: Columns may not add to totals due to rounding.

Source: American Council of Life Insurance, *1987 Life Insurance Fact Book.*

margin. Additional funds to cover claims and expenses are provided by investments made by life insurance companies in bonds, stocks, mortgages, and other assets approved by law and government regulation. Figures on the volume of insurance in force in the United States are shown in Exhibit 6–1, while the principal kinds of insurance policies sold by U.S. life insurers are listed in Exhibit 6–2.

Exhibit 6–2   The Principal Kinds of Insurance Policies Sold by Life Insurance Companies

Ordinary or whole life insurance	Insurance protection covers the entire lifetime of the policyholder whose designated beneficiaries are paid whenever the policyholder dies. Premiums are payable throughout the policyholder's lifetime or for a limited time period and build up cash values that may be borrowed by the policyholder.
Term life insurance	Insurance coverage for a certain number of years so that the policyholder's beneficiaries receive benefit payments only if death occurs within the period of coverage.
Endowment policy	Benefits are payable to the living policyholder on a specified future date or to the policyholder's beneficiaries if death occurs before the date specified in the policy. Premium payments build up cash value for the policyholder as with whole life insurance.
Group life insurance	Master insurance policy covering a group of people (usually all working for the same employer or members of the same organization) and sold normally without a required health examination.
Industrial life insurance	Small denomination life policies with premium payments collected monthly or weekly by a company agent calling at the insured's place of residence.
Universal life insurance	Insurance protection with premium payments whose amount and timing can be changed by the policyholder to increase or decrease the policy benefit. These policies include a savings account with a flexible rate of return.
Variable life insurance	Insurance protection whose benefits vary in amount with the value of assets pledged behind the policy contract.
Adjustable life insurance	A flexible form of insurance protection which permits the policyholder to alter some of the policy contract's terms, the time period of coverage, or the face value of the policy.
Credit life insurance	A type of term insurance contract pledged to pay off a loan or other form of debt in the event the borrower dies before the debt is paid off.

The Insurance Principle

The insurance business is founded upon the Law of Large Numbers. This mathematical principle states that a risk that is not predictable for one person can be forecasted accurately for a sufficiently large group of people with similar characteristics. No insurance company can accurately forecast when any one person will die, but its actuarial estimates of the total number of policyholders who will die in any given year are usually quite accurate.

Life insurance companies today insure policyholders against three basic kinds of risk: premature death, the danger of living too long and outlasting one's accumulated assets, and serious illness or accident. Many policies combine financial protection against death, disability, and retirement with savings plans to help the policyholder prepare for some important future financial need, such as the purchase of a home or meeting the costs of a college education. Actually, most benefit payments are made to living, rather than deceased, policyholders who receive annuities, disability checks, and other health insurance benefits. U.S. life companies are among the leading sources of retirement (pension) benefit payments for older Americans, and today more than 45 million U.S. citizens are enrolled in pension programs managed by life insurance companies. These companies are heavily regulated by the states to guarantee adequate compensation to the companies themselves and to ensure that the public is not overcharged or poorly served.

Investments of Life Insurance Companies

Life insurance companies invest the bulk of their funds in long-term securities—bonds, stocks, and mortgages, thus helping to fund real capital investment by businesses and government. They are inclined to commit their funds long term due to the high predictability of their cash inflows and outflows. Moreover, this predictability normally would permit a life insurance company to accept considerable risk in the securities it acquires. However, both law and tradition require a life insurer to act as a "prudent man." This restriction is imposed to ensure that sufficient funds are available to meet all legitimate claims from policyholders or their beneficiaries at precisely the time those claims mature.

Life companies pursue income certainty and safety of principal in their investments. The majority of the corporate securities they purchase are in the top four credit-rating categories.[1] Moreover, life insurers frequently follow a "buy and hold" strategy, acting as long-term holders of securities rather than rapidly turning over their portfolios. This investment approach reduces the risk of fluctuations in income and avoids having to rely on

---

[1]See Chapter 10 and Appendix A for an explanation of security ratings.

forecasting interest rates. We should note, however, that in recent years some life companies have become more active traders in securities. Emphasizing *performance* more than permanence in their investments, the larger life companies have set up trading rooms to more closely monitor the performance of their investment holdings, selling out and reinvesting in higher yielding alternatives when circumstances warrant. Because this new investment strategy creates additional risk, some of the larger companies have begun to trade in financial futures contracts and more closely match asset and liability maturities to protect themselves against losses from fluctuating interest rates.

Exhibit 6–3 shows the kinds of investments held by U.S. life insurance companies as of year-end 1986. The primary investment is in corporate bonds, the majority of which are issued by domestic companies, though purchases of foreign bonds are also important. Holdings of common and preferred stock, though much smaller, have become significant in recent years. Life insurance companies have shown renewed interest in corporate stock due to inflation and the growing importance of variable annuity policies and variable life insurance plans in their sales programs.

Exhibit 6–3   **Assets of U.S. Life Insurance Companies, 1986**

Item	Amounts ($ billions)	Percent of Total Assets
Government securities		
U.S. Treasury obligations	$ 59.0	
Federal agency securities	60.0	
State and local debt obligations	11.7	
Debt of foreign governments and international agencies	13.9	
Total government securities	$144.6	15.4%
Corporate securities		
Bonds	$342.0	
Common stocks	81.4	
Preferred stocks	9.5	
Total corporate securities	$432.9	46.2
Mortgages		
Farm	$ 11.0	
Nonfarm	182.9	
Total mortgages	193.9	20.6
Loans to policyholders	54.1	5.8
Real estate owned	31.6	3.4
Miscellaneous assets	74.8	8.6
Total Assets	$937.6	100.0%

Note: Columns may not add to totals due to rounding.

Source: American Council of Life Insurance, *1987 Life Insurance Fact Book.*

The second most important asset held by life insurance companies comprises mortgages on farm, residential, and commercial properties. Substantial changes have occurred in life insurance company mortgage investments in recent years. The industry has reduced its holdings of farm and residential mortgages on one- to four-family homes and increased its holdings of commercial mortgages, including loans on retail stores, shopping centers, office buildings, apartment buildings, hospitals, and factories. The higher yields and generally shorter maturities of the latter loans explain much of the recent rapid growth of commercial mortgage lending by the life insurance industry.[2] However, life insurers continue to provide indirect support to the residential mortgage market by making heavy purchases of federal agency securities, most of which come from government agencies aiding the home mortgage market.

Government securities play a secondary but still important role in the portfolios of life insurance companies. These securities serve the important function of providing a reservoir of *liquidity*, because they may be sold with little difficulty when more funds are required. Recently investments in government securities have been rising as industry cash flows have become more volatile, increasing demands for liquid reserves. Life insurance companies buy mostly federal government securities rather than state and local government obligations. The industry has only a limited need for the tax-exempt income provided by state and local bonds because its tax rate is relatively low.

One asset whose importance increased dramatically during the 1960s and 1970s and then declined when interest rates fell in the 1980s is *loans to policyholders*. The holder of an ordinary (whole life) insurance policy usually is entitled to borrow against the accumulated cash value of the policy, which increases every year. The interest rate on such loans is stated in the contract accompanying the policy and is usually quite low. For example, many policies issued not long ago carry an 8 percent loan rate. Policy loans tend to follow the business cycle, rising significantly in periods when economic activity and interest rates are increasing rapidly and declining when the economy or interest rates are headed down or growing more slowly. Because of this cyclical characteristic, policy loans are a volatile claim on the industry's resources. When loan demand is high, life insurance companies frequently are forced to reduce their purchases of bonds and stocks. Since 1982, however, many new whole life policies sold have had floating loan rates, and policyholder borrowing has generally declined.

---

[2]In granting mortgage credit, life insurance companies often employ *advance commitments*. These consist of promises to provide long-term mortgage funds to a real estate developer before a residential or commercial construction project begins. The developer will use that financing commitment as an aid in obtaining short-term cash (usually from commercial banks) to complete construction. Later, when the project is completed, the insurance company will loan the funds promised and the proceeds of the long-term loan will be used to repay any short-term borrowings.

Sources of Life Insurance Company Funds

The primary income source for life insurers is premium receipts from sales of insurance policies. Premiums from sales of annuity plans and health insurance policies have actually grown faster than sales of traditional life insurance policies. Annual net income from investments in bonds, stocks, and other assets average only about a third of premium receipts. The industry's net earnings after expenses roughly equal its investment income each year because virtually all premiums from the sale of policies are ultimately returned to policyholders or their beneficiaries. This means that, on balance, the industry hopes to "break even" from its insurance underwriting operations (with premiums flowing in eventually balanced by benefits paid out), while earning profits from its investment income (see Exhibit 6–4 for a statement of sources and uses of life insurance industry funds).

Regulating the Industry

The life insurance business has been heavily regulated by the states since its inception. It is generally thought to be "vested with the public interest,"

Exhibit 6–4 **The U.S. Life Insurance Company Dollar: Sources and Uses of Funds in 1986** (in Cents)

Sources of Income:	
Policyholder premiums	71.5¢
Earnings from investments and other income	28.5
	100.0¢
How used:	
Benefit payments during year	50.6¢
Additions to policy reserves	32.0
Additions to special reserves and surplus funds	1.3
	83.9¢
Operating expenses:	
Commissions paid to agents	5.9¢
Home and field office expenses	9.0
	14.9¢
Taxes*	2.7¢
Dividends to stockholders of stock life insurance companies†	1.4
	100.0¢

*Direct investment taxes (such as real estate) are excluded from taxes and are deducted, with other investment expenses, from investment income. Federal income taxes, however, are included in total taxes.

†If only stockholder-owned companies are included, then the dividend ratio becomes 2.4 cents per dollar.

Source: Adapted from the American Council of Life Insurance, *1987 Life Insurance Fact Book.*

and therefore its activities are carefully monitored by state insurance commissions and the courts. Field representatives must be licensed and policy forms approved by state agencies. All funds must be invested in accordance with court decisions and with state laws and regulations. Only commercial banking appears to be as heavily regulated as the life insurance business, though unlike banks, life insurers face little federal government regulation.

Structure and Growth of the Life Insurance Industry

The majority of the more than 2,000 American life insurance companies are corporations owned by their stockholders. The rest are mutuals, which issue ownership shares to their policyholders. However, mutual firms are much bigger on average and generally were established much earlier. Most new companies in recent years have been stockholder owned, and a few mutuals have converted to stockholder organizations to gain greater financial flexibility.

Earlier in the 1970s the number of life insurance companies declined for several years. Many smaller companies were absorbed by other insurers to counteract growing expenses and provide a broader range of services. However, in recent years many new companies have been formed to meet specialized local and regional insurance needs, leaving the older and larger companies to cover the national and international market for insurance. Then, too, the U.S. life insurance industry has grown rapidly in the 1980s as millions of Americans from the post–World War II baby boom have reached the middle-aged group where most life insurance and retirement plan purchases are made. In 1986 alone, life insurance purchases exceeded $1.3 trillion for the first time in history—a volume of business that has supported the growth of older, established companies and of many new companies as well.

New Services

Life insurers are under increasing pressure to develop new services due to a long-term decline in their share of household savings and pressure on earnings due to high-cost service delivery systems. Increasing competition from other financial intermediaries also has played a major role in encouraging the development of new services. Among the most important recent developments are the creation of separate accounts, universal and adjustable life insurance, variable premium and variable life insurance, mutual funds, tax shelters, venture capital loans, corporate cash management systems, and deferred annuities.

A *separate account* is an asset account which a life insurance company holds on behalf of a customer (usually a pension fund) apart from its other assets. Separate accounts have enabled life companies to compete successfully for the growing volume of pension savings from an aging population. Funds stored in these accounts are subject to more liberal investment rules, permitting a larger portion of these monies to be placed in common stock and other more risky investments.

Begun in 1979, *universal life insurance* allows the customer to change the face amount of his or her policy and the size and timing of the premium payments, as well as earn higher investment returns from any premiums paid in. Premium payments on a universal life insurance policy usually are invested in a money market fund.

Universal life is just one example of the more flexible types of insurance policies developed by life companies in recent years, each designed to deal with inflation and changing economic conditions. Another example of the newer flexible life insurance products is *adjustable life insurance*, which permits the policyholder to change periodically from a whole life policy to term insurance (which offers protection only for a designated period) and back again in order to match his or her changing circumstances. Adjustable policies allow the policyholder to increase or decrease the face value of the policy, the period of insurance protection, and the size of premium payments within the limits spelled out in the policy contract. A variation on this idea is *variable premium life insurance*, which grants the policyholder lower premium payments when investments made by the life insurance company earn a greater return due to rising interest rates.

Variable life insurance pays benefits according to the value of assets pledged behind the policy (primarily common stock), rather than paying a fixed amount of money. There is, however, normally a guaranteed minimum benefit for the policyholder's designated beneficiary. It is a form of inflation-hedged life insurance now authorized in all 50 states. Universal and variable life insurance sales combined accounted for about one third of all policy sales in the United States in 1986.

Life insurers have also been active in loans to help start new businesses and in offering professional funds management services to many businesses who haven't the time or experience to manage their own cash accounts and earn the best rates of return. They have also found success in attracting *deferred annuity* accounts. Here, an individual will deposit funds with the life insurer under an agreement to receive a future stream of income flowing from those deposited funds beginning on a stipulated future date. The life insurer agrees to invest the funds in earning assets that will grow over time and escape any taxation until the customer actually begins receiving income.

New services offered by life insurance companies in future years will depend heavily on changes in government laws and regulations, something that is also true of other financial intermediaries. Life insurers must also find lower-cost ways of marketing and delivering their services (such as increased use of automation and joint-venture sales through banks' and stockbrokers' branch offices).

PROPERTY CASUALTY INSURANCE COMPANIES

Property casualty insurers offer protection against fire, theft, bad weather, negligence, and other acts and events that result in injury to persons or property. So broad is the range of risk for which these companies provide protection that property casualty insurers are sometimes referred to as *insurance supermarkets*. In addition to their traditional insurance lines— automobile, fire, marine, personal liability, and property coverage—many of these firms have branched into the health and medical insurance fields, clashing head-on with life insurance companies offering the same services (see Exhibit 6–5 for a list of the major types of policies written by property casualty insurers).

Makeup of the Property Casualty Insurance Industry

The property casualty insurance business has grown rapidly in recent years due to the effects of inflation, rising crime rates, and a growing volume of lawsuits arising from product liability and professional negligence claims. There were almost 3,500 property casualty companies in the United States in 1986, holding more than $300 billion in assets. Stockholder-owned companies are dominant, holding about three fourths of the industry's total resources. Mutual companies—owned by their policy holders—hold roughly a fourth of all industry resources.

Changing Risk Patterns in Property Liability Coverage

Property casualty insurance is a riskier business than life insurance. The risk of policyholder claims arising from crime, fire, bad weather, personal negligence, and similar causes is much less predictable than is the risk of death. Moreover, inflation has had a potent impact on the cost of property and services for which this form of insurance pays. For example, the cost of medical care and for repair of automobiles has more than doubled over the past decade.

Equally important, basic changes now seem to be under way in the risk patterns of many large insurance programs, creating problems in forecasting policyholder claims and in setting new premium rates. Examples include a rapid rise in medical malpractice suits, a virtual explosion in product liability claims against manufacturers of automobiles, tires, home appliances, and other goods, and the emergence of billions of dollars in claims from so-called *toxic torts*. These are claims arising from civil court decisions favoring individuals suffering from illness or injury caused by exposure to asbestos, nuclear radiation, and other hazardous substances. In order to reduce risk, more property casualty insurers have become *multiple-line companies,* diversifying into many different lines of insurance.

Exhibit 6–5   **Principal Lines of Insurance Coverage Provided by U.S. Property-Casualty Companies, 1986** ($ Millions)

Insurance Lines	Net Premiums Written by U.S. Companies*	Insurance Lines	Net Premiums Written by U.S. Companies*
Auto liability	$44,081	Worker's compensation	$20,431
Auto physical damage	29,306	Accident and health	2,930
Medical malpractice	3,492	Inland marine	3,899
Other nonauto liability insurance	19,365	Ocean marine	1,225
Fire insurance and allied lines†	6,933	Surety and Fidelity	2,116
Homeowners multiple peril insurance	15,222	Boilers and Machinery	531
Commercial multiple peril insurance	16,190	Aircraft insurance	712
Farm owners' multiple peril insurance	828	Burglary and theft	121
		Glass	27

*Net premiums written represent premium income earned by insurance companies, direct or through reinsurance, less payments made for business reinsured.

†Allied lines include crop-hail insurance premiums.

Source: Insurance Information Institute, *Property/Casualty Fact Book*, 1987–88 edition.

Investments by Property Casualty Companies

The majority of funds received by property casualty companies are invested in state and local government bonds and common stock. Property casualty companies, unlike most financial institutions, are subject to the full federal corporate income tax rate (except that policyholder dividends are tax deductible). Faced with a potentially heavy tax burden, these companies find tax-exempt state and local government bonds an attractive investment. As shown in Exhibit 6–6, industry holdings of state and local bonds represented about one third of total financial assets, although property casualty insurers have placed less emphasis on purchases of municipal bonds in recent years due, in part, to their sluggish earnings and recent changes in income tax laws. Their second most important asset, common stock, is intended to protect industry earnings and net worth against inflation. Other important investments include U.S. government securities, federal agency securities, and corporate bonds. Property casualty insurers have stepped up their purchases of federal government securities in recent years due to their high yields (reflecting the government's large deficits) and their safety.

It is interesting to compare the distribution of the assets held by life insurance companies and by property casualty companies. The net cash flows of the two industries—their annual premium income—are roughly comparable. Yet life insurers hold about three times the assets of property casualty insurers. Much of the difference is explained by the fact that life insurance is a highly predictable business, whereas property and personal

Exhibit 6–6   **Financial Assets and Liabilities of U.S. Property Casualty Insurance Companies, December 31, 1986**

Asset and Liability Items	Amounts ($ billions)	Percent of Total Assets or Liabilities
Demand deposits and currency	$ 4.9	1.4%
Security repurchase agreements (RPs)	22.9	6.6
Corporate stock	68.3	19.7
U.S. Treasury securities	46.2	13.3
Federal agency obligations	31.4	9.1
State and local government securities	91.9	26.5
Corporate and foreign bonds	44.3	12.8
Commercial mortgages	4.5	1.3
Trade credit	31.9	9.2
Total financial assets	$346.4	100.0%
Policy payables	$253.2	99.9%
Profit taxes payable	0.1	0.1
Total liabilities	$253.3	100.0%

Note: Columns may not add to totals due to rounding.

Source: Board of Governors of the Federal Reserve System, *Flow of Funds Accounts: Financial Assets and Liabilities Outstanding, 1963–86*

injury risks are not. Most life insurance policies are long-term contracts, and claims against the insurer are not normally expected for several years. In contrast, property casualty claims are payable from the day the policy is written, because an accident or injury may occur at any time. Therefore, while life insurance companies can stay almost fully invested, property casualty insurers must be ready at all times to meet the claims of policyholders. In addition, claims against property casualty companies are directly affected by inflation, which drives up repair costs. Most life insurance policies, in contrast, pay the policyholder or a designated beneficiary a fixed sum of money.

Sources of Income

Like life insurance firms, property casualty insurers plan to break even on their insurance product lines and earn most of their net return from investments. Achieving the breakeven point in insurance underwriting has been difficult in recent years, however, due to rising costs, increased litigation, and new forms of risk. For example, in 1986 the industry ran a net underwriting loss of $15.9 billion. It was the sixth consecutive year of record underwriting losses. Investment income, however, usually offsets underwriting losses. For example, during 1986 U.S. property casualty insurers reported investment income of almost $22 billion, resulting in net income before taxes of about $6.6 billion. But industry profits are highly volatile from year to year, due to unexpected losses and expenses, and to the refusal of many state insurance commissions to let premiums rise as fast as industry expenses.

Business Cycles, Inflation, and Competition

This is an industry whose earnings and sales revenue reflect the ups and downs of the business cycle. This cyclical sensitivity, coupled with the vulnerability of property casualty insurers to inflation, has created a difficult environment for insurance managers. Inflation has pushed up claims costs, while intense competition holds premium rates down. Foreign insurance underwriters are more active in domestic markets today, and many U.S. corporations recently have started their own captive insurance companies. In order to improve their situation in future years, property casualty insurers must become more innovative in developing new services and more determined to eliminate those services which have resulted in underwriting losses. This will not be easy due to extensive state government regulations and public pressure for lower insurance rates.

PENSION FUNDS

Pension funds protect individuals and families against loss of income in their retirement years by allowing workers to set aside and invest a portion of their current income. A pension plan will place current savings in a portfolio of stocks, bonds, real estate, and other assets in the expectation of building an even larger pool of funds in the future. In this way, the pension plan member can balance planned consumption after retirement with the amount of savings set aside today.

Growth of Pension Funds

Pension funds have been among the most rapidly growing of all American financial intermediaries. Between 1980 and 1986 the assets of all private and public pension funds more than doubled (see Exhibit 6–7). Approximately half of all full-time workers in commerce and industry and three quarters of all government civilian employees are protected by pension plans other than the social security program (OASDI). Nearly 170 million persons are insured under social security.

Pension fund growth in the United States in the past has been spurred on by the relatively few retirees drawing pensions compared to the number of people working and contributing to a pension program. That situation is changing rapidly, however; individuals over 65 years of age now represent

Exhibit 6–7   Total Assets of U.S. Private and Public Pension Funds, Selected Years ($ Billions)

Type of Pension Plan or Program	Year					
	1940	1950	1960	1970	1980	1986
Private pension programs:	$2.0	$12.1	$ 52.0	$138.2	$422.7	$1,266.9
Insured plans	0.6	5.6	18.8	41.2	165.8	440.6
Noninsured plans	1.4	6.5	33.2	97.0	286.8	826.3
Government pension programs:	$4.3	$25.8	$ 56.1	$125.9	$289.8	$ 657.9
State-local retirement systems	1.6	5.3	19.3	60.3	185.2	437.2
Federal civilian systems	0.6	4.2	10.5	23.1	75.8	167.4
Railroad retirement program	0.1	2.6	3.7	4.4	2.1	6.4
Social security program (OASDI)	$2.0	$13.7	$ 22.6	$ 38.1	$ 26.5	$ 46.9
Total assets of all funds	$6.3	$37.9	$108.2	$262.0	$712.3	$1,924.8

Note: Columns may not add to totals due to rounding.

Source: Securities and Exchange Commission; Railroad Retirement Board; U.S. Department of Health and Human Services; and the American Council of Life Insurance, *Life Insurance Factbook 1987*, p. 24.

one of the fastest growing segments of the U.S. population. The growing proportion of retired individuals will threaten the solvency of many private pension funds and has, in fact, already created major funding problems for various federal government programs (such as Medicare) designed primarily to aid the elderly.[3]

Intense competition among employers for skilled management personnel has also spurred pension fund growth as firms have tried to attract top-notch employees by offering attractive fringe benefits. This growth factor is likely to persist in the 1990s and beyond due to a developing shortage of young, skilled entry-level workers. Some experts foresee a real problem in this area, however, stemming from the recent difficulties pension plans have had in keeping up with inflation and with the increasing numbers of retirees. Workers in the future are likely to demand both better performance from their pension plans and greater control over how their long-term savings are invested.

Investment Strategies of Pension Funds

Pension funds are long-term investors with limited need for liquidity. Their incoming cash receipts are known with considerable accuracy because a fixed percentage of each employee's salary is usually contributed to the fund. At the same time, cash outflows are not too difficult to forecast because the

---

[3]The present ratio of working adults to retired persons in the U.S. population is about 3:1. This ratio is projected to shrink to about 2:1 by the turn of the century. When the Social Security Act was passed in 1935, there were 11 working adults for each retired individual.

formula for figuring benefit payments is stipulated in the contract between the fund and its members. This situation encourages pensions to purchase common stock, long-term bonds, and real estate and hold these assets on a more or less permanent basis. In addition, interest income and capital gains from investments are exempt from federal income taxes, while pension plan members are not taxed on their contributions unless cash benefits are paid out.

While favorable taxation and predictable cash flows favor longer term, somewhat riskier investments, the pension fund industry is closely regulated in all its activities. The Employee Retirement Income Security Act (ERISA) requires all private plans to be *funded*, which means that any assets held plus anticipated investment income must be adequate to cover all promised benefits. ERISA also requires that investments must be made in a "prudent" manner, which is usually interpreted to mean highly diversified holdings of high-grade common stock, corporate bonds, and government securities and limited real estate investments.

While existing regulations do emphasize conservatism in pension fund investments, the private plans have been under intense pressure in recent years by both management and employees of sponsoring companies to be more liberal in their investment policies. The sponsoring employer has a strong incentive to encourage its affiliated pension plan to reduce operating expenses and earn the highest possible returns on its investments. This permits the company to minimize its contributions to the plan. Both sponsoring employers and employees have a keen interest in seeing that the pension plan earns a high enough return on its investments to at least keep pace with inflation. Otherwise, the employees will tend to seek other jobs whose pension programs offer more lucrative returns.

Pension Fund Assets

The particular assets held as investments by pension funds depend heavily on whether the fund is government controlled or private. As shown in Exhibit 6–8, private funds emphasize investments in corporate stock, which represent about three quarters of their assets. Corporate bonds ranked a distant second, accounting for about one fifth of all private pensions' financial investments. A growing volume of these securities are purchased overseas, where both risk and rates of return are generally higher. With few liquidity needs, private pensions held relatively small amounts of cash and bank deposits, though their holdings of U.S. government securities have increased significantly in recent years due to the relatively high yields and safety of these investments.

Corporate stock is far less important in the portfolios of government pensions than among private plans. As Exhibit 6–8 shows, state and local government pension programs held about one third of their financial assets in corporate stock. Stock investments were almost matched in government

Exhibit 6–8   **Financial Assets Held by Private, Noninsured Pension Funds and State and Local Government Employee Retirement Funds, December 31, 1986** ($ Billions at Year-End)

Asset Items	Private Noninsured Pension Funds		State and Local Government Employee Retirement Funds	
	Amount	**Percent**	**Amount**	**Percent**
Cash assets	$ 6.9	1.1%	$ 2.8	0.6
Time deposits	57.2	9.0	16.1	3.4
Corporate stock	481.4	75.8	150.2	32.0
U.S. government securities	61.8	9.7	94.8	20.2
Federal agency securities	50.3	7.9	48.6	10.4
State and local government securities	—	—	0.8	0.2
Corporate and foreign bonds	128.3	20.2	140.6	29.9
Mortgages	7.3	1.1	15.6	3.3
Miscellaneous assets	−158.2	−24.9	—	—
Total	$635.0	100.0%	$469.5	100.0%

Note: Columns may not add to totals due to rounding.

Source: Board of Governors of the Federal Reserve System, *Flow of Funds Accounts—Assets and Liabilities Outstanding*, September 1987.

pension plans by holdings of corporate bonds, which represented more than a quarter of their assets. Thus, the pressure of strict regulation falls more heavily upon government (public) pension plans than on private plans. As a result, their investments tend to be more conservative, with more corporate and government bonds and less of more risky common stocks. Government pensions also place small amounts of funds in state and local government securities—often IOUs issued by their own governmental units.

Factors Affecting the Future Growth of Pension Funds

Most experts feel that pension fund growth is likely to slow significantly in future years. One reason is the rising proportion of pension beneficiaries to working contributors, related to the gradual aging of the general population. At the same time, the cost of maintaining pension programs has increased dramatically. The full funding of a plan to cover all promised benefits may place extreme pressure on corporate profits, particularly if declining stock and bond markets diminish investment returns.

Even more significant is the rapidly rising cost of government regulation. ERISA, passed by Congress in 1974, imposed costly reporting requirements on the industry and granted employees the right to join a pension program, in most cases, after only one year on the job. More rapid *vesting* of accumulated benefits was also required so that employees can recover a higher proportion of their past contributions should they decide to retire early or move to another job. Trying to eliminate the danger that pensions may not have adequate funds to pay future claims against them, Congress now requires employers eventually to cover any past liabilities not fully covered at present. In addition, a federal agency—the Pension Benefit Guaranty Corporation (PBGC)—was created in 1974 to insure some part of all vested employee benefits. PBGC is supported by premiums contributed annually by participating employers and can borrow up to $100 million from the U.S. Treasury in an emergency.

These new government regulations have forced many private pension plans to close. The control of others has been turned over to a financial institution—typically a bank trust department or life insurance company—better able to deal with the current rules. At the same time, the sharp increase in business failures in recent years has threatened the continued viability of the federal pension insurance fund (PBGC) which has guaranteed workers' retirement benefits amounting to about $1.3 trillion for approximately 40 million Americans. PBGC currently has far more liabilities than assets. Many private pension plans are in weak financial condition; yet under the law PBGC must insure all *defined-benefit plans*—that is, those promising their members a fixed amount of income at retirement and representing about three quarters of all private pensions in the United States—regardless of their financial status. PBGC assesses a flat insurance premium for each pension plan member and does not charge more risky pension plans a higher insurance fee. Moreover, PBGC currently has no legal authority to regulate pension funds, nor does it receive any financial support from the government, having only a small line of credit with the U.S. Treasury. Clearly there is a pressing need for pension plan reform so that all pension plan members can be assured of receiving their promised benefits.

FINANCE COMPANIES

Finance companies are sometimes called department stores of consumer and business credit. These institutions grant credit to businesses and consumers for a wide variety of purposes, including the purchase of inventories, business equipment, automobiles, home repairs, vacations, medical care, mobile homes, and home appliances. Most authorities divide firms in the industry into one of three groups: consumer finance companies, sales finance companies, and commercial finance companies.

Different Finance Companies for Different Purposes

Consumer finance companies, also known as small-loan companies (such as Beneficial Finance), make personal cash loans available to many individuals. The majority of their loans support the purchase of passenger cars, home appliances, recreational vehicles, and mobile homes. However, a growing proportion of consumer finance company loans center on aiding customers with medical and hospital expenses, educational costs, vacations, home repair and maintenance, and energy bills. Loans made by small loan companies are considered to be more risky than other consumer installment loans and therefore generally carry steeper finance charges than those assessed by banks and other installment lenders.

Sales finance companies (like GMAC) make indirect loans to consumers by purchasing installment paper from dealers selling automobiles and other consumer durables. Many of these firms are captive finance companies controlled by a dealer or manufacturer. Their principal function is to promote sales of the sponsoring firm's goods and services by providing credit. Companies having captive finance affiliates include General Motors, General Electric, Motorola, Sears, and Wards. Generally, sales finance companies will specify in advance to retail dealers the terms (maturities, minimum down payments, and finance charges) of installment contracts they are willing to accept. Frequently they will give the retail dealer a supply of contract forms which the dealer will fill out when a sale is made. The contract is then sold immediately to the finance company.

Commercial finance companies (such as CIT) focus principally on extending credit to business firms. Most of these companies provide accounts receivable financing or factoring services to small or medium-sized manufacturers and wholesalers. With accounts receivable financing, the commercial finance company may extend credit against the borrower's receivables in the form of a direct cash loan. Alternatively, a factoring arrangement may be used in which the finance company acquires the borrowing firm's credit accounts at an appropriate discount rate to cover the risk of loss. Most commercial finance companies today do not confine their credit-granting activities to the financing of receivables, but also make loans secured by business inventories, machinery, and other fixed assets. In addition, they offer lease financing for the purchase of capital equipment and rolling stock (such as airplanes and railroad cars) and make short-term unsecured cash loans.

We should not overdramatize the differences among these three types of finance companies. The larger companies are active in all three areas. In addition, most finance companies today are extremely diversified in their credit-granting activities, offering a wide range of installment and working-capital loans, leasing plans, and long-term credit to support capital investment. Exhibit 6–9 shows that business loans are the most important financial assets held by finance companies, accounting for almost half their total assets. Consumer loans were also significant and ran a close second to business loans in the most recent period. Much smaller amounts of funds are committed by the industry to real estate mortgages or held in cash to provide liquidity.

Growth of Finance Companies

Finance companies have been profoundly affected by recent changes in the character of competition among financial intermediaries. The lack of an extensive network of branch offices has put them at a disadvantage in reaching the household borrower who values convenience. As a result, both commercial banks and nonbank thrifts have been able to capture a larger share of the consumer installment loan market at the expense of finance companies. For example, data compiled by the Federal Reserve Board show that finance companies held about 45 percent of consumer installment loans extended by financial institutions in 1950, but only 23 percent in 1987. Over the same interval of time, credit unions tripled their share of the consumer installment loan market.

Many experts now feel that the fastest growing market for finance companies in future years will be business-oriented rather than consumer-oriented financial services. Revolving credit, second mortgages on real property, and equipment leasing are among the fastest-growing forms of credit extended by finance companies today. However, they have also made substantial gains in the auto loan market recently, wresting a larger share of this credit market away from banks and credit unions by using extensive advertising and low auto loan rates.

Methods of Industry Financing

Finance companies are heavy users of debt in financing their operations. Principal sources of borrowed funds include bank loans, commercial paper, and long-term debentures (bonds) sold primarily to banks, insurance companies, and nonfinancial corportions (see Exhibit 6–9). Which source of funds these companies emphasize most heavily at any given time depends on the structure of interest rates. When long-term rates are high, these companies tend to emphasize commercial paper and shorter-term bank loans as sources of funds. In years when long-term rates are relatively low, long-term bonds will be drawn upon more heavily.

Recent Changes in the Character of the Finance Company Industry

The structure of the finance industry has changed markedly in recent years. As in the case of credit unions and savings and loans, the number of finance companies has been trending downward, although the average size of such companies has grown considerably. A survey by the Federal Reserve Board revealed that in 1960 there were more than 6,400 finance companies operating in the United States, but by 1980 only about 2,000 independent companies could be found. A modest rise in the number of new firms occurred

Exhibit 6–9   **Financial Assets and Liabilities Held by Finance Companies, December 31, 1986**

Asset and Liability Items	Amount ($ billions)	Percent of Total
Assets:		
Demand deposits and currency	$ 7.0	1.7%
Mortgages	67.5	16.4
Consumer credit	162.8	39.5
Loans to businesses	174.8	42.4
Total financial assets	$412.1	100.0%
Liabilities:		
Corporate bonds issued	$115.6	26.3%
Bank loans, n.e.c.	18.7	4.3
Open-market paper issued	181.7	41.4
Profit taxes payable	439.2	*
Funds from parent companies	97.7	22.2
Miscellaneous liabilities	25.5	5.8
Total liabilities	$439.2	100.0%

Note: Columns may not add to totals due to rounding.

*Less than 0.1 percent.

Source: Board of Governors of the Federal Reserve System, *Flow of Funds Accounts—Financial Assets and Liabilities Outstanding,* 1963–86.

during the 1970s, however, as bank holding companies centered around some of the nation's largest banks organized new finance company subsidiaries.

This long-term trend in the industry's population reflects a number of powerful economic forces at work. Rising cost pressures, the broadening of markets, the need to innovate, and intensified competition from other financial institutions have encouraged finance companies to strive for larger size and greater efficiency. Many smaller companies have sold out to larger conglomerates. Despite their declining numbers, however, finance companies rank among the fastest growing financial intermediaries in the United States and continue to be a potent force in the markets for business and consumer credit.

INVESTMENT COMPANIES

Investment companies provide an outlet for the savings of thousands of individual investors, directing their funds into bonds, stocks, and money market securities. These companies are especially attractive to the small investor, to whom they offer continuous management services for a large and highly varied security portfolio. By purchasing shares offered by an investment company, the small saver gains greater price stability and reduced risk, opportunities for capital gains, and indirect access to higher yielding securities that can only be purchased in large blocks. In addition, most investment company stock is highly liquid, since many companies stand ready at all times to repurchase their outstanding shares at current market prices.

The Background of Investment Companies

Investment companies made their appearance in the United States after World War I as a vehicle for buying up and often for monitoring subsidiary corporations. Many were unsuccessful in the early years, and the Great Depression of the 1930s forced scores of these new firms into bankruptcy. New life was breathed into the industry after World War II, however, when investment companies began to appeal to a rapidly growing middle class of savers. They were also buoyed by rising stock prices which attracted millions of investors, most of whom had only modest amounts to invest and little knowledge of how the financial markets work. The industry launched an aggressive advertising campaign that ultimately attracted more than 40 million shareholders during the 1960s.

Then the roof fell in as the long postwar bull market in stocks collapsed in the late 1960s. During the 1970s the stock market staged modest recoveries, only to be thrown back each time as it neared highs set during the sixties. Small investors began to pull out of the stock market in droves. Total assets of the most important kind of investment company—the mutual fund—reached nearly $48 billion in 1970 but five years later had dropped significantly. In all but three years during the 1970s, redemptions of mutual funds' shares exceeded their sales.

Many investment companies disappeared in this shakeout period, most of them consolidated into larger firms. The future of the industry seemed very much in doubt until a new element appeared—*innovation*. Owners and managers began to develop new types of investment companies designed to appeal to groups of investors with specialized financial needs. By custom and tradition investment companies had stressed investments in common stock, offering investors capital appreciation as well as current income. With the stock market performing poorly, however, these firms turned their focus increasingly to other markets, especially to bonds and money market instruments. The new *bond funds*, which first became prominent in the 1960s, directed the majority of their funds into corporate debt obligations or tax-exempt municipal bonds. Their principal objectives in recent years have been to generate current income and, in the case of the municipal bond fund, a higher after-tax rate of return for the investor. Capital appreciation is normally a secondary consideration to these investment companies.

Money market funds, discussed in Chapter 5, began in 1972 with the announced intent of holding money market securities—mainly bank certificates of deposit (CDs), commercial paper, and U.S. Treasury bills. They were created in response to record-high interest rates in U.S. money markets and the desire of the small investor to skirt around federal interest rate ceilings on time and savings deposits offered by banks and nonbank thrift institutions. In addition, the money funds have offered corporations and other institutional investors professional management of their liquid funds and reduced risk through diversification.

Interestingly enough, the traditional equity (stock)-investing mutual funds began to grow rapidly again in the 1980s. While money market funds rescued the investment companies during the turbulent 1970s, the equity funds generally outpaced the money market funds in the 1980s with money flowing in from individual retirement accounts (IRAs) and from investors enamored of "bargain" stock prices. Moreover, several stock funds outperformed the market as a whole (as measured by the behavior of Standard & Poor's 500 Stock Index) by purchasing stocks from smaller, rapidly growing firms dealing in high tech products or specialty items. Nevertheless, most stock funds did *not* outperform the market, which increased the popularity of so-called *index funds* that invest in a portfolio of stocks and bonds reflective of the whole market portfolio and tend to move synchronously with the market.[4]

Another prominent trend that marked the 1980s and is likely to continue for many years is the rapid growth of *global funds*. These are stock and bond funds whose income-earning securities come from all over the world, particularly from the more rapidly growing nations in Western Europe and around the Pacific rim (including Japan). These funds have access to security trading 24 hours a day through active exchanges in London, Tokyo, Singapore, Hong Kong, and in other financial centers around the globe. Many managers of these funds believe higher returns are achievable with a balanced international portfolio, rather than just from domestic securities.

Regulation of Investment Companies

Investment companies are heavily regulated at the federal level through such laws as the Investment Company Act and the Investment Advisers Act, both passed by Congress in 1940. Registration of investment company securities and periodic reports to the Securities and Exchange Commission (SEC) are mandatory. Policies for investing funds are determined by the investment company's shareholders, who also elect at least two thirds of the company's directors. The portfolio held by an investment company is managed by a separate management company or investment advisory service, which levies a substantial fee for its services. The management fee is typically a small percentage (perhaps 1 to 2 percent) of the fund's total assets

---

[4]*Index funds* are based on the theory of efficient markets, which argues that, in the long run, active money managers cannot beat the market (i.e., outperform the market as a whole). Thus, index funds tend to hold their investments longer and charge lower brokerage and service fees than do investment companies that turn over their security portfolios more rapidly. See Chapter 21 for further discussion of market efficiency.

and is not necessarily based on fund performance. Any contractual arrangements between the investment advisory service and the investment company must be approved by the latter's stockholders and must come up for renewal or revision every two years. Most investment advisory services are provided by life insurance firms or security specialists.

Tax Status of the Industry

Investment companies have a highly favorable tax situation. As long as they conform to certain rules to qualify as an investment company, they do not pay federal taxes on income generated by their security holdings. However, no less than half their resources must be devoted to securities and cash assets. Investment companies must maintain a highly diversified portfolio— a maximum of one quarter of their total resources can be devoted to securities issued by any one firm. Only a small portion of net income (no more than 10 percent) can be retained in the business. The rest must be distributed to shareholders.

Open-End and Closed-End Investment Companies

There are two basic kinds of investment companies. *Open-end companies*— often called mutual funds—will buy back (redeem) their shares any time the customer wishes and sell open shares in any quantity demanded. Thus, the amount of their outstanding shares changes continually in response to public demand. The price of each open-end company share is equal to the net asset value of the fund—that is, the difference between the values of its assets and liabilities divided by the volume of shares issued.

Open-end companies may be either *load* or *no-load* funds. Load funds, which are in the majority, offer shares to the public at net asset value plus a commission to brokers marketing the shares. No-load funds sell shares purely at net asset value. The investor must contact the no-load company directly, however. Whether load or no-load, open-end investment companies are heavily invested in common stock, with corporate bonds running a distant second. As Exhibit 6–10 shows, corporate stock represents about two fifths of the industry's total financial assets, with government bonds and corporate bonds accounting for most of the remaining industry portfolio. However, mutual funds have added substantially to their holdings of fixed-income securities (federal, state and local government bonds and corporate bonds) in recent years due to the higher yields and relative stability of these investments compared to their traditional investments in stock.

Closed-end investment companies sell only a specific number of ownership shares. An investor wanting to acquire closed-end shares must find another investor who wishes to sell. The investment company does not take part in the transaction. In addition to selling equity shares, closed-end companies issue a variety of debt and equity securities to raise funds, including

Exhibit 6–10   **Financial Assets Held by Open-End Investment Companies (Mutual Funds), December 31, 1986**

Asset Items	Amount ($ billions)	Percent of Total
Demand deposits and currency	$ 6.5	1.6%
Corporate stock (equities)	161.2	39.0
Credit instruments:		
U.S. government securities	124.2	30.0
State and local government securities	63.8	15.4
Corporate and foreign bonds	46.9	11.3
Open-end market paper	9.4	2.3
Total financial assets	$413.5	100.0%

Note: Columns may not add to totals due to rounding.

Source: Board of Governors of the Federal Reserve System, *Flow of Funds Accounts—Financial Assets and Liabilities Outstanding, 1963–86.*

preferred stock, regular and convertible bonds, and stock warrants. In contrast, open-end companies rely almost exclusively on the sale of equity shares to the public to raise the funds they require.

Goals and Earnings of Investment Companies

Investment companies adopt many different goals. *Growth funds* are interested primarily in long-term capital appreciation and tend to invest mainly in common stocks offering strong growth potential. *Income funds* stress current income in their portfolio choices rather than growth of capital, and they typically purchase stocks and bonds paying high dividends and interest. *Balanced funds* attempt to bridge the gap between growth and income, acquiring bonds, preferred stock, and common stock which offer both capital gains (growth) and adequate current income. On average, balanced funds place about two thirds of their resources in stocks and about one third in bonds.

The majority of investment companies give priority to growth in capital over current income. However, the industry's growth in recent years has centered primarily in funds that stress current income. Prominent examples include bond funds, money market funds, and option income funds (which issue options against a portfolio of common stocks). While most investment companies hold a highly diversified portfolio of securities, a few specialize in stocks or bonds from a single industry or sector (such as precious metals or oil and natural gas).

It is not at all clear that investment companies hold a significant advantage over other investors in seeking out the highest returns available in the financial marketplace. Moreover, there is evidence that these companies may roll over their portfolios too rapidly, which runs up the cost of managing the fund and reduces net earnings. Less frequent trading activity on the part of investment companies might well result in greater long-run benefits for the saver. Research evidence has been mounting for a number of years that security markets are highly *efficient*. Overvaluation or undervaluation of securities is, at most, a temporary phenomenon.[5] In this kind of environment it is doubtful that investment companies are of significant benefit to the large investor, though they may indeed aid the small investor in reducing information and transactions costs and opening up investment opportunities not otherwise available.

OTHER FINANCIAL INSTITUTIONS

In addition to the foregoing a number of other financial institutions have developed over the years to meet the specialized financial needs of their customers. For example security dealers provide a conduit for buyers and sellers of marketable securities (such as U.S. government bills and bonds, corporate and municipal bonds, and federal agency notes and certificates) to adjust their holdings of those securities. These dealer houses stand ready at all times to buy selected private and government securities or sell from a list of securities to their customers on demand at posted "bid" and "asked" prices. The most well known of the dealers are the roughly 40 primary government securities dealers that aid the U.S. Treasury in selling new issues of federal debt and trade securities with the Federal Reserve System.

Many of these dealers also serve as investment bankers, who market large amounts of new securities on behalf of governments, governmental agencies, and corporations. These "banks" are especially prominent in the offering of new corporate securities, state and local government bonds and notes, and securities issued by federal government agencies such as the Federal National Mortgage Association (Fannie Mae) and the Farm Credit System. They *underwrite* new offerings of these securities, purchasing them from the original issuer and placing them in the hands of interested investors at a higher price. When a new issue of securities involves substantial risk, several investment banking firms will usually band together to form a *syndicate* to bid for and market the issue, thus spreading the market risk. Investment banks also give financial advice on the best terms and times to sell new securities and on how to finance corporate mergers and acquisitions. Investment banking firms are among the best known names on Wall Street, and include such prominent companies as Salomon Brothers, Goldman Sachs, First Boston Corporation, Merrill Lynch Capital Markets, Morgan Stanley, Drexel Burnham Lambert, Kidder Peabody, Blyth Eastman Paine

---

[5]See especially the study by Malkiel (1975).

Webber, Lehman Brothers, Shearson-American Express, and E. F. Hutton.

A related type of dealer firm is the mortgage bank. Mortgage bankers commit themselves to take on new mortgage loans used to fund the construction of homes, apartments, office buildings, shopping centers, and other structures. They will carry these loans for a short time—perhaps weeks or months—until the mortgages can be sold to a long-term (permanent) lender of mortgage funds, such as an insurance company or savings bank. As is the case with other dealer operations, the financial risks to the mortgage banker are substantial. A rise in interest rates will sharply reduce the market value of existing fixed-rate mortgage loans, presenting the mortgage banker with a loss when it sells the loans out of its portfolio. This risk of rising interest rates and falling mortgage prices encourages mortgage banks to turn over their portfolios rapidly and to arrange lines of credit from commercial banks to backstop their operations. These firms also service the mortgage loans they sell to other lenders, collecting loan payments and inspecting mortgaged property.

Authorized by federal law in 1960, real estate investment trusts (REITS) are publicly held, tax-exempt corporations that must receive at least three quarters of their gross income from real estate transactions (such as rental income, mortgage interest, and sales of property). They also must devote at least three quarters of their assets to real estate property or loans, cash, and U.S. government securities. REITS raise funds by selling stock and debt securities, and invest most of their available funds in mortgage loans to finance the building of apartments and other multifamily housing developments, and of commercial structures such as office buildings and shopping centers.

Leasing companies represent still another kind of specialized financial institution that provides customers with access to productive assets, such as airplanes, automobiles, equipment, furniture, and real estate, through the writing of leases. These leases allow a business or household to use assets, sometimes at a lower cost than borrowing and owning these same assets without having to raise money for a down payment. Moreover, the lease payments are a current operating expense and therefore tax deductible for the business lessee. The leasing company, on the other hand, benefits from the stream of lease payments and gains substantial tax benefits in the form of an investment tax credit from purchasing the asset for its customer and from depreciating the asset. In recent years, these tax benefits have been especially attractive to commercial banks, which often tax shelter a significant proportion of their earnings via leasing activities. While there are numerous independent leasing companies serving national, regional and local markets, competition is intense in this industry because of the entry of scores of commercial banks and bank holding companies, insurance companies, and manufacturing firms which have either opened leasing departments or formed subsidiary leasing companies.

A unique financial institution that emerged in the 1970s and 1980s combined several different institutions under the same corporate umbrella. This dynamic and increasingly important financial institution is the symbiotic—a conglomerate financial firm that frequently merges insurance sales, security brokerage, real estate brokerage, financial counseling, and credit services under the same roof in an effort to become a financial department store. Usually each unit within the symbiotic attempts to sell its customers not only its own services, but services offered by other units in the conglomerate. Moreover, the same top management team may oversee all or most parts of the conglomerate organization. Prominent examples include Sears, Roebuck & Company, which in 1981 acquired control of Coldwell Banker, the leading U.S. real estate brokerage firm, and major security broker, Dean Witter Reynolds; Prudential Insurance Company, which acquired Bache Group, Inc., a leading security broker; and the well-known credit card company, American Express, which acquired the broker Shearson Loeb Rhodes. We could add to this list of prominent financial conglomerates General Motors, General Electric, International Harvester, Ford Motor Company, and J. C. Penney—all of which control major finance companies designed to help finance and sell their manufactured products and gain a share of the rapidly expanding market for financial services.

The symbiotics possess an advantage over banks and other financial institutions with which they compete because at least some aspects of their business are *unregulated*. However, a major uncertainty that surrounds their operations is whether their managements can successfully control and market such a diverse range of products and services.

TRENDS AFFECTING ALL FINANCIAL INSTITUTIONS TODAY

The emergence of the symbiotics is but a reflection of the major trends which affect all financial institutions today. One of these trends is *increasing cost pressures,* due to the rising expense of raising funds for lending and investing and burgeoning labor and equipment costs that have narrowed profit margins. Another trend is *consolidation* in which each financial institution tries to expand its size to improve efficiency and ease its growing cost burden. Certainly the new symbiotics represent a move to consolidate financial resources into a large conglomerate organization and utilize existing managerial talent, labor, and physical facilities more efficiently. A key result of the consolidation movement is declining numbers of independent financial institutions, but institutions that average much larger in size and organizational complexity.

Still a third trend is *service diversification* as all major financial institutions have invaded each other's traditional markets with new services in an effort to offset rising costs and protect thinning profit margins. Service diversification has led to a blurring of functions among the different institutions so that it becomes increasingly difficult to distinguish between different financial institutions. The symbiotics are a good example of this trend toward diversification, but so are commercial banks, nonbank thrifts, insurance companies, finance companies, mutual funds, and many other financial institutions today.

The offering of many new services over wider market areas has been made possible by another trend in the financial institutions' sector—a *technological revolution,* particularly in the growing adoption of computers and automated electronic equipment for making payments and transferring financial information. Soon there may be little need to walk into the offices of most financial institutions because many transactions will be handled more accurately and efficiently via home and office computers linked online to each financial institution's computer network. The technological revolution has made possible a global financial system and unleashed a trend toward *global competition* in which all financial institutions find themselves increasingly in a common market, competing for many of the same customers. Distance and geography no longer shelter and insulate financial institutions from the forces of demand and supply in the financial system as they once did.

Many of the new services and technological innovations, and the development of global competition, have come into existence because of a sixth trend—*deregulation,* in which the content and prices of financial services increasingly are being determined by the marketplace rather than by government rules. As we noted in Chapter 5, most of the deregulation movement thus far has centered in banking and among nonbank depository institutions. However, as depository institutions continue to receive new powers and expand their markets, it is quite likely that the whole panoply of financial institutions, such as insurance companies and pension plans, will seek to loosen the regulatory rules that bind them as well. Hopefully the public will be the ultimate beneficiary in terms of more and better financial services at lower cost.

STUDY QUESTIONS

1. Against what kinds of risk do life insurance companies protect their policyholders? How about property casualty insurers?

2. What is the Law of Large Numbers? What is its relationship to the insurance business?

3. Compare and contrast the asset portfolios of life insurance companies and property casualty insurers. Try to explain any differences you observe.

4. What is the principal function of pension funds? Explain why these institutions have been among the most rapidly growing financial institutions in recent years. Do you expect their growth to be faster or slower in the future? Why?

5. What are the principal assets acquired by pension funds? What factors guide their selection of securities?

6. What role do finance companies play in providing funds to the financial markets? How many different kinds of finance companies are there?

7. What advantages do investment companies offer the small saver? Why has their growth been so erratic in recent years?

8. Define the following terms:
    a. Open-end company.   e. Growth funds.
    b. Closed-end company.   f. Balanced fund.
    c. Bond fund.   g. Global funds.
    d. Money market fund.   h. Index funds.

9. What is a REIT? A mortgage bank? A leasing company? Why do you think these specialized financial institutions came into being? In your opinion, are they likely to survive as independent entities in an era when most financial institutions appear to be invading each other's territory with new services? Why or why not?

10. How do symbiotics (financial conglomerates) differ from more traditional financial institutions? What advantages do they have in the race for customer financial accounts?

11. In the concluding section of this chapter six major trends affecting all financial institutions today are discussed. Identify these trends. Which ones do you expect to continue over the next decade, and which do you think might be short lived? Explain your reasoning.

PROBLEMS

1. The manager of a life insurance company is trying to decide what annual premium to charge a group of policyholders, each of whom has just reached their 40th birthday. A check of mortality tables indicates that, for every million persons born 40 years ago, 3 percent die, on average, sometime during their 40th year. If the company has 10,000 policyholders in this age bracket and each has taken out a $50,000 life insurance policy, estimate the probable amount of death benefit claims against the company. How much must be charged in premiums from each policyholder just to cover these expected claims? Suppose the company has operating expenses (plus a target profit) on sales to these policyholders of $500,000. What annual premium must be charged each policyholder to recover expenses and meet expected benefit claims?

2. A pension fund has accumulated $1 million in a retirement plan for James B. Smith, who retires this month at age 65. If Mr. Smith has a life expectancy of 75 years, what is the minimum size of annual annuity check the pension plan will be able to send him each year (assuming that the value of the pension fund's investments remain stable)? Should he insist on receiving that size payment each year? Why or why not? What other kinds of information would be helpful in analyzing Mr. Smith's financial situation at retirement? (*Note:* see Chapter 8 for a discussion of annuity payments.)

SELECTED REFERENCES

American Council of Life Insurance. *1986 Life Insurance Fact Book,* 1987.

Antoncil, Madelyn, and Paul Bennet. "Corporate Use of Pension Overfunding." *Quarterly Review,* Federal Reserve Bank of New York, Spring 1984, pp. 17–30.

Babble, David F. "The Price Elasticity of Demand for Whole Life Insurance." *The Journal of Finance* 40, no. 1 (March 1985), pp. 225–39.

Board of Governors of the Federal Reserve System. "Survey of Finance Companies, 1980." *Federal Reserve Bulletin,* May 1981, pp. 398–409.

Curry, Timothy, and Mark Warshawsky. "Life Insurance Companies in a Changing Environment." *Federal Reserve Bulletin,* July 1986, pp. 449–60.

Insurance Information Institute. *Property-Casualty Fact Book,* 1986–87 edition.

Malkiel, Burton G. *A Random Walk Down Wall Street.* New York: W. W. Norton, 1975.

Rose, Peter S. "Symbiotics: Financial Supermarkets in the Making." *The Canadian Banker & ICB Review,* April 1982, pp. 77–84.

Warshawsky, Mark J. *The Funding of Private Pension Plans.* Staff Economic Study No. 155, Board of Governors of the Federal Reserve System, November 1987.

Part Three

Interest Rates and Security Prices

Chapter 7

Interest Rates in the Financial System

Learning Objectives in This Chapter

- To determine the roles that interest rates play in the economy and financial system.
- To explore the most important explanations (theories) of what determines the level of and changes in interest rates.

Key Terms and Concepts in This Chapter

Rate of interest
Price of credit
Risk-free rate of interest
Classical theory of interest rates

Substitution effect
Liquidity preference theory of interest rates
Loanable funds theory of interest rates

Income effect
Wealth effect
Rational expectations theory of interest rates

IN the opening chapter we described the money and capital markets as one vast pool of funds, depleted by the borrowing activities of households, businesses, and governments and replenished by the savings which these sectors of the economy also provide. The financial markets make saving possible by offering the individual saver a wide menu of choices where funds may be placed at attractive rates of return. By committing funds to one or more securities, the saver, in effect, becomes a lender of funds. The financial markets also make borrowing possible by giving the borrower a channel through which securities can be issued to lenders. And the financial markets make investment and economic growth possible by providing the funds needed for the purchase of machinery and equipment and the construction of buildings, highways, and other productive facilities.

Clearly, then, the acts of saving and lending, borrowing and investment are intimately linked through the financial system. And one factor that significantly influences all of them is the rate of interest. The rate of interest is the price a borrower must pay to secure scarce loanable funds from a lender for an agreed-upon period. It is the price of credit. But unlike other prices in the economy, the rate of interest is really a *ratio* of two quantities— the money cost of borrowing funds to the amount of money actually borrowed, usually expressed on an annual percentage basis.

Interest rates send *price signals* to borrowers, lenders, savers, and investors. For example, higher interest rates generally bring forth a greater volume of savings and stimulate the lending of funds. Lower rates, on the other hand, tend to dampen the flow of savings and reduce lending activity. Higher interest rates tend to reduce the volume of borrowing and capital investment, while lower rates stimulate borrowing and investment spending. In this chapter we will discuss in more detail the forces which are believed by economists and financial analysts to determine prevailing rates of interest in the financial system.

FUNCTIONS OF THE RATE OF INTEREST IN THE ECONOMY

The rate of interest performs several important roles or functions in the economy:

- It helps guarantee that current savings will flow into investment to promote economic growth.
- The rate of interest rations the available supply of credit, generally providing loanable funds to investment projects with the highest expected returns.
- It brings into balance the nation's supply of money with the public's demand for money.
- The rate of interest is also an important tool of government policy

through its influence upon the volume of saving and investment. If the economy is growing too slowly and unemployment is rising, the government can use its policy tools to lower interest rates to stimulate borrowing and investment. An overheated economy experiencing rapid inflation has traditionally called for a government policy of higher interest rates to slow both borrowing and spending.

In the pages of the financial press, the phrase "the interest rate" is frequently used. In truth, there is no such thing as "the interest rate," for there are thousands of different interest rates in the financial system. Even securities issued by the same borrower will often carry a variety of interest rates. In Chapters 9 and 10 the most important factors that cause rates to vary among different securities and over time are examined in detail. In this chapter our focus is upon those basic forces that influence the level of *all* interest rates.

To uncover these general and pervasive rate-determining forces, however, we must make a simplifying assumption. We will assume in this chapter that there is one fundamental interest rate in the economy known as the *pure* or risk-free rate of interest, which is a component of *all* rates. The closest approximation to this pure rate in the real world is perhaps the market yield on U.S. Treasury bonds. It is a rate of return presenting little or no risk of financial loss to the investor and represents the opportunity cost of holding idle money because the investor can always invest in Treasury bonds and earn this minimum rate of return.

Once the pure rate of interest is determined, all other interest rates may be determined from it by examining the special characteristics of the securities issued by individual borrowers. For example, only the government can borrow at approximately the pure, risk-free interest rate; other borrowers pay higher rates than this, due in part to the greater risk of loss attached to their securities. Differences in liquidity, marketability, and maturity are other important factors causing interest rates to differ from the pure, risk-free rate. First, however, we must examine the forces that determine the pure, risk-free rate itself.

THE CLASSICAL THEORY OF INTEREST RATES

One of the oldest theories concerning the determinants of the risk-free interest rate is the classical theory of interest rates, developed originally during the eighteenth and nineteenth centuries by a number of British economists, refined by the Austrian economist Bohm-Bawerk, and elaborated by Irving Fisher early in this century.[1] The classical theory argues that the rate of

---

[1]See especially Bohm-Bawerk (1891) and Fisher (1930).

interest is determined by two forces: (1) the supply of savings, derived mainly from households, and (2) the demand for investment capital coming mainly from the business sector. Let us examine these rate-determining forces of saving and investment demand in more detail.

Saving by Households

What is the relationship between the rate of interest and the volume of saving in the economy? Most saving in modern industrialized economies is carried out by individuals and families. For these households, savings is simply abstinence from consumption spending. *Current savings, therefore, are equal to the difference between current income and current consumption expenditures.*

In making the decision on the timing and amount of saving to be done, households typically consider several factors: the size of current and long-run income; the desired savings target; and the desired proportion of income to be set aside in the form of savings (i.e., the propensity to save). Generally, the volume of household savings rises with income. Higher-income families and individuals tend to save more and consume less relative to their total income than families with lower incomes.

While income levels probably dominate savings decisions, interest rates also play an important role. Interest rates affect an individual's choice between current consumption and saving for future consumption. The classical theory of interest assumed that individuals have a definite *time preference* for current over future consumption. A rational individual, it was assumed, would always prefer current enjoyment of goods and services over future enjoyment. Therefore, the only way to encourage an individual or family to consume less now and save more was to offer a higher rate of interest on current savings. If more were saved in the current period at a higher rate of return, future consumption and future enjoyment would be increased. For example, if the current rate of interest is 10 percent and a household saves $100 instead of spending it on current consumption, it will be able to consume $110 in goods and services a year from now.

The classical theory thus considers the payment of interest a *reward for waiting*—that is, the postponement of current consumption in favor of greater future consumption. Higher interest rates presumably increase the attractiveness of saving relative to consumption spending, encouraging more individuals to substitute saving (and future consumption) for some quantity of current consumption relative to savings. This so-called substitution effect calls for a *positive* relationship between interest rates and the volume of saving. Higher interest rates bring forth a greater volume of saving. Exhibit 7–1 illustrates the substitution effect: If the rate of interest in the financial markets rises from 5 to 10 percent, the volume of current saving by households is assumed to increase from $100 to $200 billion.

Exhibit 7–1   **The Substitution Effect Relating Saving and Interest Rates**

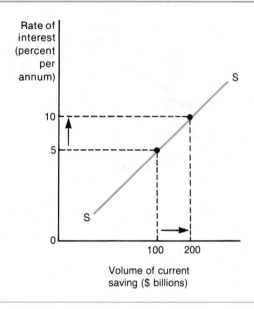

Volume of current
saving ($ billions)

Saving by Business Firms

Our principal focus to this point has been on the determinants of saving by households. Businesses also save, however, and direct a portion of their savings into the financial markets to purchase securities and make loans. Most business firms have temporary cash surpluses from week to week or month to month, and these frequently will be invested in money market instruments, such as U.S. Treasury bills or bank certificates of deposit. Most businesses hold long-run savings balances in the form of retained earnings (as reflected in equity or net worth accounts). In fact, the increase in retained earnings reported by business corporations each year is a key measure of the volume of current business saving. And these retained earnings supply most of the money for annual investment spending by businesses.

The volume of business saving depends upon two key factors—the level of business profits and the dividend policies of corporations. These two factors are summarized in the *retention ratio*—the ratio of retained earnings to net income after taxes. This ratio indicates the proportion of business profits retained in the business for investment purposes rather than paid out as dividends to the owners. Experience has shown that dividend policies of major corporations do not change often. Many corporations prefer to keep their dividend payments level or increase them slightly each year, regardless of current earnings. Any shortfalls in earnings needed for dividend payments are made up through borrowing or by drawing upon previously accumulated funds. The critical element in determining the amount of business savings is, therefore, the level of business profits.

If profits are expected to rise, businesses will be able to draw more heavily upon earnings retained in the firm and less heavily upon the money and capital markets for funds. The result is a reduction in the demand for credit and a tendency toward lower interest rates. On the other hand, when profits fall but firms do not cut back on their investment plans, they are forced to make heavier use of the money and capital markets for investment funds. The demand for credit rises, and interest rates usually rise as well.

While the principal determinant of business saving is profits, interest rates also play a role in the decision of what proportion of current operating costs and long-term investment expenditures should be financed internally and what proportion externally. Higher rates in the money and capital markets typically encourage firms to use internally generated funds more heavily in financing projects. Conversely, lower interest rates encourage greater use of external funds from the money and capital markets.

Saving by Government

Governments also save, though less frequently and generally in smaller amounts than the household and business sectors. In fact, most government saving (i.e., a budget surplus) appears to be unintended saving that arises when government receipts unexpectedly exceed the actual amount of expenditures. Income flows in the economy (out of which government tax revenues arise) and the pacing of government spending programs are the dominant factors affecting government saving; interest rates are probably not a key factor here.

The Demand for Investment Funds

Business, household, and government saving are important determinants of interest rates according to the classical theory of interest, but not the only ones. The other critical rate-determining factor in the classical theory is *investment spending by business firms.*

Businesses require huge amounts of funds each year for the purchase of equipment, machinery, and inventories and to support the construction of new buildings and other physical facilities. The majority of business expenditures for these purposes consists of what economists call *replacement investment;* that is, expenditures to replace equipment and facilities which are wearing out or are technologically obsolete. A smaller, but more dynamic, form of business capital spending is labeled *net investment*—expenditures to acquire additional equipment and facilities in order to increase output. The sum of replacement investment plus net investment equals *gross investment.*

Replacement investment usually is more predictable and grows at a more even rate than net investment. This is due to the fact that such expenditures are financed almost exclusively from inside the firm and frequently follow a routine pattern based on depreciation formulas. Expenditures for new equipment and facilities (net investment), on the other hand, depend on the business community's outlook regarding future sales, changes in technology, industrial capacity, and the cost of raising funds. Because these factors are subject to frequent changes, it is not surprising that net investment (particularly inventory investment) is highly volatile.

Net investment, because of its total size and volatility, is a driving force in the economy. Changes in net investment are closely linked to fluctuations in the nation's output of goods and services, employment, and prices. A significant decline in net investment frequently leads to a business recession, a decline in productivity, and a rise in unemployment unless offset by increased consumer or government spending. In fact, substantial cutbacks in inventory investment and long-term capital spending occur, on average, every three to four years in the United States, usually precipitating a recession. Two recent examples occurred in 1980 and 1982 when sharply higher interest rates and other factors combined to slow the pace of domestic net investment, leading to significant declines in industrial production and a sharp rise in the U.S. unemployment rate.

The Investment Decision-Making Process. The process of investment decision making by business firms is complex and depends on a host of qualitative and quantitative factors. The firm must compare its current level of production with the capacity of its existing facilities and decide whether it has sufficient excess capacity to handle anticipated demand for its product. If expected future demand will strain the firm's existing facilities, it will consider expanding operating capacity through net investment.

Most business firms have several investment projects under consideration at any one time. While the investment decision-making process varies from firm to firm, each business generally makes some estimate of net cash flows (i.e., revenues minus all expenses including taxes) which each project will generate over its useful life. From this information plus knowledge of each investment project's acquisition cost, management can calculate its expected rate of return and compare that projected return with anticipated returns from alternative projects.

One of the more popular methods of performing this calculation is the *internal rate of return method,* which equates the total cost of an investment project with the future net cash flows (NCF) expected from that project discounted back to their present values. Thus,

$$\text{Cost of project} = \frac{\text{NCF}_1}{(1+r)^1} + \frac{\text{NCF}_2}{(1+r)^2} + \cdots + \frac{\text{NCF}_n}{(1+r)^n} \qquad (7-1)$$

where each NCF represents the expected annual net cash flow from the project and r is its expected internal rate of return. The internal rate performs two functions: (1) it measures the annual yield the firm expects from an investment project; and (2) it reduces the value of all future cash flows expected over the useful economic life of the project down to their present value to the firm. In general, if the firm must choose among several mutually exclusive projects, it will choose the one with the *highest* expected internal rate of return.

While the internal rate of return provides a yardstick for selecting potentially profitable investment projects, how does a business executive decide how much to spend on investment at any point in time? How many projects should be chosen? It is here that the financial markets play a key role in the investment decision-making process.

Suppose a business firm is considering the following projects with their associated expected internal rates of return:

Project	Expected Annual Rate of Return (Internal)
A	15%
B	12
C	10
D	9
E	8

How many of these projects will be adopted? The firm must compare each project's expected rate of return with the cost of raising capital to finance the project.

Assume that funds must be borrowed in the financial marketplace to complete any of the above projects and the current cost of borrowing is 10 percent. Which projects are acceptable from an economic standpoint? As shown in Exhibit 7–2, projects A and B clearly are acceptable because their expected returns exceed the cost of borrowing capital to finance them. The firm would be indifferent about project C because its expected return is no more than the cost of borrowed funds. Projects D and E, on the other hand, are unprofitable at this time.

It is through changes in the cost of raising funds that the financial markets can exert a powerful influence on the investment decisions of business firms. As credit becomes scarcer and more expensive, the cost of borrowed capital rises, eliminating some investment projects from consideration. For example, if the cost of borrowed funds rises from 10 to 13 percent, it is obvious that only project A in our earlier example would then be economically viable. On the other hand, if credit becomes more abundant and less costly, the cost of capital for the individual firm will tend to decline and more projects will become profitable. In our example, a decline in the cost of borrowed funds from 10 to 8½ percent would make all but project E economically viable and probably acceptable to the firm.

Exhibit 7–2   **The Cost of Capital and the Investment Decision**

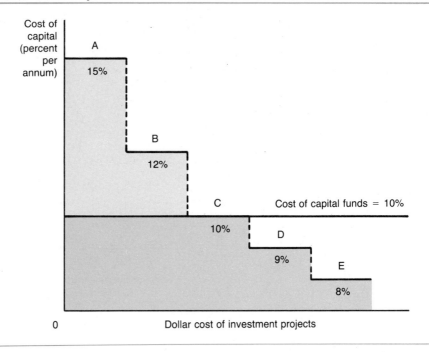

Investment Demand and the Rate of Interest. This reasoning explains, in part, why the demand for investment capital by business firms was regarded by the classical economists as *negatively* related to the rate of interest. Exhibit 7–3 depicts the business investment demand curve as drawn in the classical theory. This demand curve slopes downward and to the right, reflecting the declining net marginal productivity of capital as more and more capital funds are invested by firms.[2] At low rates of interest more investment projects become economically viable and firms require more funds to finance a longer list of projects. On the other hand, if the rate of interest rises to high levels, fewer investment projects will be pursued and less funds will be required from the financial markets. For example, at a 12 percent rate of interest, only $150 billion in funds for investment spending might be demanded by business firms in the economy. If the rate of interest

---

[2]As the quantity of investment capital is increased relative to land, labor, and other productive factors, the laws of production in economics suggest that output will increase at a decreasing rate. Therefore, with technology held constant, the marginal cost of capital rises as more of it is employed by the individual firm and the net marginal productivity of additional capital declines. As a firm spends more funds for investment purposes, it expects its return to capital to decline. For this reason, the investment demand schedule shown in Exhibit 7–3 slopes downward with an increasing volume of investment spending.

Exhibit 7–3   **The Investment Demand Schedule in the Classical Theory of Interest Rates**

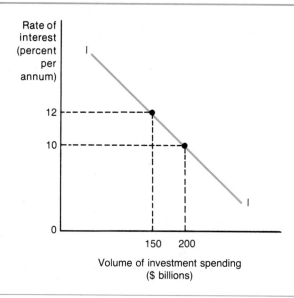

Volume of investment spending
($ billions)

drops to 10 percent, however, the volume of desired investment by firms might rise to $200 billion.

The Equilibrium Rate of Interest in the Classical Theory of Interest

The classical economists believed that interest rates in the financial markets were determined by the interplay of the supply of saving and the demand for investment. Specifically, the equilibrium rate of interest is determined at the point where the quantity of savings supplied to the market is exactly equal to the quantity of funds demanded for investment. As shown in Exhibit 7–4, this occurs at point E, where the equilibrium rate of interest is i_E and the equilibrium quantity of capital funds traded in the financial markets and invested is Q_E.

To illustrate, suppose the total volume of savings supplied by businesses, households, and governments in the economy at an interest rate of 10 percent is $200 billion. Moreover, at this same 10 percent rate businesses would also demand $200 billion in funds for investment purposes. Then 10 percent must be the equilibrium rate of interest and $200 billion is the equilibrium quantity of funds that would be traded in the money and capital markets.

The market rate of interest always moves toward its equilibrium level. However, supply and demand forces change so fast that the interest rate rarely has an opportunity to settle in at a specific equilibrium level. At any

Exhibit 7–4   **The Equilibrium Rate of Interest in the Classical Theory**

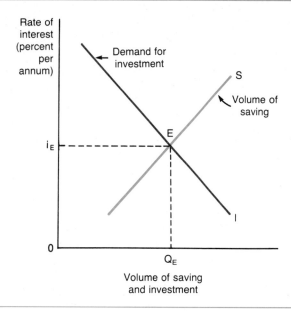

given time the rate is probably above or below its true equilibrium level, but moving *toward* that equilibrium. If the market rate is temporarily above equilibrium, the volume of savings exceeds the demand for investment capital, creating an excess supply of savings. Savers will offer their funds at lower and lower rates until the market interest rate approaches equilibrium. Similarly, if the market rate lies temporarily below equilibrium, investment demand exceeds the quantity of savings available. Business firms bid up the interest rate until it approaches the level at which the quantity saved equals the quantity of funds demanded for investment purposes.

Limitations of the Classical Theory of Interest

The classical theory sheds considerable light on the factors affecting interest rates. However, it has some serious limitations. The central problem is that the theory ignores several factors other than saving and investment which affect interest rates. For example, commercial banks have the power to create money by making loans to the public. When borrowers repay their bank loans, money is destroyed. The amount of money created or destroyed affects the total amount of credit available in the financial marketplace and therefore must be considered in any explanation of the factors determining interest rates.

In addition, the classical theory assumes that interest rates are the principal determinant of the quantity of savings available. Today, economists recognize that *income* is far more important in determining the volume of saving. Finally, the classical theory contends that the demand for borrowed funds comes principally from the business sector. Today, however, both consumers and governments are important borrowers, significantly affecting credit availability and cost. As we will see in the rest of this chapter, more recent theories of the interest rate address a number of these limitations of the classical theory.

THE LIQUIDITY PREFERENCE THEORY

The classical theory of interest has been called a long-run explanation of interest rates because it focuses upon the public's thrift habits and the productivity of capital—factors that tend to change slowly. During the 1930s British economist John Maynard Keynes developed a short-run theory of the rate of interest which, he argued, was more relevant for policymakers and for explaining near-term changes in interest rates. This theory is known as the liquidity preference theory of interest rates.

The Demand for Liquidity

Keynes argued that the rate of interest is really a payment for the use of a scarce resource—money. Businesses and individuals prefer to hold money for carrying out daily transactions and also as a precaution against future cash needs even though its yield is low or nonexistent. Investors in fixed-income securities, such as corporate and government bonds, frequently desire to hold money as a haven against declining security prices. Interest rates, therefore, are the price that must be paid to induce money holders to surrender a perfectly liquid asset and hold other assets that carry more risk. At times the preference for liquidity grows very strong. Unless the government expands the nation's money supply, interest rates will rise.

In the theory of liquidity preference, only two outlets for investor funds are considered—bonds and money (including bank deposits). Money provides perfect liquidity (i.e., instant spending power), while bonds pay interest but cannot be spent until converted into cash. If interest rates rise, the market value of bonds paying a fixed rate of interest will fall; the investor would suffer a capital loss if those bonds were converted into cash. On the other hand, a fall in interest rates results in higher bond prices; the bondholder will experience a capital gain if his or her bonds are sold for cash. To the classical theorists, it was irrational to hold money because it provided little or no return. To Keynes, however, the holding of money could be a perfectly rational act if interest rates were expected to rise, because rising rates could result in substantial losses from investing in bonds.

---

[3]See especially J. M. Keynes (1936).

Motives for Holding Money. Keynes observed that the public demands money for three different purposes (motives). The *transactions motive* represents the demand for money in order to purchase goods and services. Because inflows and outflows of money are not perfectly synchronized in either timing or amount and it is costly to shift back and forth between money and other assets, businesses, households, and governments must keep some cash in the till or in demand accounts simply to meet daily expenses. Some money also must be held as a reserve for future emergencies and to cover extraordinary expenses. This *precautionary motive* arises because we live in a world of uncertainty and cannot predict exactly what expenses or opportunities will arise in the future.

Keynes assumed that money demanded for transactions and precautionary purposes was dependent upon the level of national income, business sales, and prices. Reflecting money's role as a medium of exchange, higher levels of income, sales, or prices increased the need for money to carry out transactions and to respond to future expenses and opportunities. However, neither the precautionary nor the transactions demand for money was assumed to be affected by changes in interest rates. In fact, Keynes assumed money demand for precautionary and transactions purposes to be fixed in the short run. In a longer-run period, however, transactions and precautionary demands change as national income changes.

Short-run changes in interest rates were attributed by Keynes to a third motive for holding money—the *speculative motive* which stems from uncertainty about the future prices of bonds. As noted earlier, rising interest rates result in falling prices for bonds. To illustrate, suppose an investor has recently purchased a corporate bond for $1,000. The company issuing the bond promises to pay $100 a year in interest income. In order to simplify matters, assume the bond is a *perpetual security*. This means the investor will receive $100 a year for as long as he or she wishes to hold the security. The annual rate of return (or yield) on the bond, then, is 10 percent ($100/$1,000). Suppose now that the interest rate on bonds of similar quality rises to 12 percent. What happens to the price of the 10 percent bond? Obviously, its price in the marketplace will fall because its annual promised yield at a price of $1,000 is *less* than 12 percent.

How far will the bond's price fall? It will approach $833 because at this price the $100 annual interest payment gives the investor an approximate annual yield of 12 percent ($100/$833). In the reverse situation, if interest rates were to decline—say, to 9 percent—the 10 percent bond would become more attractive and its market price would rise.[4]

---

[4]The price of a perpetual bond (P) is related to its market interest rate (r) by the formula

$$P = R/r$$

where R is the annual income in dollars paid by the security. Clearly, as interest rate r increases, market price P falls. As we will see in Chapter 8, the same *inverse* relationship between the price and interest yield on a fixed-income security holds even if we assume that the security is not perpetual, but has a finite maturity.

Exhibit 7–5   **Speculative Demand for Money**

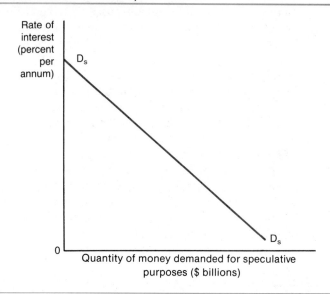

If investors expect rising interest rates, many of them will demand money or near-money assets instead of bonds because they believe bond prices will fall. As the expectation that interest rates will rise grows stronger and stronger in the marketplace, the demand for money as a secure store of value increases. We may represent this speculative demand for money by a curve that slopes downward and to the right, as shown in Exhibit 7–5, reflecting a *negative* relationship between the speculative demand for money and the level of interest rates. At low rates of interest, many investors feel that interest rates are soon to rise (i.e., bond prices are going to fall), and therefore more money is demanded. At high rates of interest, on the other hand, many investors will conclude that rates soon will fall and bond prices rise, so the demand for money decreases while the demand for bonds increases.

From another vantage point, when interest rates are high, the opportunity cost (loss) from holding idle cash increases. Thus, high interest rates encourage investors to reduce their cash balances and buy bonds. In contrast, when interest rates are low, the opportunity cost of holding idle cash is also low, but the expected capital loss from holding bonds is high should interest rates rise. Thus, there is more incentive to hold money rather than buy bonds when interest rates are low.

Total Demand for Money. The total demand for money in the economy is simply the sum of transactions, precautionary, and speculative demands.

Exhibit 7–6   The Total Demand for Money in the Economy

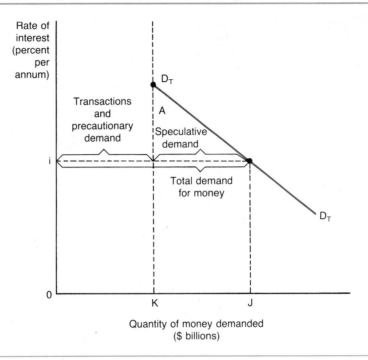

Because the principal determinant of transactions and precautionary demands is income, not interest rates, these money demands are fixed at a
certain level of national income. Let this demand be represented by the
quantity 0K shown along the horizontal axis in Exhibit 7–6. Then, any
amount of money demanded in excess of 0K represents speculative demand.
The total demand for money is represented along curve D_T. Therefore, if the
rate of interest at the moment is at i, Exhibit 7–6 shows that the speculative
demand for money is KJ and the total demand for money is 0J.

The Supply of Money

The other major element determining interest rates in liquidity preference
theory is the supply of money. In modern economies the money supply is
controlled or at least closely regulated by government. Because government
decisions concerning the size of the nation's money supply presumably are
guided by the public welfare and not by the level of interest rates, we assume
that the supply of money is *inelastic* with respect to the rate of interest.
Such a money supply curve is represented in Exhibit 7–7 by the vertical
line M_S.

Exhibit 7–7   **The Equilibrium Rate of Interest in the Liquidity Preference Theory**

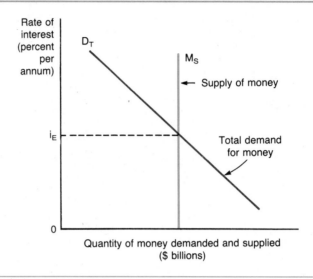

Quantity of money demanded and supplied
($ billions)

The Equilibrium Rate of Interest in Liquidity Preference Theory

The interplay of the total demand for money and the supply of money determines the equilibrium rate of interest in the short run. As shown in Exhibit 7–7, the equilibrium rate of interest is found at point i_E where the quantity of money demanded by the public equals the quantity of money supplied. Above this equilibrium rate, the supply of money exceeds the quantity demanded, and some businesses, households, and units of government will try to dispose of their unwanted money balances by purchasing bonds. The prices of bonds will rise, driving interest rates down toward equilibrium at i_E. On the other hand, at rates below equilibrium, the quantity of money demanded exceeds the supply. Some decision makers in the economy will sell their bonds to raise additional cash, driving bond prices down and interest rates up toward equilibrium.

Liquidity preference theory provides some useful insights into investor behavior and the influence of government policy on the economy and financial system. For example, it suggests that it is rational at certain times for the public to hoard money and at other times to "dishoard" (spend away) unwanted cash. If the public disposes of some of its cash balances by purchasing securities, this action increases the quantity of loanable funds available in the nation's financial markets. Other things equal, interest rates will fall. On the other hand, if the public tries to hoard more money, expanding its cash balances by selling securities, less money will be available for loans. Interest rates will rise, *ceteris paribus.*

Liquidity preference illustrates how central banks such as the Federal Reserve System can influence interest rates in the financial markets, at least in the short run. For example, if higher interest rates are desired, the central bank can contract the size of the nation's money supply and rates will tend to rise, assuming the demand for money is unchanged. If the demand for money is increasing, then the central bank can bring about higher interest rates by ensuring that the money supply grows more slowly than money demand. In contrast, if the central bank expands the nation's money supply, interest rates will decline in the short run if the demand for money does not increase as well.

Subsequent research by Friedman (1968), Cagan (1972), and others suggests that three dynamic effects on the equilibrium interest rate follow when the money supply changes: (1) an initial *money supply liquidity effect:* (2) a subsequent *money supply income effect;* and, over a longer time horizon, (3) a *money supply price expectations* effect. For example, an increase in the nation's money supply creates excess liquidity, at least temporarily, and interest rates fall. However, the excess liquidity will generate additional spending in the economy, driving up income and increasing the demand for money. Unless the money supply expands further, the downward trend in rates will be reversed and interest rates will begin rising. Finally, an increasing money supply coupled with rising incomes may generate inflationary expectations. Businesses and consumers come to expect rising prices, as do lenders of funds who therefore raise interest rates on loans. Thus, it is argued, given sufficient time the liquidity effect of money supply changes will be offset by income and price-expectations effects. Interest rates may end up higher or lower than their initial level after a money supply change, depending on the relative strengths of these three effects.

Limitations of the Liquidity Preference Theory

Like the classical theory of interest, liquidity preference theory has important limitations. It is a short-run approach to interest rate determination because it assumes that income remains stable. As we have seen in the longer run, interest rates are affected by changes in the level of income and price (inflationary) expectations. Indeed, it is impossible to have a stable equilibrium interest rate without also reaching an equilibrium level of income, saving, and investment in the economy. Then too, liquidity preference considers only the supply and demand for the stock of money, whereas business, consumer, and government demands for credit clearly have an impact upon the cost of credit to these borrowers. A more comprehensive view of interest rates is needed which considers the important roles played by *all* actors in the financial system—that is, businesses, households, and government.

THE LOANABLE FUNDS THEORY

An explanation of interest rates that overcomes many of the limitations of earlier theories is the loanable funds theory of interest rates. This view argues that the risk-free interest rate is determined by the interplay of two forces— the demand for and the supply of loanable funds. The demand for loanable funds consists of credit demands from domestic businesses, consumers, and units of government and also borrowing in the domestic market by foreigners. The supply of loanable funds stems from four sources: domestic saving, hoarding demand for money, money creation by the banking system, and lending in the domestic market by foreign individuals and institutions. We consider each of these demand and supply factors in turn.

Consumer Demand for Loanable Funds

Domestic consumers demand loanable funds in order to purchase a wide variety of goods and services on credit. Recent research indicates that consumers are not particularly responsive to the rate of interest when they seek credit, but focus instead principally on the nonprice terms of a loan, such as the down payment, maturity, and size of installment payments. This implies that consumer demand for credit is relatively *inelastic* with respect to the rate of interest. Certainly a rise in interest rates leads to some reduction in the quantity of consumer demand for loanable funds (particularly where home mortgage credit is involved), whereas a decline in rates stimulates some additional consumer borrowing. However, along the consumer's relatively inelastic demand schedule, a substantial change in the rate of interest must occur before the quantity of consumer demand for funds changes significantly.

Business Demand for Loanable Funds

The credit demands of domestic businesses generally are more responsive to changes in the rate of interest than is consumer borrowing. Most business credit is for such investment purposes as the purchase of inventories and new plant and equipment. As noted earlier in our discussion of the classical theory of interest, a high interest rate eliminates some business investment projects from consideration because their expected rate of return is lower than the cost of funds. On the other hand, at lower rates of interest many investment projects look profitable, with their expected returns exceeding the cost of funds. Therefore, the quantity of loanable funds demanded by the business sector increases as the rate of interest falls.

Government Demand for Loanable Funds

Government demand for loanable funds is a growing factor in the nation's financial markets but does not depend significantly on the level of interest rates. This is especially true of borrowing by the federal government. Federal decisions on spending and borrowing are made by Congress in response to social needs and the public welfare, not the rate of interest. Moreover, the federal government has the power both to tax and to create money in order to pay its debts. State and local government demand, on the other hand, is slightly interest-elastic because many local governments are limited in their borrowing activities by legal interest rate ceilings. When open market rates rise above these legal ceilings, some state and local units of government are prevented from offering their securities to the public.

Foreign Demand for Loanable Funds

Increasingly in recent years foreign banks and corporations, as well as foreign governments, have entered the huge U.S. financial marketplace to borrow billions of dollars. Leading foreign borrowers have included corporations (both bank and nonbank) and government agencies from Japan, Korea, Canada, Great Britain, and West Germany, to name but a few. This huge foreign credit demand is sensitive to the spread between U.S. lending rates and interest rates in foreign markets. If U.S. interest rates decline relative to foreign rates, foreign borrowers will be inclined to borrow more in the United States and less abroad. At the same time, with higher interest rates overseas, U.S. lending institutions will increase their lending abroad and reduce the availability of loanable funds to domestic borrowers. The net result, then, is a *negative* or *inverse relationship* between foreign borrowing in the United States and U.S. interest rates relative to foreign interest rates.

Total Demand for Loanable Funds

The total demand for loanable funds is the sum of domestic consumer, business, and government credit demands plus foreign credit demands. This demand curve slopes downward and to the right with respect to the rate of interest, as shown in Exhibit 7–8. Higher rates of interest lead some businesses, consumers, and governments to curtail their borrowing plans, while lower rates bring forth more credit demand. However, the demand for loanable funds does not determine the rate of interest by itself; the supply of loanable funds must be added to complete the picture.

The Supply of Loanable Funds

Loanable funds flow into the money and capital markets from at least four different sources: (1) domestic saving by businesses, consumers, and governments; (2) dishoarding (spending down) of excess money balances held by the public; (3) creation of money by the domestic banking system; and (4) lending to domestic borrowers by foreigners. We consider each of these sources of funds in turn.

Exhibit 7–8   **Total Demand for Loanable Funds**

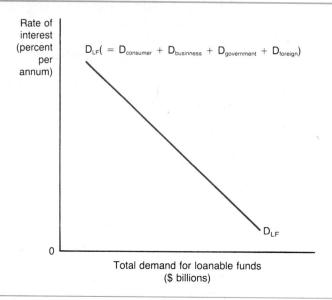

Domestic Saving. The supply of domestic savings is the principal source of loanable funds. As noted earlier, most saving is done by households and is simply the difference between current income and current consumption. Businesses, however, also save by retaining a portion of current earnings and by adding to depreciation reserves. Government saving, while relatively rare, occurs when current revenues exceed current expenditures.

Earlier in the chapter we noted that most economists today believe that income levels, rather than interest rates, are the dominant factor in the decision of how much and when to save.[5] There is also evidence that business and household saving may be goal-oriented—the so-called income effect. That is, some business firms and households set target levels of total savings as a long-run goal. For example, suppose an individual wishes to accumulate $100,000 in anticipation of retirement. Interest rates subsequently rise from 5 to 10 percent. Will this individual save more out of each period's income or less? Probably less, because the higher interest rate will enable the saver to reach the goal with less sacrifice of current income. On the other hand, a lower interest rate might lead to a greater volume of saving because a business or household must accumulate more funds to achieve its savings goal.

---

[5]There is, however, considerable controversy as to just what measure of income determines the annual volume of savings. Some economists argue that current saving is determined not by current income levels, but by a long-run view of income, perhaps adjusted for the stage of life of the income recipient. See, for example, Ando and Modigliani (1963).

Clearly, then, the goal or income effect would have the opposite effect on the volume of saving from the substitution effect, described earlier in our discussion of the classical theory of interest. These two effects pull aggregate saving in opposite directions as interest rates change. It should not be surprising, therefore, that the annual volume of saving in the economy is an extremely difficult quantity to forecast.

Recent research using econometric models of the U.S. economy has suggested the importance of another factor—the wealth effect—in influencing savings decisions.[6] Individuals accumulate wealth in many different forms: real assets (automobiles, furniture, houses, land), and financial assets (stocks, bonds). What happens to the value of financial assets as interest rates change? If rates rise, the market value of financial assets will fall until their yield approaches market-determined levels. On the other hand, with a decline in interest rates the market value of financial assets will rise until their yield approaches market-determined levels. Then again, a decline in interest rates tends to increase the value of financial assets, especially long-term bonds. In general, then, a rise in interest rates will result in decreases in the value of wealth held in financial assets, forcing the individual to save more to protect his or her wealth position. Conversely, a decrease in interest rates will increase the value of financial assets, increasing wealth and perhaps necessitating a lower volume of current saving.

For businesses and individuals heavily in debt, however, the opposite effects may ensue. When interest rates rise, debt contracted in earlier periods, when interest rates were lower, seems less of a burden. For example, a home mortgage taken on by a family when rates in the mortgage market were 10 percent seems a less burdensome drain on income when rates on new mortgages have risen to 15 percent. Therefore, a rise in interest rates tends to make those economic units carrying a large volume of debt relative to their financial assets feel better off, and they may tend to save less as a result. A decrease in interest rates, on the other hand, may result in more savings due to the wealth effect.

The *net* effect of the income, substitution, and wealth effects leads to a relatively interest-inelastic supply of savings curve. Substantial changes in interest rates usually are required to bring about any significant changes in the volume of aggregate saving in the economy.

Dishoarding of Money Balances. Still another source of loanable funds is centered on the public's demand for money relative to the available supply of money. As noted in our earlier discussion of liquidity preference theory, the public's demand for money varies with interest rates and income levels. The supply of money, on the other hand, is closely controlled by government. Clearly the two—money demand and money supply—need not be the same. The differences between the public's total demand for money and the money

---

[6]See especially Boskin (1978) and Justen and Taylor (1975).

supply is known as *hoarding.* When the public's demand for money exceeds the supply, *positive hoarding* of money takes place as individuals and businesses attempt to increase their money holdings at the expense of others. Hoarding *reduces* the volume of loanable funds available in the financial markets. On the other hand, when the public's demand for money is less than the supply available, *negative hoarding (dishoarding)* occurs. Some individuals and businesses will dispose of their excess money holdings, increasing the supply of loanable funds available in the financial system.

Creation of Credit by the Domestic Banking System. Commercial banks and nonbank thrift institutions offering payments accounts have the unique ability to create credit by lending and investing excess reserves. Credit created by the domestic banking system represents an additional source of loanable funds, which must be added to the amount of savings and the dishoarding of money balances (or minus the amount of hoarding demand) to derive the total supply of loanable funds in the economy.

Foreign Lending to the Domestic Funds Market. Finally, foreign banks and other institutions abroad have provided rapidly growing amounts of credit to borrowers in the United States. Key sources of this fourth component of the supply of loanable funds include leading banks and industrial firms in Western Europe and around the Pacific rim. These inflowing loanable funds are particularly sensitive to the difference between U.S. credit-market interest rates versus interest rates overseas. If U.S. rates rise relative to interest rates offered abroad, the supply of foreign funds to U.S. markets will tend to rise. Foreign lenders will simply find it more attractive to make loans in the United States. At the same time, U.S. borrowers will turn more to foreign markets for loanable funds when U.S. interest rates climb relative to foreign rates. The combined result is to make the foreign supply of loanable funds to the U.S. credit market *positively* related to the spread between U.S. and foreign rates of interest.

Total Supply of Loanable Funds

The total supply of loanable funds, including domestic and foreign savings, dishoarding of money, and new credit created by the banking system, is depicted in Exhibit 7–9. This curve rises with higher rates of interest, indicating that a greater supply of loanable funds will flow into the money and capital markets when the returns from lending increase.

The Equilibrium Rate of Interest in the Loanable Funds Theory

The two forces of supply and demand for loanable funds determine not only the volume of lending and borrowing going on in the economy, but also the rate of interest. The interest rate tends toward the equilibrium point at

Exhibit 7–9   **Supply of Loanable Funds**

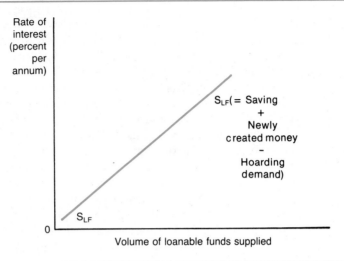

Exhibit 7–10   **The Equilibrium Rate of Interest in the Loanable Funds Theory**

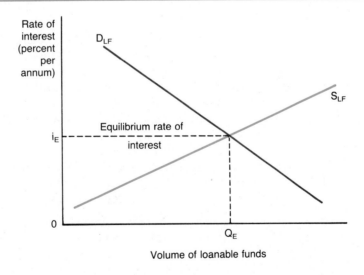

which the supply of loanable funds equals the demand for loanable funds. This point of equilibrium is shown in Exhibit 7–10 at i_E.

If the interest rate is temporarily *above* equilibrium, the quantity of loanable funds supplied by domestic and foreign savers, by the banking system, and from the dishoarding of money balances (or minus hoarding demand) exceeds the total demand for loanable funds, and the rate of interest will be bid down. On the other hand, if the interest rate is temporarily *below* equilibrium, loanable funds demand from businesses, consumers, and governments will exceed the supply. The interest rate will be bid up by borrowers until it settles at equilibrium once again.

The equilibrium depicted in Exhibit 7–10 is only a *partial* equilibrium position, however. This is due to the fact that interest rates are affected by conditions in the domestic and world economies. For the economy to be in equilibrium, planned saving must equal planned investment across the whole economic system. For example, if planned investment exceeds planned saving at the equilibrium rate shown in Exhibit 7–10, investment demands will push interest rates higher in the short run. However, as additional investment spending occurs incomes will rise, generating a greater volume of savings. Eventually, interest rates will fall. Similarly, if exchange rates between dollars, francs, pounds, yen, and other world currencies are not in equilibrium with each other, there will be further opportunities for profit for foreign and domestic lenders by moving loanable funds from one country to another.

Only when the economy, the money market, the loanable funds market, and the foreign currency markets are *simultaneously* in equilibrium will interest rates remain stable. Thus, a stable equilibrium interest rate will be characterized by:

1. Planned saving = Planned investment (including both business and government investment) across the whole economic system (i.e., equilibrium in the economy).
2. Money supply = Money demand (i.e., equilibrium in the money market).
3. Quantity of loanable funds supplied = Quantity of loanable funds demanded (i.e., equilibrium in the loanable funds market).
4. The difference between foreign demand for loanable funds and the volume of loanable funds supplied by foreigners to the domestic economy = The difference between current exports from and imports into the domestic economy (i.e., equilibrium in the nation's balance of payments and the foreign currency markets).

This simple demand-supply framework is useful for analyzing broad movements in interest rates. For example, if the total supply of loanable funds from savings and other sources is increasing and the total demand for loanable funds remains unchanged or rises more slowly, the volume of credit extended in the financial markets must increase, and interest rates will fall. This is illustrated in Exhibit 7–11A, which shows the supply curve sliding downward and to the right when S_{LF} increases to S'_{LF}, resulting in a decline in the equilibrium rate of interest from i_1 to i_2. The equilibrium quantity of loanable funds traded in the financial system increases from C_1 to C_2.

What happens when the demand for loanable funds increases with no

Exhibit 7–11   **Changes in the Demand for and Supply of Loanable Funds**

A. Effects of increased supply of loanable funds with demand unchanged

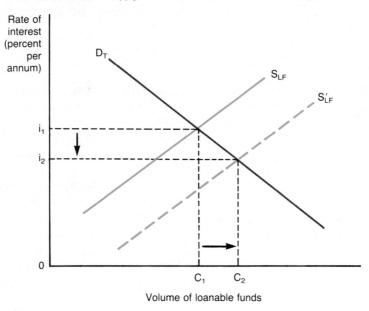

Volume of loanable funds

B. Effects of increased demand for loanable funds with supply unchanged

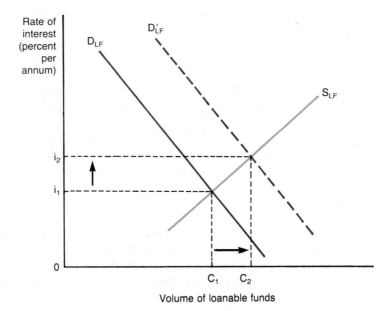

Volume of loanable funds

change in the total supply of funds available? In this instance, the volume of credit extended will increase, but loans will be made at higher interest rates. Exhibit 7–11B illustrates this. The loanable funds demand curve rises from D_{LF} to D'_{LF}, driving the interest rate upward from i_1 to i_2.

THE RATIONAL EXPECTATIONS THEORY

In recent years a fourth major theory about the forces determining interest rates has appeared and now appears to be gaining supporters. This is the rational expectations theory of interest rates. It builds upon a growing body of research evidence that the money and capital markets are highly efficient institutions in digesting and reacting to new information affecting interest rates and security prices.

For example, when new data appear about business investment, household saving, or growth in the nation's money supply, investors begin immediately to translate that new information into decisions to buy or sell securities, borrow or lend funds. In a short space of time—perhaps in minutes or seconds—security prices and interest rates change to reflect the new information. So rapid is this process of the market digesting and using new information that security prices and interest rates presumably already impound the new data from virtually the moment the data appear. In a perfectly efficient market it is impossible to snare excess profits by trading on publicly available information. Interestingly enough, this concept of the rapid response of interest rates and security prices to new information runs counter to much of the traditional interest rate literature and counter to many interest-rate forecasting models which assume that weeks or months must pass before a new development affecting rates and prices will exert its full effect on the financial marketplace.

The important assumptions and implications of the rational expectations-efficient markets view are that: (1) the prices of securities and interest rates should reflect all available information and the market uses this information correctly in establishing the probability distribution of future prices and rates; (2) changes in rates and security prices are correlated only with unanticipated, not anticipated information; (3) the correlation between rates of return in successive time periods is zero; (4) no unexploited opportunities for profit (above a normal return) can be found in the securities' markets; (5) transactions and storage costs for securities are negligible and information costs are small relative to the value of securities traded; and (6) expectations concerning future security prices and interest rates are formed rationally and used efficiently. This last assumption means that businesses and individuals are assumed to be *rational agents* who form expectations about the distribution of future security prices and interest rates that do not differ significantly from optimal forecasts made from using all the available information the marketplace provides. Rational agents attempt to make optimal use of the resources at their disposal in order to maximize their returns. They do not ignore or inefficiently employ available information in their attempts at return maximization. A rational agent would tend to make unbiased forecasts of future security prices, interest rates, and other variables, rather than make systematic forecasting errors.

If the money and capital markets are highly efficient in the way we have described above, this implies that interest rates will always be at or very near their equilibrium levels. Any deviation from the equilibrium rate level dictated by demand and supply forces will be almost instantly eliminated. Security traders or speculators who hope to *consistently* earn windfall profits from correctly guessing whether interest rates are "too high" and therefore will probably fall or are "too low" and therefore will probably rise are unlikely to be successful in the long run. Interest rate fluctuations around equilibrium are likely to be random and momentary. Moreover, knowledge of *past* interest rates—for example, those that prevailed yesterday or last month—will not be a reliable guide to where those rates are likely to be today or in the future.

The rational expectations view also suggests that interest rates do not stray permanently from their current equilibrium levels *unless new information appears*. Old news will not affect today's interest rates because those rates already have impounded that information. Rates will only change if entirely *new* and *unexpected* information appears. For example, if the federal government announces for several weeks running that it must borrow an additional $10 billion next month, interest rates probably reacted to that information only the first time it appeared. In fact, interest rates probably *increased* at that time because many investors would view the government's additional need for credit as adding to other demands for credit in the economy and, with the supply of credit unchanged, interest rates would be expected to move higher. However, if the government merely repeated that same announcement again, interest rates probably wouldn't change a second time; it would be old information already reflected in today's interest-rate level.

Imagine a new scenario, however. The government suddenly reveals that, contrary to expectations, tax revenues are now being collected in greater amounts than first forecast and therefore no new borrowing will, in fact, be needed next month. Interest rates probably will fall immediately as market participants are forced to revise their borrowing and lending plans to deal with a new situation. How do we know which *direction* rates will move? Clearly the path rates will take depends on *what market participants expected to begin with*. Thus, if market participants were expecting increased demand for credit (with supply unchanged), an unexpected announcement of reduced credit demand implies lower interest rates in the future. Similarly, a market expectation of less credit demand in the future (again, supply unchanged), when confronted with an unexpected announcement of higher credit demand, implies that interest rates will rise.

The rational expectations view, then, argues that forecasting interest rate changes requires knowledge of the public's *current set of expectations.* If new information is sufficient to alter those expectations, interest rates must change. If correct, this portion of the rational expectations theory creates significant problems for government policymakers. It implies that policymakers cannot cause interest rates to move in any particular direction without knowing what the public already expects to happen and, indeed, cannot change interest rates at all unless government officials can convince the public that a new set of expectations is warranted. Moreover, because guessing what the public's expectations are is treacherous at best, rational expectations theorists suggest that *rate hedging*—using various tools (such as financial futures) to reduce the risk of loss from changing interest rates— is preferable to rate forecasting.

A growing number of studies today imply that at least some elements of the rational expectations–efficients markets view do show up in actual market behavior. For example, studies by Mishkin (1978) and Phillips and Pippenger (1976) find that past interest rate movements are not significantly related to current rates of return for bonds or for stock, as the theory predicts. Other studies [e.g., Rozeff (1974)] find that past information on economic conditions and money supply movements also appear to bear little correlation to today's interest rate levels or to observed changes in current interest rates. However, *unanticipated* growth in the nation's money supply and in income, production, and the price level do appear to be correlated with bond and stock returns. Moreover, adjustments in interest rates and security prices to new information appear to be very rapid—far more rapid than implied by econometric models based upon the more traditional interest rate theories.

Nevertheless, the rational expectations view still is in the development stage and provides, at this time, little help for such practical problems as trying to forecast interest rates. One key problem here is that we do not know very much about how the public forms its expectations—what data are used, what weights are applied to individual bits of data, and so on. Moreover, there are several characteristics of real world markets that seem at odds with the assumptions of the expectations theory. For example, the cost of gathering and analyzing information relevant to the pricing of loans and securities is not always negligible, as assumed by the theory, tempting many lenders and borrowers of funds to form their expectations by rules of thumb (trading rules) that are not fully rational. While rationally formed expectations appear to exist in large auction markets (such as the markets for U.S. government securities or listed common stock), it is not clear that such is the case for other financial markets such as those for consumer and small business loans. Finally, some current interest rates—for example, those on short-term securities such as Treasury bills—do exhibit correlations with past interest rate movements. Thus, not all interest rates and security prices appear to display the kind of behavior implied by the expectations theory.

SUMMARY

Each theory of the determinants of interest rates reviewed in this chapter offers useful insights into the functioning of the financial system. Collectively, the various views of interest rate determination point to those forces in the economy which should be studied carefully if we are to understand current trends in interest rates and anticipate future trends. In the chapters that follow we consider various factors that cause the interest rate on one security or loan to be different from the rate on another security or loan. These factors include expectations of inflation, the maturity or length of a security or loan, the risk of borrower default, the risk of calling in a security in advance of its maturity, taxes, and security convertibility. We will find that a thorough understanding of the entire structure of interest rates in the economy requires us to be aware of all these factors as well as the interest rate theories we have reviewed in this chapter.

STUDY QUESTIONS

1. What are the different roles of the rate of interest in the economy?
2. What is the risk-free, or pure, interest rate? Explain its relationship to other interest rates in the economy.
3. What factors determine the rate of interest in the classical theory? Explain why the supply of savings curve has a positive slope. What determines the shape of the demand curve in this theory?
4. Define the following: transactions motive, precautionary motive, and speculative motive. How is the total demand for money determined in the liquidity preference theory? Why does the demand for money curve slope downward and to the right?
5. What is the liquidity effect associated with changes in the money supply? The money supply income effect? The money supply price-expectations effect? Explain how these effects cause interest rates to change when the money supply expands (demand for money unchanged). Suppose the money supply contracts (again with money demand unchanged).
6. What factors make up the demand for loanable funds? The supply of loanable funds? How is the equilibrium rate of interest determined in the loanable funds theory?
7. Trace through what happens to the equilibrium rate of interest when the demand for loanable funds increases with supply unchanged. What happens to the equilibrium rate if the supply of loanable funds expands with demand unchanged?
8. Describe the rational expectations theory of interest rate determination. What is assumed in this theory? Can you see any problems in trying to use this theory to anticipate future trends in rates?

PROBLEMS

1. Construct a supply of savings curve (with all curves and axes correctly labeled) which illustrates the *income effect*. Do the same to illustrate the *wealth effect*. Explain the differences you observe.

2. Suppose the going market rate of interest on high-quality (AAA rated) corporate bonds is 12 percent. FORTRAN Corporation is considering an investment project which will last 10 years, requires an initial cash outlay of $1.5 million, but will generate estimated revenues of $500,000 per year for 10 years. Would you recommend that this project be adopted? Explain why.

3. A government securities dealer has purchased a Treasury long-term bond bearing a coupon rate of 9 percent. The bond was purchased at par ($1,000). Interest rates on *new* bonds with comparable terms rise to 11 percent. What will happen to the 9 percent bond's market price? What price will it approach? Answer these same questions in the case where bond rates decline to 7 percent. Explain the price changes you have calculated.

4. The statements listed below were gathered from recent issues of financial newssheets. Read each statement carefully and then *(a)* identify which theory or theories of interest rate determination is implicit in each statement; and *(b)* indicate which *direction* interest rates should move if the statement is a correct analysis of the current market situation. Use appropriate supply-demand diagrams, where possible, to show the reasoning behind your answers to part b.

   "The factor which is likely to dominate interest-rate changes in the weeks ahead is a tighter credit policy at the Federal Reserve."

   "The White House unexpectedly disclosed today that budget negotiations with Capitol Hill have broken down. Market analysts are fearful of the effects on the bond and stock markets when trading begins tomorrow morning."

   "Corporate profits have declined significantly in the quarter just concluded, following a year of substantial growth. Financial experts expect this negative trend to continue for at least the next six months."

   "Personal consumption expenditures are rising rapidly, fueled by an unprecedented level of borrowing. Personal savings is up in real dollar terms, but the national savings rate dropped significantly this past year and further declines are expected. Economists believe this recent change in the savings rate explains the current trend in interest rates—a trend likely to continue into next autumn."

SELECTED REFERENCES

Ando, A., and Franco Modigliani. "The Life Cycle Hypothesis of Saving." *American Economic Review,* March 1963, pp. 55–84.

Bohm-Bawerk, Eugen von. *The Positive Theory of Capital.* New York: Macmillan, 1891.

Boskin, M. J. "Taxation, Savings and the Rate of Interest." *Journal of Political Economy,* April 1978, pp. S3–S27.

Cagan, Phillip. *The Causes of Monetary Effects on Interest Rates.* New York: National Bureau of Economic Research, 1972.

Fama, Eugene F., and Merton H. Miller. *The Theory of Finance.* New York: Holt, Rinehart & Winston, 1972.

Fisher, Irving. *The Theory of Interest.* New York: Macmillan, 1930.

Friedman, Milton. "Factors Affecting the Level of Interest Rates." *Proceedings of the Conference on Savings and Residential Financing.* U.S. League of Savings Associations, 1968, pp. 11–27.

Justen, F. T., and L. D. Taylor. "Towards a Theory of Saving Behavior." *American Economic Review,* May 1975, pp. 203–9.

Keynes, John M. *The General Theory of Employment, Interest and Money.* New York: Harcourt Brace Jovanovich, 1936.

Mishkin, Frederick. "Efficients-Markets Theory: Implications for Monetary Policy." *Brookings Papers on Economic Activity* 3 (1978), pp. 707–52.

Phillips, Llad, and John Pippenger. "Preferred Habitat vs. Efficient Market: A Test of Alternative Hypotheses." *Review,* Federal Reserve Bank of St. Louis (May 1976), pp. 11–19.

Rozeff, Michael S. "Money and Stock Prices: Market Efficiency and the Lag in Effect of Monetary Policy." *Journal of Financial Economics* 1 (September 1974), pp. 245–302.

Chapter 8

Relationships between Interest Rates and Security Prices

Learning Objectives in This Chapter

- To examine the ways used today to measure and calculate interest rates and the prices of securities and other financial assets.
- To understand the relationship between the interest rate on a bond or other debt security and its market price.
- To see how banks and other lending institutions calculate the interest rates they charge borrowers for loans and the interest rates they pay on deposits.

Key Terms and Concepts in This Chapter

Interest rate	Holding period yield	Discount method
Coupon rate	Simple interest method	Annual percentage rate (APR)
Current yield	Add-on rate	
Yield to maturity		Compound interest

THEORIES of the rate of interest help us to understand the forces that cause interest rates and prices of securities to change. They provide clues on the future direction of interest rates. However, these theories provide little or no information on how interest rates should be measured in the real world. As a result, many different measures of interest rates on securities and loans have been developed, leading to some confusion, especially for small borrowers and investors. In this chapter the methods most frequently used to measure interest rates and security prices in today's financial markets are examined. We also consider the relationship between security prices and interest rates and how they influence each other.

UNITS OF MEASUREMENT FOR INTEREST RATES AND SECURITY PRICES

Definition of Interest Rates

The interest rate is, of course, the price charged a borrower for the loan of money. As noted in Chapter 7, this price is unique because it is really a *ratio* of two quantities—the total required fee that a borrower must pay a lender to obtain the use of credit for a stipulated period divided by the amount of credit actually made available to the borrower. By convention, the interest rate is usually expressed in *percent per annum*. Thus:

$$\begin{array}{l} \text{Annual rate} \\ \text{of interest} \\ \text{on loanable} \\ \text{funds} \\ \text{(in percent)} \end{array} = \dfrac{\begin{array}{c}\text{Fee required by the} \\ \text{lender in order for the} \\ \text{borrower to obtain credit}\end{array}}{\begin{array}{c}\text{Amount of credit made} \\ \text{available to the borrower}\end{array}} \times 100 \qquad (8\text{--}1)$$

For example, an interest rate of 10 percent per annum on a $1,000 one-year car loan implies that the lender of funds has received a borrower's promise to pay a fee of $100 (10 percent of $1,000) in return for the use of $1,000 credit for a year. The promised fee of $100 is in addition to the repayment of the loan principal ($1,000) which must occur sometime during the year.

Interest rates are usually expressed as *annualized percentages* even for investments that are shorter than a year. For example, in the federal funds market commercial banks frequently loan reserves to each other overnight, with the loan being repaid the next day. Even in this market the interest rate quoted daily by lenders is expressed in percent per annum as though the loan were for a year's time. As we will soon see, however, various types of loans and securities carry important differences in how interest fees and amounts borrowed are valued or accounted for, leading to several different methods for determining interest rates. In addition, some interest rate measures use a 360-day year and others, a 365-day year. Some employ compound rates of return, with interest income earned on accumulated interest, and some do not use compounding.[1]

Basis Points

Interest rates on securities traded in the open market rarely are quoted in whole percentage points, such as 5 percent or 8 percent. The typical case is a rate expressed in hundredths of a percent—for example, 5.36 percent or 7.62 percent. Moreover, most interest rates change by only fractions of a whole percentage point in a single day or week. To deal with this situation, the concept of the basis point was developed. A *basis point* equals 1/100 of a percentage point. Thus an interest rate of 10.5 percent may be expressed as 10 percent plus 50 basis points, or 1,050 basis points. Similarly, an increase in a loan or security rate from 5.25 percent to 5.30 percent represents an increase of 5 basis points.

Security Prices

The prices of common and preferred stock in the United States are measured in dollars and eighths of a dollar. Thus, a stock price of $5\frac{1}{8}$ is a quote of $5.125 (because one eighth of a dollar = $0.125), while $40\frac{1}{4}$ means each share of a particular stock is selling for $40.25.

Bond prices are expressed in points and fractions of a point, with each point equal to $1 on a $100 basis. Thus, a U.S. government bond with a price quotation of 97 points is selling for $97 for each $100 in par (face) value. A $1,000 par value bond, therefore, would be selling for $970. Fractions of points are typically measured in 32nds, 8ths, quarters, or halves, and occasionally even 64ths. Note that one-half point equals $0.50, while $\frac{1}{32}$ equals $0.03125 on a $100 basis. Thus, a price quote on a bond of $97\frac{4}{32}$ (sometimes expressed as 97.4 or 97–4) is $97.125 for each $100 or $971.25 for a $1,000 bond. Quotations expressed in 64ths usually will be indicated by a plus (+) sign added to the nearest 32nd. Thus, 100.2+ means $100\frac{5}{64}$.

As we noted in Chapter 3, security dealers quote two prices for a security rather than one. The higher of the two is the *asked* price, which indicates what the dealer will sell the security for. The *bid* price is the price at which the dealer is willing to purchase the security. The difference between bid and asked prices—known as the *spread*—provides the dealer's return for creating a market for the security. Generally, the longer the maturity of a security, the greater the spread between its bid and asked prices. This is due to the added risks associated with trading in long-term securities. Short-

---

[1]Interest rates on U.S. Treasury bills, commercial paper, and few other short-term financial instruments are based on a 360-day year and do not compound interest. See Part Four for a discussion of these instruments and the basis for calculating their rates of return to the investor, known as the *bank discount method.*

term securities may trade with a spread as low as $\frac{1}{32}$ (equal to $312.50 for a sale of $1 million in securities). Purchases and sales of intermediate maturities may carry spreads of $\frac{4}{32}$ (equal to $1,250 on a $1 million trade), while long-term bonds may be trading on spreads of $\frac{8}{32}$ (or about $2,500 for every $1 million sold). For small transactions, a commission fee is usually added to cover the cost of executing the transaction. On very large sales, however, dealers often forego commissions and quote a net price.

MEASURES OF THE RATE OF RETURN, OR YIELD, ON A LOAN OR SECURITY

The interest rate on a loan is the annual rate of return promised by the borrower to the lender as a condition for obtaining the loan. However, that rate is not necessarily a true reflection of the yield or rate of return actually earned by the lender during the life of the loan. Some borrowers will default on all or a portion of their promised payments. The market value of the security evidencing the loan may rise or fall, adding to or subtracting from the lender's total rate of return (yield) on the transaction. Thus, while the interest rate measures the "price" the borrower has promised to pay for a loan, the actual *yield* or rate of return on the loan from the lender's viewpoint may be quite different. In this section a number of the most widely used measures of the yield or rate of return on a loan or security are discussed.

Coupon Rate

One of the best-known measures of the rate of return on a debt security is the coupon rate, which appears on corporate, U.S. government, and municipal bonds and notes. The coupon rate is the contracted rate which the security issuer agrees to pay at the time a security is issued. If, for example, a company issues a bond with a coupon rate printed on its face of 9 percent, the borrower has promised the investor an annual interest payment of 9 percent of the bond's par value. Most bonds are issued with $1,000 par values, and interest payments are semiannual.

The amount of promised annual interest income paid by a bond is called its *coupon*. The annual coupon may be determined from the formula

$$\text{Coupon rate} \ \times \ \text{Par value} = \text{Coupon} \qquad (8-2)$$

Thus, a bond with par value of $1,000 bearing a coupon rate of 9 percent pays an annual coupon of $90.

The coupon rate is not an adequate measure of the return on a bond or other debt security unless the investor purchases the security at a price equal to its par value, the borrower makes all of the promised payments on time, and the investor sells or redeems the bond at its par value. However, the prices of bonds fluctuate with market conditions; rarely will a bond trade exactly at par.

Current Yield

Another popular measure of the return on a loan or security is its current yield. This is simply the ratio of the annual income (dividends or interest) generated by the loan or security to its current market value. Thus a share of common stock selling in the market for $30 and paying an annual dividend to the shareholder of $3 would have a current yield calculated as follows:

$$\text{Current yield} = \frac{\text{Annual income}}{\text{Market price of security}} = \frac{\$3}{\$30} = 0.10, \text{ or } 10\% \tag{8-3}$$

Frequently, the yields reported on stocks and bonds in the financial press are current yields. Like the coupon rate, the current yield is usually a poor reflection of the rate of return actually received by the lender or investor. It ignores the stream of actual and anticipated payments associated with a loan or security and the price at which the investor will be able to sell or redeem it.

Yield to Maturity

The most widely accepted measure of the rate of return on a loan or security is its yield to maturity. It is the rate of interest the market is prepared to pay for a financial asset in order to exchange present dollars for future dollars. Specifically, the yield to maturity is the rate which equates the purchase price of a security or other financial asset (P) with the present value of all its expected annual net cash inflows (income). In general terms

$$P = \frac{I_1}{(1 + y)^1} + \frac{I_2}{(1 + y)^2} + \cdots + \frac{I_n}{(1 + y)^n} \tag{8-4}$$

where y is the yield to maturity and each I represents the expected annual income from the security, presumed to last for n years and terminate when the financial asset is retired. The I terms in the formula include both receipts of income and repayments of principal.

To illustrate the use of this formula, assume the investor is considering the purchase of a bond due to mature in 20 years, carrying a 10 percent coupon rate. This security is available for purchase at a current market price of $850. If the bond has a par value of $1,000 which will be paid to the investor when the security reaches maturity, the bond's yield to maturity, y, may be found by solving

$$\$850 = \frac{\$100}{(1 + y)^1} + \frac{\$100}{(1 + y)^2} + \cdots + \frac{\$100}{(1 + y)^{20}} + \frac{\$1,000}{(1 + y)^{20}} \tag{8-5}$$

In this instance y equals 12 percent—a rate higher than its 10 percent coupon rate because the bond is currently selling at a *discount* from par.

Suppose this same $1,000, 10 percent coupon bond were selling at a *premium* over par. For example, if this 20-year security has a current market price of $1,200, its yield to maturity would be

$$\$1,200 = \frac{\$100}{(1 + y)^1} + \frac{\$100}{(1 + y)^2} + \cdots + \frac{\$100}{(1 + y)^{20}} + \frac{\$1,000}{(1 + y)^{20}} \qquad (8–6)$$

In this case y equals 8 percent. Because the investor must pay a higher current market price than par value (the amount the investor will receive back when the bond matures), this bond's yield to maturity must be *less* than its coupon rate.

From the two examples above it should be clear that the value of a debt security depends on the size of its promised rate of return (coupon rate) relative to prevailing market interest rates on securities of comparable quality and terms. If a security's coupon rate equals the current market interest rate on comparable securities that security will trade at *par*. If the security's coupon rate is less than the prevailing market rate it will sell at a *discount* from par. Finally, if the security's coupon rate exceeds the current interest rate in the market it will sell at a *premium* above its par value.

The yield to maturity carries a number of significant advantages as a measure of the rate of return or yield on a financial asset. In fact, security dealers and brokers typically use the yield to maturity in quoting rates of return to investors. Unlike the current yield, this return measure considers the time distribution of expected cash flows from a security or other financial asset. Of course, the yield-to-maturity measure does assume the investor will hold a security until it reaches final maturity. Moreover, yield to maturity is not an appropriate measure for stocks, which are perpetual instruments, and even for some bonds, because the investor may sell them prior to their termination date or the bonds may pay a variable return each year which is unpredictable. Another problem is that this measure assumes all cash flowing to the investor can be reinvested at the computed yield to maturity.[2] And we have not yet considered the impact of taxes on the investor's true return from a security—a subject taken up in Chapter 10.

---

[2]The examples shown above assume that interest is paid once a year; however, most bonds sold in the United States pay interest semiannually and some even more frequently. In this instance the yield to maturity formula needs to be modified slightly with the inclusion of the parameter k—the number of times during the year that interest is paid to the bondholder. The formula then becomes:

$$\text{Purchase price} = \frac{I_1/k}{(1 + y/k)^1} + \frac{I_2/k}{(1 + y/k)^2} + \cdots + \frac{I_{nk}/k}{(1 + y/k)^{nk}} + \frac{\text{Final price}}{(1 + y/k)^{nk}}$$

Thus, for a 10-year government bond paying $50 interest twice each year, k = 2 and there would be 20 periods (n × k = 10 × 2) in which the investor receives $50 in interest income. Solution of the yield-to-maturity formula proceeds the same way as before except that you need to look up y/k percent in the present value and annuity tables (instead of y) and discount over n × k rather than n time periods.

Holding Period Yield

A slight modification of the yield-to-maturity formula results in a return measure for those situations where an investor holds a security or other financial asset for a time and then sells it to another investor in advance of the asset's maturity. This so-called holding period yield is simply

$$P = \frac{I_1}{(1 + h)^1} + \frac{I_2}{(1 + h)^2} + \cdots + \frac{I_m}{(1 + h)^m} + \frac{P_m}{(1 + h)^m} \tag{8–7}$$

where h is the holding-period yield, and the total length of the investor's holding period covers m time periods. Thus, the holding period yield is simply the rate of discount (h) equalizing the market price of a financial asset (P) with all net cash flows between the time the asset is purchased and the time it is sold (including the selling price, P_m). If the asset is held to maturity, its holding period yield equals its yield to maturity.

Calculating Yields to Maturity and Holding Period Yields

Holding period yields and yields to maturity can be calculated in several different ways. One method is to employ present value tables identical to those presented in most basic finance and accounting texts.[3]

Suppose, for example, that an investor is contemplating the purchase of a corporate bond, $1,000 par value, with a coupon rate of 10 percent. To simplify the problem, assume the bond pays interest of $100 just once each year. Currently the bond is selling for $900. The investor plans to hold the bond to maturity, which occurs in five years. We have:

$$\$900 = \frac{\$100}{(1 + y)^1} + \frac{\$100}{(1 + y)^2} + \frac{\$100}{(1 + y)^3} \tag{8–8}$$
$$+ \frac{\$100}{(1 + y)^4} + \frac{\$100}{(1 + y)^5} + \frac{\$1,000}{(1 + y)^5}$$

It is useful at this point to consider what each term in Equation 8–8 means. Both the yield-to-maturity and holding period yield formulas are based on the concept of *present value*—funds to be received in the future are worth less than funds received today. Present dollars may be used to purchase and enjoy goods and services today, but dollars to be received in the future are only promises to pay and force us to postpone consumption until the funds actually are received. Equation 8–8 indicates that a bond promising to pay $100 for five successive years in the future plus a lump sum of $1,000 at maturity is worth only $900 in present value dollars. The yield, y, serves as a rate of discount reducing each payment of future dollars

---

[3]See, for example, Weston and Brigham (1985) or any other good basic finance or accounting textbook.

back to its present value in today's market. The further in the future the payment is to be made, the larger the discount factor, $(1 + y)^n$, becomes.

Turning the concept around, the purchase of a security in today's market represents the investment of present dollars in the expectation of a greater return in the form of future dollars. The familiar *compounded interest formula* (discussed later in this chapter) applies here. This formula

$$FV = P(1 + y)^t \qquad (8\text{--}9)$$

indicates that the amount of funds accumulated t years from now (FV) depends on the principal originally invested (P), the investor's expected rate of return or yield (y), and the number of years the funds are invested (t). Thus, a principal of $1,000 invested today at a 10 percent annual rate will amount to $1,100 a year from now [i.e., $1,000 \times (1 + 0.10)^1$]. Rearrangement of the compound interest formula gives

$$P = \frac{FV}{(1 + y)^t} \qquad (8\text{--}10)$$

Equation 8–10 states that the present value of FV dollars to be received in the future is P if the promised interest rate is y. If we expect to receive $1,100 one year from now and the promised interest rate is 10 percent, the present value of that $1,100 must be $1,000.

Each term on the right-hand side of the yield-to-maturity and holding period yield formulas is a form of Equation 8–10. Solving Equation 8–8 for the yield to maturity of a bond simply means finding a value for y, which brings both right- and left-hand sides of the yield formula into balance, equating the current price (P) of a security or other financial asset with the stream of future dollars it will generate for the investor. When all expected annual cash flows are not the same in amount, trial and error may be used to find the solution. Fortunately, in the case of the bond represented in Equation 8–8, the solution is not complicated. Rewrite Equation 8–8 in the following form:

$$\$900 = \$100 \left[\frac{1}{(1 + y)^1} + \frac{1}{(1 + y)^2} + \cdots + \frac{1}{(1 + y)^5} \right] \qquad (8\text{--}11)$$

$$+ \$1,000 \left[\frac{1}{(1 + y)^5} \right]$$

This indicates that the bond will pay an annuity of $1 per year (multiplied by $100) for five years, plus a lump-sum payment of $1 (multiplied by $1,000) at the end of the fifth year.

Use of Present Value Tables.   What is the yield on this bond? A reasonable initial guess is 10 percent. To determine how accurate a guess it is, we need to consult the present value and annuity tables in Appendix B. The annuity table in Appendix B indicates the present value of $1 received annually for five years at a discount yield of 10 percent is $3.791. The present value table in Appendix B shows that the present value of $1 to be received five years from today at 10 percent is $0.621. Inserting these figures into Equation 8–11 yields

$$\$100[3.791] + \$1,000[0.621] = \$1,000.1 > \$900 \qquad (8\text{–}12)$$

An annual yield of 10 percent is obviously too small because it results in a present value for the bond far in excess of its current price of $900. A 12 percent yield gives a present value of $927.50, while a 14 percent yield results in a present value for the bond of $862.30. Clearly, the true yield to maturity of this $900 bond lies between 12 percent and 14 percent, but closer to 12 percent. Linear interpolation fixes this yield at 12.84 percent.[4] The investor interested in maximizing return would compare this yield to maturity with the yields to maturity available on other assets of comparable risk.

Present value tables may also be used to calculate the holding period yield on corporate stock. To illustrate, suppose an investor is considering the purchase of common stock issued by Gulf Oil Corporation currently selling for $40 per share. He plans to hold the stock for two years and sell out at an expected price of $50 per share. If dividends of $2 per share are expected each year, what holding period yield does the investor expect to earn? Following the form of Equation 8–6, we have

$$\$40 = \frac{\$2}{(1 + h)^1} + \frac{\$2}{(1 + h)^2} + \frac{\$50}{(1 + h)^2} \qquad (8\text{–}13)$$

The reader may wish to verify from the present value and annuity tables that the holding period yield on Gulf Oil's stock is 16.54 percent.

Bond Yield Tables. Present value tables provide a reasonably accurate method for calculating maturity and holding-period yields. However, use of the tables is a trial and error process and can be quite time-consuming. To

---

[4]The present value and annuity tables in Appendix B provide the following information:

Difference in Yield to Maturity	Difference in Present Value of Bond
14%	$862.3
12	927.5
2%	$ – 65.2

There is a difference of $27.5 between the current $900 price of the bond and its present value at a yield of 12 percent, which is $927.50. Therefore, the bond's approximate actual yield to maturity may be found from:

$$12\% + \frac{27.5}{65.2} \times 2\% = 12\% + 0.8436\% \approx 12.84\%$$

Linear interpolation of this sort must be used with care, especially where yield differentials are substantial, because the yield-price relationship is *not* linear.

Exhibit 8–1   **Bond Yield Table (prices of a bond with a 10 percent coupon rate)***

Yield to Maturity in Percent	Maturity of a Bond in Years				
	5	10	15	20	25
5%	121.88	138.97	152.33	162.76	170.91
6	117.06	129.75	139.20	146.23	151.46
7	112.47	121.32	127.59	132.03	135.18
8	108.11	113.59	117.29	119.79	121.48
9	103.96	106.50	108.14	109.20	109.88
10	100.00	100.00	100.00	100.00	100.00
11	96.23	94.02	92.73	91.98	91.53
12	92.64	88.53	86.24	84.95	84.24
13	89.22	83.47	80.41	78.78	77.91
14	85.95	78.81	75.18	73.34	72.40
15	82.84	74.51	70.47	68.51	67.56

*Prices expressed on the basis of $100 par value.

save time, securities dealers and experienced investors use bond yield tables, which give the appropriate yield for bonds of a given coupon rate, maturity, and price. An example of a page from a bond yield table is shown in Exhibit 8–1.

To illustrate, suppose the investor holds a corporate bond, bearing a 10 percent coupon rate, with 10 years remaining until maturity. The bond's purchase price may be found in the table under the correct number of years (or, for more detailed bond yield tables, number of months and years) to maturity. The correct yield to maturity will then be found along the same line as the price in the extreme left-hand column of the table. For example, if the 10-year bond's purchase price were $88.53 (on a $100 basis), then its yield to maturity would be 12 percent.

The Yield Approximation Formula. When tables or computer programs are unavailable, the yield approximation formula can be used to estimate the rate of return on a security. This formula simply assumes that

$$\begin{matrix}\text{Approximate} \\ \text{average} \\ \text{annual} \\ \text{yield on a security}\end{matrix} = \frac{\text{Average annual income from the security}}{\text{Average amount of funds invested in the security}} \qquad (8\text{--}14)$$

In the case of a bond, for example, the approximate yield would be composed of annual interest income plus the average amount of price appreciation (or minus price depreciation) which occurs each year. The average amount of funds invested can be represented by the simple arithmetic average of the purchase price and the expected selling price of the security. That is,

$$\begin{array}{c} \text{Approximate} \\ \text{average} \\ \text{annual} \\ \text{yield} \end{array} = \dfrac{\text{Annual interest} \\ \text{income} \pm \dfrac{\begin{array}{c}\text{Price appreciation} \\ \text{(or depreciation)}\end{array}}{\begin{array}{c}\text{Years remaining until} \\ \text{sold or redeemed}\end{array}}}{\dfrac{\text{Purchase price} + \text{Selling price}}{2}} \qquad (8\text{--}15)$$

To illustrate the use of this formula, suppose an investor is considering the purchase of a bond with a current market price of $900, a coupon rate of 10 percent, and the bond will be sold or redeemed in 10 years at an expected price of $1,000. The approximate expected yield would be:

$$\begin{array}{c} \text{Approximate} \\ \text{average annual} \\ \text{yield on bond} \end{array} = \dfrac{\$100 + \dfrac{(\$1,000 - 900)}{10}}{\dfrac{\$900 + \$1,000}{2}} = \dfrac{\$110}{\$950} = 11.58\% \qquad (8\text{--}16)$$

Note that the investor expects a price appreciation of $100 over the remaining life of this bond because it sells currently for $900 and will be redeemed in 10 years for $1,000. The average gain in price, therefore, is $10 per year.

The same formula may be used in the case of a security that is expected to experience a depreciation in price between time of purchase and time of sale or redemption. Suppose, for example, the investor wishes to purchase a $1,000 par value bond currently selling for $1,200 with a coupon rate of 10 percent. If the bond matures in 10 years and is held to maturity,

$$\begin{array}{c} \text{Approximate} \\ \text{average annual} \\ \text{yield on bond} \end{array} = \dfrac{\$100 + \dfrac{(\$1,000 - \$1,200)}{10}}{\dfrac{\$1,200 + \$1,000}{2}} \qquad (8\text{--}17)$$

$$= \dfrac{\$100 - \$20}{\$1,100} = 7.27\%$$

The expected price depreciation of the bond partially offsets the annual interest income it will pay to the investor, thus reducing the investor's approximate average yield.

YIELD-PRICE RELATIONSHIPS

The foregoing yield-to-maturity and holding period yield formulas illustrate a number of important relationships between security prices and yields or interest rates which prevail in the financial system. One of these important relationships is:

The price of a security and its yield or rate of return are inversely related—a rise in yield implies a decline in price; conversely, a fall in yield is associated with a rise in the security's price.

Recall that investing funds in financial assets can be viewed from two different perspectives—the borrowing and lending of money or the buying and selling of securities. As noted in Chapter 7, the rate of interest from the lending of funds is determined by the interaction of the supply of loanable funds and the demand for loanable funds. Demanders of loanable funds (borrowers) supply securities to the financial marketplace, while suppliers of loanable funds (lenders) demand securities as an investment. Therefore, the rate of return or yield on a security and the price of that security are determined at one and the same instant and are simply different aspects of the same phenomenon—the borrowing and lending of loanable funds.

This point is depicted in Exhibit 8–2, which shows demand and supply curves for both the rate of interest (yield) and the price of securities. The supply of loanable funds curve (representing lending) in the interest rate diagram (Exhibit 8–2A) is analogous to the demand for securities curve (also representing lending) in the price of securities diagram (Exhibit 8–2B). Similarly, the demand for loanable funds curve (representing borrowing) in the interest-rate diagram is analogous to the supply of securities curve (also representing borrowing) in the price of securities diagram.

Exhibit 8–2   Equilibrium Security Prices and Interest Rates (Yields)

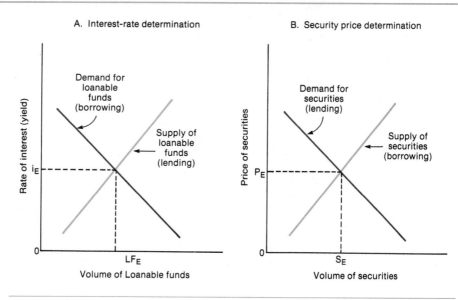

A. Interest-rate determination

B. Security price determination

We note in Exhibit 8–2B that borrowers are assumed to issue a larger volume of securities at a higher price and that lenders will demand more securities at a lower price. In Exhibit 8–2A, on the other hand, borrowers demand a smaller quantity of loanable funds at a higher interest rate while lenders supply fewer loanable funds at a lower interest rate (yield). The *equilibrium interest rate* (yield) in Exhibit 8–2A is determined, as discussed in Chapter 7, at point i_E where the demand for loanable funds equals the supply of loanable funds. Similarly, in Exhibit 8–2B the *equilibrium price* for securities lies at point P_E, where the demand for and supply of securities are equal. Only at the equilibrium interest rate and equilibrium security price will both borrowers and lenders be content with the volume of lending and borrowing taking place.

The *inverse* relationship between interest rates and security prices can be seen quite clearly when we allow the supply and demand curves depicted in Exhibit 8–2 to change. This is illustrated in Exhibit 8–3. For example, suppose that, in the face of continuing inflation, consumers and business firms accelerate their borrowings, increasing the demand for loanable funds. As shown in the upper left-hand portion of Exhibit 8–3, the demand for loanable funds curve slides upward and to the right with the supply of loanable funds unchanged. This increasing demand for loanable funds also means that the supply of securities must expand, shown in the upper right-hand portion of Exhibit 8–3 by a shift in the supply curve from S to S'. Both a new *lower* equilibrium price for securities and a *higher* equilibrium interest rate for loanable funds result.

Conversely, suppose consumers decide to save more, expanding the supply of loanable funds. As shown in the lower left-hand panel of Exhibit 8–3, the supply of loanable funds curve slides downward and to the right from S to S'. But, with more savings, the demand for securities curve must rise, sliding upward and to the right from D to D', as those added savings are invested in securities. The result is a *rise* in the equilibrium price of securities and a *decline* in the equilibrium interest rate (yield) on loanable funds.

INTEREST RATES CHARGED BY INSTITUTIONAL LENDERS

In this chapter we have examined several different measures of the rate of return, or yield, on securities traded in the financial marketplace. Our list is not complete, however, for institutional lenders of funds—commercial banks, credit unions, savings banks, insurance companies, and finance companies, to name the most important—often employ very different methods to calculate the rate of interest charged on their loans. Four commonly used methods for calculating institutional loan rates are discussed on the following pages.

Exhibit 8–3 **Effects of Changing Supply and Demand on Security Rates (Yields) and Prices**

A. Effects of an increase in the demand for loanable funds: higher interest rates and lower security prices

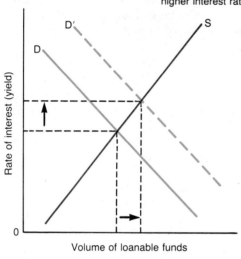

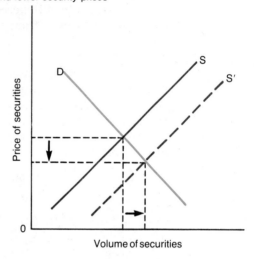

B. Effects of an increase in the supply of loanable funds: lower interest rates and higher security prices

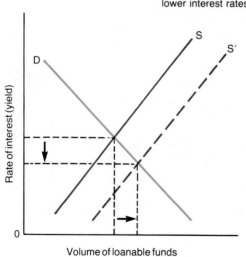

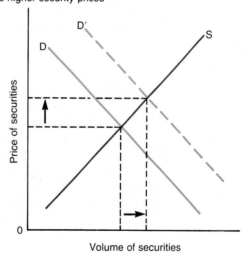

The Simple-Interest Method

The widely used simple interest method assesses interest charges on a loan only for the period of time the borrower actually has use of borrowed funds. The total interest bill *decreases* the more frequently a borrower must make payments on a loan.

For example, suppose you borrow $1,000 for a year at simple interest. If the interest rate is 10 percent, your interest bill will be $100 for the year. This figure is derived from the well-known formula

$$I = P \times r \times t \qquad\qquad (8\text{--}18)$$

where I represents the interest charge (in dollars), P is the principal amount of the loan, r is the annual rate of interest, and t is the term (maturity) of the loan expressed in years or fractions of a year. (In this example, $1,000 \times 0.10 \times 1 = \$100$.)

If the $1,000 loan is repaid in one lump sum at the end of the year, you will pay a total of

$$\frac{\text{Principal} + \text{Interest}}{\$1,000 + \$100} = \frac{\text{Total payment}}{\$1,100}$$

Suppose, however, that this loan principal is paid off in two equal installments of $500 each every six months. Then, you will pay

	Principal + Interest	= Total payment
First installment:	$500 + $50 (i.e., 6 months' interest on $1,000 at 10%)	= $ 550
Second installment:	$500 + $25 (i.e., 6 months' interest on $500 at 10%)	= $ 525
		$1,075

Clearly, you pay a lower interest bill ($75 versus $100) with two installment payments instead of one. This happens because with two installment payments on the loan's principal you effectively have use of the full $1,000 for only six months. For the remaining six months of the year, you have use of only $500. A shorthand formula for determining the total payment (interest plus principal) on a simple-interest loan is

$$\text{Total payment due} = P + P \times r \times t = P(1 + r \times t) \qquad (8\text{--}19)$$

The simple interest method is still popular with many mortgage lenders, credit unions, and commercial banks.

Add-On Rate of Interest

A method of calculating loan interest rates often used by finance companies and commercial banks is the add-on rate approach. In this instance, interest is calculated on the full principal of the loan, and the sum of interest and principal payments is divided by the number of payments to determine the dollar amount of each payment. For example, suppose you borrow $1,000 for one year at an interest rate of 10 percent. You agree to make two equal installment payments, six months apart. The total amount to be repaid is, then, $1,100 ($1,000 principal + $100 interest). At the end of the first six months you will pay half ($550), and the remaining half will be paid at the end of the year.

If the money is borrowed and repaid in one lump sum (a single-payment loan), the simple interest and add-on methods give the same interest rate. However, as the number of installment payments increases, the borrower pays a higher effective interest rate under the add-on method. This happens because the average amount of money borrowed for the term of the loan declines with the greater frequency of installment payments, yet the borrower pays the *same* total interest bill. In fact, the effective rate of interest nearly doubles when monthly installment payments are required. For example, if you borrow $1,000 for a year at 10 percent simple interest but repay the loan in 12 equal monthly installments, you have only about $500 available for use, on average, over the course of the year. Because the total interest bill is $100, the interest rate exceeds 18 percent.

Discount Method

Many commercial loans, especially those used to raise working capital, are extended on a discount basis. This so called discount method for calculating loan rates determines the total interest charge to the customer on the basis of the amount to be repaid. However, the borrower receives as proceeds of the loan only the *difference* between the total amount owed and the interest bill. For example, suppose you borrow $1,000 for one year at 10 percent, for a total interest bill of $100. Using the discount method, you actually receive for your use only $900 (i.e., $1,000 − $100) in net loan proceeds. The effective interest rate, then, is

$$\frac{\text{Interest paid}}{\text{Net loan proceeds}} = \frac{\$100}{\$900} \times 100 = 11.11\% \qquad (8\text{--}20)$$

Some lenders will grant the borrower the full amount of money required, but add the amount of discount to the face amount of the borrower's note. For example, if you need the full $1,000, the lender under this method will multiply the effective interest rate (11.11 percent) times $1,000 to derive a total interest bill of $111.11. The face value of the borrower's note and therefore the amount that must be repaid becomes $1,111.11. However, the borrower actually receives only $1,000 for use during the year. Most discount loans are for terms of one year or less and usually do not require installment payments. Instead, these loans generally are settled in a lump sum when the note comes due.

Home Mortgage Interest Rate

One of the most confusing of all rates charged by lenders of funds is the interest rate on a home mortgage loan. Many home buyers have heard that, under the terms of most fixed and variable rate mortgage loans, their monthly payments early in the life of the loan go almost entirely to pay the interest on the loan. Only later is a substantial part of each monthly payment devoted to reducing the principal amount of a home mortgage loan. Is this true?

Yes, and we can illustrate it quite easily. Suppose you find a new home you want to buy and must borrow $100,000 to close the deal. The mortgage lender quotes you an annual interest rate of 12 percent on the loan. If we divide this annual interest rate by 12 months, we derive a *monthly* mortgage loan rate of 1 percent. The lender tells you that your monthly payment will be $1,100 each month (to cover estimated property taxes, insurance premiums, interest and principal on the loan, and other fees). This means that the first month's payment of $1,100 will be divided up by the lender as follows: (1) $1,000 for the interest payment (or 1% per month × $100,000). (2) $100 to be applied to the principal of the loan, home insurance premiums, taxes, etc. For simplicity, let's assume the $100 left over after the $1,000 interest payment goes entirely to help repay the $100,000 loan principal. This means that next month your loan now totals just $99,900 (or $100,000 − $100). When you send in that next monthly payment of $1,000, the interest payment will drop to $999 and therefore $101 will now be left over to help reduce the loan principal and meet other fees. Gradually, the monthly dollar interest payment will fall and the amount left over to help retire the loan's principal will rise. After several years, as the mortgage loan's maturity date gets very near, each subsequent monthly payment will consist mostly of repaying the loan's principal amount.

Annual Percentage Rate (APR)

The wide diversity of rates quoted by lenders is often confusing and discourages shopping around for credit. With this in mind, Congress passed the Consumer Credit Protection Act in 1968. More popularly known as Truth in Lending, this law requires institutions regularly extending credit to consumers to tell the borrower what interest rate he or she is actually paying and to use a prescribed method for calculating that rate.[5] Specifically, banks, credit unions, and other lending institutions are required to calculate an annual percentage rate (APR) and inform the loan customer what this rate is before the loan contract is signed. The actuarial method is used to determine the APR, and loan officers usually have tables at hand to translate simple interest or add-on rates into the APR.

---

[5]See Chapter 18 for a discussion of consumer credit laws.

The constant ratio formula, shown below, usually gives a good approximation to the true APR:

$$\text{APR} = \frac{\begin{array}{c}2 \times \text{Number of payment periods in a year} \\ \times \text{ Annual interest cost in dollars}\end{array}}{\begin{array}{c}(\text{Total number of loan payments} + 1) \\ \times \text{ Principal of the loan}\end{array}} \times 100 \qquad (8\text{--}21)$$

To illustrate, suppose you borrow \$1,000 at 10 percent simple interest (as defined in Equation 8–18) but must repay your loan in 12 equal monthly installments. The APR for this loan is calculated as follows:

$$\text{APR} = \frac{2(12)(\$100)}{(12 + 1)(\$1,000)} \times 100 = 18.46\% \qquad (8\text{--}22)$$

This formula slightly overstates the true APR. The actual APR on this loan is closer to 18 percent.

Regulatory agencies, such as the Federal Reserve System, have developed annual percentage rate tables (such as the one shown in Appendix B of this text) to aid lenders in figuring a borrower's required monthly payment and total finance charge on an installment loan. For example, consider the loan described above. The borrower is asked to pay a 10 percent simple interest rate on a loan of \$1,000, or \$100, in annual interest for the use of the borrowed funds. The APR table in Appendix B shows that an annual percentage rate of 18 percent (last column in the table) comes closest to the true annual interest rate for this loan. At an 18 percent APR, the borrower must pay \$10.02 per \$100 loaned if repayment is to be made in 12 equal monthly payments. On a \$1,000 loan this means the total finance charge will be \$10.02 × \$1,000/100 = \$10.02 × 10 = \$100.20. Therefore, the borrower's required monthly payment will be:

$$\text{Monthly payment} = \frac{\begin{array}{c}\text{Total finance} \\ \text{charge}\end{array} + \begin{array}{c}\text{Total amount} \\ \text{of loan}\end{array}}{\text{Number of payment periods}}$$

$$= \frac{\$100.02 + \$1,000}{12}$$

$$= \$91.67$$

Congress expected that introduction of the APR would encourage consumers to exercise greater care in the use of credit and to shop around to obtain the best terms on a loan. It is not at all clear that either goal has been realized, however. Most consumers continue to give primary weight to the size of the installment payments in deciding how much, when, and where to borrow. If their budget can afford the principal and interest charges on a loan, most consumers seem little influenced by the reported size of the APR and are not usually inclined to ask other lenders for their rates on the same loan. While consumer education is vital to intelligent financial decision making, progress in that direction has been slow.

Compound Interest

Some lenders and loan situations require the borrower to pay compound interest on a loan. In addition, most interest-bearing deposits at banks, savings and loans, and credit unions pay compound interest on the balance in the account as of a certain date. The compounding of interest simply means that the lender or depositor earns interest income on both the principal amount and on any accumulated interest. Thus, the longer the period of time over which interest earnings are compounded, the more rapidly does interest earned on interest and interest earned on principal grow.

The conventional formula for calculating the future value of a loan or deposit earning compound interest is simply

$$FV = P(1 + r)^t \qquad (8\text{--}23)$$

where FV is the sum of principal plus all accumulated interest over the life of the loan or deposit, P is the loan or deposit's principal value, r is the annual rate of interest or APR, and t is the time expressed in years. For example, suppose $1,000 is borrowed for three years at 10 percent a year, compounded annually. Using an electronic calculator or a compound interest table (see Appendix B) to find the compounding factor, $(1 + r)^t$, gives

$$FV = \$1,000(1 + 0.10)^3 = \$1,000(1.331) = \$1,331 \qquad (8\text{--}24)$$

which is the lump-sum amount the borrower must pay back at the end of three years.[6] The amount of accumulated compound interest on this loan must be

$$\text{Compound interest} = FV - P = \$1,331 - \$1,000 = \$331 \quad (8\text{--}25)$$

Increased competition in the financial institution's sector in recent years has encouraged most deposit-type institutions to offer their depositors interest compounded more frequently than annually, as assumed in the formula above. To determine the future value of accumulated interest from such a deposit two changes must be made in the formula: (1) the quoted annual interest rate (r) must be divided by the number of periods during the year for which interest is compounded; and (2) the number of years

---

[6]The compound interest table in Appendix B may be used to derive the compound interest factor in this problem. Simply check along the top row of the table for the appropriate annual percentage rate (10 percent in the above problem) and then check the number of time periods (in this case, three years) in the extreme left-hand column. The figures in the body of the compound interest table indicate the total future value (FV)—principal plus interest—repaid or earned per $1 of principal at alternative annual interest rates and time periods.

involved (t) must be multiplied by the number of compounding periods within a year. For example, suppose you hold a $1,000 deposit, earning a 12 percent annual rate of interest, with interest compounded monthly and you plan to hold the deposit for three years. At the end of three years you will receive back the lump sum of

$$FV = P(1 + r/12)^{t \times 12} = \$1,000(1 + 0.12/12)^{3 \times 12} \qquad (8\text{--}26)$$
$$= \$1,000(1.431) = \$1,431$$

Total interest earned clearly will be $1,431 − $1,000 or $431. Compounding on a more frequent basis increases the depositor's total accumulated interest and therefore the deposit's future value.[7]

SUMMARY

Interest rates and security prices are among the most important ingredients of financial decisions. Over the years a number of methods have been developed for measuring interest rates and security prices. The intelligent investor must learn to distinguish one method from another. From a conceptual point of view, the yield-to-maturity and holding period methods are among the best for measuring the true return from lending and investing funds because both consider the time value of money. From the borrower's point of view, the annual percentage rate (APR) is an effective technique for measuring the true cost of credit.

In this chapter we have highlighted one of the fundamental principles of finance. This is the mandatory *inverse* relationship between the prices of debt securities and interest rates. Falling bond prices, for example, are associated with rising interest rates, while rising bond prices imply falling interest rates. We also frequently observe stock prices falling during a period of rising interest rates, though this is not always the case because stock prices are also sensitive to other factors such as the size of corporate earnings. In the next two chapters various factors that significantly influence the interest rate attached to a loan or security are reviewed. These factors— inflation, maturity, marketability, default risk, taxation, and other influences—have a significant impact on the price of credit in the money and capital markets.

---

[7]The reader can look up the 1.431 compounding factor in the compounded interest table, Appendix B, simply by checking under the 1 percent (i.e., 12%/12 months) annual percentage rate column and checking the row for 36 (3 × 12 months) periods.

Many financial institutions quote deposit rates compounded *daily*. In this case, the annual interest rate (r) is divided by 360 for simplicity and the number of years (t) in the formula is multiplied by 365. Thus, the formula for *daily* interest rate compounding is simply

$$FV = P(1 + r/360)^{t \times 365}$$

See Appendix B for a table of compounding factors for daily interest rate compounding.

STUDY QUESTIONS

1. What is a basis point? How are stock and bond prices measured?
2. Do you think the coupon rate and the current yield are good measures of the true rate of return on a bond? Why?
3. What is the difference between yield to maturity and holding period yield? Why are bond yields typically quoted on a yield-to-maturity basis? Why are stock yields usually expressed in terms of current yield?
4. Explain why debt security prices and interest rates are *inversely* related. Illustrate with a diagram.
5. Explain the meaning of the following terms:
   a. Simple interest.   d. APR.
   b. Add-on interest.   e. Compounding of interest
   c. Discount method.

PROBLEMS

1. Suppose a bond is issued with a coupon rate of 8 percent when the market rate of interest is also 8 percent. If the market rate rises to 9 percent, what happens to the price of this bond? What happens to the bond's price if the market rate falls to 6 percent? Explain why.
2. An issue of preferred stock for XYZ corporation is issued at par for $50 per share. If stockholders are promised an 8 percent annual dividend, what was the stock's current yield at time of issue? If the stock's market price has risen to $60 per share, what is its new current yield?
3. An AAA-rated corporate bond has a current market price of $800 and will pay $100 in interest for 10 years. If its par value is $1,000, what is its yield to maturity? Suppose the investor plans to sell it in five years for $900. What would his holding period yield be?
4. Using the yield approximation formula, calculate the average yield on a $1,000 bond six years from final maturity with a 12 percent coupon rate, selling today for $1,100. What would the bond's yield be if it were selling for $940?
5. You plan to borrow $2,000 in order to take a vacation and want to repay the loan in a year. The banker offers you a simple interest rate of 12 percent with repayment of principal in two equal installments, 6 months and 12 months from now. What is your total interest bill? What is the APR? Would you prefer an add-on interest rate with one payment at the end of the year? If the bank applies the discount method to your loan, what are the net proceeds of the loan? What is your effective rate of interest?
6. An investor is interested in purchasing a new 20-year government bond carrying a 10 percent coupon rate. The bond's current market price is

$875 for a $1,000 par value instrument. If the investor buys the bond at the going price and holds to maturity, what will be his yield to maturity? Suppose the investor sells the bond at the end of 10 years for $950. What is the investor's holding period yield?

7. You discover a $1,000 par value bond just issued by XYZ corporation that pays interest *semiannually* at a coupon rate of 12 percent. The bond will mature in 10 years and can be purchased today at a price of $900 including the broker's commission. What is the bond's yield to maturity if all interest payments are made on time?

8. You borrow $2,500 for five years at a rate of 12 percent per annum, compounded annually. What is the lump-sum amount due at the end of five years? What is the total amount of interest that must be paid?

9. In problem 8 above, if interest were compounded monthly, instead of annually, what lump-sum amount would be due in five years and how much total interest must be paid?

10. You have just placed $1,500 in a bank savings deposit and plan to hold that deposit for eight years, earning 5½ percent per annum. If the bank compounds interest *daily*, what will be the total value of the deposit in eight years? How does your answer change if the bank switches to monthly compounding? Quarterly compounding?

SELECTED REFERENCES

The First Boston Corporation. *Handbook of Securities of the U.S. Government and Federal Agencies.* 30th ed. New York: The First Boston Corporation, 1978.

Freund, William C. *Investment Fundamentals.* Washington, D.C.: American Bankers Association, 1970.

Homer, Sidney, and Martin L. Leibowitz. *Inside the Yield Book.* Englewood Cliffs, N.J.: Prentice-Hall, 1972.

LaPorte, Anne Marie. "ABCs of Figuring Interest." *Business Conditions,* Federal Reserve Bank of Chicago, September 1973, pp. 3–11.

Trainer, Richard D. C. *The Arithmetic of Interest Rates,* Federal Reserve Bank of New York, 1980.

Weston, J. Fred, and Eugene F. Brigham. *Essentials of Managerial Finance,* 7th ed. New York. CBS College Publishing, 1985.

Chapter 9

Inflation, Yield Curves, and Duration: Their Relationship to Interest Rates and Security Prices

Learning Objectives in This Chapter

- To understand what inflation is and how it can affect interest rates and the prices of loans and securities in the financial markets.
- To see how yield curves are created and understand the forces at work in the financial markets that determine the shape (slope) of yield curves.
- To see how yield curves can be a useful tool for investors.
- To explore the concept of duration as a measure of the length or maturity of a loan or security and show how it can be used to aid investors in making choices.

Key Terms and Concepts in This Chapter

Inflation
Nominal interest rate
Real interest rate
Inflation premium
Fisher effect
Inflation-caused wealth
    effect
Inflation-caused income
    effect

Inflation-caused
    depreciation effect
Inflation-caused income
    tax effect
Maturity
Yield curve
Expectations
    hypothesis
Liquidity premium

Market segmentation
    argument
Preferred habitat
Price elasticity
Coupon effect
Duration
Portfolio immunization

IN Chapter 7 we examined the demand and supply forces believed to determine the rate of interest on a loan or security. We know, however, that there is not just one interest rate in the economy—there are thousands. And many of these rates differ substantially from one another. For example. in February 1988 the going market rate on one-year U.S. Treasury bills averaged 6.15 percent, while the market rate on seasoned corporate bonds was 9.45 percent. At the same time, major U.S. commercial banks were quoting average loan rates to their largest and most financially sound customers of 8½ to 8¾ percent. Meanwhile, investors in the market for high-grade state and local government bonds were receiving an annual rate of return of about 7.50 percent.

Why are all these rates so different from one another? Are these rate differences purely random, or can we attribute them to a limited number of factors that can be studied and perhaps predicted? Understanding the factors that cause interest rates to differ among themselves is an indispensable aid to the investor in choosing securities for a portfolio. It is not always advisable, for example, to reach for the highest rate available in the financial marketplace. The investor who does so may assume unacceptable levels of risk, have the securities called in by the issuer in advance of maturity, pay an unacceptably high tax bill, accept a rate of return whose value is seriously eroded by inflation, or suffer other undesirable consequences. Without question, the intelligent investor must have a working knowledge of the factors affecting interest rates and be able to anticipate future changes in those factors.

For example, what role does inflation play in accounting for differences between one interest rate and another? What influence do changes in the maturity (term) of a loan or security have on the rate of return that a financial instrument pays to the investor? Why are default risk and marketability important determinants of relative interest rates? What is call risk and how does it influence the interest rate (yield) on callable securities? What role do taxes and convertibility play in accounting for rate differences? In this chapter and the next we address each of these important questions.

INFLATION AND INTEREST RATES

One of the most serious problems confronting the U.S. economy and, indeed, many economies in recent years is inflation. Inflation is defined as a rise in the average level of prices for all goods and services. Some prices of individual goods and services are always rising, while others are declining. However, inflation occurs when the *average* level of all prices in the economy rises.[1] Interest rates represent the "price" of credit. Are they also affected

---

[1]See Chapter 24 for a discussion of the nature, causes, and recent public policy responses to inflation.

by inflation? The answer is yes, though there is considerable debate as to exactly *how* and by *how much* inflation affects interest rates.

The Correlation between Inflation and Interest Rates

To be sure, the apparent correlation in recent years between the rate of inflation in the United States and both long- and short-term interest rates is high. Exhibit 9–1, which tracks two popular measures of the rate of inflation—the consumer price index and the GNP deflator—and a money market interest rate—the yield on six-month prime commercial paper—suggests a close association between inflation and interest rates, especially during the 1970s. Note, for example, the sharp run-up in the rate of inflation between 1971 and 1974 and the parallel upward surge in the commercial paper rate, which reached an average yield of nearly 10 percent in 1974. Similarly, between 1974 and 1980 the inflation rate soared into double digits before falling back in the early 1980s and interest rates did the same.

In reality, however, the correlation between these two data series has not always been so high. During the 1950s and early 1960s, for example, a relatively calm economic environment prevailed, with modest annual price increases. Interest rates too were more stable and the simple correlation between inflation and interest rates was not statistically significant. Late in the 1960s and during the 1970s, however, spurred by the Vietnam war, increasing government deficits, and rising price expectations, inflation soared and so did interest rates before both cooled off during the 1980s. Thus, more recently interest rates and inflation have tended to become more closely correlated.

The Nominal and Real Interest Rates

To explore the relationship between inflation and interest rates, several key terms must be defined. First, we must distinguish between nominal and real interest rates. The nominal rate is the published or quoted interest rate on a security or loan. For example, an announcement in the financial press that major commercial banks have raised their prime lending rate to 10 percent per annum indicates what nominal interest rate is now being quoted by banks to their best customers. In contrast, the real rate of interest is the return to the lender or investor measured in terms of its actual purchasing power. In a period of inflation, of course, the real rate will be lower than the nominal rate. Another important concept is the inflation premium, which measures the rate of inflation expected by investors in the marketplace during the life of a financial instrument.

These three concepts are all related. Obviously, a lender of funds is most interested in the real rate of return on a loan; that is, the purchasing power of any interest earned. For example, suppose you loan $1,000 to a business firm for a year and expect prices of goods and services to rise 10 percent

Exhibit 9–1   **Inflation and Interest Rates** (Annual Rates, Percent)

Year	Rate of Inflation Measured by Percentage Change in		Interest Rate on Prime Commercial Paper (Six-Month Maturities)
	Consumer Price Index	**GNP Deflator**	
1960	1.6%	1.7%	3.85%
1961	1.0	0.0	2.97
1962	1.1	1.8	3.26
1963	1.2	1.5	3.55
1964	1.3	1.6	3.97
1965	1.7	2.2	4.38
1966	2.9	3.3	5.55
1967	2.9	2.9	5.10
1968	4.2	4.5	5.90
1969	5.4	5.0	7.83
1970	5.9	5.4	7.72
1971	4.3	5.1	5.11
1972	3.3	4.1	4.69
1973	6.2	5.9	8.15
1974	10.7	9.7	9.84
1975	9.4	9.5	6.32
1976	5.8	5.3	5.35
1977	6.5	5.8	5.60
1978	7.6	7.3	7.99
1979	11.5	8.8	10.91
1980	13.5	8.8	12.29
1981	8.9	8.9	14.76
1982	3.9	4.4	11.89
1983	3.8	3.8	10.16
1984	4.1	3.4	10.16
1985	3.6	3.1	8.01
1986	1.3	2.2	6.39
1987	3.2	4.0	6.84
1988*	3.9	NA	6.58

*Consumer price index for 1988 measured from February 1987 through February 1988. The commercial paper rate is for February 1988.

Sources: U.S. Department of Commerce, *Survey of Current Business*, selected issues; and Board of Governors of the Federal Reserve System, *Federal Reserve Bulletin*, selected issues.

during the year. If you charge a nominal interest rate of 12 percent on the loan, your real rate of return on the $1,000 face amount of the loan is only 2 percent, or $20. However, if the actual rate of inflation during the period of the loan turns out to be 13 percent, you have actually suffered a real decline in the purchasing power of the monies loaned. In general, lenders will attempt to charge nominal rates of interest that give them desired *real* rates of return on their loanable funds. And nominal interest rates will change as frequently as lenders alter their expectations regarding inflation.

The Fisher Effect

In a classic article written just before the turn of the century, economist Irving Fisher (1896) argued that the nominal interest rate was related to the real rate by the following equation:

$$\begin{array}{l}\text{Nominal}\\\text{interest}\\\text{rate}\end{array} = \begin{array}{l}\text{Expected}\\\text{real}\\\text{rate}\end{array} + \begin{array}{l}\text{Inflation}\\\text{premium}\end{array} + \left[\begin{array}{l}\text{Expected}\\\text{real}\\\text{rate}\end{array} \times \begin{array}{l}\text{Inflation}\\\text{premium}\end{array}\right] \quad (9\text{-}1)$$

Clearly if the expected real interest rate is held fixed, changes in nominal rates would reflect shifting inflation premiums (i.e., changes in the public's views on expected inflation). The cross-product term in the above equation (expected real rate × inflation premium) is often eliminated because it is usually quite small except in countries experiencing severe inflation.[2]

Does the above equation suggest that an increase in expected inflation *automatically* increases nominal interest rates? Not necessarily. There are several different views on the matter. Fisher argued that the expected real rate of return tended to be stable over time because it depends on such long-run factors as the productivity of capital and the volume of savings in the economy. Therefore, a change in the inflation premium is likely to influence only the nominal interest rate, at least in the short run. The nominal rate will rise by the full amount of the expected increase in the rate of inflation and decline by the full amount of any expected decline in inflation. For example, suppose the expected real rate is 3 percent and the expected rate of inflation is 10 percent. Then the nominal rate would be:

$$\text{Nominal interest rate} = 3\% + 10\% = 13\% \quad (9\text{-}2)$$

According to Fisher's hypothesis, if the expected rate of inflation now rises to 12 percent, the expected real rate will remain unchanged at 3 percent, but the nominal rate will rise to 15 percent.

If this view (known today as the Fisher effect) is correct, it suggests a method of judging the *direction* of future interest rate changes. To the extent that a rise in the actual rate of inflation causes investors to expect greater inflation in the future, higher nominal interest rates will soon result. Conversely, a decline in the actual rate of inflation may cause investors to revise downward their expectations of future inflation, leading to lower nominal interest rates.

Alternative Views on Inflation and Interest Rates

The simple one-to-one relationship between the expected inflation rate and the nominal rate of interest posited by Irving Fisher was the majority view

---

[2]For example, if inflation is running 5 percent a year and the real rate of interest is 3 percent, the cross-product term in the above equation is only 0.05 × 0.03 or 0.0015. Equation 9–1 is derived from the relationship: (1 + nominal rate) = (1 + real rate) × (1 + inflation premium).

for several decades until researchers began to find problems with it. For example, the Fisher effect assumes that inflation is *fully anticipated*. As an example, let us imagine that both borrowers and lenders of funds expect that the inflation rate for the next year will be 10 percent and the real interest rate is 3 percent. Then the supply and demand curves for loanable funds will both shift upward just enough to ensure that the going nominal interest rate on a one-year loan is 3 percent plus 10 percent, or 13 percent. Lenders would be unwilling to lend out money at any lower rate than 13 percent because they expected the prices of goods and services they plan to purchase to increase by 10 percent during the life of the loan. Suppose, however, that all or a portion of the increase in inflation is *unanticipated*. In this case there is no way to be certain about what the equilibrium nominal interest rate will be, for the nominal rate may not fully reflect the full amount of inflation. The simple one-for-one change in the nominal rate in response to changing inflationary expectations breaks down.

The Inflation-Caused Wealth Effect. Another problem with the Fisher effect centers on its assumption that people will borrow and lend the *same* amount of funds at any expected real interest rate, regardless of the expected inflation rate. However, inflation can affect incomes, wealth holdings, the attractiveness or unattractiveness of business investment, the burden of taxes, and so on. Suppose, for example, that people come to expect a higher inflation rate and they perceive this change as lowering the value of their inflation-adjusted (real) wealth. In response to this inflation-caused wealth effect people may decide to save more, lowering the equilibrium expected real rate of interest. Therefore, the nominal interest rate would rise less than the expected increase in inflation because of the offsetting decline in the expected real interest rate. Similarly, a decrease in expected inflation might lead to a perceived increase in the real value of wealth holdings, reduce current saving, and cause the real interest rate to rise. Thus, the nominal interest rate will fall by less than the decrease in expected inflation. Clearly, with the inflation-caused wealth effect there is *less* than a one-to-one relationship between changes in expected inflation and nominal interest rates.

The Inflation-Caused Income Effect. The wealth effect of changing inflation may be joined by an inflation-caused income effect. A rise in the expected inflation rate, for example, may lead to an increase in real (inflation-adjusted) income. This may happen because a declining real interest rate associated with the reduced value of wealth may cause consumers to reduce their supply of savings to the financial markets and to step up their spending on goods and services. At the same time businesses borrow more heavily to increase production and stock their shelves with additional goods to sell. The expanded consumption and production increases employment, and both businesses and consumers experience a rise in their income. Out of the higher income more savings will eventually flow into the financial system, expanding the aggregate supply of loanable funds. Other factors held equal, borrowing and lending will take place at a lower real rate of interest and the nominal rate will again rise by *less* than the increase in expected inflation.

Similarly, a decrease in expected inflation may stimulate more saving and less consumption, reducing business investment, employment, and incomes. Eventually savings flowing into the financial markets will begin to fall, and the real interest rate will rise even as nominal rates fall due to lower expected inflation. As before, there is *less* than a one-to-one relationship between changes in the expected rate of inflation and nominal interest rates.

Both the inflation-caused income effect and wealth effect take *time* to exert their influence on real and nominal rates, and this time factor can distort the inflation-interest rate linkage. Unless we adopt a pure rational expectations–efficient markets approach to explaining interest rates (as discussed in Chapter 7), nominal interest rates will reach final equilibrium only after a series of rate-determining adjustments have been made. For example, suppose the Federal Reserve increases the nation's money supply. The liquidity preference theory of interest discussed in Chapter 7 suggests that nominal rates will fall at first due to the expansion in the available money stock relative to the public's money demand. However, the growing money stock may kindle both expectations of inflation and rising incomes, putting upward pressure on nominal rates. Thus, the nominal interest rate we observe at any point in time may not fully reflect inflationary expectations in the financial system because it is being buffeted by several other factors in its journey toward equilibrium.

The Inflation-Caused Depreciation Effect. Still another factor possibly leading to smaller changes in nominal rates than occur in the expected inflation rate is the inflation-caused depreciation effect. Inflation drives up the cost of new capital goods, such as buildings, machinery, equipment, cars, trucks, and ships, which must be purchased to replace old capital items that are wearing out. However, old capital must be depreciated by formulas (such as straight-line or sum-of-the-years' digits methods) dictated by federal and state tax laws. Thus, in periods of rapid inflation the true cost of using up existing capital equipment is understated, so that taxable business income is inflated. As a result, *after-tax* income from business investment projects is less than would be true with lower or no inflation. Experiencing reduced real returns after taxes, businesses cut back on their plans to purchase new capital goods, and the resulting fall in the demand for loanable funds decreases the equilibrium real interest rate. Clearly, then, if the expected rate of inflation rises and the real rate falls at the same time, the nominal interest rate is likely to rise by *less* than the increase in expected inflation. The exact opposite effects ensue if the expected rate of inflation declines, with nominal rates dropping by less than the decrease in expected inflation.

The Inflation-Caused Income Tax Effect. The depreciation effect brings taxes into the picture. Recent research suggests that the tax impact may work in both directions; that is, while the depreciation effect tends to dampen changes in the nominal rate, the inflation-caused income tax effect may so widen movements in the nominal rate that it changes by *more* than any given change in the rate of inflation. The heart of this argument is that lenders and investors not exempt from federal and state income taxes make lending and investing decisions on the basis of their expected real rate of return after taxes. If an investor desires to protect (i.e., hold constant) his or her expected real after-tax rate of return, then the nominal rate has to increase by a *greater* amount than any rise in the expected inflation rate because otherwise the investor's real after-tax return will decline when inflation increases.

To see the validity of this argument, we observe that

$$\begin{array}{c}\text{Expected after-tax} \\ \text{real rate of return} \\ \text{earned by a} \\ \text{taxpaying} \\ \text{investor}\end{array} = \begin{array}{c}\text{Nominal} \\ \text{rate}\end{array} - \begin{array}{c}\text{Nominal} \\ \text{rate}\end{array} \times \begin{array}{c}\text{Taxpayer's income} \\ \text{tax bracket rate}\end{array}$$

$$- \text{ Inflation premium}$$

(9–3)

Suppose an individual investor is in the 28 percent income tax bracket so that a little more than a quarter of any additional income he or she earns is taxed away. Moreover, suppose the current nominal interest rate on a one-year taxable security this investor is interested in buying is 12 percent, and the inflation premium (expected inflation rate) over the coming year is 5 percent. Then, this investor's expected real after-tax return from the security must be

$$\begin{array}{c}\text{Expected after-tax} \\ \text{real rate of return} \\ \text{earned by a tax-} \\ \text{paying investor}\end{array} = 12\% - 12\% \,(0.28) - 5\% = 3.64\%$$

(9–4)

Now suppose the expected rate of inflation rises from 5 to 6 percent. By how much must the *nominal interest rate* on the taxable security rise to yield this investor the *same* expected real rate of return after taxes? The answer must be 13.39 percent for

$$\begin{array}{c}\text{Expected after-tax} \\ \text{real rate of return} \\ \text{earned by a tax-} \\ \text{paying investor}\end{array} = 13.39\% - 13.39\% \,(0.280) - 6\% = 3.64\%$$

(9–5)

Thus, a change of 1 percent in the expected inflation rate required a 1.39 percent change in the nominal rate to leave this taxed investor in the same place in terms of a real (purchasing-power) return from his or her investment.

Clearly the arithmetic shown above works both ways—a *reduction* in expected inflation by 1 percent requires a 1.39 percent *decline* in the nominal rate to leave the real after-tax return where it is. While investors in lower tax brackets would not require as numerically large a change in nominal rates to leave after-tax real returns unaltered, inflation tends to force most investors into higher and higher tax brackets as both prices and nominal incomes rise, unless government tax schedules are indexed to change with changing inflation—something Congress mandated for U.S. taxpayers beginning in 1985.

Conclusions from Recent Research. With all of the foregoing possible effects from inflation, what actually happens to nominal rates when the expected rate of inflation shifts? Do nominal rates rise more or less than the change in expected inflation? The bulk of recent research suggests *nominal rates rise by less than any given increase in the expected inflation rate and decline by less than any given decrease in the expected inflation rate.* In essence, the inflation-caused income, wealth, and depreciation effects appear to outweigh influences pulling in the opposite direction, such as the income tax effect. Estimates vary from study to study but generally suggest that nominal rates change by 60 to perhaps 90 percent of the calculated change in the expected inflation rate, depending on the period examined and the particular measure of expected inflation chosen.[3]

While it is reassuring to embrace such a sweeping conclusion, the reader should retain a healthy skepticism about research in this field. The topic of inflation and interest rates is plagued by numerous problems of methodology and measurement. For example, there are no direct, widely accepted measures of two key factors in the drama—the real rate and the expected rate of inflation. Because the underlying theory speaks of *expected* inflation and the *expected* real market-clearing rate of return, there is the obvious problem of measuring people's expectations. We cannot, as a practical matter, survey all investors, and the results of such a survey would soon be irrelevant anyway, because expectations change. Most research studies have represented expected inflation by a survey of market experts or by employing a weighted average of past inflation rates. Both are admittedly crude proxies for the underlying concept. Note too that we cannot automatically derive the expected real interest rate merely by subtracting the current inflation rate from the current nominal rate; this gives us a measure of the *actual* real rate at a single point in time, not necessarily the *expected* rate. Moreover, none of these approaches takes into account the impact of *time lags* as interest rates, buffeted by numerous forces, strive to reach long-run equilibrium. We know for sure only that the relationship between inflation and interest rates is a positive one—more rapid inflation tends to push interest

---

[3]Prominent studies in the field include those by Fama (1975), Pindyck (1984), Sargent (1982), Tanzi (1980), and Taylor (1982).

rates higher; however, the magnitude of that relationship remains in dispute.

Inflation and Stock Prices

The discussion so far has centered on the public's inflationary expectations and their possible impact on interest rates attached to bonds, bank loans, and other debt securities. However, another interesting and largely unanswered question centers on the relationship (if any) between expectations of inflation and stock prices. Does inflation, expected or otherwise, cause the prices of corporate stock (equities) to rise? The conventional wisdom says yes. Common stock, for example, is widely viewed as a hedge against inflation—a place to park your money if you want to preserve the purchasing power of your savings.

Unfortunately, the facts often contradict what everybody knows. For example, the stock market rose to unprecedented highs in the mid-1980s, breaking price record after price record, yet the U.S. inflation rate *fell* during this period. One useful way to view this issue is to decide what factors determine the prices of corporate stock and see if those factors are likely to be affected by inflation. In basic terms, the stock price of any corporation is positively related to the dividends investors expect the company to pay to shareholders in future periods and negatively related to the risk attached to that stream of expected dividends. That is:

$$\text{Price per share of corporate stock } (P_s) = \sum_{t=0}^{\infty} \frac{E(D_t)}{(1 + r)^t}$$

where $E(D_t)$ are expected dividend payments in each period t and r is the rate of discount applied to those expected dividends to express them in terms of their present value. The more risky the corporation's dividend stream, the higher the required rate of discount, r, because market investors demand a higher rate of return to compensate them for the added risk of holding the stock.

Clearly, if a rise in expected inflation is to raise stock prices, it must either increase the amount of dividends shareholders expect each company to pay them [E(D)] or lower the perceived risk of holding stock (r), or both. On the other hand, stock prices will tend to fall with more inflation if investors lower their dividend expectations, inflation increases the perceived risk to stockholders, or both. Is there any evidence on which way the relationship goes?

There are several conflicting views. One line of argument says that if the inflation is fully expected by all investors and fully taken into account, nominal (published) stock prices may rise but *real* stock prices will not change at all. This is because both company revenues and expenses will grow equally fast, and thus the size of the firm's net income and dividend payments probably will not be affected (assuming the company's board of directors does not change the dividend rate). On the other hand, if inflation is only partly expected, the amount of unexpected inflation may be captured by company shareholders as opposed to debtholders in the form of increased earnings, and real stock prices will rise. Conversely, if the company's depreciation expenses on worn-out equipment are inadequate to offset the rising cost of new equipment in a period of inflation, current before-tax corporate income will be overstated, resulting in higher taxes against the firm, lowering its after-tax income and stockholder dividend payments. In this instance more rapid inflation would tend to lower stock prices, other factors being equal.

Some authorities (e.g., Malkiel, 1979, and Pindyck, 1984) believe that inflation increases the risk premium associated with corporate profits, perhaps because the government no longer can "fine tune" the economy and corporate planning seems less effective. The credit quality of firms may fall as more firms take on added debt and profit performance varies more widely across firms. Thus, stock prices may decline with advancing inflation because of increasing risk.

On the other hand, with falling prices businesses may be unable to cut their expenses fast enough. Business profits will then decline and credit risk will rise, leading to more business failures and declining stock values with lower inflation. In this instance, inflation contributes to higher stock prices, while a weakening economy and lower inflation force stock prices down. Either way, the issue of stock prices and inflation remains in grave doubt, awaiting further research to find the right answers.

THE MATURITY OF A LOAN

One of the most important factors causing interest rates to differ from one another is differences in the maturity (or term) of securities and loans. Financial assets traded today in the world's financial markets have a wide variety of maturities. In the federal funds and U.S. government securities markets, for example, some loans are overnight or over-the-weekend transactions, with the borrower repaying the loan in a matter of hours. At the other end of the spectrum, mortgages used to finance the purchase of new homes often stretch out 25 to 30 years. Corporate stocks are perpetual securities and will be traded as long as the issuing corporation continues to operate or until the stock is repurchased by the issuer and retired. Between these extremes lie thousands of securities issued by large and small borrowers with a tremendous variety of maturities.

The Yield Curve and the Term Structure of Interest Rates

The relationship between the rates of return (or yields) on financial instruments and their maturity is called the term structure of interest rates. This

Exhibit 9–2

Yields on Treasury Securities, March 31, 1980 (Based on Closing Bid Quotations)

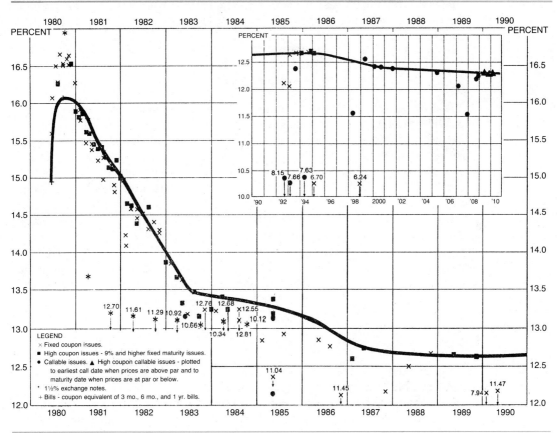

Source: *Treasury Bulletin,* April 1980, p. 84.

term structure may be represented visually by drawing a yield curve for all securities having the same credit quality. An example of a yield curve for U.S. government securities as it appeared in a recent issue of the *Treasury Bulletin* is shown in Exhibit 9–2. We note that yield to maturity (measured by the annual percentage rate of return) is plotted along the vertical axis, while the horizontal scale shows the length of time (term) to final maturity (measured in months and years).

The yield curve considers only the relationship between the maturity or term of a loan or security and its yield at one moment in time, with all other possible influential factors held constant. For example, we cannot draw a yield curve for securities bearing different degrees of risk or subject to different tax laws because both risk and tax laws affect relative yields along with maturity. We may, however, draw a yield curve for U.S. government securities of varying maturity because they all have minimal default risk, the same tax status, and so on. Similarly, yield curves could be constructed for all corporate bonds or for all municipal bonds having the same credit rating.

Types of Yield Curves

Yield curves change their shape over time in response to changes in the public's interest-rate expectations, fluctuations in the demand for liquidity in the economy, and other factors. Several different shapes have been observed, but most yield curves may be described as upward sloping, downward sloping, or horizontal (flat). An upward-sloping yield curve, of course, indicates that borrowers must pay higher interest rates for longer-term loans than for shorter-term loans. A downward-sloping yield curve means that longer-term loans and securities presently carry lower interest rates than shorter-term financial assets. Exhibit 9–2 illustrates a downward-sloping yield curve, while Exhibit 9–4 pictures an upward-sloping curve. Exhibit 9–3 depicts a recent horizontal or flat yield curve. Each shape of the yield curve has important implications for lenders and savers, borrowers and investors, and the financial institutions that serve them.

The Expectations Hypothesis

What determines the shape or slope of the yield curve? One view (with considerable research evidence to support it) is the expectations hypothesis, which argues that investor expectations regarding future changes in short-term interest rates determine the shape of the curve.[4] For example, a rising yield curve is presumed to be an indication that investors expect short-term interest rates to rise above their current levels in the future. A declining yield curve suggests declining short-term rates in the future. Finally, a horizontal yield curve implies that investors in the market expect interest rates to remain essentially unchanged from their present levels. If the expectations hypothesis is true, then the yield curve becomes an important forecasting tool for the investor because it suggests the direction of future movements in short-term interest rates as viewed by the financial marketplace today.

The unbiased expectations hypothesis assumes that investors act as *profit maximizers* over their planned holding periods and have no maturity preferences. All securities in a given risk class, regardless of maturity, are perfect substitutes for each other in the minds of investors. Each investor

---

[4]Key research studies in the development and testing of the expectations hypothesis include works by Hicks (1946), Lutz (1940), Malkiel (1966), Meiselman (1962), and Walsh (1985).

Exhibit 9–3   **Yields on Treasury Securities, April 30, 1980** (Based
on Closing Bid Quotations)

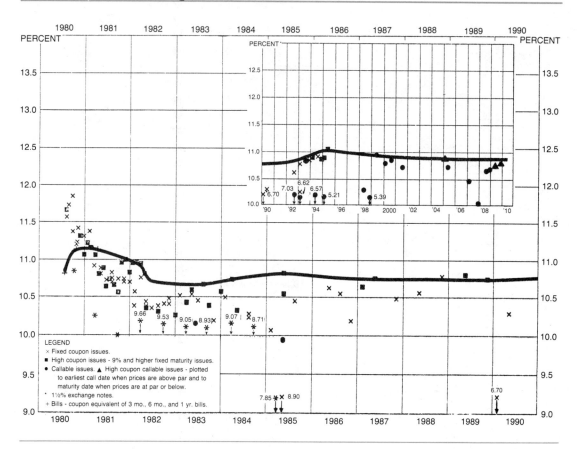

Source: *Treasury Bulletin*, May 1980, p. 86.

will seek those individual securities or combinations of securities offering
the highest rates of return. For example, it is immaterial to investors with
a planned 10-year investment horizon whether they buy a 10-year security,
two 5-year securities, or a series of 1-year securities until the 10-year holding
period terminates. Each investor will pursue that investment strategy which
offers the greatest rate of return or yield over the length of his or her planned
holding period.

Profit-maximizing behavior on the part of many thousands of investors
interacting in the marketplace ensures that holding period yields on all
securities move toward equality. Once equilibrium is achieved, and assuming no transactions costs, the investor should earn the same yield from

Exhibit 9–4   **Yields on Treasury Securities, June 28, 1985** (Based on Closing Bid Quotations)

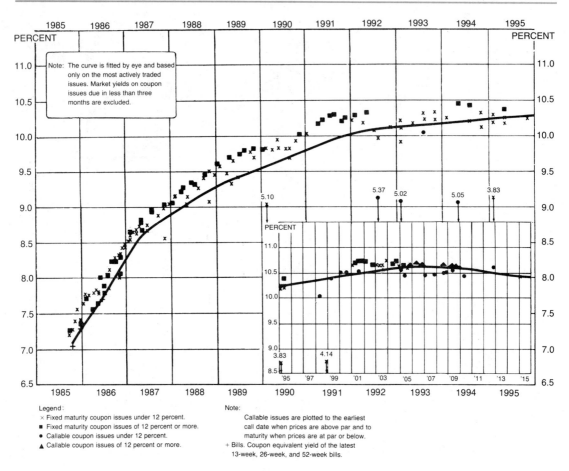

Legend:
× Fixed maturity coupon issues under 12 percent.
■ Fixed maturity coupon issues of 12 percent or more.
● Callable coupon issues under 12 percent.
▲ Callable coupon issues of 12 percent or more.

Note:
Callable issues are plotted to the earliest call date when prices are above par and to maturity when prices are at par or below.
+ Bills. Coupon equivalent yield of the latest 13-week, 26-week, and 52-week bills.

Source: *Treasury Bulletin*, First Quarter, Fiscal 1985, Winter Issue, p. 33.

buying a long-term security as from purchasing a series of short-term securities whose combined maturities equal that of the long-term security. If the rate of return on long-term securities rises above or falls below the return the investor would receive from buying and selling several short-term securities, forces are quickly set in motion to restore equilibrium. Investors at the margin will practice *arbitrage* (moving funds from one security market to another) until long-term yields once again are brought into balance with short-term yields.

The Role of Expectations in Shaping the Yield Curve

How can a factor as intangible as expectations determine the shape of the yield curve? Expectations are a potent force in the financial marketplace because investors act on their expectations. For example, if interest rates are expected to rise in the future, this is disturbing news to investors in long-term bonds. As we noted in Chapter 8, rising interest rates mean falling prices for bonds and other debt securities. Moreover, the longer the term of a bond, the more sensitive its price is to changes in interest rates. Faced with the possibility of falling bond prices, many investors will sell their long-term bonds and buy short-term securities or hold cash. As a result, the prices of long-term bonds will plummet, driving their rates (yields) higher. At the same time, increased investor purchases of short-term securities will send the prices of these securities higher and their yields lower. With rising long-term rates and falling short-term rates, the yield curve will gradually assume an upward slope. The yield curve's prophecy of rising interest rates will have come true simply because investors responded to their expectations by making changes in their security portfolios.

Relative Changes in Long-Term Interest Rates

The expectations theory does help to explain an interesting phenomenon in the financial markets. Long-term rates tend to change slowly over time, while short-term interest rates are highly volatile and often move over wide ranges. The expectations hypothesis argues that the long-term interest rate may be represented as a *geometric* average of a series of rates on current and future (forward) short-term loans whose combined maturities equal that of the long-term loan. In terms of conventional symbols:

$$(1 + {}_tR_n)^n = (1 + {}_tR_1)(1 + {}_{t+1}r_{1t})(1 + {}_{t+2}r_{1t}) \ldots (1 + {}_{t+n-1}r_{1t}) \quad (9\text{--}6)$$

where

$_tR_n$ = The rate of interest prevailing at time t on a long-term loan covering n periods of time

$_tR_1$ = The one-period loan rate prevailing at time period t.

$_{t+1}r_{1t}$ = Forward interest rate as quoted at time t on a one-period loan to start in time period t + 1.

$_{t+2}r_{1t}$ = Forward interest rate as quoted at time t on a one-period loan to start in time period t + 2.

.

.

.

$_{t+n-1}r_{1t}$ = Forward interest rate as quoted at time t on a one-period loan to start in time period t + n − 1.

The expectations hypothesis presumes that each of the forward rates—$_{t+1}r_{1t}, _{t+2}r_{1t}, \ldots, _{t+n-1}r_{1t}$—are equal to the future interest rates the market *expects* to exist at each indicated future time period from t + 1 through t + n − 1. Equation 9–6 illustrates a fundamental principle in the expectations theory: *An investor expects the same holding period yield regardless of whether he or she purchases one long-term security or a series of short-term securities whose combined maturities make up the long-term security. This is true because all markets are presumed to be perfectly competitive without significant barriers between them and all securities, whatever their maturity, are presumed to be perfect substitutes for each other.*

According to the expectations theory, the rate of interest on a 20-year bond, for example, may be viewed as equivalent to the geometric average of the interest rate on a current 1-year loan plus the rates expected to be attached in future periods to a series of 19 1-year loans, altogether adding up to 20 years. Experience teaches us that an average changes much more slowly than the individual components making up that average. If the long-term interest rate is really a geometric *average* of current and expected future short-term rates, then this helps to explain why in real world markets long-term rates tend to lag behind short-term rates and are less volatile. As we will see more fully in Chapter 11, the assumption that the long-term interest rate embodies the market's expectation regarding expected future short-term interest rates suggests an important clue on forecasting future rate movements in the financial marketplace.

Policy Implications of the Expectations Hypothesis

The expectations hypothesis has important implications for public policy. The theory clearly implies that changes in the relative amounts available of long-term versus short-term securities do not influence the shape of the yield curve *unless* investor expectations also are affected. For example, suppose the U.S. Treasury decided to refinance $100 billion of its maturing short-term IOUs by issuing $100 billion in long-term bonds. Would this government action affect the shape of the yield curve? Certainly the supply of long-term bonds would be significantly increased, while the supply of short-term securities would be sharply reduced. However, according to the expectations theory, the yield curve itself would not be changed unless investors altered their expectations about the future course of short-term interest rates.

To cite one more example, the Federal Reserve System buys and sells U.S. government securities almost daily in the money and capital markets in order to promote the nation's economic goals.[5] Can the Fed influence the

---

[5] Federal Reserve open-market operations are discussed at length in Chapter 23.

shape of the yield curve by buying one maturity of securities and selling another? Once again, the answer is no unless the Federal Reserve can influence the interest rate expectations of investors. Why? The reason lies in the underlying assumption of the unbiased expectations hypothesis: Investors regard all securities, whatever their maturity, as perfect substitutes. Therefore, the relative amounts of long-term bonds versus short-term securities simply should not matter to investors.

The Liquidity Premium View of the Yield Curve

The strong assumptions underlying the unbiased expectations theory coupled with the real world behavior of investors have caused many financial analysts to question the theory's veracity. Securities dealers and analysts who trade actively in the financial markets frequently argue that other factors besides rate expectations also exert a significant impact on the character and shape of the yield curve.

For example, in recent years most yield curves have sloped upward. Is there a built-in bias toward positively sloped yield curves due to factors other than interest rate expectations? The liquidity premium view of the yield curve suggests that such a bias exists.

Longer-term securities tend to have more volatile market prices than short-term securities. Therefore, the investor faces greater risk of capital loss when buying long-term financial instruments. To overcome this risk, it is argued, investors must be paid an extra return in the form of an interest rate premium to encourage them to purchase long-term issues. If it exists, this additional rate or yield premium for giving up liquidity—known as the liquidity premium—would tend to give yield curves a bias toward a positive slope.

Why then do some yield curves slope downward? In such instances, expectations of declining interest rates plus other factors simply overcome the liquidity premium effect. The liquidity premium view does not preclude the important role of interest rate expectations in influencing the shape of the yield curve. Even though expectations may be the dominant factor influencing the yield curve, however, other factors such as liquidity play an important role as well.

Moreover, the liquidity argument may help explain why yield curves tend to flatten out at the longest maturities. (Note that this flattening out at the long-term end of the maturity spectrum is characteristic of all three yield curves shown in Exhibits 9–2, 9–3, and 9–4.) There are obvious differences in liquidity between a 1-year and 10-year bond, but it is not clear that major differences in liquidity exist between a 10-year bond and a 20-year bond, for example. Therefore, the size of the required liquidity premium paid to long-term investors may decrease for securities of the longest maturities.

The Segmented-Markets or Hedging-Pressure Argument

A strong theoretical and empirical challenge to the expectations theory of the yield curve appeared in the 1950s and 1960s in the form of the market segmentation argument or *hedging-pressure theory* of the term structure of interest rates.[6] The underlying assumption is that all securities are *not* perfect substitutes in the minds of investors. Maturity preferences exist among major investor groups. Moreover, these investor groups will not stray from their desired maturity spectrum unless induced to do so by higher yields or other favorable terms on longer- or shorter-term securities.

Why would certain investors strongly prefer one maturity of security over another? Market segmentation theorists find the answer in a fundamental assumption concerning investor behavior, especially the investment behavior of financial intermediaries such as investment companies, savings and loan associations, pension funds, and commercial banks. These investor groups, it is argued, often act as *risk minimizers* rather than as profit maximizers as assumed in the expectations hypothesis. They prefer to *hedge* against the risk of fluctuations in the prices and yields of securities by balancing the maturity structure of their assets with the maturity structure of their liabilities.

For example, pension funds have stable and predictable long-term liabilities. Therefore, these intermediaries prefer to invest in bonds, stocks, and other long-term assets. Credit unions and commercial banks, on the other hand, with volatile deposits and volatile short-term money market liabilities, prefer to confine the majority of their investments to short-term loans and securities. These important investor groups use the *hedging principle* of portfolio management—that is, correlating the maturity of liabilities with the maturity of assets to ensure the ready availability of liquid funds when those funds are needed. This portfolio strategy reduces the risks of fluctuating income and loss of principal.

The existence of maturity preferences among important investor groups implies that the financial markets are not one large pool of loanable funds, but rather are segmented or divided into a series of submarkets. Thus, the market for securities of medium maturity (5- to 10-year securities) attracts different investor groups than the market for long-term (over 10-year) securities. And demand and supply curves within each maturity range are held to be the dominant factors shaping the level and structure of interest rates within that maturity range. However, interest rates prevailing in one maturity range are little influenced by demand and supply forces at work setting rates in other maturity ranges.

The segmented-markets or hedging-pressure theory does not rule out

---

[6]Important research studies contributing to the development and investigation of the segmentation or hedging-pressure theory include: Culbertson (1957), Dobson, Sutch and Vanderford (1976), Elliott and Echols (1976), Kessell (1965), and Malkiel (1966).

the possible influence of expectations in shaping the term structure of interest rates, but it argues that other factors related to maturity-specific demand and supply forces are of dominant importance.

Policy Implications of the Segmented-Markets Theory

The segmented-markets theory, like the expectations theory, has significant implications for public policy. If markets along the maturity spectrum are relatively isolated from each other due to investor preferences, government policymakers can alter the shape of the yield curve merely by influencing supply and demand curves in one or more market segments.

For example, if a positively sloped yield curve were desired, with long-term interest rates higher than short-term rates, the government and the central bank could flood the market with long-term bonds. Simultaneously, the government could purchase large quantities of short-term securities. The expanded supply of bonds would drive long-term rates higher, while purchases of short-term securities would push short-term rates down, other factors held equal. Therefore, government economic policy could alter the shape of the yield curve merely by shifting the supplies available of different maturities of securities relative to the demand for those securities. This policy conclusion directly contradicts the expectations hypothesis.

The Preferred Habitat or Composite Theory of the Yield Curve

During the 1960s and 1970s an expanded theory of the yield curve appeared which attempted to combine the expectations, liquidity premium, and market segmentation arguments into a single theory. This composite view argues that investors, particularly institutional investors, such as insurance companies or pension funds, seek out their preferred habitat along the scale of varying maturities of securities that matches their risk preferences, tax exposure, liquidity needs, regulatory requirements, and planned holding periods. Normally an investor will not stray from his or her preferred habitat unless rates of return on longer- or shorter-term securities are high enough to overcome each investor's menu of preferences. The result is that security markets are divided up into distinct submarkets by these multifaceted investor preferences. Thus, factors other than just expectations play a key role in shaping the character of the yield curve at any given moment.[7]

Proponents of the preferred habitat view typically argue that investors derive their expectations about future interest rates on the basis of *historical experience*—the recent trend of rates and what history suggests is a normal range for interest rates. In the short run the majority of investors generally expect current rate trends to persist into the future; thus, rising interest

---

[7]Key research studies either developing the theory of preferred habitat or testing its implications include Dobson, Sutch, and Vanderford (1976), and Modigliani and Sutch (1966).

rates in recent weeks often lead to the expectation that rates will continue to rise in the near term. However, investors generally expect that, given sufficient time (months or years), interest rates will return to their historical averages. An important research implication here is that more recent movements in interest rates and yield spreads are linked to *past* interest rate behavior—a conclusion that tends to contradict the expectations and efficient markets theories of how the financial markets operate.

Research Evidence on Yield-Curve Theories

Which view of the yield curve is correct? Existing research evidence tends to support the *expectations* view. Studies by Sargent (1982), Meiselman (1962), Buse (1965), and others find rate expectations to be a significant factor in shaping the maturity structure of interest rates. While all investors clearly do not regard all maturities of securities as perfect substitutes, there are sufficient numbers of traders in the financial marketplace who do not have specific maturity preferences. These investors are guided principally by relative yields on different securities. They bring about the results generally predicted by the expectations theory.

Nevertheless, there is evidence that other factors, especially the demand for liquidity, do affect the shape of the yield curve. Studies by Kessel (1965), Van Horne (1965), Walsh (1985), and others suggest the existence of a liquidity premium attached to the yields on longer-term securities, compensating investors for the risks associated with all but the shortest-term investments. The size of the liquidity premium does appear to decline (though not necessarily at an even rate) with increasing maturity, however. There is also evidence provided by Elliott and Echols (1976), Modigliani and Sutch (1966), Terrell and Frazer (1972) and others that changes in the supply of securities in any particular maturity range can, at least temporarily, alter the shape of the yield curve, offering some support for the segmented-markets or hedging-pressure argument. For example, at certain phases of the business cycle, commercial banks become heavy sellers of medium-term U.S. government securities in order to raise cash and make more loans. During these periods, the yield curve frequently has a bowed or humped shape, with the highest yields offered by medium-term securities. In this instance, a sudden and massive increase in the supply of medium-term bonds appears to change the yield curve's overall shape for a brief period of time.

Uses of the Yield Curve

The controversy surrounding the determinants of the yield curve should not obscure the fact that this curve can be an extremely useful tool for investors.

Forecasting Interest Rates. First, if the expectations hypothesis is correct, the yield curve gives the investor a clue concerning the future course of interest rates. If the curve has an upward slope, for example, the investor may be well advised to look for opportunities to move away from bonds and other long-term securities into investments whose market price is less sensitive to interest-rate changes. A downward-sloping yield curve, on the other hand, suggests the likelihood of near-term declines in interest rates and a rally in bond prices if the market's forecast of lower rates turns out to be true. Under the terms of the pure or unbiased expectations hypothesis the yield curve prevailing at any given point in time actually generates a very precise forecast of what the market expects interest rates to be in any future period. We will see exactly how in Chapter 11.

Uses for Financial Intermediaries. The slope of the yield curve is critical for financial intermediaries, especially commercial banks, savings and loan associations, and savings banks. A rising yield curve is generally favorable for these institutions because they borrow most of their funds by selling short-term deposits and lend a major portion of those funds long term. The more steeply the yield curve slopes upward, the wider the spread between borrowing and lending rates and the greater the potential profit for a financial intermediary. However, if the yield curve begins to flatten out or slope downward, this should serve as a warning signal to portfolio managers of these institutions.

A flattening or downward-sloping yield curve squeezes the earnings of financial intermediaries and calls for an entirely different portfolio management strategy than an upward-sloping curve. For example, if an upward-sloping yield curve starts to flatten out, portfolio managers of financial institutions might try to lock in relatively cheap sources of funds by getting long-term commitments from depositors and other funds-supplying customers. Borrowers, on the other hand, might be encouraged to take out long-term loans at fixed rates of interest. Of course, the financial institution's customers also may be aware of impending changes in the yield curve and resist taking on long-term loans or deposit contracts at unfavorable interest rates.

Detecting Overpriced and Underpriced Securities. Yield curves can be used as an aid to investors in deciding which securities are temporarily overpriced or underpriced. This use of the curve derives from the fact that, in equilibrium, the yields on all securities of comparable risk should come to rest along the yield curve at their appropriate maturity level. In an efficiently functioning market, however, any deviations of individual securities from the yield curve will be short lived, so the investor must act quickly to profit from the deviations.

If a security's rate of return lies above the yield curve, this sends a signal to investors that that particular security is temporarily *underpriced* relative to other securities of the same maturity. Other things equal, this is a *buy* signal some investors will take advantage of, driving the price of the purchased security upward and its yield back down toward the yield curve. On the other hand, if a security's rate of return is temporarily below the yield curve, this indicates a temporarily *overpriced* financial instrument, because its yield is below that of securities bearing the same maturity. Some investors holding this security will *sell* it, pushing its price down and its yield back up toward the curve.

Indicating Trade-Offs between Maturity and Yield. Still another use of the yield curve is to indicate the current trade-off between maturity and yield confronting the investor. If the investor wishes to alter the maturity of a portfolio, the yield curve indicates what gain or loss in rate of return may be expected for each change in the portfolio's average maturity.

With an upward-sloping yield curve, for example, an investor may be able to increase a bond portfolio's expected annual yield from 9 percent to 11 percent by extending the portfolio's average maturity from six to eight years. However, the prices of longer-term bonds are more volatile, creating greater risk of capital loss. Moreover, longer-term securities tend to be less liquid and less marketable than short-term securities. Therefore, the investor must weigh the gain in yield from extending the maturity of his or her portfolio against added price, liquidity, and marketability risk. Because yield curves tend to flatten out for the longest maturities, the investor bent on lengthening the average maturity of a portfolio eventually discovers that gains in yield get smaller and smaller for each additional unit of maturity. At some point along the yield curve it clearly does not pay to further extend the maturity of an investor's security portfolio.

Riding the Yield Curve. Finally, some active security investors, especially dealers in U.S. government securities, have learned to "ride" the yield curve for profit. If the curve is positively sloped, with a slope steep enough to offset transactions costs from buying and selling securities, the investor may gain by timely portfolio switching.

For example, if a security dealer purchases U.S. Treasury bills six months from maturity, holds them for three months, converts the bills into cash, and buys new six-month bills, he or she can profit in two ways from a positively sloped yield curve. Because the yield is lower (and price higher) on three-month than on six-month bills, the dealer experiences a capital gain on the sale. Second, the purchase of new six-month bills replaces a lower-yielding security with a higher-yielding one at a lower price. Riding the yield curve can be risky, however, because yield curves are constantly changing their shape. If the curve gets flatter or turns down, a potential gain can be turned into a realized loss. In this case a rise in interest rates may make riding the yield curve less profitable than a simple buy and hold strategy. Experience and good judgment are indispensable in using the yield curve for profitable investment decision making.

DURATION: A DIFFERENT APPROACH TO MATURITY

The Price Elasticity of a Debt Security

Theories of the yield curve remind us that longer-maturity debt securities tend to be more volatile in price. That is, for the same change in interest rates, the price of a longer-term bond generally changes more than the price of a shorter-term bond. A popular measure of how responsive a debt security's price is to changes in interest rates is its price elasticity —thus:

$$\text{Price elasticity of a debt security (E)} = \frac{\text{Percentage change over time in a security's price}}{\text{Percentage change over time in a security's yield}} = \frac{\dfrac{P_1 - P_0}{P_0}}{\dfrac{y_1 - y_0}{y_0}} \tag{9-7}$$

where P_0 and y_0 represent a security's price and yield at some initial point in time, while P_1 and y_1 represent the security's price and yield at a subsequent point in time. Price elasticity is generally measured from the security's par value and coupon rate and is larger for downward price movements than for upward price movements.[8] Security price elasticity must be negative because rising interest rates (yields) result in falling security prices, and conversely.

For example, suppose we are interested in purchasing a 10-year bond, par value of $1,000, promising its holder a 10 percent annual coupon rate ($100 a year in interest). Looking this bond up in a bond yield table (see Chapter 8) tells us that if interest rates on comparable securities sold in the open market are at 10 percent, this bond will sell for exactly $1,000. If rates fall to 5 percent, this 10-percent bond will have a price of $1,389.70, and if rates climb to 15 percent, the bond's price will drop to just $745.10. What is the price elasticity of this bond, measured from par? From Equation 9–7 we have for the downward movement in interest rates from 10 to 5 percent:

$$\text{Price elasticity of 10 percent bond (E)} = \frac{\dfrac{(\$1,389.70 - \$1,000)}{\$1,000}}{\dfrac{5\% - 10\%}{10\%}} = \frac{0.3897}{-0.5} = -0.779 \tag{9-8}$$

On the other hand, for an upward movement in rates from 10 to 15 percent this bond's elasticity is -0.510. (The reader should verify this.) Clearly E is greater in absolute terms for the down movement in interest rate or yield

---

[8]That is, for the same change in yield, capital gains generally are larger than capital losses on the same debt security.

(from 10 to 5 percent) than it is for the rise in rate or yield (from 10 to 15 percent).

Greater price elasticity means a security goes through a greater price change for a given change in market rates of interest. And, as we noted above, longer-term securities generally carry greater price risk (their price elasticity, E, is larger) than for shorter-term securities. However, this relationship between time to maturity and price elasticity is not linear (i.e., not strictly proportional). It is not true, for example, that 10-year bonds are twice as price elastic (and price volatile) as 5-year bonds. One important reason for this nonlinear relationship is that the price volatility and elasticity of a security depend upon the size of its *coupon rate*—the annual rate promised by the borrower—as well as its maturity.

The Impact of Varying Coupon Rates

The lower a security's annual coupon rate, the more volatile (and elastic) its price tends to be; thus, investors buying lower-coupon securities generally take on greater risk of price fluctuations. In effect, a security promising lower annual coupon payments to the holder behaves as though it has a longer maturity even if it is due to mature on the same date as a security carrying a higher coupon rate. With a low-coupon (promised) rate the investor must wait longer for a substantial return of his or her funds because a greater proportion of the low-coupon security's total dollar return lies in the final payment at maturity when the bond's face value is returned to the investor. And the farther in the future cash payments are to be received, the more sensitive is the present value of that stream of payments to changes in interest rates.

The relationship we have been describing is usually called the coupon effect. It says simply that the prices of low coupon rate securities tend to rise *faster* than the prices of high coupon rate securities when market interest rates decline. Similarly, a period of rising interest rates will cause the prices of low coupon securities to fall *faster* than the prices of high coupon securities. Thus, the potential for capital gains and capital losses is greater for low coupon than for high coupon securities.

An Alternative Maturity Index for a Security: Duration

Knowledge of the impact of varying coupon rates on security price volatility and elasticity resulted in the search for a new index of maturity other than simply straight calendar time (years and months)—the maturity measure used in conventional yield curves. What was needed was a measure of the term or length of a bond that would allow financial analysts to construct a *linear* (strictly proportional) relationship between term to maturity and security price volatility or elasticity, regardless of differing coupon rates. Such a measure would have the property, for example, that a doubling of the term to maturity would mean a doubling of a security's price elasticity, thereby giving us a direct measure of the interest rate risk faced by the individual investor. This maturity measure is known today as duration:

$$
D = \frac{\begin{array}{c}\text{Present value of interest and}\\ \text{principal payments from a}\\ \text{security weighted by the timing}\\ \text{of those payments}\end{array}}{\begin{array}{c}\text{Present value of the security's}\\ \text{promised stream of interest and}\\ \text{principal payments}\end{array}} = \frac{\sum\limits_{t=1}^{n} \dfrac{I_t(t)}{(1+y)^t}}{\sum\limits_{t=1}^{n} \dfrac{I_t}{(1+y)^t}}
\tag{9 - 9}
$$

In the formula above I represents each expected payment of principal (face value) and interest income from the security and t represents the time period in which each payment is to be received. The discount factor, y, is the security's yield to maturity, with final maturity reached at the end of n periods. As the formula indicates, D is a *weighted average* measure of term to maturity in which each payment of interest and principal is multiplied by the time period in which it is received by the investor. Strictly speaking, duration reflects the price elasticity of a debt instrument with respect to changes in the instrument's yield to maturity.

We can explain the use of the duration formula by giving a numerical example. Let us imagine that an investor is interested in purchasing a $1,000 par value bond that has a term to maturity of 10 years, a 10 percent annual coupon rate (with interest paid once a year), and a 12 percent yield to maturity based on its current price. Then its duration must be:

$$
\text{Duration (D)} = \frac{\dfrac{\$100(1)}{(1.12)} + \dfrac{\$100(2)}{(1.12)^2} + \cdots + \dfrac{\$100(10)}{(1.12)^{10}} + \dfrac{\$1,000(10)}{(\$1.12)^{10}}}{\dfrac{\$100}{(1.12)} + \dfrac{\$100}{(1.12)^2} + \cdots + \dfrac{\$100}{(1.12)^{10}} + \dfrac{\$1,000}{(1.12)^{10}}}
\tag{9-10}
$$

or

$$
D = \frac{5810.90}{887.10} = 6.55 \text{ years}
$$

A number of duration's features are evident from this example. For example, duration is always *less* than the time to maturity for a coupon-paying security.[9] Duration increases with a longer stream of future payments (i.e., when the time until final cash payment is longer), but the rate of increase

---

[9]See Chapter 8 for a discussion of yield to maturity and calculating discounted present values such as required in this duration formula. Any security carrying installment payments of principal and/or interest will have a duration shorter than its calendar maturity. Only for zero coupon bonds or for any loan where principal and accumulated interest are paid in a lump sum at maturity, without any intervening installment payments, will duration and maturity be the same.

in D decreases as time to maturity stretches out. Moreover, the larger a security's yield to maturity, y, the lower its duration.

As Equation 9–10 shows, duration reflects the amount and timing of *all* payments expected during the life of a security, unlike the conventional measure of maturity—calendar time—which shows only the length of time until the final cash payment. In simplest terms, duration is an index of the average amount of time required for the investor to recover the original cash outlay used to buy the security. It has the essential property that securities with higher values of D are more volatile in price and therefore carry increased price risk. Moreover, lower coupon bonds have longer duration and therefore display more price risk than higher coupon bonds.

Uses of Duration

Because duration is related in linear fashion to the price volatility of a debt security, there is a useful approximate relationship between changes in interest rates and percentage changes in debt security prices. This relationship may be written:

$$\text{Percent change in the price of a debt security} \approx -D\left|\frac{\Delta r}{1 + r}\right| \times 100\%$$

where D is duration and Δr is the change in interest rates. For example, consider the bond whose duration was calculated above to be 6.55 years. The bond's price at the coupon rate of 10 percent is $1,000; and at an r of 12 percent, its price is $887.10. Thus, if the interest rate changes from 10 to 12 percent, the bond's approximate percentage decline in price would be:

$$\text{Percent change in bond's price} \approx -6.55 \times \left|\frac{.02}{1 + 0.10}\right| \times 100\% = -11.91\%$$

In this instance interest rates rising by two percentage points would bring about a decline in the bond's price of almost 12 percent measured from its par value and coupon rate. An investor who expects interest rates to rise would find this information helpful in deciding whether or not to continue to hold this bond.

Today duration has aroused great interest among portfolio managers for major financial institutions such as commercial banks. The reason is its possible usefulness as a device to insulate (or, in the terminology of finance, immunize) security portfolios against the risk of changing interest rates. In theory, portfolio immunization against interest rate changes can be achieved by simply acquiring a portfolio of securities whose average duration equals the investor's desired holding period. If this is done, the effect is to hold the investor's earnings *constant* regardless of whether interest rates rise or fall. In the absence of borrower default the investor's realized return can be no less than the return he or she has been promised by the borrower. Only if the future course of interest rate movements is known for certain would portfolio immunization be a less than optimal investor strategy.[10]

How does portfolio immunization work? Suppose an investor buys a portfolio of bonds with an average yield to maturity of 12 percent and an average duration of six years which exactly matches the investor's planned holding period. If interest rates rise *above* 12 percent and remain there over this six-year period, the market value of the bonds will decline and they must be sold at a capital loss at the end of the holding period. However, the investor will be able to reinvest the periodic interest payments from the bonds at the higher interest rates. In this case added interest earnings during the holding period will offset the capital loss suffered on the sale of the bonds if the portfolio's average duration equals six years, the same length as the investor's holding period. Conversely, if interest rates fall *below* 12 percent and remain low for the six-year period, the investor will be forced to reinvest the interest earnings from the bonds at lower rates. Thus, interest income will decline; *but* the lower interest rates mean the 12 percent bonds will rise in market value and can be sold for a capital gain at the conclusion of the investor's holding period. Again, if portfolio duration equals the length of the investor's holding period, the lower interest income will be fully offset by the capital gain on the bonds and the investor's total dollar return will be protected.

All this sounds easy: *To protect the return from a portfolio of securities against changes in interest rates, merely select a portfolio whose duration equals the time remaining in your planned holding period.* In practice it does not work out quite this easily, however. For example, it is usually very difficult to identify and purchase a collection of securities whose average portfolio duration exactly matches the investor's holding period. And because many bonds are callable in advance of maturity, investors may find themselves with a sudden and unexpected change in their portfolios' average duration. Moreover, duration is sensitive to the particular tax treatment of capital gains. Another problem arises if the slope of the yield curve changes over the holding period. In general, different patterns of interest rate movements require somewhat different measures of duration—a complex problem. However, there is evidence that investors can achieve reasonably accurate immunization against changing interest rates by approximately matching portfolio durations with their planned holding periods.

SUMMARY

While theories of interest rate determination typically assume there is a single interest rate in the economy, there are in fact thousands of different interest rates confronting investors at any one time. This chapter has focused

---

[10]Important studies dealing with the development of the duration and immunization concepts and the exploration of their properties and uses include: Bierwag, Kaufman, and Toevs (1983), Marshall and Yawitz (1982), Kalotay (1985), Kolb and Chiong (1982), and Macaulay (1938).

upon two major factors: (1) the maturity, term, or duration of a loan; and (2) inflationary expectations, which cause interest rates to vary on different types of securities. Knowledge of each of these factors is of critical importance to security investors in making intelligent portfolio decisions.

One key factor affecting interest rates considered in this chapter is *inflation*. Increases in the general level of prices for all goods and services affect interest rates because lenders are unwilling to commit funds to borrowers unless they are adequately protected against any expected future losses in purchasing power. If lenders expect a higher rate of inflation during the life of a credit contract, they will adjust upward the nominal rate on a loan in order to achieve their desired real rate of return. Modern financial theory argues that the nominal (published) rate on a loan or security equals the sum of the expected real rate of return (measured in terms of the real purchasing power of any income earned from the financial instrument) and the inflation premium (or expected rate of inflation). According to the so-called Fisher effect, if the expected inflation rate rises, the nominal interest rate on a loan or security must also rise by exactly the same amount, point for point.

Lesser known views usually referred to as the inflation-caused wealth, income, and depreciation effects contend that a rise in the expected inflation premium reduces the real rate of return to lenders as well as pushing nominal rates higher. However, because of the offsetting decline in the real rate, nominal rates rise *less* than the increase in expected inflation. A contrasting view argues that taxation of interest income from loans and securities forces the nominal interest rate to rise more than expected inflation in order for lenders and investors to protect their expected after-tax real rate of return. Existing research tends to give support to the idea that interest rates do respond to inflation in the *direction* predicted by the Fisher effect, but by *less* than the change in the inflation rate due to income, wealth, and other effects. However, dispute over the true magnitude of the inflation effect points to the need for further research in future years.

This chapter also emphasizes the key importance of the *yield curve* in explaining and predicting interest rate movements. The yield curve expresses the relationship between the annual rate of return on a financial instrument and its term to maturity when all other factors are held constant. Yield curves reflect the interest rate *expectations* of the marketplace and hint at the direction, if not the magnitude, of future rate movements. They are a key tool in the management of financial intermediaries who borrow a substantial proportion of their funds at the short end of the maturity spectrum and lend heavily at the long-term end. Knowledge of what and how the yield curve is determined is vital, therefore, to the long-term profitability of financial institutions.

In recent years financial analysts have become somewhat dissatisfied with one of the two key variables making up the yield curve relationship— the term to maturity, or number of months and years until a security must finally be paid off. After all, the term to maturity of a security conveys no information on the timing or size of payments received by an investor over the life of a security, but only gives the date of the final payment. An alternative measure of maturity called *duration* has become popular in recent years because it is a weighted average capturing both the size and timing of all cash payments from an individual security or portfolio of securities. Duration has grown in popularity among portfolio managers because it can be used to at least partially immunize a portfolio of securities against changing interest rates.

STUDY QUESTIONS

1. Explain how inflation affects interest rates. What is the Fisher effect? The inflation-caused income effect? Wealth effect? Depreciation effect? Tax effect?

2. The correlation between the inflation rate and market interest rates appears to have increased considerably in recent years. Can you explain why?

3. How are stock prices affected by inflation?

4. Explain the meaning of the phrase "term structure of interest rates." What is a yield curve? What assumptions are necessary to construct a yield curve?

5. Explain the differences between the expectations, market segmentation, preferred habitat, and liquidity-premium views of the yield curve. Depending upon which of these views is correct, what are the implications of each for investors? For public policy?

6. What is the *coupon effect?* How does it relate to the concept of *security price elasticity?* What is the relationship between the coupon rate on a security and the volatility of its price as interest rates change?

7. Explain the meaning and importance of the concept of *duration.* How can duration be used to aid a security portfolio manager in protecting investments against fluctuating interest rates?

8. What is *portfolio immunization?* How does it work? What are its problems?

PROBLEMS

1. According to the Fisher effect, if the real interest rate is presently equal to 3 percent and the nominal interest rate is 8 percent, what rate of inflation is the financial marketplace predicting? Explain the reasoning behind your answer. If the nominal rate rises to 11 percent and following

the assumptions of the Fisher effect, what would you conclude about the expected inflation rate? The real rate?

2. Suppose the real interest rate in the economy is 4 percent and the nominal interest rate is 9 percent. Now investors in the financial marketplace expect a sudden doubling in the rate of inflation. According to the Fisher effect, what new rate of inflation is expected? If the depreciation, income, or wealth effects are at work, what do you conclude is the new expected rate of inflation? Explain your answer.

3. Calculate the expected after-tax real rate of return for an investor in the 28 percent marginal income tax bracket if he or she purchases a bond whose nominal rate is 12 percent and the expected rate of inflation is 4 percent.

4. An investor buys a U.S. Treasury bond whose current yield to maturity as reported in the daily newspaper is 10 percent. The investor is subject to a 33 percent federal income tax rate on any new income received. His real after-tax return from this bond is 2 percent. What is the expected inflation rate in the financial marketplace?

5. Calculate the price elasticity of a 15-year bond around its $1,000 par value and 10 percent coupon rate if market interest rates on comparable securities drop to 6 percent. The market price of the bond at a 6 percent yield to maturity is $1,392. Suppose now the yield to maturity climbs to 14 percent. If the bond's price falls to $751.80, what is the bond's price elasticity?

6. Calculate the value of duration for a 20-year, $1,000 par value U.S. government bond purchased today at a yield to maturity of 15 percent. The bond's coupon rate is 12 percent, and it pays interest once a year at year's end. Now, suppose the market interest rate on comparable securities falls to 14 percent. What percentage change in this bond's price will result?

SELECTED REFERENCES

Bierwag, G.O.; George G. Kaufman; and Alden Toevs. "Duration: Its Development and Use in Bond Portfolio Management." *Financial Analysts Journal,* July–August 1983, pp. 15–35.

Buse, A. "The Expectations Hypothesis, Yield Curves, and Monetary Policy." *Quarterly Journal of Economics,* November 1965, pp. 666–68.

Chew, I. Keong, and Ronnie J. Clayton. "Bond Valuation: A Clarification." *The Financial Review* 18, no. 2 (May 1983), pp. 234–36.

Culbertson, John M. "The Term Structure of Interest Rates." *Quarterly Journal of Economics,* November 1957, pp. 485–517.

Dobson, Steven W.; Richard C. Sutch; and David E. Vanderford. "An Evaluation of

Alternative Empirical Models of the Term Structure of Interest Rates." *Journal of Finance,* September 1976, pp. 1035–65.

Elliott, J.W., and M.E. Echols. "Market Segmentation, Speculative Behavior, and the Term Structure of Interest Rates." *Review of Economics and Statistics,* February 1976, pp. 40–49.

Fama, Eugene F. "Short-Term Interest Rates as Predictors of Inflation." *American Economic Review* 65 (June 1975), pp. 269–82.

Fisher, Irving. "Appreciation and Interest." *Publication of the American Economic Association,* August 1896.

Friedman, Benjamin M. "Price Inflation, Portfolio Choice, and Nominal Interest Rates." *American Economic Review* 70 (March 1980), pp. 12–21.

Gibson, William E. "Interest Rates and Inflationary Expectations: New Evidence." *American Economic Review,* December 1972, pp. 854–65.

Hicks, John R. *Value and Capital.* 2nd ed. New York: Oxford University Press, 1946.

Kalotay, Andrew J. "The After-Tax Duration of Original Issue Discount Bonds." *Journal of Portfolio Management,* Winter 1985, pp. 70–72.

Kessel, Reuben H. *The Cyclical Behavior of the Term Structure of Interest Rates.* New York: National Bureau of Economic Research, 1965.

Kolb, Robert W., and Raymond Chiong. "Duration, Immunization, and Hedging with Interest Rate Futures." *The Journal of Financial Research* 5, no. 2 (Summer 1982), pp. 161–70.

Lutz, Friedrich A. "The Structure of Interest Rates." *Quarterly Journal of Economics,* November 1940, pp. 36–63.

Macaulay, Frederick R. *Some Theoretical Problems Suggested by the Movements of Interest Rates, Bond Yields, and Stock Prices in the United States Since 1856.* New York: National Bureau of Economic Research, 1938.

Malkiel, Burton G. *The Term Structure of Interest Rates.* Princeton, N.J.: Princeton University Press, 1966.

———. "The Capital Formation Problem in the United States." *Journal of Finance* 34, no. 2 (May 1979), pp. 291–306.

Marshall, William J., and Jess B. Yawitz. "Lower Bounds on Portfolio Performance: An Extension of the Immunization Strategy." *Journal of Financial and Quantitative Analysis* 17, no. 1 (March 1982), pp. 101–70.

Meiselman, David A. *The Term Structure of Interest Rates.* Englewood Cliffs, N.J.: Prentice-Hall, 1962.

Modigliani, Franco, and Richard Sutch, "Innovations in Interest Rate Policy." *American Economic Review,* May 1966, pp. 178–97.

Mundell, Robert. "Inflation and Real Interest," *Journal of Political Economy,* June 1963.

Pindyck, Robert S. "Risk, Inflation, and the Stock Market." *The American Economic Review,* June 1984, pp. 335–51.

Sargent, Thomas J. "Anticipated Inflation and Nominal Interest." *Quarterly Journal of Economics,* May 1982.

Tanzi, Vito. "Inflationary Expectations, Economic Activity, Taxes and Interest Rates." *American Economic Review* 70 (March 1980), pp. 12–21.

Taylor, Herbert. "Interest Rates: How Much Does Expected Inflation Matter?" *Business Review,* Federal Reserve Bank of Philadelphia, July–August 1982, pp. 3–12.

Terrell, William T., and William J. Frazer, Jr. "Interest Rates, Portfolio Behavior, and Marketable Government Securities." *Journal of Finance,* March 1972, pp. 1–35.

Van Horne, James. "Interest-Rate Risk and the Term Structure of Interest Rates." *Journal of Political Economy,* August 1965, pp. 344–51.

Walsh, Carl E. "A Rational Expectations Model of Term Premia with Some Implications for Empirical Asset Demand Equations." *The Journal of Finance* 60, no. 1 (March 1985), pp. 63–83.

Chapter 10

Marketability, Default Risk, Call Privileges, Taxes, and Other Factors Affecting Interest Rates

Learning Objectives in This Chapter

- To explore the impact of several different characteristics of loans and securities—marketability, liquidity, default risk, call privileges, convertibility, and taxability—upon their attached interest rates or yields.

- To see why there is not one but in fact thousands of different interest rates in the economy.

Key Terms and Concepts in This Chapter

Marketability	Call privilege	Marginal tax rate
Liquidity	Tax-exempt securities	Convertibility
Default risk	Tax Reform Act of 1986	Interest rate structure
Expected yield		
Junk bonds		

IN the preceding chapter we examined two factors that cause the interest rate or yield on one security to be different from the rate or yield on another. These factors included the maturity or term of a loan and expected inflation. In this chapter our focus is on a different set of elements influencing relative interest rates: (1) marketability, (2) default risk, (3) call privileges, (4) taxation of income from securities, and (5) convertibility. While the impact of each of these factors is analyzed separately, it should be noted that yields on securities typically are influenced by several factors acting simultaneously. For example, the market yield on a 20-year corporate bond may be 12 percent, while the yield on a 10-year municipal bond may be 8 percent. The difference in yield between these two securities reflects not only the difference in their maturities, but also any differences in degree of default risk, marketability, callability prior to maturity, and tax status. To analyze yield differentials between securities, therefore, we must understand thoroughly *all* the factors that shape and direct interest rates in the money and capital markets.

MARKETABILITY

One of the most imporant considerations for an investor is: Does a market exist for those assets he or she would like to acquire? Can an asset be sold quickly, or must the investor wait some time before suitable buyers can be found? This is the question of marketability, and financial instruments vary widely in terms of the ease and speed with which they can be sold and converted into cash.

For example, U.S. Treasury bills, notes, and bonds have one of the most active and deepest markets in the world. Large lots of marketable Treasury securities in multiples of a million dollars are bought and sold daily, with the trades taking place in a matter of minutes. Small lots (under $1 million) of these same securities are more difficult to sell. However, there is usually no difficulty in marketing even a handful of Treasury securities provided the seller can wait a few hours or a few days. Similarly, common stock actively traded on the New York and American exchanges typically can be moved in minutes, hours, or overnight, depending on the number of shares being sold and how far removed the investor is from the center of trading activity. In active markets like these, negotiations are usually conducted by telephone and confirmed by wire, and frequently payment for any securities purchased is made the same day by wire or within one or two days by check.

For the thousands of lesser-known securities not actively traded each day, however, marketability is frequently a problem. Stocks, bonds, and notes issued by smaller companies usually have a narrow market, often confined to the local community or region. Trades occur infrequently, and it is difficult to establish a consistent market price. A seller may have to wait weeks or months to secure a desired price or, if the security must be sold immediately, its price may have to be discounted substantially from the expected figure. Marketability is positively related to the size (total sales or total assets) and reputation of the institution issuing the securities and to the number of similar securities outstanding. Not surprisingly, stocks and bonds issued in large blocks by the largest corporations and governmental units tend to find more ready acceptance in the market. With a greater number of similar securities available, buy-sell transactions are more frequent, and a consistent market price can be established.

Marketability is a decided advantage to the security purchaser (lender of funds). In contrast, the issuer of securities is not particularly concerned about any difficulties the purchaser may encounter in the resale (secondary) market unless lack of marketability significantly influences security sales in the primary market. And where marketability is a problem, it does influence the yield the issuer must pay in the primary market. In fact, there is a negative, or inverse, relationship between marketability and yield. More marketable securities generally carry lower expected returns, other things being equal. Purchasers of securities that can be sold in the secondary market only with difficulty must be compensated for this inconvenience by a higher promised rate of return.

LIQUIDITY

Marketability is closely related to another feature of financial assets that influences their interest rate or yield—their degree of liquidity. A liquid financial asset is readily marketable. In addition, its price tends to be stable over time and it is *reversible,* meaning the holder of the asset can usually recover his or her funds upon resale with little risk of loss. Because the liquidity feature of financial assets lowers their risk, liquid assets generally carry lower interest rates or yields than illiquid assets. Investors strongly interested in maximum profitability usually try to minimize their holdings of liquid assets.

DEFAULT RISK AND INTEREST RATES

Another important factor causing one interest rate to differ from another is the degree of default risk carried by individual securities. Investors in securities face many different kinds of risk,[1] of course, but one of the most important is default risk—that is, the risk that a borrower will not meet all promised payments at the times agreed upon. All securities except U.S. government securities are subject to varying degrees of default risk. If you

---

[1]See Chapter 13 for a discussion of the principal types of risk confronting investors in financial instruments.

purchase a 10-year corporate bond with $1,000 par value and a coupon rate of 9 percent, the issuing company promises in the indenture (bond contract) that it will pay you $90 a year (or more commonly, $45 every six months) for 10 years plus $1,000 at the end of the 10-year period. Failure to meet *any* of these promised payments on time puts the borrower in default, and the investor may have to go to court to recover at least some of the monies owed him or her.

The Premium for Default Risk

The yield on a risky security is positively related to the risk of borrower default as perceived by investors. Specifically, the yield on a risky security is composed of at least two elements:

$$\text{Yield on risky security} = \text{Risk-free interest rate} \qquad (10\text{--}1)$$
$$+ \text{ Default risk premium}$$

where:

$$\text{Default risk premium} = \text{Promised yield on a risky security} \qquad (10\text{--}2)$$
$$- \text{ Risk-free interest rate}$$

The *promised yield* on a risky security is the yield to maturity that will be earned by the investor if the borrower makes all the payments pledged when they are due. The higher the degree of default risk associated with a risky security, the higher the default risk premium on that security and the greater the required rate of return (yield) that must be attached to that security as demanded by investors in the marketplace. Any adverse development, such as a downturn in the economy, a natural disaster, ill health, serious financial difficulties, that makes a borrower appear more risky will lead the market to assign a higher default risk premium to his or her security. And if the risk-free rate remains unchanged, the security's risky yield must rise and its price must decline.

The Expected Rate of Return or Yield on a Risky Security

Increasingly in recent years, some of the nation's largest firms (such as Braniff Airlines and Franklin National Bank of New York) and even some local government units (such as the huge Washington Public Power Supply System) have been forced into bankruptcy and into default on their bonds. Others, like Chrysler Corporation and Continental Illinois Corporation, have experienced highly publicized financial problems and required government help to survive. Volatile changes in business and consumer spending, interest rates, and commodity prices frequently have led to serious miscalculations by both large and small firms with sometimes fatal results. For this reason, many investors today have learned to look at the *expected* rate of return, or yield, on a security as well as its *promised* yield.

The expected yield is simply the weighted average of all possible yields to maturity from a risky security. Each possible yield is weighted by the probability that it will occur. Thus, if there are m possible yields from a given risky security:

$$\text{Expected yield} = \sum_{i=1}^{m} p_i y_i \tag{10-3}$$

where y_i represents the ith possible yield on a risky security and p_i is the probability that the ith possible risky yield will be obtained.

Anticipated Loss and Default-Risk Premiums

For a risk-free security held to maturity, the expected yield equals the promised yield. However, in the case of a risky security, the promised yield may be greater than the expected yield, and the yield spread between them is usually labeled the *anticipated loss due to default*. That is:

Anticipated loss due to default on a risky security   (10–4)
= Promised yield − Expected yield

The concept of anticipated loss due to default is important because it represents each investor's view of what the appropriate risk premium on a risky security should be. Let's suppose that an investor carries out a careful financial analysis of a company in preparation for purchasing its bonds and decides that the firm is a less risky borrower than perceived by the market as a whole. Perhaps the market has assigned the firm's bonds a default risk premium of 4 percent; the investor feels the true anticipated loss due to default is only 3 percent. Because the market's default risk premium exceeds this investor's anticipated loss, he would be inclined to *buy* that security. As he sees it, the risky security's yield (including its market-assigned default risk premium) is too high and therefore its price is too low. To this investor, the security appears to be a bargain—a temporarily underpriced financial asset.

Consider the opposite case. An investor calculates the anticipated loss due to default on bonds issued by a state toll road project. She concludes that a default risk premium of 5 percent is justified because of a significant number of uncertainties associated with the future success of the project. However, the current yield on the risky security is only 10 percent, and the risk-free interest rate is 6 percent. Because the market has assigned only a 4 percent default risk premium, and the investor prefers a 5 percent premium, it is unlikely that she will purchase the bond. As the investor views this bond, its risky yield is too low, and therefore its price is too high.

Major financial institutions, especially insurance companies and commercial banks, employ a large number of credit analysts for the express purpose of assessing the anticipated loss due to default on a wide range of

Exhibit 10–1   **Bond-Rating Categories Employed by Moody's Investor Service and Standard & Poor's Corporation**

Quality Level of Bonds	Moody's Rating Category	Standard & Poor's Rating Category	Default Risk Premium
High-quality or high-grade bonds	Aaa Aa A	AAA AA A	Lowest
Medium-quality or medium-grade bonds	Baa Ba B	BBB BB B	
Lowest grade, speculative or poor quality bonds	Caa Ca C	CCC CC C	
Defaulted bonds and bonds issued by bankrupt companies	— — —	DDD DD D	Highest

securities they would like to acquire. These institutions feel they have a definite advantage over the average investor in assessing the true degree of default risk associated with any particular security. This high level of technical expertise may permit major institutional investors to take advantage of underpriced securities where, in their judgement, the market has overestimated the true level of default risk.

Factors Influencing Default-Risk Premiums

What factors influence the risk premiums assigned by the market to different securities? For many years in the United States, privately owned rating companies have exercised a dominant influence on investor perceptions of the riskiness of individual security issues. The two most widely consulted investment rating companies are Moody's Investor Service—a division of Dun and Bradstreet, Inc.—and Standard & Poor's Corporation—a subsidiary of McGraw-Hill, Inc. Both companies rate individual security issues according to perceived probability of default (based on the borrower's financial condition and business prospects) and publish the ratings as letter grades. A summary of the letter grades used by these companies for rating corporate and municipal bonds is shown in Exhibit 10–1.[2]

---

[2] While Moody's and Standard & Poor's currently dominate the security rating business, a number of smaller but rapidly growing rating agencies have come into prominence recently. The oldest of these is Fitch Investors Service, Inc., of New York, but in 1982 Duff & Phelps, Inc. of Chicago was recognized as an acceptable nationwide credit-rating firm by the Securities and Exchange Commission (SEC). SEC recognition was also granted to McCarthy, Crisanti & Maffei, Inc. of New York in 1983. The recent rapid growth of these smaller national firms is a reflection of the increased number of corporate bankruptcies and near-bankruptcies over the last few years that led many investors to seek multiple credit opinions on any given security before committing their funds.

Exhibit 10–2 **Long-Term Bonds Yields** (Quarterly Averages)

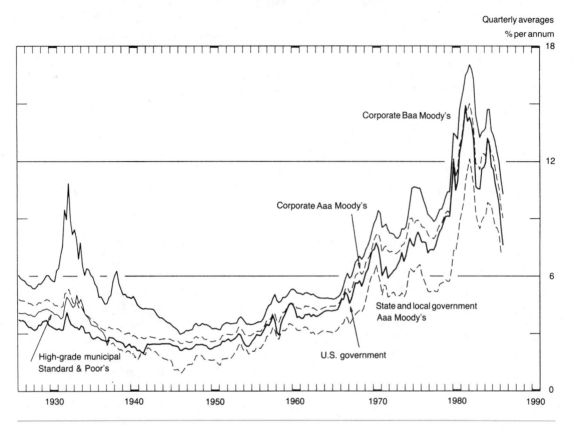

Source: Board of Governors of the Federal Reserve System, *Historical Chart Book,* 1986.

Moody's investment ratings range from Aaa for the highest-quality securities with negligible default risk to C for those securities deemed to be speculative and carrying a significant prospect of default. Quality ratings assigned by Standard & Poor's range from AAA for high-grade ("gilt-edged") securities to those financial instruments actually in default (D) or issued by bankrupt firms. Bonds falling in the four top rating categories—Aaa to Baa for Moody's and AAA to BBB for Standard & Poor's—are called *investment-grade issues*. State and federal laws frequently require commercial banks, insurance companies, and other financial institutions to purchase only those securities rated in these four categories. Lower-rated securities are referred to as *speculative issues*.

Exhibit 10–2 illustrates how the yield on bonds in two different Moody's categories—Aaa and Baa—have fluctuated in recent years, and it high-

Exhibit 10–3   **Market Yields on Rated Corporate Bonds and 20-Year U.S. Treasury Bonds, 1981–1987**

Type of bond*	Average Yields (Percent Per Annum)						
	1981	1982	1983	1984	1985	1986	1987†
20-year U.S. Treasury	13.72%	12.92%	11.34%	12.48%	10.97%	7.85%	NA
Aaa corporate	14.17	13.79	12.04	12.71	11.37	9.02	9.32
Aa corporate	14.75	14.41	12.42	13.31	11.82	9.47	9.65
A corporate	15.29	15.43	13.10	13.74	12.28	9.95	9.98
Baa corporate	16.04	16.11	13.55	14.19	12.72	10.39	10.52

*Corporate bond ratings are from Moody's Investor Service.
†Figures are for June 1987.

Source: Board of Governors of the Federal Reserve System. *Federal Reserve Bulletin,* selected issues.

lights the spread between the yields on these risky securities and those on riskless long-term U.S. government bonds. Exhibit 10–3 compares market yields on 20-year U.S. Treasury bonds with those on corporate bonds in the four top-rating categories—Aaa to Baa. It is interesting to note that these yield relationships are all in the direction theory would lead us to expect. For example, the yield on Aaa corporate bonds—the least risky of the securities rated by Moody's and Standard & Poor's—is consistently lower than yields attached to lower-rated (Baa) bonds. Moreover, the graph lines representing Aaa and Baa bonds in Exhibit 10–2 never cross each other; this suggests that investors in the marketplace tend to rank securities in the same relative default risk order as the rating agencies do. This is perhaps an appropriate strategy because there is evidence of a high correlation between the ratings assigned by the agencies and the actual default record of marketable corporate bonds.

We note, however, that the spreads between yields in different rating categories vary significantly over time. There is, for example, a pronounced association between market-assigned default risk premiums and fluctuations in business activity between recessions and expansions or boom periods. The yield spread between Aaa- and Baa-rated securities shown in Exhibit 10–2 tends to increase during recessions and decrease during periods of economic expansion. Note, for example, the marked increase in the yield spread between Aaa and Baa corporate bonds at the time of the 1969–70, 1974–75, and 1980–82 recessions and the significant decrease in that spread after these recessions ended. The correlation is not perfect, of course. Fluctuations in the nation's output and income do not always influence the default risk premium on one security versus another in the same way or to the same degree. But it is evident that, when economic and financial conditions suggest to investors that uncertainty has increased and that business prospects are less robust, the market translates these opinions into higher default risk premiums.[3]

Several studies in recent years have addressed the question of what factors influence default risk premiums on securities (especially corporate bonds) and the factors that rating companies use to evaluate default risk. Among the factors identified for corporate securities are variability in company earnings, the period of time a firm has been in operation, and the amount of leverage employed (the amount of debt relative to equity).[4] A company with volatile earnings runs a greater risk of experiencing periods when losses will exceed the firm's ability to raise funds. Moreover, the longer a firm has been operating without a default, the more investors come to expect continued successful performance. Greater use of financial leverage (debt) in the capital structure of a firm offers the potential for greater earnings per share of stock, because debt is a relatively cheap source of funds (measured on an after-tax basis). However, financial leverage is a two-edged sword. As the proportion of borrowed funds rises relative to equity, the risk of significant declines in net earnings is increased.

The Rise of Junk Bonds

The decade of the 1980s ushered in the rapid growth and development of the market for junk bonds—debt security issues with ratings below BBB (from Standard & Poor's) or Baa3 (from Moody's). The term junk bonds arose years ago when many large companies that were suddenly trapped in serious financial problems and low credit ratings (fallen angels) were forced to issue inferior quality bonds to stay alive. More recently, new companies and relatively small established companies have also been able to reach the bond market, which previously was closed to them, by issuing these speculative-grade securities. Junk bonds have also been issued to facilitate mergers and, in the opposite situation, to prevent a corporate takeover. Such low-rated bonds often trade at interest yields of 5 percentage points or more over yields on otherwise comparable U.S. government securities.

The number of individual investors and financial institutions interested

---

[3]This conclusion is supported by research studies prepared by Hickman (1958), Fisher (1959), and Jaffee (1975).

[4]See especially the study by Fisher (1959). While we do not know for sure what factors the security rating companies use to assign default risk ratings, we do know that they consider at least three levels of factors: (1) condition of the economy, (2) industry conditions, and (3) borrower-specific factors, including coverage ratios (earnings before interest and taxes to interest and principal payments owed), leverage ratios (debt to equity ratios), liquidity indicators (such as the current ratio), and profitability measures (such as return on assets and return on equity). Recent studies of corporate bankruptcy, as noted by Scott (1981), have found some of these factors—especially liquidity or cash flow variables, earnings, debt exposure, and stock prices—to be effective discriminators between corporations eventually declaring bankruptcy and healthy firms. Moreover, a recent study by Holthausen and Leftwich (1986) finds that when Moody's or Standard & Poor's downgrades a security's credit rating, the affected company's stock returns tend to fall significantly immediately following the announcement.

in purchasing junk bonds appears to have grown rapidly in recent years due to the few actual defaults on these bonds. At the same time, a leading investment banking firm, Drexel Burnham Lambert, Inc., has pioneered new techniques to issue and sell junk bonds that have rapidly expanded the scope and appeal of this market. A diversified portfolio of junk bonds (for example, at least 12 different issues) appears to have lower risk than many higher rated bonds. Thus, the yields offered on junk bonds appear to be higher than their actual degree of default risk would appear to justify. (Current estimates place the actual default rate on such bonds in the range of 1 to 4 percent of total par values.) Moreover, the development of an active market for such bonds has given many smaller and new firms access to another source of financing other than borrowing from banks or venture capitalists.

On the negative side, however, the rapid growth of junk bonds has aroused concern among policymakers and legislators over the declining credit quality of corporate debt securities. For example, insurance regulators in New York state recently moved to limit junk bond investments by insurance companies selling policies in that state. The use of junk bonds in financing hostile takeovers has also caught the attention of U.S. congressional investigators. The tax deductibility of interest expenses on corporate debt and the development of hedging instruments to offset market risks (such as financial futures, options, currency and interest rate swaps) appear to have encouraged corporations to make greater use of these bonds and other similar forms of debt. If junk bonds continue to grow in importance, both investors and those who regulate the securities markets will need to look closely at trends in the quality of corporate bonds and proceed cautiously.

A Summary of the Default Risk, Interest Rate Relationship

In summary, careful study of the relationship between default risk and interest rates points to a fundamental principle in the field of finance: Default risk and expected return are positively related. The investor seeking higher expected returns must also be willing to accept greater risk of ruin. Moreover, default risk is correlated with both *internal* (borrower-specific) factors associated with a loan and *external* factors, especially the state of the economy and changing demands for a particular industry's product or service.

CALL PRIVILEGES

Nearly all corporate bonds and mortgages, most municipal revenue bonds, and some U.S. government bonds issued in today's financial markets carry a call privilege. This provision of the bond contract, or indenture, permits the borrower to retire all or a portion of a bond issue by buying back the securities in advance of maturity. Bondholders usually are informed of a call through a notice in a newspaper of general circulation, while holders of record of registered bonds are notified directly. For most bonds there is usually a period of *call deferment* (often 5 to 10 years) during which the security cannot be called in, thus giving the bondholder some call protection. Normally, when the call privilege is exercised, the security issuer will pay the investor the call price, which equals the securities' face value plus a call penalty. The size of the *call penalty* is set forth in the indenture (contract) and generally varies inversely with the number of years remaining to maturity and the length of the call deferment period. In the case of a bond, one year's worth of coupon income is often the minimum call penalty required.

Calculating the Yields on Called Securities

Bonds may be callable immediately or the privilege may be deferred (postponed) for a time. In the corporate sector, bonds usually are not eligible for call for a period of 5 to 10 years after issue in order to give investors at least some protection against early redemption. Of course, calling a security at any point in advance of its final maturity has an impact on the investor's effective yield.

To demonstrate this, we recall from Chapter 8 that the yield to maturity of any security is that discount rate, y, which equates the security's price, P, with the present value of all future cash flows, I_i, expected from holding the security. In symbols:

$$P = \frac{I_1}{(1 + y)^1} + \frac{I_2}{(1 + y)^2} + \cdots + \frac{I_n}{(1 + y)^n} \qquad (10-5)$$

where n is the number of periods until maturity. Suppose that after k periods (with k < n) the borrower exercises the call option and redeems the security. The investor will receive the call price (C) for the security, which can be reinvested at the current market interest rate, i. If the investor's planned holding period ends in time period n, the expected holding period yield (h) can be calculated using the following formula:

$$P = \frac{I_1}{(1 + h)^1} + \frac{I_2}{(1 + h)^2} + \cdots + \frac{I_k}{(1 + h)^k} + \frac{i \times C_{k+1}}{(1 + h)^{k+1}} \qquad (10-6)$$

$$+ \frac{i \times C_{k+2}}{(1 + h)^{k+2}} + \cdots + \frac{i \times C_n}{(1 + h)^n} + \frac{C}{(1 + h)^n}$$

Using summation signs, this reduces to:

$$P = \sum_{j=1}^{k} \frac{I_j}{(1 + h)^j} + \sum_{j=k+1}^{n} \frac{i \times C_j}{(1 + h)^j} + \frac{C}{(1 + h)^n} \qquad (10-7)$$

The first term in Equation 10–7 gives the present value of all expected cash flows (I) from the security until it is called in time period k. The second term captures the present value of income received by the investor after he or she reinvests at interest rate i the call price (C) received from the security issuer. The third and final term in the equation shows the current discounted value of the call price the investor expects to receive when the holding period ends in time period n.

As an example, let's suppose that a corporate bond, originally offering investors an 8 percent coupon rate for 10 years and issued at $1,000 par, is called 5 years after the issue date when going market interest rates on investments of comparable risk are 6 percent. What is this bond's 10-year holding period yield (h), if its call price equals par ($1,000) plus one year's worth of coupon income ($80)? We have:

$$\$1,000 = \sum_{t=1}^{5} \frac{\$80}{(1+h)^t} + \sum_{t=6}^{10} \frac{\$1,080 \times .06}{(1+h)^t} + \frac{\$1,080}{(1+h)^{10}} \qquad (10–8)$$

The reader, using the present value and annuity tables in Appendix B, should verify that h, the 10-year holding-period yield, is 7.94 percent in this instance. Thus, the investor holding this bond received 0.06 percent less in yield than if the bond had not been called and had been held to maturity.

Equation 10–7 shows quite clearly that the investor in callable securities encounters two major uncertainties:

1. The investor does not know if or when the securities might be called (i.e., the value of k).

2. The investor does not know the market yield (reinvestment rate, i) that might prevail at the time the security is called.

Therefore, how aggressively the investor chooses to bid for a callable instrument will depend on:

1. The investor's expectations regarding future changes in interest rates, especially decreases in rates, during the term of the security.

2. The length of the deferment period before the security is eligible to be called.

3. The call price (face or par value plus call penalty) the issuer is willing to pay to redeem the security.

Advantages and Disadvantages of the Call Privilege

Clearly, the call privilege is an advantage to the security issuer because it grants greater financial flexibility and the potential for reducing future interest costs. On the other hand, the call privilege is a distinct disadvantage to the security buyer, who may suffer a decline in the expected holding period yield if the security is in fact called. The issuer will call in a security if the market rate of interest falls far enough so that the savings from issuing a new security at lower interest rates more than offset the call penalty plus flotation costs of a new security issue. This means, however, that the investor who is paid off will be forced to reinvest the call price in lower yielding securities.

Another disadvantage for the investor is that call privileges limit the potential increase in a security's market price. In general, the market price of a security will not rise significantly above its call price, even when interest rates fall. The reason is that the issuer can call in a security at its call price, presenting the investor with a loss equal to the difference between the prevailing market price and the call price. Thus, callable securities have a more limited potential for capital gains than noncallable securities.

The Call Premium and Interest Rate Expectations

For all of these reasons, securities that carry a call privilege generally sell at lower prices and higher interest rates than noncallable securities. Moreover, there is an inverse relationship between the length of the call deferment period and the required rate of interest on callable securities. The longer the period of deferment and therefore the longer the investor is protected against early redemption, the lower the interest rate the borrower must pay. Issuers of callable securities must pay a call premium in the form of a higher rate of interest for the option of early redemption and for a shorter period of deferment.

The key determinant of the size of the call premium is the *interest rate expectations* of investors in the marketplace. If interest rates are expected to rise over the term of a security, the risk that the security will be called is low. Borrowers are highly unlikely to call in their securities and issue new ones at higher interest. As a result, the yield differential between callable and noncallable securities normally will be minimal. The same conclusions apply even if interest rates are expected to decline moderately but not enough to entice borrowers to call in securities and issue new ones.

It is when interest rates are expected to fall substantially that securities are most likely to be called. In this instance security issuers can save large amounts of money—more than enough to cover the call penalty plus flotation costs of new securities—by exercising the call privilege. Thus, the call premium is likely to be significant as investors demand a higher yield on callable issues to compensate them for increased call risk. Moreover, the yield spreads between bonds with long call deferments versus those with short or no call deferments widen during such periods as investors come to value more highly the deferment feature.

Research Evidence

Is there evidence of an *inverse* relationship between interest rate expectations and the value of the call privilege? Recent research answers in the affirmative. For example, Cook (1973) finds that, when interest rates are high, the call premium rises because investors expect interest rates to fall in the future. Moreover, he points out that call provisions also influence yield spreads between corporate bonds, nearly all of which have the call privilege attached, and municipal and U.S. government bonds, which generally are not subject to call. For example, when interest rates are expected to fall, the spread between corporate and U.S. government bond rates tends to widen. Pye (1966, 1967) and Jen and Wert (1966, 1967, 1968) find additional evidence that bonds carrying a call deferment have lower rates of return than bonds that are callable immediately.

Effect of Coupon Rates on Call Risk

Finally, we should note that the coupon rate on a bond is closely related to the investor's call risk. We recall from Chapter 8 that a bond's coupon rate is the rate of return against the security's par value promised by the borrower. High coupon rates mean that a bond issuer is forced to pay high interest costs as long as the bond is outstanding. Therefore, there is a strong incentive to call in such bonds and replace them with lower coupon securities.

Another problem is that bonds bearing high coupons have less opportunity for capital gains than bonds carrying lower coupon rates. This is true because the market value of a high coupon security is usually close to its call price ceiling. In contrast, bonds with more modest coupon rates sell at lower prices and carry considerably more potential for capital gains before hitting the call price. This means there is more risk of call and less potential capital gain to the investor who chooses high coupon securities. As a result, the issuer of such securities must pay a higher yield to induce investors to buy them and accept greater call risk.

TAXATION OF SECURITY RETURNS

Taxes imposed by federal, state, and local governments have a profound effect on the returns earned by investors on financial assets. The income from most securities—interest or dividends and capital gains—is subject to taxation at the federal level and by many state and local governments as well. Government uses its taxing power to encourage purchases of certain financial assets and thereby redirect the flow of savings and investment toward areas of critical social need.

In 1986 Congress enacted the Tax Reform Act, which resulted in major changes in personal and business tax rates in the United States and could have major redistributive effects on the financial markets, the supply of savings, and the demand for loanable funds. Exhibit 10–4 summarizes a number of the most important provisions of the revised federal tax code. The new law reduced personal and corporate tax rates substantially, which

Exhibit 10–4   **Changes in Federal Tax Laws: The 1986 Tax Reform Act**

Purpose: To bring about greater tax equity, resulting in corporations paying more taxes and individuals and families generally less in taxes. Overall, the new tax code was designed to be revenue neutral.

Changes in Personal Tax Rates: A complicated schedule of 15 different tax rates and income brackets was replaced by two basic tax rates of 15 percent and 28 percent plus a 5 percent surtax on high-income taxpayers.

Changes in Corporate Tax Rates: The largest corporations will pay a new basic tax rate of 34 percent for any net income over $235,000 instead of the old rate of 46 percent. The minimum corporate tax rate is 15 percent. Earnings losses may be carried backward for 3 years and then forward for up to 15 years. Stock dividends received from another corporation are 80 percent tax-exempt instead of 85 percent exempt under the old tax code.

Capital Gains: All capital gains must be treated as ordinary income taxable at standard personal and corporate tax rates, replacing the old preferential tax rate on long-term capital gains. Capital losses may be used to offset capital gains up to a maximum of $3,000 per year.

Personal Deductions: Home mortgage interest is deductible from taxable income, but nonmortgage loan interest payments will not be deductible after 1990. State and local sales taxes no longer are deductible expenses, and many unprofitable tax shelters are restricted or eliminated. The standard deduction for those individuals not itemizing deductible items is $5,000 on joint returns and $3,000 for singles.

Depreciation: The estimated useful life of structures and equipment is increased, reducing the annual tax deduction for depreciation of capital goods.

Investment Tax Credit: Eliminated.

State and Local Government (Municipal) Securities: Interest earnings on municipal notes and bonds are still federal income-tax-exempt and exempted by most states as well for issuers within their borders. However, state and local government debt issued for private benefit (such as to build facilities for business firms) is generally not tax-exempt. Moreover, commercial banks can no longer deduct the interest cost of borrowed funds used to purchase municipal notes and bonds.

---

has tended to increase the after-tax cost of borrowing money. Moreover, favorable capital gains tax rates (previously a maximum of 20 percent) have been eliminated, and capital gains are now taxable at ordinary income tax rates.

The Tax Treatment of Capital Gains

Under current tax rules administered by the Internal Revenue Service, an increase in the value of a capital asset (including stocks and bonds) which the taxpayer converts into cash is subject to federal income taxation. For example, if you had purchased stock in XYZ Corporation for $1,900 and sold it at a later date for $3,100, you would have experienced a capital gain of $1,200. Under the Tax Reform Act of 1986, the capital gain of $1,200 is taxable as ordinary income at your current income tax rate. Thus, a $1,200 capital gain for an investor in the 28 percent tax bracket would result in a tax liability of $336 ($1,200 × 0.28).

Treatment of Capital Losses

Net losses on security investments are deductible for tax purposes within well-defined limits. For the individual taxpayer, a net capital loss is deductible up to the amount of the capital loss, the size of the ordinary income, or $3,000, whichever is smaller. For example, suppose an investor experiences a net loss on securities held and then sold of $8,000. Suppose this person receives other taxable income of $20,000. How much of the capital loss can be deducted? What is this taxpayer's total taxable income? The maximum loss deduction in this case is $3,000, and therefore the taxpayer's net taxable income is $17,000 ($20,000 minus the $3,000 in deductible losses). Current federal law does allow the taxpayer to carry forward into subsequent years the remaining portion of the loss ($5,000 in this example) until all the loss has been deducted from ordinary income, but the loss cannot be carried backward.

Tax-Exempt Securities

One of the most controversial tax rules affecting securities is the tax-exemption privilege granted investors in state and local government (municipal) bonds. The interest income earned on municipal bonds is exempt from federal income taxes, and most states exempt interest on their own securities from state income taxes. Tax-exempt securities represent a subsidy to induce investors to support local government by financing the construction of schools, highways, bridges, airports, and other needed public projects. The exemption privilege shifts the burden of federal taxation from buyers of municipal bonds to other taxpayers.

What investors benefit from buying municipals? The critical factor here is the marginal tax rate (tax bracket) of the investor—the tax rate he or she must pay on the last dollar of income received during the tax year. For individual investors, these marginal tax rates range from zero for nontaxpayers to as high as 28 percent (plus a surtax of 5 percent in some cases) for the highest income earners (see Exhibit 10–5 for an example of marginal tax rates applying to individuals and corporations). The marginal rate for corporations is 15 percent on the first $50,000 in taxable profits up to as high as 34 percent on net income above $335,000. In recent years, marginal tax rates of around 20 percent have represented a breakeven level for investors interested in municipal bonds. Investors carrying marginal tax rates

Exhibit 10–5   **Examples of Marginal Federal Income Tax Rates (Tax Brackets)**

Married Individual Taxpayers Filing Joint Returns		Corporations Subject to Income Taxes	
Taxable Income	**Applicable Tax Rate**	**Taxable Income**	**Applicable Tax Rate**
Up to $29,750	15%	Less than $50,000	15%
$29,750–$71,900	28	$50,000–$75,000	25
$71,900–$149,250	33	$75,000–$100,000	34
Over $149,250	28	$100,000–$335,000	39
		Over $335,000	34

above this range generally receive higher after-tax yields from buying tax-exempt securities instead of taxable securities. Below this range, taxable securities generally yield a better after-tax return.

The Effect of Marginal Tax Rates on After-Tax Yields. To illustrate the importance of knowing the investor's marginal tax rate in deciding whether to purchase tax-exempt securities, consider the following example. Assume the current yield to maturity on taxable corporate bonds is 12 percent, while the current tax-exempt yield on municipal bonds of comparable quality and rating is 9 percent. The after-tax yield on these two securities can be compared by using the following formula:

$$\text{Before-tax yield } (1 - \text{Investor's marginal tax rate}) \qquad (10\text{--}9)$$
$$= \text{After-tax yield}$$

For an investor in the 28-percent tax bracket (see Exhibit 10–5), the after-tax yields on these bonds are:

Taxable Corporate Bond	Tax-Exempt Municipal Bonds
12% (1 − 0.28) = 8.64%	9% before and after taxes

On the basis of yield alone, the investor in the 28 percent tax bracket would prefer the tax-exempt municipal bond.[5]

At what rate would an investor be *indifferent* to whether securities are taxable or tax exempt? In other words, what is the breakeven point between these two types of financial instruments?

This point is easily calculated from the formula

$$\text{Tax-exempt yield} = (1 - t) \times \text{Taxable yield} \qquad (10\text{--}10)$$

where t is the investor's marginal tax rate. Solving for the breakeven tax rate gives

---

[5]The particular tax brackets favoring the purchase of municipals versus taxable securities change over time due to changes in tax laws and variations in the yield spread between taxable and tax-exempt securities.

$$t = 1 - \frac{\text{Tax-exempt yield}}{\text{Taxable yield}} \qquad (10\text{–}11)$$

Clearly, if the current yield on tax-exempt securities is 8 percent and it is 10 percent on taxable issues, the breakeven tax rate is $1 - 0.80$, or 20 percent. An investor in a marginal tax bracket *above* 20 percent would prefer a tax-exempt security to a taxable one, other factors held equal.

Comparing Taxable and Tax-Exempt Securities. The existence of both taxable and tax-exempt securities complicates the investor's task in trying to choose a suitable portfolio to buy and hold. In order to make valid comparisons between taxable and tax-exempt issues, the investor must convert all expected security yields to an after-tax basis.

In the case of the yield to maturity on a security, this can be done by using the following formula:

$$P_o = \sum_{i=1}^{n} \frac{I_i(1-t)}{(1+a)^i} + \frac{(P_n - P_o)(1-t)}{(1+a)^n} + \frac{P_o}{(1+a)^n} \qquad (10\text{–}12)$$

which equates the current market value (P_o) of the security to the present value of all after-tax returns promised in the future. If the security is to be held for n years, I_i is the amount of interest or other income expected each year and t is the marginal income tax rate of the investor. If we assume the security will be sold or redeemed for price P_n at maturity, then $(P_n - P_o)$ measures the expected capital gain on the instrument which, of course, will be taxed at the taxpayer's ordinary income tax rate under the terms of the 1986 Tax Reform Act. Provided investors know their marginal income tax rate, the current price of the security, and the expected distribution of future income from the security, they can easily calculate discount rate a—the after-tax yield to maturity.

For example, consider the case of a $1,000 corporate bond selling for $900 (with par equal to $1,000), maturing in 10 years, with a 10 percent coupon rate. If an investor in the 28 percent federal income tax bracket buys and holds the bond to maturity, his after-tax yield, a, could be found from evaluating:

$$\$900 = \sum_{t=1}^{10} \frac{\$100(1-0.28)}{(1+a)^t} + \frac{(\$1,000 - \$900)(1-0.28)}{(1+a)^{10}} + \frac{\$900}{(1+a)^{10}}$$

In this instance the reader should verify, using the annuity and present value tables in Appendix B, that the after-tax yield, a, is 8.57 percent.

Certainly the tax-exempt privilege has lowered the interest rates at which municipals can be sold in the open market relative to taxable bonds, and therefore the amount of interest cost borne by local taxpayers. For example, in February 1988, Aaa-rated municipal bonds carried an average yield to maturity of 7.05 percent compared to 9.40 percent on comparable quality seasoned (taxable) corporate bonds—a yield spread of just over 2 percentage points. However, the primary beneficiaries of the exemption privilege are *investors* who can profitably purchase municipals and escape some portion of the federal tax burden. Other taxpayers must pay higher federal taxes in order to make up for those lost tax revenues. Moreover, by limiting the municipal market to these high tax bracket investors, the tax-exemption feature has probably increased the unpredictability of municipal bond interest rates and made the job of state and local government fiscal management more difficult.

CONVERTIBLE SECURITIES

Another factor that affects relative rates of return on different securities is convertibility. Convertible securities consist of special issues of corporate bonds or preferred stock which entitle the holder to exchange these securities for a specific number of shares of the issuing firm's common stock. Convertibles are frequently called hybrid securities because they offer the investor the prospect of both stable income in the form of interest or dividends plus capital gains on common stock once conversion takes place. The timing of a conversion is purely at the option of the investor; however, the contract agreed to at time of purchase specifies the terms under which conversion may take place. An issuing firm often can "force" conversion of its securities by either calling them in or by encouraging a rise in the price of its common stock (such as by announcing a merger offer), because conversion is most likely to occur in a rising market. Conversion is a one-way transaction—once convertibles are exchanged for common stock, there is no way back for the investor.

Investors generally pay a premium for convertible securities over nonconvertible securities in the form of a higher price and reduced yield. Thus, convertibles will carry a lower rate of return than other securities of comparable quality and maturity issued by the same company. This occurs because the investor in convertibles is granted a hedge against future risk. If security prices fall, the investor still earns a fixed rate of return in the form of interest income from a convertible bond or dividend income from each share of convertible preferred stock. On the other hand, if stock prices rise, the investor can exercise his or her option and share in any capital gains earned on the company's common stock. Of course, convertibles are most attractive in a period of rising stock prices and declining interest rates.

Bonds with the convertible feature are nearly always issued as debentures. A *debenture* is a long-term corporate IOU that is unsecured in the sense that no specific collateral is pledged to support the security in the event of financial problems. Instead, the debenture is backed by the general earning power of the issuing corporation, which promises to pay interest at specified times and return the principal (par) value of the security at maturity. The interest and principal amount owed on a convertible bond must be paid before any dividends are paid on the issuing company's preferred and common stock. Most convertibles are callable bonds and, like other callable bonds, are worth no more than their call price on the day of redemption.

Convertible bonds offer several significant advantages to the issuing company. Due to the conversion feature they can be issued at a lower net interest cost than conventional (nonconvertible) bonds. Convertibles offer an alternative to issuing more common stock which a firm may wish to avoid because the additional stock could dilute the equity interest of current stockholders and reduce earnings per share. Moreover, dividends on stock are not deductible from federal income taxes, but interest on convertible bonds *is* a tax-deductible expense.

Key advantages to the investor include the fact that convertible bonds guarantee the payment of interest (as long as the issuing company remains solvent) and generally appreciate in value when the company's common stock is rising in price. Moreover, there is a floor under the price of a convertible bond—known as its *investment value*—below which its price normally will not fall. This is the price which would produce a yield on the convertible equal to the yield on nonconvertible bonds of the same quality and credit rating. However, investors are often counseled by financial analysts not to buy convertibles unless they would be happy holding the issuing company's stock because the issuer may call in the securities early, thereby forcing conversion. (Many convertible issues are accompanied by a sinking fund provision that requires the issuer to call in a few securities each year.) This situation may present the investor with a substantially reduced return on investment, especially if the convertibles are called within a few years of their issue date, because when new, they usually sell at substantial premiums above their conversion value. It normally takes at least a few months and sometimes a few years for the investor to recover the purchase premium.

Convertible bonds have been exceedingly popular securities in recent years. The number of convertibles listed on the New York Stock Exchange nearly doubled during the 1970s, for example. Firms issuing convertible bonds in recent years number among the largest corporations in the United States, including such firms as Alcoa, American Motors, Chase Manhattan Corporation, General Telephone, RCA, U.S. Steel Corporation, and United Airlines. Innovative types of convertibles have appeared in recent years, including floating-rate securities with interest returns linked to dividends on the issuing company's stock. Convertibles are generally regarded as a more conservative investment than purchasing the stock of the same company because they offer less risk than stock. They also provide less potential return, of course; nevertheless, convertibles permit an investor to get a piece of the action in the stock market without actually holding stock.

THE STRUCTURE OF INTEREST RATES

As we conclude this chapter, it is important to gain some perspective on the fundamental purpose of this section of the book. In reality, Chapters 7, 8, 9, and 10 should be viewed as a unit, tied together by a common subject— what determines the level of and changes in interest rates and security yields. In Chapter 7 we argued that there is *one* interest rate which underlies all interest rates and is a component of all rates. This is the *risk-free* (or pure) rate of interest, which is a measure of the opportunity cost of holding money and a measure of the reward for saving money rather than spending all of our income on consumption. All other interest rates are scaled upward by varying degrees from the risk-free rate, depending on such factors as the term (maturity) of a loan, the risk of borrower default, and the marketability, liquidity, callability, convertibility, and tax status of the securities to which those rates apply. However, the interest rates attached to all securities have the risk-free rate in common.

There is, then, a structure to interest rates whose foundation is the risk-free rate (as determined by the demand and supply for loanable funds described in Chapter 7). Perhaps one picture of that interest rate structure is worth a thousand words. Recently, the yield to maturity on long-term U.S. Treasury bonds was reported as 8.25 percent, while corporate BAA bonds were quoted at an average yield of 10.43 percent. As Exhibit 10–6 indicates, each of these rates, like *all* interest rates, is really a summation of rewards (premiums) paid to investors (lenders of funds) to get those investors to hold a particular security. Each reward or premium is merely compensation for bearing some kind of *risk;* for example, (1) the risk of giving up liquidity and accepting greater price risk from buying a longer maturity security; (2) the risk of inflation over the term of a security; (3) the risk the borrower will default on some or all of his or her promised payments; (4) the risk that some securities can be called in before they mature and the investor may have to reinvest his or her money at a lower interest rate; and (5) the risk of taking on a security with a weak resale market (low marketability). Each interest rate or yield that we see in today's market is the *sum* of some or all of these risk-premium factors plus the real risk-free interest rate. And, when interest rates change, that change may be due to a change in the risk-free rate or to a change in any of the risk-premium factors cited above.

Truly, interest rates are a complex phenomenon, affected by many factors and influences. We need to keep this complexity in mind as we proceed to the next chapter and take on the difficult tasks of trying to anticipate and forecast interest rate changes and to hedge against any possible losses from interest rate movements.

Exhibit 10–6   An Example of the Structure of Interest Rates in the Financial System

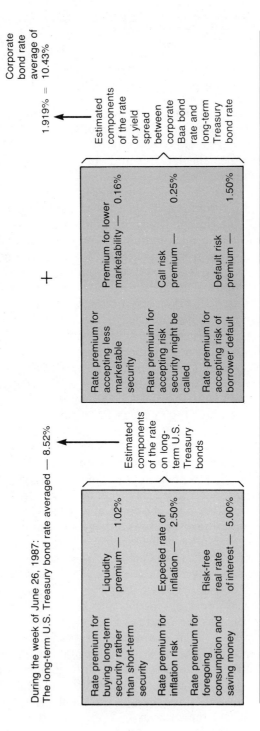

During the week of June 26, 1987:
The long-term U.S. Treasury bond rate averaged — 8.52%

← Estimated components of the rate on long-term U.S. Treasury bonds

Rate premium for buying long-term security rather than short-term security	Liquidity premium — 1.02%
Rate premium for inflation risk	Expected rate of inflation — 2.50%
Rate premium for foregoing consumption and saving money	Risk-free real rate of interest — 5.00%

+

1.919% = Corporate bond rate average of 10.43%

← Estimated components of the rate or yield spread between corporate Baa bond rate and long-term Treasury bond rate

Rate premium for accepting less marketable security	Premium for lower marketability — 0.16%
Rate premium for accepting risk security might be called	Call risk premium — 0.25%
Rate premium for accepting risk of borrower default	Default risk premium — 1.50%

Source: Bond rates from the *Federal Reserve Bulletin*, September 1987; components of rates estimated by the author.

STUDY QUESTIONS

1. Define the term *marketability*. Explain its importance to the securities investor and its relationship to the yield on a financial instrument.

2. Explain the meaning of the phrase *default risk*. What factors appear to influence the degree of default risk displayed by a security? In what ways are security ratings designed to reflect default risk?

3. What is a *call privilege?* Why is this privilege an advantage to the security issuer and a disadvantage to the investor?

4. What types of risk are encountered by the investor in callable securities? Does the coupon rate on a bond influence its call risk?

5. Which kinds of securities are favored by current U.S. tax laws? Explain why these particular financial instruments are given favorable tax treatment.

6. What portion of the income generated by municipal bonds is tax-exempt, and what portion is taxable under federal law? Why do you think the law is structured in this way? Should it be?

7. Explain the relationship between the investor's marginal tax rate and after-tax yields on corporate and municipal bonds. Would municipal bonds be a worthwhile investment for you today? Why?

8. Define the term *convertibility*. Why are convertibles sometimes called hybrid securities? Convertible bonds typically carry lower yields than nonconvertible bonds of the same maturity and risk class. Explain why this is true.

PROBLEMS

1. In a recent Federal Reserve publication, the following market interest rates or yields were reported:

Three-month Treasury bills	10.22%
One-year Treasury bills	10.38
Five-year Treasury bonds	12.52
Long-term Treasury bonds	12.38
Corporate Ba bonds	14.24
Aaa municipal bonds	10.15

Calculate the difference in percentage points and basis points between these rates. *Explain* the rate differences you derive in terms of the factors discussed in Chapters 9 and 10.

2. The market yield to maturity on a risky bond is currently listed at 14.50 percent. The risk-free interest rate is estimated to be 9.25 percent. What is the default risk premium, all other factors removed? The promised yield on this bond is 15 percent. A certain investor, looking at this bond,

estimates there is a 25 percent probability the bond will pay 15 percent at maturity, a 50 percent probability it will pay a 10 percent return, and a 25 percent probability it will yield only 5 percent. What is the bond's expected yield? What is this investor's anticipated default loss? Will the investor buy this bond?

3. A 10-year corporate bond was issued on January 1, 1982 with call privilege attached. The bond was sold to investors at $1,000 par value with a 10 percent coupon rate. The bond was called on January 1, 1985, at a price to holders of par plus one year's coupon income. At the time prevailing market interest rates on securities of comparable quality and term was 8 percent. If a holder of this bond reinvested the call price at 8 percent for 7 years, calculate this investor's holding period yield for the entire period of 10 years. How much yield did the investor lose as a result of the call?

4. Aaa-rated municipal bonds are carrying a market yield today of 5.25 percent, while Aaa-rated corporate bonds have current market yields of 11.50 percent. What is the breakeven tax rate that would make a taxable investor indifferent between these two types of bonds?

5. An investor purchases a 10-year U.S. government bond for $800. The bond's coupon rate is 10 percent and at time of purchase it still had five years remaining till maturity. If the investor holds the bond until it matures and collects the $1,000 par value from the Treasury and his marginal tax rate remains at 28 percent, what will be his after-tax yield to maturity?

SELECTED REFERENCES

Altman, Edward I. "The Success of Business Failure Prediction Models." *Journal of Banking and Finance* 8 (1984), pp. 171–98.

Cook, Timothy Q. "Some Factors Affecting Long-Term Yield Spreads in Recent Years." *Monthly Review,* Federal Reserve Bank of Richmond, September 1973, pp. 2–14.

Fisher, Lawrence. "Determinants of Risk Premiums on Corporate Bonds." *Journal of Political Economy,* June 1959, pp. 217–37.

Hickman, W. Braddock. *Corporate Bond Quality and Investor Experience.* New York: National Bureau of Economic Research, 1958.

Jaffee, Dwight, M. "Cyclical Variations in the Risk Structure of Interest Rates." *Journal of Monetary Economics,* July 1975, pp. 309–25.

Jen, Frank C., and James E. Wert. "The Value of the Deferred Call Privilege." *The National Banking Review,* March 1966, pp. 269–78.

———. "The Effect of Call Risk on Corporate Bond Yields." *Journal of Finance,* December 1967, pp. 637–51.

————. "The Deferred Call Provision and Corporate Bond Yields." *Journal of Financial and Quantitative Analysis,* June 1968, pp. 157–69.

Mehra, Yash. "The Tax Effect, and the Recent Behavior of the After-Tax Real Rate: Is It Too High?" *Economic Review,* Federal Reserve Bank of Richmond, July/August 1984, pp. 8–20.

Holthausen, Robert W., and Richard W. Leftwich. "The Effect of Bond Rating Changes on Common Stock Prices." *Journal of Financial Economics* 17 (1986), pp. 57–89.

Pye, Gordon. "The Value of the Call Option on a Bond." *Journal of Political Economy,* April 1966, pp. 200–05.

————. "The Value of Call Deferment on a Bond: Some Empirical Results." *Journal of Finance,* December 1967, pp. 623–36.

Scott, James. "The Probability of Bankruptcy: A Comparison of Empirical Predictions and Theoretical Models." *Journal of Banking and Finance* 5 (1981), pp. 317–44.

Chapter 11

Interest Rate Forecasting and Hedging against Interest Rate Risk

Learning Objectives in This Chapter

- To examine the effect that the business cycle of expansions (boom periods) and recessions has on interest rates.
- To determine if interest rates display seasonal movements.
- To review the most popular methods used to forecast interest rates in recent years.
- To examine several important ways used today to hedge a borrower or a lender against the risk of loss from changes in interest rates.

Key Terms and Concepts in This Chapter

Business cycle
Seasonality
Money supply liquidity
    effect
Money supply
    expectations effect

Money supply income
    effect
Fisher effect
Econometric models
Forward calendar
Implied Rate forecast
Consensus forecast
Rate hedging methods
Duration
GAP Management

Financial futures
Put and call options
Rate cap
Rate collars
Interest rate insurance
Loan options
Interest rate SWAP

IN this section of the book we have looked at a few of the most important factors that cause interest rates and security prices to change over time. Included in our survey have been such powerful rate- and price-determining factors as savings, investment demand, inflation, maturity, default risk, taxes, marketability, convertibility, and call features. Yet even this impressive list of influential factors does not account for all the changes in interest rates and security prices that we observe daily in the real world. Political developments at home and abroad, changes in government economic policy, news reports of changes in corporate earnings or business conditions, announcements of new security offerings, and thousands of other bits of information flood the financial markets daily and bring fluctuations in interest rates and security prices. In fact, for actively traded securities (such as stocks listed on the New York Stock Exchange or U.S. government bonds) demand and supply forces are continually shifting, minute by minute, so that investors interested in these securities must constantly stay abreast of the latest developments in the financial marketplace. Prices and interest rates sometimes change so fast that even a few minutes' delay in receiving new information can mean substantial losses for the uninformed investor.

THE INFLUENCE OF THE BUSINESS CYCLE IN SHAPING INTEREST RATES

Amid the turmoil of daily movements in interest rates and security prices there are certain long-run factors that seem to create trends or patterns in both rates and prices. One of the most obvious of these patterns relates to the condition of the nation's economy—whether the economy is in a period of expansion, with production, jobs, and income rising (often accompanied by rising inflation) or in a period of recession, with falling production and rising unemployment. These phases of the business cycle may last for months or years, in some cases, and interest rates tend to move with them (with short leads or lags), because the demand for and supply of loanable funds changes with the business cycle. *Interest rates tend to fall* (and the prices of bonds and other debt securities rise) *during a business recession, while interest rates typically rise* (and debt security prices fall) *during a period of economic expansion.*

None of this should be particularly surprising. An expansion period encourages both businesses and consumers to borrow more relative to the available supply of loanable funds, and the resulting increase in the demand for loanable funds drives up interest rates. In contrast, during recessions businesses and consumers become more cautious, reducing their borrowings relative to the available supply of loanable funds and building up their savings as a precaution against possible unemployment, declining sales, and loss of income. Interest rates usually fall during such periods, then, under the combined pressure of reduced credit demands and a larger supply of savings.

The typical cyclical movement in interest rates is illustrated in Exhibit 11–1 which tracks changes in rates (yields) on long-term U.S. Treasury, corporate, and municipal bonds. The U.S. economy entered a recession as the 1970s began, and bonds yields declined sharply after mid-1970, reaching a low point in late 1971. As business sales and employment recovered from this recession, interest rates climbed to new highs, peaking in mid-1974 just after the oil embargo. There followed in 1975 one of the worse business

Exhibit 11–1   Average Yields on Long-Term Treasury, Corporate, and Municipal Bonds

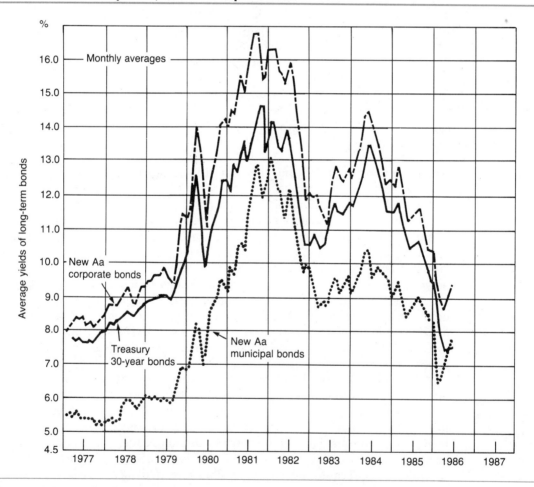

Source: *U.S. Treasury Bulletin*, Third Quarter, Fiscal 1987, p. 38.

recessions since World War II. Declining industrial production and a sharp rise in unemployment were accompanied by a long-term decline in interest rates, which did not cease until the latter half of 1977 in the market for municipal bonds. Then a sharp rebound in economic activity during 1978 and 1979, accompanied by soaring double-digit inflation, sent interest rates to unprecedented highs early in 1980. However, reflecting once again the powerful influence of the business cycle upon the financial markets, interest rates plummeted rapidly beginning in the spring of 1980 as the economy entered the next business recession, rising during the brief recovery in 1981 before declining sharply in 1982 as another recession occurred. Then interest rates rose in 1983 and through most of 1984 as the economy recovered and grew rapidly. However, interest rates began to retreat in late 1984 and early 1985 as the economy's growth rate slowed, inflation moderated, and loan demand tapered off. More rapid economic growth then set in during 1986 and 1987, and interest rates correspondingly edged higher again.

Relative Movements in Short- and Long-Term Interest Rates and Security Prices over the Business Cycle

The cyclical movements in the economy do not fall evenly across the broad spectrum of interest rates. In general, short-term interest rates (those attached to money market securities) are more volatile and sensitive to business cycle changes than are long-term interest rates on bonds and other capital market securities. Exhibit 11–2 depicts the typical pattern displayed by long- and short-term interest rates during the course of the business cycle.

During an expansion period, when the economy is growing at a rapid pace, *all* interest rates—both long- and short-term—tend to rise. However, short-term interest rates typically rise faster than long-term rates and at some point, in the later stages of the expansion, may climb above long-term rates. This means, of course, that at certain phases of the business cycle, especially around cyclical peaks, borrowers negotiating a loan for, say, six months will actually pay higher annual interest rates than for the same loan stretched over 5 or 10 years. Thus, the yield curve typically has a positive slope during most of the expansion phase of the business cycle, probably due to the expectations of rising interest rates on the part of investors. Around the cyclical peak and in the early stages of the ensuing business recession, however, yield curves usually assume a negative slope as investors come to expect declining interest rates. Once the expansion phase of the cycle is over and the economy starts down into a recession, however, *all* rates begin to fall. But short-term interest rates typically drop faster than long-term rates and fall below long-term rates as the recession deepens. Thus, at some point midway in a recession the yield curve typically will again assume a *positive* slope. Once the trough (low point) of the reces-

Exhibit 11–2   **Interest Rates over the Course of a Business Cycle**

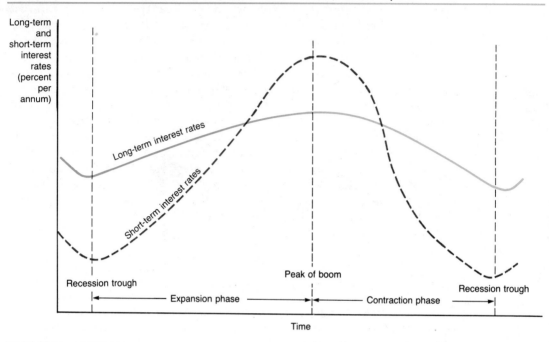

sion is reached and recovery begins, the process is repeated with short-term interest rates rising more rapidly than long-term rates.

Why do long-term and short-term interest rates behave in this way? Their behavior reflects another important relationship which exists between security prices and interest rates in the financial system:

> Long-term security prices tend to be more volatile than the prices of short-term securities. In contrast, short-term interest rates tend to be more volatile than long-term interest rates.

Fluctuations in market prices, then, will tend to be greater the longer the maturity of a security. This conclusion follows logically if we examine the yield to maturity formula discussed in Chapter 8. This formula indicates that the market price of any security equals the present value of all its promised future payments, but each future payment is discounted by the security's yield. With a long-term security there are more future payments affected by any change in yield than is true for a short-term security. Therefore, a given increase in interest rates will bring about a greater decrease in the price (present value) of a long-term security than in the price of a short-term security. Similarly, for the same decrease in interest rates, the price (present value) of a short-term security will be less affected than the price of a long-term security.

The greater volatility of long-term security prices means that investors in bonds and other long-term financial instruments face greater risk of capital loss (increased *principal risk*) than investors in short-term securities. Partly as a result, interest rates charged on long-term loans are usually higher than those charged for short-term credit, other things being equal. Lenders must be compensated for the added risk of price fluctuations associated with long-term financial instruments. Of course, the long-term investor has the offsetting advantage of receiving a more stable rate of return (reduced *income risk*) than the short-term investor. Long-term securities generally provide a more stable cash flow over an extended period until they are sold or redeemed than is true of short-term securities.

SEASONALITY

Just as interest rates change with cycles in business activity there is some evidence that interest rates also display seasonality — tending to be higher at some times of the year than at others. If seasonal rate patterns were consistent and predictable this would be extremely important information for both borrowers and lenders, for it would suggest the best times of the year to borrow and lend money. While there is a diversity of opinion on the subject, most studies seem to agree that interest rates do display seasonal patterns. In particular, short-term rates tend to be pushed higher through the summer and fall months due to rising seasonal demand for short-term funds, especially as businesses stock their shelves with inventory for the fall. From January through May, on the other hand, slackening demand for short-term credit encourages short-term interest rates to fall, *other factors held equal.* Long-term interest rates, on the other hand, tend to experience upward pressure in the late spring through midsummer (June or July), perhaps related to the higher level of construction activity normally occurring during this time of the year, and then long-term rates approach seasonal lows in the winter months.

Several notes of caution should be added here, however. First, these seasonal patterns are easily overridden by other factors such as changes in the economy or in government economic policy. For example, the Federal Reserve System frequently uses its monetary policy tools to counteract seasonal changes in the supply and demand for loanable funds. Second, limited evidence suggests the observed seasonal patterns are not stable over time.[1] Third, unpredictable events, such as droughts, changes in laws and regulations, political turmoil, and energy crises, often create false signals of seasonal interest rate pressures. In general, we can say that seasonal in-

---

[1]See, for example, Kohn (1974) and Barth and Bennett (1975).

terest rate patterns probably exist, but they are usually of minor importance in explaining interest rate changes.

FORECASTING INTEREST RATES: ADVANTAGES AND PROBLEMS[2]

The tendency of interest rates to move up and down with the business cycle and to some extent with seasonal pressures has led economists and financial analysts to believe that many rate movements can be predicted. By using variables that reflect changing economic conditions—GNP, employment, industrial production, savings flows, consumer prices, and so on—it seems logical to expect that at least broad, longer-term movements in interest rates can be forecast successfully (assuming, of course, that the forecaster has confidence in the forecast of the economy itself).

Advantages of Rate Forecasting

Clearly it would be an advantage to almost everyone (businesses, consumers, and governments) to be able to forecast interest rates accurately. Borrowers could plan to seek loans at those times when rates were supposed to be the lowest, saving hundreds or thousands of dollars in interest costs. A family considering the purchase of a new home with a variable-rate mortgage would be able to estimate how its monthly payments would change over time and whether the family budget could withstand future rate shifts. The same advantage would accrue to a business firm seeking a variable-rate bank loan to purchase inventories or fund a new warehouse. Banks and other lenders of funds could reduce their exposure to earnings risk and default risk by charging loan rates that were in line with their forecast of deposit rates. They would also be able to assess their borrowing customers' ability to service (meet future payments on) new floating-rate loans. When a large borrowing customer cannot repay a loan because of rising interest charges, both the customer and the bank are subject to greater risk of failure.

Problems in Forecasting Interest Rates

Unfortunately, while the ability to forecast interest rates would be enormously useful to almost everyone at one time or another, the problem is far from easy to solve. For one thing, as we saw in Chapter 7, there is a continuing controversy over which of several possible theories—loanable funds, rational expectations, and so on—explains how and why rates change. Clearly this matters greatly because each theory suggests that we gather

---

[2]This section is based, in part, on Rose's earlier article in the *Canadian Banker* (1984) and is used with the permission of that journal.

somewhat different information about the economy in order to predict which way rates are headed and suggests a different structuring of our forecasting equations. Moreover, if the financial markets are highly efficient, as much research evidence now suggests, all data relevant to where security prices and rates should be is already captured in those prices and rates. The theory of efficient markets implies that to be consistently right, the forecaster must either have access to data the market does not now possess or outguess the market on the implications of new information that has yet to be revealed. This is a difficult assignment!

An added problem is that the statistical forecasting tools currently at our disposal may be too crude to generate a consistently accurate forecast of rate movements. The reason should be obvious: We live in an economy composed of millions of households, businesses, and units of government who borrow money and generate savings. Each year tens of thousands of these individuals and institutions enter the financial markets to save (supply loanable funds) or borrow money (demand loanable funds). Each and every individual financial decision affects either the demand for or supply of loanable funds and therefore influences the price of credit. To really know for sure which way interest rates are headed, we would need a working model which incorporates those thousands of individual financial decisions. Even the largest, most sophisticated econometric forecasting models today—some of which contain several hundred equations and forecast 1,000 or more variables—cannot consistently deal with the enormity of detail in today's financial markets.[3] Perhaps as business and household computers are increasingly linked to each other and a majority of money flows in the economy are handled electronically we may be better able to track credit demand and supply forces and anticipate future rate changes; but that era still lies ahead of us.

APPROACHES TO MODERN INTEREST RATE FORECASTING

The inherent difficulties in interest rate and security price forecasting have not stopped economists and financial analysts from attempting to predict the future. They are impressed by the continual presence of broad trends in interest rates, particularly those related to the business cycle, to seasons of the year, and to Federal Reserve monetary policy. A number of forecasting models have been developed in recent years, and some have performed at least better than pure chance for short periods of time. Several of the more popular forecasting models are reviewed below.

---

[3]Another problem plaguing forecasters of interest rates is measurement errors in economic data, especially in national income and production data and money supply statistics. Often large errors are not picked up until revisions are made months later. Unfortunately, the largest econometric forecasting models in use today probably face the most serious data measurement problems because they rely on such huge amounts of current economic data.

Money Supply Approaches

Many financial analysts attempt to forecast short-run changes in interest rates, particularly short-term money market rates, by tracking weekly, monthly, and quarterly money supply figures. Each week the Federal Reserve System releases estimates of recent rates of growth in its various measures of the U.S. money supply. The most prominent of these measures are M1, the sum of currency and coin held by the public plus transaction (payments) accounts (such as non-interest-bearing checkbook (demand) deposits and interest-bearing NOW accounts); M2, the sum of M1 plus passbook savings deposits and other small-denomination thrift accounts and deposits; and M3, the sum of M2 plus large-denomination (over $100,000) savings accounts at banks, savings and loans, money market funds, and other nonbank institutions.[4]

Recall from Chapter 7 that changes in the money supply can be linked in theory to interest rate changes in several different ways. For example, the so-called money supply liquidity effect suggests that an increase in money supply growth (relative to money demand) results in lower interest rates in the short run. On the other hand, slower money growth (relative to money demand) should lead to short-run rises in interest rates. A contrary force, the money supply expectations effect, argues that, when the actual money supply growth rate exceeds the public's expected rate of money growth, interest rates will tend to rise, perhaps due to the public's fear of more inflation. Conversely, a slower than expected money growth rate will lead to lower interest rates as investors come to expect either less inflation or accelerated money growth in the future as government stimulates the money supply to grow faster. Many financial analysts believe the expectations effect has become more important than the liquidity effect since the Federal Reserve System announced in October 1979 that it would begin to concentrate its efforts on meeting preannounced money supply targets during the year. Thus, when actual money growth exceeds the Fed's announced target growth range, the public may fear that the Fed will attempt to slow future growth and drive up interest rates. In contrast, actual money supply growth below the Fed's target range may lead the public to predict lower interest rates in the future as the Federal Reserve accelerates growth to catch up to its target.

Recall from our discussion of interest rate theories in Chapter 7 that money supply changes can also influence interest rates through a money supply income effect. Specifically, an increase in total spending and income in the economy increases the public's demand for money, other factors held constant. If the nation's money supply remains fixed or grows more slowly than money demand, the relative increase in money demand will lead to

---

[4]See Chapter 24 for a more complete discussion of these and other measures of the nation's money supply or money stock.

higher interest rates. Conversely, a decline or slower growth in money demand—perhaps related to a slowing of income growth in the economy—will put downward pressure on interest rates, other factors held constant. Clearly, there should be a *positive* correlation between income and spending in the economy and market interest rates through income-caused changes in the demand for money with the money supply income effect. And such a positive relationship between total spending and interest rates does seem to hold over the course of most business cycles, as we noted at the beginning of this chapter.

How might an interest rate forecaster use the money supply income effect? Let's suppose the federal government or a professional forecasting firm has just released an estimate that nominal GNP—a widely used barometer of total spending in the economy—will increase at an 8 percent annual rate next year. However, the Federal Reserve System has just announced that its target range for growth in the nation's money supply (something it must reveal at least twice a year) is going to be just 4 to 6 percent next year. If the money supply does in fact grow this slowly while the public plans to increase its aggregate spending (GNP) by 8 percent, what must happen to interest rates? Clearly, they must *rise* to bring about a faster rate of turnover (velocity) in the money supply in order to accomodate the higher volume of planned spending.[5]

Of course, if the Fed achieves its relatively low money growth target, it is highly unlikely that GNP will be able to increase a full 8 percentage points because the resulting higher interest rates will discourage some borrowing and spending by the public. However, the point is that we can get a clue about the *direction* of future interest rate changes by comparing money supply growth estimates for a future period with forecasts of economic activity for that *same* period (assuming, of course, that we have confidence in both the money supply and economic forecasts). Thus,

1. If projected money supply growth > projected GNP growth, interest rates are likely to *fall*.
2. If projected money supply growth < projected GNP growth, interest rates are likely to *rise*.

Inflation and the Fisher Effect

In Chapter 9 we discussed still another possible approach to interest rate forecasting; that is, the Fisher effect, which asserts that *the nominal (published) interest rate charged by a lender of funds must equal the lender's expected real rate of return on the loan plus the expected rate of inflation over the life of the loan.* Many economists, including Irving Fisher, have

---

[5]For a detailed discussion of the theoretical and empirical linkages between money supply growth and fluctuations in income and production in the economy, see especially Poole (1975).

argued that the expected real rate is relatively constant—perhaps in the 3 to 3.5 percent range—in the long run. If true, observed changes in nominal interest rates will tend to reflect changes in the rate of inflation expected by lenders in the financial marketplace.

The table below suggests a simple forecasting strategy using the Fisher effect:

Forecasting Interest Rates Using the Fisher Effect

If lenders in the marketplace expect the inflation rate over the coming year to average	And the real rate of interest is expected to be	Then the nominal interest rate on a one-year loan according to the Fisher effect will be
1%	3 to 3.5%	4 to 4.5%
2	3 to 3.5	5 to 5.5
3	3 to 3.5	6 to 6.5
4	3 to 3.5	7 to 7.5
5	3 to 3.5	8 to 8.5
6	3 to 3.5	9 to 9.5

Of course, a key problem with this approach is estimating the rate of inflation expected by lenders over the life of a loan or security. Unfortunately there is little agreement at this point on the most accurate method of making such an estimate. One commonly used approach is to calculate a weighted average of past rates of inflation (often with declining weights so that more recent inflation news is more heavily weighted) and use that average as a proxy for expected inflation. This is a crude approximation because we do not know exactly what factors the public considers in formulating its inflation forecast. Undoubtedly, past rates of inflation do influence public expectations concerning future inflation, but other factors (such as the outcome of presidential elections, unemployment, and the performance of the stock market) also are likely to play a role in such forecasts. More recently, periodic surveys of economists and investors have been used to represent inflationary expectations in the marketplace, but such an approach suffers from being incomplete and possibly irrelevant. Expectations often change so fast that any opinion survey can be outdated even before its results are published.

Econometric Models

The four interest rate relationships we have discussed to this point—the liquidity, expectations, income, and Fisher effects—have been used in a large number of interest rate forecasting models consisting of one or more equations. These so-called econometric models developed by economists and financial analysts over the years often employ current and lagged values of money, income or total spending, and past rates of inflation to predict short-

and long-term interest rates through the application of least-squares regression techniques.[6] The larger models simultaneously measure changes in total spending for goods and services, consumption and investment, inflation, exports and imports, employment, wages and salaries, credit demands, supplies of securities and capital goods, and a broad spectrum of interest rates, forecasting several variables simultaneously and considering interactions among both predictor and predicted variables. Among the best known of such models are those used by Chase Econometric Associates (CHASE), Data Resources, Inc. (DRI), and Wharton Econometric Forecasting Associates, Inc. (WEFA). Such models are truly impressive in their complexity and detail; for example, the DRI model forecasts approximately 1,000 financial and economic variables, while the Wharton model in use since 1963 forecasts about 10,000 different variables. The complex interactions in such models between forecast variables (such as interest rates and the nation's income) and causal factors (such as government monetary and fiscal policy, and the supply of securities) are illustrated in Exhibit 11–3.

An example of a relatively simple econometric model prepared by the Federal Reserve Bank of St. Louis is shown in Exhibit 11–4. This simple model contains only eight basic equations and generates quarterly forecasts for seven essential economic and financial variables: *(a)* the level of nominal (current dollar) GNP; *(b)* the annual rate of change in nominal GNP; *(c)* the annual rate of change in real (constant dollar) GNP; *(d)* the annual rate of

Exhibit 11–3   Linking Interest Rates to the Economy in Major Econometric Models

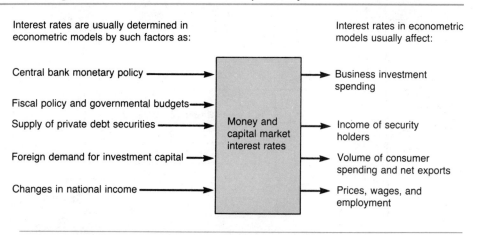

Source: Peter S. Rose, "Interest Rates, Economic Forecasting and Bank Profits," *Canadian Banker*, June 1984.

---

[6]For readers unfamiliar with the regression technique, see Cooley and Lohnes (1971) or any comprehensive statistics text.

Exhibit 11–4   An Example of an Econometric Forecasting Model: The Monetarist Model of the Federal Reserve Bank of St. Louis

Equations Making up the Model

1. Total spending:
$$\Delta Y_t = f_1[\Delta M_t, \cdots, \Delta M_{t-n}, \Delta E_t, \cdots, \Delta E_{t-n}]$$
2. Price equation:
$$\Delta P_t = f_2[D_t, \cdots, D_{t-n}, \Delta P_t^A]$$
3. Demand pressure identity:
$$D_t = \Delta Y_t - (X_t^F - X_{t-1})$$
4. Total spending identity:
$$\Delta Y_t = \Delta P_t + \Delta X_t$$

5. Interest-rate equation:
$$R_t = f_3(\Delta M_t, \Delta X_t, \cdots, \Delta X_{t-n}, \Delta P_t, \Delta P_t^A)$$
6. Anticipated price equation:
$$\Delta P_t^A = f_4(\Delta P_{t-1}, \cdots, \Delta P_{t-n})$$
7. Unemployment rate equation:
$$U_t = f_5(G_t, G_{t-1})$$
8. GNP gap identity:
$$G_t = \frac{X_t^F - X_t}{X_t^F}$$

Endogenous (Forecast) Variables

ΔY_t = Change in total spending (nominal GNP)

ΔP_t = Change in price level (GNP price deflator)

D_t = Demand pressure

ΔX_t = Change in the nation's output (real GNP)

R_t = Market interest rate

ΔP_t^A = Anticipated change in price level

U_t = Unemployment rate

G_t = GNP gap

Exogenous Variables

ΔM_t = Change in nation's money stock

ΔE_t = Change in high-employment federal expenditures

X_t^F = Potential (full-employment) output of goods and services in the U.S.

Exhibit 11–4 *(concluded)*   Flow diagram of the St. Louis Econometric Model

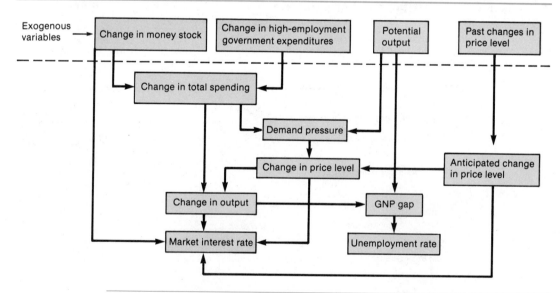

Source: Leonall C. Anderson and Keith M. Carlson, "A Monetarist Model for Economic Stabilization," *Review,* Federal Reserve Bank of St. Louis, April 1970, pp. 7–25.

change in the general price level; *(e)* the U.S. unemployment rate; and two interest rates—*(f)* the rate (or yield) on Aaa corporate bonds; and *(g)* the four- to six-month commercial paper rate. The type of interest rate forecasting equations used in this short econometric model is illustrated by the equation below, which tracks the long-term Aaa corporate bond rate—a key capital market interest rate:

$$
\begin{aligned}
\text{Moody's seasoned} \\
\text{corporate Aaa} \\
\text{bond rate in} \\
\text{quarter t}
\end{aligned}
= 1.28 - .06
\begin{Bmatrix}
\text{Annual rate} \\
\text{of change in} \\
\text{money stock, t}
\end{Bmatrix}
+ 1.42
\begin{Bmatrix}
\text{Dummy variable} \\
\text{representing} \\
\text{specific time} \\
\text{periods}
\end{Bmatrix}
$$

$$
+ \sum_{i=1}^{16} a_i
\begin{Bmatrix}
\text{Annual rate of} \\
\text{change in real} \\
\text{output in the} \\
\text{economy, t} - \text{i}
\end{Bmatrix}
+ \sum_{i=0}^{16} b_i
\begin{Bmatrix}
\text{Annual rate of} \\
\text{change in the} \\
\text{U.S. price level} \\
\text{(GNP deflator)} \\
\text{divided by the} \\
\text{U.S. unemploy-} \\
\text{ment rate index,} \\
\text{t} - \text{i}
\end{Bmatrix}
$$

Careful inspection of the equation reveals the prominent role that changes in the nation's money stock (reflecting primarily the liquidity effect), changes in the nation's income or output (reflecting primarily the income effect), and changes in the price level relative to unemployment (reflecting expectations and Fisher effects among other influences) are believed to play today in influencing interest rates.

While econometric models are all somewhat different from one another and their forecasts are often at odds, a few generalizations can be made about their content and interest rate predictions. For example, econometric models nearly always contain a money supply or monetary policy variable and show that an easier money and credit policy by the government leads to lower interest rates for periods stretching from about six months to one year. In contrast, when credit tightens up, interest rates (especially money market rates) climb higher for roughly 6 to 12 months. In most models interest rates (particularly short-term rates) react quickly, if not immediately, to the change toward tight or easy money policy, but as the months go by rates begin to move back toward their original levels. And, if the public believes inflation will increase, interest rates may rebound higher than they were at the beginning of the forecast period. Much depends on how much excess capacity there is in the economy at the time a government policy change occurs. And, of course, there are always feedback effects from the economy to the financial markets. Thus, higher interest rates reduce business investment spending, the building and buying of new homes, and spending by consumers (especially for durable items). Ultimately, this slowdown in spending reduces credit demands and eventually leads to lower interest rates, according to the structure of most econometric models.

There has been much dissatisfaction in the business community in recent years with the relatively poor track record of econometric models in spotting major turning points in the economy and at handling external shocks, such as the oil embargo of 1973–74. Despite the enormous complexity of some of these models, the economy and the financial markets they are designed to mirror are infinitely more complex. As the U.S. experience with the 1973-74 oil embargo suggests, the real world economy is subject to unexpected political and social changes that no mathematical model can adequately duplicate. Indeed, it is surprising that many econometric models work as well as they do.

The Flow of Funds Accounts as a Source of Forecasting Information

Still another forecasting approach that depends upon forecasts of other variables is the loanable-funds or flow of funds approach. The basic idea is to estimate total demand for credit from different borrowing sectors in the economy *assuming that interest rates remain at current levels.* This might be done, for example, by extrapolating past growth trends in the volume of business loans, consumer loans, government borrowing, and foreign borrowing into future time periods. The Flow of Funds Accounts (discussed in Chapter 3) can be used to provide historical data with which to make such future estimates. Similarly, we can estimate the projected supply of credit from key financial institutions such as commercial banks, savings and loan associations, insurance companies, finance companies, and pension funds. An example of such estimates is shown in Exhibit 11–5.

Once derived, the total projected demand for credit in the economy can be compared to total estimated credit supply. If, at today's level of interest rates,

1. Projected credit demand > projected credit supply, interest rates will tend to *rise.*
2. Projected credit demand < projected credit supply, interest rates will tend to *fall.*
3. Projected credit demand = projected credit supply, interest rates will remain essentially *unchanged.*

This approach is used with variations today by such well-known institutions as Bankers Trust Company and Salomon Brothers. It provides a useful benchmark for other forecasts, particularly in suggesting the direction of future rate changes, and can be used to predict yield spreads between various sectors of the economy. One obvious drawback is that numerous estimates of various sources of credit supply and credit demand must be made, increasing the opportunities for error.

Exhibit 11–5 **Using the Loanable Funds Theory of Interest Rates and the Federal Reserve's Flow of Funds Accounts to Forecast Interest Rates**

	Predicted Amounts ($ billion)
1. Estimate ex ante *demands* for credit in the economy at today's interest rates from:	
a. Domestic business firms:	
Estimated short-term (working capital) loans	$ 70
Estimated long-term (plant and equipment) loans	40
Nonresidential mortgage credit demand	30
b. Households:	
Estimated nonmortgage installment loans	50
Estimated residential mortgage credit demand	100
c. Governmental units:	
Estimated federal government credit demand	160
Estimated federal agency borrowings	20
Estimated state and local government borrowings	50
d. Foreign units (businesses and governments):	
Estimated foreign borrowing in U.S. financial markets	60
Total estimated credit demands	$580
2. Estimate ex ante *supplies* of credit in the economy at today's interest rates from:	
a. Depository institutions:	
Estimated commercial bank credit supplied	$100
Estimated savings and loan and savings bank credit	50
Estimated credit union loans	10
b. Pension funds and insurance companies:	
Estimated credit provided by private and public pensions	40
Estimated credit provided by life and property-casualty insurers	50
c. Estimated credit supplied by other financial institutions:	
Investment company credit supplied	30
Finance company credit supplied	20
Miscellaneous lending institutions	30
d. Estimated direct loans from nonfinancial sectors of the economy	120
e. Estimated residual funds sources and statistical discrepancy	50
Total estimated credit supplies	$500
3. Estimated excess credit demand (+) or excess credit supply (−) at today's interest rates	+$ 80

Interpretation: Excess credit demand (+) implies *rising* interest rates; excess credit supply (−) implies *falling* interest rates.

Following the Forward Calendar of New Security Offerings

One of the rate-determining variables included in the larger econometric models is the supply of debt securities being offered in the open market at any given time. Theory suggests that an increase in offerings of *new* corporate, municipal, or U.S. Treasury notes and bonds would drive interest rates higher, because these offerings represent additional demand for credit. Conversely, when the volume of new debt offerings declines, the lessened demand for credit should lead to lower interest rates, *ceteris paribus*.

This is the reason many market analysts follow the announced forward calendar of new security offerings expected to come to market in coming weeks. Such information is regularly reported in *The Wall Street Journal* and other leading financial newssheets and magazines. For example, *The Wall Street Journal* might report that:

· The Treasury will be issuing $22 billion in 5-year notes this week, about $4 billion more than this time last year, plus $20.5 billion in 13-week and 26-week bills, which is $3 billion above last week's auction.

· Offerings of new state and local government bonds are scheduled to reach $3.7 billion due to heavy school system and utility construction cash needs.

· In corporate issues market offerings will top an estimated $2.5 billion, with Textron selling $175 million in notes and debentures, Hospital Corporation offering $300 million of convertible debentures, and Chase Manhattan Corporation selling $150 million in floating-rate notes.

Any indication that the market is becoming clogged with increased quantities of unsold notes and bonds, especially when security dealers are reporting heavy inventories of already issued but unsold securities, usually triggers a forecast of rising interest rates and falling security prices in the near term. Similarly, the huge federal government budget deficits in recent years have led many financial analysts to scrutinize congressional reports, press releases, and budget data from the U.S. Treasury (as reported, for example, in *The Treasury Bulletin)* to estimate whether the government's need for new cash appears to be rising or falling. Increased Treasury borrowing requirements frequently lead to near-term increases in government security rates and increases in other market yields as well.

Market Expectations and Implied Rate Forecasting

Our discussion of the rational expectations theory of interest rates in Chapter 7 and the expectations hypothesis of the yield curve in Chapter 9 suggests the critical role that shifting public opinion about the future can play in influencing the financial markets. Recall from our earlier discussion of the expectations hypothesis, for example, that the slope of the yield curve itself *implies* a forecast of interest rate changes expected by the public.

For example, suppose that 30-day maturity U.S. Treasury bills are currently selling in the market to yield 10 percent, while 60-day bills carry current yields of 10.5 percent. This obvious upward slope in the short-term yield curve carries an implied rate forecast of what investors in the market expect Treasury bill rates to be in the next 30 days. Specifically, the 30-day bill rate 30 days from now is expected to be

$$\frac{\begin{array}{l}\text{Current 30-day}\\\text{Treasury bill rate}\end{array} + \begin{array}{l}\text{30-day forward (expected)}\\\text{Treasury bill rate}\end{array}}{2} = \begin{array}{l}\text{Current}\\\text{60-day}\\\text{Treasury}\\\text{bill rate}\end{array}$$

or

$$\frac{10.0\% + \begin{array}{l}\text{30-day forward (expected)}\\\text{Treasury bill rate}\end{array}}{2} = 10.50\%$$

and, thus,

$$\text{30-day forward (expected) rate on bills} = 11.00\%.$$

The yield curve is projecting an 11 percent, 30-day Treasury bill rate one month from today. Why? Because, according to the expectations hypothesis about the yield curve, investors in an efficient market should earn the same average return over the next 60 days whether they buy a 10.5 percent, 60-day Treasury bill today or a 10 percent, 30-day Treasury bill today followed by an 11 percent, 30-day bill purchased one month from now.

Actually, a more accurate forecast of the forward rate implied by the current slope of the yield curve can be found by using the formula

$$_{t+n}r_{kt} = \left| \frac{(1 + {_t}R_{n+kt})^{n+k}}{(1 + {_t}R_{nt})^n} \right|^{1/k} - 1$$

where the security whose rate is being forecast covers k periods and the loan to the borrower begins at time t + n. (This formula is derived from solving Equation 9–4 in Chapter 9 for any future k-period loan rate.) For the Treasury bill whose rate we were trying to forecast in the example above, we are working with a loan period of length 30 days, beginning 30 days from now. Therefore, we can let k = 1, meaning one 30-day loan period, and n = 1, meaning the 30-day loan whose rate we wish to forecast begins one 30-day period after the current 30-day loan period. Thus, with a current 30-day bill rate of 10 percent and a rate at the end of the forecast period of 10.50 percent, the predicted interest rate must be:

$$_{t+1}r_{1t} = \left| \frac{(1.1050)^2}{(1.10)^1} \right|^{1/1} - 1 = \frac{1.221}{1.10} - 1 = 0.11 \text{ or } 11\%$$

which matches our prediction above.

Another implied market forecast of future changes in interest rates is conveyed by current prices on financial futures contracts—a subject discussed more fully in Chapter 12. A *financial futures contract* is an agreement between a buyer and a seller to deliver a designated amount and type of securities days, weeks, or months in the future, but at a price agreed upon today. Thus, we might assume that current prices on such contracts reflect security traders' and investors' expectations about the levels of interest rates and security prices around the future delivery date of the securities named in the futures contract. In general, the interest rate (or yield) in the futures market will be higher than the interest rate (or yield) on the same security in the current (cash) market if interest rates are expected to rise; conversely, the futures market rate (or yield) will be below the rate (or yield) on the same security in the cash market if interest rates are expected to fall.

For example, *The Wall Street Journal* reported that contracts for the delivery of $1 million in U.S. Treasury bills in December 1987 were selling for $92.34 (assuming a $100 face value) on October 12, 1987. This price translated into an interest yield of 7.66 percent if the Treasury bill were held to maturity. In contrast, Treasury bills of comparable maturity available for immediate (cash) delivery were selling in the open market on October 12 for a yield of about 6.60 percent. Clearly, investors in Treasury bill futures contracts were signaling an expectation of *rising* short-term interest rates between October and December 1987.

The Consensus Forecast

While expectations models are useful barometers of current market opinion, the financial market forecaster must recognize their inherent limitations. They give us a reading only on what the marketplace—the average investor—expects, but not necessarily on what will happen. Expectations are often disappointed; other factors often intrude to upset the most convincing of forecasts. Indeed, no one forecasting method has yet demonstrated its consistent superiority over the others. Perhaps the safest approach is for the forecaster to use several different methods, checking to see if there is a consensus forecast that emerges from a variety of different approaches. Still, the forecasting process is laden with difficulties and uncertainties. Many analysts today confine their forecasts to rate predictions only one or two months in advance, with constant checking and revision as new information appears.

INTEREST RATE RISK HEDGING STRATEGIES

The increasingly volatile interest rates in recent years coupled with the inherent difficulties of rate forecasting have led many individuals and institutions to find ways to insulate themselves from interest rate changes. If rate changes cannot be accurately or reliably forecast, it may be possible to *hedge* against the damaging effects of increasing or decreasing interest rates. While several rate hedging methods have been developed, there is a price for such interest rate insurance: *Hedging lowers interest rate risk, but also reduces the potential profits that could be earned by correctly anticipating the direction and magnitude of interest rate changes.*

Duration

In Chapter 9 we discussed the concept of duration—a time-weighted present value measure of the maturity of a loan or security portfolio. In that chapter we pointed out that an investor could *immunize* his or her portfolio against interest rate changes simply by setting the

$$
\begin{array}{l}
\text{Duration of} \\
\text{a loan or} \\
\text{security} \\
\text{portfolio}
\end{array}
=
\begin{array}{l}
\text{Length of the} \\
\text{investor's} \\
\text{planned holding} \\
\text{period}
\end{array}
$$

With this investment strategy, a rise in interest rates will reduce the market value of our investor's portfolio, but the interest return on reinvested cash flows from the portfolio will increase by a corresponding amount. Thus, the investor's *total return* from the loan or security portfolio will be stabilized. Similarly, falling interest rates reduce interest returns from reinvesting the earnings from loans or securities, but with duration set equal to holding period length, the market value of those loans or securities will rise by a corresponding amount. Again, the total return will be stabilized.

For a financial institution (such as a bank) that both borrows and lends funds simultaneously, a good immunizing strategy is to set:

$$\text{Asset duration} = \text{Liability duration}$$

In this case, changes in interest rates should affect the institution's assets and liabilities *equally*. Thus, changes in revenues generated by the institution's assets and in the market values of those assets due to fluctuating interest rates should be offset by changes in interest costs on liabilities (such as deposits) issued by the institution and in the market values of those liabilities. If the changes in revenues, costs, and values are fully offsetting, the financial institution's *net interest margin* (or interest revenues minus interest expenses) will be protected no matter which way interest rates move.

Unfortunately, as we also saw in Chapter 9, duration has its limitations. It is often difficult to find desirable loans or securities with durations exactly matching the investor's holding period. Moreover, the theory of duration assumes parallel changes in all interest rates (both short and long term), and it is not clear how effective this hedging strategy will be if interest rates do not behave in such a lock-step fashion. Fortunately, other hedging devices can serve as a backstop to duration.

GAP Management

A very popular hedging strategy among banks and other financial institutions is known as interest-sensitivity analysis (ISA) or GAP management. The basic strategy is to set

$$\frac{\text{Interest-sensitive}}{\text{asset holdings}} = \frac{\text{Interest-sensitive}}{\text{liabilities}}$$

For example, a commercial bank holding deposits whose interest rates rise along with increases in market rates could hold an equal volume of floating-rate loans. Thus, when the bank's deposit interest costs increased in a rising rate period, interest revenues from loans would increase by a similar amount, thereby protecting the bank's net interest margin (or gap) between revenues and expenses.

To take a specific example, suppose a commercial bank has $100 million in loans and securities maturing or being renegotiated in the next 30 days so their attached interest rates can be adjusted to the latest market conditions. However, interest-bearing deposits and nondeposit borrowings coming due or subject to renegotiation amount to just $50 million (see Exhibit 11–6). This bank has a positive GAP between interest-sensitive assets and liabilities of $50 million ($100 million − $50 million). The bank is *asset-sensitive*. If rates rise over the next 30 days, asset revenues should go up faster than interest expenses on deposits and nondeposit liabilities. Profits will rise. However, if interest rates decline, the bank's profits will suffer because asset revenues will drop faster than liability costs.

A *liability-sensitive* position, in contrast, would find the bank having more interest-sensitive deposits and other liabilities than rate-sensitive assets. The bank is going to experience rising profits if rates fall; however, rising interest rates will send liability costs soaring relative to asset revenues, and profits will decline. Only if interest-sensitive assets equal interest-sensitive liabilities is the bank perfectly hedged.

There are several problems with "gapping," however. Borrowers may resist accepting loans whose rate continually fluctuates with market conditions. In practice, it is often difficult to match interest-sensitive assets with interest-sensitive liabilities exactly at every maturity. And any mismatches threaten the institution's net return from lending. Moreover, the choice of the time horizon over which to measure the interest rate sensitivity of assets and liabilities seems to affect the measurement of each institution's exposure to interest rate changes and therefore management's response to the problem.

Financial Futures Contracts

In the middle and late 1970s still another hedging device was developed—trading in financial futures. The basic futures rate-hedging strategy calls for offsetting purchases (sales) of securities in the cash (spot) market with sales

**Exhibit 11–6   Using GAP Management to Hedge a Bank's Cash
Flows against Changing Interest Rates**

The bank esti-mates that it has:	Time Periods That Assets or Liabilities Are Maturing or When Their Interest Rates Can Be Renegotiated:				
	Next 24 Hours	Next 30 Days	Next 6 Months	Next Year	Beyond One Year
Loans and securities reaching maturity or whose interest rates can be re-negotiated up or down of	$110 million	$100 million	$340 million	$550 million	$465 million
Deposits and other borrowings reach-ing maturity or whose interest rates can be re-negotiated up or down of	$155 million	$50 million	$370 million	$560 million	$430 million
Interest-sensitivity GAP is	− $45 million	+ $50 million	− $30 million	− $10 million	+ $35 million
Bank's interest-sen-sitive position is	Liability sensitive	Asset sensitive	Liability sensitive	Liability sensitive	Asset sensitive
Bank's net interest margin and profit-ability will likely decline if	Interest rates rise	Interest rates fall	Interest rates rise	Interest rates rise	Interest rates fall
Management strategy	Use financial futures contracts, options, rate collars, or shifts in assets and/or liabilities, etc. to protect against interest rate risk				

(purchases) of an equal amount of contracts on a futures exchange. Then, if interest rates rise, securities purchased in the cash market will fall in price, but an offsetting profit will be made in the futures market because the futures contract can be fulfilled with lower-priced securities or canceled out with a lower-priced futures contract. We will explore the details of futures trading in Chapter 12.

Interest Rate and Stock Options

Investors in securities or borrowers concerned about adverse rate movements can use put and call options. With a put, the option buyer receives the right (but not the obligation) to sell and deliver debt securities, loans, or futures contracts to the option-writer at an agreed upon strike price up to a certain date. If interest rates rise, the market value of the optioned securities, loans, or contracts may fall. Exercise of the put leads to a gain for the option buyer because delivery can be made to the option writer by purchasing the securities in question at a lower price.

A call option, in contrast, grants the buyer the right to purchase ("call away") from the option writer securities, loans, or futures contracts at an agreed-upon strike price on or before expiration. Falling interest rates will raise the value of the optioned instruments, allowing the buyer to purchase them at the original low price and receive a gain once he or she sells the optioned securities. Options are discussed in greater detail in Chapter 12.

Interest Rate Caps and Collars

A simpler approach to rate hedging is to take out a loan with an agreed-upon maximum interest rate. This so-called rate cap limits how far the loan rate can be adjusted upward by the lender if market interest rates rise. The lender will only agree to imposing a cap on the loan rate in return for a fee to compensate partially for the risk interest rates will rise above the cap. For example, the borrower may be asked to pay $2 million in fees to receive a three-year loan of $100 million whose rate is capped at 10%. The lender then may use financial futures or other rate-hedging techniques to offset the interest rate risk inherent in such a loan. Rarer, but still widely used, are rate collars when both a rate cap and rate floor (minimum loan rate) are placed around the contracted loan rate. Thus, the borrower is protected against rates going too high, while the lender is sheltered from loan rates dropping too low.

Interest Rate Insurance

Borrowers who need very large loans may seek out interest rate insurance that protects against losses due to rising loan interest rates. The insurer agrees to reimburse the borrower for any additional interest expenses the borrower must pay if rates climb above some maximum figure. For example, the borrower may take out an insurance policy for a premium of $25,000 that reimburses the borrower for any interest costs above a 10 percent loan rate. If loan rates climb to 12 percent, the 2 percent excess interest cost will be returned to the borrower. Banks and insurance companies often deal in such interest-rate insurance policies.

Loan Options

Related to rate insurance are loan options entitling a borrower to take out a loan at a guaranteed interest rate over a stipulated period of time. If rates rise above the guaranteed rate and borrowing is necessary, the borrower will use the loan option and borrow at the guaranteed rate. On the other hand, if loan rates stay below the guaranteed rate, funds will be borrowed as needed at market rates and the option will not be used. An option fee is assessed by the lending institution regardless of whether or not the option is exercised.

Interest Rate SWAPs

Finally, early in the 1980s a new interest rate hedging strategy—the interest rate SWAP—became popular. In a SWAP the two participating firms exchange interest payments, each paying off the interest owed by the other firm. The result is usually a lower interest expense for both firms and a better balance between cash inflows and outflows for both firms.

SWAPs are based on the fact that rate spreads related to default risk are generally greater in the long-term capital market than they are in the short-term money market. Moreover, interest rate SWAPs enable a lender to earn a stable rate of return merely for "intermediating" a credit deal between borrowers with different credit ratings without committing large amounts of funds to a full-scale loan.

Consider the case where a top-rated corporation can borrow in the bond market at the lowest AAA bond rate, while a company with a lower credit rating is charged perhaps prime or LIBOR plus a full 1.50 percent or more on a short-term loan from a bank (see Exhibit 11–7).[7] A bank or other lending institution might aid these two firms by helping the top-rated firm sell long-term bonds in the open market at a low coupon rate and getting the lower-rated company to agree to make the top-rated firm's bond interest payments. At the same time the top-rated firm pays the lower-rated company's LIBOR or prime-based borrowing rate which, because it is a short-term interest rate, often is lower than bond rates and certainly is more flexible. *Both* firms may wind up with lower interest costs, and the lower-rated company has, in effect, replaced a variable loan rate with a fixed loan rate. And, the lending institution bringing the two firms together earns a fee based on the difference in loan rates between the top-rated and lower-rated firms.

SUMMARY

In this chapter we have discussed the close relationship between changes in interest rates and the cycle of business expansion and recession in the economy. Interest rates tend to rise in periods of economic expansion, with short-term rates generally increasing faster than long-term rates. Conversely, recessions typically bring falling interest rates with, again, short-term rates declining more rapidly than long-term rates. This cyclical pattern in rates suggests to many economists and financial analysts that interest rates can be forecast by looking at factors reflecting the state of the economy plus other determining variables. However, as we have discovered in this

---

[7]LIBOR stands for London Interbank Offer Rate and is the basic deposit interest rate in the Eurodollar market, used as the basis for setting loan rates to major corporations. See Chapter 16 for a discussion of the Eurodollar loan and deposit markets.

Exhibit 11–7   Using Interest-Rate SWAPs to Hedge against Fluctuating Interest Rates

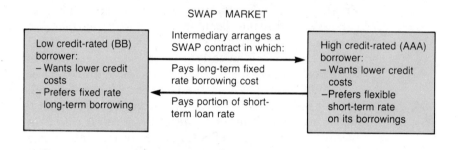

SWAP MARKET

| Low credit-rated (BB) borrower:
 – Wants lower credit costs
 – Prefers fixed rate long-term borrowing | Intermediary arranges a SWAP contract in which:

 Pays long-term fixed rate borrowing cost

 Pays portion of short-term loan rate | High credit-rated (AAA) borrower:
 – Wants lower credit costs
 –Prefers flexible short-term rate on its borrowings |

An example of a SWAP transaction

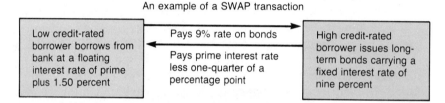

| Low credit-rated borrower borrows from bank at a floating interest rate of prime plus 1.50 percent | Pays 9% rate on bonds

 Pays prime interest rate less one-quarter of a percentage point | High credit-rated borrower issues long-term bonds carrying a fixed interest rate of nine percent |

Result: Both save on interest costs, with the high-rated borrower paying the prime bank loan rate minus one quarter percentage point (i.e., prime − 0.25 percent) instead of borrowing at prime, and the low-rated borrower borrowing at 9 percent plus 1.75 percent (i.e., 0.25 percent less than prime plus 1.50 percent over prime). Because the low-rated borrower probably will save more, that borrower may agree to pay the high-rated borrower's underwriting cost of selling new bonds.

Note: The two borrowers actually swap only the net *difference* in borrowing rates, with the party owing the highest rate in the market on the payment date paying the other party the rate difference.

chapter, interest rate forecasting is at best a difficult art. No single theory of interest rate changes and no single factor accounts for all the changes in security prices and rates we observe all the time. And no forecast, however well constructed, is likely to be completely accurate or totally reliable. The economy and the millions of individual decision-making units—businesses, households, and governments—that make it up offer too many opportunities for the most carefully drawn assumptions to go awry.

Still, interest rate theory focuses our attention upon a limited set of factors that need to be watched in conjunction with any rate forecast. These key rate-influencing factors include the *liquidity effect* of changes in the nation's money supply, suggesting that money supply expansion may produce lower rates in the near term if money demand is fixed or changes slowly. The *expectations effect* of money supply changes contends that, if money growth exceeds the public's expectations, interest rates may well rise because the public may fear worsening inflation and more restrictive government policies. The *income effect* of money supply changes suggests that the growth of income and spending raises money demand and ultimately interest rates. The *supply effect* of new security offerings argues that an increase in planned new security offerings is an indicator of added credit demands and, other things equal, tends to push interest rates higher in the short run.

Expected inflation also affects interest rates because, according to the *Fisher effect,* a rise in the rate of inflation expected by lenders of funds over the life of a loan or security causes a rise in the nominal (published) rate of interest attached to that security or loan, especially for longer-term financial instruments. Another factor in rate forecasting is *estimated credit demands* captured by changes in gross national product, personal income, factory output, retail sales, consumption spending, business investment plans, and other measures of spending and production in the economy. Rising credit demands suggest the onset of higher interest rates unless offset by an increasing supply of credit funds. Finally, *public expectations* regarding future interest rates, security prices, unemployment, spending, and future government policies all exert powerful effects on the bond and stock markets and must be weighed in the forecasting process.

The great difficulties inherent in forecasting interest rates have led many borrowers and lenders of funds to practice *interest rate hedging,* insulating themselves at least partially from the ravages of fluctuating interest costs and returns. Among the more popular rate-hedging devices are the use of *duration* analysis, which weights the maturity of loans and securities by the timing of their cash payments, and *GAP management.* Interest rate hedging with duration requires that a lender match the length of his or her holding period to the duration of the securities he or she holds. GAP management, on the other hand, requires an individual or institution to match the volume of their interest-sensitive assets to the volume of liabilities they hold that are also sensitive to interest rate changes. The goal of GAP management is to protect a lender's net interest margin—that is, the difference between his or her returns on assets and the cost of borrowed funds. Interest rate hedging may also be done using *financial futures contracts* in which cash transactions are matched by futures contracts calling for the future sale or purchase of the same securities or with *option contracts* where securities may be sold ("put") or purchased ("call") in the future at prices agreed upon today. Still other hedging devices center around *interest rate caps,* which put ceiling rates on loans, or *collars* that prevent rates from rising too far or falling too low. Other borrowers use *interest rate insurance* and *loan options* to avoid the highest loan rates. Finally, hedging has also been used by banks making large corporate loans and by major borrowers through *interest rate SWAPs* which give a borrower either fixed rates no matter which way interest rates move, or more flexible borrowing costs. Each hedging method has important limitations, but those limitations may be outweighed in those cases where borrowers and lenders are significantly exposed to the uncertainties of a volatile financial marketplace.

STUDY QUESTIONS

1. Describe the relationship between changes in economic activity and interest rates. Why do interest rates often rise during a period of economic expansion and fall when the economy is in a recession?

2. How do long- and short-term rates usually behave over the course of a business cycle? Which rises or falls at a faster rate? Can you explain why?

3. Why are interest rates so difficult to forecast? What advantages can you identify from being able to forecast rates successfully?

4. Explain the meaning of the following terms:
   a. Liquidity effect.   c. Income effect.
   b. Expectations effect.   d. Fisher effect.
   Describe how each might be used to forecast or predict future increases or decreases in the level of interest rates.

5. What factors or variables are used more frequently to forecast interest rates in econometric models? What are some of the weaknesses or limitations of these models?

6. What is the forward calendar? Explain how it could be useful as an indicator of future security prices and rates.

7. How can market expectations be used as a guide to future changes in interest rates? What pitfalls are there in such an approach?

8. Explain the meaning of the term *consensus forecast*.

9. What is hedging? Explain briefly how each of the following rate-hedging devices work:
   a. Interest rate caps.   f. Interest rate and stock options.
   b. Rate collars.   g. Financial futures.
   c. Interest-rate insurance.   h. GAP management.
   d. Loan options.   i. Interest rate SWAPs.
   e. Rate cap.

PROBLEMS

1. Suppose that today the one-year U.S. Treasury bond rate is 6 percent, the two-year Treasury bond rate is 7 percent, and the three-year bond rate is 8 percent. Plot a yield curve from this data. What interest rate is this yield curve forecasting on a one-year loan one year from now? What is the expected one-year loan rate two years from now? What is the expected two-year bond rate one year from now?

2. Current interest rates in the corporate bond market on AAA-rated bonds are as follows: one-year bonds, 8 percent; two-year bonds, 9 percent; three-year bonds, 10 percent; four-year bonds, 11 percent; and five-year

bonds, 12 percent. What is the slope of the yield curve in the one- to five-year range? Calculate the implied one-year expected rate one year from now. What one-year loan rate is expected two years from now? three years from now? four years from now?

SELECTED REFERENCES

Anderson, Leonall C. and Keith M. Carlson. "A Monetarist Model for Economic Stabilization." *Review,* Federal Reserve Bank of St. Louis, April 1970, pp. 7–25.

Barth, James R., and James T. Bennett. "Seasonal Variation in Interest Rates." *Review of Economics and Statistics,* February 1975, pp. 80–83.

Brick, John R., and Howard E. Thompson. "Time-Series Analysis of Interest Rates: Some Additional Evidence." *Journal of Finance* 33, no. 1 (March 1978), pp. 93–103.

Cooley, William W., and Paul R. Lohnes. *Multivariate Data Analysis.* New York: John Wiley & Sons, 1971.

Elliott, J. Walter, and Jerome R. Baier. "Econometric Models and Current Interest Rates: How Well Do They Predict Future Rates?" *Journal of Finance* 34, no. 4 (September 1979), pp. 975–86.

Emory, John T., and Robert H. Scott. "Evidence on Expected Yields Implied from the Term Structure and the Futures Market." *Business Economics,* May 1979.

Hafer, R.W., and Scott E. Hein. "Monetary Policy and Short-Term Real Rates of Interest." *Review,* Federal Reserve Bank of St. Louis, March 1982, pp. 13–19.

Kohn, Donald L. "Causes of Seasonal Variation in Interest Rates." *Monthly Review,* Federal Reserve Bank of Kansas City, February 1974, pp. 3–12.

Lang, Richard W. "Using Econometric Models to Make Economic Policy: A Continuing Controversy." *Business Review,* Federal Reserve Bank of Philadelphia, January–February 1983, pp. 3–13.

McNees, Stephen K. "The Optimists and the Pessimists: Can We Tell Whose Forecast Will Be Better?" *New England Economic Review,* Federal Reserve Bank of Boston, May–June 1981, pp. 5–14.

Murphy, J.E., and M.F.M. Osborne. "Predicting the Volatility of Interest Rates." *Journal of Portfolio Management,* Winter 1985, pp. 66–69.

Poole, William. "The Relationship of Monetary Decelerations to Business Cycle Peaks: Another Look at the Evidence." *The Journal of Finance,* June 1975, pp. 697–712.

Roley, V. Vance, and Rick Troll. "The Impact of New Economic Information on the Volatility of Short-Term Interest Rates." *Economic Review,* Federal Reserve Bank of Kansas City, February 1983, pp. 3–15.

Rose, Peter S. "Interest Rates, Economic Forecasting, and Bank Profits." *Canadian Banker* 91, no. 3 (June 1984), pp. 38–44.

Walmsley, Julian K. "Understanding Interest-Rate SWAPs?" *The Bankers Magazine,* June 1984, pp. 44–47.

Chapter 12

Financial Futures Contracts and Options on Futures

Learning Objectives in This Chapter

- To examine the nature and characteristics of two of the most popular financial instruments—financial futures and options on futures—for protecting against the risk of changing interest rates.
- To see *how* financial futures and futures options can be used to combat the market risks associated with making loans, purchasing and selling securities, and borrowing money.
- To explain the concept of "hedging" more fully.

Key Terms and Concepts in This Chapter

Hedging	Long hedge	Call options
Basis	Short hedge	Strike price
Financial futures contracts	Cross hedge	Put options
	Option contracts	Option premium
Stock index arbitrage		

AMONG the most innovative markets to be developed in recent years and also among the most rapidly growing are the markets for financial futures and futures options. Futures and options trading are designed to protect the investor against interest rate risk. In the financial futures and options markets, the risk of future changes in the market prices or yields of securities is transferred to someone—an individual or an institution—willing to bear that risk. Financial futures and options are used in both the short-term money market and the long-term capital market to protect both borrowers and lenders of funds against changes in interest rates.

While relatively new in the field of finance, risk protection through futures and options trading is an old concept in commodities trading. As far back as the Middle Ages, traders in farm commodities developed contracts calling for the future delivery of farm produce at a guaranteed price. Trading in rice futures began in Japan in 1697. In the United States, the Chicago Board of Trade established a futures market in grains in 1848. Later, the Board of Trade developed futures and options markets for metals and wood products; more recently, it has done so for selected kinds of financial instruments.[1]

THE NATURE OF FUTURES TRADING

In the futures market, buyers and sellers enter into contracts for the delivery of commodities, securities, or cash at a specific location and time and at a price that is set when the contract is made. The principal reason for the existence of a futures market is hedging; that is, the act of coordinated buying and selling of a commodity or a financial claim in order to protect against the risk of future price fluctuations. Adverse movements in prices can result in increased costs and lower profits and, in the case of financial instruments, reduced value and yield. Many business firms and investors today find that even modest changes in prices, interest rates, and other costs can lead to magnified changes in their net earnings. Some investors see the futures market as a means to ensure that their profits depend more on planning and design than on the dictates of a treacherous and volatile market.

Hedging may be compared to insurance. Insurance protects an individual or business firm against risks to life and property. Hedging protects against the risk of fluctuations in market price. However, there is an important difference between insurance and hedging. Insurance rests on the

---

[1]The major commodities currently traded on various exchanges in the United States include: wheat, corn, soybean oil, cattle, hogs, pork bellies, barley, flaxseed, copper, platinum, oats, rye, eggs, iced broilers, lumber, plywood, sugar, coffee, orange juice, cotton, cocoa, potatoes, silver, gold, crude oil, distillate oil, and gasoline. As we will soon see, there is now an active futures market for U.S. Treasury bills, bonds, and notes; Eurodollar certificates of deposit (CDs); common stock and selected corporate and municipal bond indices; and selected foreign currencies. Exchange-traded options include corn, soybeans, livestock, and other agricultural products; oil; selected metals; foreign currency options; Treasury bill, bond, and note options; Eurodollar deposits; and bond and stock index options.

principle of sharing or *distributing* risk over a large group of policyholders. Through an insurance policy the risk to any one individual or institution is reduced. Moreover, the risks covered by most insurance plans are highly predictable, especially the risk of death.

In contrast, hedging does not reduce risk. It is a relatively low-cost method of *transferring* the risk of unanticipated changes in interest rates from one investor or institution to another. Ultimately, some investor must bear the risk of fluctuations in the prices of commodities or securities. Moreover, that risk is generally less predictable than would be true of most insurance claims. The hedger who successfully transfers risk through a futures contract can protect an acceptable selling price for a commodity or a desired yield on a security weeks or months ahead of the sale or purchase of that item. In the financial futures market, the length of such contracts normally ranges from three months to two years.

GENERAL PRINCIPLES OF HEDGING

The basic principles of hedging may be described most easily through the use of a model. In this section we will examine the model of a *complete* or *perfect* hedge. Such a hedge contracts away all risk associated with fluctuations in the price of an asset. The hedger creates a situation in which any change in the market price of a commodity or security is exactly offset by a profit or loss on the futures contract. This enables the hedger to lock in the price or yield that he or she wishes to obtain.

Opening and Closing a Hedge

Suppose an agricultural firm produces a commodity such as wheat and is anticipating a decline in wheat prices. This unfavorable price movement can be hedged by *selling futures contracts* equal to the current value of the wheat. Sale of these contracts, which promise the future delivery of wheat days, weeks, or months from now, is called "opening a hedge."[2] When the firm does sell its wheat, it can buy back the same number of futures contracts as it sold originally and "close the hedge."

Of course, the firm could deliver the wheat as specified in the original futures contract. However, this is not usually done. If the price of wheat does decline as expected, then it costs the firm less to repurchase the futures contract than the price for which it originally sold that contract. Thus, the profit on the repurchase of wheat futures offsets the decrease in the price of wheat itself. The firm would have perfectly hedged itself against any adverse change in wheat prices over the life of the futures contract.

What would happen if wheat *rose* in price instead of declined? A perfect hedge would result in a profit on the sale of the wheat itself, but a loss on

---

[2]Opening a hedge represents the forward sale of an asset.

Exhibit 12–1   **Price Changes on Assets Can Be Offset by
Profits or Losses on Futures Contracts**

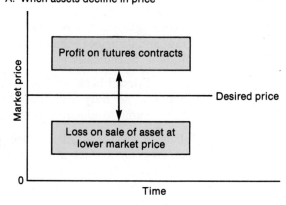

A. When assets decline in price

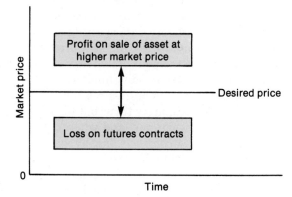

B. When assets rise in price

the futures contract. This happens because the firm must repurchase its futures contract at a higher price than its original cost due to the higher price for wheat. Exhibit 12–1 summarizes how a profit (or loss) on a futures contract can be used to *offset* a decrease (or increase) in the market price of an asset, helping the hedger to achieve a desired price level.

Why Hedging Can Be Effective

The hedging process can be effective in transferring risk because prices in the *spot* (or cash) market for commodities and securities are generally cor- related with prices in the *futures* (or forward) market. Indeed, the price of a futures contract in today's market represents an estimate of what the spot (or cash) market price will be on the contract's delivery date (less any storage, insurance, and financing costs). Hedging essentially means adopting equal and opposite positions in the spot and futures markets for the same asset.

The relationship between the price of a commodity or security in the cash or spot market and its price in the forward or futures market is captured in the concept of basis. Specifically:

Basis for   Spread between the cash (spot) price of a commodity
a futures contract = or security and the futures (forward) price for that
                       same commodity or security at a point in time.

For example, if long-term Treasury bonds are selling in today's cash market for immediate delivery at a price of $98 per bond (assuming a $100 par value), but are selling in the futures market today for forward delivery in three months at $88 per bond, the *basis* for this T-bond futures contract purchased today is $98 − $88 or $10. We can also define basis in terms of interest rates; it is the difference between the interest rate attached to a security in the cash market and the interest rate on that same security in the financial futures market.

One important principle of futures trading is the *principle of convergence*. As the delivery date specified in a futures contract grows nearer, the gap between the futures and spot price for the same security or commodity narrows. At the moment of delivery, the futures price and spot price on the same security or commodity must be identical (except for transactions costs), so that the basis of the futures contract becomes *zero*. Whether or not a futures trade ultimately turns out to be profitable depends on what happens to its basis between now and when the contract ends. *It is changes in the basis for futures contracts that create risk in the trading of commodities and financial futures contracts.*

Hedging through futures converts price or interest rate risk to basis risk. One useful measure of basis risk in financial futures is the *volatility ratio*:

$$\text{Volatility ratio for a futures contract (basis risk measure)} = \frac{\text{Percentage change in cash (spot) price of a commodity or security}}{\text{Percentage change in the price of the futures instrument used for hedging the commodity or security}}$$

The more stable the basis associated with a given futures trade—that is, the closer the volatility ratio is to 1—the greater the reduction of risk achieved by the futures trader. When cash and futures prices (or cash and futures interest rates) move in parallel, basis risk is *zero*. The futures markets "work" to reduce risk because the risk of changes in basis is generally less than the risk of changes in the price of a commodity or security. However, as we will soon see, there are both risks and costs to futures trading and losses can mount rapidly, especially for the unwary and uninformed investor. Moreover, U.S. tax laws require that income taxes be collected on any futures gains realized.

Risk Selection through Hedging

In the wheat example discussed earlier we described a complete (perfect) hedge. In a perfect hedge the basis remains constant throughout the contract period. Profits (losses) in the cash market exactly offset losses (profits) in the futures market. Such a hedge is essentially a profitless hedging position and is rare; in most futures trades, the basis fluctuates, introducing at least some degree of risk. Many speculators and investors, however, are willing to take on added risk by not fully closing a hedge, believing they can guess correctly which way prices are going. Through the futures markets, the investor can literally "dial" the degree of risk he or she wishes to accept. If the investor wishes to take on all the risk of price fluctuations in the hope of achieving the maximum return, no hedging will take place at all.[3]

FINANCIAL FUTURES

Beginning in October of 1975, the Chicago Board of Trade opened active trading in financial futures contracts for GNMA mortgage-backed certificates. In the ensuing months, futures contracts for U.S. Treasury securities, commercial paper, bank CDs, Eurodollar deposits, and even common stock appeared on the scene.

The development of futures markets for these securities was motivated by the extremely volatile interest rate movements that have characterized the financial markets for the past two decades. Repeatedly, interest rates have risen to record levels under the pressure of tight money policies and inflation, shutting out important groups of borrowers from ready access to credit. These high and volatile rates reduce the value of securities held by financial institutions, threatening them with a liquidity crisis and, in some cases, ultimate failure. Some members of the regulatory community have favored the growth of financial futures as a way to reduce the risks associated with security investments. However, as we will soon see, other regulatory authorities feel that the development of the futures markets may have encouraged speculation and increased the riskiness of those financial institutions participating in futures trading. These regulatory agencies have

---

[3]Hedging in the futures and options markets is not a costless exercise. There are brokerage commissions with each futures transaction and options carry a market price (premium) which rises with the probability the options will be used (exercised). Moreover, a complete hedge denies the investor the benefits of any unanticipated but favorable movements in the price of a security or commodity. Reducing the risk of losses also limits potential gains.

placed tight restrictions on the use of the futures markets, especially by commercial banks.

The Purpose of Trading in Financial Futures

The basic principle behind trading in financial futures is the same as in the commodity markets. A securities dealer, commercial bank, or other investor may sell futures contracts on selected securities in order to protect against the risk of falling security prices (rising interest rates) and, therefore, a decline in the rate of return or yield from an investment. If the price of the security in question does fall, the investor can lock in the desired yield because a profit on the futures contract may fully offset the capital loss incurred when selling the security itself. On the other hand, a rise in the market price of a security (fall in interest rates) may be fully offset by a loss in the futures market. Either way, the investor or institution is able to maintain its desired holding period yield. (These points are illustrated in Exhibit 12–2.) Many financial institutions prefer to use the futures market to hedge against interest rate fluctuations rather than passing interest rate risk on to their customers through floating-rate loans.

Financial futures may also be used by financial institutions and other investors to reduce the risk of interest rate fluctuations when borrowing money. For example, suppose that a commercial bank is planning to raise funds by issuing certificates of deposit (CDs) and borrowing in the Eurodollar market one year from today. However, the bank's economics department forecasts that interest rates are likely to rise significantly by the time the borrowing takes place. The adverse impact of these expected higher borrowing costs on the bank's profit position could be reduced by a sale and then a purchase of financial futures contracts. For example, management could sell one-year Treasury bill futures contracts now and then "zero out" this sale by purchasing a like amount of T-bill contracts when the delivery date arrives. Provided interest rates on Treasury bills, bank CDs, and Eurodollars increase by about the same magnitude, the added CD and Eurodollar borrowing costs would be offset by a profit on the futures position in T-bills. Using financial futures the bank can lock in its desired borrowing cost.[4] A recent study of Western banks and savings and loans by Booth, Smith and Stotz (1984) finds that insuring against future increases in the cost of funds was the principal use of futures trading by these financial institutions, followed by insuring against future decreases in investment returns and the ability to offer fixed-rate loans to customers safely.

---

[4]Note that even if interest rates fall, thereby *reducing* the bank's borrowing costs, the use of financial futures still stabilizes the bank's position. In this instance, losses would be incurred on the sale and purchase of financial futures but could be fully offset by reduced borrowing costs. However, if interest rates do fall, the bank would have been better off without its position in financial futures because its profits would have been greater. In addition, gains or losses on futures contracts are taxable, and there are brokerage commissions to consider.

Exhibit 12–2   **Changes in the Yield on Securities Can Be Offset by Profits or Losses on Futures Contracts**

A. When interest rates rise and security prices fall

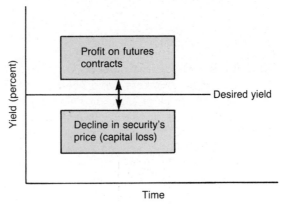

B. When interest rates fall and security prices rise

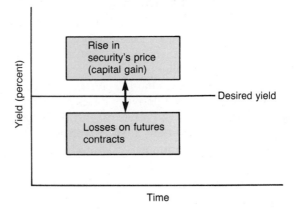

Under a financial futures contract, the seller agrees to deliver a specific security at a fixed price at a specific time in the future. Delivery under the shortest contracts is usually in 3 months from today's date, while a few contracts stretch out to 18 months or even 2 years. When the delivery date arrives, the security's seller can do one of three things: (1) make delivery of the security if he or she holds it; (2) buy the security in the spot (cash) market and deliver it as called for in the futures contract; or (3) purchase a futures contract for the same security with a delivery date exactly matching the first contract. This last option would result in a buy and a sell order maturing on the same day, which "zero out" and clear the market. In reality, settlement of contracts generally occurs in the futures market through offsetting buy and sell orders rather than by using spot (cash) transactions and making actual delivery of securities.

SECURITIES USED IN FINANCIAL FUTURES CONTRACTS

The number of futures markets and the types of securities and contracts traded in those markets have been expanding rapidly in recent years. In 1975 only one type of contract was traded at the Chicago Board of Trade. By the beginning of the 1980s, 25 different futures contracts were being traded on several different exchanges. However, most trading in financial futures today centers around six types of securities: (1) U.S. Treasury bills; (2) Treasury bonds and notes; (3) Eurobank certificates of deposit (CDs); (4) common stock indices; (5) corporate and municipal bond indices; and (6) such major foreign currencies as the British pound, Canadian dollar, Japanese yen, Swiss franc, and West German mark.[5] The Chicago Board of Trade first offered interest rate futures contracts for GNMA mortgage-backed securities in October 1975. Soon other commodity exchanges—the International Monetary Market of the Chicago Mercantile Exchange (IMM), the Amex Commodities Exchange, Inc. (ACE), and the Commodity Exchange, Inc. (Comex)—began offering futures trading in T-bills and GNMA certificates. Then, in August 1980, the New York Stock Exchange opened its own futures floor.

Each of these exchanges controls which security contracts may be offered for sale, acceptable delivery dates, delivery methods, posting of prices, contract par values, and other essential terms of trade. Current terms of trade for several prominent futures contracts now represented on the various exchanges are summarized below.[6]

U.S. Treasury Bonds and Notes

The futures market for U.S. Treasury bonds and notes is one of the most active markets for the forward delivery of an asset to be found anywhere in the world. As we will see in Chapter 25, Treasury bonds and notes are a popular investment medium for individuals and financial institutions because of their safety and liquidity. Nevertheless, there is substantial market risk involved with longer-term Treasury bonds and notes due to their

---

[5] Foreign currency futures are examined in Chapter 28.

[6] The contract exchanges carry a heavy burden of responsibility in preserving the integrity of futures trading and the orderliness of the markets. Each exchange stands behind the transactions conducted on its floor and imposes strict rules to minimize risk to the investor. For example, daily price fluctuations are not permitted to go beyond well-defined limits. Qualifications of floor traders and financial standards for member firms are set and monitored on a continuing basis by management and the governing board. The federal government also regulates futures trading through the Commodity Futures Trading Commission.

lengthy maturities and relatively thin market. Because the market for Treasury bonds is thinner than for bills and their durations are longer, T-bond prices are more volatile, creating greater uncertainty for investors. Not surprisingly, then, Treasury bonds were among the first financial instruments for which a futures market was developed to hedge against the risk of price fluctuations.

Only those Treasury bonds that either have maturities of at least 15 years or cannot be called for at least 15 to 20 years from their date of delivery (depending on the exchange selected) are eligible for futures contracts. Moreover, all Treasury bonds delivered under a futures contract must come from the same issue. The basic trading unit is $100,000 (measured at par), with a coupon rate of 8 percent. Bonds with coupon rates above or below 8 percent are deliverable at a premium or discount from their par values. Delivery of Treasury bonds is accomplished by book entry and accrued interest is prorated. Price quotes in the market are expressed as a percentage of par value.

The minimum price change that is recorded on published lists or in dealer quotations is $\frac{1}{32}$ of a point, or $31.25 per futures contract.[7] For example, *The Wall Street Journal* reported the following price information on Treasury bond futures contracts traded on the Chicago Board of Trade on November 11, 1987:

Prices on T-Bond Futures

	Open	High	Low	Settle	Change	Settle	Change	Open Interest
December	89–06	89–14	88–30	88–31	−12	9.218	+.046	252,258
Mr-88	88–10	88–15	88–01	88–01	−13	9.332	+.050	69,897
June	87–12	87–18	87–07	87–07	−13	9.432	+.050	9,795
Sept	86–19	86–27	86–15	86–15	−13	9.526	+.051	4,770
Est Vol 90,000		Vol. Tues 298,714			Open int 342,952		+1,298	

The first column reports the months in which each contract matures and delivery is to be made, while the next four columns show the opening price, high and low prices, and the closing (settlement) price that day. We note that Treasury bonds for delivery in December opened at 89–06 (or $89 $\frac{6}{32}$ on a $100 par or about $89,187.50 for a security with $100,000 in par value) and closed at 88–31 (or about $88,968.75). The price change over the last two trading sessions was $\frac{12}{32}$ ($37.50), and the interest rate implied by the most recent settlement price on December T-bond futures was 9.218 percent, an increase of about 5 basis points (+.046) over the last two trading days. The final "open interest" column shows the number of outstanding T-bond contracts, which is usually greatest for the most recent contract to be delivered and then decreases for successive, more distant delivery dates. Total trading volume for the most recent and previous day appears at the bottom, along with the sum of all outstanding T-bond contracts and the change in contracts over the previous two days.

---

[7]See Chapter 8 for a discussion of the meaning of 32ds and points and how security prices are measured.

Contracts for U.S. Treasury notes and noncallable bonds with maturities of four to six years also are traded today. Like Treasury bond contracts, T-note contracts are priced as a percentage of their par (or face) value, based on an 8 percent coupon rate. The basic trading unit is $100,000 in face value. Trading in Treasury note futures began at the Chicago Board of Trade in June 1979, while Treasury bond contracts were first traded in August 1977.

U.S. Treasury Bills

In January 1976, U.S. Treasury bills (which are described fully in Chapter 14) were declared eligible for trading in the financial futures market. The International Monetary Market (IMM), now a division of the Chicago Mercantile Exchange (CME), announced that contracts for future delivery would be written on T-bills of 90-day and one-year maturities. Ninety-day T-bill contracts are for $1 million each, while single contracts on one-year bills carry denominations of $250,000. T-bill contracts mature once each quarter of the year in March, June, September, and December.

Eurodollar Time Deposits

Futures trading in Eurobank dollar-denominated time deposits (which are described in Chapter 17) began in 1981 at the International Monetary Market (IMM) of the Chicago Mercantile Exchange (CME). The next year the London International Financial Futures Exchange (LIFFE) introduced a similar contract. The Eurodollar time deposit futures market offers investors the opportunity to hedge against changing interest rates on commercial loans, bank deposits, and other money market instruments. Eurodollar futures contracts are obligations to deliver or receive a $1 million deposit maturing in approximately 90 days, except that open contracts are settled *in cash* with the clearinghouse. Prices are expressed as an index which is equal to 100 minus the prevailing London Interbank Offer Rate (LIBOR) on short-term Eurodollar deposits that day, as identified by a survey of leading banks.

Stock and Bond Index Futures

In February 1982 futures contracts on the index value of those common stocks making up the Value Line Stock Index (covering 1,700 stocks) were first offered by the Kansas City Board of Trade. These contracts promised delivery of the *cash value* of a group of stocks at a set price on a specified future date. Two months later the Chicago Mercantile Exchange offered its own version of these so-called pin-stripe pork bellies by opening trading in a contract whose value was tied to daily fluctuations in the Standard & Poor's 500 Stock Index. And in May 1982, the New York Futures Exchange inaugurated trading in the New York Stock Exchange's (NYSE's) Composite

Stock Price Index (which includes all stock traded on the NYSE). These popular futures indices were followed by the establishment of a municipal bond index (based on the Bond Buyer's bond rate index) and, in 1987, by a corporate bond index using Moody's index rate for investment-grade corporate debt exceeding five years to maturity.

The advantage of these composite contracts is that they permit an investor to participate in the "action" of the stock and bond markets without buying individual stocks; the investor merely risks his or her cash on whether the stock or bond index will rise or fall in value. This is accomplished, for example, by buying or selling a futures contract a few points above or below the current stock index value (multiplied by $500). If the stock index gains or loses a point, the associated futures contract will change by a greater amount, presenting the investor with gains or losses until he or she either cancels or makes delivery.[8] Buyers of stock index futures bet on rising stock prices causing the stock price index to fall, while sellers are forecasting declining stock prices and a rising stock index.

Stock index futures contracts have figured prominently in a form of computerized "program trading" called stock index arbitrage.[9] Program traders seek to profit from any significant temporary disparity that occurs between the price of a stock index futures contract and the price of a basket of stocks representative of that stock index (such as those stocks listed in the S&P 500 stock index). For example, if the stock index futures price rises above the cash value of stocks that make up that particular index by more than the net carrying cost of the futures contracts (approximated by the current rate of return on U.S. Treasury bills or another riskless investment), program traders will spot an opportunity for profit. They will buy stocks representative of the basket of stocks in the index in the cash (spot) market and sell stock index contracts in the futures market. The result will be a profit when stock prices subsequently rise and futures contract prices fall back toward their usual positions relative to each other. On the other hand, if the stock index futures price temporarily falls below its parity with comparable stock bought in the cash (spot) market (adjusted for carrying costs and dividend yields on any stock purchased), program traders will arbitrage between the two markets, selling stock for cash and buying the momentarily underpriced futures contracts. These buy-sell pressures will quickly push cash market (spot) stock prices and futures contract prices back to their normal relative positions.

Arbitrageurs using these futures-related program trading strategies can earn a hedged rate of return that tends to be higher than the return earned by simply purchasing a portfolio of riskless securities. Some analysts believe such rapid portfolio switching between stock and futures markets makes

---

[8]Because of the inherent problems of trying to deliver the entire basket of stocks represented in any given index, a stock index contract is settled *in cash* if it has not been "zeroed out" before maturity.

[9]See Chapter 21 for a discussion of program trading.

both markets more volatile and treacherous, especially for the small investor. Other analysts argue, however, that stock index arbitrageurs are simply following the age-old rule to "buy cheap and sell dear" which ultimately leads to a fairer set of prices for all participants in the market. Moreover, the tremendous growth of stock index arbitrage activity has probably generated greater liquidity for both stocks and futures contracts, especially for financial futures. Today the dollar value of daily stock index futures trading routinely outstrips the daily volume of trading on the New York Stock Exchange.

TYPES OF HEDGING IN THE FINANCIAL FUTURES MARKET

There are basically three types of hedges used in the financial futures market today: the long hedge, the short hedge, and the cross hedge. Cross hedges, as we will see, may be either long or short. Each type of hedge meets the unique trading needs of a particular group of investors. All three types have become increasingly popular as interest rates and security prices have become more volatile in recent years.

The Long (or Buying) Hedge

A long hedge involves the purchase of futures contracts today, before the investor must buy the actual securities desired at a later date. The purpose of the long hedge is to guarantee (lock in) a desired yield in case interest rates decline before securities are actually purchased in the cash market.

As an example of a typical long hedge transaction, suppose that a commercial bank, life insurance company, pension fund, or other institutional investor anticipates receiving $1 million 90 days from today.[10] Assume that today is April 1 and the funds are expected on July 2. The current yield to maturity on securities the investor hopes to purchase in July is 12.26 percent. We might imagine that these securities are long-term U.S. Treasury bonds, which appeal to this investor because of their high liquidity and zero default risk. Suppose, however, that interest rates are expected to decline over the next three months due to a recession in the economy. If the investor waits until the $1 million in cash is available 90 days from now, the yield on Treasury bonds may well be lower than 12.26 percent. Is there a way to lock in the higher yield available now even though funds will not be available for another three months?

Yes, if a suitable long hedge can be negotiated with another trader. In this case the investor can purchase ("go long") 10 September Treasury bond futures contracts at their current market price. Recall that Treasury bond

---

[10]This example of the long hedge and the subsequent examples of short and cross hedges are drawn from examples developed by the Chicago Board of Trade in its instructional pamphlet, *An Introduction to Financial Futures,* February 1981, and are used with CBT's permission.

futures are sold in $100,000 denominations. The number of bond futures contracts needed is simply:

$$\frac{\text{Value of securities to be hedged}}{\text{Denomination of the appropriate futures contract}}$$

$$= \frac{\$1 \text{ million}}{\$100,000} = 10 \text{ contracts}$$

Cash payment on these contracts will not be due until September.[11]

Suppose their price currently is 68–10, or $68,312.50 on a $100,000 face-value contract. Assume too that, as expected, bond prices rise and interest rates fall. At some later point, the investor may be able to sell the bond futures contracts at a profit, because prices on these contracts tend to rise along with rising bond prices in the cash market. Selling the bond futures contracts at a profit will help this investor offset the lower yields on Treasury bonds that will prevail in the cash market once the $1 million actually becomes available on July 2.

The details of this long hedge transaction are given in Exhibit 12–3. We note that on July 2 the investor goes into the spot market and buys $1 million in 8¼ percent, 20-year U.S. Treasury bonds at a price of 82–13. At the same time, the investor sells 10 September Treasury bond futures contracts at 80–07. Due to higher bond prices (lower yields) in July, the investor loses $139,687.50 because the market price of Treasury bonds has risen from 68–14 to 82–13. This represents an *opportunity loss* because the $1 million in investable funds was not available in April when interest rates were high and bond prices low. However, this loss is at least partially offset by a gain in the futures market of $119,062.50, because the 10 September bond futures purchased on April 1 were sold at a profit on July 2. Over this period, bond futures contracts rose in price from 68–10 to 80–07. In effect, this investor will pay only $705,000 for the Treasury bonds bought in the cash market on July 2. The market price of these bonds will be $824,062.50 (or 82–13)

---

[11]In many practical situations the security to be hedged and the needed time of risk protection will not match up exactly to available futures contracts. These differences introduce additional uncertainty into the process of determining exactly how many futures contracts will be needed. A useful formula which takes many of these problems into account is:

$$\begin{array}{c}\text{Number of}\\\text{futures}\\\text{contracts}\\\text{needed}\end{array} = \frac{\begin{array}{c}\text{Value of}\\\text{securities}\\\text{or loans}\\\text{to be hedged}\end{array}}{\begin{array}{c}\text{Denomination}\\\text{of futures}\\\text{contracts}\end{array}} \times \frac{\begin{array}{c}\text{Volatility ratio}\\\text{of price movements}\\\text{in the cash (spot)}\\\text{security relative}\\\text{to the price of}\\\text{the futures}\\\text{contract}\end{array}}{} \times \frac{\begin{array}{c}\text{Days exposed to risk}\\\text{in cash (spot) market}\end{array}}{\text{Term of futures contract}}$$

where the volatility ratio is the percentage change in market price of the cash (spot) security relative to the percentage change in the price of the desired futures contract over the most recent period. For example, if we wish to hedge $1 million in corporate bonds for 60 days with a $100,000 denomination Treasury bond futures contract covering 90 days and the recent relative price movements of corporate bonds and T-bond futures contracts have displayed a volatility ratio of 0.75, the number of T-bond futures contracts needed is about:

$$\text{Number of contracts needed} = \frac{\$1 \text{ million}}{\$100,000} \times 0.75 \times 60/90 \approx 5$$

Exhibit 12–3 **An Example of a Long Hedge Using U.S. Treasury Bonds**

Spot (or Cash) Market Transactions	Futures (or Forward) Market Transactions
April 1:	**April 1:**
A portfolio manager for a financial institution wishes to "lock in" a yield of 12.26 percent on $1 million of 20-year, 8¼ percent U.S. Treasury bonds at 68–14.	The portfolio manager purchases 10 September Treasury bond futures contracts at 68–10.
July 2:	**July 2:**
The portfolio manager purchases $1 million of 20-year, 8¼ percent U.S. Treasury bonds at 82–13 for a yield of 10.14 percent.	The portfolio manager sells 10 September Treasury bond futures contracts at 80–07.
Results:	**Results:**
Opportunity loss of $139,687.50 due to lower Treasury bond yields and higher bond prices.	Gain of $119,062.50 on futures trading (less brokerage commissions, interest cost on funds tied up in required cash margin, and taxes).

Source: Based on an example developed by the Chicago Board of Trade in *An Introduction to Financial Futures*, February 1981. Reprinted by permission of the Chicago Board of Trade.

per bond, but the investor's *net* cost is lower by $119,062.50 due to a gain in the futures market.

The Short (or Selling) Hedge

A financial device of growing popularity is the short hedge. This hedge involves the immediate sale of financial futures contracts until the actual securities must be sold in the cash market at some later point. Short hedges are especially useful to investors who may hold a large portfolio of securities which they plan to sell in the future but, in the meantime, must be protected against the risk of declining security prices. We examine a typical situation where a securities dealer might employ the short hedge.

Suppose the dealer holds $1 million in U.S. Treasury bonds, carrying an 8¾ percent coupon and a maturity of 20 years. The current price of these bonds is 94–26 (or $948.125 per $1,000 par value), which amounts to a yield of 9.25 percent. However, the dealer is concerned that interest rates may rise. Any upward climb in rates would bring about lower bond prices and therefore reduce the value of the dealer's portfolio. A possible remedy in this case is simply to sell bond futures contracts in order to counteract the anticipated decline in bond prices. For example, suppose the dealer decides to sell 10 Treasury bond futures contracts at 86–28, and 30 days later is able to sell $1 million of 20-year, 8¾ percent Treasury bonds at a price of 86–16 for a yield of 10.29 percent. At the same time the dealer goes into

Exhibit 12–4   **An Example of a Short Hedge Using U.S. Treasury Bonds**

Spot (or Cash) Market Transactions	Futures (or Forward) Market Transactions
October 1:	October 1:
A securities dealer owns $1 million of 20-year, 8¾ percent U.S. Treasury bonds priced at 94–26 to yield 9.25%.	The dealer sells 10 Treasury bond futures contracts at 86–28.
October 31:	October 31:
The dealer sells $1 million of 20-year 8¾ percent U.S. Treasury bonds at 86–16 to yield 10.29%.	The dealer purchases 10 Treasury bond futures contracts at 79–26.
Results:	Results:
Loss of $83,125 in spot (cash) market.	Gain of $70,625 on futures trading (less brokerage commissions, interest cost on cash margin maintained, and tax obligation).

Source: Based on an example developed by the Chicago Board of Trade in *An Introduction to Financial Futures*, February 1981. Reprinted by permission of the Chicago Board of Trade.

the futures market and buys 10 Treasury bond futures contracts at 79–26 to offset the previous forward sale of bond futures.

The financial consequences of these combined trades in the spot and futures markets are offsetting, as shown in Exhibit 12–4. The dealer has lost $83,125 in the cash market due to the price decline in the bonds held. However, a gain of about $70,625 (less brokerage commissions, interest on cash margins maintained, and any tax liability) has resulted from the gain in the futures price. This dealer has helped to insulate the value of his or her security portfolio from the risk of price fluctuations through a short hedge.

Cross Hedging

Another approach to minimizing risk is the cross hedge—a combined transaction between the spot market and the futures market using different types of securities in each market. This device rests on the assumption that the prices of most financial instruments tend to move in the same direction and by roughly the same proportion. Because this is only approximately true in any real-world situation, cross hedging does not usually result in forming a perfect hedge. Profits or losses in the cash market will not exactly offset losses or profits in the futures market because basis risk is greater with a cross hedge. Nevertheless, if the investor's goal is to minimize risk, cross hedging is often preferable to a completely unhedged position.

As an example, consider the case of a commercial bank that holds good-quality corporate bonds carrying a face value of $5 million with an average maturity of 20 years. The bank's portfolio manager anticipates a rise in interest rates, which will reduce the value of the corporate bonds. Unfortunately, there is only a limited futures market for corporate bonds, and the portfolio manager fears that he cannot construct an effective hedge involving these securities. However, futures contracts can be negotiated in U.S. Treasury bonds, providing either a long or a short hedge against the risk of a decline in the value of the corporate bonds.

To illustrate how such a cross hedge transaction might take place, suppose that on January 2 the total market value of the bank's corporate bonds is $3,673,437.50. This means that each $1,000 par value bond currently carries a market price of $734.69 (or 73–15 on a $1,000 basis). The portfolio manager decides to sell 50 Treasury bond futures contracts at 81–20 (or $816.25 per $1,000 face value). About two and a half months later, on March 14, interest rates have risen significantly. The value of each corporate bond has fallen to 64–13 (or $644.06 per $1,000 bond). At this point the bank's portfolio manager decides to sell the bonds, receiving $3,220,312.50 from the buyer. This represents a loss on the bonds of $453,125. At the same time, however, the portfolio manager buys back 50 U.S. Treasury bond futures contracts at 69–20. The result is a gain from futures trading of $600,000. In this particular transaction the gain from futures trading more than offsets the loss in the cash market. (See Exhibit 12–5 for a summary of this transaction.)

Of course, this example of a cross hedge and the preceding examples of long and short hedges are simplified considerably to make the fundamental principle of futures trading easier to understand. In the real world the placing and removal of hedges is an exercise requiring detailed study of the futures market and, in most cases, a substantial amount of trading experience.

THE MECHANICS OF FUTURES TRADING

The mechanics of purchasing a futures contract are simple and straightforward. The investor chooses the commodity or security he or she wishes to trade and the preferrred maturity date for a futures contract calling for delivery of that commodity or security. Then the investor contacts a futures broker or commission salesman, usually through a local brokerage house or service. The broker or salesman indicates today's available prices and denominations and the investor can then place an order. Such a request must be accompanied by the posting of a cash margin (often 5 percent or more of the contract value) with the broker which will be returned at the end of the trade less the broker's commission.

The investor's order then will go from a brokerage firm to a floor trader working at the commodity exchange which handles that particular kind of futures contract. The floor trader will repeatedly call out the investor's offer to determine if there are any takers (a trader representing a buyer who is

Exhibit 12–5   **An Example of a Short Cross Hedge Involving
Corporate and U.S. Treasury Bonds**

Spot (or Cash) Market Transactions	Futures (or Forward) Market Transactions
January 2:	**January 2:**
A commercial bank holds a diversified portfolio of $5 million in high-grade corporate bonds with an average maturity of 20 years and a current market value of 73–15 per bond. The market value of the total portfolio is, therefore, $3,673,437.50.	The bank's portfolio manager sells 50 U.S. Treasury bond futures contracts at 81–20.
March 14:	**March 14:**
The market price per bond falls to 64–13, for a total value of the portfolio of $3,220,312.50 when sold.	The portfolio manager purchases 50 U.S. Treasury bond futures contracts at 69–20.
Results:	**Results:**
The total loss in value of the corporate bonds is $453,125.	Gain of $600,000 on the Treasury bond futures contracts (less brokerage commissions, interest cost on cash margins maintained, and taxes owed).

Source: Based on an example developed by the Chicago Board of Trade in *An Introduction to Financial Futures*, February 1981. Reprinted by permission of the Chicago Board of Trade.

willing to take a contract at the seller's quantity and price or a trader with a seller client willing to dispose of his or her contracts at the buyer's proposed purchase price) on the exchange floor. When two floor traders agree on the proposed quantity and price, the contract is made and each writes on a card the price, quantity, and delivery month of the contract and passes the card to a clerk who will turn it in to the clearinghouse for recording at the close of the trading day. The floor traders will also notify observers situated around the trading pit of the terms of each new trade so that this information can be communicated to those outside the exchange interested in buying or selling futures contracts.

Once a contract is made, if you are the seller, you must deliver the commodity or security specified in the invoice on the date specified. Similarly, if you are the buyer, you must pay the commodity exchange's clearinghouse the invoice amount on the date spelled out in the futures contract. However, most contracts (well over 80 percent in financial futures trading) are "zeroed out" by going back through a broker and floor trader with an opposite order that offsets and cancels the first order on or before the first contract's due date.

What is the purpose of the cash margin that each investor must post? It protects customers, brokers, and traders against market risk. At the end of each trading day, the clearinghouse is required to *mark to market* each contract outstanding based on its closing price. The cash margin covers the loss when a contract falls in price. If the price decline is more than a specified percentage of the margin, the investor may get a *margin call* to post additional cash or securities for protection.

OPTION CONTRACTS ON FINANCIAL FUTURES

In addition to financial futures contracts themselves, there is also active trading in options on financial futures contracts. An option contract is an agreement between a buyer and seller to grant the holder of the contract the right to buy or sell a security, commodity, or other item at a specified price on or before the day the contract expires. Options on farm commodities and on selected common stock have been traded in the United States and in selected markets abroad for decades. However, in 1985 the International Monetary Market (IMM), a division of the Chicago Mercantile Exchange, began trading on the floor of that exchange option contracts on financial futures for Eurodollar deposits. The following year the IMM opened floor trading in options on U.S. Treasury bill futures contracts. As more and more investors (including both borrowers and lenders of funds) began to take an interest in options trading, the major futures and stock exchanges began developing many new option contracts on stock, foreign currencies, and financial futures. The options market also has spread overseas. For example, options on futures contracts for Eurodollar deposits are also traded on the London International Financial Futures Exchange (LIFFE).

Basic Types of Option Contracts

There are two basic types of option contracts. Call options give the contract buyer the right, but not the obligation, to buy ("call away") financial futures contracts or other items at a set price called the strike price. The seller of the contract is called the option *writer*. Under the terms of American options the buyer may *exercise* the option and purchase the futures contracts or other items specified from the writer at any time on or before the expiration date of the option. So-called European options, on the other hand, can only be exercised on the expiration date. An option that is not used by its expiration date becomes worthless.

Put options grant the contract purchaser the right, but not the obligation, to sell ("put" or deliver) financial futures contracts or other items to the option writer at a set (strike) price on or before the contract expiration date. Buyers of both call and put options must pay a price—known as the option premium—for the privilege of being able to buy or sell futures contracts or other items at a guaranteed price. By fixing the price of a financial transaction for a stipulated period, options provide an alternative way of hedging against market risk (price or interest rate fluctuations) on securities. Their principal advantage over futures contracts as a hedging device is that hedging with futures contracts limits the hedger's profits; options, in contrast, can be used to limit losses while preserving the opportunity to make substantial profits.

Most options on financial instruments are traded today on organized exchanges such as the IMM or the Chicago Board Options Exchange (CBOE). Exchange-traded options are standardized contracts with uniform terms that control the quality of the items being traded, the permissible length (maturity) of contracts, and enhance the marketability of options. The exchange sets rules for the trading and pricing of options, while the exchange clearinghouse keeps a record of all trades and guarantees performance on all exchange-traded options. In effect, the clearinghouse becomes the ultimate seller to all option buyers and the ultimate buyer for all option sellers. As in the case of futures trading, most contracts are liquidated before they expire by the parties to the contract engaging in an offsetting purchase or sale. For example, the holder of a call option can "erase" his or her contract simply by selling a call option involving the same security with the same expiration date and strike price. Put options are liquidated in the same fashion—with the buyer (seller) of the put selling (buying) a comparable put on or before expiration day.

Option Contracts for Money Market and Capital Market Instruments

The two principal types of exchange-traded options involving short-term money market instruments are U.S. Treasury bill futures options and Eurodollar deposit futures options.[12] The IMM launched trading in T-bill futures options in April 1986. These options call for the delivery of three-month T-bill futures on or before an expiration date that is usually three to four weeks ahead of the maturity date of the futures contracts involved. The strike price is quoted in terms of a price index equal to 100 less the bill futures discount rate. For example, a call option on T-bill futures with a strike price of 94 means that bill futures must be delivered at an interest rate of 6 percent (100 − 94).

The Eurodollar deposit futures options first were traded on the IMM in March 1985. These contracts expire on the last day for trading the Eurodollar deposit futures contract that is the target of the option. This contract is somewhat unique in that an "open position" on the expiration date is settled *in cash,* not by delivering futures contracts or Eurodollar deposits.

For longer-term capital market securities, the most popular exchange-

---

[12]U.S. Treasury bills, which are discussed at length in Chapter 14, are the most widely traded of all short-term financial instruments having maturities ranging from a few days or weeks to one year. Each bill is a direct debt obligation of the U.S. government. Eurodollar deposits, in contrast, are large-denomination deposits in the world's largest banks with offices outside the United States. As Chapter 17 notes, they are traded between international banks daily at varying interest rates.

traded option is the Treasury bond option contract. This option is traded on the Chicago Board of Trade's Options Exchange in units of $100,000. The T-bond options' current price is quoted in points ($1 on a base of $100) and 64ths of a point. For example, on November 11, 1987, T-bond options for exercise on or before December, March, and June were quoted at:

T-BOND OPTIONS (CBT)

Strike Price	Calls-Last			Puts-Last		
	Dec.	**March**	**June**	**Dec.**	**March**	**June**
84	5–02	5–48	5–48	0–09	1–53	2–60
86	3–15	4–35	4–50	0–21	2–32	3–50
88	1–50	3–25	3–42	0–51	3–17	—
90	0–51	2–27	2–50	1–51	4–17	—
92	0–23	1–48	2–15	3–23	5–34	6–57
94	0–10	1–20	1–50	5–11	7–01	—

Est. Vol. 20,000   Tues. Vol.   24,736 Calls   33,906 Puts

Open Interest   Tues: 332,342 Calls   350,342 Puts

We note that the option to call Treasury bond futures contracts in December at a strike price of 84 (or $84,000 on a $100,000 contract) was trading at a price of 5–02 ($5 2/64 or $5.03125 on a $100 par or $5,031.25 for a $100,000 contract). As the strike price rose, however, the call option's market price fell due to less and less likelihood that the call option would be exercised at higher bond prices. Call options expiring in March and June were selling for higher prices due to the greater probability that they would be exercised because there is more time for bond prices to change.

Uses of Options on Futures Contracts

While options have many uses, the two most common ones involve: (1) protecting a future investment's yield against falling interest rates by using call options; and (2) protecting against rising interest rates by using a put option. Let's examine an example of each of these typical transactions using options.

Protecting Investment Yields. A major concern of most security buyers is how to protect against falling interest rates (and, therefore, falling yields and rising prices on bills, bonds, and other securities) that will be purchased in the future. Options offer a way to anticipate a future investment with a temporary transaction that helps guarantee future yields by setting a maximum price for the targeted securities.

For example, suppose a commercial bank plans to buy $100 million in United States Treasury bills in a few days and hopes to earn an interest yield of at least 7 percent. However, fearing a substantial drop in interest rates before the bank is ready to buy, the bank's portfolio manager executes a call option on T-bill futures at an index (strike) price of 93 [i.e., an interest rate of 7 percent]. If T-bill futures rise in value above 93, the bank manager will probably exercise the option because it is now "in the money." When the market price of a futures contract or a security rises above the strike price in the associated option contract, the buyer of the call option is said to be "in the money" because he or she can buy the futures contracts or securities from the option writer at the strike price (in this case, at 93) and sell at a higher price (perhaps at 93.50) in the futures or cash markets. The resulting profit (less, of course, the option's cost or *premium*) will offset the lost yield on the planned investment due to a subsequent drop in interest rates.

Now if interest rates go against the forecast and rise instead, the call option will be "out of the money." Its strike price will be above the market's current price for futures contracts or other financial instruments covered by the option. In this case the call option will not be exercised, and the bank will lose the premium it paid to secure the option. However, the fact that interest rates rose (and, therefore, Treasury bill prices fell) means the bank can now purchase T-bills at a more desirable yield.

Incidentally, the profit on an exercised call option can be found from this simple equation:

$$\text{Profit} = F - S - P$$

where F is the current futures contract price, S is the strike price agreed upon in the option contract, and P is the premium paid by the call option buyer. If the futures price, F, rises high enough, the buyer can call away the future contracts from the option writer at price S and still have some profit left over after paying the premium, P. However, if the futures price, F, declines, the option will go unexercised and the buyer's loss will equal $-P$. The seller of the unexercised call will then reap a profit of $+P$.

Protecting against Rising Interest Rates. Borrowers of funds usually have an opposite concern to investors worried about falling yields; their concern is to keep borrowing costs from rising. Consider a bank, for example, that must borrow millions of dollars daily in domestic and Eurocurrency markets and fears rising money market interest rates. Perhaps market rates on Eurodollar deposits are currently at 8 percent and the bank fears a substantial rise in deposit rates to 9 percent. Accordingly, the bank's deposit manager purchases a put option on Eurodollar deposit futures at a strike price of 92. If these futures fall below 92 in price due to rising interest rates, the bank's liability manager may well decide to exercise the put option and sell Eurodollar futures to the option writer at the strike price. The manager will then liquidate the bank's futures position by buying equivalent futures contracts at the lower market price and profit from the spread between the strike price of 92 and the current lower market price. This profit will at least partially offset the bank's higher borrowing costs.

On the other hand, if interest rates do not rise, the bank's deposit manager will not exercise the put option. This will mean losing the full amount of the option premium, but the bank's borrowing costs will stay low. In this instance it has paid the premium for interest rate insurance protection which turned out not to be needed.

The profit to the buyer of a put option can be calculated from the equation:

$$Profit = S - F - P - T$$

where S is the strike price, F the market price of the futures contracts mentioned in the option, P the premium paid for the option, and T taxes owed. If the futures price, F, falls far enough below strike price, S, the put buyer will show a profit $S - F$ which will exceed the premium paid and any resulting tax liability. On the other hand, if the futures price rises, the put will go unexercised and the buyer's loss is measured by $-P$. If this happens, the seller of the unexercised put will experience a corresponding profit of $+P$ (less commissions, taxes, and other costs).

TRADERS ACTIVE IN THE FUTURES AND OPTIONS MARKETS

A wide variety of financial institutions and individuals are active in futures and options trading today. The principal traders in financial futures and options today are individuals, commodity pools, and financial institutions. Commodity pools are like mutual funds, offering shares to individual investors who regularly purchase futures and options contracts. Commodity pools offer the advantage of diversifying risk by trading in many contracts with varied maturities; in addition, they are professionally managed. The majority of commodity pools try to limit the losses to the investor's original investment, liquidating investor holdings rather than issuing margin calls.

Firms and individual traders representing the futures and options industries run a close second to individual investors and commodity pools as participants in daily futures and options trading. Many of these industry personnel speculate on interest rate movements or arbitrage between spot and futures markets, purchasing one contract and selling another in the expectation that interest rates on purchased contracts will decline more than (or rise less than) rates on contracts sold. Alternatively, futures firms and industry traders will buy or sell futures and options contracts simultaneously with a sell or buy order in the spot market.

Financial institutions also play a prominent role in futures trading, led by securities dealers, investment bankers, commercial banks, mortgage bankers, and savings and loan associations. Securities dealers and investment bankers are interested both in risk reduction through hedging and in profitable trades arising from correctly guessing the future course of interest rates and contract prices. Savings and loan associations and mortgage bankers, not surprisingly, are most involved in futures trading to hedge the market value and yield on their mortgage loans and mortgage-backed securities. Rapid increases in long-term mortgage rates and volatile swings in the demand for new housing over the past two decades have brought substantial risk to the mortgage lending business, as we noted in Chapter 5. Under pressure from rising interest costs and deposit withdrawals, today many savings and loan associations have been forced to deeply discount and sell their old, low-yielding mortgage loans in the secondary market in order to raise funds. Losses incurred in the sale of old mortgages can be at least partially offset by gains made from trading in futures contracts. For their part, mortgage bankers frequently sell futures to hedge against interest rate changes that may occur between the time mortgage loans are taken into their portfolios and the time they are sold in packages to other investors.

Participation by commercial banks in futures trading has been quite limited to date, with only a few hundred U.S. banks active in the market on a daily or weekly basis. One major factor limiting commercial bank participation in the futures market is federal regulation which requires banks to limit their futures and options trading to hedging real risk-exposure situations and to receive regulatory approval before launching their trading programs. Another problem centers on the required accounting treatment of gains and losses from futures trading. Gains or losses on futures positions must be recorded daily, even though these position changes are not realized until the contract is concluded or zeroed out. The result may be volatile fluctuations in reported income for those banks active in futures trading.

A further barrier to bank use of futures and options is a lack of qualified personnel and resistance from top management and boards of directors who do not see any material benefits. However, it is anticipated that bank participation in the futures and options markets will expand significantly as the regulatory community becomes more comfortable with the hedging concept and bank management becomes more knowledgable about futures and options trading.

POTENTIAL BENEFITS TO FINANCIAL INSTITUTIONS FROM THE FUTURES AND OPTIONS MARKETS

Trading in security futures and options opens up several potential advantages for financial institutions and for individual investors. The prospect of hedging against changes in security prices offers the potential for reducing risk and offsetting losses stemming from adverse movements in interest rates. Financial futures and option contracts can be especially beneficial for financial institutions and individual investors heavily leveraged with debt, which makes their net earnings particularly sensitive to changes in interest rates. This is certainly true of major commercial banks, savings and loan associations, savings banks, securities dealers, investment bankers, and mortgage banking institutions. These financial intermediaries experience marked fluctuations in net income with changes in the differential between interest rates on borrowed funds and returns on loans and other assets.[13]

Moreover, if the futures and options markets do lead to a reduction of risk, this will enable many financial institutions to extend greater amounts of credit. The result could be a more efficient allocation of scarce funds within each financial institution and within the financial system. Moreover, the futures and options markets provide for a freer flow of information concerning alternative uses and outlets for funds, permitting each financial institution rapidly to adjust its risk position to changes in interest rates and other costs. As noted by Stevens (1976), the existence of a futures market, for example, may result in "increased market information, less search time, integration of markets and greater specialization of risk bearing."

SOCIAL CONSEQUENCES OF THE FUTURES AND OPTIONS MARKETS

Not all observers agree that the futures and options markets result in a net gain for society by helping financial institutions reduce risk and use scarce resources more efficiently. Some analysts believe that the futures and options markets are largely speculative and not really geared for the hedging of risks per se. They see these markets as aimed principally at providing wealthy investors with a speculative outlet for their funds, and as resulting in unnecessary risks due to excessive speculation. Some have argued that futures and options markets increase the price volatility of those securities whose contracts are actively traded and played a major role (due to computer-linked program trading between futures and spot markets) in the stock market's record decline in October 1987. If this is true, it would tend to make the impact of government economic policy, aimed at promoting high employment and low inflation, more difficult to predict. There is evidence from the commodities field that trading in futures and options tends to smooth out seasonal fluctuations, but only limited evidence exists to date on the overall impact on the securities markets of financial futures and options trading.

Certainly the mere existence of the futures and options markets and their continuing growth creates additional problems for regulatory authorities, especially those concerned with the regulation of financial institutions. Another market must be supervised and additional regulations prepared to cover new forms of risk and new fiduciary relationships. Some observers have expressed the fear that the futures markets substitute "gambling"

---

[13]It is certainly not true that every financial institution would benefit from trading in financial futures and options. The critical determining factor is the overall interest rate sensitivity of each institution's asset and liability portfolio. If both liabilities and assets carry floating interest rates, for example, hedging may be unnecessary, even in a period of rising interest rates. In fact, if an institution is already hedged, futures and options trading could increase the interest sensitivity of a financial institution's earnings and do more harm than good.

with securities for "investing" in securities.[14] If this view is correct, it suggests a withdrawal of some risk-taking activity from the traditional securities markets and a redirection of this activity toward the futures and options markets. To the extent that risk taking by securities investors is curtailed, this limits the flow of funds into venture capital and decreases the aggregate volume of investment in the economy. Other things being equal, the economy's rate of growth is reduced.

On balance, the financial futures and options markets probably have resulted in a modest net benefit to the financial system and to the economy. Those who support the development of these markets have certainly over-dramatized the positive features—alleging, for example, that interest rates tend to be lower and less volatile with a well-functioning futures and options market. There is little evidence that this is, in fact, the case. Still, it seems clear that the futures and options markets have separated the risk of changing security prices and interest rates from the lending of funds, at least for those institutions actively participating in this market. The risk of price and yield changes is transferred to investors quite willing to assume such risks. The futures and options markets have helped to reduce search costs and expand the flow of information on market opportunities for those who seek risk reduction through hedging. In this sense, the market tends to promote greater efficiency in the use of scarce financial resources. Moreover, this developing institution has tended to unify many local markets into a national forward market, overcoming geographic and institutional rigidities that tend to separate one market from another.

But futures and options trading is not without its own special risks. While the risk of price and yield fluctuations is reduced through negotiating these contracts, the investor faces the risk of changing interest rates and security prices *between* the futures and spot markets *(basis risk)*. It is rare that gains and losses from simultaneous trading in spot, futures, or options markets will exactly offset each other, resulting in a perfect hedge. There is also the risk of broker cash margin calls on the trader due to adverse price changes *(margin risk),* and possible problems in liquidating an open interest position in futures and options *(liquidity risk)*. Moreover, there are substantial brokerage fees for executing futures contracts and required minimum deposits for margin accounts that tie up cash in non-interest-bearing assets.[15] To the extent that the futures and options markets encourage speculation, do not fully offset all price and interest rate risk, and are characterized by substantial transactions costs, their net benefit to society will

---

[14]See, in particular, Wallich (1979), p. 11.

[15]Brokerage commissions and margin requirements in contract trading are not inconsequential. For example, a so-called *round trip*—buying and selling of contracts—of 100 S&P 500 stock index futures will cost approximately $2,500. Margin accounts must be maintained above a specified minimum level. Each account is evaluated daily, and additional funds must be supplied when the account declines below the minimum level. Many traders pledge securities to their margin accounts to eliminate the necessity of repeatedly supplying new funds.

remain both limited and the subject of continuing controversy and close regulatory scrutiny.

SUMMARY

The increasingly volatile interest rates of recent years have increased the risk sensitivity of many investors. With increased uncertainty concerning the future course of interest rates, managers of security portfolios find that financial planning is a far more difficult task today than in years past. Financial institutions that both borrow and lend in the money and capital markets have found that both their earnings and their cost of funds have become less predictable and subject to wide swings. It is not surprising, therefore, that many individual and institutional investors have sought new and innovative ways to insulate their investments from fluctuations in interest rates and security prices. The financial futures market, inaugurated by the Chicago Board of Trade in 1975, and the newer markets trading in options on futures and securities have become an increasingly popular form of insulation against the risks of investing in common stock and debt securities.

Futures and options markets are based upon the notion of *hedging,* which is simply the act of contracting to buy or sell a security in the future but at a price agreed upon today. By setting the price and other terms of such a contract now, the investor is at least partially insulated against the risk of future changes in interest rates and security prices. Hedging, in effect, transfers risk for one investor to another willing to bear that risk in the hope of scoring a significant gain. The hedger contracts away all or a portion of the risk of security price fluctuations in order to lock in a targeted rate of return on an investment. This is accomplished by taking equal and opposite positions in the spot (or cash) market and in the forward (or futures) market. If interest rates are expected to fall and the investor desires to lock in a current high yield on a security, he or she should buy a contract calling for the future delivery of the security at a set price (i.e., take on a long hedge) or purchase a call option which protects the purchase price of a security. Then, if interest rates do fall, the investor will earn a profit on the futures or option contract which will wholly or partially offset the lower yields available from buying the security in the spot (cash) market. An opposite set of buy-sell transactions in the futures market (i.e., a short hedge) or in the options market (i.e., a put option) would generally be used if interest rates were expected to rise.

Trading in financial futures and options is limited today to a list of high-quality financial instruments—for example, U.S. Treasury bonds, notes and bills; Eurobank CDs; and common stock and bond price indexes. But the list is growing, and the volume of daily trading in these markets is rapidly expanding. Most observers expect continued growth in futures and options markets activity due to volatile conditions in the financial markets and the growing financial sophistication of investors.

STUDY QUESTIONS

1. What is the basic purpose of futures and options trading in commodities? In securities? Where is most future and options trading carried out in the United States?

2. Explain the similarities and differences between hedging in the futures and options markets and insurance.

3. What is a perfect or complete hedge? Define the terms *opening a hedge* and *closing a hedge*.

4. How do spot (cash) markets differ from futures (forward) markets?

5. What is *basis?* Explain how the basis for a futures contract relates to trading risk.

6. For what specific kinds of securities is there now an active futures market in the United States? Who issues these securities? Describe the restrictions imposed on trading in futures contracts involving securities.

7. Define and explain the use of the following: a. Long hedge. b. Short hedge. c. Cross hedge.

8. Explain carefully and discuss the uses of: a. Call options. b. Put options.

9. What are the principal benefits to financial institutions such as commercial banks, securities dealers, investment bankers, savings and loan associations, and mortgage bankers from the use of the futures and options markets? Can you see any possible dangers?

10. What risks are inherent in futures and options trading? Costs? Evaluate the futures and options markets from a social point of view.

PROBLEMS

1. An insurance company during the month of March committed itself to buy a block of home mortgages at a fixed price from a mortgage banker in September. The mortgages have a face value of $10 million. The insurer has recently prepared a forecast which indicates that mortgage interest rates will rise between now and September by a full percentage point. What kind of futures transaction would you recommend to protect the insurance company against a sizable loss on its mortgage commitment, particularly if it has to sell the mortgages shortly after they are taken into its portfolio? Indicate specifically what buy and sell trans-

actions you would undertake in the futures market. Which futures contract would you most likely use? Why? What options contract seems best and why?

2. A large money center bank plans to offer money market CDs in substantial volume (at least $100 million) in six months due to a projected upsurge in credit demands from some of its most valued corporate customers. Unfortunately, the bank's economist has just predicted that money market interest rates should rise over the next year, with perhaps a full 1.5 percentage point increase within the next six months. Explain why the bank's management would be concerned about this development. Suppose management expects its corporate loan customers to resist any loan terms that would automatically result in loan rates being immediately adjusted upward to fully reflect any rate increases in the money market. What futures market transaction would you recommend? Please be specific, and explain why. What is the best options contract alternative for the bank? Why?

3. An investment banking firm discovers that 90 days from today the firm is due to receive a cash payment from one of its corporate clients of $972,500. The firm's portfolio manager is instructed to plan to invest this new cash for a horizon of three months, after which it will need to be liquidated. While interest rates are attractive today at 10 percent, a steep decline is forecast due to a developing economic recession. The portfolio manager decides to try to guarantee (lock in) a 9 percent rate of return today on this planned three-month investment of cash.

   A. Describe what the manager should do today in the financial futures market. Then indicate how he or she will close out the futures position eventually.

   B. What are the appropriate (buy-sell) steps for the manager if options on financial futures are to be used?

SELECTED REFERENCES

Belongia, Michael T., and G.J. Santoni. "Hedging Interest Rate Risk with Financial Futures: Some Basic Principles." *Review,* Federal Reserve Bank of St. Louis, October 1984, pp. 15–25.

Board of Trade of the City of Chicago. *Hedging Interest Rate Risks.* 1st rev. ed. Chicago, 1977.

———. *An Introduction to Financial Futures.* Chicago, 1981.

Booth, James R., Richard L. Smith, and W. Stotz. "Use of Interest Rate Futures by Financial Institutions." *Journal of Bank Research,* Spring 1984, pp. 15–20.

Comptroller of the Currency, Federal Deposit Insurance Corporation, and Federal Reserve Board. "Regulators Adopt Revisions to Policy on Futures, Forward and Standby Contracts." *Joint News Release,* March 12, 1980.

Jaffe, Naomi, and Ronald B. Hobson. *Survey of Interest-Rate Futures Markets*. Commodity Futures Trading Commission, 1979.

Kolb, Robert W. *Understanding Futures Markets*. Glenview, Ill.: Scott, Foresman and Company, 1985.

Koppenhaver, G.D. "A T-Bill Futures Hedging Strategy for Banks." *Economic Review,* Federal Reserve Bank of Dallas, March 1983, pp. 15–28.

———. "Bank Funding Risks, Risk Aversion, and the Choice of Futures Hedging Instrument." *The Journal of Finance* 40, no. 1 (March 1985), pp. 241–55.

Merrick, John J., Jr. "Fact and Fantasy About Stock Index Futures Program Trading." *Business Review,* Federal Reserve Bank of Philadelphia, September–October 1987, pp. 13–25.

Stevens, Neil A. "A Mortgage Futures Market: Its Development, Uses, Benefits, and Costs." *Review,* Federal Reserve Bank of St. Louis, April 1976, pp. 12–19.

Wallich, Henry C., Member, Board of Governors of the Federal Reserve System. Speech before the Commodities and Financial Futures Conference, Federal Bar Association and Commerce Clearing House, Washington, D.C., November 1, 1979.

Part Four

The Money Market

Chapter 13

━━━━━━━━━━━━━━━━━━━

Characteristics of the Money Market

Learning Objectives in This Chapter

- To explain the many essential roles and functions performed by the money market in the financial system.
- To see who the key actors—individuals and institutions—are in the workings of the money market.
- To understand how money market loans and securities differ from other financial services and instruments in the financial marketplace.

Key Terms and Concepts in This Chapter

Money market	*Inflation risk*	*Original maturity*
Market risk	*Currency risk*	*Actual maturity*
Reinvestment risk	*Political risk*	*Federal funds*
Default risk	*Liquidity*	*Clearinghouse funds*

To the casual observer, the financial markets appear to be one vast cauldron of borrowing and lending activity in which some individuals and institutions are seeking credit while others supply the funds needed to make lending possible. All transactions carried out in the financial markets seem to be basically the same—borrowers issue securities which lenders purchase. When the loan is repaid, the borrower retrieves the securities and returns funds to the lender. Closer examination of our financial institutions reveals, however, that beyond the simple act of exchanging securities for funds, there are major differences between one financial transaction and another. For example, you may borrow $100,000 for 30 years to purchase a new home, whereas my financing need may be for a 6-month loan of $3,000 to cover my federal income-tax obligation. A corporation may enter the financial markets this week to offer a new issue of 20-year bonds to finance the construction of an office building, and next week, find itself in need of funds for 60 days to purchase raw materials so that production can continue without interruption.

Clearly, then, the *purposes* for which money is borrowed within the financial system vary greatly from person to person, institution to institution, and transaction to transaction. And the different purposes for which money is borrowed result in the creation of different kinds of financial assets, having different maturities, yields, default risks, and other features. In this chapter and the others in Part Four, we will be focusing on a collection of financial markets which share a common purpose in their trading activity and deal in financial instruments with similar features. Our particular focus is on the money market—the market for short-term credit.

In the money market, loans have an original maturity of one year or less. Money market loans are used to help corporations and governments pay the wages and salaries of their workers, make repairs, purchase inventories, pay dividends and taxes, and satisfy other short-term, working-capital needs. In this respect the money market stands in sharp contrast to the capital market. The capital market deals in long-term credit—that is, loans and securites over a year to maturity typically used to finance capital investment projects. There are important similarities between the money and capital markets, as we will see in subsequent chapters, but also important differences that make these two markets unique.

CHARACTERISTICS OF THE MONEY MARKET

The money market, like all financial markets, provides a channel for the exchange of financial assets for money. However, it differs from other parts of the financial system in its emphasis upon loans to meet purely short-term cash needs. The money market is the mechanism through which holders of temporary cash surpluses meet holders of temporary cash deficits. It is designed, on the one hand, to meet the short-run cash requirements of corporations, financial institutions, and governments, providing a mechanism for granting loans as short as overnight and as long as one year to maturity. At the same time, the money market provides an investment outlet for those spending units (also principally corporations, financial institutions, and governments) that hold surplus cash for short periods of time and wish to earn at least some return on temporarily idle funds. The essential function of the money market, of course, is to bring these two groups into contact in order to make borrowing and lending possible.

The Need for a Money Market

Why is such a market needed? There are several reasons. First, for most individuals and institutions inflows and outflows of cash are rarely in perfect harmony with each other. Governments, for example, collect taxes from the public only at certain times of the year, such as in April, when personal and corporate income tax payments are due. Disbursements of cash must be made throughout the year, however, in order to cover such items as wages and salaries of government employees, office supplies, repairs, and fuel costs as well as unexpected expenses. When taxes are collected, governments usually are flush with funds that far exceed their immediate cash needs. At these times they frequently enter the money market as lenders and purchase Treasury bills, bank deposits, and other attractive financial assets. Later on, however, as cash runs low relative to current expenditures, these same governmental units must once again enter the money market as borrowers of funds, issuing short-term notes attractive to money market investors.

Business firms too collect sales revenue from customers at one point in time and dispense cash at other points in time to cover wages and salaries, make repairs, and meet other operating expenses. The checking account of an active business firm fluctuates daily between large surpluses and low or nonexistent balances. A surplus cash position frequently brings such a firm into the money market as a net *lender* of funds, investing idle funds in the hope of earning at least a modest rate of return. Cash deficits force it onto the *borrowing* side of the market, however, seeking other institutions with temporary cash surpluses. Clearly, then, the money market serves to bridge the gap between receipts and expenditures of funds, covering cash deficits with short-term borrowings when current expenditures exceed receipts, and providing an investment outlet to earn some interest income for units whose current receipts exceed current expenditures.

To fully appreciate the workings of the money market, we must remember that money is one of the most perishable of all commodities. The holding of idle surplus cash is expensive, because cash balances earn little or no income for the owner. When idle cash is not invested, the holder incurs an *opportunity cost* in the form of interest income which is foregone.[1] Moreover, each day that idle funds are not invested is a day's income lost forever. When large amounts of funds are involved, the income lost from not profitably investing idle funds for even 24 hours can be substantial. For example, the interest income from a loan of $10 million for one day at a 10 percent annual rate of interest amounts to about $2,800.[2] In a week's time close to $20,000 in interest would be lost from not investing $10 million in idle funds. Many students of the financial system find it hard to believe that investment outlets exist for loans as short as one day or even two or three days. However, billions of dollars in credit are extended in the money market for as little as 24 hours to securities dealers, commercial banks, and nonfinancial corporations to cover temporary shortfalls of cash. As we will see in Chapter 15, one important money market instrument—the federal funds loan—is designed mainly for extending credit overnight or over a weekend.

Borrowers and Lenders in the Money Market

Who are the principal lenders of funds in the money market? Who are the principal borrowers? These questions are difficult to answer because the same institutions frequently operate on *both sides* of the money market. For example, a large commercial bank operating in the money market (such as Chase Manhattan or Manufacturers Hanover) will be borrowing short-term funds aggressively in the market through CDs, federal funds, and Eurodollars, while simultaneously lending short-term funds to corporations that have temporary cash shortages. Frequently, large nonfinancial corporations borrow millions of dollars on a single day, only to come back into the money market later in the week as a lender of funds due to a sudden upsurge in cash receipts. Institutions which typically play both sides of the money market include large commercial banks, major nonfinancial corporations, state and local units of government, finance companies, and savings banks. Even the central bank, in the U.S. the Federal Reserve System, may be an aggressive supplier of funds to the money market on one day and

---

[1] The nationwide spread of interest-bearing checking accounts (such as NOW accounts) has reduced the opportunity cost of holding cash balances for some units in the economy. However, the yields on these transactions balances are still among the lowest available in the financial system, and some interest-bearing payments accounts such as NOWs may be held only by individuals and nonprofit institutions. Thus, the money market offers a convenient, low-risk way to earn competitive interest returns on money needed in the near-term for transactions.

[2] As we saw in Chapter 8, the amount of interest income from a simple-interest loan may be calculated from the formula:

$$I = P \times r \times t$$

where I is interest income, P is the principal amount loaned, r is the annual rate of interest, and t is the maturity of the loan. In the example given above, we have:

$$I = (\$10,000,000)(0.10)(1/360) = \$2,777.78$$

Note that for purposes of simplifying the calculation we have assumed a 360-day year—a common assumption in determining yields on money market instruments.

reverse itself the day following, demanding funds through the sale of securities in the open market. One institution that is virtually always on the demand side of the market, however, is the U.S. Treasury—the largest of all money market borrowers worldwide.

The Goals of Money Market Investors

Investors in the money market seek mainly *safety* and *liquidity* plus the opportunity to earn some interest income. This is because funds invested in the money market represent only temporary cash surpluses and are usually needed in the near future to meet tax obligations, cover wage and salary costs, pay stockholder dividends, and so on. For this reason, *money market investors are especially sensitive to risk.*

The strong aversion to risk among money market investors is especially evident when there is even a hint of trouble concerning the financial conditions of a major money market borrower. For example, when the huge Penn Central Transportation Company collapsed in 1970 and defaulted on its short-term commercial notes, the short-term commercial paper market virtually ground to a halt because many investors refused to buy even the notes offered by top-grade companies. Similarly, in 1974, when Franklin National Bank of New York, holding nearly $4 billion in assets, closed its doors, the rates on short-term certificates of deposit (CDs) issued by other big New York banks surged upward due to fears on the part of money market investors that all large-bank CDs had become more risky.

Types of Investment Risk

What kinds of risk do investors face in the financial markets? And how do money market instruments rank in terms of these different kinds of risk?

First, all securities, including money market instruments, carry market risk (sometimes called interest rate risk), which refers to the danger that their prices will fall (and interest rates rise), subjecting the investor to a capital loss. Even U.S. Treasury notes and bonds decline in price when interest rates rise. Only the dollar bill escapes market risk in the domestic economy because, of course, a dollar always exchanges for a dollar.

Not only can security prices fall, but so can interest rates. This latter development increases an investor's reinvestment risk; that is, the risk that earnings from a loan or security will have to be reinvested in lower-yielding loans and securities at some point in the future. Even government securities carry reinvestment risk.

Securities issued by private firms and state and local governments carry default risk. For such securities there is always some positive probability that the borrower will fail to meet some or all of his promised principal and/or interest payments.

Lenders of funds face the possibility that increases in the average level of prices for all goods and services will reduce the purchasing power of their income; this is known as inflation risk (sometimes called purchasing-power risk). Of course, lenders usually attempt to offset anticipated inflation by charging higher contract rates on their loans.[3]

International investors also face currency risk—possible loss due to unfavorable changes in the value of foreign currencies. For example, if an American investor purchases British Treasury bills in the London money market, the return from these bills may be severely reduced if the value of the British pound falls relative to the dollar during the life of the investment.[4]

Finally, political risk refers to the possibility that changes in government laws or regulations will result in a diminished rate of return to the investor or, in the extreme case, a total loss of invested capital. For example, the windfall profits tax on U.S. petroleum companies levied by Congress in 1980 generally reduced the earnings of petroleum stockholders. Investors in industries that are closely regulated, such as banking, insurance, and public utilities, continually run the risk that new price controls, output quotas, or other restrictions will be imposed, reducing their earnings potential. In some foreign countries, facilities and equipment owned by U.S. corporations have been expropriated by national governments, resulting in total loss for the investors involved. A summary of each of the foregoing kinds of risk is shown in Exhibit 13–1.

Money market instruments generally offer more protection against such risks than most other investments. For example, the prices of money market securities tend to be remarkably stable over time compared to the prices of bonds, stocks, real estate, and actively traded commodities, such as wheat, corn, gold, and silver. Money market instruments generally do not offer the prospect of significant capital gains for the investor, but neither do they normally raise the specter of substantial capital losses. Similarly, default risk is minimal in the money market. In fact, money market borrowers must be well-established institutions with impeccable credit ratings before their securities can even be offered for sale in this market.

Few investments today adequately protect the investor against inflation risk. Money market securities are no exception. However, they do offer superior liquidity, allowing the investor to quickly cash them in when a promising inflation-hedged investment opportunity comes along.

Currency risk concerns the international investor who frequently must convert one currency into another. That risk has increased dramatically in recent years due to the advent of foreign exchange rates that float with market conditions. Investors who purchase securities in foreign markets cannot completely escape currency risk, but they are probably less prone to such losses when buying money market instruments, due to the short-term

---

[3] Inflation risk and default risk are discussed in greater detail in Chapters 9 and 10.

[4] See Chapters 27 and 28 for a further examination of currency or exchange-rate risk.

Exhibit 13–1   **Types of Risk Confronting Investors in the
Money and Capital Markets**

Type of Risk	Definition
Market risk	The risk that the market price (value) of an asset will decline, resulting in a capital loss when sold. Sometimes referred to as interest rate risk.
Reinvestment risk	The risk that an investor will be forced to place earnings from a loan or security into a lower-yielding investment because interest rates have subsequently fallen.
Default risk	The probability that a borrower will fail to meet one or more promised principal or interest payments on a loan or security
Inflation risk	The risk that increases in the general price level will reduce the purchasing power of investor earnings from a loan or security.
Currency risk	The risk that adverse movements in the price of one national currency vis-à-vis another will reduce the net rate of return from a foreign investment. Sometimes called exchange-rate risk.
Political risk	The probability that changes in government laws or regulations will reduce the investor's expected return from an investment.

nature of these securities. Money market instruments also provide some hedge against political risk because they are short-term investments and fewer changes in government policy are likely over brief intervals of time.

Money Market Maturities

Despite the fact that money market securities cover a narrow range of maturities—one year or less—there are maturities available within this range to meet just about every short-term cash and investment need. We must distinguish here between original maturity and actual maturity, however. The interval of time between the issue date of a security and the date on which the borrower promises to redeem it is the security's original maturity. Actual maturity, on the other hand, refers to the number of days, months, or years between today and the date the security is actually redeemed or retired.

Original maturities on money market instruments range from as short as one day on many federal funds transactions and loans to security dealers to a full year on some Eurodollar deposits, bank certificates of deposit, and Treasury bills. Obviously, once a money market instrument is issued, it grows shorter in actual maturity every day. Because there are thousands of money market securities outstanding, some of which reach maturity each day, investors have a wide menu from which to select the precise number of days they need to invest cash.

Depth and Breadth of the Money Market

The money market is extremely broad and deep, meaning it can absorb a large volume of transactions with only small effects on security prices and interest rates. Investors can easily sell most money market instruments on short notice, often in a matter of minutes. This is one of the most *efficient* markets in the world, containing a vast network of securities dealers, major banks, and funds brokers in constant touch with one another and alert to any bargains. The slightest hint that a security is underpriced (carries an exceptionally high yield) usually brings a flood of buy orders, while money market traders are quick to dump or avoid overpriced securities. This market is dominated by active traders who constantly search their video display screens for opportunities to arbitrage funds; that is, they move money from a corner of the market with relatively low yields to one where investments offer the highest returns available. And overseeing the whole market is the Federal Reserve System, and other central banks, which try to ensure that trading is orderly and prices are reasonably stable.

There is no centralized trading arena in the money market as there is on a stock exchange, for example. The money market is a *telephone market,* in which participants arrange trades over the phone and usually confirm by wire. Speed is of the essence in this market because, as we observed earlier, money is a highly perishable commodity. Each day that passes means thousands of dollars in lost interest income if newly received funds are not immediately invested. Most business between traders, therefore, is conducted in seconds or minutes, and payment is made almost instantaneously.

Federal Funds versus Clearinghouse Funds

How can funds move so fast in the money market? The reason is that money market traders usually deal in federal funds. These funds are mainly deposit balances of commercial banks held at the regional Federal Reserve banks and at larger correspondent banks across the nation. When a dealer firm buys securities from an investor, for example, it immediately contacts its bank and requests that funds be transferred from its account to the investor's account at another bank. Many of these transactions move through the Federal Reserve's wire transfer network. In this case the Fed removes funds from the reserve account of the buyer's bank and transfers these reserves to the seller's bank. The transaction is so quick that the seller of securities has funds avaialble to make new investments, pay bills, or for other purposes the same day a trade is carried out or a loan is made. Federal funds are often called "immediately available funds" because of the speed with which money moves from one bank's reserve account to that of another.

Contrast this method of payment with that used generally in the capital market and by most businesses and households. When most of us purchase goods and services—especially purchases involving a large amount of money—the *check* is the most desirable means of paying the bill. Funds transferred by check are known as clearinghouse funds. This is because, once the buyer writes a check, it goes to the seller's bank, which forwards that check eventually to the bank upon which it was drawn. If the two banks are in the same community, they exchange bundles of checks drawn against each other every day through the local clearinghouse—an agreed-upon location where checks and other cash items are delivered and passed from one bank to another.

Clearinghouse funds are an acceptable means of payment for most purposes, but *not* in the money market, where speed is of the essence. It takes at least a day to clear local checks and two to three days for checks moving between cities. For money market transactions this is far too slow, because no interest can be earned until the check is collected. Clearinghouse funds also have an element of risk because a check may be returned as fraudulent or for insufficient funds. Federal funds transactions, however, are not only speedy but safe.

A Market for Large Borrowers and Lenders

The money market is dominated by a relatively small number of large financial institutions. No more than a few hundred banks in New York, Chicago, San Francisco, London, Tokyo, Singapore, and a handful of other money centers are at the heart of the market. These large institutions account for the bulk of federal funds trading through which many money market transactions are carried out. In addition, securities move readily from sellers to buyers through the market-making activities of major government security dealers and dealers and brokers in commercial paper, bankers' acceptances, certificates of deposit, and federal funds. And, of course, the U.S. government in consultation with governments and central banks abroad plays a major role in this market as the largest borrower and as regulator, setting the rules of the game. The Federal Reserve System, operating principally through the trading desk at the Federal Reserve Bank of New York, is in the market nearly every day, either supplying funds to banks and security dealers or absorbing funds through security sales.

Individual transactions in the money market involve huge amounts of funds. Most trading occurs in multiples of a million dollars. For this reason the money market is often referred to as a *wholesale market* for funds, as opposed to the retail market where consumers and small businesses borrow and save.

THE VOLUME OF MONEY MARKET SECURITIES

The principal financial instruments traded in the money market are U.S. and other Treasury bills, federal agency securities, dealer loans, repurchase agreements, bank certificates of deposit (CDs), federal funds, commercial paper, bankers' acceptances, financial futures, and Eurodollar deposits. Each of these instruments is discussed in detail in the next several chapters, but it is useful at this point to examine the relative importance, measured by the dollar volume outstanding, of each of these instruments in the American portion of the money market.

In fact, the volume of money market securities has grown rapidly in recent years. One reason is the international economy's growing need for liquid, readily marketable investment securities. Another factor in the money market's growth has been the attractive yields offered investors. As shown in Exhibit 13–2, two of the most important money market instruments (measured by dollar volume) are Treasury bills and certificates of deposit (CDs). By 1988 over $400 billion in U.S. Treasury bills were outstanding, representing about one quarter of the federal government's debt. Somewhat less in total amount were $100,000-plus certificates of deposit issued by U.S. banks and thrift institutions. These large-denomination CDs totaled nearly $400 billion in 1988. We should note, however, that the volume of CDs fluctuates widely with credit market conditions, corporate earnings, and changes in interest rates available on other securities.

Nearly as large as Treasury bills and CDs is the total volume of secu-

Exhibit 13–2   **Volume of Selected Money Market Instruments, 1981–1987 ($ Billions at Year-End)**

Financial Instruments	1981	1982	1983	1984	1985	1986	1987
U.S. Treasury bills	$245.0	$311.8	$343.8	$374.4	$399.9	$426.7	$426.7
Federal agency securities	211.9	237.1	239.7	261.3	293.9	307.4	341.4
Commercial paper	165.8	166.7	185.9	239.1	300.9	331.0	357.1
Bankers' acceptances	69.2	79.5	78.3	75.5	68.4	65.0	70.6
Federal funds borrowings and repurchase agreements	111.8	127.7	140.5	140.9	NA	164.0	161.9
Net Eurodollar borrowings by domestic banks from their own foreign branches	18.1	47.7	42.7	31.4	NA	30.7	15.2
Certificates of deposit ($100,000 or more)	325.4	347.9	283.1	325.8	NA	345.6	387.0

NA = not available.

Source: Board of Governors of the Federal Reserve System, *Federal Reserve Bulletin,* selected issues.

rities issued by U.S. federal agencies. These high-quality securities, nearly half of which fall due within a year and therefore are true money market instruments, approached $350 billion by 1988. Three quarters of all agency IOUs are issued by just three federally sponsored organizations—the Federal Home Loan banks, the Federal National Mortgage Association, and the Farm Credit banks. The remaining agency issues come from a variety of government-related enterprises and organizations, including the Department of Defense, the Export-Import Bank, the Postal Service, the Tennessee Valley Authority, and the Student Loan Marketing Association.

Commercial paper issued by top-flight corporations totaled over $350 billion in 1988 and represented one of the most rapidly growing money market instruments. Many large corporations have found the commercial paper market a cheaper and more flexible place to obtain credit than borrowing from banks. Bankers' acceptances—time drafts against large multinational banks—have also fluctuated with the growth of world trade, but stood between $60 and $70 billion in 1988.

The volume of federal funds loans—the principal means of payment in the money market—is difficult to estimate because thousands of banks are active in this market every day and not all transactions are reported. Moreover, the federal funds market is extremely volatile, reflecting wide swings in the flow of funds through the banking system. Estimates by the Federal Reserve System indicate that Fed funds loans outstanding (including repurchase agreements) totaled around $170 billion in 1988.

The true size of the Eurodollar market (dollar deposits in banks abroad) is also unknown, principally because this market spans so many nations and is not regulated. The amount shown in Exhibit 13–2 of about $15 billion at year-end 1987 includes only the net amount of Eurodollar borrowings by U.S. banks from their foreign branches. Conservative estimates of total Eurodollar deposits worldwide place the net figure in the neighborhood of $1 trillion.

THE PATTERN OF INTEREST RATES IN THE MONEY MARKET

The rates of return on money market securities vary over time and among different securities. The foundation of the market's structure is the level of yields on Treasury bills. These securities are considered to have zero default risk and minimal market risk as well. Moreover, the resale market for Treasury bills is the most active and deep of all securities markets, making bills readily marketable should the investor need cash in a hurry. Because of this combination of low risk and ready marketability, Treasury bills typically carry the lowest yields in the money market.

Other yields in the money market are scaled upward from Treasury bill rates. One set of yields which hovers very close to T-bill rates is the yield on federal agency securities, considered virtually riskless by many investors.

Exhibit 13–3   Yield Relationships in the Money Market, Week of March 25, 1988

Security	Yield (percent per annum)	Yield Spread Over Three-month U.S. Treasury Bills (basis points)
U.S. Treasury Bills:*		
Three-month	5.77%	—
Six-month	5.98	+ 21
One-year	6.35	+ 58
Federal funds rate	6.51	+ 74
Commercial paper (prime):†		
One-month	6.58	+ 81
Three-month	6.64	+ 87
Six-month	6.68	+ 91
Certificates of Deposit (CDs)		
($100,000 or more):††		
One-month	6.57	+ 80
Three-month	6.64	+ 87
Six-month	6.84	+107
Bankers' acceptances, three-month†	6.53	+ 76
Eurodollars	6.75	+ 98
Prime bank lending rates§	8.50	+273
Federal Reserve discount rate	6.00	+ 23

*Based on daily closing bid prices in the secondary market and the bank discount method.

†Interest yield figured by the bank discount method explained in Chapter 14.

††Secondary market as quoted by five dealers.

§Average for March 1988.

Source: Board of Governors of the Federal Reserve System, *Federal Reserve Bulletin,* June 1988.

Nevertheless, agency securities are less marketable than bills, though their quantity has increased rapidly in recent years. As a result, the yield spread between agencies and bills in recent periods averages about 1 percentage point in favor of agency securities.

Another yield in the money market which stays fairly close to the Treasury bill rate is the rate charged on federal funds loans. The low risk of these loans, coupled with their short maturities, helps to explain their relatively low yields. As shown in Exhibit 13–3, the federal funds rate in March 1988 was less than one percentage point above the market rate of return on three-month Treasury bills.

The interest rates on two bank-related financial instruments—negotiable CDs and bankers' acceptances—also tend to follow changes in the market yield on Treasury bills and hover close to prevailing bill rates for the same maturities. As shown in Exhibit 13–3, the secondary market yield on three-month CDs was just under one percentage point higher than the three-month T-bill rate, while the spread between this rate and the rate of return on three-month bankers' acceptances was just over one percentage point above the bill rate. CDs issued by the largest U.S. banks are rated *prime* and carry the lowest yields in the CD market. The same is true of prime-rated bankers' acceptances. Acceptances are considered to be a high-quality investment nearly as riskless as Treasury bills. However, the resale market for acceptances is not as active or as deep as the T-bill market, and this difference in marketability helps to explain why acceptances must carry a slightly higher yield.

Large, well-established corporations in need of credit can, of course, draw upon many different sources of funds. However, when short-term credit is needed, two of the most popular sources are borrowing from commercial banks and issuing marketable IOUs in the commercial paper market. The largest and best-known corporations generally qualify for the prime bank lending rate. Thus, the market for prime-rate bank loans is a direct competitor with the commercial paper market. As shown in Exhibit 13–3, for those corporations able to tap either market, it is generally cheaper to borrow in the commercial paper market. This spread in rates on short-term corporate loans favoring commercial paper helps explain why the commercial paper market has been one of the most rapidly growing segments of the U.S. money market in recent years.

The final money interest rate shown in Exhibit 13–3 is the discount rate charged depository institutions when they borrow from the Federal Reserve banks. In contrast to the other yields discussed to this point, the discount rate is not determined by demand and supply forces in the marketplace, but is set by the Federal Reserve banks with the approval of the Board of Governors of the Federal Reserve System. The level of the discount rate is governed by the Federal Reserve's assessment of the state of the economy and credit market conditions. Where possible, however, the Fed tries to keep the discount rate reasonably close to rates on Treasury bills. An unusually low discount rate may result in excessive borrowing at the Fed's discount window. In contrast, an excessively high discount rate forces banks to borrow heavily in the open market, increasing the volatility of interest rates and sometimes creating unstable market conditions.

SUMMARY

This chapter has presented a broad overview of one of the most important components of any financial system—the money market. By convention, money markets are defined as the collection of institutions and trading relationships that move short-term funds from lenders to borrowers. All money market loans have an original maturity of one year or less. Most loans extended in the money market are designed to provide short-term working capital to businesses and governments so they can purchase inventories, meet payrolls, pay dividends and taxes, and deal with other immediate needs for cash. There short-run cash needs arise from the fact the inflows and outflows of cash are not perfectly synchronized. In the real world, even with the best of planning, temporary cash deficits and temporary cash surpluses are more the rule rather than the exception.

The money market at one and the same time answers the needs of borrowers for short-term credit and the needs of lenders for temporary interest-bearing outlets for their surplus funds. In a period of rapid inflation and high interest rates, it is too costly to let cash lie idle for even a few days. At the same time, however, money market investors are extremely conservative when it comes to investing their funds. They will accept little or no risk of borrower default, prefer financial instruments whose prices are stable, and usually require an investment where their funds can be recaptured quickly as the need arises. For this reason nearly all money market instruments are of prime quality—among the safest, most liquid, and most readily marketable in the financial system. In the remaining chapters of Part Four we examine in detail the characteristics of each of the money market's key financial instruments.

STUDY QUESTIONS

1. What is the money market? Explain why there is a critical need for money market instruments.

2. Who are the principal lenders and borrowers active in the U.S. money market?

3. Define the following:
   a. Money risk.
   b. Default risk.
   c. Inflation risk.
   d. Currency risk.
   e. Political risk.

   Which of these risks are minimized by investing in money market instruments? Does a money market investor avoid all of these risk factors? Why or why not?

4. What are federal funds? Clearinghouse funds? Explain which is more important in the money market, and why.

5. Describe the structure of interest rates in the money market. Which instrument anchors the market and appears to be the foundation for other interest rates? Can you explain why this is so?

PROBLEMS

1. How much interest would be earned (on a simple-interest basis) from a three-day money market loan for $1 million at an interest rate of 12

percent (annual rate)? Suppose the loan were extended on the third day for an additional day at the going market rate of 11 percent. How much total interest income would the money market lender receive?

2. Check the most recent issue of *The Wall Street Journal* you can find. Calculate the *yield spreads* in basis points between U.S. Treasury bills of varying maturity, the federal funds rate, and commercial paper, CD, and bankers' acceptance rates. How do your calculated yield spreads compare with those shown in Exhibit 13–3? Can you explain the observed differences in yield spreads using your knowledge of the factors explaining movements in interest rates discussed in Chapters 7–11?

SELECTED REFERENCES

Federal Reserve Bank of Richmond. *Instruments of the Money Market,* 1977.

Lucas, Charles M.; Marcos T. Jones; and Thom B. Thurston. "Federal Funds and Repurchase Agreements." *Quarterly Review,* Federal Reserve Bank of New York, Summer 1977, pp. 33–48.

McCurdy, Christopher J. "The Dealer Market for U.S. Government Securities." *Quarterly Review,* Federal Reserve Bank of New York, Winter 1977–78.

Melton, William C. "The Market for Large Negotiable CDs." *Quarterly Review,* Federal Reserve Bank of New York, Winter 1977–78, pp. 22–34.

Chapter 14

Treasury Bills, Dealer Loans, and Repurchase Agreements

Learning Objectives in This Chapter

- To examine the nature of Treasury bills—one of the most important of all money market instruments—and the workings of the government securities market.
- To see how U.S. Treasury bills are auctioned each week and how their yield to the investor is determined.
- To determine why government securities dealers are so important to the functioning of the money market and how these dealers finance their operations using loans and repurchase agreements.

Key Terms and Concepts in This Chapter

Treasury bills	Primary dealers	Long position
Auction	Demand loan	Short position
Bank discount method	Repurchase agreement (RP)	

AS we noted in the previous chapter, the money market is an institution designed to supply the cash needs of short-term borrowers and provide investors who hold temporary cash surpluses with an interest-bearing outlet for their funds. In this chapter we focus on one of the most important of all money market instruments—the U.S. Treasury bill. Purchases and sales of Treasury bills represent the largest volume of daily transactions in the money market. Interest rates on bills are the anchor for all other money market interest rates. Trading in T-bills, as these instruments are usually called, is one component of a vast domestic and international market for securities issued by the U.S. government. These government IOUs, which include bills, notes, and long-term bonds, carry great weight in the financial system due to their zero default risk, ready marketability, and high liquidity. At the heart of the market for Treasury bills, notes, and bonds is a handful of securities dealers who make the market go and aid the federal government in selling billions of dollars in new securities each year. In this chapter we examine the activities of these securities dealers and how they finance their daily trading operations in T-bills and other financial instruments.

U.S. TREASURY BILLS

U.S. Treasury bills are direct obligations of the U.S. government. By law, they must have an original maturity of one year or less. T-bills were first issued by the U.S. Treasury in 1929 in order to cover the federal government's frequent short-term cash deficits.

The federal government's fiscal year runs from October 1 to September 30. However, individual income taxes—the largest single source of federal revenue—are not fully collected until April of each year. Therefore, even in those rare years when a sizable federal budget surplus is expected, the government is likely to be short of cash during the fall and winter months and often in the summer as well. During the spring, personal and corporate tax collections are usually at high levels, and the resulting inflow of funds can be used to retire some portion of the securities issued earlier in the fiscal year. T-bills are suited to this seasonal ebb and flow of Treasury cash because their maturities are short, they find a ready market among banks and other investors, and their prices adjust readily to changing market conditions.

Volume of Bills Outstanding

The volume of U.S. Treasury bills outstanding has grown rapidly in recent years, especially since the mid-1960s. As shown in Exhibit 14–1, the total volume of bills outstanding climbed to more than $400 billion in 1987, compared to slightly over $200 billion in 1980, and just $88 billion in 1970. The major factors behind the recent growth of T-bills have been record

Exhibit 14–1   **U.S. Treasury Bills: Total Amount Outstanding and Their Proportion of the Marketable Public Debt, 1960–1987**

End of Year	Volume of Bills Outstanding ($ billions)	Total Marketable Public Debt of the United States ($ billions)	T-Bills as a Percent of the Total Marketable Public Debt
1960	$ 39.4	$ 189.0	20.8%
1965	60.2	214.6	28.1
1970	87.9	247.7	35.5
1975	157.5	363.2	43.4
1980	216.1	623.2	34.7
1985	399.9	1,437.7	27.8
1987	426.7	1,619.0	26.4

Source: Board of Governors of the Federal Reserve System, *Federal Reserve Bulletin,* selected issues.

federal budget deficits, deep recessions which have reduced government tax revenues, and the rapid expansion of certain federal programs such as national defense. Moreover, the U.S. and global economies have grown rapidly at times in recent years, creating a greater need for liquid assets such as bills to aid commercial banks and other investors in the efficient management of their cash positions. Interestingly enough, however, bills have declined as a percentage of the U.S. federal debt due to the more rapid growth of longer-term Treasury notes (1-year to 10-year IOUs).

Types of Treasury Bills

There are several different types of Treasury bills. *Regular-series* bills are issued routinely every week or month in competitive auctions. Bills issued in the regular series have original maturities of three months, six months, and one year. New three- and six-month bills are auctioned weekly, while one-year bills normally are sold once each month. Of these three maturities, the six-month bill provides the largest amount of revenue for the Treasury.

On the other hand, *irregular-series* bills are issued only when the Treasury has a special cash need. These instruments include strip bills and cash management bills. A package offering of bills requiring investors to bid for an entire series of different bill maturities is known as a *strip bill.* Investors who bid successfully must accept bills at their bid price each week for several weeks running. *Cash-management* bills, on the other hand, consist simply of reopened issues of bills that were sold in prior weeks. The reopening of a bill issue normally occurs when there is an unusual or unexpected Treasury need for more cash.

How Bills Are Sold

Treasury bills are sold using the auction technique. The marketplace, not the U.S. Treasury, sets bill prices and yields. A new regular bill issue is announced by the Treasury on Tuesday of each week, with bids from investors due the following Monday at 1 P.M. New York time. Interested investors fill out a form tendering an offer to the Treasury for a specific bill issue at a specific price. These forms must be filed by the Monday deadline with one of the 37 regional Federal Reserve banks or branches. The interested investor can appear in person at a Federal Reserve bank or branch to fill out a tender form, submit the form by mail, or place an order through a security broker, bank, or other depository institution.

The Treasury will entertain both competitive and noncompetitive tenders for bills. *Competitive* tenders typically are submitted by large investors, including commercial banks and government securities dealers, who buy several million dollars' worth at one time. Institutions submitting competitive tenders bid aggressively for bills, trying to offer the Treasury a price high enough to win an allotment of bills but not too high, because the higher the price bid, the lower the rate of return. *Noncompetitive* tenders (normally less than $1 million each) are submitted by small investors who agree to accept the average price set in the weekly or monthly bill auction. The investor must pay the full par value price of the bill at the time the tender is made and, on the issue date, receives a refund check from the Federal Reserve representing the difference between the amount paid in by the investor and the auction price. Generally, the Treasury tries to fill all noncompetitive tenders for bills.

In the typical bill auction, Federal Reserve officials open all the bids at the designated time and array them from the lowest yield (and highest price) to the highest yield (and lowest price). Since April 18, 1983, all competitive bids must be expressed on a bank discount basis with not more than two decimal places. For example, a typical series of bids in a Treasury auction might appear as follows:

Hypothetical Yields Bid for Three-Month U.S. Treasury Bills

Treasury Bill Yields Bid	Their Equivalent Prices
3.54%	$99.115
3.55	99.113
4.06	98.985
4.07	98.982
9.08	97.729
9.34	97.664
9.37	97.657

Note that all the prices associated with each yield bid are expressed on a $100 basis as though T bills have a $100 par value.[1] In fact, the minimum denomination for bills is $10,000, and they are issued in multiples of $5,000 above that minimum. The highest bidder (in this case the one offering 3.54 percent or a price of $99.115) receives bills, and those who bid successively lower prices also receive their bills until all available securities have been allocated.

The lowest price at which at least some bills are awarded is called the *stop-out price*. Let's suppose this is a yield of 9.08 percent (or a price of $97.729), the third yield from the bottom in the array of prices shown above. No one bidding less than the stop-out price will receive any bills in this particular auction. However, once bills are acquired by successful bidders, many of them will be sold right away in the secondary market, giving the unsuccessful bidders a chance to add to their own T-bill portfolios. Payments for bills won in the auction must be made in federal funds, cash, by redeeming maturing Treasury securities or coupon payments, cashier's check, certified personal check, or when permitted by the Treasury, through crediting Treasury tax and loan accounts at banks.[2] All bills today are issued only in *book-entry form*—a computerized record of ownership maintained in Washington, DC—with the owner receiving a statement of account about four to six weeks after purchase. The Treasury Department automatically sends a check to the investor the day the bill matures unless reinvestment of the maturing bill's proceeds into new Treasury securities has been requested.

Results of a Recent Bill Auction

A summary of the results from each T-bill auction is published in *The Wall Street Journal*. The results from an actual bill auction are presented in Exhibit 14–2. In this particular auction, held during October 1987, two maturities of bills—13 and 26 weeks—were offered to the public, and both issues were heavily oversubscribed. Almost $20 billion in both 13-week bills and 26-week bills were requested by the public; however, the Treasury awarded only $6.4 billion of each. Just 6 percent of the bids offering the low (or stop-out) price on the 13-week issue received bills, while 59 percent of the bids offering the low price for the 26-week issue were awarded some bills. Noncompetitive tenders in the amount of $699 million for the 13-week issue and about $801 million for the 26-week issue received their bills.

---

[1] The prices of Treasury Bills usually are expressed on the basis of 100 and contain not more than three places to the right of the decimal point.

[2] These so-called T&L accounts are Treasury deposits kept in about 12,000 of the nation's 15,000 commercial banks. The purpose of these accounts is to minimize the impact on the financial system of Treasury tax collections and debt-financing operations. As taxes are collected or securities are sold, the Treasury deposits the funds received in these T&L accounts and gradually withdraws money from them as needed into its checking accounts held at the Federal Reserve banks.

Exhibit 14–2   **Report of Results from a Typical Weekly Auction of U.S. Treasury Bills, October 19, 1987**

Item	13-Week Bill Issue	26-Week Bill Issue
Applications for bills	$19,971,620,000	$19,753,170,000
Accepted bids	$ 6,416,740,000	$ 6,405,765,000
Percent accepted at low price	6%	59%
Noncompetitive bids accepted	$699,465,000	$801,170,000
Average auction price (rate)	98.271 (6.84%)	96.355 (7.21%)
High price (rate)	98.301 (6.72%)	96.400 (7.12%)
Low price (rate)	98.256 (6.90%)	96.335 (7.25%)
Coupon-equivalent yield	7.08%	7.61%

Notes: The 13-week bills matured January 21, 1988, and the 26-week bills matured April 21, 1988. The interest rates (yields) reported under each price are determined by the difference between the purchase price and the face value and assume a 360-day year. The coupon-equivalent yield is based on a 365-day year.

Source: *The Wall Street Journal*, October 20, 1987.

The dollar-weighted average auction price for the 13-week bills was $98.271 per $100, or $9,827.10 for a $10,000 denomination bill. The 26-week issue sold for an average price of $9,635.50. This works out to a 6.84 percent return on the 13-week bill and a 7.21 percent return on the 26-week issue.[3] On a yield to maturity (or coupon-equivalent) basis, the 13-week bill carried an average return of 7.08 percent, while the 26-week bill had an average return of 7.61 percent. The highest competitive bidders paid a price of $9,830.10 for the 13-week security and $9,640 for the 26-week, $10,000 par value instrument. The lowest successful bidders received their 13-week bills for only $9,825.60 and their 26-week bills for $9,633.50 per $10,000 par bill. Those who bid less than these prices underbid in the auction and received no bills. If these unsuccessful bidders wish to purchase bills of this particular issue, they must buy them in the secondary market, usually from a government securities dealer.

Calculating the Yield on Bills

Treasury bills do not carry a promised interest rate, but instead are sold at a discount from par. Thus, their yield is based on their appreciation in price between the time the bills are issued and the time they mature or are sold by the investor. Any price gain actually realized by the investor is treated not as a capital gain, but as ordinary income received during the year the bill matures for federal tax purposes.[4] We saw in Chapter 8 that the rate

---

[3]These rates of return are figured on a bank discount basis, as discussed on the following pages.

[4]While the income earned from investing in T-bills is not exempt from federal taxes, it is exempt from state and local income taxes.

or yield on most debt instruments is calculated as a yield to maturity. However, bill yields are determined by the bank discount method, which ignores the compounding of interest rates and uses a 360-day year for simplicity.

The bank discount rate (DR) on bills is given by the following formula:

$$DR = \frac{\text{Par value} - \text{Purchase price}}{\text{Par value}} \times \frac{360}{\text{Number of days to maturity}} \quad (14\text{--}1)$$

For example, suppose you purchased a Treasury bill at auction for $97 on a $100 basis (par value) and the bill matured in 180 days. Then the discount rate on this bill would be:

$$DR = \frac{(100 - 97)}{100} \times \frac{360}{180} = 6\%$$

Because the rate of return on T-bills is figured in a different way than the rate of return on most other debt instruments, the investor must convert bill yields to an investment (or coupon-equivalent) yield in order to make realistic comparisons with other securities. The investment yield or rate (IR) on Treasury bills is given by the following formula:

$$IR = \frac{365 \times DR}{360 - (DR \times \text{Days to maturity})} \quad (14\text{--}2)$$

For example, the investment yield on the bill discussed above, which has a discount rate (DR) of 6 percent, would be calculated as follows:

$$IR = \frac{365 \times 0.06}{360 - (0.06 \times 180)} = 6.27\%$$

Because of the compounding of interest rates and the use of a 365-day year, the investment yield on a bill will always be higher than its discount rate. Several other formulas have become popular among investors for calculating yields on Treasury bills when the bills are not held to maturity. Both Equations 14–1 and 14–2 assume that the investor buys a T-bill and ultimately redeems it with the Treasury on its due date. But what if the investor needs cash right away and sells bills to a dealer or other investor in advance of their maturity? In this instance we may use the following formulas:

$$\text{Holding-period yield on bill} = \text{DR when purchased} \\ \pm \text{Change in DR over the holding period} \quad (14\text{--}3)$$

where:

Change in DR over the investor's holding period

$$= \frac{\text{(Days to maturity when purchased} - \text{Days held)}}{\text{Days held}} \quad (14\text{–}4)$$

$$\times \text{ Difference in DR on date purchased and date sold}$$

For example, suppose the investor buys a new six-month (180-day) bill at a price which results in a discount rate (DR) of 6 percent. As is typical, the bill's price begins to rise (and DR to fall) as the bill approaches maturity. Thirty days after purchase, the investor needs immediate cash and is forced to sell at a price which results in a DR of 5.80 percent. What is the investor's holding-period yield? Using Equation 14–4:

$$\text{Change in DR over holding period} = \frac{(180 - 30)}{30} \times (6.00\% - 5.80\%)$$

$$= \frac{150}{30} \times 0.20\% = 1.00\%$$

Then, using Equation 14–3:

$$\text{Holding-period yield on bill} = 6.00\% + 1.00\% = 7.00\%$$

Because this T-bill rose in price, the investor experienced a gain that increased the bill's holding period yield by 1 percent over the original discount rate of 6 percent.

Consider another problem that frequently confronts the T-bill investor. Suppose a corporation has just purchased some bills to serve as a temporary reserve of liquidity, but it knows that sometime in the next few weeks it will need those funds to help finance a building project. However, the firm wants to hold the bills long enough to earn a specific *target yield*. How many days must the bills be held to hit the target yield? The correct formula is as follows:[5]

Number of days to hold bill for target yield =

$$\frac{\text{Days to maturity when purchased} \times \text{Difference in DR on date purchased and date sold}}{\text{Desired Change in DR over holding period}} \quad (14\text{–}5)$$

$$+ \text{ Difference in DR on date purchased and date sold}$$

To illustrate the use of this formula, we can draw upon the figures in the preceding example and assume the investor wants to achieve a 7 percent target yield. We have:

---

[5]Sometimes interest rates rise sharply after a Treasury bill auction, and the market price of bills falls below their original purchase price. An investor unloading bills in such a market will take a loss unless they can be held until prices rise again. Equation 14–5 can also be used to determine the number of days bills must be held to avoid a loss, provided the change in DR over the holding period is replaced by the DR on the date the bills were purchased.

$$\frac{\text{Numbers of days to hold bills}}{\text{for 7 percent target yield}} = \frac{180 \times (0.20\%)}{1.00\% + 0.20\%} = \frac{36\%}{1.20\%} = 30 \text{ days}$$

Therefore, a 180-day bill purchased at a discount rate of 6 percent must be held for 30 days if the investor desires a 7 percent annual yield and expects the bill's discount rate to decline by 20 basis points.

Market Interest Rates on Treasury Bills

Due to the absence of default risk and because of the superior marketability of T-bills, the yields on these popular financial instruments are typically the lowest in the money market. And because of the tremendous size of the bill market, conditions there tend to set the tone in all other segments of the money market. A rise in T-bill rates, for example, usually is quickly translated into increases in interest rates attached to bankers' acceptances, commercial paper, CDs, and other money market instruments. Easier conditions in the bill market that lead to lower T-bill rates rapidly spread to other segments of the short-term market, and conditions there usually ease as well.

While the prices of Treasury bills, like those attached to all money market instruments, tend to be quite stable, yields on bills fluctuate widely in response to changes in economic conditions, government policy, the demand for credit, and a host of other factors. This can be seen quite clearly in Exhibit 14–3, which gives annual averages for the secondary market yields on 3-, 6-, and 12-month bills. T-bill rates typically fall during periods of recession and sluggish economic activity as borrowing and spending sag. Note, for example, the decline in bill yields in 1975 and 1982–83, as shown in Exhibit 14–3. All of these years were periods in which the economy reached the peak of a boom period and then dropped into a recession. During periods of economic expansion, on the other hand, T-bill rates frequently surge upward, as happened between 1976 and 1981. Inflationary expectations also appear to have a potent impact on bill market yields, as evidenced by the sharp run-up in T-bill rates during the late 1970s and early 1980s— both periods when price increases accelerated rapidly and, in the latter case, soared to double-digit levels.

It is interesting to examine the shape of the *yield curve* for bills. As Exhibit 14–3 suggests, that curve usually slopes upward, with 12-month bill maturities generally carrying the highest yields, 6-month the next highest, and 3-month maturities the lowest yields. This is not always the case, however. During certain periods—1974 and 1979–81 are good examples— the bill yield curve seems to signal the onset of a recession by sloping downward. Occasionally too, the yield curve for bills assumes a pronounced humped or inverted U shape, with middle maturities carrying the highest rates of return. This happened during the 1973–74 period. It is difficult to

Exhibit 14–3   Market Interest Rates on U.S. Treasury Bills, 3-, 6-, and 12-Month Maturities (Annual Percentage Rates)

Year	3-Month	6-Month	12-Month	Year	3-Month	6-Month	12-Month
1971	4.33%	4.52%	4.60%	1980	11.43	11.37	10.89
1972	4.07	4.49	4.77	1981	14.03	13.80	13.14
1973	7.03	7.20	7.01	1982	10.61	11.07	11.07
1974	7.84	7.95	7.71	1983	8.61	8.73	8.80
1975	5.80	6.11	6.30	1984	9.52	9.76	9.92
1976	4.98	5.26	5.52	1985	7.48	7.65	7.81
1977	5.27	5.53	5.71	1986	5.98	6.02	6.07
1978	7.19	7.58	7.74	1987	5.78	6.03	6.33
1979	10.07	10.06	9.75	1988*	5.69	5.91	6.30

*Average for March, 1988.

Source: Board of Governors of the Federal Reserve System, *Federal Reserve Bulletin,* selected monthly issues.

assign any particular cause to this phenomenon. Sometimes the bend in the curve in the middle maturities appears to reflect heavy Treasury issues of new six-month bills or heavy commercial bank sales of T-bills as bankers try to accommodate customer loan demand by converting their bills into loanable funds. It is noteworthy that the humped yield curve has generally appeared near the end of a boom period and shortly before the onset of a recession. During these periods investors in the financial marketplace are especially uncertain as to which way interest rates are headed.

Recent research has found that the yield curve for Treasury bills is not determined exclusively by the expectations of investors (as implied, for example, by the rational expectations interest rate theory discussed in Chapter 7 or the expectations hypothesis of the yield curve discussed in Chapter 9). Studies by Rowe, Lawler, and Cook (1986) and by Jones and Roley (1982) indicate that Treasury bill yield curves usually slope upward because of the existence of liquidity (or term) premiums on longer-term bills—an extra yield paid to investors who buy longer-term bills to compensate them for the greater price risk. Investors cannot eliminate these extra yields on longer-term bills by borrowing short and lending long, it is argued, because private investors cannot borrow at interest rates as low as the U.S. government's borrowing rate. Private rates are necessarily higher than interest rates on government securities due to default risk. In contrast, yield curves on private money market securities (such as on bank CDs) usually have much less of an upward slope than do Treasury bill yield curves and do not appear to contain significant liquidity (term) premiums. Investors *can* eliminate term premiums on *private* securities by borrowing and lending at roughly equal interest rates.

Investors in Treasury Bills

Principal holders of Treasury bills include commercial banks, nonfinancial corporations, state and local governments, and the Federal Reserve banks. Commercial banks and private corporations hold large quantities of bills as a reserve of liquidity until cash is needed. The most attractive feature of bills for these institutions is their ready marketability and relatively stable price. The Federal Reserve banks conduct the bulk of their open-market operations in T-bills because of the depth and volume of activity in this market. In fact, T-bills play a crucial role in the conduct of monetary policy by the Federal Reserve System. The Fed purchases and sells bills in an effort to influence other money market interest rates and thereby alter the volume and growth of bank credit and ultimately the total amount of investment spending and borrowing in the economy.[6]

DEALER LOANS AND REPURCHASE AGREEMENTS

The money market depends heavily upon the buying and selling activities of securities dealers to move funds from cash-rich units to those with cash shortages. Today, about 40 primary dealers in government securities trade in both new and previously issued Treasury bills, bonds, and notes. Many of these dealers also buy and sell other money market instruments, such as commercial paper, CDs, and bankers' acceptances. They are the principal points of contact with the money market for thousands of individual and institutional investors and are essential to the efficient functioning of that market.

While the dealers supply a huge volume of securities daily to the financial marketplace, they also depend heavily on the money market for borrowed funds. Most dealer houses invest little of their own equity in the business. The bulk of operating capital is obtained through borrowings from commercial banks, nonfinancial corporations, and other institutions. A major dealer firm carries hundreds of millions of dollars in securities in its trading portfolio, with 95 percent or more of that portfolio supported by short-term loans, some carrying only 24-hour maturities.

The two most heavily used sources of dealer funds are demand loans from the largest banks and repurchase agreements (RPs) with banks and other lenders. Every day, the major New York banks post rates at which they are willing to make short-term loans to dealers. Generally, one rate is quoted on new loans and a second (lower) rate is posted for renewals of existing loans. A demand loan may be called in at any time if the banks need cash in a hurry. Such loans are virtually riskless, however, because

---

[6] We will examine Federal Reserve open market operations and the role of Treasury bills in those operations in Chapter 23.

they usually are collateralized by U.S. government securities, which may be transferred temporarily to the lending bank or its agent.

Repurchase Agreements

An increasingly popular alternative to the demand loan is the repurchase agreement (RP). Under this arrangement, the dealer sells securities to a lender but makes a commitment to buy back the securities at a later date at a fixed price plus interest. Thus, RPs are simply a temporary extension of credit collateralized by marketable securities. Some RPs are for a set length of time (term), while others, known as *continuing contracts,* carry no explicit maturity date but may be terminated by either party on short notice. Larger commercial banks provide both demand loans and RPs to the dealers, while nonfinancial corporations have provided a growing volume of funds to dealers through RPs in recent years. Other lenders active in the RP market include state and local governments, insurance companies, and foreign financial institutions who find the market a convenient, relatively low-risk way to invest temporary cash surpluses that may be retrieved quickly and easily when the need arises. On some trading days the volume of RP loans approaches a trillion dollars or more.

The typical RP loan transaction can be described quite easily through the use of T accounts (an abbreviated balance sheet) for a security dealer and for the lender of funds. Exhibit 14–4 presents a typical example of such a loan. In this case we assume a manufacturing company has a temporary $1 million cash surplus. The manufacturer is eager to loan its temporary

Exhibit 14–4   Example of a Typical RP Loan Transaction

	Security Dealer		Manufacturing Company	
	Assets	**Liabilities**	**Assets**	**Liabilities**
a. Lender of funds—a manufacturing company—has a $1 million surplus in its cash account.			Deposit at bank + $1 million	
b. A security dealer and the manufacturing company settle on an RP with the dealer using the borrowed funds to buy securities.	Securities held + $1 million	RP borrowing from manufacturer + $1 million	Deposit at bank − $1 million RP loan to security dealer + $1 million	
c. The RP agreement is concluded and the funds returned (plus interest).	Deposit at bank − $1 million	RP borrowing from manufacturer − $1 million	Deposit at bank + $1 million RP loan to security dealer − $1 million	

cash surplus right away to avoid losing even a single day's interest, while the dealer wishes to borrow at the low-cost RP loan rate in order to purchase interest-bearing securities. The borrowing dealer and the lending company agree on a $1 million RP loan—the minimum loan usually made in this market—collateralized by Treasury bills, with the dealer agreeing to buy back the T-bills within a few days plus pay the interest on the loan. Normally the securities that form the collateral for the RP loan are supposed to be placed in a custodial account at a bank.[7] When the loan is repaid, the dealer's RP liability is automatically canceled and the securities are returned to the dealer.

Until recently, RPs were principally overnight transactions or expired in a few days. Today, however, there is a substantial volume of one- to three-month agreements and some carry even longer maturities. Longer-term RPs are known as *term agreements*. Many recent RPs have built-in flexibility to benefit both borrower and lender. For example, *dollar repos* permit the seller of securities (borrower) to repurchase securities from the lender that are similar to, but not necessarily the same as, the securities originally sold. So-called *flex repos,* usually involving a securities dealer and a state or local unit of government, are very similar to deposits. In this case the lender can withdraw part of the loan when he or she needs cash (such as to start construction on a new building), and the remaining funds continue being loaned to the borrowing dealer.

The interest rate on RPs is the return that a dealer must pay a lender of short-term funds for the temporary use of money and is closely related to other money market interest rates. Usually the securities pledged behind an RP are valued at their current market prices plus accrued interest (on coupon-bearing securities), less a small "haircut" (discount) to reduce the lender's exposure to market risk. The longer the term, the riskier and the less liquid the securities pledged, the larger the "haircut" will be to protect the lender in case security prices fall. Periodically, RPs are "marked to market," and if the price of the pledged securities has dropped, the borrower may have to pledge additional collateral.

Interest rates on repurchase agreements are usually add-on rates determined from this formula:

$$\begin{array}{c} \text{RP interest} \\ \text{income} \end{array} = \begin{array}{c} \text{Amount} \\ \text{of loan} \end{array} \times \begin{array}{c} \text{Current} \\ \text{RP rate} \end{array} \times \frac{\text{Number of days loaned}}{360 \text{ days}}$$

For example, a loan of $100 million to a dealer overnight at a 7 percent RP rate would yield interest income of $19,444.44. That is:

---

[7] There is evidence that this safety device of placing securities involved in an RP agreement in a separate bank-held custodial account is not always scrupulously followed. Moreover, because the majority of outstanding RP loans are simply recorded as book entries at the Federal Reserve banks, verification of what has been done with the pledged securities is difficult. The result is that if a government securities dealer goes out of business, customers may have difficulty recovering the collateral behind some of the loans they have made to the dealer.

$$\begin{array}{c} \text{RP interest} \\ \text{income} \end{array} = \$100,000,000 \times .07 \times \frac{1}{360} = \$19,444.44$$

Under a continuing contract RP, the rate changes daily so the calculation above would be made for each day the funds were loaned, and the total interest owed paid to the lender when the contract is ended by either party.

In order to promote a smoothly functioning market, the Federal Reserve System through its trading desk at the New York Fed frequently participates with a Fed-approved list of about 40 primary (recognized) government security dealers in RPs. In a straight RP transaction, the Federal Reserve buys securities from a dealer on a short-term basis and then sells them back at the end of the agreed-upon period. The Fed may also enter into a reverse RP transaction with one or more approved dealers. In this case, the Federal Reserve Bank of New York will sell securities to a dealer with an agreement to buy them back after a short period of time, thus temporarily absorbing dealer funds and reducing the ability of the dealer's bank to make loans. Whereas the dealers use the RP to protect or increase their earnings from security trading, the Federal Reserve uses RPs to steady the money market and to promote national economic goals.[8]

Sources of Dealer Income

Securities dealers take substantial risk in order to make a market for Treasury bills and other financial instruments. To be sure, the securities they deal in are among the highest-quality instruments available in the financial marketplace. However, the prices of even top-quality securities can experience rapid declines if interest rates rise. Moreover, established dealer houses cannot run and hide, but are obliged to stand ready at all times to buy and sell on customer demand, regardless of the condition of the market. In contrast to securities brokers, who merely bring buyers and sellers together, dealers take a position of risk, which means that they act as principals in the buying and selling of securities. Dealers add any securities purchased to their own portfolios.

Dealers stand ready to buy specified types of securities at an announced *bid* price and to sell them at an announced *ask* price. This is called *making a market* in a particular financial instrument. The dealer hopes to earn a profit from such market-making activities—in part from the positive spread between bid and asked prices for the same security. This spread varies with market activity and the outlook for interest rates, but is very narrow on bills (often about $50 per $1 million or less) and wider on more volatile notes and bonds (often 1/32 to 4/32 or $312.50 to $1,250 per $1 million). Spreads range higher on longer-term securities than on shorter-term securities, on small versus large transactions, and on securities not actively traded due

---

[8] We will discuss Federal Reserve RP transactions in more detail in Chapter 23.

to both greater risk and greater costs.[9] Dealers do not usually charge commissions on their trades.

As we have seen, the dealers' holdings of securities are financed by loans, so their portfolio positions are extremely sensitive to fluctuations in interest rates. For this reason dealers frequently will shift from long positions to short positions, depending on the outlook for interest rates. A long position means that dealers purchase securities outright, take title to them, and hold them in their portfolios as an investment or until a customer comes along. Long positions typically increase in a period of falling interest rates. A short position, on the other hand, means that dealers sell securities they do not presently own for future delivery to a customer. In so doing, they hope the prices of those securities will fall (and interest rates rise) before they must be delivered to the buyer. Obviously, as interest rates fall (and security prices rise), the dealer will experience capital gains on a long position but losses on a short position. On the other hand, if interest rates rise (resulting in a drop in security prices), the dealer's long position will experience capital losses, while the short position will post a gain.

In periods when interest rates are expected to rise, dealers typically reduce their long positions and go short. Conversely, expectations of falling rates lead dealers to increase their long positions and avoid short sales. By correctly anticipating rate movements, the dealer can earn sizable *position profits*. Dealers also receive *carry income,* which is the difference between interest earned on securities they hold and their cost of borrowing funds. Generally, dealers earn higher rates of return on the securities they hold than the interest rates they pay for loans, but this is not always so. Because most dealer borrowings are short term, securities dealers normally are better off if the yield curve is positively sloped.

Dealer Positions in Securities

As reflected in the first section of Exhibit 14–5, dealer holdings of U.S. government and other securities are both huge and subject to erratic fluctuations. For example, in 1985 and 1986, dealer positions in U.S. government securities rose sharply, following relatively modest government security holdings in 1983 and 1984. Why was there such a tremendous difference in

---

[9] We recall from Chapter 8 that 1/32 of a point is equal to $0.03125 for each $100. On a $1 million trade in Treasury bills, the dealer's spread would normally be $50 to $60. For shorter-term coupon issues the spread usually lies in the range of $312.50 to $1,250 for each $1 million in par value. However, dealer spreads are difficult to predict in advance because they vary with the nature and total size of each transaction and current demand and supply conditions in the marketplace.

Generally, dealers will deliver securities sold the next business day after a sale has been made (known as *regular delivery*), though smaller odd-lot transactions are usually completed within five business days— a method of delivery used for most Treasury bill trades. Large customers or dealers themselves may demand same-day settlement (known as *cash delivery*). In recent years an increasing number of dealer transactions have been *forward transactions* in which securities are purchased or sold for delivery after 5 business days from the date of the transaction if U.S. government securities are involved or after 30 days when mortgage-backed agency securities are the subject of the trade. Payment for all deliveries is usually made in federal funds.

Exhibit 14–5 **Positions and Sources of Financing for U.S. Government Security Dealers** (Averages of Daily Figures Expressed in $ Millions at Par)

Item	1981	1982	1983	1984	1985	1986	1987*
Net immediate positions:							
U.S. Treasury securities	$ 9,033	$ 9,328	$ 6,263	$ 5,543	$ 7,391	$ 13,055	$ −7,950
Bills	6,485	4,837	4,282	5,504	10,075	12,723	2,296
Other securities within 1 year	−1,526	−199	−177	63	1,050	3,699	2,105
1–5-year issues	1,488	2,932	1,709	2,159	5,154	9,297	371
5–10-year issues	292	−341	−78	−1,119	−6,202	−9,504	−7,524
Over 10 years	2,294	2,001	528	−1,174	−2,686	−3,161	−5,197
Federal agency securities	2,277	3,712	7,172	15,294	22,860	33,066	31,981
Certificates of deposit	3,435	5,531	5,839	7,369	9,192	10,533	8,612
Bankers' acceptances	1,746	2,832	3,332	3,874	4,586	5,535	3,777
Commercial paper	2,758	3,317	3,159	3,788	5,570	8,087	7,203
Futures positions:							
Treasury bills	−8,934	−2,508	−4,125	−4,525	−7,322	−18,062	−579
Treasury coupons	−2,733	−2,361	−1,032	1,795	4,465	3,489	3,182
Federal agency securities	522	−224	170	233	−722	−153	−100
Forward positions:							
U.S. Treasury securities	−603	−788	−1,935	−1,643	−911	−2,304	−921
Federal agency securities	−451	−1,190	−3,561	−9,204	−9,420	−11,909	−19,236
Sources of dealer financing:							
Reverse repurchase agreements: Overnight and continuing term agreements	14,568 32,048	26,754 48,247	29,009 52,493	44,078 68,357	68,035 −80,509	98,954 108,693	124,791 148,033
Repurchase agreements: Overnight and continuing term agreements	35,919 29,449	49,695 43,410	57,946 44,410	75,717 57,047	101,410 70,076	141,735 102,640	170,840 120,980

*1987 figures are averages for the month of June.

Source: Board of Governors of the Federal Reserve System, *Federal Reserve Bulletin,* various monthly issues.

the size of dealer portfolios during those years? Money market interest rates began falling late in 1984, creating opportunities for sizable dealer profits on short-term securities held in long positions as market prices rose. Thus, dealer holdings of short- and medium-term government securities as well as other short-term money market instruments (federal agency securities, certificates of deposit, acceptances, and commercial paper) rose substantially. In their futures and forward positions—contracts promising future delivery of securities—the dealers moved aggressively to protect themselves against fluctuating interest rates, however. The use of futures contracts and other interest rate hedging devices became especially important in the period after October 1979 when the Federal Reserve System announced that it would allow interest rates and security prices to fluctuate more freely while it concentrated on controlling money-supply growth.[10]

Sources of Dealer Financing

Where do government security dealers derive most of their funds to purchase and carry securities? As the second section of Exhibit 14–5 shows, the dealers make heavy use of repurchase agreements, usually collateralized by securities held in their portfolios. Commercial banks are also a major source of dealer borrowed funds, year in and year out. Indeed, a dozen of the primary U.S. government security dealers are really dealer departments housed in some of the nation's largest banks and the remaining two dozen are nonbank dealers. However, nonfinancial business corporations are the most rapidly growing source of funds for major securities dealers. Many industrial corporations today find the dealer loan market a convenient and safe way to dispose of temporarily idle monies. With wire transfer of funds between banks readily available, a company can lend a dealer millions of dollars in idle cash and recover those funds in a matter of hours if a cash emergency arises.

Dealer Transactions

Trading among securities dealers and between dealers and customers amounts to billions of dollars a day. For example, average daily transactions in the U.S. government securities market were in the neighborhood of $50 to $60 billion in the 1980s. Indeed, so large is the government securities market that the volume of trading often exceeds several times over the total volume of trading on the major U.S. stock exchanges. About half the trades in this market involve Treasury bills. Government securities dealers trade heavily among themselves, usually through *brokers*. Government security brokers do not take investment positions themselves, but try to match bids and offers placed with them by dealers and other investors. There are just four main brokers of Treasury securities today, each of which operates a closed-circuit TV network showing dealer prices and quantities available.

Dealerships are a cutthroat business in which each dealer firm is out to maximize its returns from trading, even if gains must be made at the expense of competing dealers. Indeed, market analysts housed within each dealer firm study the daily price quotations of competitors. If one dealer firm temporarily underprices some securities (offers excessively generous

---

[10] See Chapter 12 for an explanation of financial futures contracts and Chapter 24 for a discussion of Federal Reserve money supply control procedures.

yields), other dealers are likely to rush in before the offering firm has a chance to correct its mistake. It is a business with little room for the inexperienced or slow-moving trader and fraught with low margins, risk, and unstable earnings. For example, in 1982 two major firms—Drysdale Government Securities, Inc., and Lombard-Wall, Inc.—collapsed. These closings were followed by four more dealer failures: Lion Capital Group and RTD Securities in 1984, and E.S.M. Government Securities and Bevill, Bresler & Schulman Asset Management Corporation in 1985. Large losses in the hundreds of millions of dollars can be recorded in a few days or weeks, and huge security positions are often amassed with little cash and heavy, unregulated borrowing. Dealers may buy large quantities of bonds that are not yet issued—"when-issued" securities—without any money down and payment not due until delivery a week or so later. Yet, as we have seen, the government securities dealers are essential to the smooth functioning of the financial markets and to the successful placement of billions of dollars in new securities issued each year by the U.S. Treasury.

SUMMARY

In this chapter we examined one of the most important of all securities markets—the market for Treasury bills and other U.S. government securities. This market has grown rapidly in recent years in response to huge Treasury borrowing needs and the needs of investors for highly liquid, readily marketable financial instruments. It is difficult to overestimate the importance of the government securities market in the functioning of the global financial system. This market sets the tone for the whole financial system in terms of interest rates, security prices, and availability of credit. And it is in this market today that most U.S. government economic policy measures begin in the form of U.S. Treasury issues of new securities and Federal Reserve open market operations. A thorough knowledge of the workings of the market for government securities tells us much about the "how" and "why" of the financial system.

STUDY QUESTIONS

1. Why has the volume of Treasury bills grown so rapidly in recent years? Explain why the T-bill is so popular with money market investors.
2. List and define the various types of Treasury bills. Why are there so many different varieties?
3. Explain how a T-bill auction works. Can you cite some advantages of this method of sale? Disadvantages?

4. How are the yields on U.S. Treasury bills calculated? How does this method differ from the method used to calculate bond yields? Why is this difference important?

5. What is the normal, or typical, slope of the yield curve for T-bills? Why? What other slopes have been observed, and why do you think these occur?

6. Who are the principal investors in U.S. Treasury bills? What factors motivate these investors to buy bills?

7. Explain why dealers are essential to the smooth functioning of the securities markets. Where do most dealer funds come from?

8. What is a demand loan? An RP? Explain their role in dealer financing.

9. In what ways do dealers earn income and possibly make a profit? To what risk is each source of dealer income subject?

10. Are the majority of government security dealers' positions in short-term or long-term securities? What causes their positions to change?

PROBLEMS

1. From the following sets of figures: (1) calculate the bank discount rate on each T-bill; and (2) convert that rate to the appropriate investment (or coupon-equivalent) yield.
   a. A new three-month T-bill sells for $98.25 on a $100 basis.
   b. The investor can buy a new 12-month T-bill for $96 on a $100 basis.
   c. A 30-day bill is available from a U.S. government securities dealer at a price of $97.50 (per $100).

2 Calculate the holding-period yield for the following situations:
   a. The investor buys a new 12-month T-bill at a discount rate of 7½ percent. Sixty days later the bill is sold at a price which results in a discount rate of 7 percent.
   b. A large manufacturing corporation acquires a T-bill in the secondary market 30 days from its maturity but is forced to sell the bill 15 days later. At time of purchase the bill carried a discount rate of 8 percent, but it was sold at a discount rate of 7¾ percent.

SELECTED REFERENCES

Bowsher, Norman H. "Repurchase Agreements." *Review,* Federal Reserve Bank of St. Louis, September 1979, pp. 17–22.

Federal Reserve Bank of Richmond. *Instruments of the Money Market.* 7th ed., 1986.

Jones, David S., and V. Vance Roley. "Rational Expectations, The Expectations Hypothesis, and Treasury Bill Yields: An Econometric Analysis." Research Working Paper 82-01, Federal Reserve Bank of Kansas City, February 1982.

The First Boston Corporation. *Handbook of Securities of the United States Government and Federal Agencies*. 32nd ed., 1986.

McCurdy, Christopher J. "The Dealer Market for United States Government Securities." *Quarterly Review*, Federal Reserve Bank of New York, Winter 1977–78, pp. 35–47.

Rowe, Timothy D.; Thomas A. Lawler; and Timothy Q. Cook. "Treasury Bill Versus Private Money Market Yield Curves." *Economic Review*, Federal Reserve Bank of Richmond, July–August 1986, pp. 3–12.

Simpson, Thomas D. *The Market for Federal Funds and Repurchase Agreements*. Staff Study, Board of Governors of the Federal Reserve System, July 1979.

Chapter 15

Federal Funds, Negotiable CDs, and Loans from the Discount Window

Learning Objectives in This Chapter

- To examine the critical roles banks play in the workings of the money market.

- To illustrate three important ways that banks borrow funds in the money market—from the federal funds and certificate of deposit (CD) markets and by requesting loans from the discount windows of the Federal Reserve banks.

- To see what changes the technique known as "liability management" has made in bank performance and practice.

Key Terms and Concepts in This Chapter

Federal funds

Legal reserves

Contemporaneous
reserve accounting

Negotiable certificates
of deposit (CDs)

Liability management

Eurodollar CD

Discount window

Discount rate

THE single most important financial institution in the money market is the commercial bank. Large money center banks, such as those headquartered in New York City, Chicago, San Francisco, London, Tokyo, and a handful of other major cities around the globe, provide billions of dollars in funds daily through the money market to governments and corporations in need of cash. As we saw in the previous chapter, bank loans and repurchase agreements are a principal source of financing for dealers in government securities, while banks also make large direct purchases of Treasury bills and other money market securities. Commercial banks support private corporations borrowing in the money market both by purchasing their securities and by granting lines of credit to backstop a new security issue. Banks conduct acceptance financing to support the movement of goods in international trade, resulting in the creation of a high-grade money market instrument—the bankers' acceptance.[1] And both large and small banks today readily lend their cash reserves to other financial institutions and to industrial corporations overnight or for a few days to cover short-term liquidity needs.

In order for commercial banks to lend huge amounts of funds daily in the money market, they must also borrow heavily in that market. As we saw in Chapter 4, the owners (stockholders) supply only a minor portion of a commercial bank's total resources; the bulk of bank funds must be borrowed. While the majority of borrowed funds (close to 80 percent for most banks) comes from deposits, a growing portion of the industry's financing needs are supplied by the money market. However, bank managers today are more cautious in their use of money market borrowings than was true even a few years ago. Such funds are relatively expensive to use, and their interest cost is more volatile than for most kinds of deposits. Many large banks today follow the strategy of maintaining a roughly equal balance between their lending and borrowing activities in the money market. The volume of short-term bank debt is counterbalanced by a nearly equal volume of short-term bank assets.[2]

In this chapter we examine three of the most important money market sources of funds for banks and other deposit-type financial institutions— federal funds, certificates of deposit (CDs), and loans from the Federal Reserve's discount window. In Chapter 17 we discuss still another important source of funds for many of the largest depository institutions— Eurodollars.

---

[1] Bankers' acceptances are discussed in Chapter 17.

[2] The idea of maintaining a roughly *equal* balance between borrowing and lending in the money market follows one of the oldest concepts in the field of finance—the *hedging principle*. As discussed in Chapter 9, in a world of uncertainty, borrowers of funds can reduce risk by matching the maturity of their assets and liabilities. This approach reduces the risk of borrowing when funds are not needed and also lowers the risk of not having sufficient cash when interest payments and other bills come due.

FEDERAL FUNDS

As we saw in the introductory chapter to the money market (see Chapter 13), federal funds are among the most important of all money market instruments for one key reason: Fed funds are the principal means of making payments in the money market. By definition, federal funds are any monies available for immediate payment ("same-day money"). They are generally transferred from one depository institution to another by simple bookkeeping entries requested by wire or telephone after a purchase of securities is made or a loan is granted.

The Nature of Federal Funds

The name *federal funds* came about because early in the development of the market the principal source of immediately available money was the reserve balance which each bank must keep at the Federal Reserve bank in its region of the United States. If one bank needs to transfer funds to another, it need only contact the Federal Reserve bank in its district, and money is readily transferred into the appropriate reserve account—a transaction accomplished in minutes or seconds by computer.

Today, however, the Fed funds market is far broader in scope than just reserves on deposit with the Federal Reserve banks. For example, virtually all banks maintain deposits with large correspondent banks in the principal U.S. cities, and these deposits may be transferred readily by telephone and by wire from the account of one bank to that of another. They may also be borrowed by the institution that holds the correspondent deposit, simply by transferring funds from the correspondent deposit to an account titled "Federal funds purchased" and reversing the entries when the loan matures. Savings and loan associations, credit unions, and savings banks maintain deposits with commercial banks that also are available for immediate transfer to a customer or to another financial institution.[3] Business corporations and state and local governments can lend federal funds by executing repurchase agreements with securities dealers, banks, and other funds traders. Securities dealers who have received payment for securities sold can turn around and make their funds immediately available to borrowers through the federal funds market. Borrowers of federal funds include securities dealers, corporations, state and local governments, and nonbank financial intermediaries, such as savings and loan associations and insurance companies. Without question, however, the most important of all borrowers in the Fed funds market are commercial banks, who use this instrument as the

---

[3] As we saw in Chapters 4 and 5, nonbank thrift institutions that offer transactions accounts must also keep reserve balances at the Federal Reserve banks or at approved depository institutions under the terms of the Depository Institutions Deregulation and Monetary Control Act of 1980. These reserve balances are available for borrowing and lending in the federal funds market.

principal way to adjust their legal reserve account at the Federal Reserve bank in their district.

Use of the Federal Funds Market to Meet Deposit Reserve Requirements

As we saw in Chapter 4, commercial banks and other depository institutions must hold liquid assets in a special reserve account, equal to a fraction of the funds deposited with them by the public. Only vault cash held on the premises and reserve balances kept with the Federal Reserve bank in the district count in meeting a U.S. bank's requirement to hold legal reserves. Frequently, commercial banks (especially small banks) hold more legal reserves than the law requires. Because these reserves earn little or no income, most bankers active in the money market try to dispose of any excess legal reserves in their possession, even if they only lend the funds overnight.

Banks are aided in this endeavor by the fact that their legal reserve requirement is calculated on a daily average basis over a two-week period, known as the *reserve computation period*. For example, the reserve computation period for *transaction deposits* (e.g., checking accounts and NOWs) stretches from a Tuesday through a Monday two weeks later. The Federal Reserve calculates the daily average level of transaction deposits held by each depository institution over this two-week period and then multiplies that average by the required reserve percentage (3 percent for smaller banks, for example) to determine the amount of legal reserves (vault cash and deposits with the Federal Reserve bank in the district) that must be held by each depository institution. These legal reserves must average the required amount over a two-week period known as the *reserve maintenance period*. For transaction deposits the reserve maintenance period starts on a Thursday—two days after the transaction-deposit reserve computation period begins—and ends on a Wednesday two weeks later. Thus, the reserve computation and reserve maintenance periods for transaction deposits overlap each other except for *two days*. This overlapping feature explains why this deposit reserve accounting system is often called contemporaneous reserve accounting (CRA).[4]

In theory at least, contemporaneous reserve accounting promotes a closer correspondence between the growth of deposits, which reflect bank lending, and the volume of legal reserves which can be controlled by the Federal Reserve System. Interestingly enough, however, the Federal Reserve allows depository institutions to calculate the legal reserves they must hold on *nonpersonal time deposits* (principally business CDs) and *other non-*

---

[4]The CRA system replaced the old lagged reserve accounting (LRA) system in February 1984. Under the old LRA system there was a two-week gap between the reserve computation and reserve maintenance periods.

transaction liabilities on the basis of the average level of these liabilities over a two-week period ending 16 days before the reserve maintenance period begins. Furthermore, each depository institution is allowed to count its average vault cash holdings over the same two-week computation period and then deduct that daily average vault cash figure from its required reserves.

Exhibit 15-1 illustrates the contemporaneous reserve accounting system now in use. As this exhibit illustrates, the manager of each depository institution's money desk—the department responsible for keeping track of the institution's legal reserve position—must adjust each deposit institution's reserve balance at the district Federal Reserve bank to the right level over the two-week reserve maintenance period.[5] The federal funds market is an indispensable tool for this kind of daily reserve management, especially for the largest and most aggressive banks, which hold few reserves of their own. Indeed, many large U.S. banks today borrow virtually all of their legal reserve requirement on a more or less permanent basis from the federal funds market.

Mechanics of Federal Funds Trading

The mechanics of federal funds trading vary depending on the locations of the buying (borrowing) and selling (lending) institutions. For example, suppose two commercial banks involved in a federal funds transaction are located in the heart of the New York money market. These banks can simply exchange checks. The borrowing bank is given a check drawn on the lending bank's reserve account at the Federal Reserve Bank of New York or drawn on a correspondent balance held at some other bank in New York City. This check is payable immediately ("same-day money") and therefore Fed funds are transferred to the borrower's reserve account before the close of business that same day. The lender, on the other hand, receives a check drawn on the borrower. This last check is "one-day money" (payable the following day) because it must pass through the New York Clearinghouse for settlement. Thus, funds flow instantly to the borrowing bank's reserve account and are automatically returned to the lending bank's reserve account the next day or whenever the loan agreement terminates. Interest on the loan may be included when the funds are returned, paid by separate check, or settled by debiting and crediting correspondent balances.

If the transacting institutions are not both located within the New York Federal Reserve District, the loan transaction proceeds in much the same way except that two Federal Reserve banks are involved. Once borrower and lender agree on the terms of a federal funds loan, the lending institution

---

[5] Actually, the money desk manager receives a little leeway under existing regulations because each depository institution is allowed to fall up to 2 percent below its required reserve level in a given reserve maintenance period, provided it runs a corresponding excess reserve position during the next maintenance period.

Exhibit 15-1   **The Contemporaneous Reserve Accounting (CRA) System for Calculating Deposit Reserve Requirements of Commercial Banks and Other U.S. Depository Institutions**

Week 1–Week 2	Week 3–Week 4	Week 5–Week 6
Reserve computation period for nonpersonal time deposits and other nontransaction liabilities	Skip over	Reserve computation period for transaction deposits
Tues. Mon. Mon.		Tues. Mon. Mon.
↑_____↑		↑_____↑
Calculate daily average levels of nonpersonal time deposits and other (nontransaction) liabilities and daily average holdings of vault cash over this two-week period		Reserve maintenance period for holding required daily average levels of legal reserves at the district Federal Reserve bank
		Thur. Thur. Wed.
		↑_____↑

Example of Required Deposit Reserve Calculation

First National Bank holds a daily average of $10 million in nonpersonal time deposits and $100,000 in vault cash over weeks 1 and 2. Transaction deposits at First National Bank averaged $20 million daily during weeks 5 and 6 (Tuesday through Monday 14 days later). The reserve requirement percentage on nonpersonal time deposits and on transaction deposits as set by the Federal Reserve Board is 3 percent. Therefore, First National must hold $800,000 in its required daily average reserve balance over a two-week period (week 5–week 6, Thursday through Wednesday, 14 days hence). This required reserve figure was derived as follows:

Legal reserves required behind nonpersonal time deposits	= $10 million × 3% =	$300,000
Legal reserves required behind transaction deposits	= $20 million × 3% =	600,000
Total legal reserve requirement	=	$900,000
Less: Average vault cash holdings in weeks 1 and 2	=	− 100,000
Required daily average deposit to be held at the Federal Reserve bank during weeks 5 and 6		$800,000

will directly, or indirectly through a major correspondent bank, contact the Federal Reserve bank in its district, requesting a wire transfer of funds. The Federal Reserve bank then merely transfers reserves through the Fed's wire network to the Federal Reserve bank serving the region of the country where the borrowing institution is located. Funds travel the reverse route when the loan is terminated.

Incidentally, how do Fed funds borrowers and lenders contact each other to find out who has surplus funds to lend and who is short funds? The telephone is the most common medium of communication with institutions in need of funds and those with surplus funds calling their regular Fed funds customers. In addition, a handful of Fed funds *brokers* active in the New York money market work to bring buying and selling institutions together.

Volume of Borrowings in the Funds Market

Commercial banks borrow billions of dollars each day in the funds market. Total federal funds borrowings by banks in all 50 states (including security resale agreements from nonbank institutions) stood at more than $170 billion early in 1988. Borrowings between banks themselves can only be estimated, though figures released by the Federal Reserve Board indicate that the money center banks (with $1 billion or more in assets) borrowed an average of between $120 and $130 billion daily from other commercial banks. Thus, the federal funds market probably extends close to $300 billion in credit *daily*. The large banks in New York City, by virtue of their strategic location at the heart of the domestic money market, still account for a disproportionate share of Fed funds transactions. However, the market has broadened considerably in recent years to include both domestic and foreign banks in Atlanta, Chicago, Dallas, San Francisco, and other major U.S. cities, as well as thousands of smaller banks in outlying areas. Member banks of the Federal Reserve System, despite their smaller total numbers, are more important in this market than nonmember banks due to their greater average size and strategic locations.

Most federal funds loans are overnight (one-day) transactions or continuing contracts that have no specific maturity date and can be terminated without advance notice by either party. One-day loans carry a fixed rate of interest, but continuing contracts often do not. There is a growing volume of loans lasting beyond one day, often arising from security repurchase agreements. These longer-maturity interbank loans are usually called *term* federal funds and are being supplied increasingly by foreign banks and savings and loan associations as a safe, easy, and profitable way to warehouse funds until they are needed for long-term loan commitments.

Rates on Federal Funds

The federal funds interest rate is highly volatile from day to day and week to week, though on an annual basis it tends to move roughly in line with

Exhibit 15-2 **Effective Interest Rates on Federal Funds Transactions, 1971–1988** (Percent per Annum)*

Year	Average Daily Rate on Federal Funds	Year	Average Daily Rate on Federal Funds
1971	4.67%	1980	13.36%
1972	4.44	1981	16.38
1973	8.74	1982	12.26
1974	10.51	1983	9.09
1975	5.82	1984	10.22
1976	5.05	1985	8.10
1977	5.54	1986	6.80
1978	7.94	1987	6.77
1979	11.20	1988†	6.58

*Figures in the table are averages of daily effective rates for each week ended on Wednesday during the indicated year. The daily effective rate is an average of the interest rates on a given day weighted by the volume of transactions at these rates.

†Average for the month of March 1988.

Source: Board of Governors of the Federal Reserve System, *Federal Reserve Bulletin*, selected monthly issues.

other money market rates (see Exhibit 15-2). The short-run volatility of the rate arises from substantial variations in the volume of funds made available by lenders each day and the size of daily cash deficits experienced by banks and other money market participants. The funds rate tends to be most volatile toward the close of the reserve maintenance period (especially on the last day), depending on whether larger banks across the nation are flush with reserves or are short of reserves. There are also definite seasonal patterns, with the funds rate tending to rise around holiday periods when loan demand and deposit withdrawals are heavy.

Federal Funds and Government Policy

The federal funds market is an easy and riskless way to invest excess reserves for short periods and still earn some interest income. It is essential to the daily management of bank reserves, because credit can be obtained in a matter of minutes to cover emergency situations. As we have seen, the market is also critical to the whole money market because these funds serve as the principal means of payment for securities and loans. Moreover, the funds market transmits the effects of Federal Reserve monetary policy quickly throughout the banking system.

Prior to 1979 the Federal Reserve routinely set target levels for the federal funds rate and raised or lowered those targets depending on whether the Fed wished to slow down borrowing and spending in the economy or speed it up. Using daily open market operations—buying and selling securities—the Fed was able to push the funds rate in the desired direction on any given day. However, fearing accelerating inflation, the Fed announced in October 1979 that it would pay less attention to daily federal funds rates and try to control the nation's money supply. Since that time the federal funds rate appears to have become *more volatile* from day to day.

NEGOTIABLE CERTIFICATES OF DEPOSIT

One of the largest of all money market instruments, measured by dollar volume, is the negotiable certificate of deposit (CD). A CD is an interest-bearing receipt for funds deposited in a bank or other depository institution for a set period of time.[6] While banks, savings and loan associations, and other deposit-type institutions issue many types of CDs, the true money market CDs are negotiable instruments that may be sold any number of times before reaching maturity and carry minimum denominations of $100,000. The usual round-lot trading unit for CDs bought and sold in the money market is $1 million.

The interest rate on a large negotiable CD is set by negotiation between the issuing institution and its customer and generally reflects prevailing market conditions. Therefore, like the rates on other money market securities, CD rates rise in periods of tight money when loanable funds are scarce and fall in periods of easy money when loanable funds are more abundant.

The negotiable CD is one of the youngest of all American money market instruments. It dates from 1961, when First National City Bank of New York began offering the instrument to its largest corporate customers. Simultaneously a small group of securities dealers agreed to make a secondary (resale) market for CDs of $100,000 or more. Other money center banks soon entered the competition for corporate funds and began to offer their own CDs.

The decision to offer this new money market instrument was agonizing for the nation's major banks, because CDs have sharply raised the average cost of bank funds. However, commercial banks had little choice but to offer the new instrument or face the loss of billions of dollars in interest-sensitive deposits. The cash management departments of major corporations have become increasingly aware of the many profitable ways available today to invest their short-term funds. Prior to the introduction of the negotiable CD, many bankers found that their biggest corporate customers were reducing their deposits (especially demand accounts) and buying U.S. Treasury bills, bankers' acceptances, RPs, and other money market instruments. The CD was developed to attract those lost deposits back into the banking system.

---

[6]The minimum maturity permitted for CDs under federal regulation is 7 days though as a practical matter 14 days is usually the minimum. There is no legal upper limit on maturities, however. CDs must be issued at par and trade on an interest-bearing basis, unlike Treasury bills. Payment is made in federal funds on the day the CD matures.

Growth of CDs

Negotiable CDs are a real success story for most banks. In 1988, large ($100,000 +) time deposits outstanding at banks operating in the United States totaled nearly $400 billion. This compares with only about $100 billion in large CDs a decade earlier. Until the Penn Central crisis in 1970, large negotiable CDs were subject to legal interest rate ceilings as specified in the Federal Reserve Board's Regulation Q. However, the bankruptcy of the huge Penn Central Transportation Company rocked the money market, and many large corporations could not sell their commercial notes to raise short-term funds. To ease this serious liquidity crunch, the Fed suspended interest rate ceilings on large short-term (30–89-day) CDs in June 1970 and lifted the ceilings on longer-term CDs in May 1973. Freed from legal interest rate ceilings, the volume of large CDs has soared, especially during periods of rapid economic growth.

Terms Attached to CDs

Negotiable CDs may be *registered* on the books of the issuing bank or other depository institution or issued in *bearer form* to the investor purchasing them. CDs issued in bearer form are more convenient for resale in the secondary market because they are in the hands of the investor who owns them. Denominations range from $25,000 to $10 million, though as we noted previously, CDs traded in the money market carry minimum denominations of $100,000. Maturities range from 1 to about 18 months, depending on the customer's needs. However, most negotiable CDs have maturities of 6 months or less.

Interest rates in the CD market are computed as a yield to maturity but quoted on a 360-day basis (except in secondary market trading, where the bank discount rate is used as a measure of CD yields). For example, if your business firm purchases a $100,000 negotiable CD for 6 months at an interest rate of 7.50 percent, you would receive back at the end of 180 days:

$$\$100,000 \times (1 + \frac{180}{360} \times 0.075) = \$103,750.$$

To convert the yield on newly issued CDs to a coupon-equivalent (or yield-to-maturity) basis, we must multiply their yield by the ratio 365:360. The yield on CDs normally is slightly above the Treasury bill rate due to greater default risk, a thinner resale market, and the state and local government tax exemption of earnings on Treasury bills. CD rates are sometimes lower than going rates on federal funds and Eurodollars as alternative sources of bank funds, due in part to the fact that CDs sold to businesses carry reserve requirements and federal funds borrowings do not. Because many money market investors can easily *arbitrage* between short-term markets, moving funds toward the highest yields, the CD interest rate adjusted for reserve requirement hovers very close to the average of current and future federal funds interest rates expected by investors to prevail over the life of the CD. However, as Exhibit 15-3 shows, in 1984 and again in 1987, following severe problems at some of the nation's largest banks, risk premiums attached to large bank CDs rose, driving them well above the federal funds rate and closer to Eurodollar deposit rates. The yield spread between CDs and other money market instruments varies over time, depending upon investor preferences, the supply of CDs and other money market instruments, and the changing financial condition of issuing banks.

One of the most interesting developments in recent years is the appearance of a *multitiered* (segmented) market for CDs. Investors have grouped issuing banks into different risk categories, and yields in the market are scaled accordingly. This development is a legacy of the collapse of such banking giants as United States National Bank of San Diego in October 1973, Franklin National Bank of New York in October 1974, Penn Square Bank in Oklahoma City in 1982, and Continental Illinois Bank in Chicago in 1984. Faced with the specter of major bank failures, banks viewed as less stable by investors were forced to issue their CDs at significantly higher interest rates.

CDs from the largest and most financially sound banks are rated *prime*, while smaller banks or those viewed as less stable issue *nonprime* CDs at higher interest rates. As is true for any depositor in a U.S. insured bank, the holder of a CD is covered against loss up to a maximum of $100,000 if the issuing bank fails. Unfortunately, this insurance protection is of limited value to a corporation holding a million-dollar or larger CD.

Buyers of CDs

The principal buyers of large negotiable CDs include nonfinancial corporations, state and local governments, foreign central banks and governments, wealthy individuals, and a wide variety of financial institutions. The latter include insurance companies, pension funds, investment companies, savings banks, credit unions, and especially money market funds. Large CDs appeal to these investors because they are readily marketable at low risk, may be issued in any desired maturity, and carry a somewhat higher yield than that on Treasury bills. However, the investor gives up some marketability in comparison with T-bills because the resale market for CDs averages $3 to $4 billion a day—well below the average daily volume of trading in bills.

Most buyers hold CDs until they mature. However, prime-rated CDs issued by billion-dollar banks are actively traded in the secondary market, centered in New York City. The purpose of the secondary market is principally to accommodate corporations that need cash quickly or see profitable opportunities from the sale of their deposits. Also, buyers of CDs who desire

Exhibit 15-3 **Recent Interest Rates on Money Market CDs ($100,000 or More) versus Rates on Treasury Bills, Federal Funds, and Eurodollars**

Instrument	Period (percent)							
	1981	**1982**	**1983**	**1984**	**1985**	**1986**	**1987**	**1988***
Certificates of deposit:								
Three-month	15.91%	12.27%	9.07%	10.37%	8.05%	6.52%	6.87%	6.63%
Six-month	15.77	12.57	9.27	10.68	8.25	6.51	7.01	6.78
U.S. Treasury bills:								
Three-month	14.03	10.61	8.61	9.52	7.48	5.98	5.78	5.70
Six-month	13.80	11.07	8.73	9.76	7.65	6.03	6.03	5.91
Federal funds	16.38	12.26	9.09	10.22	8.10	6.80	6.66	6.58
Eurodollars, three-month	16.79	13.12	9.56	10.73	8.28	6.71	7.06	6.74

*Rates as of March 1988.

Note: Based on five-day average rates for each week of the period as quoted by five dealers in CDs. All rates expressed in percent per annum. Bill yields in the secondary market are quoted on a bank discount basis from daily closing bid prices.

Source: Board of Governors of the Federal Reserve System, *Federal Reserve Bulletin,* selected issues.

shorter maturities or higher yields than are available on new issues will enter the secondary market. No U.S. bank is allowed to purchase its own CDs in the secondary market or redeem them in advance of maturity, except under special circumstances. Moreover, banks usually will not lend money using their own CDs as collateral because of the risk of borrower default.

CDs in Liability Management

Commercial banks and other depository institutions use the CD as a supplement to federal funds when additional reserves are needed. A depository institution in need of funds simply raises the rate it is currently offering on CDs to attract new deposits. Financial institutions may also trade CDs (not their own) in the secondary market to raise funds, much as they might sell Treasury bills for cash. Today the negotiable CD plays a prominent role in the strategy of liability management, where banks control their funds sources as well as their funds uses to achieve each bank's goals.

New Types of CDs

Bankers are becoming increasingly innovative in packaging CDs to meet the needs of customers. One notable innovation occurred in 1975 when the *variable-rate CD* was introduced. Variable-rate CDs issued by major banks today generally carry maturities of 18 months to 2 years, with an interest rate that is adjusted every 30 to 90 days (known as a *leg* or *roll* period). The rate is usually based on a fixed premium over the average secondary market rate for major bank CDs. Variable-rate CDs give the investor a higher return than normally will be obtained by continually renewing shorter-term CDs and is a particularly popular investment for money market mutual funds. These CDs represent about one fifth of the domestic CD market and generally pay higher rates than fixed-rate CDs due to the absence of reserve requirements on CDs with maturities longer than 18 months. The market interest rate on variable-rate CDs is usually a few basis points above the secondary market rate on comparable-maturity fixed-rate CDs.

Another important development occurred in 1976 when Morgan Guaranty Trust in New York City introduced the *rollover CD* (also known as the rolypoly CD). Because 6-month CDs are the maximum maturity traded in the secondary market, Morgan offered its customers longer-term CDs with higher rates, but in packages composed of a series of 6-month CDs extending over a period of at least 2 years. Thus, the rolypoly CD promised higher returns plus the ability to market some CDs in the package in advance of maturity to meet emergency cash needs. However, the bank's customer is still obligated to purchase the remaining certificates on each 6-month anniversary date until the contract expires. Some rolypoly CDs are issued with fixed rates, while others carry floating rates that change every 6 months.

Another variation on the CD theme is the Eurodollar CD, developed in 1966. Eurodollar CDs are negotiable, dollar-denominated time deposits issued by the foreign branches of major U.S. banks and foreign-owned banks. These instruments generally carry higher yields than comparable domestic CDs due to greater perceived risk. Most Eurodollar CDs carry fixed rates, but floating-rate instruments were introduced in 1977. These CDs carry maturities over one year with a rate adjusted every three to six months to match changes in the London Interbank Offer Rate (LIBOR). There is now an active secondary market for Eurodollar CDs centered in New York City and in London.

Recent years have ushered in still more CD innovations; for example, *Asian Dollar CDs, Jumbo CDs, Yankee CDs,* and *Brokered CDs.* Offered by U.S., Japanese, and other banks operating in Singapore, *Asian Dollar CDs* carry both fixed and floating interest rates based on the current level of the Singapore interbank offer rate, known as SIBOR. Payable in New York Clearinghouse funds, Asian CDs normally trade in $1 million units like domestic CDs, but at higher yields. *Jumbo CDs,* on the other hand, are large ($100,000 +), negotiable CDs issued by nonbank thrift institutions such as savings and loan associations and savings banks. *Yankee CDs* are issued in the United States by foreign banks (mainly Japanese, Canadian, British, and West European institutions) that usually have branch or agency offices in one or more major U.S. cities. *Brokered CDs* consist of CDs sold through security brokers in maximum $100,000 denominations in order to qualify for federal deposit insurance. Many brokers participate in exchanges where their investing customers can purchase packages of the highest-yielding CDs issued by banks and thrifts. Further innovations in CDs are likely in the future as banks face increasingly stiff competition for funds.

LOANS FROM THE FEDERAL RESERVE'S DISCOUNT WINDOW

A money market source of funds available to commercial banks and other depository institutions is the Federal Reserve's discount window. Each of the 12 Federal Reserve banks has a department where banks and other qualified borrowers can come to borrow reserves for short periods.[7] Most discount window loans are short term (a maximum of 15 days), though longer-term credit can be arranged upon presentation of acceptable collateral and adequate reasons for the request. Today the Fed grants three types of loans: (1) adjustment credit, designed to cover short-term deficiencies in required legal reserves; (2) seasonal credit, designed to aid small depository institutions experiencing seasonal fluctuations in loans and deposits; and (3) extended credit, aimed mainly at institutions facing serious financial problems of a long-term nature. Normally, adjustment credit to cover short-term reserve deficiencies accounts for the majority of loans granted by the Federal Reserve banks. However, the other forms of discount window credit can be extremely important in emergency situations, such as the recent financial crisis experienced by Continental Illinois Bank in Chicago.

The mechanics of borrowing from the discount window are relatively simple. A depository institution granted a loan merely receives an increase in its reserve account at the Federal Reserve Bank in its district. When the loan comes due, the Fed merely removes the amount owed from the borrowing institution's reserve account.[8]

Causes and Effects of Borrowing from the Discount Window

Borrowing from the Fed *increases* the total volume of reserves available in the banking system until the loan is repaid. Many banks and other depository institutions come to the Federal Reserve near the end of their reserve settlement week when they find themselves short of legal reserves. Frequently, the funds available from the Federal Reserve carry a lower interest rate than prevails in the federal funds market, on CDs, or on other money market sources of funds. This is especially true in periods of rapidly rising

---

[7] Until 1980 only member banks could borrow from the Federal Reserve banks except under special circumstances. However, with passage of the Monetary Control act of 1980, nonmember commercial banks, savings banks, savings and loan associations, and credit unions offering transaction accounts or nonpersonal time deposits were authorized to borrow from the Fed's discount window on the same basis as member banks.

[8] See Chapter 23 for a more complete discussion of the methods used by depository institutions to borrow from the Federal Reserve.

Exhibit 15–4   **Volume of Borrowings from the Federal Reserve Banks, 1975–1988** ($ Millions at Year-End)

Year	Discount Window Loans to Depository Institutions	Year	Discount Window Loans to Depository Institutions
1975	$ 211	1982	$ 697
1976	25	1983	774
1977	265	1984	3,186
1978	1,174	1985	1,318
1979	1,454	1986	827
1980	1,617	1987	777
1981	642	1988*	396

*As of February 1988.

Source: Board of Governors of the Federal Reserve System, *Federal Reserve Bulletin,* selected issues.

interest rates because the Fed changes its loan rate infrequently. As the gap between open market rates (especially on federal funds) and the Fed's rate widens, demands on the discount window increase. In contrast, a period of falling rates usually brings about a decline in borrowings from the Fed.

This last point is illustrated by the figures shown in Exhibit 15-4. Money market interest rates rose to record levels in 1979 and 1980, spurred on by high rates of inflation. The federal funds rate averaged just over 11 percent in 1979 and more than 13 percent in 1980, rising to a high of almost 20 percent in December 1980. Nevertheless, the Federal Reserve kept the rate on its loans around 10 percent until late 1979 and held it in the 10 to 12 percent range through most of 1980. With discount window loans much cheaper than other money market sources of funds, borrowers predictably turned to the Federal Reserve banks for huge amounts of funds. Discount window loans averaged more than $1.5 billion during the 1979–80 period and climbed to well over $2 billion in the fall of 1980. Much the same pattern developed in 1983 and 1984 when open market interest rates in the money market climbed to double-digit levels, while the Fed kepts its discount rate in the 8.5 to 9 percent range. The result was a sharp upsurge in borrowings from the Federal Reserve banks which reached a peak of more than $8 billion (on a daily average basis) in August of 1984 before falling back as market interest rates eased down. Lower interest rates and moderate growth in bank loan demand kept Federal Reserve borrowings down in 1987 and 1988.

Collateral for Discount Window Loans

Most loans granted through the Fed's discount window are secured by U.S. government securities. However, the Federal Reserve also will make loans against commercial or farm paper, bankers' acceptances, and bills of exchange. Discount window loans may be for terms as long as 90 days if the collateral used consists of U.S. government securities or eligible paper, and up to 4 months on other forms of collateral. However, as we noted earlier, most loans from the discount window are for a maximum of 15 days. To make the borrowing process as simple as possible, many depository institutions keep U.S. government securities in the vaults of the Federal Reserve banks and sign loan authorization agreements with the Fed's discount department in advance so they can borrow over the telephone. Such requests must be confirmed in writing, however.

Restrictions on Federal Reserve Credit

Large money center banks are the heaviest users of the discount window because they incur reserve deficits most frequently. However, less than 10 percent of all institutions eligible regularly borrow from the Federal Reserve System, despite the fact that it is often the cheapest source of reserves. In part, this is due to an uneasy feeling experienced by most bankers about being in debt to a government regulatory agency. The Fed's own regulations discourage heavy and frequent use of the window. For example, Federal Reserve officials stress that borrowing is a "privilege, not a right" and that no depository institution should come to rely on Federal Reserve credit. Borrowing institutions are required to alternate between the window and other money market sources, especially federal funds.

The Federal Reserve's Discount Rate

The discount rate is the interest rate charged by the Fed on loans of reserves secured by U.S. government securities or other acceptable collateral. In reality, there are four different discount rates. The cheapest rate applies to loans (advances) for short-term liquidity adjustment or seasonal needs, secured by U.S. government securities or high-grade commercial ("eligible") paper. A slightly higher interest rate is levied against discount window loans secured by collateral of lesser quality. In times of national emergency, the Fed may also extend credit to individuals, partnerships, and even nonfinancial corporations, but the interest rate is much higher on such loans.[9]

The individual Federal Reserve banks often recommend that the discount rate be changed; however, a change in that rate must be approved by the Federal Reserve Board in Washington, DC. In recent years the Fed has levied a higher interest rate for emergency borrowings when a bank is in serious financial trouble. Large, continuous borrowings over a prolonged period of time may be approved at a rate of 1 to 2 percent above the regular Federal Reserve discount rate.

---

[9]See Chapter 23 for a schedule of rates charged on various types of discount-window loans.

The spread between the Fed's discount rate and the market rate on federal funds has a profound effect on the amount of borrowing from the discount windows of the Federal Reserve banks. The federal funds rate usually stays *above* the discount rate because most banks prefer to borrow reserves from private sector lenders rather than deal with a government agency (the Federal Reserve System) that regulates them. Many bankers fear that heavy use of direct loans from the Fed rather than from the impersonal funds market would subject them to closer scrutiny by the regulatory authorities.

The exact relationship between the federal funds rate and the discount rate is depicted in Exhibit 15–5. Banks cannot determine by themselves the total supply of reserves available; that supply consists of nonborrowed reserves (which the Fed expands or reduces through its operations) and borrowed reserves (which the Fed chooses to loan or not to loan to banks through the discount window). If the Federal Reserve expands the total supply of reserves, the federal funds rate will fall, other things being equal. In contrast, greater bank demand for reserves (due perhaps to rising loan demand) will drive the equilibrium federal funds rate higher.

If the federal funds rate drops *below* the discount rate, banks will not borrow from the discount window. All their reserves will come from federal funds, CDs, and other private market sources. However, if the federal funds rate rises above the discount rate, banks will begin to step up their discount window borrowings until the added cost in the form of closer surveillance and scrutiny by Federal Reserve officials matches the net benefit of discount window borrowing (equal to the federal funds rate minus the discount rate). At that point, borrowing from the discount window should stop.

A CONCLUDING COMMENT ON BANK ACTIVITY IN THE MONEY MARKET

In this chapter we focused on the major money market sources of funds used by commercial banks and other depository institutions. As we have seen, banks operate on both sides of the money market, supplying billions of dollars in credit to governments, corporations, securities dealers, and financial intermediaries each day while also borrowing huge amounts daily from many of the same institutions.

The money market has not always been as important a source of funds for banks and other depository institutions as it is today. Prior to the 1960s, even many of the largest money center banks in the United States regarded short-term deposits and nondeposit borrowings from the money market as a secondary, supplementary source of funds. Bankers were aware that heavy dependence on money market borrowing would make their earnings more sensitive to fluctuations in interest rates. When interest rates rose rapidly,

Exhibit 15–5   **The Relationship between Discount Window Borrowing and the Interest Rates on Federal Funds and Discount Window Loans**

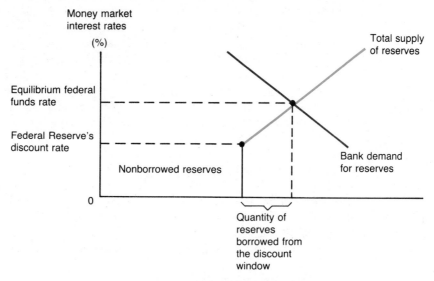

Volume of reserves available to the banking system ($)

bank profit margins would be squeezed. However, the force of competition intervened in the 1960s and 1970s, and many banks were compelled to draw more heavily upon the money market simply to protect their share of credit and deposit markets.

The real catalyst for growing money market borrowing by U.S. banks and other depository institutions has been the growing financial sophistication of their largest customers. When major corporations began to seek alternative investments for their short-term funds, especially the purchase of commercial paper and Treasury bills, rather than holding most of their money in bank deposits, bankers were forced to turn to the money market for additional funds. As we have seen in this chapter, the banking community approached the problem in two ways. One was to offer a new financial instrument—the negotiable certificate of deposit—to compete directly for short-term corporate funds. The other approach was to draw more intensively upon existing sources of money market funds, especially the federal funds market.

Prior to the 1960s and 1970s, the federal funds market was confined principally to the nation's largest banks, who swapped reserves. As bankers turned more and more to the fund market, however, it broadened tremendously. Thousands of small banks and other nonbank financial institutions in cities, towns, and rural areas across the United States began supplying their excess reserves to larger banks in the central cities, hoping to boost their earnings. In turn, the greater supply of Fed funds encouraged the nation's largest banks to rely even more heavily on the money market and less upon customer deposits as a source of reserves. The federal funds market had become an accepted institution for both the smallest and the largest financial institutions in the nation.

As we will see in subsequent chapters, the rapid expansion of the CD and federal funds markets was just the beginning of banking's *money market strategy*. When the Federal Reserve became concerned over the rapid growth of CDs and federal funds, especially in periods of severe inflation, and clamped down with tight-money policies and a slower growth in available reserves, innovative financial managers were forced to find new sources of reserves or face a real cutback in their lending activities. Many turned to the Eurodollar market, borrowing deposits from abroad or organizing holding companies and issuing commercial paper through subsidiary corporations. Still others found innovative ways to use repurchase agreements backed by Treasury bills and other government securities to raise additional funds.

All of these clever maneuvers form part of what has been called the technique of *liability management*. For decades prior to the 1960s and 1970s, bankers devoted most of their time and attention to the management of assets—mainly loans and security investments—and assumed their deposits and other liabilities would take care of themselves. Many financial analysts argued that deposits were essentially beyond management's control, determined by such external factors as interest rates, economic conditions, and government policy. Heavier dependence on the money market for funds changed all that, however. Bankers very quickly came to realize that simply by varying the daily interest rates (yields) they were willing to offer on CDs, federal funds, Eurodollars, commercial paper, and other funds sources, they could gain a measure of control over the volume of incoming funds. If more funds were needed on a given day to accommodate customer loan demand, for example, a bank active in the money market would simply offer a higher yield on the particular money market instrument it desired to use. If a smaller volume of funds was required at another time, the institution might simply lower its offer rate on money market borrowings.

What is especially fascinating about the growth of liability management strategies is that they have had precisely the effects many financial analysts predicted from the start. The earnings of banks and other financial institutions *have* become more sensitive to fluctuations in interest rates; and in periods of rapidly escalating rates, profit margins have been squeezed. The use of liability management strategies appears to have fundamentally altered the earnings-size relationship in banking. Until the 1970s the largest banks generally reported the highest earnings rates, but no more! Today the most profitable banks are generally those of only moderate size. The heavier use of expensive and often highly volatile money market borrowings has contributed in many instances to more rapid increases in bank expenses than in revenues.

Whether this adverse impact on the earnings of major banks will continue into the future remains to be seen. The great innovative abilities of these institutions freed in recent years by deregulation of the industry will do much to shape their earnings performance in the years ahead. But, whatever the future holds, bankers have transformed the money market into a far larger, more dynamic, and more vital institution than at any other time in history. The future rapid growth of money market transactions, with banks at the very center of trading activity, seems assured.

STUDY QUESTIONS

1. Define the term *federal funds*. Why are federal funds so important to the functioning of the money market?

2. Who are the principal borrowers in the federal fund market? Principal lenders?

3. Describe the process of reserve position adjustment for commercial banks and other depository institutions. What role does the federal funds market play in the management of depository institutions' money (reserve) position?

4. Why do you suppose the funds market is so important to the Federal Reserve in the conduct of monetary policy?

5. What is a large negotiable CD? When and why were CDs first offered in the U.S. money market?

6. What factors appear to influence the interest rate offered on the CDs issued by any particular depository institution? Explain the meaning of the term *multitiered market*.

7. What role do large negotiable CDs play in liability management?

8. What is a variable-rate CD? Rolypoly CD? Eurodollar CD? Many financial experts expect banks and other deposit institutions to continue to develop new and more innovative forms of CDs in the future. Can you explain why?

9. What is a discount window loan? What types of loans do the Federal Reserve banks make? How are those loans made and repaid?

10. What role does the discount window play in managing the reserves of depository institutions?

PROBLEMS

1. Security State Bank has just verified by checking its legal reserve account on the computer of the Federal Reserve bank in its district that its daily average reserve balance for the current reserve maintenance period is $1.25 million. Today is the final day of the current reserve maintenance period and the bank's money market officer is concerned that Security might be running a large deficit in its legal reserve account. Checking the bank's own computer records, the officer discovers that nontransaction deposits and other liabilities averaged $16 million and transaction deposits averaged $31 million over the relevant two-week reserve computation period. Vault cash holdings over the same reserve computation period as that for nonpersonal time deposits averaged $250,000. Currently the Federal Reserve imposes a 3 percent reserve requirement on the total of a depository institution's transaction deposits below $29 million and 12 percent for any amount of transaction deposits over $29 million. Nontransaction deposits are subject to a 3 percent required reserve. Does Security State have a reserve deficiency? If so, is it required to cover the reserve shortfall before this current reserve maintenance period ends today? Explain your answer. If Security State must borrow, what is the cheapest source of legal reserves currently available?

SELECTED REFERENCES

Federal Reserve Bank of Richmond. *Instruments of the Money Market.* 6th ed., 1986.

Melton, William C. "The Market for Large Negotiable CDs." *Quarterly Review,* Federal Reserve Bank of New York, Winter 1977–78, pp. 22–24.

Simpson, Thomas D. *The Market for Federal Funds and Repurchase Agreements.* Staff Study, Board of Governors of the Federal Reserve System, July 1979.

Tarhan, Vefa. "Individual Bank Reserve Management." *Economic Perspectives,* Federal Reserve Bank of Chicago, May–June 1984, pp. 17–23.

Chapter 16

Commercial Paper and Federal Agency Securities

Learning Objectives in This Chapter

- To highlight the important role large corporations and government agencies play in the money market.
- To examine the characteristics of the oldest of all U.S. money market instruments—commercial paper.
- To see how federal agencies, by borrowing funds in the money market, help a number of sectors in the economy (such as agriculture, home buyers, and small businesses) to find lower-cost credit.

Key Terms and Concepts in This Chapter

Commercial paper	Master note	Federal Financing
Direct paper	Government-sponsored	Bank
Dealer paper	agencies	Solicitation method
	Federal agencies	

IN the previous chapter we discussed the vital role played by banks as major borrowers and lenders in the money market. However, banks have had to share the limelight in recent years with two other groups of money market borrowers—federal government agencies and large corporations. Indeed, the largest of all borrowers in the American money market is not a bank, but a unit of government—the U.S. Treasury Department. Moreover, in the 1960s and 70s, other units within the federal government's huge structure, known as federal agencies, came to be major demanders of money market funds. Many of these agencies, such as the Federal Land Banks, Small Business Administration, and Federal National Mortgage Association, have become familiar names to active investors worldwide, who are regularly offered a menu of attractive notes and bonds so that these agencies can carry out their mission of assisting "disadvantaged" sectors of the economy.

The ranks of *private* money market participants have also grown rapidly in recent years due to the borrowing and lending activities of some of the largest corporations. Each year companies like American Telephone & Telegraph, General Motors, and Philip Morris borrow billions of dollars in the money market through the sale of unsecured promissory notes, known as commercial paper. A 1982 study by the Federal Reserve Board found that, at that time, about 1,200 corporations were regularly selling their commercial notes to money market investors.[1] Commercial paper issued by large corporations and bought principally by other large corporations has become one of the most dynamic and rapidly growing segments of the money market. In this chapter we take a close look at both commercial paper and federal agency securities and their important roles within the financial system.

COMMERCIAL PAPER

What Is Commercial Paper?

Commercial paper is one of the oldest of all money market instruments, dating back to the 18th century in the United States. By definition, commercial paper consists of short-term, unsecured promissory notes issued by well-known companies that are financially strong and carry high credit ratings.[2] The funds raised from a paper issue normally are used for current

---

[1] See Hurley (1982).

[2] As a further backstop to reduce investor risk, borrowers in the commercial paper market nearly always secure a line of credit at a commercial bank and pay a small fee (about ⅛ percent) or hold a compensating deposit at the bank. However, because the line of credit cannot be used to directly guarantee payment if the company goes bankrupt, many commercial note issuers today also take out irrevocable letters of credit prepared by their banks. Such a letter makes the bank responsible for repayment if the corporation defaults on its commercial paper. In today's uncertain markets, investors frequently need reassurance that a borrowing corporation can pay its bills either from current cash flow or by drawing upon an existing bank credit line. The bank charges a fee of ½ percent to 1½ percent of the amount of the guarantee it issues. Insurance companies and parent companies of issuing firms also guarantee commercial paper.

transactions—that is, to purchase inventories, pay taxes, meet payrolls, and cover other short-term obligations. However, a growing number of paper issues today are used to provide "bridge financing" for such long-term projects as the building of pipelines, ships, office buildings, nuclear power plants, and manufacturing assembly lines. In these instances issuing companies usually plan to convert their short-term paper issues into long-term, more permanent financing when the capital market is more favorable.

Commercial paper is generally issued in multiples of $1,000 and in denominations designed to meet the needs of the buyer. It is traded mainly in the *primary market*. Opportunities for resale in the secondary market are limited, though some dealers will redeem the notes they sell in advance of maturity and others trade paper issued by large finance companies and bank holding companies. Because of the limited resale possibilities, investors are usually quite careful to purchase those paper issues whose maturity matches their planned holding periods.

Types of Commercial Paper

There are two major types of commercial paper—direct paper and dealer paper.

The main issuers of direct paper are large finance companies and bank holding companies that deal directly with the investor rather than using a securities dealer as an intermediary and that borrow money continuously. These companies, which regularly extend installment credit to consumers and large working capital loans and leases to business firms, announce the rates they are currently paying on various maturities of their paper. For example, not long ago, General Motors Acceptance Corporation (GMAC), the largest finance company borrower in this market, offered the following yields to interested investors:

Paper Maturity	Offered Yield (Percent)
30 to 59 days	9.40%
60 to 89 days	9.30
90 to 119 days	9.25
120 to 209 days	9.05
210 to 270 days	9.50

Investors select the maturities that most closely approximate their expected holding periods and buy the securities directly from the issuer. Interest rates may be adjusted during the day the paper is being sold in order to regulate the inflow of investor funds.

Leading finance company borrowers in the direct paper market include GMAC, CIT Financial Corporation, Commercial Credit Corporation, and General Electric Credit Corporation. The leading U.S. bank holding companies which issue commercial paper are centered around the largest banks in New York, Chicago, San Francisco, and other major U.S. cities.[3] Today, about 70 financially oriented U.S. companies account for nearly all the directly placed paper, with finance companies issuing approximately three fourths of the total. All these firms have an ongoing need for huge amounts of short-term money, possess top credit ratings, and have established working relationships with major institutional investors in order to place new note issues rapidly.

Directly placed paper must be sold in large volume to cover the substantial costs of distribution and marketing. On average, each direct issuer has between $600 and $700 million outstanding at any one time and will usually borrow at least $1 billion per month. While issuers of direct paper do not have to pay dealers' commissions and fees, these companies must operate a marketing division to maintain constant contact with active investors. Sometimes direct issuers must sell their paper even when they have no need for funds as the price of maintaining a good working relationship with active investor groups. These companies also cannot escape paying fees to banks for supporting lines of credit, to rating agencies who rate their paper issues, and to agents (usually banks) who dispense required payments and collect funds.

The other major variety of commercial paper is dealer paper, issued by security dealers on behalf of corporate customers. Also known as industrial paper, dealer paper is issued mainly by nonfinancial companies (including public utilities, manufacturers, retailers, wholesalers, and transportation companies), as well as by smaller bank holding companies and finance companies, all of whom borrow less frequently than firms issuing direct paper. The issuing company may sell the paper directly to the dealer, who buys it less discount and commission and then attempts to sell it at the highest possible price in the market. Alternatively, the issuing company may carry all the risk, with the dealer agreeing only to sell the issue at the best price available less commission (often referred to as a best efforts basis). Finally, the open-rate method may be used in which the borrowing company receives some money in advance, but the balance depends on how well the issue sells in the open market. Companies using dealers to place their paper are generally smaller and less frequent borrowers than issuers of direct paper.

Recent Growth of Commercial Paper

As Exhibit 16–1 indicates, the volume of commercial paper more than tripled between 1980 and 1988. By the end of the period more than 700 com-

---

[3]Bank holding companies issue both direct and dealer paper, with the largest companies going the direct placement route. Much of this so-called bank-related paper comes from finance company subsidiaries of large bank holding companies. Frequently, a holding company will issue paper through a nonbank subsidiary and then funnel the proceeds to one or more of its subsidiary banks by purchasing some of the banks' assets. This gives the banks additional funds to lend and may be especially helpful when a bank is having difficulty attracting deposits through normal channels.

Exhibit 16–1   **Volume of Commercial Paper Outstanding** ($ Billions, End of Period)

Instrument	1980	1982	1984	1986	1988*
All issuers	$124.4	$166.4	$237.6	$331.0	$389.0
Finance companies:					
Dealer-placed paper					
Total	19.6	34.6	56.5	100.2	121.4
Bank-related	3.6	2.5	2.0	2.3	1.7
Directly placed paper					
Total	67.9	84.4	110.5	152.4	174.6
Bank-related	22.4	32.0	42.1	40.9	44.0
Nonfinancial companies	36.9	47.4	70.6	78.4	93.1

*For February 1988.

Note: Includes public utilities and firms engaged primarily in communications, construction, manufacturing, mining, wholesale and retail trade, transportation, and similar activities.

Source: Board of Governors of the Federal Reserve System, *Federal Reserve Bulletin,* selected issues.

panies had nearly $400 billion in commercial notes outstanding. Slightly less than half the total was placed directly with investors by larger finance companies and bank holding companies, while the rest reached the market through the efforts of security dealers.

What factors explain the rapid growth in commercial paper? One key factor is the relative cost of other sources of credit compared to interest rates prevailing on current commercial paper issues. For the largest, best-known corporations, commercial paper is often an efficient, cost-effective substitute for bank loans and other forms of borrowing. This is especially true for nonfinancial companies issuing notes through dealers. These firms usually come to the commercial paper market when it is significantly cheaper to borrow there than to tap bank lines of credit. In recent years the paper market has also frequently been a cheaper alternative source of funds than issuing long-term bonds and selling stock in a depressed market. Many companies have begun to use the paper market in interest rate swaps designed to hedge against losses due to fluctuating interest rates.[4] Another reason for the market's rapid growth is the high quality of most commercial paper obligations. Many investors regard this instrument as a close substitute for Treasury bills, bank CDs, and other money market instruments. As a result, market yields on commercial notes tend to move in the same direction and by similar amounts as do the yields on other money market securities.

This fact is shown clearly in Exhibit 16–2, which compares the market yields on three-month maturities of commercial paper, Treasury bills, negotiable CDs, and bankers' acceptances. Rates on these four money market

---

[4]See Chapter 11 for a discussion of the nature and purpose of interest rate swaps.

Exhibit 16–2   **Market Yields on Commercial Paper Compared to Yields on Other Money Market Instruments** (Average Yields on Three-Month Maturities; Percent per Annum)

Instruments	1981	1982	1983	1984	1985	1986	1987	1988*
Commercial paper	15.32%	11.89%	8.88%	10.10%	7.95%	6.49%	6.82%	6.62%
U.S. Treasury bills	14.03	10.61	8.62	9.52	7.48	5.98	5.78	5.70
Certificates of deposit	15.91	12.27	9.07	10.37	8.05	6.52	6.87	6.63
Prime bankers' acceptances	15.32	11.89	8.90	10.14	7.92	6.39	6.75	6.51

*As of March 1988.

Note: Commercial paper yields are unweighted averages of rates quoted by at least five dealers. Treasury bills are secondary-market yields computed from daily closing bid prices. CD rates are secondary-market yields quoted as five-day averages by five dealers. Bankers' acceptance rates are on 90-day maturities and are an average of the midpoint of the range of daily dealer closing rates offered for domestic issues. All yields except CDs are quoted on a bank discount basis.

Source: Board of Governors of the Federal Reserve System, *Federal Reserve Bulletin*, selected issues.

instruments tend to stay within roughly a percentage point or two of each other. We note that commercial paper yields are always higher than market rates on comparable maturity Treasury bills, due to the greater risk and lower marketability of commercial notes and the fact that Treasury bills are exempt from state and local taxation.

Still another key factor in the market's recent growth is the expanding use of letters of credit and other *payment guarantees*. For example, a commercial bank or other lending institution may issue a certificate promising payment of principal and/or interest if the borrowing company fails to do so. The result is that such paper usually carries the higher credit rating of the guarantor rather than the lower credit rating of the issuing firm. Through these guarantees, mortgage companies, utilities, and small manufacturers in large numbers have been attracted into a market otherwise closed to them, while still saving on interest costs even after paying the guarantor's fee. A related development inaugurated by Merrill Lynch in 1984 allowed smaller or lower-rated institutions (such as savings and loans or retail firms) to issue commercial paper collateralized by holdings of Treasury or federal agency securities or even accounts receivable.

Other groups recently entering the market on the borrowing side include foreign banks and industrial companies, international financial conglomerates, and state and local governments (which offer tax-exempt commercial paper). Paper issued in the United States by foreign firms is called *Yankee paper,* and frequently can be sold at lower rates in America than abroad. Recently the market has expanded overseas with the rapid rise of European commercial paper. The Europaper market began in the mid-1980s, and volume soared as borrowing firms tapped a large reservoir of short-term foreign investor cash. Japanese banks and securities firms have begun to enter this market as investors and probably will issue yen-denominated notes in significant volume in the years ahead.

Maturities of Commercial Paper

Maturities of commercial paper range from 3 days ("weekend paper") to 9 months. Most commercial notes carry an original maturity of 60 days or less, with an average maturity ranging from 20 to 45 days. Commercial paper is generally not issued for longer maturities than 270 days because, under the provisions of the Securities Act of 1933, any security sold in the U.S. open market for a longer term must be registered with the Securities and Exchange Commission.

Yields to the investor are calculated by the *bank discount method*, as in the case of Treasury bills. Like T-bills, most commercial paper is issued at a discount from par, and the investor's yield stems from the price appreciation of the security between purchase date and maturity date. However, coupon-bearing paper is also available. The minimum denomination is usually $25,000, though among institutional investors, who dominate the market, the usual denomination is $1 million. The notes typically are issued in bearer form, which makes their resale easier. Payment is made at maturity upon presentation to the particular bank listed as agent on the note. Settlement in federal funds is usually made the same day the note is presented for payment by its holder.

Changing Yields on Paper Issues

Because yields on commercial paper are open market rates, they fluctuate with the daily ebb and flow of supply and demand forces in the marketplace. In the wide swings between easy and tight money, between depressed and resurgent economic activity in recent years, commercial paper rates have fluctuated between extreme highs and lows. For example, in 1983 and 1985–88—years of moderate credit demands and moderate inflation—paper rates averaged less than 9 percent (see Exhibit 16–2). In 1981, however, when intense credit demands and rapid inflation characterized the economic situation, paper rates ranged upward to nearly 18 percent and averaged about 15 percent for the year.[5] The commercial paper market is highly volatile and difficult to predict. This is why many corporations eligible to borrow there still maintain close working relationships with commercial banks and other institutional lenders.

---

[5] In most years, yields on longer-term paper issues are higher than on the shortest-term notes, resulting in an upward-sloping yield curve. However, near the peak of an economic boom, yield curves on commercial paper often slope downward.

Exhibit 16–3 **Spread between the Average Prime Rate Quoted by Major U.S. Banks and the Six-Month Commercial Paper Rate, Selected Months in 1988**

Month	Bank Prime Rate	Six-Month Commercial Paper Rate	Rate Spread
1988:			
January	8.75%	6.92%	+1.83%
February	8.51	6.58	+1.93
March	8.50	6.64	+1.86

*The prime rate is the average of rates posted by major U.S. banks. The commercial paper rate is an unweighted average of offering rates quoted by at least five dealers. Both rates are measured on a bank discount basis.

Source: Board of Governors of the Federal Reserve System, *Federal Reserve Bulletin,* selected issues.

Advantages of Issuing Commercial Paper

There are several financial advantages to a company able to tap the commercial paper market for funds. Generally, rates on paper are lower than on corporate loans extended by commercial banks. This is evident from the data shown in Exhibit 16–3. In 1988, for example, the bank prime rate was consistently at least a full percentage point higher than the rate on six-month dealer paper. This spread between the bank prime rate and the six-month paper rate at times has widened to 3 or 4 full percentage points.

Moreover, the effective rate on most commercial loans granted by banks is even higher than the quoted prime rate, due to the fact that corporate borrowers usually are required to keep a percentage of their loans in a bank deposit. This so-called *compensating balance requirement* is generally 15 to 20 percent of the amount of the loan. Suppose a corporation borrows $100,000 at a prime interest rate of 15 percent but must keep 20 percent of this amount on deposit with the bank granting the loan. Then the effective loan rate is 18.75 percent (or $15,000/$80,000).

Another advantage of borrowing in the commercial paper market is that interest rates there are often more flexible than bank loan rates. Moreover, a company in need of funds can raise money quickly through either dealer or direct paper. Dealers maintain close contact with the market and generally know where cash may be found. Frequently, notes can be issued and funds raised the same day or within a day or two.

Generally, larger amounts of funds may be borrowed more conveniently through the paper market than from other sources, particularly bank loans. This situation arises due to federal and state regulations that limit the amount of money a bank can lend to any single borrower. For national banks, the maximum unsecured loan is 15 percent of the bank's capital and surplus account. Frequently, corporate credit needs exceed an individual bank's loan limit, and a group of banks (consortium) has to be assembled to make the loan. However, this takes time and often requires lengthy and complicated negotiations. Using the paper market is generally much faster than trying to hammer out a loan agreement among several parties. Moreover, the ability to issue commercial paper gives a corporation considerable leverage when negotiating with banks. A banker who knows that the customer can draw upon the commercial paper market for funds is more likely to offer advantageous terms on a loan and be more receptive to future customer credit needs.

Possible Disadvantages of Issuing Commercial Paper

Despite the advantages, there are some risks for corporations that choose to borrow frequently in the commercial paper market. One of these is the risk of alienating banks whose loans might be needed when a real emergency develops. The paper market is volatile and sensitive to financial and economic problems. This fact was demonstrated quite convincingly in 1980 when Chrysler Financial, the finance company subsidiary of Chrysler Corporation, was forced to cut back its borrowings in the commercial paper market due to the widely publicized troubles of its parent company. At times, it is extremely difficult even for companies in sound financial condition to raise funds in the paper market at reasonable rates of interest. It helps to have a loyal and friendly banker available to supply emergency credit when the market turns sour. Another problem lies in the fact that commercial paper cannot be paid off at the issuer's discretion, but generally must remain outstanding until it reaches maturity. In contrast, many bank loans permit early retirement without penalty.

Principal Investors

The most important investors in the commercial paper market include non-financial corporations, money market mutual funds, bank trust departments, smaller commercial banks, pension funds, insurance companies, and state and local governments. In effect, this is a market in which corporations borrow from other corporations. These investor groups regard commercial paper as a low-risk outlet for their surplus funds.

A recent innovation in the direct paper market is the master note, most frequently issued to bank trust departments and other permanent money market investors by finance companies. Under a master note agreement, the investing company notifies the issuing company how much paper it will purchase each day for immediate payment. The investor agrees to take some paper each day up to an agreed-upon maximum amount. Interest owed is figured on the average daily volume of paper taken on by the investor during the current month. The prevailing interest rate on six-month commercial paper generally is used to determine the appropriate rate of return.

Commercial Paper Ratings

Commercial paper is generally rated as prime, desirable, or satisfactory, depending on the credit standing of the issuing company. Firms desiring to issue paper generally will seek a credit rating from one or more of five rating services—Moody's Investor Service, Standard & Poor's Corporation, Fitch Investor Service, Duff and Phelps, and McCarthy, Crisanti, and Maffei—with the first two especially prominent. Moody's assigns a rating of Prime-1 (P-1) for the highest-quality paper, with lower-quality issues designated as Prime-2 (P-2) or Prime-3 (P-3). Standard & Poor's assigns ratings of A-1, A-2, or A-3, while Fitch uses F-1, F-2, or F-3. Any issue rated below P-2, A-2, or F-2 usually sells poorly or not at all.

It is extremely difficult in today's volatile conditions to market unrated commercial paper. Indeed, paper available is mainly from top-quality issuers; about three quarters of the firms currently selling notes carry A-1 or P-1 ratings. Generally, commercial notes bearing credit ratings from at least two rating agencies are preferred by both investors and dealers. The rating assigned to an issue often depends heavily on the liquidity position and the amount of backup lines of credit held by the issuing company.

Dealers in Paper

The market is relatively concentrated among a handful of dealers who account for the bulk of all trading activity. The top commercial paper dealers today include Goldman Sachs & Co.; A. G. Becker, Inc.; the First Boston Corporation, Lehman Brothers; Kuhn Loeb, Inc.; Salomon Brothers; and Merrill Lynch, Pierce, Fenner & Smith, Inc. Dealer firms charge varying fees to borrowing companies, depending on the size of an issue and how much paper the company has issued through the dealer recently (such as within the past year). Dealers maintain inventories of unsold new issues or repurchased paper, but they usually expect to turn over most of a new issue in 24 hours or less. Like dealers in government securities, commercial paper dealers draw upon repurchase agreements (RPs) and demand loans from banks to help finance their inventory positions. They pay interest rates only a few basis points higher than on RPs collateralized by government securities.

FEDERAL AGENCY SECURITIES

For at least the past 50 years, the federal government has attempted to aid certain sectors of the economy that appear to have an unusually difficult time raising funds in the money and capital markets. These so-called disadvantaged sectors include agriculture, housing, and small businesses. Dominated by smaller, less creditworthy borrowers, these sectors allegedly get pushed aside in the race for scarce funds by large corporate borrowers and governments, especially in periods of tight money. Beginning in the 1920s, the federal government created several agencies to make loans to or guarantee private loans for these disadvantaged borrowers. These agencies also buy selected assets from private lenders which gives these lenders added funds to make new loans to financially disadvantaged borrowers. Today, the federal credit agencies are large enough and, with the government's blessing, financially sound enough to compete successfully for funds in the open market and channel those funds to areas of critical social need.

Types of Federal Credit Agencies

There are two types of federal credit agencies: government-sponsored agencies and the true federal agencies. Government-sponsored agencies are not officially a part of the federal government's structure, but are quasi-private institutions. They are federally chartered but privately owned; in fact, in some instances their stock is traded on major securities exchanges. The borrowing and lending activities of government-sponsored agencies are *not* reflected in the federal government's budget. This has aroused the ire of many fiscal conservatives who regard the credit-granting operations of government-sponsored agencies as a disguised form of federal government spending. Because these agencies are omitted from the federal government's books, annual federal budget deficits look considerably smaller and conceal the full extent of federal deficit financing.[6] True federal agencies, on the other hand, are legally a part of the government structure, and their borrowing and lending activities are included in the federal budget. Exhibit 16-4 lists the principal federal and government-sponsored agencies that borrow in the money and capital markets.

In their borrowing and lending activities, federal and government-sponsored agencies act as true financial intermediaries. They issue attractively packaged certificates, notes, and bonds to capture funds from savers, and they direct the resulting flow of funds into loans and loan guarantees to farmers, ranchers, small business owners, financial institutions, and

---

[6]Public concern over the growth of federal agency activities has increased in recent years, perhaps with some justification. To the extent that agency borrowing and lending activities increase the total amount of credit available in the economy and add to aggregate spending for goods and services, they may add to inflationary pressures. Agency borrowing is not limited by the debt ceiling or interest-rate restrictions that apply to direct obligations of the U.S. government.

Moreover, there is a tendency to create a new agency each time a new financial problem rears its head, increasing the cost of government activities. A prominent example is the Chrysler Corporation Loan Guarantee Board established by Congress in 1979. This board, whose voting members consisted of the Secretary of the Treasury, the chairman of the Federal Reserve Board, and the Comptroller General of the United States, was authorized to guarantee with the "full faith and credit of the United States" notes issued by financially troubled Chrysler Corporation and other eligible borrowers. The board's creation raised a number of significant issues concerning government involvement in the private sector of the economy. How many other firms should the federal government guarantee against failure in the future? Upon what basis are such guarantees to be made? What happens to the efficiency of the market system when some firms are not allowed to fail?

Exhibit 16-4   Principal Borrowers in the Federal Agency Market

---

Agencies of the Federal Government

Export-Import Bank (EXIM)
U.S. Railway Association
Farmers Home Administration
  (FMHA)
General Services Administration
  (GSA)

Government National Mortgage Association
  (GNMA, or Ginnie Mae)
Postal Service (PS)
Tennessee Valley Aurthority (TVA)

Government-Sponsored Agencies

Banks for Cooperatives (BC)
Federal Farm Credit Banks (FFCB)
Federal Home Loan Banks (FHLB)
Federal Home Loan Mortgage Corpo-
  ration (FHLMC, or Freddie Mac)
Federal Intermediate Credit Banks
  (FICB)

Federal Land Banks (FLB)
Federal National Mortgage Association
  (FNMA, or Fannie Mae)
Student Loan Marketing Association (SLMA
  or Sallie Mae)

---

mortgage borrowers. While the securities issued by government-sponsored agencies are usually not guaranteed by the federal government, most investors feel that the government is "only a step away" in the event any agency gets into trouble.[7]

Growth of the Agency Market

Armed with this implied government support, the agency market has grown rapidly, with the volume of outstanding securities climbing from about $2 billion during the 1950s to more than $300 billion today (see Exhibit 16–5). Agency debt today equals about one sixth of the huge U.S. public debt and is roughly one third the amount of corporate bonds outstanding.

The agency market is dominated by the government-sponsored agencies, which have restricted access to federal government coffers and must rely mainly on the open market to raise money. The federal agencies, in contrast, are financed through the Federal Financing Bank (FFB), which borrows money from the Treasury. The FFB is closely aupervised by the Treasury Department and, in fact, is staffed by Treasury employees. If present trends con-

---

[7] The government-sponsored agencies are permitted to draw upon the U.S. Treasury for funds up to a specified limit with Treasury approval. For example, FNMA has a $2.25 billion line of credit with the U.S. Treasury. However, neither the principal nor the interest on the debt of government-sponsored agencies is guaranteed by the federal government, though the issuing agency guarantees its own securities. In contrast, securities of agencies operated by the federal government are fully guaranteed by the credit of the U.S. government.

Exhibit 16–5   **Growth of Agency Market Debt** ($ Billions)

Year-End	Total Agency Debt Outstanding
1961	$ 8.6
1966	22.7
1971	50.7
1976	103.8
1980	193.2
1987	341.4

Source: Board of Governors of the Federal Reserve System, *Federal Reserve Bulletin*, selected issues; and U.S. Treasury Department, *Treasury Bulletin*, selected issues.

tinue, all outstanding federal agency debt will be FFB securities issued to the Treasury, and only the government-sponsored agencies, which cannot borrow through the FFB, will tap the open market directly for funds.[8]

Terms on Agency Securities

Agency securities are generally short to medium term (to 10 years), and about 20 percent have original maturities under 1 year. Money market borrowing is usually done by issuing *discount notes* which, like Treasury bills and commercial paper, have no promised interest rate but are sold at a price below their par value. Five to 10 dealers sell the notes for a small fee with banks, mutual funds, insurance companies, thrifts, and pension funds purchasing most of them. The sponsored agencies also issue short-term coupon securities and variable-rate notes. Long-term borrowing in the capital market is usually accomplished by issuing *debentures*, either on a monthly basis or at irregular intervals as the need for funds arises.

Longer-term agency securities are available in denominations as small as $1,000, while the shorter-term notes traded actively in the money market generally come in minimum denominations of $50,000 or more. They are subject to federal income taxes, but many are exempt from state and local income taxes (except for FNMA and FHLMC securities). However, state and local government estate, gift, and inheritance taxes do apply to all agency

[8] Due to FFB activities, the Treasury has to add a certain amount to its regular borrowings each year in order to cover any FFB drawings. As of February 1988, the Federal Financing Bank had borrowed a total of $150 billion from the Treasury to fund the agencies.

The FFB was created by Congress in 1973. Up to that time, each federal agency did its own borrowing. As a result, the number of different federal agency issues was proliferating at a rapid rate, creating confusion among investors as to the terms and characteristics of each issue. There were also fears expressed in Congress that agency borrowing was out of control. Centralization of borrowing in one agency, it was hoped, would increase efficiency in the fundraising process, improve the marketability of agency securities, and give Congress a more adequate measure of the growth of agency activities. All FFB obligations are fully guaranteed by the U.S. government. The FFB, in turn, purchases only those securities fully guaranteed as to principal and interest by the issuing agency.

obligations. Depository institutions may use the agency securities they acquire as collateral for loans from the Federal Reserve's discount window and as legal backing for government deposits. National banks may act as dealers in agency securities.

One of the most popular agency securities is the certificate of participation (PC) or pass-through security used by the Federal National Mortgage Association (FNMA or Fannie Mae) and the Federal Home Loan Mortgage Corporation (FHLMC). PCs represent an interest in a pool of securities which entitles the holder to receive a portion of any income earned by the pool. In 1983 FHLMC developed a new instrument—the Collateralized Mortgage Obligation (CMO), which is backed by residential mortgages or pass-through securities. CMOs are divided into classes based upon the degree of certainty about the maturity (length of time), principal, and interest payments received by the investor, thus reducing somewhat the risk that early repayments of home mortgages backing the CMO will reduce the investor's expected yield.

The heaviest agency borrowers in recent years, as indicated in Exhibit 16–6, have been Fannie Mae, the Federal Home Loan Banks (FHLB), and the Farm Credit Banks. These three agencies accounted for about 80 percent of the outstanding debt issued by all federal and government-sponsored

Exhibit 16–6   Total Debt Outstanding of Federal and Government-Sponsored Agencies, April 1987 ($ Billions)

Agency	Total Debt Outstanding
Federal agencies:	
Export-Import Bank	$ 13.8
Federal Housing Administration	0.2
Government National Mortgage Association	2.0
Postal Service	3.1
Tennessee Valley Authority	17.4
Other agencies	0.0*
Total federal agency debt	$ 36.5
Government-sponsored agencies:	
Federal Home Loan Banks	$ 94.6
Federal Home Loan Mortgage Corporation	13.1
Federal National Mortgage Corporation	89.7
Farm Credit Banks†	57.3
Student Loan Marketing Association	13.9
Total government-sponsored agency debt	$268.6

*Less than $100 million.
† In January 1979 the Farm Credit Banks began issuing consolidated bonds to replace those securities previously issued by the Federal Land Banks, Federal Intermediate Credit Banks, and the Banks for Cooperatives.

Source: Board of Governors of the Federal Reserve System, *Federal Reserve Bulletin*, September 1987.

agencies, and an active secondary market exists for the short-term debt of these three agencies. Clearly, most agency borrowing goes to support the housing market and agriculture.

The securities of all government-sponsored agencies are regarded as highly similar by investors, and therefore comparable maturities tend to have about the same yield, regardless of the issuing agency. Each agency is able to borrow at interest rates below the average yield on its asset portfolio due to government support and control. Generally, the yield on agency securities is close to the yield on U.S. government securities of comparable maturity, but slightly higher. Most of this small difference in yield is due to the fact that agency securities are less marketable than Treasury IOUs. The Treasury issues a security homogeneous in quality and other financial characteristics, while the agency market is splintered into many small pieces due to differences among the agencies themselves. The yields on agency securities are lower than yields on private debt issues, however, due to their superior credit standing. Agency yields are calculated on a 360-day basis like Treasury bills, with their prices quoted in 32nds of a point like corporate and U.S. government notes and bonds.

The Marketing of Agency Issues

Most agency issues are sold through the solicitation method. A fiscal agent in New York City assembles a group of banks, dealers, and brokers to bring each issue to market. This *solicitation group* conveys to potential investors information on the size, denomination, and maturity of a new issue and asks the investors on its list to make a firm commitment to buy a certain amount of agency securities. Investors are not told the price of the new securities, but are asked for their views on what the price should be. This pricing information is conveyed to the fiscal agent. The day after order books close, the fiscal agent prices the new securities and delivery to committed investors then occurs normally a few days later. Investors do *not* know the prices or yields on the securities they buy until after the sale, but must rely on the agent's knowledge and experience to price each issue correctly. A recent study by Puglisi and Vignola (1983) suggests that the fiscal agents generally are highly accurate in choosing competitive equilibrium yields on new issues of agency debt. When their price decisions are off the mark, they tend to err on the side of underpricing rather than overpricing a new issue. The solicitation group of bank and nonbank dealers receives a commission from the fiscal agent for gathering investor orders and pricing information.

Among the most active buyers of agency securities are commercial banks, savings banks, state and local governments, savings and loan associations, government trust funds, and the Federal Reserve System. The Federal Reserve has been authorized to conduct open market operations in agency IOUs since 1966. Fed buying and selling of these securities has helped to improve their marketability and stature among private investors.

Major securities dealers who handle U.S. government securities also generally trade in agency issues.

Government-sponsored agencies have become innovative borrowers in recent years. For example, FNMA and SLMA have sold securities in foreign markets, some of these denominated in foreign currencies or in "dual currency" form where interest is paid in a foreign currency and the principal is repaid at maturity in U.S. dollars. These agencies have also used interest rate swaps and currency swaps to protect themselves against the risks of fluctuating interest rates and currency prices.[9]

SUMMARY

In this chapter we looked at two of the most rapidly growing securities markets of the past decade—commercial paper and agency securities. Major industrial corporations, faced with rapidly growing demands for their products and services, have turned increasingly to the market for short-term commercial notes to meet pressing cash needs. The commercial paper market offers a flexible avenue for borrowing, often at lower interest rates than those available from commercial banks and other institutional lenders. At the same time, commercial banks and finance companies, faced with burgeoning demand for credit from households, business firms, and federal, state, and local governments, have found the commercial paper market an excellent avenue for raising large amounts of short-term funds quickly, at minimum cost and with minimum inconvenience. The pressure of demand from these large groups of industrial and financial firms caused the volume of commercial paper outstanding to increase fivefold during the 1960s and to nearly quadruple during the 1970s. Further rapid expansion of commercial paper issues has occurred in the 1980s.

Equally impressive has been the growth of debt securities issued by agencies created by the U.S. government. Their extensive borrowing and lending activities in the financial markets channel billions of dollars in funds to farmers, ranchers, commercial fishers, small businesses, mortgage borrowers, and mortgage-lending institutions on more generous terms than the open market often provides. Many of these agencies, especially those aiding agriculture and the mortgage market, have been operating since the 1920s and 1930s, but their growth in recent years has been unprecedented. Federal agency debt increased more than threefold during the 1970s, and the rapid growth continued in the 1980s.

All federal agencies are creatures of Congress and may be destroyed, in theory at least, at the stroke of a pen. In reality, however, with continuing rapid growth in the number of new families formed in the United States each year and the rising costs of housing, food, and fuel, the role of the

---

[9]See Chapter 11 for a discussion of interest rate swaps and Chapter 28 for an explanation of currency swaps.

federal agencies in the financial markets probably will continue to expand. Agency securities will continue to be an attractive investment for commercial banks, savings and loan associations, credit unions, industrial corporations, and other investors who seek competitive rates of return with minimal risk.

STUDY QUESTIONS

1. What is commercial paper? What features make it attractive to money market investors?

2. Describe the role dealers play in the functioning of the commercial paper market.

3. How is the yield (or rate of return) on commercial paper calculated?

4. What are the principal advantages accruing to a company large enough to tap the commercial paper market for funds? Are there any disadvantages to issuing commercial paper?

5. Who are the principal investors in commercial paper? How and why is this paper rated?

6. What are disadvantaged sectors of the economy? Give some examples.

7. What is the difference between a government-sponsored agency and a federal agency? Give some examples of each.

8. Are federal or government-sponsored agencies really financial intermediaries? Why?

9. What are the principal investment characteristics of agency securities?

10. How are agency securities marketed? What is a *solicitation group?* What is unusual about the *pricing* of agency securities?

PROBLEMS

1. A new issue of 90-day commercial paper is available from a dealer in New York City at a price of $97.60 on a $100 basis. What is the bank discount yield on this note if held to maturity?

2. A note traded in the commercial paper market will mature in 15 days. The dealer will sell it to you at $98.35 on a $100 basis. What is the note's discount rate of return?

3. Commercial paper is purchased in the secondary market 30 days from maturity at a bank discount yield of 9 percent. Ten days later, it was sold to a dealer at an 8 percent discount rate. What was the investor's holding period yield?

SELECTED REFERENCES

Banks, Louis. "The Market for Agency Securities." *Quarterly Review,* Federal Reserve Bank of New York, Spring 1978.

Board of Governors of the Federal Reserve System. "Survey of Finance Companies, 1975." *Federal Reserve Bulletin,* March 1976.

Federal Reserve Bank of Richmond. *Instruments of the Money Market.* 6th ed., 1986.

Hurley, Evelyn M. "The Commercial Paper Market since the Mid-Seventies." *Federal Reserve Bulletin,* June 1982, pp. 327–34.

Puglisi, Donald J., and Anthony J. Vignola, Jr. "An Examination of Federal Agency Debt Pricing Practices." *The Journal of Financial Research.* 6, no. 2 (Summer 1983), pp. 83–92.

Resler, David, and Richard Lang. "Federal Agency Debt: Another Side of Federal Borrowing." *Review,* Federal Reserve Bank of St. Louis, November 1979, pp. 10–19.

Chapter 17

International Money Market Instruments: Bankers' Acceptances and Eurodollars

Learning Objectives in This Chapter

- To see how the money market and its institutions now cover the globe, reaching across national borders to make possible global short-term borrowing and lending of funds.

- To understand how financial instruments, such as bankers' acceptances and Eurodollars, are used to provide the credit needed in international trade and commerce.

- To determine how the ownership of money can be transferred across international boundaries and what the effects of these funds transfers are likely to be on the domestic economy.

Key Terms and Concepts in This Chapter

Bankers' acceptance	*Third-country bills*	*Eurodollars*
Time draft	*Eurocurrency market*	*LIBOR*

THE money market today is not confined within the boundaries of a single nation. Money flows around the globe, seeking out those investments offering the highest expected returns for a given degree of risk. Moreover, world trade has expanded in recent years at a rapid pace, especially between the United States, Japan and the Pacific Basin, Western Europe, and the Middle East. Further rapid increases in international trade and commerce are expected in the decade ahead, including a significant expansion of trade between East and West. China, the Soviet Union, and the Eastern European nations are developing close economic ties with several Western countries. The exporting of agricultural products and advanced technology by the United States, Japan, and Western Europe to Third World countries and, in some cases, to the Communist bloc constitutes one of the major avenues for international trade in the modern world.

And, of course, the growth and development of international commerce requires a concomitant expansion in both long- and short-term sources of financing. Long-term capital is needed to build new factories, transport systems, dams, deep-water ports, and energy producing and refining facilities. Short-term capital from the money market is needed to finance the annual export and import of goods, the carrying of inventories, and the payment of tax obligations, and to provide other working-capital needs. In this chapter we focus upon two of the most widely used international money market instruments—bankers' acceptances and Eurodollars.

BANKERS' ACCEPTANCES

A banker's acceptance is a *time draft* drawn on a bank by an exporter or an importer to pay for merchandise or to buy foreign currencies.[1] If the bank honors the draft, it will stamp "accepted" on its face and endorse the instrument. By so doing, the issuing bank has unconditionally guaranteed to pay the face value of the acceptance at maturity, shielding exporters and investors in international markets from default risk. Acceptances carry maturities ranging from 30 to 270 days (with 90 days being the most common) and are considered prime-quality money market instruments. They are actively traded among bank and nonbank financial institutions, manufacturing and industrial corporations, and securities dealers as a high-quality investment and source of ready cash. An illustration of a typical banker's acceptance, prepared at the Federal Reserve Bank of New York, is shown in Exhibit 17–1.

Why Acceptances Are Used in International Trade

Acceptances are used in the import and export trade because most exporters are uncertain of the credit standing of the importers to whom they ship

---

[1] See Chapter 29 for a discussion and explanation of time drafts.

Exhibit 17–1   **Illustration of a Banker's Acceptance**

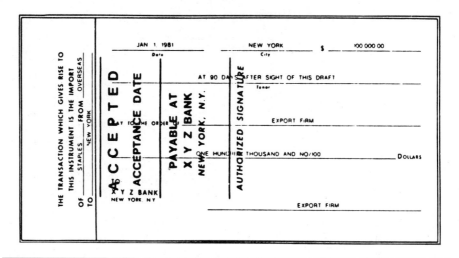

goods. Exporters may also be concerned about business conditions or political developments in foreign countries. Nations experiencing terrorist violence or even civil war have serious problems in attracting financing for imports of goods and services because of the obvious risks of extending credit to them. However, exporters usually are quite content to rely upon acceptance financing by a foreign bank. Thus, an acceptance is a financial instrument designed to shift the risk of international trade to a third party willing to take on that risk for a known cost. Banks are usually willing to take on such risk because they are specialists in granting credit, assessing credit risk, and spreading that risk over thousands of different loans.

How Acceptances Arise

Trade acceptances usually begin when an importer goes to a bank to secure a line of credit to pay for a shipment of goods from abroad. (See Exhibit 17–2 for a flowchart illustrating how acceptances can be created.) Once the line of credit is approved, the bank will issue a letter of credit in favor of the foreign exporter. This document authorizes the exporter to draw a time draft for a specified amount against the issuing bank, provided the exporter agrees to send appropriate shipping documents giving the issuing bank temporary title to the exported goods.

Because the letter of credit authorizes the drawing of a *time draft* and not a sight draft (which is payable immediately upon presentation), the exporter must wait until the draft matures (perhaps as long as six months) to be paid. Such a delay is unacceptable for most export firms. They must

Exhibit 17–2 **The Creation of a Banker's Acceptance**

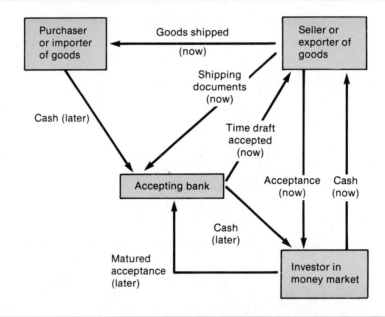

Effect of an Acceptance: Reduces risk to seller from shipping goods on credit because the purchaser has received a bank's guarantee of future payment, thus transferring risk from the seller to the accepting bank and the seller can receive his or her funds right away by discounting the acceptance before it matures.

Source: Adapted from William C. Melton and Jean M. Mahr, "Banker's Acceptances," *Quarterly Review*, Federal Reserve Bank of New York, Summer 1981.

meet payrolls, purchase inventories, pay taxes, and satisfy other obligations. Moreover, the time draft will generally be redeemed in the home currency of the issuing bank, and this particular currency may not be needed by the exporter. A French exporter holding a time draft from a U.S. bank, for example, would be paid in dollars on its maturity date, even though the exporter probably needs francs to pay employees and meet other expenses. Typically, then, the exporter will discount the time draft in advance of maturity through his/her principal bank. The exporter then receives timely payment in local currency and avoids the risk of trading in foreign currencies.

The foreign bank that has now acquired the time draft from the exporter will forward it (plus shipping documents if goods are being traded) to the bank issuing the original letter of credit. The issuing bank checks to see that the draft and any accompanying documents are correctly drawn and then stamps "accepted" on its face. Two things happen as a result of this action: (1) a banker's acceptance—a high-quality, negotiable money market instrument—has been created; and (2) the issuing bank has acknowledged an absolute liability which must be paid in full at maturity. Frequently, the issuing bank will discount the new acceptance for the foreign bank which

Exhibit 17–3   **The Growth of Bankers' Dollar Acceptances**

Year-End	Volume Outstanding at End of Period ($ millions)
1950	$ 394
1960	2,027
1970	7,058
1980	54,744
1985	68,413
1988*	62,419

*Figures as of February 1988.

Source: Board of Governors of the Federal Reserve System, *Federal Reserve Bulletin* and *Banking and Monetary Statistics*, selected issues.

sent it and credit that bank's correspondent account for the proceeds. The acceptance may then be held by the issuing bank as an asset or sold to a dealer. Meanwhile, shipping documents for any goods that accompanied the acceptance are handed to the importer against a trust receipt, permitting the importer to pick up and market the goods. However, under the terms of the letter of credit, the importer must deposit the proceeds from selling those goods at the issuing bank in sufficient time to pay for the acceptance. When the time draft matures, the acceptance will be presented to the issuing bank for payment by its holder.

It should be clear that all three principal parties to the acceptance transaction—the exporter, importer, and issuing bank—benefit from this method of financing international trade. The exporter receives good funds with little or no delay. The importer may delay payment for a time until the related bank line of credit expires. The issuing bank regards the acceptance as a readily marketable financial instrument that can be sold before maturity through an acceptance dealer in order to cover short-term cash needs. In fact, 85 to 90 percent of all acceptances created by U.S. banks are sold in the secondary market each year.

However, there are costs associated with all these benefits. A discount fee is charged off the face value of the acceptance whenever it is discounted in advance of maturity. And the accepting bank earns a commission (usually 50 to 100 basis points), which may be paid by either exporter or importer, in addition to the fees associated with the original line of credit.

Recent Growth of Acceptance Financing

Given the significant advantages of acceptance financing for exporters, importers, and banks, it is not surprising that the volume of bankers' acceptances outstanding has grown in recent years. As Exhibit 17–3 shows, the volume of acceptances increased from less than $400 million in 1950 to just over $2 billion in 1960 and then tripled in 1970 to slightly more than $7

Exhibit 17–4   **Uses of Acceptance Financing** ($ Millions)

Uses of Acceptance Financing	Year-End		
	1975	**1980**	**1988***
Imports into the United States	$ 3,726	$11,536	$14,354
Exports from the United States	4,001	11,339	13,891
All other uses	11,000	31,480	34,173

*As of February 1988.

Source: Board of Governors of the Federal Reserve System, *Federal Reserve Bulletin,* selected issues.

billion outstanding. However, even these rapid rates of growth look pale compared with the virtual explosion of acceptance financing during the 1970s and early 1980s. By December 1987, the volume of bankers' acceptances outstanding exceeded $70 billion—a tenfold increase in about 15 years. Then, as world commodity prices declined or leveled out in the late 1980s and U.S. banks began to offer below prime-rate loans, acceptance growth flattened out.

What factors account for this impressive long-term growth in acceptances? Exhibit 17–4 helps us find the answer. The majority of acceptances created by U.S. banks arise from four types of financial transactions: (1) the financing of imports into the United States; (2) the financing of exports from the United States; (3) the acquisition of dollars to add to foreign exchange reserves; and (4) the financing of goods stored in or transported between other countries. Acceptances arising from the last source are called third-country bills. While these various types of acceptances have grown rapidly in recent years, it is the third-country bills which have dominated the growth in volume of acceptance financing by U.S. bankers, led by dollar acceptance financing and trade with Japan, South Korea, and nations in the Middle East whose export and import trade have increased rapidly in recent years.

Despite their rapid growth abroad, however, acceptances are not widely used inside the United States for purely domestic trade. A small amount of domestic acceptance financing is carried out to support the storage of staple commodities such as cotton, grain, rice, wood, or tobacco, or the domestic shipment of goods. However, if a company can borrow from a bank at or close to the prime interest rate, that is generally a cheaper source of funds than acceptance financing. Moreover, it is usually much easier for a domestic firm to assess the financial condition of its domestic customer than to evaluate the credit standing of a foreign firm thousands of miles away. For this reason, suppliers of goods in the domestic market usually extend short-term credit (accounts receivable) directly to customers rather than insisting on time drafts against a bank (acceptances). Moreover, in domestic commerce no exchange of foreign currencies is necessary, eliminating one important type of business risk.

Exhibit 17–5   **Interest Rates on Bankers' Acceptances, Bank CDs, and U.S. Treasury Bills*** (Average, Percent per Annum)

Instrument	1981	1982	1983	1984	1985	1986	1987	1988†
Prime 90-day bankers' acceptances	15.32%	11.89%	8.90%	10.14%	7.92%	6.39%	6.75%	6.51%
Three-month negotiable CDs	—	—	—	10.37	8.05	6.52	6.87	6.63
Three-month U.S. Treasury Bills	14.03	10.61	8.61	9.52	7.48	5.98	5.78	5.70

*Both bankers' acceptances and Treasury bill yields are quoted on a bank discount basis. Acceptance yields are averages of the midpoint of the range of daily dealer closing rates offered for domestic issues. Bill rates are auction averages for the week in which bills were issued.

†Averages for March 1988.

Source: Board of Governors of the Federal Reserve System, *Federal Reserve Bulletin*, selected issues.

Acceptance Rates

Acceptances do not carry a fixed rate of interest, but are sold at a discount in the open market like Treasury bills. The prime borrower under an acceptance contract is charged a commitment fee for this line of credit, which is usually 1½ percent (⅛ of 1 percent per month) for top-quality customers. U.S. banks are limited in the dollar amount of acceptances they can create to 150 percent of their paid-in capital and surplus, or by special permission, up to 200 percent of capital and surplus.

If the bank wishes to sell the acceptance in advance of its maturity, the rate of discount it must pay is determined by the current bid rate on acceptances of similar maturity in the open market. The yield on acceptances is usually only slightly higher than on Treasury bills because banks that issue them are among the largest and have solid international reputations (see Exhibit 17–5). Acceptance rates hover close to negotiable CD rates offered by major banks because both acceptances and CDs are unconditional obligations to pay. Adding to the stature and marketability of acceptances, depository institutions are permitted to borrow reserves from the Fed's discount window using eligible acceptances (six months or less to maturity) as collateral.[2]

---

[2]The banker's acceptance is one of the safest of all financial instruments. It is an irrevocable primary debt of the bank stamping "accepted" on its face, as well as a contingent liability of the drawing firm and of any other bank, firm, or individual who endorses the document. Moreover, domestic banks are limited in the volume of acceptances they can have outstanding relative to the size of their capital and surplus. At the same time, the customer (usually an importer) who has requested the initiating letter of credit which gives rise to the acceptance has guaranteed payment by the maturity date. Then too, any goods shipped under the letter of credit are nearly always insured and accompanied by trust and warehouse receipts and other documents specifying value and ownership. There is no record of a defaulted acceptance in the U.S. banking system, though of course the value of discounted acceptances does fluctuate with market conditions.

Exhibit 17–6   **Holders of Bankers' Acceptances** ($ Millions)

Holders	Year-End						
	1981	**1982**	**1983**	**1984**	**1985**	**1986**	**1987**
Accepting banks:	$10,857	$10,910	$ 9,355	$ 9,811	$11,197	$13,423	$10,943
Own bills	9,743	9,471	8,125	8,621	9,471	11,707	9,464
Bills bought	1,115	1,439	1,230	1,191	1,726	1,716	1,479
Federal Reserve banks:							
Own accounts	195	1,480	418	0	0	0	0
Foreign corre- spondents	1,442	949	729	671	937	1,317	965
Other holders	41,614	66,204	67,807	67,881	56,279	50,234	58,658

Source: Board of Governors of the Federal Reserve System, *Federal Reserve Bulletin,* selected issues.

Investors in Acceptances

Commercial banks regard acceptances as high-grade negotiable instruments suitable for liquidity management purposes. In addition, the essential safety of acceptances is recognized by the U.S. Treasury, which permits banks to use acceptances as collateral to back the Treasury's tax and loan accounts held in a majority of the nation's commercial banks. Smaller banks often participate in acceptance financing with money center banks to gain added income, spread out their risk, and accommodate their largest international customers.

As shown in Exhibit 17–6, U.S. bank holdings of acceptances amounted to about $11 billion in 1987 (consisting mostly of their own drafts), which was about one fifth of the total amount of acceptances outstanding.

Other important investors in the acceptance market include industrial corporations, savings banks, money market funds, foreign banks, local governments, federal agencies, and insurance companies. To many investors, acceptances are a close substitute for Treasury bills, negotiable CDs, or commercial paper in terms of quality, though the acceptance market is far smaller in volume of trading.

Only a few dealers—today there are about 20 major ones—regularly trade in acceptances, usually as an adjunct to their trading activities in Treasury bills and government notes and bonds. Trading is carried out purely on a negotiated basis, with most daily volume accounted for by swaps of holdings among accepting banks. The dealers usually call accepting banks and place bids for acceptances on behalf of their buying customers. Dealers' inventories of acceptances available for purchase are small, especially of acceptances created by the 10 largest U.S. banks that are prime rated. While a wide variety of denominations is available for both large and small investors, nonbank investors usually find the menu of fresh offerings very limited.

Nevertheless, an investor who is willing to accept the odd-lot denominations in which acceptances are issued will generally find the investment quite rewarding in terms of a competitive rate of return, low risk, and brisk resale demand, especially from bank and foreign nonbank investors.

EURODOLLARS

Comparable to the domestic market, a chain of international money markets trading in deposits that are denominated in the world's most convertible currencies stretches around the globe. This so-called Eurocurrency market has arisen because of a tremendous need worldwide for funds denominated in dollars, marks, pounds, francs, yen, and other relatively stable currencies. For example, as American corporations have expanded their operations in Europe, Asia, and the Middle East, they have needed huge amounts of U.S. dollars to purchase machinery and other goods in the United States and to pay federal and state taxes. The same companies have also required huge amounts of other national currencies to carry out transactions in the countries where they are represented. To meet this kind of need, in the 1950s large international banks headquartered in the world's key financial centers—London, Paris, Zurich, Tokyo, and other major cities—began to accept deposits from businesses, individuals, and governments denominated in currencies other than that of the host country and to make loans in those same foreign currencies. Thus, the Eurocurrency market was born.

What Is a Eurodollar?

Because the dollar is the chief international currency today, the market for Eurodollars dominates the Eurocurrency markets. What are Eurodollars? They are deposits of U.S. dollars in banks located outside the United States or in U.S.-based banking facilities free of United States deposit regulations.[3] The banks in question record the deposits on their books in U.S. dollars, not in the home currency. While the large majority of Eurodollar (and other Eurocurrency) deposits are held in Europe, these deposits have spread worldwide, and Europe's share of the total is actually declining.[4]

Frequently, banks accepting Eurodollar deposits are foreign branches of American banks. For example, in London, the center of the Eurocurrency market today, branches of American banks outnumber British banks and

---

[3] In 1981 the Federal Reserve Board allowed banks operating in the United States to establish International Banking Facilities (IBFs)—computerized recordkeeping centers for international transactions—which can accept deposits from nonresidents of the United States that are not subject to regulations governing the taking of domestic deposits. Thus, any deposit by a U.S. nonresident recorded in an IBF is counted as a Eurodollar deposit.

[4] Among the most important non-European centers for Eurocurrency trading are the Bahamas, Bahrain, Canada, the Cayman Islands, Hong Kong, Japan, Panama, and Singapore.

bid aggressively for deposits denominated in U.S. dollars.[5] Many of these funds will then be loaned to the home office in the United States to meet reserve requirements and other liquidity needs. The remaining funds will be loaned to private corporations and governments abroad who need U.S. dollars. No one knows exactly how large the Eurodollar market is. One reason is that the market is almost completely unregulated. Moreover, many international banks refuse to disclose publicly their deposit balances in various currencies. Another reason for the relative lack of information on market activity is that Eurocurrencies are merely bookkeeping entries on a bank's ledger and not really currencies at all. You cannot put Eurodollars in your pocket like bank notes.

Moreover, Eurodollar deposits are continually on the move in the form of loans. They are employed to finance the import and export of goods, to supplement government tax revenues, to provide working capital for the foreign operations of U.S. multinational corporations, and as we noted earlier, to provide liquid reserves for the largest banks headquartered in the United States.

One estimate for year-end 1986 drawn from figures compiled by Morgan Guaranty Trust Company in New York gave the *gross* size of the entire Eurocurrency market at more than $3.5 trillion. The term *gross* in this instance means the sum of all foreign-currency-denominated liabilities outside the country of the currency's origin. Because Eurodollars represent about 70 percent of all Eurocurrency liabilities, the gross size of the Eurodollar market would have been in the vicinity of $2.5 trillion. Figures of this magnitude would make the Eurodollar market the largest of all money markets.

The Creation of Eurodollars

To illustrate how Eurodollar deposits arise, we trace through a simple but typical example. While our discussion will be in terms of Eurodollars, the reader should be aware that the process being described really applies to any Eurocurrency.

Suppose a French exporter of fine wines ships cases of champagne to a New York importer, accompanied by a bill for $10,000. The importing firm pays for the champagne by issuing a check drawn on its local bank in the requested amount. Because the French exporter deals regularly in the United States, frequently buying American equipment and securities, it is happy to accept the importer's check denominated in dollars and deposits it right away in a U.S. bank—First American Bank—where the French firm maintains a commercial checking account. After this check clears, the results of the transaction are shown below.

---

[5] U.S. banks are prohibited from accepting deposits or making loans in currencies other than U.S. dollars in the domestic market. However, banks in other countries, branches of U.S. banks abroad, and IBFs (see note 3) can accept foreign-currency-denominated accounts.

French Exporter		First American Bank	
Assets	Liabilities	Assets	Liabilities
Demand +$10,000 deposit in U.S. bank			Demand +$10,000 deposit owed French exporter

Is the deposit a Eurodollar deposit? *No,* because the deposit of dollars occurred in the United States, where the dollar is the official monetary unit. Suppose, however, that the French exporter is offered an attractive rate of return on its dollar deposit by its own local bank in Paris and decides to move the deposit there. The Paris bank wants to loan these dollars to other customers who need them to pay bills or make purchases in the United States. After the wine exporter and its Paris bank exchange letters setting the terms of the deposit, the French exporter will receive a receipt for a dollar-denominated time deposit in its Paris bank. That bank will now hold claim to the original dollar deposit in the United States. The Paris bank will have at least one U.S. correspondent bank and will ask to have the original dollar deposit transferred there. We show these transactions as follows:

French Exporter		First American Bank	
Assets	Liabilities	Assets	Liabilities
Demand −$10,000 deposit in U.S. bank		Reserves −$10,000 trans- ferred to U.S. corre- spondent bank	Demand −$10,000 deposit owed French exporter
Time +$10,000 deposit in Paris bank			

U.S. Correspondent Bank		Paris Bank	
Assets	Liabilities	Assets	Liabilities
Reserves +$10,000 received from First American Bank	Demand +$10,000 deposit owed Paris bank	Deposit +$10,000 with U.S. corre- spondent bank	Time +$10,000 deposit owed French exporter

Do we now have a Eurodollar deposit? *Yes,* in the form of a $10,000 time deposit in a Paris bank. The wine exporter's deposit has been accepted and recorded on the Paris bank's books in U.S. dollars, even though the official monetary unit in France is the franc.[6]

Let us follow this Eurodollar deposit through one more step. Assume

---

[6]The $10,000 time deposit is used here for illustrative purposes only. The vast majority of Eurocurrency deposits are far larger. In fact, the normal trading unit in this market is 1 million currency units.

now that the Paris bank makes a loan of $10,000 to a small oil company based in Manchester, England. The British company needs dollars to pay for a shipment of petroleum drilling equipment from Houston, Texas. By securing a dollar credit from the Paris bank, the British oil firm, in effect, receives a claim against dollars deposited in U.S. banks. The appropriate accounting entries would be:

Paris Bank		British Oil Company	
Assets	**Liabilities**	**Assets**	**Liabilities**
Loan to British oil company +$10,000		Demand deposit in U.S. correspondent bank +$10,000	Loan owed to Paris bank +$10,000
Deposit in U.S. correspondent bank −$10,000			

U.S. Correspondent Bank	
Assets	**Liabilities**
	Deposit owed to Paris bank −$10,000
	Deposit owed to British oil company +$10,000

Note that we have assumed the British oil company held a deposit account in the same U.S. bank where the Paris bank held its correspondent deposits. This, of course, is often not the case, but it was done here to reduce the number of accounting entries. If another U.S. bank was involved, we would simply transfer deposits and reserves to it from the U.S. correspondent that held the account of the Paris bank. The result would be exactly the same as in our example: *The total amount of dollar deposits and U.S. bank reserves remains unchanged.* These funds are merely passed from U.S. bank to U.S. bank as loans are extended and deposits made in the Eurodollar market. Thus, Eurodollar activity does not alter the total reserves of the U.S. banking system. In fact, the workings of the Eurodollar market remind us of a fundamental principle of international finance: *Money itself usually does not leave the country where it originates; only the ownership of money is transferred across international boundaries.*

The chain of Eurodollar loans and deposits started in our example by the wine exporter's bank in Paris will go on unbroken as long as dollar loans are in demand and the funds are continually redeposited somewhere in the international banking system. Some economists believe that Eurobanks, like domestic U.S. banks, can create a multiple volume of deposits and loans for each dollar deposit they receive. However, this view has recently been disputed by a number of analysts (e.g., Niehans and Hewson, (1976)). They point out that major Eurobanks in their borrowing and lending activities are closer to nonbank financial institutions in the United States than to U.S. commercial banks. Eurobanks appear to closely match the maturities of their assets (principally loans) with the maturities of their liabilities (principally Eurocurrency deposits and borrowings); thus, funds raised in the Eurocurrency markets flow through the bank back into those same markets. Rather than creating money or liquidity, Eurobanks appear to function more as "efficient distributors of liquidity." If there is any actual credit or money creation in the Eurosystem, leading to a multiplication of deposits, the deposit multiplier must be very small (close to one).[7]

Of course, just as Eurodollars are created by making loans, they are also destroyed as loans are repaid. In our example above, suppose the British oil company trades pounds for dollars with a foreign currency dealer and uses the dollars purchased to repay its loan from the Paris bank. At about the same time, the dollar time deposit held by the French exporter matures, and the exporter spends those dollars in the United States. As far as U.S. banks are concerned, total deposits and reserves remain unchanged. However, as a result of these transactions, all dollar deposits are now held in the United States and therefore have ceased to be Eurodollars.

Eurodollar Maturities and Risks

Most Eurodollar deposits are short-term time deposits (ranging from overnight to call money loaned for a few days out to one year) and therefore are true money market instruments. However, a small percentage are long-term time deposits, extending in some instances to about five years. Most Eurodollar deposits carry one-month maturities to coincide with payments for shipments of goods. Other common maturities are 2, 3, 6, and 12 months.[8] The majority are interbank liabilities that pay a fixed interest rate.

Even though Eurobanks do not issue demand deposits, funds move rap-

---

[7]See Chapters 4 and 23 for a discussion of the deposit multiplier. The granting of a Eurodollar loan to a borrower does not give the borrower "money" in a strict sense. Eurodollars are not generally acceptable as a medium of exchange to pay for goods and services. They are more like time deposits. The holder of a Eurodollar deposit must convert that deposit into some national currency unit before using it for spending. Thus, Eurodollars and other Eurocurrency deposits are not negotiable instruments. The Eurocurrency system does not create money in the traditional sense. A lender of Eurocurrency who needs liquid funds before a deposit matures must go back into the market and negotiate a separate loan.

Interest usually is paid only at maturity unless the Eurodollar deposit has a term of more than one year. Most deposit interest rates are tied to the London Interbank Offer Rate (LIBOR)—the rate at which major international banks offer term Eurodollar deposits to each other. The rate is usually fixed for the life of the deposit, though floating rates tied to semi-annual changes in LIBOR are not uncommon on longer-term deposits, with promised rates reset every three to six months at a spread over LIBOR.

[8]Banks active in the Eurodollar market for liquidity-adjustment purposes use so-called short-date deposits. Comparable to federal funds transactions in the domestic U.S. money market, short dates represent deposits available for as long as 14 days, though generally they are weekend or 2-day money, with some 7-day maturities as well. Short dates may carry fixed maturities or simply be payable on demand with minimal notice (such as 24 or 48 hours).

idly in the Eurocurrency market from bank to bank in response to demands for short-term liquidity from corporations, governments, and Eurobanks themselves. There is no central trading location in the market. Traders thousands of miles distant from each other may conduct negotiations by cable, telephone, or telex, with written confirmation coming later. Funds normally are transferred on the second business day after an agreement is reached through correspondent banks.

Eurocurrency deposits are known to be volatile and highly sensitive to fluctuations in interest rates. A slight difference in interest rates or currency values between two countries can cause a massive flow of Eurocurrencies across national boundaries. One of the most famous examples of this phenomenon occurred in West Germany in 1971, when speculation that the German mark would be upvalued brought an inflow into Germany of billions in dollar deposits in a few days, forcing the West German government to cut the mark loose from its official exchange value and allow the currency to float.

As Goodfriend (1981) observes, Eurodollars are not without risk. There is *political risk* because governments may restrict or prohibit the movement or repatriation of funds across national borders as the United States did for a time during the Iranian crisis. There may be disputes between nations over the legal jurisdiction and control of deposits. *Default risk* may also be a factor because banks in the Eurobank system may fail and Eurocurrency deposits usually are not insured. This problem is compounded by the fact that it is more costly to secure information on the financial condition of foreign banks than on domestic banks. However, on the positive side, Eurobanks are among the largest and most stable banking institutions in the world. Moreover, most foreign nations have tried to encourage the growth of the Eurocurrency markets through lenient regulation and taxation.

The Supply of Eurodollars

Where do Eurodollars come from? A major factor in the market's growth has been the enormous balance-of-payments deficits which the United States has run since the late 1950s.[9] American firms building factories and purchasing goods and services abroad have transferred ownership of dollar deposits to foreign companies, banks, and governments. Domestic shortages of oil and natural gas have forced the United States to import from 30 to 40 percent of its petroleum needs, generating enormous outflows of dollars to oil-producing nations. The OPEC countries, for example, accept dollars in payment for crude oil and use the dollar as a standard for valuing the oil they sell. American tourists visiting Europe, Japan, Singapore, and the Middle East frequently use dollar-denominated traveler's checks or take U.S. currency with them and convert it into local currency overseas. Dollar

---

[9]See Chapter 27 for a discussion of the causes and effects of U.S. balance-of-payment deficits.

loans made by U.S. corporations and foreign-based firms have added to the vast Eurodollar pool. Many of these dollar deposits have gravitated to foreign central banks, such as the Bank of England and the Bundesbank in the Federal Republic of Germany, as these institutions have attempted to support the dollar and their own currencies in international markets.

Eurodollars in Domestic Bank Operations

Since the late 1960s American banks have drawn heavily upon Eurodollar deposits as a means of adjusting their domestic reserve positions. Thus, the manager of the money desk at a large U.S. bank, knowing the bank will need extra cash reserves in a few days, can contact foreign banks holding dollar deposits and arrange a loan. The manager can also contact other U.S. banks with branches abroad and borrow Eurodollars from them. Alternatively, if the money manager's own bank operates foreign branches accepting dollar deposits, these can be placed at the disposal of the home office.

Eurodollar borrowing of bank reserves has been especially heavy during periods of rapidly rising interest rates in the United States. For example, during the credit crunches of 1969–70 and 1979–80, when domestic money market rates rose to record levels, major U.S. banks tapped the Eurodollar market for billions of dollars in short-term funds. In the midst of the 1969–70 credit crunch, U.S. bank dollar liabilities to their foreign branches reached $15 billion—a record not surpassed until 1979, when net Eurodollar borrowings by U.S. commercial banks totaled nearly $35 billion. Such borrowings are highly volatile, however, and extremely interest-rate-sensitive. For example, when U.S. money market rates fell precipitously from all-time record highs in the spring of 1980 and domestic sources of reserves became much less expensive, American banks repaid their Eurodollar borrowings nearly as fast as they borrowed these international deposits months earlier. The volume of U.S. bank net Eurodollar borrowings from foreign-related institutions, which totaled $28 billion in December 1979, stood at only about $8 billion by the end of 1980 (see Exhibit 17–7).

Eurodollars usually carry *higher* reported interest rates than other sources of bank reserves, such as the federal funds market, or domestic deposits (see Exhibit 17–8). However, there are fewer legal and regulatory restrictions on the borrowing of Eurodollars. For example, Eurodollar deposits, in most periods, have been free of reserve requirements. Moreover, U.S. banks must pay assessments to the Federal Deposit Insurance Corporation on domestic nonbank deposits to cover the costs of deposit insurance. Eurodollar deposits, however, are not insured.

In addition to meeting their own reserve needs from the Eurodollar market, U.S. banks have actively aided their corporate customers in acquiring and transmitting Eurocurrency deposits. Direct loans in Eurodollars and other Eurocurrencies are made by U.S. banks, and these banks will readily swap Eurocurrencies at the customer's request. While most Euro-

Exhibit 17–7   Eurodollar Borrowings by Commercial Banks Operating in the United States, Monthly Averages for December ($ Billions)

Item	1980	1981	1982	1983	1984	1985	1986	1987
Net balance due to foreign-related institutions	$ −8.2	$ −18.1	$ −47.7	$ −42.7	$ −32.0	$ −33.1	$ −19.0	$ 15.2
Domestic chartered U.S. banks' net position with their own foreign branches	−14.7	−22.4	−39.6	−39.7	−31.4	−31.8	−30.6	−14.1
Gross due from balances	37.5	54.9	72.2	75.2	69.0	70.6	73.3	69.6
Gross due to balances	22.8	32.4	32.6	35.5	37.6	38.8	42.7	55.5

Source: Board of Governors of the Federal Reserve System, *Federal Reserve Bulletin,* selected issues.

Exhibit 17–8   Interest Rates on Eurodollar Deposits and Other Money Market Instruments (Percent)

Period	Eurodollar Deposits, Three-Month Maturities	U.S. Treasury Bills, Three-Month Maturities	Federal Funds Rate
1975	6.00%	5.84%	5.82%
1976	5.00	4.99	5.05
1977	7.25	5.27	5.54
1978	11.69	7.22	7.94
1979	14.94	10.04	11.20
1980	14.00	11.43	13.36
1981	16.79	14.03	16.38
1982	13.12	10.61	12.26
1983	9.56	8.61	9.09
1984	10.73	9.52	10.22
1985	8.28	7.48	8.10
1986	6.71	5.98	6.80
1987	7.06	5.77	6.66

Source: U.S. Department of Commerce, *Business Statistics,* selected editions; and Board of Governors of the Federal Reserve System, *Federal Reserve Bulletin,* selected monthly issues.

currency loans to nonbank customers are short-term credits to provide working capital, a sizable percentage in recent years have consisted of medium-term (one- to five-year) loans for equipment purchases, frequently set up under a revolving credit agreement. The total amount of Eurodollar and other Eurocurrency loans is unknown, though fairly reliable estimates are available concerning Eurodollar activity by branches of U.S. banks operating abroad. For example, foreign branches of U.S. banks reported holding dollar claims of about $330 billion in 1987, of which $67 billion represented claims on foreign banks, $16 billion were claims on public borrowers, and another $40 billion were claims on other nonbank foreigners.

Eurodollar loan rates have two components: (1) the cost of acquiring Eurodollar deposits (usually measured by the London Interbank Offer Rate (LIBOR) on three- or six-month Eurodeposits); and (2) a profit margin ("spread") based on the riskiness of the loan and degree of competition. Profit margins generally are very low on Eurodollar loans (often ⅛ percentage point or less) because the market is highly competitive, the cost of lending operations is low, and the risk is normally low. Borrowers are generally well-known institutions with substantial net worth and solid credit standing. Market transactions are usually carried out in large, even denominations ranging from about $500,000 to $5 million or more.

Recent Innovations in the Eurodollar Market

Since 1984 the Eurodollar market has witnessed rapid growth in medium-term credit arrangements between international banks and their large corporate and governmental customers. These so-called NIFs—Note Issuance Facilities—span five to seven years in most cases and allow the customer to borrow in his/her own name by selling short-term IOUs (typically maturing in three to six months) to investors. The bank, for its part, backstops this customer paper, either by purchasing any that remains unsold or by providing standby credit at an interest rate spread over LIBOR or some other base interest rate. The notes issued are usually denominated in American dollars with par values of $100,000 or even higher. With bank support, NIFs are roughly equivalent to Eurodollar CDs and compete with them for investor funds.

Benefits and Costs of the Eurodollar Market

For the most part, the development of Eurodollar trading has resulted in substantial benefits to the international community and especially to U.S. banks and multinational corporations. The market ensures a high degree of funds mobility between international capital markets and provides a true international market for bank and nonbank liquidity adjustments. It has provided a mechanism for absorbing huge amounts of U.S. dollars flowing overseas and generally lessened international pressure to forsake the dollar for gold and other currencies. The market reduces the cost of international trade by providing an efficient method of economizing on transaction balances in the world's most heavily traded currency, the dollar.[10] Moreover, it acts as a check on domestic monetary and fiscal policies, especially on the European continent, and encourages international cooperation in economic

---

[10] See Balbach and Resler (1980) on this point. In effect, the Eurodollar market lowers the cost of dollar-denominated financial intermediation.

policies because interest-sensitive traders in the market will quickly spot interest rates that are out of line and move huge amounts of funds to any point on the globe. Central banks, such as the Bank of England, the Bundesbank, and the Federal Reserve System, monitor the Eurodollar market continuously in order to moderate heavy inflows or outflows of funds that may damage their domestic economies.

The capacity of the Eurocurrency market to mobilize massive amounts of funds has brought severe criticism of this market from central bankers in Europe and from certain government officials, economists, and financial analysts in the United States. They see the market as contributing to instability in currency values, particularly when Eurocurrency trading places severe downward pressure on the dollar and other key trading currencies. The market can wreak havoc with monetary and fiscal policies designed to cure domestic economic problems. This is especially true if a nation is experiencing severe inflation and massive inflows of Eurocurrency occur at the same time. The net effect of Eurocurrency expansion, other things being equal, is to push domestic interest rates down, stimulate credit expansion, and accelerate the rate of inflation. The ability of local authorities to deal with inflationary problems might be overwhelmed by a Eurocurrency glut. This danger is really the price of freedom, for an unregulated market will not always conform to the plans of government policymakers.[11]

It is not surprising that certain European central banks have for more than a decade called for controls on Eurocurrency trading. One of the most frequently heard proposals is to impose reserve requirements on Eurodollar deposits. For example, during the 1970s France levied a 9.5 percent reserve requirement on Eurodollar loans. But such controls have not really been effective because of lack of unanimity among foreign governments and central banks. Funds tend to flow away from areas employing controls and toward free and open markets. The key to the future of controls in this market probably rests with the Bank of England, because London is the heart of the Eurodollar market. Thus far, the Old Lady of Threadneedle Street, as that bank is often called, remains firmly against significant government restraints on Eurocurrency trading.

SUMMARY

"The world is getting smaller all the time"—a familiar and trite phrase. It is also true. Travel time between distant cities and even across oceans is neasured today in hours and minutes instead of days. Supersonic jet trans-

---

[11] There is little evidence that the rapid growth of the Eurodollar market has had any adverse effects on U.S. economic policies, however. For example, a recent study by Balbach and Resler (1980) concludes: "Eurodollar flows . . . have only minor effects on the U.S. money stock. This evidence warrants the conclusion that the Eurodollar market does not pose a serious threat to the ability of the Federal Reserve to control the money supply" (p. 11).

ports, such as the British Concorde, have cut in half jet travel time between London and New York and between the major European and American financial centers and their counterparts in Asia, the Middle East, and the Far East.

However, the great speed at which people can travel today is far outclassed by the velocity of funds and information transfers worldwide. Communications satellites, orbiting thousands of miles above the earth's surface, speed financial and other data to their destination in minutes, seconds, and microseconds. On the ground telex, telephone, and microwave transmissions link large and small financial centers and permit financial transactions between traders separated by thousands of miles, oceans, mountain ranges, and deserts almost as conveniently as among those traders who meet on the floor of the New York Stock Exchange. The financial world is shrinking rapidly in size, and it is becoming intensely more competitive, better informed, and more sensitive to the receipt of relevant information.

It is within this environment of change, which emphasizes speed and the availability of relevant information, that the international money market instruments we have discussed in this chapter—bankers' acceptances and Eurodollars—have grown to a position of dominance. The vast improvements in information flow and speed have broadened markets for the products and services of all businesses and linked national economies into an interdependent network—a multinational economic and financial system. That system requires a fluid market for the flow of loanable funds from those businesses and governments with cash surpluses, and therefore a need to invest idle funds, to those business and governmental institutions with cash deficits and a need to borrow money as briefly as overnight or for periods covering months and years.

And, as in any money market, there is great concern for *risk* within the multinational financial and economic system. Will the borrower be able to repay a loan and make the interest payments on it? What is the borrower's true credit position? These burgeoning international needs—for financial and credit information, for credit to support trade and commerce, and for low-risk investment outlets—have led to the development and growth of both bankers' acceptances and Eurodollars. Both instruments provide large amounts of credit to businesses engaged in international trade and commerce, and at the same time offer an attractive, high-quality investment. Moreover, both acceptances and Eurodollars are traded in large unregulated and efficient markets where interest rates are highly responsive to changing demand and supply forces and investor expectations. This is why thousands of corporations, including the largest commercial banks, have entered these international markets as both borrowers and lenders of funds. And, in the absence of government regulation and control, markets linking financial systems should continue to grow in size and relative importance, exerting an ever-widening influence on the character of economic and political relationships in the international community.

STUDY QUESTIONS

1. What is a banker's acceptance? What does the word *accepted* mean?

2. Explain why acceptances are popular with exporters and importers of goods. Why are these instruments not as widely used within the United States as they are in financing international trade?

3. Evaluate bankers' acceptances as a security investment. What are their principal advantages and disadvantages from an investment point of view?

4. What is a Eurocurrency market? Why is it needed?

5. Define the term *Eurodollar*. Can a U.S. bank create Eurodollars? Why?

6. Describe the process by which Eurodollars are created. Explain what happens to the total volume of U.S. bank reserves and deposits in the creation process.

7. Can Eurodollars be destroyed? How?

8. List the sources of Eurodollar deposits. List their principal uses.

9. What role do Eurodollar deposits play in the reserve management operations of major U.S. banks? What are the advantages of Eurodollar borrowings over other sources of bank reserves?

10. Evaluate the Eurocurrency markets from a social point of view. What are the major benefits and costs of this rapidly growing institution? Would you support closer regulation of the Eurocurrency markets? Why or why not?

PROBLEMS

1. A West German manufacturer of furniture sells a large order of home furnishings to a furniture outlet in Houston. The Houston firm pays for the shipment by wiring funds from its local bank through Fedwire to the West German firm's account at Chase Manhattan Bank in New York City. Subsequently, the West German manufacturer decides to invest half the funds received in a dollar deposit offered by a bank in London, Barclays Bank, where interest rates are particularly attractive. No sooner are the funds deposited in London when a Japanese auto company, shipping cars to the U.S. and to Western Europe, asks the London bank for a loan to purchase raw materials in the United States.

   Later, when the loan falls due, the Japanese auto firm will go into the foreign currency market to purchase dollars to retire its Eurodollar loan at Barclays Bank, receiving a dollar deposit at a U.S. bank. When the loan is repaid, Barclays gains the dollar deposit in the United States and uses that deposit to pay off the West German firm when its time deposit matures. The West German firm chooses to deposit the funds received from Barclays in its demand deposit account at Chase Manhattan Bank in New York City because it now needs to buy goods and services in the United States.

Construct T accounts which reflect the foregoing transactions at each step. In particular, show the proper entries for: (1) payment by the Houston firm to the German furniture company; (2) deposit of the funds in London; (3) the loan to the Japanese automaker; (4) repayment of the loan; and (5) return of the funds to the United States. Indicate which deposit is a Eurodollar deposit and if any Eurodollars are destroyed at any particular stage.

2. A company known as Standard Quality Importing ships videocassette recorders made in Japan to retail dealers in the United States and Western Europe. It decides to place an order with its Japanese supplier for 10,000 Hi-Fi VCRs at $575 each after securing a line of credit from Guaranty Security Bank in Los Angeles. Guaranty issues a credit letter to the Japanese supplier promising payment in U.S. dollars 90 days hence. However, the Japanese firm needs the promised funds within seven days from receipt of the credit letter to make purchases of technical components from an electronics firm in Phoenix, Arizona. Explain and illustrate with T accounts and diagrams how a banker's acceptance could arise from the foregoing transactions, how the Japanese supplier could receive the dollars he needs in timely fashion, and what would happen to the acceptance at the end of the 90-day period. Use T account entries to show the movement of funds from the importer to the Japanese supplier to the electronics firm and to money market investors.

SELECTED REFERENCES

Balbach, Anatol B., and David H. Resler. "Eurodollars and the U.S. Money Supply." *Review,* Federal Reserve Bank of St. Louis, June–July 1980, pp. 2–12.

Dufey, Gunter, and Ian H. Giddy. "Eurocurrency Deposit Risk." *Journal of Banking and Finance,* 8 (1984), pp. 567–89.

Einzig, Paul. *The Eurodollar System.* 5th ed. New York: St. Martin's Press, 1973.

Feder, Gershon, and Knud Ross. "Risk Assessments and Risk Premiums in the Eurodollar Market." *Journal of Finance,* June 1982, pp. 679–91.

Goodfriend, Marvin. "Eurodollars." *Economic Review,* Federal Reserve Bank of Richmond, May–June 1981, pp. 12–18.

Goodman, Laurie S. "The Pricing of Syndicated Eurocurrency Credits." *Quarterly Review,* Federal Reserve Bank of New York, Summer 1980, pp. 39–49.

Hervey, Jack L. "Bankers' Acceptances Revisited." *Economic Perspectives,* Federal Reserve Bank of Chicago, May–June 1983, pp. 21–31.

Kreichen, Lawrence L. "Eurodollar Arbitrage." *Quarterly Review,* Federal Reserve Bank of New York, Summer 1982, pp. 10–22.

Morgan Guaranty Trust Company of New York. *World Financial Markets,* selected issues.

Niehans, Jung, and John Hewson. "The Eurodollar Market and Monetary Theory." *Journal of Money, Credit, and Banking,* 1976, pp. 1–27.

Resler, David H. "Does Eurodollar Borrowing Improved the Dollar's Exchange Value?" *Review,* Federal Reserve Bank of St. Louis, August 1979, pp. 10–16.

Part Five

The Consumer in the Financial Markets

Chapter 18

Consumer Lending and Borrowing

Learning Objectives in This Chapter

- To demonstrate the vital role played by consumers—individuals and families—in *supplying* loanable funds to the money and capital markets.
- To examine the principal characteristics of consumers as *borrowers* of funds in the financial system.
- To explore the principal characteristics of consumer lending institutions—commercial banks, savings banks, credit unions, and finance companies.

Key Terms and Concepts in This Chapter

NOW account
Share draft
Consumer cash-management services
Universal life insurance
Residential mortgage credit
Installment credit

Noninstallment credit
Home equity loan
Credit card
Debit card
Truth-in-lending
Fair Credit Billing Act
Fair Credit Reporting Act

Competitive Banking Equality Act
Community Reinvestment Act
Equal Credit Opportunity Act
Bankruptcy Reform Act

AMONG the most important of all financial markets are the markets providing savings instruments and credit to individuals and families. Many financial analysts have referred to the period since World War II as the age of consumer finance because individuals and families not only are the principal source of loanable funds flowing into the financial markets today, but also are one of the largest borrowing groups in the entire financial system. Moreover, the market for consumer financial services is the one financial market which *everyone,* regardless of income or social status, will enter at one time or another during their lifetime. In this chapter we examine the major characteristics of the consumer market for financial services, the principal lenders active in this market, and some of the more important rules and regulations applying to consumer borrowing and lending today.

CONSUMERS AS LENDERS OF FUNDS

Each of us is a consumer of goods and services virtually every day of our lives. Scarcely a single day passes that we do not enter the marketplace to purchase food, shelter, entertainment, books, newspapers, and thousands of other "essentials" of modern living. We are also well aware, perhaps from personal experience, that consumers often borrow heavily in the financial marketplace to achieve their desired standard of living. U.S. consumers borrowed about $245 billion in 1987, for example, and by the end of that year owed close to $3 trillion to various lending institutions.

What is not nearly so well known or so often recognized, however, is the fact that consumers as a group are also the most important *lenders of funds* in the economy. Loanable funds are supplied by consumers when they purchase financial assets from other units in the economy. In 1987 gross saving by U.S. households totaled $706 billion, of which nearly $320 billion flowed into commercial bank deposits, savings deposits at nonbank financial institutions, bonds, stocks, and direct cash loans to others in the economy. By comparison, nonfinancial businesses recorded gross savings of only $448 billion, the federal government had negative savings (a budget deficit) of about $170 billion, and state and local governments racked up a paltry $ − 2.2 billion in savings. Clearly, the consuming public is the chief source of the raw material—loanable funds—exchanged in the financial markets.[1]

Financial Assets Purchased by Consumers

If consumers make loanable funds available to other units in the economy by purchasing financial assets, what kinds of *financial assets* do they buy? And what are the principal sources of borrowed funds for consumers? The

---

[1] These figures were taken from the Federal Reserve Board's Flow of Funds Accounts as discussed in Chapter 3. Portions of this chapter are drawn from Rose (1978, June 1979, and September 1979).

Exhibit 18–1 **Principal Financial Assets Held by U.S. Households, Year-End 1960, 1970, 1980, and 1986** ($ Billions)

Financial Assets Held	1960		1970		1980		1986	
	Amount	Percent	Amount	Percent	Amount	Percent	Amount	Percent
Demand deposits and currency	$ 70.2	7.3%	$ 118.2	4.7%	$ 270.7	4.1%	$ 503.7	4.7%
Time and savings accounts:	165.3	17.1	426.3	17.1	1,272.8	19.4	2,099.5	19.5
At commercial banks	62.0	6.4	—	—	—	—	—	—
At nonbank thrift institutions	103.3	10.7	—	—	—	—	—	—
Shares in money market mutual funds	—	—	—	—	64.9	1.0	257.1	2.4
U.S. government securities	73.5	7.6	102.8	4.1	246.9	3.8	547.5	5.1
State and local government securities	30.8	3.2	46.0	1.8	88.4	1.3	236.6	2.2
Open market paper	0.1	0.0	11.8	0.5	41.3	0.6	63.8	0.6
Corporate and foreign bonds	9.8	1.0	35.6	1.4	58.8	0.9	95.3	0.9
Mortgages	31.8	3.3	52.1	2.1	116.5	1.8	147.1	1.4
Corporate stock:	396.1	40.9	727.2	29.1	1,173.1	17.9	2,210.2	20.5
Investment companies	17.0	1.8	44.5	1.8	52.1	0.8	365.5	3.4
Other corporate shares	279.0	39.2	682.7	27.3	1,121.0	17.1	1,844.8	17.1
Life insurance reserves	85.2	8.8	130.7	5.2	216.4	3.3	274.2	2.5
Pension fund reserves	90.7	9.4	240.8	9.6	830.0	12.6	1,750.9	16.2
Security credit	1.1	0.1	4.4	0.2	14.8	0.2	39.3	0.4
Other assets	13.3	1.4	603.5	24.1	2,168.6	33.0	2,560.0	23.7
Total financial assets	$967.9	100.0%	$2,499.3	100.0%	$6,563.3	100.0%	$10,785.3	100.0%

Note: Columns may not add to totals due to rounding.

Source: Board of Governors of the Federal Reserve System, *Flow of Funds Accounts: Financial Assets and Liabilities Outstanding,* indicated years.

Federal Reserve Board's Flow of Funds Accounts provide us with a wealth of information on the borrowing and lending habits of households. Exhibit 18–1 summarizes information contained in recent Flow of Funds reports on the kinds of financial assets acquired by households. One fact immediately evident is the wide diversity of financial assets purchased by individuals and families, ranging from those of very low risk and short maturity (such as bank deposits and government securities) to long-term, high-risk investments (such as mortgages and corporate stock).

The most important household financial asset today is deposits held at commercial banks, savings and loan associations, credit unions, savings banks, and other thrift institutions. These checkable demand deposits and time and savings deposits represented about one quarter of the total financial asset holdings of American consumers at year-end 1986. Moreover, as Exhibit 18–1 reveals, the importance of deposits in consumer financial investments has generally increased as bank and nonbank thrift institutions have offered higher returns and greater convenience to savers.

While household investments in thrift deposits have been growing, purchases of corporate stock have declined in relative terms. Exhibit 18–1 shows that individuals and families held as much as 40 percent of their financial investments in corporate stock in 1960 and nearly 30 percent in 1970. However, the stock market's often volatile performance, coupled with attractive returns available elsewhere, have driven thousands of small investors out of the stock market. By year-end 1986, only one fifth of household financial investments remained committed to corporate stock. Offsetting these stock investment changes, however, has been a dramatic rise in household investments in small businesses, which are often owned and operated by a single family. By year-end 1986, household investments in the equity of unincorporated business firms (listed under Other Assets in Exhibit 18–1) totaled almost $2.6 trillion.

Other financial assets—corporate bonds, mortgages, life insurance policies, and cash itself—also have fallen in favor with the average consumer in comparison with bank and thrift deposits. Faced with uncertain economic conditions and inflation, households have come to emphasize safety, liquidity, and long-term financial security in choosing financial assets. This is evidenced by the growing importance of consumer investments in time and savings deposits, shares in money market mutual funds, and pension plans in recent years.

The Growing Menu of Savings Instruments Available to Consumers Today

One of the most important of all trends affecting consumer savings and lending today is a veritable explosion of new financial instruments. Banks, brokerage houses, thrift institutions, and other financial institutions began in the 1970s to compete aggressively for consumer savings not only by offering higher returns where the law allowed, but also by proliferating new financial services. Like a Baskin-Robbins' ice cream store, leading financial institutions began to offer household customers 31 or more flavors of savings and transactions accounts as well as credit plans to meet a wide variety of personal financial needs (for some examples, see Exhibit 18–2).

This trend toward financial service proliferation began with the introduction of the NOW account in New England in 1970. NOWs are checkbook deposits which, like any checking account, can be used to make payments for purchases of goods and services. But NOWs also pay interest—something currently prohibited regular checking accounts by federal law. Initially confined to the six New England states NOWs were permitted nationwide beginning in 1981 as a result of passage of the Depository Institutions Deregulation and Monetary Control Act of 1980. This law, as we saw in Chapters 4 and 5, also called for the gradual phasing out of federal interest rate

Exhibit 18–2 **Examples of Key Financial Services Offered to Consumers by U.S. Financial Institutions**

Payments services:

NOW accounts	Interest-bearing checking accounts offered by banks and thrift institutions that may be held by individuals and nonprofit institutions.
Super NOW accounts	An interest-bearing checking account without restrictions on the number of withdrawals, number of checks written, or on the interest rate that can be paid.
Money market deposit accounts (MMDAs)	An interest-bearing checkbook deposit with up to six preauthorized third-party transfers out of the account, only three of which may be by check. No legal restrictions are imposed, however, on withdrawals in person, by mail, or through a messenger or automated teller machine. A seven-day notice of withdrawal may be imposed by the offering financial institution.
Share drafts	Interest-bearing checking accounts offered by credit unions to members only.
Share accounts	Shares in a money market mutual fund, representing an ownership interest in a pool of money market securities held by the fund; minimums are required to open an account and make deposits; checks may be written provided they are equal to or larger than some minimum amount (e.g., $500).
Automatic transfer service (ATS)	Allows the customer of a depository institution to transfer funds between checking and savings accounts, thus earning interest on unused balances until the funds are needed for expenditures.

Savings instruments:

Passbook or regular savings accounts	Savings plan allowing withdrawals or deposits at any time; while technically a seven-day withdrawal notice may be required, this is usually not requested by the offering institution.
Certificates of deposit, at least seven days to maturity	A time account with a set maturity or with a required notice of withdrawal of 7 to 31 days; may carry a penalty for premature withdrawal; and the interest rate may be fixed or variable.
Market-index certificates of deposit	A deposit account whose rate of return to the holder is tied to the performance of the stock market, but some minimum rate of return usually is promised in case the stock market declines.
Universal life insurance plans	A combination risk-protection and savings instrument offering the customer money market interest rates

continued

Exhibit 18–2 *(continued)*

	on savings accumulated in a mutual fund plus the convenience of automatic withdrawals to cover premium payments on a life insurance policy.
IRAs and Keogh plans	Retirement funds which some wage earners (in the case of IRAs) or self-employed persons (in the case of Keoghs) can open up at local banks or non-bank thrifts, brokerage firms, insurance companies, or mutual funds and contribute limited amounts of annual income free of federal income taxes.
Combined brokerage (either full-service or discount) and cash-management services	A comprehensive financial management package offered primarily by brokerage companies and some banks and thrift institutions which may offer share accounts in money market funds and stock and bond funds, credit card and checkwriting services, automatic funds transfers into and out of the customer's account, and low-cost execution of desired security trades along with option and margin accounts.
Credit plans: Credit cards	A plastic identification card that permits the user to charge purchases and therefore delay payment for days, weeks, or months.
Installment credit	A loan of money accompanied by an agreement that the borrower will gradually pay back the principal of the loan over time.
Home equity loans	Credit extended to the borrower that is collateralized by the residual value over and beyond any mortgage debt on the borrower's residence.

ceilings on all bank and thrift institution deposits so that consumers could receive competitive, market-determined interest rates on their deposits.

The Depository Institutions Deregulation Act of 1980 (DIDMCA) also authorized two services that compete directly with NOWs. One of these — automatic transfers (ATS)—permits the consumer to preauthorize a bank to move funds from a savings account to a checking account in order to cover overdrafts. The net effect is to pay interest on transactions balances at the savings account rate. Credit unions are permitted to offer their own version of the NOW, known as the share draft. These interest-bearing checkbook plans give the consumer the advantage of a duplicate record system for any checks written, frequently offer extra float time, and potentially pay higher interest rates on liquid funds.

In 1973 money market mutual funds appeared, offering consumers *share accounts* with low denominations (most allowing accounts to be opened for as little as $1,000), but paying interest rates reflecting current rates in the money market. Like NOWs, share accounts at money funds were developed originally to get around federal deposit interest rate ceilings and give smaller savers access to competitive rates of return on their funds. Later, several prominent brokerage houses began offering consumer cash-management services in which funds could be held in an interest-bearing money market fund until transferred into stocks, bonds, or other securities or accessed via check or credit card. Life insurance firms began offering a related service known as universal life insurance in which savings contributed by the policyholder are placed in a money market fund, with the life insurer making periodic preauthorized withdrawals to pay the premiums on the life insurance policy. The consumer is offered life insurance protection plus a higher return on savings.

Finally, in 1981 with passage of the Economic Recovery Tax Act of 1981, wage earners and salaried individuals were granted the right to make limited contributions each year, tax free, to an individual retirement account (IRA) offered by local banks, savings institutions, brokerage firms, insurance companies, and mutual funds or by employers with qualified pension, profit-sharing, or savings plans. Similarly, Keogh Plan retirement accounts have been open to self-employed persons since 1962 and may be offered by the same institutions that sell IRAs.

Beginning in the late 1970s, flexible interest rate savings plans became popular as many consumers fought to stay ahead of inflation through savings instruments whose rates of return were sensitive to changes in the cost of living. Money market certificates of deposit were authorized by federal regulation in 1978 with interest rates that changed as market yields on U.S. government securities fluctuated. Unfortunately, such accounts often carried high minimum deposits and stiff penalties for early withdrawal. Nevertheless, their popularity with consumers stirred Congress to act and, as we noted above, federal interest rate ceilings were ordered gradually phased out beginning in 1981. In 1982 the Garn–St Germain Depository Institutions Act allowed banks and nonbank thrift institutions to offer deposits competitive with shares offered by money market mutual funds. The result was the appearance of money market deposit accounts (MMDAs) and Super NOWs, each offering flexible money market interest rates but accessible via check and preauthorized draft to pay for purchases of goods and services. The great success of the MMDAs is reflected in the fact that they exceeded $300 billion within six months of their inauguration. Finally, in 1987 several banks and savings associations, led by Chase Manhattan of New York, introduced market-index certificates of deposit whose return was linked to stock market performance.

These recent innovations have been designed largely to attract consumer savings and to bring individuals and families into the financial markets as

Exhibit 18–3 **Principal Liabilities of U.S. Households Outstanding at Year-End 1960, 1970, 1980, and 1986** ($ Billions)

Liabilities	1960 Amount	1960 Percent	1970 Amount	1970 Percent	1980 Amount	1980 Percent	1986 Amount	1986 Percent
Home mortgages	$136.8	60.5%	$290.0	57.9%	$ 943.3	62.6%	$1,645.1	60.1%
Other mortgages	9.2	4.1	19.0	3.8	31.5	2.1	46.1	1.7
Consumer installment credit	43.0	19.0	105.5	21.1	300.4	19.9	586.3	21.4
Other consumer credit	13.2	5.8	37.6	7.5	74.0	4.9	136.7	5.0
Bank loans n.e.c.*	7.2	3.2	6.9	1.4	29.5	2.0	51.5	1.9
Other loans	7.0	3.1	20.9	4.2	54.7	3.6	88.4	3.2
Security credit	5.4	2.4	10.4	2.1	27.2	1.8	59.9	2.2
Trade credit	2.3	0.9	5.3	1.1	17.2	1.1	30.5	1.1
Deferred and unpaid life insurance premiums	2.4	1.1	5.1	1.0	12.9	0.9	13.9	0.5
Other Liabilities	—	—	0.2	—	16.6	1.1	79.8	2.9
Total liabilities	$226.2	100.0%	$500.9	100.0%	$1,507.3	100.0%	$2,738.2	100.0%

*Not elsewhere classified.

Note: Columns may not add to totals due to rounding.

Source: Board of Governors of the Federal Reserve System, *Flow of Funds Accounts: Financial Assets and Liabilities Outstanding,* indicated years.

more active lenders of funds. The newest financial services offer the consumer greater *financial flexibility*—easier access to liquid funds for transactions purposes and the ability to move funds more easily from one type of savings instrument to another. The newest savings instruments offer the potential for higher effective rates of return more closely tied to changing interest rates and security prices in the open market.

CONSUMERS AS BORROWERS OF FUNDS

We have noted that consumers provide most of the savings out of which loans are made and financial assets created in the money and capital markets. However, it is also true that consumers are among the most important borrowers in the financial system. For example, in 1987 households borrowed about $245 billion in U.S. credit markets, while nonfinancial businesses raised just under $266 billion. Equally impressive is the total amount of debt owed by households relative to other sectors of the economy. For example, total credit market debt owed by U.S. households exceeded $2.7 trillion by year-end 1986 (see Exhibit 18–3). This was just slightly more than the total indebtedness of all nonfinancial businesses in the U.S. economy, and substantially exceeded the total amounts owed by the federal government and all state and local governments combined.

Exhibit 18–4   The Household Sector as a Net Lender of Funds

	Amounts Outstanding at Year-End ($ billions)				
Item	1950	1960	1970	1980	1986
Total financial assets held by households	$447.5	$967.9	$2,499.3	$6,563.3	$10,785.3
Total financial liabilities of households	77.4	226.2	500.9	1,507.3	2,738.2
Difference: Financial assets – liabilities	$370.1	$741.7	$1,998.4	$5,056.0	$ 8,047.1
Ratio of household liabilities to financial assets	17.3%	23.4%	20.0%	29.8%	25.4%

Source: Board of Governors of the Federal Reserve System, *Flow of Funds Accounts: Financial Assets and Liabilities Outstanding*, indicated years.

Is Consumer Borrowing Excessive?

Are consumers too heavily in debt today? Have they jumped in over their heads? Certainly, the total volume of household debt outstanding is huge in both absolute terms and relative to most other sectors of the economy. However, to judge whether consumer borrowing is really excessive, that debt should be compared to the financial assets consumers hold. These assets, presumably, can be drawn upon to meet any interest and principal payments that come due on consumer borrowings. Exhibit 18–4 shows that, while the volume of consumer debt has increased rapidly in recent years, the volume of household financial assets has also grown rapidly. For example, in 1986 financial assets held by U.S. households exceeded their outstanding liabilities by $8 trillion. Moreover, the absolute dollar size of that financial asset cushion has increased dramatically over the past three decades.

When we measure the ratio of consumer liabilities to financial assets, however, the picture is not quite so optimistic. As shown in Exhibit 18–4, this liability-to-asset ratio has risen from less than 20 percent in 1950 to more than 25 percent in the most recent year. Whether the household liability-financial asset ratio has reached an excessive level depends, of course, on economic conditions and the educational level and degree of financial sophistication of individuals and families. If the average consumer today is better educated and more capable of managing a larger volume of debt, a higher ratio of liabilities to financial assets in household portfolios is probably not an alarming development. Moreover, the total wealth held by consumers includes not just their financial assets, but also their real assets, such as homes, automobiles, and furniture. While we have no really reliable measure of the value of real assets held by consumers, it is obvious that the total wealth of individuals and families (including both real and financial assets) far exceeds their debt obligations.

Categories of Consumer Borrowing

The range of consumer borrowing needs is enormous. Loans to the household sector support a more diverse group of purchases of goods and services than is true of any other sector of the economy. Consumers borrow *long term* to finance purchases of durable goods, such as single-family homes, automobiles, mobile homes, recreational vehicles, repair and modernization of existing homes, boats, and home appliances. They usually borrow *short term* to cover purchases of nondurable goods and services, such as medical care, vacations, fuel, food, and clothing. Financial analysts frequently divide the credit extended to consumers into three broad categories: (1) residential mortgage credit to support the purchase of new or existing single-family homes, duplexes, and other permanent dwellings; (2) installment credit used primarily for long-term nonresidential purposes; and (3) noninstallment credit for shorter-term cash needs.

Which of these forms of consumer borrowing is most important? Exhibit 18–3 provides a clear answer. Far and away the dominant form of consumer borrowing is aimed at providing shelter for individuals and families through mortgage loans. Home mortgage indebtedness by U.S. households reached more than $1.6 trillion at year-end 1986, representing 60 percent of all household debt. Moreover, the volume of home mortgage credit flowing to households has grown rapidly in recent years with the increasing attractiveness of home ownership as a tax shelter and with recent tax law reforms that favor loans secured by the borrower's home.

Installment credit is the second major component of consumer debt in the United States. Installment debt consists of all consumer liabilities other than mortgages that are retired in two or more consecutive payments, usually made monthly or quarterly. Four major types of installment credit are extended by lenders in this field: automobile credit, revolving credit, mobile homes, and other consumer installment loans. An incredibly wide variety of consumer goods and services is financed by this kind of credit, including the purchase of furniture and appliances, payment of medical and dental expenses, vacations, the purchase of transportation and recreational vehicles, and the consolidation of outstanding debts. As shown in Exhibit 18–3, consumer installment debt totaled nearly $590 billion at year-end 1986, nearly double the amount in 1980.

The final major category of consumer debt is noninstallment credit, which is normally paid off in a lump sum. This form of consumer credit includes single-payment loans, charge accounts, and credit for services, such as medical care and utilities. The total amount of noninstallment loans outstanding is difficult to estimate because many such loans are made by one individual to another or by department stores, oil and gas companies, and professional service firms that do not report their lending activities. Commercial banks, however, make a substantial volume of noninstallment loans to consumers and are considered the leading lender in this field.

HOME EQUITY LOANS

One new form of consumer borrowing that is closely related to residential mortgage credit is the home equity loan. Unlike traditional home mortgages, many home equity loans consist of a prearranged revolving credit line the borrower can draw upon for purchases in varying amounts over the life of the credit line. Thus, the consumer can literally write himself or herself a loan simply by writing a check or presenting a credit card for purchases made up to a stipulated maximum amount, known as the *borrowing base*. The borrowing base typically amounts to 75 to 85 percent of the owner's equity interest in his or her home (which equals the home's market value less the amount of any mortgage loans outstanding). The maturities of these credit lines usually range from 10 to 20 years without prepayment penalties. Because the loan is secured by pledging the borrower's home, interest rates charged on home equity loans typically are lower than those assessed on other types of nonmortgage consumer credit.

If a home equity loan is taken out by the consumer in order to purchase or improve a residence, to pay for education, or to cover medical expenses, any interest paid usually is tax-deductible, unlike interest on nonmortgage loans, which will no longer be tax deductible after 1990 under current tax law. Most home equity loans carry floating interest rates, adjustable monthly with changes in the bank prime interest rate or in some other base rate. Because most home equity credit lines are revolving credits, the borrower can repeatedly borrow, repay, and borrow again. Moreover, most homeowners have substantial equity and therefore borrowing capacity in their homes—more than $3 trillion, according to some estimates. There is a real danger here, however, because if the borrower cannot make the loan payments, his or her home may be repossessed and sold to pay back the lender. Many financial experts recommend that consumers use home equity lines of credit with considerable caution, particularly when their future employment prospects appear highly uncertain.

CREDIT AND DEBT CARDS

One of the most popular forms of installment credit available to consumers today comes through the credit card. Through this encoded piece of plastic, the consumer has instant access to credit for any purchase up to a prespecified limit. More recently, another piece of plastic—the debit card—has made instant cash available and check cashing much easier. The growth of credit and debit cards has been truly phenomenal, and the future looks equally promising. Current estimates suggest that there are about 1 trillion credit and debit cards in use worldwide.

In the future a wide array of new consumer financial services will be offered through plastic credit and debit card programs. Such services will include consumer revolving credit lines and preauthorized borrowing, interest paid on surplus credit card balances, optional credit repayment plans, and the payment of other household bills. Many of these consumer-oriented financial services are already offered on a limited basis in selected markets across the United States. In the future customers will need to make fewer trips to their bank or other financial institution, because transactions will be handled mainly over the telephone or through a conveniently located computer terminal, either in the home or in easily accessible public locations. The hometown financial institution will lose much of its convenience advantage for local customers. It will be nearly as convenient for the customer to maintain a checking, savings, or loan account in a city hundreds of miles away as to keep it in a local financial institution. In short, the ticket to many consumer financial services will be a plastic credit or debit card, with the capability of electronic processing of consumer financial data across great distances.

Credit Cards

Credit cards are used for very different purposes today, depending upon the social class, education, income, and lifestyle of the user. Customers who use credit cards merely as a substitute for cash are referred to as *convenience users*. These people tend to be in the upper-middle or top income-earning brackets and do not necessarily seek stores accepting their cards. Customers who purchase large items (such as furniture, appliances, and gifts) and generally maintain large outstanding credit card balances are referred to as *installment users* because they pay only a portion of their outstanding balances each month. These individuals frequently are in lower-and middle-income brackets and tend to be the most profitable credit card customers for card-issuing firms.

For both convenience and installment users, the principal advantage of credit cards is *convenience*. The installment loan feature of the credit card is a major attraction because it functions as a revolving line of credit. In addition, the card itself serves to identify the customer and makes pertinent information available when the privilege of using the card is exercised. Most merchants know that charge cardholders tend to have higher incomes and better payment records than the general population.

Debit Cards

Until recently, commercial banks were the only major financial institution actively involved in the plastic card field. This situation changed rapidly during the 1970s and early 1980s, however, as nonbank financial institutions (principally credit unions, savings banks, and savings and loan associations) successfully invaded the plastic card market using debit cards. While a credit card permits the customer to buy now and pay later, debit cards are merely a convenient way of paying now. A debit card enables users to make deposits and withdrawals from an automated teller (money machine) and also to pay for purchases by direct electronic transfer of funds from their own accounts to the merchant's account. Debit cards are also used for identification and check-clearing purposes and to access remote computer terminals for information or for the transfer of funds. An important feature of debit cards is their potential for the elimination of checkbook float. Electronic funds transfer systems activated with a debit card will take only seconds instead of days (as checks now do) to move money from one account to another.

THE DETERMINANTS OF CONSUMER BORROWING

As we noted earlier, consumers represent one of the largest groups of borrowers in the financial system. Yet individual consumers differ widely in their use of credit and in their attitudes toward borrowing money. What factors appear to influence the volume of borrowing carried out by households?

Recent research points to a number of factors that bear on the consumer's decision of when and how much to borrow.[2] Leading the list is the size of *individual or family income* and *accumulated household wealth*. Families with larger incomes and greater accumulated wealth use greater amounts of debt, both in absolute dollar amounts and relative to income and wealth holdings. In part, the debt-income-wealth relationship reflects the high correlation between income levels, wealth, and education. Families whose principal breadwinners have made a significant investment in education are most often aware of the advantages (as well as the dangers) of using debt to supplement current income. Moreover, there is a high positive correlation between level of education and income-earning power of the principal breadwinners in a family.

The *stage in life* in which adult income-earning members of a family find themselves is a major influence on household borrowing. The so-called life cycle hypothesis contends that young families just starting out tend to be heavy users of debt.[3] The purchase of a new home, automobile, appliances, and furniture follow soon after a new family is formed. As children come along, living costs rise and a larger home may be necessary, resulting in additional borrowing. Later the family's income usually rises, children leave home, and saving increases, while borrowing typically falls relative to income.

---

[2] An excellent discussion of the factors influencing household borrowing is presented in the study by Katona, Mandell, and Schiedeskamp (1971).

[3] See especially Ando and Modigliani (1963) and Chen and Jensen (1985).

Research suggests families with children tend to borrow more heavily relative to current income than either singles or childless couples. Moreover, the more volatile a family's income, the more debt it tends to use relative to current income. Similarly, a family that holds a low proportion of liquid assets (such as insurance policies, stocks, bonds, and deposits) tends to use more debt per dollar of income than a household with a high proportion of liquid assets

Consumer borrowing is correlated with the *business cycle*. During periods of economic expansion, the number of jobs increases, and households become more optimistic about the future. New borrowings usually outstrip repayments of outstanding loans, and the total volume of household debt rises. When an economic expansion ends and a recession begins, however, unemployment rises and many households become pessimistic about the future. Some, fearing a drop in income or even loss of jobs, will attempt to build up savings and cut back on borrowing. Loan repayments rise relative to new borrowings, and total household debt declines.

One factor that accentuates the cyclical behavior of consumer borrowing is fluctuations in the *demand for durable goods*.[4] When the economy turns down into a recession, many households postpone replacement of worn-out furniture, home appliances, and automobiles. Repairing the old automobile, for example, is often viewed as a safer, less expensive alternative than incurring additional debt and committing uncertain future income to buy a new one. Therefore consumers are likely to cut back on purchases of durables and on the debt used to finance them when a recession hits. However, new furniture, appliances, and automobiles become more attractive in boom periods, and consumer debt used to buy these items usually increases during such periods.

In recent years, *price expectations* have influenced consumer borrowing heavily. This has been especially the case since the late 1960s, when the rate of inflation began to accelerate. Postponing the purchase of an automobile, a new home, furniture, or appliances usually means these goods will simply cost more in the future. If family incomes are not increasing at least as fast as consumer prices, it often pays to "buy now" through borrowing rather than postpone purchases.

Fluctuations in *interest rates* also play a role in shaping the volume and direction of consumer borrowing. Interest rates rise as the economy expands and gathers momentum. At first, the rising rates are not high enough to offset strong consumer optimism, and household borrowing continues to increase. As the period of economic expansion reaches a peak, however, the rise in interest rates becomes so significant that consumer borrowing begins to decline. The drop in borrowing also leads to a decline in consumer spending, which may worsen the impending recession.

---

[4] For a discussion of the factors influencing purchases of consumer durables, see Dunkelberg and Stevenson (1972).

CONSUMER LENDING INSTITUTIONS

Financial intermediaries—commercial banks, savings banks and savings and loan associations, credit unions, and finance companies—account for most of the loans made to consumers in the American economy. For example, of the $625 billion in nonmortgage installment loans owed by consumers in February 1988, financial intermediaries accounted for $578 billion, or about 90 percent. Intermediaries also dominate the market for noninstallment credit and make the bulk of home mortgage loans. While each type of financial institution prefers to specialize in one type or a few selected areas of consumer lending, there has been a tendency in recent years for institutions to diversify their lending operations. One important result of this diversification has been to bring all major consumer lenders into direct competition.

Commercial Banks

The single most important consumer lending institution is the commercial bank. Commercial banks approach the consumer in three different ways — by direct lending, through purchases of installment paper from merchants, and by making loans to other consumer lending institutions. Roughly half of all bank loans to consumers (measured by dollar volume) consist of mortgages to support the purchase, construction, or improvement of residential dwellings, while the rest consists of installment and noninstallemnt credit to cover purchases of goods and services and debt retirement. In the mortgage field, commercial banks usually prefer to provide short-term construction financing rather than making long-term permanent loans for family housing.

Banks make a wider variety of consumer loans than any other lending institution. They grant about half of all auto loans extended by financial institutions to consumers each year. However, most bank credit in the auto field is indirect—installment paper purchased from auto dealers—rather than being made directly to the auto-buying consumer. Moreover, banking's lead in auto lending is seriously threatened by finance companies, which are rapidly closing in. Commercial banks have lost their number one position to finance companies in lending to support the purchase of mobile homes. Indeed, in most forms of consumer installment credit today, the lead of commercial banks is narrower and the share of other consumer lending institutions is on the rise.

Finance Companies

Finance companies have a long history of active lending in the consumer installment field, providing funds directly to the consumer through thousands of small loan offices and indirectly by purchasing installment paper from appliance dealers. These active household lenders provide auto loans, credit for home improvements and for the purchase of appliances and furniture, and revolving credit arrangements. Finance companies often face legal limits on the interest rates they can charge for household loans and on the maximum size of such loans as set by state law.

Other Consumer Lending Institutions

Other consumer installment lenders include credit unions, savings and loan associations, and savings banks. Credit unions make a wide variety of loans for such diverse purposes as purchases of automobiles, vacations, medical expenses, home repair and modernization, and more recently, mortgage credit for the purchase of new homes. Also making sizable inroads into the consumer loan field in recent years have been savings and loan associations and savings banks. While these institutions have long been dominant in residential mortgage lending, they have aggressively expanded their portfolios of credit card, education, home improvement, furniture, appliance, and mobile home loans over the past decade. This expansion in the consumer credit field is due to recent federal deregulation of the services offered by savings institutions.

FACTORS CONSIDERED IN MAKING CONSUMER LOANS

Consumer loans are considered one of the most profitable uses of funds for most financial institutions. There is evidence, however, that such loans usually carry greater risk than most other kinds of loans, and they are more costly to make per dollar of loan.[5] On the other hand, the lender often can offset these costs by charging higher interest rates. Consumer credit markets in many communities are less competitive than the market for business loans or for marketable securities, giving the lender something of an advantage.

Making consumer loans is one of the most challenging aspects of modern financial management. It requires not only a thorough knowledge of household financial statements, but also an ability to assess the character of the borrower and the likelihood that he or she will honor financial commitments in the future. Over the years, most loan officers have developed decision "rules of thumb" as an aid to processing and evaluating consumer loan applications. These decision rules often vary greatly with the financial institution doing the lending and the experience of each loan officer, but a few of the more common practices may be noted.

For example, many consumer loan officers insist that household debt

---

[5] Credit investigations and recordkeeping are the principal costs associated with consumer lending.

(exclusive of housing costs) should not exceed a certain critical percentage of a family's monthly or annual gross income. A maximum of 15 to 20 percent of gross income is a common standard in this instance. For younger borrowers, without substantial assets to serve as collateral for a loan, a cosigner may be sought whose assets and financial standing represent more adequate security. The duration of employment of the borrower is often a critical factor, and many institutions will deny a loan request if the customer has been employed at his or her present job for less than a year.

The past payment record of a customer usually is the key indicator of *character* and the likelihood that the loan will be repaid in timely fashion. Many lenders refuse to make loans to consumers who evidence "pyramiding of debt;" that is, borrowing from one financial institution to pay another. Evidence of sloppy money handling, such as unusually large balances carried on charge accounts or a heavy burden of installment payments, is regarded as a negative factor in a loan application. Loan officers are particularly alert to evidence of a lack of credit integrity as reflected in frequent late payments or actual default on past loans. The character of the borrower is the single most important issue in the decision to grant or deny a consumer loan. Regardless of the strength of the borrower's financial position, if the customer lacks the willingness to repay debt, then the lender has made a bad loan.

Most lenders feel that those who own valuable property, such as land, buildings, or marketable securities, are a better risk than those who do not own such property. For example, homeowners are usually considered better risks than those who rent. Moreover, a borrower's chance of getting a loan usually goes up if he or she does other business (such as maintain a deposit) with the lending institution. If more than one member of the family works, this is often viewed as a more favorable factor than if the family depends on one breadwinner who may become ill, die, or simply lose a job. Having a telephone at home is another positive factor in evaluating a loan application because the telephone gives the lender an inexpensive way to contact the borrower. One way to lower the cost of a loan is for the consumer to pledge a bank deposit, marketable securities, or other liquid assets as security behind the loan. The disadvantage here is that such security ties up the asset pledged until the loan is repaid.

FINANCIAL DISCLOSURE AND CONSUMER CREDIT

A number of important new laws have appeared in recent years designed to protect the consumer in dealings with lending institutions. One major area of emphasis in recent consumer legislation is *financial disclosure*— making all relevant information about the terms of a loan available to the borrower before a commitment is made. The assumption is that an informed

---

Financial Planning for Consumers

One of the most rapidly growing of all consumer-oriented industries is *financial planning*—rendering professional advice to the consumer on how to manage money. While there are literally thousands of paid and volunteer financial planners in business today, each offering their own brand of financial advice, many financial planners seem to agree on certain principles of good money management for the consumer:

1. Use borrowing cautiously, especially where your home is pledged as collateral and your income is volatile or highly uncertain.
2. In choosing which financial assets to acquire as investments or how much to borrow:
    a. Decide what your personal goals are—adequate retirement income? a vacation home? extra car? college education?
    b. Classify your goals into short-term, medium-term, and long-term and estimate how much money will be required for each.
    c. Target each personal investment in assets and each borrowing to match each of the short-, medium-, and long-term goals you have set, so that the money is there exactly when it is needed.
    d. Make sure any debt taken on is comfortably covered (both principal and interest) by your expected income plus financial investments.
    e. Diversify your investments—keep a roughly equal balance of funds invested in different stocks, bonds, deposits, mutual fund shares, and real estate to spread your risk.
3. Seek competent, unbiased professional advice, particularly where large purchases are to be made, large borrowings are contemplated, or when planning for retirement.

---

borrower will be a wise user of credit. Moreover, if all important information is laid out before a loan agreement is reached, this may encourage the consumer to shop around to find the cheapest and most convenient sources of credit. However, there is considerable debate today on whether consumer protection legislation has really accomplished its goals. Both lenders and borrowers are confronted with a confusing array of laws and regulations which encourage violations and may be of little net benefit to the consumer.[6]

---

[6] Recent studies by Day and Brandt (1974), Mandell (1974), and Parker and Shay (1974) suggest that many of the goals sought by recent consumer-oriented financial legislation have *not* been achieved. Many consumers do not shop for credit and appear more concerned about the affordability of monthly payments on a loan than with how one lender's interest charge compares with that quoted by another. Survey evidence suggests that the majority of consumers are unaware of the rights and privileges granted them under recent federal financial legislation and see little practical benefit from these laws. See also Rose (June 1979).

Truth in Lending

In 1968 Congress passed a watershed piece of legislation in the consumer credit field—the Consumer Credit Protection Act, more widely known as Truth-in-Lending. However, the Consumer Credit Protection Act covered more than just truthful disclosure by lenders of the terms of a loan. It defined and prohibited extortionate credit practices, limited garnishment of wages, and created a National Commission on Consumer Finance to oversee enforcement of the law. Shortly after the act was passed, federal regulatory agencies prepared new rules to implement and enforce the principles of truth in lending, such as the Federal Reserve Board's Regulation Z.

Truth-in-Lending simply requires banks and other lenders to provide sufficient information about a credit contract, in easily understood terms, so that the consumer can make an intelligent decision about purchasing credit. The law does not tell creditors how much to charge or to whom they may lend money. Rather, the lenders are required to tell the customer the true cost of a loan and any other terms of the loan that might have an impact on the consumer's financial well-being.

At the same time the consumers were granted certain rights. For example, they have the right to sue the lender for failure to conform to the Consumer Credit Protection Act and its supporting regulations. Consumers have the right to cancel or rescind a credit agreement within three business days if their home is included as part of the collateral for a loan. This so-called *right of rescission* usually applies to the repair or remodeling of a home or the taking out of a second mortgage on an existing home. It does not cover an application for a first mortgage to make the initial purcahse of a home, however. And, the credit requested must be intended for personal, family, household, or agricultural purposes and result in a debt obligation repayable in more than four installments.

The most widely known provision of Truth-in-Lending is the requirement that a lender must tell the customer the annual percentage rate of interest (APR) charged on a loan. Lenders must disclose the total dollar cost associated with granting a loan—known as the finance charge—which is the sum of all charges the customer must pay as a condition for securing the loan. These charges may include credit investigation fees, insurance to protect the lender, and points on a mortgage loan. Once the finance charge is determined, it must be converted into the APR by comparing it with the amount of the loan. The APR is really the ratio of the dollar finance charge to the declining unpaid balance of a loan, determined by the actuarial method.[7] Because all lenders must quote the APR, computed by the same method, this makes its easier (at least in theory) for the consumer to shop around and purchase credit from the cheapest source available.

The concept of Truth-in-Lending has been extended in a number of

---

[7] See Chapter 8 for a discussion of how the APR can be figured and Rose (June 1979).

directions in recent years. One important dimension concerns *advertising*. A lender who advertises one attractive feature of a credit package to consumers must also disclose other relevant credit terms. For example, if a car dealer advertises low down payments, he or she must also disclose other aspects of the loan, such as how many payments are required, what the amount of each payment is, and how many months or years are involved.

Fair Credit Billing Act

In 1974 Congress passed the Fair Credit Billing Act, which amended the original Truth-in-Lending law. The new amendment came in response to a torrent of consumer complaints about credit billing errors, especially on credit cards. Many individuals found they were being billed for items never purchased or received, that some merchants would not respond when contacted about billing errors, and that finance charges were frequently assessed even though the consumer claimed no responsibility for charges listed on the billing statement.

The Fair Credit Billing Act requires a creditor to respond to a customer's billing inquiry within 30 days. In most cases, the dispute must be resolved within 90 days. The customer may withhold payment of any amounts in dispute, though he or she must pay any portions of a bill that are not in dispute. However, no creditor can report a customer as "delinquent" over amounts of a bill that are the subject of disagreement. A creditor who fails to respond to the customer's inquiry or makes no effort to settle the dispute may forfeit the disputed sum up to $50.

Fair Credit Reporting Act

A further extension of Truth-in-Lending occurred when the Fair Credit Reporting Act was passed by Congress in 1970. This law entitles consumers to have access to their credit files, which are kept by hundreds of credit bureaus active in the United States. These credit bureaus supply subscribing lenders with vital information on amounts owed and the payment records and credit ratings of individuals and families. They aid greatly in reducing the risks inherent in consumer lending. However, because the information credit bureaus supply has a substantial impact on the availability of credit to individuals and families, their activities and especially the accuracy of the information they provide have been brought under closer scrutiny in recent years by federal and state regulatory authorities.

Under the provisions of the Fair Credit Reporting Act, the consumer is entitled to review his or her other credit file at any time (after paying a required fee). Moreover, he or she may challenge any items that appear in the file and demand an investigation. The credit bureau must respond and, if inaccuracies exist, remove or modify the incorrect information. If the consumer determines that an item in the credit file is damaging and requires clarification, he or she may insert a statement of 100 words or less explaining the consumer's version of the matter. Data in the file may be shown only to properly identified individuals for approved purposes or upon direct written request from the consumer. No information may be disclosed to anyone after a period of seven years unless the consumer is seeking a loan of $50,000 or more, purchasing life insurance, applying for a job paying $20,000 or more per year, or has declared personal bankruptcy. The consumer may sue if damaged by incorrect information in a credit file. Many financial analysts today recommend that consumers check their credit bureau report several months before applying for a major loan.

Consumer Leasing Act

In 1976 Congress passed the Consumer Leasing Act, which requires disclosure by leasing companies of the essential terms of any lease involving personal property. Short-term leases are excluded, but all those with terms over four months are covered by the law provided the property is leased for personal, family, or household use. The customer must be told about all charges, any insurance required, the terms under which the lease may be canceled, any penalties for late payment, and any express warranties that go with the property. The lease customer is entitled to sue for damages plus court costs if the requirements of the law are not met.

Competitive Banking Equality Act

On August 10, 1987, President Ronald Reagan signed the Competitive Banking Equality Act into law. It requires banks and other depository institutions to more fully disclose to customers the terms on various deposit services they offer. One major change was the required disclosure of how many days a depositor must wait before a check that is deposited in an account becomes available for spending. Some depository institutions had previously delayed the granting of credit for some deposits for a week to ten days or sometimes even longer. The new law stipulates that by 1990 no more than one business day can intervene between the day of deposit of a local check and the customer receiving credit for that deposit. Nonlocal checks must be credited to the customer's account in no more than four business days.

CREDIT DISCRIMINATION LAWS

The civil rights movement has had an impact on the granting of consumer loans. Among the most important civil rights laws involving consumer credit are the Equal Credit Opportunity Act of 1974 and its amendments in 1976, the Fair Housing Act of 1968, the Home Mortgage Disclosure Act of 1975, and the Community Reinvestment Act of 1977. The fundamental purpose of these laws is to outlaw discrimination in the granting of credit due to the age, color, marital status, national origin, race, religious affiliation, or sex of the borrower. Today, lenders must be able to justify in terms of fairness and objectivity, not only the loans that are made, but also those that are not made.

Community Reinvestment Act

One of the most important and controversial pieces of financial legislation in recent years is the Community Reinvestment Act, signed into law by President Carter on October 12, 1977. Under its terms financial institutions are required to make an "affirmative effort" to meet the credit needs of low- and middle-income customers, including households, small businesses, farms, and ranches. Each commercial and savings bank must define its own local "trade territory" and describe the services it offers or is planning to offer in that local area. Once a year each institution must prepare an updated map which delineates the trade territory served, without deliberately excluding low- or moderate-income neighborhoods, and lists the principal types of credit offered in that territory. Customers are entitled to make written comments, which must be available for public inspection, concerning the lender's performance in meeting local credit needs. The basic purpose of the Community Reinvestment Act is to avoid gerrymandering out low-income neighborhoods and other areas that a lender may consider undesirable.

Equal Credit Opportunity Act

The Equal Credit Opportunity Act of 1974 forbids discrimination against credit applicants on the basis of age, sex, marital status, race, color, religion, national origin, receipt of public assistance, or good-faith exercise of rights under the federal consumer credit protection laws. Women, for example, may receive credit under their own signature, based on their own personal credit record and earnings, without having their husband's joint signature. Credit applicants must be notified, in writing, of the approval or denial of a loan request within 30 days of filing a completed application. The lender may not request information on the borrower's race, color, religion, national origin, or sex, except in the case of residential mortgage loans.

Fair Housing and Home Mortgage Disclosure Act

Two other important antidiscrimination laws are the Fair Housing Act, which forbids discrimination in lending for the purchase or renovation of residential property, and the Home Mortgage Disclosure Act (HMDA). The latter requires financial institutions to disclose to the public the amount and location of their home mortgage and home improvement loans. HMDA was designed to eliminate *redlining,* in which some lenders would mark out areas of a community as unsuitable for mortgage loans because of low income, high crime rates, or other negative factors.

Both HMDA and the Fair Housing Act require nondiscriminatory advertising by lenders. No longer can a consumer lending institution direct its advertisements solely to high-income neighborhoods to the exclusion of other potential customers. On written advertising the Equal Housing symbol must be attached. Clearly, then, in advertising the availability of credit and in the actual granting of credit, the principles of civil rights and nondiscrimination apply. Lenders are free to choose who will receive credit, but that decision must be made within the framework of social goals.

CONSUMER BANKRUPTCY LAWS

Over the past decade the number of households filing for personal bankruptcy and relief from personal debts has soared. In 1984, for example, a record 60 out of every 100,000 U.S. adults legally declared personal bankruptcy. One reason for this upsurge in household bankruptcies was certainly the rapid growth of consumer borrowing. Another reason lay in the deep back-to-back recessions in the early 1980s with protracted high levels of unemployment. However, the principal reason for these record bankruptcy filings appeared to be more lenient federal and state bankruptcy laws, especially the Bankruptcy Reform Act of 1978. This law allowed virtually any consumer to file a bankruptcy petition even if he or she could pay off outstanding debts from current income or savings or from future earnings. In addition, once bankruptcy was declared, the consumer could keep substantial personal assets (such as a home or personal clothing) that could not be sold or repossessed to repay outstanding debts. These lenient provisions in federal and state statutes reduced the cost of consumer bankruptcy and encouraged more households to attempt to make a fresh start in managing their financial affairs.

Responding to the record explosion of consumer bankruptcy filings, Congress passed the Bankruptcy Amendments and Federal Judgeship Act of 1984. This new law significantly increased bankruptcy costs and restricted the amount and types of household debt that could be discharged with the filing of a bankruptcy petition. For example, federal rules now exempt no more than $4,000 in household furniture and appliances, clothing, and other personal items from forced sale to pay debts. These recent revisions in applicable federal and state statutes have slowed consumer bankruptcy applications significantly. The new personal bankruptcy rules serve simply as a reminder to consumers to think carefully before borrowing money and to read closely the terms of any credit agreement before "signing on the dotted line."

SUMMARY

One of the most remarkable developments in the financial system over the past century is the awakening of the consumer as a borrower and lender of funds. Better educated and more aware of their financial opportunities today, householders have become the principal source of loanable funds flowing into the financial markets and also one of the most important borrowers. Reflecting their key influence on the financial system and financial institutions, new consumer-oriented financial services have appeared in profusion in recent years in an effort to attract and hold consumer accounts. Examples include NOWs, money market deposits, share accounts in money market mutual funds, universal life insurance, consumer cash-management services, and home equity loans.

The growing role of the consumer in the financial system has brought with it greater political influence. The 1960s and 1970s ushered in landmark pieces of federal legislation to aid the consumer in borrowing and lending funds. On the borrowing side, such laws as the Consumer Credit Protection Act of 1968 (Truth-in-Lending), the Fair Credit Billing Act (1974), the Consumer Leasing Act (1976), and the Fair Credit Reporting Act (1971) have supported the rights of consumers to know what they are being charged for credit and that their credit complaints are heard and acted upon. As a result of such laws as the Community Reinvestment Act (1977), the Equal Credit Opportunity Act (1974), the Fair Housing Act (1968), and the Home Mortgage Disclosure Act (1975), lenders must make an "affirmative effort" to make credit available to all segments of their local communities without regard to age, sex, marital status, race, color, religion, or national origin of the borrower. Consumers with the support of the federal government are asking today not only to be told more about the cost of credit, but also why credit is denied to some and granted to others.

Until the 1980s consumers were largely neglected on the financial asset side of the ledger. Interest rate ceilings severely limited the yields banks and other deposit-type financial institutions could pay on consumer savings deposits. Moreover, due to restrictive interest rate ceilings (usury laws) imposed by the states on installment and mortgage loans, consumers found that the credit they needed to supplement their incomes was simply not available. A rising chorus of consumer complaints led to passage of the Depository Institutions Deregulation and Monetary Control Act of 1980 and the Garn–St Germain Depository Institutions Act of 1982. These sweeping pieces of consumer-oriented financial legislation legalized interest-bearing checking accounts (NOWs), authorized automatic transfers of funds from savings to checking accounts, set up regulatory machinery for a phaseout of deposit interest rate ceilings, lifted ceiling rates on home mortgage loans, increased the amount of federal insurance behind the public's deposits, and expanded the number of borrowing alternatives open to consumers by granting broader consumer credit powers to nonbank thrift institutions.

Unquestionably, there is more to come. Consumers have awakened financially to an awareness not only of the critical role credit and savings play in determining their own well-being, but to their powerful collective influence on the whole financial system. The consumer now seems well aware that decisions made in the financial sector help to determine how many and what kinds of jobs are available, the rate of inflation and economic growth, and even the outcome of the great social issues of modern-day society—better housing, improved educational facilities, equality and justice under the law, and freedom of economic opportunity. For the most part, modern governments have shown a strong determination to ensure that the individual consumer is treated fairly in the financial marketplace and that the financial system contributes to, rather than impedes, the progress of peaceful social change. Unfortunately, we cannot yet determine whether the recent plethora of consumer-oriented financial laws have brought the laudable benefits hoped for by their authors, or simply threaten to mire our financial system in a debilitating swamp of red tape. If the new rules reduce incentives in the financial community to compete, to offer new services, and to price existing financial services commensurate with the dictates of the marketplace, then both the consumer and society as a whole may have lost more than they have gained. On that important issue, we must await the impartial verdict afforded by time.

STUDY QUESTIONS

1. Which sector of the economy provides the largest amount of loanable funds for borrowers to draw upon? Does this sector make primarily direct loans or indirect loans to borrowers?

2. What is the most important financial asset held by households? What proportion of total household financial investments does this asset represent? What financial asset is in second place in household portfolios?

3. Define the following terms
   a. NOWs.
   b. ATS.
   c. Share drafts.
   d. MMDAs.
   e. Universal life.
   f. Money market share accounts.
   g. Home equity loans.

   In what ways do these financial services benefit consumers?

4. How much money do U.S. households owe today? Do you believe consumers are too heavily in debt? Why or why not?

5. Into what broad categories is consumer borrowing normally divided? Which is most important, and why?

6. Discuss the factors that influence the volume of borrowing by individuals and families. What role do you believe inflation plays in the borrowing and saving decisions of households today?

7. What factors do consumer lending institutions usually look at when evaluating a loan application? Why?

8. What is Truth-in-Lending? Describe the law's major features and explain why it was enacted.

9. What protections are offered the consumer under the Fair Credit Billing Act? Consumer Leasing Act? Fair Credit Reporting Act? Why?

10. What are the principal purposes of the Community Reinvestment Act? Equal Credit Opportunity Act? Fair Housing Act? Home Mortgage Disclosure Act? Assess the benefits and costs of these pieces of social responsibility legislation.

SELECTED REFERENCES

Ando, Albert, and Franco Modigliani. "The 'Life Cycle' Hypothesis of Savings: Aggregate Implications and Tests." *American Economic Review,* March 1963, pp. 55–84.

Avery, Robert B.; Gregory E. Elliehausen; and Arthur B. Kennichell. "Changes in Consumer Installment Debt." *Federal Reserve Bulletin,* October 1987, pp. 761–778.

Board of Governors of the Federal Reserve System. *Consumer Handbook to Credit Protection Laws.* Washington, DC: 1978.

Chen, Alexander, and Helen H. Jensen. "Home Equity Use and the Life Cycle Hypothesis." *The Journal of Consumer Affairs* 19, no. 1 (Summer 1985), pp. 37–56.

Day, George S., and William K. Brandt. "Consumer Research and the Evaluation of Information Disclosure Requirements: The Case of Truth in Lending." *Journal of Consumer Research,* June 1974, pp. 21–32.

Dunkelberg, William C., and James Stevenson. *Durable Goods Ownership and the Rates of Return.* Washington, DC: National Commission on Consumer Finance, 1972.

Katona, George; Lewis Mandell; and Joy Schiedeskamp. *1970 Survey of Consumer Finances.* Ann Arbor: University of Michigan Press, 1971.

Kowalewski, K. J. "Recent Changes in the Consumer Bankruptcy Laws." *Economic Commentary,* Federal Reserve Bank of Cleveland, February 1, 1985.

Mandell, Lewis. "Consumer Perception of Incurred Interest Rates: An Empirical Test of the Efficiency of the Truth-in-Lending Law." *Journal of Finance,* March 1974, pp. 217–25.

Ownes, Raymond E., and James F. Tucker. "Home Equity Loans: A Way of Financing Consumer Purchases." *Cross Sections,* Federal Reserve Bank of Richmond, 4, No. 2 (Summer 1987).

Parker, George G.D., and Robert P. Shay. "Some Factors Affecting Awareness of Annual Percentage Rates in Consumer Installment Credit Transactions." *Journal of Finance,* March 1974, pp. 217–25.

Rose, Peter S. "Bank Cards: The Promise and the Peril." *The Canadian Banker and ICB Review,* December 1978, pp. 62–67.

———. "Social Responsibility in Banking: Pressures Intensify in the U.S." *The Canadian Banker and ICB Review,* June 1979, pp. 70–75.

———. "Credit Discrimination Under Attack." *The Canadian Banker and ICB Review,* June 1979, pp. 70–75.

Weinstein, Michael. "Home Equity Credit Lines Expected to Boom." *American Banker,* August 5, 1986, p. 14.

Chapter 19

The Residential Mortgage Market

Learning Objectives in This Chapter

- To describe how the largest of all financial markets—the residential mortgage market—functions to provide credit to build and buy homes, apartments, and other dwellings.

- To understand the problems faced by individuals and families in finding credit to finance the purchase of their homes.

- To understand the problems faced by lenders of residential mortgage money in designing new loan agreements that will protect them against inflation and other risks.

- To describe the role played by the federal government and government agencies, such as Fannie Mae (FNMA) and Ginnie Mae (GNMA), in supporting the mortgage market.

Key Terms and Concepts in This Chapter

Conventional home
  mortgage loans
Residential mortgages
Nonresidential
  mortgages
Savings and loan
  associations
Federal Housing
  Administration
  (FHA)
Federal National
  Mortgage
  Association
  (FNMA)

Government National
  Mortgage
  Association
  (GNMA)
Mortgage-backed
  securities
Pass-throughs
Federal Home Loan
  Mortgage
  Corporation
  (FHLMC)
Securitized mortgages

Fixed-rate mortgage
  (FRM)
Variable-rate mortgage
  (VRM)
Adjustable mortgage
  instrument (AMI)
Creative financing
Second mortgage

ONE of the most important goals for many American families is to own their own home. Besides the psychic benefits of privacy and a feeling of belonging to the local community, home ownership has conferred important financial and economic benefits upon those families and individuals both able and willing to make the investment. The market value of single-family residences has risen substantially faster than the rate of inflation over the long term, offering individuals and families of even modest means one of the few effective long-term hedges against inflation. Moreover, the interest cost on home mortgages is tax deductible, reducing significantly the *after-tax* interest rate levied on residential mortgage loans.

Unfortunately for families seeking home ownership, the residential mortgage market is often treacherous, swinging quickly from low interest rates and ample credit to high and rising rates with little credit available. In this highly volatile market home ownership often becomes an impossible dream for thousands of individuals and families. Moreover, the wide swings characteristic of the residential mortgage market send reverberations throughout the economy, contributing to the cycles of "boom" and "bust" that often characterize economic activity.

RECENT TRENDS IN NEW HOME PRICES AND THE TERMS OF MORTGAGE LOANS

We can get a glimpse of the tremendous pressures buffeting the market for residential mortgages today by looking at recent trends in the prices of new homes and the cost of financing them. Exhibit 19–1 provides us with recent data on the average terms quoted on conventional home mortgage loans in the United States. A conventional mortgage loan is *not* guaranteed by the government, but is purely a private contract between the home buyer and the lending institution. In this case, the lender of funds bears the risk that the home buyer will default on principal or interest payments associated with a mortgage loan, forcing foreclosure and resale of the home, though today about half of conventional loans are insured by private insurance companies. In contrast, mortgage loans issued through the Federal Housing Administration (FHA) or Veterans Administration (VA) are partially guaranteed as to principal and interest by the federal government and are generally used to finance low-cost and moderately-priced housing.

As shown in Exhibit 19–1, the average purchase price of a conventional single-family residence in the United States more than doubled between 1974 and 1980, climbing above $83,000 in the latter year. Early in the 1980s, however, back-to-back recessions, coupled with high interest rates and high energy prices, significantly reduced the demand for new homes. The rise in new home prices slowed and then gained momentum again late in the decade as interest rates moderated, with the median-price U.S. home climbing well over $100,000. Lenders of funds compensated for the slowing demand for

Exhibit 19–1 **Prices and Yields of Conventional Home Mortgage Loans**

	Terms and Yields						
Item	1974	1976	1978	1980	1982	1984	1986
Primary market:							
Conventional mortgages on new homes:							
Purchase price ($000)	$40.10	$48.40	$62.60	$83.50	$94.60	$96.80	$118.10
Amount of loan ($000)	29.80	35.90	45.90	59.30	69.80	73.70	86.20
Loan/price ratio (percent)	74.30	74.20	75.30	73.30	76.60	78.70	75.20
Maturity (years)	26.30	27.20	28.20	28.20	27.60	27.80	26.60
Fees and charges (percent of loan)	1.30	1.44	1.39	2.10	2.95	2.64	2.48
Contract interest rate (percent)	8.71	8.76	9.30	12.25	14.47	11.87	9.82
Yield—FHLBB series	8.92	8.99	9.54	12.65	15.12	12.37	10.25
Yield—HUD series	9.22	8.99	9.68	13.95	15.79	13.80	10.07

Source: Board of Governors of the Federal Reserve System, *Federal Reserve Bulletin*, July 1987.

home mortgages and rising home prices by increasing the percentage of a new home's purchase price they were willing to lend in the 1980s, after doing exactly the opposite during the hectic home-buying spree of the late 1970s. Home buyers were forced to come up with larger down payments both in total dollars and relative to the market value of a new home during the 1970s, but were able to buy with smaller down payments as builders and lenders tried to move homes in a more sluggish market during the 1980s.

We note also from Exhibit 19–1 that mortgage lenders were willing to extend credit for longer periods as a partial offset to the higher cost of new homes. The average maturity of conventional home mortgage loans climbed from about 26 years in 1974 to about 28 years in the mid-1980s. Extra fees and charges ("points") levied by lenders as a condition for making mortgage credit available also rose sharply in the surging housing market of the 1970s, and then eased back in the 1980s to accommodate the softer demand. The average contract interest rate on conventional mortgage loans climbed above 14 percent in the early 1980s before falling back late in the decade.

The combination of relatively high home mortgage interest rates and high market prices for new homes in recent years has greatly increased monthly mortgage payments and shut many families out of the housing market. For example, a family putting 10 percent down on a $40,000 home in 1974, when conventional home mortgage rates ranged from 8½ to 9 percent, would have faced monthly payments (including taxes and insurance) in the $350 to $400 range. During the 1980s, however, the same house would have cost $100,000 or more with mortgage rates 10 percent or higher, so that mortgage payments would have averaged close to $1,000 per month, depending on the terms of the loan.

Several factors account for this dramatic escalation in the cost of home ownership. Certainly, inflation has played a key role in driving up building costs, especially the prices of lumber and other building materials, and this increase has been passed on to the consumer. On the demand side, a substantial rise in the number of new family formations has occurred in recent years. Children born during the great postwar baby boom of the 1940s and 1950s began to establish their own families in the 1970s and 1980s. Added to this has been a rapid increase in individuals living alone and in single-parent households. Therefore, while the U.S. birth rate dropped to the lowest level in history, the sharp increase in new families, in the numbers of children born into those new families, and in single-adult households dramatically increased the demand for housing, especially for low- and medium-priced homes.

At the same time, the proportion of the U.S. population represented by Americans in their forties and fifties began to decline. Historically, this group has provided the bulk of savings out of which home mortgage lenders can make new loans. In fact, during the 1980s, the ratio of savings to personal income in the United States fell to the lowest level since World War II.

Finally, the Tax Reform Act of 1986 appears to have increased both the after-tax cost of owner-occupied housing and the rents landlords will be forced to charge to recover their investment in apartments and other multifamily residences. These housing costs will rise primarily because of lower personal tax rates which makes home ownership a less attractive after-tax investment, longer required depreciation of property, and higher capital gains taxes. This combination of tax law changes, increased demand for new family residences, and a smaller savings flow has sharply raised the cost of housing and diminished the financial attractiveness of investing in housing. Financial analysts project that in future years, as the population continues to age and new family formations slow, new housing demand will drop and increases in housing costs will moderate.[1]

THE STRUCTURE OF THE MORTGAGE MARKET

Volume of Mortgage Loans

Mortgages are among the most important securities in the financial system. The total of all mortgages outstanding in the United States is approaching

---

[1]See, for example, the discussion by Freund (1983) and Crone (1987).

Exhibit 19–2   Total Mortgage Debt Outstanding in the United States, Year-End ($ Billions)

Year	Amount
1950	$ 72.8
1960	206.8
1970	451.7
1980	1,451.8
1987	2,906.4

Sources: Board of Governors of the Federal Reserve System, *Annual Statistical Digest,* 1971–75, and *Federal Reserve Bulletin,* selected issues.

$3 trillion (see Exhibit 19–2). This total represented over half the nation's gross national product (GNP) and made the mortgage market the largest primary security market in the United States. Moreover, the mortgage market has grown rapidly in recent years under the combined pressures of inflation and economic growth. Thus, an enormously important market within the financial system became even more important as time progressed.

Residential versus Nonresidential Mortgage Loans

The mortgage market can be divided into two major segments: (1) residential mortgages, which encompass all loans secured by single-family homes and other dwelling units; and (2) nonresidential mortgages, which includes loans secured by business and farm properties. Which of these two sectors is the more important? As Exhibit 19–3 shows, loans to finance the building and purchase of homes, apartments, and other residential units dominate the American mortgage market. In 1987 residential mortgage loans on one- to four-family properties and multifamily structures represented about three fourths of all mortgage loans outstanding. Mortgages on commercial and farm properties accounted for the remaining one fourth of all mortgages issued.

In recent years, loans to support the construction of single-family homes and other small residential structures and commercial mortgages to fund everything from shopping centers to office buildings, shipping ports, and factories have grown the most rapidly. In contrast, farm mortgages have declined drastically in relative terms, reflecting severe problems in the agricultural sector and the closing of many farming operations. The proportion of one- to four-family residential mortgage loans increased slightly in the 1980s to a secure two thirds of all U.S. mortgage loans outstanding. This category of mortgages is dominated by single-family home loans, which increased due to the rapid growth of new family formations and the effects of inflation. Because residential mortgages dominate the market, it should

Exhibit 19–3   **Mortgage Loans Outstanding, Fourth Quarter of 1987** ($ Billions)

Type of Property	Amount	Percent
Residential properties (one- to four-family and multifamily structures)	$2,162.0	74.4%
Nonresidential properties (commercial and farm)	744.4	25.6
All properties	$2,906.4	100.0%

Source: Board of Governors of the Federal Reserve System, *Federal Reserve Bulletin*, June 1988.

not be surprising that households are the leading mortgage borrower, accounting for about two thirds of outstanding mortgage debt. The next largest group of mortgage borrowers—unincorporated businesses—is a distant second.

MORTGAGE-LENDING INSTITUTIONS

In the years before World War II, mortgages were one of the most widely held securities in the financial system, comparable to stock in the great diversity of investors who chose to add these securities to their portfolios. Individuals were then the dominant mortgage investors, with financial institutions in second place. However, the rapid growth of commercial banks, savings and loan associations, savings banks, and insurance companies as major mortgage lenders during the past three decades has forced individual investors into the background. There is evidence, though, that wealthier individuals have recently stepped up their investments in housing for low-income families through syndicates and partnerships due to tax credits granted by the 1986 Tax Reform Law.

Exhibit 19–4 shows the total amounts of mortgage loans held by various lender groups in 1987. Savings and loan associations are the principal mortgage-lending institution in the United States, accounting for about one fifth of all mortgage loans outstanding. Mortgage pools, which represent collections of similar mortgages that are used as collateral for issuing new securities, rank second, while commercial banks are in third place. In general, the relative share of the mortgage market accounted for by traditional private mortgage-lending institutions, such as savings and loans, savings banks, commercial banks, and insurance companies, has declined, while pension funds and government agencies have accounted for a growing share of outstanding loans. Noteworthy in this regard has been the expanding role of mortgage pools—that is, continuing groups of high-quality residential mortgages insured or guaranteed by a government agency and in which investors hold shares, entitling them to a portion of interest and principal payments generated by the pool. We will have more to say about mortgage

Exhibit 19–4   **Principal Lenders in the U.S. Mortgage Market, Second Quarter 1987**

Lender Group	Volume of Mortgage Loans Held ($ billions)	Percent of Total
Savings and loan associations and savings banks	$ 823.2	30.0%
Commercial banks	542.6	19.8
Life insurance companies	198.1	7.2
Mortgage pools or trusts	612.4	22.3
Federal and related government agencies	196.5	7.2
Individuals and others*	372.1	13.6
Totals	$2,744.9	100.0%

*Includes mortgage companies, REITs, state and local credit agencies, state and local government retirement funds, noninsured pension funds, credit unions, and U.S. government agencies for which amounts are small or separate data are not available.

Source: Board of Governors of the Federal Reserve System, *Federal Reserve Bulletin,* July 1987.

pools later in the chapter when we discuss the expanding role of the federal government in the nation's mortgage market.

THE ROLES PLAYED BY FINANCIAL INSTITUTIONS IN THE MORTGAGE MARKET

Mortgage lenders tend to specialize in the types of loans they grant, and some are far more important to the residential market than to commercial mortgage lending. Moreover, even within the residential lending field, different institutional lenders will favor one type of mortgage (e.g., conventional versus government guaranteed) over another and also desire a certain range of maturities. Some lenders are organized to deal with home mortgage borrowers one at a time, while others may prefer to acquire large packages of mortgages associated with major residential building projects.

Savings and Loan Associations

Savings and loan associations are predominantly local lenders, making the majority of their mortgage loans in the communities where their offices are located. Moreover, S&Ls usually service the mortgage loans they make rather than turning that task over to a mortgage bank or trust company. Servicing a mortgage involves maintaining ownership and financial records on the mortgaged property, receiving installment payments from the borrower, checking on the mortgaged property to ensure that its value is maintained, and in the event of borrower default, foreclosing on the property to collect any unpaid balance on the loan. While historically S&Ls have preferred single-family home mortgages, they have diversified their portfolios in recent years to include many new kinds of assets, some mortgage-related and some not. Prominent on that list are mobile home loans, mortgage credit for the purchase of duplexes and other multifamily housing units, apartment loans, and consumer installment loans for the purchase of automobiles, furniture, and home appliances, and commercial credit. Most financial analysts expect savings and loans to expand the proportion of their portfolios devoted to consumer and commercial nonmortgage loans in future years and decrease the proportion devoted to residential mortgage loans due to federal deregulation of the industry.

Commercial Banks

In recent years commercial banks have expanded their market share of nearly every type of mortgage loan. Overall, they rank second to savings and loans among all private mortgage lenders, but hold more commercial mortgages than any other lender. The bulk of bank mortgage credit, however, goes for shorter-term loans to finance the *construction* of new commercial and residential projects, with other lenders taking on the long-term mortgage loans from these projects.

Commercial banks as a group have shown a strong interest in financing the so-called upscale homes purchased by higher-income families in recent years. Many of the individuals and families who purchased their first homes in the 1960s and 1970s with low down payments and limited living space have now become more affluent, two-earner families ready to trade up to a larger house with more amenities. These often custom-designed homes command significantly higher prices and larger down payments. Moreover, banks usually view such loans as less risky than lower-priced housing because the homeowner is typically in a higher-income category, with substantial savings to back up his or her income.

Life Insurance Companies

Life insurance companies make substantial investments in commercial as well as residential mortgage properties. These companies will search national and international markets for good mortgage investments instead of focusing on only one or a few local areas. They often prefer to purchase residential mortgages in large blocks rather than one at a time.

In the past, life insurers preferred government-guaranteed home mortgages. In recent years, however, the higher yields available on conventional mortgages have caused some shift of emphasis toward these more risky loans. Despite the greater flexibility of conventional single-family home mortgages, however, life insurance companies have been gradually reducing their holdings of single-family home mortgages and emphasizing commercial and apartment mortgages. Commercial and apartment loans often carry "equity kickers," which permit the lender to receive a portion of project earnings as well as a guaranteed interest rate.[2]

Savings Banks

Another lender of great importance in the residential mortgage market is the savings bank, headquartered mainly in the New England area and in the Middle Atlantic states of New York, New Jersey, and Pennsylvania.[3] These institutions invest in both government-guaranteed and conventional mortgage loans. While single-family homes constitute the bulk of savings bank mortgage loans, their loans supporting multifamily units (including large apartment projects) have grown rapidly in recent years. Like life insurance companies, mutuals often prefer to acquire residential mortgages in large blocks, such as a whole subdivision, rather than loan by loan.

Mortgage Bankers

Mortgage banking houses act as a channel through which builders or contractors in need of long-term funds can find permanent mortgage financing. In providing this service, mortgage bankers take on portfolios of mortgages from property developers, using mainly bank credit to carry their inventories of mortgages. Then, within a relatively short time span, these mortgages are placed with long-term institutional investors. Mortgage bankers supply important services to *both* institutional investors and property developers. The developers receive a commitment for permanent financing, which allows them to proceed with planned real estate projects. Institutional investors, especially life insurance companies and savings banks, receive mortgages appropriately packaged to match the timing of their cash flows and risk-return preferences. The mortgage banker often secures servicing fees from institutional investors who purchase the mortgages he packages and sells. Many savings and loan associations and savings banks have become more active in mortgage banking in recent years.

GOVERNMENT ACTIVITY

Adequate housing for all U.S. citizens is a major goal of the federal government. One of the steps taken by Congress to achieve this goal was the establishment of the Federal Housing Administration (FHA) in 1934. FHA has sought to promote home ownership by reducing the risk to private

---

[2]See Chapter 20 for a discussion of equity kickers in commercial mortgage lending.

[3]See Chapter 5 for a more complete discussion of the structure and characteristics of the savings bank industry.

lenders of residential mortgage contracts. At the same time efforts have been made to encourage the development of an active secondary market for existing mortgage lenders to raise cash to make new loans and to attract new investors into the mortgage business, such as pension funds, investment companies, individuals, and foreign buyers. The combination of government guarantees (FHA–VA) and the development of a secondary market has led to greater participation in mortgage lending by so-called long-distance lenders—particularly insurance companies, pension funds, and savings banks. (Exhibit 19–5 provides an overall view of the role of private lenders and federal government agencies in the mortgage market.)

The Impact of the Great Depression on Government Involvement in the Mortgage Market

Any attempt to understand how the mortgage market operates today must begin with the Great Depression and the enormous impact that economic calamity had upon the market for property loans. The Great Depression generated massive, unprecedented unemployment; an estimated one quarter to one third of the civilian labor force was thrown out of work between 1929 and 1933. Moreover, the scarcity of jobs lasted not just a few months, as in recent recessions, but for years. Few new mortgage loans were made during this period, and thousands of existing mortgages were foreclosed. With so many forced sales, property values declined precipitously, endangering the financial solvency of thousands of mortgage lenders. Indeed, scores of banks and S&Ls were forced into bankruptcy or into mergers with larger institutions.

The federal government elected to tackle the mortgage market's problems by moving in several directions at once: (1) it provided mortgage insurance through FHA for low- and medium-priced homes; (2) it insured the deposits of mortgage-lending institutions through such agencies as the Federal Deposit Insurance Corporation and the Federal Savings and Loan Insurance Corporation; (3) it placed more rigid controls on lending by banks, savings and loans, and other institutional lenders, but also provided them with easier access to credit through direct government loans; and (4) it created several new federal agencies to buy and sell residential mortgages.

For example, in 1932 the Federal Home Loan Bank System (FHLB) was created to supervise the activities of savings and loan associations and make loans to those S&Ls in trouble. In 1934, the National Housing Act was passed, setting up a system of federal insurance for qualified home mortgage loans. The Federal Housing Administration (FHA) was authorized to guarantee repayment of up to 90 percent of acceptable home loans, encouraging private lenders to lend more of a home's market value, accept longer terms on home mortgages, and charge lower interest rates.

Shortly before the end of World War II, the Veterans Administration (VA) was created with passage of the Servicemen's Readjustment Act (1944).

Exhibit 19–5 **The Structure of the Mortgage Market**

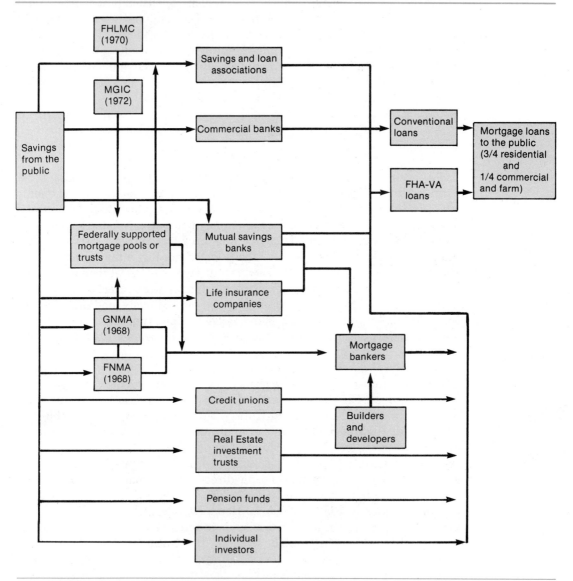

Source: Based on a diagram in "Structure of the Residential Mortgage Market," *Monthly Review,* Federal Reserve Bank of Richmond, September 1972, and modified by the author.

The VA was designed to aid military servicemen returning to civilian life in finding jobs and adequate housing. Like FHA, VA offered to insure residential mortgages. This program permitted mortgage lenders to commit their funds at low risk and reduced the required down payment on a new home.

The Creation of Fannie Mae (FNMA)

The FHA–VA insurance program was an almost instant success, and home mortgage lending grew rapidly following its inception. Federal government efforts to create a resale (secondary) market for residential mortgages took a little longer, however. The first successful federal agency set up to buy and sell residential mortgages was Fannie Mae—the Federal National Mortgage Association (FNMA). Fannie Mae was established in 1938 for the purpose of buying and selling FHA-guaranteed mortgages in the secondary market. Later, in 1948, it was authorized to trade in VA-guaranteed mortgages as well. Adjusting to the changing character of the mortgage market, FNMA began to exert a potent impact on mortgage trading in the 1950s. One reason was the launching of its standby commitment program.

Standby Commitments. Under the terms of a standby commitment, Fannie Mae agrees to purchase a specific mortgage within a stipulated period of time at a set price. The standby commitment aids builders and property developers because it provides a floor price for a mortgage and allows the holder to sell the instrument at a higher price if market conditions prove favorable. Such commitments usually are made for 4-month or 12-month periods and are sold at auction. Following reorganization as a privately owned corporation in 1968, Fannie Mae announced that it would begin issuing commitments for and buying conventional home mortgages as well as FHA- and VA-guaranteed loans. Fannie Mae raises funds for its mortgage purchases by selling discount notes and debentures in the open market.

Purchase Options. A second innovation developed by FNMA was the purchase option. The opposite of a standby commitment, a purchase option allows the seller of a mortgage to repurchase that mortgage from FNMA within nine months at the original price paid by the agency. FNMA conducts biweekly auctions where mortgage lenders indicate the interest rates at which they are willing to sell various amounts of mortgages. Based on its cost of funds and market conditions, FNMA will issue both standby commitments and purchase options to those institutions offering the best terms.

Mortgage-Backed Securities Program. In 1981 FNMA began to issue and guarantee securities backed by conventional mortgage loans purchased from lenders. FNMA mortgage-backed securities are marketed by lenders that deal with FNMA or through security dealers, with many bought in recent years by pension funds.

The Mortgage Guarantee Insurance Corporation (MGIC)

Fannie Mae is the world's largest mortgage bank and, until recently, had a virtual monopoly in secondary market trading activities. Early in the 1970s, however, the Mortgage Guarantee Insurance Corporation (MGIC) was organized by a private group in Milwaukee, Wisconsin. Known as Maggie Mae, this corporation insures conventional home mortgage loans carrying down payments as low as 5 percent. Of course, Fannie Mae has a significant advantage over Maggie Mae and other more recently formed private mortgage insurance companies because it operates as a federally sponsored agency with a privileged borrowing status and normally can raise funds at lower cost. Today, mortgage insurance is usually required by lending institutions when the borrower makes a down payment of less than 20 percent of the purchase price of a home.

The Creation of Ginnie Mae (GNMA)

Efforts by Congress to make the federal government's budget look better resulted in the splitting of Fannie Mae into two agencies in 1968. Fannie Mae itself became a private, shareholder-owned corporation devoted to secondary market trading. At the same time, loan programs requiring government subsidies or direct government credit were handed over to a new corporation set up within the Department of Housing and Urban Development, known as the Government National Mortgage Association (GNMA) or Ginnie Mae. This federal agency pursues a two-part program to aid the nation's mortgage market. Under one portion of its program, Ginnie Mae purchases mortgages to finance housing for low-income families at below-market interest rates. These "assistance mortgages" are eventually sold to FNMA or to private investors at current market prices.

Far more important for the secondary market, however, is GNMA's mortgage-backed securities program. Backed by the full faith and credit of the U.S. government, Ginnie Mae agrees to *guarantee* principal and interest payments on securities issued by private mortgage institutions if those securities are backed by pools of government-guaranteed mortgages. These so-called pass-throughs are popular with savings and loan associations, pension funds, commercial banks, and even individual investors as safe, readily marketable securities with attractive rates of return. They are issued mainly by mortgage bankers, though substantial quantities of pass-throughs also come from savings and loan associations, savings banks, and commercial banks. The issuing institutions raise cash to make new loans by selling the pass-throughs against mortgages that they place in a pool, and they continue to earn servicing income on those pooled mortgages. Today most newly originated FHA-VA mortgages on single-family dwellings are in mortgage pools supporting pass-throughs or are sold directly to Fannie Mae.[4]

The Federal Home Loan Mortgage Corporation (FHLMC)

Another federal agency created to aid the secondary mortgage market appeared in 1970. The Emergency Home Finance Act passed that year gave birth to the Federal Home Loan Mortgage Corporation (FHLMC), more popularly known as Freddie Mac. FHLMC is a branch of the Federal Home Loan Bank System which, like Ginnie Mae, may combine the mortgages it buys (primarily from savings and loans) into pools and issue bonds against them. Securities issued by Freddie Mac are guaranteed by that agency and are very popular with individual and institutional investors, particularly savings and loan associations and savings banks.

The creation of Freddie Mac reflected a desire by the federal government to develop a stronger secondary market for *conventional* home mortgages. About 80 percent of the conventional mortgage loans bought by Freddie Mac come from savings and loan associations; the remainder are supplied by mortgage banking houses, commercial banks, and savings banks.

To raise funds to support these purchases, Freddie Mac sells mortgage participation certificates (PCs) and guaranteed mortgage certificates (GMCs). PCs represent an ownership interest in a pool of conventional mortgages bought and held by Freddie Mac. PCs are sold through Freddie Mac directly and through major security dealers, who also make an active resale market in these instruments. Freddie Mac guarantees the investor's monthly interest and principal payments passed through from the mortgage pool, but PCs are not guaranteed directly by the federal government.

Guaranteed mortgage certificates (GMCs), like PCs, are claims against a pool of mortgages. They are similar to corporate bonds in that interest is paid semi-annually to investors. Repayments of principal are made once a year. While not guaranteed by the federal government, GMCs are guaranteed as to principal and interest by Freddie Mac and are available in minimum denominations of $100,000.

Another recent innovation in mortgage-backed securities is the CMO— the collateralized mortgage obligation, which has many of the attributes of a conventional bond. CMOs are issued in different classes based on a projected schedule for repaying the mortgage loans that are pooled to back each CMO. Thus, CMOs offer investors a range of different maturities from long term to short term and overcome some of the cash-flow uncertainty investors face when buying home mortgages themselves because a homeowner may

---

[4] All mortgages placed in a pool against which GNMA-guaranteed pass-throughs are issued must carry the same interest rate and have issue dates no older than one year. The coupon rate on pass-through securities must be one-half percentage point below the contract interest rate on the pooled mortgages, with a small fee paid to GNMA for its guarantee. Pass-throughs are registered securities with coupons, and pay interest and principal each month.

pay off the loan early. More recently, some mortgage-backed securities have been issued in "strips" in which the investor can receive principal payments from a pool of home mortgages or interest payments, depending upon his or her preferences for maturity and risk.

The development of securitized mortgages—pass-throughs, participation certificates, mortgage certificates, and CMOs—by Ginnie Mae, Fannie Mae, and other lending institutions has had a profound effect on the mortgage market and the mortgage lending process in recent years. These new instruments have made mortgage securities more competitive with government securities and corporate stocks and bonds, allowing many mortgage lenders to invade national and international capital markets for funds. They have also made it much easier to get old, low-yielding mortgages off lenders' books to make room for higher-yielding investments. On the negative side, however, these new financial instruments have increased the sensitivity of mortgage interest rates to national and international market conditions. Home mortgage rates are today much more volatile, often changing significantly in a single day, instead of weeks or months. The residential mortgage market has broadened geographically, embracing many more lenders and borrowers in one competitive cauldron, but only at the price of a far less predictable environment for loan rates and availability of credit for the home buyer.

Remaining Problems in Developing a Secondary Market for Mortgages

Though considerable progress has been made in the development of an active secondary mortgage market, there is still substantial room for improvement. Among the major obstacles are differences between one mortgage and another in the quality of property and borrower credit standing, which crucially affect each instrument's risk and market value. In addition, different lenders have their own particular preferences for certain kinds of mortgage instruments. Differences in foreclosure laws among the states complicate the picture, as do different state rules concerning the taxation of mortgage-lending institutions.

Other securities traded in the open market typically carry larger denominations than residential mortgages, are usually more uniform in quality, and are not amortized through installment payments. Moreover, on-site inspection of mortgaged property is often necessary to judge the quality of the mortgage instrument. Government guarantee programs serve to lower mortgage risk, but of course do not aid the purchaser of conventional mortgages unless a private firm guarantees these. The packaging of individual mortgages into pools by Freddie Mac, Ginnie Mae, and some private lenders is a positive development that tends to standardize the mortgage instrument and make it more attractive to investors. However, offsetting this positive factor is a negative one—the new adjustable-term mortgages developed in recent years have appeared in such profusion that further progress toward standardization of mortgage loans is now in doubt, thus inhibiting the continued growth of the secondary (resale) market. Overall, the secondary market for mortgages is still less well developed than the markets for corporate, municipal, and U.S. government securities, though recent estimates suggest that at least two out of every three new home mortgages today wind up in the secondary market, with the original lender selling out his or her interest to a new holder. However, substantially greater progress will be needed if we are to grapple effectively with the nation's enormous housing demands in the years ahead.

SENSITIVITY OF THE MORTGAGE MARKET TO MONETARY POLICY AND CREDIT CONDITIONS

The mortgage market is one of the most sensitive of all financial markets to changing interest rates and money and credit conditions. For example, as interest rates rise, the mortgage market is affected from two different directions. Lenders are forced to reduce their mortgage commitments in the face of rising interest rates due to *usury laws* in some states which impose maximum interest rate ceilings on new loans. In addition, commercial banks, savings and loan associations, and savings banks often lose deposits due to disintermediation as their more interest-sensitive depositors seek more attractive investment opportunities elsewhere.[5] With fewer deposits coming in, a smaller volume of funds is available for mortgage loans, and what funds *are* available usually carry higher rates. Finally, the total cost of a home goes up as interest rates rise, and this depresses the demand for housing. In many ways the mortgage market is a "boom-and-bust" affair, growing rapidly in easy money periods when interest rates are relatively low and contracting sharply in high-rate, tight money periods.

Fannie Mae, Ginnie Mae, Freddie Mac, and other government mortgage agencies have helped to stabilize the market to some extent by purchasing mortgages in tight-money periods and selling them in times of easy money and rapid credit expansion. One obvious problem, however, is that this approach frequently goes against Federal Reserve monetary policy designed to stabilize the economy and fight inflation. In tight money periods, for example, the Federal Reserve System attempts to reduce the volume of borrowing and spending in the economy through high interest rates and slower growth of the nation's money supply. However, because these developments would tend to depress the mortgage market, government mortgage agencies will respond by purchasing mortgages and making more loans to private mortgage-lending institutions.

Conversely, when the Federal Reserve attempts to pull the economy out

---

[5] See Chapter 2 for a discussion of the causes and effects of disintermediation.

of a recession by promoting low interest rates and more rapid money supply growth, the government mortgage-lending agencies tend to sell mortgages in the secondary market and cut back on loans to the housing sector. Thus, the activities of the government mortgage agencies probably contribute to economic instability. This is a clear example of a conflict in the nation's goals—stabilizing the economy versus supporting the housing industry.

INNOVATIONS IN MORTGAGE INSTRUMENTS

To this point in the chapter we have described a number of problems that have impaired the functioning of the mortgage market and limited the availability of funds for housing. The extreme sensitivity of the mortgage market to monetary policy and changing credit conditions and the struggle to develop a viable and active secondary mortgage market represent major difficulties that decades of work have only partially resolved. Still another problem with mortgages reared its head in the tumultuous economic and financial environment of the 1970s and 1980s. This problem centers on the *inflexibility* of the conventional fixed-rate mortgage (FRM) in the face of inflation and rising interest rates.

Repeatedly in recent years interest rates have climbed to record levels, only to fall back during brief recessions and then surge upward again. Each upward movement in interest rates forced mortgage lenders to cut back on the availability of funds for housing. In part, these cutbacks in mortgage funds were a response to the widespread use of fixed-rate mortgages (FRMs). Following the economic debacle of the 1930s, long-term home mortgages with 20- to 30-year maturities became popular. Until recently, the large majority of these carried *fixed* interest rates for the life of the loan. FRMs return to the lender the same annual interest income (cash flow) regardless of what is happening to inflation or to interest rates in the open market. When savings and loan associations, commercial banks, and other depository institutions are forced to pay higher rates on their deposits to attract funds, their profits tend to be squeezed because the revenues from FRMs remain unchanged. Of course, these lending institutions are able to charge higher rates on *new* mortgage loans, but new loans are always a small fraction of an institution's total loan portfolio. The bulk of that portfolio is in *old* mortgages granted during an era when interest rates often were much lower.

In short, the FRM amplifies the normal up and down cycle of earnings for a mortgage-lending institution, leading to low or even negative earnings in periods of rising interest rates and positive earnings in periods of falling rates. FRMs require the *lender* to bear the risk of interest rate fluctuations. An alternative to the FRM was needed that both guaranteed lenders a satisfactory real rate of return on mortgage loans and made funds available to home buyers on reasonable terms. (Various new and old types of mortgage instruments are described in Exhibit 19–6.)

Exhibit 19–6   Types of Mortgage Instruments

Fixed-Rate Mortgage (FRM). The contract interest rate is set at the time a mortgage loan is made and does not change over the life of the loan. The maturity (term) and the size of the monthly payment called for by the mortgage usually is fixed as well.

Variable-Rate Mortgage (VRM). The contract interest rate specified in the mortgage loan is tied to another interest rate which is sensitive to current supply and demand conditions in the open market. Higher interest rates usually result in higher monthly mortgage payments.

Adjustable Mortgage Instrument (AMI). Changes in the interest rate attached to the mortgage loan can be passed along to the borrower by changing the loan principal, loan maturity, or monthly payment, or by varying some combination of these credit terms.

Convertible Mortgage Instrument (CMI). A variable-rate home mortgage loan that allows the borrower to convert the loan to a fixed-rate mortgage (FRM) when interest rates become more favorable to the borrower.

Graduated-Payment Mortgage (GPM). Installment payments required under a mortgage contract are set lower than those required under a comparable fixed-rate mortgage but rise over time with inflation, borrower income, or some other index.

Canadian Rollover Mortgage (CRM). This mortgage loan is of much shorter term than a conventional fixed-rate mortgage and usually requires the borrower to renegotiate and refinance the loan on the due date.

Renegotiated-Rate Mortgage (RRM). With this long-term residential mortgage loan, the interest rate is set for a period shorter than the term of the mortgage and must be renegotiated between borrower and lender on a periodic basis.

Deferred-Interest Mortgage (DIM). This mortgage loan has interest rates that are generally lower than on conventional fixed-rate mortgages, but at a later point the borrower must reimburse the lender for accumulated interest not paid earlier.

Flexible-Payment Mortgage (FPM). The borrower pays only the interest on a mortgage loan for the first five years; subsequent payments must be high enough to fully amortize the loan, however.

Shared-Appreciation Mortgage (SAM). The borrower agrees to give the lender a portion of the profits from the sale of mortgaged property in return for a lower contractual interest rate and lower monthly payments.

Reverse-Annuity Mortgage (RAM). This is a device to raise money by borrowing against an existing home or other structure (usually a property whose original mortgage loan has been paid off), with the borrower receiving fixed annuity payments based on the value of the mortgaged property.

Variable-Rate and Other Adjustable Mortgages

The problems created by fixed-rate mortgages led to the development of several new mortgage instruments, led by the variable-rate mortgage or VRM, which permits the lender to vary the contractual interest rate on a mortgage loan as market conditions change. Generally, the VRM loan rate is linked to a reference interest rate *not* determined by the lender. For example, the yield on long-term U.S. Treasury bonds may be used as a reference rate so that, if Treasury bonds yields rise, the homeowner pays a higher contractual interest rate and makes a higher monthly payment on the mortgage. Alternatively, under a broader adjustable mortgage instrument (AMI), the maturity of the mortgage loan may be lengthened or a combination of rate increases and maturity changes may be made as interest rates rise.[6] In some cases the loan principal can be increased with interest rate increases, reducing the growth of the homeowner's equity — a process known as negative amortization. In effect, VRMs and other adjustable mortgage instruments shift the *risk* of interest rate fluctuations, partially or wholly, from the lender to the borrower.

The broader adjustable mortgage instruments (AMIs) mentioned above are more flexible and have more lenient regulations than pure VRMs. Under most state and federal laws, changes in the interest rates attached to VRMs are limited as to frequency and amount. However AMIs, with their options of varying monthly payments, the maturity of a mortgage loan, or the loan principal as interest rates change, face few legal restrictions on their terms and have grown rapidly in recent years. Part of the reason for the growth of AMIs is their usually lower initial loan rate compared to FRMs, with many mortgage lenders offering *teaser rates* to attract AMI customers.

Convertible Mortgages

The volatile interest rates of recent years have led to the development of a combination variable-rate, fixed-rate home mortgage loan that some home buyers find attractive today. This so-called convertible mortgage instrument (CMI) starts out with an adjustable interest rate, but later the home buyer can switch to a fixed-rate mortgage if interest rates look more favorable. There is a fee charged (usually a few hundred dollars) to make the switch; moreover, some loan contracts carry a mandatory holding period (such as one year) before conversion to a fixed-rate loan is permitted and also prohibit switching after a certain length of time has elapsed (such as five years).

---

[6]The loan rate on an AMI usually is tied to U.S. government security rates, the national average mortgage contract rate, or some index of the lender's cost of funds, though the majority of such loans today impose a cap (ceiling) on how high rates or monthly payments can go.

CMIs have attracted the interest of home buyers because their initial adjustable interest rates are usually much lower than those on new fixed-rate mortgages and the switch to a fixed-rate loan in the future typically is much cheaper than refinancing an old mortgage. Fannie Mae (FNMA) agreed in 1987 to begin creating a resale market for CMIs, improving their liquidity for private mortgage lenders.

Canadian Rollover and Other Renegotiated Mortgage Loans

Recently, there has been interest in the United States in Canadian rollover mortgages (CRMs). These instruments are usually issued for short to medium terms (5- to 10-year maturities are common), at the end of which the note falls due. The borrower must then pay off the note or negotiate a new loan. A related variety of loan is the renegotiated rate mortgage (RRM). Unlike the Canadian rollover mortgage, it carries a longer maturity, but its interest rate must be renegotiated periodically—usually every three to five years.

Still another renegotiated-type property loan is the deferred-interest mortgage (DIM), in which the borrower pays a lower interest rate than with a conventional FRM and thus has lower mortgage payments. However, the borrower must reimburse the lender for any accumulated interest that is postponed during the life of the loan plus an additional fee. This reimbursement may occur through a refinancing of the loan at the end of a certain period or when the property is sold or transferred to another owner.[7]

Reverse-Annuity Mortgages

A mortgage-financing device which may be of help to older families and retired individuals is the reverse-annuity mortgage (RAM). This financial instrument is designed to provide additional income to those who may have already paid off their home mortgage but intend to keep their present home. The lender determines the current value of the home and pays the borrower a fixed monthly annuity, amounting to a specified percentage of the property's value. The loan is secured by a gradually increasing mortgage on the

---

[7]A new type of mortgage related to CRMs, RRMs, and DIMs is the *flexible-payment mortgage* (FPM). This instrument requires the borrower to pay only the interest on the loan and no principal during the first five years. After the initial five-year period, however, the mortgage loan must be fully amortized as to both principal and interest. Since the bulk of the early payments on conventional mortgage instruments go to pay interest anyway, with very little reduction of principal, the monthly savings from FPMs are usually small.

Another relatively new mortgage instrument developed in the western United States is the *shared-appreciation mortgage* (SAM). The borrower is offered substantially smaller monthly payments and a contractual interest rate well below rates prevailing on conventional mortgages in return for a commitment to turn over a fraction of any capital gain resulting from the sale of the mortgaged property. One popular SAM contract requires the borrower to pay the lender one third of any profit earned on the sale of a home.

borrower's home. Repayment of the loan occurs when the annuity holder dies, with the loan being discharged against the deceased's estate, or when the home is sold.

Graduated-Payment Mortgages

A relatively new mortgage instrument developed in recent years to help lower-income families is the graduated-payment mortgage (GPM), which FHA began insuring in 1977. With the GPM, initial monthly payments on a new home are lower at first, then rise for a time before leveling off after several years. The idea is to tailor the debt service payments on a home mortgage to the financial needs and improving financial position of the borrower. GPMs have proved popular with young families who otherwise might be stymied by high mortgage payments until their earning power has increased.

Of course, the total amount of interest paid by the borrower will be much larger with a GPM than it would be under a conventional FRM. In part, this occurs because the low initial monthly payments do not cover the full amount of interest owed each month, forcing the lender to increase the amount of the mortgage loan in the early years. Moreover, due to the delayed receipt of income, lenders generally raise the interest rate on GPMs above rates prevailing on level-payment mortgages.

Epilogue on the Fixed-Rate Mortgage

It is interesting that, with all the new mortgage instruments developed during the 1970s and 1980s, fixed-rate mortgages (FRMs) continue to hold a substantial share of the residential loan market. This is true even though FRMs usually carry an interest rate at least 1 to 2 percentage points higher than an adjustable mortgage and often carry higher origination fees and prepayment penalties. One reason appears to be public mistrust of many of the new instruments, coupled with fears of renewed inflation which would push up the interest rate on a variable-rate loan. Another factor is competition. Where FRMs and VRMs are offered in the same market, the fixed-rate loans threaten to drive out the variable loans. It is likely, therefore, that both FRMs and VRMs will continue to exist side by side in the home mortgage market, each serving the special needs of individual mortgage lenders and new homeowners.

CREATIVE FINANCING TECHNIQUES

Soaring prices of new homes and high mortgage interest rates have frequently put a damper on the demand for single-family homes in recent years. Homeowners and real estate agents have sought innovative financing techniques—creative financing —to make single-family homes more affordable for the average home buyer.

Second Mortgages

One of the most popular creative financing techniques is the second, or junior, mortgage. A second mortgage is a claim against real property which is subordinated to a first mortgage claim and usually payable in monthly installments. Its maturity typically is much shorter than that of a first mortgage loan—5- to 10-year terms are common. Because the second mortgage holder has a subordinated claim, the interest rate is often significantly higher than on a first mortgage loan.

The shorter maturities and higher interest rates attached to second mortgages have made them attractive to many lenders, particularly savings and loan associations, commercial banks, and finance companies. Historically, second mortgages have been used by homeowners to draw upon the growing equity investment in their home in order to pay for improvements (such as adding an extra bedroom) or to raise cash to make other purchases or investments. More recently, second mortgages have been used as a form of seller financing to speed up home sales.

For example, a homeowner who has placed his or her house on the market with an $80,000 price tag may find few buyers due to high interest rates and many young families lacking the funds for a down payment. A financial institution or the homeowner may be willing to take a second deed of trust in lieu of a portion of the required down payment. The home buyer benefits, even though the interest rate is usually higher on this second mortgage, by being able to more completely leverage the home purchase and gain a bigger tax deduction in the form of interest payments.

Home-Leasing Plans

In addition to second mortgages, *lease-purchase agreements* are used in certain markets. Under this arrangement, the buyer leases a home while retaining the option to buy for a period of at least one year. The seller receives monthly lease payments plus option money, which the buyer may later apply toward a down payment on the home. The advantage of this financing technique is that it permits the buyer to move in right away and still have time to accumulate enough savings to make the required down payment. Meantime, the seller is receiving cash payments while still enjoying the tax advantages of owning and renting a home.

Land-Leasing Plans and Property Exchanges

A related lease-financing option is the *land lease*. In this case the buyer acquires title only to the house and any improvements on the land, and the seller retains title to the land on which the house stands. In return for monthly lease payments, the buyer will receive a long-term lease (sometimes 100 years) on the land, frequently with an option to buy. This creative financing technique reduces monthly payments and results in a lower initial down payment

A simpler but equally effective aproach is a *property exchange* of homes between two parties. Any difference in value between the two houses exchanged can be handled by a promissory note issued by the owner of the cheaper property. Sometimes the difference in value will be made up by swapping personal property, such as savings deposits, stocks, bonds, jewelry, or automobiles.

The Message of Creative Financing Techniques

These and other creative financing techniques illustrate one favorable aspect of periods when interest rates are high and credit is tight: such conditions frequently stimulate the invention of new financial instruments to better serve the public's needs and to more efficiently utilize scarce capital. Creative financing techniques also serve as a reminder to government agencies responsible for regulating the financial system: *Rules and regulations that ignore or try to suppress the basic forces of supply and demand in the financial marketplace soon will be outmoded by the ever-changing technology of finance.*

SUMMARY

This chapter focused on one of the most important and also one of the most troubled markets in the American financial system—the residential mortgage market. Huge by almost any standard, the total volume of mortgage debt outstanding in the United States is approaching $3 trillion, or more than half the size of the United States GNP and far larger than any other financial instrument. The health and vitality of this market has a powerful impact on the nation's standard of living, social welfare, and public attitudes. It is inextricably intertwined with the political sphere and has been the object of government intervention, supervision, and regulation for decades.

Three major problems have affected the performance of the mortgage market in recent years. One concerns the relatively weak resale market for existing mortgages. When lenders have difficulty selling their old mortgages in order to make new loans, the availability of financial capital for the construction of new homes, apartments, shopping centers, office buildings, and other structures is curtailed. However, federal government efforts to deal with this problem through the creation of special agencies actively buying and selling mortgages in the open market have begun to bear fruit.

An active and increasingly broad secondary market for both government-guaranteed and conventional mortgages has developed, with many new buyers of old mortgages, including pension funds, banks, mutual funds, insurance companies, individuals, and foreign investors, entering the market.

Government and private efforts to deal with a second major problem—the redesigning of the basic mortgage instrument itself—also appear to be making progress. Years of inflation and high interest rates have rendered the conventional fixed-rate mortgage inappropriate in today's financial environment. As a result, lenders have turned to new forms of mortgage credit whose cash flows vary with interest rates and general market conditions. Included in this list are graduated-payment mortgages, variable-rate mortgages, Canadian rollover mortgages, renegotiated-rate mortgages, deferred-interest mortgages, and reverse-annuity mortgages.

The third major problem that marks mortgage trading activity is the extreme volatility and sensitivity of this market. It tends to be a counter-cyclical market, expanding rapidly in periods when the economy is in a recession or experiencing a slow recovery and declining in expansion periods when the rest of the economy is buoyant. When the mortgage market is depressed, the building of new homes and other structures virtually grinds to a halt, and unemployment in the construction industry soars.

The federal government's response to these problems has been to create federal agencies with the power to borrow money and buy mortgages in the open market or to guarantee them against default. The buying and selling of mortgages has been carried out by such government agencies as the Federal National Mortgage Association (FNMA), the Government National Mortgage Association (GNMA), and the Federal Home Loan Mortgage Corporation (FHLMC). Government guarantees for residential mortgages are issued by the Federal Housing Administration (FHA) and the Veterans Administration (VA). Most recently, federal and state interest rate ceilings which restrict both loan and deposit growth have been attacked and eliminated in many cases.

These serious problems in the mortgage market will not be solved overnight, as the record of the past several decades suggests. The best that can be said to date is that progress *is* being made. The residential mortgage market is slowly being released from the many artificial constraints which have limited the free interplay of demand and supply forces and prevented an optimal allocation of scarce resources. And none too soon, for the thousands of new families formed in the United States each year are placing unprecedented pressures on this huge and volatile market. Indeed, for many families seeking new homes, the changes may be coming too late. Inflation, heavy tax burdens, and relatively high interest rates have all but destroyed the dream of home ownership for many families and individuals of modest means.

STUDY QUESTIONS

1. What has happened in recent years to the prices of new homes? To interest rates and other terms on conventional home mortgage loans? What are the causes of these trends?

2. Mortgages may be classified in several different ways. Describe the structure of the mortgage market as it relates to:
   a. Type of mortgage contract—conventional versus government guaranteed.
   b. Residential versus nonresidential mortgages.
   c. Type of mortgage borrower.

3. List the principal mortgage lending institutions in the United States. Which is most important? In what areas?

4. Compare and contrast the mortgage lending activities of savings and loan associations, savings banks, insurance companies, commercial banks, and mortgage banking houses. How are these institutions alike, and how do they differ in their mortgage lending activities?

5. Why is it important to have a viable and active secondary market for mortgages? Discuss the efforts of the federal government to develop a secondary mortgage market.

6. Identify the following federal agencies and describe their function:
   a. FHA.   d. FNMA.
   b. VA.   e. GNMA.
   c. FHLB.   f. FHLMC.

7. Why is the mortgage market particularly sensitive to monetary policy and changing credit conditions?

8. A number of new mortgage instruments have been developed in recent years to replace the conventional fixed-rate mortgage (FRM). These new financial instruments include:
   a. Graduated-payment mortgages (GPM).
   b. Variable-rate mortgages (VRM).
   c. Adjustable mortgage instruments (AMI).
   d. Canadian rollover mortgages (CRM).
   e. Renegotiated-rate mortgages (RRM).
   f. Flexible-payment mortgages (FPM).
   g. Shared-appreciation mortgages (SAM).
   h. Deferred-interest mortgages (DIM).
   i. Reverse-annuity mortgages (RAM).
   Describe how each of these instruments work. Why have these alternatives to the fixed-rate mortgage been developed?

9. What is creative financing? What factors have given rise to its growth and development?

10. Explain what the following terms mean:
    a. Second mortgage.
    b. Lease-purchase agreement.
    c. Land lease.
    d. Property exchange.

SELECTED REFERENCES

Berkman, Neil G. "Mortgage Finance and the Housing Cycle." *New England Economic Review,* Federal Reserve Bank of Boston, September–October 1979, pp. 54–76.

Buynak, Thomas M. "Will Adjustable Rate Mortgages Survive?" *Economic Commentary,* Federal Reserve Bank of Cleveland, January 15, 1985.

Crone, Theodore. "Housing Costs After Tax Reform." *Business Review,* Federal Reserve Bank of Philadelphia, March–April 1987, pp. 3–12.

Davidson, Philip H. "Structure of the Residential Mortgage Market." *Monthly Review,* Federal Reserve Bank of Richmond, September 1972, pp. 2–6.

Esaki, Howard. "Economic Effects of Enforcing Due-on-Sale Clauses." *Quarterly Review,* Federal Reserve Bank of New York, Winter 1982–83, pp. 33–36.

Estrella, Arturo, and Andrew Silver. "Collateralized Mortgage Obligations: Do They Reduce Uncertainty?" *Quarterly Review,* Federal Reserve Bank of New York, Summer 1984, pp. 58–60.

Freund, James L. "The Housing Market: Recent Developments and Underlying Trends." *Federal Reserve Bulletin,* February 1983, pp. 61–69.

Gabriel, Stuart A. "Housing and Mortgage Markets: The Post 1982 Expansion." *Federal Reserve Bulletin,* December 1987, pp. 893–903.

Sivesind, Charles M. "Mortgage-Backed Securities: The Revolution in Real Estate Finance." *Quarterly Review,* Federal Reserve Bank of New York, Autumn 1979, pp. 1–10.

United States League of Savings Associations. *Savings and Loan Fact Book '86.* Chicago, 1986.

Part Six

Businesses in the Financial Markets

Chapter 20

Business Borrowing in the Money and Capital Markets

Learning Objectives in This Chapter

- To examine the different ways business firms issue securities and negotiate loans in order to borrow loanable funds in the money and capital markets.
- To explore the factors that cause business firms to increase or decrease the amount of funds they seek to borrow or raise in the money and capital markets.
- To see the powerful impact business borrowing has upon interest rates and credit conditions in the economy.

Key Terms and Concepts in This Chapter

Corporate bonds	Mortgage bonds	Private or direct
Corporate notes	Industrial development	placement
Indenture	bond (IDB)	Leveraged buyouts
Debenture	Zero-coupon bonds	Base rate
	Public sale	Commercial mortgages

BUSINESS firms draw upon a wide variety of sources of funds in order to finance their daily operations and to carry out long-term investment. In 1987, for example, nonfinancial business firms in the United States raised more than $700 billion in funds to carry out long-term investment, purchase inventories of goods and raw material, and acquire financial assets. Of this total, about $240 billion (about 30 percent) was supplied from the financial markets through issues of bonds, stocks, notes, and other financial instruments. In this chapter we look at sources of borrowed (debt) funds used by businesses today. In the next chapter we consider the advantages and disadvantages of stock (equity) as a source of business funds.

FACTORS AFFECTING BUSINESS ACTIVITY IN THE MONEY AND CAPITAL MARKETS

Many factors affect the extent to which business firms draw upon the money and capital markets for funds. One prominent factor is *the condition of the economy and the demand for goods and services*. A booming economy will generate rapidly growing sales, encouraging business people to borrow to expand inventories and to issue stocks and bonds in order to purchase new plant and equipment. In contrast, a sagging economy normally will be accompanied by declining sales and a reduction in both inventory purchases and long-term investment. Other factors held equal, the need for external fundraising declines when the economy grows more slowly or heads down into a recession. In contrast, rising demand for business goods and services is usually translated into rising demand for short- and long-term capital supplied from the financial markets.

Credit availability and interest rates also have powerful effects on the level of business activity in the financial markets. Rising interest rates that typically accompany a period of economic prosperity or rapid inflation eventually choke off business borrowing and spending plans because of the increasing cost of carrying inventories, floating new securities, and renewing existing credit lines. Falling interest rates, on the other hand, can stimulate business borrowing and spending, leading to a restocking of inventories and to an expansion of long-term business investment financed by bonds, stocks, and direct loans.

Because the financial markets are largely a *supplemental* funds source for business firms, drawn upon to backstop internal cash flows when credit availability, interest rates, and economic conditions are favorable, it should not surprise us to learn that business fundraising activity in the financial system is highly volatile. Heavy business borrowings and new stock issues in one year often are followed by a dearth of new offerings and even significant paydowns of outstanding loans and securities in succeeding years.

These marked fluctuations in business fundraising in the financial markets result in wide swings in interest rates and security prices. Much of the volatility in stock and bond prices reported in the daily financial press may be attributed to the on-again–off-again character of financial market activity by the business sector. The key actors in this rapidly changing drama are, of course, the largest industrial and manufacturing corporations who have the reputation and financial stature to tap both the open market and negotiated loan markets for debt and equity funds. Skillful security analysts often can read which way the wind is blowing as far as interest rates and security prices are concerned by watching what is happening to the current earnings and investment plans of major corporations.

CHARACTERISTICS OF CORPORATE NOTES AND BONDS

If a corporation decides to use long-term funds to finance its growth, the most popular form of long-term financing is the corporate bond or corporate note. This is especially true for the largest corporations whose credit standing and reputation is so strong they can avoid dealing directly with an institutional lender such as a bank, finance company, or insurance company and sell their long-term IOUs in the open market. Smaller companies without the necessary standing in the eyes of security investors usually must confine their long-term financing operations to negotiated loans with an institutional lender, an occasional stock issue, and heavy use of internally generated cash.

Principal Features of Corporate Notes and Bonds

A distinction needs to be drawn here between notes and bonds. By convention, a *note* is a corporate debt contract whose original maturity is five years or less; a *bond* carries an original maturity of more than five years. Both securities promise the investor an amount equal to the security's par value at maturity plus interest payments at specified intervals until maturity is reached. Because both securities have similar characteristics other than maturity, we will use the term *bond* to refer to both notes and bonds in the discussion that follows.

Corporate bonds are generally issued in units of $1,000 and earn income that, in most cases, is fully taxable to the investor. Each bond is accompanied by an indenture, which is a contract listing the rights, privileges, and obligations of the borrower and the investor. Indentures usually contain at least some *restrictive covenants* designed to protect bondholders against actions by a borrowing firm or its shareholders that might tend to weaken the value of the bonds. For example, typical restrictive covenants in an indenture may prohibit increases in a borrowing corporation's dividend rate (which would reduce the growth of its net worth), limit additional borrowing, restrict merger agreements, or limit the sale of the borrower's assets. These and other terms in a bond indenture are enforced by a third party—the trustee (often a bank trust department)—who represents the entire group of investors holding the bonds.

Term Bonds versus Serial Bonds

The majority of corporate bonds issued today are *term bonds,* which means that all the bonds in a particular issue mature on a single date. In contrast, most bonds issued by state and local governments (municipals) and a few corporate bonds are *serial bonds*, carrying a range of maturity dates.[1]

Recent Trends in Original Maturities of Bonds

There is a trend today toward shorter and shorter original maturities for corporate bonds due to inflation, rapid changes in technology, and uncertainty about future nominal interest rates. During the 1950s and 1960s corporations usually found a ready market for 20- to 30-year bonds. Such long-term debt contracts were extremely desirable from the borrowing company's standpoint because they locked in relatively low interest costs for many years and made financial planning much simpler. Today, with inflation and a volatile economy frequently sending market interest rates to record or near-record levels, bonds and notes with 1- to 15-year maturities have become more common as corporate managers shy away from the future uncertainties associated with long-term debt.

One positive factor that has encouraged greater use of short-term debt by borrowing corporations is the development of new interest rate hedging tools. These new hedging instruments permit companies to use short-term borrowings with reduced exposure to loss from sudden increases in market interest rates. Among the most widely used hedging devices are interest rate swaps, futures, and option contracts (discussed in Chapters 11 and 12 of this book).

Call Privileges

Nearly all corporate bonds issued today carry *call privileges* allowing early redemption (retirement) of the bonds if market conditions prove favorable. The call privilege represents a way to shorten the average maturity of corporate bonds in an era of rapid inflation and high borrowing costs. As we saw in Chapter 10, the redemption (or call) price decreases as a callable bond approaches maturity. Depending on the call premium and market conditions, investors generally prefer that the redemption of a bond be de-

---

[1] See Chapter 26 for a discussion of the serial feature of municipal bonds.

ferred as long as possible to protect them against loss of income due to lower interest rates. And most corporate bonds issued today defer the call privilege for 5 to 10 years, with utility company bonds usually callable after 5 years and industrial bonds after 10 years. The call feature gives the firm greater flexibility in financing its operations, but can be expensive to a company when interest rates are high and expected to fall. Investors realize that the bond is likely to be called if interest rates fall far enough and therefore demand a higher yield as compensation for the risk that the bond will be called in and retired.

Sinking Fund Provisions

Most corporate bonds issued in the United States are backed by *sinking funds* designed to ensure that the issuing company will be able to pay off the bonds when they come due. Periodic payments are made into the sinking fund on a schedule which usually is related to the depreciation of the assets supported by the bonds. The trustee is charged with the responsibility of making sure the user actually places the right amount of money in the sinking fund each time a payment is due. Periodically, a portion of the bonds outstanding may be retired from monies accumulated in the fund. The trustee will call in selected bonds at their par value, even though the market prices of those bonds may have risen well above par due to falling interest rates.

Yields and Costs of Corporate Bonds

Yields on corporate bonds tend to move in line with general business conditions and respond to swings in the credit market between tight and easy money. Yields on the highest-grade corporate issues tend to move closely with yields on government bonds. In contrast, yields carried by lower-grade corporate bonds are more closely tied to conditions in the economy and to factors specifically affecting the risk position of each borrowing firm. Bonds issued by the largest U.S. industrial, manufacturing, and utility companies are, with few exceptions, listed and traded on the New York or American Stock exchanges, though the largest volume of bond trading passes through dealers operating off exchanges.[2]

As noted in Chapter 8, there are several different ways to measure the rate of return to the investor or the cost to the firm of issuing a bond, note, or other debt security. From the point of view of the issuing company, one widely quoted measure of the cost of a bond is its *coupon rate*—that is, the rate of interest the company promises to pay as printed on the face of the bond. However, the coupon rate may understate or overstate the true cost

---

[2] See Chapter 21 for a description of the workings of these major securities exchanges.

of a bond to the issuing company, depending on whether the bond was issued at a discount or at a premium from its par value. A better measure of the cost of issuing a bond is to compare the *net proceeds* available for the borrowing company's use from a bond sale to the present value of the stream of cash payments the firm must eventually make to the bondholders.

For example, suppose a corporation issues $1,000 par bonds, but flotation costs reduce the net proceeds to the company from each bond to $950.[3] If the bonds mature in 10 years and carry a 10 percent coupon rate, then the before-tax cost, k, to the issuing company is:

$$\text{Net proceeds per bond} = \frac{\text{Interest cost in year 1}}{(1+k)} + \frac{\text{Interest cost in year 2}}{(1+k)^2}$$
$$+ \cdots + \frac{\text{Interest cost in year 10}}{(1+k)^{10}}$$
$$+ \frac{\text{Principal payments in year 10}}{(1+k)^{10}}$$

In this example:

$$\$950 = \frac{\$100}{(1+k)^1} + \frac{\$100}{(1+k)^2} + \cdots + \frac{\$100}{(1+k)^{10}} + \frac{\$1,000}{(1+k)^{10}}$$

A check of the present value tables in Appendix B indicates that k is 10.85 percent.

However, interest charges on debt are *tax deductible,* making the after-tax cost considerably less than the before-tax cost, especially for the largest and most profitable firms. For the largest corporations with annual earnings in the top tax bracket, the marginal federal income tax rate is 34 percent. Thus, a large company issuing the bond described above would incur an after-tax cost (k') of

$$k' = k(1 - t)$$

where k is the before-tax cost and t is the firm's marginal tax rate. In this example:

$$k' = 10.85\%(1 - 0.34) = 7.16\%$$

Of course, if the firm were in a lower tax bracket, the after-tax cost of its debt would be higher; and in the case of an unprofitable company (whose effective tax rate is zero), the after-tax cost of debt would equal its before-tax cost.

The before- and after-tax costs of debt vary not only with each firm's tax rate, but also with conditions in the financial markets. During periods

---

[3]The major elements of flotation cost for a new bond issue are the underwriting spread of the securities dealer who agrees to sell the issue, registration fees, paper and printing charges, and legal fees.

of rapid economic expansion when the supply of credit is scarce relative to the demand for credit, the cost of borrowing debt capital will rise. Bonds and notes must be marketed at lower prices and higher yields. Conversely, in periods when the economy contracts and easier credit conditions prevail, the cost of borrowing debt capital tends to decline. The prices of bonds and notes will rise and their yields will fall. It should not surprise us to learn that the volume of long-term corporate borrowings tends to increase markedly during business recessions as companies attempt to lock in the relatively low interest rates available at that time.

The Most Common Types of Corporate Bonds

Debentures. There are many different types of corporate bonds issued every day in the financial markets (see Exhibit 20–1). Among the most common is the debenture, which is not secured by any specific asset or assets owned by the issuing corporation. Instead, the holder of a debenture is a general creditor of the company and looks to the earning power and reputation of the borrower as the main source of the bond's value.

Subordinated Debentures. A related form of bond is the subordinated debenture, frequently called a *junior security*. If a company goes out of business and its assets are liquidated, the holders of subordinated debentures will be paid only after all secured and unsecured senior creditors receive the monies to which they are entitled.

Mortgage Bonds. Debt securities representing a claim against specific assets (normally plant and equipment) owned by a corporation are known as mortgage bonds. These bonds may be either *closed end* or *open end*. Closed-end mortgage bonds do not permit the issuance of any additional debt against the assets already pledged under the mortgage. Open-end bonds, on the other hand, do allow additional debt to be issued against pledged assets, and this may dilute the position of the current bondholders. For this reason, open-end mortgage bonds typically carry higher yields than closed-end bonds. Sometimes several different mortgage bonds with varying priorities of claim will be issued against the same assets. For example, the initial issue of bonds against a corporation's fixed assets may be designated first mortgage bonds, and later second mortgage bonds may be issued against those same assets. If the company were liquidated and the pledged assets sold, holders of second mortgage bonds would receive only funds left over after holders of the first mortgage bonds were paid off.

Collateral Trust Bonds. A debt instrument secured by stocks, bonds, and notes issued by units of government or by other corporations is called a collateral trust bond. Such a bond is really an interest in a pool of securities

Exhibit 20–1   **The Most Common Types of Corporate Notes and Bonds**

Debentures. Long-term debt instruments secured only by the earning power of the issuing corporation and not by any specific property owned.

Subordinated Debentures. Unsecured bonds whose holders receive a claim on the issuing company's assets that ranks behind holders of senior debt securities but ahead of common and preferred stockholders.

Mortgage Bonds. Long-term debt secured by a lien on specific assets (normally plant and equipment) held by the issuing corporation.

Equipment Trust Certificates. A type of lease financing in which the title to certain assets (normally equipment or rolling stock) is held by a trustee and the company issuing the certificates makes lease payments to certificate holders through the trustee.

Collateral Trust Bonds. Long-term debt representing an interest in a pool of securities held by the issuing corporation.

Industrial Development Bonds. Debt securities issued by a local government agency to aid a private company in the construction of a plant and/or the purchase of equipment or land.

Convertible Bonds. Long-term debt securities that can be exchanged for a specific number of shares of common stock at the option of the bondholder.

Income Bonds. Debt instruments used mainly in corporate reorganizations that earn interest for the holder only when the issuing company has sufficient earnings.

Pollution Control Bonds. Long-term debt securities issued by a local government agency (often on a tax-exempt basis) to assist a private company in purchasing pollution-control equipment or facilities.

---

held by the bond issuer. The pledged securities are held in trust for the benefit of the bondholders, though the borrowing company usually receives any interest and dividend payments generated by the pledged securities and retains voting rights on any stock that is pledged.

Income bonds. Bonds often used in corporate reorganizations and in other situations when a company is in financial distress are known as income bonds. Interest on these bonds is paid only when enough income is actually earned, making an income bond similar to common stock. However, holders of income bonds do have a prior claim on earnings over both stockholders and holders of subordinated debentures. Moreover, some income bonds carry a cumulative feature under which unpaid interest accumulates and must be fully paid before the stockholders receive any dividends.

Equipment Trust Certificates. Resembling a lease in form, equipment trust certificates are used most frequently to acquire industrial equipment or rolling stock (such as trucks, railroad cars, or airplanes). Title to the assets acquired is vested in a trustee (often a bank trust department) who leases these assets to the company issuing the certificates. Periodic lease payments are made to the trustee who passes them along to certificate holders. Title to the assets passes to the borrowing company only after all lease payments are made.

Industrial Development Bonds. In recent years state and local governments have become much more active in aiding private corporations to meet their financial needs. One of the most controversial forms of government-aided, long-term business borrowing is the industrial development bond (IDB), developed originally in the southern states during the Great Depression of the 1930s and used today by local governments throughout the United States. These bonds are issued by a local government borrowing authority in order to provide buildings, land, and/or equipment to a business firm. Because governmental units can borrow more cheaply than most private corporations, the lower debt costs may be passed along to the firm as an added inducement to move to a new location, bringing new jobs to the local economy. The business firm normally guarantees both interest and principal payments on the IDBs by renting the buildings, land, and/or equipment at a rental fee high enough to cover debt service costs.

Pollution Control Bonds. Related to industrial development bonds, pollution control bonds are used to aid private companies in financing the purchase of pollution control equipment. In this case, local governments frequently will purchase pollution control equipment with the proceeds of a bond issue and lease that equipment to business firms in the area.[4]

New Types of Corporate Notes and Bonds

Corporate bonds are traditionally called *fixed-income* securities because most bonds pay a fixed amount of interest each year, as determined by their coupon rate and par value. This creates a problem for bondholders when interest rates rise, inflation increases, or both, because then the real market value of fixed-income securities falls. In recent years, repeated bouts with

---

[4]Another important type of corporate bond (discussed previously in Chapter 10) is the *convertible bond*. Convertibles may be exchanged for a specific number of shares of common stock at the option of the bondholder. These securities lie midway between stock and corporate debt in their financial characteristics. The value of convertibles to the investor stems as much from the value of the issuing company's stock as it does from the value of the bonds themselves.

inflation and high interest rates and reduced quality ratings on corporate bonds have spurred borrowers and investment bankers to develop new types of corporate bonds whose return to the investor is sensitive to changing inflation and changing bond values and interest rates. Among the most popular of these innovative securities are discount bonds, stock-indexed bonds, floating-rate bonds, commodity-backed bonds, and warrant bonds.

Discount bonds, first used extensively in 1981, are sold at a price well below par and appreciate toward par as maturity approaches. Thus, the investor earns capital gains as well as interest, while the issuing corporation usually can issue discount bonds at a lower after-tax cost than on conventional bonds. Some discount bonds, known as zero coupon bonds, pay no interest at all. First used by J.C. Penney in 1981, "zeros" pay a return based solely on their appreciation in market price as they approach maturity. However, the annual price increase in zeros is taxable as ordinary income, not as capital gains, under current IRS regulations.

Stock-indexed bonds have an interest rate tied to stock market trends. For example, one $25 million issue sold in 1981 had its annual interest rate tied to the annual trading volume on the New York Stock Exchange. A rise in stock trading volume (on the theory that stocks are more eagerly sought by investors as a hedge when inflation increases) raises the bond's promised rate of return to the holder.

Floating-rate bonds have their annual promised rate tied to changes in long-term or short-term interest rates or both. Many investors regard floaters as realistic alternatives to buying money market securities. *Commodity-backed bonds* carry a face value tied to the market price of an internationally traded commodity, such as gold, silver, or oil, which presumably is sensitive to inflation.

Finally, *warrant bonds* permit an investor to purchase additional bonds at the same yield as the original bonds or sell the detachable warrants to another investor. A related bond, called a *usable bond,* has warrants to purchase at par the issuing company's stock, and those warrants can be traded separately from the bonds themselves. Warrant and usable bonds are obviously most valuable when interest rates are expected to decline. While many of these new types of bonds do reasonably well in inflationary periods, they often prove difficult to sell when inflation decreases or when investors become very risk conscious.

The development of new financial instruments inside the United States has been paralleled by the growth of new corporate borrowing instruments abroad. One successful innovation is the *Euronote*—a short-term unsecured corporate IOU underwritten by a bank or group of banks. If the company cannot sell all of its notes to investors, the bank or banks will buy them or provide credit at a stipulated yield spread over current market interest rates. *Eurobonds* have also expanded rapidly, with many firms now choosing to

Exhibit 20–2   **Principal Investors in Corporate and Foreign Bonds, 1986**
($ Billions Outstanding at Year-End)

	1986	
Investor Group	Amount	Percent of Total
Households	$ 95.3	9.4%
Rest of the world	137.0	13.6
Commercial banks	47.3	4.7
Savings and loan associations	20.3	2.0
Mutual savings banks	16.1	1.6
Life insurance companies	321.4	31.9
Property–casualty insurance companies	44.3	4.4
Private pension funds	128.3	12.7
Government pension funds	140.6	13.9
Mutual funds	46.9	4.7
Security brokers and dealers	10.8	1.1
Totals	$1,008.6	100.0%

Note: Columns may not add to totals due to rounding.

Source: Board of Governors of the Federal Reserve System, *Flow of Funds Accounts: Assets and Liabilities Outstanding, 1963–86.*

issue long-term bearer bonds directly to foreign investors in overseas markets at lower cost.

INVESTORS IN CORPORATE NOTES AND BONDS

Today, the investor market for corporate notes and bonds is dominated by insurance companies and pension funds (see Exhibit 20–2). The latter prefer buying corporate bonds in the open market, while insurance companies frequently purchase their corporate securities directly from the issuing company in an off-the-market transaction. The stability of cash flows experienced by pension funds and insurance companies permits them to pursue corporate debt obligations with long maturities and lock in their high market yields.

Commercial banks are *not* heavy investors in corporate bonds. Generally, a banker would prefer to deal personally with a business customer and grant a loan specifically tailored to the borrower's needs, rather than enter the highly impersonal bond market. Increasingly in recent years commercial banks have become direct competitors with the corporate note and bond markets through the granting of *term loans*. A term loan is any loan granted by a commercial bank for business purposes which has a maturity of more than one year. Responding to inflation and the soaring cost of business equipment and facilities, bankers have gradually extended the maturity of term loans, with many now falling in the 5- to 10-year maturity range. Rates on such loans generally exceed the interest cost on corporate debt sold in the open market, however, especially when banks also insist that the borrowing firm keep funds on deposit equal to a specified percentage of the loan.

THE SECONDARY MARKET FOR CORPORATE BONDS

The resale (secondary) market for corporate notes and bonds is relatively limited compared to the resale markets for common stock, municipal bonds, and other long-term securities. Trading volume is thin, even for some bonds issued by the largest and best-known companies. Part of the reason is the small number of individuals active as investors in this market. Individuals generally have limited investment time horizons (holding periods) and tend to turn over their portfolios rapidly when attractive alternative investments appear. In the past secondary market trading in corporate bonds was also held back by the "buy and hold" strategy of major institutional investors, especially insurance companies and pension funds. Many of these firms purchased corporate bonds exclusively for interest income and were content to purchase the longest-term issues and simply hold them to maturity. Today, however, under the pressure of volatile interest rates and inflation, many institutions buying corporate bonds have shifted into a new and aggressive strategy often labeled *total performance*. Institutional portfolio managers are more sensitive today to changes in bond prices and look for near-term opportunities to trade bonds and make capital gains. In fact, a number of insurance companies, pension funds, and mutual bond funds operate their own trading departments and keep constant tab on developments in the corporate bond market.

Unlike the stock market, no one central exchange for bond trading dominates the market. While corporate bonds are traded on all major exchanges, including the New York (NYSE) and American (AMEX) exchanges and at other exchanges around the world, most secondary market trading in bonds is conducted over the telephone through brokers and dealers. Bond brokers act as middlemen by arranging trades between dealers in return for a small commission. Dealers, on the other hand, commit themselves to take on large blocks of bonds either from other dealers or from pension funds, insurance companies, and other clients. Due to rapid and often unpredictable changes in interest rates, many dealers now try to close out positions taken in individual corporate bond issues in just a few days, frequently act only as middlemen in trades between major institutional investors without committing their own capital, and often hedge against the risk of large trading losses by using the financial futures market.

THE MARKETING OF CORPORATE NOTES AND BONDS

New corporate bonds may be offered publicly in the open market to all interested buyers or sold privately to a limited number of investors. The first route, known as public sale, accounts for the largest proportion of corporate bond sales each year. Among smaller companies and those firms with unique financing requirements, however, the second route, known as private (or direct) placement, has become popular.

The Public Sale of Bonds

The sale of new corporate bonds and notes in the open market is handled principally by investment bankers. The term *investment banker* is somewhat misleading, because these firms have little or nothing to do with banking as we know it. In fact, the Glass-Steagall Act of 1933 prohibits commercial banks from underwriting most corporate securities. This law was passed out of fear that commercial bank underwriting of corporate securities would lead to bank failures or to control of nonfinancial businesses by the banking community.

In contrast to commercial banks, which accept deposits from the public, investment bankers underwrite new issues of corporate stocks and bonds and give advice to corporations on their financing requirements. An investment banking firm may singly take on a new issue of corporate securities or band together with other underwriters to form a *syndicate*. Either way, the investment banker's game plan is to acquire new corporate securities at the lowest possible price and sell them to other investors as quickly as possible in order to turn a profit. An investment banker may purchase the securities from the issuing company directly or merely guarantee the issuer a specific price for his securities. With either approach, it is the investment banker who carries the risk of substantial gains or significant losses when the securities are marked for sale in the open market.

The largest issues of corporate bonds and notes sold in the open market are usually bid on by several syndicates (groups of underwriters). Competition among syndicates to win a large underwriting contract is usually intense. Investment bankers hope to acquire a new issue at the lowest possible bid price and place the securities with investors at a significantly higher retail price, maximizing the banker's *spread* or return on invested capital. Unfortunately, each new bond issue is always somewhat different from those that have traded before and may involve hundreds of millions of dollars. Moreover, a decision on what price to bid for new securities must be made *before* the bonds are released for public trading; in the interim, the prices of bonds may change drastically. If the underwriter bids too high a price for the new issue, the firm may not be able to resell the securities at a price high enough to recover the cost and secure an adequate spread. To cite an example, in October 1979 IBM Corporation offered $1 billion in notes and debentures through a collection of Wall Street underwriters. Unfortunately, just as the IBM issue was coming to market, bond prices tumbled (due, in part, to an announcement made by the Federal Reserve implying that credit conditions would be tightened to deal with inflation). The underwriters reportedly suffered a massive loss.

Competition in the bidding process tends to narrow the underwriter's spread between bid price and retail (asked) price. If several investment banking houses band together in a syndicate, a consensus bid price must be hammered out among the participants. Disagreements frequently arise within a syndicate due to different perceptions on the probable future direction of interest rates and market conditions. Because more than a hundred underwriters may be included in a single syndicate, the task of reaching a compromise and placing a unified bid for a new security issue may prove impossible. The old syndicate will break apart with those bidders still interested in the issue hurriedly piecing together a new syndicate and a new bid.

A number of factors are considered in pricing a new corporate bond issue. Certainly the rating assigned by Moody's or Standard & Poor's Corporation is a key item, because many investors rely on such agencies for assessing the degree of risk carried by a new security.[5] Another critical factor is the "forward calendar" of security offerings which lists new issues expected to come to market during the next few weeks. Obviously, if a heavy volume of new offerings is anticipated in the near-term, prices will decline unless additional demand appears. Changes in government monetary and fiscal policy also must be anticipated because both can have profound effects on security prices and interest rates. Other factors considered by investment bankers include the overall size of the issue, how aggressive other bidders are likely to be, and the strength of the "book," which consists of indications of advance investor interest in the particular security being offered.

Once the securities are received from the issuing company, the underwriting syndicate will advertise their availability at the price agreed upon by all members of the syndicate. Exhibit 20–3 illustrates an announcement of a public offering of corporate bonds. *Delay* in selling new securities is one of the investment banker's worst enemies because additional financing must be obtained to carry the portfolio of unsold securities. Also there is the added risk of price declines as time stretches out. To speed the process of selling newly acquired bonds, many investment banking firms today are affiliated with retail brokerage companies that maintain close working relationships with large bond buyers, such as insurance companies and pension funds.

What happens to the market prices of securities being sold by investment banking syndicates is, of course, the key determinant of the success or failure

---

[5] See Chapter 9 and Appendix A for a discussion of security ratings.

Exhibit 20–3   An Announcement of a Public Offering of Corporate Bonds

---

This announcement is neither an offer to sell nor a solicitation of an offer to buy these securities.
The offer is made only by the Prospectus.

$75,000,000

Leucadia National Corporation

14% Senior Subordinated Notes due May 15, 1993
(Interest payable May 15 and November 15)

Price 100%

----

*Copies of the Prospectus are obtainable in any State from the undersigned
and such other dealers as may lawfully offer these securities in such State.*

Drexel Burnham Lambert
INCORPORATED

May 23, 1985

Source: *The Wall Street Journal*, May 23, 1985, p. 38.

of the underwriting process. If the market price at which a new issue can be sold falls far enough, the syndicate will disband, and individual underwriters will scramble to sell their allotments of securities at whatever price the market dictates. The spread between the selling (retail) price of corporate bonds and the proceeds paid to the issuing company (the flotation cost of a new issue) is usually less than one point.[6] It obviously takes only a small decline in the retail price of a security before the underwriter's profit is eliminated. Moreover, unfavorable price movements can damage the reputation of the investment banker with both investors and the client companies that issue securities for public sale. Clearly, the investment banking business is risky, highly competitive, and subject to numerous uncertainties.

---

[6]See Chapter 8 for a discussion of *points* in the pricing of bonds.

Private Placements of Corporate Bonds

In recent years, private placements of bonds with one or a limited group of investors have declined relative to public sales, following a period of rapid growth during the 1970s. For example, in 1986, the latest year with complete data, private placements accounted for about one quarter of public market sales, compared to 40 to 50 percent in the late 1970s. However, the ratio of private to public sales is sensitive to the changing composition of borrowing companies and to economic conditions. Usually periods of rising interest rates and reduced credit availability bring more borrowing companies into the public market, while falling rate periods often bring a rise in private placements. For the largest corporations, public sales and private placements are *substitutes*. When interest rates are high or credit is tight in one of these markets, the largest borrowers shift freely and easily to the other market.

Who buys privately placed bonds? Life insurance companies and pension funds are the principal investors in this market. These institutions hope to secure higher yields and protection against call privileges on bonds by engaging in *direct negotiation* with borrowing corporations. The avoidance of call privileges on corporate securities is of special benefit to life insurance companies and pension funds because these institutions prefer the stable income which comes from purchasing long-term bonds and holding them to maturity. In fact, institutional investors active in the private placement market frequently impose extra fees in a sales contract containing an allowance for early retirement or refunding of a security by the issuing corporation. Investors other than life insurance companies and pension funds tend to be shut out of the private market due to their lack of financial expertise, small portfolio size, and the absence of a resale market for privately placed securities.[7]

Most private placements are concentrated in the hands of the largest life insurance companies. So dominant are life insurance companies in private placements that their financial condition at any particular point in time sets the tone of the whole private market. When these companies are highly liquid and the demand for funds from other sectors of the economy (especially the mortgage market) is weak, life insurers will bid aggressively for new privately placed bonds, and business borrowing costs will drop. During such periods, many borrowers will switch from public to private bond sales to take advantage of the ready availability of relatively cheap credit.

---

[7] Most security offerings in the private placement market are less than $20 million. In contrast, new issues sold in the open market typically range from $20 million on up. Experience has shown that $20 million is just about the minimum amount necessary to develop a good secondary market and give a new security adequate liquidity. At the other extreme, a security issue can be too large for public sale, with few investment bankers willing to accept the risks involved. For example, several utility bond and stock offerings have exceeded a billion dollars and many of these have been positioned through private sale to avoid market risks and large underwriting commissions.

There are several advantages to the borrower from a private placement. One is the lower cost of distribution because there are no legal registration fees or expenses associated with the issuance of a prospectus as there would be with a public sale. Generally, a more rapid placement of bonds takes place in the private market because only one or a few buyers are involved and the loan is confidential. Special concessions can often be secured through a private sale, such as a commitment for future borrowing. For example, a corporate borrower may negotiate a private sale of $15 million in bonds to an insurance company but also may be granted a line of credit in the amount of $2 million a year over the next five years. This kind of future commitment is simply not possible in the impersonal public market, where most bonds are highly standardized. Moreover, lenders in the private market try to tailor the terms of a loan to match the specific cash flow and maturity needs of borrowers. This may involve offering a conventional fixed-rate, single-sum credit contract at the prevailing interest rate, a floating-rate loan that can be retired early if cash flows permit, or even a participating loan in which the lender charges a lower interest rate in return for a share of net income from the project financed.

One obvious disadvantage is that interest costs are higher in private sales than in public sales for bonds of comparable quality and maturity. However, private sale bonds are less liquid and carry more risk. One indication of this is that privately placed debt issues tend to have more restrictive covenants written into their accompanying indentures in order to protect lenders. Still, the larger the size of a corporate issue, the smaller the cost differential between public and private placements.

THE VOLUME OF BORROWING IN THE CORPORATE BOND MARKET

The volume of borrowing through new issues of corporate notes and bonds has grown rapidly in recent years (see Exhibit 20–4). For example, annual offerings of new corporate debt securities nearly quadrupled between 1960 and 1970, nearly doubled between 1970 and 1980, and then more than quadrupled in the 1980s. Much of this growth in long-term corporate borrowing could be traced to inflation, which reduced the real cost of debt, to increased use of financial leverage to boost returns to corporate stockholders, and to the development of international capital markets where the largest firms could raise low-cost funds. Faced with record interest rates and two back-to-back recessions in 1980 and 1982, however, long-term corporate borrowing leveled out in the early 1980s before surging ahead again in the middle and late 1980s with a stronger economy and lower interest rates. This track record reveals quite clearly that the corporate debt market is very sensitive to economic conditions (particularly fluctuations in corporate earnings, sales, and prices) and to changes in the cost of long-term credit.

Another factor that has spurred the private bond market's growth in

Exhibit 20–4 **Growth of Corporate Notes and Bonds Sold in the United States ($ Millions)***

Year	New Issues of Corporate Bonds and Notes
1950	$ 4,920
1960	8,081
1970	30,321
1980	53,199
1983	68,370
1985	203,500
1987	233,578

*Figures are gross proceeds of issues maturing in more than one year, sold for cash in the United States. Excluded are issues of less than $100,000 and secondary offerings.

Source: U.S. Department of Commerce, *Business Statistics,* 1975 ed.; and Board of Governors of the Federal Reserve System, *Federal Reserve Bulletin,* selected issues.

the 1980s is a rash of corporate takeovers and merger proposals. Targets for these corporate raids have included such well-known companies as CBS, Hilton Hotels, Crown Zellerbach, Pennzoil, and Uniroyal, to name just a few. Many of these mergers have been motivated by deregulation of key industries in recent years, including the airlines, trucking, communications, the railroads, and commercial banking, and more liberal antitrust rules followed by the U.S. government. Frequently, these proposed mergers include plans to offer billions of dollars in so-called *junk bonds*—that is, high-yield, often unsecured debt obligations with low credit ratings.[8] With the expanded use of debt, resulting in much heavier use of financial leverage by corporations and a heavier drain on their earnings from borrowing costs, the credit ratings of scores of corporations have been reduced in recent years. At the same time, low-rated (speculative) corporate bond and note issues have mushroomed to become a growing share of the corporate debt-security market.

A substantial proportion of recent takeovers have been in the form of leveraged buyouts in which a single investor or small group of investors (frequently including senior management of the target company) propose to buy the publicly owned stock of a business firm by borrowing 80 to 90 percent or more of the purchase price from banks and the bond market. In this instance, the takeover group is counting on faster growth and improved profitability of the targeted company to pay off the huge volume of acquisition debt. Because such expectations are fraught with risk, leading financial analysts have expressed concern over many of the proposed mergers and buyouts, fearing they may undermine public confidence in the financial system and in financial institutions.

---

[8] See Chapter 10 for a discussion of the causes, effects, and characteristics of junk bond issues.

Exhibit 20–5   **Industry Source of Bonds and Notes Publicly Offered**
by U.S. Corporations in 1986 ($ Millions)

Issuers	Amount	Percent of Total
Totals	$355,293	100.0%
Industry group:		
Manufacturing	$ 91,548	25.8%
Commercial and miscellaneous	40,124	11.3
Transportation	9,971	2.8
Public Utilities	31,426	8.8
Communications	16,659	4.7
Real estate and financial	165,564	46.6

Notes: Figures are gross proceeds of issues maturing in more than one year. Offerings exclude secondary market sales, intracorporate transactions, open-end investment companies, and employee stock plans.

Source: Securities and Exchange Commission and Board of Governors of the Federal Reserve System.

These debt-funded mergers have generated much proposed federal and state legislation to prevent "corporate raiders" from taking over some companies. Some targeted firms have developed so-called shark repellents or poison pills, such as favorable deals for outside investors not affiliated with a corporate raider or revisions in corporate charters that make it more difficult for undesirable outsiders to take over the firm. Surprisingly, as noted by Ott and Santoni (1985), available research evidence tends to show that the stockholders of the companies targeted for acquisition tend to benefit from mergers and takeover activity, even when the planned takeover is unsuccessful. Investors in the securities markets apparently believe that, as a rule, such takeovers will improve the efficiency and profitability of the target companies beyond what their existing management has been able to do and, as a result, the stock of the target firm rises in value.

Substantial changes have occurred in recent years in the types of firms issuing bonds and notes (see Exhibit 20–5). The manufacturing and commercial sectors have generally declined in relative importance as bond issuers. Many of these firms have turned instead to commercial banks and the short-term commercial paper market to handle a growing portion of their credit needs. On the other hand, the rapid expansion of communications firms, commercial banks, finance companies, mortgage banking houses, securities dealers, and real estate development corporations has resulted in significantly larger bond issues from these sectors of the economy.

BANK LOANS TO BUSINESS

Commercial banks are direct competitors with the corporate note and bond markets in making both long- and short-term loans to business. By the fall

Exhibit 20-6   **Terms of Lending at U.S. Commercial Banks (Federal Reserve survey of loans made May 2–4, 1988)**

Types of Loans and Terms	Average for Loans of All Sizes
Short-term commercial and industrial loans:	
Average loan size ($000s)	$340
Weighted-average maturity in days	49 days
Weighted-average interest rates	8.49%
Percentage carrying floating rate	47.7%
Long-term commercial and industrial loans:	
Average loan size ($000s)	$227
Weighted-average maturity in months	49 months
Weighted-average interest rates	9.05%
Percentage carrying floating rate	70.3%

Source: Board of Governors of the Federal Reserve System.

of 1987, total commercial and industrial loans extended by commercial banks operating in the United States exceeded $560 billion, or about one third of all U.S. commercial bank loans. Banks grant their loans to a wide variety of firms covering all major sectors of the business community.

In recent years the Federal Reserve Board has carried out surveys of business lending practices by banks across the United States. A summary of the findings from a recent business loan survey is shown in Exhibit 20–6. The Federal Reserve survey indicates that bank loans to business firms tend to be short- or medium-term in maturity. For example, short-term commercial and industrial loans averaged only about one to two months to maturity, while long-term business loans averaged just about four years. Moreover, the short-term loans, which are used principally to purchase inventories, pay wages and salaries, and meet other current expenses, average considerably larger at most banks than long-term business loans, which are taken out mainly to purchase equipment and to expand physical facilities.

The Federal Reserve survey suggests that longer-term busines loans tend to carry *higher* average interest rates than short-term busines loans. This is due, in part, to the greater risk associated with long-term credit. Moreover, yield curves have usually sloped upward in recent years, calling for higher average rates on long-term loans.[9] Especially interesting is the high proportion of business loans today that carry *floating* rather than fixed interest rates. The larger and longer-term a business loan is, the more likely its rate will float with market conditions. For example, almost half of the short-term business loans included in the May 1988 Federal Reserve Survey

---

[9] See Chapter 9 for a discussion of recent patterns in yield curves and the factors which appear to cause them.

of U.S. banks carried floating interest rates, while roughly 70 percent of the long-term business loans had floating rates. Clearly, banks become more determined to protect themselves against unexpected inflation and other adverse developments through floating interest rates as the maturity and size of a business loan increase.

The Prime or Base Interest Rate

One of the best known and most widely followed interest rates in the financial system is the prime bank interest rate, sometimes called the base rate or reference rate.[10] The prime rate is the annual percentage interest rate that banks quote on loans made to their most creditworthy customers. Most prime loans are unsecured, but the borrower often is required to keep a deposit at the lending bank equal to a specified percentage of the loan. This so-called *compensating balance* normally is 15 to 20 percent of the amount loaned. Even for a prime borrower, therefore, the true cost of a bank loan is normally significantly higher than the prime rate itself. Most prime loans are short term—one year or less—taken out to finance purchases of inventory and meet other working capital needs or to support construction projects.

Each bank must set its own prime or base rate, following a vote by its board of directors. Beginning in the 1930s, however, a uniform nationwide prime rate began to appear, with differences in rates from bank to bank quickly eliminated by competition. Split primes do occur for brief periods, however, due to differences in the formulas used by individual banks to calculate their rates and differences in the availability of bank funds. Thus, a bank strapped for loanable funds may keep its prime temporarily above rates posted by other banks in order to ration the available supply of credit. Similarly, a bank with ample funds to lend may post a prime temporarily below market to encourage its best customers to borrow more frequently and in larger amounts.

Traditionally, the prime rate was set by one or more of the nation's leading banks and other banks followed the leader in setting their own prime rate. However, a major innovation in the market for prime rate loans occurred in October 1971 when First National City Bank of New York

---

[10]*Base rate* is a more general term than prime, referring to that loan interest rate used as the basis for determining the current rate charged a business borrower. Most business loan rates are scaled upward from the base rate. Many commercial loans today, especially those made to the largest corporations, are tied to base rates other than prime, however. This is frequently the case for large multinational companies that have ready access to the Eurodollar market and other credit markets abroad. For example, the London interbank offering rate (LIBOR) on short-term Eurodollar deposits is often used as a base rate for large corporate loans. In some cases the commercial paper rate, the federal funds rate, or the secondary market rate on bank CDs is also used as a loan base rate. The smaller numbers of borrowers today who remain tied to the prime rate are less mobile customers with fewer alternatives than many of the largest corporations, who not only maintain accounts with several different banks, but also have numererous alternative sources of funds and therefore can frequently demand credit at rates significantly less than prime. Such large loans are often made today at contract rates only fractions of a percentage point above a bank's actual cost of raising funds in the money market.

Exhibit 20–7　**The Prime Rate Charged by Banks on Short-Term Business Loans** (Percent per annum)

Effective Date	Announced Rate
1987:	
April 7	7.75%
May 1	8.00
May 15	8.25
September 4	8.75
October 7	9.25
October 22	9.00
November 5	8.75
1988:	
February 2	8.50

Source: Board of Governors of the Federal Reserve System, *Federal Reserve Bulletin,* June 1988.

(Citibank) announced that it would float its prime. Citibank's basic lending rate was pegged on a weekly basis at 1/2 percentage point above the yield on 90-day commercial paper. Other major banks soon followed, pegging their prime rates to prevailing yields on U.S. Treasury bills, negotiable CDs, and other money market instruments.

Linking the prime to such active money market rates as those attached to Treasury bills, negotiable CDs, and commercial paper resulted in a more flexible, rapidly changing base lending rate, illustrated by the frequent prime rate changes shown in Exhibit 20–7. The prime has come to reflect somewhat more accurately the forces of shifting credit demands, fluctuations in government policy, and inflation. A more flexible prime, while disconcerting to borrowers, has enabled banks to better protect their interest margins—the difference between the return on loans and the cost of bank funds—and to make credit more readily available to customers willing to pay the price.

Many business loans today, especially for smaller firms, are priced at *premiums* above the prime or other base rate because only the largest, most financially sound customers qualify for prime or even below-prime loans. Nevertheless, commercial loan rates typically are tied to the base rate— prime or other reference rate—through a carefully worked out formula. One popular approach, known as *prime-plus,* adds on a rate premium for default risk and often an additional premium for longer maturities (term risk). Thus, the banker may quote a commercial customer "prime plus 2" with a 1 percent premium above the base rate for default risk and another 1 percent premium for term risk. Other banks use the *times-prime* method, which multiplies the base rate by a risk factor. For example, the business customer may be quoted a loan at 1.5 times prime. If the current prime is 10 percent, this customer will pay 15 percent initially. If the loan carries a

Exhibit 20–8   **Recent Growth of Commercial Mortgage Loans**
(End-of-period figures)

Year	Volume of Commercial Mortgages Outstanding ($ billions)
1970	$ 82.3
1980	258.3
1982	301.4
1984	418.3
1986	556.5
1987	654.3

Source: Board of Governors of the Federal Reserve System, *Federal Reserve Bulletin,* selected issues.

floating rate, then the interest rate in future periods can always be calculated by multiplying the base rate by 1.5.

Which of these formulas the banker uses often depends on his or her forecast of interest rates. In a period of falling rates, interest charges on floating-rate loans figured on a times-prime basis decline faster than those based on prime-plus. When interest rates are on the rise, times-prime pricing results in more rapid increases in business loan rates. Therefore, times-prime financing is more sensitive to the changing cost of bank funds over the course of the business cycle.

COMMERCIAL MORTGAGES

The construction of office buildings, shopping centers, and other commercial structures is generally financed with an instrument known as the commercial mortgage. Short-term mortgage loans are used to finance the construction of commercial projects, while longer-term mortgages are employed to pay off short-term construction loans, purchase land, and cover property development costs. The majority of long-term commercial mortgage loans are made by life insurance companies, savings and loan associations, and pension funds, while commercial banks are the predominant short-term commercial mortgage lender. Banks support the construction of shopping centers, office buildings, and other commercial projects with loans secured by land and building materials. These short-term mortgage credits usually fall due when construction is completed with permanent mortgage financing of the project then passing to insurance companies, savings and loans, and other long-term lenders.

The growth of commercial mortgages has been rapid in recent years, as reflected in Exhibit 20–8. The dollar volume of such loans more than tripled during the 1970s. However, the market was buffeted by severe problems as the decade of the 1980s began and the growth of commercial mortgages slowed until the mid-1980s, when lower interest rates stimulated a higher volume of commercial mortgage financing. Up to that point, most commercial real estate financing was provided through fixed-rate mortgages. Faced with inflation and a more volatile economy, however, commercial mortgage lenders began searching for new financial instruments to protect their rates of return.

Many mortgage lenders today combine both debt and equity financing in the same credit package. The best-known example is the *equity kicker*, where the lending institution grants a fixed-rate mortgage but also receives a share of any net earnings from the project. For example, a life insurance company may agree to provide $10 million to finance the construction of an office building. It agrees to accept a 15-year mortgage loan bearing a 12 percent annual interest rate against the property. However, as a hedge against inflation and higher interest rates, the insurance company may also insist on receiving 10 percent of any net earnings generated from office rentals over the 15-year period.

Another device used recently in commercial mortgage financing is *indexing*. In this case, the annual interest rate on a loan may be tied to the prevailing yields on high-quality government or public utility bonds of comparable maturity. Lender and borrower may agree to renegotiate the interest rate at certain intervals—every three to five years is common. There is also a trend toward shorter maturity commercial mortgage loans—many as short as five years—with the borrower paying off the debt or refinancing the unpaid principal with the same or another lending institution.

SUMMARY

The majority of funds drawn upon by business firms to meet their working capital and long-term investment needs come not from the financial markets, but from inside the individual firm. In most years well over half of business capital requirements are supplied by net earnings and noncash depreciation expenses—internal cash flow. However, a quarter to half of business investment needs in recent years have been met by selling debt and equity securities in the financial markets. The financial system is a backstop for the operations of business firms for those periods when internally generated cash fails to increase fast enough to support the growth of sales and meet customer demands.

The financial markets provide both short-term working capital to purchase inventories and meet current expenses and long-term investment funds to support the purchase of buildings and equipment. The principal external sources of working capital include trade credit (accounts payable), bank loans and acceptances, short-term credits from nonbank financial institutions (such as finance companies and life insurance firms), and sales of commercial paper in the open market. For businesses in need of long-term funding the principal funds sources are the sale of bonds and notes to non-bank financial institutions and other investors, term loans from banks, and the issuance of common and preferred stock and commercial mortgages.

Corporate bonds have original maturities of more than five years, while notes carry maturities of five years or less. There is a trend today toward shorter maturities of corporate debt securities due to inflation, more rapid changes in technology, and huge government deficits that force corporations into intense competition for funds with the government. Indexing of corporate bond rates to broader movements in the economy has also become more common. A wide variety of different bond and note issues have been developed to provide investors with varying degrees of security and risk protection, including debentures, mortgage bonds, equipment trust certificates, convertible bonds, and government-supported industrial development and pollution control bonds. Each type of bond is accompanied by an indenture spelling out in detail the rights and obligations of borrowers and investors. Corporate notes and bonds are purchased by a wide range of investors today, but the dominant buyers are life insurance companies and public and private pension funds.

New corporate bonds may be offered publicly in the open market, where competitive bidding takes place, or in a private sale to a limited group of investors. Public sales typically account for the largest portion of annual long-term borrowings, but the private market appeals to many smaller firms unable to tap the open market for funds and to companies with unique financing needs. Private sales offer the advantages of speed, lower distribution costs, and financing tailor-made to each company's special cash requirements. Public sales offer the advantage of competition as investment bankers, who underwrite new issues of stocks and bonds, bid against each other to win the right to market a new security issue. The process of competitive bidding tends to result in higher security prices and lower interest costs to corporations in need of funds.

The corporate bond market has faced aggressive competition in recent years from commercial banks making long-term business loans. These so-called term loans are generally used to purchase equipment. Most such loans carry floating, rather than fixed, interest rates tied to the prime lending rate—the interest rate levied on loans made to a bank's most creditworthy customers. Commercial banks also are the leading financial institution in extending mortgage loans to business. These loans support the construction of office buildings, shopping centers, and other commercial structures. Banks generally specialize in short-term mortgages that finance the construction of commercial facilities, while long-term commercial mortgage financing is provided mainly by insurance companies, savings banks, and pension funds.

STUDY QUESTIONS

1. Explain what is meant by the phrase, "the financial markets are a supplemental funds source for business." What factors appear to affect the volume of business fundraising from the money and capital markets?

2. List the principal external sources of business working capital. Of long-term business investment funds. What factors influence which of these various funds sources a business firm will draw upon?

3. Carefully define each of the following terms:
   a. Indenture.
   b. Trustee.
   c. Term bond.
   d. Call privilege.
   e. Sinking fund.
   f. Debenture.
   g. Subordinated debenture.
   h. Mortgage bond.
   i. Collateral trust bond.
   j. Income bond.
   k. Equipment trust certificate.
   l. Convertible bond.
   m. Industrial development bond.
   n. Pollution control bond.

4. Explain how the true cost of a corporate bond to the issuing company may be determined.

5. Who are the principal investors in corporate bonds and notes? Why?

6. Describe the role of investment bankers in the corporate bond market. What are the principal risks encountered by these firms? Discuss the factors that must be considered in pricing a new bond issue.

7. What is a *private placement?* Who buys privately placed bonds and why? What are the principal advantages to the borrower in a private placement of securities?

8. What is a leveraged buyout? Junk bond? Shark repellent? What are the dangers associated with these practices?

9. Provide a definition for each of the following terms:
   a. Term loan.
   b. Floating rate.
   c. Prime rate.
   d. Compensating balance.

10. For what purposes are commercial mortgages issued? What changes have occurred recently in the terms on commercial mortgages? What is an *equity kicker?*

11. Explain the term *indexing.* Why is this device necessary in today's economy?

PROBLEMS

1. A corporation sells $5,000 par value bonds at par in the open market, bearing an 8 percent coupon rate. Costs of marketing the issue, including dealer's commission, amounted to $200 per bond. If the bonds are due

to mature in 15 years, what is their before-tax cost to the corporation? If the issuing company is in the 34 percent tax bracket, what is the bonds' after-tax cost to the firm?

2. A corporation borrows $5 million from a bank at a 12 percent prime rate. If the bank requires the company to hold 15 percent of the amount of the loan on deposit as a compensating balance, what is the effective rate of interest on the loan?

3. A bank quotes one of its corporate customers a loan at prime plus 4 percentage points when prime is 12 percent. Another bank, posting the same prime rate, quotes this same customer a loan at 1¼ times prime. Which loan would you recommend the corporation take? Suppose both loans carry floating rates. Prime increases to 16 percent. Which loan is the better deal? Which would be the better deal if prime rises to 18 percent? Explain what is happening.

SELECTED REFERENCES

Arak, Marcell; A. Steven Englander; and Eric M. P. Tong. "Credit Cycles and the Pricing of the Prime Rate." *Quarterly Review,* Federal Reserve Bank of New York, Summer 1983, pp. 12–18.

Block, Earnest. "Pricing a Corporate Bond Issue: A Look Behind the Scenes." *Monthly Review,* Federal Reserve Bank of New York, October 1961.

Brady, Thomas F. "Changes in Loan Pricing and Business Lending at Commercial Banks." *Federal Reserve Bulletin*, January 1985, pp. 1–13.

Jensen, Frederick H. "Recent Developments in Corporate Finance." *Federal Reserve Bulletin,* November 1986, pp. 747–56.

Mitchell, Karlyn. "Interest Rate Uncertainty and Corporate Debt Maturity." *Journal of Economics and Business* 39 (1987), pp. 101–14.

Ott, Mack, and G. J. Santoni. "Mergers and Takeovers—The Value of Predators' Information." *Review,* Federal Reserve Bank of St. Louis, December 1985, pp. 16–28.

Silver, Andrew. "Original Issue Deep Discount Bond." *Quarterly Review,* Federal Reserve Bank of New York, Winter 1981–82, pp. 18–28.

Smith, Clifford W., and Jerold B. Warner. "On Financial Contracting: An Analysis of Bond Covenants." *Journal of Financial Economics* 7 (1979), pp. 117–61.

Zwick, Burton. "The Market for Corporate Bonds." *Quarterly Review,* Federal Reserve Bank of New York, Autumn 1977, pp. 27–36.

Chapter 21

Corporate Stock

Learning Objectives in This Chapter

- To learn about the characteristics of common and preferred corporate stock.
- To understand how the stock market operates today and what its component parts are.
- To compare and contrast the roles and functions of the organized stock exchanges and the over-the-counter market.
- To explore the question of market efficiency and examine the evidence for and against the efficiency of the stock market.

Key Terms and Concepts in This Chapter

Common stock	Third market	Stock index arbitrage
Preferred stock	Call option	Dynamic hedging
Organized exchanges	Put option	Random walk
Over-the-counter (OTC) market	Program trading	Efficient markets hypothesis
	Portfolio insurance	

Iℕ the preceding chapters we focused exclusively on debt securities and the extension of credit. In this chapter we examine a unique security that is not debt, but equity. It is a certificate of *ownership* in a corporation—a residual claim against both the assets and the earnings of a business firm. Corporate stock grants the investor no promise of return as debt does but only the right to share in the firm's net assets and net earnings, if any.

Corporate stock is unique in one other important respect. All the securities markets we have discussed to this point are intimately bound up with the process of moving funds from ultimate savers to ultimate borrowers in order to support investment and economic growth. In the stock market, however, the bulk of trading activity involves the buying and selling of securities already issued rather than the exchange of financial claims for new capital. Thus, trading in the stock market, for the most part, is not closely linked to the saving and investment process in the economy unless *new* stock is involved.

A small portion of trading in corporate shares does involve the sale of new stock to support business investment. Moreover, the stock market has a significant impact on the *expectations* of businesses when planning future investment and households when planning future expenditures. Therefore, stock trading indirectly affects employment, growth, and the general health of the economy.[1] In this chapter we take a close look at the basic characteristics of corporate stock and the markets where that stock is traded.

CHARACTERISTICS OF CORPORATE STOCK

All corporate stock represents an ownership interest in a corporation, conferring on the holder a number of important rights and privileges as well as risks. In this section we examine the two types of corporate stock issued today—common and preferred shares.

Common Stock

The most important form of corporate stock is common stock. Like all forms of equity, common stock represents a *residual* claim against the assets of the issuing firm, entitling the owner to a share in the net earnings of the

---

[1] One broad index of stock market prices—Standard & Poor's Composite Index—is considered to be a *leading indicator* of subsequent changes in economic conditions, especially of future developments in industrial production, employment, and total spending (GNP). Thus, the stock market often turns in its greatest gains in the deepest part of a recession and turns down before a boom is over. There appear to be several reasons for this. The stock market seems to provide a forecast of business capital spending plans, perhaps reflecting the fact that it captures the expectations of the business community. Stock prices anticipate future changes in corporate profits and, of course, these profits are a major source of capital spending which affects employment and economic growth. In addition, stock prices affect interest rates, which eventually influence business activity. In fact, there is a high *negative* correlation between interest rates (particularly short-term rates) and stock prices. As interest rates on bonds and other fixed-income securities decline, many investors rapidly switch their funds into the stock market.

firm when it is profitable and to a share in the net market value (after all debts are paid) of the company's assets if it is liquidated. By owning common stock the investor is subject to the full risks of ownership, which means that the business may fail or its earnings may fall to unacceptable levels. However, the risks of equity ownership are limited because the stockholder is liable only for the amount of his or her investment of funds.

If a corporation with outstanding shares of common stock is liquidated, the debts of the firm must be paid first from any assets available. The preferred stockholders then receive their contractual share of any remaining funds. The residual, whatever is left, accrues to common stockholders on a pro rata basis. Unlike many debt securities, common stock is generally a registered instrument with the holder's name recorded on the issuing company's books.

The volume of stock a corporation may issue is limited by the terms of its charter of incorporation (see Exhibit 21–1 for an announcement of a new stock offering). Additional shares beyond those authorized by the company's charter may be issued only by amending the charter with the approval of the current stockholders. Some companies have issued large numbers of corporate shares, reflecting not only their need for large amounts of equity capital, but also a desire to broaden their ownership base. For example, American Telephone and Telegraph (AT&T) has more than 700 million shares of common stock listed on the New York Stock Exchange.

The *par value* of common stock is an arbitrarily assigned value printed on each stock certificate. Par is usually set low relative to the stock's current market value. In fact, today some stock is issued without any par value. Originally, par was supposed to represent the owner's initial investment per share in the firm. The only real significance of par today is that the firm cannot pay any dividends to stockholders that would reduce the company's net worth per share below the par value of its stock.

Common stockholders are granted a number of rights when they buy a share of equity in a business corporation. Stock ownership permits them to elect the company's board of directors, which, in turn, chooses the officers responsible for day-to-day management of the company. Common shareholders have a *preemptive right* when stock is purchased (unless specifically denied by the firm's charter) which gives the individual shareholder the right to purchase any new voting stock, convertible bonds, or preferred stock issued by the firm in order to maintain his or her *pro rata* share of ownership. For example, if a stockholder holds 5 percent of all shares outstanding and 500 new shares are issued, this stockholder has the right to subscribe to 25 new shares.

While most common stock grants each stockholder one vote per share, nonvoting common is also issued occasionally. Some companies issue Class A common which has voting rights and Class B common which has a prior claim on earnings but no voting power. The major stock exchanges do not encourage publicly held firms to issue classified common stock, but classified shares are used extensively by privately held firms.

Exhibit 21–1   Example of the Announcement of a New Stock Offering in *The Wall Street Journal*

This announcement constitutes neither an offer to sell nor a solicitation of an offer to buy these securities. The offering is made only by the Prospectus, copies of which may be obtained in any State from such of the undersigned and others as may lawfully offer these securities in such State.

May 24, 1985

2,400,000 Shares

Anitec
Image Technology Corp.

Common Stock

Price $11 per Share

Smith Barney, Harris Upham & Co.
Incorporated

Donaldson, Lufkin & Jenrette
Securities Corporation

Bear, Stearns & Co.   The First Boston Corporation   Alex. Brown & Sons
Incorporated

Dillon, Read & Co. Inc.   Drexel Burnham Lambert   Goldman, Sachs & Co.   Hambrecht & Quist
Incorporated   Incorporated

E. F. Hutton & Company Inc.   Kidder, Peabody & Co.   Lazard Frères & Co.
Incorporated

Merrill Lynch Capital Markets   Montgomery Securities   PaineWebber
Incorporated

Prudential-Bache   L. F. Rothschild, Unterberg, Towbin   Salomon Brothers Inc
Securities

Shearson Lehman Brothers Inc.   Wertheim & Co., Inc.   Dean Witter Reynolds Inc.

Source: *The Wall Street Journal*, May 24, 1985, p. 28.

A right granted to all common stockholders is the right of access to the minutes of stockholder meetings and to lists of existing shareholders. This gives the stockholders some power to reorganize the company if existing management or the board of directors is performing poorly. Common stockholders may vote on all matters that affect the firm's property as a whole, such as a merger, liquidation, or the issuance of additional equity shares.

Preferred Stock

The other major form of stock issued today is preferred stock. Each share of preferred stock carries a stated annual dividend expressed as a percent of the stock's par value. For example, if preferred shares carry a $100 par value with an 8 percent dividend rate, then each preferred shareholder is entitled to dividends of $8 per year on each share owned, provided the company declares a dividend.[2] Common stockholders receive whatever dividends remain *after* the preferred shareholders receive their stated annual dividend.

Preferred stock occupies the middle ground between debt and equity securities, including advantages and disadvantages of both forms of raising long-term funds. Preferred stockholders have a prior claim over the firm's assets and earnings relative to the claims of common stockholders. However, bondholders and other creditors must be paid before either preferred or common stockholders receive anything. Unlike creditors of the firm, preferred stockholders cannot press for bankruptcy proceedings against a company that fails to pay them dividends. Nevertheless, preferred stock is part of a firm's equity capital and strengthens a firm's net worth account, allowing it to issue more debt in the future. It also is a more flexible financing arrangement than debt because dividends may be passed if earnings are inadequate or uncertain and there is no fixed maturity date when the securities must be retired.

Generally, preferred stockholders have no voice or vote in the selection of management unless the corporation "passes" dividends (fails to pay dividends at the agreed-upon time) for a stipulated period. A frequent provision in corporate charters gives preferred stockholders the right to elect some members of the board of directors if dividends are passed for a full year. Dividends on preferred stock, like those paid on common stock, are not a tax-deductible expense. This makes preferred shares nearly twice as expensive to issue as debt for companies in the top-income bracket. However, IRS regulations specify that 80 percent of the dividends on preferred stock received by a corporate investor are not taxable. This tax-exemption feature makes preferred stock especially attractive to companies seeking to acquire ownership shares in other firms and sometimes allows preferred stock to be issued at a lower net interest cost than debt securities. In fact, corporations themselves are the principal buyers of preferred stock issues.

Most preferred stock is *cumulative,* which means that the passing of dividends results in an arrearage which must be paid in full before the common stockholders receive anything. A few preferred shares are *participating,* allowing the holder to share in the residual earnings normally accruing entirely to common stockholders. To illustrate how the participating feature might work, assume that an investor holds 8 percent participating preferred stock with a $100 par value. After the issuing company's board of directors votes to pay the preferred shareholders their stated annual dividend of $8 per share, the board also declares a $20 a share common stock dividend. If the formula for dividend participation calls for common

---

[2]Recently Dutch-auction-rate preferred stock has become very popular as a cash-management device for corporate investors. This equity security carries a flexible dividend rate that can be changed frequently (for example, at the end of each 7-week period) to reflect current market conditions.

and preferred shareholders to share equally in any net earnings, then each preferred shareholder will earn an additional $12 to bring its total dividend to $20 per share as well. Not all participating formulas are this generous, however, and most preferred issues are nonparticipating because the participation feature is detrimental to the interests of common stockholders.

Most corporations plan to retire their preferred stock, even though it carries no stated maturity. In fact, the bulk of preferred shares issued today have call provisions. When interest rates decline, the issuing company may exercise the call privilege at the price (which usually includes a premium over par) stated in the formal agreement between the firm and its shareholders. A few preferred issues are *convertible* into shares of common stock at the investor's option. The company retires all converted preferred shares and may force conversion by simply exercising the stock's call privilege. New preferred issues today are often accompanied by a sinking fund provision whereby funds are gradually accumulated and set aside for eventual retirement of preferred shares. A trustee is appointed (usually a bank trust department) who collects sinking fund payments from the company and periodically calls in preferred shares or occasionally purchases them in the open market. While sinking fund provisions allow the issuing firm to sell preferred stock with lower dividend rates, payments into the fund drain earnings and reduce dividend payments flowing to common stockholders.

From the standpoint of the investor, preferred stock represents an intermediate investment between bonds and common stock. Preferred shares often provide more income than bonds, but also carry greater risk. Preferred share prices fluctuate more widely than bond prices for the same change in interest rates. Compared to common stock, preferred shares generally provide less total income (considering both capital gains and dividend income) but are, in turn, less risky. They appeal to the investor who is looking for a favorable but moderate rate of return.

STOCK MARKET INVESTORS

Corporate stock is one of the most widely held financial assets in the United States and around the world. Only one other financial asset—government securities—is held by as large and as diverse a group of individuals and institutions as are common and preferred stock. One important source of information on stockholders in the United States is the Federal Reserve Board's Flow of Funds Accounts.[3] Exhibit 21–2 gives the names of major investor groups and their total holdings of common and preferred stock as of year-end 1970, 1980, and 1986. The exhibit makes clear that *households*—individuals and families—are the dominant holders of corporate stock in

---

[3]See Chapter 3 for an explanation of the method of construction and types of information presented in the Flow of Funds Accounts.

Exhibit 21–2   **Principal Investors in U.S. Corporate Stock**
($ Billions Outstanding at Year-End)*

Investor Group	1970		1980		1986	
	Amount	Percent of Total	Amount	Percent of Total	Amount	Percent of Total
Households	$728.6	80.4%	$1,188.2	72.6%	$2,210.3	65.8%
Rest of the world	27.2	3.0	64.2	3.9	167.4	5.0
Commercial banks	0.1	—	0.1	—	0.1	—
Mutual savings banks	2.8	0.3	4.2	0.3	7.0	0.2
Life insurance companies	15.4	1.7	47.4	2.9	90.0	2.7
Property–casualty insurance companies	15.4	1.5	32.3	2.0	68.3	2.0
Private pension funds	67.1	7.4	209.5	12.8	481.4	14.3
Government pension funds	10.1	1.1	44.3	2.7	150.2	4.5
Mutual funds	39.7	4.4	42.2	2.6	161.2	4.8
Security brokers and dealers	2.0	0.2	2.9	0.2	9.7	0.3
Total market value of holdings	$906.2	100.0%	$1,635.6	100.0%	$3,361.5	100.0%

*Investor holdings valued at market.

Source: Board of Governors of the Federal Reserve System, *Flow of Funds Accounts: Assets and Liabilities Outstanding,* 1963–86.

the United States. At year-end 1986, for example, households held about two thirds of all corporate shares outstanding. Pension funds—both private and government—were a distant second, holding about 19 percent of available shares. Foreign investors—principally foreign banks, brokers, trusts, and individuals—ranked third with 5 percent of the total. Life insurance companies, mutual funds, and property-casualty insurers each held about 2 to 5 percent of all corporate shares outstanding. The deposit-type financial intermediaries—commercial banks and savings banks—collectively held less than 1 percent of the total. State laws severely limit savings bank investment in corporate stock, while both state and federal laws prohibit commercial banks from purchasing or underwriting most corporate stock. Commercial banks do acquire stock pledged as collateral for loans when the borrower defaults, but such holdings usually must be worked out of the bank's portfolio at the earliest opportunity.

While individuals hold a majority of all equity shares outstanding, their interest in corporate stock has ebbed and flowed with market conditions. For example, as shown in Exhibit 21–3, households were *net sellers* of equity shares in most years from 1980 to 1988. However, in 1986 individuals and families made record additions to their stock holdings, adding nearly $22 billion to their stock investments in that year before a massive selloff occurred in 1987 and 1988 in the wake of a record plunge in stock prices. Foreign investors also have purchased huge amounts of corporate equities

Exhibit 21–3   **Net Purchases of U.S. Corporate Stock by Investor Groups**
($ Billions at Seasonally Adjusted Rates)

Investor Groups	1980	1981	1982	1983	1984	1985	1986	1987	1988†
Households	$ −6.3	$ −29.0	$ 2.1	$14.8	$ −36.4	$ −0.8	$ 21.8	$ −54.1	$ −59.2
Rest of the world	5.4	5.8	3.9	5.4	−3.0	5.0	17.8	15.4	4.1
Commercial banks	*	−0.1	*	*	−0.1	0.1	*	−0.1	0.3
Mutual savings banks	−0.5	−0.6	−0.5	0.3	−0.2	−0.1	0.9	0.2	0.5
Life insurance companies	0.5	2.9	3.4	3.1	0.7	6.0	8.1	3.5	*
Private pension funds	15.0	6.4	13.4	2.3	−4.3	−2.4	−3.8	−24.8	−41.8
State and local government pension funds	5.3	7.1	6.0	20.0	7.3	28.6	23.1	29.4	21.1
Property–casualty insurance companies	3.1	2.0	2.7	2.1	−4.3	−2.0	3.7	5.8	6.4
Mutual funds	−1.8	−0.6	3.5	13.7	5.9	10.3	20.2	26.9	−9.0
Security brokers and dealers	0.7	2.7	−0.9	5.3	3.3	0.5	−2.2	2.0	9.8

*Less than $50 million.

†Figures are for the first quarter of the year.

Source: Board of Governors of the Federal Reserve System, *Flow of Funds Accounts,* selected quarters.

in the United States recently, adding about $15 billion in stock during 1987 and $4 billion in 1988.

Fluctuations in the volume of stock purchases have been accompanied by marked changes in the number and composition of shareholders. Periodically, the New York Stock Exchange conducts ownership surveys to determine the number and financial characteristics of stock market investors. Until recently, the NYSE surveys reported a flight of individual shareowners away from the market. However, the number of individual shareholders rose in the late 1970s and 1980s, paralleling the rapid growth of new households in recent years. At the same time, as we have seen, the market posted strong rallies during each year in the mid-1980s. Other factors arousing recent investor interest in the stock market include a reduction in federal income and estate taxes and a perception on the part of many investors that common stocks are an effective long-run hedge against inflation.

Several financial institutions have increased their participation in the stock market in recent years. As Exhibit 21–2 shows, institutional shareholders held about 28 percent of all equity shares outstanding in 1986. This compares to only 23 percent in 1980 and 17 percent in 1970. Among the various financial institutions, private and public pension funds have expanded their share of the equities market the most, with pension-held shares climbing from about 8 percent of the total value in 1970 to almost 19 percent in 1986. Over the same period, insurance companies increased their holdings

Exhibit 21–4   **Leading Stock Exchanges around the World**

New York Stock Exchange	Stockholm Exchange
American Stock Exchange	Brussels Exchange
Tokyo Exchange	Sydney Exchange
London Exchange	Hong Kong Exchange
Frankfurt Exchange	Singapore Exchange
Zurich Exchange	Johannesburg Exchange
Paris Exchange	Taipei Exchange
Manila Exchange	Toronto Exchange
Milan Exchange	Wellington Exchange
Amsterdam Exchange	

from just 3 percent of all equity shares to about 5 percent. Toward the end of the 1980s mutual funds—traditional stock buyers on behalf of their customers—dramatically added to their stock holdings as a soaring market captured the interest of scores of individual investors. Mutual funds have been especially attractive to middle-income investors who cannot afford to buy a large number of shares on their own.

CHARACTERISTICS OF THE CORPORATE STOCK MARKET

There are two main branches of the market for trading corporate shares. One is the organized exchanges, which in the United States include the New York (NYSE) and American (AMEX) exchanges plus regional exchanges, including the Pacific (PSE), Midwest (MSE), Philadelphia (PHLX), Boston (BSE), and Cincinnati (CSE) exchanges. The regional exchanges historically have served to promote trading mainly in securities of interest to investors in their particular region of the nation. Today, however, the regional exchanges have penetrated the national market and rely to a significant degree on transactions in securities listed on both AMEX and the NYSE. Overseas, the Tokyo, Singapore, and London exchanges have grown in importance as major centers for trading corporate shares worldwide (see Exhibit 21–4). All the exchanges today, foreign and domestic, use similar procedures for controlling membership, regulating trade, and recording purchases and sales of stock.

Trading on the exchanges is governed by regulations and formal procedures designed to ensure both competitive pricing of shares and an active market for the stock of the largest, financially stable companies. In contrast, the second branch of the equities market—the over-the-counter (OTC) market—involves trading of stock through brokers operating off the major exchanges. This "over the telephone" market is much more informal and fluid than exchange trading and includes the stocks and bonds of many small-

and medium-sized companies and large numbers of banks, mutual funds, and other financial institutions.

The Major Organized Exchanges

Approximately three quarters of all trading in U.S. corporate shares occurs on the organized exchanges. By far the largest and best known of these is the Big Board—the New York Stock Exchange. In recent years the Big Board has accounted for four fifths or more of both the number of shares and total market value of all equities traded on U.S. exchanges. The American Stock Exchange (ASE or AMEX) ranks a distant second among the U.S. exchanges. The NYSE, AMEX, and the regional exchanges overlap in trading and function and therefore are competitive markets for the most actively traded U.S. stocks. For example, more than four fifths of the volume of trading on the regional exchanges is in stocks listed on the New York Stock Exchange. Moreover, in 1978 the Intermarket Trading System (ITS) was set up to link the Big Board with five other exchanges electronically and create additional intermarket competition. Stock brokers and specialists on one exchange thereafter could contact traders on the other exchanges directly in order to find the best prices for their customers.

Each exchange provides a physical location for trading, and trading by member firms must be carried on at that location. On the floor of the NYSE, for example, there are 18 counters, each with several windows or *trading posts*. A handful of the more than 1,500 common stocks listed and available for trading on the NYSE are traded from each post as prescribed by the Exchange's Board of Governors. The exchanges permit the enforcement of formal trading rules in order to achieve an efficient and speedy allocation of available equity shares.

In order to be eligible for trading on an organized exchange, the stock must be issued by a firm *listed* with the exchange. A substantial number of major U.S. corporations are listed simultaneously on several different exchanges. The listing qualifications demanded by the New York Stock Exchange are the most comprehensive and difficult to fulfill, which serves to limit NYSE trading to stocks issued by the largest and most financially stable companies. The most important listing requirements of the NYSE are summarized in Exhibit 21–5. The basic intent of these rules is to ensure that the listed company has a sufficient volume of shares available to create an active national market for its stock and discloses sufficient data so that interested investors can make informed decisions. Even if a company meets all the formal listing requirements shown in Exhibit 21–5, its stock must still be approved for admission by the NYSE board of directors, which includes 10 members elected by firms with seats on the exchange.[4] Corpora-

---

[4] Listing of a company which meets all of the NYSE requirements shown in Exhibit 21–5 is not automatic. The NYSE's board of directors also considers the degree of national interest in the company, whether it is in an expanding industry and is likely to at least retain its relative position, and the stability of the industry involved.

Exhibit 21–5 **Requirements for Listing a Company on the New York Stock Exchange**

Minimum Requirements for Initial Listing on the Exchange

A. Demonstrated earning power, with before-tax earnings of at least $2.5 million in the most recent year and at least $2 million during the previous two years.
B. Adequate size of company operations, with net tangible assets of at least $16 million.
C. Adequate minimum market value of publicly held shares, adjusted for market conditions.
D. A sufficient number (currently 1 million) of common shares held by the public.
E. Shares which are held widely enough to promote an active market—currently at least 2,000 shareholders with 100 or more shares each are required to qualify.

Requirements for Continued Listing

A. Periodic public disclosure of financial condition and earnings.
B. Maintenance of an adequate number of publicly traded shares outstanding. The Exchange would consider suspending or removing a company's security from the trading list if there are fewer than 1,200 round-lot investors, 600,000 or fewer shares in public hands, and the aggregate market value of publicly held shares falls below acceptable limits.

Source: New York Stock Exchange.

tions that are successful in listing their stock must make an annual disclosure of their financial condition, limit trading by insiders, publish quarterly earnings reports, and help maintain an active and deep public market for their shares. If trading interest in a particular firm's stock falls off significantly, the firm may be *delisted*. Under some circumstances a firm may be granted "unlisted trading privileges" if its stock has been listed previously on another exchange.

One of the most important advantages claimed for listing on an exchange is that it improves the *liquidity* of a corporation's stock. If a stock is liquid, a relatively large volume of shares can be sold at any given time without significantly depressing its price. This feature is of special concern to large institutional investors (such as pension funds) that have come to dominate daily trading in the equities market, because these institutions typically trade in large blocks, rather than a few shares at a time. Allegedly, a corporation can improve the market for its stock by getting it listed on a securities exchange.

Member firms of the exchange are the only ones who may trade in listed securities on the exchange floor, either for their own account or for their customers. Most members actually own "seats" on the exchange and hold claims against the exchange's net assets. The majority of seat owners are directors or partners of brokerage firms, and some of these firms own several seats. Member firms are allowed to sell or lease their seats with the approval of the exchange's governing board.

Member firms fulfill a variety of roles on an exchange. Some act as *floor traders* who buy and sell only for their own account. Floor traders are really speculators whose portfolios turn over rapidly as they drift from post to post on the exchange floor looking for profitable trading opportunities. Other members serve as *commission brokers,* employed by member brokerage firms to represent the orders of their customers on the exchange floor, or *floor brokers,* who are usually individual entrepreneurs carrying out buy and sell orders from other brokers not present on the exchange floor.

A few traders holding exchange seats are *specialists* who trade in one or a limited number of stocks. The specialist firms operating on the New York Stock Exchange act as *both* brokers and dealers, buying and selling for other brokers and for themselves when there is an imbalance between supply and demand for the stocks in which they specialize. For example, when sell orders pile up for the stocks a specialist firm is responsible for, it will move in to buy some of the offered shares. Specialists help to create orderly and continuous markets and stabilize prices by agreeing to undertake immediate trading to cover unfilled customer orders. However, in return for this service of immediate trading, specialists profit by purchasing stocks from public sellers at discounts from the market price and by selling stocks at a premium above the market price. Finally, a few *odd-lot traders,* typically representing large brokerage firms dealing with the public, also are active on the exchange floor. Odd lots are buy or sell orders involving less than 100 shares that come primarily from small individual investors. The odd-lot trader typically will purchase 100 or more shares—a *round lot*—and retain any extra shares that are not needed by customers in his or her portfolio.

Stock exchanges are among the oldest financial institutions. The New York Stock Exchange, for example, was set up following an agreement among 24 Wall Street brokers in May 1792, just three years after the U.S. Constitution was adopted. The exchanges provide a continuous market centered in an established location for buying and selling equity shares, with rigid rules to ensure fairness in the trading process. By bringing together buyers and sellers, the exchanges, at one and the same time, make stock a liquid investment, promote efficient pricing of securites, and make possible the placement of huge amounts of financial capital.

The Informal Over-the-Counter Market

The large majority of securities bought and sold around the globe, especially debt securities, are traded over-the-counter (OTC) and not on organized exchanges. The customer places a buy or sell order with a bank, broker, or dealer which is then relayed via telephone, by wire, or by computer terminal to the particular dealer or broker with securities to sell or an order to buy. In this system of electronically linked market-makers each broker or dealer seeks the best possible price on behalf of himself or his customer, and the resulting competition to find the best deal brings together traders located hundreds or thousands of miles apart. The prices of actively traded securities respond almost instantly to the changing forces of demand and supply so that security prices constantly hover at or near competitive, market-determined levels.

All money market instruments are traded in the over-the-counter markets, as are the large majority of government bonds and corporate bonds. While most common stocks are traded on exchanges, an estimated one quarter to one third of all stocks are traded OTC. The OTC market is generally preferred by financial institutions, especially commercial banks, bank holding companies, mutual funds, and insurance companies, because in many cases their shares are not actively traded and OTC trading and disclosure rules are less restrictive. The presence of financial institutions tends to give the OTC market a more conservative tone than the exchanges.

Many dealers in the OTC market act as *principals* instead of brokers as on the organized exchanges. That is, they take "positions of risk" by buying securities outright for their own portfolios as well as for retail customers. Several dealers will handle the same stock so that customers can shop around. All prices are determined by negotiation with dealers acquiring securities at *bid* prices and selling them at *asked* prices. The U.S. OTC market is regulated by a code of ethics established by the National Association of Security Dealers, a private organization that encourages ethical behavior among its members. Trading firms or their employees who break NASD's regulations may be fined, suspended, or thrown out of the organization.

One of the most important contributions of NASD has been the development of NASDAQ (the National Association of Security Dealers Automated Quotations system). NASDAQ displays bid and asked prices for nearly 4,000 OTC-traded securities on video screens connected electronically to a central computer system. All NASD member firms trading in a particular stock report their bid-ask price quotations immediately to NASDAQ. This nationwide communications network allows dealers, brokers, and customers to determine instantly the terms currently offered by major securities dealers.

THE THIRD MARKET: TRADING IN LISTED SECURITIES OFF THE EXCHANGE

The market for securities listed on a stock exchange but traded over the counter is known as the third market. Broker and dealer firms not members of an organized exchange are active in this market, which in the United States deals mainly in NYSE-listed stocks. The original purpose of the third market was to supply large blocks of shares to institutional investors, especially mutual funds, bank trust accounts, and pension funds. These investors engage mainly in *block trades,* defined as transactions involving 1,000 shares or more. Presumably, the largest block traders possess the technical knowhow to make informed investment decisions and then carry out transactions without assistance from a stock exchange and the high brokerage commissions that may entail. By trading with third market broker and dealer firms, who, in effect, compete directly with specialists on the exchanges, a large institutional investor frequently can lower transactions costs and trade securities faster.

The third market provides additional competition for the organized exchanges, especially the New York Stock Exchange. Moreover, along with the other over-the-counter markets, the third market has been a catalyst in reducing brokerage fees and promoting trading efficiency. For example, the growth of the third market and other OTC trading during the 1970s encouraged the unbundling of commissions at many U.S. broker and dealer firms to more accurately reflect the true cost of each security trade. Many brokerage firms, especially those active in odd-lot trading, offer customers an array of peripheral services, such as research on market trends and security credit accounting for purchases and sales, and often the customer pays for these services whether or not he or she uses them. The largest institutional investors have little need for such services, however, and they seek brokers and dealers offering their services at minimum cost.

The flight of major stock investors into the third market and into other OTC markets brought about pricing policies in the industry geared more directly to actual services used. As a result, the third market itself declined in importance. While major stockbrokers and dealers used to quote set commissions, the practice of charging fixed brokerage commissions to stock investors ended on the New York Stock Exchange on May 1, 1975. The result was an upward surge in the volume of trading on the organized exchanges; in fact, stock trading on Wall Street multiplied fivefold between 1975 and 1985. In the latter year average daily trading on the New York Stock Exchange exceeded 100 million shares. More recently numerous "discount" brokerage houses[5] have appeared, leading many institutional customers to abandon the third market and return to more traditional channels for executing their security orders as trading prices continue to decline.

THE MARKET FOR STOCK OPTIONS

Paralleling the exchange and over-the-counter markets for common and preferred stock is a market for *stock options*. As we saw in Chapter 12, an option is an agreement between two parties granting one party the right (but not the obligation) to purchase an asset from or sell an asset to the

---

[5]*Discount brokerage firms* offer trading services at commission rates as much as 80 percent less than the rates quoted by so-called full-service firms. The more than 600 discount houses currently operating (many organized by banks) cut costs by not giving investment advice or offering personal account management to customers.

other party under specified conditions. The price of an option is known as the *option premium*—the cost to the option buyer of insuring against an adverse change in the price of a stock. In the stock market both *call* and *put* options are sold, with the call option generally predominant. Both are designed as techniques to manage the risk of fluctuating security prices and interest rates.

Call Options

A call option on stock grants the buyer the right to purchase ("call away") a specified number of shares of a given stock at a specified price up to an expiration date. Call options become attractive when the investor expects the price of a given stock to rise above the price specified in the option contract (known as the striking price or exercise price). Thus, an option may be available to buy 500 shares of the common stock of Caledonia Manufacturing Company at $6 per share. If the stock rises to a price of $7.50 in the open market, the holder of the option can buy $3,750 worth of stock for only $3,000. Even if the option buyer does not wish to hold the stock, he or she can resell it in the open market and receive a nice short-term gain.

Another potential advantage of options is the amount of financial *leverage* they grant the investor. Less money is required to control a specified number of equity shares than would be necessary if the stock were purchased outright. However, the risk of loss is greater with options; even small changes in the price of a stock can lead to magnified changes in the value of an option. For example, it is not uncommon for an option to double or triple in price even though the price of the stock itself may increase by only 15 to 20 percent. And, of course, losses can double or triple as well. For this reason stockbrokers usually prefer options customers who have greater net worth and market knowledge than the average investor.

Trading in options gained widespread interest among U.S. investors early in the 1970s, and many corporations today offer stock options to employees. In 1973, the Chicago Board Options Exchange initiated trading in options for selected stocks listed on the major exchanges. Today, *listed* or exchange-traded options are popular, along with over-the-counter or negotiated options purchased through brokers and dealers. Listed options and their current holders are all recorded on computerized records maintained by the Options Clearing Corporation, which also guarantees delivery of the stock in the event the seller defaults.

Puts

The opposite of a call option is know as a put option. Puts grant the investor the right to *sell* a specified number of equity shares at a set price on or before the expiration date. Unlike a call, the investor in puts hopes the associated stock will *decline* in price so that he or she can sell at a price higher than is currently available in the market. In fact, the more market prices fall, the more money the holder of a put option expects to collect. In this sense, puts are similar to selling a stock *short* (the sale of borrowed stock) in the hope that its price will fall. However, puts require less capital and usually result in a lower total brokerage commission than short sales of stock. Also, the investor's potential loss is limited to the price of the put plus brokerage commission, regardless of what happens to the price of the underlying stock. Puts often become popular in bear markets or near the peak of a bull market when the long-run outlook is eventually for significant declines in stock values. Like calls, puts are traded both over-the-counter and on major organized exchanges.

Straddles

Some investors will combine put and call options to establish a *straddle* on a given stock. A straddle is simply a combination trade in which the investor purchases a put and a call on the same stock, both carrying the same exercise price and maturing on the same date. For example, suppose the stock of Caledonia Manufacturing is selling for $7.50, but the market is so volatile the investor is highly uncertain as to its future direction. To protect against an unexpected move, the investor buys a call option with a strike price of $8 and an $8 put option, each costing $1. Profits will be made if either the call or the put increase in value by more than $2. A rise in the market value of Caledonia's stock will cause the call option to rise in value; a fall in the stock's price will cause the put's value to increase. Sometimes, if the market fluctuates violently, *both* the put and call options will turn out to be profitable, though usually one or the other will expire without being used. An option that expires without being exercised is worthless.

The Growth of Options Markets

Until 1982, only options for common stock were traded in organized markets such as the American Stock Exchange or the Chicago Board Options Exchange. However, beginning in 1982 new options markets appeared for *stock indexes* (such as the S&P 500, the Amex Market Value Index, the Value Line Composite Index, and the New York Stock Exchange Composite Index); and for futures contracts for the S&P 500 and NYSE Composite Stock Index. Stock index options are based on a basket (collection) of common stocks that are thought to be representative of the whole market. No securities are delivered to settle a stock index option contract; instead, all transactions must be settled in cash on the one day each month that contracts normally expire. The purpose of a stock index option is to permit speculative investors to bet on which way the stock market as a whole is likely to go, while simultaneously allowing risk-averse investors to protect against an adverse movement in the stock market as a whole. Recently *subindex* options have appeared for small baskets of stocks, such as the AMEX's computer technology stock index.

While options and futures contracts (discussed at length in Chapter 12) can serve as devices for hedging against security price or interest-rate risk, options have certain advantages over futures for hedging purposes, especially when an investor desires to hedge a transaction that may or may not actually occur in the future. The recent rapid growth of new options contracts and markets reflects a desire among many financial market participants to protect themselves against the wide swings in security prices and interest rates that have characterized the money and capital markets in recent years. Options allow a risk-averse investor to shift market risk to someone else willing to bear that risk and hoping to profit from risk-taking.

Options and Stock Prices

In the past two decades, financial theory on how options are priced has developed. The key contribution in the options pricing field was made in 1973 when Black and Scholes developed a model linking options prices to the risk-free interest rate. These researchers observed that an investor could achieve a riskless hedge combining options and stocks as long as the hedge could be modified at any time to reflect changing market conditions. The price of a call option reaches equilibrium when a hedge's return approaches the risk-free or pure rate of interest. Later, the Black-Scholes model was extended to tracking stock prices. The value of equity shares issued by a corporation with outstanding debt was shown to be dependent on the market value of the company's assets, the variability of asset returns, the remaining term (maturity) of its debt obligations, and the amount of debt outstanding.

The Rise of Program Trading: Portfolio Insurance and Stock Index Arbitraging

Many analysts believe that stock markets worldwide have become more volatile and unpredictable due to the widespread use of computerized program trading. This computer-assisted investment decision-making strategy represents an attempt to shield a security investor against loss from changing prices and interest rates by making continuous changes in an investor's holdings as the relative prices between two or more financial instruments change. It is used extensively today by major banks, brokerage firms, insurance companies, and pension funds.

There are at least two types of program trading today: (1) portfolio insurance arrangements and (2) stock index arbitrage. One of the simplest types involves buying and selling stock index futures contracts (as described in Chapter 12). The most popular such contract is the Standard & Poor's 500 stock-index contract, which is bought and sold on the Chicago Mercantile Exchange (CME). A buyer of this futures contract (who, by definition, takes a long position in futures) promises to take future delivery of the cash value of the S&P 500 index when the futures contract expires unless he or she cancels out the contract before it expires by selling a similar contract. Similarly, a seller of the S&P 500 index contract (who, by definition, takes a short position in futures) promises to pay the contract buyer the cash value of the S&P index when the futures contract runs out. However, the contract seller can also cancel out his or her obligation by simply buying a similar contract. The clearinghouse at the futures exchange will simply "zero out" the sell and buy orders from the same trader, freeing him or her from the obligation to deliver or accept payment.

How can these futures contracts be used to protect against stock price declines? The interested investor could simply *sell* stock index futures contracts that will expire on or about the date he or she plans to sell their stock holdings. If stock prices decline, the loss on any shares held will be partially or wholly offset by a gain on the stock index futures because, with a falling stock market, those contracts can be bought back to "zero out" the futures position at a lower price than their original purchase price. Unfortunately, the use of pure stock index futures as just described limits profits as well as losses. For example, if stock prices rise rather than fall, the investor will suffer a loss on his or her futures position that reduces any profits earned on the stock itself.

An investor can preserve the profit potential on stock while still hedging against losses by using a *put option contract* on a stock index, such as the S&P 500 stock index. Under this arrangement, the buyer of a put option gains the right (but not the obligation) to *sell* units of the S&P stock index contract at a set (strike) price on the date the option contract expires. If stock prices fall below the strike price spelled out in the option contract, the put option goes up in value, wholly or partially offsetting the loss on the stock itself. However, if the stock itself goes up in value, the option contract will not be exercised and the investor will pocket a nice capital gain on selling the stock, minus only the relatively small price paid for the put option. In this case, paying the price of the put option is equivalent to buying an insurance policy against declining stock prices. In essence, portfolio insurance of the type just described gives an investor protection against security price declines, with at least some reduction in potential gains.

More complicated portfolio insurance strategies are also in use today employing so-called replicating or synthetic security portfolios. These portfolios are built using portfolio insurance techniques—that is, dynamic hedging strategies that continuously adjust an investor's holdings to limit exposure to adverse stock market developments. Dynamic hedging programs attempt to take into account the current prices of stock, options, futures, options and futures expiration dates, interest rates, and how volatile stock prices appear to be. Replicating portfolios may consist of a basket of stocks that represent a major stock index (such as the S&P 500 stock index), index futures contracts, Treasury bills, or other financial instruments. If stock prices begin to fall, a common strategy is to sell off some stocks held by the investor and move into other financial instruments that are safer, such as U.S. Treasury bills or stock index futures contracts. If the selloff of stocks makes them appear to be underpriced, stocks may then be purchased until once again all financial asset prices are aligned and there is no further reason for arbitrageurs to move funds from one security market to another. Program trading systems, including portfolio insurance techniques, generally work well at limiting an investor's exposure to risk except in periods when stock prices change very rapidly, as in the crash of October 19, 1987, when the value of corporate stock fell by more than $500 billion in a single trading session, or when trading is not smooth and continuous.[6]

THE DEVELOPMENT OF A UNIFIED INTERNATIONAL MARKET FOR STOCK

It is clear from the foregoing discussion that the stock market is fractured into several different parts, each with its own unique collection of brokers and dealers and, in some cases, its own unique collection of customers. However, one of the most significant developments during the 1970s and 1980s was a movement spurred by government action and industry competition to weld all parts of the equities market together into a single national and even international market. In 1975 Congress passed the Securities Act Amendments—the most sweeping and potentially significant piece of securities legislation since the Great Depression of the 1930s. The amendments instructed the Securities and Exchange Commission to "facilitate the establishment of a national market system for securities" in order to further the development of widespread trading in equities and bring the fresh breath of open competition to stock trading, rather than confining most such trading to the floor of an exchange.

While the 1975 amendments did not specify what the proposed *national market system* would look like or what kinds of securities would be involved, the intent of Congress was to ensure that all investors, regardless of location, would have ready access to information on security prices and could transact business at the best available price, wherever that might be. Moreover, with greater mobility of funds from one exchange to another or between the exchanges and the over-the-counter market, the resulting increase in competition in stock trading might reduce the cost to corporations of raising new equity capital.

Shortly after the Securities Act Amendments became law, the New York Stock Exchange announced that it would begin reporting daily trades of NYSE-listed stocks as they occurred on the principal exchanges. This meant that up-to-the-minute information on the latest stock trades would be re-

---

[6]See Abken (1987) for a discussion of recent problems with portfolio insurance techniques.

ported on a *consolidated* or *composite tape,* available through the familiar stock ticker machines, regardless of which of the major American exchanges handled the transaction. While the invention of the consolidated tape was an important step in developing a national and ultimately international market system, it only provided investors with an indication of current trends in the market. No information was provided on the best bid and asked prices available anywhere in the market, even for the most actively traded stocks. The Securities and Exchange Commission responded to this need shortly after the Securities Act Amendments were passed by asking each U.S. stock exchange to make its quotations more readily available to brokers and dealers everywhere.

The first major step in that direction occurred in April 1978 with the development of the Intermarket Trading System (ITS). Through this electronic medium, brokers and specialists could compare bid and ask prices on all the major U.S. exchanges for about 700 different stocks through a central computer system that stores and dispenses price information. If the Philadelphia Exchange, for example, is offering a better price for AT&T stock than prevails on the NYSE, a broker or market specialist could immediately place an order through the Philadelphia Exchange without any additional cost. In effect, ITS brought major U.S. equities markets into direct price competition with one another for trades in the most popular corporate stocks.

Paralleling the development of ITS, the Cincinnati Stock Exchange created the National Securities Trading System (NSTS). This system permitted automated purchases and sales from the offices of member brokerage firms as well as from the floor of the exchange. Also aiding the unified market's spread was a decision by the Securities and Exchange Commission, issued as Rule 19c-3. This rule stated that any stock not being traded on an organized exchange before April 26, 1979, could be traded off the exchange by member firms. Previously, a broker or securities dealer with membership on a particular exchange could not trade listed stocks anywhere but on the floor of that exchange. Under Rule 19c-3, however, exchange members could trade *newly listed* stocks over the counter or on the exchange itself. This SEC decision brought the U.S. exchanges and OTC market into direct competition for the trading of *new* stock.

In 1979 and 1980 the National Association of Security Dealers (NASD) moved to promote an even broader market system by further automating price quotations on over-the-counter stock. Computer terminals with greatly expanded capacity were set up to include a wide array of information on bid and asked prices offered by traders who may be hundreds or thousands of miles apart. At the same time, NASD and representatives of the ITS moved to link quotations and trading on the six major U.S. exchanges electronically with OTC quotations and trading.

In February 1980, the Securities and Exchange Commission adopted new regulations aimed at improving the flow of stock price information to both brokers and investors. Previously, the NASDAQ system for securities traded over the counter had carried only "representative" bid and asked prices. Effective in 1980, however, NASDAQ was required to display on its terminals the highest bid prices and the lowest asked price present in the market. The new rule aided investors in determining what price brokers were actually paying to execute a customer purchase order or what the true sales price is when the customer places his or her shares on the market. In theory, at least, the rule promoted competition among OTC brokers and made it easier for customers to negotiate low commission rates. Another SEC rule, which took effect in October 1980, required that the consolidated tape carrying price quotations for stock listed on the major exchanges always include the best price available on *any* stock, regardless of which exchange is quoting that price.

The trend toward deregulation of the U.S. financial sector began to exert its effects on stock purchases and sales in the 1980s. On March 5, 1982, the SEC put Rule 415—the Shelf Registration Rule—into operation. This allowed many large firms selling *new* corporate stocks and bonds to register an issue with the SEC and then sell securities from the issue at any time during the next two years. *Shelf registration* substantially reduced the cost of offering new stocks and bonds and gave offering companies greater flexibility in selecting when to enter the financial marketplace to sell new securities. There is also evidence that shelf registration increased competition among investment bankers in the underwriting of new security issues, further reducing the cost of preparing and marketing new stocks and bonds.

These developments in the United States leading toward a unified national market for corporate stock were joined in the 1980s by the development of a true international equities market in which the sun would never set on purchases and sales of stock. The trading of both American corporate stock and shares of foreign companies on exchanges in Hong Kong, Singapore, Tokyo, and Sydney soon began to rival or even surpass in volume stock trading in America and in Western Europe on the London, Paris, Zurich, and Frankfurt exchanges (see Exhibit 21–4). Satellite, cable, and wire communications networks now girdle the globe, allowing traders in distant financial centers to seek out the best prices wherever they might be. Some U.S. trading firms "pass the book" to their overseas branch offices as the sun moves west to keep abreast of the growing 24-hour stock and debt markets. Other market traders have taken to hiring "all-nighters" who remain in the home office at overnight desks to monitor market movements overseas and execute trades as needed.

The efficiency of this growing worldwide security market network was demonstrated convincingly in October 1987 when stock prices on the New York Stock Exchange and the other American exchanges crashed, recording the largest one-day slide in history. Within a few hours, this stock price collapse spread around the globe with the Pacific Rim exchanges in Sydney, Hong Kong, Singapore, and Tokyo also reporting record losses. The worldwide stock price decline appeared to be worsened in the view of some market analysts by the spreading use of *program trading* in which computers at leading firms constantly monitor the thousands of prices in stock, debt, and futures markets, looking for opportunities to simultaneously buy and sell in two or more different markets and profit from any price differences they discover.

Thus, while the growing worldwide market for stock and debt securities has and will have tremendous benefits for borrowers and other users of financial services, making more funds available at lower cost, it has brought some disadvantages as well. Most notably, world financial markets appear to be less stable and predictable. Panic selling in one market soon spreads to all markets. Domestic and foreign businesses are forced to monitor the global capital markets daily to protect their sources of funding and assess their future prospects for raising new capital.

RANDOM WALK AND EFFICIENT MARKETS

Stock market behavior has figured prominently in the development of modern theories of what determines the market price and value of securities. One of the most popular of modern theories regarding the valuation of stocks and other securities is the random-walk hypothesis.

Random walk is a term used in mathematics and statistics to describe a process in which successive elements in a data series are independent of each other and therefore are essentially random and unpredictable. The theory of random walk applied to the valuation of stocks says that the future path of individual stock prices is no more predictable than the path of a series of random numbers. Each share of stock is assumed to have an *intrinsic value* based on investor expectations of the discounted value of future cash flows generated by that stock. The market price per share is an unbiased estimator of a stock's intrinsic value and reflects the latest information available concerning the issuing company's condition and future prospects. Successive changes in the price of a stock are random fluctuations around that stock's intrinsic value, and these changes are independent of the sequence of price changes which occurred in the past. In effect, stock price changes act as though they were independent random drawings from an infinite pool of possible prices. Therefore, it is not possible to predict this week's stock price from last week's stock price. Knowledge of the sequence of past price changes prior to the current time period is of little or no help in defining the probability distribution of price changes in any current or future period.

The random walk notion is not accepted by all stock market analysts. Many analysts still subscribe to chartist or *technical analysis* theories, which assume that the past behavior of a security's price is rich in information concerning the future behavior of that price. Patterns of past price behavior, technical analysts argue, will tend to reoccur in the future. For this reason, careful analysis of stock price averages and the prices of individual shares will reveal important data concerning future price movements.[7] Unfortunately, recent empirical evidence does not indicate any meaningful degree of dependence of future stock price movements on those occurring in the past. Important research studies by Fisher and Lorie (1964), Mandelbrot (1963), Fama (1965), Granger and Morgenstern (1970), and others show that recent changes in stock prices are not significantly related to past price changes. Stock price changes act as though they were independent random drawings.

Another test performed on the technical analysis theory has been to try various mechanical trading or "filter" rules to see if the investor is better off using these rules instead of a simple buy and hold strategy. Filter rules usually require the investor to buy if a security's price goes up at least Y percent and sell when the security's price declines by Y percent or more. Research studies by Alexander (1961), Fama and Blume (1966), Chang and Lewellen (1985) and others have found results that generally favor the simple buy and hold strategy, especially after brokerage commissions are considered. Average earnings generated by trading rules appear to be no better and often considerably worse than those achieved if the investor randomly selected a group of stocks representative of the market as a whole and held them for the full holding period.[8] Trading rules do not generate above-normal rates of return.

The random walk notion has been supplemented in recent years by a broader theory of stock price movements known as the efficient markets hypothesis. A market is "efficient" if scarce resources are allocated to their most productive uses. In each case those buyers willing and able to pay the highest prices for each resource must receive the resources they require. In a perfectly efficient securities market the prices of securities will fluctuate randomly around their intrinsic values and are always in equilibrium. Any temporary deviations from equilibrium prices are quickly (indeed, instantly) corrected. Information relevant to the valuation of securities is simultaneously available to all investors at virtually no cost, and existing security prices fully reflect the latest information available bearing on the future

---

[7]See, for example, Edwards and Magee (1958) and Levy (1968). Technical analysts focus upon a study of the stock market itself and not upon external factors (such as economic conditions) which influence the market. External factors are presumed to be fully reflected in share prices and the volume of stock exchange trading. Thus, all the relevant information for analyzing and predicting stock price behavior is assumed to be provided by the market itself.

[8]Technical analysts are not the only group which argues that stock price behavior is inherently predictable. Another approach, *fundamental analysis,* attempts to forecast returns from holding certain types of securities or from securities of specific firms or industries. Initially, forecasts are made of general economic conditions and then of supply and demand for the products of certain firms and industries. Complex econometric models may be used that consider such diverse factors as government monetary and fiscal policy, consumer spending and saving, inflation rates, and unemployment. The results provided by economic models are usually supplemented by a detailed analysis of individual firm financial statements and a comparison of key financial ratios for the firm with industrywide ratios.

profitability and risk of business firms. Moreover, security market prices adjust instantaneously to *new* information, and a new set of intrinsic values results, leading some investors to adjust their portfolios. All of this happens almost instantaneously, so that market price always equals intrinsic value in a state of continuous equilibrium. As a result, it is impossible in a perfectly efficient market to make economic profits by trading on the information available because, as Davidson and Froyen (1982) observe, an efficient market is one that quickly processes all relevant information.

In recent years the efficient markets hypothesis has been tested on three different levels—each representing a different assumption about how efficient the securities markets really are. In its so-called *weak form,* the efficient markets hypothesis suggests that successive changes in stock prices are independent. In other words, past stock price movements are *not* a reliable guide to future price movements. Investors cannot use historical price data to earn above-normal profits.

At a somewhat higher level of abstraction, the *semi-strong form* of the efficient markets hypothesis declares that all relevant information concerning security prices that is available to the public is fully reflected in the prices actually observed in the marketplace. Thus, security prices hover around their intrinsic equilibrium values, which reflect the latest publicly available information. Above-normal profits cannot be earned by trading on publicly available information.

Finally, the *strong form* of the efficient markets theory says that *all* forms of information—that which is publicly available and that which is available to securities analysts through private inquires—will be reflected fully in the existing set of security prices. This strong form hypothesis suggests that such groups as stock specialists, security brokers and dealers, and corporate insiders, who often have access to concealed information, cannot earn greater profits than investors who do not have access to such information. Investors should expect to earn only a normal rate of return for the amount of risk they are willing to bear.

What does available research evidence have to say about these various levels of market efficiency? How efficient are securities markets? Research studies generally find that security prices respond promptly to new, publicly available information, including government policy actions. Prices do appear to fluctuate around a base (or intrinsic) value in an essentially random and unbiased manner, as noted in excellent reviews by Fama (1970, 1976) and Pearce (1987). Moreover, studies of the performance of mutual funds, such as the recent project by Chang and Lewellen (1985), and of other professional portfolio management firms indicate that these firms do *not* consistently outperform randomly selected portfolios of securities bearing comparable risk. In general, the weak and semi-strong forms of the efficient markets hypothesis are validated by recent research findings. However, there is disagreement and some contrary evidence regarding the strong form of the efficient markets theory. For example, some researchers (such as Givoly and Palmon, 1985) find evidence that traders who possess inside information (including corporate executives, brokers, and stock specialists) have been able to score impressive gains beyond those available to the average investor. The strong form of the efficient markets hypothesis, therefore, is not consistent with all the facts for all time periods. Moreover, there is evidence that the stock of smaller firms tends persistently to earn higher returns than the stock of larger firms (as reported, for example by Lustig and Leinbach, 1983).

Nevertheless, on balance, the securities markets must be regarded as efficient channels for directing the flow of savings into investment. Changes in security prices do appear to conform generally to a form of the random walk process in which daily price quotations cluster about a security's intrinsic value, reflecting the latest information available. Thus, above-normal profits from using publicly available information as a guide for security trades are most unlikely, because that information is already included in current security prices.

A buy and hold strategy coupled with random selection of securities from the entire market's portfolio will, in most cases, yield returns at least as good as those earned by professional traders who rapidly turn over their portfolios. Of course, financial analysts with extraordinary ability to uncover new information and act quickly are likely to achieve above-average rates of return, at least for short periods. Moreover, individual investors differ in their financial goals and circumstances, and professional advice is frequently required to meet those specialized needs.

SUMMARY

The market for corporate stock is the best known to the general public and the most widely followed of all securities markets. U.S. corporations alone have outstanding well over a trillion dollars in equity shares, with millions of shares changing hands each day. Prices of the most actively traded stocks worldwide are quoted daily in the financial press and watched avidly by millions of investors around the globe.

Though one of the oldest of the securities markets, the market for corporate shares even now is in a period of transition. Spurred by legislation and competition within the securities industry, electronic links between the major exchanges and over-the-counter markets today help to ensure that investors, regardless of location, can transact business at competitive prices. Rapid developments in the technology of information transfer are breaking down the barriers to free and open trading posed by geography and outmoded practices and regulations. Centralized computer systems, coupled with cheaper electronic methods of data transfer and display, have paved the way for integrating existing markets into a new international system, retaining the benefits of experience while allowing ample room for innovation. A true global market for trading in common and preferred stock and stock options is emerging. And the benefits of stronger competition and a freer flow of information to all market participants are not likely to be confined to equities alone. Ultimately, all securities markets, all investors, and the financial system as a whole will benefit from the era of change and innovation through which the stock market is now passing.

STUDY QUESTIONS

1. In what important ways does the stock market differ from the other securities markets we have dealt with up to this point?

2. What are the essential characteristics of *common stock?* What priority do common stockholders have in the event a corporation is liquidated? What limits the amount of shares a company may issue?

3. Discuss the nature of *preferred stock.* In what ways are preferred shares similar to "debt" and in what ways are they "equity" securities?

4. What are the principal differences between trading in stocks OTC and trading on the organized exchanges? How would you rate these two markets in terms of their advantages for the small investor? The large investor?

5. Explain the possible link between economic conditions and the performance of the stock market. Why do stock price movements tend to *lead* changes in general economic conditions?

6. What is *shelf registration?* What benefits does it offer to security issuers and the financial markets?

7. What is the *random walk* hypothesis? Does available research evidence tend to support or deny the validity of this hypothesis?

8. Explain the difference between fundamental security analysis and technical analysis. Which approach is likely to yield the best returns to the investor in today's markets, according to recent research findings?

9. What is an *efficient market?* What are the consequences of market efficiency for the behavior of security prices?

10. Recent research concerning the implications of the *efficient markets hypothesis* focuses on three different theories concerning the degree of market efficiency. These are known as the weak, semi-strong, and strong form hypotheses. Explain the basic differences among these hypotheses. Which of the three is supported by recent research?

SELECTED REFERENCES

Abken, Peter A. "An Introduction to Portfolio Insurance." *Economic Review,* Federal Reserve Bank of Atlanta, November–December 1987, pp. 2–25.

Alexander, S. "Price Movements in Speculative Markets: Trends or Random Walks." *Industrial Management Review,* May 1961, pp. 7–26.

Black, Fischer, and Myron Scholes. "The Pricing of Options and Corporate Liabilities." *Journal of Political Economy* 81 (1973), pp. 637–59.

Chang, Eric C., and Wilbur G. Lewellen. "An Arbitrage Pricing Approach to Evaluating Mutual Fund Performance." *The Journal of Financial Research* 8, no. 1 (Spring 1985), pp. 15–30.

Corrigan, E. Gerald. "Coping with Globally Integrated Markets." *Quarterly Review,* Federal Reserve Bank of New York, Winter 1987, pp. 1–5.

Cootner, Paul H. "Stock Prices: Random versus Systematic Changes." *Industrial Management Review,* Spring 1962, pp. 24–45.

Edwards, R. D., John Magee, Jr. *Technical Analysis of Stock Trends.* 4th ed. Springfield, MA: Magee, 1958.

Fama, Eugene F. "The Behavior of Stock Market Prices." *Journal of Business,* January 1965, pp. 34–105.

———. "Efficient Capital Markets: A Review of Theory and Empirical Work." *Journal of Finance* 25 (1970), pp. 383–417.

———. *Foundations of Finance.* New York: Basic Books, 1976.

Fama, E. F., and M. E. Blume. "Filter Rules and Stock Market Trading." *Journal of Business,* January 1966, pp. 226–41.

Fisher, L., and J. Lorie. "Rates of Return on Investments in Common Stock: The Year-by-Year Record, 1926–1965." *Journal of Business,* January 1964.

Givoly, Dan, and Dan Palmon. "Insider Trading and the Exploitation of Inside Information: Some Empirical Evidence." *Journal of Business,* January 1985, pp. 69–87.

Granger, C. W., and D. Morgenstern. *Predictability of Stock Market Prices.* Lexington, MA: Lexington Books, 1970.

Jensen, Michael C. "Some Anomalous Evidence Regarding Market Efficiency." *Journal of Financial Economics* 6 (1978), pp. 95–101.

Levy, R. A. *The Relative Strength Concept of Common Stock Forecasting.* Larchmont, NY: Investors Intelligence, 1968.

Lustig, Ivan L., and Philip A. Leinbach. "The Small Firm Effect." *Financial Analysts Journal,* May–June 1983, pp. 46–49.

Mandelbrot, Benoit. "The Variation of Certain Speculative Prices." *Journal of Business,* October 1963, pp. 394–419.

Merrick, John J. "Fact and Fantasy about Stock Index Futures Program Trading," *Business Review,* Federal Reserve Bank of Philadelphia, September–October 1987, pp. 13–25.

Mulhern, John J. "The National Stock Market: Taking Shape." *Business Review,* Federal Reserve Bank of Philadelphia, September–October 1980, pp. 3–11.

Pearce, Douglas K. "Challenges to the Concept of Stock Market Efficiency." *Economic Review*, Federal Reserve Bank of Kansas City, September–October 1987, pp. 16–23.

Rogowski, Robert J., and Eric Sorensen. "Deregulation in Investment Banking: Shelf Registrations, Structure, and Performance." *Financial Management*, Spring 1985, pp. 5–15.

Part Seven

Government in the Financial Markets

Chapter 22

Central Banking and the Role of the Federal Reserve

Learning Objectives in This Chapter

- To explore the many roles played by central banks in general (and the Federal Reserve System in particular) in the economy and financial system of a nation.

- To understand how and why the Federal Reserve System came to be established as the U.S. central bank.

- To examine how the Federal Reserve System is organized to carry out its many roles in the economy and the financial system.

Key Terms and Concepts in This Chapter

Central bank	Federal Open Market Committee (FOMC)	Member banks
Federal Reserve System		Fiscal agent
Board of Governors	Federal Reserve banks	Monetary policy

ONE of the most important financial institutions in any modern economy is the central bank. Basically, a central bank is an agency of government which has important public policy functions in monitoring the operation of the financial system and controlling the growth of its money supply. Central banks ordinarily do not deal directly with the public; rather they are "bankers' banks," communicating with commercial banks and securities dealers in carrying out their essential policymaking functions. The central bank of the United States is the Federal Reserve System, a creature of Congress charged with issuing currency, regulating the banking system, and taking measures to protect the value of the dollar and promote full employment. In this and the two succeeding chapters we examine in detail the nature and impact of central bank operations and the major problems of policymaking faced by Federal Reserve money managers today.

THE ROLE OF CENTRAL BANKS IN THE ECONOMY
Control of the Money Supply

Central banks, including the Federal Reserve System, perform several important functions in a modern economy. The first and most important of their functions is *control of the money supply*.

What is money? Money is anything that serves as a *medium of exchange* in the purchase of goods and services. Money has another important function, however—serving as a *store of value,* for money is a financial asset that may be used to store purchasing power until it is needed by the owner.[1] If we define money exclusively as a medium of exchange, then the sum of all currency and coin held by the public plus the value of all publicly held checking accounts and other deposits against which drafts may be made (such as NOWs and money market accounts) would constitute the money supply. If we define money as a store of value, on the other hand, then time and savings accounts at commercial banks and other nonbank financial intermediaries, such as credit unions and savings banks, would also be considered important components of the money supply. In Chapter 24 we will note that several different definitions of the money supply may be useful for the purpose of implementing and monitoring central bank policies.

However we define money, the power to regulate its quantity and value was delegated by Congress early in this century to the Federal Reserve System. The Fed has become not only the principal source of currency and coin (pocket money) used by the public, but also the principal government agency responsible for stabilizing the value of the dollar and protecting its integrity in the international financial markets. Why is control of the money supply so important? One reason is that changes in the money supply are closely linked to changes in economic activity. A number of studies in recent

---

[1]See Chapter 2 for a discussion of the functions performed by money in the economy.

years have found a statistically significant relationship between current and lagged changes in the money supply and movements in gross national product (GNP).[2] The essential implication of these studies is that, if the central bank carefully controls the rate of growth of money, it can influence the growth rate of the economy as a whole. We will have more to say on this important issue in Chapter 24.

Another important reason for controlling the money supply is that, in the absence of effective controls, money in the form of paper notes or bank deposits could expand virtually without limit. The marginal cost of creating additional units of money is close to zero. Therefore, the banking system, the government, or both are capable of increasing the money supply well beyond the economy's capacity to produce goods and services. Because this action would bring on severe inflation, disrupt the payments mechanism, and eventually bring business activity to a halt, it is not surprising that modern governments have come to rely so heavily on central banks as guardians of the quantity and value of their currencies. The Federal Reserve System enters the financial markets frequently in an attempt to control domestic price inflation in order to protect the purchasing power of the dollar at home, while occasionally intervening in foreign currency markets to protect the dollar abroad.

Stabilizing the Money and Capital Markets

A second vital function of central banking is *stabilization of the money and capital markets.* As we have seen, the financial system must transmit savings to those who require funds for investment so that the economy can grow. If the system of money and capital markets is to work efficiently, however, the public must have confidence in financial institutions and be willing to commit its savings to them. If the financial markets are unruly, with extremely volatile fluctuations in interest rates and security prices, or if financial institutions are prone to frequent collapse, public confidence in the financial system might well be lost. The flow of capital funds would dry up, resulting in a drastic slowing in the rate of economic growth and a rise in unemployment. All central banks play a vital role in fostering the mature development of financial markets and in ensuring a stable flow of funds through those markets.

Pursuing this objective, the Federal Reserve System will, from time to time, provide funds to major securities dealers when they have difficulty financing their portfolios so that buyers and sellers may easily acquire or sell securities. When the money supply and interest rates rise or fall more rapidly than seems consistent with economic goals, the Fed will again intervene in the financial markets. The central bank may change the rates

---

[2]See, for example, the studies by Burger (1971), Carlson (1980), Carlson and Hein (1980), and Poole and Lieberman (1972).

it charges banks on direct loans or engage in securities trading in an attempt to moderate changes occurring in the money and capital markets.

Lender of Last Resort

Another essential function of central banks is to serve as a *lender of last resort*. This means providing liquid funds to those financial institutions in need, especially when alternative sources of funds have dried up. For example, as discussed in Chapter 15, the Federal Reserve through its discount window will provide funds to selected deposit-type financial institutions, upon their request, to cover short-term cash deficiencies. As we will see, before the Fed was created, one of the weaknesses in the financial system of the United States was the absence of a lender of last resort to aid financial institutions squeezed by severe liquidity pressures.

Maintaining and Improving the Payments Mechanism

Finally, central banks have a role to play in *maintaining and improving a nation's payments mechanism*. This involves clearing checks, providing an adequate supply of currency and coin, wiring funds, and preserving confidence in the value of the fundamental monetary unit. A smoothly functioning and efficient payments mechanism is vital for carrying on business and commerce. If checks cannot be cleared in timely fashion or if the public cannot get the currency and coin it needs to carry out transactions, business activity will be severely curtailed. The result might well be large-scale unemployment and a decline in both capital investment and the rate of economic growth.

THE GOALS AND CHANNELS OF CENTRAL BANKING

Central banking is goal-oriented. Since World War II, the United States and several other industrialized nations have accepted the premise that government is responsible to its citizens for maintaining high levels of employment, combating inflation, and supporting sustained growth in the economy. This is a relatively new idea. In earlier periods, governments were assigned a much smaller role in the economic system and much less was expected of them by their citizens. It was felt that "automatic" mechanisms operated within the economy to provide stability and high employment in the long run. One of the bitter lessons of the Great Depression of the 1930s was that these mechanisms can break down and that innovative and skillfully managed government policies may be needed to restore the economy's stability and growth.

Central banking in the United States and in most other nations is directed toward four major goals:

1. Full employment of resources.
2. Reasonable stability in the general price level of all goods and services.
3. Sustained economic growth.
4. A stable balance-of-payments position for the nation vis-à-vis the rest of the world.

Through its influence over interest rates and the growth of the money supply, the central bank is able to influence the economy's progress toward each of these goals. Achievement of all of these goals simultaneously has proved to be exceedingly difficult, however, as the recent track record of the economy demonstrates. One reason is that the goals often *conflict*. Pursuit of price stability and an improved balance-of-payments position, for example, may require higher interest rates and restricted credit availability— policies which tend to increase unemployment and slow investment spending and growth. Central bank policymaking is a matter of accepting *tradeoffs* (compromises) among multiple goals. For example, the central bank can pursue policies leading to a lower rate of inflation and a stronger dollar in international markets, but probably at the price of some additional unemployment and slower economic growth in the short run.

Central banking in most Western nations, including the United States, operates principally through the *marketplace*. Modern central banks operate as a balance wheel in promoting and stabilizing the flow of savings from surplus-spending units to deficit-spending units. They try to assure a smooth and orderly flow of funds through the money and capital markets so that adequate financing is available for worthwhile investment projects. This means, among other things, avoiding panics due to sudden shortages of available credit or sharp declines in security prices. However, most of the actions taken by the central bank to promote a smooth flow of funds are carried out through the marketplace rather than by government order. For example, the central bank may encourage interest rates to rise in order to reduce borrowing and spending and combat inflation, but it does not usually allocate credit to particular borrowers. The private sector, working through supply and demand forces in the marketplace, is left to make its own decisions about how much borrowing and spending will take place at the current level of interest rates and who is to receive credit.

The Channels through Which Central Banks Work

Later on we will examine in some detail how the Federal Reserve System affects domestic and international economic conditions. It is useful at this point, however, to give a brief overview of the channels through which modern central banks influence conditions in the economy and financial system. Central bank policy affects the economy as a whole by making:

Exhibit 22–1   **The Channels of Central Bank Policy**

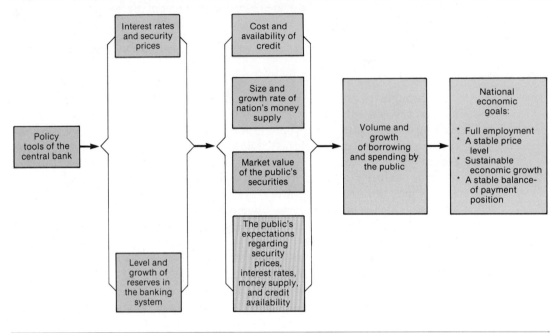

1. Changes in the cost and availability of credit to businesses, consumers, and governments.
2. Changes in the volume and rate of growth of the money supply.
3. Changes in the wealth of investors as reflected in the market value of their security holdings.
4. Changes in the public's expectations regarding future money and credit conditions (see Exhibit 22–1).

The central bank has a number of policy tools at its command that it can use to influence the cost of credit (interest rates), the value (prices) of securities, money supply volume and growth, and the public's expectations regarding future security prices, interest rates, and credit conditions. In the United States the principal policy tools used by the central bank are open-market operations, changes in required reserves held by depository institutions, and changes in the discount rate on central bank loans.[3] In turn,

---

[3] Different central banks emphasize different policy tools. For example, the Bank of England relies principally on changes in its basic lending rate to influence economic and financial conditions, while the Bank of Canada uses changes in reserve requirements as its main policy tool. As we will see in Chapter 23, the Federal Reserve System relies mainly on open-market operations to pursue the goals of U.S. economic policy.

changes in interest rates, security prices, and bank reserves influence the cost and availability of credit. If borrowers find that credit is less available and more expensive to obtain, they are likely to restrain borrowing and reduce spending for both capital and consumer goods. This results in a slowing in the economy's rate of growth and perhaps a reduction in inflationary pressures. Second, if the central bank can reduce the rate of growth of the money supply, this policy will eventually slow the growth of income and production in the economy due to a reduction in the demand for goods and services. Finally, if the central bank raises interest rates and therefore lowers security prices, this will tend to reduce the market value of the public's holdings of stocks, bonds, and other securities. The result is a decline in the value of investors' wealth, altering borrowing and spending plans and ultimately influencing employment, prices, and the economy's rate of growth.

In recent years economic research has suggested a fourth channel for central bank policy to affect the economy—its impact on the public's expectations regarding credit costs, money supply growth, and the future value of loans and securities. If the central bank's operations result in shifting public expectations, businesses and consumers will alter their borrowing, spending, and investing plans (unfortunately not always in the direction the central bank wishes), which can have profound effects on the economy's rate of growth, jobs, and inflation. We will have more to say about these important channels of central bank policy in Chapters 23 and 24.

THE HISTORY OF THE FEDERAL RESERVE SYSTEM

The United States was one of the last major nations in the Western world to charter a central bank. The Bank of England was established in 1694; the Bank of France and the central banks of Switzerland and Italy were founded during the 18th century. Most major industrialized nations early in their history recognized the need for an institution that would provide a measure of stability and control over the growth of money and credit. Public officials in the United States were hesitant to charter a central bank, however, out of fear that it would possess great financial power, restrict the availability of credit to a growing nation, and be difficult to control. However, a series of economic and financial crises in the late 19th and early 20th centuries forced Congress to act.

Problems in the Early U.S. Banking System

To fully understand why the Federal Reserve System was created, we must understand the problems that plagued the U.S. financial system throughout much of the nation's early history. Many of these problems were born in the years prior to the Civil War when the states, not the federal government, regulated and controlled the nation's banking system. Unfortunately, with a few notable exceptions, the states did a poor job. Charters for new banks were awarded by state legislatures and were therefore subject to political lobbying and influence peddling. If a new bank's organizers had the right political connections, a charter could be obtained by individuals with little banking experience and with minimal capital invested in the business.

Deposit banking was not as popular then as it is today. Most people preferred hard money (currency and coins) to deposits. As a result, banks made loans simply by printing and issuing their own paper notes, which circulated as currency. Because few controls existed, there was a tendency to issue these notes well beyond the financial strength of the bank making the loan. Frequently charters were granted to "wildcat banks" that would issue a large quantity of notes and then disappear. Some banks, promising to redeem their notes in gold or silver coin, would set up "redemption centers" in locations nearly impossible for the public to reach, such as in the middle of a swamp. Needless to say, there was a high failure rate among these poorly capitalized, ill-managed institutions, resulting in substantial losses to unlucky depositors.

Responding to these problems and also to the tremendous financial strain imposed by the Civil War, Congress passed the National Banking Act in 1863. This act and its subsequent amendments authorized the open establishment of federally licensed commercial banks, subject to regulations imposed by a newly created office, the Comptroller of the Currency—a part of the U.S. Treasury Department. Any group of businesspeople could organize a so-called *national bank,* provided they could show that the new bank would be profitable within a reasonable period of time (usually within three years), meet the minimum equity capital requirements imposed by the Comptroller's office, and not endanger the viability of banks already operating in the local area. Under the provisions of the National Banking Act, the chartering of commercial banks was, in the main, removed from the political sphere and made subject to carefully spelled-out rules. At the same time, Congress attempted to drive state-chartered banks into the national banking system by imposing a 10 percent tax on state bank notes. It was argued that most bankers would prefer the more liberal state regulations and avoid seeking national bank charters unless they were forced to do so.

In order to help finance the Civil War, Congress authorized national banks to issue their own notes as circulating currency. However, these notes had to be collateralized by U.S. government securities. Under the terms of the National Banking Act, federally chartered banks could issue notes up to 90 percent of the value of Treasury securities they deposited with the Comptroller of the Currency. The result was to create a money or cash medium under federal control and help pay for the Civil War by creating a demand from banks for U.S. government securities.

Even more important, the National Banking Act created a *dual banking system,* with both federal and state authorities having important regulatory powers over commercial banks. Unfortunately, these authorities were given overlapping powers, and in recent years competition between federal and state bank regulatory agencies has sometimes resulted in actions detrimental to the public interest. Moreover, one of the principal aims of the federal program—to drive out state-chartered banks—was not achieved. The state banks survived only because of the growing popularity of deposit banking which swept the nation in the years following the Civil War. Instead of issuing paper notes, commercial banks increasingly began to make loans by simply creating a deposit on their books in the borrower's name—the practice followed today. Acceptance by the public of deposits instead of notes led to the disappearance of state bank notes, making the federal government's tax on them ineffective.

Although the number of state-chartered banks had dwindled to only about 500 out of an estimated bank population of 10,000, state banks made a dramatic comeback late in the 19th century and soon outnumbered national banks. As we saw in Chapter 4, there are about twice as many state-chartered banks as national banks today, though the federally chartered institutions average much larger in size and include most of the United States's largest banking institutions.

Creation of the Federal Reserve System

Several festering problems (including some traceable to the provisions of the National Banking Act) resulted in the creation of the Federal Reserve System. For one thing, the new national bank notes proved to be unresponsive to the growing need for a money or cash medium. The need for money and credit grew rapidly as the United States became more heavily industrialized and the Midwest and Far West opened up to immigration. Farmers and ranchers in these areas of the nation demanded an "elastic" supply of money and credit—adequate to their needs at relatively low cost. As we will soon see, the new Federal Reserve System would attempt to deal with this problem by issuing a currency of its own and by closer control over the growth of the nation's supply of money and credit.

As deposit banking and the writing of checks became increasingly popular, another serious problem appeared. The process of clearing and collecting checks was slow and expensive. Then as now, most checks written by the public were local in character, moving funds from the account of one local customer to that of another. These checks normally are cleared routinely through the local clearinghouse, which is simply a location where representatives of local banks meet daily to exchange bundles of checks drawn on each other's banks. For checks sent outside the local area, however, the collection process is more complicated, with some checks passing through several banks before reaching their final destination.

Before the Federal Reserve System was created, many banks, especially smaller, outlying institutions, charged a fee (exchange charge) for the clearing and redemption of checks. This fee was usually calculated as a percentage of the par (or face) value of each check. Banks levying the fee were called *no-par* banks because they refused to honor checks at their full face value. To avoid exchange fees, bankers would route nonlocal checks they received only through banks accepting and redeeming them at par. Often this meant routing a check through scores of banks in distant cities until days or weeks had elapsed before the check was finally cleared. Such a delay was not just annoying, but served as an impediment to commercial transactions and the speedy allocation of funds within the financial system. Exchange charges resulted in needless inefficiency and increased the true cost of business transactions far above their nominal cost. A new national check-clearing system was needed which honored checks at par and moved them swiftly between payee and payer. As we will soon see, this responsibility too was given to the Federal Reserve System, which insisted that all checks cleared through its system be honored at full face (par) value without exchange charges.

A third problem with the banking and financial system of that time was recurring liquidity crises. Then as now, money and bank reserves tended to concentrate in the nation's leading financial centers, such as New York City, Chicago, Dallas, and San Francisco, where the greatest need for loanable funds existed. Bank reserves flowed into the major cities as smaller banks in outlying areas deposited their reserves with larger banking institutions to earn greater returns. However, when the pressures for agricultural credit increased in rural areas, many country banks were forced to draw upon their reserves in the cities, and the larger city banks, in turn, had to sell securities and call loans in order to come up with the necessary funds. When the reserve demands of country banks were larger than expected, security prices in the nation's major financial centers plummeted due to massive forced selling of bank-held securities. Panic selling by other investors soon followed, leading to chaos in the financial marketplace.

The nation's banking system clearly needed a lender of ready cash to provide liquidity to those banks with heavy cash drains and to protect the stability and smooth functioning of the financial system. A serious financial panic in 1907 finally led to the creation of the Federal Reserve System. In 1908 Congress created a National Monetary Commission to study the financial needs of the nation. The commission's recommendations were forwarded to Congress and ultimately resulted in passage of the Federal Reserve Act, signed into law by President Wilson in December 1913. The Federal Reserve banks opened for business as World War I began in Europe.

The Early Structure of the Federal Reserve System

The first Federal Reserve System was quite different from the Fed of today. The original Federal Reserve Act reflected a mix of diverse viewpoints—an effort to reconcile competing political and economic interests. There was, on the one hand, great fear that the Fed would have too much control over the nation's financial affairs and operate against the best interests of important segments of American society. For example, small businesses, consumer groups, farmers, and ranchers were concerned that the Fed might pursue restrictive credit policies leading to high interest rates. In addition, it was recognized that the Federal Reserve would become a major financial institution wherever it was located. Any city or state that housed a Federal Reserve bank was likely to become a major financial center.

Responding to these various needs and interest groups, Congress created a truly "decentralized" central bank. Not 1 but 12 Federal Reserve banks were chartered, stretching across the continental United States but located predominantly in the East, where the largest cities and banks were situated. Each bank was assigned its own district, over which it possessed important regulatory powers. In addition, 24 branch banks were created to serve local areas and satisfy those not fortunate enough to have a full-fledged Federal Reserve bank in their area. A supervisory board of seven members was set up in Washington, DC, to promote a common monetary policy for the nation. In fact, however, the regional Federal Reserve banks possessed the essential monetary tools and made the key policy decisions during the Fed's early history.

Goals and Policy Tools of the Federal Reserve System

To deal with the economic and financial problems of that day, the Federal Reserve Act permitted each regional Reserve bank to open up a discount window where eligible banks could borrow reserves for short periods of time. However, borrowing banks were required to present high-quality, short-term business loans (commercial paper) to the discount window to secure the loans they needed. The Fed's chief policy tool of the day was the *discount rate* charged on these loans, with each Reserve bank having the authority to set its own discount rate. By varying this rate, the Reserve banks could encourage or discourage commercial banks' propensity to discount commercial paper and borrow reserves from the Fed. Central bankers could promote easy or tight credit conditions and indirectly influence the overall volume of bank loans.

The Federal Reserve banks were given authority to issue their own paper notes to serve as a circulating currency, but these notes had to be 100 percent backed by Fed holdings of commercial paper, plus a 40 percent gold reserve. Almost as an afterthought, Congress authorized the Reserve banks to trade

U.S. government securities in the open market, known as *open market operations*—the Fed's principal policy tool today. Reserve requirements were imposed on deposits held by member banks of the system, but the Fed could not change these requirements. In contrast to the provisions of the earlier National Banking Act, required reserves had to be held on deposit at the Federal Reserve banks instead of in correspondent balances (deposits) with other commercial banks.

Slowly but surely, economic, financial, and political forces combined to amend the original Federal Reserve Act and remake the character and methods of the central bank. The leading causes of change were war, economic recessions, and more recently, persistent inflation. For example, in order to combat economic recessions, fight wars, and pursue desired spending programs, the U.S. government issued billions of dollars in debt. As the debt began to grow, it seemed only "logical" to permit greater use of U.S. government securities in Federal Reserve operations. Banks were quickly authorized to use government securities as backing for loans from the Fed's discount window. The Fed itself was called upon to play a major role in smoothing and stabilizing the market for U.S. government securities to ensure that the Treasury would have little difficulty in refinancing its maturing debt. Government securities were made eligible as collateral for the issue of new Federal Reserve bank notes.

More than any other historical event, however, it was the Great Depression of the 1930s that changed the character of the Federal Reserve. Faced with the collapse of the banking system and unprecedented unemployment—some estimates suggest that a quarter of the nation's labor force was thrown out of work during the 1930s—Congress entrusted the Fed with sweeping monetary powers. Significant changes were made in the central bank's operating structure and lines of authority.

The seven-member Board of Governors in Washington, DC, became the central administrative and policymaking group for the Fed. From 1933 on, any changes in discount rates charged by the Reserve banks have had to be approved in advance by the Board of Governors. The board was granted authority to set minimum reserve requirements on deposits and maximum interest rates that member banks could pay on those deposits. In order to control speculative buying of stocks, the Reserve Board was empowered to set margin requirements specifying what proportion of a security's market value the investor could borrow against to purchase the security. Recognizing that open market operations in U.S. government securities were rapidly becoming the Fed's main policy tool, a powerful policymaking body—the Federal Open Market Committee—was created to oversee the conduct of open market operations. And the majority of voting seats on this committee were given to the Federal Reserve Board. In summary, the Great Depression brought about a *concentration of power* within the Federal Reserve System so that the Fed could pursue a single unified policy and speak with one voice concerning the nation's monetary affairs.

Exhibit 22–2   **How the Federal Reserve System Is Organized**

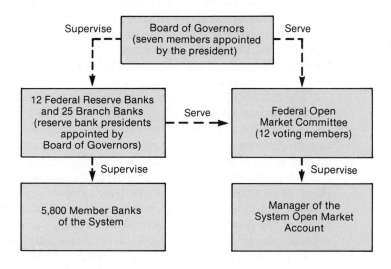

HOW THE FED IS ORGANIZED

The Federal Reserve System today has an organizational structure that resembles a *pyramid*. As Exhibit 22–2 shows, the apex of that pyramid is the Board of Governors—the Federal Reserve's chief policymaking and administrative group. At the middle level of the pyramid are the Federal Reserve banks, which carry out system policy and provide essential services to banks and other depository financial institutions in their region, and the Federal Open Market Committee. The bottom of the pyramid contains the member banks of the system, which the Fed supervises and regulates, and the manager of the System Open Market Account, who is responsible for buying and selling securities to achieve the goals of Fed monetary policy.

Board of Governors of the Federal Reserve System

The key administrative body within the Federal Reserve System is the Board of Governors. The board consists of seven persons appointed by the president of the United States and confirmed by the Senate for maximum 14-year terms. Terms of office are staggered, with one board member's appointment ending every two years. When a member of the Federal Reserve Board resigns or dies, the president may appoint a new person to complete the remainder of the unexpired term, and that member may be reappointed to a subsequent full term. However, no member who completes a full term can be reappointed to the Board of Governors. The president designates one member of the board as its chairman and another, as vice chairman, and both serve four-year terms in those positions. In selecting new board members the president is required to seek a "fair representation of the financial, agricultural, industrial, and commercial interests and geographical divisions of the country" and may not choose more than one member from any one Federal Reserve district.

The powers of the Federal Reserve Board are extensive. The board sets reserve requirements on deposits held by member banks and other depository institutions subject to its rules,[4] reviews and determines the discount rate charged on loans to depository institutions, sets margin requirements on purchases of securities, and provides leadership in the conduct of open-market operations through the Federal Open Market Committee. Besides its monetary policy functions, the board supervises the activities of the 12 Reserve banks and has supervisory and regulatory control over member banks of the system. It regulates all bank holding companies, foreign banks entering the United States, and the overseas activities of U.S. banks.

In principle, the board is independent of both the Congress and the executive branch of the federal government. This independence is supported by terms of office much longer than the president's and by the fact that the Fed does not depend on Congress for operating funds. The Federal Reserve supports itself from revenue generated by selling its services (such as clearing checks and shipping currency and coin), making loans through the discount window, and trading securities in the open market. These monies are not retained by the Fed, because it is operated in the public interest and not for profit. All net income left over after expenses, dividends, and minimal allocations to equity reserves is transferred to the U.S. Treasury. For example, in 1986 the Fed reported net earnings of just over $18 billion, of which $17.8 billion was paid to the U.S. Treasury, helping to reduce tax collections from the private sector.

The Federal Open Market Committee and Manager of the System Open Market Account

Aside from the Federal Reserve Board, the other key policymaking group within the system is the Federal Open Market Committee (FOMC). It has been called the most important committee of individuals in the United States because its decisions concerning the conduct of monetary policy and the cost and availability of credit affect the lives of millions of people. Membership on the FOMC consists of the seven members of the Federal Reserve Board

---

[4] Any depository institution—commercial bank, savings and loan association, mutual savings bank, or credit union—accepting transaction accounts (such as checking accounts, NOWs, or money market deposits) or nonpersonal time deposits (mainly business CDs) must hold legal reserves behind those accounts as specified by the Federal Reserve Board.

and the presidents of the Reserve banks. Only members of the board and five of the Reserve bank presidents may vote when a final decision is reached on the future conduct of monetary policy, however. The president of the Federal Reserve Bank of New York is a permanent voting member of the FOMC, while the other 11 Reserve bank presidents rotate the four remaining voting seats among themselves. Each Reserve bank president serves a voting term of one year beginning on March 1.

By tradition, the chairman of the Federal Reserve Board and the president of the New York Federal Reserve bank serve as chairman and vice chairman of the FOMC. The law stipulates that the FOMC will meet in Washington, DC, at least four times a year. In practice, however, the committee meets at least once every four to six weeks and more frequently if emergencies develop. Between regularly scheduled meetings, telephone conferences may occur, and the members of the FOMC may be asked to cast votes by telephone or telegram. FOMC meetings are not open to the public because confidential financial information frequently is discussed and also because the Fed wants to avoid sending false signals to the financial marketplace. Only Federal Reserve Board members, selected board staff, the Reserve bank presidents and their aides, and the manager and deputy manager of the System Open Market Account are permitted to attend FOMC meetings.

The name Federal Open Market Committee implies that this committee's sole concern is with the conduct of Federal Reserve open market operations in securities, the most important policy tool of the system. In fact, the FOMC reviews current economic and financial conditions and considers all aspects and tools of monetary policy at its meetings. Once a consensus is reached concerning the appropriate future course for monetary policy, a directive is given orally and in writing to the manager of the System Open Market Account (SOMA), who is a vice president of the Federal Reserve Bank of New York. The SOMA manager is told in general terms how open market operations should be conducted in the weeks ahead, and the FOMC's targets for money-supply growth and interest rates.[5] Decisions made by the FOMC and actions of the SOMA manager at the securities trading desk in New York are binding on the entire Federal Reserve System.

The Federal Reserve Banks

When the Federal Reserve System was created in 1913, the nation was divided into 12 districts, with one Federal Reserve bank in each district responsible for supervising and providing services to the member banks located there. Reserve banks were established in the cities of Atlanta, Boston, Chicago, Cleveland, Dallas, Kansas City, Minneapolis, New York, Philadelphia, Richmond, San Francisco, and St. Louis. In addition, 24 branches

---

[5] See Chapter 23 for an example of a recent FOMC policy directive.

(later expanded to 25) were created to serve particular regions within each of the 12 districts. (Figure 22–2 indicates the boundaries of each Federal Reserve District and the locations of the 12 Reserve banks and their branch offices.) The Reserve banks and their branches are an integral part of the Fed's efforts to supervise and regulate the banking system, ensure a smooth flow of payments, and control the growth of money and credit.

Using computers and high-speed sorting machines, the regional Reserve banks route checks and other cash items drawn on financial institutions in one city and deposited in another. While most checks are not cleared through the Fed, it handles billions of checks and other paper information items each year. The Federal Reserve maintains a nationwide electronic network (known as Fed wire) to transfer funds and securities in minutes. Approximately 30 automated clearinghouses (ACHs) are operated by the Reserve banks and their branches to handle the direct deposit of payrolls, mortgage payments, and other funds transfer requests by electronic means instead of through pieces of paper. The Reserve banks ship currency and coin to banks and other depository institutions at those times when the public needs more pocket money and store excess currency and coin in their vaults when less pocket money is needed.

The Reserve banks serve as the federal government's *fiscal agent*. This involves keeping the operating financial account of the U.S. Treasury, delivering and redeeming U.S. government securities, and paying interest on securities issued by the Treasury and various federal agencies. The Reserve banks also accept deposits of federal income, excise, and unemployment taxes and honor checks drawn against the Treasury. In addition to serving as the federal government's fiscal agent, the Reserve banks closely supervise the activities of member banks within their districts. They conduct field examinations of all state-chartered member banks and supervise bank holding companies headquartered in their region of the nation.

The Reserve banks play a significant role in the conduct of the nation's money and credit policy. Each reserve bank houses a research division to study regional economic and financial developments and convey this information to the Board of Governors and to the Federal Open Market Committee. While only 5 of the 12 Reserve bank presidents are voting members of the FOMC, all 12 Reserve bank presidents attend FOMC meetings to report on conditions and events in their region and give their views on the appropriate course for monetary policy. The Reserve banks also administer the discount windows where loans are made to financial institutions in their district, and therefore have a direct impact on the growth of money and credit.

Each Federal Reserve bank is a corporation chartered by Congress. Officially, the Reserve banks are owned by the member banks of their districts, who select a majority of each bank's board of directors. In fact, the regional Reserve banks are closely controlled by the Federal Reserve Board, which appoints three of their nine directors and approves appointments of all officers. While under the terms of the original Federal Reserve Act the Reserve banks could set the discount rate on loans to depository institutions, these rate changes must now be approved by the board in Washington. The regional banks are required to participate in all open market transactions on behalf of the system. These purchases and sales are centered in the FOMC, but the Reserve banks must provide the securities needed for open market sales and also take their pro rata share of any purchases the system makes.

The Member Banks of the Fed's System

The member banks of the Federal Reserve System consist of national banks, which are required to join the system, and state-chartered banks that agree to conform to the Fed's rules. Today, Federal Reserve member banks constitute a minority of all U.S. banks—about 40 percent of the total. In 1988 there were about 4,700 national banks and close to 1,100 state-chartered banks registered as members of the Federal Reserve System, compared to approximately 8,000 nonmember banks.

Member banks must subscribe to the stock of the Reserve bank in their district in volume equal to 6 percent of their paid-in capital and surplus accounts. However, only half this amount must actually be paid, with the rest payable on call from the system. Member banks are bound by Federal Reserve rules regarding capital structure, deposits, loans, branch operations, formation of holding companies, and policies regarding the conduct of officers and boards of directors. These banks are subject to supervision and examination by the Federal Reserve at any time, though most banks are examined only once a year. Moreover, member banks must hold reserves behind their deposits at levels specified by the Federal Reserve Board.

A number of important privileges are granted to member banks. Legally, they are "owners" of the Federal Reserve banks because they hold the stock of these institutions and may elect six of their nine directors. A 6 percent annual dividend is paid to member banks on their holdings of Federal Reserve bank stock. Member banks may borrow reserves through the discount window of the Reserve bank in their district, though the majority of these loans cover only a few days.[6]

Member banks may also use the nationwide check-clearing system to process checks coming from distant cities. However, this is not a particularly distinctive privilege, since nonmember financial institutions may also use the Fed's check-clearing facilities, provided they agree to maintain a clearing account with the Reserve bank in the region. An intangible benefit of membership is the prestige that comes from belonging to the Federal Reserve

---

[6]As a result of the passage of the Monetary Control Act of 1980, any depository institution that holds transaction accounts or nonpersonal time deposits subject to mandatory reserve requirements may borrow from the Fed's discount window on the same terms as member banks.

System. Many bankers feel that membership in the system attracts large business deposits and correspondent accounts from smaller banks that otherwise might go elsewhere.

ROLES OF THE FEDERAL RESERVE SYSTEM TODAY

In the course of this chapter we have talked about the many roles the Federal Reserve must play in the financial system of the United States and how these roles have changed over time. In this final section of the chapter we attempt to pull together all of the Fed's responsibilities and roles to give a more complete view of how the central bank interfaces and interacts with the financial markets and the banking system.

The Clearing and Collection of Checks and Other Means of Payment

As we saw earlier in this chapter, one of the earliest tasks of the Federal Reserve System was to establish a nationwide system for clearing and collecting checks. When a depository institution receives a check drawn on another institution in a distant city, it can route this check directly through the Federal Reserve banks. The Fed credits an account called Deferred Availability Items on behalf of the institution sending in the check and routes that check toward the institution upon which it was drawn for eventual collection. At the end of a specified period, the depository institution sending in the check will receive credit in its legal reserve account for the amount of that check. Eventually, the check reaches the institution on which it was drawn and is deducted from that institution's reserve account.

Sometimes delays in the clearing system result in the creation of *float*. This occurs when a depository institution receives credit for a check deposited with the Federal Reserve before the institution on which the check was drawn actually loses reserves. When there are strikes or bad weather affecting surface or air transportation, the clearing of checks is delayed, and the volume of float rises. Because float is, in effect, an interest-free loan of reserves that banks can use to create credit, the Fed often has to take action through its open market operations to offset fluctuations in the volume of float.

Issuing Currency and Coin and Providing Other Services

The Fed helps to promote an efficient payments mechanism not just through the clearing of checks, but also by issuing its own currency in response to public need. Today nearly all the paper money in circulation consists of Federal Reserve notes, issued by all 12 of the Reserve banks and backed mainly by Federal Reserve holdings of government securities. These notes are liabilities of the Federal Reserve bank issuing them. In fact, Federal Reserve notes are a lien against the assets of the Fed, payable to the holder in the event the Reserve banks are ever liquidated. When the public demands more currency, financial institutions request a shipment of new currency and coin from the Federal Reserve bank in the region, which maintains an ample supply in its vault. Payment for the shipment is made simply by charging the legal reserve account of the institution requesting the shipment. In the opposite situation, when depository institutions receive deposits of currency and coin from the public beyond what they wish to hold in their vaults, the surplus is shipped back to the Reserve banks. Depository institutions receive credit for these return shipments through an increase in their legal reserve accounts at the Reserve bank.

Prior to 1981, most Federal Reserve services, including the clearing of checks and shipments of currency and coin, were provided free of charge. However, the Depository Institutions Deregulation Monetary Control Act (DIDMCA) of 1980 required the Fed to publish a set of pricing principles and to assess fees for such services as transportation of currency and coin, coin wrapping, check clearing and collection, wire transfer of funds, the use of Federal Reserve automated clearinghouse facilities, and book entry, safekeeping, and other services connected with the purchase and sale of government securities. All fees set by the Fed are to be reviewed annually and set at levels that, over the long run, simply recover the total costs of providing each service.

Why did Congress order the Fed to switch from free services to a fee basis? One reason was the rapid increase in the number of users of Federal Reserve services. DIDMCA of 1980, for the first time in U.S. history, provided for access by all nonmember depository institutions to the Fed's facilities and services. With so many new financial institutions eligible to receive Fed services, their total cost would soar. Second, Congress wanted to encourage as much competition as possible in the provision of these services so that the Fed would not be the only source of supply. Still another motivating factor was a feared loss of revenue to the Treasury. All of these developments together would have substantially reduced the Fed's annual net income, most of which flows to the Treasury, if the central bank had not begun charging for its services.

Maintaining a Sound Banking and Financial System

Another important function of the Federal Reserve System today is to maintain a sound banking and financial system. It contributes to this goal by serving as a lender of last resort, providing reserves to depository institutions through the discount window of each Reserve bank. The window represents a source of funds which can be drawn upon without taking reserves away from other banks, and it helps to avoid a liquidity squeeze brought about by sudden changes in economic and financial conditions. The Fed also promotes a sound banking system by regular examinations of member banks, reviewing the quality and quantity of their assets and capital and making sure that federal and state laws are followed.

Serving as the Federal Government's Fiscal Agent

The Fed serves as the government's chief fiscal agent. In this role, it holds the Treasury's checking account and clears any checks written against that account. The Fed supervises the thousands of Tax and Loan Accounts maintained in banks across the United States which hold the bulk of the Treasury's cash balances until the Treasury needs these monies for spending. The Federal Reserve banks receive bids when new Treasury securities are offered and provide securities to the purchasers. They redeem maturing U.S. government securities as well. In general, the Fed is responsible for maintaining reasonable stability in the government securities market so that any new Treasury offerings sell quickly and the government raises the amount of money that it needs.

Carrying Out Monetary Policy

The most critical job of the Federal Reserve is to carry out monetary policy. Monetary policy may be defined as the use of various tools by the central bank to control the availability of loanable funds in an effort to achieve national economic goals, such as full employment and reasonable price stability. The policy tools reserved for the Federal Reserve include deposit reserve requirements, discount rates, open market operations, and margin requirements on purchases of securities. We will examine the Fed's policy tools in detail in Chapter 23.

Providing Information to the Public

Another critical function which the Federal Reserve has performed particularly well in recent years is the provision of information to the public. Each Reserve bank has its own research staff, and the Board of Governors maintains a large staff of economists who follow current economic and financial developments and recommend changes in policy. The Fed makes available on a daily, weekly, and monthly basis an impressive volume of statistical releases, special reports, and studies concerning the financial markets, the nation's money supply, long- and short-term interest rates, the volume and composition of borrowing by the public, and national economic developments. In the international sector, the Federal Reserve supplies, on request, information dealing with developments in foreign currency markets, international loans and capital flows, and the U.S. foreign trade and balance-of-payments position. In addition, as we noted in Chapter 3, the Fed prepares the Flow of Funds Accounts each quarter, providing extensive data on borrowing and lending activities among major sectors of the U.S. economy. This information function is often overlooked in discussions of the Federal Reserve's role within the nation's financial system, but it is one of the more important contributions of the central bank.

SUMMARY

In this chapter we examined the important role played by central banks, and in particular, the Federal Reserve System in the financial system and the economy. Central banks must function to control the nation's money supply, maintain stable conditions in the financial markets, serve as a lender of last resort to aid financial institutions in trouble, and maintain and improve the mechanism for making payments for goods and services. In most industrialized countries, including the United States, central banking is goal-oriented, aimed principally at the major economic goals of full employment, reasonable price stability, sustainable economic growth, and a strong and stable balance-of-payments position with the rest of the world. In the Western world, central banks operate mainly through the marketplace, influencing credit conditions but leaving to private borrowers and lenders the basic decisions of whether to create credit, borrow, and spend.

While there is much disagreement today as to how central banks influence the economy through their actions, economists generally argue that these institutions affect the spending, saving, and borrowing decisions of millions of individuals and businesses through at least four interrelated channels. Central bank policies influence the cost and availability of credit, the volume and rate of growth of the money supply, the market value of securities held by the public, and the public's expectations. Each of these policy channels ultimately affects the borrowing, consumption, and investment spending decisions of businesses, consumers, and governments.

Central banks around the world use a variety of tools to influence economic and financial decisions. The Bank of Canada, for example, relies heavily on changes in deposit reserve requirements, while the Bank of England uses its discount rate on loans as a major policy tool. In contrast, the Federal Reserve System depends principally on open market operations—the buying and selling of securities—to achieve its policy objectives. As we will see in the next chapter, the Fed's reliance on open market operations reflects both the great flexibility of this policy tool and the great breadth and depth of security markets in the United States compared to the limited market systems that exist in many other nations.

Just as the Federal Reserve System's heavy reliance on open market operations is distinctive among the world's central banks, its organizational structure is also uniquely American. The main administrative body within the system is the Board of Governors, composed of seven persons appointed by the president of the United States and headquartered in Washington,

DC. The Federal Reserve Board appoints officers and staff of the system, sets budgets, and controls such important policy tools as deposit reserve requirements, margin requirements on stock, and changes in the discount rate on loans to banks and other deposit-type financial institutions. However, the board's authority over the future course of economic policy and the implementation of that policy is shared with other departments within the Federal Reserve System.

For example, the Federal Open Market Committee, composed of the seven members of the Federal Reserve Board and five presidents of the Federal Reserve banks, discusses all major policy initiatives by the Fed and closely controls the system's major policy tool—open market operations. The 12 Federal Reserve banks, located in major financial centers across the United States, determine which banks and other depository financial institutions can borrow from the Fed and on what terms. These regional Reserve banks also supervise banks and bank holding company activities within their districts and provide important services, including the clearing and collection of checks, shipment of currency and coin, transfer of funds by wire, and the safekeeping of securities. Moreover, each of the Reserve banks serves as the federal government's fiscal agent, dispensing and collecting government funds, selling and redeeming government securities, and helping to maintain orderly market conditions so that the federal government can borrow new money and refinance its debt as smoothly as possible.

Each part of the Federal Reserve System, therefore, has a key role to play in the operation of the financial system and the functioning of the economy. In the next two chapters we explore more fully what is generally considered the Federal Reserve's most important job, *monetary policy*—the regulation of money and credit conditions in order to achieve major economic goals.

STUDY QUESTIONS

1. What functions do central banks perform in a market-oriented economy? Explain why each is important to the efficient functioning of the financial and economic system.

2. What are the principal goals of the Federal Reserve System in its pursuit of monetary policy? To what extent are these goals consistent or inconsistent with each other?

3. What major problems in the late 19th and early 20th centuries led to the creation of the Federal Reserve System? What problems did the National Banking Act solve, and what problems did it create? How did the creation of the Fed help to solve these problems?

4. In what ways did the early Federal Reserve System differ from the Fed of today? Consider in your answer such factors as the goals pursued, structure, and policy tools used.

5. List the principal functions of the Federal Reserve System today and explain why each is important.

6. What are the principal responsibilities assigned to:
   a. The Board of Governors of the Federal Reserve System?
   b. The Federal Open Market Committee?
   c. The Federal Reserve Banks?
   d. The Manager of the System Open Market Account?

SELECTED REFERENCES

Board of Governors of the Federal Reserve System. *The Federal Reserve System— Purposes and Functions*. Washington, DC, 1974.

Burger, Albert E. *The Money Supply Process*. Belmont, CA: Wadsworth, 1971, pp. 52–56.

Carlson, Keith M. "Money, Inflation, and Economic Growth: Some Updated Reduced-Form Results and Their Implications." *Review*, Federal Reserve Bank of St. Louis, April 1980.

Carlson, Keith M., and Scott E. Hein. "Monetary Aggregates as Monetary Indicators." *Review*, Federal Reserve Bank of St. Louis, November 1980.

Federal Reserve Bank of Chicago. "The Depository Institutions Deregulation and Monetary Control Act of 1980." *Economic Perspectives*, September–October 1980, pp. 3–23.

Poole, William, and Charles Lieberman. "Improving Monetary Control." In *Brookings Papers on Economic Activity*, 1972; 2, ed. Arthur M. Okun and George L. Perry. Washington, DC: The Brookings Institution, 1972.

Chapter 23

The Tools of
Monetary Policy

Learning Objectives in This Chapter

- To examine the tools available to the nation's central bank, the Federal Reserve System, to control the growth of money and credit in the economy.

- To understand the concept of legal reserves and how actions taken by the Federal Reserve influence the level and rate of growth of legal reserves.

- To compare the strengths and weaknesses of each of the Federal Reserve's policy tools—reserve requirements, the discount rate, open market operations, moral suasion, and margin requirements.

Key Terms and Concepts in This Chapter

Legal reserves	Monetary base	Open market
Required reserves	General credit controls	operations
Excess reserves	Selective credit	Moral suasion
Deposit multiplier	controls	Regulation Q ceilings
Money multiplier	Reserve requirements	Margin requirements
	Discount rate	

AS we saw in the preceding chapter, the Federal Reserve System has been given the task of regulating the money and credit system in order to achieve the nation's economic goals. Prominent among these goals are the achievement of full employment, a stable price level, sustainable economic growth, and a strong balance-of-payments position with the rest of the world. As recent experience has demonstrated, these objectives are not easy to achieve and frequently conflict. Still, the central bank has powerful policy tools at its disposal with which to pursue the nation's economic goals. Our purpose in this chapter is to examine the policy tools available to the Federal Reserve in carrying out its task of controlling the supply of money and credit.

RESERVES AND MONEY—TARGETS OF FEDERAL RESERVE POLICY

The principal immediate target of Federal Reserve policy is the *reserves of the banking system,* consisting mainly of deposits held at the Federal Reserve banks plus currency and coin. These reserves are the raw material out of which banks and other depository institutions create credit and cause the money supply to grow. And because the growth of the money supply is closely linked to changes in income, production, prices, and employment, the Fed pays close attention on a daily basis to fluctuations in the quantity of reserves depository institutions have at their disposal. The total supply of reserves can be changed directly by Federal Reserve open market operations and by making loans to depository institutions through the Fed's discount window. The Fed can also exert a powerful effect on the growth of money and credit by changing the legal reserve requirements applicable to deposits held by commercial banks and other depository institutions.

While the Fed's primary concern is the volume and rate of growth of reserves held by depository institutions, all of its policy tools have an impact on *interest rates* as well. Whenever the supply of reserves is reduced relative to the demand for reserves, interest rates tend to rise as funds are rationed among competing financial institutions. Conversely, an expansion in the supply of reserves usually leads to lower interest rates because of the increased availability of loanable funds. Why do these changes occur? What are the specific links between bank reserves and the money supply? Between reserves and interest rates?

THE COMPOSITION OF RESERVES

To answer these questions, we need to look closely at what makes up the supply of reserves at depository institutions. We recall from Chapters 4 and 15 that all depository institutions offering transaction accounts (principally demand deposits and NOWs) and nonpersonal time deposits are required to hold a small percentage of those deposits in an asset account known as legal reserves. Legal reserves consist of the amount of deposits each institution keeps with the Federal Reserve bank in its district plus the amount of currency and coin held in its vault.

We noted in Chapter 4 that legal reserves may be divided into two parts: required reserves and excess reserves. In particular

$$
\begin{aligned}
\text{Total legal reserves} &= \text{Required reserves} + \text{Excess reserves} \quad (23\text{–}1) \\
&= \text{Deposits at the Federal Reserve banks} \\
&\quad + \text{Vault cash held on the} \\
&\quad\quad \text{premises of} \\
&\quad\quad \text{depository institutions}
\end{aligned}
$$

Required reserves are those holdings of cash and deposits at the Fed that a depository institution must hold in order to back the public's deposits or face a legal penalty. Excess reserves consist of cash and Fed deposits owned by depository institutions that are not needed to back the public's deposits and may be used to make loans, purchase securities, repay debts, or serve other purposes. Because legal reserve assets earn little or no income, most depository institutions try to keep their excess reserves close to zero. For example, the largest commercial banks today frequently run reserve deficits and must borrow additional legal reserves in the money market to avoid costly penalties.

The Deposit Multiplier

The distinction between excess and required reserves is important because it plays a key role in the growth of money and credit in the economy. As we observed in Chapter 4, depository institutions offering checkable deposits have the unique ability to create and destroy deposits—which are the bulk of the money supply—at the stroke of a pen. While an individual depository institution cannot create more deposit money than the volume of excess reserves it holds, the banking system as a whole can create a multiple amount of deposit money from any given injection of reserves by using excess reserves to make loans and purchase securities.

How much deposit money can the banking system create if it has excess reserves available? The banking system's deposit-creating potential can be estimated using a concept known as the deposit multiplier, or coefficient of deposit expansion. The deposit multiplier indicates how many dollars of deposits (and loans) will result from any given injection of new excess reserves into the system. If we assume the existence of a very simple financial system in which the public makes all of its payments by check and does not convert any checkbook (demand deposit) money into thrift deposits, and where depository institutions do not wish to hold any excess reserve but rather loan out immediately all funds received, then:

The transaction deposit multiplier, or coefficient of expansion

$$= \frac{1}{\text{Reserve requirement on transaction deposits}} \qquad (23-2)$$

For example, if the Federal Reserve insists that depository institutions keep $0.12 in required reserves for each new dollar of demand deposits and other transaction deposits they receive, the deposit multiplier must be 1/0.12, or 8.33.

Then how much in new deposit money can the banking system create under these circumstances? If all depository institutions continually make loans with any excess reserves they receive, the maximum amount of new deposits (and loans) that can be created by the entire banking system may be found from the following equation:

Transaction deposit multiplier × Excess reserves   (23-3)
                         = Maximum volume of new deposits and loans

If banks and other depository institutions receive additional excess reserves in the amount of $1 million and the reserve requirement behind transaction deposits is 12 percent, we have:

$$1/0.12 \times \$1 \text{ million} = 8.33 \times \$1 \text{ million}$$
$$= \$8.33 \text{ million in new deposits and loans}$$

A *withdrawal* of reserves from depository institutions can work in the opposite direction, destroying deposits and loans. For example, a withdrawal of deposits by the public that causes depository institutions to have a $1 million deficiency in their required reserves would eventually lead to an $8.33 million *decline* in deposits, assuming a 12 percent reserve requirement.

Of course, the real world is quite different from the simple deposit expansion model outlined above. Leakages of funds from the banking system greatly reduce the size of the deposit multiplier, so that its actual value is probably somewhat less than 2. Among the most important leakages are the public's desire to convert some portion of new checkbook money into pocket money (currency and coin) or into thrift deposits, and the presence of unutilized lending capacity. Banks and other depository institutions may choose to hold substantial excess reserves and not lend out all their excess funds because they cannot find enough qualified borrowers or wish to hold a protective "cushion" of reserves.

These various leakages of funds from transaction balances suggest the need for a slightly more complex model of the deposit and loan expansion process. In this model the deposit multiplier would be represented by the following expression:

Transaction deposit multiplier assuming drains of funds
into cash, time and savings deposits, and excess reserves

$$= \frac{1}{RR_D + CASH + EXR + (RR_T \times TIME)} \qquad (23\text{--}4)$$

In this instance, RR_D represents the required legal reserve ratio for demand deposits and other transaction accounts, while RR_T is the required legal reserve ratio for time and savings deposits. CASH and TIME represent the amounts of additional currency and coin and time and savings deposits the public wishes to hold for each dollar of new transaction deposits they receive, while EXR stands for the quantity of excess reserves depository institutions desire to hold for precautionary purposes out of each dollar of new transaction deposits. The largest amount of transaction deposits and loans that the banking system can create, assuming all of the above drains of funds occur, would be given by this formula:

$$\frac{1}{RR_D + CASH + EXR + (RR_T \times TIME)} \times \text{Excess reserves} \qquad (23\text{--}5)$$

$$= \text{Maximum volume}$$
$$\text{of new deposits}$$
$$\text{and loans}$$

To illustrate the use of the formula, assume depository institutions have just received an additional \$1 million in excess reserves from some source outside the banking system. (One possible source is actions by the Federal Reserve lowering legal reserve requirements or buying securities from the public.) We further assume that, for each new dollar of transaction deposits received, the public will convert \$0.25 into pocket money (CASH = 0.25), and \$0.60 will be placed in time and savings deposits (TIME = 0.60). Further, suppose depository institutions elect to hold \$0.05 of every new checkable deposit dollar received as excess reserves (EXR = 0.05) to protect against future contingencies. The reserve requirement on transaction deposits (RR_D) is assumed to be 12 percent, and on time and savings deposits (RR_T), 3 percent. Then the maximum amount of new deposits and loans that depository institutions as a group can create with \$1 million in excess reserves is calculated as follows:

$$\frac{1}{0.12 + 0.25 + 0.05 + (0.03 \times 0.60)} \times \$1 \text{ million} = \frac{1}{0.438} \times \$1 \text{ million}$$

$$= 2.28 \times \$1 \text{ million}$$
$$= \$2.28 \text{ million in}$$
$$\text{new deposits}$$
$$\text{and loans}$$

Clearly, the deposit multiplier is far smaller when we allow for the conversion of checkable deposits into currency, coin, and thrift deposits and when banks and other depository institutions are unwilling to lend all their excess reserves. This would appear to be good news for the central bank charged with controlling the rate of growth of the money supply and deposits. A numerically small deposit multiplier implies that the banking system will not be able significantly to increase the size of the deposit money supply unless the supply of excess reserves is also greatly increased. But the central bank has a potent influence on the quantity of excess reserves available to financial institutions.

Unfortunately the existence of cash drains, time and savings deposits, and other reserve-absorbing factors, while reducing the size of the deposit multiplier, also makes the forecasting of deposit flows much more difficult. The central bank must be constantly alert to shifts in the public's demand for currency and coin and time and savings deposits and also alert to the changing demands of depository institutions for excess reserves and other liquid assets. If the central bank cannot accurately forecast changes in the public's money and deposit preferences, control of the money supply will be less precise and subject to erratic fluctuations, so that achievement of the nation's economic goals will be much more difficult.

The Money Multiplier

While the concept of the deposit multiplier is useful for some purposes, central bankers are more interested in a related concept known as the money multiplier, which defines the relationship between the size of the money supply (including deposits, currency and coin, and other readily spendable funds) and the size of the total reserve base available to depository institutions. The money multiplier is defined as follows:

$$\text{Money multiplier} = \frac{1 + \text{CASH}}{\text{RR}_\text{D} + \text{CASH} + \text{EXR} + (\text{RR}_\text{T} \times \text{TIME})} \quad (23\text{--}6)$$

The terms CASH, EXR, RR_D, RR_T, and TIME are defined just as they were in the deposit multiplier formula.

We note that the money multiplier differs from the deposit multiplier only in the addition of CASH—the proportion of new transaction deposits the public desires to hold in the form of currency and coin—to the numerator of the multiplier ratio. This change is made because currency and coin held by the public also forms an important component of the money supply and must be accounted for in measuring how fast the money supply grows over time. With the rapid spread of coin-operated machines, the amount of currency and coin outstanding actually has been growing faster than the volume of regular checking accounts.

Another important point to note about currency and coin is that fluctuations in the volume held by the public have a direct bearing on the reserves held by depository institutions. For example, when the public wishes to increase its holdings of pocket money—something that routinely occurs around holidays and over weekends—it will write checks against transaction deposits in depository institutions, drawing down both demand accounts and reserves. If the public desires to hold less pocket money, the excess currency and coin typically will be redeposited in transaction accounts, increasing both reserves and demand deposits. Recognizing this important link between currency and bank reserves, economists have developed the concept of the monetary base, which is simply the sum of legal reserves plus the amount of currency and coin held by the public.[1] Currency and coin represent almost 85 percent of the monetary base, and legal reserves account for about 15 percent.

Why is the monetary base important? It is one of the principal determinants of the money supply. Specifically:

$$\text{Money multiplier} \times \text{Monetary base} = \text{Money supply} \qquad (23\text{--}7)$$

or,

$$\frac{1 + \text{CASH}}{\text{RR}_\text{D} + \text{CASH} + \text{EXR} + (\text{RR}_\text{T} \times \text{TIME})} \times$$
$$\text{Monetary base} = \text{Money supply}$$

We may use this formula as a device to estimate the size of the money multiplier. For example, in February 1988 the U.S. monetary base was $261 billion, while the sum of transaction deposits (e.g., demand deposits, NOWs, Super NOWs, and travelers checks) and currency and coin stood at almost $760 billion.[2] The money multiplier, therefore, was as follows:

$$\text{Money multiplier} = \frac{\$760 \text{ billion}}{\$261 \text{ billion}} = 2.91$$

On average, each $1 increase in the monetary base resulted in a rise in the U.S. money supply of about $2.91. This is one reason the monetary base is frequently referred to as *high-powered money;* a change in the base, working through the money multiplier, produces a magnified change in the money supply.

The monetary base–money multiplier relationship identifies for us the most important factors that explain changes in the money supply, and it also helps us to understand how the Federal Reserve can influence the money-supply creation process. The Fed is one of the principal determinants of the size of the monetary base, along with the public and the U.S. Treasury.

---

[1] To be more precise, the Federal Reserve defines the monetary base as equal to total reserve balances plus currency and coin held outside the U.S. Treasury, Federal Reserve banks, and the vaults of commercial banks.

[2] The definition of the money supply used in the formula above is the one labeled M-1 by the Federal Reserve System. The Fed has developed several other money supply definitions, which we will examine in Chapter 24. Each concept can be linked directly to the monetary base, provided the components of the money multiplier are altered to reflect the different kinds of deposits or financial assets available to the public under each definition.

It can increase or decrease the total supply of reserves to change the size of the base. Alternatively, the Fed may choose merely to offset actions taken by the public or the Treasury in order to keep the size of the monetary base unchanged. Finally, the central bank can change the required reserve ratios behind transaction (RR_D) and time (RR_T) deposits, which will affect the magnitude of the money multiplier. Occasionally, when the central bank wishes to exert a potent impact on economic and financial conditions, it will make changes in *both* the monetary base and the money multiplier. In the next section we take a close look at the tools the Federal Reserve System uses to influence the size of the monetary base, the money multiplier, and ultimately the money supply.

GENERAL VERSUS SELECTIVE CREDIT CONTROLS

In order to change the volume of reserves available to depository institutions for lending and investing and to influence interest rates in the economy, the Federal Reserve System uses a variety of policy tools. Some of these tools are general credit controls, which affect the entire banking and financial system. Included in this list are reserve requirements, the discount rate, and open market operations. A second set of policy tools may be labeled selective credit controls because they affect specific groups or sectors of the financial system. Moral suasion, legal interest rate ceilings, and margin requirements on the purchase of listed securities are examples of selective credit controls. Of course, all the central bank's policy tools have as their ultimate goal the promotion of full employment, sustainable economic growth, price stability, and a stable balance-of-payments position for the United States. Our objective in this section is to look first at the Fed's general credit controls and then at its selective credit controls.

THE GENERAL CREDIT CONTROLS OF THE FED

Reserve Requirements

Since the 1930s the Federal Reserve Board has had the power to vary the amount of required legal reserves member banks must hold behind deposits they receive from the public. With passage of DIDMCA in 1980, nonmember banks and all nonbank depository financial institutions (including credit unions, mutual savings banks, and savings and loan associations) were required to conform to the deposit reserve requirements set by the Fed. Early in the Fed's history it was felt that the primary purpose of reserve requirements was to safeguard the public's deposits. More recently we have come to realize that their principal use is to give the central bank a powerful tool for emergency situations. Indeed, reserve requirements are probably the most potent policy tool the Federal Reserve System has at its disposal today.

However, changes in reserve requirements are a little-used tool, as we will soon see.

Effects of a Change in Deposit Reserve Requirements. A change in deposit reserve requirements has at least *three* different effects on the financial system. First of all, it *changes the deposit multiplier* (or coefficient of expansion) which, as we saw earlier, affects the amount of deposits and new loans the banking system can create for any given injection of new reserves. A change in reserve requirements also affects the size of the money multiplier, influencing the rate of increase in the money supply. If the Fed increases reserve requirements, the deposit multiplier and the money multiplier are *reduced,* slowing the growth of money, deposits, and loans. On the other hand, a decrease in reserve requirements increases the size of both the deposit multiplier and the money multiplier. In this instance each dollar of additional reserves available to the banking system will lead to accelerated growth in money, deposits, and loans.

A change in reserve requirements also affects the *mix* between excess and required legal reserves. Suppose all depository institutions are fully loaned up, and excess reserves are zero. If reserves requirements are *reduced,* a portion of what were required reserves now become excess reserves. Depository institutions will soon convert all or a portion of these newly created excess reserves into loans and investments, expanding the money supply. Similarly, if all institutions are fully loaned up, with zero excess reserves, an *increase* in reserve requirements will mean that some depository institutions will be short required legal reserves. These institutions will be forced to sell securities, cut back on loans, and borrow reserves from other financial institutions in order to meet their reserve requirements. The money supply will grow more slowly and may even decline.

Interest rates also respond to a change in reserve requirements. A move by the Fed toward higher deposit reserve requirements soon leads to higher interest rates, particularly in the money market, as depository institutions scramble to cover any reserve deficiencies. Credit becomes less available and more costly. In contrast, a lowering of reserve requirements tends to bring interest rates down as well. Flush with excess reserves, depository institutions are willing to make more loans at lower interest rates, and fewer institutions will have to sell securities or borrow to meet their reserve requirements.

An illustration. Exhibit 23–1 illustrates the effects of changes in deposit reserve requirements. Suppose depository institutions are required to keep 12 percent of their deposits in legal reserves. Then, $120 of legal reserves will be needed to support each $1,000 in deposits. If there is sufficient demand for loanable funds, institutions will probably loan or invest the remaining $880. Suppose that the Federal Reserve increases reserve requirements from 12 to 15 percent. As a result, more legal reserves are necessary

Exhibit 23–1   Effects of Changes in Reserve Requirements on Deposits, Loans, and Investments

	Commercial Bank		
	Assets	Liabilities	
With a 12 percent reserve requirement, $120 of reserves are needed to support each $1,000 of deposits.	Loans and investments $ 880	Deposit	$1,000
	Legal reserves 120		
	⌈ Required 120 ⌉		
	⌊ Excess 0 ⌋		
	$1,000		$1,000

Increase in reserve requirements:

	Commercial Bank		
	Assets	Liabilities	
If required reserves are increased from 12 to 15 percent, more reserves are needed against the same volume of deposits. Any deficiencies (negative excess reserves) must be covered by liquidating loans and investments or by borrowing.	Legal reserves $ 120	Deposits	$1,000
	⌈ Required 150 ⌉		
	⌊ Excess −30 ⌋		
	Loans and investments 880		
	$1,000		$1,000

Decrease in reserve requirements:

	Commercial Bank		
	Assets	Liabilities	
If required reserves are reduced from 12 to 10 percent, excess reserves are created which can be loaned to the public or invested in securities.	Legal reserves $ 120	Deposits	$1,000
	⌈ Required 100 ⌉		
	⌊ Excess 20 ⌋		
	Loans and investments 880		
	$1,000		$1,000

to support the same volume of deposits, and institutions have a $30 reserve deficit for each $1,000 of deposits. This deficit may be covered by selling loans or investment securities, borrowing funds, or reducing deposits.

On the other hand, suppose required reserves are lowered from 12 to 10 percent. There now are $20 in excess reserves for each $1,000 in deposits, and that excess can be loaned or invested, creating new deposits. We should note that *total* legal reserves available to the banking system are *not* affected by changes in reserve requirements. A shift in deposit reserve requirements affects only the *mix* of legal reserves between required and excess.

Current Levels of Reserve Requirements. Today deposit reserve requirements are imposed by the Federal Reserve Board on all depository institutions that are federally insured or eligible to apply for federal insurance, including commercial banks, mutual savings banks, savings and loan associations, and credit unions. Under the terms of DIDMCA of 1980, three types of deposits are subject to legal reserve requirements:

1. Transaction accounts, which are deposits used to make payments by negotiable or transferable instruments and include regular checking accounts, NOW accounts, and any account subject to automatic transfers of funds.
2. Nonpersonal time deposits, which are interest-bearing time deposits [including savings deposits and money market accounts (MMDAs)] held by businesses and governmental units but not individuals.
3. Eurocurrency liabilities, which are borrowings of deposits from banks and branches located outside the United States.

As shown in Exhibit 23–2, the current reserve requirement on transaction accounts of $40.5 million or less is 3 percent, while the net amount of transaction deposits over $40.5 million is subject to a 12 percent reserve requirement.[3] Personal time and savings deposits carry no reserve requirement, but nonpersonal time deposits owned by businesses and units of government currently have a 3 percent required reserve. Average reserve requirements are higher on transaction accounts than on time and savings accounts because transaction balances are considered to be less stable deposits than time and savings deposits.

The largest depository institutions, holding more than $40.5 million in net transaction balances, carry the heaviest reserve requirements. This is due to the fact that larger financial institutions hold the deposits of thousands of smaller banks and other deposit-type intermediaries. Moreover, the failure of a large bank or other depository institution can send shock waves through the entire financial system and threaten the economic viability of many other institutions and individuals as well.[4]

Changes in reserve requirements, combined with other monetary policy measures, can be used to carry out major shifts in government economic policy. The reserve requirement tool is exceedingly powerful, however—even a small change affects hundreds of millions of dollars in legal reserves. Moreover, it is an *inflexible* tool. Required reserve ratios cannot be changed frequently because this would disrupt the banking system. Not surprisingly, changes in reserve requirements do not occur very often, averaging about once every two years since World War II.

---

[3]The Federal Reserve Board is empowered under the Monetary Control Act to vary reserve requirements on transaction accounts over $40.5 million between 8 and 14 percent. The $40.5 million dividing line (known as the *tranche*) is indexed and will change each calendar year by 80 percent of the percentage change in total transaction accounts of all depository institutions during the previous year ended June 30. In addition, the Garn–St Germain Depository Institutions Act of 1982 stipulated that $2 million of reservable liabilities (transaction accounts, nonpersonal time deposits, and Eurocurrency liabilities) of each depository institution be subject to a zero reserve requirement, adjusted each year by 80 percent of the percentage increase in total reservable liabilities.

[4]See, for example, Laurant (1979), Poole (1976), and Woodworth (1972).

Exhibit 23–2   **Reserve Requirements of Depository Institutions** (Percent of Deposits)

Type of Deposit and Deposit Interval	Percentage Reserve Requirement	Permissible Statutory Range
Net transaction accounts:		
$0–$40.5 million	3%	3%
Over $40.5 million	12	8–14
Nonpersonal time deposits:		
Original maturity of:		
Less than 1½ years	3	0–9
1½ years or more	0	0–9
Eurocurrency liabilities:		
All types	3	None

Source: Board of Governors of the Federal Reserve System, *Federal Reserve Bulletin,* January 1988, Table 1.15.

Changes in the Federal Reserve's Discount Rate

Any depository institution that accepts transaction accounts or nonpersonal time deposits may borrow reserves from the discount window of the Federal Reserve bank in its region. The Fed's Regulation A states, however, that these loans must be a *temporary* source of funds. In fact, Federal Reserve regulations require depository institutions to alternate their borrowings from the discount window with drawings from other sources, such as the federal funds market. Frequent borrowing is discouraged and may be penalized with a higher interest rate.[5]

The discount rate is the percentage interest charge levied against those institutions choosing to borrow from the Fed. The board of directors of each Federal Reserve bank votes to determine what the discount rate should be in its region of the country. However, the Federal Reserve Board in Washington, DC, must approve the rate charged in each of the 12 Federal Reserve districts. As shown in Exhibit 23–3, the basic rate on short-term loans of reserves in September 1988 was 6.50 percent. Depository institutions with marked seasonal movements in deposits could apply for extended credit at rates ranging from 6.50 to more than 8 percent, depending on how long funds were to be borrowed and current market conditions.

Borrowing and Repaying Discount Window Loans. Depository institutions that borrow regularly at the discount window keep a signed loan authorization form at the Federal Reserve bank in their district and also keep U.S. government securities or other acceptable collateral on deposit there. When a loan is needed, the officer responsible for managing the bor-

---

[5]For a discussion of the use of the Federal Reserve's discount window as a reserve adjustment device for banks and other depository institutions, see Chapter 15.

Exhibit 23–3   **The Discount Rates Charged by the Federal Reserve Banks on Loans to Depository Institutions, Effective August 1988**
(Percent per Annum)

Type of Loan	Short-Term Adjustment Credit and Seasonal Credit	Extended Credit	
		First 30 Days of Borrowing	After 30 Days of Borrowing*
Discount Rates	6.50%	6.50%	8.45%

*Credit may be extended for longer periods of time when a particular borrowing institution needs support due to exceptional circumstances at a flexible rate that varies with market conditions.

Source: Board of Governors of the Federal Reserve System, *Federal Reserve Bulletin,* September 1988, Table 1.14.

rowing institution's legal reserve position will merely contact the district Federal Reserve bank and request that the necessary funds be deposited in that institution's reserve account.

In Exhibit 23–4 we illustrate the borrowing process by supposing that a bank has requested a loan of $1 million and the Fed has agreed to make the loan. The borrowing bank receives an increase in its account, Reserves Held at Federal Reserve Bank, of $1 million. At the same time, the bank's liability account, Bills Payable, increases by $1 million. On the Federal Reserve bank's balance sheet, the loan shows up as an increase in Bank Reserves of $1 million—a liability of the Federal Reserve System—and also as an increase in a Fed asset account, Discounts and Advances. When the loan is repaid, the transaction is reversed.

Quite clearly, borrowings from the Fed's discount window *increase* the total reserves available to the banking system. Repayments of those borrowings cause total reserves to fall.

Effects of a Discount Rate Change. Most observers today feel that at least three effects follow from a change in the Federal Reserve's discount rate. One is the *cost effect*. An increase in the discount rate means that it is more costly to borrow reserves from the Federal Reserve than to use some other source of funds. Other things being equal, loans from the discount window and the total volume of borrowed reserves will decline. Conversely, a lower discount rate should result in an acceleration of borrowing from the Federal Reserve and more reserves flowing into the banking system.

Of course, the strength of the cost effect depends on the spread between the discount rate and other money market interest rates. If the Fed's rate remains well below other interest rates even after it is increased, then it would still be cheaper, relatively speaking, to draw upon the Fed for funds. There would be little reduction in loans from the discount window. This has

Exhibit 23–4   Borrowing and Repaying Loans from the Fed's Discount Window

Borrowing from a Federal Reserve Bank:

Federal Reserve Bank				Commercial Bank or Other Depository Institution			
Assets		Liabilities		Assets		Liabilities	
Discounts and advances	+ $1 million	Bank Reserves	+ $1 million	Reserves held at Federal Reserve bank	+ $1 million	Bills payable	+ $1 million

Repayment of Borrowings from the Fed:

Federal Reserve Bank				Commercial Bank or Other Depository Institution			
Assets		Liabilities		Assets		Liabilities	
Discounts and advances	− $1 million	Bank Reserves	− $1 million	Reserves held at Federal Reserve bank	− $1 million	Bills payable	− $1 million

happened frequently in recent years, with the discount rate usually lagging well behind other interest rates in the money market.

A second consequence of changes in the discount rate is called the *substitution effect.* A change in the discount rate usually causes other interest rates to change as well. This is due to the fact that the Federal Reserve is one source of borrowed reserves, but certainly not the only source. An increase in the discount rate, for example, will make borrowing from the Fed less attractive, but borrowing from other sources such as the Federal funds and Eurodollar markets will become relatively more attractive. Banks and other borrowers will shift their attention to these other markets, causing interest rates there to rise as well.

A lowering of the discount rate, on the other hand, frequently causes a downward movement in money market rates and ultimately capital market rates. This happens because deposit-type financial institutions will begin borrowing more from the Federal Reserve, reducing the demand for credit in other segments of the financial marketplace.

The final effect of a discount rate change is called the *announcement effect.* The discount rate has a psychological impact on the financial markets because the Fed's rate is widely regarded as an indicator of monetary policy. If, for example, the Federal Reserve raises the discount rate, many observers regard this as a signal that the Fed is pushing for tighter credit conditions.

Market particpants may respond by reducing borrowing and curtailing spending plans.

Unfortunately, the psychological impact of the discount rate may work *against* the Fed as well as for it. It is quite likely, for example, that if the Federal Reserve raises the discount rate, borrowers will respond by accelerating their borrowings in an effort to secure the credit they need before interest rates move even higher. Such an action would thwart the Fed's objective of slowing the growth of borrowing and spending. Because of the possibility of *negative psychological effects,* the discount rate is changed infrequently and often lags behind rates in the open market. The Fed, however, must often make a technical adjustment in the rate just to bring it closer into line with other interest rates. Even so, market participants are likely to "read into" discount rate changes a new policy position or more aggressive pursuit of existing policies by the Fed.

Open Market Operations

The limitations of the discount rate and reserve requirement policy tools have led the Federal Reserve to rely more heavily in recent years upon open market operations to accomplish its goals. By definition, open market operations consist of the buying and selling of U.S. government and other securities by the Federal Reserve System to affect the quantity and growth of legal reserves and ultimately general credit conditions. Open market operations are the most flexible policy tool available to the Fed, and suitable for "fine tuning" of the financial markets when this is necessary.

Effects of Open Market Operations on Interest Rates. The open market tool has two major effects upon the banking system and credit conditions. First of all, it has an *interest rate effect* because the Fed usually buys or sells a large quantity (several hundred million dollars worth) of securities in the financial marketplace at any one time. If the Fed is *purchasing* securities, this adds additional demand for these securities in the market, which tends to increase their prices and lower their yields. If the Federal Reserve is *selling* securities from its portfolio, this action increases the supply of securities available in the market, tending to depress their prices and raise their yields. The Fed has claimed for many years, however, that its principal objective is not to influence interest rates, but to alter the volume of *legal reserves* available to the banking system and, through reserves, the growth of money and credit. Nevertheless, interest rate effects do follow from open market operations.

Effects of Open Market Operations on Reserves. Most authorities agree, however, that the principal day-to-day effect of open market operations is to change the level and growth of *legal reserves*. Generally, a Federal

Reserve *purchase* of securities will *increase* the reserves of the banking system and expand its ability to make loans and create deposits, increasing the growth of money and credit. In contrast, a *sale* of securities by the Federal Reserve will *decrease* the level and growth of reserves and reduce the growth of money and credit. The impact of Federal Reserve open market operations on the reserve position of banks and other deposit-type institutions is illustrated in Exhibit 23–5.

Fed Purchases. In the top portion of Exhibit 23–5 we assume that the Fed is making *purchases* of U.S. government securities in the open market from either deposit-type financial institutions, which keep their reserve

Exhibit 23–5   Federal Reserve Open Market Operations

The Fed Buys Securities

Open market purchase from a bank or other deposit-type financial institution:

Depository Financial Institution		Federal Reserve Bank		Effects
Assets	Liabilities	Assets	Liabilities	Total and excess
U.S. securities − 1,000		U.S. securities + 1,000	Reserves + 1,000	legal reserves increase.
Reserves + 1,000				
at Fed				

Open-market purchase not from a depository financial institution:

Depository Financial Institution		Federal Reserve Bank		Effects
Assets	Liabilities	Assets	Liabilities	Total and excess
Reserves + 1,000	Deposits + 1,000	U.S. securities + 1,000	Reserves + 1,000	legal reserves increase. Deposits
at Fed				increase.

The Fed Sells Securities

Open market sale to a bank or other deposit-type financial institution:

Depository Financial Institution		Federal Reserve Bank		Effects
Assets	Liabilities	Assets	Liabilities	Total and excess
U.S. securities + 1,000		U.S. securities − 1,000	Reserves − 1,000	legal reserves
Reserves − 1,000				decrease.
at Fed				

Open market sale not to a depository financial institution:

Depository Financial Institution		Federal Reserve Bank		Effects
Assets	Liabilities	Assets	Liabilities	Total and excess
Reserves − 1,000	Deposits − 1,000	U.S. securities − 1,000	Reserves − 1,000	legal reserves
at Fed				decrease. Deposits decrease.

accounts at the Federal Reserve banks, or from other institutions and individuals.[6] In the case of purchases from deposit-type institutions, the Federal Reserve records the acquisition of securities in the system's asset account—U.S. securities—and pays for the securities by increasing the reserve account of the selling institution. Thus, reserves of depository institutions at the Fed rise, while institutional holdings of securities fall by the same amount. Note that *both* total and excess reserves rise in the wake of a Fed purchase, assuming that depository institutions have no reserve deficiencies to begin with. With these extra reserves, additional loans can be made and deposits created that will have an expansionary impact on the availability of credit in the economy.

An expansionary effect also takes place when the Federal Reserve buys securities from an institution or individual other than a deposit-type financial institution. Legal reserves increase, but total deposits—a component of the money supply—increase as well. Deposits rise because the Fed issues a check to pay for the securities it purchases, and that check will be deposited in some financial institution. Excess reserves rise, making possible an expansion of deposits and loans on the part of depository institutions. Note, however, that the rise in excess reserves is *less* in this case than would occur if the Fed bought securities only from institutions that maintain reserve accounts with the Federal Reserve banks. This is due to the fact that some of the new legal reserves created by the Fed purchase must be pledged as required reserves behind the newly created deposits. Therefore, Federal Reserve open market purchases of securities have less of an effect on total credit and deposit expansion if the Fed's transaction involves only nondeposit financial institutions and individuals.

Fed Sales. Federal Reserve *sales* of securities reduce the growth of reserves, deposits, and loans. As shown in the bottom half of Exhibit 23–5, when the Fed sells U.S. government securities out of its portfolio to a depository financial institution, that institution must pay for those securities by letting the Fed deduct the amount of the purchase from its reserve account. Both total reserves and excess reserves fall. If deposit institutions were fully loaned up with no excess reserves available, the open market sale would result in a reserve deficiency. Some institutions would be forced to sell loans and securities or borrow funds, reducing deposits and the availability of credit.

The Federal Reserve may also sell securities to an individual or a nondeposit institution. As Exhibit 23–5 reveals, in this instance *both* reserves and deposits fall. Credit becomes less available and usually more expensive.

---

[6]In reality, all Fed security transactions are conducted with one or more of approximately forty primary dealers in U.S. government securities. However, as we will soon see, the effects of each transaction spread rapidly through the money market, affecting the financial position of many individuals and institutions.

How Open Market Operations Are Conducted. All trading in securities by the Federal Reserve is carried out through the system's Trading Desk, located at the Federal Reserve Bank of New York. The Trading Desk is supervised by the manager of the System Open Market Account (SOMA)— a vice president of the New York Fed. The SOMA manager's activities are, in turn, supervised and directed by the Federal Open Market Committee, which meets periodically in Washington, DC. All Fed security purchases and sales are made through a select list of primary U.S. government securities dealers who agree to buy or sell in amounts called for by the Trading Desk at the time the Fed wishes to trade. About a dozen of these dealers are commercial banks that have securities departments. The rest—about two dozen—are exclusively dealers in U.S. government and selected private securities.

The Policy Directive. How does the manager of SOMA decide whether or not to buy or sell securities in the open market on a given day? The manager is guided, first of all, by a policy directive issued to the Federal Reserve Bank of New York following the conclusion of each meeting of the Federal Open Market Committee (FOMC). The manager of SOMA attends each FOMC meeting and participates in its policy discussions. He or she listens to the views of each member of the Federal Reserve Board and the Reserve bank presidents, who describe economic conditions in their region of the country. The manager also receives the benefit of a presentation by staff economists of the Federal Reserve Board that analyzes current economic and financial developments.

An example of a recent Federal Reserve policy directive to the SOMA manager is shown in Exhibit 23–6. This directive summarizes the Federal Reserve's view of current economic developments, particularly those that pertain to the growth of output in the economy and to movements in prices and employment. In line with the Fed's concern over international affairs and especially the value of the dollar in international markets, the directive also contains a synopsis of recent developments in the international money market.

Prominently mentioned in every directive are the *monetary aggregates*—M1, M2, and M3—all measures of the money supply.[7] The FOMC usually sets target ranges for growth in the money supply and asks the SOMA manager to use the open-market policy tool in an effort to achieve those targeted growth rates. In addition, a target range for a key money market interest rate—the average rate on federal funds loans—also is often specified. In the event that rates of growth in the money supply or the federal funds rate drift outside these ranges, the SOMA manager is to notify the chairman of the Federal Reserve Board for further instructions.

We note that the directive issued to the SOMA manager is extremely

---

[7]These and other money supply measures are discussed in Chapter 24.

Exhibit 23–6   Domestic Policy Directive Issued to the Federal Reserve Bank of New York Following the Federal Open Market Committee Meeting, August 19, 1987

At the conclusion of the meeting the following domestic policy directive was issued to the Federal Reserve Bank of New York:

The information reviewed at this meeting suggests on balance that economic activity is expanding at a moderate pace in the current quarter. In July, total nonfarm payroll employment rose considerably further; the increase included continuing large gains in the service-producing sector and a sizable advance in manufacturing. The civilian unemployment rate fell slightly further to 6.0 percent. Industrial production increased strongly in July after rising moderately on balance in the first half of the year. Consumer spending grew at a reduced pace earlier in the year but retail sales posted large increases in June and July. Housing starts were unchanged in July and remained at their reduced second-quarter level. Recent indicators of business capital spending point to some strength, particularly in equipment outlays. The rise in consumer and producer prices has been moderate in recent months, but for the year to date prices generally have risen more rapidly than in 1986, primarily reflecting sizable increases in prices of energy and non-oil imports. Wage increases have remained relatively moderate in recent months.

In foreign exchange markets, the trade-weighted value of the dollar in terms of the other G-10 currencies was unchanged on balance since the meeting of the Committee on July 7. In the second quarter the merchandise trade deficit in current dollars was about the same as in the first quarter.

The monetary aggregates grew slowly in July. For 1987 through July, expansion of both M2 and M3 has been below the lower ends of the ranges established by the Committee for the year, while growth in M1 has been well below its pace in 1986. Expansion in total domestic nonfinancial debt has moderated this year. Most long-term interest rates have risen somewhat since the July meeting; in short-term markets, Treasury bill rates also have increased somewhat while private rates are little changed. Stock prices have risen substantially since the latest meeting.

The Federal Open Market Committee seeks monetary and financial conditions that will foster reasonable price stability over time, promote growth in output on a sustainable basis, and contribute to an improved pattern of international transactions. In furtherance of these objectives the Committee agreed at its meeting in July to reaffirm the ranges established in February for growth of 5½ to 8½ percent for both M2 and M3, measured from the fourth quarter of 1986 to the fourth quarter of 1987. The Committee agreed that growth in these aggregates around the lower ends of their ranges may be appropriate in light of developments with respect to velocity and signs of the potential for some strengthening in underlying inflationary pressures, provided that economic activity is expanding at an acceptable pace. The monitoring range for growth in total domestic nonfinancial debt set in February for the year was left unchanged at 8 to 11 percent.

For 1988, the Committee agreed on tentative ranges of monetary growth, measured from the fourth quarter of 1987 to the fourth quarter of 1988, of 5 to 8 percent for both M2 and M3. The Committee provisionally set the associated range for growth in total domestic nonfinancial debt at 7½ to 10½ percent.

With respect to M1, the Committee recognized that, based on experience, the behavior of that aggregate must be judged in the light of other evidence relating to economic activity and prices; fluctuations in M1 have become much more sensitive in recent years to changes in interest rates, among other factors.

Exhibit 23–6   *(concluded)*

Because of this sensitivity, which has been reflected in a sharp slowing of the decline in M1 velocity over the first half of the year, the Committee again decided at the July meeting not to establish a specific target for growth in M1 over the remainder of 1987 and no tentative range was set for 1988. The appropriateness of changes in M1 this year will continue to be evaluated in the light of the behavior of its velocity, developments in the economy and financial markets, and the nature of emerging price pressures. The Committee welcomes substantially slower growth of M1 in 1987 than in 1986 in the context of continuing economic expansion and some evidence of greater inflationary pressures. The Committee in reaching operational decisions over the balance of the year will take account of growth in M1 in the light of circumstances then prevailing. The issues involved with establishing a target for M1 will be carefully reappraised at the beginning of 1988.

In the implementation of policy for the immediate future, the Committee seeks to maintain the existing degree of pressure on reserve positions. Somewhat greater reserve restraint would, or slightly lesser reserve restraint might, be acceptable depending on indications of inflationary pressures, the strength of the business expansion, developments in foreign exchange markets, as well as the behavior of the aggregates. This approach is expected to be consistent with growth in M2 and M3 over the period from June through September at annual rates of around 5 percent. Growth in M1, while picking up from recent levels, is expected to remain well below its pace during 1986. The Chairman may call for Committee consultation if it appears to the Manager for Domestic Operations that reserve conditions during the period before the next meeting are likely to be associated with a federal funds rate persistently outside a range of 4 to 8 percent.

Votes for this action: Messrs. Greenspan, Corrigan, Angell, Boehne, Boykin, Heller, Johnson, Keehn, Kelley, Ms. Seger, and Mr. Stern. Votes against this action: None.

Source: Board of Governors of the Federal Reserve System, *Federal Reserve Bulletin,* November 1987, pp. 867–868.

general in nature, giving specific targets or target ranges but recognizing the need for flexibility as market conditions change. This is a reflection of the crude state of the art in trying to control money market conditions and the money supply. Many factors other than Federal Reserve operations affect both interest rates and the money supply. While the Federal Reserve can have a significant impact on the *direction* of change, it has considerable difficulty in trying to hit specific targets, especially money supply targets. The Federal Open Market Committee must be flexible and trust the SOMA manager's judgment in responding to daily conditions in the money market, which subsequently may be quite different from those anticipated when the FOMC held its last meeting.

The Conference Call. As an added check on the decisions of the SOMA manager, a conference call between staff economists at the Federal Reserve Board, a member of the FOMC, and the SOMA manager is held each day before trading occurs. The SOMA manager will update those sitting in on the conference call concerning current conditions in the money market and then make a recommendation on the type and volume of securities to be bought or sold that day. At this point the conference call participants may make alternative recommendations for security purchases or sales. Usually, however, the SOMA manager's recommendation is taken, and trading proceeds.

Types of Open Market Operations. There are four basic types of Federal Reserve open market operations. The so-called *straight* or *outright transaction* refers to the sale or purchase of securities in which outright title passes to the buyer on a permanent basis. In this case, a permanent change occurs in the level of legal reserves, up or down. Thus, when the Federal Reserve wants to bring about a once-and-for-all change in reserves, it will tend to use the straight or outright type of transaction.

In contrast, when the Fed wishes to have a temporary effect on bank reserves, it will employ a *repurchase agreement* with a securities dealer. Under a repurchase agreement (REPO or RP), the Fed will *buy* securities from dealers but agree to sell them back after a few days.[8] The result is a temporary increase in legal reserves which will be reversed when the Fed sells the securities back to the dealers. Such RPs frequently are used during holiday periods or when other temporary factors are at work that have resulted in a shortfall in reserves.

The Fed can also deal with a temporary excess quantity of reserves by using a matched-sale purchase transaction—commonly called a reverse RP or reverse REPO. In this instance the Fed will agree to sell securities to dealers for a brief period and then to buy them back. Frequently, when mail deliveries are slowed by weather or strikes, the result is a sharp increase in the volume of uncollected checks (float), giving banks and other depository institutions hundreds of millions of dollars in excess reserves until the checks are cleared. The Fed can absorb these excess reserves using RPs until the situation returns to normal.

The third type of open market operation is the *runoff*. The Federal Reserve may deal directly with the U.S. Treasury in purchasing and redeeming securities. Suppose the Fed has some U.S. Treasury securities that are about to mature. It may redeem these for new securities that are being offered by the Treasury in its latest public auction. The amount of securities that the Fed takes will not then be available to the public, reducing the quantity of securities sold in the marketplace. Other things being equal, this would tend to raise security prices and lower interest rates.

On the other hand, the Fed may decide not to acquire new securities from the Treasury to replace those that are maturing. This would mean the Treasury would be forced to sell an increased volume of securities in the

---

[8]See Chapter 14 for an explanation of how these repurchase agreements are used as a source of funds for securities dealers.

open market in order to raise cash to pay off the Fed. Other things being equal, security prices would fall and interest rates rise. The banking system would, at least temporarily, lose additional reserves to the Treasury.

Finally, the Fed also conducts purchases and sales of securities on behalf of foreign central banks and other foreign institutions that hold accounts with the New York Federal Reserve Bank. The Fed may buy or sell securities from its own portfolio to accommodate these foreign accounts or merely act as an intermediary between the foreign accounts and security dealers in the money market. For example, suppose the Federal Reserve Bank in New York has just received a request from the Bank of Japan to purchase U.S. government securities with its excess cash balance. To pay for the securities, the Bank of Japan will transfer a portion of its deposit at a U.S. bank to its deposit account at the New York Fed. The Fed's trading desk may contact private dealers and make the purchase on behalf of the Bank of Japan, crediting the dealers' banks for the purchase price of the securities and reducing the Bank of Japan's Fed deposit. In this case, the total reserves of the U.S. banking system will not change. Reserves fall initially, but then rise back to their original levels.

However, the Fed may decide to sell the Bank of Japan securities from its *own* portfolio. In this case, bank reserves fall initially but do not rise again. In general, sales of Federal Reserve-held securities to foreign accounts reduce U.S. bank reserves; purchases of securities from foreign accounts for the Fed's own account increase U.S. bank reserves.

Goals of Open Market Operations: Defensive and Dynamic. In the use of any of its policy tools, the Federal Reserve always has in mind the basic economic goals of full employment, a stable price level, sustainable economic growth, and a stable international balance of payments position for the United States. However, only a portion of the Federal Reserve's daily open market activity is directed toward those particular goals. The Fed is also responsible on a day-to-day basis for stabilizing the money and capital markets and avoiding sharp changes in interest rates and credit conditions. A substantial portion of its operations is devoted to making fine adjustments in credit conditions and interest rates to keep the financial markets functioning smoothly. These technical adjustments in market conditions are often referred to as *defensive* open market operations. Their basic purpose is to preserve the status quo and to keep the present pattern of interest rates and credit availability about where it is by keeping reserves of depository institutions steady. For example, suppose the Fed feels that the current level of reserves held by the banking system of about $50 billion is just right to hold interest rates and credit conditions where they are. However, due to changes in other factors affecting bank reserves (such as the public demanding more currency and coin from banks to spend over the holidays), total reserves in the system are expected to fall to $49 billion. The Fed is likely to buy about $1 billion in securities over the next couple of weeks (during the reserve maintenance period for depository institutions) so that total reserves average $50 billion.

In contrast, when the Federal Reserve is more interested in the pursuit of broader economic goals, it will engage in *dynamic* open market operations. These operations are designed to upset the status quo and to change money and credit conditions to a level the Fed believes to be more consistent with its economic goals. For example, if the Fed believes the economy needs to grow faster to create more jobs, it may come to the conclusion that total reserves in the banking system must increase from $50 to $55 billion. In this case, the Fed's trading desk is likely to launch an aggressive program of buying securities until reserve levels reach $55 billion. Open market operations have now become *dynamic,* not merely defensive.

The fact that open market operations are carried out for a wide variety of purposes makes it difficult to follow the Fed's daily transactions in the marketplace and draw any firm conclusions about the direction of monetary policy. On any given day, the Fed may be buying or selling securities merely to stabilize market conditions without any longer-term objectives in mind. For example, even in periods when the Federal Reserve is pursuing a tight money policy, it frequently is in the market *buying* securities because (in the Fed's judgment) other factors have been tightening the market too rapidly. The Fed will attempt to slow things down.

The central bank is really a balance wheel in the financial system, supplying or subtracting reserves as needed on any given day. While experienced Fed watchers find the daily pattern of open market operations meaningful, many observers argue that, unless the investor possesses inside information on the motivation of Federal Reserve actions, it is exceedingly difficult to "read" daily open market operations. A longer-term view is usually needed in order to see the direction in which the central bank is trying to move the financial system.

SELECTIVE CREDIT CONTROLS USED BY THE FED

The discount rate, reserve requirements, and open market operations are often called *general credit controls* because each has an impact on the whole financial system. Another set of policy tools available to the Federal Reserve, however, is more *selective* in its impact, focusing on particular sectors of the economy. Nevertheless, use of these selective tools does contribute toward the overall objectives of the Fed to minimize unemployment, stabilize prices, sustain economic growth, and protect the U.S. international payments position.

Moral Suasion by Federal Reserve Officials

A selective policy tool that has been used more frequently in recent years is moral suasion. This refers to the use of "arm twisting" or "jawboning" by

Federal Reserve officials in order to encourage banks and other lending institutions to conform with the spirit of its policies. For example, if the Fed wishes to tighten credit controls and slow the growth of credit, Fed officials will issue letters and public statements urging financial institutions to use more restraint in granting loans. These public statements may be supplemented by personal phone calls from top Federal Reserve officials to individual lending institutions, stressing the need for more conservative policies. There is evidence that the Federal Reserve has made greater use of moral suasion in recent years, perhaps out of a sense that its general policy tools have become less effective.[9]

Deposit Interest Rate Ceilings

Another selective policy tool used frequently in the past consisted of manipulating legal interest rate ceilings on deposits. These maximum legal deposit rates, usually called Regulation Q ceilings after a set of deposit regulations enforced by the Board of Governors of the Federal Reserve System, were begun during the Great Depression. The Banking Act of 1933 prohibited interest payments on regular checking accounts, for example. Later, interest rates on time and savings deposits offered by any depository institution were restricted to a maximum (or ceiling) level as set by the regulatory agency responsible for each depository institution.

On March 31, 1980, the regulation of deposit interest rate ceilings was turned over to the Depository Institutions Deregulation Committee (DIDC). Created by the Depository Institutions Deregulation Act of 1980, this committee included the chairpersons of the Federal Reserve and other federal agencies regulating banks and thrift institutions. The committee was asked to phase out these federal deposit-rate ceilings no later than 1986 so that the public could earn a market rate of return on its savings. The phaseout was to be gradual to protect the safety and soundness of individual depository institutions. However, DIDC worked fairly rapidly, so that by 1986 regular checking accounts were the only major type of deposit with a mandatory interest rate ceiling (in this case, a ceiling of zero percent).

Why were deposit rate ceilings set in the first place? The original reason for limiting the interest rates financial institutions could pay on their deposits was to safeguard the public's funds and prevent failures among financial institutions. Thousands of banks and savings associations failed during the Great Depression, and many experts felt at the time that excessive competition for deposits had contributed to their collapse. Allegedly, smaller financial institutions, which are more prone to failure even today, are less able to compete for both checking and savings deposits than larger institutions. Thus, the legal rate ceilings were aimed at limiting competition to protect the most vulnerable depository intermediaries. Still another purpose was to ensure an adequate flow of funds to the housing industry by

---

[9]See especially Kane (1974).

protecting the mortgage-lending activities of savings and loans and savings banks.

Several times in the past, the rate ceilings have been used as a tool of monetary policy. If interest rates on securities sold in the open market were rising rapidly but the ceilings were not adjusted upward, interest-sensitive savers would pull their funds out of time and savings deposits. Commercial banks, savings and loans, and savings banks would experience a significant loss of funds, limiting their ability to make loans. Therefore, in theory the rate ceilings could be used to regulate the flow of credit from depository financial institutions.

Unfortunately, it is not at all certain that the rate ceilings really could control the total volume of credit available in the economy. To be sure, when market interest rates rose above the legal ceilings, depository institutions were forced to reduce their loans to their principal customers—small businesses, households, and state and local governments; but other borrowers who could readily tap the open market probably had little difficulty in raising funds. Thus, the ceiling rates, more than likely, resulted in credit discrimination rather than credit control. Then too, the ceilings were damaging to small savers, who were often forced to place their money in a regulated time or savings deposit because they could not afford or lacked the knowledge to purchase higher-yielding unregulated securities in the open market. Hopefully, with deregulation, the use of deposit interest rate ceilings as a central bank policy tool has been ended once and for all.

Margin Requirements

A selective credit control still under the exclusive control of the Federal Reserve Board is margin requirements on the purchase of stocks and convertible bonds and on short sales of those same securities. Margin requirements were enacted into law with passage of the Securities Exchange Act of 1934. This federal law limited the amount of credit that could be used as collateral for a loan. Regulations G, T, and U of the Federal Reserve Board prescribe a maximum loan value for marginal stocks, convertible bonds, and short sales. That maximum loan value is expressed as a specified percentage of the market value of the securities at the time they are used as loan collateral. The margin requirement on a regulated security, then, is simply the difference between its market value (100 percent) and the maximum loan value of that security.

For example, as shown in Exhibit 23–7, the current margin requirement on stock is 50 percent. This means that common and preferred stock can be purchased on credit with the stock itself used as collateral. However, the purchaser can only borrow up to a maximum of 50 percent of the stock's current market value. He or she must put up the remainder of the stock's purchase price in cash money.

As Exhibit 23–7 suggests, margin requirements are not changed very

Exhibit 23–7   **Federal Reserve Margin Requirements on Stocks, Convertible Bonds, and Short Sales** (Percent of Market Value and Effective Date)

Security	March 11, 1968	June 8, 1968	May 6, 1970	Dec. 6, 1971	Nov. 24, 1972	Jan. 3, 1974
Margin stocks	70%	80%	65%	55%	65%	50%
Convertible bonds	50	60	50	50	50	50
Short sales	70	80	65	55	65	50

Note: Regulations G, T, and U published by the Board of Governors of the Federal Reserve System, in accordance with the Securities Exchange Act of 1934, limit the amount of credit to purchase or carry margin stocks when the securities to be purchased are used as collateral. Margin requirements specify the maximum loan value of the securities expressed as a percentage of their market value at the time a loan is made. Margin requirements, therefore, are the difference between the market value of the securities and their maximum loan value.

Source: Board of Governors of the Federal Reserve System, *Federal Reserve Bulletin,* January 1988, Table 1.36.

often. The current margin requirements on stocks, convertible bonds, and short sales of these securities have remained unchanged since January 1974. Most observers of the financial markets feel that the imposition of margin requirements was unnecessary. These requirements arose out of the turmoil of the Great Depression, when many felt that speculative buying and selling of stocks had contributed to the economy's sudden collapse. While this was probably not the case, margin requirements do ensure that a substantial amount of cash must be contributed by the buyer of securities and that borrowing against these securities is kept within reasonable limits. One serious limitation of this selective tool is that it does not cover purchases of all types of stocks and bonds. For this reason, its future use as a tool of Federal Reserve monetary policy is likely to remain very limited.

SUMMARY

The policy tools used by the Federal Reserve System affect the quantity and rate of growth of legal reserves in the banking system which, in turn, have an impact on the capacity of financial institutions to make loans and investments. Central bank policy also influences the level of and direction of change in interest rates. For example, a policy of tight money and restricted growth in reserves usually results in higher interest rates and a diminished supply of credit available to borrowers. An easy money policy is usually accompanied by lower interest rates and an expanded supply of credit available. Working through both interest rates and legal reserves, the Federal Reserve has a direct impact on the size and rate of growth of the money supply. Because changes in the money supply are highly correlated with changes in economic activity, the Fed ultimately influences *both* the level of economic activity and economic growth.

Over the years the Federal Reserve has developed a number of tools for carrying out the objectives of monetary policy. The Fed's primary policy tool is open market operations—buying and selling of securities. Open market operations are used not only to carry out major shifts in policy toward tighter or easier credit conditions (known as dynamic operations), but also to make technical adjustments in market conditions to preserve the status quo (known as defensive operations). Open market operations are carried out by the Trading Desk of the New York Federal Reserve Bank on behalf of all 12 Federal Reserve banks. Policy guidelines for the conduct of open market operations are set by the Federal Open Market Committee, which meets every few weeks in Washington, DC.

When the Federal Reserve wishes to have a quick and powerful impact on the financial system, it may change the amount of legal reserves deposit-type financial institutions must hold behind their deposits. Changes in legal reserve requirements have a direct effect on the volume of funds available to financial institutions for lending and investing and therefore affect both the growth of the money supply and interest rates. However, the impact of reserve requirement changes is so potent that the Fed uses this tool infrequently. A third policy tool—changes in the discount rate charged by Federal Reserve banks on loans made to depository institutions—is also used infrequently. While this tool affects interest rates in the short run, it has a psychological impact on credit uses that often works against the aims of the Fed. Nevertheless, loans to depository institutions provide an important safety valve for the Federal Reserve in the event its policies threaten the safety and soundness of individual financial institutions.

Other tools of monetary policy have been used by the Federal Reserve from time to time to carry out its objectives. Through public speeches and testimony before Congress, private letters, and phone calls, the Fed frequently tries to persuade individuals and groups of the wisdom of its policies. Often called "jawboning" or moral suasion, this policy tool has seen increasing use in recent years to deal with the psychological aspects of major economic problems, especially inflation. Policy tools recently phased out include deposit interest rate ceilings and margin requirements on the purchase of selected stocks and convertible bonds. These infrequently used tools can affect the flow of credit available from selected financial institutions and discourage speculative borrowing. However, like many regulatory controls, these selective policy tools can lead to distortions in the allocation of scarce resources and discrimination in access to credit, especially for borrowers of limited means.

While it is useful to know what tools the Federal Reserve has at its disposal to deal with economic problems and what effects these policy tools are likely to have, the student of the financial system needs to know more. When is the Fed likely to use its policy tools? What factors indicate whether a change in monetary policy has occurred or perhaps soon will occur? How successful has the central bank been in helping to achieve the nation's economic goals? We address these important questions in the next and final chapter on the Federal Reserve System.

STUDY QUESTIONS

1. What is the principal target of Federal Reserve monetary policy? Why?

2. What are legal reserves? Required reserves? Excess reserves? Explain why these concepts are important.

3. Why are commercial banks and other deposit-type intermediaries able to create money? What factors increase the amount of deposits the banking system can create with any given injection of new reserves? What factors reduce the money-creating capabilities of the banking and financial system?

4. In what ways can the Federal Reserve influence the money creation process? The public? The U.S. Treasury?

5. How does the reserve requirement tool affect the ability of deposit-type institutions to create money? What are the principal advantages and disadvantages of the reserve-requirement tool?

6. How and why does a depository institution borrow from the Federal Reserve? Explain what happens when the Fed changes the discount rate. What are the principal advantages and disadvantages of the discount mechanism as a policy tool?

7. Why are open market operations the Fed's most popular and frequently used policy tool? What are the principal effects of open market operations on the financial system?

8. Describe the relationship between the SOMA manager and the FOMC. What is a policy directive? What types of policy targets does the Fed use?

9. Explain the difference between an RP and a straight (or outright) open market transaction. Why is each used? What is a runoff?

10. Explain the difference between defensive and dynamic open market operations.

11. What is moral suasion? Do you believe this tool can be effective? Explain.

12. Explain how margin requirements affect the financial system. Why were these requirements instituted by Congress? Could they be effective in promoting the nation's economic goals?

PROBLEMS

1. Suppose the public wishes to hold $0.40 in pocket money (currency and coin) and $0.25 in time deposits (especially CDs), while depository institutions plan to keep $0.15 in excess reserves for each new dollar of transaction money received. If reserve requirements on transaction deposits and time and savings are 3 percent, what is the size of

the transaction deposit multiplier? The money multiplier? Suppose $5 million in new excess reserves appear in the banking system. How much will be created in the form of new deposits and loans?

2. Total legal reserves currently amount to $40 billion, while currency and coin in public hands total $160 billion. The narrowly defined (transaction) money supply is $525 billion. How large is the money multiplier?

3. A bank holds $130 million in the form of transaction and time and savings deposits. Its reserve deposit at the Federal Reserve bank during the current reserve maintenance period contains a daily average balance of $4 million and its vault cash holdings have averaged daily $0.40 million for several weeks running. Calculate its required reserves and excess reserves if deposits are subject to a 5 percent legal reserve requirement. Now suppose the bank elects to buy $1 million in Treasury bills from the Fed. Do you see any problems with this? Explain.

SELECTED REFERENCES

Board of Governors of the Federal Reserve System. *The Federal Reserve System— Purposes and Functions.* Washington, DC, 1974.

Cacy, J. A.; Bryon Higgins; and Gordon H. Sellon, Jr. "Should the Discount Rate Be a Penalty Rate?" *Economic Review,* Federal Reserve Bank of Kansas City, January 1981, pp. 3–10.

Federal Reserve Bank of Chicago. "The Depository Institutions Deregulation and Monetary Control Act of 1980." *Economic Perspectives,* September–October 1980, pp. 3–23.

Kane, Edward. "The Re-politicization of the Fed." *Journal of Financial and Quantitative Analysis,* Proceedings, November 1974, pp. 743–52.

Laurant, Robert. "Reserve Requirements: Are They Lagged in the Wrong Direction?" *Journal of Money, Credit, and Banking,* August 1979, pp. 171–76.

Lombra, R. E., and R. G. Torto. "Discount Rate Changes and Announcement Effects." *Quarterly Journal of Economics,* February 1977, pp. 171–76.

Poole, William. "A Proposal for Reforming Bank Reserve Requirements in the United States." *Journal of Money, Credit, and Banking,* May 1976, pp. 137–47.

Roth, Howard L. "Federal Reserve Open Market Techniques." *Economic Review,* Federal Reserve Bank of Kansas City, March 1986, pp. 2–15.

Sellon, Gordon H., Jr. "The Role of the Discount Rate in Monetary Policy: A Theoretical Analysis." *Economic Review,* Federal Reserve Bank of Kansas City, June 1980, pp. 3–15.

Thorton, Daniel L. "An Early Look at the Volatility of Money and Interest Rates under CRR." *Review,* Federal Reserve Bank of St. Louis, October 1984, pp. 26–34.

Woodworth, G. Walter. *The Money Market and Monetary Management.* 2nd ed. New York: Harper & Row, 1972.

Chapter 24

Indicators and Goals of Monetary Policy

Learning Objectives in This Chapter

- To explain what an indicator of monetary policy is.
- To define and illustrate the most important indicators of monetary policy in use today.
- To explain how the Federal Reserve System attempts to control money supply growth today.
- To examine the ways in which monetary policy actions can affect the nation's economic goals of achieving full employment, controlling inflation, sustaining adequate economic growth, and achieving a stable balance of payments position.

Key Terms and Concepts in This Chapter

Legal reserves	*M3*	*The Monetarist view*
Federal Reserve	*L*	*The credit availability*
statement	*D*	*or neo-Keynesian*
M1		*view*
M2	*Borrowed reserves*	*Supply-side economics*
	Nonborrowed reserves	

THE Federal Reserve System exerts a powerful impact on the availability and cost of credit in the financial markets. Because the Fed has a great deal to do with the broad changes that occur in interest rates, prices of securities, and the availability of credit, economists and financial analysts spend enormous amounts of time analyzing Federal Reserve actions in an attempt to predict the future course of monetary policy. Indeed, if the experts are able to guess correctly which way the Fed is going, they can make appropriate adjustments in their security portfolios and in their borrowing and spending plans in order to reduce costs and maximize earnings.

It should be noted, however, that understanding the Federal Reserve's intentions and predicting the direction of monetary policy are not easy tasks. Many factors influence interest rates, security prices, and the flow of loanable funds in the financial markets. For example, if we see interest rates on money market instruments rising, there is often a temptation to assume that this trend reflects government policy and, in particular, the actions of the Federal Reserve. In fact, interest rates are subject to all the forces of demand and supply operating in the financial marketplace. An upward surge in rates may reflect a sharp rise in borrowings by units of government and private investors, the impact of inflation, changes in the public's money-using habits, and a host of other factors. The Federal Reserve System is an extremely important influence on the financial system, to be sure, but only one of *many* influences.

FACTORS INFLUENCING THE RESERVES OF THE BANKING SYSTEM

To fully understand the role of the Federal Reserve in the complex environment of the financial marketplace, we need to focus on the principal target of Federal Reserve policy—legal reserves. Recall from the previous chapter that the reserves of the banking system consist of deposits kept at the Federal Reserve banks plus currency and coin held in the vaults of depository institutions. These reserves are the raw material out of which lenders create credit and cause the money supply to grow. This is why the total supply of reserves is the main target of Federal Reserve monetary policy. However, numerous factors affect the supply of reserves available to banks and other lenders. As shown in Exhibit 24–1, these factors fall into three groups: (1) actions of the public; (2) Federal Reserve operations; and (3) operations of the U.S. Treasury Department and foreign investors.

Actions of the Public Affecting Reserves

For example, suppose the public desires to increase its holdings of currency and coin (pocket money). It will do so by writing checks or drafts against deposits held in banks and thrift institutions, reducing the legal reserves of these lending institutions. If these institutions were already fully loaned up, with no excess reserves, then the withdrawal of currency and coin would

Exhibit 24–1   Factors Affecting the Supply of Legal Reserves in the Banking System

Factors	Effect on Total Legal Reserves of the Banking System
Actions of the public:	
Increase in holdings of currency and coin	−
Decrease in holdings of currency and coin	+
Federal Reserve operations:	
Purchase of securities	+
Sale of securities	−
Loans to depository institutions	+
Repayment of loans made to depository institutions	−
Increase in Federal Reserve float	+
Decrease in Federal Reserve float	−
Increase in other assets of the Federal Reserve banks	+
Decrease in other assets of the Federal Reserve banks	−
Increase in other liabilities of the Federal Reserve banks	−
Decrease in other liabilities of the Federal Reserve banks	+
Increase in capital accounts of the Federal Reserve banks	−
Decrease in capital accounts of the Federal Reserve banks	+
U.S. Treasury and foreign operations:	
Increase in Treasury deposits at the Federal Reserve banks	−
Decrease in Treasury deposits at the Federal Reserve banks	+
Gold purchases	+
Gold sales	−
Increase in Treasury currency outstanding	+
Decrease in Treasury currency outstanding	−
Increase in Treasury cash holdings	−
Decrease in Treasury cash holdings	+
Increase in foreign and other deposits in Federal Reserve banks	−
Decrease in foreign and other deposits in Federal Reserve banks	+

force them to raise additional reserves by selling securities, calling loans, and borrowing. The stock of total reserves and the nation's money supply would begin to contract. On the other hand, if the public wishes to reduce its holdings of currency and coin, pocket money will be redeposited in banks and thrift institutions, increasing the total reserves of these institutions. The volume of bank lending and investing will rise, resulting in an increase in the money supply, unless, of course, the Federal Reserve uses its policy tools to counteract the inflow of currency and coin.

Operations of the Treasury and Foreign Investors Affecting Reserves

Actions of the U.S. Treasury and foreign investors also affect the level and growth of legal reserves. The Treasury, foreign central banks, and international financial institutions keep large deposits with the Federal Reserve banks. Any increase in these deposits generally results in a decline in the reserves of deposit-type financial institutions. This is due to the fact that both the Treasury and foreign institutions frequently receive payments from domestic businesses and households. These payments are nearly always made by check and drain reserves from private banks and thrift institutions as the checks are cleared at the Fed. Federal income tax payments by the public, which periodically flow out of private checkable deposits and into the Treasury's checking accounts at the Fed, are good examples of this process. Similarly, when the Treasury sells securities in the open market, investors write checks against their accounts that are eventually credited to the Treasury's deposits with the Federal Reserve banks. In both instances, the public's deposits and total reserves of the banking system fall. Conversely, whenever the Treasury or a foreign depositor write checks against their accounts, these are normally deposited somewhere in the banking system, causing total reserves to rise.

Occasionally, the Treasury buys and sells *gold* at the request of foreign governments or to hold in reserve. Payment for Treasury gold purchases is made by checks drawn on the Treasury's accounts at the Fed. Those individuals and institutions selling the gold will deposit the Treasury's checks somewhere in the banking system, leading to an increase in reserves and deposits. Conversely, if the Treasury sells gold, buyers write checks against their deposits, which forces a decline in both reserves and deposits of the banking system when those checks are collected. If the decline in reserves is too great, the Federal Reserve may have to offset the impact of Treasury gold transactions through open market operations.

The Treasury's minting of new currency and coin also has an impact on reserves and deposits. Newly minted currency and coin are shipped to the vaults of the Federal Reserve banks in return for credit to the Treasury's checking accounts. When the Treasury spends these funds by issuing checks to the public, deposits and reserves in the banking system will rise. Similarly, when there is a decrease in Treasury currency outstanding as currency and coin are retired, total reserves must fall. This happens because the Treasury must pay for the redeemed currency and coin by writing checks against its deposits at the Fed. To cover those checks, it must draw down its deposits kept in private banks, which reduces total reserves available to the banking system.[1]

The Treasury does hold small amounts of currency and coin in its own vaults. When these vault deposits rise, the increase in Treasury cash holdings must have come from funds kept somewhere in the private banking system, leading to a decline in total reserves. Similarly, when Treasury cash holdings decline, the released currency and coin flow into the private banking system and both deposits and total reserves rise.

---

[1] As we noted in Chapter 14, the Treasury keeps deposits—known as Tax and Loan Accounts—in a majority of the nation's banks. The majority of Treasury receipts flow initially into these accounts before they are transferred to the Federal Reserve banks.

Federal Reserve Operations Affecting Reserves

The Federal Reserve System can offset any of the foregoing actions by the public, foreign institutions, or the U.S. Treasury, keeping total reserves of the banking system at roughly the level it desires. As we observed in the preceding chapter, the Fed can increase total reserves by purchases of securities in the open market, or it can reduce total reserves by sales of securities. Loans made to depository institutions through the discount windows of the Reserve banks will increase reserves, while repayments of those loans will cause reserves to fall.

The Fed often increases reserves unintentionally when the volume of float from uncollected checks rises. Banks and other depository institutions that route their checks through the Federal Reserve banks for collection receive credit in their reserve accounts after a specified period (usually two or three days). However, many of those checks have not been collected at the time the Fed grants credit for them due to delays in processing, transportation, or other problems. Checkbook float is essentially an interest-free loan of reserves from the Fed and has the same effect on the total reserves of the banking system as a loan made through the Fed's discount window.

Finally, when the Federal Reserve banks acquire assets of any kind or issue checks to pay their debts or cover expenses, total reserves of the banking system will rise. In contrast, when the Fed receives payments from banks, securities dealers, and others, total reserves fall as checks written against financial institutions are sent to the Federal Reserve banks. Similarly, when a bank joins the Federal Reserve System, it must purchase Federal Reserve stock. This action increases the Fed's capital accounts and lowers the reserves available to private banks. Generally speaking, any Federal Reserve expenditure increases reserves, while any receipt of funds by the Fed reduces the reserves available to the banking system.

The Heart of the Monetary Policy Process—Controlling Reserves

The heart of the monetary policy process is correctly to anticipate changes in all of the foregoing factors that affect the legal reserves of the banking system. The Federal Reserve then tries to achieve a level and rate of growth in total reserves that is consistent with its targeted rate of growth in the money supply and with the nation's economic goals.

THE FEDERAL RESERVE STATEMENT

One of the most widely followed indicators of what the Federal Reserve System is doing to influence conditions in the financial markets and the economy is known as the Federal Reserve Statement. It is published each week in the financial press and lists the factors that supply reserves to depository institutions and those that absorb reserves. The total amount of reserves held by depository institutions at any time equals the difference between the factors supplying reserves and the factors absorbing reserves. The Federal Reserve Statement shows levels of each reserve-supplying or reserve-absorbing factor for the current and previous month or week and any changes between the two time periods. It is the changes in each reserve factor that analysts concentrate on in attempting to understand what the Federal Reserve is trying to accomplish in the financial marketplace.

Factors Supplying Reserves

A Federal Reserve Statement for the months of February and March 1987 is shown in Exhibit 24–2. The first item listed on the statement is Reserve Bank Credit, including Federal Reserve purchases of securities, loans from the discount windows of the Reserve banks, float, and other Federal Reserve assets. If each of these items increases, reserves available to depository institutions rise. Other factors being equal, the ability of financial institutions to make loans and investments and expand the money supply also increases. A *decrease* in any component of Reserve bank credit, on the other hand, results in a decline in the reserves of depository institutions.

Looking more closely at the statement, we note that the Federal Reserve held outright $195,619 million in U.S. government securities and $7,719 million in federal agency securities in March 1987. In addition, $306 million in U.S. government securities and $53 million in federal agency securities were held under repurchase agreements with securities dealers. The column marked "Change" tells us that the Fed, on balance, *bought* securities between February and March 1987. Its total security holdings rose net $924 million ($709 + $193 + $22) over this one-month time span.

Because Federal Reserve purchases expand the supply of reserves, does this mean the Fed was moving toward an easier, less restrictive monetary policy in the spring of 1987? Perhaps, but we also know that much Federal Reserve activity is *defensive* in nature; that is, an effort to offset the effects of other factors on reserves and preserve the status quo in the financial markets.[2] Were other factors at work in this case, draining reserves from depository institutions and forcing the Fed to supply more reserves through security purchases just to keep total reserves reasonably stable? Exhibit 24–2 suggests the answer is yes. For example, checkbook float fell $1,619 million, costing the banking system that much in available reserves. In total, the factors supplying reserves actually *reduced* the total pool of reserves available for lending and investing by the banking system by $1,227 million, as shown in the third column of Exhibit 24–2.

---

[2]See Chapter 23 for a discussion of defensive open market operations.

Exhibit 24–2 **Reserves of Depository Institutions** ($ Millions)

Item	Monthly Averages of Daily Figures for:		
	February 1987	March 1987	Change
Factors Supplying Reserve Funds:			
Reserve Bank Credit:			
U.S. government securities:			
Bought outright	$194,910	$195,619	+709
Held under repurchase agreement	113	306	+193
Federal agency obligations:			
Bought outright	7,719	7,719	0
Held under repurchase agreement	31	53	+22
Acceptances	0	0	0
Loans	554	535	−19
Float	2,085	466	−1,619
Other Federal Reserve assets	17,470	16,885	−585
Gold stock	11,070	11,083	+13
Special drawing rights certificate account	5,018	5,018	0
Treasury currency outstanding	17,652	17,711	+59
Total of factors supplying Reserve funds	$256,622	$255,395	−1,227
Factors Absorbing Reserve Funds:			
Currency in circulation	$206,450	$207,265	+815
Treasury cash holdings	484	506	+22
Deposits (other than reserve balances with Federal Reserve banks):			
Treasury	4,834	3,161	−1,673
Foreign	228	238	+10
Service-related balances and adjustments	2,519	2,026	−493
Other deposits	424	442	+18
Other Federal Reserve liabilities and capital	6,602	6,345	−257
Total of factors absorbing Reserve funds	$221,541	$219,983	−1,558
Reserve Balances with Federal Reserve Banks	$ 35,081	$ 35,412	+331

Source: Board of Governors of the Federal Reserve System, *Federal Reserve Bulletin,* May 1987.

Factors Absorbing Reserves

There is more to the story, however, because most of these new reserves were absorbed by a second set of factors. As we can see in Exhibit 24–2, the second half of the Federal Reserve Statement looks at those factors that reduce reserves, including increases in currency in circulation, Treasury holdings of cash, miscellaneous deposits at the Fed, and the liability and capital accounts of the Federal Reserve banks. If these factors increase, reserve balances held by depository institutions must decline unless offset by reserve supplying factors such as Federal Reserve Credit. However, a decrease in reserve-absorbing factors results in an increase in total reserves. Careful inspection of Exhibit 24–2 shows that a sizable change occurred in the amount of currency and coins in circulation between February and March 1987. The public had greater need for pocket money and withdrew from banks and other depository institutions a net of $815 million in currency and coin. Without any offsetting action, the supply of reserves would have decreased as depository institutions surrendered their vault cash to meet the public's need for pocket money.

However, a major factor increasing reserves was a $1,673 million decrease in Treasury deposits at the Federal Reserve banks. These funds were spent by the Treasury, putting new deposits and reserves into commercial banks scattered across the country. In total, reserve-draining factors fell a net $1,558 million, which meant that total reserves of the banking system would have *increased* that much unless reserve-supplying factors went down.

Interpreting the Federal Reserve Statement

If we compare the sum of changes in factors supplying reserves with changes in factors absorbing reserves, the net change is about $330 million. Because the factors absorbing reserves decreased, on balance, this would have added $1,558 million to the reserves of depository institutions. However, reserve-supplying factors fell $1,227 million. The net difference between these two amounts of approximately $330 million resulted in an increase in the total reserves of depository institutions from $35,081 in February to $35,412 in March of 1987, as shown in the last line of Exhibit 24–2.

The Fed can use open market operations to bring about any change in total reserves that it wishes. Why did it permit the reserves of the banking system to grow by about $330 million over the period shown in Exhibit 24–2? Probably because growth in the money supply had declined sharply in the preceding month and rose only slightly in the current month. The decrease in money growth brought this policy indicator below the minimum acceptable money-growth target as planned by the Fed for 1987. Faced with these developments, the Fed allowed the reserves of depository institutions to rise temporarily as a stimulus to money growth.

MEASURES OF THE NATION'S MONEY SUPPLY

The Federal Reserve Statement is an important indicator of monetary policy, but by no means the only one. Economists, business leaders, and investors look even more closely at weekly, monthly, quarterly, and annual changes in various measures of the money supply. The money supply is the subject of widespread interest and attention for two reasons: (1) changes in money are highly correlated with changes in economic conditions; and (2) the Federal Reserve has a significant impact on money supply growth through its control over the reserves of depository institutions.

Today economists and other students of the financial system follow not one definition of the money supply, but several, each reflecting a slightly different view of what money is. The public's money-using habits are changing rapidly, and many new financial instruments have recently appeared, complicating measurement of the money supply. Examples of recent money-related financial instruments include automatic transfers of funds from savings to checking accounts (ATS), shares in money market mutual funds, interest-bearing negotiable-order-of-withdrawal (NOW) accounts, Super NOWs, and money market deposit accounts (MMDAs). Moreover, Eurodollar deposits and repurchase agreements, once the exclusive property of the largest banks, securities dealers, and corporations, now are available to individuals and smaller institutions for the rapid investment and transfer of funds. These innovations in money-related assets force the Federal Reserve Board occasionally to revise old definitions of the money supply and announce new ones.

Money Supply Measures

The narrowest definition of the money supply in use today is known as M1 — the sum of checking accounts, other checkable deposits (such as NOWs and share drafts), and currency and coin held by the public. This definition views money exclusively as a *medium of exchange* and includes mostly non-interest-bearing assets. It excludes demand deposits owned by domestic banks (called "due from" or correspondent deposits), the U.S. government, and foreign banks and official institutions. Similarly, currency and coin held in the vaults of commercial banks, the U.S. Treasury, and the Federal Reserve banks are also excluded from M1. As shown in Exhibit 24–3, the narrow M1 definition of the money supply totaled about $760 billion in February 1988.

While all forms of money serve as a medium of exchange, the newer forms of money today bear interest and therefore serve partly as a *store of value* or *temporary repository of savings*. Prominent examples include Super NOW accounts, money market deposit accounts (MMDAs), and shares in money market mutual funds held by the public that can be as accessible for making payments as conventional non-interest-bearing checking accounts. Other near-money accounts that are a temporary repository of savings but frequently accessible for spending include savings deposits and small time deposits (with denominations of less than $100,000) at all depository institutions, overnight RPs issued by commercial banks, and overnight Eurodollars issued to U.S. nonbank residents by foreign branches of U.S. banks worldwide. These liquid funds plus everything in M1 make up the M2 definition of money.

An even broader measure of the money supply is M3, which includes all

Exhibit 24–3 **Money-Supply Measures**

Symbol	Definition	Amounts as of February 1988 ($ billions)
M1	Demand deposits at commercial banks (except those due other domestic banks, the U.S. government, and foreign banks and official institutions) less cash items in the process of collection and float + NOW accounts and automatic transfer service accounts at banks and thrift institutions + credit union share draft accounts + demand deposits at mutual savings banks + currency and coin held by the public outside bank and government vaults.	$ 759.6
M2	M1 + savings and small-denomination time deposits at all depository institutions + overnight and continuing contract repurchase agreements at commercial banks + overnight Eurodollars issued to U.S. residents by foreign branches of U.S. banks worldwide + money market mutual funds shares not held by institutions + MMDAs.	$2,946.3
M3	M2 + large-denomination ($100,000+) time deposits at all depository institutions + term Eurodollars and term RPs + institutional money market funds.	$3,717.5
L	M3 + nonbank holdings of bankers' acceptances, commercial paper, U.S. Treasury bills and other liquid Treasury securities, and U.S. savings bonds.	$4,398.4
D	Debt of domestic nonfinancial sectors (U.S. government, state and local governments, and private nonfinancial units) as of the end of each month.	$8,457.6

Source: Board of Governors of the Federal Reserve System, *Federal Reserve Bulletin,* June 1988, Table 1.21.

the components of M2 plus time deposits issued by depository institutions in denominations of $100,000 or more, term RPs offered by commercial banks and thrifts, term Eurodollar deposits held by U.S. residents at foreign banks and U.S. banks worldwide and at banking offices in Canada and Great Britain, and large-denomination institutional deposits in money market funds. Financial institutions, governments, and corporations are the principal holders of these additional financial instruments, most of which are negotiable, with an active resale market. Thus, M3 focuses on *liquid working balances.*

One of the broadest money supply measures is L, which represents total liquid assets. The critical difference between L and other measures of the money supply is the addition of various money market securities: bankers' acceptances, commercial paper, U.S. Treasury bills and other short-term marketable Treasury obligations, and U.S. savings bonds. The fifth and last money supply measure, D or debt, serves as an approximate measure of the total supply of credit resulting from lending funds to federal, state, and local governments, corporations and other private businesses, and consumers. It excludes the debt of financial institutions, however.

Federal Reserve Control of Money Supply Growth

The Federal Reserve attempts to regulate the growth of these measures of the money supply, particularly M2 and M3. As we will soon see, changes in the money supply have been found to be closely correlated with changes in the economy's level of production (GNP) and, through production, both employment and prices. The problem is that the Fed is by no means the only factor determining the size and rate of growth of the money supply. Changes in the public's money-using habits, income levels, and savings habits, and the credit policies of financial institutions also play key roles in money growth.

How does the Fed attempt to control the growth of the money supply? The Fed's method of money supply control has been called the *money-supply-reserve aggregates approach.*[3] This approach focuses on the legal reserves of the banking system, whose level and rate of growth are regulated through open market operations. Three steps are involved. First, the Federal Open Market Committee (FOMC) sets target growth rates for selected money supply measures (usually M2 and M3) for the coming year and for shorter periods within the year.[4] These targets are stated in the form of annual percentage growth rate ranges. For example, in 1987 the Fed called for growth in M2 and M3 between 5½ and 8½ percent during the year. As the year progressed and money growth fell above or below the annual target, shorter-run targets were set, covering calendar quarters or periods between FOMC meetings, in an effort to bring money's growth back into line with the annual target.

The second step in money supply control is to *determine the growth paths for the legal reserves of the banking system.* As we saw in Chapter 23, the total legal reserves of the banking system are linked to the money supply through the money multiplier:

$$\text{Money supply} = \text{Money multiplier} \times \text{Monetary base} \qquad (24\text{-}1)$$

---

[3]See especially Cacy (1980).

[4]Under the terms of the Full-Employment and Balanced Growth Act of 1978 (known also as the Humphrey-Hawkins Act), the FOMC is required to establish calendar year growth ranges for money and credit aggregates by February of each year and review these at midyear. These ranges, which must be reported to Congress in February and July, are based on the period running from the fourth quarter of the previous year to the fourth quarter of the current year. The FOMC is at liberty to change the target growth ranges at any time, however, if it feels that new circumstances warrant a change.

where the money multiplier tells us how many dollars of money result from each dollar increase in the monetary base; and the monetary base includes both total legal reserves and currency and coin held by the public. The size of the money multiplier reflects the public's demand for currency and coin, shifts in deposits between transaction accounts and savings accounts, legal reserve requirements, and the credit-granting policies of financial institutions. The money-multiplier relationship suggests that the growth rate of the money supply will be approximately equal to the growth rate of the multiplier plus the rate of growth in the monetary base (including growth in bank reserves). Therefore, if the Fed is to control the money supply, it must control or influence the growth of the monetary base and project how the money multiplier will change over time. A staff paper released by the Board of Governors on January 31, 1980, sheds a little light on how the Fed makes its projections in order to control money growth:

> After the objective for money supply growth is set, reserve paths expected to achieve such growth are established for a family of reserve measures. These measures consist of total reserves, the monetary base (essentially total reserves of member banks plus currency in circulation), and nonborrowed reserves. Establishment of the paths involves projecting how much of the targeted money growth is likely to take the form of currency, of deposits at nonmember institutions, and of deposits at member institutions (taking account of differential reserve requirements by size of demand deposits and between the demand and time and savings deposit components of M2). Moreover, estimates are made of reserves likely to be absorbed by expansion in other bank liabilities consistent with money supply objectives and also takes account of tolerable changes in bank credit. . . . Estimates are also made of the amount of excess reserves banks are likely to hold.
>
> The projected mix of currency and demand deposits, given the reserve requirements for deposits and banks' excess reserves, yields an estimate of the increase in total reserves, and the monetary base consistent with FOMC monetary targets.[5]

Clearly, the Fed does not completely control either the monetary base or the size of the money multiplier. The public, by making decisions on how much currency and coin, demand deposits, and time and savings deposits it wishes to hold, and depository institutions, in deciding what excess reserves they choose to hold, exert a powerful influence on the growth of the monetary base and the money multiplier. The Federal Reserve must *estimate* what the public and depository institutions will do and try to offset those actions by manipulating the legal reserves of the banking system—the sum of reserves held on deposit at the Federal Reserve banks plus vault cash held

---

[5]See Board of Governors of the Federal Reserve System (1980).

by depository institutions—an important component of the monetary base. Unfortunately, the Fed does not fully control total legal reserves either. This is due to the fact that

Total legal reserves = Borrowed reserves + Nonborrowed reserves

Borrowed reserves are supplied through the discount windows of the Federal Reserve banks and depend on the demand for loans from depository institutions that hold their reserve accounts with the Fed as well as Fed regulations and policy decisions. Nonborrowed reserves are all remaining total legal reserves that are not borrowed.

Since October 1982 the Federal Reserve has aimed to keep the amount of *borrowed reserves* at or near a desired target. To achieve this target level of borrowed reserves, the Federal Reserve must determine what quantity of nonborrowed reserves it must provide to the banking system from this relationship:

$$\text{Amount of nonborrowed reserves that must be supplied} = \text{Estimated amount of total reserves that will be available} - \text{Target level of borrowed reserves}$$

Borrowed reserves have been targeted since 1982 in order to promote more stable interest rates and to allow the Fed to take a longer-run view of money supply growth rather than making many short-term adjustments.

The third step in the money supply control process is to undertake daily and weekly open market operations through the Trading Desk of the Federal Reserve Bank of New York to supply just enough nonborrowed reserves to achieve the desired growth path for borrowed reserves. At each of its periodic meetings the Federal Open Market Committee issues a policy directive to the Trading Desk specifying its desired level of restraint in controlling the growth of reserves and calling either for more restraint, less restraint, or unchanged restraint. The staff of the Trading Desk must interpret that policy directive as to the right amount of reserve restraint each day in terms of the desired average level of borrowings from the Federal Reserve banks.

If *more* restraint on the growth of reserves appears to be needed, the Trading Desk will begin selling and buying securities to change nonborrowed reserves in such a way as to cause the level of borrowings by depository institutions from the Federal Reserve banks to *increase*. If *less* restraint seems needed, the staff of the Trading Desk will use a combination of purchases and sales of securities until the level of borrowings from the Reserve banks *decreases* to the desired level. The Federal Reserve's key focus in controlling the money supply, then, is *reserve availability*.

The manager of the Fed's Trading Desk will continue to add more nonborrowed reserves or take nonborrowed reserves away until both money supply growth and borrowed reserves move toward desired levels.[6] The Federal Reserve banks, with the approval of the Board of Governors, may also decide to change the discount rate or be more or less restrictive in granting loans in order to change the volume of bank borrowing from the discount window. These actions will also affect money market interest rates which will affect the demand for reserves by depository institutions and the public's demand for money.

Achieving the Fed's Money Supply Targets

How well has the Fed done in achieving its targeted growth rates for money? Overall, the Fed has held quite close to its target ranges on an annual basis. However, from month to month and quarter to quarter, the Fed is frequently well outside its annual money growth targets. A good example is presented in Exhibit 24–4 that shows selected actual monthly M2 and M3 growth rates in 1987, along with Fed's targets for that year. Note that some monthly growth rates are well below or significantly above the target 5½ to 8½ percent range. And, we don't know for sure how much damage is done to the achievement of the nation's economic goals from the deviations themselves and from the often hurried adjustments the Fed makes to get back on target.

Exhibit 24–4   **Money Supply Growth, Actual and Planned, in 1987**
(Annualized Percentage Changes)

	M2	M3
January	9.5%	9.2%
February	−0.3%	1.4%
March	1.8%	1.8%
April	5.6%	5.3%
May	0.3%	4.6%
June	0.5%	5.8%
July	2.7%	2.7%
August	6.5%	7.7%
September	5.7%	6.0%
October	6.8%	7.9%
November	0.8%	1.9%
December	4.8%	1.4%
Planned target range	5½ to 8½%	5½ to 8½%

Sources: Board of Governors of the Federal Reserve System and Federal Reserve Bank of St. Louis.

---

[6]The specific procedures used by the Federal Reserve and the System Open Market Account Manager to control the growth of the money supply are described in more detail by Long (1980), Sellon (1980), Wallich (1984), Gilbert (1985), and Sellon (1986).

The Fed does face a number of serious problems as it attempts to achieve its announced money supply targets. Continuing changes in the public's money-using habits, especially shifts from conventional time and savings deposits to NOWs, MMDAs, and other interest-bearing transaction accounts, distort the money supply measures. Moreover, judging by the rapid pace of financial innovation over the past decade, many new types of savings and transaction instruments will be developed in the years ahead, forcing the Fed frequently to readjust its money supply definitions, growth targets, and operating procedures.

Indeed, the Fed has made several important changes in recent years. For example, when more volatile interest rates seemed to be causing too much instability in the early 1980s, the Fed began to modify its money supply control methods. During the fall of 1982 the Board of Governors announced that it would no longer simply make automatic corrections in the growth of reserves when money supply growth deviated from the targeted path. Henceforth, policy judgement would be used, taking into account market conditions, before major adjustments in reserves were carried out. Thus, market forces were granted a larger role in affecting short-term Federal Reserve monetary policy actions. The key results of this policy shift appear to have been: (1) somewhat less variability in interest rates (especially in the key federal funds interest rate); (2) a greater role for money market interest rates in influencing Federal Reserve policy; and (3) somewhat greater variability in month-to-month growth in the nation's money supply.[7]

Controlling the money supply, whatever method is used, is an extremely difficult process. We must keep in mind that Federal Reserve policy is not the sole determinant of the money supply or of total reserves. Fluctuations in the public's demand for money can lead to enormous changes in the amount of credit creation and interest rates in the financial system. Moreover, many of these changes cannot be anticipated. The Fed frequently is forced to react after the fact, leading to sudden surges or sudden declines in the growth of the money supply.

MONEY MARKET INDICATORS

While control of the money supply and reserves are now the principal focus of central bank policymaking in the United States, the Fed also keeps close watch on conditions in the financial markets, especially *the cost and availability of credit in the money market.* Indeed, there is evidence that the Federal Open Market Committee also sets target levels or ranges for the interest rate on federal funds loans. One reason is that the Fed is charged with the responsibility for stabilizing conditions in the financial markets to

---

[7]For a description of this policy shift and its effects see, for example, Wallich (1984) and Sellon (1986).

assure a smooth flow of funds from savers to investors. In addition, it must ensure that the government securities market functions smoothly so that adequate supplies of credit are available to security dealers and the federal government can market its billions of dollars in debt securities without serious difficulty. This is a burdensome responsibility because the Treasury is in the market every week refunding and offering new bills, and both the Treasury and several federal agencies sell billions of dollars worth of notes and bonds each quarter of the year.

The Federal Funds Rate

We can often gather important clues about the magnitude and direction of Federal Reserve policy by watching changes in the cost of credit in the money market. A key money market indicator for many financial analysts is the *daily average rate on federal funds transactions*. This interest rate is usually the first to feel the impact of Federal Reserve open market operations because it reflects the "price" of reserves in the banking system. When the Fed sells securities, the supply of available legal reserves is reduced and, other things held equal, the Fed funds rate will tend to rise. On the other hand, a Federal Reserve purchase of securities will increase available reserves, which tends to push the Fed funds rate down. Because the Federal Reserve does not announce its interest rate targets in advance, however, market watchers try to guess the Fed's target ranges for the federal funds rate by following hourly and daily quotations of that interest rate.

Other Money Market Interest Rates

Other money market rates watched carefully by investors and financial analysts include yields on U.S. Treasury bills, rates charged securities dealers by major New York banks on short-term security loans, and the Federal Reserve's discount rate. When interest rates rise, this is often regarded as an indicator of tightening credit conditions resulting from the Fed's restricting the growth of credit. When rates on T-bills and other money market securities fall, however, this may be regarded as a sign the Fed is easing up, with even lower interest rates soon to follow.

Dealer loans rates and the availability of credit for security dealers are especially sensitive to Federal Reserve policy. As we saw in Chapter 14, dealers in U.S. government securities require millions of dollars in financing each day to carry their extensive inventories. These dealers use relatively little of their own equity capital to finance their operations, relying heavily on borrowed funds from major banks and large nonfinancial corporations. Dealer loans rates, like the federal funds rate, are sensitive to market conditions and fluctuate daily as credit conditions change. Nevertheless, the Fed has a powerful influence on interest rates in the economy, especially money market rates. It is safe to say that interest rates are unlikely to move very far up or down unless the Federal Reserve sanctions the move.

Free Reserves

Another popular indicator of money market conditions is the free reserve position of the banking system. *Free reserves* are excess reserve balances of depository institutions held at the Federal Reserve banks minus borrowings from the discount window. (Recall that excess reserves are legal reserve balances kept at the Reserve banks plus vault cash less required reserves.) Both the level and direction of changes in free reserves are thought to have meaning.

The dynamic element in free reserves is borrowings by depository institutions from the discount windows of the Federal Reserve banks. When these borrowings increase, depository institutions feel more restricted in their lending and investing until they can repay their debt to the Fed. Credit becomes more difficult to obtain and more expensive. On the other hand, when discount window borrowings fall relative to excess reserves, depository institutions feel less pressure against their reserves and may become more liberal in extending credit.

Free reserves can be either positive or negative, depending on whether excess reserves are larger or smaller than borrowings from the Reserve banks. When borrowings exceed excess reserves, a condition of *net borrowed reserves* prevails. On the other hand, if borrowings are less than excess reserves, the banking system has *net free reserves*. Movement from week to week toward deeper net borrowed reserves generally implies that tighter credit conditions are developing. In contrast, a change toward greater net free reserves is usually regarded as an indicator of easier credit conditions. One problem with the free reserve indicator is that many forces affect free reserves other than just Federal Reserve policy. For example, individual depository institutions decide what volume of excess reserves they wish to hold and whether or not to borrow from the Federal Reserve banks. This indicator, then, is subject to much the same criticism as the other monetary policy indicators we have discussed—it is influenced by many factors other than Federal Reserve policy.

Interpreting Money Market Indicators

The use of money market indicators to interpret the current course of monetary policy may be illustrated using the information given in Exhibit 24–5. Movements in the effective federal funds rate, market yields on U.S. Treasury bills, the Federal Reserve of New York's discount rate, and free reserves between January and March 1987 are shown in this exhibit. We note that money market interest rates at first declined over the period shown in the exhibit and then rose slightly. At the same time, deposit institutions experienced a rising net free reserve position early in the period, with free reserves increasing from $488 to $655 million. This was a signal to many money market analysts that the Federal Reserve was easing credit conditions and credit was becoming more available and less expensive. Later, in

Exhibit 24–5   **Money Market Indicators of Federal Reserve Policy**

	1987		
Money Market Indicator	**January**	**February**	**March**
Effective federal funds rate	6.43%	6.10%	6.13%
Interest rate on U.S. Treasury bills, secondary market:			
Three-month	5.43	5.59	5.59
Six-month	5.44	5.59	5.60
Federal Reserve Bank of New York discount rate	5.50	5.50	5.50
Net free (or net borrowed) reserves ($ millions)	$488	$655	$389

Notes: Figures for the federal funds rate are averages of daily effective rates weighted by the volume of transactions at these rates. Treasury bill rates are computed on a bank discount basis from daily closing bid prices. Discount rates are averages supplied by the Federal Reserve Bank of New York. Free reserves are the difference between excess reserve balances with the Federal Reserve banks less total borrowings from the discount windows of the Reserve banks.

Source: Board of Governors of the Federal Reserve System, *Federal Reserve Bulletin,* selected issues.

the last month, free reserves declined and interest rates rose slightly as the Fed tightened credit somewhat. In part, the Fed appeared to be reacting against unusually heavy credit demands from the federal government, a sharp resurgence in consumer borrowing which was fueling something of a consumer "spending spree" following the last recession, and investors' fears that inflation might be rekindled.

THE FEDERAL RESERVE AND NATIONAL ECONOMIC GOALS

For many years now, the Federal Reserve System has played an active role in the stabilization of the economy and the pursuit of economic goals. These goals include controlling inflation, promoting full employment and sustainable economic growth, and achieving a stable balance of international payments position for the United States. In recent years these goals have proved to be extremely difficult to achieve in practice and in fact have often required conflicting policies. Nevertheless, the Fed remains committed to them and sets its policies accordingly.

The Goal of Controlling Inflation

Inflation—a rise in the general price level of all goods and services produced in the economy—has been among the more serious economic problems of the United States in recent years. Indeed, inflation has been a worldwide problem, with many nations experiencing far higher annual rates of inflation

Exhibit 24–6   **Measures of the Rate of Inflation in the United States**
(Compound Annual Rates of Change)

Price Level Index	Period						
	1960–65	1965–70	1970–75	1975–80	1980–85	1986-87	1988*
Consumer price index (CPI)	1.3%	4.2%	6.7%	8.9%	5.5%	2.8%	4.2%
Producer price index, finished goods (PPI)	0.4	2.9	8.6	8.6	3.5	0.3	3.1
Implicit price deflator for gross national product	1.6	4.2	6.6	7.2	5.4	2.8	NA

*The rate of change in the consumer price index and the producer price index are for the 3 months ending in March 1988.

Source: Federal Reserve Bank of St. Louis, *Annual U.S. Economic Data,* Compound Rates of Change, 1967–1986; U.S. Department of Commerce; and Board of Governors of the Federal Reserve System, *Federal Reserve Bulletin.*

than those currently prevailing in the United States. Moreover, inflation is *not* new; price levels have been generally rising since the beginning of the Industrial Revolution in Europe nearly 300 years ago. There is also evidence of outbreaks of rampant inflation during the Middle Ages and in ancient times.

What is particularly alarming about inflation is its tendency to *accelerate* in the absence of strong efforts to control it. For example, between 1960 and 1965 the U.S. consumer price index (the CPI or cost-of-living index) rose an average of only 1.3 percent a year. Then, between 1965 and 1970, in the middle of the Vietnam war, large federal budget deficits, and rapid expansion of the money supply, the average annual growth rate of consumer prices more than tripled, to a 4.2 percent annual rate. From 1970 through 1975, the CPI's annual growth rate climbed to almost 7 percent and then soared to nearly 9 percent through 1980. Finally, large-scale unemployment and back-to-back recessions in the 1980s helped reverse the accelerating trend and significantly lowered the inflation rate. More recently, however, inflation has risen somewhat with faster growth in the economy (see Exhibit 24–6).

What are the causes of inflation? During the 1960s and 1970s, war and government spending were certainly contributing factors. Soaring energy and food costs, higher home mortgage rates, and rapid increases in labor and medical care costs also played key roles until the 1980s brought a turnaround. Another contributing factor was the decline in the value of the U.S. dollar in international markets. The dollar's weakness relative to other major currencies (particularly the German mark and the Japanese yen) raised the prices of imports into the United States and lessened the impact of foreign competition on domestic producers.

Still another causal factor is inflationary expectations—the anticipation of continued inflation by businesses and households. Once underway, inflation seems to develop a momentum of its own as consumers spend more and borrow more freely to stay ahead of rising prices, sending those prices still higher. Businesses and labor unions begin to build inflation into price and wage decisions, passing higher costs along in the form of higher prices for goods and services. The result is a wage-price spiral where each plateau of increased costs is used as a basis for justifying further price increases.

Inflation creates distortions in the allocation of scarce resources and definitely hurts certain groups. For example, it tends to discourage saving and encourages consumption at a faster rate to stay ahead of rising prices. Moreover, the decline in the savings rate tends to discourage capital investment. Unfortunately, this means that the economy's growth in productivity (output per worker-hour) tends to slow. The fall in productivity means that the supply of new goods and services cannot keep pace with rising demands, putting further upward pressure on prices. At the same time, workers usually seek cost-of-living adjustments in wages and salaries, leading to a dramatic increase in labor costs. While some workers represented by strong unions or in growth industries manage to keep pace with inflation, other groups, including many savers, lenders of funds, retired persons, and government employees, whose income is fixed or rises slowly, often experience a decline in their real standard of living.

The Goal of Full Employment

The Employment Act of 1946 committed the federal government for the first time to minimizing unemployment as a major national goal. The Federal Reserve, as part of the government's structure, is therefore committed to this goal as well. In recent years, the U.S. unemployment rate as determined from monthly surveys conducted by the U.S. Department of Labor has hovered in the 5 to 10 percent range. In terms of numbers of people, between 7 and 11 million workers have been actively seeking jobs but have been unable to find them. The nation's output of goods and services and its real standard of living are reduced by unemployment, which also breeds social unrest, increased crime, and higher tax burdens on those who are working.

In some years the U.S. economy has experienced rising plateaus of unemployment. As the 1960s ended, unemployment affected less than 5 percent of the civilian labor force. However, a recession in 1970–71 led to substantial increases in the number of jobless workers, and there was little improvement until 1973, when the jobless rate fell below 5 percent. Following the Arab oil embargo and a deep recession in 1974–75, the nation's unemployment rate rose to a postwar record of almost 9 percent. The recovery of the economy between 1976 and 1979 brought the unemployment rate down to just under 6 percent midway in 1979. However, the double recessions of 1980 and 1982 sent it soaring again to about 10 percent. In the middle and late 1980s the U.S. unemployment rate fell back and eventually dipped under 6 percent for a time (see Exhibit 24–7).

Exhibit 24–7 **U.S. Civilian Unemployment Rate** (Percent of Civilian Labor Force)

1970	4.9%	1979	5.8%
1971	5.9	1980	7.1
1972	5.6	1981	7.6
1973	4.9	1982	9.7
1974	5.6	1983	9.6
1975	8.5	1984	7.5
1976	7.7	1985	7.2
1977	7.1	1986	7.0
1978	6.2	1987	6.2
		1988*	5.6

*As of March 1988.

Source: Economic Report of the President, February 1984; and *Federal Reserve Bulletin,* selected issues.

Is it possible to have zero unemployment? What is full employment? In a market-oriented economy, where workers are free to change jobs and businesspeople are free to hire and fire, some unemployment is inevitable. There is a minimum level of unemployment, known as *frictional unemployment,* which arises from the temporary unemployment of persons who are changing jobs in response to higher wages or better working conditions. Full employment, therefore, refers to a situation in which the only significant amount of unemployment is frictional in nature. In a fully employed economy, everyone actively seeking work will find it in a relatively short period. During the 1960s the President's Council of Economic Advisers defined full employment as a situation in which only 4 percent of the civilian labor force was unemployed.

In recent years, however, economists have raised their estimates of the amount of irreducible frictional unemployment. A key factor is the massive shifts which have occurred in the composition of the American labor force in recent years, especially the rapid increase in the number of adult women seeking jobs. Women 20 years of age and older, in fact, have accounted for more than half the net increase in the U.S. labor force in recent years. This upward surge in women's employment may be attributed to a decline in fertility rates, more varied jobs available to women, and the erosion of family incomes due to inflation. Teenage participation in the labor force also has expanded sharply since the late 1970s under the pressure of inflation, the rising cost of college training, and the spread of vocational schools. Historically, these two groups (women and teenagers) have reported higher average unemployment rates than those of most other workers. Both women and teenagers move in and out of the job market with much greater fluidity than do adult male workers, due to family needs and schooling opportunities, thus raising the average unemployment rate.

Other groups also increasing in importance who traditionally report high unemployment rates include nonwhite workers and unskilled labor. One of the most conspicuous shortcomings of U.S. economic policy has been its inability to significantly lower the unemployment rate among minority workers and the unskilled. Structural unemployment—joblessness due to a lack of necessary skills—has not been reduced to any appreciable extent in the U.S. economy since the mid-1960s.

The Goal of Sustainable Economic Growth

The Federal Reserve has declared that one of its most important long-run goals is to keep the economy growing at a relatively steady and stable rate— that is, high enough to absorb increases in the labor force and prevent the unemployment rate from rising, but slow enough to avoid runaway inflation. Most economists believe that this implies a rate of growth in GNP of close to 4 percent annually on a real (inflation-adjusted) basis. Periodically, however, the economy grows more slowly than this or turns down into a recession, resulting in rising unemployment.

While most recessions have been relatively brief and mild, they have averaged two each decade, or about once every three to four years. For example, during the 1970s the nation's real output of new goods and services declined in 1973–75 and again in 1979–80 (Exhibit 24–8). The 1980 recession was the shortest downturn ever recorded, lasting only six months, but was followed by a deep recession in 1982 when real GNP dropped about 2 percent. However, during the mid-1980s a strong economic recovery produced accelerated GNP growth in 1983 and 1984 toward the 7 percent range, only to be followed by a slowdown late in the 1980s, when GNP grew in the 3 to 4 percent range.

Exhibit 24–8   Rates of Growth in Real U.S. GNP (Compounded Annual Rates of Change)

Period	Annual Rate of Change in GNP (1972 dollars)	Period	Annual Rate of Change in GNP (1972 dollars)
1960–69	3.9%	1979–80	−0.3%
1970–79	3.5	1980–81	2.5
1980–87	2.6	1982–83	3.7
		1983–84	6.8
		1984–85	2.7
		1985–86	2.5
		1986–87	4.0

Source: Federal Reserve Bank of St. Louis, *National Economic Trends,* and *Annual U.S. Economic Data,* various issues; and Board of Governors of the Federal Reserve System, *Federal Reserve Bulletin,* various issues.

Forecasting the actual starting point of each recession and its duration has proved to be an exceedingly difficult problem for the Federal Reserve. Each downturn in the economy springs from somewhat different causes, though most recessions involve a sharp cutback in investment in inventories as business decisionmakers come to anticipate lower sales volume. Fears of being caught with a large quantity of unsold goods lead to periodic cutbacks in new orders, throwing people out of work. At the same time, interest rates usually rise to peak levels shortly before a recession begins, gradually choking off private investment.

Traditional economic theory suggests that a decline in the rate of economic growth should lead to a lower rate of inflation. This follows from the observation that recessions are marked by reduced demand for goods and services and falling incomes. Thus, in theory at least, a recession and slower economic growth are short-run cures for severe inflation, though for those without jobs they are certainly high-cost cures. Interestingly enough, however, recent recessions have been accompanied by substantial inflation. Many observers believe the bias in the U.S. economy toward inflation even during recessionary periods may be due to the rapid growth of service industries relative to the manufacturing sector, to welfare payments (especially unemployment compensation) that sustain money incomes, escalator clauses in wage contracts, and the expectation that government policy will always respond quickly to protect jobs whenever economic problems appear.

Equilibrium in the U.S. Balance of Payments and Protecting the Dollar

The Federal Reserve must be concerned not only with domestic economic conditions, but also with developments in the international sector. In this area, the Fed pursues two interrelated goals: protecting the value of the dollar in foreign currency markets, and achieving an equilibrium position in the U.S. balance of payments.

When the United States buys more of the goods, services, and securities offered by other nations than those countries spend for what the United States sells, the difference must be made up by giving foreigners claims against U.S. reserves and resources. If the United States persists in purchasing or acquiring more abroad than foreigners purchase or acquire here, a disequilibrium position in the nation's balance of payments results. This means that the United States cannot continue to draw down its reserve assets (primarily gold, foreign currencies, and Special Drawing Rights at the International Monetary Fund) indefinitely, nor will it find foreigners willing to accept unlimited amounts of dollars.[8] At some point the federal government and the Federal Reserve must adopt policies that slow down

---

[8]See Chapter 27 for a discussion of reserve assets and disequilibrium problems in the U.S. balance of payments.

Exhibit 24–9   **Merchandise Trade Balance of the United States**

Billions of Dollars	FOB Exports-CIF Imports
1965	$ 4.3
1970	0.5
1975	2.2
1980	−36.2
1981	−39.7
1982	−36.4
1983	−67.1
1984	−112.5
1985	−122.1
1986	−144.3
1987	−159.2

Source: U.S. Department of Commerce.

the outflow of U.S. dollars and encourage foreigners to buy more U.S. goods, services, and securities. Failing this, the value of the dollar in international markets will begin to weaken.

In recent years the United States has experienced some deep deficits in its merchandise trade with other nations and in its international balance-of-payments position (see Exhibit 24–9). One cause of these international deficits, as we will see in Chapter 27, has been massive imports of foreign oil. Petroleum imports now account for about one third of total U.S. merchandise imports each year. Other foreign imports into the United States experiencing considerable growth in recent years include European and Japanese autos, steel products, building materials, natural gas, and crude rubber. At the same time foreign investors have sharply increased their investments in the United States, making the United States a debtor nation and leading to large outflows of investment earnings to foreign investors.

The sizable trade deficits and current net debtor position of the United States has presented Federal Reserve policymakers with a major dilemma. Should they push up domestic interest rates and limit credit growth to protect the dollar, slow imports, and prevent future inflation? Perhaps, but this would probably slow domestic economic growth and increase unemployment. This is not an easy dilemma to unravel; there are substantial costs no matter which way the Federal Reserve chooses to go.

WHAT POLICIES SHOULD WE PURSUE TO ACHIEVE NATIONAL AND INTERNATIONAL ECONOMIC GOALS?

The four key economic goals we have discussed—avoidance of inflation, reducing unemployment, achieving healthy and sustainable economic growth, and achieving a strong international payments position—cannot be achieved by wishful thinking. They require carefully constructed and consistent national and international economic policies. Unfortunately, there is a long-standing controversy over what these policies should be. Three different views have emerged over the years on what public policy strategies contribute most to low inflation, high employment, strong growth, and stable international payments. These three competing viewpoints on public policy are known as:

1. The Monetarist view.
2. The credit availability (neo-Keynesian) view.
3. Supply-side economics.

We will look briefly at each one and how it proposes to solve economic problems.

The Monetarist View

An approach to economic policy growing rapidly in popularity in recent years is the Monetarist view. Among the most important proponents of this particular approach to government policy are economists Milton Friedman, Karl Brunner, Alan Meltzer, David Meiselman, Anna Schwartz, Christopher Sims, and others.[9] These economists argue that the *money supply* is a dominant influence on prices, spending, production, and employment. Friedman and Schwartz, for example, after analyzing money and business cycles dating back to the Civil War, concluded that

> Appreciable changes in the rate of growth of the money stock are a necessary and sufficient condition for appreciable changes in the rate of growth of money income.[10]

Moreover, changes in the rate of money supply growth appear to precede changes in economic activity and inflation, suggesting that money exerts an independent causal influence on economic conditions. They believe the economy is inherently stable and tends toward full employment and sustainable growth without inflation if left to its own devices. One of the ways in which government can aid the economy in achieving noninflationary growth and full employment is to avoid "fine tuning" the system. Allegedly, attempts at fine tuning do more harm than good, causing instability in the economy.

According to the Monetarist view, Federal Reserve monetary policy affects the economy mainly through changes in the rate of monetary growth. For example, if the money supply grows too rapidly, exceeding the public's

---

[9]See especially Friedman and Schwartz (1963), Friedman and Meiselman (1963), Keran (1967), Anderson and Carlson (1970), and Sims (1972) in the references list at the end of this chapter.

[10]See Friedman and Schwartz (1963), p. 53.

expectations, an excess stock of money results. Money demand for goods and services will rise rapidly and put upward pressure on prices.[11] In contrast, when the money supply grows too slowly relative to the demand for money, the public attempts to restore its desired money balances by cutting back on spending and purchases of financial assets. The result is a drop in income and demand in the economy and a rise in interest rates, so that employment and growth are slowed. The Federal Reserve can exert its most favorable effect on the economy simply by allowing the money supply to grow at a relatively constant rate (preferably about 4 to 6 percent a year), which approximates the rate of growth in the economy's capacity to produce goods and services.

The Credit Availability, or Neo-Keynesian, View

A more traditional approach to fighting inflation is known as the credit availability, or neo-Keynesian, view.[12] Adherents to this view believe that a wide range of factors—monetary and nonmonetary—influence employment, growth, and prices. They argue that the money supply is an important factor in generating business cycles, but not necessarily the most important factor. Government spending and taxation (fiscal policy) as well as money and credit policy also play critical roles in creating or reducing inflation, unemployment, and other problems because of their impact on investment spending.

We recall from Chapter 7 that investment spending includes household expenditures for housing, automobiles, and other durable goods and business expenditures for plant, equipment, and inventories. Investment spending is the most volatile component of the total demand for goods and services in the economy. When investment falls, a recession usually follows, while rising investment often precipitates an economic boom. Changes in investment expenditures have a multiplier effect on total income in the economy because new investment generates income, which leads to increased consumption and still more income. Thus, even small changes in the volume and mix of investment expenditures can lead to magnified changes in income, spending, employment, and prices.

How can government fiscal and monetary policy affect investment spending and ultimately exert an impact on inflation, employment, and

---

[11]Monetarists base this conclusion on the assumption that each unit (individual or business) in the economy desires to hold a certain quantity of money. If the money supply grows so large that it exceeds desired levels, then the cost of holding additional money exceeds its benefits. Businesses and individuals will attempt to spend away their excess money balances by purchasing goods, services, and other assets. With the economy at or near full employment, prices must rise due to the added spending.

[12]The term *neo-Keynesian* is often used to describe economists who have adopted, amplified, and further refined many of the ideas of British economist John Maynard Keynes. While Keynes wrote several books and many articles covering the period from World War I through World War II, his views on the causes of unemployment, inflation, and other economic problems appear in his *The General Theory of Employment, Interest, and Money* (1936). Leading economists who have further refined and developed the original Keynesian theories include Patinkin (1976), Tobin (1965), Smith (1969), and Samuelson (1979).

growth? According to the neo-Keynesian view, the volume of investment spending is affected directly by the cost and availability of credit, monetary growth, and total wealth. The rate of interest is especially important here because it is a measure of the cost of financing new investment spending. A rise in interest rates, other things being equal, will reduce the demand for investment funds, slowing not only investment spending but also the growth of employment, income, and prices. Higher rates will tend to increase unemployment but usually strengthen the dollar in international markets. In contrast, lower interest rates stimulate the demand for investment, which increases income and employment and may cause more inflation (if the economy is at or near full employment). The Federal Reserve can bring about changes in interest rates, up or down, by changing the real money supply (money adjusted for changes in the price level). For example, rising inflation can be countered by slower monetary growth. If the money supply grows more slowly than the public's demand for real money balances, interest rates will rise, leading to a decline in investment spending. Income and spending in the economy will grow more slowly, and inflationary pressures will be reduced.

We can illustrate these hypothesized effects of changes in the money supply on interest rates and income by using a familiar methodology in economics—IS-LM analysis. This well-known tool of economic analysis is based on two key relationships: (1) the effects of changing money supply and money demand on both interest rates and income, and (2) the effects of changing saving and investment decisions (including government borrowing) on both interest rates and income. IS-LM analysis assumes there are *two* equilibrium relationships between all these factors, each represented in Exhibit 24–10 below. The *LM curve* is a locus (collection) of equilibrium interest rates for which money demand (L) equals money supply (M). For each level of income specified along the horizontal axis in Exhibit 24–10, the point on the LM curve directly above that level of income gives the equilibrium interest rate at which L = M. Similarly, the *IS curve* is a locus (collection) of equilibrium levels of income at which the volume of planned savings (S) equals the volume of planned investment (I), including government borrowing. For any given interest rate along the vertical axis of Exhibit 24–10, the IS curve will show that level of income at which point the economy is in equilibrium (with S = I). At the exact point where the IS and LM curves cross, *both* the economy and interest rates in the financial markets are in *equilibrium*.

But, suppose the Federal Reserve *increases the money supply*. In the short run, at least, the LM curve shifts outward and to the right to LM', resulting in a *lower equilibrium interest rate* (i'). Moreover, because the lower equilibrium interest rate will stimulate new investment spending, there is a rise in economic activity to a new and *higher equilibrium level of income* (y'). Thus, a monetary policy action by the Fed affects *both* interest rates and income (production and spending).

Exhibit 24–10   **How Equilibrium Interest Rates and Income Change
with Shifts in the Money Supply**

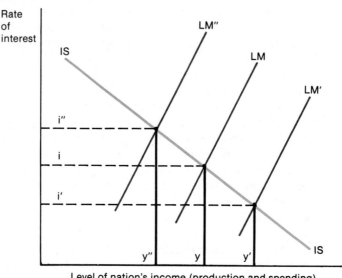

Level of nation's income (production and spending)

Suppose the Federal Reserve *decreases the money supply*. The LM curve
contracts backward and to the left to LM″, resulting in a *higher equilibrium
interest rate* (i″). Moreover, with higher interest rates, some investment
spending is discouraged, reducing the level of overall economic activity. A
lower equilibrium level of income (y″) results.

Fiscal policy—government taxing and spending—also has a significant
role to play in cooling inflation and promoting high employment and growth,
according to the neo-Keynesian view. If total spending in the private sector
of the economy grows too rapidly, generating inflation, government spending
can be reduced, which will soon lead to less consumption spending and
ultimately decrease private investment. In other words, government spending, like private investment spending, has a multiplier effect, up or down,
on employment, income, and prices. Alternatively, private consumption and
investment spending can be choked off by higher taxes. Through increased
tax revenues, federal, state, and local governments can reduce budget deficits
or even run budget surpluses so that the government sector actually withdraws funds from the private spending stream. Demand for goods and services will fall, leading to reduced inflationary pressures but also probably
some increase in unemployment and slower economic growth.

Thus, the neo-Keynesian, or credit availability, view stresses the necessity of using *both* monetary and fiscal policy to achieve economic goals. Neo-Keynesians question whether merely maintaining a constant rate of growth in the money supply will, by itself, solve the problems of inflation and unemployment. The appropriate growth rate for money depends on economic conditions, the status of government fiscal policy, and especially the public's demand for money. Under some circumstances (especially if the demand for money were falling), a 4 percent rate of growth in the money supply could be highly inflationary. Under other circumstances (such as following a rapid rise in money demand), 4 percent money growth could lead to severe recession and higher unemployment. In either case, suggest the neo-Keynesians, the key factors to watch in gauging the direction and impact of monetary policy are interest rates and the growth of the real money supply. To fight inflation, reduce the growth rate of the real money supply and increase interest rates; to stimulate employment and economic growth, speed up money growth and lower interest rates.

Supply-Side Economics

Shortly after President Ronald Reagan took office in January 1981, the administration announced a new approach to economic problems. It was labeled supply-side economics, to differentiate this strategy from methods employed during most of the postwar period that attacked inflation and unemployment from the demand side of the marketplace. Just as logically, supply-siders claimed, we could solve inflation and unemployment problems from the supply side—by increasing the output of goods and services. If the economy produces more goods and services relative to the public's demand, there is less reason for prices to rise and more jobs open up.

How can this be done? Basically, by stimulating private investment and increasing savings to finance that investment. As Tatom notes, "supply-side economics is growth- and efficiency-oriented."[13] It argues that economic policy has a direct impact on the rate of growth in the supply of productive resources and upon technological innovation—factors that determine the economy's capacity to produce. The economy's productive capacity is lowered by government regulations which require the use of inefficient technologies or reduce incentives to save, invest, and use resources. The same is true of an excessive tax burden which transfers resources from the private to the public sector. In an effort to avoid high tax rates, resource owners will divert their resources to lower-taxed but less efficient uses, such as by substituting labor for capital, retaining rather than replacing old equipment, and spending more on consumption instead of saving. Supply-siders in recent years have recommended:

---

[13]See Tatom (1981), p. 18.

1. A lower and more stable rate of monetary expansion.
2. Less government regulation of business to stimulate competition and technological innovation.
3. Reduced tax rates on individual incomes and business profits to stimulate saving.
4. Accelerated depreciation of business equipment to stimulate investment.
5. A reduction in the size of the government sector in order to divert more resources into the private sector and into free markets.

Can the supply-side approach really work to simultaneously subdue inflation, bring about stable long-term economic growth with low unemployment, and improve the U.S. international payments position? The jury is still out on this question. The U.S. inflation rate *has* dropped significantly since its record high levels in the late 1970s, but at the price of slower economic growth. And the U.S. balance-of-payments situation, as we saw earlier, worsened in the early and mid-1980s. Much depends on the *psychological effects* of supply-side economics—its ability to persuade business to increase investment in plant and equipment and to convince savers to spend less on current consumption and save more. Moreover, the lowering of tax rates in the 1980s contributed to higher federal budget deficits which, combined with other factors, kept interest rates at relatively high levels and limited growth in capital investment. Thus, it is not at all clear that supply-side economics, like Monetarism or the neo-Keynesian approach, can ensure progress toward all of society's economic goals.

THE TRADEOFFS AMONG ECONOMIC GOALS

As we have seen in this chapter, the United States and other nations face some serious economic problems. Inflation is less severe today than in the turbulent 1970s, but unemployment and balance-of-payments problems present imposing difficulties. Does this mean the Federal Reserve System and other government policymaking agencies have simply failed to do their jobs?

Unfortunately, the problem is not that simple. For one thing, economic goals *conflict*. For example, controlling inflation and stabilizing the U.S. international payments situation usually require the Fed to slow down the economy through restricted money growth and higher interest rates. However, this policy threatens to generate more unemployment and subdued economic growth. Evidence that economic goals frequently conflict was provided by British economist A. W. Phillips and American economists Paul Samuelson and Robert Solow nearly three decades ago.[14] These economists uncovered an *inverse* relationship between price-level increases (inflation)

---

[14]See, in particular, Phillips (1958) and Samuelson and Solow (1960).

and unemployment. For example, Samuelson and Solow, using data collected from the 1950s, found that stable prices could only be achieved if unemployment remained as high as 5 to 6 percent of the civilian labor force. And their estimate may prove to be conservative in today's economy. As we have seen, in the 1980s U.S. unemployment hovered in the 5 to 10 percent range, while prices continued to rise about 3 to 4 percent a year on average. Such a policy tradeoff may not be *inevitable* in the long run, but it is clear that the process of attaining economic stability can be a difficult and painful one.

THE LIMITATIONS OF MONETARY POLICY

In addition to conflicts among the nation's economic goals, the Federal Reserve finds that it cannot completely control financial conditions or the money supply. Changes in the economy itself feed back upon the money supply. It becomes exceedingly difficult, especially on a weekly or monthly basis, to sort out the effects of monetary policy from the impact of broad economic forces.

Moreover, the Fed has received only limited cooperation from Congress in the pursuit of effective taxing and spending programs. Most economists agree that fiscal policy—the taxing and spending activities of the federal government—can have a potent impact on economic conditions. Unfortunately, changes in tax rates and federal spending programs require the cooperation of both the executive and legislative branches of the government. This kind of cooperation between Congress and the president has been difficult to achieve on a long-term basis. Frequently the Federal Reserve System has been forced to carry the burden of economic policy almost totally alone. Under these circumstances, we should not be too surprised that the Fed's past track record leaves much to be desired.

STUDY QUESTIONS

1. Why are indicators of Federal Reserve policy important to the Fed itself and to managers of financial institutions, corporate treasurers, and the public?

2. What is a *money market indicator?* Give examples and explain how these indicators reflect changes in credit conditions. What problems can you see in the use of money market indicators to gauge the direction of monetary policy?

3. List and define the various measures of the money supply. Why do we need several different measures of money? Do you really think it matters which form of the money supply the Federal Reserve controls?

4. What are the principal items on the Federal Reserve Statement? Which of these items reflect Federal Reserve activities?

5. Define what is meant by *net free reserves* and *net borrowed reserves*. How would you interpret changes in these money market indicators?

6. Explain how the actions of the U.S. Treasury can influence the reserves of depository institutions.

7. What is *float?* Why is it of concern to Federal Reserve policymakers?

8. List the principal economic goals of Federal Reserve monetary policy and define each. Which of these goals have been reasonably well achieved in recent years, and which have not? Try to explain why.

9. Explain the basic similarities and differences between the Monetarist and neo-Keynesian approaches to monetary policy. How would each deal with inflation? With unemployment?

10. What is supply-side economics? Can you foresee any problems in trying to implement the supply-side approach?

11. Outline the steps that the Federal Reserve System goes through in trying to control the growth rate of the money supply and hit its money growth targets. What difficulties do you see in the Fed's approach?

12. What tradeoffs appear to exist among the key economic goals? Why do you think these tradeoffs exist?

SELECTED REFERENCES

Anderson, Leonall C., and Keith Carlson. "A Monetarist Model for Economic Stabilization." *Review,* Federal Reserve Bank of St. Louis, April 1970.

Board of Governors of the Federal Reserve System. "The New Federal Reserve Technical Procedures for Controlling Money." *Staff Memorandum,* January 31, 1980.

Cacy, J. A. "Monetary Policy in 1980 and 1981." *Economic Review,* Federal Reserve Bank of Kansas City, December 1980, pp. 18–25.

Friedman, Milton, and David Meiselmen. "The Relative Stability of Monetary Velocity and the Investment Multiplier in the United States, 1897–1958." In *Stabilization Policies,* ed. Commission on Money and Credit. Englewood Cliffs, NJ: Prentice-Hall, 1963.

Friedman, Milton, and Anna Jacobson Schwartz. "Money and Business Cycles." *Review of Economics and Statistics,* February 1963.

————. *A Monetary History of the United States, 1867–1960.* Princeton, NJ: Princeton University Press, 1963.

Gilbert, R. Alton. "Operating Procedures for Conducting Monetary Policy." *Review,* Federal Reserve Bank of St. Louis, February 1985, pp. 13–21.

Higgins, Bryan. "Free Reserves and Monetary Policy." *Economic Review,* Federal Reserve Bank of Kansas City, July–August 1980.

Keran, Michael. "Economic Theory and Forecasting." *Review,* Federal Reserve Bank of St. Louis, March 1967.

Keynes, John M. *The General Theory of Employment, Interest and Money.* London: Macmillan, 1936.

Long, Richard W. "The FOMC in 1979: Introducing Reserve Targeting." *Review,* Federal Reserve Bank of St. Louis, March 1980.

Patinkin, Don. *Keynes' Monetary Thought: A Study of Its Development.* Durham, N.C.: Duke University Press, 1976.

Phillips, A. W. "The Relation between Unemployment and the Rate of Change of Money Wage Rates in the United Kingdom, 1961–1957." *Economica,* November 1958.

Samuelson, Paul A., and Robert M. Solow. "The Problem of Achieving and Maintaining a Stable Price Level: Analytical Aspects of Anti-Inflation Policy." *American Economic Review,* May 1960.

Sellon, Gordon, Jr. "The Role of the Discount Rate in Monetary Policy: A Theoretical Analysis." *Economic Review,* Federal Reserve Bank of Kansas City, June 1980.

————. *The Recent Evolution of Federal Reserve Operating Procedures.* Research Working Paper 86–13, Federal Reserve Bank of Kansas City, December 1986.

Sims, Christopher. "Money, Income, and Causality." *American Economic Review,* September 1972, pp. 540–52.

Smith, Warren L. "A Neo-Keynesian View of Monetary Policy." In *Controlling Monetary Aggregates,* ed. Federal Reserve Bank of Boston, 1969.

Tatom, John A. "We Are all Supply-Siders Now!" *Review,* Federal Reserve Bank of St. Louis, May 1981, pp. 18–30.

Tobin, James. "The Monetary Interpretation of History." *American Economic Review,* June 1965.

Wallich, Henry. Member of the Board of Governors of the Federal Reserve System. "Recent Techniques of Monetary Policy." Speech to the Midwest Finance Association, Chicago, April 5, 1984.

Chapter 25

The Treasury in the Financial Markets

Learning Objectives in This Chapter

- To examine the many important roles played by the Treasury Department in supporting federal government programs and pursuing the federal government's goals and objectives.

- To see how the federal government raises funds and how it spends the funds that it raises.

- To understand how the activities of the Treasury Department affect the financial markets and the economy.

- To explore the meaning, purpose, and impact of two key government policy tools: fiscal policy and debt management.

Key Terms and Concepts in This Chapter

Fiscal policy	*Public debt*	*Exchange offering*
Debt management policy	*Cash offering*	*Auction method*
	Tax Reform Act of 1986	*Book-entry form*
Budget deficit		
Budget surplus		

ONE of the most important financial institutions in any nation's economy is the government treasury. In the United States, the Treasury Department exerts a powerful impact on the financial system because of two activities that it pursues on a continuing basis. One of these is fiscal policy, which refers to the taxing and spending programs of the federal government designed to promote high employment, sustainable economic growth, and other worthwhile economic goals. A second area in which the Treasury exerts a potent effect on financial conditions is debt-management policy, which involves the refunding or refinancing of the federal government's huge debt in a way that contributes to broad national goals and minimizes the burden of the federal debt. These Treasury policymaking activities influence interest rates, the prices of securities traded in the open market, and the availability of credit to both private and public sectors of the economy. In general, the Treasury pursues policies designed to achieve its economic goals, but not to disturb the functioning of the financial markets and not to unduly interfere with the operations of the Federal Reserve System.

THE FISCAL POLICY ACTIVITIES OF THE U.S. TREASURY

Congress dictates the amount of funds the federal government will spend each year for a variety of programs ranging from welfare to national defense, education, the preservation of the environment, and the construction of highways and buildings. Congress also determines the sources of tax revenue and the tax rates that must be paid by individuals and businesses. Frequently, Congress will vote for a greater amount of spending than can be supported by tax revenues and other governmental receipts. Alternatively, due to a slowdown in the economy, tax revenues may fall short of projections and not be sufficient to cover planned expenditures. Either way, the result is a budget deficit, requiring the U.S. Treasury to borrow additional funds in the financial markets. On the other hand, government revenues may exceed expenditures, resulting in a budget surplus, which the Treasury may use to build up its cash balances or to retire debt previously issued.

As shown in Exhibit 25–1, U.S. Treasury budget surpluses have been very rare in recent years. In fact, the federal budget has been in surplus in only three fiscal years since 1931. The last federal budget surplus occurred during the 1969 fiscal year, when revenues exceeded expenditures by about $3 billion. Since that time, the federal budget has been continually in deficit. It seems safe to assume at this point that federal budget deficits will continue to be frequent occurrences in the future, forcing the Treasury to borrow huge amounts annually in the financial markets.

Sources of Federal Government Funds

It is interesting to analyze what sources of revenue the federal government draws upon to fund its activities. Exhibit 25–2 presents information on the

Exhibit 25-1   **Federal Government Revenues, Expenditures, and Net Budget Surplus or Deficit, Selected Fiscal Years 1960–1988** ($ Millions)

Fiscal Year	Total Revenues	Total Expenditures	Net Budget Surplus or Deficit
1960	$ 92,492	$ 92,223	$ 269
1965	116,833	118,430	−1,597
1969	187,784	184,548	3,236
1970	193,743	196,588	−2,845
1975	280,997	326,151	−45,154
1979	463,302	503,464	−40,162
1980	517,112	590,920	−73,808
1981	599,272	678,209	−78,936
1982	617,766	745,706	−127,940
1983	600,562	808,327	−207,764
1984	666,457	851,781	−185,324
1985	734,057	946,316	−212,260
1986	769,091	989,815	−220,725
1987*	842,390	1,015,572	−173,182
1988*	916,571	1,024,328	−107,756

*Estimated by Office of Management and Budget and the U.S. Department of the Treasury.

Note: Figures based on the unified budget for fiscal years. Prior to 1977 fiscal years ran from July 1 through June 30. Thereafter, the federal budget year runs from October 1 through September 30.

Sources: U.S. Department of Commerce; Business Statistics, 1977 ed.; Survey of Current Business, September 1979; Board of Governors of the Federal Reserve System, Banking and Monetary Statistics, 1941–1970; and Council of Economic Advisors, Economic Report of the President, selected years.

principal sources of federal revenue and major spending programs. On the revenue side, the bulk of incoming funds is derived from taxes levied against individual and family incomes. In fiscal 1988, for example, individuals paid an estimated $393 billion in income taxes, representing about 43 percent of all federal revenues that year. Social security taxes supplied $333 billion—roughly a third of total federal revenue. Corporate income taxes were a distant third at 13 percent, while other taxes and fees for government services provided about 8 percent of all federal revenues.

During the 1970s and early 1980s, the share of federal revenues produced by personal income taxes declined. This was due to efforts by Congress to reduce withholding taxes and increase personal deductions against individual income taxes. At the same time, however, payroll taxes for social insurance rose as Congress attempted to rescue the social security system from ever-deepening deficits. Moreover, corporate taxes were increased in an effort to offset declining personal tax rates and reduce the government's overall budget deficit. These recent changes in tax rates suggest that the federal government has attempted in recent years to make the federal tax structure somewhat more responsive to the nation's economic problems. When the economy headed down into a recession, or inflation pushed in-

Exhibit 25–2   **Federal Government Revenues, Expenditures, and Net Budget Surplus or Deficit, 1988** (Estimate; $ Millions)

Budget Item	Amounts	Percent of Total
Budget revenues by source:		
Individual income taxes	$ 392,821	42.86%
Corporation income taxes	117,207	12.79
Social insurance taxes and contributors	333,184	36.35
Excise taxes	33,406	3.64
Estate and gift taxes	5,817	0.63
Customs duties	15,274	1.67
Miscellaneous receipts:		
Deposits of Earnings by the Federal Reserve System	15,450	1.69
All other	3,413	0.37
Total Budget Revenue	$ 916,571	100.00%
Budget expenditures by function:		
National defense	$ 297,550	29.05%
International affairs	15,209	1.48
General science, space and technology	11,439	1.12
Energy	3,344	0.33
Natural resources and environment	14,241	1.39
Agriculture	26,333	2.57
Commerce and housing credit	2,533	0.25
Transportation	25,523	2.49
Community and regional development	5,463	0.53
Education, training, employment, and social services	28,429	2.78
Health	38,865	3.79
Medicare	73,032	7.13
Income security	124,784	12.18
Social security	219,388	21.42
Veteran benefits and services	27,160	2.65
Administration of justice	9,170	0.90
General government	7,528	0.73
General-purpose fiscal assistance	1,475	0.14
Net interest on federal debt	139,032	13.57
Allowances	−770	−.08
Undistributed offsetting receipts	−45,399	−4.43
Total budget expenditures	$1,024,328	100.00%

Note: Columns may not add to totals due to rounding.

Sources: Office of Management and Budget and U.S. Department of the Treasury.

dividuals into higher tax brackets, Congress generally responded with in-come tax reductions.[1] There has also been a trend toward income tax sim-plification to make personal tax accounting and tax decisions both fairer and less burdensome.

Federal Government Expenditures

Reflecting the effects of rising taxes and inflation, the federal government collects today an enormous volume of revenue from its citizens. For example, federal revenues were expected to exceed $900 billion in 1988. Where does the federal government spend this money? What programs account for the bulk of federal expenditures?

Exhibit 25–2 indicates that more than half of all federal spending goes for national defense and various income security programs, including social security, Medicare, and unemployment compensation. The latter programs are designed to sustain the spending power and standard of living of indi-viduals who are retired, disabled, or temporarily unemployed. For example, outlays for federal income security programs and federal grants to states and localities for these purposes climbed from about 9 percent of the U.S. GNP in 1970 to about 13 percent in the 1980s. Federal benefit payments under the social security program more than tripled during the 1970s alone, while outlays under the federal food stamp program increased almost 10 times over the same period. However, the growth of income security pro-grams leveled off significantly in the 1980s, while a major national defense buildup was under way. Expenditures for defense climbed from just under 24 percent of federal outlays in 1980 to nearly 30 percent in 1988.

Viewing the federal government's budget as a whole, the share of the nation's economic activity accounted for by federal programs has been on a gradual long-term uptrend. Federal expenditures accounted for about 22 percent of the nation's GNP in 1987, up from less than 20 percent in 1970. This growth relative to other sectors of the American economy represents both an expansion of existing programs, particularly national defense since 1980, and the birth of several new programs designed to deal with pressing social, economic, and environmental needs.

Recent Tax and Expenditure Legislation

Confronted with inflation and deepening federal deficits Congress and the president responded in the 1980s with a number of major pieces of fiscal

---

[1]One of the most serious limitations of fiscal policy in the past has been the long lag between the recognition of a need for new fiscal policies and the passage of new legislation. For example, it may take several months before tax cuts or budgetary changes are made. By that time, the underlying economic problems might have changed so that the wrong kind of policy is being pursued. For example, a tax cut proposed to stimulate an economy mired in the depths of a recession may be passed several months later when a strong economic recovery is under way, adding fuel to inflation. There is some evidence, however, that fiscal policy lags have shortened in recent years and that Congress has become somewhat more flexible in this area of legislative decisionmaking.

legislation—legislation that continues to affect the financial markets today. For example, in August 1981 Congress passed the Economic Recovery Tax Act, which brought about significant cuts in individual income tax rates. In addition, new accelerated depreciation allowances, investment tax credits, and tax incentives for business research expenditures were included in the Recovery Act in an attempt to increase investment spending and create jobs. The Economic Recovery Act reduced the maximum individual income tax rate from 70 percent to 50 percent. Income tax brackets and personal exemptions were adjusted for the effects of inflation. This last provision, known as *indexing,* is designed to eliminate bracket creep—that is, the tendency for inflation to push individual incomes into higher and higher tax brackets. One purpose of the changes was to stimulate added saving by individuals and families, provide additional funds for business investment and reduce inflationary pressures in the economy.

While the Economic Recovery Act may have made a significant contribution toward reducing inflation, it probably also contributed to deepening federal budget deficits. As Exhibit 25–1 shows, the federal budget deficit nearly tripled between 1980 and 1986, forcing the U.S. Treasury to borrow unprecedented amounts in the financial markets and confronting private borrowers with both higher interest rates and more limited availability of credit funds. One bill, the Deficit Reduction Act of 1984, made a partial contribution to this problem by calling for about $50 billion in combined spending reductions and tax increases. And, in 1985 and again in 1987, Congress and the administration agreed on a new budget that called for a slowing in the rate of growth in defense spending and selected cuts in domestic programs, resulting in some planned moderation of the deficit. The most notable legislation during this period was the Gramm-Rudman-Hollings bill, which mandated reduced budget deficit targets in each year until the federal deficit was brought down significantly from its all-time record level of well over $200 billion in 1985 and 1986.

Tax Reform

A strong drive for federal income tax reform was launched in the mid-1980s. Proponents of basic changes in federal tax laws and IRS regulations cited numerous abuses of the existing tax system, such as pseudo-business ventures begun exclusively to shelter income from taxation and many wealthy individuals and corporations paying no taxes at all. Moreover, there was considerable pressure from individual taxpayers and consumer lobby groups to simplify the tax code so the average taxpayer could more fully understand tax laws and make more rational spending and saving decisions. The result of months of debate and compromise was the Tax Reform Act of 1986.

While the 1986 Tax Reform Act is exceedingly complex, covering literally thousands of pages, and has already undergone numerous corrections, its principal provisions may be summarized here:

- Personal tax rates are reduced and simplified from 15 different tax brackets and tax rates under the old law to only 2 basic individual income tax rates—15 percent for lower-income taxpayers and 28 percent for upper-income families and individuals. For certain individuals in the top-earning group a tax surcharge will apply, bringing the top bracket rate to 33 percent.

- The top tax rate for corporations is reduced from 46 percent to 34 percent.

- All capital gains on securities and other assets will be taxed as ordinary income, subject to the tax rates reported above, doing away with the old favorable capital gains tax rate.

- Many personal deductions formerly available to individuals and families will no longer be permitted—notably interest payments on non-housing-related (mortgage) debt and sales taxes imposed by states and local governments. Moreover, the deductibility of several tax shelter items such as real estate depreciation has been sharply reduced.

- There will no longer be any investment tax credit for purchases of business capital goods.

- While the accelerated depreciation rules set up by the 1981 Economic Recovery Act were kept, businesses and individuals purchasing depreciable assets must, in most cases, depreciate them over longer intervals, which reduces their annual savings in taxes. For example, buildings must generally be depreciated in 31½ years instead of just 18 years, while most equipment must be depreciated over a 7-year period instead of 5 years as allowed previously.[2]

The Tax Reform Act was designed to be *neutral* in its impact on economic and financial conditions. While personal tax rates were reduced, resulting in an expected decline in tax payments by individuals, tax collections from corporations were expected to rise, bringing total federal revenues roughly back to where they started. Thus, the Tax Reform Act was not designed to deal with the massive federal budget deficit or to reduce the Treasury's need to borrow money frequently from the financial markets.

Effects of Federal Borrowing and Budget Deficits on the Financial System and the Economy

What are the effects of government borrowing on the economy and the financial markets? If the federal government runs a *small* budget deficit, it is possible for the Treasury to cover the shortfall in revenues by drawing upon its accumulated cash balances held at the Federal Reserve banks or

---

[2]However, some of the reduction in the annual tax benefit from depreciation that these longer required asset lifetimes brought about was offset by basing depreciation rates on a 200-percent declining balance method instead of 150 percent as stipulated in earlier tax law and regulation.

even by issuing new currency. In recent years, however, federal deficits have been so large that substantial amounts of new debt securities have been issued in the money and capital markets. The impact of these massive borrowings on the money and capital markets and the economy depends, in part, on the *source* of borrowed funds. Exhibit 25–3 summarizes the probable effects of government borrowing designed to cover a budget deficit.

Borrowing from the Nonbank Public. For example, suppose the Treasury needs to borrow $20 billion, which it raises by selling government bonds to the nonbank public. As the public pays for these securities, it writes checks against its deposits held with depository institutions, initially reducing the size of the money supply. As the checks are cleared and deposited in the Treasury's accounts at the Federal Reserve banks, legal reserves held by depository institutions decline by $20 billion.

To gauge the full effects of government borrowing, however, we must consider the fact that the government plans to *spend* its borrowed funds. In our example the Treasury will write checks totaling $20 billion against its Federal Reserve accounts and distribute these checks to the public. Deposits of the public rise by $20 billion, also increasing the legal reserves held by depository institutions.

On balance, after all transactions are completed, there is *no change* in the money supply or in the total amount of reserves held by the banking system. However, there is likely to be an *increase* in total spending and income in the economy due to the fact that funds are transferred from those who purchase securities to members of the public receiving government checks. Presumably, recipients of government checks have a higher propensity to spend new income than security investors, who have a higher marginal propensity to save any new income received. Aggregate consumption spending will probably increase, and if the economy is at or near full employment, inflation may rise. Initially, the increased sale of Treasury securities should put upward pressure on interest rates. Over a longer-run period, however, it is quite possible that interest rates will fall due to the higher levels of income and increased saving out of that income.

Borrowing from Depository Institutions. The effects of government borrowing are somewhat different if the borrowing takes place entirely from depository institutions. If we assume, once again, that the Treasury borrows $20 billion, deposit-type institutions will pay for the securities they purchase by drafts against their legal reserve accounts held at the Federal Reserve banks. Reserves of depository institutions drop by $20 billion, as shown in Exhibit 25–3, and the Treasury's deposits, of course, rise by a like amount. Once again, however, the Treasury spends these borrowed funds, resulting in an increase in deposits held by the public and in legal reserves. The money supply rises because the public's deposit holdings increase.

On balance, after all transactions are completed, total legal reserves

Exhibit 25–3   Effects of Government Borrowing on the Financial Markets and the Economy

Borrowing from the Nonbank Public

	Federal Reserve Banks		Depository Financial Institutions	
	Assets	Liabilities	Assets	Liabilities
Sale of securities		Legal reserves of depository institutions −20 Government deposits +20	Legal reserves −20	Deposits of the public −20
Spending of borrowed funds		Government deposits −20 Legal reserves of depository institutions +20	Legal reserves +20	Deposits of the public +20

EFFECTS: No change in the money supply or total reserves; total spending in the economy and interest rates rise.

Borrowing from Depository Institutions

	Federal Reserve Banks		Depository Financial Institutions	
	Assets	Liabilities	Assets	Liabilities
Sale of securities		Legal reserves of depository institutions −20 Government deposits +20	Government securities +20 Legal reserves −20	
Spending of borrowed funds		Legal reserves of depository institutions +20 Government deposits −20	Legal reserves +20	Deposits of the public +20

EFFECTS: The money supply increases; total reserves are unchanged, but excess reserves fall due to increases in deposits; total spending and interest rates rise.

Borrowing from the Federal Reserve Banks

	Federal Reserve Banks		Depository Financial Institutions	
	Assets	Liabilities	Assets	Liabilities
Sale of securities	Government securities +20	Government deposits +20		
Spending of borrowed funds		Government deposits −20 Legal reserves of depository institutions +20	Legal reserves +20	Deposits of the public +20

EFFECTS: The money supply and total reserves increase, while total spending in the economy rises and interest rates tend to fall.

remain unchanged, but excess reserves fall because of the increase in deposits. There is also likely to be an increase in total spending and income in the economy as the public gains additional funds. Prices may rise if unemployment is low. Interest rates will increase in the short run with the increased quantity of government securities available. However, the gain in total spending should lead eventually to a decline in interest rates.

Borrowing from the Federal Reserve Banks. Still a third route for government borrowing would be to secure credit directly from the central bank. In the United States this could be done by having the Treasury issue securities directly to the Federal Reserve banks. However, borrowing directly from the Federal Reserve is a highly *inflationary* way for the federal government to raise money. Financially speaking, it is the equivalent of printing money. Therefore, borrowing from the Fed is restricted by law. Nevertheless, in a severe national emergency such as a serious depression, it would probably be called upon to support a sagging economy.

How would borrowing from the central bank work, and what would its effects be? The Federal Reserve banks acquire securities and increase the Treasury's deposits by the same amount. Initially, there is no withdrawal of reserves from the banking system, nor does the public lose deposits. Instead, both legal reserves and the public's deposits rise by the amount of any borrowed funds actually spent by the Treasury. In the example shown in Exhibit 25–3, the Treasury sells $20 billion in securities to the Federal Reserve banks, and its deposit accounts at the Fed rise by a like amount. As the Treasury spends the $20 billion, public deposits and reserves rise, causing increases in the money supply, total spending, and income. Interest rates tend to fall due to the increase in the money supply.

Effects of the Retirement of Government Debt from a Budget Surplus on the Financial System and the Economy

Occasionally, the federal government collects more in revenue than it spends, running a budget *surplus*. By definition, a budget surplus implies that the government withdraws a greater amount of funds from the economy in the form of tax collections than it puts back into the economy through government expenditures. The Treasury could save these surplus funds to cover deficits in later years. However, this is usually unpopular from a political standpoint. It is more likely that a government budget surplus would be used to retire debt previously issued. But the impact of government debt retirement on the economy and the financial system depends, in part, on who happens to hold the debt securities the government plans to retire.

Retiring Government Debt Held by the Nonbank Public. Suppose the securities scheduled for retirement are held by individuals and institutions that are not a part of the banking system. In this case, there will be little

**Exhibit 25–4   Effects of Retiring Government Debt on the
Financial Markets and the Economy**

Retiring Government Securities Held by the Nonbank Public

	Federal Reserve Banks			Depository Financial Institutions		
	Assets	Liabilities		Assets		Liabilities
Collection of tax surplus		Legal reserves of depository institutions	−20	Legal reserves −20		Deposits of taxpayers −20
		Government deposits	+20			
Retiring government securities		Government deposits	−20	Legal reserves +20		Deposits of security holders +20
		Legal reserves of depository institutions	+20			

EFFECTS: No change in money supply or in bank reserves; but total spending tends to fall, because funds move from active to passive spenders; interest rates decline.

Retiring Government Securities Held by Depository Institutions

	Federal Reserve Banks			Depository Financial Institutions		
	Assets	Liabilities		Assets		Liabilities
Collection of tax surplus		Legal reserves of depository institutions	−20	Legal reserves −20		Deposits of taxpayers −20
		Government deposits	+20			
Retiring government securities		Legal reserves of depository institutions	+20	Government securities −20		
		Government deposits	−20	Legal reserves +20		

EFFECTS: Money supply falls in short run, while total bank reserves are unchanged. Excess reserves increase due to a fall in deposits. Total spending and interest rates decline.

or no change in the money supply or in the reserves held by depository institutions.

This is illustrated in Exhibit 25–4, where the act of retiring government debt is separated into two steps. In the first step we assume the U.S. Treasury collects a surplus of $20 billion in tax revenues. This might arise, for ex-

Exhibit 25–4   *(concluded)*

Retiring Government Securities Held by the Federal Reserve Banks

	Federal Reserve Banks		Depository Financial Institutions	
	Assets	Liabilities	Assets	Liabilities
Collection of tax surplus		Legal reserves of depository institutions −20	Legal reserves −20	Deposits of taxpayers −20
		Government deposits +20		
Retiring government securities	Government securities −20	Government deposits −20		

EFFECTS: Money supply and total reserves decrease by the amount of the budget surplus; total spending and interest rates decline.

ample, if the federal government spent $100 billion but collected $120 billion in taxes from the public. Clearly, the public's deposits will drop a *net* $20 billion. Moreover, as members of the public write checks against their transaction deposits to pay taxes, legal reserves of depository institutions will also fall a net $20 billion. The Treasury's deposits at the Federal Reserve banks will rise by a like amount.

Assume now that the Treasury uses its surplus funds to retire securities held by the nonbank public. Security holders receive government checks totaling $20 billion, which are deposited in bank and nonbank thrift institutions. Legal reserves of these institutions rise by $20 billion. Of course, the Treasury now loses the same amount of money from its deposits at the Federal Reserve as the government's checks are cleared. The public's deposits and therefore its money supply first decline and then rise by $20 billion, with reserves following the same path. Is there no effect, then, from retiring securities held by the nonbank public? Not likely, because the government has transferred money from the general public (taxpayers), with a high propensity to spend, to security investors who, as a group, tend to be heavy savers. The net effect is probably to *reduce* total spending in the economy. Prices of goods and services may fall and unemployment may rise. It is likely, too, that interest rates will decline because the total supply of securities is being reduced.

Retiring Government Debt Held by Depository Institutions. What happens if the government uses its budget surplus to retire securities held by banks and other depository institutions? Initially, the effects are much the same. Funds are withdrawn from taxpayer deposit accounts and transferred to the U.S. Treasury's deposits at the Federal Reserve. Legal reserves of depository institutions fall by the amount of the tax surplus (in Exhibit 25–4 by $20 billion). Now, however, the surplus funds are paid to depository institutions, who turn their securities in to the Treasury. Legal reserves rise as the government spends down its $20 billion deposit.

In the short run, the money supply is reduced due to the drain on taxpayer funds. Total legal reserves are unchanged, first falling and then rising. Note, however, that excess reserves must increase because total legal reserves are unchanged when deposits fall. In the long run the money supply expands due to the gain in excess reserves. With fewer taxpayer funds, however, spending in the economy should decline, which may increase unemployment. Interest rates, too, will probably decline because fewer securities are now available to investors.

It should be clear from the example that budget surpluses and the retirement of government debt tend to slow down economic activity and therefore could be used as a vehicle to combat inflation. If the federal government wanted to have a maximum deflationary impact on the economy, whose government securities should it retire? The banking system's? No! The Treasury could have the greatest anti-inflationary impact by retiring government securities held by the Federal Reserve banks. This approach would be the equivalent of destroying money.

Retiring Government Debt Held by the Federal Reserve Banks. As the bottom panel of Exhibit 25–4 shows, retiring government securities held by the Federal Reserve drains funds from taxpayers. However, those funds are *not* returned to the private spending stream. Instead, the government uses its increased deposits to pay off the Federal Reserve banks and retrieve the securities they hold. Legal reserves of the banking system and the money supply decline by the full amount of the budget surplus. Spending, interest rates, and the prices of goods and services are likely to fall as well.

Overall Impact of Government Borrowing and Spending

We may summarize all these impacts of government borrowing and spending with an IS-LM diagram. We recall our earlier discussion of IS-LM analysis in Chapter 24 (see Exhibit 24–10), which links determination of equilibrium interest rates with equilibrium income (spending). In this analysis the LM curve represents a collection of *equilibrium interest rates* [where money demand (L) = money supply (M)] for various levels of income (Y). We can also draw an IS curve, representing a collection of points at different levels of interest rates at which *income is in equilibrium;* that is, the volume of

**Exhibit 25–5   Effects of Additional Government Borrowing and Deficit
Spending on Income and Interest Rates**

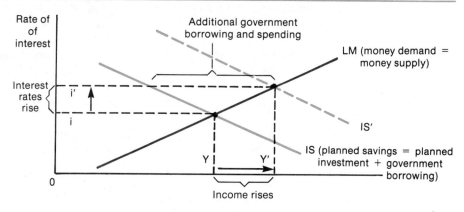

Level of national income (production and spending)

planned saving (S) by the public exactly equals the volume of planned
investment plus government borrowing (I). As shown in Exhibit 25–5,
the point where the IS and LM curves intersect yields *both* an equilibrium interest rate and an equilibrium level of income and spending for the
economy.

What happens, then, when the government runs a deficit and increases
its borrowing to finance it? As Exhibit 25–5 suggests, the added government
borrowing adds to planned investment spending and, with the money supply
and money demand unchanged, equilibrium interest rates *rise* and income
and production also *rise*. Of course the higher interest rates discourage some
additional private borrowing and spending—the so-called *crowding out*
effect—even as government borrowing and spending increases. If there is
substantial unemployment, more jobs probably will be made available and
the unemployment rate will fall. If the economy is already close to full
employment, the added income and spending may drive the prices of goods
and services higher, generating inflation.

This conventional view of government deficits and borrowing adding to
income and possibly driving up interest rates and inflation has been chal-
lenged in recent years. One counterargument is that interest rates and
security prices in an *efficient* market simply may not respond to increased
government borrowing, either because an equal amount of *private* borrowing
and spending are crowded out of the marketplace, or because the added
government borrowing is already anticipated by the market and has been
discounted by investors. Thus, there may be little *net* gain in terms of
economic activity or change in interest rates from deficit spending.

Several recent studies tend to support these arguments. For example, Plosser (1982) and Roley (1981) find that security prices and interest rates do not respond significantly to the presence or absence of government deficits or to the sheer size of those deficits. While interest rates may tend to rise as government borrowing increases, the demand for money tends to fall at the same time which reduces the pressure of total credit demands on the financial markets. Canto and Rapp (1982) found that information on past budget deficits did not improve forecasts of current interest rates, nor was the current budget deficit significantly correlated with future changes in rates. And, finally, Dwyer (1982) finds that government budget deficits did not appear to cause the rising U.S. inflation rate over the 1952–81 period. Rather, Dwyer suggests that current budget deficits appear to be more influenced by past inflation, rather than the other way around. Thus, there is considerable controversy today about the true effects of government deficits and borrowing on the financial markets and the economy. More research on this important issue clearly is needed.

MANAGEMENT OF THE FEDERAL DEBT

As we noted at the beginning of this chapter, one of the most important activities of the Treasury today is managing the huge public debt of the United States. The U.S. public debt is the largest single collection of securities available in the financial system today. Securities issued directly by the Treasury, which make up the bulk of the public debt, are regarded by investors as having zero *default risk* because the federal government possesses both taxing power and the power to create money. The government, unless it is overthrown by war or revolution, can always pay its bills.

Government securities do carry *market risk,* however, because their prices fluctuate with changes in demand and supply. In fact, the longer the term to maturity of a government security, the more market risk it possesses.

The principal role of government securities in the financial system is to provide *liquidity*. Corporations, commercial banks, insurance companies, and other major institutional investors rely heavily on government securities as a readily marketable reserve to be drawn upon when cash is needed quickly. While private debt securities do carry higher explicit yields than government debt of comparable maturity, the greater liquidity of government securities represents an added return to the investor.

The Size and Growth of the Public Debt

How much money does the federal government owe? As shown in Exhibit 25–6, the gross public debt of the United States totaled over $2.3 trillion in 1987. On a per capita basis the public debt amounts to about $10,000 for every man, woman, and child living in the United States.

Exhibit 25–6 The Public Debt of the United States, 1987 ($ Billions)*

Types of Securities			Amount
Interest-bearing public debt			$2,306.7
Marketable debt		$1,659.0	
Bills	$391.0		
Notes	984.4		
Bonds	268.6		
Nonmarketable debt		$ 647.7	
Foreign issues	5.1		
Savings bonds and notes	95.2		
Government account series	421.6		
Other	125.4		
Non-interest-bearing debt			2.6
Total gross public debt			$2,309.3

*As of the end of the second quarter of 1987.

Note: Columns may not add to totals due to rounding.

Source: Board of Governors of the Federal Reserve System, Federal Reserve Bulletin, and Economic Report of the President, selected issues.

How did the federal debt become so huge? Wars, recession, inflation, and the rapid expansion of military expenditures and social programs have been the principal causes. The federal government's debt was insignificant until the Great Depression of the 1930s, when the administration of President Franklin Roosevelt chose to borrow heavily to fund government programs and provide jobs. Even so, the public debt amounted to scarcely more than $50 billion at the beginning of World War II. The public debt multiplied five times over during the war years, however, approaching $260 billion by the end of World War II. (See Exhibit 25–7.) Embroiled in the most destructive and costly war in history, the U.S. government borrowed and taxed away resources from the private sector to build tanks, planes, ships, and other war materials in enormous quantities.

For a brief period following World War II, it appeared that much of the public debt might be repaid. However, the Korean war intervened in the early 1950s, followed by a series of deep recessions when government tax revenues declined. The advent of the Vietnam war and rapid inflation during the late 1960s and 1970s sent the debt soaring above its earlier levels. Between 1970 and 1980 the public debt of the United States more than doubled and then more than doubled again to climb near $2.5 trillion during the 1980s. This latest surge could be traced to the combined effects of slower economic growth that lowered tax collections, inflationary increases in government costs, a strong national defense buildup, and federal tax cuts.

Is this much debt simply too much? Have we as a society borrowed beyond our means? Or was Alexander Hamilton, the first Treasury secretary, accurate when he wrote: "A national debt, if it is not excessive, will be to

Exhibit 25–7   **The Public Debt of the U.S. Government, Selected Years, 1946–1987** ($ Billions)

Year	Total Gross Public Debt
1946	$ 259.1
1950	225.4
1960	287.7
1970	388.3
1980	930.2
1985	1,945.9
1987	2,309.3
1988*	2,492.6

* First quarter only.

Source: Board of Governors of the Federal Reserve System, *Banking and Monetary Statistics, 1941–70;* and *Federal Reserve Bulletin,* various monthly issues.

us a national blessing"? The answer depends, in part, on the standard (or base) used to gauge the size of the public debt. Measured against the national income (the earnings of individuals and businesses which can be taxed to repay the debt), the public debt is lower now than it was a generation ago. For example, in 1988 the gross public debt amounted to about 50 percent of the U.S. GNP, compared to well over 100 percent at the end of World War II. Moreover, other forms of debt in the U.S. economy totaled as much or more than the public debt. For example, total mortgage debt outstanding in 1987 was about $2.7 trillion. It should be remembered that U.S. government securities are at one and the same time debt obligations and also readily marketable, liquid assets to the millions of investors who hold them.

Another problem to keep in mind about today's huge federal debt and its possible burden on the economy is the difficulties we face in trying to accurately *measure* the true size of the debt. It turns out that the answer to the question—How big is the federal debt?—is not all that easy. For example, *inflation* tends to increase the size of the debt because it tends to increase government budget deficits. Thus, in an inflationary period the government typically must borrow more, but this does not necessarily mean that the burden of the debt has increased; that is, government may not be exerting a greater impact on the economy. An interesting study by Eisner and Pieper (1984), for example, concludes that the real size of the U.S. federal debt (adjusted for inflation) actually fell between 1946 and 1980. Moreover, the size of the public debt is typically measured in terms of the *par value* of government securities outstanding. But, when interest rates rise, the *market value* of government debt falls. Thus, a significant rise in interest rates will cause the value of that portion of the government's debt held by private investors to decline and may result in increased saving in the private sector.

Accurate measurement of the burden imposed by government debt probably also means that we must consider the value of the assets held by government. For example, most national governments hold a reserve of gold, foreign currencies, and securities. We might also add to these financial assets the estimated value of government buildings, military hardware, highways, and airports. Thus, we may distinguish between the *gross liabilities* of the federal government—the total amount of its debt outstanding—and its *net liabilities*—government debt minus government assets. Including all of the government's assets at their fair market value would yield substantially smaller net government liabilities. Of course, to be fair we would also have to consider the amount of total indebtedness of off-budget federal agencies (such as the farm credit agencies or federal mortgage agencies) which now amounts to about one fifth of the gross public debt. And, there are *contingent liabilities* that might be added to the government's debt total, such as deposit insurance like that offered by the FDIC to guarantee bank deposits or the Social Security fund which must eventually pay retirement benefits to millions of citizens. Clearly, measuring the true size of the government's debt is an extremely difficult job. For this reason, we must be careful before jumping to any hasty conclusions about how large or significant the debt is or what its impact on the economy and financial markets might be.

The Composition of the Public Debt

The public debt as it is traditionally measured consists of a wide variety of government IOUs with differing maturities, interest rates, and other features. A small amount—less than 1 percent—carries no interest rate at all. This *non-interest-bearing public debt* consists of paper currency and coins issued by the U.S. Treasury Department, including silver certificates and greenbacks that are gradually being retired as they are turned in by the public. Virtually all paper money in circulation today is Federal Reserve notes, which are not officially a part of the public debt, but obligations of the Federal Reserve banks.

More than 99 percent of all federal debt securities are *interest bearing* and may be divided into two broad groups—marketable securities and nonmarketable securities. By definition, *marketable* securities may be traded any number of times before they reach maturity. In contrast, *nonmarketable* securities must be held by the original purchaser until they mature or are redeemed by the Treasury. It is the marketable debt over which the Treasury exercises the greatest measure of control and which has the greatest impact on the cost and availability of credit in the financial markets.

Marketable Public Debt

The marketable public debt totaled over $1.6 trillion in 1987, representing about three quarters of all interest-bearing U.S. government obligations. As Exhibit 25–8 reveals, the marketable public debt today is composed of

Exhibit 25–8   **Volume of Marketable U.S. Government Debt by Type of Security, Year-End 1987** ($ Billions)

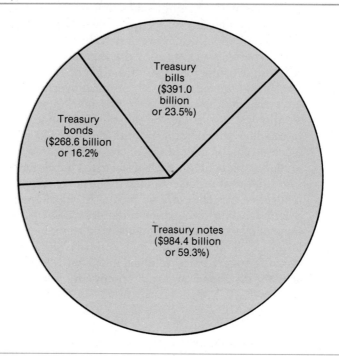

Treasury bills ($391.0 billion or 23.5%)

Treasury bonds ($268.6 billion or 16.2%

Treasury notes ($984.4 billion or 59.3%)

Source: Board of Governors of the Federal Reserve System, *Federal Reserve Bulletin,* various issues.

just three types of securities—Treasury bills, notes, and bonds. By law, a U.S. Treasury bill must mature in one year or less. In contrast, U.S. Treasury notes range in original maturity from 2 years to 10 years, while Treasury bonds may carry any maturity, though generally they have a maturity at issue of more than 10 years.[3]

Under federal law, Treasury bonds can carry a maximum interest rate of 4¼ percent, unless special exemption from this legal interest-rate ceiling is granted by Congress. Because only limited exemptions have been granted and interest rates have been far higher than 4¼ percent in recent years, the proportion of long-term bonds making up the Treasury's marketable debt has declined significantly. In contrast, Treasury bills and notes carry

---

[3]Both Treasury notes and bonds bear interest at a fixed rate payable semi-annually, while bills do not carry a fixed rate. Bonds can carry a call option, allowing the Treasury to redeem them before maturity with four months' notice. Notes and bonds are issued in denominations and in multiples of $1,000, $5,000, $10,000, $100,000, and $1 million, while bills are available in denominations and in multiples of $10,000, $15,000, $50,000, $100,000, $500,000, and $1 million. Payment for purchases of Treasury securities generally must be made in cash, immediately available funds, the exchange of eligible securities (accepted at par value), or by check to the Federal Reserve banks or to the Treasury.

no legal interest-rate ceiling. Moreover with their greater liquidity and marketability, bills and notes have been especially attractive to investors in recent years. Bills and notes represented about 40 percent of all marketable government obligations in 1960; by 1987, however, these securities accounted for more than 80 percent of the marketable public debt.

Concealed within the totals for Treasury notes and bonds reported above are relatively new hybrid securities known as Treasury *zeros* or *strips*. Beginning in the 1970s, major investment houses began offering customers stripped Treasury notes and bonds—that is, selling the principal (face value) of the bond or note separately from its stream of promised interest payments. Both the principal value and the interest stream were sold at deep discounts, resulting in substantial tax savings and permitting investors to more accurately hedge against interest rate risk (because, once purchased and held to maturity, the zeros' yield is fixed). While many of the tax benefits of Treasury strips were removed by subsequent changes in tax law, the zero coupon issues have grown in popularity and in daily trading volume, expanding the market for U.S. Treasury securities, especially among institutional investors. Viewing this new instrument as a way to reduce the burden of interest costs, the Treasury announced in January 1985 that it would allow all future note and bond issues over 10 years to maturity to be stripped and transferred by wire among interested investors over the Federal Reserve's electronic wire network.

Nonmarketable Public Debt

The nonmarketable public debt consists mainly of Government Account series securities issued by the Treasury to various government agencies and trust funds (see Exhibit 25–6). These agencies and trust funds include the Social Security Administration, the Rural Electrification Administration, the Tennessee Valley Authority, and several smaller government agencies. As these governmental units accumulate funds, they turn them over to the Treasury in exchange for special, nonmarketable IOUs, thus reducing the federal government's borrowing activity in the open market. Another significant component of the nonmarketable debt is U.S. Savings Bonds and Notes, sold to the general public in small denominations and representing only about 4 percent of the public debt.

As we will note in Chapter 27, holdings of U.S. dollars by foreign governments and foreign investors have expanded enormously in recent years due to oil imports and the flow of American capital to Europe, Asia, the Middle East, and the Far East. Because large foreign holdings of dollars and dollar deposits represent a constant threat to the value of the U.S. dollar in international markets, the Treasury periodically issues small amounts of nonmarketable dollar-denominated securities to attract these overseas funds. In order to increase U.S. government holdings of foreign currencies that can be used to settle international claims, the Treasury can issue foreign-currency-denominated securities to investors abroad. The Treasury also issues special securities to state and local governments. These securities provide a temporary investment outlet for the funds raised by local governments when they borrow in the open market.

Investors in U.S. Government Securities

Who *holds* the public debt of the United States? Each month the Treasury makes estimates of the distribution of its securities among various groups of investors, drawing upon data supplied by the Federal Reserve banks, U.S. government agencies and trust funds, banking associations, trade organizations, and government security dealers. The results from a recent Treasury ownership survey are shown in Exhibit 25–9.

It is evident from the survey that most Treasury debt—almost three quarters—is held by private individuals and institutions in the domestic economy and abroad. Rather surprising to many observers, however, is the large proportion of the public debt—more than one quarter—held by the federal government itself. For example, in 1987, U.S. government agencies and trust funds, including the Social Security Trust Fund, Tennesseee Valley Authority, and other federal departments, held about one fifth of the total debt. The Federal Reserve banks hold almost 10 percent of all public debt securities outstanding.

Exhibit 25–9   **Principal Investors in the U.S. Public Debt, 1987** ($ Billions, End of Period)

Investor Group	Amount Held, Second Quarter 1987		Percent Total Holdings
Federal government:			
U.S. government agencies and trust funds		$ 438.1	19.0%
Federal Reserve banks		212.3	9.2
Private investors:			
Commercial banks	$237.1		10.3%
Money market funds	20.6		0.9
Individuals:			
Savings bonds	96.8		4.2
Other securities	63.4		2.7
Foreign and international	269.9		11.7
Other investors*	969.9		42.0
Total for private investors		$1,657.7	71.8%
Total for all investor groups		$2,308.1	100.0%

*Includes savings and loan associations, nonprofit institutions, corporate pension trust funds, dealers and brokers, certain government deposit accounts, government-sponsored agencies, insurance companies, and state and local governments.

Source: Board of Governors of the Federal Reserve System, *Federal Reserve Bulletin,* December 1987.

The sheer size of the government's holdings of its own debt is viewed with alarm by some analysts. A large volume of government debt held out of circulation in federal vaults tends to thin out the market for government securities, reducing the volume of trading. Other factors held constant, interest rates and security prices become more volatile and unpredictable, discouraging investment. This could be critical because the market for government securities is the anchor of the whole financial system.

Among private holders of the public debt, commercial banks and individuals are at or near the top of the list. In 1987, for example, individual investors held about 7 percent of the public debt—the majority in U.S. Savings Bonds. Commercial banks held an even larger government portfolio, with more than $200 billion in government issues. Other financial institutions with significant holdings of U.S. government securities included insurance companies, pension funds, savings banks and savings and loan associations, and nonfinancial corporations that hold these securities as a ready reserve of liquid funds.

The proportion of the public U.S. debt held by foreign and international investors, including foreign central banks, foreign governments, and other international investors, has increased in recent years and totaled about $270 billion in 1987. Foreign holdings of government securities result from a rise in U.S. imports of goods and services, especially oil imports, that lead foreign investors to build up substantial dollar deposits in banks abroad. These investors have converted many of their dollars into purchases of Treasury securities in the money market and into foreign-currency-denominated securities purchased directly from the U.S. Treasury.

A Trend toward Shorter Maturities

One of the most serious problems the Treasury has faced in the debt management field is a long-term trend since World War II toward shorter and shorter maturities. The percentage of marketable federal securities over five years to maturity held by private investors was a full 40 percent in 1950. By 1987, however, this long-term component of the public debt was scarcely more than a quarter of all marketable issues. The average maturity of the entire marketable public debt in 1987 was about 5 years, or about two thirds what it was at the end of World War II. Today, just over one third of the debt comes due each year, though it should be noted the public debt has lengthened significantly in recent years.

A short-term public debt is a potentially serious problem because it requires the Treasury to come to market more frequently to retire or refund debt as securities pile up in shorter maturities. Moreover, in recent years the Federal Reserve has been especially cautious about making significant changes in the posture of monetary policy at a time when the Treasury is actively in the market selling notes and bonds. If the Treasury must refund and issue more frequently, this reduces the period of time over which the

Federal Reserve can comfortably make significant changes in monetary policy. Suppose, for example, that the Fed wanted to increase interest rates and reduce the availability of credit at precisely the time the Treasury was coming to market with a new issue of bonds. Clearly, the government would have difficulty in selling its bonds in an environment of rising interest rates and falling bond prices. If maturing securities were coming due and had to be paid off, the Treasury might not be able to raise enough cash to meet its obligations. Conditions in the financial marketplace might border on panic. Therefore, a public debt of short maturity tends to reduce the flexibility of monetary policy. It limits the options open to the Federal Reserve.

Many analysts believe as well that a substantial buildup of short-term government debt contributes to inflation. Of special concern is the proportion of government securities maturing within one year—the so-called *floating debt*. These short-term issues are the most liquid and readily marketable of all securities in the financial system. Most are held by commercial banks and other lenders of funds, who use them as an extra source of funds when reserves are scarce and credit demand is high. If the Federal Reserve wishes to reduce the growth of money and credit, it must wrestle with the problem that banks and other financial institutions can sell off their floating-debt issues and generate still more credit. It is perhaps more than just coincidence that both inflation and the short-term federal debt have tended to grow rapidly together.

Methods of Offering Treasury Securities

Management of the public debt is a complicated task. Treasury debt managers are called upon continually to make decisions about raising new money and refunding maturing securities. They must decide what kinds of securities to issue, which maturities would appeal to investors, and the form in which an offering of securities should be made.

Cash Offerings and Exchange Offerings. For example, the Treasury can make a cash offering in which buyers simply pay cash for any securities they receive. On the other hand, if some existing securities must be refunded (rolled over), the Treasury can offer new securities just to holders of the maturing issues. This is called an exchange offering. In this type of sale, investors who want to acquire a portion of the new issue must purchase securities from those who hold the maturing issue. The maturing securities are known as "rights" to the new debt being offered.

The choice between a cash offering and an exchange offering can be a difficult one because of changing market conditions. For example, if interest rates rise, holders of maturing securities may not wish to acquire any new Treasury securities offered in exchange; instead, they will seek the higher yields available on other securities sold in the open market. Those investors electing not to exchange with the Treasury will demand cash payment instead. The Treasury may find itself with a substantial amount of unsold securities and in the embarrassing position of not having sufficient cash to pay off holders of maturing issues. A cash offering usually solves this *attrition* problem. However, cash offerings have a far more powerful impact on interest rates and security prices than exchange offerings do because they represent a net withdrawal of funds from the financial system. Nevertheless, since 1973 the Treasury has elected to use cash offerings rather than exchange offerings, due primarily to the enormous volume of new securities it has needed to sell.

The Auction Method. Today the auction method is the principal means of selling Treasury notes, bonds, and bills. While there are several different auction methods in use, all such techniques have a number of features in common. Both competitive and noncompetitive tenders are accepted from the public. All noncompetitive bidders receive an allotment of securities from the auction up to a maximum amount determined by the Treasury. As we have seen, federal government agencies and trust funds and the Federal Reserve banks purchase and hold large amounts of Treasury issues. These agencies participate in virtually every auction but pay the price charged noncompetitive bidders. They receive a special allotment of securities in exchange for their maturing issues after the regular auction is concluded.

Types of Treasury Auctions. The Treasury has used three different auction methods in recent years:

1. Yield auctions.
2. Dutch auctions.
3. Price auctions.

The auction method used most often for Treasury bills, notes, and bonds is known as a *yield auction*.[4] Neither the price nor the coupon rate on the new securities is set in advance by the Treasury. Instead, it merely announces the amount of securities available and calls for yield bids. Investors submitting competitive bids must express their offers on a bank discount basis (in the case of Treasury bills) or on an annual percentage yield basis (for notes and bonds), accurate to two decimal places. For example, we might place a yield bid of 11.75 percent in the current auction. When the auction closes, noncompetitive bidders will first receive their securities at the average auction price; then those bidding the lowest annual percentage yield (the highest price) will be awarded their securities. Awards will continue to be made at successively higher yields (lower prices) until the issue is exhausted. (See Exhibit 25–10 for an example of an announcement of a recent Treasury yield auction of new bonds.)

The *price auction* has been used on occasion for note and bond sales.

---

[4]See Chapter 14 for a more detailed discussion of the weekly auctions for U.S. Treasury bills.

Exhibit 25–10   **The U.S. Treasury Auctions Off Another Bond**

DEPARTMENT OF THE TREASURY
OFFICE OF THE SECRETARY
[Department Circular—Public Debt Series—No. 22–87]
Treasury Bonds of 2017
Washington, August 11, 1987.

1. INVITATION FOR TENDERS

1.1. The Secretary of the Treasury, under the authority of Chapter 31 of Title 31, United States Code, invites tenders for approximately $9,000,000,000 of United States securities, designated Treasury Bonds of 2017 (CUSIP No. 912810 DZ 8), hereafter referred to as Bonds. The Bonds will be sold at auction, with bidding on the basis of yield. Payment will be required at the price equivalent of the yield of each accepted bid. The interest rate on the Bonds and the price equivalent of each accepted bid will be determined in the manner described below. Additional amounts of the Bonds may be issued to Government accounts and Federal Reserve Banks for their own account in exchange for maturing Treasury securities. Additional amounts of the Bonds may also be issued at the average price to Federal Reserve Banks, as agents for foreign and international monetary authorities.

2. DESCRIPTION OF SECURITIES

2.1. The Bonds will be dated August 15, 1987, and issued August 17, 1987. Payment for the Bonds will be based on the price equivalent to the bid yield determined in accordance with this circular, plus accrued interest from August 15, 1987, to August 17, 1987. Interest on the Bonds is payable on a semiannual basis on February 15, 1988, and each subsequent 6 months on August 15 and February 15 through the date that the principal becomes payable. They will mature August 15, 2017, and will not be subject to call for redemption prior to maturity. In the event any payment date is a Saturday, Sunday, or other nonbusiness day, the amount due will be payable (without additional interest) on the next business day.

2.2. The Bonds are subject to all taxes imposed under the Internal Revenue Code of 1954. The Bonds are exempt from all taxation now or hereafter imposed on the obligation or interest thereof by any State, any possession of the United States, or any local taxing authority, except as provided in 31 U.S.C. 3124.

2.3. The Bonds will be acceptable to secure deposits of Federal public monies. They will not be acceptable in payment of Federal taxes.

2.4. The Bonds will be issued only in book-entry form, and in denominations of $1,000, $5,000, $10,000, $100,000, and $1,000,000, and in multiples of those amounts. They will not be issued in registered definitive or in bearer form.

2.5. A Bond may be held in its fully constituted form or it may be divided into its separate Principal and Interest Components and maintained as such on the book-entry records of the Federal Reserve Banks, acting as fiscal agents of the United States. The provisions specifically applicable to the separation, maintenance, transfer, and reconstitution of Principal and Interest Components are set forth in Section 6 of this circular. Subsections 2.1. through 2.4. of this section are descriptive of Bonds in their fully constituted form; the description of the separate Principal and Interest components is set forth in Section 6 of this circular.

2.6. The Department of the Treasury's general regulations governing United States securities, i.e., Department of the Treasury Circular No. 300, current revision (31 CFR Part 306), as to the extent applicable to marketable securities issued in book-entry form, and the regulations governing book-entry Treasury Bonds, Notes, and Bills, as adopted and published as a final rule to govern securities held in the TREASURY DIRECT Book-Entry Securities System in 51 FR 18260, *et seq.* (May 16, 1986), apply to the Bonds offered in this circular.

3. SALE PROCEDURES

3.1. Tenders will be received at Federal Reserve Banks and Branches and at the Bureau of the Public Debt, Washington, D.C. 20239, prior to 1:00 p.m.,

Exhibit 25–10 *(concluded)*

Eastern Daylight Saving time, Thursday, August 13, 1987. Noncompetitive tenders as defined below will be considered timely if postmarked no later than Wednesday, August 12, 1987, and received no later than Monday, August 17, 1987.

3.2. The par amount of Bonds bid for must be stated on each tender. The minimum bid is $1,000, and larger bids must be in multiples of that amount. Competitive tenders must also show the yield desired, expressed in terms of an annual yield with two decimals, e.g., 7.10%. Fractions may not be used. Noncompetitive tenders must show the term "noncompetitive" on the tender form in lieu of a specified yield.

Source: U.S. Treasury Department.

Under this method, the Treasury sets the coupon rate and minimum price it is willing to accept on notes and bonds and announces the amount of securities available for public sale. Competitive bids are accepted with prices above or below par, accurate to two decimal places (assuming a par value of $100). Securities are allotted first to the highest bidder and then to investors submitting successively lower bids until the amount available (less any noncompetitive tenders) has been exhausted.

The Treasury also has employed the *uniform price,* or *Dutch auction,* method to sell new notes and bonds. After all competitive bids are in, the Treasury proceeds to award the available securities (once noncompetitive orders are filled), beginning with the highest bidder, until all securities are allocated. However, the price actually paid by all bidders may be the average price bid in the auction. Therefore, all investors receiving securities in a Dutch auction pay the same price.

Marketing Techniques. Unlike borrowers in the corporate and municipal bond markets, the Treasury does *not* use dealers to underwrite its new debt issues (though dealers play a key role, as noted in Chapter 14, in purchasing new Treasury securities in the auctions and reselling a portion of their holdings to other investors). The Treasury places new securities *directly* with the investing public. New Treasury bills, notes, and bonds can be bought directly from the Treasury Department or from the Treasury's agents—the Federal Reserve banks and their branches. Bids or tender offers are accepted from private and government investors at the Federal Reserve banks until 1 P.M., Eastern Standard Time, the day the new securities are sold. Individuals may also file bids for new Treasury securities with the Bureau of Public Debt in Washington, DC. Many investors place orders for new Treasury issues through a security broker or dealer, commercial bank, or nonbank financial institution that offers such a service.

Before issuing new notes and bonds, the Treasury will consult Federal Reserve officials and government securities dealers as to the appropriate terms to be offered. It also frequently is necessary to tailor the terms of a new issue to appeal to investor groups who have the necessary funds to spend.

Book Entry. The marketable public debt is issued today in book-entry form. This means that the investor does not receive an engraved certificate representing the Treasury's debt obligation. Instead, the investor's name and amount of securities purchased are recorded in the automated TREASURY DIRECT System. Member banks of the Federal Reserve System are permitted to hold security safekeeping accounts at the Federal Reserve banks where their own security holdings and those of their customers are recorded. As interest is received or securities are sold or purchased, banks will credit or debit their own or their customers' accounts accordingly. Book entry is the safest form in which to hold any security, because this method significantly reduces the risk of theft. Some investors still prefer *bearer* securities. With this system, engraved certificates are actually kept in the investor's possession, and he or she must send in a coupon to receive interest payments. All new Treasury securities must now be sold in book-entry form, however.

Other Services Offered Investors. In order to encourage greater participation in the government securities market and stimulate demand for new Treasury issues, both the Federal Reserve and the Treasury offer a number of other services to investors. For example, securities held in book-entry accounts at the Federal Reserve banks may be transferred by wire almost anywhere using the Fed's electronic wire transfer network. This device makes it easy to sell Treasury securities before maturity on a same-day basis. Moreover, as discussed earlier, in 1985 the Treasury announced a STRIPS program in which the principal and interest payments on longer-term Treasury securities can be separately owned and traded, in effect making them zero coupon instruments and broadening their appeal to investors. However, in order to be eligible for "stripping," the investor must keep the securities in a book-entry account at a Federal Reserve bank.

The Goals of Federal Debt Management

Over the years the Treasury has pursued several different goals in the management of the public debt. These goals may be divided into two broad groups: (1) *housekeeping goals,* which pertain to the cost and composition of the public debt; and (2) *stabilization goals,* which have to do with the impact of the debt on the economy and the financial markets.

Minimize Interest Costs. The most important housekeeping goal is to keep the interest burden of the public debt as low as possible. The Treasury has not always been successful in the pursuit of this goal, however. Today, the interest burden on the public debt is the third largest category of federal expenditures, after welfare payments and national defense. As Exhibit 25–2 reveals, net interest on the debt reached nearly $140 billion, or about

14 percent of total federal government spending, in fiscal 1988. This interest burden on the American taxpayer has increased in recent years.

Reduce the Frequency of Refundings. The Treasury also tries to minimize the number of trips it must make to the market to refund old securities or issue new ones. As we have seen, this housekeeping goal is particularly important to the Federal Reserve's conduct of monetary policy.

Frequently in the past the Fed has followed a loosely defined policy known as *even keel* when the Treasury is in the market offering a substantial volume of notes or bonds. Even-keel policy calls for the Fed to exert a *steadying* influence on the financial markets, making sure that security trading is orderly and that changes in interest rates are moderate. In principle, the even keel policy protects the Treasury's financing operations from catastrophic failure, as might occur if interest rates rose sharply and security prices plunged at the time of a Treasury refunding, but it can limit the Fed's freedom of action.

Economic Stabilization. A much broader goal of debt management is to stabilize the economy—promoting high employment and sustainable growth while avoiding rampant inflation. In strict terms this would involve issuing long-term Treasury securities in a period of economic expansion and issuing short-term securities in a period of recession. The long-term securities would tend to increase long-term interest rates and therefore act as a brake on private investment spending, slowing the economy down. On the other hand, issuing short-term securities during a recession may take the pressure off long-term interest rates and avoid discouraging investment spending that is needed to provide jobs.

Unfortunately, the goal of economic stabilization often conflicts with other debt management goals, particularly the goal of minimizing the interest burden of the public debt. If the Treasury sells short-term securities in a period of expansion when interest rates are high and then rolls over those short-term securities into long-term bonds during a recession when rates are low, this strategy will tend to minimize the debt's average interest cost. The Treasury will be able to lock in cheap long-term rates. From a stabilization point of view, however, this is exactly the wrong thing to do. The short-term debt may fuel inflation during an economic expansion, while long-term debt issued during a recession may drive up interest rates and reduce private investment. Treasury debt managers are often confronted with tough choices among conflicting goals.

The Impact of Federal Debt Management on the Financial Markets and the Economy

What effect do Treasury debt management activities have on the financial markets and the economy? This is a subject of heated debate among economists and financial analysts. Most experts agree that in the short run the financial markets become more agitated and interest rates tend to rise when the Treasury is borrowing, especially when new money is involved. A mere exchange of new for old securities usually has minimal effects, however, unless the offering is very large.

The longer-run impact of Treasury debt management operations is less clear. Certain the *liquidity* of the public's portfolio of securities changes, though we are uncertain by how much or what the exact impact might be. For example, suppose $10 billion in Treasury bonds are maturing next month. Treasury debt managers decide to offer investors $10 billion in 10-year notes in exchange for the maturing bonds. The bonds, regardless of what their original maturity might have been, are now short-term securities (with one-month maturities). If investors accept the new 10-year notes in exchange for the one-month bonds, the average maturity of the public's security holdings obviously has lengthened, all else being equal. Longer-term securities, as a rule, are less liquid than shorter-term securities.

Will this reduction in public liquidity affect spending habits and interest rates? The research evidence on this question is conflicting, with many studies finding little or no effect from debt management activities.[5] However, there is some evidence that *lengthening debt maturities* in investor portfolios increases the public's demand for money and *raises interest rates*. In contrast, if the Treasury offers shorter-term securities, this tends to make the public's portfolio of securities more liquid and may reduce the demand for money. The result would be an increase in total spending for goods and services and, for a time, *lower* interest rates.

Still another possible debt management impact is on the *shape of the yield curve*. *Lengthening* the average maturity of the debt tends to increase long-term interest rates relative to short rates. The yield curve assumes a *steeper positive slope*, favoring short-term investment over long-term investment. On the other hand, *shortening* the debt's maturity would tend to reduce longer-term interest rates and raise short-term rates. The yield curve would tend to *flatten out*, if positively sloped, or even turn down, favoring long-term investment over short-term investment. The net impact on total investment spending would depend on whether private investment is more responsive to short-term interest rates or to long-term interest rates. We believe that long-term rates are more critical than short-term rates for most business investment decisions.

On balance, most authorities are convinced that the debt management activities of the Treasury do *not* have a major impact on economic conditions. The effects of debt management operations appear to be secondary compared to the powerful impact of monetary and fiscal policy on the economy and financial markets. The optimal policy is probably one that makes Treasury refunding operations as *unobtrusive* as possible, especially where these operations might interfere with the activities of the Federal Reserve System.

---

[5] See especially the studies of Lang and Rasche (1977), and Smith (1960).

Nevertheless, debt management represents yet another policy tool that can be used by the federal government in the face of serious economic problems.

SUMMARY

In this chapter we examined the many roles played by the Treasury Department in financing federal expenditures and managing the huge public debt of the United States. The federal government affects the financial system through its taxing and spending activities (fiscal policy) and through refunding or refinancing the government's debt (debt management policy). Both tasks involve enormous amounts of money today. The public debt of the United States now is well over $2 trillion, while annual federal expenditures hover around the trillion dollar mark. It should certainly come as no surprise that spending and borrowing of such magnitude can have powerful effects on interest rates, security prices, and the pursuit of economic goals.

We have observed in this chapter that government borrowing tends to raise interest rates, increase the money supply, and add to total spending and demand in the economy. In general, the economy will grow faster, with reduced unemployment, when the government borrows and spends additional funds, but often at the price of more rapid inflation and threats to the dollar abroad. Government budget surpluses, especially where these surpluses are used to retire government debt, often lead to lower interest rates, a decline in the money supply, and reduced spending. A move toward more conservative fiscal policy and toward budget surpluses tends to dampen inflation and strengthen the dollar abroad, but increases the risk of high unemployment and slower economic growth at home.

Management of the public debt can also be used to alter economic conditions, reduce unemployment, and counter inflation. We have noted that, if the Treasury refunds maturing short-term securities with longer-term debt, it can reduce the liquidity of the public's security holdings. Interest rates tend to rise, credit becomes more difficult to obtain, and spending and employment tend to fall. Long-term Treasury borrowing, therefore, tends to slow the economy's rate of growth and reduces inflationary pressures. In contrast, a debt management policy that emphasizes short-term government borrowing often leads to more rapid economic expansion and reduced unemployment, but these are sometimes purchased at the price of higher inflation.

As we saw in the preceding chapter on the Federal Reserve System, government policymakers face few happy choices. The goals of full employment, reasonable stability in prices, sustainable economic growth, and a stable balance of payments position are elusive targets. Successful fiscal, monetary, and debt management policies require careful coordination among all branches of government.

STUDY QUESTIONS

1. What exactly is fiscal policy? Debt management policy?

2. Explain how fiscal policy and debt management policy might be used to fight inflation. How about unemployment?

3. How frequently have budget surpluses occurred during the past three decades? Can you explain why?

4. List from largest to smallest the principal sources of federal government revenue. What are the principal federal spending programs?

5. Describe the effects of government borrowing on the financial system and the economy. If the federal government wished to increase total spending in the economy the most, from whom should it borrow funds?

6. Describe the effects of retiring government securities on the financial system and the economy. Whose securities should be paid off if the federal government wants to have the maximum contractionary impact on the economy?

7. What is the crowding-out theory? What does recent research say about the link between government deficits, interest rates, and inflation?

8. What are the principal reasons investors purchase and hold U.S. government securities?

9. Describe the principal types of securities that make up the public debt of the United States. What portions of the debt can the Treasury most closely control?

10. What problems exist in trying to measure the size of the public debt?

11. List the principal holders of the public debt. What are the most important trends in the ownership of federal securities?

12. Define the following methods of selling U.S. Treasury securities and explain under what circumstances each might be used:
   a. Cash offering.   d. Dutch auction.
   b. Exchange offering.   e. Yield auction.
   c. Price auction.

13. List the *goals* of Treasury debt management. What is the essential difference between the so-called housekeeping goals and the stabilization goals? To what extent do these goals conflict?

14. Explain how changes in the maturity structure of the public debt can affect interest rates, the yield curve, and spending for goods and services in the economy.

PROBLEMS

1. Due to an unexpected decline in the federal income tax collections, the Treasury will be compelled to borrow an extra $40 billion to cover planned expenditures in the current government budget. Using T ac-

counts and IS-LM analysis discussed in this chapter trace through the likely effects of this additional borrowing on the financial markets and on the economy. Assume that 50 percent of the securities to be issued will be absorbed by nonbank institutions and private individuals and 50 percent by depository institutions. How would your analysis change if the economy were at full employment?

2. Due to drastic cuts in federal spending and strong economic growth, it now appears that the federal government will experience a $10 billion budget surplus during the current fiscal year. If the Treasury plans to retain $2 billion of this surplus in its cash account at the Federal Reserve and to use the balance to retire $5 billion in government securities held by depository institutions and $3 billion held by the general public, use T accounts to show the effects of this debt-retirement operation. Using IS-LM analysis and the results from your T account analysis, what effects do you predict for interest rates, security prices, total spending, and employment?

SELECTED REFERENCES

Barro, Robert. "Are Government Bonds Net Wealth?" *Journal of Political Economy,* November–December 1984.

Canto, Victor A., and Donald Rapp. "The 'Crowding Out' Controversy: Arguments and Evidence." *Economic Review,* Federal Reserve Bank of Atlanta, August 1982.

Dwyer, Gerald P., Jr. "Is Inflation a Consequence of Government Deficits?" *Economic Review,* Federal Reserve Bank of Atlanta, August 1982.

Eisner, Robert, and Paul J. Pieper. "A New View of the Federal Debt and Budget Deficits." *The American Economic Review,* March 1984, pp. 11–29.

Lang, Richard W., and Robert H. Rasche. "Debt Management Policy and the Own-Price Elasticity of Demand for U.S. Government Notes and Bonds." *Review,* Federal Reserve Bank of St. Louis, September 1977, pp. 8–22.

Plosser, Charles I. "Government Financing Decisions and Asset Returns." *Journal of Monetary Economics,* 9 (1982), pp. 325–52.

Roley, V. Vance. "The Financing of Federal Deficits: An Analysis of Crowding Out." *Economic Review,* Federal Reserve Bank of Kansas City, July–August 1981, pp. 16–29.

Smith, Warren L. "Debt Management in the United States." In *Study of Employment, Growth, and Price Levels,* ed. Joint Economic Committee. Washington, DC: U.S. Government Printing Office, 1960.

Tanner, J.R. "Fiscal Policy and Consumer Behavior." *Review of Economics and Statistics,* August 1979.

Chapter 26

State and Local Governments in the Financial Markets

Learning Objectives in This Chapter

- To explore the various ways in which state, county, city, and other local units of government raise the funds they need in order to provide services to the public.

- To understand why state and local government borrowing has grown rapidly in recent years and to examine the financial instruments these governments use to raise money.

- To explore the marketing process by which state and local government bonds and notes are sold.

- To understand the problems faced by the municipal market today and to explore some of its options for the future.

Key Terms and Concepts in This Chapter

Municipals	Bond-anticipation notes (BANs)	Revenue bonds
Tax-anticipation notes (TANs)	General obligation bonds (GOs)	Tax-exemption privilege
Revenue-anticipation notes (RANs)		Serialization

$\mathbf{T}$HE borrowing and spending activities of state and local governments have been one of the most dynamic, rapidly growing segments of the financial system in recent years. Pressured by rising population and inflated costs, states, counties, school districts, and other local units of government have been forced to borrow in growing numbers in order to meet increased demands for their services. As we will see later in this chapter, the volume of state and local government debt has more than doubled over the past decade.

Despite the rapid growth in borrowing by state and local governments, many investors consider state and local debt obligations a highly desirable investment medium due to their high quality, ready marketability, and tax-exemption feature. The interest income generated by state and local securities is exempt from federal income taxes, and most states exempt their own securities from state income taxes. As a result, these high-quality debt obligations—known to investors as municipals—appeal to such heavily taxed investors as commercial banks, top-income-bracket individuals, and large corporations. In addition, an active secondary market permits the early resale of many state and local government bonds.

GROWTH OF STATE AND LOCAL GOVERNMENT BORROWING

The rapid growth of state and local government borrowing is reflected in Exhibit 26–1, which shows the total volume of municipal securities outstanding between the years 1940 and 1986. State and local government indebtedness grew slowly until the 1950s, when it nearly tripled. The volume of municipal debt doubled again during the 1960s and more than doubled during the 1970s. In 1986 state and local debt outstanding had climbed to almost $500 billion.

Exhibit 26–1   **Total Debt Issued by State and Local Governments in the United States, 1940–1986** ($ Billions)

Year	Debt Outstanding at Year-end
1940	$ 20.3
1950	24.1
1960	70.8
1970	144.4
1980	287.7
1986	495.0

Sources: U.S. Department of Commerce, Bureau of the Census, *1977 Census of Governments;* and Board of Governors of the Federal Reserve System, *Flow of Funds: Assets and Liabilities Outstanding,* 1960–83 and 1963–86.

What factors account for this strong record of growth in municipal borrowing? *Rapid population and income growth* are two of the most important causes. The U.S. population, spurred by a postwar baby boom, rose from less than 132 million in 1940 to an estimated 230 million in the 1980s, a gain of about 100 million people in four decades. Rapid population growth implies that many local government services, such as schools, highways, and fire protection, must also expand rapidly. Tax revenues cannot provide all the moneys needed to fund these facilities and services.

Another factor pushing state and local borrowings higher is the *uneven distribution of population growth across the nation*. Beginning in the 1950s, a massive shift of the U.S. population began to take place out of the central cities into suburban areas. This demographic change was augmented during the 1970s and 1980s by a movement of population and industry into small towns and rural areas to escape the social and environmental problems of urban living. Smaller outlying communities were rapidly transformed into moderate-sized cities with a corresponding need for new streets and schools as well as new airports and freeways to commute back to the central cities for work, recreation, and shopping. The result was an upsurge in borrowing by existing local units of government and the creation of thousands of new borrowing units in the form of sewer and lighting districts, power and water authorities, airport and toll-road boards, and public housing authorities. There are more than 80,000 state, county, municipal, and other units of local government in the United States. And, the majority of these governmental units have the authority to issue debt.

Accompanying the growth and shifting of the U.S. population has come an *upgrading of citizens' expectations* concerning the quality of government services. We expect much more from government today than even 10 years ago. Particularly noticeable is an increased demand for government services that directly affect the quality of life, such as more modern and better designed schools, parks, auditoriums, and football stadiums. Instead of gravel roads and narrow highways, local citizens demand paved and guttered streets and all-weather, controlled-access highways. Many municipal governments are active in providing cultural facilities, such as libraries, museums, and convention centers, and are expected to play leading roles in the control of environmental pollution.

All of these public demands have had to be financed in an era of rapid inflation in construction and labor costs, exacerbating the money burdens of local governments. The rapid growth of local government borrowing is expected to continue in future years, with the federal government making smaller contributions to local funding. Adding to local financial needs will be a continuing expansion of suburban and rural communities, especially in the southern and western regions of the United States.

SOURCES OF REVENUE FOR STATE AND LOCAL GOVERNMENTS

Borrowing by state and local governments supplements their tax revenues and income from fees charged users of government services. When tax and fee revenues decline or fail to grow as fast as public demands, municipal borrowings rise. Moreover, when long-term capital projects are undertaken, long-term borrowing rather than taxation is the preferred method of governmental finance.

As we study state and local government borrowing in the financial markets, it is useful to have in mind the principal sources and uses of state and local funds. Where do the majority of state and local government revenues come from? And where does most of the money go? Exhibits 26–2 and 26–3, drawn from a recent census of state and local units of government, provide some answers to these questions.

As expected, most state and local government *revenues* are derived from

Exhibit 26–2   **Sources of Revenue for State and Local Governments, 1981–1982**
(Percent of Total General Revenues)

Source	State and Local Governments	State Governments	Local Governments
General revenue from own sources	80.9%	74.9%	58.5%
Taxes	58.4	59.1	37.1
Property	18.0	1.1	28.2
Sales and gross receipts	20.5	28.6	5.3
General sales and gross receipts	13.3	18.3	3.7
Selective sales and gross receipts	7.2	10.3	1.6
Motor fuel	2.3	3.8	0.1
Alcoholic beverages	0.6	1.0	0.1
Tobacco products	0.9	1.4	—
Public utility	1.7	1.8	1.0
Other	1.7	2.3	—
Income	14.4	21.7	2.2
Individual	11.1	16.6	1.8
Corporate	3.3	5.1	0.4
Motor vehicle license	1.4	2.2	0.1
Death and gift	0.5	0.9	—
All other taxes	3.5	4.6	1.2
Current charges	12.3	7.6	12.5
Miscellaneous general revenue	10.3	8.1	8.8
Intergovernmental revenue	19.1	25.1	41.5
General revenue, total	100.0%	100.0%	100.0%

Note: Blank items are either zero or round to zero.

Columns may not add to totals due to rounding.

Source: U.S. Department of Commerce, Bureau of the Census, *1982 Census of Governments.*

Exhibit 26–3   **Annual Expenditure by State and Local Governments, 1981–1982**
(Percent of Total General Expenditures)

Function	State Governments	Local Governments
Education and library services	24.9%	45.4%
Social Services and income maintenance:		
Public welfare	24.3	5.6
Hospitals	8.1	6.0
Health	3.2	2.0
Social insurance administration	1.3	*
Veterans' service	*	—
Transportation:		
Highway	11.8	5.5
Air transportation	0.2	0.9
Other	0.3	0.5
Public safety:		
Police protection	1.4	5.4
Fire protection	—	2.6
Correction and other	4.4	1.5
Environmental and housing:		
Sewerage	0.2	4.0
Natural resources	3.0	0.5
Housing and urban renewal	0.8	2.9
Parks and recreation	—	2.3
Other	—	1.6
Governmental administration:		
Financial administration	2.1	1.7
General control	2.2	2.7
General public buildings	0.5	0.9
Interest on general debt	5.3	4.2
Other and unallowable	5.6	5.9
Direct general expenditures, total	100.0%	100.0%

Note: Columns may not add to totals due to rounding.

*Indicates that the percentage figure is less than half the unit of measurement shown.

Source: U.S. Department of Commerce, Bureau of the Census, *1982 Census of Governments.*

local sources of funds, that is, from the citizens these governmental units serve. For example, more than 70 percent of state government revenues and nearly 60 percent of local government revenues were derived from local sources, according to a 1982 Department of Commerce census. However, intergovernmental transfer of funds, including state aid to local schools, also provides a significant share of total revenues. For example, local governments received more than 40 percent of their revenues and state governments about 25 percent from other governmental units in 1982.

Not surprisingly, *taxes* are the largest single revenue source for state and local governments. Property taxes are the mainstay of local government support, providing about 30 percent of general revenues. State governments, in contrast, rely principally on sales and income taxes. Selective sales taxes on alcoholic beverages, entertainment, gasoline, tobacco, and other specialized products and services are levied almost entirely at the state level. Income taxes also are imposed almost exclusively at the state level and are levied mainly against individuals rather than corporations. Income taxes contributed about 20 percent of state government revenues but only about 2 percent of local government revenues during the 1981–82 fiscal year.

State and Local Government Expenditures

Where do state and local governments spend most of their funds? As Exhibit 26–3 suggests, *education* is the number one item on the budgets of local governmental units and ranks number two on state budgets. The U.S. Department of Commerce reported that during the 1981–82 fiscal year, nearly 45 percent of local government funds and about one quarter of state revenues flowed into education and library services. *Social services,* including public welfare and medical care, occupied a distant second place in local government spending, representing about one eighth of total outlays, but ranked first in state budgets at about 40 percent of total spending. *Transportation services,* especially highway construction and maintenance, ranked third in the volume of state spending and fourth for local governments.

It is interesting that some of the most important local government services account for only a minor share of annual public budgets. For example, the cost of insuring public safety—principally police and fire protection— accounted for less than 10 percent of local government expenditures. Sewer services, protection of the environment and natural resources, and housing programs to aid the poor and the disadvantaged represented only about 11 percent of local government costs and less than 6 percent of state government spending.

State and local government expenditures have grown rapidly in recent years. During 1987, expenditures by state and local units totaled more than $600 billion, as shown in Exhibit 26–4. This figure was more than four times larger than the level of state and local government spending in 1970. In fact, state and local outlays have more than doubled in each decade since World War II. Local tax revenues have simply been inadequate to handle this kind of growth in current (short-term) and capital (long-term) expenditures. Moreover, while state and local governments showed substantial budget surpluses in the 1970s and 1980s, a growing perception across the nation has been that many municipal facilities, especially highways and electrical and service systems, need upgrading and modernizing. Accordingly, borrowing in the money and capital markets against future revenues surged upward in the 1980s to accommodate local needs for renovation and

Exhibit 26–4   State and Local Government Receipts and Expenditures, NIA Accounts ($ Billions)

Year	Total Receipts	Total Expenditures	Surplus or Deficit
1946	$ 13.0	$ 11.1	$ 1.9
1950	21.3	22.5	−1.2
1955	31.7	32.9	−1.3
1960	49.9	49.8	0.1
1965	75.1	75.1	−0.0
1970	135.4	133.5	1.9
1975	237.7	232.2	5.5
1980	386.1	355.5	30.6
1985	577.5	515.8	61.7
1986	618.8	557.9	60.8
1987	652.3	607.0	45.4

Source: U.S. Department of Commerce, Bureau of Economic Analysis.

modernization and for expansion of facilities. However, in the late 1980s the total volume of municipal borrowing fell back due to lower federal income tax rates that reduced the value of tax-exempt securities to many investors and to new federal restrictions on tax-exempt borrowing.

MOTIVATIONS FOR STATE AND LOCAL GOVERNMENT BORROWING

There are several reasons why state and local governments borrow money. The first is *to satisfy short-run cash needs*—that is, to meet payrolls, make repairs, purchase supplies and equipment, cover fuel costs, and maintain adequate levels of working capital. Most state and local governments will use tax-anticipation notes (to be discussed later) and other forms of short-term borrowing from local sources as a supplement to tax revenues to meet these immediate cash needs. Frequently, the construction phase of a building project will be financed out of short-term funds, and then permanent financing will be obtained by selling long-term bonds.

The second major reason for state and local government borrowing is *to finance long-term capital investment*—that is, the building of schools, water, gas and electric systems, highways, public buildings, and similar permanent facilities. Long-term projects of this sort account for the bulk of all municipal securities issued each year. Some governmental units try to anticipate future financial needs by borrowing when interest rates are low even though project construction will not begin for a substantial period of time. Funds raised through anticipatory borrowing will then be "warehoused" in various investments (such as Treasury bills) until actual construction begins.

In recent years local governments have occasionally employed *advance refunding* of securities. Advance refundings occur when a governmental unit has been granted a higher credit rating on its bonds by a rating agency, such as Moody's Investors Service or Standard & Poor's Corporation.[1] Bonds issued previously with lower credit ratings (higher interest rates) will be called in and new securities issued at lower cost. Any significant decline in market interest rates usually gives rise to more advance refunding activity by state and local governments.

TYPES OF SECURITIES ISSUED BY STATE AND LOCAL GOVERNMENTS

There are many different types of securities issued by state and local governments today and, as we will soon see, the variety of municipal securities available to investors is expanding rapidly. One useful distinction is between short-term securities, which are generally issued to provide working capital and support construction, and long-term securities, used to fund capital projects.

Short-Term Securities

The two most popular short-term securities issued by state and local governments are tax-anticipation notes and bond-anticipation notes.

Tax-Anticipation and Revenue-Anticipation Notes. These notes, also called TANs and RANs, are used to attract funds in lieu of tax receipts or other sources of revenue expected to be received in the near future. Governments, like businesses and households, have a daily need for cash to meet payrolls, purchase supplies, make repairs, and so on. However, funds raised through taxes usually flow in only at certain times of the year. In order to satisfy their continuing need for cash between tax dates, state and local governments will issue short-term notes with maturities ranging from a few days to a few months. Most of these short-term issues are acquired by local banks. When tax funds are received, the issuing government simply pays off note holders and retires any outstanding securities.

Bond-Anticipation Notes. These short-term IOUs, also called BANs, are used to provide temporary financing of a long-term project until the time is right to sell long-term bonds. A school district, for example, may need to get construction started on new school facilities due to pressure from rising

---

[1]See Appendix A for a discussion of municipal and other security ratings.

student enrollments. If interest rates currently are too high to permit the issue of bonds, then construction will be started out of funds raised with bond-anticipation notes. Once the project is under way and interest rates decline to more modest levels, the school district will then sell its long-term bonds and retire the bond-anticipation notes.

The majority of short-term notes issued by state and local governments are backed by the "full faith and credit" of the issuing governmental unit. They sell at interest rates competitive with current money market yields and reflect the credit rating of the issuer. Like municipal bonds, interest on short-term local government notes is exempt from federal income taxes. These notes range in original maturity from one month to the more common six-month and one-year maturities. These short-term IOUs are usually sold through underwriting syndicates who file competitive bids for the securities. Short-term tax-exempt notes are issued in marketable bearer form, with denominations ranging typically from $5,000 to $1 million. Both principal and interest are paid at maturity.[2]

Long-Term Securities

The most common type of municipal borrowing is through long-term bonds. There are two major types of municipal bonds issued today—general obligation and revenue bonds—and both are used principally to finance public construction.

General Obligation Bonds. These bonds, known as GOs, are the safest and most secure form of municipal borrowing from the standpoint of the investor, because they are backed by the "full faith and credit" of the issuing government and may be paid from *any* revenue source. State, county, and city governments, along with school districts, have the power to tax citizens in order to meet principal and interest payments on any debt issued. GOs are fully backed by this taxing power and usually must be approved by public referendum before issue. The quality or level of risk of GOs depends, therefore, on the economic base (income and property values) of local communities and the total amount of debt issued.

Revenue Bonds. In contrast, revenue bonds are payable only from a specified source of revenue, such as a toll road or toll bridge or user fees from a water, sewer, electrification, or other revenue-gathering project, and usually do not require a public referendum before they can be issued. These securities are not guaranteed or backed by the taxing power of the local unit of

---

[2]Tax-exempt notes with maturities longer than a year generally bear coupons. For most tax-exempt notes, interest is computed on the basis of a 30-day month or a 360-day year, like the interest on Treasury bills and bank CDs.

Exhibit 26–5 **New Security Issues of State and Local Governments** ($ Billions)

Types of Issue, Issuer, or Use of Funds	Years					
	1981	1982	1983	1984	1985	1986
All issues	$47.7	$79.0	$86.4	$106.6	$214.2	$134.6
Type of Issue:						
General obligation	12.4	21.1	21.6	26.5	52.6	44.8
Revenue	35.3	58.0	64.9	80.2	161.6	89.8
U.S. government loans	0.1	0.7	0.3	NA	NA	NA
Type of Issuer						
State	5.3	8.4	7.1	9.1	13.0	14.9
Special district and statutory authority	27.5	45.1	51.3	63.6	134.4	79.3
Municipalities, counties, and townships	14.9	25.6	28.0	34.0	66.8	40.4
Uses of Funds Raised from Issues for New Capital						
Education	4.5	6.5	8.1	7.6	16.7	16.9
Transportation	3.4	6.3	4.4	7.6	12.1	11.7
Utilities and conservation	10.0	14.3	13.6	17.8	26.9	35.4
Social welfare	12.7	26.6	26.9	29.9	63.2	17.2
Industrial aid	7.7	8.3	7.8	15.4	12.9	5.6
Other purposes	8.1	12.8	11.6	15.8	24.4	47.4

Notes: Figures include all state and local government security issues to raise new capital and to refund outstanding debt. Securities are valued at par based on date of sale. School districts are classified under municipalities, counties, etc., until April 1986, and then are classified as special districts.

Source: Board of Governors of the Federal Reserve System, *Federal Reserve Bulletin,* selected issues.

government. Instead, revenue bonds depend for their value on the revenue-generating capacity of the particular project they support.[3]

The total amount of general obligation bonds outstanding today exceeds the total supply of revenue bonds. However, as shown in Exhibit 26–5, revenue issues have been increasing faster in recent years. For example, during 1986, nearly $90 billion in revenue bonds reached market, while only $45 billion in GOs were issued. There has been a virtual explosion of different types of revenue bonds within the past decade. Much of the growth in amount and variety of revenue issues is due to welfare programs of the federal government designed to provide housing for low-income groups, improved medical care facilities, and student loans. In addition, the passage

---

[3]Some municipal bonds display characteristics of both GO and revenue securities. For example, a *special tax bond* is payable from the revenues generated by a special tax, such as on gasoline. Many special tax bonds are backed by the full faith, credit, and taxing power of the issuing governmental unit, giving them the character of GOs. *Special assessment bonds* are payable only from assessments against property constructed or purchased from the proceeds of the bonds issued and arise from water and sewer projects, street construction, and similar projects. As in the case of special tax bonds, however, special assessment issues may take on the character of GOs when backed by the taxing power of the issuer. *Authority bonds* are issued by special governmental units set up by states, cities, or counties to construct and manage certain facilities, such as airports or water and sewer projects. Authority bonds may be either GOs or revenue issues.

of Proposition 13 in California in 1978 and the enactment of similar laws by other states in subsequent years has encouraged many local authorities to substitute revenue bonds for GOs. Many of the newer revenue bonds are not well known to the majority of investors and may, in some cases, provide a higher rate of return to the well-informed buyer.

Types of Revenue Bonds

One of the most popular revenue issues is *student-loan bonds* (SLROs) which are issued by state government agencies that lend money to college students. The federal government guarantees 100 percent of the principal and interest of an SLRO, provided the issuing agency's loan-default ratio is low. If a high percentage of students default on their loans, federal guarantees are limited to only a certain portion (usually 80 to 90 percent) of principal and interest payments on the bonds. SLROs are issued in minimum denominations of $1,000.

In the housing field several new forms of guaranteed and nonguaranteed state and local revenue bonds have appeared in recent years. For example, *life-care bonds,* also known as retirement community bonds, are issued by state and local development agencies to provide housing for the elderly. The housing is not government subsidized but supported by rental fees paid by the tenants. Frequently, nonprofit agencies organized by religious groups administer the property. Investor funds are secured by lease rentals and mortgages against the property. Life-care bonds are issued in minimum denominations of $5,000.

A related security is the *Section 8 bond* issued under the terms of the Federal Housing Act. These bonds finance low- and middle-income rental housing, usually designed for elderly citizens. Section 8s are not federally guaranteed, but the U.S. Department of Housing and Urban Development (HUD) must accumulate a cash reserve for each project that protects against the failure of project residents to pay their rent. Security for Section 8s is provided by rent subsidies and a mortgage on the housing project. Section 8 bonds carry a minimum denomination of $5,000.

Joint federal and state support for low-income housing is frequently provided through *public housing authority notes* (PHAs). These securities are used to finance the construction of public housing projects for low-income families, many of whom live on welfare. PHAs are attractive to many investors because they are guaranteed by the federal government as well as being tax exempt.

Construction of hospital facilities is frequently supported by *hospital revenue bonds*. These bonds are not guaranteed but are issued by state authorities to build hospitals for lease to public or private operating agencies. Issued in minimum denominations of $1,000, hospital revenue bonds have their principal and interest secured by lease rentals and a mortgage against hospital property.

An unusual type of municipal security which serves both public and private interests is the *industrial development bond* (IDB). These securities originally were used to finance plant construction and the purchase of land which is then leased to a private company. More recently, IDBs have financed the construction of industrial parks, electric-generating plants, commuter systems, rental properties, and pollution-control equipment. The purpose is to attract industry into the local area and increase both the number of jobs available and local tax revenues. IDBs were first issued by the state of Mississippi during the Great Depression. Soon the concept of using government credit to promote local industry became common practice across the nation, especially in those areas experiencing declining population or the exodus of large firms. However, the use of public funds raised through the tax-exempt borrowing privilege for private purposes disturbed many members of Congress. The Deficit Reduction Act of 1984 listed several prohibited uses of IDB money, placed a ceiling of $40 million on small IDBs from a single issuer, and restricted the total amount that could be issued from each state based on statewide population.

Innovations in Municipal Securities

The vast majority of state and local securities promise the investor a *fixed* rate of return. Unfortunately, this reduces the attractiveness of GOs and revenue bonds in periods of rising interest rates and inflation. During the 1970s and 1980s, several new municipal instruments were developed to deal with this "inflexibility" problem. For example, several tax-exempt revenue bonds have recently been issued as *floaters*. In one case, U.S. Steel issued $48 million in government-sponsored pollution-control bonds with a flexible (floating) interest rate to protect investors against future rate changes. Buyers were so attracted by this novel idea that an additional $500 million in floating-rate bonds soon came to market, promising a yield tied to changes in the weekly rates on 13-week Treasury bills and 30-year Treasury bonds.

Still another recent innovation is the *option bond*. Option bonds bear a fixed rate of interest but can be sold back to the issuer or his agent at par after a specified period. One example was a $43 million issue of 9 percent, single-family mortgage bonds offered by Denton County, Texas, in December 1980. While these bonds do not come due until the year 2013, a trustee with the backing of First National City Bank of New York guaranteed to buy back eligible bonds beginning December 1, 1985. More recently, several municipal borrowers have reduced the maturities of their bonds from 30 years into the 10- to 15-year range to improve their flexibility to investors.

These innovations in state and local government borrowing are not without risks. Other things being equal, they will require more frequent borrowing by municipal governments and, more than likely, increase the average cost of government funds, further burdening the taxpayer. In effect, floaters, option bonds, and shorter-maturity financial instruments shift risk from investors to borrowers and ultimately to taxpayers. Financial planning becomes more difficult for those local governments electing to use these new financial instruments. Perhaps fortunately for municipal planners, investor interest in flexible-return municipal securities dampened significantly when the rate of inflation declined during the 1980s.

Types of Securities Issued by Different Governmental Units

Whether a state or local unit of government issues general obligation or revenue bonds depends upon the type of governmental unit involved. For example, special districts which provide such services as water, sanitation, bridges and toll roads, street lighting, and electricity tend to use revenue bonds. City and state governments are about evenly split between GO and revenue issues, while counties generally borrow using revenue bonds.

KEY FEATURES OF MUNICIPAL DEBT

Tax Exemption

Certainly the outstanding and unique feature of municipal securities is the tax-exemption privilege. The interest income from qualified municipal securities is exempt from federal income taxes; in addition, state law usually exempts municipals from income taxes levied by the state of issuance. This exemption feature was created so that federal, state, and local governments would not interfere with each other in raising funds and providing services to their citizens. Capital gains on municipal securities are not tax exempt, however, unless the security is issued at a discount from par. In that special case, any increase in price up to par value is considered part of the security's interest return and is tax exempt. However, if the security continues to rise in price, that portion of the gain above par is subject to taxation once the investor realizes the gain.

An Interest Subsidy to High-Income Investors. The tax-exempt feature has been a controversial issue for many years. Clearly, it is a government subsidy to high-tax-bracket investors. This is true because the value of the exemption privilege increases with the investor's marginal income tax rate. Exhibit 26–6 illustrates the impact of the investor's marginal income tax rate (or tax bracket) on the relative attractiveness of municipals compared to taxable securities. This exhibit compares the approximate after-tax yield on high-grade corporate bonds, which are fully taxable, with the yield on comparable-quality municipal bonds, assuming that Aaa-rated corporate bonds are trading currently at a 10 percent before-tax yield and Aaa municipal bonds are trading at 7.75 percent. Because the 10 percent corporate bond yield is a before-tax rate of return, we must adjust it using the investor's

Exhibit 26–6   **The Impact of the Tax-Exemption Feature on the after-Tax Yields of Long-Term Corporate and Municipal Bonds**

Investor Group	Before-Tax Yield on Seasoned AAA Corporate Bonds	Appropriate Federal Income Tax Bracket for Investor Group	After-Tax Yield on Seasoned AAA Corporate Bonds	Before-Tax and After-Tax Yield on AAA Municipal Bonds
Individuals in the highest income bracket (with surcharge)	10%	33%	6.67%	7.75%
Large corporate investors:				
Manufacturing and industrial corporations	10	34	6.66	7.75
Property–casualty insurance companies	10	34	6.66	7.75
Commercial banks	10	34	6.66	7.75
Individuals in middle income-tax brackets	10	28	7.20	7.75
Individuals and institutions in the lowest income-tax brackets	10	15	8.50	7.75
Tax-exempt investors: Governments, pension funds, charities, foundations, and credit unions	10	0	10	7.75

marginal income tax rate to derive the after-tax rate of return. The before-tax corporate yield is multiplied by $(1 - t)$ where t is the investor's applicable federal tax rate.[4]

Exhibit 26–6 illustrates the effect of this calculation for individual investors with marginal tax rates ranging from 0 to 33 percent and for corporations whose marginal tax rates range from 0 to 34 percent as a result of the 1986 Tax Reform Act.[5] For an individual investor in the top 33 percent tax bracket, the after-tax return on Aaa corporate bonds was 10 percent $\times$ $(1 - 0.33)$, or 6.67 percent. Clearly, an investor in this high-income group would prefer to purchase municipal bonds yielding 7.75 percent rather than corporate bonds returning just 6.67 percent after taxes, other factors being equal. The same conclusion holds true for larger manufacturing and industrial corporations, property–casualty insurance companies, and commercial

---

[4] See Chapter 10 for further discussion of the impact of tax exemption on security yields.

[5] See Chapter 25 for a discussion of recent changes in federal income tax laws.

banks confronted with the top 34 percent corporate federal tax rate.[6] Even for middle-bracket investors facing a 28 percent rate, the municipals would be more attractive in terms of after-tax return.

Of course, the foregoing analysis focuses exclusively on after-tax rates of return, ignoring differences in liquidity and other features of taxable and tax-exempt securities. A corporation that needs to hold securities for liquidity purposes, for example, might well hold taxable issues, such as U.S. government securities, which usually can be converted into cash quickly and with little risk of loss, even though their after-tax yields may be lower than the yields on municipal bonds.

For income tax brackets below the top rung, corporate bonds and other taxable securities compare more favorably with municipals. For example, many small private investors whose applicable federal income tax rate is 15 percent often find taxable securities more lucrative and purchase fewer municipals. In effect, the tax-exempt feature limits the demand for state and local government securities to high-income individuals, commercial banks, property–casualty insurers, and large nonfinancial corporations. This limitation may represent a serious problem in future years when local governments in some areas of the nation must raise an enormous volume of new funds to accommodate rapidly expanding populations.

The tax exemption feature is an advantage to municipal governments because it keeps their interest cost low relative to interest rates paid by other borrowers. These savings can be passed on to local citizens in the form of lower local tax rates. Of course, the U.S. Treasury is able to collect less revenue from high-bracket investors as a result of the exemption privilege and must tax lower-bracket taxpayers more heavily to make up the difference. Therefore, the *total* tax bill from all levels of government is probably little affected by the tax-exempt feature of municipals.

Exemption Contributes to Market Volatility. Because the market for municipal bonds is limited by the tax-exempt privilege to top-bracket investors, prices and interest rates on municipal bonds tend to be highly volatile and unpredictable. Prices of tax-exempt bonds tend to rise during those periods when corporate and individual incomes are rising, because top-

---

[6] Recent federal tax laws have reduced the attractiveness of municipal securities to commercial banks and other top tax-bracket investors. The Tax Equity and Fiscal Responsibility Act of 1982 ruled that banks borrowing funds (such as through issuing deposits) to buy municipals could only deduct 85 percent of the interest cost on any borrowed funds that were invested in municipals. Then, the Deficit Reduction Act of 1984 stipulated that just 80 percent of borrowing costs could be deducted from taxable bank income when those borrowings were placed in tax-exempt municipal securities. In 1986, the Tax Reform Act lowered the top corporate tax rate from 46 percent to 34 percent, forcing the after-tax yield on municipal bonds closer to the after-tax return on corporate bonds and other taxable securities. Moreover, the volume of tax-exempt borrowing was legally restricted. Federal tax reform, therefore, made municipal bonds less attractive relative to all taxable securities. When bank earnings declined in the 1980s, fewer banks benefitted from buying municipals because their taxes were already reduced due to declining income. Nonbank investors in the top tax brackets also found municipal and taxable securities more nearly equal in after-tax yields and began to buy fewer municipals. Many investors, especially individuals, still found municipals attractive, however, because they were one of only a few tax shelters left after federal tax reforms were enacted.

bracket investors have greater need to shelter their earnings from taxation at those times. However, a fall in individual or corporate earnings often leads to sharp reductions in the demand for municipal bonds. Prices of tax-exempt issues may plummet, and interest costs confronting borrowing governments may rise dramatically during those periods when corporate profits are squeezed. This makes financial planning in the state and local government sector more difficult.

A Market of "Fair Weather" Investors. Another problem that exacerbates the volatility of municipal bond prices is the limited investment horizon of many tax-exempt bond buyers. For the most part, investors active in the tax-exempt market are "fair weather" friends. Commercial banks, for example, build up their state and local bond holdings when customer loan demand is weak, only to sell off substantial quantities of municipals when loan demand revives. Another major group of tax-exempt investors (high-income individuals) have finite life spans, and therefore their bonds are often sold after only a short holding period. The net result is to create an active secondary market and relatively high turnover rate for the larger, better-known municipal issues.

Credit Ratings

A feature of municipal securities that makes them especially attractive to investors is their high credit rating. About 10 percent of all municipal securities are AAA-rated by Moody's Investors Service and Standard & Poor's Corporation, while close to 60 percent are AA or A rated. Only about 10 percent of all state and local government securities are rated BA or lower or carry no published rating. This means that the large majority of municipal issues are considered to be of investment quality rather than speculative buys.[7]

Factors behind Setting Credit Ratings. In assigning credit ratings to municipals, Moody's and other rating services consider the past repayment record of the borrowing unit of government, the quality and size of its tax base, the volume of debt outstanding, local economic conditions, and future prospects for growth in the local economy. The fact that many municipal issues are backed by taxing authority or may draw upon several different sources of revenue for repayment of principal and interest helps to keep the investment quality of most tax-exempt issues high. This is particularly important for one of the largest buyers of new municipal bonds and notes— commercial banks. Federal regulations applying to national banks, and most state banking regulations as well, prohibit commercial banks from acquiring

---

[7]See Chapter 10 and Appendix A for a discussion of published credit ratings for corporate and municipal bonds.

debt securities rated below BAA (so-called speculative issues). These re-strictive rules encourage state and local governments to keep their credit ratings high in order to encourage active participation by banks in bidding for new municipal bonds.

Recent Credit Quality Problems. Until recently, state and local govern-ments possessed virtually unblemished credit records. No major defaults on municipal securities had occurred since the Depression. However, the tur-bulent economic and financial environment of the 1970s and 1980s caused many investors to reassess the credit standing of municipals, especially the bonds and notes issued by some of the largest cities in the nation and those associated with special local government projects, such as nuclear power production.

This problem first surfaced dramatically in the financial crisis experi-enced by New York City in the 1970s. Soaring costs for municipal services, excessive reliance on short-term debt, and high unemployment combined to threaten that city with record-high interest costs and financial default. And in the wake of New York City's fiscal crisis, other northeastern cities—Boston, Buffalo, Cleveland, Detroit, Philadelphia, and Newark—also found their credit costs rising to unprecedented levels. Even though there have been few actual defaults on municipal bonds in recent years (though about 6,000 have occurred in U.S. history) and the investors involved usually received back the principal value of their bonds (with some loss of interest), risk premiums demanded by investors purchasing lower-grade municipal bonds have at times exceeded risk premiums on comparable-quality cor-porate bonds, setting in motion a periodic "flight to quality" by high-tax-bracket investors.

This fundamental concern about the investment quality of municipal issues was heightened in December 1978 when Cleveland became the first major U.S. city to default on its debt since the Great Depression. However, Cleveland was able to work out an acceptable agreement with local banks to pay off approximately $15 million in short-term notes. This favorable outcome in the Cleveland case unfortunately did not carry over to the case of Washington Public Power Supply System (WPPSS), a nuclear power con-sortium. This company was caught in an environmental squabble, coupled with serious project delays and cost overruns on nuclear power facilities under construction. The result in the summer of 1983 was the largest default on a local government bond issue in American history, amounting to more than $2 billion. Since that time utility companies with large nuclear power plants in the construction phase have frequently seen their bond interest rates rise sharply as market investors came to fear greater risk of default.

Insurance for Municipal Bonds. Investor concern over the quality of some municipal securities and the potential failure of some state and local government projects led to the creation of "sleep insurance" for selected municipal notes and bonds. First offered by Ambac Indemnity Corp. in the early 1970s, these insurance policies, which guarantee timely payment of principal and interest, now cover approximately one quarter of all long-term state and local government bonds. Such insurance protection normally is requested and paid for by the bond issuer, not the investor. However, buyers of the bonds usually receive lower yields on insured bonds (typically a half to a tenth of a percentage point less) compared to noninsured bonds. Therefore, issuers benefit from insurance policies because they can usually sell their bonds at lower interest cost. The rating agencies, such as Standard & Poor's Corporation and Moody's Investors Service, generally give higher credit ratings to insured municipal securities. Interestingly enough, however, if the credit rating of the insurance company falls, the interest rates on municipal bonds insured by that particular company also tend to rise as investors become more concerned about the insurer's ability to pay if the state or local government issuing the securities defaults on its obligation.

Serialization

Most municipal bonds are *serial* securities. Serialization refers to the splitting up of a single bond issue into several different maturities. Thus, an issue of $20 million in bonds to build a municipal auditorium might include the following securities:

Amount	Due in
$1 million	1 year
$1 million	2 years
$1 million	3 years
•	•
•	•
•	•
$1 million	20 years

Splitting a single issue of municipals into multiple maturities contrasts with the practice employed by most corporate borrowers and the federal government. Corporations, for example, generally issue *term* bonds in which all securities in the same issue come due on the same date. In effect, serialization of municipal bonds is a way of *amortizing* state and local debt.

Why has serialization become so popular in the municipal field? Before serial bonds were widely adopted, state and local bonds were generally term securities. A sinking fund was usually created at the time of issue, and annual contributions were made to the fund until sufficient monies were accumulated to pay off the bond issue at maturity. However, sinking funds proved irresistible to unscrupulous politicians and to governments facing financial emergencies. Accumulated funds often disappeared, leaving virtually nothing to retire municipal debt when it came due. The serial feature seemed to offer an ideal solution to this problem.

Unfortunately, serialization has created as many problems as it has solved. For one thing, splitting a security issue into a number of different maturities reduces the liquidity and marketability of municipal securities. The average-sized municipal issue sold publicly contains about $20 to $30 million in securities. Therefore, when such an issue is split into multiple maturities, there is only a small amount outstanding in any one maturity class. The potential volume of trading for particular maturities is therefore extremely limited. Serialization also complicates the offering of new securities because a number of different investor groups must be attracted into the bidding. For example, commercial banks generally prefer the shorter-term (1- to 10-year) securities, while insurance companies, individuals, and other investors often want only the longest-term bonds.

HOW MUNICIPAL BONDS ARE MARKETED

The selling of municipals is usually carried out through a syndicate of commercial banks, investment banks, and securities dealers. These institutions underwrite municipals by purchasing them from issuing units of government and reselling the securities in the open market, hopefully at a higher price. Commercial banks dominate the underwriting of general obligation bonds, while investment banks (dealers) handle most of the revenue issues.[8] Prices paid by the underwriting firms may be determined either by competitive bidding among several syndicates or by negotiation with a single securities dealer or syndicate. Competitive bidding normally is employed in the marketing of general obligation bonds, while revenue bonds more frequently are placed through negotiation.

In competitive bidding, syndicates (which may contain from 2 to upwards of 50 underwriters) interested in a particular bond issue will estimate its potential reoffer price in the open market and what their desired underwriting commisssion must be. Each syndicatee wants to bid a price high enough to win the bid, but low enough so that the securities later can be sold in the open market at a price sufficient to protect the group's commission. That is,

Bid price + Underwriting commission = Market reoffer price

The winning bid carries the lowest *net interest cost* (NIC) to the issuing unit of government. The NIC is simply the sum of all interest payments that will be owed on the new issue divided by its principal amount.

---

[8]Commercial banks are permitted to underwrite for resale only GOs and revenue bonds used to finance university, dormitory, or housing projects or those revenue bonds collateralized at least indirectly by the "full faith and credit" of a state or local unit of government. Investment banks, however, legally can underwrite any form of municipal bond or note. More recently, selected subsidiaries of large bank holding companies have been permitted to underwrite selected municipal revenue bond issues.

Bidding for new issues of municipal bonds is a treacherous business. Prices, interest rates, and market demand for municipals all change rapidly, often without warning. In fact, the tax-exempt securities market is one of the most volatile of all financial markets. This is due in part to the key role of commercial banks, whose demand for municipals fluctuates with their net earnings and loan demand. Legal interest rate ceilings, which prohibit some local governments from borrowing when market interest rates climb above those celings, also play a significant role in the volatility of municipal trading. These combined factors render the tax-exempt market highly sensitive to the business cycle, monetary policy, inflation, and a host of other economic and financial factors. The specter of high interest rates often forces the postponement of hundreds of millions of dollars of new issues, while the onset of lower rates may unleash a flood of new security offerings. Still another problem is federal tax reform which has reduced the volume and attractiveness of many municipal securities to investors—a structural shift in this market which, in 1987, led the largest municipal bond underwriter, Salomon Brothers, Inc., to largely withdraw from the market.

There is a trend today away from competitive bidding and toward negotiated sales of new state and local bonds, due partly to the treacherous character of the tax-exempt market. This trend has aroused some concern among financial analysts because competitive bidding should result in the lowest net interest cost, reducing the burden on local taxpayers. On the other side of the coin, underwriting firms argue that they provide extra services to borrowing governments during the negotiation process—services not generally available through competitive bidding. These include preparing legal offering statements, scheduling the sale of new securities, helping to secure desirable credit ratings, and contacting potential buyers.

PROBLEMS IN THE MUNICIPAL MARKET

Problems and Proposals Regarding Tax Exemption

The municipal market has been plagued by a number of problems over the years, some related to its unique tax-exempt character. Many observers question the social benefit of the tax-exemption privilege. As we noted earlier, while state and local governments can borrow more cheaply as a result of tax exemption, the federal government must tax nonexempt groups more heavily to make up the lost revenue. Also, many important investor groups, such as pension funds, life insurance companies, and mutual funds, display little interest in municipal bonds because they have little need for this type of tax shelter. A number of proposals have been advanced over the years for improving the depth and stability of the municipal market and eliminating the tax-exempt feature. One interesting idea calls for reimbursing state and local governments for loss of the tax-exempt privilege through federal interest subsidies. A related idea calls for paying a subsidy directly to investors who choose to buy municipal securities. An *Urbank* has also been proposed which, under federal sponsorship, would issue its own bonds, and direct the proceeds of bonds sales to municipal governments. One criticism of this approach is the danger of increased federal controls over state and local governments.

California's Proposition 13

The municipal market was rocked to its foundations in 1978 when California voters approved Proposition 13. This law set maximum real property tax rates in California at 1 percent of the full cash value of taxable property, except for those bonds which had already been approved by the voters. The state of California was prohibited from enacting a statewide property tax or property transfer tax, and any increase in state taxes required a two-thirds vote of the legislature. In effect, Proposition 13 called for a 60 percent decline in real-property tax collections without making provision for other sources of funds to take up the slack.

The success of Proposition 13 in California resulted in the creation of taxpayer lobby groups in other states intent on enacting similar legislation. A taxpayer revolt continuing into the 1980s resulted subsequently in more than 30 states passing legislation to limit the growth of local government or directly reduce taxes. Budget balancing was required in 49 of the 50 states. Many financial analysts predicted dire consequences for the municipal market stemming from such laws. General obligation bonds were expected to fade away if other states joined California in a move to limit state and local taxing authority. While the new law certainly did not prohibit the issue of municipal bonds, it did prevent increases in taxes to finance many new bond issues. This fact suggested to many observers that revenue bonds rather than GOs would be more heavily used in the future, especially for utilities, lighting districts, and other revenue-generating services—a trend that has, in fact, occurred.

Laws like Proposition 13 might well encourage the shifting of the local tax base from real property to personal property. Moreover, Proposition 13 appeared to shift a substantial measure of fiscal authority away from state governments toward local governments. Beyond this, there was great concern in California about layoffs of public employees, reduced school hours, and severe limitations on the availability of essential services due to the lack of available funds. However, few of these "calamities" materialized. Indeed, the prospect of lower taxes appears to have stimulated additional private investment. The added jobs and tax revenues springing from expanded private investment activity appear to have filled in much of the gap left by Proposition 13's fiscal restrictions.

The Growing Burden of Local Taxes and Debt

California's passage of Proposition 13 and strong voter interest in similar laws in other states reflects the tremendous growth in state and local taxes and debt in recent years. The tax burden faced by the average taxpayer today has been worsened by inflation, which pushes individuals into higher and higher tax brackets at both federal and state levels. Moreover, rising property values subject taxpayers to increased tax payments against their homes and other forms of real and personal property.

Local property taxes are particularly onerous to the average citizen because they are so *visible.* Each year, the homeowner is confronted with a large lump-sum property assessment to cover the cost of local schools, street improvements, and other essential services. The fact is that income and sales taxes have increased more rapidly than property taxes, but they are less visible to the taxpayer and therefore often ignored. An added problem is that many citizens do not see a direct correlation between the size of their tax burdens and the quantity and quality of government services available to them. Moreover, the public has come to question the wisdom of both higher taxes and increased borrowing in the face of a favorable trend in state and local government revenues and large budget surpluses run up by several states in recent years.

In short, with rising taxes and growing investor concern over the credit quality of many municipal issues it seems clear that the market for state and local government debt has an "image problem" to deal with in the years ahead. The need for more local government services is not likely to fade, but the continued willingness of taxpayers to authorize new construction and new borrowing and the continued willingness of large numbers of investors to fund those needs in a volatile and uncertain economic environment are the key issues in municipal finance for the period ahead.

STUDY QUESTIONS

1. The market for state and local government bonds has been one of the most rapidly growing financial markets in the United States since World War II. Why has this been the case? Can you foresee any serious problems on the horizon for the continued growth of the municipal market?

2. What are the principal sources of revenue for state and local governments today? Where do they spend the bulk of their incoming funds?

3. For what reasons do state and local governments borrow short- and long-term funds?

4. Give a concise definition of each of the following state and local government securities, and explain how each is used:
   a. Tax-anticipation notes.
   b. Revenue-anticipation notes.
   c. Bond-anticipation notes.
   d. General obligation (GO) bonds.
   e. Revenue bonds.
   f. Special tax bonds.
   g. Special assessment bonds.
   h. Authority bonds.

5. Revenue bonds issued by local governments and public agenices have grown more rapidly than any other type of municipal security in recent years. Moreover, many new kinds of revenue bonds have been developed to deal with specialized public needs. Several different kinds of revenue bonds are listed below. Please explain the principal purpose or function of each of these securities:
   a. SLROs.
   b. Life-care bonds.
   c. Section 8 bonds.
   d. PHAs.
   e. Hospital revenue bonds.
   f. Mortgage revenue bonds.
   g. IDBs.

6. What are the principal features of municipal bonds that have made them attractive to many groups of investors? What factors or features often limit the demand for these bonds?

7. How has recent federal tax reform legislation affected the municipal market?

8. Describe how municipal bonds are marketed. What risks do syndicates face? What advantages do you see for competitive bidding versus negotiated sales?

9. What recommendations would you make to improve the functioning of the municipal bond market? Carefully explain the purpose and probable effects of each of your recommendations.

10. In what ways is the municipal bond market dealing with the problem of "inflexibility"? What is a "floater"? An option bond? How might these devices assist the marketability of municipals in future years?

SELECTED REFERENCES

Advisory Commission on Intergovernmental Relations. *State and Local Finances in Recession and Inflation: An Economic Analysis.* Washington, DC: U.S. Government Printing Office, 1979.

Aronson, J. Richard, and John L. Hilley. *Financing State and Local Governments,* 4th Edition. Washington, DC: The Brookings Institution, 1986.

Beek, David C. "Rethinking Tax-Exempt Financing for State and Local Governments." *Quarterly Review,* Federal Reserve Bank of New York, Autumn 1982, pp. 30–40.

Bradbury, Katherine L. "Structural Fiscal Distress in Cities—Causes and Conse-quences." *New England Economic Review,* Federal Reserve Bank of Boston, February, 1983, pp. 32–43.

Browne, Lynn E., and Richard F. Syron. "Big City Bonds after New York." *New England Economic Review,* Federal Reserve Bank of Boston, July–August 1977.

————. "How Much Government Is Too Much?" *New England Economic Review,* Federal Reserve Bank of Boston, March–April 1981, pp. 21–34.

Fortune, Peter. "Tax-Exemption of State and Local Interest Payments: An Economic Analysis of the Issues and an Alternative." *New England Economic Review,* Federal Reserve Bank of Boston, March–April 1978, pp. 21–31.

Kaufman, George G. "Municipal Bond Underwriting: Market Structure." *Journal of Bank Research,* Spring 1981, pp. 24–31.

Rubin, Lamar S. "Recent Developments in the State and Local Government Sector." *Federal Reserve Bulletin,* November 1984, pp. 791–801.

Part Eight

The International Financial System

Chapter 27

The Balance of Payments and International Transactions

Learning Objectives in This Chapter

- To explore the functions and roles of the international financial markets within the financial system.

- To see how international payments for goods and services and international lending and borrowing are tracked through the balance-of-payments accounts.

- To examine the problems created by different monetary units (standards of value) used by different nations.

- To see how the values of national currencies (such as the dollar and the yen) are determined in the modern world.

Key Terms and Concepts in This Chapter

Balance-of-payments (BOP) accounts	Basic balance	The managed floating currency standard
Current account	Official reserve transactions	Peggers
Merchandise trade balance	The gold standard	Special drawing rights
Balance in invisibles	The gold exchange standard	Managed float
Unilateral transfers	The modified exchange standard	
Capital account		

IN many ways the world we live in is rapidly shrinking in size. Jet planes such as the British Concorde can race across the Atlantic between New York and London in less than four hours, about the same time it takes a Boeing 747 jetliner to travel across the United States. Teletype, telex, and transoceanic cable can move financial information and instructions from one spot on the globe to another in minutes. Orbiting satellites can bring news of major international significance to home television sets the same day an event takes place and make possible video as well as voice communication between those involved in international business transactions.

Accompanying these dramatic improvements in communication and transportation is an enormous growth in world trade and international investment. For example, in 1965 total exports of goods and services worldwide reached $190 billion. By the 1980s, the estimated dollar value of world trade had reached the neighborhood of $2 trillion, or almost half the U.S. GNP. Moreover, the United States itself has become increasingly dependent upon world trade; for example, imports into the United States represented just 4.6 percent of GNP in 1960, but had jumped to nearly 13 percent of GNP by 1988, while U.S. exports climbed from 6 percent to 10 percent of GNP over the same period. Thus, more than one fifth of the value of production and spending in the U.S. economy stems directly from foreign trade. The international financial markets have had to grow enormously in recent years just to keep up with the burgeoning in world trade and finance.

Actually, the international financial markets perform the same basic functions as do the domestic financial markets. They bring international lenders of funds (savers) into contact with borrowers, thereby permitting an increased flow of scarce funds toward their most productive uses. The volume of capital investment worldwide is made larger because of the workings of the global financial system. And, with increased capital investment, the productivity of individual firms and nations is increased and economic growth in the international sector accelerates. The international financial markets also facilitate the flow of consumer goods and services across national boundaries, making possible an optimal allocation of resources in response to consumer demand on a global scale. With increased efficiency in resource use, the output of consumer goods and services in the international sector is increased and costs of production are minimized.[1]

Just as the domestic financial markets have given rise to a unique collection of financial institutions and methods for transferring funds, so the international financial system has spawned institutions and practices

---

[1]These benefits from international trade and finance are most likely to occur if each nation involved follows the principle of *comparative advantage*. This principle argues that each country will have a higher real standard of living if it specializes in the production of those goods and services in which it has a comparative advantage in resource costs, while importing those goods and services where it is at a comparative resource-cost disadvantage. In simplest terms, a country should acquire goods and services from those sources—foreign or domestic—which result in the lowest cost in terms of its own resources. The principle of comparative advantage works best, of course, in an environment of free international trade which permits nations to specialize in their most efficient productive activities.

unique to that system. As we will see later in this chapter and in the two chapters to follow, the global financial markets are dominated by huge multinational corporations, central banks, government agencies, the largest commercial banks and financial conglomerates, investment banking houses, security and foreign exchange dealers, and major brokerage houses. Our purpose in this section of the book is to examine the unique roles played by each of these institutions within a rapidly expanding international financial system.

THE BALANCE OF PAYMENTS

One of the most widely used sources of information concerning flows of funds, goods, and services between nations is each country's balance-of-payments (BOP) accounts. This annual statistical report summarizes all the economic and financial transactions between residents of one nation and the rest of the world during a specific period of time. It is a report capturing flows (rather than stocks) of payments between nations. Thus, the BOP accounts reflect *changes* in the assets and liabilities of units, such as businesses, individuals, and governments, involved in international transactions, rather than the levels of their assets and liabilities.[2] The major transactions captured in the BOP accounts include exports and imports of goods and services; tourist expenditures; income from debt and equity investments made abroad; government loans, grants, and military expenditures overseas; and net private capital flows between nations.

In a statistical sense, a nation's BOP accounts always "balance" because a system of double-entry bookkeeping is used. For example, every payment made for goods and services imported from abroad simultaneously creates a claim on the home country's resources or extinguishes an existing liability. Similarly, every time a domestic business firm receives payment from overseas, either it acquires a claim against resources in a foreign country, or a claim that firm held against a foreign individual or institution is erased. In practice, however, imbalances frequently show up in the BOP accounts due to unreported transactions or inconsistencies in reporting. These errors and omissions are handled through a Statistical Discrepancy account.

The U.S. Balance of International Payments

The U.S. BOP accounts are prepared and published quarterly by the Department of Commerce. The quarterly figures usually are then *annualized* to permit comparisons across years. The transactions recorded in the U.S.

---

[2]In this sense the balance-of-payments accounts are analogous to the Flow of Funds Accounts discussed in Chapter 3. The BOP accounts are really sources and uses of funds statements for a whole nation vis-à-vis the rest of the world.

balance of payments (and those for other countries as well) fall into three broad groups:

1. *Transactions on current account,* which include imports and exports of goods and services and unilateral transfers (gifts).

2. *Transactions on capital account,* which include both long- and short-term investment at home and abroad and usually involve the transfer of financial assets (acceptances, bonds, deposits, stock, etc.).

3. *Official reserve transactions,* which are used by monetary authorities (the Treasury, central bank, exchange stabilization fund, etc.) to settle BOP deficits, usually through transferring the ownership of official reserve assets to countries with BOP surpluses.

Transactions that bring about an inflow of foreign currency into the home country are recorded as *credits* (+). Transactions resulting in an outflow of foreign currency from the home country are listed as *debits* (−). Thus, credit (+) items in the BOP represent sources of funds—an increase in a nation's external buying power or ability to command goods and services from abroad or to invest abroad. Debit (−) items represent uses of funds, which decrease a nation's buying power abroad. If a country sells goods and services or borrows abroad, these transactions are credit items because they increase a nation's external buying power. On the other hand, a purchase of goods and services abroad or a paydown of a nation's international liabilities is a debit item because that country is surrendering part of its external buying power. A summary of the major credit and debit items making up the BOP accounts is shown in Exhibit 27–1.

Exhibit 27–1   Principal Credit and Debit Items Recorded in a Nation's Balance of Payments (BOP)

Credit entries (inflows of funds, +)	Debit entries (outflows of funds, −)
Exports of merchandise	Imports of merchandise
Services provided to foreign countries	Services provided to domestic citizens by foreign countries
Interest and dividends due domestic citizens from business firms abroad	Gifts of money sent abroad by domestic citizens
Remittances received from domestic citizens employed in foreign countries	Capital invested abroad by domestic citizens
Foreign purchases of securities issued by domestic firms and units of government	Dividend and interest payments to foreign countries on investments made in the domestic economy
Repayments by foreigners of funds borrowed from domestic lending institutions	

The actual U.S. BOP accounts for the years 1985 and 1986 as reported by the Department of Commerce are shown in Exhibit 27–2. We have subdivided these international accounts into the three major categories discussed above—the current account, capital account, and official reserve transactions account—to more fully understand how the BOP bookkeeping system operates.

The Current Account

One of the most highly publicized components of the U.S. BOP is the current account, which contains three elements:

1. The *merchandise trade balance*, comparing the volume of goods exported to those imported.
2. The *service balance*, comparing exports and imports of services.
3. *Unilateral transfers*, reflecting the amount of gifts made to foreigners by domestic citizens.

The Merchandise Trade Balance. Prior to the 1970s the United States reported a positive merchandise trade balance with exports exceeding imports in most years due to substantial demand for American agricultural products and machinery overseas. However, rapid inflation and a dramatic increase in crude oil prices turned U.S. trade surpluses into substantial deficits. In general, U.S. *sources* of external buying power have generally been less than its *uses* of external buying power. Moreover, American merchandise trade deficits generally deepened over time. For example, in 1980 the U.S. merchandise trade balance was − \$25.5 billion; and in 1986 almost − \$148 billion before declining somewhat in the late 1980s. These huge trade deficits have been attributed widely to such factors as declining competitiveness of American goods abroad, sluggish economic growth, and federal budget deficits.

The Service Balance. Because Americans have purchased more goods from abroad in recent years than they have sold to other countries, how has this deficit (debit balance) in the merchandise trade account been paid for? Funds must be acquired from some other source to finance the excess of merchandise imports over exports. Part of the needed funds have come from the service balance, which has been in surplus for many years. Services counted in the BOP accounts include insurance policies covering foreign shipments of goods, the shipping of ocean freight and other transportation services, hotel accommodations for foreigners visiting the United States, and property management services, entertainment, and medical care for foreign residents. Also included in the service balance are receipts of income from U.S. direct investments abroad (usually in the form of interest and

Exhibit 27–2 **The Balance of Payments of the United States, 1985 and 1986 ($ Billions)**

Credit (+) and Debit (−) Items	1985	1986
The Current Account		
Merchandise:		
Exports of merchandise	$ 214.4	$ 221.8
Imports of merchandise	− 338.9	− 369.5
Balance on merchandise trade	− 124.4	− 147.7
Services:		
Military transactions, net	− 2.9	− 2.4
Investment income, net	25.2	22.9
Other service transactions, net	− 0.5	1.8
Service balance	+ 21.8	+ 22.3
Balance on goods and services	− 102.6	− 125.4
Unilateral transfers and government grants	− 15.0	− 15.1
Balance on Current Account	− 117.7	− 140.6
The Capital Account		
Change in U.S. citizens' private assets abroad (increase, −):		
Bank—reported claims	− 0.7	− 57.3
Nonbank—reported claims	1.7	− 4.2
U.S. purchase of foreign securities, net	− 8.0	− 4.8
U.S. direct investments abroad, net	− 18.8	− 31.9
Private capital outflows from the U.S.	− 25.8	− 98.1
Change in foreign private assets inside the U.S. (increase, +):		
U.S. bank-reported liabilities	40.4	77.4
U.S. nonbank-reported liabilities	− 1.2	− 3.1
Foreign private purchases of U.S. Treasury securities, net	20.5	9.3
Foreign purchases of other U.S. securities, net	50.9	70.7
Foreign direct investments in the U.S., net	17.9	25.6
Private capital flows into the U.S.	+ 128.4	+ 179.9
Total private capital flows, net (net capital inflow, +)	+ 102.6	+ 81.8
Changes in Official Reserve Assets		
Changes in U.S. official reserve assets (increase, −):		
Gold	0	0
Special drawing rights (SDRs)	− 0.9	− 0.2
Reserve position in International Monetary Fund (IMF)	0.9	1.5
Foreign currencies	− 3.9	− 0.9
Increase (−) or decrease (+) in U.S. Official Reserve Assets	− 3.9	0.3
Changes in foreign official assets in the U.S. (increase, +):		
U.S. Treasury securities	− 0.5	34.5
Other U.S. government obligations	− 0.3	− 1.2
Other U.S. government liabilities	0.5	1.1
Other U.S. liabilities reported by U.S. banks	0.5	− 0.1
Other foreign official assets	− 1.5	− 0.8
Increase (+) or Decrease (−) in foreign official reserve assets	− 1.3	+ 33.4
Change in U.S. government assets (other than official reserve assets), net (increase, −)	− 2.8	− 2.0
Allocation of SDRs	0	0
Statistical discrepancy	23.0	27.1

Notes: Details may not add to column totals due to rounding error. The current account is seasonally adjusted. Investment income in the current account includes reinvested earnings. The "other foreign official assets" category includes investments in U.S. corporate stocks and in debt securities of private corporations and state and local governments.

Source: Board of Governors of the Federal Reserve System, *Federal Reserve Bulletin,* selected issues, and U.S. Department of Commerce, Bureau of Economic Analysis.

dividends).[3] These income flows are created when U.S. residents purchase foreign securities and acquire equity interests in foreign businesses. When exports of services exceed service imports, the result is a credit (+) balance in the services account. The balance in the service accounts is sometimes called the balance in invisibles, because services are intangible items. In 1986 the U.S. service balance, or balance in invisibles, was in surplus by $22.3 billion, helping to offset about one sixth of the U.S. merchandise trade deficit.

Balance on Goods and Services. If we combine the merchandise trade balance with the service balance, the resulting figure is labeled the *balance on goods and services*. In 1986 the United States reported a merchandise trade deficit of $147.7 billion and a credit balance in services of $22.3 billion, resulting in a debit balance on goods and services of $125.4 billion.

Unilateral Transfers. The third category of transaction recorded in the current account, labeled unilateral transfers, consists of gifts of goods and money from U.S. residents to foreigners. Gifts of food, clothing, money, and other items are referred to as unilateral transfers because they represent a *one-way flow* of resources to the recipient; nothing is expected in return. Of course, foreigners send gifts to U.S. residents as well, but American gift-giving abroad far exceeds the return flow. For example, gifts to foreigners from Americans were about $15 billion larger than foreign gifts flowing into the United States in 1986 (see Exhibit 27–2). Each gift sent overseas represents the *use* of the nation's external buying power and therefore is recorded as a *debit* (−) item.

The Balance on Current Account. When we put the three components— balance on merchandise trade, balance on services, and net unilateral transfers together—we derive the *balance on current account*. As Exhibit 27–2 reveals, the U.S. balance on current account in 1986 was a debit balance of $140.6 billion—the largest current account deficit in American history. The United States experienced such a huge debit balance primarily because of the rising value of the U.S. dollar in international markets for part of the period that discouraged sales of U.S. goods abroad. Lagging economic recovery abroad added further to the record current account deficit.

The Capital Account

Flows of funds destined for investment abroad are recorded in the capital account. Investments abroad may be long term, as in the case of an American automobile company building an assembly plant in West Germany, or short

---

[3]In effect, interest and dividend payments received by domestic residents from international investments reflect services that the nation's capital is providing overseas. The interest and dividend payments increase a nation's external buying power.

term, such as the purchase of six-month British Treasury bills by U.S. citizens. Of course, capital investment flows both ways across national boundaries. For example, in 1986 U.S. citizens and private organizations invested more than $98 billion overseas, but foreign individuals and private institutions, attracted by relatively high interest rates here, invested about $180 billion in U.S. assets. The result was a *net private capital inflow* into the United States of almost $82 billion.

Investments by foreigners in the United States are growing faster today than U.S. investments overseas. The relative prosperity experienced by the American economy over the past decade and the attractiveness of the dollar in international markets coupled with political upheavals abroad have brought forth an increasing volume of foreign investment within the continental United States. American banks, hotels, insurance companies, traders in motor vehicles and farm products, energy companies, and numerous other firms have all been acquisition targets for foreign investors.[4] In effect, these huge foreign-capital inflows have financed a substantial portion of the U.S. trade deficit.

Components of the Capital Account. The capital account in the balance of payments includes three different types of international investment: (1) short-term capital flows, (2) direct investments, and (3) portfolio investments. The latter two—direct and portfolio investments—represent a long-term commitment of funds, involving the purchase of stocks, bonds, and other financial assets having a maturity of more than one year. Short-term capital flows, on the other hand, reflect purchases of financial assets with maturities of less than one year. These short-term financial assets are mainly government notes and bills, bank deposits, bills of exchange, and foreign currencies.

What is the essential difference between direct investment and portfolio investment? The key factor is *control*. Portfolio investment merely involves purchasing securities to hold in order to receive interest, dividends, or capital gains. Direct investment, on the other hand, refers to the purchase of land or the acquisition of ownership shares in an attempt to control a foreign business firm.[5]

Claims against Foreigners. In addition to direct investment and purchases of foreign securities, the capital account also records claims against foreigners reported by domestic banks and nonbanking concerns. The bulk

---

[4]The leading foreign nations with ownership interests in U.S.-based firms are Japan, the United Kingdom, Canada, the Netherlands, and West Germany. Most of the remaining foreign-controlled U.S. assets are held by Latin American companies.

[5]The U.S. Department of Commerce defines direct investment as ownership of 10 percent or more of the voting stock or the exercise of other means of control over a foreign business enterprise by an individual or corporation. Ownership of less than 10 percent of a foreign firm's stock is referred to as portfolio investment.

of these claims comprise loans extended by domestic banks to firms and governments abroad.

In 1986, U.S. bank claims on foreigners rose $57 billion. Most of the gain was due to loans made by U.S. banks in the global Eurocurrency markets.[6] However, U.S. banks also borrowed heavily abroad to sustain their domestic and international lending operations, giving foreign investors substantial claims against American banks. For example, short- and long-term liabilities to foreigners reported by U.S. banking concerns rose $77 billion in 1986.

Interestingly enough, U.S. bank loans abroad have declined sharply from what they had been in earlier years. What reversed this trend? Several foreign countries, notably in Central and South America and in Eastern Europe, have been unable to service their huge loans from American banks, and many international energy and commodity loans nosedived in value due to continuing weakness in the oil and raw materials markets. As a result, many U.S. banks began to sell off their nonperforming foreign credits and to reduce sharply their foreign lending activities. Then too, many U.S. corporations have brought the earnings of their foreign affiliates home (known as *repatriation of funds*) to take advantage of relatively high domestic interest rates.

The Basic Balance

If the current account balance is added to the long-term investment balance in the nation's international accounts, the net figure is known as the basic balance. We can calculate this for the United States in 1986 as follows:

	$ Billions	
U.S. balance on current account		− 140.6
Long-term capital flows:		
Net direct investment[7]	− 6.3	
Net portfolio investment[7]	+ 88.0	
Net capital inflow		+ 81.7
Basic balance		− 58.9

Therefore, when merchandise trade, services, gifts, and capital flows are taken into consideration, the United States had a $58.9 billion deficit in its basic balance account. This deficit has to be covered by giving up U.S. reserves of gold, foreign currency, and other assets, or by giving foreigners larger claims (in the form of securities, bank deposits, etc.) against U.S. resources.

---

[6]See Chapter 17 for a discussion of borrowing and lending activity in the Eurodollar and other Eurocurrency markets.

[7]The net figure is derived by subtracting foreign investments in the United States from investments by U.S. residents abroad.

Cumulative Balance in International Accounts and Short-Term Capital Flows

Actually, the total or cumulative U.S. balance-of-payments deficit may be larger or smaller than the basic balance. The principal reason is that the basic balance fails to consider short-term capital flows, which are assumed to result from temporary factors, such as the financing of current transactions, that will "net out" in the long run. Moreover, we must consider the possibility of a statistical discrepancy in the reported figures due to thousands of unreported transactions that occur across national borders each day.

As noted earlier, because the balance of payments is based on a double-entry system of bookkeeping, it should always balance out except for errors in recording and reporting transactions and the omission of many unrecorded items. Errors and omissions are captured in an account called *Statistical Discrepancy,* which is the difference between the reported current account and capital account balances. Many authorities believe that the Statistical Discrepancy reflects primarily unreported current earnings and unrecorded short-term capital flows. This account often increases in size when large amounts of short-term capital are known to be in motion from one country to another in response to differences in interest rates or currency values. The 1986 Statistical Discrepancy was a credit ($+$) balance of $27.1 billion, suggesting that U.S. security issuers were able to attract relatively large amounts of short-term foreign funds.[8] After adjusting for foreign capital flowing into the United States, therefore, the *net* amount of funds which flowed out of the country in 1986 was probably much less than the basic balance deficit we have just calculated.

Official Reserve Transactions

When a nation has a deficit in its international payments accounts, it must settle up by surrendering assets or claims to foreign individuals and institutions. Official reserve transactions, involving transfer of the ownership of gold, convertible foreign currencies, deposits in the International Monetary Fund and special drawing rights (SDRs), are usually the vehicle for settling net differences in international claims between nations.

Official reserve accounts are immediately available assets for making international payments. When these assets *increase,* this represents a use of external buying power by the nation experiencing the increase. On the other hand, a *decrease* in the official reserve accounts represents a use of external buying power by the nation experiencing the increase. On the other

---

[8]The Statistical Discrepancy account has generally increased in size in recent years. Several factors apparently have contributed to the account's growth, including political unrest abroad, secret and illegal transactions, and concealment by some governments of their true international reserve positions.

hand, a *decrease* in the official reserve accounts represents a source of external buying power. If a nation has a surplus (credit balance) in its current and capital accounts, the balance in its official reserve accounts generally rises, indicating an excess of sales abroad over foreign purchases. Conversely, a country experiencing a deficit (debit balance) in its current and capital accounts usually will find that the balance in its official reserve accounts is falling. Such a decline can be temporarily offset, however, by official borrowing by the central bank or some other designated government agency.

In 1986 offsetting movements occurred in U.S. and foreign holdings of official reserve assets. Foreign governments and central banks increased their holdings of gold, currencies, and other official assets in the United States by $33.4 billion, net. Also, reflecting its huge BOP deficit, the U.S. government lost official reserve assets in the net amount of $0.3 billion in 1986. However, as we noted earlier, most of the American BOP deficits in recent years have not been financed through changes in official reserve assets, but through capital inflows from abroad, especially massive purchases of U.S. stocks and debt securities.

Disequilibrium in the Balance of Payments

For several years running now, the United States has displayed a disequilibrium position in its balance of international payments. This means that the nation has relied on foreign credit, foreign capital inflows into the United States, and the U.S. stock of gold, foreign currencies, and other reserve assets to settle continuing BOP deficits. However, the amount of these financial devices is limited—no nation can go on indefinitely accumulating BOP deficits, borrowing abroad, and using up its reserves. Moreover, relying on foreign capital inflows is dangerous because the perceptions of foreign investors regarding the desirability of placing funds in the United States may change quite abruptly.

To this point, foreign central banks and foreign investors have regarded American securities and interest-bearing, dollar-denominated deposits as good investments and have been willing to extend an increasing volume of international credit to the United States. At some point, however, foreign governments and private investors may become satiated with dollar claims; at this point, the value of the U.S. dollar must decline in international markets. American purchases of goods and services abroad would also decline because of the dollar's reduced purchasing power. All else being equal, the nation's standard of living would begin to fall until equilibrium in its balance-of-payments position was restored.

Is this long-term disequilibrium position in U.S. international payments likely to continue? To be sure, U.S. trade deficits have had many causes— huge amounts of imported oil, declining industrial productivity, the success of several foreign nations (especially Japan) in marketing their goods in

U.S. markets, burgeoning demand for imported automobiles, computers, and other electronic devices, and domestic inflation. Among recent efforts to deal with this trade deficit, one of the most important advances was passage of the Trade and Tariff Act of 1984 (also known as the Omnibus Trade bill) to make it easier for the United States to negotiate free trade agreements and tariff reductions with other nations and to further reduce barriers to international investment. However, there is also a rising tide of protectionist sentiment arguing for tough trade barriers.

A positive factor in the U.S. international payments position is the long-term surplus in the services account. In fact, the United States has had a service account surplus each year for more than two decades. As American shipping lines and airline companies, hotels, travel agencies, insurance companies, and banks continue to expand their service offerings abroad, the U.S. service account should continue to display substantial surplus (credit) balances in the future.

Another positive factor for the American BOP lies in the *capital account* where growing investment by foreigners in the United States has offset outflows of capital funds from U.S. investors. Capital inflows into the United States have grown faster in recent years than U.S. investments abroad, making the U.S. the world's largest debtor nation. The most rapid gains in foreign investment inside the United States have been centered in service-oriented industries—banking and finance, insurance, and trade. However, investments in U.S. manufacturing industries, real estate, and petroleum affiliates have also continued to grow rapidly. A major factor accelerating foreign direct investment in the United States is the desire to avoid American import restrictions by developing production facilities inside the United States. Even more significant are relatively high returns on U.S. securities and domestic political stability offering an attractive haven for international investors. If this capital inflow continues in the future, it will do much to alleviate the serious international payments problems of the United States.

THE PROBLEM OF DIFFERENT MONETARY UNITS IN INTERNATIONAL TRADE AND FINANCE

Businesses and individuals trading goods and services in international markets encounter a problem not experienced by those who buy and sell only in domestic markets. This is the problem of different monetary units used as the standard of value from country to country. Americans, of course, use the dollar as a medium of exchange and standard of value in domestic markets. British citizens employ pounds sterling for domestic exchange, while the Swiss and the French rely on the franc as their basic monetary unit. There are more than 100 different monetary units around the world (see Exhibit 27–3). As a result, whenever goods and services are sold or

Exhibit 27–3   **Principal Monetary Units Used in International Trade and Finance**

Country	Monetary Unit	Country	Monetary Unit
Argentina	Peso	Japan	Yen
Australia	Dollar	Malaysia	Ringgit
Austria	Schilling	Mexico	Peso
Belgium	Franc	Netherlands	Guilder
Canada	Dollar	New Zealand	Dollar
Denmark	Krone	Norway	Krone
Finland	Markka	Portugal	Escudo
France	Franc	Saudi Arabia	Riyal
Germany	Deutsche mark	South Africa	Rand
Honduras	Lempira	Spain	Peseta
India	Rupee	Sri Lanka	Rupee
Iran	Rial	Sweden	Krona
Ireland	Pound	Switzerland	Franc
Italy	Lira	United Kingdom	Pound sterling
		United States	Dollar

capital flows across national boundaries, it is usually necessary to sell one currency and buy another.

Unfortunately, the act of trading currencies entails substantial *risk*. Exporters and importers may be forced to purchase a foreign currency when its value is rising, while at the same time the home country's currency is falling in value. Any profits earned on the sale of goods and services abroad may be outweighed by losses suffered in currency exchange. Differing monetary units also complicate government monetary policy aimed at curbing inflation and ensuring adequate economic growth. Repeatedly in recent years massive flows of funds surged through foreign and domestic markets from speculative buying and selling of dollars, francs, pounds, and other major currencies. These speculative currency flows greatly increased the problems of economic recovery and the control of inflation.

The Gold Standard

The problem of trading in different monetary units whose prices change frequently is one of the world's oldest financial problems. It has been dealt with in a wide variety of ways over the centuries. One of the most successful solutions prior to the modern era centered on *gold* as an international standard of value. During the 17th and 18th centuries, a period that gave birth to the Industrial Revolution and the rapid expansion of world trade, major trading nations in Western Europe made their currencies freely convertible into gold. Gold bullion and gold coins could be exported and imported from one country to another without significant restriction, and each unit of currency was defined in terms of so many grains of fine gold. Nations adopting the gold standard agreed to exchange paper money or coins for gold bullion in unlimited amounts at fixed, predetermined prices.

One advantage of the gold standard was that it imposed a common standard of value on all national currencies. This brought a measure of security to international trade and investment, dampened exchange rate fluctuations, and stimulated the expansion of commerce and investment abroad. A second advantage of the gold standard was economic discipline. Tying national currencies to gold regulated the growth and stability of national economies. A nation experiencing severe inflation or excessively rapid growth in consumption of imported goods and services soon found itself losing gold reserves. Exports declined, unemployment rose, and domestic prices soon began to fall. As a result, the volume of imports was curtailed, and the outflow of gold reduced. Eventually, export industries would recover and the country would begin to rebuild its gold reserves, providing a basis for further expansion of its international trade.

These advantages of security and economic discipline were offset by a number of limitations inherent in the gold standard. For one thing, maintenance of that standard depended crucially on *free trade*. Nations desiring to protect their industry and jobs from foreign competition through export or import restrictions could not do so. Moreover, the growth of a nation's money supply was limited by the size of its gold stock. Problems of rising unemployment or lagging economic growth might call for a stimulative monetary policy, leading to lower interest rates and rapid expansion of the domestic money supply. However, such a policy required a suspension of gold convertibility, taking the nation off the gold standard. Thus, the gold standard often conflicted with national economic goals and drastically limited the policy alternatives open to governmental authorities.

The Gold Exchange Standard

While government policymakers are mainly concerned about the effects of the gold standard on domestic economies, investors and commercial traders found that gold bullion was not a particularly convenient medium of exchange. Gold is expensive to transport and risky to handle. Moreover, the world's gold supply was limited relative to the rapidly expanding volume of international trade. These problems gave rise in the 19th century to the gold exchange standard. Central banks, governments, major commercial banks, and other institutions actively engaged in international commerce began to hold stocks of convertible currencies. Each currency was freely convertible into gold at a fixed rate, but also was freely convertible into other currencies at relatively stable prices. In practice, virtually all transactions took place in convertible currencies, while gold faded into the background as an international medium of exchange.

Without question, the gold exchange standard provided greater convenience for international traders and investors. However, this monetary standard possessed the same inherent limitations as the original gold standard. National currencies were still tied to gold, and growth in world trade depended upon growth of the international gold stock. The gold exchange standard collapsed during the economic chaos of the Great Depression.

Despite the problems inherent in the gold and gold exchange standards, there continues to be considerable interest in the United States in returning to some type of gold standard. For example, Congress created a 17-member Gold Commission in 1980 to "study and make recommendations concerning the role of gold in the domestic and international monetary systems." But at least two problems appear to stand in the way of a return to even a modified gold standard. First, while a dollar-gold link may stabilize prices in the long run, a gold standard is likely to produce substantial short-run swings in prices and domestic employment, some of which would be politically unacceptable. Second, world production of gold is expected to be essentially flat or possibly even turn downward over the next two decades. The result, in all probability, would be a sharply inflated gold price and significant instability in the international payments system.

The Modified Exchange Standard

Dissatisfaction with international monetary systems tied exclusively to gold resulted in a search for a new payments system following World War II. Major Western countries convened an international monetary conference in Bretton Woods, New Jersey, in 1944 to devise a more stable money and payments system. The conference created a new mechanism for settling international payments, a new system of currency values—known as the Bretton Woods System or modified exchange standard—and an agency for monitoring the exchange rate practices of member nations (known as the International Monetary Fund, or IMF, with headquarters in Washington, DC).[9]

The centerpiece of the Bretton Woods System was the linking of foreign currency prices to the U.S. dollar and to gold. The United States committed

---

[9]The IMF, which is headed by a Board of Governors with a representative from each member nation, establishes rules for settling international accounts between nations and grants short-term loans to member nations who lack sufficient international reserve assets to settle their BOP deficits. IMF balance-of-payments loans usually are accompanied by strict requirements that a member nation receiving credit must adopt stern economic measures to curtail the growth of its imports and expand sales of goods and services abroad. The IMF's credit guarantee often encourages banks and other nations to grant loans and aid to a member nation in trouble. The funds loaned by the IMF come mainly from *quotas* which each member nation must contribute in dollars or other reserve assets and in its own home currency. The size of the quota for each of the IMF's nearly 150-member nations determines that nation's voting power in any IMF decisions with each member of the fund's Board of Governors casting the number of votes to which his or her nation is entitled. The quota sizes also limit how much each member country may borrow from the IMF.

A companion organization to the IMF is the *World Bank*, also created under the Bretton Woods Agreement. The World Bank makes long-term loans to speed the economic development of IMF member nations.

itself to buy and sell gold at $35 per ounce upon request from foreign monetary authorities. Other IMF member nations pledged to keep their currency's price within 1 percent of its par value in terms of gold or the dollar. Central banks would use their foreign exchange reserves to buy or sell their own currency in the foreign exchange market. In practice, this usually meant that, if a foreign currency fell in value *below* par (the lower intervention point), a central bank would sell its holding of dollars and buy that currency in the market, driving its price up toward par. If the price of a nation's currency rose more than 1 percent *above* par (the upper intervention point), the central bank involved would sell its own currency and buy dollars, driving the currency's price down toward par. If a currency fell too far in value or rose too high, resulting in market disruption and threatening a massive loss of foreign exchange reserves, the country involved would simply revalue its currency, establishing a new par value.[10]

Fundamentally, the success of the Bretton Woods System depended on the ability of the United States to maintain confidence in the dollar and to protect its value. One of the weaknesses of the new system was that the U.S. dollar was in short supply early in the postwar period, as gold had been in short supply during the 18th and 19th centuries. However, the system worked well at first because the dollar was by far the most stable money medium around. Later, however, the United States began to export large amounts of capital to Western Europe and Asia (principally Japan). The result was sizeable U.S. trade deficits that were dealt with by drains on the American gold stock and by a buildup of dollar holdings abroad. In one sense, this was a favorable development because it increased the supply of dollars in foreign hands and alleviated the shortage of dollars needed to finance international trade. In another sense, however, it was an indication of fundamental problems developing in the U.S. economy.

The 1960s and 1970s ushered in a massive outflow of U.S. dollars as American investors were attracted by higher interest rates abroad. At the same time, the favorable merchandise trade surplus that the United States had enjoyed for many years began to erode in the 1960s and turned negative in the 1970s, contributing to deepening American BOP deficits. Presidents Kennedy and Johnson attempted to deal with the problem of capital outflows by creating an Interest Equalization Tax in 1963 and a Voluntary Credit Restraint Program in 1965, respectively. Unfortunately, an accelerating rate of inflation in the late 1960s and 1970s undermined government efforts to improve the American payments position. Rising prices for domestically produced goods relative to foreign products increased the volume of U.S. imports and restrained the growth of American exports. Foreign governments and both foreign and domestic investors began to lose confidence in

---

[10]A key advantage of the Bretton Woods System over the gold standard was a severing of the old link between the supply of gold and a nation's money supply. There was no commitment to redeem paper currency with gold in unlimited amounts to anyone filing a claim for gold. Only dollars held by foreign governments could be exchanged for gold (at a fixed price of $35 per ounce).

the ability of U.S. policymakers to control the American economy and subdue inflation.

Abandonment of the Bretton Woods System

Continuing inflation and other economic weaknesses forced the abandonment of the Bretton Woods System early in the 1970s. The first and most important step in the dismantling of the old system was taken by the Nixon administration in August 1971, when the dollar was devalued and the convertibility of foreign official holdings of dollars into gold suspended. Gold ceased to be an international monetary medium; it is traded today only as a commodity.

A second step toward a new monetary system was taken in March 1973, when IMF member nations agreed to allow their currencies to float over a wider range, intervening only when currency-exchange rates varied from their par values by more than 2.25 percent. However, volatile economic conditions continued to generate massive speculative flows of capital across national boundaries. Using improved communications and funds-transfer techniques, speculators anticipating changes in official exchange rates could now move huge amounts of funds from one nation to another both cheaply and quickly. Central banks, including the Federal Reserve System, soon found themselves compelled to intervene in the currency markets almost daily and to use up huge amounts of reserves. Soon, the largest IMF member countries were allowing their currencies to *float* in value, responding more actively to demand and supply forces in the marketplace.

The Managed Floating Currency Standard

In 1978 a new international payments system—often called the managed floating currency standard—was formally adopted by member nations of the IMF. Known as the Second Amendment to the International Monetary Fund's Articles of Agreement, the official rules under which today's international money system is supposed to operate allow each nation to choose its own exchange rate policy, consistent with the structure of its economy and its economic goals. There are, however, three principles that each member country must follow in establishing its exchange rate policy:

1. When a nation intervenes in the foreign exchange markets to protect its own currency, it must take into account the interests and welfare of other IMF member countries.
2. Government intervention in the foreign exchange markets should be carried out to correct disorderly conditions in those markets that are essentially short term in nature.
3. No member nation should intervene in the exchange markets in order to gain an unfair competitive advantage over other IMF members or to prevent necessary adjustments in a nation's BOP position.

DETERMINING CURRENCY VALUES IN THE MODERN WORLD

With nations now free to choose their own exchange rate policies, many different approaches to establishing the value of national currencies have been adopted around the world. Basically, two types of policies are followed today—*pegging* and *floating*.

Pegging Exchange Rates

Nations that attempt to keep the exchange value of their currencies within a fixed range around the value of some other currency or basket of currencies are known as peggers. The majority of pegging nations are developing countries that have strong commercial and financial links with one or more industrialized trading partners. Examples include the Bahamas, Ecuador, El Salvador, Egypt, Guatemala, Iraq, Korea, Panama, and Venezuela, all of which peg the exchange rate on their currency to the U.S. dollar. Madagascar and several other African republics have tied their currencies to the French franc, while Gambia's monetary unit is pegged to the value of the British pound sterling.

Frequently, when a small, developing country has strong trade relations with more than one industrialized nation, it will use a basket (group) of major currencies to set the value of its own monetary unit in order to "average out" fluctuations in the value of its exports and imports. The currency basket will reflect the current exchange rates for each major trading partner, weighted by the proportion of trade carried on with each partner. A good example is Sweden, which pegs its krona to a basket of 15 currencies, each representing a trading partner. Other nations relying on baskets of trading-partner currencies to set the value of their own currencies include Algeria, Austria, Norway, Singapore, Thailand, and Finland.

Special Drawing Rights

Several nations peg their currency's exchange rate to a basket of currencies assembled by the International Monetary Fund, known as special drawing rights (SDR). The SDR is an official international monetary reserve unit designed to settle international claims arising from transactions between the IMF, governments of member nations, central banks, and various international agencies. SDRs are really "book entries" on the ledgers of the IMF and are sometimes referred to as "paper gold." Periodically, that organization will issue new SDRs and credit them to the international reserve accounts of member nations based on each nation's IMF quota (contributions of currency and reserve assets to the IMF). To spend its SDRs, a nation simply requests the IMF to transfer some amount of SDRs from its own reserve account to the reserve account of another nation, usually one whose currency is widely accepted in the international markets. In return, the country asking for the transfer gets deposit balances denominated in the currency of the nation receiving the SDRs. These deposit balances may then be used to make international payments.

The value of SDRs today is based on a basket of currencies representing the five IMF member nations with the largest volume of exports. These five countries currently are the United States, the Federal Republic of Germany, France, Japan, and the United Kingdom. In determining the current value of SDRs, the currency of each of these five nations is weighted according to the value of their exports and currency holdings valued at current exchange rates. Countries that peg their currency's value to the value of the SDR basket include Burma, Guinea, Kenya, Jordan, Vietnam, and Zambia.

Floating Currency Values

Most of the developed nations *float,* rather than peg, their currencies. This means that the value of any particular currency is determined by demand and supply forces operating in the marketplace. Usually a managed float is used, in which governments will intervene on occasion, either by buying or selling one or more currencies, to stabilize the value of their home currency. As Carlozzi (1980) notes:

> Some nations follow a policy of leaning against the wind—intervening in order to reduce daily fluctuations in their exchange rates without attempting to adhere to any target rate. Others choose target exchange rates and intervene in order to support them. Even nations that do target exchange rates usually do not reveal their targets. Thus, they discourage speculation against these targets and retain greater flexibility to adjust them.

Three nations—Brazil, Colombia, and Portugal—employ economic indicators, such as inflation rates in various countries, to set targets for their exchange rates. Others set currency-value targets based upon the level of growth of their reserve assets or BOP position. The United States has officially adopted a managed float policy, but in practice often follows a "free" floating exchange rate policy, in which the open market determines the value of the dollar, with U.S. monetary authorities intervening only in emergency situations.[11]

In theory at least, a system of floating currency values should help the United States and other nations who are experiencing severe BOP deficits today. The theory of BOP adjustments suggests that, with floating currency values, the international marketplace will set supply and demand forces in motion to reduce and eventually eradicate any nation's balance-of-payments deficit. For example, if Americans are importing more goods from abroad

---

[11] See Chapter 28 for a discussion of recent U.S. policies in the management of the dollar's international value.

than they are able to sell to overseas customers, an excess supply of U.S. dollars should build up abroad. The result should be an eventual decline in the dollar's market value vis-à-vis other world currencies, making U.S. exports cheaper and foreign goods sold in the United States relatively more expensive. Ultimately, American exports and imports should become more evenly balanced. Only time will tell whether these theoretically expected effects will work out in practice. Much depends upon the future course of interest rates in the United States and the stability of the world and U.S. economies.

The European Monetary System

A compromise currency-valuation system, including elements of both the peg and the float, has appeared recently among the eight European nations that comprise the European Monetary System (EMS).[12] Known as a "joint float," the EMS arrangement calls for member countries to peg their exchange rates with each other, maintaining EMS currencies within 2¼ percent of their pegged exchange values. However, exchange rates with currencies outside the EMS group are subject to a managed float. EMS member countries intervene in the market as a group to maintain the purchasing power of their group's currencies vis-à-vis those of outside nations. The EMS is viewed as a further step toward economic integration (and eventual political integration) in Western Europe.

Freedom and a Flexible Exchange Rate System

It should be clear from the discussion of pegs and floats that wide diversity exists today in the manner in which national monetary units are valued. There is a strong trend today toward greater flexibility and diversity in the management of the international monetary system. That trend is reinforced by the International Monetary Fund's current rules, which allow each member nation to adjust its exchange policies in line with changing economic and financial conditions.

We must note, however, that in the international field as elsewhere, greater freedom carries greater risk. Trading nations have sought greater freedom in settling their exchange rate policies in the hope of gaining an increased measure of control over their domestic economies. However, there is now for the first time in history a true international financial system, in which the economic destinies of trading nations are inextricably linked to each other. For the most part capital flows freely across international boundaries today in response to differences in interest rates, currency values, and economic conditions. These relatively unrestricted capital flows have in-

---

[12]The eight countries are Belgium, Denmark, West Germany, France, Ireland, Italy, Luxembourg, and the Netherlands.

creased the risk that domestic policies designed to fight inflation and speed economic growth and development will be thwarted by shifting currents in a largely unregulated international marketplace. Today, successful economic policy at home requires the cooperation and coordinated action of major trading nations.

There are signs that international cooperation on global financial and economic matters *is* increasing. The emergence of the European Monetary System, the 1987 Louvre Currency Stabilization Accord involving six leading Western countries, and recent summits between leaders of major nations are all indications of a new spirit in international financial affairs. And that spirit will give rise to new institutions designed to deal with conflicts between the desire for national autonomy and independence and the urgent need for international cooperation. The International Monetary Fund—the international agency charged with the responsibility to monitor the international currency and payments policies of member nations—is likely to play an even larger role in the international financial system of the future. SDRs, the reserve asset created by the IMF to settle international claims between nations, will be more widely used to facilitate global payments. Cooperative government regulation of international capital flows, of international banking, of the vast Eurocurrency markets will be key issues of global economics and global politics for years to come.

STUDY QUESTIONS

1. What is meant by the term *balance of payments*? Describe the principal components of the balance-of-payments accounts.

2. Please supply a brief definition of each of the following terms associated with the balance of payments:
   a. Current account.
   b. Merchandise trade balance.
   c. Service transactions.
   d. Capital account.
   e. Official reserve assets.
   f. Special drawing rights.
   g. Direct investment.
   h. Errors and omissions.

3. Describe and discuss the principal trends which have occurred in the following components of the U.S. balance-of-payments accounts in recent years:
   a. Merchandise trade balance.
   b. Investment in assets abroad by U.S. residents.
   c. Investment in U.S. assets by foreign residents.

4. What is currency risk? Explain how it affects exporters, importers, and securities investors active in the international markets.

5. Why was the gold standard developed? What problems did it solve, and what problems did it create? What is the difference between the gold standard and the gold exchange standard?

6. When and where was the modified exchange standard created? Explain how this system worked to stabilize the value of foreign currencies. Why was the modified exchange standard abandoned in the 1970s?

7. The international monetary system of today has been called a managed floating currency standard. Briefly and concisely explain what this term means. Why, in your opinion, have we adopted this system today? Can you foresee any problems with this approach?

8. Explain the difference between pegging and floating currency values. What are the advantages of each? What is a basket of currencies?

9. What are SDRs? Describe their function in settling international payments and in determining certain exchange rates.

10. What is a managed float? A joint float? What advantages can you see for each? Any disadvantages?

SELECTED REFERENCES

Abrams, Richard K., and Donald V. Kimball. "U.S. Investment in Foreign Equity Markets." *Economic Review,* Federal Reserve Bank of Kansas City, April 1981, pp. 17–31.

Carlozzi, Nicholas. "Pegs and Floats: The Changing Face of the Foreign Exchange Market." *Business Review,* Federal Reserve Bank of Philadelphia, May–June 1980, pp. 13–23.

Chrystal, K. Alec and Geoffrey E. Wood. "Are Trade Deficits a Problem?" *Review,* Federal Reserve Bank of St. Louis, January/February 1988, pp. 3–10.

Kahley, William J. "Direct Investment Activity of Foreign Firms." *Economic Review,* Federal Reserve Bank of Atlanta, Summer 1987, pp. 36–51.

Kubarych, Roger M. "Financing the U.S. Current Account Deficit." *Quarterly Review,* Federal Reserve Bank of New York, Summer 1984, pp. 24–31.

Kuwayama, Patrick H. "Measuring the United States Balance of Payments." *Monthly Review,* Federal Reserve Bank of New York, August 1975, pp. 183–94.

Lees, Francis A. *International Banking and Finance.* New York: Wiley, 1973.

Chapter 28

The Markets for Foreign Exchange

Learning Objectives in This Chapter

- To explain how national currencies are priced and traded in foreign exchange markets.
- To examine who the principal players are and what their roles are in the markets where national currencies are traded.
- To understand why protecting against fluctuations in currency prices is so important, and how it can be done.
- To explore the ways in which government policymakers can influence currency prices.

Key Terms and Concepts in This Chapter

Foreign exchange markets

Commercial banks

Foreign exchange brokers

Cable transfer

Bill of exchange

Foreign exchange rates

Spot market

Forward market

Currency futures

Arbitrage

Forward contract

Covered interest arbitrage

Interest rate parity

Currency swaps

Vehicle currency

Swap agreements

THE markets where the world's major currencies are traded have changed dramatically in recent years. Major international economic and political developments (inflation, wide swings in the price of oil, political revolutions, and a growing spirit of nationalism and independence in the less developed countries), all have had profound effects on the relative value of the U.S. dollar, the British pound, the Japanese yen, and most of the world's other actively traded currencies. So unsettling have been these changes that, during the 1970s and 1980s, the U.S. government and its major trading partners were no longer able to preserve the official exchange rates among the world's major currencies. Since the early 1970s major international currencies have floated with relative freedom, their values dependent upon demand and supply forces in the marketplace.

With this newfound freedom for currency prices and the expansion of world commerce, the volume of currency trading and the number of financial institutions actively participating in that trading have virtually exploded. This is especially evident in the New York money market, where brokers have opened up their business to bring in currency trading orders from financial institutions worldwide. U.S. banks today no longer purchase foreign currencies exclusively from domestic sources, but deal with foreign exchange brokers in the world's leading financial centers. Deregulation of financial institutions has brought scores of nonbank financial companies (such as security brokerage houses and commodity traders) into the currency markets to wrest away a portion of what has always been a commercial-bank-dominated activity.

This phenomenal explosion of activity and interest in foreign currency trading and prices reflects, in large measure, a desire for self-preservation by businesses, governments, and individuals. As the international financial system has moved increasingly toward freely floating exchange rates, currency prices have become significantly more volatile and uncertain. The risks of buying and selling dollars, yen, and other currencies have increased markedly in recent years. Moreover, fluctuations in the prices of foreign currencies affect domestic economic conditions, international investment, and the success or failure of government economic policies. Governments, businesses, and individuals involved in international affairs find it is more important today than ever before to understand how foreign currencies are traded and what affects their relative values. A few examples serve to illustrate the importance of the topic.

Consider the problems faced by a corporation headquartered in the United States and selling machinery overseas. This firm frequently negotiates sales contracts with a foreign importer months before the machines are shipped and payment is made. In the meantime, the value of the foreign currency the American company expects to receive in payment for sales of its products may have declined precipitously, canceling out any expected profits. Similarly, an American importer bringing fine wines or any number of other goods into domestic U.S. markets frequently must pay for incoming shipments in the currency demanded by a foreign exporter. The American importer's profits could be significantly reduced if the value of the dollar declined relative to the values of foreign currencies used by the importer to pay for goods purchased abroad. Both exporters and importers, then, require practical knowledge of how the foreign exchange markets operate and how to use those markets to their advantage.

The same problems confront investors in foreign securities who find that attractive interest rates frequently available overseas must be protected from an erosion in currency values through suitable purchases and sales of foreign currencies. Knowledge of the foreign exchange markets is the *first step* toward successful international business and economic policy. In this chapter we examine the structure, instruments, and price-determining forces of the world's major currency markets.

THE STRUCTURE OF THE FOREIGN EXCHANGE MARKET[1]

The foreign exchange markets are among the largest markets in the world, with trading each day in excess of $200 billion. The purpose of the foreign exchange markets is to bring buyers and sellers of currencies together. It is essentially an *over-the-counter market,* with no central trading location and no set hours of trading. Prices and other terms of trade are determined by negotiation over the telephone or by wire, satellite, or telex. The foreign exchange market is *informal* in its operations; there are no special requirements for market participants, and trading conforms to an unwritten code of rules among active traders.

The Role of Banks in the Foreign Exchange Market

The central institution in modern foreign exchange markets is the commercial bank. Most transactions of any size in foreign currencies represent merely an exchange of the deposits of one bank for the deposits of another bank. That is, if an individual or business firm needs foreign currency, it will contact a bank, which in turn will secure a deposit denominated in foreign money or actually take delivery of foreign currency if the customer requires it. If the bank is a large money-center institution, it may hold inventories of foreign currency just to accommodate its customers. Smaller banks typically do not hold stocks of foreign currency or foreign-currency-denominated deposits. Rather, they will contact larger correspondent banks, who in turn will contact foreign exchange brokers or dealers.

The largest money center banks headquartered in New York, London,

---

[1]This section draws upon the booklets *The New York Foreign Exchange Market* by Alan R. Holmes, first published in 1959 and revised in 1965 by Holmes and Francis H. Schott; and *Foreign Exchange Markets in the United States,* prepared by Roger M. Kubarych for the Federal Reserve Bank of New York in 1978.

Tokyo, and other financial capitals of the world not only maintain large inventories of key foreign currencies, but trade currencies with each other simply through an exchange of deposits. For example, if a major U.S. bank needs to acquire pounds sterling, it can contact its correspondent bank in London and ask that bank to transfer an additional amount of sterling to the U.S. bank's correspondent account. In turn, the U.S. bank will increase the dollar deposit held with it by the London bank. In this way money never really leaves the country of its origin; only its ownership does, as deposits denominated in various currencies have their ownership transferred from one holder to the next.

The heart of the foreign exchange market in the United States is New York City. Approximately one dozen banks in that city plus a dozen banks headquartered in other cities keep active positions in 12 to 15 principal currencies, with smaller holdings of less traded currencies. Most large foreign exchange transactions take place between the biggest U.S. banks and major banks headquartered abroad. The largest American banks hold dollar and foreign-currency-denominated deposits in banks overseas in order to make foreign exchange trading possible. At the same time, more than 100 foreign banks maintain offices in the United States to handle the exchange accounts of foreign businesses and government agencies.

Foreign exchange trading takes place in a *three-tiered market*. Banks trade with commercial customers who need large amounts of foreign exchange for purchases of imported goods or to convert funds received from abroad into domestic currency. A second tier consists of trading mainly between domestic banks in order to make a market for foreign exchange. This tier includes exchange trading among domestic banks, foreign central banks represented in the United States, and the Federal Reserve System. The market's third tier consists of trading between U.S. banks and foreign banking institutions.

As we noted above, the largest U.S. banks with foreign exchange departments routinely keep working balances of foreign currencies with major banks abroad. These working balances rise when a bank buys currency for itself or its customers, sells dollars to foreign banks, or purchases financial documents (such as bills of exchange or traveler's checks) that are denominated in foreign currencies. Transactions affecting a bank's working currency balance are carried out by specialized traders with the aid of telephones, video screens, and teletype equipment to keep them in constant touch with other exchange dealers. The foreign exchange trader must also keep in close contact with the bank's money desk and senior management, because foreign exchange trading can have a profound effect on the bank's overall financial position.

This last point was brought home dramatically in 1974 when Franklin National Bank of New York, then the 20th-largest United States bank, was forced into bankruptcy. While numerous factors led to Franklin's demise, massive losses from foreign exchange trading was one of the primary factors in its ultimate collapse. In an era of floating exchange rates, trading in foreign currencies can be exceedingly risky, requiring considerable skill and experience.

Foreign Exchange Brokers

Frequently, currency-trading banks do not deal directly with each other, but rely on foreign exchange brokers. Less than a dozen in number, these brokerage firms are in constant communication with the exchange trading rooms of the world's major banks. Their principal function is to bring buyers and sellers of foreign exchange together.

For example, a bank wishing to sell foreign currency simply contacts a broker by telephone, indicating the amount and type of currency for sale. The broker then contacts buyers on his or her active customer list, ascertaining the preferred price and quantity of each buyer. Once a deal is struck, the selling bank is notified to initiate a transfer of funds, and the broker receives a commission for his or her efforts. The foreign exchange broker's essential contribution is to reduce the search costs associated with finding buyers and sellers of foreign exchange. By providing an essential flow of trading information, the broker makes the foreign exchange market more efficient.

Nonbank Financial Institutions

As we noted in the introduction to this chapter, security brokerage firms, commodity traders, insurance companies, and scores of other nonbank companies have come to play a growing role in the foreign exchange markets today. These institutions have entered in the wake of deregulation of the financial marketplace and the lifting of some foreign controls on international investment, especially by Japan and the United Kingdom. Nonbank currency traders now offer a wide range of services to international investors and export-import firms, including assistance with foreign mergers, currency swaps and options, hedging foreign security offerings against exchange rate fluctuations, and providing currencies needed for purchases abroad.

INSTRUMENTS OF THE FOREIGN EXCHANGE MARKET

Cable and Mail Transfers

Several financial instruments are used to facilitate foreign exchange trading by institutions and individuals. One of the most important is the cable transfer—that is, an execute order sent by cable to a foreign bank holding a currency seller's account. The cable directs the bank to debit the seller's account and credit the account of a buyer or someone the buyer designates.

For example, suppose a U.S. export firm has just received payment from one of its overseas customers in francs. The U.S. firm is paid in the form of a deposit denominated in francs residing currently in a bank in Paris. The U.S. exporter cables the Paris bank to transfer the francs to the account of a New York bank, receiving a dollar deposit from the New York bank at the current dollar-franc exchange rate. The export firm now has dollars that can be spent in the United States for raw materials, to pay taxes, and so on, while its New York bank now owns a deposit in francs that can be loaned out or used for other purposes.

The essential advantage of the cable transfer is *speed,* because the transaction can be carried out the same day or within one or two business days. Business firms selling their goods in international markets can avoid tying up substantial sums of money in foreign exchange by using cable transfers.

When speed is not a critical factor, a *mail transfer* of foreign exchange may be used. Such transfers are simply written orders from the holder of a foreign exchange deposit to a bank to pay a designated individual, firm, or institution upon presentation of a draft. A mail transfer may, of course, require days to execute, depending on the speed of mail deliveries.

Bills of Exchange

One of the oldest and most important of all international financial instruments is the bill of exchange. Frequently today the word *draft* is used instead of *bill.* Either way, a draft or bill of exchange is a written order requiring a person, business firm, or bank to pay a specified sum of money to the bearer of the bill.

We may distinguish *sight bills,* which are payable on demand (presentation), from *time bills,* which mature at a future date and are payable only at that time. There are also *documentary bills,* which typically accompany the international shipment of goods. A documentary bill must be accompanied by shipping papers allowing importers of goods to pick up their merchandise. In contrast, a *clean bill* has no accompanying documents and is simply an order to a bank to pay a certain sum of money. The most common example arises when an importer requests its bank to send a letter of credit to an exporter in another country. The letter authorizes the exporter to draw bills for payment, either against the importer's bank or against one of its correspondent banks.

Foreign Currency and Coin

Foreign currency and coin itself (as opposed to bank deposits) is an important instrument for payment in the foreign exchange markets. This is especially true for tourists who require pocket money to pay for lodging, meals, transportation, and so on. Usually this money winds up in the hands of merchants accepting it in payment for purchases and is deposited in domestic banks. For example, many U.S. banks operating along the Canadian and Mexican borders receive a substantial volume of Canadian dollars and Mexican pesos each day. These funds normally are routed through the banking system back to banks in the country of issue, and the U.S. banks receive credit in the form of a deposit denominated in a foreign currency. This deposit may then be loaned to a customer or to another bank that needs foreign currency.

Other Foreign Exchange Instruments

A wide variety of other financial instruments are denominated in various foreign currencies, most of these small in amount. For example, traveler's checks denominated in dollars and other convertible currencies may be spent directly or converted into the currency of the country where purchases are being made. International investors frequently receive interest coupons or dividend warrants denominated in various foreign currencies. These documents normally are sold to a domestic bank at the current foreign exchange rate.

FOREIGN EXCHANGE RATES

Exchange Rate Quotations

The prices of foreign currencies expressed in terms of other currencies are called foreign exchange rates. There are today three markets for foreign exchange: (1) the spot market, which deals in currency for immediate delivery; (2) the forward market, which involves the future delivery of foreign currency; and (3) the currency futures market, which deals in contracts to hedge against future changes in foreign exchange rates. Immediate delivery is defined as one or two business days for most transactions. Future delivery typically means one, three, or six months from today.

Exhibit 28–1 cites some recent foreign exchange rates between the U.S. dollar and the world's other major currencies. The exhibit shows, for example, that an American importer or investor could obtain pounds sterling (£) that could be used to buy British bonds or British goods and services at a cost of about \$1.5054 per pound (\$1.5054/£) in January 1987. Conversely, a British investor or importer seeking to make purchases in the United States would have to pay 0.6643 pounds (\$1/1.5054 or 0.664/\$) for each dollar needed. Clearly, the exchange rate between dollars and pounds is the *reciprocal* of the exchange rate between pounds and dollars, which is also true for any other pair of currencies. In truth, currencies are merely commodities, the prices of which are expressed in terms of one currency per

Exhibit 28–1   Foreign Exchange Rates (Currency Units per Dollar)

Country/Currency	1981	1982	1983	1984	1985	1986	1987*
1 Australia/dollar†	114.95	101.65	90.14	87.937	70.026	67.093	66.09
2 Austria/schilling	15.948	17.060	17.968	20.005	20.676	15.260	13.087
3 Belgium/franc	37.194	45.780	51.121	57.749	59.336	44.662	38.616
4 Brazil/cruzeiro	92.374	179.22	573.27	1841.50	6205.10	13.051	15.58
5 Canada/dollar	1.1990	1.2344	1.2325	1.2953	1.3658	1.3896	1.3605
6 China, P.R./yuan	1.7031	1.8978	1.9809	2.3308	2.9434	3.4615	3.7314
7 Denmark/krone	7.1350	8.3443	9.1483	10.354	10.598	8.0954	7.0591
8 Finland/markka	4.3128	4.8086	5.5636	6.0007	6.1971	5.0721	4.6419
9 France/franc	5.4396	6.5793	7.6203	8.7355	8.9799	6.9256	6.2007
10 Germany/deutsche mark	2.2631	2.428	2.5539	2.8454	2.9419	2.1704	1.8596
11 Greece/drachma	n.a.	66.872	87.895	112.73	138.40	139.93	134.80
12 Hong Kong/dollar	5.5678	6.0697	7.2569	7.8188	7.7911	7.8037	7.7698
13 India/rupee	8.6807	9.4846	10.1040	11.348	12.332	12.597	13.029
14 Ireland/pound†	161.32	142.05	124.81	108.64	106.62	134.14	143.90
15 Italy/lira	1138.60	1354.00	1519.30	1756.10	1908.90	1491.16	1317.17
16 Japan/yen	220.63	249.06	237.55	237.45	238.47	168.35	154.83
17 Malaysia/ringgit	2.3048	2.3395	2.3204	2.3448	2.4806	2.5830	2.5701
18 Netherlands/guilder	2.4998	2.6719	2.8543	3.2083	3.3184	2.4484	2.0978
19 New Zealand/dollar†	86.848	75.101	66.790	57.837	49.752	52.456	53.605
20 Norway/krone	5.7430	6.4567	7.3012	8.1596	8.5933	7.3984	7.1731
21 Portugal/escudo	61.739	80.101	111.610	147.70	172.07	149.80	142.90
22 Singapore/dollar	2.1053	2.1406	2.1136	2.1325	2.2008	2.1782	2.1510
23 South Africa/rand†	114.77	92.297	89.85	69.534	45.57	43.952	47.70
24 South Korea/won	n.a.	731.93	776.04	807.91	861.89	884.61	862.86
25 Spain/peseta	92.396	110.09	143.500	160.78	169.98	140.04	129.54
26 Sri Lanka/rupee	18.967	20.756	23.510	25.428	27.187	27.933	28.578
27 Sweden/krona	5.0659	6.2838	7.6717	8.2706	8.6031	7.1272	6.6188
28 Switzerland/franc	1.9674	2.0327	2.1006	2.3500	2.4551	1.7979	1.5616
29 Taiwan/dollar	n.a.	n.a.	n.a.	39.633	39.889	37.837	35.304
30 Thailand/baht	1.731	23.014	22.991	23.582	27.193	26,314	26.037
31 United Kingdom/pound†	202.43	174.80	151.59	133.66	129.74	146.77	150.54
MEMO United States dollar‡	102.94	116.57	125.34	138.19	143.01	112.22	101.13

*Average for the month of January 1987.

†Value in U.S. cents.

‡Index of weighted-average exchange value of U.S. dollar against currencies of other G–10 countries plus Switzerland. March 1973 = 100. Weights are 1972–76 global trade of each of the 10 countries.

Source: Board of Governors of the Federal Reserve System, *Federal Reserve Bulletin,* various issues.

Exhibit 28–2 Methods for Calculating Foreign Exchange Rates

Exchange Rate Conversion

Suppose the exchange rate between German deutsche marks (DM) and the U.S. dollar ($) is DM/$ = 2.500, or DM 2.50/$.

What is the $/DM exchange rate?

Answer: 1 ÷ $0.40/DM.

Exchange Rate Appreciation

Suppose the exchange rate between German marks and the U.S. dollar rises from DM/$ = 2.000, or DM 2.00/$, to DM 2.50/$.

How much has the dollar appreciated, in percent?

Answer: 2.500 ÷ 2.000 = 1.25, or 25%.

Suppose the mark-dollar exchange rate is DM/$ = 2.5000, or DM 2.50/$. If the dollar has appreciated by 3 percent, what is the new mark-dollar exchange rate?

Answer: 2.500 × 1.03 = 2.5750, or DM 2.575/$.

Exchange Rate Depreciation

Suppose the exchange rate between marks and U.S. dollars rises from DM/$ = 2.000 to DM/$ = 2.5000.

How much has the mark depreciated, in percent?

Answer: Note that the $/DM exchange rate has changed from 1 ÷ 2.000 = $0.50/DM to 1 ÷ 2.500 = $0.40/DM. The ratio of these two exchange rates is 0.4000 ÷ 0.5000, or 0.8000. Then, 1 − 0.8000 = 0.2000, or an exchange-rate depreciation of 20%.

Suppose the mark-dollar exchange rate is DM/$ = 2.50 or DM 2.50/$. If the mark has depreciated 5 percent, what is the new mark-dollar exchange rate?

Answer: Because 0.4000 × 0.95 = 0.3800, the new exchange rate is 1 ÷ 0.3800 = 2.6316, or DM 2.6316/$.

Suppose, once again, the mark-dollar exchange rate is DM/$ = 2.5000. If the U.S. dollar has depreciated 5 percent, what is the new mark-dollar exchange rate?

Answer: 2.5000 × 0.95 = 2.3750, or DM 2.375/$.

Cross Exchange Rates

Suppose the mark-dollar exchange rate is DM/$ = 2.5000, or DM 2.50/$, and the Swiss franc-dollar exchange rate is 2.000, or SF2.000/$. What is the SF/DM exchange rate?

Answer: 2.000 ÷ 2.500 = 0.8000, or SF 0.80/DM.

Suppose the mark-dollar exchange rate is DM/$ = 2.500, or DM 2.50/$ and the dollar-Swiss franc exchange rate is $/SF = 0.5000 or 0.50/SF. What, then, is the DM/SF exchange rate?

Answer: 2.5000 ÷ (1 ÷ 0.5000) = 2.5000 ÷ 2.000 = 1.25, or DM 1.25/SF.

Source: Public Information Center, Federal Reserve Bank of Chicago.

unit of another. Exhibit 28–2 illustrates the commonly accepted procedures for calculating foreign exchange rates.[2]

Dealers and brokers in foreign exchange actually post not one, but *two*

---

[2]We note that in each quotation of a foreign exchange rate, one currency always serves as a unit of account (the unit of value) and the other currency functions as the unit for which a price is stated. For example, a quote of $0.40/DM tells us that one deutsche mark costs $0.40. In this instance the dollar serves as the unit of account, and the currency whose price is quoted is the mark. It is customary to place the symbol for the currency serving as the unit of account (in this case, $) in front of the stated number and the symbol of the currency whose price is being quoted (in this case, DM) following the number.

exchange rates for each pair of currencies. That is, each trader sets a *bid* (buy) price and an *asked* (sell) price. For example, the dealer department in a large New York bank might be posting a bid price for pounds sterling of £ = \$1.5052US (or \$1.5052/£) and an asked price of £ = \$1.5056US (or \$1.5056/£). This means the dealer is willing to buy sterling at \$1.5052 per pound and sell it at \$1.5056. (These two exchange rates are sometimes referred to as "double-barreled" quotations.) The dealer makes a profit on the *spread* between the bid and asked price, though that spread is normally very small.[3]

Traders in the market continually watch exchange rate quotations in order to take advantage of any arbitrage opportunities. Arbitrage refers to the purchase of one currency in a certain market and the sale of that currency in another market in response to differences in price between the two markets. The force of arbitrage generally keeps foreign exchange rates from getting too far out of line in different markets. Thus, if pounds are selling for \$1.5053US in New York and \$1.5057US in London, professional traders will quickly eliminate this discrepancy by purchasing sterling in the New York market and selling it in London.

Factors Affecting Foreign Exchange Rates

Balance-of-Payments Position. The exchange rate for any foreign currency depends on a multitude of factors reflecting economic and financial conditions in the country issuing the currency. One of the most important factors is the status of a nation's *balance-of payments position*. When a country experiences a deficit in its balance of payments, it becomes a net demander of foreign currencies and may be forced to sell substantial amounts of its own currency to pay for imports of goods and services. Therefore, balance-of-payments deficits often lead to price depreciation of a nation's currency relative to the prices of other currencies. For example, during most of the 1970s and 1980s, when the United States was experiencing deep balance-of-payments deficits and owed substantial amounts abroad for imported oil, the value of the dollar sagged dramatically.

Speculation. Exchange rates also are profoundly affected by speculation over *future* currency values. Brokers, dealers, and investors in foreign exchange monitor the currency markets daily, looking for profitable trading opportunities. A currency viewed as temporarily undervalued will quickly bring forth numerous buy orders, driving its price higher vis-à-vis other currencies. A currency considered to be overvalued will soon be greeted by

---

[3] Dealers will usually quote the bid price first and the asked price second and, as a rule, only the last digits will be quoted to the buyer or seller. Thus, the spot bid and asked rates on pounds might be quoted by a foreign exchange dealer as 52/56. It is assumed the customer is aware of current foreign exchange rates and knows, therefore, that the bid price being quoted is \$1.5052/£ and the asked price is \$1.5056/£.

a rash of sell orders, depressing its price. Today the international financial system is so efficient and finely tuned that billions of dollars can flow across national boundaries in a matter of hours in response to speculative fever. Moreover, these massive unregulated flows can wreak havoc with the plans of economic policymakers because currency trading affects interest rates and ultimately the entire economy.

Domestic Economic and Political Conditions.   The market for a national currency is, of course, influenced by domestic conditions. Wars, revolutions, the death of a major political leader, inflation, recession, and labor strikes have all been observed to have adverse effects on the currency of a nation experiencing these problems. On the other hand, signs of rapid economic growth, industrial development, improving government finances, rising stock and bond prices, and successful economic policies to control inflation and unemployment usually lead to a stronger currency in the exchange markets.

Central Bank Intervention.   Overshadowing the currency markets today is the ever-present possibility that central banks will become active participants. Major central banks around the world, including the Federal Reserve System and the Bundesbank in West Germany, may decide on a given day that their national currency is declining too rapidly in value relative to one or more other key currencies. Thus, if the dollar falls precipitously against the German mark, support operations by the Federal Reserve Ssytem in the form of heavy sales of marks and corresponding purchases of dollars in cooperation with the Bundesbank may be employed to stabilize the currency markets. Usually, central bank intervention is temporary, designed to promote a smooth adjustment in currency values toward a new equilibrium level rather than to permanently prop up a weak currency.

Supply and Demand for Foreign Exchange

The factors influencing a currency's rate of exchange with other currencies may be expressed in terms of the market forces of demand and supply. Exhibit 28–3, for example, illustrates a demand curve and a supply curve for dollars ($) in terms of British pounds (£). Note that the demand curve for dollars is also labeled the supply curve for pounds. This is due to the fact that an individual or institution holding pounds and demanding dollars would be supplying pounds to the foreign exchange market. Similarly, the supply curve for dollars is identical to the demand curve for pounds because someone holding dollars and demanding pounds must supply dollars to the foreign currency markets in order to purchase pounds. We recall, too, that the price of dollars in terms of pounds is the reciprocal of the price of pounds in terms of dollars.

Exhibit 28–3   **Demand and Supply of U.S. Dollars in Terms of British Pounds**

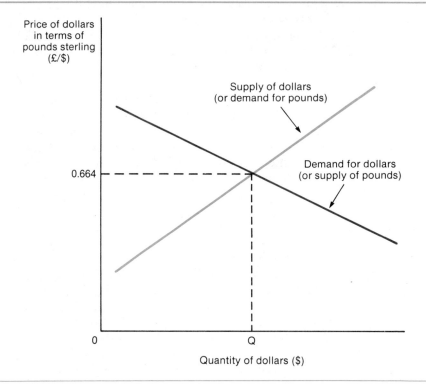

To illustrate how demand and supply forces operate in the foreign exchange markets, suppose the current exchange rate between dollars and pounds is £ = $1.5054. To purchase dollars, we would have to pay 0.664 pounds per dollar, while to purchase pounds would cost us $1.5054 per pound. This exchange rate between dollars and pounds is set in the foreign exchange markets by the interaction of the supply and demand for each currency. Exhibit 28–3 indicates that, at an exchange rate of 0.664 pounds, the quantity of dollars supplied is exactly equal to the quantity of dollars demanded.

If the price of dollars in terms of pounds were to fall temporarily *below* this exchange rate, more dollars would be demanded than supplied. Some buyers needing dollars would bid up the exchange rate toward the point where the demand for and supply of dollars were perfectly in balance. On the other hand, if the price of dollars were temporarily *above* 0.664 pounds, more dollars would be supplied to the foreign exchange markets. The price of dollars in terms of pounds would fall as suppliers of dollars willingly accepted a lower exchange rate to dispose of their excess dollar holdings. Only at that point where the exchange rate stood at 0.664 pounds per dollar

Exhibit 28–4   **Effects on the Exchange Rate for Dollars of an Increase in Foreign Demand for U.S. Goods and Services**

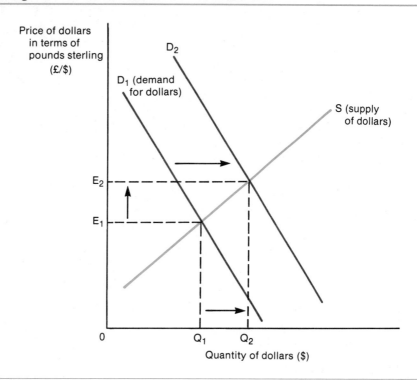

would quantity supplied equal quantity of dollars demanded. Only at that between the dollar and the pound unless changes occur in the demand or supply of either currency.

Effects of Changes in the Relative Supply and Demand for Currencies

As we noted earlier, a number of factors affect the exchange rates between national currencies, including a nation's balance-of-payments position, currency speculation, domestic political and economic developments, and central bank intervention. Each of these factors leads to a shift in the demand for or supply of one currency vis-à-vis another, which brings about a change in their relative rates of exchange.

To illustrate the impact of shifts in currency demand and supply, suppose that consumers in Great Britain increase their demand for U.S. goods and services. As Exhibit 28–4 indicates, the demand curve for dollars would

Exhibit 28–5   **Effects on the Exchange Rate for Dollars of an Increase in U.S. Demand for Foreign Goods and Services**

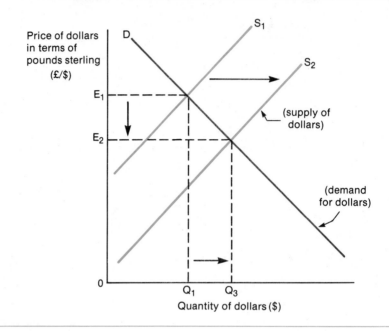

increase from D_1 to D_2. This is equivalent, as noted earlier, to an increase in the supply of pounds seeking dollars. The cost of dollars in terms of pounds, therefore, will rise from E_1 to E_2. British importers will be forced to surrender a greater quantity of pounds per dollar in order to satisfy the demands of British consumers for American goods and services. Other things being equal, the prices of imported goods from the United States will tend to rise.

The opposite effects would tend to occur if American consumers demanded a larger quantity of British goods and services. In this case the supply-of-dollars (demand-for-pounds) curve slides downward and to the right from S_1 to S_2, as shown in Figure 28–5. Reflecting the increased demand for pounds and associated sales of dollars for pounds by American importers, the dollar's price in pounds sterling falls from E_1 to E_2. At the same time, the market prices of British goods and services imported into the United States will tend to rise.

What happens if a central bank, such as the Bank of England, intervenes to stabilize the dollar-pound exchange rate at some arbitrary target level? The answer depends, among other things, on which side

Exhibit 28–6   **Effects of Central Bank Intervention to Stabilize
the Dollar-Pound Exchange Rate**

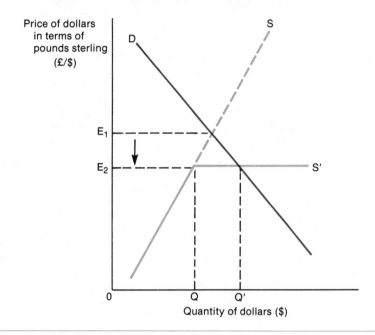

of the market the central bank intervenes, which currency is used as
the vehicle for central bank intervention, and the particular exchange-
rate target chosen.

For example, suppose that increased British demand for American goods
and services had driven the dollar-pound exchange rate up to E_1, as shown
in Exhibit 28–6. However, this surge in the dollar's value had sharply
reduced the purchasing power of the pound for dollar-denominated goods
and services and threatened to have damaging effects on British foreign
trade and industrial output. Perhaps speculators had begun to sell pounds
in anticipation of even lower exchange rates. The Bank of England might
intervene to force the dollar-pound exchange rate down to E_2 by selling
dollars out of its currency reserve and demanding pounds in the foreign
exchange market. In effect, the supply-of-dollars curve would be "kinked"
at the stabilization price, E_2. In order to peg the dollar-pound exchange rate
at E_2, the central bank would have to spend $Q'-Q$ of its dollar reserves.
Otherwise, the price of dollars would once again rise toward E_1—the level
dictated by private demand and supply forces in the foreign exchange markets. Conversely, if the dollar were falling to unacceptably low levels against

the pound, the Bank of England or the Federal Reserve System might enter on the opposite side of the market, purchasing dollars with pounds and driving the dollar's price higher.[4]

THE FORWARD MARKET FOR CURRENCIES

Knowledge of how the foreign exchange markets work and the ways in which currency risk can be reduced is indispensable for business managers today. Of course, the problem of fluctuating currency values is not so serious if payment for foreign goods, services, or securities must be made right away. Spot market prices of foreign currencies normally change little from day to day. However, if payment must be made weeks or months in the future, there is considerable uncertainty as to what the spot currency rate will be on any given future date. When substantial sums of money are involved, the rational investor or commercial trader will try to guarantee the future price at which currency can be purchased. This is the function of the *forward exchange market*—to reduce the risk associated with the future purchase and delivery of foreign currency by agreeing upon a price in advance.

Spot, Forward, and Option Contracts

Earlier in this chapter we distinguished between the spot market, or market for immediate delivery of a currency, and the forward market, where contracts were made for future currency delivery. Trading in the spot market results in agreements to deliver a specified amount of foreign currency at an agreed-upon price, usually within one or two business days and sometimes on the same day. In contrast, a forward contract is an agreement to deliver a specified amount of foreign currency at a set price on some future date (usually within 1, 2, 3, 6, or 12 months). The actual delivery date is referred to by traders as the *value date*. In the event customers do not know when they will need foreign currency, an *option forward contract* frequently is used.

---

[4] In the United States the Treasury Department is the designated agency to pursue intervention measures to protect the dollar and stabilize currency values. While the Treasury must decide what to do, however, it is the Federal Reserve System that must do the buying and selling of currencies on the Treasury's behalf. Mechanically, purchases are paid for by check or other form of draft with the buying institution generally receiving, not currency "in the hand," but rather deposit balances held in various banks overseas. Central bank intervention not only affects relative currency values, but the reserves held by the private banking system and the money supply of the nations where intervention has occurred. For example, if the Federal Reserve purchases bank deposits, it will add to the reserves of those banks which will ultimately result in an expansion of bank loans and investments. Thus, a decision by a central bank to intervene in the foreign currency markets will have both currency market and money supply effects unless an operation known as *sterilization* is carried out in which the reserve and money supply effects of central bank currency operations are neutralized (offset) by other central bank actions (such as open market operations).

Methods of Quoting Forward Exchange Rates

There are several different ways of measuring and quoting forward exchange rates. Suppose the spot exchange rate on German marks today is $0.40US (or 0.40/DM) and that dealers in foreign exchange are selling forward contracts for delivery of marks in six months at $0.3846US. (This means that the spot exchange rate for converting marks into dollars is DM/$ = 2.500 and the six-month forward rate is DM/$ = 2.600.) We may express the forward exchange rate for marks simply as $0.3846US, or $0.3846/DM— known as the *outright rate*.

Another popular method is to express the forward rate as a premium or discount from the spot rate, known as the *swap rate*. In the example above, marks are selling at a 1.54 cent *discount* in the forward market. Traders in the forward market appear to be signaling an expectation that the mark will fall in value over the next few weeks.[5]

We may also express forward exchange rates in terms of an annualized percentage rate above or below the current spot price. To use the example above, $/DM spot = 0.4000 and $/DM forward = 0.3846.[6] Then, the discount on forward DM for delivery in six months is:

$$\frac{\text{Forward rate} - \text{Spot rate}}{\text{Spot rate}} \times \frac{12}{\text{Number of months forward}} \times 100$$

$$= \frac{0.3846 - 0.4000}{0.4000} \times \frac{12}{6} \times 100$$

$$= -0.0385 \times 2 \times 100$$

$$= -7.7\%$$

Marks are selling at a 7.7 percent *discount* from spot in the forward market. Because marks are selling at a discount from their spot price, forward dollars must be selling at a *premium* over spot.

Suppose we know the current spot exchange rate between two currencies and the forward premium or discount. We want to know the actual forward exchange rate. What formula should be used? The following will suffice:

$$\text{Spot rate} + \frac{\text{Spot rate} \times [\text{Premium } (+) \text{ or Discount } (-) \text{ expressed as an annual rate}] \times \text{Number of months forward}}{100 \times \text{Number of months in a year}}$$

---

[5] We can see from the above example that the current outright rate is the current spot exchange rate adjusted by the current swap rate.

[6] This example is based on one developed by the Public Information Center, Federal Reserve Bank of Chicago in its *Exchange Rate Calculation Guide*.

Suppose that $/DM spot = 0.4000 and forward marks for delivery in three months are selling at a 4 percent premium over spot. Using the formula above, we have:

$$0.4000 + \frac{0.4000 \times 4.0 \times 3}{1,200} = 0.4040\$/DM \text{ forward}$$

This means DM/$ forward is 2.4752, or DM 2.4752/$.

FUNCTIONS OF THE FORWARD EXCHANGE MARKET

Contracts calling for the future delivery of currency are employed to cover a number of risks faced by investors and commercial traders. Some analysts group the functions or uses of forward contracts into four categories: commercial covering, hedging an investment position, speculation, and covered interest arbitrage. These four uses of the forward market are discussed below.[7]

Commercial Covering

The export or import of goods and services usually requires someone to deliver payment in a foreign currency or to receive payment in a foreign currency. Either the payor or payee, then, is subject to currency risk because no one knows for sure what the spot price will be for a currency at the time payment must be made. The forward exchange market can be used as a buffer against currency risk associated with the export or import of goods and services.

To illustrate, suppose an American importer of cameras has agreed to pay 5,000 marks to a West German manufacturer upon receipt of a new shipment. The cameras are expected to arrive dockside in 30 days. The importer has no idea at this point what 5,000 marks will cost in U.S. dollars 30 days from now. To reduce the risk that the price of marks in terms of dollars may rise significantly, the importer negotiates a forward contract with his or her bank for delivery of 5,000 marks at $0.30/DM in 30 days. When payment is due, the importer simply takes delivery of the marks (usually by acquiring ownership of a deposit denominated in marks) at the agreed-upon price and pays the West German manufacturer. Because the price is fixed in advance, the risk associated with fluctuations in foreign exchange rates has been eliminated. Today, export and import firms routinely cover their large purchases overseas with forward currency contracts.

---

[7] The discussion which follows is indebted to the excellent article by Anderson (1972).

Hedging an Investment Position

As we saw in the preceding chapter, thousands of American corporations have invested in long-term capital projects overseas, building manufacturing plants, warehouse and dock facilities, shopping centers, and office buildings. In recent years a large return flow of long-term investments by foreign firms in the United States also has occurred. Of course, the market value of these foreign investments may change drastically as the price of a foreign currency changes over time.

To illustrate, suppose an American commercial bank constructed an office building in downtown London. When completed, the office facility had an estimated market value of £ 2 million. The current spot rate on pounds is, let us say, $1.40/£. The bank values the new building on its consolidated financial statement, therefore, at $2.8 million. However, suppose the pound has declined rapidly in value in recent months due to persistent balance-of-payments problems and rapid inflation in the British economy. Some market analysts expect pounds to be selling at $1.20/£ in a few months. In the absence of a hedged position, the bank would take a loss of $400,000 on its building. This is due to the fact that, at an exchange rate of $1.20/£, the office building will have a value of only $2.4 million.

Can this kind of loss be avoided or at least reduced? Yes, provided the bank can negotiate a sale of pounds *forward* at a higher price. For example, the bank may be able to arrange with a dealer for the sale of £2 million for future delivery at $1.30 US ($1.30/£). When this forward contract matures, if the spot price has fallen to $1.20/£, the bank can buy pounds at this rate and deliver them to the dealer at $1.30 US as agreed. The result is a profit on the foreign exchange transaction of $200,000, partially offsetting the financial loss on the building due to declining currency values.[8]

Speculation on Future Currency Prices

A third use of the forward exchange market is speculative investment based on expectations concerning future movements in currency prices. Speculators will buy currency for future delivery if they believe the future spot rate will be *higher* on the delivery date than the current forward rate. They will sell currency under a forward contract if the future spot rate appears likely to be *below* the forward rate on the day of delivery. Such speculative pur-

---

[8]The problem of the exposure of corporate balance sheets, especially fixed investments, to currency risk was ameliorated somewhat in the 1980s by a ruling of the Financial Accounting Standards Board (FASB). Under a rule known as FASB 52, gains or losses on corporate balance sheets due to currency fluctuations are supposed to be reported in a specially designated item in the capital (net worth) accounts rather than as a charge against current earnings. The result has been to reduce the use of options and futures contracts to hedge against potential losses due to currency risk and to place greater emphasis upon the *economic fundamentals* of foreign investment, rather than on *translation gains or losses* (the impact of changing from one currency to another as a standard for valuing one's assets).

chases and sales carry the advantage of requiring little or no capital and no borrowing costs in advance of the delivery date. A speculator whose forecast of future spot rates turns out to be correct makes a profit on the spread between the purchase price and sale price.

Covered Interest Arbitrage

One of the most common transactions in the international financial system arises when an investor discovers a higher interest rate available on foreign securities and invests funds abroad. When the currency risk associated with the purchase of foreign securities is reduced by using a forward contract, this transaction is often referred to as covered interest arbitrage.

To illustrate the interest arbitrage process, suppose that a British auto company is selling high-grade bonds with a promised annual yield of 12 percent. Comparable bonds in the United States offer a 10 percent annual return. While the bonds are of good quality and there is probably little default risk, there is currency risk in this transaction. The U.S. investor must purchase pounds in order to buy the British bonds. When the bonds earn interest or reach maturity, the issuing auto company will pay foreign and domestic investors in pounds sterling. Then the pounds must be converted into dollars to allow the U.S. investor to spend the earnings in the United States. If the spot price of sterling falls, the U.S. investor's net yield from the bonds will be reduced.

Specifically, while the investor expects an interest spread of 2 percent a year over U.S. rates by purchasing British bonds, if the spot rate on pounds declines by 2 percent (on an annual basis), the interest gain will be offset by the loss on trading pounds. Clearly, a series of forward contracts is needed to sell pounds at a guaranteed price as the bonds generate a stream of cash payments. In this case the investor will probably purchase sterling spot in order to buy the bonds and sell sterling forward to protect his or her expected income.

The Principle of Interest Rate Parity

The foregoing example suggests an important rule regarding international capital flows and foreign exchange rates: *The net rate of return to the investor from any foreign investment is equal to the interest earned plus or minus the forward premium or discount on the price of the foreign currency involved in the transction.* The theory of forward exchange states that, under normal conditions, the forward discount or premium on one currency relative to another is directly related to the difference in interest rates between the two countries involved. More specifically, the currency of the nation experiencing higher interest rates normally will sell at a forward *discount* in terms of the currency issued by the nation with lower interest rates. And the currency of the nation with relatively low interest rates normally will sell at a *premium* forward relative to that of the high-rate country. A condition known as interest rate parity exists when the interest rate differential between two nations is exactly equal to the forward discount or premium on their two currencies. When parity exists, the currency markets are in equilibrium, and capital funds will not flow from one country to another. This is due to the fact that the gain from investing abroad at higher interest rates is fully offset by the cost of covering currency risk in the forward exchange market.

To illustrate the principle of interest rate parity, suppose interest rates in a foreign country are 3 percent above those in the United States. Then the currency of that foreign nation will, in equilibrium, sell at a 3 percent discount in the forward exchange market. Similarly, if interest rates are 1 percent lower abroad than in the United States, in equilibrium the foreign currency of the nations involved should sell at a 1 percent premium against the dollar. When such an equilibrium position is reached movements of funds between nations, even with currency risk covered, do not generate excess returns relative to domestic investments of comparable risk. Capital funds tend to stay in the domestic market rather than flowing abroad.

It is when interest parity does *not* exist that capital tends to flow across national boundaries in response to differences in domestic and foreign interest rates. For example, suppose interest rates in a foreign nation are 3 percent above U.S. interest rates on securities of comparable quality and the foreign currency involved is selling at a 1 percent discount against the dollar in the forward exchange market. In this case, investing abroad with exchange risks covered will yield the investor a net added return of 2 percent per year. Clearly, there is a positive incentive to invest overseas. In the absence of exchange controls, capital will flow abroad.

Is this situation likely to persist for a long period of time? No, because the movement of funds into a country offering higher interest rates tends to increase the forward discount on its currency and lowers the net rate of return to the investor. Other factors held constant, the flow of funds abroad eventually will subside, and capital funds will tend to stay at home until further changes in currency prices and interest rates take place.

TRADING CENTERS FOR FORWARD EXCHANGE CONTRACTS

Wherever there are major spot-currency markets operating, forward exchange contracts are usually traded as well. Leading currency markets today are situated in Amsterdam, Brussels, Frankfurt, London, Montreal, New York City, Paris, Toronto, and Zurich. London continues to be the predominant location for most spot and forward currency trading. In 1972 the Chicago Mercantile Exchange (CME) inaugurated trading in forward contracts for Canadian dollars, sterling, Swiss francs, marks, yen, lira, and pesos. As in the spot markets, most trading in forward currency contracts occurs between dealer departments of major banks and foreign exchange brokers.

THE MARKET FOR FOREIGN CURRENCY FUTURES

Forward contracts, as we have seen, call for the delivery of a specific currency on a specified date in the future at a set price. Thus, the intent of buyer and seller in a forward contract is to actually *deliver* the currency mentioned in the contract. In recent years, an important variation of the forward currency contract has developed—*foreign currency futures*. These too are contracts calling for the future delivery of a specific currency at a price agreed upon today, *but there is usually no intent to actually deliver the currencies mentioned in the contracts*. Rather, *currency futures are traded in the majority of cases to reduce the risk associated with fluctuating currency prices*. Today, currency futures contracts are traded in the United States and in a number of other world financial centers.

Foreign currency futures trading developed rapidly following the collapse in 1971 of the fixed-exchange rate system that had been established after World War II. With the world's major currencies no longer tied to gold, the value of major currencies began to freely float in international markets, buffeted by the changing demands of world trade and commerce, by political developments, and by the activities of currency speculators. In response to this new need for risk protection, commodity and security exchanges in the United States and in a few other world trade centers set up a mechanism for trading currency futures. The movement was led by the Chicago Mercantile Exchange, which established the International Monetary Market (IMM), designed primarily to appeal to businesses, individuals, and financial firms that found the traditional forward currency contracts inadequate for their specific needs. The IMM offered futures contracts in eight major currencies, with the heaviest trading now concentrated in contracts for German marks, Swiss francs, British pounds, Japanese yen, and Canadian dollars.

The operating rules and procedures of the CME and its IMM division parallel those of other commodity and financial futures exchanges around the world and are explained in detail in Chapter 12. Currency futures contract terms, sizes, and allowable price changes are set by each exchange and generally call for delivery of the currency specified in the contract on the third Wednesday of March, June, September, and December at a price quoted in U.S. dollars per unit of the foreign currency involved.

As in all futures trading, currency futures are attractive to two groups: foreign exchange hedgers and foreign exchange speculators. The *hedgers,* who typically are dealer and broker houses, commercial banks, individuals, trading companies, and multinational corporations, seek to avoid damage to their profits from normal business transactions caused by unexpected changes in currency exchange rates. Usually a hedging individual or institution will seek out, through traders or an exchange, a currency *speculator* who hopes to profit from changes in relative currency rates by taking on the risk the hedger seeks to avoid or minimize. Two basic types of transactions take place on currency futures exchanges: the buying hedge and the selling hedge.

Importers of goods typically use the *buying hedge*. In this case a domestic importer who is committed to pay in a foreign currency, such as British pounds, when goods are received from abroad fears that currency may rise in price. He therefore *purchases* a futures contract, agreeing to take delivery of pounds at a set price as near as possible to the date on which the goods must be paid for. Because the price of this contract is fixed, the importer, in effect, has "locked in" the value of the imported goods, thus helping to protect his potential profit on the business transaction. As a final step, on or close to the date the goods are paid for, the importer will "zero out" his or her futures contract purchase by *selling* a comparable currency futures contract through a broker trading on the exchange floor. The exchange's clearinghouse, which records each transaction taking place on the exchange, will automatically cancel out the importer's obligation to take delivery of or to deliver foreign currency.

How has the importer protected himself against loss due to currency fluctuations? If the pound or other currency rises in value during the life of a futures contract, the importer will experience reduced profits or increased losses on the imported goods themselves because the pound has risen in value relative to his or her home currency. However, the market value of a currency futures contract also rises when the market value of the underlying currency increases. Therefore, the importer will be able to sell currency futures contracts at a higher price than he or she originally purchased them for. The resulting profit in currency futures wholly or at least partially offsets the reduced gains or losses on purchase of the imported goods. On the other hand, if currency values fall, potential profits on the imported goods will increase because they can be bought more cheaply, but an offsetting loss will be recorded in futures trading because contracts must be sold at a lower price than they were purchased for. Cash-market gains (losses) offset futures market losses (gains).

The opposite kind of hedge in currency futures is known as the *selling hedge*. This transaction is often employed by investors who purchase foreign securities and want to protect their interest or dividend earnings from those securities from a drop in currency values. In this instance the investors could hedge their expected earnings by *selling* futures contracts in the currency involved at the time the securities are acquired in the cash (spot) market. If contracts are sold in an amount that covers both principal and interest or dividends, the investors have, in effect, "locked in" their investment return regardless of which way exchange rates go by the time they must convert foreign-denominated investment earnings into home currency. If the foreign currency involved has declined in price relative to the home currency when the security pays interest or dividends, matures, or must be sold, a loss will be incurred in cash received, but the investors will earn an offsetting futures market profit by *buying* futures contracts in an amount equivalent to those sold earlier. Conversely, if the foreign currency appreciates relative to the home currency, cash market revenues from the security will rise when the foreign currency is converted to home money, offsetting a loss from buying back futures contracts that now cost more.

In summary, the development of the currency futures market in recent years has opened up a new way for commercial traders and investors in foreign securities to hedge against volatile foreign exchange rates, stimulating both international trade and international investment. Futures markets broaden the availability of currency-hedging tools to a wider range of individuals and institutions exposed to foreign exchange risk. The result in the long run is an increase in the flow of goods and services across international boundaries, adding to each nation's standard of living.

OTHER INNOVATIVE METHODS FOR DEALING WITH CURRENCY RISK

The recent volatility of foreign exchange rates has given rise to an ever-widening circle of devices to deal with currency risk. For example, the *currency option* gives a buyer the right, though not the obligation, to either deliver or to take delivery of a designated currency at a set price any time before the option expires. Thus, unlike the forward market, actual delivery *may* not occur, but unlike futures trading, no follow-up purchases or sales are needed to stop delivery. The advantage of the currency option is that it limits downside risk, but not upside profits. However, the new instrument is available only from a limited number of banks or from a few currency exchanges and exposes the offering banks to additional risk that may limit the market's future growth.

A related hedging instrument is the *option on currency futures. Calls* on currency futures give the buyer a way to protect against rising exchange rates by buying from another investor a currency futures contract at a fixed price, thus locking in a desired currency delivery price. On the other hand, *puts* on currency futures give a hedger protection against falling exchange rates by giving him or her the right to sell currency futures contracts at a fixed price, regardless of how market prices change. These options carry their own market price, called the *exercise* or *strike* price, which rises or falls based on the probability that the currency futures option will actually be exercised by the buyer of the contract.

Another innovative device is the *swap,* which may include currency swaps or back-to-back loans. In a *back-to-back loan arrangement,* two multinational firms may agree to swap loans that are denominated in two different currencies for a specific time period. Currency risk is reduced because

Exhibit 28–7   **The Currency Swap: Converting a Foreign-Currency-Denominated Loan into a Domestic Currency Loan**

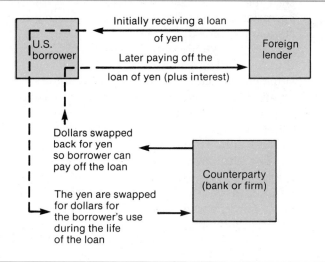

each party can service a loan denominated in its most desired currency and avoid the risk of switching currencies.

In straight currency swaps, on the other hand, a company that has borrowed foreign currency (such as yen) for a designated length of time (maturity) immediately turns around and exchanges the yen for its home currency (say, dollars) with a counterparty. The counterparty may be a bank or other business firm with an exactly opposite situation, holding dollars but needing yen. As shown in Exhibit 28–7, when the loan comes due, the borrowing company reverses the transaction with the counterparty, swapping its home currency to get back the yen needed to pay off its foreign currency loan. In this case there is no exposure to the risk of changing yen prices. The borrower has received an inflow of dollars at the beginning of the loan and experienced a dollar outflow when the loan is paid off. The currency swap has merely facilitated the borrower's ability to borrow dollars from foreign markets without currency risk. The advantage of currency swaps is that they can be arranged with much longer maturities—sometimes up to 15 years—and with more suitable terms of settlement than most standard currency exchange contracts. *Exchange-risk insurance* also has become popular and is available from selected government sources (such as the Export-Import Bank) and from some private insurers. The majority of these insurance policies are designed to cover currency losses incurred by exporters of goods or to safeguard the value of foreign investments from currency price fluctuations.

Innovative new approaches to currency risk continue to emerge each year, and many old methods have been resurrected lately. For example, many multinational firms have expanded their use of *local loans*—that is, securing credit inside the countries where they have sales or production operations. Others have resorted to issuing *dual-currency bonds* with principal and interest payments denominated in two different currencies. Some exporters now ship only if *prepayments* are made by a customer overseas that cover all or a substantial portion of the value of a shipment before that shipment is made. Some companies simply *barter* (exchange) their goods, equipment, or real property directly so that no money and therefore no currency changes hands. *Selective currency pricing* is also employed: the seller invoices the buyer with a bill denominated in a currency thought to be more stable or easier to hedge.

The ultimate economic response when other risk-reducing methods appear to be too costly, too risky, or unavailable is for a seller to use *risk-adjusted pricing* of goods and services traded across international boundaries. For example, goods sold to countries or areas where currency risk is unacceptably large may simply be priced higher in order to compensate the seller for that added risk. Ultimately, the household customer in those countries where currency risk is unusually high will wind up paying higher prices for goods and services and possibly face a lower standard of living. Currency risk, like any other form of risk in the financial system, has very real consequences for the economic welfare of both individuals and nations.

GOVERNMENT INTERVENTION IN THE FOREIGN EXCHANGE MARKETS

The value of a nation's currency in the international markets has long been a source of concern to governments around the world. National pride plays a significant role in this case because a strong currency, avidly sought by traders and investors in the international marketplace, implies the existence of a strong, vigorous, and well-managed economy at home. A strong and stable currency encourages investment in the home country, stimulating its economic growth and development. Moreover, as we observed in Chapter 27, changes in currency values affect a nation's balance-of-payments position. A weak and declining currency makes foreign imports more expensive, lowering the standard of living at home. And a nation whose currency is not well regarded in the international marketplace will have difficulty selling its goods and services abroad, giving rise to unemployment at home.

The United States has pursued an active policy of supporting the dollar in international markets for many years. In part, this policy has been motivated by concern over the condition of the U.S. economy, particularly the effects of inflation. Another factor, however, is the key role played by the U.S. dollar in the international financial system. The dollar is a vehicle currency that facilitates trade and investment between many nations in addition to the United States. For example, international shipments of crude oil, regardless of their origin or destination, are usually valued in dollars. As noted in Chapter 17, the market for dollar deposits held in banks abroad—Eurodollars—is the world's largest international money market, financing commercial projects and even providing operating funds for many foreign governments around the world. For all of these reasons, then, the United States as well as foreign governments and central banks have repeatedly intervened in the foreign exchange markets to stabilize currency values and insulate domestic economic conditions from adverse financial developments abroad.

As we observed in the preceding chapter, during the years immediately following World War II, the United States agreed to maintain a fixed exchange ratio between the dollar and gold. The Treasury Department stood ready to buy gold from or sell gold to foreign central banks and other monetary authorities at a fixed price of $35 per ounce. The secretary of the Treasury was also responsible for maintaining the U.S. Exchange Stabilization Fund, to be drawn upon when necessary to intervene in foreign currency markets and protect the dollar. While the United States committed itself to intervene in the currency markets to preserve the desired ratio of dollars to gold, other nations agreed to keep the exchange ratios between their currencies and the dollar centered about a fixed rate. Whenever a currency's exchange rate against the dollar deviated significantly from the agreed-upon rate, central banks and government agencies would intervene (either on the demand side or the supply side of the exchange market) to restore the proper dollar-currency ratio.

U.S. Intervention in the Currency Markets during the 1960s

This relatively passive U.S. foreign exchange policy, which relied mainly upon other nations to stabilize the international financial system, was modified during the 1960s because of serious economic problems. Massive outflows of capital from the United States into Western Europe, Japan, Latin America, and the Middle East weakened the dollar in foreign markets. High unemployment rates in the United States during the early 1960s, coupled with significant inflation in later years, further eroded the pivotal role of the dollar in the international financial system. Beginning in 1961, the U.S. Treasury, acting in cooperation with the monetary authorities of other Western nations, began to intervene in the currency markets to counter speculative attacks against the dollar.

Later, the Federal Reserve System joined in the cooperative effort to support the dollar and stabilize the currency system. The Fed established a network of swap agreements with foreign central banks. These agreements created lines of credit through which a participating central bank could obtain foreign currencies in order to sell them in the exchange markets and protect its home currency. Typically, any drawings against these currency credit lines were repaid within a few weeks or months. The Federal Reserve pledged to absorb excess dollars that had been accumulated by foreign central banks in their attempt to keep the dollar's value at its officially established level. The Fed would borrow foreign currencies against its swap lines and use these currencies to purchase unwanted dollars held by the Bank of England and other major central banks on a temporary basis. When the exchange markets calmed and the dollar recovered, the Fed would simply repay its swap drawings by purchasing foreign currency from private dealers.

U.S. Foreign Exchange Policy during the 1970s

Federal Reserve swap operations and Treasury intervention in the exchange markets came to an abrupt halt in August 1971, when the Nixon administration snapped the official link between the dollar and gold. Because the dollar was no longer convertible into gold at a government-guaranteed rate, there seemed little reason to interfere with supply and demand forces in the exchange marketplace. The dollar began to "float." However, concern over the stability of all exchange rates and the possible threats to world trade from unbridled speculation in foreign currencies soon brought another reversal of U.S. intervention policy. The Federal Reserve increased its currency swap lines with other central banks, while the Treasury drew on the International Monetary Fund for credit, floated foreign-currency-denominated securities to gain additional exchange reserves, and increased its sales of gold. Moreover, rising foreign interest rates, higher OPEC oil prices, and inflation at home forced even more strenuous efforts by U.S. monetary authorities to protect the dollar from erosion.

A Limited Intervention Policy for the 1980s

The inauguration of President Reagan in January 1981 ushered in another new foreign exchange policy for the United States. For want of a more convenient label, this latest official foreign exchange market approach might be called Emergency Intervention Only. In May 1981 the Reagan administration announced that U.S. monetary authorities would intervene in the foreign exchange markets only if an emergency developed that threatened to disrupt the smooth functioning of the currency markets. The new policy received its first test almost immediately after its inception when the president was shot in an assassination attempt outside a Washington hotel. The Fed and the Treasury immediately began dollar-support operations to calm the exchange markets amidst worldwide concern over the stability and continuity of U.S. government policies and programs.

Once this emergency had passed, the Federal Reserve and the Treasury were confronted with a dramatic rise in the dollar's market price vis-à-vis virtually all other major foreign currencies. A number of factors accounted for the dollar's unprecedented increase in value early in the 1980s—the cooling off of domestic inflation, the rapid economic recovery of the United States after deep recessions in the early 1980s while European recovery lagged, and continuing political and social turmoil in the Middle East and Africa. Whatever the causes of the dollar's market appreciation, the benefits and costs of that rise left few individuals and institutions untouched. Many foreign exporters rejoiced at the time because it meant that their goods could be sold more cheaply in the United States; however, American farmers and other U.S.-based exporting industries were badly damaged because the dollar's rise made U.S. exports more expensive overseas, drastically reducing their salability in foreign markets. Unemployment and business failures in U.S. export industries increased significantly; some American firms began to move their production operations overseas. The U.S. balance-of-payments accounts reflected record payments deficits. Moreover, a shortage of international financial capital began to develop as foreign investors diverted more and more of their investments into the United States.

The Treasury and the Federal Reserve were finally goaded into action by the dollar's persistent gains. The Reagan administration announced a cooperative program with central bankers in Britain, France, Japan, and West Germany to force the dollar's exchange value down against other major national currencies. This new interventionist policy was an effort to avert international trade wars and the erection of import restrictions by the U.S. and other countries. It also reflected concern over the loss of jobs in U.S. export industries and a dramatic rise in farm bankruptcies.

Early in 1985 the U.S. government was presented with a *new* problem for the dollar—a historic plunge in the dollar's value, particularly relative to European currencies and the Japanese yen. So rapid was the greenback's decline, unmatched since World War II, that the global volume of foreign exchange trading rose sharply as corporate treasurers scrambled to protect the value of their overseas investments. One estimate placed the volume of trading in dollar futures, options, swaps, and mutual funds at $150 billion a day in the wake of the dollar's plunge.[9]

Following repeated unsuccessful efforts by the Federal Reserve Bank of New York and the Bank of Japan to stop or slow the decline by buying dollars, the six leading Western trading nations—the United States, Japan, West Germany, France, Britain, and Canada—convened in Paris in February 1987 to devise a plan to stabilize the currency markets. This so-called Louvre Currency Stabilization Accord called for stabilizing foreign exchange rates among the six countries through coordinated intervention by central banks and government agencies. Japan and the European nations involved were urged to stimulate their economies in order to increase the demand for exports and make U.S. securities relatively more attractive, which would help to strengthen the dollar. At the same time, the United States was urged

---

[9]See especially *The Economist* (1985) in the references at the end of the chapter.

to pursue a policy of higher interest rates to attract foreign investors to buy U.S. securities. An earlier Tokyo economic summit (held in the summer of 1986) had developed a plan requiring major trading nations to monitor each other's economic performance as a step toward better international coordination and cooperation in economic policymaking.

There seems little doubt that government intervention to (a) stabilize the dollar or at least insure smoother increases or decreases in its international market value; and (b) coordinate more closely the economic and monetary policies of major trading nations will continue. The cost of not doing so could be extremely high. For example, a falling dollar threatens the United States with more rapid inflation because the prices of imported goods denominated in other currencies rise. Moreover, the U.S. government now depends heavily on foreign investors to purchase its debt securities to help finance the huge federal budget deficit. A falling dollar is, in part, a sign of declining foreign investor interest in U.S. securities. United States' policymakers could revive foreign investor interest by pushing for sharply higher interest rates, but this step would tend to slow U.S. economic growth and create more unemployment. Clearly, government intervention in world currency markets is neither an easy nor a riskless step. And the luxury of a single nation making economic policy decisions independent of other nations that will be significantly affected by those decisions now seems very much a relic of the past.

STUDY QUESTIONS

1. Describe the important role played by commercial banks in the operation of the foreign exchange market. Why do you think banks are so dominant in this market?

2. The foreign exchange market consists of three tiers. What are these three divisions of the market?

3. What role do foreign exchange brokers play in currency trading? Why are broker operations important to the smooth functioning of the foreign exchange market?

4. Please supply a definition of the following terms:
   a. Cable transfers.   e. Time bills.
   b. Mail transfers.   f. Documentary bills.
   c. Bills of exchange.   g. Clean bills.
   d. Sight bills.

5. What are the principal factors affecting the value of any particular currency in the international exchange markets? What role does a nation's balance-of-payments position play in affecting the value of its currency?

6. Distinguish between the spot and forward markets for foreign exchange. Why is it necessary to have two markets rather than one?

7. Describe the principal uses of forward exchange contracts today. Give an example of each use.

8. What is interest rate parity? How does it influence the flow of capital funds abroad?

9. In recent years central banks (including the Federal Reserve System) have intervened in the foreign exchange markets from time to time to support one currency or another. Why do you think central bank intervention in the market might be necessary? What impact are central-bank operations likely to have? Would you expect this impact to be temporary or long lasting?

10. What factors explain the U.S. dollar's steep rise in value early in the 1980s and then sharp decline later in the decade?

PROBLEMS

1. Suppose the exchange rate between British pounds (£) and U.S. dollars ($) is $1.35 per pound. What is the correct way to write this pound-dollar exchange rate? The dollar-pound exchange rate?

2. Suppose the pound-dollar exchange rate is now 1.3500. Then the U.S. dollar increases in value by 5 percent. What is the new pound-dollar exchange rate? What is the new exchange rate if the U.S. dollar appreciated by 10 percent?

3. If the pound-dollar exchange rate increased from £/$ = 1.3500 to 1.4000, by what percentage amount has the pound depreciated?

4. If the pound-dollar exchange rate is 1.4000 and the pound declines 10 percent in value, what is the new pound-dollar exchange rate?

5. Suppose the pound-dollar exchange rate is 1.4000 and the yen-dollar exchange rate is 2.3000. What is the yen-pound exchange rate?

SELECTED REFERENCES

Anderson, Gerald H. "The Nature and Use of Forward Exchange." *Economic Review,* Federal Reserve Bank of Cleveland, April–May 1972, pp. 7–15.

Andrews, Michael E. "Recent Trends in the U.S. Foreign Exchange Market." *Quarterly Review,* Federal Reserve Bank of New York, Summer 1984, pp. 38–47.

Boxer, Russell S. "Efficiency and the Flexible Exchange Rate System." *Economic Review,* Federal Reserve Bank of Atlanta, Summer 1987, pp. 17–34.

Chalupa, Karel V. "Foreign Currency Futures: Reducing Foreign Exchange Risk." *Economic Perspectives,* Federal Reserve Bank of Chicago, Winter 1982, pp. 3–11.

Chrystal, K. Alec. "A Guide to Foreign Exchange Markets." *Review,* Federal Reserve Bank of St. Louis, March 1984, pp. 5–18.

Holmes, Alan R., and Francis H. Schott. *The New York Foreign Exchange Market,* rev. ed. New York: Federal Reserve Bank of New York, 1965.

Humpage, Owen F. "Exchange-Market Intervention: The Channels of Influence." *Economic Review,* Federal Reserve Bank of Cleveland, Third Quarter 1986, pp. 2–13.

Kubarych, Roger M. *Foreign Exchange Markets in the United States.* Federal Reserve Bank of New York, 1978.

"Round the World on $150 Billion a Day." *The Economist,* November 30, 1985.

Chapter 29

International Banking

Learning Objectives in This Chapter

- To understand the important role that large multinational banks play in both domestic and foreign markets around the world.
- To explore the different types of offices and facilities multinational banks operate overseas and to know what financial services they offer in foreign markets.
- To trace the recent expansion of foreign banking in the United States and other parts of the globe.
- To understand how and why international banking is regulated.

Key Terms and Concepts in This Chapter

Multinational corporation

Shell branches

Representative office

Edge Acts

International banking facilities (IBFs)

Letter of credit

Trading foreign currencies (FOREX)

Bankers' acceptances

Eurocurrency deposits

Eurocurrency loans

Eurobonds

Note issuance facilities (NIFs)

International Banking Act (1978)

International Lending and Supervision Act (1983)

No review of the international financial system would be complete without a discussion of the role of international banking institutions. Through these vitally important banking institutions flow the majority of commercial and financial transactions that cross international borders. Along with British and Canadian banks, American commercial banking institutions have led in the development of international banking facilities to meet the far-flung financial needs of foreign governments and multinational corporations. Until recently, the international activities of U.S. banks were concentrated principally in foreign offices, due mainly to federal government controls over foreign lending. However, the relaxation of government controls during the 1970s and 1980s and the growth of international trade brought a veritable explosion of international banking services provided from *domestic* offices and institutions. More recently, though, international banking has retreated from its earlier gains due to problems with foreign loans and a recent slowing in the growth of world trade.

The continuing development of multinational banking over the past half century has resulted in several benefits for international trade. One obvious benefit to the public is greater competition in international financial markets, reducing the prices of financial services. It also has tied together more effectively the various national money markets into a unified international financial system, permitting a more optimal allocation of scarce resources. Funds flow quite freely today across national boundaries in response to differences in relative interest rates and currency values. While these developments undoubtedly have benefited both borrowers and investors, they also have created problems for governments trying to control the volume of credit, interest rates, and inflation.

THE SCOPE OF INTERNATIONAL BANKING ACTIVITIES

Multinational Banking Corporations

The term multinational corporation usually is reserved for large nonfinancial corporations with manufacturing or trading operations in several different countries. However, this term is equally applicable to the world's leading commercial banks, most of which have their home offices in Canada, the United States, Great Britain, and Japan, but have established offices worldwide. In terms of sheer numbers, however, it is the largest U.S. and Japanese banks that have accounted for most of the growth in multinational banking in recent decades.

Types of Facilities Operated by U.S. Banks Abroad

U.S. banks and other major banks around the world have used several vehicles to expand their international operations. All major banks have international departments, and many operate full-service branches in foreign markets as well. U.S. banks also operate Edge Act and Agreement Corporations, shell branches, and representative offices in targeted overseas markets. In addition, most multinational banks make direct investments in the stock of foreign companies, either alone or as part of a consortium with other banks.

International Banking Departments. A major bank's international department generally has 20 to 30 officers and staff and maintains close personal contact with customers and correspondent banks overseas. The larger international banking departments buy and sell foreign currencies, issue letters of credit, and engage in acceptance financing.

Shell Branches. Booking offices of major banks, also known as shell branches, are located today mainly in such offshore islands as the Bahamas and Grand Cayman Islands. These branches have been set up to attract Eurocurrency deposits from abroad by avoiding many domestic banking regulations.

Representative Offices. These offices house staff whose job is to find new loan customers and help meet the service needs of existing customers. However, a representative office cannot accept deposits, but must refer them to the home office.

Edge Acts and Agreement Corporations. These corporations are special subsidiaries of U.S. banks authorized to offer international banking services. Federal legislation passed at the end of World War I permitted American banks to seek charters through the Federal Reserve Board for Edge Act and Agreement Corporations. These subsidiaries could be set up in any location in the United States, provided the bank could come up with the required capital. Edge Acts can engage in activities such as equity financing that normally are prohibited to commercial banks themselves, but the majority of their accounts must be directly related to international transactions.

International Banking Facilities (IBFs). Authorized by the Federal Reserve Board in 1981, IBFs are a set of computerized accounts showing flows of funds through the credit and deposit accounts of foreign residents and foreign banks. However, the IBF must be located in the United States, reflecting an effort by federal regulatory authorities to bring a substantial share of U.S. foreign bank operations back home. Unlike domestic deposits received by a U.S. bank, deposits in an IBF are not subject to reserve requirements, nor can they be insured.

Choosing the Right Kind of Facility to Serve Foreign Markets. Which kind of facility is adopted by a multinational bank to serve its customers depends upon government regulations and the bank's size, goals, and location. Most banks begin with international departments or Edge Acts and

Exhibit 29–1   Geographical Distribution of Assets and Liabilities of Major Foreign Branches of U.S. Banks* as of June 30, 1984 ($ Millions)

Country of Customer	Assets	Liabilities	Country of Customer	Assets	Liabilities
Europe	$110,171	$72,010	Latin America and Caribbean	$45,098	$23,464
Austria	1,490	527	Argentina	2,939	1,391
Belgium-Luxembourg	7,752	4,683	Bahamas	4,942	5,049
Bulgaria	79	29	Bermuda	482	1,887
Czechoslovakia	68	64	Bolivia	115	80
Denmark	2,096	316	Brazil	9,195	2,180
Finland	1,286	190	Cayman Islands	4,423	2,000
France	10,180	5,113	Chile	1,963	473
Germany (East)	174	95	Colombia	452	219
Germany (West)	10,546	2,696	Costa Rica	118	81
Hungary	124	179	Ecuador	423	279
Ireland	1,043	745	Jamaica	94	12
Italy	6,553	3,579	Mexico	8,615	2,561
Netherlands	2,617	3,061	Netherlands Antilles	2,344	1,829
Norway	2,538	469	Nicaragua	260	20
Poland	637	22	Panama	4,783	2,366
Portugal	540	123	Peru	349	470
Romania	198	26	Venezuela	2,861	1,295
Spain	4,333	2,936	Others	740	1,272
Sweden	1,469	237			
Switzerland	3,462	13,059	Africa	9,017	3,189
Turkey	932	155	Egypt	887	1,179
U.S.S.R.	104	12	Liberia	2,599	509
United Kingdom	48,254	29,173	South Africa	2,143	382
Yugoslavia	975	88	Morocco	345	8
Others (including BIS)	2,721	4,433	Zaire	84	9
			African oil-exporting countries‡	1,787	602
Canada	4,228	3,413	Others	1,172	500

then, if business warrants, open shell branches, representative offices, and ultimately full-service branches and subsidiaries. A recent trend toward legal liberalization of foreign trade and international lending has stimulated the growth of *home-based offices* that send officers to call on customers overseas or serve clients by wire. However, many multinational banks argue that successful international operations require an institution to have a stable presence overseas in the form of agencies, branches, or representative offices.

Growth of U.S. International Banking Activities

U.S. international banking really began on a major scale in the early 1960s when the domestic economy was soft and loan demand abroad was strong, particularly from European and Japanese firms. Moreover, interest rate

Exhibit 29–1   *(concluded)*

Country of Customer	Assets	Liabilities	Country of Customer	Assets	Liabilities
Oceania	$ 4,203	$ 108	Unallocated§	$ 13,041	$ 53,314‖
Australia	3,650	76			
New Zealand	458	10	Total excluding the United		
Others	95	22	States, Puerto Rico,		
			and U.S. dependencies	253,096	207,983
Asia	67,338	52,485			
China (PRC)	73	139	United States	124,808	167,038
Taiwan	4,032	5,832			
Hong Kong	10,351	10,315	Puerto Rico and U.S. de-		
India	681	668	pendencies	5,850	5,808
Indonesia	3,193	3,157			
Israel	456	909	Grand total	383,754	380,829
Japan	20,072	8,911			
Korea (South)	4,660	610			
Malaysia	2,156	1,382			
Philippines	4,354	1,839			
Singapore	9,341	4,701			
Thailand	1,244	894			
Middle East oil-export-					
ing countries†	5,960	10,708			
Others	765	2,420			

*Beginning with data for June 1984, total reported assets and liabilities have been reduced by an increase in the reporting threshold for shell branches from $50 million to $150 million equivalent in total assets. Coverage thus differs from that for earlier dates described in previous releases.

†Bahrain, Iran, Iraq, Kuwait, Oman, Qatar, Saudi Arabia, and the United Arab Emirates.

‡Algeria, Gabon, Libya, and Nigeria.

§Including international organizations.

‖Beginning with data for June 1984, negotiable CDs issued by the branches are included in the "unallocated" line.

Source: Federal Reserve Bank of Chicago.

differentials in the international money market generally favored the United States as a source of loanable funds. By the late 1960s restrictive interest rate ceilings on domestic deposits encouraged the largest U.S. banks to draw more heavily on the international Eurodollar market as a source of reserves. When the administration of President Lyndon Johnson imposed restrictions on overseas lending from domestic offices through a Voluntary Foreign Credit Restraint Program in 1965, U.S. banks saw offshore facilities as a vital link to foreign deposits and loans, and bank facilities abroad expanded rapidly. By 1974, 125 American banks controlled 732 foreign branch offices. A much slower growth in the internationalization of U.S. banking then set in as global economic conditions softened due to inflation, high interest rates, and higher energy prices. Still, there were 902 U.S.-bank foreign branches in 1987.

As shown in Exhibit 29–1, the majority of assets and liabilities held by

U.S. bank branches abroad are concentrated in Western Europe (particularly the United Kingdom), Latin America, and the Caribbean. Assets held by U.S. bank branches in the United Kingdom—most of these headquartered in London, the center of the worldwide Eurodollar market—accounted for close to one third of the assets of all U.S. bank branches abroad. Other nations where U.S. bank branches hold substantial assets include Japan, France, Belgium-Luxembourg, West Germany, Brazil, Mexico, Hong Kong, and Singapore.

In terms of total offices, Latin America leads the list, with more than 200 branches and other office facilities operated by U.S. banks. Shell branches in the Bahamas and Grand Cayman Islands ranked second in total numbers, and the Far East and continental Europe were not far behind with well over 100 branches, representative offices, and other facilities of American banks stationed there. Significant numbers of U.S. banking offices may also be found today in Africa, the Middle East, and U.S. possessions and trust territories.

Laws and regulations play a major role in determining where multinational banking offices are located around the globe. For example, The People's Republic of China, India, and Saudi Arabia prohibit or restrict the operation of branches by foreign banks. In other areas of the world fears of political upheaval or outright expropriation of foreign-owned facilities have severely limited the entry of multinational banks.

For several of the largest U.S. banks, international operations yield from one third to as much as one half of their income, and a few receive more than half their earnings from international activities. Particularly noteworthy has been U.S.-bank penetration of foreign consumer banking markets, such as the "money shops" operated by New York's Citibank in Great Britain. American banks entered the consumer lending field in the 1920s, and they have developed considerable expertise in that field. Personal loans and other personal financial services often represent extremely attractive opportunities in foreign markets, and U.S. banks hold a significant share of consumer loan and deposit markets abroad, especially in Western Europe.

SERVICES OFFERED BY INTERNATIONAL BANKS

Multinational banks today offer a wide variety of international financial services to customers. These services, described briefly below, include issuing letters of credit, buying and selling foreign exchange, issuing bankers' acceptances, accepting Eurocurrency deposits, making Eurocurrency loans, and assisting in the marketing of Eurobonds. Of course, the particular services offered by each bank depend on its size, location, and the types of facilities it maintains overseas.

Issuing Letters of Credit (LC)

Most banks enter the international sector to finance trade. In trading across national borders rarely are goods and services paid for in advance. Nearly always financing is needed to bridge the gap between cash expenditures and cash receipts and to reduce the risks associated with long-distance trading. In these situations a letter of credit is often the ideal financing instrument. A letter of credit is simply an international bank's future promise to pay for goods stored overseas or goods shipped between two countries. Such letters may be issued to finance exports and imports or to provide standby credit, such as a guarantee of payment behind commercial paper issued by a corporate customer. Through a letter of credit, which is usually irrevocable, the bank merely substitutes its own future promise to pay for the promise to pay of one of its customers. By substituting its promise, the bank acts as a guarantor of payment and thereby reduces the seller's risk, facilitating the flow of goods and services through international markets. Occasionally, the seller becomes concerned about the soundness of the bank issuing the letter of credit; he may then ask his own bank to issue a confirmation letter in which his bank guarantees against foreign bank default.

Buying and Selling Foreign Exchange (FOREX)

Major multinational banks, as we saw in the preceding chapter, have dealer departments that specialize in trading foreign currencies. Major international banks will buy and sell foreign currencies on a 24-hour basis around the globe to support the import and export of goods and services, the making of investments, the distribution of earnings from foreign business ventures, the giving of gifts, and the financing of tourism. They also negotiate forward contracts for the future delivery of foreign exchange, and some speculate on future currency price movements in hope of turning a profit.

Issuing Bankers' Acceptances

Bankers' acceptances are time drafts used mainly to finance the shipment of goods or commodities.[1] With a banker's acceptance the bank agrees to pay a seller of goods when the time draft expires. For example, an exporter and importer may agree upon 60-day sight terms on the shipment of certain items. This tells us that the exporter will receive payment from a bank 60 days following the date when the issuing bank affirms that the draft and certain documents associated with the transaction are in good order. Once this is affirmed, the issuing bank will stamp "Accepted" across the face of the draft. The bank's stamp is a guarantee of future payment, and it makes

---

[1]See Chapter 17 for a detailed discussion of the creation and uses of bankers' acceptances.

the acceptance a negotiable instrument. The exporter may sell (discount) the acceptance to a bank or other investor and thereby receive payment before the draft's due date.

Accepting Eurocurrency Deposits and Making Eurocurrency Loans

As we saw in Chapter 17, international banks accept deposits denominated in currencies other than that of their home country. Thus, London banks will accept deposits denominated in dollars, francs, and other major convertible currencies. Eurocurrency deposits are used to pay for goods shipped between countries, and as a source of loanable funds for banks.

Eurocurrency deposits may be loaned in the interbank market to corporations, governments, and other large wholesale borrowers. The majority of Eurocurrency loans carry floating interest rates, in most cases, based on the London Interbank Offer Rate (LIBOR) for three-month and six-month Eurocurrency deposits. Eurocurrency credit normally goes to borrowers with impeccable credit ratings. One important innovation in this field in recent years is the *syndicated Eurocurrency credit* in which one or more large multinational banks will put together a loan package accompanied by an information memorandum. Smaller banks can then participate in the loan without direct communication with the borrower. Syndicated credits are a fast method of raising loanable funds and spreading risk.

Assisting in the Marketing of Eurocurrency Bonds and Notes

In recent years multinational banks have become active as agents, underwriters, and, in some instances, investors in the rapidly growing market for Eurobonds and Euronotes. A Eurobond is a debt security denominated in a currency other than that of the country or countries where most or all of the security is sold. For example, an American automobile company may desire to float an issue of long-term bonds to raise capital for one of its subsidiaries operating in Greece. The company might issue bonds denominated in British pounds to be sold in several countries in Western Europe through an underwriting syndicate made up of banks, securities dealers, and other firms.

Most Eurobonds are denominated in dollars, though substantial amounts are also denominated today in Deutsche marks, guilders, pounds, yen, and francs. Eurobonds normally are straight debt offerings with maturities ranging to about 15 years, though warrants and conversion features occasionally are attached to improve the marketability of a particular issue. The majority are callable bearer bonds with coupons attached.

Large multinational banks assist the Eurobond market in several ways. Major banks such as Morgan Guaranty Trust Company of New York have established international clearing systems to expedite the delivery of Eurobonds. Banks and security brokers are the principal intermediaries through which both old and new Eurobonds find their way to the long-term investor. The borrower (a government or large corporation) usually contacts a major international bank and asks it to organize a syndicate to place a new issue. At this point a *consortium* will be formed, embracing at least four or five American, British, Japanese, French, or German banks and a bank located in the borrowing country. The consortium typically agrees to subscribe to the Eurobond issue at issue price minus a commission and then organizes a large group of banks and securities dealers as underwriters. Sometimes more than 100 banks are included in the underwriting syndicate. Once formed, the underwriting group gives the borrower a firm offer for its bonds and proceeds to place the issue with investors.

Multinational banks also assist their corporate and governmental customers with medium-term financing through Note Issuance Facilities (NIFs). Under a standard NIF contract, a customer is authorized to periodically issue short-term notes (usually with three- to six-month maturities) to interested investors over a designated time span (perhaps five years). The bank or banks involved agree to provide backup funding (standby credit) at a spread over prevailing Euromarket interest rates. For an underwriting fee the bank will agree to purchase any unsold notes or advance cash to the customer until enough market funding is obtained.

Other Services Provided by International Banks

In addition to the foregoing services, international banks offer extensive *advisory services* to their customers. These include analyses of foreign market conditions, evaluation of sales prospects and plant location sites, and advice on foreign laws and regulations. International banks often prepare credit reports on overseas buyers for exporters of goods and services, and assist domestic firms interested in entering foreign markets.

International banks offer cash management services and lease capital assets for their corporate customers. They frequently engage in interest rate swaps to aid multinational corporations in dealing with the risk of fluctuating market interest rates. In recent years, many international banks have added sales of insurance, credit cards, mortgage brokering services, customer installment loans, and financing to their traditional service lines.

SMALLER BANKS ENTER THE INTERNATIONAL FIELD

One of the unique features of international banking in recent years is the opening of offshore offices by smaller, essentially regional banks. Regional banks are usually defined as large banks with a billion dollars or more in assets located in a U.S. city other than New York, Chicago, or San Francisco. Large downtown banks in Atlanta, Boston, Dallas, Houston, Miami, Los Angeles, Seattle, Portland, and New Orleans are examples of regional banks.

A study by Thompson (1979) concludes that more than half the regional banks among the top 300 American commercial banks then operated international departments. Smaller banks without formal departments still provide such international services as letters of credit and bankers' acceptances.

Expansion offshore has given some of the smaller banks an opportunity to diversify out of slowly growing domestic markets and to open up entirely new markets. Only the largest regionals actually open foreign branches or set up Edge Act Corporations. However, many regional banks have opened shell branches, mainly in the Caribbean area. These shells provide a convenient source of loanable funds when domestic reserves are scarce. Moreover, shell operations are low cost compared to most other forms of international banking. Most of the regional banks rely heavily on loan participations with better established multinational lenders. Some of the smaller banks have become quite successful in international lending by centering their activities on selected industries and developing expertise in one area or a few areas, such as ship financing and petroleum exploration.

FOREIGN BANKS IN THE UNITED STATES[2]

Banks owned by foreign individuals and companies have entered the United States in great numbers in recent years. The reasons behind the expansion of foreign banking activities in the United States reflect both the growth in international trade and investments and the opportunity for profit in the huge U.S. market. Originally, foreign-based banks penetrated U.S. markets for essentially the same reason U.S. banks established facilities overseas— to follow customers who had established operations in other countries. Once in the United States, however, foreign banks found the possibility of attracting deposits and loans from major American corporations irresistible. Moreover, the U.S. economy has been more stable and prosperous than many other national economies where foreign banks are headquartered or represented.

Recent Growth of Foreign Banks in the United States

The size of foreign bank operations in the United States is impressive. By year-end 1987, there were more than 500 foreign bank offices in the United States, including agency offices, branches, and subsidiary firms. Japanese offices led all others by a wide margin, followed by France, the United Kingdom, and Canada. Data released by the Federal Reserve Board indicates those foreign-based institutions held assets of nearly $470 billion at year-end 1987, compared to less than $150 billion in 1980. In relative terms, U.S. offices of foreign banks held about 16 percent of total assets of all banks in

---

[2]This section is based in part on an earlier article by Rose (1976) in *The Canadian Banker and ICB Review*.

the United States in 1987. The growth rate of foreign bank assets held at their U.S. offices has averaged about double the growth rate of domestic bank assets. Such rapid growth has made foreign banks a significant factor in U.S. financial markets, especially in the market for domestic business loans.

Types of Organizations Operated by Foreign Banks in the United States

Foreign banks use a variety of institutional arrangements to market their services in the United States. Of course, the particular vehicles used by foreign banks to enter U.S. markets depend on the financial services they offer, the expected volume of foreign business, and the nature of their domestic operations.

British banks generally have set up full-service banking facilities on the American continent by establishing branches and acquiring domestically chartered banks, principally in California and New York. Canadian banks were the first to enter the United States, establishing agency offices during the last century. The large Canadian-chartered banks then and now rely on the American money market as a source of liquidity. Canadian banks make loans to U.S. security brokers and dealers and hold substantial deposits with U.S. money center banks. Canadian banks in the main have used four devices to carry on their operations in the United States: (1) trust companies in New York to provide for the safekeeping of valuables and the transfer and processing of bank payments; (2) New York and San Francisco agencies; (3) wholesale-retail affiliates, principally in California; and (4) representative offices. Banks in Switzerland and Germany have used branch offices and securities affiliates. Japanese banks have established wholesale banking affiliates, retail banking offices, and agency offices that service loans, finance trade, and offer investment banking services.

Federal Regulation of Foreign Bank Activity

Until recently, no federal laws regulated foreign bank activity within U.S. borders. However, Congress has been monitoring foreign bank operations since 1966, when IntraBank, a Lebanese institution, collapsed and several U.S. banks suffered severe losses. Passage of the Bank Holding Company Act Amendments of 1970 marked an initial step toward federal regulation of foreign banking. Under the terms of these amendments, any corporation controlling one or more domestic banks became subject to regulation and supervision by the Federal Reserve Board. An additional step was taken in 1972, when the Federal Reserve began monitoring foreign bank activities by gathering monthly balance sheet reports from these banks.

However, with foreign bank operations in the United States growing more rapidly than domestic banks, the pressure on Congress for regulation of foreign banks intensified. Proponents of restrictive legislation argued that the presence of foreign banks reduced the effectiveness of domestic monetary policy, especially control over the nation's money supply. Moreover, the lack of specific regulations applying to foreign banks seemed unfair to domestic financial institutions, which must conform to an elaborate system of regulations. Perhaps more important, foreign banks could move across state lines—a privilege denied American banks since passage of the McFadden Act in 1927 unless the individual states grant express permission to branch into their territory.

There was also a disparity between foreign and domestic banks in the financial services each group of institutions was permitted to offer. American banks are prohibited from offering services in domestic markets not *closely related* to traditional banking services such as the extension of credit and the taking of deposits. Moreover, passage of the Glass-Steagall Act in 1933 prohibited American banks from investment underwriting of either corporate bonds or stock. Such a prohibition does not apply to foreign-owned banks, and several foreign banking organizations moved in to take advantage of this loophole. For example, a number of Japanese, West German, and Swiss banks established U.S. affiliates to trade equity securities.

Foreign Banks and the International Banking Act of 1978

Responding to these various arguments, Congress passed the International Banking Act (IBA) which became law on September 17, 1978 (see Exhibit 29–2). Under the terms of the IBA and subsequent regulations, branches and agencies of foreign banks with worldwide consolidated assets of $1 billion or more are subject to legal reserve requirements and federal interest rate ceilings on their deposits. Foreign banks that maintain U.S. offices other than branches or agencies are required to register with the Secretary of the Treasury upon establishment of such an office. Each foreign bank with an office accepting deposits from the public must select a "home state." If it does not do so, the Federal Reserve Board will designate the home state for the bank. No foreign bank may directly or indirectly establish and operate a federal- or state-chartered branch outside its home state unless granted permission by the states involved. This provision of the law limits a foreign bank's ability to accept deposits across state lines, especially retail (consumer-type) deposits.

The IBA proved to be a more lenient piece of legislation than many analysts had expected. It did not attempt to punish or discriminate against foreign banks relative to their U.S. counterparts. In fact, the act set down in law the principle of *mutual nondiscrimination,* used widely abroad as a regulatory standard. This principle permits foreign-owned banks to operate under the same conditions and to possess the same powers as domestic banks. It is a policy that avoids establishing two sets of banking regulations—one

Exhibit 29–2 **Purposes and Provisions of the International Banking Act (IBA) of 1978**

Purpose: To promote competitive equality between domestic and foreign banking institutions operating in the United States.

Provisions: Limited the interstate branching of foreign banks.

Provided for federal licensing of branches and agencies of foreign banks.

Authorized the Federal Reserve Board to impose reserve requirements on branches and agencies of foreign banks.

Provided for foreign bank access to Federal Reserve services such as the discount window.

Provided for federal deposit insurance for branches of foreign banks.

Granted broader powers to Edge Act Corporations of U.S. banks so they can compete more effectively with branches and agencies of foreign banks.

Subjected foreign banks operating branches and agencies to the prohibitions against non-bank business ventures of the U.S. Bank Holding Company Act.

Source: Federal Reserve Bank of Chicago, *International Letter,* May 22, 1981.

for domestic institutions and the other for foreign-owned banks. Foreign banks can even acquire majority control of U.S. Edge Acts under the terms of the IBA.

Federal regulation of foreign banks was extended a step further in 1980 when the Depository Institutions Deregulation and Monetary Control Act (DIDMCA) was passed. All foreign banking organizations offering services to U.S. residents became eligible for deposit insurance from the Federal Deposit Insurance Corporation and all such organizations, regardless of size, were required to conform to deposit reserve requirements set by the Federal Reserve Board. Moreover, when a foreign bank opens an agency, branch, or loan production office in the United States, it must register as a bank holding company and conform with all holding company laws and regulations as administered by the Federal Reserve System. These new legal requirements even more firmly reflected Congress's intention to place all banks (foreign and domestic) on the same regulatory footing and in the same field of competition.

REGULATION OF THE INTERNATIONAL BANKING ACTIVITIES OF U.S. BANKS

A far more significant problem than regulating foreign banking activities in the United States is the regulation, supervision, and control of U.S. banks offering their services overseas. What limits should be placed on U.S. banks operating overseas? Who should enforce those limits?

The first of these questions is not yet fully resolved, but the second has a ready answer. The Federal Reserve Board has been designated as the chief regulatory agency for international banking activities, especially where Fed member banks are involved. A member bank choosing to expand its activities abroad through the creation of foreign branches or through investments in foreign firms must secure the approval of the Federal Reserve Board. In contrast, state laws govern the foreign operations of state-chartered banks. However, with the exception of a handful of states, state governments have exerted only nominal control over foreign banking activities.

Of prime concern to the Federal Reserve is the protection of domestic deposits and the stability of the domestic banking system. The Fed has argued that it is difficult to separate a bank's foreign operations from its domestic activities. If a foreign subsidiary gets into trouble, the danger exists that public confidence in the soundness of the domestic bank will be undermined. For this reason, the Fed, in passing upon applications of American banks to expand abroad, examines closely the condition of their domestic offices to determine if their home-based operations are adequately capitalized and if the bank has sufficient management skill to support both foreign and domestic operations.

The regulatory authorities would like to develop ways to insulate the foreign activities of U.S. banks from their domestic operations. Such insulation would grant wider latitude to banking activities abroad and at the same time shield domestic banks from the hazards associated with foreign operations. Legally, one subsidiary is not liable for the debts of another. However, in practice a domestic bank might feel compelled to aid at least its wholly owned affiliates operating in foreign markets. The practical, if not legal, links between foreign and domestic subsidiaries of multinational banks force regulators to keep close tabs on the foreign operations of all commercial banks.

One central problem the Federal Reserve Board faces in regulating multinational banking activities is the wider latitude given most foreign commercial banks by the regulatory authorities of other countries. For example, banks outside the United States frequently are permitted to make equity investments in nonfinancial corporations, but domestic U.S. banks are not. The Board, therefore, typically allows U.S. banks to offer a greater variety of services in foreign markets than at home, including investment banking services and noncontrolling equity investments in nonfinancial corporations. While American banks do not play an important direct role in our own capital markets, the broader powers available to them for international operations have brought them into the long-term Eurobond market, as we saw earlier. The Fed argues that banking regulations in the United States reflect this nation's views on how much competition there should be in the financial system. However, competition in foreign markets depends on the policies of other nations, and Federal Reserve officials have preferred to leave such questions to the host country. The Fed tries to balance freedom against risk in deciding on the proper scope of multinational banking activities.

PROBLEMS AND THE FUTURE OF INTERNATIONAL BANKING

The future of international banking is clouded at this time due to the many cross-currents of economics and politics that pervade our world. Sluggish economic growth, trade barriers, and political struggles threaten the flow of international commerce in parts of the globe and make bank lending across national boundaries inherently more risky. In this section we take a brief look at these problems and their implications for the future of international banking.

The Risks of International Lending

For one thing, lending funds in the international arena is risky business—probably more risky, on average, than domestic lending. *Political risk*—the risk that government laws and regulations will change to the detriment of business interests—is particularly significant in international operations. Governments are frequently overthrown and confiscation of private property is a common occurrence in many parts of the world.[3] There is also *currency risk*—that is, the risk associated with changing relative prices of foreign currencies. The value of property pledged behind an international loan will fall if the currency of the home country is devalued, thus eroding the lender's collateral. Geography too works against the international lender of funds. The larger distances that frequently separate lender and borrower make it more difficult for the bank loan officer to see that the terms of a loan are being followed.

The risks of international lending by banks became of much greater concern in the 1970s and 1980s because commercial banks became the principal source of borrowed funds for developing countries. Unfortunately, when international commodity prices declined precipitously in the 1980s, many developing countries could not meet the terms of their existing loans. Many

---

[3]Many financial analysts often lump political and other risks in international lending under the general term *country risk*. This is the possibility that governments borrowing money from multinational banks may be unable or unwilling to repay and that private borrowers may, because of law and regulation, be unable to pay on their loans. For example, private borrowers may be prevented from paying due to *transfer risk*—a component of country risk in which a nation prohibits outflows of capital, dividends, or interest payments due to an internal shortage of foreign exchange. The other component of country risk—*political risk*—arises when loans cannot be repaid due to war, revolution, or changes in regulatory philosophy that adversely affect the ability of a borrower to fulfill a debt obligation.

of these debts were rescheduled by agreement between multinational banks and debtor countries. Simultaneously, the International Monetary Fund and World Bank moved to supply more funds to give these debtor nations time to adjust their domestic economies to a harsher economic climate.

Frequently such adjustments resulted in reduced demands for imports, slower economic growth, and increased unemployment. Some nations threatened to repudiate their international debt or unilaterally alter the terms of repayment and some (such as Mexico) offered only partial payment deals stretched out over several years. At the same time, some multinational banks began to withdraw or scale down their international lending operations by selling old loans at deep discounts, which further weakened the availability of needed liquidity in international markets and slowed the growth of world trade. Industrialized countries reduced their purchases of exports from developing countries, which resulted in these nations having even less in spendable reserves to pay off their debts. Many multinational banks with heavy loan exposure to developing countries saw the prices of their stock and their credit ratings plummet.

Some banks pioneered *debt-for-equity swaps* in which they accepted stock investments in certain overseas projects as a substitute for holding loans. This promising innovation was aimed at replacing nonperforming assets with performing assets. These swaps also provided more flexible funding arrangements for developing countries.

Beginning in the late 1970s the Federal Reserve Board, the Comptroller of the Currency, and the Federal Deposit Insurance Corporation inaugurated semi-annual surveys of foreign lending by U.S. banking organizations. The principal concern of these regulatory agencies was that U.S. multinational banks were overly committed to loans in certain countries where the political and economic risks were unusually high. If this were the case, it might threaten the confidence of the public in the stability and soundness of some of the world's largest banks. These recent regulatory surveys show that most loans extended by U.S. multinational banks are made to industrially developed nations and to countries in Central and South America. However, close to a third of all foreign loans are made to less developed countries, a number of which have been in serious financial difficulty in recent years. Examples include Argentina, Brazil, and Mexico.

Fortunately, the majority of loans to distant nations are short term (maturity of one year or less) and many are to banks themselves. On the whole, multinational banks are relatively conservative lenders, directing their credits mainly to large bank, corporate, and governmental borrowers situated mainly in Western Europe and in rapidly growing Asian markets such as Japan. Moreover, the bulk of such loans are concentrated in the largest U.S. banks. This is a potentially troublesome situation, however, because hundreds of smaller banks keep sizable deposits with those leading multinationals and would be themselves threatened if any of the top banks became insolvent.

Public Confidence and Bank Failures

The key problem in the international banking field today is the preservation of public confidence in the banking system. Essentially, this means protecting the major multinationals against failure. This problem charged into the headlines in 1974 when both Franklin National Bank in New York, then the 20th largest U.S. bank, and Bankhaus Herstatt of West Germany were forced into bankruptcy. In the 1980s, Continental Illinois Bank of Chicago had to be bailed out by a $4 billion-plus loan from the Federal Deposit Insurance Corporation. In the wake of these major problems, public confidence in virtually all of the world's multinational banks was shaken. International lending, particularly in the Eurodollar market, was often limited to the largest, prime-quality borrowers, and smaller banks were forced to pay substantially higher rates to attract funds. Many loan syndicates disbanded, and business investment slowed.

In order to avert future failures and serious financial difficulties among the world's largest banks, regulatory authorities in the United States and elsewhere today look closely at the *capital positions* of multinational banks. Regulators have urged a slower, more considered expansion of international loans, avoiding excessive credit exposure in loans to any one country, especially to non-oil-producing nations of the Third World. This is coupled today with an insistence on adequate levels of equity capital, adjusted for differences in loan risk among major banks. For example, in June 1983 the Federal Reserve and the Comptroller of the Currency issued minimum capital guidelines for major U.S. multinational banks. And in 1988 the Federal Reserve System, the Bank of England, the Bank of Japan, and the central banks of nine other countries adopted a cooperative plan to monitor the capital positions of international banks falling under their jurisdiction and to impose joint minimum capital requirements. Unfortunately, determining what is an adequate capital position to support foreign banking activities is a complicated problem. Fluctuations in foreign exchange rates, barriers to the flow of information, and foreign political developments add to the unique risks inherent in international banking.

To further ensure that U.S. multinational banks adhere to more stringent regulatory standards in making foreign loans, Congress passed the International Lending Supervision Act in 1983. This law ordered federal bank regulatory agencies to prepare new rules requiring U.S. banks to:

1. Maintain special reserves against foreign loans in those instances where the quality of a bank's assets has been impaired by protracted borrower inability to pay out loans.

2. Limit loan rescheduling fees that may be charged troubled foreign borrowers.

3. Disclose a bank's exposure to foreign borrowers.

4. Hold minimum levels of capital as protection for an international bank's depositors.

5. Conduct feasibility studies of large foreign projects involving mining, metal, or mineral primary processing operations before approving a loan.

Many members of Congress saw this law as an essential precondition before the United States approved any additional contributions to the International Monetary Fund to support further growth in world trade and finance.

The Spread of Deregulation: How Fast Should We Go?

As we saw in earlier chapters (especially Chapters 4 and 5), the United States began an aggressive program of deregulating domestic banking in the 1980s. Other nations—like Great Britain with its Big Bang deregulation of selected banking and security dealer services in 1987—have also made significant strides toward lifting confining rules and regulations, permitting their banks as well as foreign banks operating within their borders to compete more equally with other financial institutions. Unfortunately, the pattern of international banking deregulation has been spotty, with some nations (such as Japan) lowering the barriers to competition very slowly in order to protect domestic institutions. The real losers here are domestic consumers of financial services who have fewer options and probably pay higher prices until deregulation takes place. The key issue is how to allow deregulation of financial services on an international scale to proceed rapidly without wholesale bank failures that destroy public confidence. No one has yet found a convincing solution to this perplexing and enormously challenging global issue.

PROSPECTS AND ISSUES IN THE 1980s

These recent trends suggest a much different future for international banking than seemed likely in earlier years. Growth—limited by capital and the availability of experienced management—should be more gradual and loan quality more of a factor in future extensions of credit to businesses and governments abroad. However, continuing expansion of foreign banking activities in the United States and in Asia and the Pacific Basin can be anticipated.

Certainly a number of critical questions lie ahead for international banking. For example, to what extent can and will the regulatory authorities of different nations cooperate to control foreign banking activities? How can we reconcile different banking rules from one country to the next so as to promote competition and innovation, but also public safety? What is an appropriate capital position for banks engaged in foreign lending, and how does this relate to domestic capital needs? Where must regulation end and the free play of market forces be allowed to operate in international banking? Should multinational banks be subject to the same rigid controls as domestic banks? What impact are developments in multinational banking, especially in the Eurocurrency market, likely to have on domestic financial markets, and how can domestic monetary policy best deal with that impact?

These are perplexing issues that have few clear answers. However, the importance of international banking and the penetration of domestic markets all over the globe by foreign banking institutions demand that effective answers be found that strengthen the system and provide a basis for future growth and development.

STUDY QUESTIONS

1. What are the essential differences between the following types of banking organizations?
   a. International banking departments.
   b. Edge Act Corporations.
   c. Agreement Corporations.
   d. Shell branches.
   e. Representative offices.
   f. Full-service branches.
   g. Consortiums.

2. In what parts of the world are most U.S. banking offices located? Can you explain why?

3. Explain why many smaller U.S. regional banks have entered the international banking field in recent years. What specific problems is management likely to encounter in trying to establish banking facilities and offer financial services abroad?

4. Explain why foreign banks have entered the United States in such large numbers in recent years. What types of organizations do these banks operate in the United States?

5. What federal regulations apply to foreign banks operating in the United States today? What factors motivated Congress to pass the International Banking Act of 1978?

6. What federal agency is the chief regulator of international banking in the United States? What are its principal powers?

7. What is the principle of mutual nondiscrimination? Do you agree with this principle? What problems could it create for regulators?

8. What major problems have been encountered by the international banking community in recent years? How have these problems been dealt with?

SELECTED REFERENCES

Board of Governors of the Federal Reserve System. "Implementation of the International Banking Act." *Federal Reserve Bulletin,* October 1979, pp. 785–96.

Chrystal, K.A. "International Banking Facilities." *Review*, Federal Reserve Bank of St. Louis, April 1984, pp. 5–11.

Edwards, Franklin R. *Regulation of Foreign Banking in the United States: International Reciprocity and Federal-State Conflicts.* New York: Columbia University, Graduate School of Business, 1974.

Heller, H. Robert. "The Debt Crisis and the Future of International Bank Lending." Speech by a Member of the Board of Governors of the Federal Reserve System before the Annual Convention of the American Economic Association, New Orleans, December 29, 1986.

Houpt, James V., and Michael G. Martinson. *Foreign Subsidiaries of U.S. Banking Organizations.* Staff Economic Study, Board of Governors of the Federal Reserve System, 1982.

Houpt, James V. *International Trends for U.S. Banks and Banking Markets.* Staff Economic Study, Board of Governors of the Federal Reserve System, 1988.

Klopstock, Fred H. "Foreign Banks in the United States: Scope and Growth of Operations." *Monthly Review*, Federal Reserve Bank of New York, June 1973, pp. 140–54.

Lees, Francis A. *International Banking and Finance.* New York: Wiley, 1973.

Rose, Peter S. "Foreign Banking in the United States." *The Canadian Banker and ICB Review,* May–June 1976, pp. 58–61.

Rose, Peter S., and Habib G. Bassoul, "Edge Acts: Outside-In." *The Canadian Banker and ICB Review,* April 1980, pp. 52–56.

Segala, John P. "A Summary of the International Banking Act of 1978." *Economic Review*, Federal Reserve Bank of Richmond, January–February 1979, pp. 16–21.

Teeters, Nancy H. "The Role of Banks in the International Financial System." *Federal Reserve Bulletin,* September 1983, pp. 663–71.

Thompson, I.B. "The International Banking Activities of Regional Banks." *American Banker,* March 23, 1979, pp. 14, 36, and 38.

White, Betsy Butrill. "Foreign Banking in the United States: A Regulatory and Supervisory Perspective." *Quarterly Review,* Federal Reserve Bank of New York, Summer 1982, pp. 48–58.

Chapter 30

The Future of the Financial System

Learning Objectives in This Chapter

- To understand the economic, demographic, social, and technological forces reshaping financial institutions, financial markets, and the financial system today.

- To gain a perspective on recent trends in the financial system and to see how those trends could affect all of us personally and professionally in the future.

Key Terms and Concepts in This Chapter

Financial innovation
Market broadening
Aging population
Service-oriented economy
Information revolution
Public confidence
Interstate operations
Risk-management tools

Fiber optics
Video conferences
Securitization
Home-equity loans
Consumer cash management services
Franchising

Deregulation
Financial disclosure
Social responsibility
Tax Reform Act

THE TRENDS SWEEPING THROUGH TODAY'S FINANCIAL SYSTEM

The financial system of markets and institutions is passing through an era of *revolutionary* changes, as we have seen in earlier chapters. As shown in Exhibit 30–1, which summarizes the most important changes, new financial services and new financial instruments are proliferating, exploding in volume and variety. Variable-rate mortgages (VRMs), collateralized mortgage obligations (CMOs), stripped bonds, SWAPs and interest rate options, home equity loans, cash management accounts, and universal life insurance are only the vanguard of a wave of financial innovation sweeping through the financial system today. A trend toward deregulation of the financial sector and greater reliance upon private decision-making, rather than government fiat, has unleashed the force of competition on a scale never seen before. Banks and insurance companies, security brokers and thrift institutions are

Exhibit 30–1   Changes and Trends in the Financial System That Point to the Future

1. Increasing proliferation of new financial services offered to the public with increased product development and research activity and heavy emphasis on sales techniques, including sales by satellite and video conference.

2. Further deregulation of the financial sector of the economy with the private marketplace playing a greater role in determining the type and character of services offered.

3. Increasing nationalization and internationalization of financial markets and services with commercial, consumer, mortgage, and agricultural loans developing broader and broader resale markets, providing new sources of liquidity for lenders of funds.

4. Growing competition in the production and distribution of *all* financial services as more financial institutions establish interstate offices and sell their services in broader regional, national, and international markets.

5. Increasing consolidation, through mergers and acquisitions, of the structure of key financial service industries—banking, insurance, security brokerage, investment banking, pension plans—with larger financial institutions continuing to emerge with the broadening of markets and the need for greater efficiency.

6. Increased attention by financial institutions and financial managers to the control of operating costs and to improving the productivity of labor and other resources needed to produce financial services.

7. Continuing updating of service production and delivery techniques with the latest technological methods, including networking, fiber optics, video conferences, and many other new technologies.

8. Increased risk of failure for individual institutions due to greater competition, service innovation, cost pressures, and technological change.

9. Rapid growth of new job and career opportunities in developing and marketing financial services, in information processing, and in planning and financial advising.

10. Rapid growth and development in selected areas for the future, especially the evolution of an integrated national market and eventual exchange trading of mortgage loans, substantial increases in home remodeling loans and home equity loans, and the expansion of consumer cash management services.

locked in an intense competitive struggle for the customer's business that is unparalleled in history.

And that competitive struggle has given rise not only to new services and new financial instruments, but also to new financial institutions—larger, multiproduct, multimarket, more technologically and marketing oriented organizations that should be better able to deal with the greater risks inherent in today's intensively competitive and volatile financial marketplace. More and more, today's financial institutions look *alike*—they offer many of the same services and they are organized in many of the same ways. Traditional distinctions between one type of financial institution and another are becoming hopelessly blurred and functionally irrelevant.

More financial institutions are establishing interstate operations and expanding their marketing and sales programs to cover whole regions, if not the whole globe. The result is falling geographic barriers to interinstitutional competition and pressure to consolidate banks and other financial institutions with a wave of mergers and acquisitions. At the same time, intensified interinstitutional competition has increased the risk of failure for both large and small institutions and decreased their profit margins.

Financial markets that traditionally have been predominantly local are expanding to regional, national, and international horizons. This market broadening phenomenon reflects recent advances in communications technology and transportation methods, with the most significant technological breakthroughs in the gathering and processing of information. These breakthroughs offer the prospect of substantially reducing service delivery costs, improving employee productivity, bringing new services on line more rapidly, and expanding the effective marketing area for both old and new services. Such an expansion of effective marketing areas will bring profound changes in how financial services are sold and in the options available to customers and to financial institution managers.

One of the most dramatic examples of the trend toward market broadening was the Federal National Mortgage Association's recent announcement of a plan to establish a *national mortgage exchange* to provide a more efficient interstate channel for secondary market trading of mortgage loans—currently the largest of all financial markets. Many more commercial, consumer, and farm loans will be actively traded in national and international markets in the not-too-distant future, providing new sources of liquidity for financial institutions making these loans and improving the availability of credit to the public.

Of course, what is happening to the financial system and financial institutions today is not a completely new story; its roots lie deep in our history. The trend toward deregulation of financial institutions today is, in a sense, a counterreaction to the excesses of an earlier era—the Great Depression of the 1930s—when comprehensive regulation of financial institutions and financial services promised *safety* from the turmoil of a free market by stifling both competition and innovation. Today's emphasis in the financial sector on new product development and research, frequent technological updating, elaborate marketing programs to "sell" financial services, and the use of strategic planning is a carryover from manufacturing and industrial firms, which have used such techniques for decades. There is a growing awareness in the financial marketplace that the challenges and techniques of managing a financial institution are not fundamentally different from those of managing any other business firm. The products are different, but the methods of control and decision-making are essentially the same.

SOCIAL, ECONOMIC, AND DEMOGRAPHIC TRENDS AFFECTING THE FINANCIAL SYSTEM OF THE FUTURE

We must recognize too that much of what is happening in the financial sector today is a response to broad social, economic, and demographic trends that span generations. These trends are affecting not just financial institutions, but *all* institutions in every corner of society and in nearly every nation on the globe. As summarized in Exhibit 30–2, these fundamental social, economic, and demographic forces today include an aging population with new attitudes toward investing and borrowing money and new financial service requirements. The fastest growing segment of the U.S. population, for example, is middle-aged adults over 45 years old, led by dramatic increases expected in numbers of people over 65 years of age. In contrast, people in younger age groups, especially those under 30 years of age, are expected to decline significantly as a percentage of the U.S. and world populations.

The basic family unit is also changing, with reduced numbers of adults choosing marriage and traditional two-parent households as their preferable life style. More and more women (including women with young children) are entering the labor force each year and more households are choosing not to have children or not to have large families. The U.S. fertility rate (measured by the number of children the average adult woman will bear) declined about 35 percent between the 1960s and the 1980s. The highest divorce rate in history marks many industrialized nations, and more people are choosing to live alone or to marry much later in life. Single-parent families have soared in numbers and as a percentage of the population with associated increases in the poverty rate.

While many of these demographic trends—for example, the high divorce rate and falling birth rate—have slowed recently, most demographers do not anticipate a significant reversal anytime soon. So there will be demands for new forms of housing, for day care facilities and childcare programs, for flexible work schedules, and for both improved and less expensive medical care. The result is a new matrix of financial-service needs and demands, including new long-term savings vehicles, smaller and shorter-term mortgage and installment loans, more venture capital for small new businesses,

Exhibit 30–2   **Key Economic, Social, and Demographic Trends Affecting Financial Markets and Institutions Today and Tomorrow**

1. Aging of the population worldwide, altering public attitudes toward saving, investment, borrowing, and consumption.
2. More and more women entering the labor force and fewer people choosing marriage and two-parent families with children as their preferred life style. With lower birth rates, fewer entry-level workers will be available in the future, and there will be more older workers in the labor force.
3. Increasingly service-oriented economies in the United States and other industrialized nations, with significant shifts in employment and capital and changing needs for credit and other financial services to match the unique needs of service industries.
4. Accelerated technological change and increasing use of automation and computer-assisted production and delivery of goods and services, requiring wide dissemination of computer skills.
5. An explosion of information related to the ongoing technological revolution, bringing the results of research and new ideas more rapidly to businesses and their customers.
6. An increasing emphasis on college education and advanced technical and professional training (especially in management, auditing, marketing and sales, financial services, electrical engineering, public relations, technical writing and editing, and health management), with declining numbers of jobs available for clerical and blue collar workers.
7. Increasing internationalization of economies and societies, related to the acceleration in technology and improvements in communication and transportation systems, promoting increased interdependence among businesses and governments in all parts of the world. More coordination in the policies and programs of individual nations will be needed.
8. Intensified competition in all industries and occupations, related to improvements in communication and transportation, leading to a proliferation of new goods and services and to consolidation—mergers and acquisitions—in business organizations and governmental institutions for greater stability and to withstand the risks of introducing new products, methods, and services.
9. Decentralization of political power and business decision-making toward leaner, more efficient, and more localized business and governmental units, with key decisions increasingly being made by interacting groups or coalitions of managers, workers, and citizens who will be affected by those decisions.
10. Increased role for the private marketplace in directing resources, production, career choices, and the allocation of goods and services.

and new credit packages to meet transportation, medical, and educational needs.

Added to the demographic changes are broad *economic* trends. For example, manufacturing industries are being displaced in importance by service industries that are creating most of the new jobs and have their own unique financing needs. In this increasingly service-oriented economy we are seeing accelerated technological changes in the form of automation, telecommunications, and biotechnology that have created the need for new kinds of credit and risk protection. These recent technological innovations have led to an explosion of information and research, with increasingly rapid dissemination of information around the globe. The computer and related electronic devices have transformed the economy from primary reliance on manufacturing to a system centered around the processing and transfer of information—literally an information revolution. In turn, the wider and faster dissemination of information has contributed to a growing internationalization of markets that spurs competition even more and heightens the need for international political cooperation. Increasingly, too, there is an emphasis on decentralized decision-making and group consensus to guide critical political and business decisions, and pressure for a stronger role for free markets to make many decisions that in the past were left to government.

These social, economic, and demographic trends offer new opportunities and new markets but also new risks to financial service institutions trying to position themselves for the future. So powerful are these trends that none can be ignored by management and owners of financial institutions today. The choice now for those who work in or use the services of the financial system is to recognize and adapt to these trends or be swept away in their wake. More than ever before, it is a time for careful consideration and effective planning.

THE CHALLENGES AND OPPORTUNITIES PRESENTED BY RECENT TRENDS IN THE ECONOMY, SOCIETY, AND THE FINANCIAL SYSTEM

There seems little question now that the trends mentioned above will continue into the foreseeable future. Their momentum is strong now; it will take a major cataclysm, such as another Great Depression, a major war, or perhaps a resurgence of severe inflation, to turn them around. But we must recognize that these changes and trends have unleashed new problems of their own—great unresolved issues that must somehow be dealt with by the financial system of the future.

Among the most pressing issues that will shape tomorrow's financial institutions and markets are these:

1. How can we assure the financial strength of major financial institutions and restore ailing institutions to health in order to preserve and promote public confidence in both financial institutions and the financial markets?

2. If, in contrast to the 1970s and early 1980s, inflation and interest rates remain relatively low and moderate in the future, how can financial institutions and markets adjust to this new environment, preserving their profitability and sustaining their growth.

3. How will new technology affect the design and delivery of future financial services, and how can financial institutions prepare for technological change?

4. Which financial services will be supplied by different financial institu-

tions in the future (will banks be selling insurance, while insurance companies market checking accounts)?

5. If financial institutions continue to grow in size and complexity, offering more services in more markets, how can such diversity be successfully coordinated and managed?

6. As technology changes, what methods of distributing financial services will be most effective and efficient, and which will fall by the wayside? For example, must *all* financial institutions offer a full range of services and "one-stop" convenience for the customer?

7. What role must the vestiges of regulation play in the future? Will there be a need in some quarters for more regulation to promote equity, safety, or other social objectives? What exactly should the regulator's role be?

8. As the tax system is changed (as happened to the U.S. federal income tax system in 1986, for example), how will financial institutions be affected? What adjustments will they need to make?

We turn to these critical issues in the sections that follow.

Dealing with Risk in the Financial System: Assuring the Strength and Viability of Financial Institutions

Importance of Public Confidence. The money and capital markets and the financial institutions that operate within them depend crucially upon public confidence. The financial system works to channel scarce loanable funds (credit) to their most productive uses only if a substantial proportion of individuals and businesses are willing to save and entrust those savings to one or more financial institutions and if other businesses and individuals are willing to rely upon the financial system to provide funding to support their consumption and investment activities.

When any financial institution fails or develops serious financial problems that reach public notice, the public's confidence in *other* financial institutions locally, regionally, even globally, is damaged. If the institution is large relative to its market area or if its problems are believed by the public to be general in nature, rather than specific to one institution, they can result in a smaller flow of savings through *all* financial institutions and restrictions on the total availability of credit. Jobs and economic growth will be threatened.

Consequences of Reduced Public Confidence. There seems little question that the public regards financial institutions as less secure today than was true even a decade ago. Periodic recessions, the stresses and strains of recurring bouts of severe inflation, the record numbers of failed banks, S&Ls, and other financial institutions, and volatile swings in stock prices have all taken their toll in public esteem. Periodic "flights to quality" by investors have been more and more frequent—as evidenced, for example, by the successful marketing of new safety-oriented financial products (such as government-security money market funds, insured brokerage accounts, reinsurance contracts, and broker-placed deposits). Financial service customers are more sensitive to both price and the risk of losing their funds and therefore less loyal in dealing with any one institution. They are more inclined to withdraw their funds at the slightest hint of trouble.

Loss of public confidence not only produces adverse consequences for the individual financial institution, but also damages the *efficiency* of the financial service process itself. A flight of funds from financial institutions reduces their operating volume and makes them less efficient in using resources. That portion of the public continuing to rely on the financial system for credit, insurance, savings, and other services is forced to pay a higher price for less quantity and quality.

Ways to Promote Public Confidence. How can we assure the continued strength and viability of existing institutions and restore public confidence? Both governmental and private responses *may* offer effective remedies. Governments, especially the federal government, have taken steps in recent years to ensure the safety and soundness of major financial institutions and to protect the public's funds. For example, when federal deregulation of depository institutions was launched nationwide in 1980 with passage of the Depository Institutions Deregulation and Monetary Control Act, Congress anticipated public concern for the safety of its funds and raised federal deposit insurance maximums from $40,000 to $100,000 per depositor. These insurance maximums surely will have to be increased in the future, and perhaps even indexed to inflation.

Why couldn't the federal insurance idea be extended to include other financial instruments in which the public saves its money, such as life insurance policies or hospitalization insurance coverage? This is *not* a revolutionary idea. For example, there is already a federal guarantee program for pension plans that was launched in 1974 with passage of the Employee Retirement Income and Security Act (ERISA). There are federal guarantees of pools of securities purchased or assembled by financial institutions, such as the mortgage-backed securities program that has helped bolster the ailing S&L industry in recent years.

One problem with the insurance idea must first be resolved: how can we avoid distorting private risk-taking decisions by managers of financial institutions that often result from government insurance programs? Federal deposit insurance programs, for example, have protected small depositors, but led many banks and thrifts to accept greater risk because deposit insurance premiums are the same for *all* depository institutions. Thus, more risky institutions tend to be subsidized by less risky institutions, encouraging greater risk-taking and more failures. One idea currently being debated is to tie the size of government insurance premiums directly to the amount of risk taken on so that risk exposure to the federal insurance fund becomes the determinant of the cost of the federal insurance. One unresolved problem here is that we don't know for sure how to measure the failure risk of a financial institution accurately. Moreover, private entrepreneurs have a high degree of skill, judging by past history, in finding loopholes in regulatory formulas and procedures.

Another step government can take is to impose *minimum equity capital requirements* on all or most financial industries. The stockholders' equity in each financial institution provides a cushion to absorb short-term losses until management can correct weaknesses or develop new strategies to deal with external problems that may have caused the losses. In this instance the burden of controlling risk would be vested in the stockholders of a financial institution, who must supply high-cost capital if the institution suffers too many losses and face increased risk to their capital funds.

Minimum statutory capital requirements have already been imposed upon U.S. commercial banks as a result of the passage of the International Lending and Supervision Act of 1983. Prior to passage of this law, banks were expected to hold capital roughly in line with "average" levels for the industry and size group in which each bank fell. However, because the average ratio of capital to assets tended to decline over time, many banks were taking advantage of this trend and allowing their capital to erode relative to the assets and deposits it was designed to protect. While setting minimum requirements for all or most financial institutions is arbitrary and tends to punish more conservatively managed institutions for the "sins" of the more reckless ones, it does help to avoid weakening the cushion of financial protection that capital affords a financial institution. One compromise plan is to require only those financial institutions with excessive risk to add additional capital protection. Such a solution, however, presumes we really do know how to measure the portfolio risk of a financial institution—a fact not yet in evidence.

Private Sector Responses to the Safety Issue. Can the private financial sector satisfactorily ensure its own financial strength (and the public confidence that supports it)? Is the *market* a competent police mechanism? In theory at least, the private marketplace *is* its own regulator. Financial institutions choosing to accept greater risk in managing and using their customers' funds must pay the penalty for risk that the market imposes— a higher cost for any funds raised and often a less reliable supply of funds when capital market investors display a heightened sensitivity to risky investments. Thus, the financial markets will squeeze the earnings of more risky institutions as their funding costs rise.

One of the most important ways the private market is dealing with greater risk of failure and loss of customer funds today is by encouraging the development of *larger* institutions that diversify themselves, both geographically and by service line, to spread risk over a greater number of markets and a larger customer base. This has been most evident lately in the rise of interstate banking in the United States. By the late 1980s more than 40 states had authorized entry, now or in the future, by outside banking organizations, usually with reciprocal agreements that their own banks would be extended the same interstate branching privileges. Many financial experts predict that within a decade all the remaining federal and state barriers to interstate banking will fall and the nation will move rapidly toward a system of two or three dozen dominant banking organizations.

This trend toward interstate operations will encompass not only banks and other financial firms that traditionally have served broad regional and national markets (such as insurance companies, finance companies, and brokerage firms), but also smaller and more locally oriented institutions, such as credit unions and savings and loan associations. The result will be to intensify competition in thousands of local markets, often with the *same* competitors meeting each other in one market after another. Smaller financial service companies, lacking the capital to expand, will gradually be absorbed, though firms in rural areas and smaller towns are likely to survive as independent organizations.

Developing Better Tools to Deal with Risk. A second way for private financial institutions to deal with risk in the financial system is to develop and use better risk-management tools. Managers of successful institutions today must become intimately familiar with such risk management tools as these:

1. *Zero coupon securities,* which do not pay interest, but can be tailored in maturity to the investor's investment horizon.
2. *Gap management,* which permits a financial manager to compare the maturities and repricing opportunities that exist between an institution's asset portfolio and its portfolio of liabilities.
3. *Duration analysis,* which offers the financial manager a more complete picture of the exposure to interest rate changes faced by his or her institution.
4. *Interest rate swaps,* which permit two or more institutions to trade interest payments on some of their debt obligations in order to better match inflows and outflows of cash.
5. *Financial futures,* which allow financial institutions' managers to hedge the yields on their loans and investments and the interest costs of their sources of funds against fluctuating interest rates.
6. *Option contracts,* which protect both hedging and profit opportunities from fluctuating interest rates.

While these existing tools are useful, *more* new tools must be added to the financial manager's arsenal in order to provide more effective hedging against the many different forms of risk that will confront financial institutions in the years ahead.

The Information Problem. Unfortunately, relying exclusively on the marketplace to assure the strength of financial institutions is open to serious question. Given adequate information, the market can correctly value the securities of individual financial institutions and correctly rank-order the minimum returns each of those securities must earn to retain capital and remain viable in the long run. But does the financial marketplace receive all the information it needs to generate optimal decisions? The answer clearly is no. Depository institutions, for example, still provide only limited information to depositors and buyers of their securities. Key information regarding the quality of their loans and security investments and the adequacy of their capital is classified and known in detail only to federal and state supervisory agencies.

Capital market investors can only approximately price the securities of financial institutions that do not fully disclose their financial condition and prospects. A classic case in point was the $4 billion Franklin National Bank of New York City, whose weakened financial condition apparently was not fully known by many large depositors for a period of several months before it failed. Serious consideration needs to be given to greater disclosure to the public of the risk exposure of individual financial institutions, especially for depositories and those institutions holding retirement savings. In combination with a strong, risk-adjusted insurance program, increased public disclosure would let in the searchlight of public opinion and unleash the powerful economic force of informed investing to more effectively control risk-taking by financial institutions.

The Implications of Relatively Low Interest Rates and Inflation for Financial Institutions

Like any business firm, a financial institution must adapt to a changing market environment if it is to survive and prosper. Perhaps nowhere in the financial marketplace has this been more evident than in the area of interest rates and inflation. The 1950s and early 1960s were a period of low to nonexistent inflation (with the exception of the Korean war period) and low interest rates that were also relatively stable. The late 1960s and 1970s, however, ushered in a period of rampant inflation, exacerbated by the Vietnam war and record federal government budget deficits. Financial institutions and the customers they served were faced with a whole new economic and financial environment—one that tended to favor consumption spending and penalize saving, to favor borrowers, and to present greater risks to lenders. The yields on financial instruments, especially corporate bonds and stocks, did not generally keep pace with inflation, and thousands of savers turned from financial assets to real assets, including diamonds, rare paintings, farmland, crude oil, and gold.

The declining attractiveness of financial instruments to many savers, coupled with inflated credit demands, created a serious "funding gap" for financial institutions. Conventional savings plans and other fundraising services were less attractive to the public, forcing banks, insurance companies, and other credit-granting institutions to develop new and more expensive fundraising services and to offer higher and higher yields on conventional savings instruments in order to bring in more funds. Many institutions were forced to rely more heavily upon expensive short-term borrowings in the money market (liability management techniques). Inflation raised the cost of funds for financial institutions and narrowed the profit margin between asset yields and borrowing costs. It also created a *capital shortage* problem for banks and other financial institutions because the squeeze on margins limited the availability of retained earnings to strengthen equity capital. With thinner capital positions, more financial institutions were prone to failure.

Inflation not only increased the risk of failure among financial institutions, but also generated another element of uncertainty in financial institutions' management—the risk of unexpected changes in interest rates due to unexpected inflation. When inflation is expected, lenders simply raise their loan rates high enough to offset the decline in the purchasing power of their earnings. But what about *unexpected* inflation? A lender might suffer an erosion in both the real value of funds loaned to a borrower and in any interest payments due because he or she was unable to adjust for unexpected inflation. This proved to be a serious problem in the 1970s and early 1980s because the interest costs on funds sources drawn upon by financial institutions, spurred upward by inflation, rose much faster than anticipated. Financial institutions' net earnings were not only squeezed, but became significantly more volatile.

A New Reduced-Inflation Environment. The middle and late 1980s ushered in a very different inflation scenario—a markedly lower annual rate of price increases. In some sectors, particularly in farm commodities and petroleum, actual deflation set in, with significant price-level decreases that benefitted buyers of these commodities but resulted in numerous business bankruptcies and substantial unemployment. In theory, just as financial institutions earlier were adversely affected by rapid inflation, it might be expected that the much slower inflation and sporadic deflation of the 1980s would be beneficial to them, widening or at least stabilizing the profit margins and stock values of financial institutions. Moreover, the credit risk exposure of lending institutions presumably would be lessened because their borrowing customers should experience both lower average borrowing costs and more stable borrowing costs.

Unfortunately, the lower inflation of recent years has ushered in its own unique set of problems. These problems have arisen because of the fundamental *causes* of this slowing in inflationary pressures. One key causal factor is a more slowly growing economy. While the costs of deposits and other funds sources have fallen dramatically in recent years, the demand for credit has also declined, so that loan revenues grow more slowly. This limits potential earnings and makes cost control by financial institutions operating in a deflationary environment as important as cost controls were in an inflationary environment.

The burden of reducing inflation has not fallen evenly upon all sectors of the economy. Some sectors, especially agriculture, oil and natural gas, mining, and basic manufacturing (especially steel and autos), have borne more than their share. Indeed, most of the dramatic decline in the U.S. inflation rate in the mid-1980s was traceable to two elements—declining food prices and collapsing world petroleum prices. These declining sectors presented severe credit risk problems for many banks and other financial institutions, resulting in an acceleration in their failure rates. And the long-term outlook for these sectors continues to be depressed due to increased foreign competition, slower economic growth worldwide, and a huge oversupply problem exacerbated by advancing technology.

Will subdued inflation continue into the future? Many economists and financial analysts fear that the answer to that question is no. For one thing, the current period of deflation seems to rest on a comparatively narrow base—market weakness in selected commodities and a glut in residential and commercial structures. Once these sectors recover, it is argued, there will be little except the determination of government policymakers (particularly the Federal Reserve System) to stem the tide of renewed inflation. Of course, all the evidence does not point in the same direction. An aging population and a more slowly growing economy, for example, would seem to suggest a period of relative price stability into the foreseeable future. Still, it is difficult to argue with the broad sweep of history. The Western world has been experiencing rapid and more or less continuous inflation since the beginning of the Industrial Revolution, nearly three centuries ago. The building blocks of that inflation—expanding consumer demand, concentrations of economic power, and the growth of government activity in the economy—are still with us.

Importance of Financial Flexibility. If rapid inflation rekindles itself, financial institutions will need to be better prepared for it than was true of the last inflationary round. The key to weathering future inflationary storms is *financial flexibility*—the ability of financial institutions to shift portfolios and operating strategies to stay abreast of price-level changes. Investments will need to be shifted toward inflation-hedged assets (such as selected common stock, real estate, commodities, and collectibles), minimizing losses in that process and maximizing opportunities. Operating costs, especially wages and salaries and interest costs, will soar out of control once again unless they are skillfully managed with particular attention to more effective use of electronic technology, productivity enhancement, and strategic planning.

Impact of New Technology on the Design and Delivery of Financial Services

The Information Revolution. Providing financial services to the public involves nothing more nor less than the storage and transfer of *financial information*. A checking account, for example, merely conveys the information that an individual or business firm has claim to the assets managed by a bank or thrift institution. The writing of a check is simply a new information item designating what amount of funds are to be removed from one account and transferred to another account. Similarly, an insurance policy is nothing more than a collection of bits of information on the rights and obligations of the policyholder and the rights and obligations of the insurer. The advent of the computer has taught us that all these pieces of information can be stored and transferred in microseconds via computer and through electronic wire and satellite networks which, in addition to speed, offer the potential for greater accuracy and completeness of information and lower cost.

The current technological revolution in information storage and transfer is not only here to stay, but is continuing to develop at an accelerating pace. Newer, smaller, and faster computer systems appear almost daily, and new techniques for transferring information, such as fiber optics, are constantly under development and refinement.

Recent Technological Advances. One area of strong future growth will be in *networking* (systems integration) in which computers are linked to each other. A related development is the fifth generation computer which will use parallel processing—the simultaneous execution of many different programming instructions with multiple processors—rather than the traditional sequential processing that characterizes most computer systems today. Once compatible software is developed, these new machines will store and process information several thousand times faster than today's sequential systems. Still more promising is the continuing research on artificial intelligence (AI) systems which would permit computers to make judgmental decisions once they are properly programmed with logic systems and probability tables.

The wave of the future in carrying out financial transactions and in sending and receiving information between financial institutions and their customers seems clearly at this point to be fiber optics. Finger-width fiber optic cables transmit large volumes of data and images (nearly 600,000 bits of information per second with current technology) through bursts of laser light, with virtually no distortion over great distances. Computers can be networked and large databases as well as TV and motion pictures can be transferred in seconds along a fiber optic network. Plans announced thus far call for in excess of 60,000 miles of fiber networks in the United States alone and a similar rapid expansion abroad. Because of the fidelity, speed, low installation costs, and virtually inexhaustible capacity of fiber optics, this technique should gradually displace older payments and data transfer systems used by financial institutions, allowing managers more easily to reach distant financial customers, to keep track of far-flung branches, and to react more quickly to economic and financial problems.

Communications through fiber optics will increasingly be supplemented by video conferences via satellite involving both financial institution managers and their customers. Management strategy meetings and presentations to corporate and individual customers can be beamed into local hotels, business meeting rooms, and corporate offices. This medium will make it easier for financial institutions to bring in outside experts to help sell their services to promising customers, using an information approach to product advertising. Through this space age communications channel, managers of financial institutions will have less need to travel to conferences and to have direct contacts with customers.

Public Attitudes and Cost. Admittedly, the adjustment of people and institutions to the unfolding technological revolution is much slower than the revolution itself. Many consumers and businesses still prefer the security and privacy of cash and checkbook transactions. *Personal* communications between financial institutions and their customers will always be a significant element in the delivery of services. However, the cost of these traditional methods is rising, and their advantages relative to electronic methods are becoming less significant (e.g., the long-standing advantage to the check-writer of float, which delays the loss of funds from a checking account, is gradually being eliminated by recent Federal Reserve actions).

Preparing for New Technologies. *All* financial institutions, large and small, must be prepared for the continuing spread of new information technology. Otherwise, their competitors will wrest the high ground of new markets and new services from them. But there are major challenges in this technological high ground for financial institutions. The challenges include these:

1. Customer access to financial information and the transfer of financial information must be as user-friendly and as nonthreatening as possible, with the stress on convenience and compatibility with customer needs for information and for privacy.

2. Operating costs and therefore service prices must be kept low relative to more conventional, paper-based and in-person information transfers so that there is sufficient economic incentive for the customer to use the most cost-efficient information systems.

3. Sufficient technological flexibility must be built in and sunk costs minimized so that, as new and improved technologies of service production and delivery appear, they can be quickly and smoothly

pressed into service in order to keep each institution current and competitive.

4. Finally, auditing and internal control programs must be upgraded and strengthened to reduce the probability of loss due to computer errors or computer fraud.

The Changing Mix of Suppliers of Financial Services

The Walls Come Tumbling Down. Who will offer the financial services of the future? When the customer wishes to purchase a life insurance policy or a checking account, who will be the most likely provider? One thing that is clear now is that the traditional walls between different financial industries, between different suppliers of financial services, have already crumbled. For example, Travelers Insurance sells cash management accounts to its customers competitive with those offered by banks and securities' firms, while the Dreyfus Corporation, a securities firm, offers consumer loans, an array of credit card plans, insurance coverage, checkable deposits, a nationwide automated teller network, mutual fund investments, and financial counseling through personal financial centers. Sears Roebuck has its feet solidly planted in consumer credit, insurance, security and real estate brokering, and property development. Most of the remaining vestiges of the traditional distinctions between one type of financial institution and another undoubtedly will be swept away in the years ahead, leading to further blurring of function in the financial institutions' sector.

Price Sensitivity and Intense Local Competition. Life insurance policies, checking accounts, and other financial services will be purchased from the financial firm offering the lowest price and best nonprice features (including the lowest transactions and information costs). That low-cost supplier may be different from market area to market area, depending upon the level and intensity of competition in each local marketplace. In smaller cities and rural communities the local bank or banks may turn out to be the most likely and most advantageous supplier of many of the financial services needed, as was the case in many local communities before elaborate regulatory restrictions were placed on the banking industry in the 1930s. Larger urban markets, in contrast, will continue to be characterized by multiple suppliers locked in an intense competitive struggle, with frequent changes of price and nonprice terms offered to the consumer. Moreover, financial service firms will face a customer increasingly sensitized to differing terms of sale and more ready to transfer his or her business to the cheapest source of the quality of service desired.

Importance of Established Delivery Systems. Because cost-control and productivity will be key factors for the future success of financial service firms, financial institutions with extensive service delivery systems already in place will have a distinct competitive advantage. This feature will clearly favor banking institutions with established networks of branch offices, ATMs, point-of-sale terminals, and home and office computer–financial institution linkages. These cost and productivity advantages will lead to still more mergers and consolidations of smaller financial companies, especially in the most intensely competitive urban markets.

Bank and Insurance Companies: A Possible Alliance?   Because of the superior delivery capabilities of many branch bank and holding company systems, some financial experts, such as McDonald (1985) and Randall (1985), have argued that bankers and insurance companies are "logical allies" for the future. Bankers can contribute an established customer base for distributing insurance services and perhaps higher retail margins, while insurers can offer essential product and marketing expertise. Bankers may be in a good position to supply insurance services in local communities because of their credibility, frequent customer contact, low-cost delivery systems, and conveniently located offices. Several options may be open to banks in delivering insurance products in a given local market, such as acquiring insurance companies, becoming partners with insurance companies, renting lobby space to insurers, creating insurance brokerage departments, or selling lists of customers' names and addresses to insurance firms. McDonald and other financial analysts believe that, whatever delivery method becomes popular in the future, insurance will become the biggest new profit center for both banks and nonbank thrift institutions by the turn of the century.

New Financial Institutions and Instruments.   We must also recognize that the future, like the past, will usher in new financial institutions to deal with the emerging needs of the public. For example, secondary (resale) markets for many traditionally illiquid loans and securities will emerge so that lenders of funds can readily sell their older assets and gain the cash needed to make new loans. Prominent examples will include resale of better-quality loans to businesses (including small and medium-size business credits), consumer loans, and farm loans. Just as high-grade common stocks are traded on national exchanges, exchange trading of top-quality mortgages will also become a reality. These unfolding new markets will require new financial institutions and new financial services from existing institutions, especially brokers and dealers to facilitate the marketing of many types of loans and installment contracts.

Securitization.   There will be a parallel need for new institutions to facilitate the continuing trend toward securitization of many of the assets held by lending institutions. The success of mortgage-backed securities, first offered in 1970, and collateralized mortgage obligations (CMOs), first offered in 1983, has spurred interest in raising loanable funds by selling shares in other assets held by lending institutions, such as pools of high-quality commercial and consumer loans, agricultural notes, and government securities. A good example of this explosive trend was First Boston Corporation's 1986 offering through a special purpose subsidiary of $3.2 billion in securities backed by GMAC's low-interest car loans—the biggest single security offering in U.S. history. Today there are loan-backed securities collateralized by commercial and residential mortgage loans, credit card receivables, auto loans, mobile home loans, computer and truck leases, and Small Business Administration loans. The future is likely to bring even greater use of loan-backed securities because this device opens up an additional funding source for financial institutions, adding liquidity and diversification to the loan portfolio even for small loans that often do not have a ready resale market.

Housing-Secured Credit. Other financial services and financial instruments expected to see rapid growth in the future include home equity loans and housing-secured credit lines (stimulated by new federal tax laws and the impact of inflation on residential property values) and home-remodeling loans (spurred on by the fact that close to one third of permanent residences in the United States are now more than 40 years old). Not only will these expanding lending opportunities encourage the development of new financial firms, but they will spur on existing institutions, especially banks and savings and loans, who have accumulated years of experience in property appraisals, real estate law, and the revolving housing-secured credit lines that many consumers will demand in the years ahead. Indeed, these institutions are likely to tie home equity lending to their established credit card and checking-account programs, giving consumers access to instant revolving credit at lower interest rates and in larger volume than is currently available under conventional consumer loan programs.

Consumer Cash Management Services. A related development will be an upsurge in the demand for consumer cash management services. Patterned after the highly successful Cash Management Account (CMA) developed by Merrill Lynch in the 1970s, both new and existing financial institutions are moving rapidly to develop lower-cost consumer cash management services that combine access to a credit line, security brokerage services, and financial planning options with checking-account privileges. While today's successful programs have been confined largely to high-income households, advancing technology, falling geographic and legal barriers, the greater interest sensitivity of households, and the growth of larger consumer-oriented financial institutions will combine to produce low-cost cash management packages for middle-income customers. The potential market in this field is enormous, but the keys to tapping that market successfully will be efficiency and effective cost control.

Management Coordination within Diversified Financial Institutions: The Problem of Bigness. As more and more financial firms offer wider menus of financial services, they will become more complex businesses. The span of management control will have to increase to encompass more departments and more affiliated and subsidiary firms offering different services. Management problems will multiply, centering upon difficulties in coordination and control over such facets of daily operations as service quality, pricing, production costs, management objectives, employee benefits, recruiting, and portfolio selection. Failure to coordinate and control these activities will weaken the diversified financial institution's performance at a time when competition is increasing. Many diversified firms will have difficulty attracting new capital and some will fail, forcing the sale of more marketable subsidiaries and service lines (downsizing). Indeed, we are already seeing a trend in this direction among major diversified bank holding companies and financial conglomerates as unprofitable affiliates are spun off into the hands of new owners who may be able to manage them more efficiently.

Steps toward Better Management Coordination. The difficulties of coordination and control among what are likely to be much larger and more diversified financial institutions in the future will necessitate a number of key steps for financial institutions' managers. These include:

1. The necessity of seeking management and staff personnel more thoroughly trained in coordination and control skills, including a continuation of the trend evident in recent years of hiring more college graduates and people with advanced professional business degrees.

2. The necessity for strengthening internal auditing procedures and improving management information systems (MIS) as each institution grows in size and/or expands its service menu.

3. The continuing evaluation of all affiliate and subsidiary firms, profit centers, and service functions to determine their contribution to the financial firm's goals.

Not all diversified financial service companies will be successful in an intensely competitive, increasingly unforgiving marketplace. Not all customers will demand and pay for "one-stop" convenience. Not all customers will willingly acquiesce in the depersonalization of delivery systems. There will remain numerous profitable opportunities for narrowly focused financial firms that do a few jobs well, that recognize the economic value of sensitivity and responsiveness to the unique service needs of each individual customer, and that find better methods for improving employee productivity and keeping operating costs under a tight rein. The most successful financial service suppliers—both those highly diversified and those narrowly focused—will be those who do not hesitate to dispose of service firms and service lines that are not contributing positively to their planned objectives.

The Future of Alternative Distribution Systems

The channels through which financial services are delivered and distributed to the public are changing rapidly. There is, on the one hand, the rapid spread of electronic delivery systems, represented by automated tellers in stores and shopping centers, point-of-sale terminals, and video banking and shopping services at home, in the office, and in other convenient locations. But other service-delivery systems, including traditional personalized ones, are likely to exist side by side with electronic delivery methods.

What Future Service Delivery Systems Must Do. Financial service delivery and distribution systems in the future will depend for their growth and survival upon several factors:

1. Their ability to keep transactions and information costs low for their users.
2. Their ability to protect customer privacy.
3. Their ability to ease the information burden faced by the customer who is confronted by a diverse and ever-widening range of service options and service providers.
4. Their ability to deliver speed and accuracy and simplify customer recordkeeping.
5. Their capacity for personalization in dealing with the individual customer.

The Continued Spread of Franchising. The franchising of financial services, with larger companies producing financial services and smaller firms delivering them to the customer, will grow in popularity. This will be true especially of services dependent on high volume for profitability. Examples include security brokerage, security and insurance underwriting, credit evaluation and information processing, and real estate brokerage. Franchising will allow smaller firms to update their service menus and avoid complete erosion of their market shares in thousands of neighborhood and community markets across the nation.

Electronic Delivery. At the same time, teleconferences and satellite-associated video conferences will permit even the most remote financial institutions to reach into innumerable local markets, explaining their services, answering questions, and moving to "close the deal." Increasingly durable electronic sales vehicles will pose a growing challenge to locally oriented financial institutions, especially smaller banks, credit unions, and thrifts, forcing them to broaden their service menus, and become more efficient and more conscious of changing customer needs.

The Future Need for Regulation

More Deregulation. The trend toward deregulation of the financial sector is likely to continue, driven by the capacity and desire of unregulated financial firms to grow and expand their beachhead within the financial system. In the U.S., Congress and the states will be under continuing pressure to amend and relax regulations against product-line diversification (the development of new services) and against geographic diversification (the ability of banks and other financial service firms to cross state borders and other territorial boundaries to offer their services in distant markets). If Congress and the states do not act to free the financial institutions they supervise from many of today's restrictions, nonregulated financial intermediaries will move in and eventually drive the more closely regulated institutions from one market after another.

The most likely fields where deregulation will occur will be these:

1. Reducing barriers to geographic diversification, including restrictions against branching across state, city, and county lines and against penetrating foreign markets.

2. Reducing barriers to product line diversification, allowing banks to offer security underwriting and brokerage services, insurance underwriting and sales, and real estate development and brokerage services and insurance companies to offer more payments services and credit plans to individuals and businesses.

3. Liberalizing some portfolio restrictions on assets, liabilities, and capital that lead to regulatory inequities among financial institutions and dampen their profitability and growth of capital, while maintaining strict national and international standards for minimum amounts of capital in order to protect customers.

Regulations That Could Grow. But all the regulations will not be done away with. Indeed, regulation is shifting to new ground, with a new emphasis in some cases and a reemphasis on traditional regulatory goals in others. There will continue to be great concern for the safety of the public's savings and for maintaining public confidence in the smooth and efficient functioning of financial institutions and the markets in which they operate.

Disclosure. One important area of emphasis for the future will be financial disclosure. Financial institutions will be expected to divulge their financial condition and performance to investors and to the customers they serve in order to promote better financial decision-making. A good example of this trend is the U.S. Competitive Equality Banking Act of 1987 that requires increased public disclosure of deposit terms and withdrawal penalties, credit card charges, and home equity credit terms, thus extending the loan dis-

Exhibit 30–3   **Key Areas Where Regulation of Financial Services and Institutions Probably Will Continue to Be Important**

Financial disclosure to savers, investors, and borrowers in order to encourage greater market discipline

Fair and equal legal and regulatory treatment of different financial institutions, especially in the services they may offer, capital requirements, tax exposure, and mix of assets and liabilities permitted

Social responsibility in allocating scarce funds and supplying other financial services

Protection of disadvantaged groups that could be significantly damaged by concentrated financial power and reduced competition for financial services, especially household customers, small businesses, and agriculture

closure principles first laid down during the 1960s in the Truth-in-Lending Act.

There is potential gain here as well as potential risk. With greater disclosure more financial institutions will be subject to the risk of public disfavor, the withdrawal of capital, and the loss of customer accounts. Ultimately the discipline of the market will be unleashed to help insure prudent management and to control risk-taking, especially in making loans. However, more disclosure will enable both investors in and customers of financial institutions to make more intelligent decisions about expected return and risk and the most economical uses of available resources.

Social Responsibility. Another area of regulatory emphasis likely to grow in the future is the social responsibility of financial institutions. Even as conventional regulations are eased, the industry will find itself under increasing regulatory scrutiny concerning the equity and fairness of its use of resources and the availability and distribution of its services, particularly access to credit. For example, are all loan customers, particularly small businesses and consumers, treated the same way, given the same consideration, and subjected to the same credit standards? Is there any evience that the age, race, religion, neighborhood, or other irrelevant characteristics of a credit customer have entered into the decisions of what loans a financial institution has chosen to make and what loans it has chosen *not* to make?

Promoting a Level Playing Field. Fair and equal regulatory treatment of all financial institutions offering essentially the same services will continue to be a burning issue for law and regulation in future years. Bankers have labeled this the "level playing field" issue, and they will continue to be among its strongest advocates, pressing for more equal taxation of the earnings of different financial institutions and more equal powers to expand geographically without regard to territorial boundaries. This will require more international cooperation in regulation in the future as governments and central banks increasingly recognize their mutual dependence.

Crisis-Induced Regulation. As in the past, financial crises will undoubtedly usher in new forms of regulation. For example, concern over the "liability insurance crisis"—with property–casualty insurers saddled with record claims and suits from victims of toxic substances, professional negligence, and environmental damage—threatens to bring federal regulation to the insurance industry. Concern is growing in Congress over the degree of both the availability and the affordability of insurance coverage. Not unlikely for the future is the repeal of the McCarran-Ferguson Act, which prohibits federal oversight of private insurers.

Effects of New Federal Tax Laws

Goals of Tax Reform. The long and often acrimonious debate over federal income tax reform bore fruit in 1986 with the adoption of a comprehensive tax bill. The federal Tax Reform Act of 1986 had two widely advertised purposes:

1. To promote simplicity and equity in the income tax burdens borne by businesses and individuals so that tax rules are easy to understand and result in more individuals and institutions carrying their "fair share" of the rising cost of government.

2. To make tax rules less a factor in the public's saving and investment decisions, which have such a profound impact on growth and jobs in the economy, so that tax shelters will have a sound economic basis in the future and the nation's resources will be allocated more efficiently.

Both objectives are evident in all sections of the new tax law. For example, the goals of simplicity and equity are behind such provisions of the new law as the reduction of individual tax brackets from a dozen to only three and the requirement of a minimum tax for all covered individuals and businesses. The elimination of abusive tax shelters also serves both objectives, requiring all taxpayers to evaluate investments on their economic, not tax-avoidance, merits, with tax-sheltering deductions allowable only as an offset to real investment earnings.

The second goal of making taxes a less significant factor in saving and investment decisions may be seen in the new rules that limit the tax deductibility of individual retirement accounts (IRAs) and restrict the use of accelerated depreciation. Overall, personal savings should be stimulated due to lower personal tax rates. However, tax reform will probably not reduce the federal budget deficit because cuts in personal taxes are roughly counterbalanced by increases in corporate taxes.

Gainers and Losers. Recent changes in tax rules will affect financial institutions from many different directions. They will almost assuredly slow the growth of tax-sheltered savings plans and long-term savings programs. By lowering tax brackets it will make tax-exempt investments, such as municipal bonds and municipal bond funds, less attractive relative to taxable investments, though many analysts think municipals may be more attractive to some investors because they are one of the few tax shelters still available. Financial instruments offering greater capital gains potential, such as long-term and deeply discounted bonds and common stock, will become less attractive relative to new debt securities and other investments with limited capital gains potential.

Securities with high dividend and interest payouts will look better to individual investors with lower personal tax rates. This means that such financial instruments as corporate bonds, mortgage-backed securities, and federal and government-sponsored agency notes and certificates will experience gains in after-tax returns due to a combination of higher cash payouts and lower taxes on those payouts. Nonmortgage consumer loans will represent a less attractive market because their interest payments are no longer deductible, but interest payments on business loans, home mortgages, and investor margin accounts (if offset against investment income) will be tax deductible.

Lending institutions will need to reconsider the future direction of their loan programs. The attractiveness of lending to support the construction of single-family homes will increase relative to longer-term commercial real estate projects. Vacation homes will be less desirable lending targets. Shorter-term commercial loans will become more attractive relative to consumer cash and installment loans. Smaller businesses, too, look more desirable as loan customers because many are taxed at the personal marginal tax rates of their owners, and personal tax rates will be lower.

Possible Negative Effects of Tax Reform. Despite its sweeping changes, the 1986 tax bill did not solve all the problems of the nation's income tax code—nor even many of them. Respected economists fear that the new law will severely depress business investment and perhaps increase the chances of a prolonged recession. Other economists argue that the near-term effects of tax reform are largely unpredictable because it will set in motion behavioral changes, and no one can foresee confidently what these changes will be. In the long run, however, there should be beneficial effects on the economy due to better investment decisions, increased savings, and a more efficient allocation of resources. The greatest impact will probably fall on the manufacturing sector, which employs the largest volume of capital equipment and which will lose valuable depreciation allowances and investment tax credits. Cyclically sensitive industries, such as those producing capital goods, recreational vehicles, steel, and autos, will be at something of a disadvantage due to the loss of income-averaging benefits. The services sector (particularly retailing, computer software, and security brokerage) as a whole apparently will benefit, making service industry customers more desirable loan customers. However, financial service firms such as banks, real estate companies, and many insurance companies will lose key tax incentives.

Large banks (over $500 million in assets), for example, will no longer be able to take a direct tax deduction from operating revenues to build their bad-debt reserves (loan-loss provisions). Now such deductions can be made only when a loan is actually written off. Moreover, the larger banks must recapture loan-loss deductions made in earlier years over a four-year adjustment period. This change comes at a particularly inopportune moment when bank capitalization has been weakened for several years running due to slow-paying or uncollectible loans to energy producers, farmers, real estate developers, and international borrowers. Moreover, there is concern that these newest loan-loss rules will encourage banks to press for faster foreclosure on delinquent borrowers when they need bigger tax deductions.

Other potentially damaging provisions of the tax bill for banks include the loss of the permissible interest deduction for deposits and other borrowed funds used to buy municipal bonds. Because banks are one of the leading buyers of these state and local securities, this provision adversely affects local governments because it makes banks less avid buyers of their notes and bonds, driving up local government borrowing costs. Bank leasing programs will also be affected significantly by a loss of the investment tax credit on the equipment they buy and lease to business customers. Some portion of the traditional deduction banks were allowed to make against foreign income by deducting from that income the sum total of any taxes paid overseas (except for exempted nations) will be lost, which should reduce U.S. bank financing overseas (including support of U.S. exports) and hurt domestic banks in competition with foreign banks for a slice of global credit markets.

Possible Beneficial Effects. Offsetting at least some of these damages will be a possible increase in total domestic business investment due to lower corporate income tax rates, including the possibility that more foreign businesses will relocate to the United States, creating new customers for American banks. Moreover, the elimination of the favorable capital gains tax rate should make bank deposits more attractive relative to stocks and bonds. The result could be a sizable expansion of bank deposits, possibly at lower interest costs to the banks themselves. Deposits, stocks, bonds, and other financial assets will benefit over land, commodities, precious stones, and other hard assets as investment vehicles under tax reform.

Possible Impact on Thrifts and Mortgages. Tax reform is likely to have a major impact on the services offered by and the portfolio makeup of thrift institutions, such as savings and loan associations. For one thing, it will encourage nonbank thrifts to become even more like banks in their lending policies and loan portfolios. The new law gives thrifts only a 5 percent deduction from net income if they devote at least 60 percent of their assets to residential mortgage credit, compared to a 40 percent deduction (if more than 80 percent of their assets were dedicated to home mortgage loans) under the old law. Yet, by preserving the tax deduction for mortgage interest payments on a home and not for nonmortgage consumer borrowing, the public will be encouraged to buy new homes and borrow against the equity in their existing homes to make other purchases. Because this will tend to spur the demand for new homes while at the same time reducing the enthusiasm of traditional mortgage lending institutions for making home loans, tax reform may set in motion a sizable "funding gap" in the nation's housing market.

Residential mortgage rates will tend to rise higher than would otherwise be the case, spurring the entry of other financial institutions into home mortgage lending and into purchases of mortgage-backed securities (such as Ginnie Maes). Insurance companies, for example, which for a generation have been gradually reducing the overall size of their residential mortgage programs, may begin to expand these portfolios once again. At the same time, competition for nonmortgage consumer loans should intensify, making this market less attractive for new entrants and for lending institutions that historically have supplied most of the consumer installment and cash loans.

Insurance Companies and Tax Reform. Life insurers appear to have gained relative to other major financial institutions as a result of federal tax reform, though their tax burdens were increased significantly in earlier years.

Life insurers were largely left alone under the latest tax bill, letting the premiums paid by policyholders buying whole life policies accumulate as tax-sheltered cash values—one of the few remaining tax shelters left untouched by the latest tax law. However, the industry will need to be vigilant in future years on this issue, for tax proposals have a tendency to reappear again, particularly in periods when the government faces severe cash strains.

Property–casualty insurers should experience significantly higher taxes in the wake of the new law. The ability of these high-risk insurance carriers to defer premium income will be seriously eroded with speeded-up recognition of some premiums and delayed recognition of some claims. Several of that industry's firms will now face the minimum corporate tax, and others will be forced to pay some tax on their earnings from municipal bonds—features which, along with those mentioned above, are likely to slow the growth of the industry. This comes at a most inopportune moment, because the casualty insurance business has been struggling in recent years against a rising tide of claims and litigation involving medical malpractice, product liability, workers' compensation, nuclear accidents, and other insurance hazards that have ballooned costs and drained away earnings. It is likely that the revised tax code will simply make it harder for domestic insurers to attract capital and to fend off the growing numbers of foreign insurers striving to enter U.S. markets.

Regional Effects. Finally, there will be significant regional effects, with some parts of the nation benefitting and other regions losing, on balance, as the tax reform provisions are fully phased in. For example, the East and West Coasts, with their higher proportions of service firms, will probably be net gainers. The nation's troubled midsection, on the other hand, will likely face more tax problems due to its heavy involvement with the less favored manufacturing industries. Clearly these regional differences will set in motion shifts in the lending programs and services offered by financial institutions.

SUMMARY AND A LOOK FORWARD

We have spent a considerable portion of this chapter exploring the broad trends that are reshaping financial markets and institutions today—service innovation and proliferation, spreading deregulation, growing competition, and the evolution and consolidation of financial institutions. We have also glimpsed the broad social, economic, and demographic changes that are and will continue in the future to restructure financial services and the institutions that produce and deliver them—a changing population that is growing older; the expansion of service-oriented industries; advances in automation, telecommunications, and biotechnology; the information explosion; the internationalization of markets and business and political institutions; political and business decision-making by group consensus; and a growing role for market-based decisions regarding the distribution of resources and incomes.

Each of these trends must be dealt with by both management and investors in the financial sector and by the customers they serve. These trends call for new approaches and new skills—for example, greater knowledge of marketing and planning techniques, awareness of new technologies, and the capacity to filter and analyze a growing volume of information and translate that information into sound business decisions.

No one knows for sure what the financial system or financial institutions of the future will look like. Only the broadest outline seems reasonably clear at this point; the details remain hidden from view. It seems a reasonable guess to predict fewer, but larger and more highly diversified financial service firms, survivors of growing competition but more capable of withstanding the volatile fluctuations of an uncertain economy. Financial institutions must and will pay more attention to risk management and to the sales orientation of managements and employees. They will need to work harder to control expenses, to improve productivity, and to retain a more price-sensitive and quality-conscious customer. It will be an era of challenges and competition, of testing and turmoil, of openness and opportunity. An old Chinese curse says simply: "May you live in interesting times." Financial markets and institutions, the people they hire, and the people they serve will have many occasions to remember those prophetic words in the years that lie ahead.

STUDY QUESTIONS

1. List the principal trends in the economy, in society, and in population (demographics) that you believe will affect financial institutions and financial services the most over the next 5 years. How about the next 10 years? For each trend listed, describe at least one response the management of a financial service firm might make.

2. If you were managing a small bank or insurance agency in your local community, what future trends in financial services and financial institutions are likely to have the greatest impact on your institution? Why? What response or responses could you make to each trend you have listed?

3. Please prepare a good definition for each of the following key terms:
   a. Consolidation.
   b. Financial disclosure.
   c. Networking.
   d. Blurring of function.
   e. Securitization.
   f. Franchising.
   g. Downsizing.

SELECTED REFERENCES

Berry, Leonard L., and Thomas W. Thompson. "Relationship Banking Keeps Clients Returning." *Trusts and Estates*, November 1985, pp. 27–35.

Kane, Edward J. *The Gathering Crisis in Federal Deposit Insurance*. Cambridge, MA: MIT Press, 1985.

MacDonald, Robert. "Bankers and Insurers: Logical Allies." *The Bankers' Magazine*, January–February 1985, pp. 11–16.

Pavel, Christine. "Securitization." *Economic Perspectives*, Federal Reserve Bank of Chicago, 1986, pp. 16–31.

Randall, Ronald K. "Insurance Strategies for Profit." *The Magazine of Bank Administration*, October 1985, pp. 40, 42, and 44.

Roll, Richard. "Banking on the Consumer." *Marketing Communications*, October 1985, pp. 27–40.

Appendix A: Security Credit Ratings

SECURITY CREDIT RATINGS

What Are Credit Ratings?

Corporate and municipal debt securities sold in the financial markets today generally must carry a credit rating assigned by one or more rating agencies. The two most widely respected credit-rating agencies in the United States are Moody's Investors Service and Standard & Poor's Corporation, both headquartered in New York City. The ratings assigned by these private companies are generally regarded in the investment community as an objective evaluation of the probability that a borrower will *default* on a given security issue.

Default occurs whenever a security issuer is late in making one or more payments that it is legally obligated to make. In the case of a bond, when any interest or principal payment falls due and is not made on time, the bond is legally in default. While many defaulted bonds ultimately resume the payment of principal and interest, others never do, and the issuing company winds up in bankruptcy proceedings. In most instances, holders of bonds issued by a bankrupt company receive only pennies on each dollar invested, once the company's assets are sold at auction. It is no wonder, then, that security ratings are followed so closely by investors.

Factors Affecting Assigned Ratings

Each rating assigned to a security issue is a reflection of at least three factors: (1) the character and terms of the particular security being issued;

797

(2) the probability that the issuer will default on the security and the ability and willingness of the issuer to make timely payments; and (3) the degree of protection afforded investors if the security issuer is liquidated, reorganized, and/or declares bankruptcy. As a matter of practice, the investment agencies focus principally upon: (1) the past and probable future cash flows of the security issuer as an indication of the institution's ability to service its debt; (2) the volume and composition of outstanding debt; and (3) the stability of the issuer's cash flows over time. Other factors influencing quality ratings are the value of assets pledged as collateral and the security's priority of claim against the issuing firm's assets.

The rating agencies stress that their evaluations of individual security issues are not recommendations to buy or sell or an indication of the suitability of any particular security for the investor. The agencies do not act as financial advisers to the businesses or units of government whose securities they rate, which helps to promote objectivity in assigning quality ratings.[1]

Standard & Poor's Corporate and Municipal Bond Ratings

The credit ratings assigned to corporate and municipal bonds by Standard & Poor's Corporation are listed below along with the definitions used by S&P for each rating category.[2]

1. AAA—Bonds rated AAA have the highest rating assigned by Standard & Poor's to a debt obligation. Capacity to pay interest and repay principal is extremely strong.

2. AA—Bonds rated AA have a very strong capacity to pay interest and repay principal and differ from the highest-rated issues only in small degree.

3. A—Bonds rated A have a strong capacity to pay interest and repay principal, although they are somewhat more susceptible to the adverse effects of changes in circumstances and economic conditions than bonds in higher-rated categories.

4. BBB—Bonds rated BBB are regarded as having an adequate capacity to pay interest and repay principal. Whereas they normally exhibit adequate protection parameters, adverse economic conditions or changing circumstances are more likely to lead to a weakened capacity to pay interest and repay principal for bonds in this category than for bonds in higher-rated categories.

5. BB, B, CCC, CC—Bonds in these categories are regarded, on balance,

---

[1]Fees are assessed for ratings according to the time and effort expended in gathering sufficient information to determine an appropriate rating. These fees are usually paid either by the security issuer or by the firm or syndicate underwriting the security issue.

[2]See Standard & Poor's Corporation, *Bond Guide*, October 1980, p. 6.

as predominantly speculative with respect to capacity to pay interest and repay principal. While such bonds will likely have some quality and protective characteristics, these are outweighed by large uncertainties or major risk exposures to adverse conditions.

6. C—The rating C is reserved for income bonds on which no interest is being paid.

7. D—Bonds rated D are in default, and payment of interest and/or repayment of principal is in arrears.

The ratings from AA to B may be modified by the addition of a plus (+) or minus (−) sign to show relative standing within the major rating categories. A plus (+) sign indicates a bond of better-than-average quality in the particular rating category chosen, while a minus (−) sign denotes a bond that is worse than average in that category. Provisional ratings may also be assigned, as indicated by the letter *P*. According to Standard & Poor's, this may be interpreted as follows:

> A provisional rating assumes the successful completion of the project being financed by the bonds being rated and indicates that payment of debt service requirements is largely or entirely dependent upon the successful and timely completion of the project. This rating, however, while addressing credit quality subsequent to completion of the project, makes no comment on the likelihood of, or the risk of default upon failure of, such completion. The investor should exercise his own judgment with respect to such likelihood and risk. When no rating is requested for a security or the agency feels that insufficient information exists to assign a rating, it will designate the security as NR.[3]

S&P publishes a *Bond Guide* each month that contains data revised through the last business day of the preceding month. The S&P *Bond Guide* gives a brief description of each security issue, including its yield, listing status, form, and redemption provisions.

Moody's Investors Service

Beginning in 1909, John Moody developed and published a simple system of letter grades which indicated the relative investment quality of corporate bonds. Today, Moody's Investors Service rates thousands of issues of corporate and municipal bonds, commercial paper, short-term municipal notes, and preferred stock. These security ratings are reported in *Moody's Bond Record,* which is published monthly. In addition to assigning issue ratings, Moody's also notes for its subscribers the essential characteristics of each security issue and the dates when interest, principal, or dividend payments are due.

---

[3]Standard & Poor's Corporation, *Bond Guide*, October 1980, p. 6.

Moody's Corporate and Municipal Bond Ratings

The credit ratings assigned by Moody's to corporate and state and local government (municipal) bonds are listed below with the definitions of each rating category:[4]

Aaa

Bonds which are rated Aaa are judged to be of the best quality. They carry the smallest degree of investment risk and are generally referred to as "gilt edge." Interest payments are protected by a large or by an exceptionally stable margin and principal is secure. While the various protective elements are likely to change, such changes as can be visualized are most unlikely to impair the fundamentally strong position of such issues.

Aa

Bonds which are rated Aa are judged to be of high quality by all standards. Together with the Aaa group they comprise what are generally known as high-grade bonds. They are rated lower than the best bonds because margins of protection may not be as large as in Aaa securities or fluctuation of protective elements may be of greater amplitude or there may be other elements present which make the long-term risks appear somewhat larger than in Aaa securities.

A

Bonds which are rated A possess many favorable investment attributes and are to be considered as upper-medium-grade obligations. Factors giving security to principal and interest are considered adequate but elements may be present which suggest a susceptibility to future impairment.

Baa

Bonds which are rated Baa are considered as medium-grade obligations. Interest payments and principal security appear adequate for the present but certain protective elements may be lacking or may be characteristically unreliable over any great length of time. Such bonds lack outstanding investment characteristics and have speculative characteristics as well.

Ba

Bonds which are rated Ba are judged to have speculative elements; their future cannot be considered as well assured. Often the protection of interest and principal payments may be very moderate and thereby not well safe-guarded during both good and bad times over the future. Uncertainty of position characterizes bonds in this class.

B

Bonds which are rated B generally lack characteristics of a desirable

---

[4]See *Moody's Bond Record*, October 1979.

investment. Assurance of interest and principal payments or of maintenance of other terms of the contract over any long period of time may be small.

Caa

Bonds which are rated Caa are of poor standing. Such issues may be in default and there may be present elements of danger with respect to principal or interest.

Ca

Bonds which are rated Ca represent obligations which are speculative in some degree. Such issues are often in default or have marked shortcomings.

C

Bonds which are rated C are the lowest rated class of bonds, having extremely poor prospects of ever attaining any real investment standing.

Con. (−)

Bonds for which the security depends on the completion of some act or the fulfillment of some condition are rated conditionally. These are bonds secured by (a) earnings of projects under construction, (b) earnings of projects unseasoned in operation experience, (c) rentals which begin when facilities are completed, or (d) payments to which some other limiting condition attaches. Parenthetical rating denotes probable credit stature upon completion of construction or elimination of basis of condition.

Like Standard & Poor's Corporation, Moody's Investors Service will sometimes affix an additional symbol to its bond ratings to denote finer gradations of quality. For example, an A-rated municipal bond that appears to be superior to other bonds in this category may be designated as A1.

Moody's Commercial Paper Ratings

Promissory notes sold in the open market by large corporations and having an original maturity of nine months or less are known as commercial paper. Moody's assigns those commercial notes it is willing to rate to one of three quality categories:

- Prime-1 (or P-1)—Highest quality
- Prime-2 (or P-2)—Higher quality
- Prime-3 (or P-3)—High quality

Moody's Ratings of Short-Term Municipal Notes

Short-term securities issued by states, cities, counties, and other local governments are also rated by Moody's as to their investment quality. For these short-term issues Moody's uses the rating symbol MIG, meaning Moody's

Investment Grade. Only four rating categories are used and speculative issues or those for which adequate information is not available are not rated. The rating categories are:

MIG 1

Loans bearing this designation are of the best quality, enjoying strong protection from established cash flows of funds for their servicing or from established and broad-based access to the market for refinancing, or both.

MIG 2

Loans bearing this designation are of high quality, with margins of protection ample though not so large as in the preceding group.

MIG 3

Loans bearing this designation are of favorable quality, with all security elements accounted for but lacking the undeniable strength of the preceding grades. Market access for refinancing is likely to be less well established.

MIG 4

Loans bearing this designation are of adequate quality, carrying specific risk but having protection commonly regarded as required of an investment security and not predominantly speculative.

Moody's Preferred Stock Ratings

Beginning in 1973, Moody's extended its rating system to include preferred stock issues. As discussed in Chapter 21, preferred stock dividend payments are not required as are interest payments on bonds and, in the event of liquidation, preferred stockholders can recover their funds only after bondholders and other creditors are paid. Because preferred stock does have a different status than bonds, Moody's stresses that preferred stock ratings should not be compared in absolute terms with bond ratings. The preferred stock ratings currently assigned by Moody's are:

aaa

An issue which is rated "aaa" is considered to be a top-quality preferred stock. This rating indicates good asset protection and the least risk of dividend impairment within the universe of preferred stocks.

aa

An issue which is rated "aa" is considered a high-grade preferred stock. This rating indicates that there is reasonable assurance that earnings and asset protection will remain relatively well maintained in the foreseeable future.

a

An issue which is rated "a" is considered to be an upper-medium-grade preferred stock. While risks are judged to be somewhat greater than in the "aaa" and "aa" classifications, earnings and asset protection are expected to be maintained at adequate levels.

baa

An issue which is rated "baa" is considered to be medium grade, neither highly protected nor poorly secured. Earnings and asset protection appear adequate at present but may be questionable over any great length of time.

ba

An issue which is rated "ba" is considered to have speculative elements and its future cannot be considered well assured. Earnings and asset protection may be very moderate and not well safeguarded during adverse periods. Uncertainty of position characterizes preferred stocks in this class.

b

An issue which is rated "b" generally lacks the characteristics of a desirable investment. Assurance of dividend payments and maintenance of other terms of the issue over any long period of time may be small.

caa

An issue which is rated "caa" is likely to be in arrears on dividend payments. This rating designation does not purport to indicate the future status of payments, however.

Appendix B: Present Value, Annuity, Compound Interest, and Annual Percentage Rate (APR) Tables

Present Value Table

Present Value of $1 to Be Received N Years in the Future

Years Hence	1%	2%	4%	6%	8%	10%	12%	14%	15%	16%	18%	20%	22%	24%	25%	26%	28%	30%	35%	40%	45%	50%
1	0.990	0.980	0.962	0.943	0.926	0.909	0.893	0.877	0.870	0.862	0.847	0.833	0.820	0.806	0.800	0.794	0.781	0.769	0.741	0.714	0.690	0.667
2	0.980	0.961	0.925	0.890	0.857	0.826	0.797	0.769	0.756	0.743	0.718	0.694	0.672	0.650	0.640	0.630	0.610	0.592	0.549	0.510	0.476	0.444
3	0.971	0.942	0.889	0.840	0.794	0.751	0.712	0.675	0.658	0.641	0.609	0.579	0.551	0.524	0.512	0.500	0.477	0.455	0.406	0.364	0.328	0.296
4	0.961	0.924	0.855	0.792	0.735	0.683	0.636	0.592	0.572	0.552	0.516	0.482	0.451	0.423	0.410	0.397	0.373	0.350	0.301	0.260	0.226	0.198
5	0.951	0.906	0.822	0.747	0.681	0.621	0.567	0.519	0.497	0.476	0.437	0.402	0.370	0.341	0.328	0.315	0.291	0.269	0.223	0.186	0.156	0.132
6	0.942	0.888	0.790	0.705	0.630	0.564	0.507	0.456	0.432	0.410	0.370	0.335	0.303	0.275	0.262	0.250	0.227	0.207	0.165	0.133	0.108	0.088
7	0.933	0.871	0.760	0.665	0.583	0.513	0.452	0.400	0.376	0.354	0.314	0.279	0.249	0.222	0.210	0.198	0.178	0.159	0.122	0.095	0.074	0.059
8	0.923	0.853	0.731	0.627	0.540	0.467	0.404	0.351	0.327	0.305	0.266	0.233	0.204	0.179	0.168	0.157	0.139	0.123	0.091	0.068	0.051	0.039
9	0.914	0.837	0.703	0.592	0.500	0.424	0.361	0.308	0.284	0.263	0.225	0.194	0.167	0.144	0.134	0.125	0.108	0.094	0.067	0.048	0.035	0.026
10	0.905	0.820	0.676	0.558	0.463	0.386	0.322	0.270	0.247	0.227	0.191	0.162	0.137	0.116	0.107	0.099	0.085	0.073	0.050	0.035	0.024	0.017
11	0.896	0.804	0.650	0.527	0.429	0.350	0.287	0.237	0.215	0.195	0.162	0.135	0.112	0.094	0.086	0.079	0.066	0.056	0.037	0.025	0.017	0.012
12	0.887	0.788	0.625	0.497	0.397	0.319	0.257	0.208	0.187	0.168	0.137	0.112	0.092	0.076	0.069	0.062	0.052	0.043	0.027	0.018	0.012	0.008
13	0.879	0.773	0.601	0.469	0.368	0.290	0.229	0.182	0.163	0.145	0.116	0.093	0.075	0.061	0.055	0.050	0.040	0.033	0.020	0.013	0.008	0.005
14	0.870	0.758	0.577	0.442	0.340	0.263	0.205	0.160	0.141	0.125	0.099	0.078	0.062	0.049	0.044	0.039	0.032	0.025	0.015	0.009	0.006	0.003
15	0.861	0.743	0.555	0.417	0.315	0.239	0.183	0.140	0.123	0.108	0.084	0.065	0.051	0.040	0.035	0.031	0.025	0.020	0.011	0.006	0.004	0.002
16	0.853	0.728	0.534	0.394	0.292	0.218	0.163	0.123	0.107	0.093	0.071	0.054	0.042	0.032	0.028	0.025	0.019	0.015	0.008	0.005	0.003	0.002
17	0.844	0.714	0.513	0.371	0.270	0.198	0.146	0.108	0.093	0.080	0.060	0.045	0.034	0.026	0.023	0.020	0.015	0.012	0.006	0.003	0.002	0.001
18	0.836	0.700	0.494	0.350	0.250	0.180	0.130	0.095	0.081	0.069	0.051	0.038	0.028	0.021	0.018	0.016	0.012	0.009	0.005	0.002	0.001	0.001
19	0.828	0.686	0.475	0.331	0.232	0.164	0.116	0.083	0.070	0.060	0.043	0.031	0.023	0.017	0.014	0.012	0.009	0.007	0.003	0.002	0.001	
20	0.820	0.673	0.456	0.312	0.215	0.149	0.104	0.073	0.061	0.051	0.037	0.026	0.019	0.014	0.012	0.010	0.007	0.005	0.002	0.001	0.001	
21	0.811	0.660	0.439	0.294	0.199	0.135	0.093	0.064	0.053	0.044	0.031	0.022	0.015	0.011	0.009	0.008	0.006	0.004	0.002	0.001		
22	0.803	0.647	0.422	0.278	0.184	0.123	0.083	0.056	0.046	0.038	0.026	0.018	0.013	0.009	0.007	0.006	0.004	0.003	0.001	0.001		
23	0.795	0.634	0.406	0.262	0.170	0.112	0.074	0.049	0.040	0.033	0.022	0.015	0.010	0.007	0.006	0.005	0.003	0.002	0.001			
24	0.788	0.622	0.390	0.247	0.158	0.102	0.066	0.043	0.035	0.028	0.019	0.013	0.008	0.006	0.005	0.004	0.003	0.002	0.001			
25	0.780	0.610	0.375	0.233	0.146	0.092	0.059	0.038	0.030	0.024	0.016	0.010	0.007	0.005	0.004	0.003	0.002	0.001	0.001			
26	0.772	0.598	0.361	0.220	0.135	0.084	0.053	0.033	0.026	0.021	0.014	0.009	0.006	0.004	0.003	0.002	0.002	0.001				
27	0.764	0.586	0.347	0.207	0.125	0.076	0.047	0.029	0.023	0.018	0.011	0.007	0.005	0.003	0.002	0.002	0.001	0.001				
28	0.757	0.574	0.333	0.196	0.116	0.069	0.042	0.026	0.020	0.016	0.010	0.006	0.004	0.002	0.002	0.001	0.001	0.001				
29	0.749	0.563	0.321	0.185	0.107	0.063	0.037	0.022	0.017	0.014	0.008	0.005	0.003	0.002	0.002	0.001	0.001	0.001				
30	0.742	0.552	0.308	0.174	0.099	0.057	0.033	0.020	0.015	0.012	0.007	0.004	0.003	0.001	0.001	0.001						
40	0.672	0.453	0.208	0.097	0.046	0.022	0.011	0.005	0.004	0.003	0.001	0.001										
50	0.608	0.372	0.141	0.054	0.021	0.009	0.003	0.001	0.001	0.001												

Source: Robert N. Anthony and James S. Reece, Accounting Principles, 4th ed. (Homewood, IL: Richard D. Irwin, 1979).

Annuity Table

Present Value of $1 Received Annually for N Years Running

Years (N)	1%	2%	4%	6%	8%	10%	12%	14%	15%	16%	18%	20%	22%	24%	25%	26%	28%	30%	35%	40%	45%	50%
1	0.990	0.980	0.962	0.943	0.926	0.909	0.893	0.877	0.870	0.862	0.847	0.833	0.820	0.806	0.800	0.794	0.781	0.769	0.741	0.714	0.690	0.667
2	1.970	1.942	1.886	1.833	1.783	1.736	1.690	1.647	1.626	1.605	1.566	1.528	1.492	1.457	1.440	1.424	1.392	1.361	1.289	1.224	1.165	1.111
3	2.941	2.884	2.775	2.673	2.577	2.487	2.402	2.322	2.283	2.246	2.174	2.106	2.042	1.981	1.952	1.923	1.868	1.816	1.696	1.589	1.493	1.407
4	3.902	3.808	3.630	3.465	3.312	3.170	3.037	2.914	2.855	2.798	2.690	2.589	2.494	2.404	2.362	2.320	2.241	2.166	1.997	1.849	1.720	1.605
5	4.853	4.713	4.452	4.212	3.993	3.791	3.605	3.433	3.352	3.274	3.127	2.991	2.864	2.745	2.689	2.635	2.532	2.436	2.220	2.035	1.876	1.737
6	5.795	5.601	5.242	4.917	4.623	4.355	4.111	3.889	3.784	3.685	3.498	3.326	3.167	3.020	2.951	2.885	2.759	2.643	2.385	2.168	1.983	1.824
7	6.728	6.472	6.002	5.582	5.206	4.868	4.564	4.288	4.160	4.039	3.812	3.605	3.416	3.242	3.161	3.083	2.937	2.802	2.508	2.263	2.057	1.883
8	7.652	7.325	6.733	6.210	5.747	5.335	4.968	4.639	4.487	4.344	4.078	3.837	3.619	3.421	3.329	3.241	3.076	2.925	2.598	2.331	2.108	1.922
9	8.566	8.162	7.435	6.802	6.247	5.759	5.328	4.946	4.772	4.607	4.303	4.031	3.786	3.566	3.463	3.366	3.184	3.019	2.665	2.379	2.144	1.948
10	9.471	8.983	8.111	7.360	6.710	6.145	5.650	5.216	5.019	4.833	4.494	4.192	3.923	3.682	3.571	3.465	3.269	3.092	2.715	2.414	2.168	1.965
11	10.368	9.787	8.760	7.887	7.139	6.495	5.937	5.453	5.234	5.029	4.656	4.327	4.035	3.776	3.656	3.544	3.335	3.147	2.752	2.438	2.185	1.977
12	11.255	10.575	9.385	8.384	7.536	6.814	6.194	5.660	5.421	5.197	4.793	4.439	4.127	3.851	3.725	3.606	3.387	3.190	2.779	2.456	2.196	1.985
13	12.134	11.343	9.986	8.853	7.904	7.103	6.424	5.842	5.583	5.342	4.910	4.533	4.203	3.912	3.780	3.656	3.427	3.223	2.799	2.468	2.204	1.990
14	13.004	12.106	10.563	9.295	8.244	7.367	6.628	6.002	5.724	5.468	5.008	4.611	4.265	3.962	3.824	3.695	3.459	3.249	2.814	2.477	2.210	1.993
15	13.865	12.849	11.118	9.712	8.559	7.606	6.811	6.142	5.847	5.575	5.092	4.675	4.315	4.001	3.859	3.726	3.483	3.268	2.825	2.484	2.214	1.995
16	14.718	13.578	11.652	10.106	8.851	7.824	6.974	6.265	5.954	5.669	5.162	4.730	4.357	4.033	3.887	3.751	3.503	3.283	2.834	2.489	2.216	1.997
17	15.562	14.292	12.166	10.477	9.122	8.022	7.120	6.373	6.047	5.749	5.222	4.775	4.391	4.059	3.910	3.771	3.518	3.295	2.840	2.492	2.218	1.998
18	16.398	14.992	12.659	10.828	9.372	8.201	7.250	6.467	6.128	5.818	5.273	4.812	4.419	4.080	3.928	3.786	3.529	3.304	2.844	2.494	2.219	1.999
19	17.226	15.678	13.134	11.158	9.604	8.365	7.366	6.550	6.198	5.877	5.316	4.844	4.442	4.097	3.942	3.799	3.539	3.311	2.848	2.496	2.220	1.999
20	18.046	16.351	13.590	11.470	9.818	8.514	7.469	6.623	6.259	5.929	5.353	4.870	4.460	4.110	3.954	3.808	3.546	3.316	2.850	2.497	2.221	1.999
21	18.857	17.011	14.029	11.764	10.017	8.649	7.562	6.687	6.312	5.973	5.384	4.891	4.476	4.121	3.963	3.816	3.551	3.320	2.852	2.498	2.221	2.000
22	19.660	17.658	14.451	12.042	10.201	8.772	7.645	6.743	6.359	6.011	5.410	4.909	4.488	4.130	3.970	3.822	3.556	3.323	2.853	2.498	2.222	2.000
23	20.456	18.292	14.857	12.303	10.371	8.883	7.718	6.792	6.399	6.044	5.432	4.925	4.499	4.137	3.976	3.827	3.559	3.325	2.854	2.499	2.222	2.000
24	21.243	18.914	15.247	12.550	10.529	8.985	7.784	6.835	6.434	6.073	5.451	4.937	4.507	4.143	3.981	3.831	3.562	3.327	2.855	2.499	2.222	2.000
25	22.023	19.523	15.622	12.783	10.675	9.077	7.843	6.873	6.464	6.097	5.467	4.948	4.514	4.147	3.985	3.834	3.564	3.329	2.856	2.499	2.222	2.000
26	22.795	20.121	15.983	13.003	10.810	9.161	7.896	6.906	6.491	6.118	5.480	4.956	4.520	4.151	3.988	3.837	3.566	3.330	2.856	2.500	2.222	2.000
27	23.560	20.707	16.330	13.211	10.935	9.237	7.943	6.935	6.514	6.136	5.492	4.964	4.524	4.154	3.990	3.839	3.567	3.331	2.856	2.500	2.222	2.000
28	24.316	21.281	16.663	13.406	11.051	9.307	7.984	6.961	6.534	6.152	5.502	4.970	4.528	4.157	3.992	3.840	3.568	3.331	2.857	2.500	2.222	2.000
29	25.066	21.844	16.984	13.591	11.158	9.370	8.022	6.983	6.551	6.166	5.510	4.975	4.531	4.159	3.994	3.841	3.569	3.332	2.857	2.500	2.222	2.000
30	25.808	22.396	17.292	13.765	11.258	9.427	8.055	7.003	6.566	6.177	5.517	4.979	4.534	4.160	3.995	3.842	3.569	3.332	2.857	2.500	2.222	2.000
40	32.835	27.355	19.793	15.046	11.925	9.779	8.244	7.105	6.642	6.234	5.548	4.997	4.544	4.166	3.999	3.846	3.571	3.333	2.857	2.500	2.222	2.000
50	39.196	31.424	21.482	15.762	12.234	9.915	8.304	7.133	6.661	6.246	5.554	4.999	4.545	4.167	4.000	3.846	3.571	3.333	2.857	2.500	2.222	2.000

Source: Robert N. Anthony and James S. Reece, Accounting Principles, 4th ed. (Homewood, IL: Richard D. Irwin, 1979).

Compound Interest Rate Table

Annual Percentage Rate

(Future Value of $1—Principal Plus Accumulated Interest)

Number of Periods	1.00%	1.50%	2.00%	2.50%	3.00%	3.50%	4.00%	4.50%	5.00%	6.00%	7.00%	8.00%	9.00%	10.00%	12.00%	14.00%	16.00%	18.00%
1	1.010	1.015	1.020	1.025	1.030	1.035	1.040	1.045	1.050	1.060	1.070	1.080	1.090	1.100	1.120	1.140	1.160	1.180
2	1.020	1.030	1.040	1.051	1.061	1.071	1.082	1.092	1.103	1.124	1.145	1.166	1.188	1.210	1.254	1.300	1.346	1.392
3	1.030	1.046	1.061	1.077	1.093	1.109	1.125	1.141	1.158	1.191	1.225	1.260	1.295	1.331	1.405	1.482	1.561	1.643
4	1.041	1.061	1.082	1.104	1.126	1.148	1.170	1.193	1.216	1.262	1.311	1.360	1.412	1.464	1.574	1.689	1.811	1.939
5	1.051	1.077	1.104	1.131	1.159	1.188	1.217	1.246	1.276	1.338	1.403	1.469	1.539	1.611	1.762	1.925	2.100	2.288
6	1.062	1.093	1.126	1.160	1.194	1.229	1.265	1.302	1.340	1.419	1.501	1.587	1.677	1.772	1.974	2.195	2.436	2.700
7	1.072	1.110	1.149	1.189	1.230	1.272	1.316	1.361	1.407	1.504	1.606	1.714	1.828	1.949	2.211	2.502	2.826	3.185
8	1.083	1.126	1.172	1.218	1.267	1.317	1.369	1.422	1.477	1.594	1.718	1.851	1.993	2.144	2.476	2.853	3.278	3.759
9	1.094	1.143	1.195	1.249	1.305	1.363	1.423	1.486	1.551	1.689	1.838	1.999	2.172	2.358	2.773	3.252	3.803	4.435
10	1.105	1.161	1.219	1.280	1.344	1.411	1.480	1.553	1.629	1.791	1.967	2.159	2.367	2.594	3.106	3.707	4.411	5.234
11	1.116	1.178	1.243	1.312	1.384	1.460	1.539	1.623	1.710	1.898	2.105	2.332	2.580	2.853	3.479	4.226	5.117	6.176
12	1.127	1.196	1.268	1.345	1.426	1.511	1.601	1.696	1.796	2.012	2.252	2.518	2.813	3.138	3.896	4.818	5.936	7.288
14	1.149	1.232	1.319	1.413	1.513	1.619	1.732	1.852	1.980	2.261	2.579	2.937	3.342	3.797	4.887	6.261	7.988	10.147
16	1.173	1.269	1.373	1.485	1.605	1.734	1.873	2.022	2.183	2.540	2.952	3.426	3.970	4.595	6.130	8.137	10.748	14.129
18	1.196	1.307	1.428	1.560	1.702	1.857	2.026	2.208	2.407	2.854	3.380	3.996	4.717	5.560	7.690	10.575	14.463	19.673

20	1.220	1.347	1.486	1.639	1.806	1.990	2.191	2.412	2.653	3.207	3.870	4.661	5.604	6.727	9.646	13.743	19.461	27.393
22	1.245	1.388	1.546	1.722	1.916	2.132	2.370	2.634	2.925	3.604	4.430	5.437	6.659	8.140	12.100	17.861	26.186	38.142
24	1.270	1.430	1.608	1.809	2.033	2.283	2.563	2.876	3.225	4.049	5.072	6.341	7.911	9.850	15.179	23.212	35.236	53.109
26	1.295	1.473	1.673	1.900	2.157	2.446	2.772	3.141	3.556	4.549	5.807	7.396	9.399	11.918	19.040	30.167	47.414	73.949
28	1.321	1.517	1.741	1.996	2.288	2.620	2.999	3.430	3.920	5.112	6.649	8.627	11.167	14.421	23.884	39.204	63.800	102.967
30	1.348	1.563	1.811	2.098	2.427	2.807	3.243	3.745	4.322	5.743	7.612	10.063	13.268	17.449	29.960	50.950	85.850	143.371
32	1.375	1.610	1.884	2.204	2.575	3.007	3.508	4.090	4.765	6.453	8.715	11.737	15.763	21.114	37.582	66.215	115.520	199.629
34	1.403	1.659	1.961	2.315	2.732	3.221	3.794	4.466	5.253	7.251	9.978	13.690	18.728	25.548	47.143	86.053	155.443	277.964
36	1.431	1.709	2.040	2.433	2.898	3.450	4.104	4.877	5.792	8.147	11.424	15.968	22.251	30.913	59.136	111.834	209.164	387.037
38	1.460	1.761	2.122	2.556	3.075	3.696	4.439	5.326	6.385	9.154	13.079	18.625	26.437	37.404	74.180	145.340	281.452	538.910
40	1.489	1.814	2.208	2.685	3.262	3.959	4.801	5.816	7.040	10.286	14.974	21.725	31.409	45.259	93.051	188.884	378.721	750.378
42	1.519	1.869	2.297	2.821	3.461	4.241	5.193	6.352	7.762	11.557	17.144	25.339	37.318	54.764	116.723	245.473	509.607	1044.827
44	1.549	1.925	2.390	2.964	3.671	4.543	5.617	6.936	8.557	12.985	19.628	29.556	44.337	66.264	146.418	319.017	685.727	1454.817
46	1.580	1.984	2.487	3.114	3.895	4.867	6.075	7.574	9.434	14.590	22.473	34.474	52.677	80.180	183.666	414.594	922.715	2025.687
48	1.612	2.043	2.587	3.271	4.132	5.214	6.571	8.271	10.401	16.394	25.729	40.211	62.585	97.017	230.391	538.807	1241.605	2820.567
50	1.645	2.105	2.692	3.437	4.384	5.585	7.107	9.033	11.467	18.420	29.457	46.902	74.357	117.391	289.002	700.233	1670.704	3927.357
52	1.678	2.169	2.800	3.611	4.651	5.983	7.687	9.864	12.643	20.697	33.725	54.706	88.344	142.043	362.524	910.023	2248.099	5468.452
54	1.711	2.234	2.913	3.794	4.934	6.409	8.314	10.771	13.939	23.255	38.612	63.809	104.962	171.872	454.751	1182.666	3025.042	7614.272
56	1.746	2.302	3.031	3.986	5.235	6.865	8.992	11.763	15.367	26.129	44.207	74.427	124.705	207.965	570.439	1536.992	4070.497	10602.113
58	1.781	2.372	3.154	4.188	5.553	7.354	9.726	12.845	16.943	29.359	50.613	86.812	148.162	251.638	715.559	1997.475	5477.260	14762.381
60	1.817	2.443	3.281	4.400	5.892	7.878	10.520	14.027	18.679	32.988	57.946	101.257	176.031	304.482	897.597	2595.919	7370.201	20555.140

Source: Federal Reserve Bank of New York, *The Arithmetic of Interest Rates*, pp. 26–27.

Interest Rate Table for Daily Compounding (360-Day Basis Year)

Number of Years	Annual Percentage Rate					
	5.00%	5.25%	5.50%	5.75%	6.00%	6.25%
	(What a $1 Deposit Will Grow to in the Future)					
1	1.0520	1.0547	1.0573	1.0600	1.0627	1.0654
2	1.1067	1.1123	1.1180	1.1237	1.1294	1.1351
3	1.1642	1.1731	1.1821	1.1911	1.2002	1.2094
4	1.2248	1.2373	1.2499	1.2626	1.2755	1.2885
5	1.2885	1.3049	1.3215	1.3384	1.3555	1.3727
6	1.3555	1.3762	1.3973	1.4187	1.4405	1.4625
7	1.4259	1.4515	1.4774	1.5039	1.5308	1.5582
8	1.5001	1.5308	1.5622	1.5942	1.6268	1.6601
9	1.5781	1.6145	1.6518	1.6899	1.7288	1.7687
10	1.6602	1.7028	1.7465	1.7913	1.8373	1.8844
15	2.1391	2.2219	2.3080	2.3975	2.4904	2.5868
20	2.7561	2.8994	3.0502	3.2087	3.3756	3.5511
25	3.5512	3.7834	4.0309	4.2946	4.5755	4.8747
30	4.5756	4.9370	5.3270	5.7478	6.2019	6.6918

Number of Years	Annual Percentage Rate					
	8.25%	8.50%	8.75%	9.00%	9.25%	9.50%
	(What a $1 Deposit Will Grow to in the Future)					
1	1.0872	1.0900	1.0928	1.0955	1.0983	1.1011
2	1.1821	1.1881	1.1941	1.2002	1.2063	1.2124
3	1.2852	1.2950	1.3049	1.3148	1.3249	1.3350
4	1.3973	1.4115	1.4259	1.4404	1.4551	1.4699
5	1.5192	1.5386	1.5582	1.5781	1.5982	1.6186
6	1.6517	1.6770	1.7027	1.7288	1.7553	1.7822
7	1.7958	1.8279	1.8607	1.8940	1.9279	1.9624
8	1.9525	1.9924	2.0333	2.0749	2.1174	2.1607
9	2.1228	2.1718	2.2219	2.2731	2.3255	2.3792
10	2.3080	2.3672	2.4279	2.4903	2.5542	2.6197
15	3.5062	3.6421	3.7832	3.9298	4.0820	4.2402
20	5.3267	5.6036	5.8949	6.2014	6.5238	6.8629
25	8.0922	8.6215	9.1854	9.7861	10.4261	11.1080
30	12.2937	13.2648	14.3125	15.4430	16.6628	17.9790

Source: Federal Reserve Bank of New York.

Annual Percentage Rate						
6.50%	**6.75%**	**7.00%**	**7.25%**	**7.50%**	**7.75%**	**8.00%**
(What a $1 Deposit Will Grow to in the Future)						
1.0681	1.0708	1.0735	1.0763	1.0790	1.0817	1.0845
1.1409	1.1467	1.1525	1.1584	1.1642	1.1702	1.1761
1.2186	1.2279	1.2373	1.2467	1.2562	1.2658	1.2755
1.3016	1.3149	1.3282	1.3418	1.3555	1.3693	1.3832
1.3903	1.4080	1.4259	1.4441	1.4625	1.4812	1.5001
1.4850	1.5077	1.5308	1.5543	1.5781	1.6022	1.6268
1.5861	1.6145	1.6434	1.6728	1.7027	1.7332	1.7642
1.6941	1.7288	1.7642	1.8004	1.8373	1.8749	1.9133
1.8095	1.8513	1.8940	1.9377	1.9824	2.0281	2.0749
1.9328	1.9824	2.0333	2.0855	2.1390	2.1939	2.2502
2.6871	2.7912	2.8993	3.0117	3.1284	3.2496	3.3755
3.7357	3.9299	4.1343	4.3492	4.5753	4.8132	5.0634
5.1936	5.5333	5.8952	6.2807	6.6915	7.1292	7.5955
7.2204	7.7907	8.4061	9.0701	9.7866	10.5596	11.3937

Annual Percentage Rate						
9.75%	**10.00%**	**10.25%**	**10.50%**	**11.00%**	**12.00%**	**13.00%**
(What a $1 Deposit Will Grow to in the Future)						
1.1039	1.1067	1.1095	1.1123	1.1180	1.1294	1.1409
1.2186	1.2248	1.2310	1.2372	1.2498	1.2754	1.3016
1.3452	1.3554	1.3658	1.3762	1.3973	1.4404	1.4849
1.4849	1.5001	1.5153	1.5308	1.5621	1.6268	1.6941
1.6392	1.6601	1.6813	1.7027	1.7464	1.8372	1.9327
1.8095	1.8372	1.8654	1.8939	1.9524	2.0748	2.2049
1.9975	2.0332	2.0696	2.1067	2.1827	2.3432	2.5155
2.2050	2.2502	2.2962	2.3433	2.4402	2.6463	2.8698
2.4341	2.4902	2.5477	2.6064	2.7281	2.9886	3.2741
2.6870	2.7559	2.8266	2.8992	3.0499	3.3752	3.7353
4.4044	4.5751	4.7523	4.9364	5.3263	6.2009	7.2191
7.2197	7.5950	7.9899	8.4053	9.3019	11.3922	13.9522
11.8345	12.6085	13.4331	14.3116	16.2447	20.9295	26.9651
19.3990	20.9313	22.5845	24.3683	28.3697	38.4513	52.1150

Annual Percentage Rate Table for Monthly Payment Plans

Number of Payments	Annual Percentage Rate							
	10.00%	10.50%	11.00%	11.50%	12.00%	12.50%	13.00%	13.50%
	(Finance Charge Per $100 of Amount Financed)							
1	0.83	0.87	0.92	0.96	1.00	1.04	1.08	1.12
2	1.25	1.31	1.38	1.44	1.50	1.57	1.63	1.69
3	1.67	1.76	1.84	1.92	2.01	2.09	2.17	2.26
4	2.09	2.20	2.30	2.41	2.51	2.62	2.72	2.83
5	2.51	2.64	2.77	2.89	3.02	3.15	3.27	3.40
6	2.94	3.08	3.23	3.38	3.53	3.68	3.83	3.97
7	3.36	3.53	3.70	3.87	4.04	4.21	4.38	4.55
8	3.79	3.98	4.17	4.36	4.55	4.74	4.94	5.13
9	4.21	4.43	4.64	4.85	5.07	5.28	5.49	5.71
10	4.64	4.88	5.11	5.35	5.58	5.82	6.05	6.29
11	5.07	5.33	5.58	5.84	6.10	6.36	6.62	6.88
12	5.50	5.78	6.06	6.34	6.62	6.90	7.18	7.46
18	8.10	8.52	8.93	9.35	9.77	10.19	10.61	11.03
24	10.75	11.30	11.86	12.42	12.98	13.54	14.10	14.66
30	13.43	14.13	14.83	15.54	16.24	16.95	17.66	18.38
36	16.16	17.01	17.86	18.71	19.57	20.43	21.30	22.17
42	18.93	19.93	20.93	21.94	22.96	23.98	25.00	26.03
48	21.74	22.90	24.06	25.23	26.40	27.58	28.77	29.97
54	24.59	25.91	27.23	28.56	29.91	31.25	32.61	33.98
60	27.48	28.96	30.45	31.96	33.47	34.99	36.52	38.06
66	30.41	32.06	33.73	35.40	37.09	38.78	40.49	42.21
72	33.39	35.21	37.05	38.90	40.76	42.64	44.53	46.44
78	36.40	38.40	40.41	42.45	44.49	46.45	48.64	50.74
84	39.45	41.63	43.83	46.05	48.28	50.54	52.81	55.11
90	42.54	44.91	47.29	49.70	52.13	54.58	57.05	59.54
96	45.67	48.22	50.80	53.40	56.03	58.68	61.35	64.05
102	48.84	51.59	54.36	57.16	59.98	62.83	65.71	68.62
108	52.05	54.99	57.96	60.96	63.99	67.05	70.14	73.26
114	55.30	58.43	61.61	64.81	68.05	71.32	74.63	77.96
120	58.58	61.92	65.30	68.71	72.17	75.65	79.17	82.73
180	93.43	98.97	104.59	110.27	116.03	121.85	127.74	133.70
240	131.61	139.61	147.73	155.94	164.26	172.67	181.18	189.77
300	172.61	183.25	194.03	204.94	215.97	227.11	238.35	249.69
360	215.93	229.31	242.84	256.50	270.30	284.21	298.23	312.35

Source: Federal Reserve Bank of New York.

			Annual Percentage Rate					
14.00%	**14.50%**	**15.00%**	**15.50%**	**16.00%**	**16.50%**	**17.00%**	**17.50%**	**18.00%**
			(Finance Charge Per $100 of Amount Financed)					
1.17	1.21	1.25	1.29	1.33	1.37	1.42	1.46	1.50
1.75	1.82	1.88	1.94	2.00	2.07	2.13	2.19	2.26
2.34	2.43	2.51	2.59	2.68	2.76	2.85	2.93	3.01
2.93	3.04	3.14	3.25	3.36	3.46	3.57	3.67	3.78
3.53	3.65	3.78	3.91	4.04	4.16	4.29	4.42	4.54
4.12	4.27	4.42	4.57	4.72	4.87	5.02	5.17	5.32
4.72	4.89	5.06	5.23	5.40	5.58	5.75	5.92	6.09
5.32	5.51	5.71	5.90	6.09	6.29	6.48	6.67	6.87
5.92	6.14	6.35	6.57	6.78	7.00	7.22	7.43	7.65
6.53	6.77	7.00	7.24	7.48	7.72	7.96	8.19	8.43
7.14	7.40	7.66	7.92	8.18	8.44	8.70	8.96	9.22
7.74	8.03	8.31	8.59	8.88	9.16	9.45	9.73	10.02
11.45	11.87	12.29	12.72	13.14	13.57	13.99	14.42	14.85
15.23	15.80	16.37	16.94	17.51	18.09	18.66	19.24	19.82
19.10	19.81	20.54	21.26	21.99	22.72	23.45	24.18	24.92
23.04	23.92	24.80	25.68	26.57	27.46	28.35	29.25	30.15
27.06	28.10	29.15	30.19	31.25	32.31	33.37	34.44	35.51
31.17	32.37	33.59	34.81	36.03	37.27	38.50	39.75	41.00
35.35	36.73	38.12	39.52	40.92	42.33	43.75	45.18	46.62
39.61	41.17	42.74	44.32	45.91	47.51	49.12	50.73	52.36
43.95	45.69	47.45	49.22	51.00	52.79	54.59	56.40	58.23
48.36	50.30	52.24	54.21	56.18	58.17	60.17	62.19	64.22
52.85	54.98	57.13	59.29	61.46	63.66	65.86	68.09	70.32
57.42	59.75	62.09	64.46	66.84	69.24	71.66	74.10	76.55
62.05	64.59	67.14	69.72	72.31	74.93	77.56	80.22	82.89
66.77	69.51	72.28	75.06	77.88	80.71	83.57	86.44	89.34
71.55	74.51	77.49	80.50	83.53	86.59	89.67	92.78	95.91
76.40	79.58	82.78	86.01	89.27	92.56	95.87	99.21	102.57
81.33	84.73	88.15	91.61	95.10	98.62	102.17	105.74	109.35
86.32	89.94	93.60	97.29	101.02	104.77	108.56	112.37	116.22
139.71	145.79	151.93	158.12	164.37	170.67	177.02	183.42	189.88
198.44	207.20	216.03	224.93	233.90	242.94	252.03	261.19	270.39
216.13	272.65	284.25	295.92	307.67	319.47	331.34	343.26	355.23
326.55	340.84	355.20	369.63	384.11	398.65	413.24	427.88	442.55

Money and Capital Markets Dictionary

Actual maturity The number of days, months, or years between today and the date a loan or security is redeemed or retired. *(Chapter 13)*

Add-on rate A method for calculating the interest charge on a loan where the interest bill is added to the principal amount of the loan. That sum is then divided by the number of installment payments required to determine the amount of each payment needed to eventually pay off the loan. *(Chapter 8)*

Adjustable mortgage instrument (AMI) A home mortgage loan under which some of the terms of the loan, such as the contract loan rate or the maturity (term) of the loan, will vary as financial market conditions change. *(Chapter 19)*

Aging population A long-term increase in the average age of people in many countries is resulting in changes in their saving habits and in their demands for financial services, thus putting added pressure on financial institutions to develop new financial services. *(Chapter 30)*

Annual percentage rate (APR) The actuarially determined rate on a consumer loan which the federal Truth-in-Lending law requires lenders to calculate and communicate to their borrowing customers. *(Chapter 8)*

Arbitrage The purchase of a security or currency in one market and the sale of that security or currency in another market in response to differences in price or yield between the two markets. *(Chapters 1, 9, and 28)*

Asked price The price at which a securities dealer is willing to sell securities held in his or her portfolio to the public. *(Chapters 3 and 14)*

Auction A method used to sell securities in which buyers file bids and the highest-price bidders receive securities. *(Chapters 14 and 25)*

Auction method The principal means by which U.S. Treasury securities are sold to the public today *(Chapters 14 and 25)*

Balanced-budget unit An individual, business firm, or unit of government whose current expenditures equal its current receipts of income and therefore is neither a borrower nor a lender of funds. *(Chapter 2)*

Balance-of-payments (BOP) accounts A double-entry bookkeeping system recording a nation's transactions with other nations, including exports, imports, and capital flows. *(Chapter 27)*

Balance in invisibles Difference between services supplied by a nation to residents of other nations less services supplied from abroad. *(Chapter 27)*

Bank discount method The procedure by which yields on U.S. Treasury bills, commercial paper, and bankers' acceptances are calculated; a 360-day year is assumed and there is no compounding of interest income. *(Chapters 14, 16, and 17)*

Bankers' acceptance A time draft against a bank that the bank has agreed to pay unconditionally on the date the draft matures. *(Chapter 4)*

Bank holding company A corporation that owns stock in one or more commercial banks. *(Chapter 4)*

Banking structure The number, relative sizes, and types of banks and bank services offered in a given market or in the industry as a whole. *(Chapter 4)*

Bankruptcy Reform Act A federal law originally passed in 1978 and subsequently amended that made it easier for consumers to file bankruptcy petitions and keep substantial personal assets that cannot be sold or repossessed to repay outstanding debts. *(Chapter 18)*

Base rate A loan rate used as the basis or foundation for determining the size of the current interest rate to be charged a business borrower, such as the prime rate or LIBOR. *(Chapters 16, 17, and 20)*

Basic balance The sum of the current-account balance and the net long-term capital flows recorded in a nation's balance of payments accounts. *(Chapter 27)*

Basis The spread between the cash (spot) price of a commodity or security and its futures (forward) price at any given point in time. *(Chapter 12)*

Bid Price The price a securities dealer is willing to pay to buy securities from his or her customers. *(Chapters 3, 14, and 26)*

Bill of exchange A written order requiring a person, business firm, or bank to pay a specified sum of money under stipulated conditions to the bearer of the bill. *(Chapter 28)*

Board of Governors The chief policymaking and administrative body of the Federal Reserve System, composed of no more than seven persons appointed by the president of the United States and confirmed by the Senate for maximum 14-year terms. *(Chapters 4, 22, 23, and 24)*

Bond A debt obligation issued by a business firm or unit of government that covers several years, usually over five years. *(Chapters 3 and 19)*

Bond anticipation notes Shorter-term securities issued by a state or local government to raise funds to begin a project that eventually will be funded by issuing long-term bonds. *(Chapter 26)*

Book-entry form The method by which marketable U.S. Treasury securities are issued today with the buyer receiving only a receipt, rather than an engraved certificate, indicating that the purchase is recorded on the Treasury's books or recorded in another approved location. *(Chapter 25)*

Borrowed reserves Legal reserves loaned to depository institutions through the discount windows of the Federal Reserve banks. *(Chapters 15, 22, 23, and 24)*

Borrowing The change in liabilities outstanding reported by a sector or unit in the economy over a specified time period. *(Chapter 3)*

Branch banking A type of banking organization in which services are sold through multiple offices, all owned and operated by the same banking corporation. *(Chapter 4)*

Budget deficit A government's financial position in which current expenditures exceed current revenues. *(Chapter 25)*

Budget surplus A government's financial position in which current revenues exceed current expenditures. *(Chapter 25)*

Business cycle Fluctuations in economic activity, with the economy passing alternately through expansionary (boom) and recessionary (depressed) periods. *(Chapter 11)*

Cable transfers Orders transferred by cable or wire to a foreign bank holding the account of a seller of currency directing that a stipulated amount of a particular currency be moved into another account. *(Chapter 28)*

Call option Grants its buyer the right to purchase a specified number of shares of a given stock or volume of debt securities at a specified price up to an expiration date. *(Chapters 12 and 21)*

Call privilege The provision often found in a bond's contract (indenture) that permits the borrower to retire all or a portion of a bond issue by buying back the securities in advance of their maturity. *(Chapter 10)*

Capital account A record of flows of short-term and long-term funds into a nation and out of a nation and included in its balance-of-payments accounts. *(Chapter 27)*

Cash offering A method used by the U.S. Treasury to sell securities in which buyers must pay cash to acquire new securities. *(Chapter 25)*

Central bank An agency of government that has public policy functions such as monitoring the operation of the nation's financial system and controlling the growth of the money supply. *(Chapter 22)*

Classical theory of interest rates An explanation of the level of and changes in interest rates that relies upon the interaction of the supply of savings and the demand for investment capital. *(Chapter 7)*

Clearinghouse funds Money transferred by writing a check and presenting it for collection. *(Chapter 13)*

Commercial bank A business corporation that accepts deposits, makes loans, and sells other financial services, especially to other business firms, but also to households and governments. *(Chapter 4)*

Commercial mortgage A debt obligation whose purpose is to finance the construction of office buildings, shopping centers, and other business structures. *(Chapter 20)*

Commercial paper A short-term, high-grade debt security issued by a corporation that is not tied to any specific collateral, but secured only by the general earning power of the issuing corporation. *(Chapter 16)*

Community Reinvestment Act A federal law passed in 1977 that requires depository institutions to designate the market areas they will serve and to provide those services without discrimination to all neighborhoods and regions within their designated market areas. *(Chapter 18)*

Common stock A residual claim against the assets and earnings of the issuing corporation evidencing a share of ownership in that company. *(Chapters 2, 3, and 21)*

Competitive Equality Banking Act A 1987 federal law that required depository institutions to speed up giving customers credit for deposits made in their checking accounts, placed a moratorium on the offering of new banking services, and gave federal insurance agencies additional tools to deal with failing depository institutions. *(Chapters 4 and 18)*

Compound interest The payment of additional interest earnings on previously earned interest income. *(Chapter 8)*

Consolidation A trend among banks and other financial institutions in which smaller institutions are being combined through merger and acquisition into larger institutions. *(Chapter 4)*

Consensus forecast A prediction of interest rates or economic conditions based on a variety of projections derived from several different forecasting methods. *(Chapter 11)*

Consumer cash management service A financial service in which an individual can hold surplus cash funds in an interest-bearing payments account until investments in higher-yielding assets can be made and through which credit can be obtained. *(Chapter 18)*

Contemporaneous reserve accounting The method of determining the amount of legal reserves a bank or other depository institution must hold behind its deposits and other reservable liabilities in which the reserve computation and reserve maintenance periods overlap. *(Chapter 15)*

Contractual institutions Financial institutions that attract savings from the public by offering contracts that protect the saver against risk in the future, such as insurance policies and pension plans. *(Chapter 2)*

Conventional home mortgage loan Credit funds extended to a home buyer by a private lender without a government guarantee behind the loan to insure that the lender is repaid. *(Chapter 19)*

Convertibility A feature of some preferred stocks and bonds which entitles the holder to exchange those securities for a specific number of shares of common stock. *(Chapter 10)*

Corporate bond A debt contract (IOU) of a corporation whose original maturity is more than five years. *(Chapter 20)*

Corporate note A debt contract (IOU) of a corporation whose original maturity is five years or less. *(Chapter 20)*

Coupon effect The size of a debt security's promised interest rate (coupon) influences how rapidly its price moves with changes in market interest rates. *(Chapter 9)*

Coupon rate The promised interest rate on a bond or note consisting of the ratio of the annual interest income promised by the security issuer to the security's face (par) value. *(Chapter 8)*

Covered interest arbitrage Using forward exchange contracts to protect the yield from an investment in foreign securities against the risk of fluctuating currency prices. *(Chapter 28)*

Creative financing Innovative financing techniques used to make single-family homes more affordable for the average home buyer. *(Chapter 19)*

Credit A loan of funds in return for a promise of future payment. *(Chapter 1)*

Credit availability (neo-Keynesian) view A view of economic policy which contends that both fiscal policy (government spending and taxation) and monetary policy (activities of the central bank) are needed to influence employment, growth, and prices and achieve a nation's economic goals. *(Chapter 24)*

Credit bureaus Institutions holding information on the credit histories of individuals who have borrowed money, reporting the credit ratings of these individuals to lending institutions and others legally authorized to receive such information. *(Chapters 3 and 18)*

Credit card A plastic card (sometimes equipped with a microprocessor) that allows the holder to borrow cash or to pay for goods and services with credit. *(Chapter 18)*

Credit unions Nonprofit associations accepting deposits from and making loans to their members, all of whom have a common bond, such as working for the same employer. *(Chapter 5)*

Currency futures Contracts that allow businesses or individuals acquiring or selling a foreign currency to protect against future fluctuations in currency prices by shifting the risk of those price changes to someone else willing to bear that risk. *(Chapter 28)*

Currency risk Possible losses to a borrower or lender in foreign markets or to a holder of non-

financial assets in foreign markets due to adverse changes in currency prices. *(Chapters 13 and 28)*

Currency swaps A contract designed to reduce the risk of loss due to changes in currency prices by exchanging one nation's currency for another that is of more use to a borrower. *(Chapter 28)*

Current account A component of a nation's balance-of-payments accounts that tracks purchases and sales of goods and services (trade) and gifts made to foreigners by domestic citizens. *(Chapter 27)*

Current saving The change in net worth recorded by a sector or unit in the economy over the current time period. *(Chapter 3)*

Current yield The ratio of a security's promised or expected annual income to its current market price. *(Chapter 8)*

D Definition of the U.S. money supply that includes the total debt of domestic nonfinancial sectors, consisting of credit market debt of the U.S. government, state and local governments, and private nonfinancial sectors. *(Chapter 24)*

Dealer paper Short-term commercial notes sold by borrowing corporations and issued through security dealers who contact interested investors to determine if they will buy the notes. *(Chapter 16)*

Debentures Long-term debt instruments secured only by the earning power of the issuing corporation and not by any specific assets pledged by the issuing firm. *(Chapter 20)*

Debit cards Plastic cards that are used to identify the owner of the card or to make immediate payments for goods and services. *(Chapter 18)*

Debt management policy The refunding or refinancing of the federal government's debt in a way that contributes to broad national goals and minimizes the burden of the federal debt. *(Chapter 25)*

Debt securities Financial claims against the assets of a business firm, individual, or unit of government, represented by bonds, notes, deposits, and other contracts evidencing a loan of money. *(Chapter 2)*

Default risk The risk to the holder of bonds or other debt securities that a borrower will not meet all promised payments at the times agreed upon. *(Chapter 10)*

Deficit-budget unit An individual, business firm, or unit of government whose current expenditures exceed its current receipts of income, forcing it to become a net borrower of funds in the money and capital markets. *(Chapter 2)*

Demand loan A borrowing of funds (usually by a security dealer) subject to recall of those funds on demand by the lender. *(Chapter 14)*

Deposit multiplier Also called the coefficient of deposit expansion because it indicates how many dollars of new deposits will result from an injection of one more dollar of excess reserves into the banking system. *(Chapters 4 and 23)*

Depository institutions Financial institutions that raise loanable funds by selling deposits to the public. *(Chapter 2)*

Depository Institutions Deregulation and Monetary Control Act (DIDMCA) Law passed in 1980 by the U.S. Congress to deregulate interest rate ceilings on deposits and grant new services to nonbank thrift institutions as well as to impose common reserve requirements on all depository institutions. *(Chapters 4, 5, 22, and 23)*

Deregulation The lifting or liberalization of government rules that restrict what private businesses (especially those in the financial markets) can do to serve their customers. *(Chapters 4 and 30)*

Direct finance Any financial transaction in which a borrower and a lender of funds communicate directly and mutually agree on the terms of a loan. *(Chapter 2)*

Direct paper Short-term commercial notes issued directly to investors by borrowing companies without the aid of a broker or dealer. *(Chapter 16)*

Direct placement Sale of corporate securities to one or a small group of investors following private negotiations. *(Chapter 20)*

Discount method A method for calculating the interest charge on a loan that deducts the interest owed from the face amount of the loan, with the borrower receiving only the net proceeds after interest is deducted for his or her use. *(Chapter 8)*

Discount rate The interest charge (in annual percentage terms) set by the Federal Reserve banks for borrowings by depository institutions from the discount windows of these Reserve banks. *(Chapters 15, 22, and 23)*

Discount window The department in a Federal Reserve bank that grants credit to banks and other depository institutions in need of short-term loans of legal reserves. *(Chapters 15, 22, and 23)*

Disintermediation The withdrawal of funds from a financial intermediary by ultimate lenders (savers) and the lending of those funds directly to ultimate borrowers. *(Chapter 2)*

Duration A weighted average measure of the maturity of a loan or security which takes into account the amount and timing of all promised interest and principal payments associated with that loan or security. *(Chapters 9 and 11)*

Econometric models The use of systems of equations and statistical estimation methods to explain or forecast changes in interest rates or other variables. *(Chapter 11)*

Edge Acts Special subsidiaries of U.S. banking organizations authorized by federal law and regulation to offer international banking services. *(Chapter 29)*

Efficient market A competitive market in which the prices of financial instruments traded there fully reflect all the latest information available. *(Chapters 1, 7, and 21)*

Efficient markets hypothesis A theory of the financial markets which argues that security prices tend to fluctuate randomly around their intrinsic values, return quickly toward equilibrium, and fully reflect the latest information available. *(Chapter 21)*

Equal Credit Opportunity Act A federal law passed in 1974 forbidding lending institutions from discriminating in the granting of credit based on the age, race, ethnic origin, religion, or receipt of public assistance of the borrowing customer. *(Chapter 18)*

Equities Shares of both common and preferred stock, with each share representing a certificate of ownership in a business corporation. *(Chapters 2 and 21)*

Eurobond A long-term debt security denominated in a currency other than that of the country or countries where most or all of the security is sold. *(Chapter 29)*

Eurocurrency deposits Deposits of funds in a bank that are denominated in a currency foreign to the bank's home country. *(Chapters 17 and 29)*

Eurocurrency loans Loans made by a multinational bank in a currency other than that of the bank's home country. *(Chapter 29)*

Eurocurrency market An international money market where bank deposits denominated in the world's most convertible currencies are traded. *(Chapter 17)*

Eurodollars Deposits of U.S. dollars in foreign banks abroad or in foreign branch offices of U.S. banks or in U.S. international banking facilities (IBFs). *(Chapter 17)*

Eurodollar CDs Certificates of deposit denominated in dollars but issued by a bank or bank branch office located outside U.S. territory. *(Chapters 15 and 17)*

Excess reserves Cash and deposits at the Federal Reserve banks held by depository institutions that are in excess of their legal reserve requirements. *(Chapters 4 and 23)*

Exchange offering A method used in the past by the U.S. Treasury to sell new securities by offering them to investors who hold maturing Treasury securities. *(Chapter 25)*

Expectations hypothesis A theory of the determinants of the yield curve which argues that the curve's slope is determined by investor expectations about the course of future interest rates. *(Chapter 9)*

Expected yield The weighted average return on a risky security composed of all possible yields from the security multiplied by the probability that each possible yield will occur. *(Chapter 10)*

Fair Credit Billing Act A federal law giving customers the right to question entries on bills sent to them for goods and services purchased on credit and giving them the right to expect that billing errors will be corrected as quickly as possible. *(Chapter 18)*

Fair Credit Reporting Act A federal law that gives credit customers the right to view their credit record held by a credit bureau and to secure quick correction of any errors in that record. *(Chapter 18)*

Federal agencies Departments or divisional units of the federal government empowered to borrow funds in the open market in order to make loans to private businesses and individuals or otherwise subsidize private lending or borrowing. *(Chapters 16 and 19)*

Federal Financing Bank A unit of the federal government created in 1973 which borrows money from the U.S. Treasury Department and channels these funds to federal agencies. *(Chapter 16)*

Federal funds Funds that can be transferred immediately from their holder to another party for immediate payment for purchases of securities, goods, or services. *(Chapters 13 and 15)*

Federal Home Loan Mortgage Corporation (FHLMC) A federal agency created in 1970 to improve the resale (secondary) market for home mortgages, which is part of the Federal Home Loan Bank System. *(Chapter 19)*

Federal Housing Administration (FHA) An agency of the federal government established in 1934 to guarantee mortgage loans for low-priced and medium-priced homes, thereby reducing the risks of lending by financial institutions making qualified home mortgage loans. *(Chapter 19)*

Federal National Mortgage Association (FNMA) A federal agency created in 1938 to buy and sell selected residential mortgages in the secondary market and thus encourage the development of a resale market for home loans. *(Chapters 16 and 19)*

Federal Open Market Committee (FOMC)
The chief body for setting and monitoring money
and credit policy within the Federal Reserve
System, consisting of the seven members of the
Federal Reserve Board and the presidents of the
12 Federal Reserve banks, only 5 of whom may
vote. *(Chapters 22 and 23)*

Federal Reserve Statement A weekly listing
of the factors supplying reserves to and absorbing the reserves of depository institutions.
(Chapter 24)

Federal Reserve System The central bank of
the United States, created by Congress to issue
currency and coin, regulate the banking system,
and take measures to protect the value of the
dollar and promote full employment. *(Chapters
4, 22, 23, and 24)*

**Federal Savings and Loan Insurance Cor-
poration (FSLIC)** The federal agency charged
with insuring the deposits accepted by member
savings and loan associations up to a maximum
of $100,000 for each account. *(Chapter 5)*

Fiber optics Electronic cables capable of transmitting data and images over great distances
using bursts of laser light. *(Chapter 30)*

Finance companies Financial service firms
that provide both business and consumer credit
in the form of loans and leases to their customers. *(Chapters 6 and 16)*

Financial asset A claim against the income or
wealth of a business firm, household, or unit of
government usually represented by a certificate,
receipt, or other legal document. *(Chapter 2)*

Financial disclosure The provision of relevant financial information to the public to aid
individuals and institutions in making sound
financial decisions. *(Chapter 30)*

Financial futures contracts Contracts that
call for the future delivery or sale of designated
securities at a price agreed upon the day the
contract is made and that are used mainly to
hedge (protect) against changing interest rates.
(Chapters 11 and 12)

Financial innovation A trend in the financial
system toward developing new services and new
service delivery methods. *(Chapter 30)*

Financial investment The net change in financial assets held by a sector or unit in
the economy over a specified time period.
(Chapter 3)

Financial market An institutional mechanism created by society to channel savings and
other financial services to those individuals
and institutions willing to pay for them.
(Chapter 1)

Financial system The collection of markets,
individuals, institutions, laws, regulations, and
techniques through which bonds, stocks, and
other securities are traded, financial services
produced and delivered, and interest rates determined. *(Chapter 1)*

Fiscal agent A role of the Federal Reserve System in which it provides services to the federal
government, such as clearing and collecting
checks on behalf of the U.S. Treasury and conducting auctions for the sale of new Treasury
securities. *(Chapter 22)*

Fiscal policy The taxing and spending programs carried out by government in order to
promote high employment, reasonable price stability, economic growth, and other economic
goals. *(Chapter 25)*

Fisher effect The theory of inflation and interest rates which argues that nominal interest
rates respond one-for-one to changes in the expected rate of inflation over the life of a loan.
(Chapters 9 and 11)

Flow of Funds Accounts A system of social
accounts prepared quarterly by the Board of
Governors of the Federal Reserve System that
reports the amount of saving and borrowing in
the U.S. economy by major sectors and how those
savings and borrowings are allocated to different kinds of financial instruments. *(Chapter 3)*

Flow of Funds matrix The combined sources
and uses of funds statements for all sectors in
the economy as reported in the Federal Reserve
Board's Flow of Funds Accounts. *(Chapter 3)*

Foreign exchange brokers Business firms
that, in return for a commission, bring buyers
and sellers of various currencies together to
carry out currency trading. *(Chapter 28)*

Foreign exchange markets Channels for trading national currencies and determining relative currency prices. *(Chapter 28)*

Foreign exchange rates The prices of foreign currencies expressed in terms of other currencies. *(Chapter 28)*

FOREX Foreign exchange services offered by multinational banks that trade in various currencies and hold inventories of currencies for the convenience of their customers. *(Chapter 29)*

Forward calendar The anticipated supply of new bonds or other securities expected to come to market over the next week, month, or other calendar period. *(Chapter 11)*

Forward contract An agreement to deliver a specified amount of currency, securities, or other goods or services at a set price on some future date. *(Chapter 28)*

Forward market Channel through which currencies, securities, commodities, or other goods and services are traded for future delivery to the buyer with the terms of trade set in advance of delivery. *(Chapter 28)*

Franchising A method of producing and delivering financial services in which a financial institution sells the services it produces through locally licensed suppliers. *(Chapter 30)*

FRMs Home mortgage loans carrying an interest rate that is fixed for the life of the loan. *(Chapter 19)*

GAP management A technique for protecting a bank's or other financial institution's earnings from losses due to changes in interest rates by matching the volume of interest-sensitive assets held to the volume of interest-sensitive liabilities taken on. *(Chapter 11)*

Garn–St Germain Depository Institutions Act A law passed by the U.S. Congress in 1982 to further deregulate the depository institutions sector, especially the services offered by nonbank thrift institutions, and to give the federal deposit insurance agencies additional tools to deal with failing institutions. *(Chapter 5)*

General credit controls Monetary policy tools that affect the entire banking and financial system, such as open market operations or changes in the Federal Reserve's discount rate. *(Chapter 23)*

General obligation bonds Debt obligations issued by state and local governments and backed by the "full faith and credit" of the issuing government (i.e., may be repaid from any available revenue source). *(Chapter 26)*

Gold exchange standard A system for making international payments in which each national currency is freely convertible into gold bullion at a fixed price and also freely convertible into other currencies at relatively stable prices. *(Chapter 27)*

Gold standard A system of payments for purchases of goods and services in international markets in which nations agree to exchange paper money or coins for gold bullion at predetermined prices without significant restrictions and allow gold bullion and gold coins to be exported or imported freely from one nation to another. *(Chapter 27)*

Government intervention in the foreign exchange market Buying or selling currencies, domestic or foreign, by a government agency or central bank in order to protect the value of the home currency in international markets. *(Chapter 28)*

Government National Mortgage Association (GMNA) A federal government agency created in 1968 to assist the nation's home mortgage market through such activities as purchasing mortgages to finance low-income family housing projects and guaranteeing principal and interest payments on securities issued by private mortgage lenders that are backed by pools of selected home mortgages. *(Chapter 19)*

Government-sponsored agencies Institutions originally owned by the federal government but now privately owned with the authority to borrow from and lend money to private businesses and individuals or to issue loan guarantees. *(Chapter 16)*

Hedging The act of buying and selling financial claims or using other financial tools in order to protect against the risk of fluctuations in market prices or interest rates. *(Chapters 11 and 12)*

Holding period yield The rate of return received or expected from a loan or security over the period the investor actually holds it, including the price for which the instrument is sold to another investor. *(Chapter 8)*

Home equity loans Extensions of credit to individuals who own their homes in which the borrowers' homes are pledged as collateral to support the loans and the amount of the loan is based on the difference between the market value of the home and the amount of any home mortgage debt outstanding (i.e., the owner's equity in a home); the loan proceeds may be used for a variety of purposes, including a college education or starting a new business. *(Chapters 18 and 19)*

IBFs International banking facilities located inside U.S. borders that contain a set of computerized credit and deposit accounts offered by U.S. multinational banks to their foreign customers. *(Chapters 17 and 29)*

Implied rate forecast The market's expectation about future interest rates as indicated by the shape of the yield curve or by financial futures prices. *(Chapter 11)*

Income effect The relationship between interest rate levels and the volume of saving in the economy which argues that the advent of higher interest rates may induce savers to save *less* because each dollar saved now earns a higher rate of return. *(Chapter 7)*

Indenture A contract accompanying the issue of a bond or note by a corporation or other borrower that lists the rights, privileges, and obligations of the borrower and of the investor who has purchased the bond or note. *(Chapter 20)*

Indirect finance Also known as financial intermediation, in which financial transactions (especially the borrowing and lending of money) are carried on through a financial intermediary such as a commercial bank. *(Chapter 2)*

Industrial development bonds Debt securities issued by a local government agency to aid a private company in the construction of a plant and/or the purchase of equipment or land. *(Chapters 20 and 26)*

Inflation A rise in the average level of all prices of goods and services traded in the economy over any given period of time. *(Chapters 9 and 24)*

Inflation-caused depreciation effect Changes in the expected price inflation rate may not lead to equivalent increases in nominal interest rates due to the tendency of depreciation charges on existing plant and equipment to lag behind the rising cost of new replacement plant and equipment, discouraging business investment and credit demand. *(Chapter 9)*

Inflation-caused income effect The relationship between changes in the rate of price inflation and shifts in income (including consumption and saving) that lead to changes in real and nominal interest rates. *(Chapter 9)*

Inflation-caused income tax effect The presence of a progressive income tax structure tends to cause nominal interest rates to increase by more than the expected increase in the rate of inflation. *(Chapter 9)*

Inflation-caused wealth effect Changes in inflation expectations may alter the value of wealth held in financial assets by individuals and institutions, causing a change in their savings plans and leading to offsetting movements in real and nominal interest rates. *(Chapter 9)*

Inflation premium The expected rate of price inflation which, when added to the real interest rate, equals the nominal interest rate on a loan. *(Chapter 9)*

Inflation risk (or purchasing power risk) The probability that increases in the average level of prices for all goods and services sold in the economy will reduce the purchasing power of an investor's income from loans or securities. *(Chapter 13)*

Information revolution A trend in the economy in which electronic innovation allows information to be moved faster and in greater volume between individuals and institutions. *(Chapter 30)*

Installment credit All liabilities of a borrowing customer other than home mortgages that are retired in two or more consecutive loan payments. *(Chapter 18)*

Interest rate The price of credit, or ratio of the fees charged to secure credit from a lender to the amount borrowed, usually expressed on an annual percentage basis. *(Chapter 8)*

Interest rate insurance An insurer agreeing to reimburse a borrower for additional interest expense if the borrower's loan rate climbs above some specified maximum loan rate. *(Chapter 11)*

Interest rate parity A condition prevailing in international markets where the interest rate differential between two nations matches the forward discount or premium on their two currencies. *(Chapter 28)*

Interest rate structure The concept that the interest rate or yield attached to any loan or security consists of the risk-free (or pure) rate of interest plus risk premiums for the security holder's exposure to default risk, inflation risk, call risk, and other forms of risk. *(Chapter 10)*

Interest rate SWAP A contract between two or more firms in which interest payments are exchanged so that each participating firm saves on interest costs and gets a better balance between its cash inflows and cash outflows. *(Chapter 11)*

International Banking Act A U.S. law passed in 1978 to bring foreign banks operating in the United States under federal government regulation. *(Chapters 4 and 29)*

International banking facilities (IBFs) A domestically based set of computerized accounts recording transactions of a U.S. bank with its foreign customers and created by Federal Reserve Board regulation. *(Chapters 17 and 29)*

International Lending and Supervision Act A federal law passed in 1983 requiring U.S. banks to increase their capital and to pursue more prudent international loan policies. *(Chapter 29)*

Interstate operations A trend toward financial institutions establishing facilities in more than one state. *(Chapter 30)*

Investment Expenditures on capital goods or inventories of goods or raw materials that are used to produce other goods and services, causing future production and income to rise. *(Chapter 1)*

Investment bankers Financial institutions that assist corporations and units of government in raising funds by underwriting their security offerings and rendering financial advice. *(Chapters 6, 20, and 26)*

Investment companies Financial intermediaries that sell shares to the public to raise funds and invest the proceeds in stocks, bonds, and other securities. *(Chapter 6)*

Investment institutions Financial intermediaries selling their customers securities and other financial assets in order to build up savings for retirement or for other uses. *(Chapter 2)*

Junk bonds Corporate debt securities with low credit ratings (below investment grade). *(Chapter 10)*

L The definition of the U.S. money supply that includes the M3 definition of money plus nonbank public holdings of U.S. Savings Bonds, short-term Treasury securities, commercial paper, and bankers' acceptances, net of money market mutual funds' holdings of these same assets. *(Chapter 24)*

Leasing companies Financial service firms that provide businesses and consumers access to equipment, motor vehicles, and other assets for a stipulated period of time at an agreed-upon leasing rate. *(Chapter 6)*

Legal reserves Deposits held at the Federal Reserve banks by depository institutions plus currency and coin held in the vaults of these institutions. *(Chapters 4, 15, 23, and 24)*

Letter of credit An authorization to draft funds held by a bank provided stipulated conditions are met. *(Chapters 17 and 29)*

Leveraged buyouts A form of corporate takeover in which the management of a company or other small group of investors buys the publicly owned stock of the firm, financing the transaction mainly with new debt that will be repaid from planned increases in company earnings. *(Chapter 20)*

Liability management The techniques used by banks to control the amount and composition of their borrowed funds by changing the interest rates they offer to reflect competition and the intensity and maturity of the bank's borrowing requirements. *(Chapter 15)*

LIBOR The London Interbank Offer Rate on short-term Eurodollar deposits as quoted by banks operating in the London money market and seeking to attract Eurodollar deposits from their customers. *(Chapters 17, 20, and 29)*

Life insurance companies Financial service firms selling contracts to customers that promise to reduce the financial loss to an individual or family associated with death, disability, or old age. *(Chapter 6)*

Liquidity The quality or capability of any asset to be sold quickly with little risk of loss in value when sold and possessing a relatively stable price over time. *(Chapters 2, 10, and 13)*

Liquidity preference theory of interest rates An explanation of the level of and changes in interest rates that focuses upon the interaction of the supply of and demand for money. *(Chapter 7)*

Liquidity premium The added yield (interest return) that must be paid to investors to get them to buy and hold long-term instead of short-term securities. *(Chapter 9)*

Loanable funds theory of interest rates The credit view of what determines the level of and changes in interest rates which focuses upon the interaction of the demand for and the supply of loanable funds (credit). *(Chapter 7)*

Loan option A contract entitling a borrower to take out a loan at a guaranteed interest rate over a stipulated time period. *(Chapter 11)*

Long hedge The purchase of futures contracts calling for the delivery of securities or commodities to the hedger on a specific future date at a set price. *(Chapter 12)*

Long position The purchase of securities outright from the seller in order to hold them until they mature or must be sold. *(Chapter 14)*

M1 The narrowest definition of the U.S. money supply consisting of currency outside the Trea-

sury, Federal Reserve banks, and the vaults of banks, plus checking accounts and other checkable deposits held by the nonbank public. *(Chapter 24)*

M2 The definition of the U.S. money supply that includes M1 plus savings and small-denomination (under $100,000) time deposits, money market mutual funds not held by institutions, money market deposit accounts (MMDAs), overnight Eurodollar deposits issued to U.S. residents by foreign branches of U.S. banks worldwide, and overnight and continuing-contract repurchase agreements issued by all commercial banks. *(Chapter 24)*

M3 The definition of the U.S. money supply which includes M2 plus large denomination ($100,000-plus) time deposits and term repurchase agreements issued by commercial banks and thrift institutions, term Eurodollars held by U.S. residents at foreign branches of U.S. banks worldwide and at all banking offices in the United Kingdom and Canada, and institutional-owned balances in money market mutual funds. *(Chapter 24)*

Managed float An international monetary and payments system in which the value of any currency is determined by demand and supply forces in the marketplace, but governments intervene on occasion in an effort to stabilize the value of their own currencies. *(Chapter 27)*

Managed floating currency standard System of currency valuation used today in which each nation chooses its own currency exchange rate standard or policy. *(Chapter 27)*

Marginal tax rate The federal or state tax rate that applies to the last dollar of income earned from a financial asset or other income source. *(Chapter 10)*

Margin requirements The difference between the market value of a security and its maximum loan value as specified by a regulation enforced by the Federal Reserve Board. *(Chapter 23)*

Marketability The feature of a loan or security which reflects its ability to be sold quickly to recover the purchaser's funds. *(Chapter 10)*

Market broadening A tendency for financial service markets to expand geographically over time due to advances in technology and increased customer mobility. *(Chapter 30)*

Market risk (or interest rate risk) The probability that the prices of securities or other assets will fall (due to rising interest rates), confronting the investor with a capital loss. *(Chapter 13)*

Market segmentation argument A theory of the yield curve in which the financial markets are thought to be separated into several distinct markets by the maturity preferences of various investors so that demand and supply for loans and securities in each market determine relative interest rates on long-term versus short-term securities. *(Chapter 9)*

Master note A borrowing arrangement between a corporation issuing commercial paper and an institution buying the paper in which the buying institution agrees to accept new paper each day up to a specified maxium amount. *(Chapter 16)*

Maturity Length of calendar time in days, weeks, months, and years before a security or loan comes due and must be paid off. *(Chapters 9 and 13)*

Member banks Banks that have joined the Federal Reserve System, consisting of all federally chartered (national) banks and any state-chartered U.S. banks that meet the Federal Reserve's requirements for membership. *(Chapters 4 and 22)*

Merchandise trade balance The difference between the value of a nation's exports of goods and the value of its imports of goods. *(Chapter 27)*

Modified exchange standard A system of currency exchanges and international payments in which foreign currencies were linked to gold and the U.S. dollar, with the price of gold in terms of U.S. dollars remaining fixed. *(Chapter 27)*

Monetarist view An approach to economic policy which contends that the money supply is a dominant influence on the price level, total spending, production, and employment in the economy. *(Chapter 24)*

Monetary base The sum of legal reserves in the banking system plus the amount of currency and coin held by the public. *(Chapter 23)*

Monetary policy The use of various tools by central banks to control the cost and availability of loanable funds in an effort to achieve national economic goals. *(Chapter 22)*

Money A financial asset that serves as a medium of exchange and standard of value for purchases of goods and services. *(Chapter 2)*

Money creation The ability of banks and other depository institutions to create a deposit, such as a checking account, that can be used as a medium of exchange (to make payments for purchases of goods and services). *(Chapter 4)*

Money market The institution set up by society to channel temporary surpluses of cash into temporary loans of funds, one year or less to maturity. *(Chapters 1 and 13)*

Money market deposit accounts (MMDAs) Deposits whose interest yields vary with market conditions and are subject to withdrawal by check. *(Chapters 4 and 5)*

Money market mutual fund An investment company selling shares to the public and investing the proceeds in short-term securities, such as Treasury bills, bank CDs, and other money market instruments. *(Chapter 5)*

Money multiplier The ratio of the size of the nation's money supply to the total reserve base available to depository institutions. *(Chapter 23)*

Money supply expectations effect A method for forecasting interest rates that compares actual growth of the nation's money supply with the market's expectation for money supply growth; for example, if expected money supply growth exceeds actual growth, interest rates will tend to fall. *(Chapter 11)*

Money supply income effect Increases and decreases in the nation's income and spending resulting in changes in the demand for money, and leading to corresponding increases or decreases in interest rates. *(Chapters 7 and 11)*

Money supply liquidity effect Increases or decreases in the nation's money supply causing interest rates to move in the opposite direction (assuming money demand is unchanged). *(Chapters 7 and 11)*

Mortgage-backed securities Debt obligations issued by private mortgage-lending institutions using selected residential mortgage loans they hold as collateral; the mortgage loans generate principal and interest payments to repay holders of the mortgage-backed securities. *(Chapter 19)*

Mortgage banks Financial service firms that work with property developers to provide real estate financing and then place the long-term loans with long-term lenders such as insurance companies and savings banks. *(Chapter 6)*

Mortgage bonds Long-term debt secured by a lien on specific assets, usually plant and equipment, held by the issuing corporation. *(Chapter 20)*

Moral suasion A monetary policy tool of the central bank in which its officers and staff try to persuade bankers and the public through speeches, conferences, and written communications to conform more closely to the central bank's goals. *(Chapter 23)*

Multinational bank A commercial bank engaged in selling services or conducting operations in more than one country. *(Chapter 29)*

Multinational corporation A large company with manufacturing, trading, or service operations in several different countries. *(Chapter 29)*

Municipals Debt securities issued by states, counties, cities, school districts, and other local units of government. *(Chapters 10 and 26)*

Mutuals Depository institutions owned by their depositors, such as savings banks and most savings and loan associations. *(Chapter 5)*

National banks U.S. banking institutions that received their charter of incorporation from the Comptroller of the Currency, an agency of the U.S. government. *(Chapter 4)*

National Credit Union Administration (NCUA) Federal regulatory agency that oversees the activities of federally chartered credit unions. *(Chapter 5)*

National Income Accounts A system of social accounts compiled and released quarterly by the U.S. Department of Commerce that presents data on the nation's production of goods and services, income flows, spending, and saving. *(Chapter 3)*

Negotiable certificate of deposit (CD) A marketable receipt issued by a bank or other depository institution to a customer, acknowledging the deposit of customer funds for a designated period at a specified interest rate or interest rate adjustment formula. *(Chapter 15)*

Negotiated markets Institutional mechanisms set up by society to make loans and trade securities where the terms of trade are set by direct bargaining between a lender and a borrower. *(Chapter 1)*

Nominal interest rate The published rate of interest attached to a loan or security that includes both a real interest rate component and the inflation rate (inflation premium) expected over the life of the loan or security. *(Chapter 9)*

Nonborrowed reserves The largest component of the total legal reserves of depository institutions, consisting of all those legal reserves owned by depository insitutions themselves and not borrowed from the Federal Reserve banks. *(Chapter 24)*

Nondeposit funds Borrowings of funds by banks (usually in the short-term money market) to supplement the funds they receive from selling deposits to the public. *(Chapter 4)*

Noninstallment credit A loan that is normally paid off in a lump sum rather than in a series of installment payments. *(Chapters 8 and 18)*

Nonresidential mortgages Loans secured by business and farm properties. *(Chapters 19 and 20)*

Note A shorter-term debt obligation issued by a business firm, individual, or unit of government to borrow money with a time to maturity that usually does not exceed five years. *(Chapter 3)*

Note issuance facilities A form of short-term or medium-term credit issued by multinational banks in which the banks agree to backstop a customer's notes and to provide supplemental funding for those notes the customer has difficulty selling in the open market. *(Chapters 17 and 29)*

NOW account An interest-bearing checking account available to individuals and nonprofit institutions from banks, savings and loans, and other depository institutions.

Official reserve transactions Transfer of the ownership of gold, convertible foreign currencies, deposits in the International Monetary Fund, and Special Drawing Rights (SDRs) used by a nation to settle a deficit in its balance of payments. *(Chapter 27)*

Open market Institutional mechanism created by society to make loans and trade securities in which any individual or institution can participate. *(Chapters 1 and 20)*

Open market operations The buying and selling of securities by the Federal Reserve System to affect the quantity and growth of the legal reserves of depository institutions and ultimately general credit conditions in order to achieve the nation's economic goals. *(Chapter 23)*

Option contracts Agreements between contract writers and contract buyers to accept delivery of ("call") securities or place with buyers ("put") securities at a specified price on or before the date the contracts expire. *(Chapters 12 and 21)*

Option premium The fee that the buyer of an option contract must pay to the writer of the contract for the right to deliver or accept delivery of securities at a set price. *(Chapters 12 and 21)*

Organized exchanges Locations where stocks, bonds, and other securities are traded according to the rules and regulations for trading established by members of the exchange. *(Chapter 21)*

Original maturity The interval of time between the issue date of a security and the date on which the borrower promises to redeem it. *(Chapter 13)*

Over-the-counter market A mechanism for trading stocks, bonds, and other securities through brokers or dealers operating off the major securities exchanges. *(Chapter 21)*

Pass-throughs Securities issued against a pool of mortgage loans held by a financial institution. *(Chapter 19)*

Peggers Nations that strive to keep the exchange value of their currencies within a fixed range around the value of some other currency or basket of currencies. *(Chapter 27)*

Pension funds Financial service firms selling retirement plans to their customers in which savings are set aside in accounts established in the customers' names and allowed to accumulate at interest until those customers reach retirement age. *(Chapter 6)*

Perfect market A market in which all available information affecting the value of financial instruments is freely available to everyone, transactions costs are minimal, and all participants in the market are price takers rather than price setters. *(Chapter 1)*

Political risk The probability that changes in government laws or regulations will result in a lower rate of return of the investor or, in the extreme case, a total loss of invested capital. *(Chapters 13 and 29)*

Portfolio immunization An investment strategy that tries to protect the expected yield from a security or portfolio of securities by acquiring those securities whose duration equals the length of the investor's planned holding period. *(Chapter 9)*

Portfolio insurance A strategy of making continuous adjustments in a security portfolio between risky and riskless investments so that the investor's total rate of return achieves at least some desired minimum level. *(Chapter 21)*

Preferred habitat The theory of the yield curve which holds that investors prefer certain maturities of securities over other maturities due to differences in liquidity needs, risk, tax exposure, and other factors. *(Chapter 9)*

Preferred stock A share of ownership in a business corporation that promises a stated annual dividend. *(Chapter 21)*

Price elasticity The ratio of changes in the price of a debt security to changes in its yield. *(Chapter 9)*

Price of credit The rate of interest that must be paid to secure the use of borrowed funds. *(Chapter 7)*

Primary dealers Security firms that acquire securities from the government and other borrowers and make markets for those securities, standing ready to buy and sell them at posted prices. *(Chapter 14)*

Primary markets Institutional mechanisms set up by society to trade newly issued loans and securities. *(Chapter 1)*

Primary reserves The most liquid assets held by a bank, consisting of its vault cash and the deposits it has placed with other banks. *(Chapter 4)*

Primary securities The IOUs issued by borrowers from a financial intermediary and held by the intermediary as interest-bearing assets. *(Chapter 2)*

Private pass-throughs Securities issued against a group of conventional or guaranteed home mortgages with the interest and principal payments on the securities derived from the cash flow generated by the home mortgages. *(Chapter 19)*

Private (or direct) sale Placing securities with one or a limited number of investors rather than trying to sell them in the open market. *(Chapter 20)*

Program trading Computer-assisted decisions about security purchases and sales in an effort to take advantage of temporary price differences between securities or security price indexes in different markets in order to earn above-average returns or to protect against excessive market risk. *(Chapters 12 and 21)*

Property–casualty insurance companies Financial service firms selling contracts to protect their customers against losses to person or property due to negligence, crime, adverse weather changes, fire, and other hazards. *(Chapter 6)*

Public confidence The attitude of the public toward the safety and stability of financial markets and institutions. *(Chapter 30)*

Public debt The volume of debt obligations that are the responsibility of the federal government and therefore of its taxpayers. *(Chapter 25)*

Public sale When securities are sold in the open market to any individual or institution willing to pay the price, usually through investment bankers. *(Chapter 20)*

Put option A contract granting its buyer the right to sell a specified number of equity shares or debt securities at a set price on or before the expiration date. *(Chapters 12 and 21)*

Random walk A theory of security price movements which argues that the future path of individual security prices is no more predictable than is the path of a series of random numbers. *(Chapter 21)*

Rate cap A maximum interest rate inserted into a loan agreement which limits how far the loan interest rate can rise over the term of the loan. *(Chapter 11)*

Rate collar A loan agreement containing both a minimum and a maximum loan rate level to protect both borrower and lender against excessive interest rate risk. *(Chapter 11)*

Rate-hedging methods Techniques for insulating an investor's holdings of financial assets from loss due to changes in market rates of interest. *(Chapters 11 and 12)*

Rate of interest The price of acquiring credit, usually expressed as a ratio of the cost of securing credit to the total amount of credit obtained. *(Chapter 7)*

Rational expectations theory of interest rates An explanation of the level of and changes in interest rates based on changes in investor expectations regarding future security prices and returns. *(Chapter 7)*

Real estate investment trusts (REITs) Tax-exempt corporations that receive at least three quarters of their gross income from real estate transactions and devote a high percentage of their assets to real property loans. *(Chapter 6)*

Real interest rate The rate of return from a financial asset expressed in terms of its purchasing power (adjusted for inflation). *(Chapter 9)*

Real investment The net change in real assets held by a sector or unit in the economy over a specified time period. *(Chapter 3)*

Regulation Q ceilings Maximum interest rates on certain types of deposits that are set under federal law and administered by a regulatory agency such as the Federal Reserve Board. *(Chapter 23)*

Reinvestment risk Probability that earnings from a loan or security will have to be reinvested in lower-yielding assets in the future. *(Chapters 9 and 13)*

Representative offices Facilities established in distant markets by a bank in order to sell the bank's services and assist its clients; these offices usually cannot accept deposits or make loans. *(Chapter 29)*

Repurchase agreement (RP) A loan (usually granted to a bank or security dealer) that is collateralized by high-quality securities (usually government securities). *(Chapter 14)*

Required reserves Holdings of cash and funds on deposit with the Federal Reserve banks by depository institutions that are required by law to backstop the public's deposits held by these same institutions. *(Chapter 23)*

Reserve requirements The percentage of various liabilities (such as deposits received from the public) that must be held by depository institutions, either in vault cash or on deposit at the Federal Reserve banks. *(Chapter 23)*

Residential mortgages Loans secured by single-family homes and other dwellings. *(Chapter 19)*

Residential mortgage credit Loans provided to support the purchase of new or existing single-family homes, duplexes, and other permanent dwellings. *(Chapters 18 and 19)*

Revenue-anticipation notes (RANs) Short-term debt obligations issued by state and local units of government in lieu of expected future governmental revenues in order to meet near-time cash needs. *(Chapter 26)*

Revenue bonds Debt obligations issued by state and local governments that are repayable only from a particular source of funds, such as revenues generated by a toll road or toll bridge or from user fees derived by selling water or electric power. *(Chapter 26)*

Risk-free rate of interest The rate of return on a riskless security, often called the pure rate of interest or the opportunity cost of money. *(Chapter 7)*

Risk management tools Financial devices (such as futures and options) which permit a borrower or lender of funds to protect against the risks of changing prices and interest rates. *(Chapter 30)*

Savings The amount of funds left over out of current income after current consumption expenditures are made, or for a business firm, the current net earnings retained in the business instead of paid out to the owners. *(Chapters 1, 2, and 7)*

Savings banks Depository institutions that are owned by their depositors and can be chartered by both the federal government and by some states. *(Chapter 5)*

Savings and loan associations The predominant home mortgage lender in the United States, making predominantly local loans to finance the purchase of housing for individuals and families. *(Chapters 5 and 19)*

Seasonality Patterns in the behavior of interest rates, with rate increases during certain seasons of the year and decreases during other seasons, year after year. *(Chapter 11)*

Secondary markets Institutional mechanisms set up by society to trade or exchange loans and securities that have already been issued. *(Chapter 1)*

Secondary securities Financial claims, such as deposits, issued by a financial intermediary to raise loanable funds. *(Chapter 2)*

Second mortgage A claim against real property arising from a loan which is subordinated to (comes after) the claim held by the holder of a first mortgage against the same property. *(Chapter 19)*

Securitization The selling of shares or certificates representing an interest in a pool of income-generating assets (such as mortgages, commercial loans, or consumer loans) as a method for raising funds by a financial institution. *(Chapters 5, 19, and 30)*

Security dealers Financial firms that provide a conduit for buyers and sellers of marketable securities by holding a portfolio of these securities and standing ready to buy and sell these securities at an announced price. *(Chapter 6)*

Selective credit controls Monetary policy tools that affect specific groups or sectors in the financial system. *(Chapter 23)*

Semidirect finance Any financial transaction (especially the borrowing and lending of money) that is assisted by a security broker or dealer. *(Chapter 2)*

Serialization The splitting up of a single bond issue into several different maturities (used most often for state and local government bonds). *(Chapter 26)*

Service-oriented economy An industrialized economy in which the production and delivery of services account for a growing share of national output and employment. *(Chapter 30)*

Share draft Interest-bearing checking account offered by a credit union. *(Chapters 5 and 18)*

Shell branches Booking offices of multinational banks, usually set up offshore to attract deposits and avoid certain domestic banking regulations. *(Chapter 29)*

Short hedge The sale of futures contracts promising the delivery of securities or commodities to another party (individual or institution) on a specific future date at a set price. *(Chapter 12)*

Short position Dealers and other investors promise to sell and deliver in the future securities they do not currently own, hoping security prices will fall in the interim. *(Chapter 14)*

Simple interest method A method of figuring the interest on a loan that charges interest only for the period of time the borrower actually has use of the borrowed funds. *(Chapter 8)*

Social accounting A system of recordkeeping which reports economic and financial activity for the whole economy and/or between the principal sectors of the economy, such as households and businesses. *(Chapter 3)*

Social responsibility A trend among financial institutions and their regulators to promote fair and equitable treatment of all customers and to make financial services available to all or most segments of the population. *(Chapter 30)*

Solicitation method A method for selling federal agency securities in which orders are taken from buyers and the securities are priced and then delivered to investors after the order book is closed. *(Chapter 16)*

Sources and uses of funds statements A financial report prepared for each sector of the economy in the Federal Reserve Board's Flow of Fund Accounts that shows changes in net worth and changes in holdings of financial assets and liabilities over a specific time period. *(Chapter 3)*

Special drawing rights (SDRs) An official monetary reserve unit developed by the International Monetary Fund to settle international claims between nations. *(Chapter 27)*

Spot market Channel through which currencies, securities, commodities, or other goods and services are traded for immediate delivery to the buyer once buyer and seller agree on the terms of trade. *(Chapters 12 and 28)*

State-chartered banks U.S. banking corporations that received their charter of incorporation from a board or commission appointed by a governmental body in each of the 50 states. *(Chapter 4)*

Stocks Ownership shares in a corporation, giving the holder claim to any dividends distributed from current earnings. *(Chapter 3)*

Stock-index arbitrage The program trading strategy in which professional traders look for temporary underpricing or overpricing of stock-index financial futures contracts compared to the cash market (spot) prices of comparable stocks, simultaneously buying (selling) stocks and selling (buying) futures contracts to profit from any temporary relative mispricing of these two financial instruments. *(Chapters 12 and 21)*

Strike price The price for securities specified in an option contract; also called the *exercise price*. *(Chapters 12 and 21)*

Supply-side economics An approach to economic policy which argues that the nation's economic policy should be directed toward increasing productivity and the supply of goods and services in order to combat inflation. *(Chapter 24)*

Surplus-budget unit An individual, business firm, or unit of government whose current income receipts exceed its current expenditures and therefore is a net lender of funds to the money and capital markets. *(Chapter 2)*

Swap agreements Lines of credit established between central banks to be used when any particular central bank needs foreign currency to sell in the currency markets. *(Chapter 28)*

Symbiotic A conglomerate financial firm that frequently merges insurance sales, security brokerage, real estate brokerage, financial counseling, and credit services within the same organization. *(Chapter 6)*

Tax-anticipation notes (TANs) Short-term debt obligations issued by state and local governments to provide for immediate cash needs until tax revenues come in. *(Chapter 26)*

Tax-exemption privilege A feature bestowed by law on some financial assets (such as state and local government bonds) that makes the income they generate free of taxation at federal or state and local government levels, or both. *(Chapters 10 and 26)*

Tax-exempt securities Debt securities issued by state, city, county and other local units of government or by other qualified borrowers whose interest income is exempt from federal taxation and from most state taxes as well. *(Chapter 10)*

Tax Reform Act of 1986 A legislated revision of the U.S. federal income tax code lowering individuals' tax rates and raising taxes on corporations as well as simplifying the federal tax code to make it easier to understand and to reduce the importance of tax laws in making economic and financial decisions. *(Chapters 10, 20, and 25)*

Third-country bills Bankers' acceptances issued by banks in one country that finance the transport or storage of goods traded between two other countries. *(Chapter 17)*

Third market Mechanism through which securities listed on a stock exchange are traded off the exchange in the over-the-counter market. *(Chapter 21)*

Time draft A bank's promise to pay a stipulated amount of funds upon presentation of the draft on a specific future date. *(Chapter 17)*

Transaction accounts Deposits (such as a checking account) or other accounts offered by banks and other financial institutions that can be used to make payments for purchases of goods and services. *(Chapters 4 and 23)*

Treasury bills Short-term debt securities sold by the U.S. Treasury to raise cash in order to cover seasonal shortfalls of federal government funds. *(Chapter 14)*

Truth-in-Lending A law passed by the U.S. Congress in 1968 that requires covered lenders to disclose fully all the relevant terms of a personal loan to the borrower and to report a standardized loan rate (known as the APR, or annual percentage rate). *(Chapters 8 and 18)*

Unilateral transfers Gifts of goods and money made by residents of one nation to residents of another nation, with the net amount recorded in the donor nation's balance-of-payments accounts. *(Chapter 27)*

Universal life insurance A form of life insurance policy in which savings contributed by the policyholder are placed in a money market fund, with the life insurance company making periodic withdrawals to cover the premiums owed on the life insurance policy. *(Chapter 18)*

Vehicle currency A monetary unit of a nation that is not only the standard of value (unit of account) for domestic transactions, but also used to express the prices of many goods and services traded between other nations as well. *(Chapter 28)*

Video conferences Meetings between business executives or other individuals that are conducted over great distances using satellites and other electronic communications devices. *(Chapter 30)*

VRMs Home mortgage loans carrying a loan interest rate that varies during the term of a loan, generally depending on the movement of interest rates in the open market. *(Chapter 19)*

Wealth effect (of saving and interest rates) The relationship between the volume of saving and interest rates which contends that the net wealth position of savers (the balance in their portfolios between debt and financial assets) determines how their desired levels of saving will change as interest rates change. *(Chapter 7)*

Yield curve Relationship between short-term and long-term interest rates (that is, between yield to maturity and time to maturity of a debt security) as reflected in a smooth curve with an upward, downward, or horizontal slope. *(Chapter 9)*

Yield to maturity The interest rate on a debt security that equates the purchase price of the security to the present value of all its expected annual net cash inflows (income). *(Chapter 8)*

Zero coupon bonds Long-term debt obligations that are sold at a price well below their par (or face) value and without any promised interest payments; the buyer's gain is in the form of price appreciation over time toward the debt securities' par (or face) value. *(Chapters 9 and 20)*

Index